Chapter	Topic Area	Learning-by-Doing Exercises	Graphs and Tables	Example Boxes
7: Costs and Cost Minimization (continued)	Cost Minimization and the Optimal Choice of Inputs	LBD Exercises 7.2, 7.3	Figures 7.1–7.8	Example 7.4: Oil Tankers Example 7.5 Burke Mills Revisited
	Input Demand Curves	LBD Exercise 7.4	Figure 7.11	Example 7.6: The Price Elasticity of Demand for Inputs in Manufacturing Industries
8: Cost Curves	Total Cost Curves	LBD Exercise 8.1	Figures 8.1–8.6	Example 8.1: How Would Input Prices Affect the Long-Run Total Cost for a Trucking Firm
	Average and Marginal Cost Curves	LBD Exercise 8.2	Figures 8.7–8.9	Example 8.2: The Relationship between Average and Marginal Cost in Higher Education
	Relationship between Short-Run Cost Curves and Long-Run Cost Curves	LDB Exercise 8.4	Figures 8.17–8.20	Example 8.4: The Short-Run and Long-Run Cost Curves for an American Railroad Firm
9: Perfectly Competitive Markets	Short-Run Supply Curves	LBD Exercises 9.1, 9.2	Figures 9.2–9.7	Example 9.2: The Supply Curve for an American Corn Producer Example 9.3: Short-Run Supply Curves for Copper
	Short-Run Equilibrium	LBD Exercise 9.3	Figures 9.9–9.11	Example 9.5: The Price of Electricity on Nord Pool
	Free Entry and Long-Run Equilibrium	LBD Exercise 9.4	Figures 9.16, 9.18, 9.20, 9.21	Example 9.6: Free Entry into the Internet Access Market Example 9.7: The Collapse of the Supertanker Market Example 9.8: Free Entry into an Increasing Cost Industry: The Solvent Extraction Business in India
10: Competitive Markets: Applications	Impact of an Excise Tax	LBD Exercise 10.1	Figures 10.2, 10.3, 10.5	Example 10.1: Gasoline Taxes in the United States
	Price Ceilings	LBD Exercise 10.3	Figures 10.7, 10.8, 10.9	Example 10.3: Price Ceilings in the Market for Natural Gas
	Price Floors	LBD Exercise 10.4	Figures 10.11, 10.12, 10.13	Example 10.4: Unintended Consequences of Price Regulation in Airline Markets
	Production Quotas	LBD Exercise 10.5	Figure 10.15	Example 10.5: Quotas for Taxi Cabs
11: Monopoly and Monopsony	Profit Maximization by a Monopoly and the Inverse Elasticity Pricing Rule	LBD Exercises 11.2, 11.3, 11.4	Figures 11.5, 11.7	Example 11.1: Chewing Gum, Baby Food, and the IEPR
	Monopoly Comparative Statics	LBD Exercise 11.5	Figures 11.10, 11.11	Example 11.2: Coca Cola's Smart Vending Machines
	Multi-Plant Monopoly and Cartels	LBD Exercise 11.6	Figure 11.15	Example 11.4 Allocating Production Quotas in a Cartel: The Case of OPEC
	Monopsony	LBD Exercise 11.7	Figure 11.19	Example 11.6 Monopsony Power in the Market for Nurses

(continued)

Chapter	Topic Area	Learning-by-Doing Exercises	Graphs and Tables	Example Boxes
12: Capturing Surplus	First Degree Price Discrimination	LBD Exercises 12.1, 12.2	Figure 12.1	Example 12.1: Undergraduate Financial Aid at U.S. Universities
	Second Degree Price Discrimination	LBD Exercise 12.3	Figures 12.5, 12.6	Example 12.2: Declining Block Tariff for Electricity
	Third Degree Price Discrimination	LBD Exercises 12.4, 12.5	Figures 12.8, 12.9	Example 12.3: Alcoa's Vertical Integration to Implement Price Discrimination Example 12.4: Pricing Airline Tickets
13: Market Structure and Composition	Oligopoly with Homogeneous Products	LBD Exercises 13.1, 13.2	Figures 13.1–13.5	Example 13.1: Cournot Equilibrium in the Corn Wet-Milling Industry Example 13.2: Individual versus Group Rationality in the Copper Industry
	Oligopoly with Differentiated Products	LBD Exercise 13.3	Figures 13.10–13.12	Example 13.5: Bertrand Price Competition: Eurotunnel verus the Channel Ferry Boats
14: Game Theory and Strategic Behavior	The Concept of Nash Equilibrium	LBD Exercises 14.1, 14.2	Tables 14.1–14.11	Example 14.1: Prisoners' Dilemma and the Law Example 14.2: The Game of Chicken between Sky TV and British Satellite Broadcasting in the Satellite Television Market in the U.K. Example 14.3 Bank Runs
	Sequential Move Games and Strategic Moves	LBD Exercise 14.3	Figures 14.2, 14.3	Example 14.6: Irreversibility of Business Decisions in the Airline Industry
15: Risk and Information	Bearing and Eliminating Risk	LBD Exercise 15.3	Figure 15.9	Example 15.1: Why Does Anyone Supply Insurance? A Brief History of Insurance and the Sharing of Risk
	Auctions	LBD Exercise 15.4	Figures 15.14, 15.15	Example 15.3: The Winner's Curse in the Classroom Example 15.4: "The Greatest Auction of Them All": The FCC's Broadband Spectrum Auction
16: General Equilibrium Theory	General Equilibrium Analysis: Two Markets	LBD Exercise 16.1	Figures 16.2, 16.3	Example 16.1: Internet Sales Taxes
	General Equilibrium Analysis: Many Markets	LBD Exercise 16.2	Figures 16.5–16.12	Example 16.2: The General Equilibrium Effects of the Gasoline Excise Tax
17: Externalities and Public Goods	Externalities	LBD Exercise 17.1	Figures 17.2–17.6	Example 17.1: Negative Externality: Congestion on the Internet Example 17.2: Congestion Pricing on the Highway Example 17.3: Subsidizing Mass Transit
	Public Goods	LBD Exercise 17.4	Figure 17.7	Example 17.4: The Free Rider Problem in Public Broadcasting

MICROECONOMICS

To our wives . . . Maureen and Jan . . .
and to our children
Suvarna and Eric, Justin, and Julie

MICROECONOMICS
An Integrated Approach

DAVID A. BESANKO

Northwestern University

RONALD R. BRAEUTIGAM

Northwestern University

JOHN WILEY & SONS, INC.

New York • Chichester • Brisbane • Toronto • Singapore

ACQUISITIONS EDITOR: Leslie Kraham
ASSOCIATE EDITOR: Cindy Rhoads
MARKETING MANAGER: Charity Robey
SENIOR PRODUCTION EDITOR: Valerie A. Vargas
SENIOR DESIGNER: Kevin Murphy
ILLUSTRATION EDITOR: Anna Melhorn
PHOTO EDITOR: Elyse Rieder
PRODUCTION MANAGEMENT SERVICES: Ingrao Associates
COVER ART: Victor de Vasarely, *Toroni-Nagi*, 1969. Acrylic on canvas (200 × 200cm). Private Collection/Art Resource. Reproduced with permission of Artists' Rights Society, New York.

This book was set in 10.5/12 Janson Text by TechBooks and Printed and bound by Von Hoffmann Press. The cover was printed by Von Hoffmann Press.

This book is printed on acid-free paper. ∞

Library of Congress Cataloging-in-Publication Data:
Besanko, David, 1955-
    Microeconomics: an integrated approach/David A. Besanko, Ronald R. Braeutigam.
        p. cm.
    Includes bibliographical references.
    ISBN 0-471-17064-X (cloth : alk. paper)
    1. Microeconomics. I. Braeutigam, Ronald R. (Ronald Ray) II. Title.

HB172.B49 2001
338.5--dc21

Printed in the United States of America   2001026639

1 0 9 8 7 6 5 4 3

About the Authors

David Besanko is the Alvin J. Huss Distinguished Professor of Management and Strategy at the Kellogg Graduate School of Management at Northwestern University. He is currently serving as Associate Dean for Curriculum and Teaching at the Kellogg School. He received his AB in Political Science from Ohio University in 1977, his MS in Managerial Economics and Decision Sciences from Northwestern University in 1980, and his PhD in Managerial Economics and Decision Sciences from Northwestern University in 1982. Before joining the Kellogg faculty in 1991, Professor Besanko was a member of the faculty of the School of Business at Indiana University from 1982 to 1991. In addition, in 1985, he held a post-doctorate position on the Economics Staff at Bell Communications Research.

Professor Besanko teaches courses in the fields of Management and Strategy, Competitive Strategy, and Managerial Economics. In 1995, the graduating class at Kellogg awarded Professor Besanko the L.G. Lavengood Professor of the Year, the highest teaching honor a faculty member at Kellogg can receive. At the Kellogg School, he has also received the Sidney J. Levy Teaching Award (1998, 2000) and the Chair's Core Teaching Award (1999, 2001).

Professor Besanko does research on topics relating to competitive strategy, industrial organization, the theory of the firm, and economics of regulation. He has published two books and over 35 articles in leading professional journals in economics and business. Among other places, his work has appeared in the *American Economic Review*, the *Quarterly Journal of Economics*, the *RAND Journal of Economics*, the *Review of Economic Studies*, and *Management Science*. Professor Besanko is a co-author of *Economics of Strategy* with David Dranove and Mark Shanley.

Ronald R. Braeutigam is the Harvey Kapnick Professor of Business Institutions in the Department of Economics and the Transportation Center at Northwestern University. He is Director of the Business Institutions Program. He received a Bachelor of Science in Petroleum Engineering from the University of Tulsa in 1970 and then attended Stanford University, where he received an MSc in engineering and a PhD in Economics in 1976. He has taught at Stanford University and the California Institute of Technology, and he has also held an appointment as a Senior Research Fellow at the Wissenschaftszentrum Berlin (Science Center Berlin). Since 1990, Professor Braeutigam has taught microeconomics in training programs for consultants at McKinsey & Company. He has also worked in both government and industry, beginning his career as a petroleum engineer with Standard Oil of Indiana (now BP), serving as research economist in The White House Office of Telecommunications Policy, and as an economic consultant to Congress and many government agencies. He has also served as a consultant to the World Bank and to many private firms and industry groups on matters of pricing, costing, managerial strategy, antitrust, and regulation.

Professor Braeutigam has received numerous teaching awards, including recognition as a Charles Deering McCormick Professor of Teaching Excellence at Northwestern (1997–2000), the highest teaching award that can be received by a faculty member at Northwestern University. He also received the Northwestern University Alumni Association Excellence in Teaching Award (1991).

Professor Braeutigam's research interests are in the field of microeconomics and industrial organization. Much of his work has focused on the economics of regulation and regulatory reform, particularly in the telephone, transportation, and energy sectors. He has published two books and numerous articles in leading professional journals in economics. Among other places, his work has appeared in the *American Economic Review*, the *RAND Journal of Economics*, the *Review of Economics and Statistics*, and the *International Economic Review*. Professor Braeutigam is a co-author of *The Regulation Game* with Bruce Owen.

He has also served as President of the European Association for Research in Industrial Economics.

Preface

After many years of experience teaching at the undergraduate and MBA levels, we have concluded that the most effective way to teach microeconomics is to present the content in several different forms, each one reinforcing and amplifying the other. This book introduces the subject of microeconomics the way we teach it.

Microeconomics: An Integrated Approach uses four complementary pedagogies to teach microeconomics: verbal intuition, graphs, applications, and Learning-by-Doing exercises. Our narrative *integrates* the use of algebra, graphs, and tables in the study of microeconomic problems. We *integrate* theory with applications drawn from the real world. And we *integrate* worked-out Learning by Doing exercises with verbal and graphical explanations to help students make the tools of economic analysis their own. This approach enables students to see clearly the interplay of key concepts and to understand how the fundamental tools of microeconomics work in a variety of contexts.

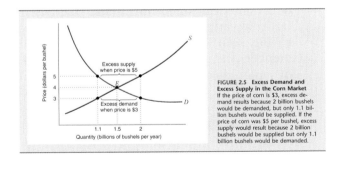

FIGURE 2.5 Excess Demand and Excess Supply in the Corn Market
If the price of corn is $3, excess demand results because 2 billion bushels would be demanded, but only 1.1 billion bushels would be supplied. If the price of corn was $5 per bushel, excess supply would result because 2 billion bushels would be supplied but only 1.1 billion bushels would be demanded.

GRAPHS TELL THE STORY ...

We use graphs and tables more abundantly than most texts, because they are central to economic analysis, enabling us to depict complex interactions simply. In economics, a picture truly *is* worth a thousand words.

... BUT WORDS DO TOO

Still, for many students, graphical explanations of economic ideas and concepts can seem convoluted and unintuitive. Tables and graphs are powerful economic tools, but many students have difficulty interpreting them at first. We have worked hard to make our exposition of the economic intuition underlying the graphs clear and easy to follow. Patient step-by-step explanations with examples enable even nonvisual learners to understand how graphs are constructed and what they mean.

Economies of Scale for "Backoffice" Activities in a Hospital **E**XAMPLE **8.4**

The business of health care was in the news a lot during the 1990s. One of the most interesting trends was the consolidation of hospitals through mergers. In the Chicago area, for example, Northwestern Memorial Hospital merged with several suburban hospitals, such as Evanston Hospital, to form a large multi-hospital system covering the North Side of Chicago and the North Shore.

Proponents of hospital mergers argue that mergers enable hospitals to achieve cost savings through economies of scale in "backoffice" operations—activities, such as laundry, housekeeping, cafeterias, printing and duplicating services, and data processing, that do not generate revenue for a hospital directly, but that the hospital cannot function without. Opponents argue that such cost savings are illusory and that hospital mergers mainly reduce competition in local hospital markets. The U.S. antitrust authorities have blocked several hospital mergers on this basis.

David Dranove recently studied the extent to which backoffice activities within a hospital are subject to economies of scale.[11] Figure 8.12 summarizes some of his findings. The figure sho~~~~~~~~~~~~~~~~three~~~~~~~~~~~~~cafeterias,

---

IT WORKS IN THEORY, BUT DOES IT WORK IN THE REAL WORLD?

Numerous real-world examples illustrate how microeconomics applies to business decision making and public policy issues. We begin each chapter with an extended example that introduces the key themes of the chapter and use real markets and companies to reinforce particular concepts and tools. Many of these examples focus on the *new economy.* Beyond the introductory chapter, each chapter contains about six examples woven into the narrative or highlighted in sidebars.

LEARN BY DOING

Our emphasis on practice exercises sets this book apart from others. Although graphs, verbal intuition, and real-world applications are essential ingredients for learning microeconomic analysis, for many students they are not sufficient. Based on our experience, in order to *really* internalize microeconomic theory students need drill. They need to work through lots of problems that are tangible, problems that have specific equations and numbers in them. Anyone who has mastered a skill or a sport, whether it be piano, ballet, or golf, understands that a fundamentally important part of the learning process involves repetitive drills that seemingly bear no relation to how one would actually execute the skill un-

---

LEARNING-BY-DOING EXERCISE 7.4

The Input Demand Curves for a Cobb–Douglas Production Function

Problem To see how the input demand curves are derived, suppose that the production function is $Q = 50L^{\frac{1}{2}}K^{\frac{1}{2}}$. What are the demand curves for labor and capital?

Solution We begin with our tangency condition $MP_L/MP_K = w/r$. As shown in Learning-By-Doing Exercise 7.2,

$$\frac{MP_L}{MP_K} = \frac{K}{L}.$$

Thus, our tangency condition is

$$\frac{K}{L} = \frac{w}{r}, \text{ or } L = \frac{r}{w}K.$$

This is the equation of the expansion path.

Let's now substitute this into the production function and solve for K in terms of Q, w, and r:

$$Q = 50\left(\frac{r}{w}K\right)^{\frac{1}{2}}K^{\frac{1}{2}},$$

which yields the demand curve for capital:

$$K = \frac{Q}{50}\left(\frac{w}{r}\right)^{\frac{1}{2}}.$$

Since $L = (r/w)K$, it follows that the demand curve for labor is

$$L = \frac{Q}{50}\left(\frac{r}{w}\right)^{\frac{1}{2}}.$$

Note from the above equation that the demand for labor is a decreasing function of w and an increasing function of r. This is consistent with the graphical analysis in Figures 7.5 and 7.11. Note also that both K and L increase when Q increases. Therefore, both capital and labor are normal inputs.

Similar Problem: 7.10

---

der "real" conditions. We believe that drill problems in microeconomics serve the same purpose. Whether or not a student ever has to do a numerical comparative statics analysis after completing the microeconomics course, having seen concretely, through the use of numbers and equations, how a shift in demand or supply affects the equilibrium, a student will have a deeper appreciation for comparative statics analysis and will be better prepared to interpret events in real markets.

Embedded in the text of each chapter are four to eight Learning-By-Doing exercises. Designed to illustrate the core ideas of the chapter, these exercises guide the student through specific numerical problems. They are integrated with the graphical and verbal exposition, so that students can clearly see, through the use of numbers and tangible algebraic relationships, what the graphs and words are striving to teach. These exercises set the student up to do similar practice problems as well as more difficult analytical problems at the end of each chapter and in the study guide that accompanies this text.

ORGANIZATION AND COVERAGE

This book is traditional in its coverage and organization. To the extent that we have made a trade-off, it is to cover traditional topics more thoroughly, as opposed to adding a broad range of additional topics that might not easily fit into a one-quarter or one-semester microeconomics course. Thus, an instructor teaching a one-semester microeconomics course could use all or nearly all of the chapters in the book, and an instructor teaching a one-quarter microeconomics or managerial economics course could use more than two-thirds of the chapters. The following chart shows how the book is organized.

Introduction to Microeconomics	Consumer Theory	Production and Cost Theory	Perfect Competition	Market Power	Imperfect Competition and Strategic Behavior	Special Topics
1 *Analyzing Economic Problems* Overview and introduction to constrained optimization, equilibrium analysis, and comparative statics analyisis	**3** *Consumer Preferences and the Concept of Utility* Introduction to consumer choice	**6** *Inputs and Production Functions* Production Functions, marginal and average product, and returns to scale	**9** *Perfectly Competitive Markets* Profit-maximizing output choice by a price-taking firm and prices in short-run v. long-run equilibrium	**11** *Monopoly and Monopsony* Theories of monopoly and monopsony price setting	**13** *Market Structure and Competition* Price determination in imperfectly competitive markets	**15** *Decision Making Under Uncertainty* Risk, uncertainty and information, including a utility-theoretic approach to uncertainty and decision-free analysis
2 *Supply and Demand Analysis* Introduction to demand curves, supply curves, market equilibrium, and elasticity	**4** *Consumer Choice* Budget Lines, utility maximization, and analysis of revealed preference	**7** *Costs and Cost Minimization* Concept of cost, input choice and cost minimization	**10** *Competitive Markets: Applications* Using the competitive market model to analyze public policy interventions	**12** *Capturing Surplus* Price discrimination	**14** *Game Theory and Strategic Behavior* Simultaneous-move games and sequential move games	**16** *General Equilibrium Theory* Overview of general equilibrium theory and economic efficiency
	5 *The Theory of Demand* Comparative statics of consumer choice and consumer surplus	**8** *Cost Curves* Construction of total, average, and marginal cost curves				**17** *Externalities and Public Goods* Market externalities, the Coase Theorem, and economic efficiency

ALTERNATIVE COURSE DESIGNS

In writing this book, we have tried to serve the need of instructors teaching microeconomics in a variety of different formats and time frames.

- **One-quarter course (10 weeks):**   An instructor teaching a one-quarter undergraduate microeconomics course that fully covers all of the traditional topics (including consumer theory and production and cost theory) would probably assign Chapters 1–11). If the instructor prefers to de-emphasize consumer theory or production theory, he or she might also be able to cover Chapters 13 and 14.

• **One-semester course (15 weeks):** In a one-semester undergraduate course, an instructor should be able to cover Chapters 1–15. If the course must in-clude general equilibrium theory, public goods, and externalities, then Chapter 15 could be dropped and the instructor could assign Chapters 1–14, 16, and 17.

• **Two-quarter course (20 weeks):** For a two-quarter sequence (the structure we have at Northwestern), the first quarter could cover Chapters 1–11, and the second quarter could pick up where the first quarter left off and cover Chapters 12–17.

• **MBA-level managerial economics course (10 weeks or 15 weeks):** For a one-quarter course, the instructor would probably want to skip the chapters on consumer theory, production functions, and cost minimization (Chapter 3–6 and the second half of Chapter 7) and cover Chapters 1–2, the first half of Chapter 7—economic concepts of cost—Chapter 8, and Chapters 9–14. Extending such a course to a full semester would allow the instructor to include the material on production and cost minimization as well as Chapter 15.

SUPPLEMENTARY RESOURCES

Available resources for students and instructors include a Study Guide, Instructor's Manual, Solutions Manual, and Test Bank. Kenneth Brown of the University of Northern Iowa prepared the Solutions Manual and co-wrote the Test Bank with Lisa Jepson, also of the University of Northern Iowa. Kate Rockett of the University of Essex, England, prepared both the Study Guide and the Instructor's Manual.

A robust Web site with support for students and instructors is available for use with the text. This Web site provides *Wall Street Journal Interactive Edition* articles related to the topics in the text, Web links to companies cited in the text, and electronic versions of the instructor's print supplements (Instructor's Manual, Test Bank, Solutions Manual) within a password-protected environment. The Web site will also provide on-line self-test tutorials and Excel templates for students to use as they work through the text problems and prepare for exams.

ACKNOWLEDGMENTS

While the book was in development, we benefited enormously from the guidance of a host of individuals both from within John Wiley & Sons and outside. We especially appreciate the vision and guidance of Joe Heider, executive publisher, and Susan Elbe, publisher, at Wiley. Their commitment to this book has remained strong from the beginning. We are grateful for their support.

Also at Wiley, Marissa Ryan, our acquiring editor during the project's formative stages, provided much needed encouragement and enthusiasm for the project. Leslie Kraham filled this role for the year prior to publication, firmly guiding the project down its "last mile." Developmental editors Judith Kromm, Johnna Barto, and Beth Bortz provided editorial support and encouraged us to stick to deadlines. Associate editor Cindy Rhoads coordinated the preparation of the

Instructor's Manual and the Study Guide for the book, and Suzanne Ingrao handled the production of the book. Others at Wiley who contributed to this project include Barbara Heaney, Charity Robey, Jeanine Furino, Anna Melhorn, Kevin Murphy, Hilary Newman, Valerie Vargas, and Sara Wight. Finally, we would like to acknowledge Whitney Blake, who encouraged us to undertake this project, and we appreciate her encouragement and her confidence in us.

The clarity of the presentation and organization in this book owes a great deal to the efforts of Gerald Lombardi, Becky Kohn, Melissa Hayes, and Nick Kreisle. Both Gerald and Becky painstakingly went through our manuscript and provided editorial and substantive advice. Melissa, a Northwestern undergraduate (and, now, alumna), made extensive suggestions for making the book readable from a student's point of view. She also carefully checked figures and equations to make sure that they agreed with what was written in the text. Nick, a Ph.D. candidate at Northwestern, has worked with our manuscript as a teaching assistant and as an instructor in his own course in intermediate microeconomics. We have greatly benefitted from his thoughtful comments, and we understand why his students attest to his unusual gift in the classroom.

The development of this book was aided by colleagues who participated in focus groups or reviewed early drafts of the manuscript. Our thanks go to all of the following individuals. The names of individuals who reviewed more than one draft or who both reviewed the manuscript and participated in a focus group are starred.

Anas Alhajji
Colorado School of Mines

Scott Atkinson
University of Georgia

Doris Bennett
Jacksonville State University

Arlo Biere
Kansas State University

Douglas Blair
Rutgers University

Michael Bognanno
Temple University

Stephen Bronars
University of Texas, Austin

Douglas Brown
Georgetown University

Kenneth Brown
University of Northern Iowa*

Don Bumpass
Sam Houston State University

Colin Campbell
Ohio State University

Corey S. Capps
University of Illinois

Manual Carvajal
Florida International University

Kousik Chakrabarti
University of Michigan, Ann Arbor

Ken Chapman
California State University

Yongmin Chen
University of Colorado–Boulder

Kui Kwon (Alice) Chong
University of North Carolina–Charlotte

Peter Coughlin
University of Maryland

Steven Craig
University of Houston

Mike Curme
Miami University

Rudolph Daniels
Florida A & M University

James Dearden
Lehigh University

Stacey Deirgerconlin
Syracuse University

John Edwards
Tulane University

Matthew Eichner
Johns Hopkins University*

Ronel Elul
Brown University

Maxim Engers
University of Virginia*

Raymond Fisman
Columbia University*

Eric Friedman
Rutgers University

Susan Gensemer
Syracuse University

Steven Marc Goldman
University of California, Berkeley*

Barnali Gupta
Miami University

Claire Hammond
Wake Forest University

Shawkat Hammoudeh
Drexel University

Lyn Holmes
Temple University

Michael Jerison
SUNY–Albany

Jiandong Ju
University of Oklahoma

David Kamerschen
University of Georgia

Donald Keenan
University of Georgia

Mark Killingsworth
Rutgers University

Philip King
San Francisco State University*

Charles Lamberton
South Dakota State University

Donald Lien
University of Kansas*

Leonard Loyd
University of Houston

Mark Machina
University of California at San Diego

Mukul K. Manjumdar
Cornell University*

Gilbert Mathis
Murray State University

Michael Mckee
University of New Mexico

Claudio Mezzetti
University of North Carolina*

Peter Morgan
University of Michigan

John Moroney
Texas A & M

Wilhelm Neuefeind
Washington University

Peter Norman
University of Wisconsin, Madison

Mudziviri Nziramasanga
Washington State University

Iyatokunbo Okediji
University of Oklahoma

Ken Parzych
Eastern Connecticut State University

Donald Pursell
University of Nebraska–Lincoln

Michael Raith
University of Chicago

Sunder Ramaswamy
Middlebury College

Jeanne Ringel
Louisiana State University*

Robert Rosenman
Washington State University

Santanu Roy
Florida International University

Jolyne Sanjak
SUNY–Albany

David Schmidt
Indiana University

Mark Schupack
Brown University

Richard Sexton
University of California, Davis

Jason Shachat
University of California, San Diego

Maxwell Stinchcombe
University of Texas, Austin

Beck Taylor
Baylor University*

Curtis Taylor
Texas A & M University

Thomas TenHoeve
Iowa State University

John Thompson
Louisiana State University

Paul Thistle
Western Michigan University*

Guogiang Tian
Texas A & M University

Theofanis Tsoulouhas
North Carolina State University*

Geoffrey Turnbull
Louisiana State University

Mich Tvede
University of Pennsylvania

Mark Walbert
Illinois University

Mark Walker
University of Arizona

Larry Westphal
Swarthmore College

Kealoha Widdows
Wabash College

Chiounan Yeh
Alabama State University

In addition, we would like especially to thank Eric Schultz, who offered suggestions for the book while at Williams College and then used a preliminary edition in his class at Northwestern in the Fall of 2000. Ken Brown at the University of Northern Iowa and Matthew Eichner at Johns Hopkins University also tested the manuscript in their classes prior to publication.

Finally, we owe a large debt of gratitude to several hundred students in Ron Braeutigam's sections of Economics 310–1 at Northwestern between 1999 and 2001. They read drafts of Chapters 1–11 and helped us eliminate some of the rough edges. Their experience of learning from the book helped make our chapters clearer and more accessible.

David Besanko
Evanston, Illinois

Ronald R. Braeutigam
Evanston, Illinois

Contents

1

Analyzing Economic Problems

In the last few years, Internet companies have raised millions of dollars from investors. Companies such as Amazon.com, eBay, etrade, and Soma.com did not exist a decade ago. Indeed, few of them existed even five years ago. The Internet is changing the way the world will do business. To keep up, consumers may have to change the way they shop, and businesses might have to change the way they set prices and sell their products. Some Internet startups took Investor money, poured it into high-tech equipment and high-profile advertising (e.g., the Super Bowl) and captured a corner of the Internet market. Others followed a similar plan—and folded when customer demand did not match expectations and the companies ran out of money.

Let's take a closer look at some qualified Internet success stories:

- The Internet auction company eBay does what traditional markets have done for centuries. It brings together sellers of goods with buyers of goods. eBay facilitates the trading of goods ranging from Beanie Babies to baseball cards to high-performance automobiles.
- The Internet book seller Amazon.com faces many of the same problems as traditional business firms. It must figure out how to set prices for the books it sells, especially in light of pressure from competitors such as Barnesandnoble.com. And it must figure out the appropriate mix of resources to employ, just as traditional business firms must do. Among other things, it must decide how many workers to hire to maintain its Web site and how much warehouse space to lease to store the books it ships to consumers. Amazon.com hopes to make a profit in the next couple of years.
  - In 1999, Soma.com, PlanetRx.com, and Drugstore.com launched online drugstores, selling prescription and nonprescription drugs and health and beauty supplies. Selling drugstore items over the Internet had the potential to be quite profitable, and the convenience of buying such items online was expected to send hordes of eager customers to the Web sites. Investors leapt at the companies' stock. But in December 2000, Soma.com had already been swallowed up by CVS and PlanetRx was hanging on by a thread, having fallen from $154 a share to less than $1 a share. Drugstore.com looked to be an e-tail survivor, however, competing with bricks-and-mortar stores and their own Web sites. To pull it off, Drugstore.com had teamed up with Rite Aid, crafted deals with insurance companies, and formed a strategic alliance with Amazon.com, adding Amazon CEO Jeffrey Bezos to its board of directors.

Microeconomic themes are prominent parts of the stories we have just described. The success of eBay illustrates just how important markets and prices are. eBay makes money because, in effect, it creates markets and allows prices to "clear" these markets. The ongoing challenges facing Amazon.com illustrate the importance of understanding the constraints that business firms face. Amazon makes decisions on the organization of its operations and on prices, recognizing that it does not fully control its own destiny. Its executives would undoubtedly love to be able to double sales every month (as Amazon did in 1997 and 1998), while maintaining a big margin between its prices and costs. But wishing these things were so does not make them so. Amazon is constrained by market demand, by the actions of competitors, and by the limitations imposed by what is feasible technologically. The saga of Drugstore.com in the online prescription drug market illustrates the power of market forces in keeping companies from capturing these profits. The competitive dynamic being played out in online retailing has occurred in numerous markets throughout history and around the world: When profit opportunities are freely available to all firms, the profits might not last, or ever be realized in the first place! This is one of the most important lessons in microeconomics.

Microeconomics can help you understand the world around you. This chapter will tell you how, first by explaining what microeconomics is and second by discussing what makes microeconomics a distinctive field of study. Nearly all microeconomic studies, whether about competition on the Internet, the purchasing behavior of individual households, or the study of social phenomena such as crime and marriage (yes, economists have studied these), rely on three powerful analytical tools that we will discuss later in this chapter—constrained optimization, equilibrium analysis, and comparative statics analysis. ■

1.1 WHY STUDY MICROECONOMICS?

Economics is the science that deals with the allocation of limited resources to satisfy unlimited human wants. Think of human wants as being all the goods and services that individuals desire, including food, clothing, shelter, and anything else that enhances the quality of life. Since we can always think of ways to improve our well-being with more or better goods and services, our wants are unlimited. However, to produce goods and services, we need resources, including labor, managerial talent, capital, and raw materials. Resources are said to be *scarce* because their supply is limited. The scarcity of resources means that we are constrained in the choices we can make about the goods and services we produce, and thus also about which human wants we will ultimately satisfy. That is why economics is often described as *the science of constrained choice*.

Broadly speaking, economics is composed of two branches, microeconomics and macroeconomics. The prefix *micro* is derived from the Greek word *mikros*, which means "small." Microeconomics therefore studies the economic behavior of individual economic decision makers, such as a consumer, a worker, a firm, or a manager. It also analyzes the behavior of individual households, industries, markets, labor unions, or trade associations. By contrast, the prefix *macro* comes from the Greek word *makros*, which means "large." Macroeconomics thus analyzes how an entire national economy performs. A course in macroeconomics would examine aggregate levels of income and employment, the levels of interest rates and prices, the rate of inflation, and the nature of business cycles in a national economy.

Constrained choice is important in both macroeconomics and microeconomics. For example, in macroeconomics we would see that a society with full employment could produce more goods for national defense, but it would then have to produce fewer civilian goods. It might use more of its depletable natural resources, such as natural gas, coal, and oil, to manufacture goods today, in which case it would conserve less of these resources for the future. In a microeconomic setting, a consumer might decide to allocate more time to work, but would then have less time available for leisure activities. The consumer could spend more income on consumption today, but would then save less for tomorrow. A manager might decide to spend more of a firm's resources on advertising, but this might leave less available for research and development.

The trade-offs illustrated in these examples of economic decisions lead us to one of the most important concepts in economic analysis, **opportunity cost.** Suppose that a decision maker is considering a choice among three alternatives (call them A, B, and C), and that any of them can be produced using the same resources. Suppose further that the decision maker attaches the highest value to alternative A, the next highest value to alternative B, and the lowest value to alternative C. By choosing alternative A, the decision maker must give up the opportunity to choose B. (C would never be chosen since it is even less attractive than B.) Thus, the opportunity cost of choosing A is the value of B. In other words, the opportunity cost of a chosen alternative is the value of the most attractive alternative that is not chosen. The notion of opportunity cost can be illustrated with two simple examples. Suppose you want to go to a concert on Saturday night. If you go, you must purchase a ticket, and take a taxi to and from the concert, all of which will cost you $200. If you do not go, you could either tutor a fellow student and earn $30 or work at a pizza parlor and earn $50. Your opportunity cost of going to the concert will be the amount of money you forgo if you choose to go: In this case, that would be expenses of $200 *and* potential earnings of $50. Therefore, your opportunity cost of attending the concert is $250. (Note that the $30 you could earn if you tutor is irrelevant because that option pays less than working at the pizza parlor.)

In the second example, you have just won a free ticket to the Super Bowl. You must now decide whether to go to the game or sell the ticket. Suppose the best offer you receive for the ticket is $400. If you go to the game, you will forgo the opportunity to sell the ticket and will also incur costs of $2,500 (these costs include airfare, lodging, and taxis between the hotel and the stadium). Thus, the opportunity cost of using the ticket to go to the game will be $2,900 (the $400 plus the $2,500 you could save by not going).

Every society has its own way of deciding how to allocate its scarce resources. Some resort to a highly centralized organization. For example, during the Cold War, governmental bureaucracies heavily controlled the allocation of resources in the economies of Eastern Europe and the Soviet Union. Other countries, such as those in North America or Western Europe, have historically relied on a mostly decentralized market system to allocate resources.

Regardless of its market system, every society must answer these questions about how to utilize its scarce resources:

- What goods and services will be produced, and in what quantities?
- Who will produce the goods and services, and how?
- Who will receive the goods and services?

Microeconomic analysis attempts to answer these questions by studying the behavior of individual economic units. By answering questions about how consumers and producers behave, microeconomics helps us understand the pieces that collectively make up a model of an entire economy. Microeconomic analysis also provides the foundation for examining the role of the government in the economy and the effects of government actions. Microeconomic tools are commonly used to address some of the most important issues in contemporary society. These include (but are not limited to) pollution, rent controls, minimum wage laws, import tariffs and quotas, taxes and subsidies, food stamps, government housing and educational assistance programs, government health care programs, workplace safety, and the regulation of private firms.

1.2
KEY
ANALYTICAL
TOOLS IN
MICROECO-
NOMICS

To study real phenomena in a world that is exceedingly complex, economists construct and analyze economic models, or formal descriptions, of the problems they are addressing. An economic model is like a roadmap. A roadmap takes a complex physical reality (terrain, roads, houses, stores, parking lots, alley ways, and other features) and strips it down to bare essentials: major streets and highways. The roadmap is an abstract model that serves a particular purpose—it shows us where we are and how we can get where we want to go. To provide a clear representation of reality, it "ignores" or "abstracts from" much of the rich detail (the location of beautiful elm trees or stately homes, for example) that makes an individual town unique and charming.

Economic models operate in much the same way. For example, to understand how a drought in Colombia might affect the price of coffee in the United States, an economist might employ a model that ignores much of the rich detail of the industry, including some aspects of its history or the personalities of the people who work in the fields. These details might make an interesting article in *Business Week*, but they do not help us understand the fundamental forces that determine the price of coffee.

Any model, whether it is used to study chemistry, physics, or economics, must specify what variables will be taken as given in the analysis, and what variables are to be determined by the model. This brings us to the important distinction between *exogenous* and *endogenous* variables. An **exogenous variable** is one whose value is taken as given in a model. In other words the value of an exogenous variable is determined by some process outside the model being examined. An **endogenous variable** is a variable whose value is determined within the model being studied.

To understand the distinction, suppose you want to build a model to predict how far a ball will fall after it is released from the top of a tall building. You might assume that certain variables, such as the force of gravity and the density of the air through which the ball must pass, are taken as given (exogenous) in your analysis. *Given* the exogenous variables, your model will describe the relationship between the distance the ball will drop and the time elapsed after it is released. The distance and time predicted by your model are endogenous variables.

Nearly all microeconomic models rely on just three key analytical tools. We believe this makes microeconomics unique as a field of study. No matter what the specific issue is—coffee prices in the United States, or decision making by firms on the Internet—microeconomics uses the same three analytical tools:

- Constrained optimization
- Equilibrium analysis
- Comparative statics

Throughout this book, we will apply these tools to microeconomic problems. This section introduces these three tools and provides examples of how they can be employed. Do not expect to master these tools just by reading this chapter. Rather, you should learn to recognize them when we apply them in later chapters.

CONSTRAINED OPTIMIZATION

As we noted earlier, economics is the science of constrained choice. The tool of **constrained optimization** is used when a decision maker seeks to make the best (optimal) choice, taking into account any possible limitations or restrictions on the choices. We can therefore think about constrained optimization problems as having two parts, an **objective function** and a set of **constraints.** An objective function is the relationship that the decision maker seeks to "optimize," that is, either maximize or minimize. For example, a consumer may want to purchase goods to maximize her satisfaction. In this case, the objective function would be the relationship that describes how satisfied she will be when she purchases any particular set of goods. Similarly, a producer may want to plan production activities to minimize the costs of manufacturing its product. Here the objective function would show how the total costs of production depend on the various production plans available to the firm.

Decision makers must also recognize that there are often restrictions on the choices they may actually select. These restrictions reflect the fact that resources are scarce, or that for some other reason only certain choices can be made. The constraints in a constrained optimization problem represent restrictions or limits that are imposed on the decision maker.

Examples of Constrained Optimization

To make sure that the difference between an objective function and a constraint is clear, let's consider three examples. See if you can identify the objective function and the constraints in each example. (Do not attempt to solve the problems. We will present techniques for solving them in later chapters. At this stage the important point is simply to understand examples of constrained optimization problems.)

LEARNING-BY-DOING EXERCISE 1.1

Constrained Optimization: The Farmer's Fence

Problem   Suppose a farmer plans to build a rectangular fence as a pen for his sheep. He has F feet of fence and cannot afford to purchase more. However, he can choose the dimensions of the pen, which will have a length of L feet and a width of W feet. He wants to choose the dimensions L and W that will maximize the area of the pen. He must also make sure that the total amount of fencing he uses (the perimeter of the pen) does not exceed F feet.

(a) What is the objective function for this problem?
(b) What is the constraint?
(c) Which of the variables in this model (L, W, and F) are exogenous? Which are endogenous? Explain.

Discussion

(a) The objective function is the relationship that the farmer is trying to maximize—in this case, the area LW. In other words, the farmer will choose L and W to maximize the objective function LW.

(b) The constraint will describe the restriction imposed on the farmer. We are told that the farmer has only F feet of fence available for the rectangular pen. The constraint will describe the restriction that the perimeter of the pen $2L + 2W$ must not exceed the amount of fence available, F. Therefore, the constraint can be written as $2L + 2W \leq F$.

(c) The farmer is given only F feet of fence to work with. Thus, the perimeter F is an exogenous variable, since it is taken as given in the analysis. The endogenous variables are L and W, since their values can be chosen by the farmer (determined within the model).

By convention, economists usually state a constrained optimization problem like the one facing the farmer is usually stated in the following way:

$$\max_{(L,W)} LW$$

$$\text{subject to: } 2L + 2W \leq F$$

The first line identifies the objective function, the area LW, and tells whether it is to be maximized or minimized. (If the objective function were to be minimized, then the "max" would instead be a "min"). Underneath the "max" is a list of the endogenous variables that the decision maker (the farmer) controls; in this example (L,W) indicates that the farmer can choose the length and the width of the pen.

The second line represents the constraint on the perimeter. It tells us that the farmer can choose L and W as long as ("subject to" the constraint that) the perimeter does not exceed F. Taken together, the two lines of the problem tell us that the farmer will choose L and W to maximize the area, but those choices are subject to the constraint on the amount of fence available.

LEARNING-BY-DOING EXERCISE 1.2

Constrained Optimization: Consumer Choice

We now illustrate the concept of constrained optimization with a famous problem in microeconomics, consumer choice. (Consumer choice will be analyzed in depth in Chapters 3, 4, and 5.)

Problem Suppose a consumer purchases only two types of goods, food and clothing. The consumer has to decide how many units of each good to purchase each month. Let F be the number of units of food that she purchases each month, and C the number of units of clothing. She chooses to maximize her satisfaction of the two goods. Suppose the consumer's level of satisfaction when she purchases F units of food and C units of clothing is measured by the product FC, but she can purchase only limited amounts of goods per month because she must live within her budget. Goods cost money and the consumer has a limited income. To keep the example simple, suppose the consumer has a fixed monthly income I, and she must not spend more than I during the month. Each unit of food costs P_F and each unit of clothing costs P_C.

(a) What is the objective function for this problem?
(b) What is the constraint?
(c) Which variables (P_F, F, P_C, C, and I) are exogenous? Which are endogenous? Explain.
(d) Write a statement of the constrained optimization problem.

Discussion

(a) The objective function is the relationship that the consumer seeks to maximize. In this example she will choose the amount of food and clothing to maximize her satisfaction, measured by FC. Thus, the objective function is FC.

(b) The constraint represents the amounts of food and clothing that she may choose while living within her income. If she buys F units of food at a price of P_F per unit, her total expenditure on food will be $(P_F)(F)$. If she buys C units of clothing at a price of P_C per unit, her total expenditure on clothing will be $(P_C)(C)$. Therefore, her total expenditure will be $(P_F)(F) + (P_C)(C)$. Since her total expenditure must not exceed her total income I, the constraint is $(P_F)(F) + (P_C)(C) \leq I$.

(c) The exogenous variables are the ones the consumer takes as given when she makes her purchasing decisions. Since her monthly income is fixed, I is exogenous. The prices of food P_F and clothing P_C are also exogenous, since she cannot control the amount she has to pay for these items. The consumer's only choices are the amounts of food and clothing to buy; hence, F and C are the endogenous variables.

(d) The statement of the constrained optimization problem is

$$\max_{(F,C)} FC$$

$$\text{subject to } (P_F)(F) + (P_C)(C) \leq I$$

The first line shows that the consumer wants to maximize FC, and that she can choose F and C. The second line describes the constraint: Total expenditure cannot exceed total income.

LEARNING-BY-DOING EXERCISE 1.3

Constrained Optimization: Cost Minimization

Another well-known problem in microeconomics describes how a producer tries to minimize the cost of production. (Producer choice and cost minimization will be analyzed in depth in Chapters 6, 7, and 8.)

Problem A firm produces cellular telephone service using equipment and labor. When it uses E units of equipment and hires L units of labor, it can provide up to Q units of telephone service. The relationship between Q, E, and L is as follows: $Q = \sqrt{EL}$. The firm must always pay P_E for each unit of machinery it uses. It must also always pay P_L for each unit of labor it employs. Suppose the production manager is told to produce $Q = 200$ units of telephone service, and that she wants to choose E and L to minimize costs while achieving that production target.

(a) What is the objective function for this problem?
(b) What is the constraint?
(c) Which of the variables (Q, P_E, E, P_L, and L) are exogenous? Which are endogenous? Explain.
(d) Write a statement of the constrained optimization problem.

Discussion

(a) The objective function is what the firm wants to minimize. In this example, the manager wants to minimize the cost of production. The expenditure on equipment will be $(P_E)(E)$, the price of a unit of machinery times the amount of machinery employed. Similarly, the expenditure on labor will be $(P_L)(L)$. The objective function in this problem is total cost (total expenditure), that is $(P_E)(E) + (P_L)(L)$.
(b) The manager must produce $Q = 200$. She must therefore use enough equipment and labor to reach that target. Since she seeks to minimize costs, she will not employ any more equipment and labor than is necessary to produce the required output. She will therefore choose E and L so that $\sqrt{EL} = 200$.
(c) The exogenous variables are the ones the production manager takes as given when she makes her decisions. She cannot control the *prices* of equipment and labor. Therefore P_E and P_L are exogenous. The production target is also beyond her control, and Q is therefore exogenous. The production manager's only choices are the amounts of equipment and labor to hire. Therefore, E and L are endogenous.
(d) The statement of the constrained optimization problem is

$$\min_{(E,L)} (P_E)(E) + (P_L)(L)$$
$$\text{subject to } \sqrt{EL} = 200$$

The first line shows that the manager can choose E and L, and that she wants to minimize expenditure. The second line describes the constraint; she must choose enough equipment and labor to be able to produce 200 units of telephone service.

***E*XAMPLE 1.1**   *The Generation of Electricity*

Examples of constrained optimization are all around us. Electric power companies, such as Commonwealth Edison, typically own and operate plants that produce electricity. A company must decide how much electricity to produce at each plant to meet the needs of its customers.

The constrained optimization problem for a power company can be complex:

- The company needs to generate enough power to ensure that its customers receive service during each hour of the day.

- To make good production decisions, the company must forecast the demand for electricity. The demand for electricity varies from one hour to another during the day, as well as across seasons of the year. For example, in the summer the highest demand may occur in the afternoon when customers use air conditioners to cool offices and homes. The demand for power may decline considerably in the evening as the temperature falls.

- Some of the company's plants are relatively expensive to operate. For example, it is more expensive to produce electricity by burning oil than by burning natural gas. Plants using nuclear fuel are even less costly to run. If the company wants to produce power at the lowest possible cost, its objective function must take these cost differences into account.

- If the company expects the demand for electricity to be low for a long period of time, it may want to shut down production at some of its plants. But there are substantial costs to starting up and shutting down plants. Thus, if the company expects the demand for electricity to be low for only a short time (for example, a few hours), it might not want to shut down a plant that will be needed again when the demand goes up.

- The company must also take into account the costs of transmitting power from the generators to its customers.

- There is a spot market for electricity during each hour of the day. A company may buy or sell power from other electric power companies. If the company can purchase electricity at a low enough price, it may be able to lower the costs of service by buying some electricity from other producers, instead of generating all of the required electricity itself. If it can sell electricity at a high enough price, the company may find it profitable to generate more electricity than its customers need. It can then sell the extra electricity to other power companies.

Electric power companies typically make production decisions on an hourly basis—that's 8760 (365 days times 24 hours per day) production decisions a year![1]   ∎

---

[1]For a good discussion of the structure of electricity markets, see P. Joskow and R. Schmalensee. *Markets for Power: An Analysis of Electric Utility Deregulation* (Cambridge, Mass: MIT Press, 1983).

Solving Constrained Optimization Problems: The Importance of Marginal Reasoning

Constrained optimization analysis can reveal that the "obvious" answers to economic questions may not always be correct. We will illustrate this point by showing how constrained optimization problems can be solved using marginal reasoning.

Imagine that you are the product manager for a small beer company that produces a high-quality microbrewed ale. You have a $1 million media advertising budget for the next year, and you have to allocate it between local television and radio spots. Although radio spots are cheaper, television spots reach a far wider audience. Television spots are also more persuasive and thus on average stimulate more new sales.

To understand the impact of a given amount of money spent on radio and TV advertisements, you have studied the market. Your research findings, presented in Table 1.1, estimate the additional new sales of your beer when a given amount of money is spent on TV advertising and on radio advertising. For example, if you spent $1 million on TV advertising, you would generate 25,000 barrels of new beer sales per year. By contrast, if you spent $1 million on radio advertising, you would generate 5,000 barrels of new sales per year. Of course, you could also split your advertising budget between the two media, and Table 1.1 tells you the impact of that decision, too. For example, if you spent $400,000 on TV and $600,000 on radio, you would generate 16,000 barrels of new sales from the TV ads and 4,200 barrels in new sales from the radio ads, for a total of 16,000 + 4,200 = 20,200 barrels of beer overall.

In light of the information in Table 1.1, how would you allocate your advertising budget if your objective is to maximize the new sales of beer?

TABLE 1.1
New Beer Sales Resulting from Amounts Spent on TV and Radio Advertising

Total Spent	New Beer Sales Generated (in barrels per year)	
	TV	Radio
$ 0	0	0
$ 100,000	4,750	950
$ 200,000	9,000	1,800
$ 300,000	12,750	2,550
$ 400,000	16,000	3,200
$ 500,000	18,750	3,750
$ 600,000	21,000	4,200
$ 700,000	22,750	4,550
$ 800,000	24,000	4,800
$ 900,000	24,750	4,950
$ 1,000,000	25,000	5,000

This is a constrained optimization problem. You want to allocate spending on TV and radio in a way that maximizes an objective (new sales of beer) subject to the constraint that the total amount spent on TV and radio must not exceed your $1 million advertising budget. Using notation similar to that introduced in the previous section, if $B(T,R)$ represents the amount of new beer sales when you spend T dollars on television advertising and R dollars on radio advertising, your constrained optimization problem is

$$\max_{(T,R)} B(T,R)$$

subject to: $T + R = 1,000,000$

A quick reading of Table 1.1 might suggest an "obvious" answer to this problem: Allocate your entire $1 million budget to TV spots and spend nothing on radio. After all, as Table 1.1 suggests, a given amount of money spent on TV always generates more new sales than the same amount of money spent on radio advertising. (In fact, a given amount of TV advertising is five times as productive in generating new sales as is the same amount of radio advertising.) However, this answer is incorrect. And the reason that it is incorrect illustrates the power and importance of constrained optimization analysis in economics.

Suppose you contemplate spending your entire budget on TV ads. Under that plan, you would expect to get 25,000 barrels of new sales. But consider, now, what would happen if you spent only $900,000 on TV ads and $100,000 on radio ads. From Table 1.1, we see that your TV ads would then generate 24,750 barrels of new beer sales, and your radio ads would generate 950 barrels of new beer sales. Thus, under this plan your $1 million budget generates new beer sales equal to 25,700 barrels. This is 700 barrels higher than before. In fact, you can do even better. By spending $800,000 on TV and $200,000 on radio, you can generate 25,800 barrels of new beer sales. Even though Table 1.1 seems to imply that radio ads are far less powerful than TV ads, it makes sense in light of your objective to split your budget between radio and TV advertising.

This example highlights a theme that comes up repeatedly in microeconomics: The solution to any constrained optimization problem depends on the *marginal* impact of the decision variables on the value of the objective function. The marginal impact of money spent on TV advertising is how much new beer sales go up for every *additional* dollar spent on TV advertising. The marginal impact of money spent on radio advertising is the rate at which new beer sales go up for every *additional* dollar spent on radio advertising. You want to allocate some money to radio advertising even though TV advertising seems to be much more productive because once you have allocated $800,000 of the $1,000,000 budget to TV, the *marginal* impact of an additional $100,000 spent on TV advertising is less than the *marginal* impact of an additional $100,000 spent on radio advertising. Why? Because the rate at which new beer sales increase when we allocate that next $100,000 to TV advertising is (24,750 − 24,000)/100,000, or 0.0075 barrels per additional dollar spent on TV advertising. But the rate at which new beer sales increase when we allocate the next $100,000 to radio advertising is (24,000 + 950 − 24,000)/100,000 or 0.0095 barrels per additional dollar spent on radio advertising. Thus, the marginal impact of radio advertising exceeds the marginal impact of TV advertising. In light of that, we now want to allocate this additional $100,000 of our advertising budget to radio, rather than TV. (In fact, as we already saw, you would want to go even further and allocate the last $200,000 in your budget to radio spots.)

In our advertising story, marginal reasoning leads to a not-so-obvious conclusion that might make you uncomfortable, or perhaps even skeptical. That's fine—that's how students often react when they first encounter marginal reasoning in microeconomics classes. But whether you realize it or not, we all use marginal reasoning in our daily lives. For example, even though pizza may be your favorite food and you may prefer to eat it rather than vegetables like carrots and broccoli, you probably don't spend all of your weekly food budget on pizza. Why not? The reason must be that at some point (perhaps after having eaten pizza for dinner Monday through Saturday nights), the additional pleasure or satisfaction that you get from spending another $10 of your food budget on a pizza is less than what you would get from spending that $10 of your budget on something else. Although you may not realize it, this is marginal reasoning in a constrained optimization problem.

The term *marginal* in microeconomics tells us how a *dependent variable* changes as a result of adding one unit of an *independent variable*. The terms *independent variable* and *dependent variable* may be new to you. To understand them, think of a relationship between two variables, such as between production volume (what economists call *output*) and the total cost of manufacturing a product. We would expect that as a firm produces more, its total cost goes up. In this example, we would classify total cost as the dependent variable because its value depends on the volume of production, which we refer to as the independent variable.

Marginal cost measures the *incremental impact* of the last unit of the independent variable (output) on the dependent variable (total cost). For example, if it costs an extra $5 to increase production by one unit, the marginal cost will be $5. Equivalently, marginal cost can be thought of as a *rate of change* of the dependent variable (again, total cost) as the independent variable (output) changes. If the marginal cost is $5, total cost is rising at a rate of $5 when a new unit of output is produced.

We will use marginal measures throughout this book. For example, we will use it in Chapters 4 and 5 to find the solution to the consumer choice problem described in Learning-By-Doing Exercise 1.2, and we will use it again in Chapters 7 and 8 to solve the cost minimization problem described in Learning-By-Doing Exercise 1.3.

EQUILIBRIUM ANALYSIS

A second important tool in microeconomics is the analysis of *equilibrium*, a concept found in many branches of science. An **equilibrium** in a system is a state or condition that will continue indefinitely as long as exogenous factors remain unchanged—that is, as long as no outside factor upsets the equilibrium. To illustrate an equilibrium, imagine a physical system consisting of a ball in a cup, as is depicted in Figure 1.1. Here the force of gravity pulls the ball downward toward the bottom of the cup. A ball initially held at point *A* will not remain at point *A* when the ball is released. Rather, it will rock back and forth until it settles at point *B*. Thus, the system is not in equilibrium when the ball is released at *A* because the ball will not remain there. It would be in equilibrium if the ball were released

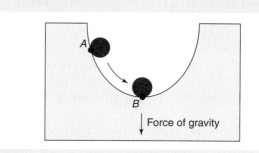

FIGURE 1.1   Equilibrium with a Ball and Cup
This physical system is in equilibrium when the ball is resting at point *B* at the bottom of the cup. The ball could remain there indefinitely. The system will not be in equilibrium when the ball is at point *A* because the force of gravity would pull the ball toward *B*.

at *B*. The system will remain in equilibrium when the ball is at *B* until some exogenous factor changes; for example, if someone were to tip the cup, the ball would move from *B* to another point.

You may have encountered the notion of an equilibrium in competitive markets early in an introductory course in economics. In Chapter 2 we will provide a more detailed treatment of markets, supply, and demand. But for now let's briefly review how the analysis of supply and demand can illustrate the concept of equilibrium in a market.

Consider the worldwide market for unprocessed coffee beans. Suppose the demand and supply curves for coffee beans are as depicted in Figure 1.2. The demand curve tells us what quantity of coffee beans (Q) would be purchased in that market at any given price. Think of a demand curve as representing the answer to a set of "what if" questions. For example, what quantity of coffee beans would be demanded if the price is $2.50 per pound? The demand curve in Figure 1.2 tells us that Q_2 pounds would be purchased if the price of coffee beans were $2.50 per pound. The demand curve also shows us that Q_4 pounds would be purchased if the price were $1.50 per pound. The negative or downward slope of the demand curve shows that higher prices tend to reduce the consumption of coffee.

When we draw a demand curve for coffee beans, we are assuming that variables other than the price and quantity of coffee beans are held constant. For example, the demand curve in Figure 1.2 is drawn for a particular level of income in the market and for given prices of other goods, such as the prices of tea, cookies, and doughnuts. Changes in these variables might shift the demand curve for coffee to the left (reduce the amount demanded at any price) or to the right (increase the amount demanded at any price). For example, if many people like to drink coffee while they eat doughnuts, then a lower price for doughnuts might stimulate coffee consumption, leading to a rightward shift (an increase in quantity demanded at any price) in the demand curve for coffee. How might a lower price of tea influence the location of the demand curve for coffee? Since many people would consider drinking tea instead of coffee if the price of tea fell, the demand curve for coffee would shift to the left with a lower price of tea.

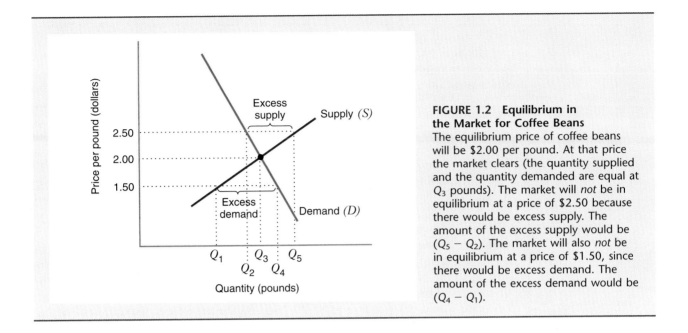

FIGURE 1.2 Equilibrium in the Market for Coffee Beans
The equilibrium price of coffee beans will be $2.00 per pound. At that price the market clears (the quantity supplied and the quantity demanded are equal at Q_3 pounds). The market will *not* be in equilibrium at a price of $2.50 because there would be excess supply. The amount of the excess supply would be ($Q_5 - Q_2$). The market will also *not* be in equilibrium at a price of $1.50, since there would be excess demand. The amount of the excess demand would be ($Q_4 - Q_1$).

The supply curve shows what quantity of coffee beans would be offered for sale in the market at any given price. You can also view a supply curve as representing the answer to a set of "what if" questions. For example, what quantity of coffee beans would be offered for sale if the price were $1.50 per pound? The supply curve in Figure 1.2 shows us that Q_1 pounds would be offered for sale at that price. The supply curve also indicates that if the price were $2.50 per pound, Q_5 pounds would be offered for sale. The positive (or upward) slope of the supply curve suggests that higher prices tend to stimulate production.

When we draw a supply curve for coffee beans, we are assuming that variables other than the price and quantity of coffee are held constant. In Figure 1.2 the supply curve is drawn for the technology that exists in the market, and for given prices of productive inputs, such as labor, land, and equipment used in coffee growing. Changes in these variables might shift the supply curve for coffee to the left or to the right. For example, suppose a new union contract increases the wages paid to coffee workers. Then the production of coffee becomes more expensive, and the supply curve for coffee shifts to the left as less coffee is produced at any given price because it costs more to produce it. The location of the supply curve will also depend on other factors, such as the weather. Better weather, including more favorable temperatures and amounts of rain, will shift the supply curve to the right; more coffee is produced because the better climate yields a bigger crop.

How is the concept of equilibrium related to this discussion of supply and demand? In a competitive market, equilibrium is achieved at a price at which the market *clears*—that is, at a price at which the quantity offered for sale just equals the quantity demanded by consumers. For the coffee market depicted in Figure 1.2, the market will clear when the price is $2.00 per pound. At that price the producers will want to offer Q_3 pounds for sale, and consumers will want to buy just that amount. All consumers who are willing to pay $2.00 per pound are able to buy it, and all producers willing to sell at that price can find buyers. The price of $2.00, therefore, could stay the same indefinitely because there is no upward or downward pressure on price. There is, in other words, an equilibrium.

To understand why one state of a system is an equilibrium, it helps to see why other states are *not* in equilibrium. If the ball in Figure 1.1, were released at some position other than at the bottom of the cup, gravity would move it to the bottom. What happens in the competitive market at non-equilibrium prices? Why, for example, would the coffee market not be in equilibrium if the price of coffee were $2.50 per pound? At that price, only Q_2 pounds would be demanded, but Q_5 pounds would be offered for sale. Thus, there would be an *excess supply* of coffee in the market. Some sellers would not find buyers for their coffee beans. To find buyers, these disappointed producers would be willing to sell for less than $2.50. The market price would need to fall to $2.00 to eliminate the excess supply.

Similarly, one might ask why a price below $2.00 is not an equilibrium price. Consider a price of $1.50. At this price the quantity demanded would be Q_4 pounds, but only Q_1 pounds would be offered for sale. There would then be *excess demand* in the market. Some buyers would be unable to obtain coffee beans. These disappointed buyers will be willing to pay more than $1.50 per pound. The market price would need to rise to $2.00 to eliminate the excess demand and the upward pressure that it generates on the market price.

LEARNING-BY-DOING EXERCISE 1.4

Exogenous and Endogenous Variables in the U.S. Market for Corn

Problem   Suppose that in the United States the quantity of corn demanded Q^d depends on two things: the price of corn P and the level of income in the nation I. Assume that the demand curve for corn is downward sloping, so that more corn will be demanded when the price of corn is lower. Assume also that the demand curve shifts to the right if income rises (i.e., higher income increases the demand for corn). The dependence of the quantity of corn demanded on the price of corn and income is represented by the demand function $Q^d(P,I)$.

Suppose the quantity of corn offered for sale, Q^s, also depends on two things: the price of corn, P, and the amount of rain that falls during the growing season, r. The supply curve is upward sloping, so that as the price of corn rises, more corn will be offered for sale. Assume that the supply curve shifts to the right (more corn is produced) if there is more rain. The relationship showing the quantity of corn supplied at any price and amount of rainfall is the supply function $Q^s(P,r)$.

In equilibrium the price of corn will adjust so that the market will clear $(Q^d = Q^s)$. Let's call the equilibrium quantity exchanged Q^* and the equilibrium price P^*. We can assume that the market for corn is only a small part of the U.S. economy, so that national income is not noticeably affected by events in the market for corn. Consider the four variables Q^*, P^*, I, and r. Which of these variables are endogenous and which are exogenous in the model?

Solution   The values of P^* and Q^* are both endogenous because they will be determined in equilibrium when the corn market clears. The amount of rain is obviously exogenous, because it is determined outside the corn market. National income in this case is not noticeably affected by the price or quantity of corn because the market for corn is a small part of the overall economy. This means that we can treat the level of national income as given (exogenous) in the model.[2] So I and r are exogenous.

COMPARATIVE STATICS

Comparative statics analysis is used to examine how a change in an exogenous variable will affect the level of an endogenous variable in an economic model. Comparative statics analysis can be applied to constrained optimization problems or to equilibrium analyses. Comparative statics allows us to do a "before-and-after" analysis by comparing two snapshots of an economic model. The first snapshot tells us the levels of the endogenous variables given a set of *initial values* of exogenous variables. The second snapshot tells us how an endogenous variable we care about has changed in response to an exogenous shock—that is, a change in the level of some exogenous variable.

Let's consider an example of how comparative statics might be applied to a model of equilibrium. In the spring of 1997, heavy rains soaked Central America, strikes disrupted Colombia, and frosts hit Brazil. All of these exogenous shocks affected the world market for coffee beans, causing coffee prices on the Coffee, Sugar & Cocoa Exchange in New York to soar to a twenty-year high. The price of coffee beans rose from about $1 per pound at the beginning of the year to more than $3 per pound in May.

We can use comparative statics to illustrate what happened in the market for coffee beans. The heavy rains, strikes, and frost all led to a decrease (a leftward shift) in the world's supply curve for coffee beans. Before these events the supply curve was S_1 and the demand curve was D_1, as shown in Figure 1.3. The first snapshot of the market shows an equilibrium price for coffee beans (an endogenous variable) of $1 per pound, and an equilibrium quantity (also an endogenous variable) of Q_1. The exogenous shocks moved the supply curve to the left, to S_2. However, because consumer demand for coffee is largely unaffected by heavy rains, strikes, and frost, it is quite reasonable to assume that the location of the demand curve did not change. The second snapshot of the market indicates an equilibrium price of coffee beans of about $3 per pound, with an equilibrium quantity of Q_2. The comparative statics analysis shows that the exogenous shocks

---

[2] Although you might initially think that the income level is always exogenous, it could be endogenous in some situations. It depends on whether the level of income will be perceptibly affected by what happens in the market being analyzed. If the market in question is a small part of the total economy, then the equilibrium price and quantity in the market will hardly effect the level of national income and it is reasonable to treat the level of income as exogenous. But, suppose the product in question, say coffee, is the primary product of a nation's or region's economy. The level of income in the economy as a whole would then almost surely be significantly affected by the market price of coffee. National income must then be regarded as an endogenous variable. To determine the equilibrium price of coffee, we would need to think further about adding to the model some description of how national income depends on price and quantity in the coffee market.

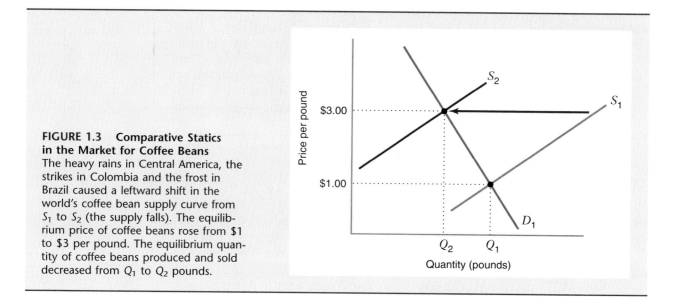

FIGURE 1.3   Comparative Statics in the Market for Coffee Beans
The heavy rains in Central America, the strikes in Colombia and the frost in Brazil caused a leftward shift in the world's coffee bean supply curve from S_1 to S_2 (the supply falls). The equilibrium price of coffee beans rose from $1 to $3 per pound. The equilibrium quantity of coffee beans produced and sold decreased from Q_1 to Q_2 pounds.

led to an increase in price ($\Delta P = \$2$ per pound, where Δ, delta, is read "the change in") and a decrease in quantity ($\Delta Q = Q_2 - Q_1$).

Almost every day you can find examples of comparative statics in *The Wall Street Journal* or in the business section of your local newspaper. Typical are items about exogenous events that influence the prices of agricultural commodities (such as corn, soybeans, wheat, coffee, and cotton), livestock, and metals (such as copper, gold, and silver). It is not unusual to see headlines such as "Coffee Prices Jump on News of Colombian Labor Strike," "Corn Prices Surge as Export Demand Increases," "Soybean Prices Leap on Dry Weather Worries," and "Silver Prices Soar on Signs of Tight Supplies." When you see headlines such as these, think about them in terms of comparative statics.

It is important to understand the kinds of questions that comparative statics analysis can address. The following exercises illustrate how comparative statics analysis might be used with a model of market equilibrium and a model of constrained optimization.

LEARNING-BY-DOING EXERCISE 1.5

Comparative Statics with Market Equilibrium

Problem   In Learning-By-Doing Exercise 1.4, we examined a model of equilibrium in the market for corn. The endogenous variables are the equilibrium price and quantity of corn, P^* and Q^*. The exogenous variables are income, I, and amount of rainfall, r, during the growing season. As before, we assume that the demand for corn increases when income is higher and the supply of corn increases if there is more rain.

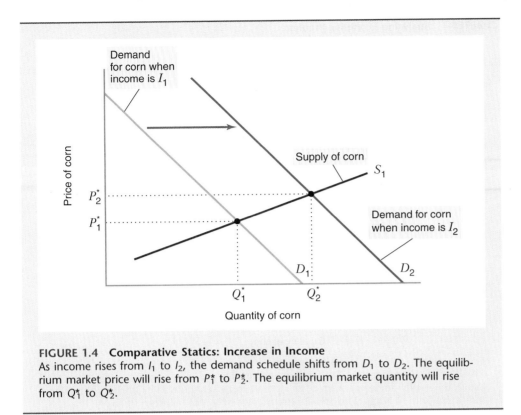

FIGURE 1.4 Comparative Statics: Increase in Income
As income rises from I_1 to I_2, the demand schedule shifts from D_1 to D_2. The equilibrium market price will rise from P_1^* to P_2^*. The equilibrium market quantity will rise from Q_1^* to Q_2^*.

(a) Suppose that income rises from I_1 to I_2. On a clearly labeled graph, illustrate how the change in this exogenous variable affects each of the endogenous variables.

(b) Suppose that income remains at I_1, but that the amount of rainfall increases from r_1 to r_2, an increase that is better for growing corn. On a second clearly labeled graph, illustrate how the change in this exogenous variable affects each of the endogenous variables.

Solution

(a) The change in income shifts the demand curve to the right (increases demand), from D_1 to D_2 in Figure 1.4. The location of the supply curve is unaffected because Q^s does not depend on I. The supply curve remains at S_1. The equilibrium price therefore rises from P_1^* to P_2^*. So the change in income $\Delta I = (I_2 - I_1)$ leads to a change in equilibrium price $\Delta P^* = (P_2^* - P_1^*)$.

The equilibrium quantity also rises from Q_1^* to Q_2^*. So the change in income leads to a change in quantity $\Delta Q^* = (Q_2^* - Q_1^*)$.

(b) The increase in rainfall shifts the supply curve to the right (increases supply), from S_1 to S_2 in Figure 1.5. The location of the demand curve is unaffected because Q^d does not depend on r. The demand curve remains at D_1. The equilibrium price therefore falls from P_1^* to P_2^*. So the change in rainfall $\Delta r = (r_2 - r_1)$ leads to a change in equilibrium price $\Delta P^* = (P_2^* - P_1^*)$.

The equilibrium quantity rises from Q_1^* to Q_2^*. So the change in rainfall leads to a change in quantity $\Delta Q^* = (Q_2^* - Q_1^*)$.

Similar Problems: 1.3, 1.4, and 1.5

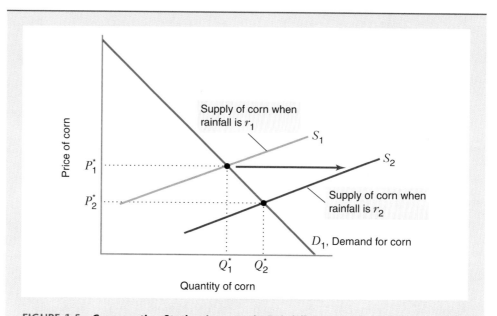

FIGURE 1.5   Comparative Statics: Increase in Rainfall
When the rainfall increases from r_1 to r_2, the supply schedule shifts to the right (supply increases) from S_1 to S_2. The equilibrium market price will fall from P_1^* to P_2^*. The equilibrium market quantity will rise from Q_1^* to Q_2^*.

LEARNING-BY-DOING EXERCISE 1.6

Comparative Statics with Constrained Optimization

Problem   In the farmer's fencing problem (Learning-By-Doing Exercise 1.1), we learned that the exogenous variable was the perimeter of the fence F, and that the endogenous variables were the length L and width W of the pen. You may have solved a problem like this one before: The area is maximized when the farmer builds a square pen. (You do not need to know how to arrive at that conclusion in this exercise. Just trust that it is correct.) If the farmer is given an extra length of fence ΔF, how will the dimensions of the pen change? In other words, how will changes in the endogenous variables ΔL and ΔW be related to a change in the exogenous variable ΔF?

Solution   Since the optimal configuration of the pen is a square, we know that the length and width of the pen will each be one-fourth of the perimeter, so $L = F/4$ and $W = F/4$. Therefore, $\Delta L = \Delta F/4$ and $\Delta W = \Delta F/4$. This comparative statics result tells us that if the farmer is given an extra four feet of fence, the length and the width of the pen will each be increased by one foot.

Similar Problems: 1.6, 1.7, and 1.8

Comparative statics are used to answer many questions that are central in microeconomics. Later we will use comparative statics to understand basic economic concepts such as demand curves, cost curves, and supply curves.

Microeconomic analysis can be used to study both positive and normative questions. **Positive analysis** attempts to explain how an economic system works or to predict how it will change over time. Positive analysis asks *explanatory* questions such as "What has happened?" or "What is happening?" It may also ask a *predictive* question: "What will happen if some exogenous variable changes?" In contrast, **normative analysis** asks *prescriptive* questions, such as "What should be done?" Normative studies typically focus on issues of social welfare, examining what will enhance or detract from the common good. In so doing, they often involve value judgments. For example, policy makers may want to consider whether we should raise the minimum wage to benefit the least skilled and least experienced workers.

We have seen illustrations of positive questions throughout this chapter. In the farmer's fencing problem (Learning-By-Doing Exercise 1.1), one positive question is, "What dimensions of the sheep's pen will the farmer choose to maximize the area of the pen?" Another is, "How will the area of the pen change if the farmer is given one more foot of fence?" In the consumer choice problem (Learning-By-Doing Exercise 1.2), positive analysis will tell us how the consumer's purchases of each good will depend on the prices of all goods and on the level of her income. Positive analysis will help the manager of the cellular telephone provider (Learning-By-Doing Exercise 1.3) or the electricity generator (Example 1.1) to produce any given level of service with the lowest possible cost. Finally, positive analysis enables us to understand why a particular price of a commodity such as coffee beans is in equilibrium, and why other prices are not. It also explains why heavy rains, strikes, and frost result in higher commodity prices.

As all of these examples suggest, applying microeconomic principles for predictive purposes is important for consumers and for managers of enterprises. Positive analysis is also useful in the study of public policy. For example, policy makers might like to understand the effect of new taxes in a market, government subsidies to producers, or tariffs or quotas on imports. They may also want to know how producers and consumers are affected, as well as the size of the impact on the government budget.

Normative studies might examine how to achieve a goal that some people consider socially desirable. Suppose policy makers want to make housing more affordable to low-income families. They may ask whether it is "better" to accomplish this by issuing these families housing vouchers that they can use on the open housing market, or by implementing rent controls that prevent landlords from charging any renter more than an amount controlled by law. Or, if government finds it desirable to reduce pollution, should it introduce taxes on emissions or strictly limit the emissions from factories and automobiles?

These examples illustrate that it is important to do positive analysis before normative analysis. A policy maker may want to ask the normative question,

"Should we implement a program of rent controls or a program of housing vouchers?" To understand the options fully, the policy maker will first need to do positive analysis to understand what will happen if rent controls are imposed, and to learn about the consequences of housing vouchers. Positive analysis will tell us who is affected by each policy, and how.

Microeconomics can help policy makers understand and compare the impacts of alternative policies on consumers and producers. It can therefore help sharpen debates and lead to enlightened public policy.

CHAPTER SUMMARY

• Economics is the study of the allocation of limited resources to satisfy unlimited human wants. It is often described as a science of constrained choice.

• Microeconomics examines the economic behavior of individual economic decision units, such as a consumer or a firm, as well as groups of economic agents, such as households or industries.

• In evaluating a choice among a set of alternatives, a decision maker needs to understand the opportunity cost associated with the alternative selected. The opportunity cost of a chosen alternative is the value of the next best alternative that is forgone.

• Economic studies are often conducted by constructing and analyzing models of a particular problem. Because the real world is complex, an economic model represents an abstraction from reality.

• In analyzing any model, one needs to understand what variables will be taken as given (exogenous variables), as well as what variables will be determined within the model (endogenous variables).

• Three essential tools of microeconomic analysis are (1) *constrained optimization*, a tool that decision makers use

to maximize or minimize some objective function subject to a constraint (**LBD Exercises 1.1, 1.2, and 1.3**); (2) *equilibrium analysis*, used to describe a condition or state that could continue indefinitely in a system, or at least until there is a change in some exogenous variable (**LBD Exercise 1.4**); and, (3) *comparative statics*, used to examine how a change in some exogenous variable will affect the level of some endogenous variable in an economic model, including equilibrium (**LBD Exercise 1.5**) and constrained optimization (**LBD Exercise 1.6**).

• The term *marginal* in microeconomics measures the amount by which a dependent variable changes as the result of adding one more unit of an independent variable.

• Microeconomics provides tools we can use to examine positive and normative issues. Positive analysis attempts to explain how an economic system works, and to predict how the endogenous variables will change as exogenous variables change. Normative analysis considers prescriptive questions such as "What should be done?" Normative studies introduce value judgments into the analysis.

REVIEW QUESTIONS

1. What is the difference between microeconomics and macroeconomics?

2. Why is economics often described as the science of constrained choice?

3. Why should a decision maker care about opportunity cost when choosing among alternatives?

4. How does the tool of constrained optimization help decision makers make choices? What roles do the objective function and constraints play in a model of constrained optimization?

5. Suppose the market for wheat is competitive, with an upward-sloping supply curve, a downward-sloping demand curve, and an equilibrium price of $4.00 per bushel. Why would a higher price (for instance, $5.00 per bushel) not be an equilibrium price? Why would a lower price (for example, $2.50 per bushel) not be an equilibrium price?

6. What is the difference between an exogenous variable and an endogenous variable in an economic model? Would it ever be useful to construct a model that contained only exogenous variables (and no endogenous variables)?

7. Why do economists do comparative statics analysis? What role do endogenous variables and exogenous variables play in comparative statics analysis?

8. What is the difference between positive and normative analysis? Consider the examples of Internet companies at the beginning of the chapter. Which of the following questions would entail positive analysis, and which normative analysis?
a) What effect will Internet auction companies have on the profits of local automobile dealerships?
b) Should the government impose special taxes on sales of merchandise made over the Internet?

PROBLEMS

1.1. You just won a free set of CDs in a radio contest. When you receive the CDs from the radio station, you notice that the suggested retail price printed on the set is $40. However, because the reviews of the CDs have not been good, you know that if you attempt to sell them to someone else, you will receive only $15. What is your opportunity cost of keeping the CDs?

1.2. Discuss the following statement: "Since supply and demand curves are always shifting, markets never actually reach an equilibrium. Therefore the concept of equilibrium is useless."

1.3. In an article entitled, "Corn Prices Surge on Export Demand, Crop Data," *The Wall Street Journal* identified several exogenous shocks that pushed U.S. corn prices sharply higher.[3] Suppose the U.S. market for corn is competitive, with an upward-sloping supply curve and a downward-sloping demand curve. For each of the following scenarios, illustrate graphically how the exogenous event described will contribute to a higher price of corn in the U.S. market.
a) The U.S. Department of Agriculture announced that exports of corn to Taiwan and Japan were "surprisingly bullish," around 30 percent higher than had been expected.
b) Some analysts projected that the size of the U.S. corn crop would hit a six-year low because of dry weather.
c) The strengthening of El Niño, the meteorological trend that brings warmer weather to the western coast of South America, reduces corn production outside the United States thereby increasing foreign countries' dependence on the U.S. corn crop.

1.4. Suppose the supply curve for wool is given by $Q^s = P$, where Q^s is the quantity offered for sale when the price is P. The demand for wool is given by $Q^d = 10 - P + I$, where Q^d is the quantity of wool demanded when the price is P and the level of income is I. Assume I is an exogenous variable.
a) Suppose the level of income is $I = 20$. Graph the supply and demand relationships, and indicate the equilibrium levels of price and quantity on your graph.
b) Explain why the market for wool would not be in equilibrium if the price of wool were 18.
c) Explain why the market for wool would not be in equilibrium if the price of wool were 14.

1.5. Consider the market for wool described by the supply and demand equations in Problem 1.4. Suppose income rises from $I_1 = 20$ to $I_2 = 24$.
a) Using comparative statics analysis, find the impact of the change in income on the equilibrium price of wool.
b) Using comparative statics analysis, find the impact of the change in income on the equilibrium quantity of wool.

1.6. You are the Video Acquisitions Officer for your dormitory. The other officers of your dorm will tell you how many videos they would like to rent during the year. Your job is to find the least expensive way of renting the required number of videos. After researching the options, you have found that there are three rental plans from which you can choose.
Plan A: Pay $3 per video, with no additional fees.
Plan B: Join the Frequent Viewer Club. Here you pay a yearly membership fee of $50, with an additional charge of $2 for each video rented.

[3]See the article by Aaron Lucchetti, August 22, 1997, page C17.

Plan C: Join the Very Frequent Viewer Club. In this club you pay a yearly membership fee of $150, with an additional charge of $1 for each video rented.

a) Which plan would you select if your instructions are to rent 75 movies a year at the lowest possible cost?

b) Which plan would you select if your instructions are to rent 125 movies a year at the lowest possible cost?

c) In this exercise, is the number of videos rented endogenous or exogenous? Explain.

d) Is the choice of plan (A, B, or C) endogenous or exogenous? Explain.

e) Are total expenditures on videos endogenous or exogenous? Explain.

1.7. Reconsider the problem of the Video Acquisitions Officer in Problem 1.6. Suppose the officers of your dorm give you a specified amount of money to spend, and want you to maximize the number of videos you can rent with that budget. You can choose from the same three plans (A, B, and C) available in Problem 1.6.

a) Which plan would you select if your instructions are to rent the most movies possible while spending $125 per year?

b) Which plan would you select if your instructions are to rent the most movies possible while spending $300 per year?

c) In this exercise, is the number of videos rented endogenous or exogenous? Explain.

d) Is the choice of plan (A, B, or C) endogenous or exogenous? Explain.

e) Are total expenditures on videos endogenous or exogenous? Explain.

1.8. Consider the comparative statics of the farmer's fencing problem in Learning-By-Doing Exercise 1.6, where L is the length of the pen, W is the width, and $A = LW$ is the area.

a) Suppose number of feet of fence given to the farmer were initially $F_1 = 200$. Complete the following table. Verify that the optimal design of the fence (the one yielding the largest area with a perimeter of 200 feet) would be a square.

L	10	20	30	40	50	60	70	80	90
W	90	80							
A	900								

b) Now suppose the farmer is instead given 240 feet of fence ($F_2 = 240$). Complete the following table. By how much would the length L of the optimally designed pen increase?

L	20	30	40	50	60	70	80	90	100
W	100	90							
A	2000								

c) When the amount of fence is increased ($\Delta F = 40$), what is the change in the optimal length (ΔL)?

d) When the amount of fence is increased ($\Delta F = 40$), what is the change in the optimal area (ΔA)? Is the area A endogenous or exogenous in this example? Explain.

1.9. Which of the following statements suggest a positive analysis and which a normative analysis?

a) If the United States lifts the prohibition on imports of Cuban cigars, the price of cigars will fall.

b) A freeze in Florida will lead to an increase in the price of orange juice.

c) To provide revenues for public schools, taxes on alcohol, tobacco, and gambling casinos should be raised instead of increasing income taxes.

d) Telephone companies should be allowed to offer cable TV service as well as telephone service.

e) If telephone companies are allowed to offer cable TV service, the price of both types of service will fall.

f) Government subsidies to farmers are too high and should be phased out over the next decade.

g) If the tax on cigarettes is increased by 50 cents per pack, the equilibrium price of cigarettes will rise by 30 cents per pack.

2

Demand and Supply Analysis

2.1 DEMAND, SUPPLY, AND MARKET EQUILIBRIUM

Demand Curves

Supply Curves

Market Equilibrium

Shifts in Supply and Demand

EXAMPLE 2.1 *The Market for Fresh-Cut Roses and the Valentine's Day Effect*

EXAMPLE 2.2 *Using Supply and Demand Curves to Understand the Market for Broilers*

2.2 PRICE ELASTICITY OF DEMAND

Elasticities Along Specific Demand Curves

Price Elasticity of Demand and Total Revenue

Determinants of the Price Elasticity of Demand

Market-Level versus Brand-Level Price Elasticities of Demand

EXAMPLE 2.3 *Brand-Level Price Elasticities of Demand in the Automobile Market*

2.3 OTHER ELASTICITIES

Income and Cross-Price Elasticities of Demand

EXAMPLE 2.4 *Cross-Price Elasticities of Demand in the Automobile Market*

EXAMPLE 2.5 *Price, Income, and Cross-Price Elasticities for Coke and Pepsi*

Price Elasticity of Supply

2.4 LONG-RUN VERSUS SHORT-RUN DEMAND AND SUPPLY

Greater Elasticity in the Long Run than in the Short Run

Greater Elasticity in the Short Run than in the Long Run

EXAMPLE 2.6 *Using Long-Run and Short-Run Supply Curves to Understand the DRAM Price Collapse of 1996*

2.5 BACK-OF-THE-ENVELOPE CALCULATIONS

"Fitting" Linear Demand Curves Using Quantity, Price, and Elasticity Information

Identifying Supply and Demand Curves from Price and Quantity Movements

Identifying the Price Elasticity of Demand from Shifts in Supply

EXAMPLE 2.7 *Using Supply Shifts to Identify the Price Elasticity of Demand for Pepper on the Back of an Envelope*

CHAPTER SUMMARY

REVIEW QUESTIONS

PROBLEMS

APPENDIX A: STRUCTURAL VERSUS REDUCED-FORM EQUATIONS

APPENDIX B: MORE ON ELASTICITY

Point versus Arc Price Elasticity

Price Elasticity of Demand along a Constant Elasticity Demand Curve

For years, the market for corn in the United States was dull and predictable. Prices hovered between $2.00 and $2.50 per bushel, and few expected them to rise much higher. But in the mid-1990s, as Figure 2.1 shows, the scenario changed. In late 1995, corn prices topped $3.00 per bushel, and by July 1996, prices were averaging nearly $4.50 per bushel! The upheaval created by rising corn prices was so great that experienced commodities traders warned investors to stay away from corn futures because prices had become too volatile.[1] Yet, as the 1990s came to a close, most news accounts of the corn market focused not on unprecedented high prices for corn, but on record low prices![2] After peaking in July 1996, corn prices fell consistently throughout 1997, 1998, and 1999. By late 1999, average corn prices had dipped to their lowest level in a decade.

This story illustrates the vagaries of prices in a competitive market. Prices rise and fall in seemingly unpredictable ways, and there is little that individual participants (e.g., corn farmers, grain elevators, commodity traders) can do about it. However, we *can* understand *why* prices in the market change as they do. In the case of corn, the pattern of prices shown in Figure 2.1 can be traced to the interaction of some important changes in supply and demand conditions in the corn market in the 1990s. In the early 1990s, several years of bad weather devastated U.S. corn harvests. By early 1996, the amount of corn in storage for sales in future years had reached a record low. With the Asian economy booming and several countries around the world experiencing significant crop failures in 1996, demand for corn from overseas rose sharply and unexpectedly. With demand for U.S. corn up and the available supply in storage down, corn prices rose dramatically in the early summer of 1996.

But in 1997, the Asian economy slowed significantly, reducing the demand for corn from overseas. The global financial crisis of 1998 and the associated rise in the value of the dollar also reduced the demand for U.S. corn by countries such as Russia and Brazil. In the late 1990s, China, which had been the world's largest importer of agricultural commodities, undertook a major initiative to achieve self-sufficiency in basic foodstuffs. As a result, by 1999, China had shifted from being a leading importer of U.S. corn to a net exporter of its own corn. This, too, had a significant impact on the demand for U.S. corn in the last half of the 1990s. Finally, since 1996, the weather during the U.S. planting season (spring and summer) has generally been good, resulting in large harvests every year since 1996. By the end of 1999, the supply of corn in storage in the United States was twice as large as it was at the end of 1995.[3] Increases in corn supplies, coupled with decreases in corn demand, explain why corn prices have fallen consistently since 1996.

The tools of supply and demand analysis that we introduced in Chapter 1 can help us understand the story that unfolded in the corn market in the 1990s. In fact, they can help us understand the pattern of prices that prevail in a variety of markets, ranging from fresh-cut roses to DRAM chips for computers. In this chapter we will develop a number of tools that we will use repeatedly throughout this text. We begin by discussing the three main building blocks of supply and demand analysis: demand curves, supply curves, and the con-

[1]"Hedge Row: As Corn Prices Soar, A Futures Tactic Brings Rancor to Rural Towns," *Wall Street Journal* (July 2, 1996), pp. A1, A6.

[2]See, for example, "Weather Goes Against the Grain: Farmers Sweat as Prices Fall to 27-Year Low," *Chicago Tribune* (July 7, 1999), Section 3, pp. 1 and 3.

[3]Frederic Suris and Dennis Shields, "The Ag Sector: Yearend Wrap-up" *Agricultural Outlook, Economic Research Service*, U.S. Department of Agriculture (December 1999).

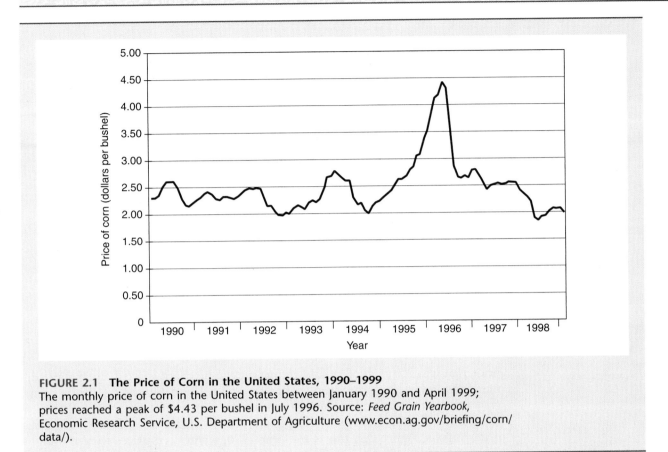

FIGURE 2.1 The Price of Corn in the United States, 1990–1999
The monthly price of corn in the United States between January 1990 and April 1999;
prices reached a peak of $4.43 per bushel in July 1996. Source: *Feed Grain Yearbook*,
Economic Research Service, U.S. Department of Agriculture (www.econ.ag.gov/briefing/corn/
data/).

cept of a market equilibrium. We then introduce an important quantitative concept for characterizing the nature of demand and supply: elasticity. Finally, we present some "back of the envelope" techniques for taking a limited amount of quantitative information about market conditions or elasticities and using it to construct simple analyses that help predict how markets might respond to changing demand or supply conditions. ■

2.1
DEMAND, SUPPLY, AND MARKET EQUILIBRIUM

Chapter 1 introduced equilibrium and comparative statics analysis. In this chapter, we apply those tools to the analysis of perfectly competitive markets. Perfectly competitive markets comprise large numbers of buyers and sellers. The transactions of any individual buyer or seller are so small in comparison to the overall volume of the good or service traded in the market that each buyer or seller "takes" the market price as given when making purchase or production decisions. For this reason, the model of perfect competition is often cited as a model of *price-taking* behavior.

Figure 2.2 illustrates the basic model of a perfectly competitive market. The horizontal axis depicts the total quantity Q of a particular good—in this case corn—that is supplied and demanded in this market. The vertical axis depicts the

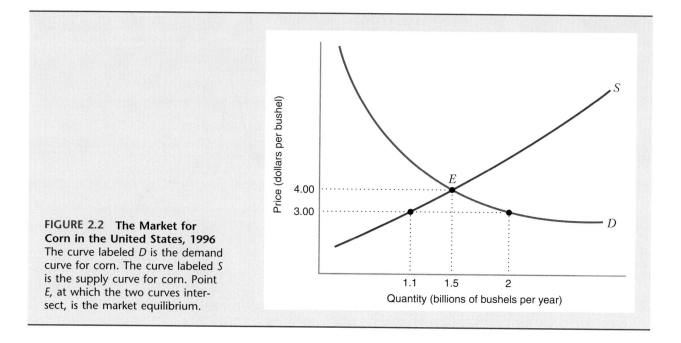

FIGURE 2.2   The Market for Corn in the United States, 1996
The curve labeled *D* is the demand curve for corn. The curve labeled *S* is the supply curve for corn. Point *E*, at which the two curves intersect, is the market equilibrium.

price P at which this good is sold. A market can be characterized along three dimensions: *commodity*—the product bought and sold (in Figure 2.2 this is corn); *geography*—the location in which purchases are being made (in Figure 2.2 this is the United States); and *time*—the period of time during which transactions are occurring (in Figure 2.2, this is the year 1996, when corn prices were the highest in a decade).

DEMAND CURVES

The curve D in Figure 2.2 is the **market demand curve** for corn. It tells us the quantity of corn that consumers are willing to buy at different prices. For example, the demand curve tells us that at a price of $3 per bushel, the annual demand for corn would be 2 billion bushels, while at a price of $4 per bushel, the annual demand for corn would be only 1.5 billion bushels.

Corn supplies are bought by companies (e.g., Archer Daniels Midland and General Mills) that process the corn into finished or intermediate products (e.g., high fructose corn syrup or corn grits), which in turn are used to make final products (e.g., soft drinks or breakfast cereal). Part of the demand depicted in Figure 2.2 is **derived demand**—that is, it is derived from the production and sale of other goods. For example, the demand for high fructose corn syrup is derived from the demand for soft drinks in which it is used as a sweetener (instead of sugar). Corn is also purchased by brokers and wholesale distributors, who then sell it to retailers who then resell it to final consumers. Thus, another part of the demand for corn depicted in Figure 2.2 is **direct demand**—demand for the good itself. The demand curve D is a market demand curve in that it represents the aggregate demand for corn from all the corn purchasers in the U.S. market.

In Figure 2.2, we have drawn the demand curve with price on the vertical axis and quantity on the horizontal axis. This representation emphasizes another useful interpretation of the demand curve that we will return to in later chapters. The demand curve tells us the highest price that the "market will bear" for a given quantity or supply of output. Thus, in Figure 2.2, if suppliers of corn offered, in total, 2 billion bushels for sale, the highest price that the corn would fetch would be $3 per bushel.

Other factors besides price affect the quantity of a good demanded. The prices of related goods, consumer incomes, consumer tastes, and advertising are among the factors that we expect would influence the demand for a typical product. However, the demand curve focuses only on the relationship between the price of the good and the quantity of the good demanded. When we draw the demand curve, we imagine that all other factors that affect the quantity demanded are fixed.

The demand curve in Figure 2.2 slopes downward, indicating that the lower the price of corn, the greater the quantity of corn demanded, and the higher the price of corn, the smaller the quantity demanded. The inverse relationship between price and quantity demanded, *holding all other factors that influence demand fixed*, is called the **law of demand**. Countless studies of market demand curves confirm the inverse relationship between price and quantity demanded, which is why we call the relationship a *law*. Still, you might wonder about so-called luxury goods, such as perfume, designer labels, or crystal. It is alleged that some consumers purchase *more* of these goods at higher prices because a high price indicates superior quality.[4] However, these examples do not violate the law of demand because all of the other factors influencing demand for these goods are *not* held fixed while the price changes. Consumers' *perceptions* of the quality of these goods have also changed. If consumers' perceptions of quality could be held constant, then we would expect that consumers would purchase less of these luxury goods as the price went up.

LEARNING-BY-DOING EXERCISE 2.1

Sketching a Demand Curve

Problem Suppose the demand for new automobiles in the United States is described by the equation

$$Q^d = 5.3 - 0.1P \qquad (2.1)$$

where Q^d is the number of new automobiles per year (in millions) when P is the average price of automobiles (in thousands of dollars).

(a) What is the quantity of automobiles demanded when the average price of an automobile is $15,000? When it is $25,000 per year? When it is $35,000 per year?
(b) Sketch the demand curve for automobiles. Does this demand curve obey the law of demand?

[4]Michael Schudson, *Advertising, The Uneasy Persuasion: Its Dubious Impact on American Society* (New York: Basic Books), pp. 113–114. 1984.

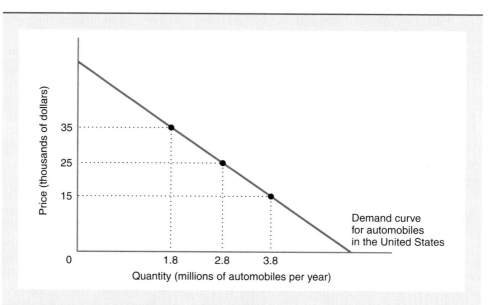

FIGURE 2.3   The Demand Curve for Automobiles
The U.S. demand curve for automobiles derived in Learning-By-Doing Exercise 2.1. The law of demand holds in this market because the demand curve slopes downward.

Solution

(a) To find the demand for automobiles when the price is $15,000, we use equation 2.1. For $P = 15$, we have

$$Q^d = 5.3 - 0.1(15) = 3.8$$

There is a demand for 3.8 million new cars when the price per car is $15,000. The demand for automobiles when the price is $25,000 ($P = 25$) is

$$Q^d = 5.3 - 0.1(25) = 2.8$$

Thus, there is a demand for 2.8 million new cars when the price per car is $25,000. Similarly,

$$Q^d = 5.3 - 0.1(35) = 1.8$$

which tells us that when the price is $35,000, the demand for new cars will be 1.8 million per year.

(b) Figure 2.3 shows the demand curve for automobiles. To sketch it, you can plot the combinations of prices and quantities that we found in part (a) and connect them with a line. The downward slope of the demand curve in Figure 2.3 tells us that as the price of automobiles goes up, consumers demand fewer automobiles. The fact that the coefficient on the price P in equation (2.1) is a negative number (-0.1) tells us the same thing.

Similar Problem: 2.1

SUPPLY CURVES

The curve labeled *S* in Figure 2.2 is the **market supply curve** for corn. It tells us the total quantity of corn that suppliers of corn are willing to sell at different prices. For example, the supply curve tells us that at a price of $3 per bushel, 1.1 billion bushels of corn would be supplied in 1996, while at a price of $4 per bushel, 1.5 billion bushels would be supplied in that year.

The supply of corn in the United States primarily comes from corn farmers around the country. The available supply in a given year consists of corn that is harvested in that year plus corn that has been stored from previous harvests. We should think of the supply curve *S* as being constructed from the sum of the supply curves of all individual suppliers of corn in the United States.

The supply curve slopes upward, indicating that at higher prices, suppliers of corn are willing to offer more corn for sale, and at lower prices they are willing to offer less for sale. The positive relationship between price and quantity supplied is known as the **law of supply.** Studies of market supply curves confirm the positive relationship between the quantity supplied and the price, which is why we call the relationship a law.

As with demand, other factors besides price affect the quantity of a good that producers will supply to the market. For example, the prices of **factors of production**—resources such as labor and raw materials that are used to produce the good—will affect the quantity of the good that sellers are willing to supply. The prices of other goods that sellers produce could also affect the quantity supplied. For example, the supply of natural gas goes up when the price of oil goes up, because higher oil prices spur more oil production, and natural gas is a byproduct of oil. When we draw a supply curve like the one in Figure 2.2, we imagine that all of the factors that affect the quantity supplied (e.g., prices of factors of production) except the price of the product itself are held fixed.

LEARNING-BY-DOING EXERCISE 2.2

Sketching a Supply Curve

Problem Suppose the supply of wheat in Canada is described by the equation

$$Q^s = 0.15 + P \qquad (2.2)$$

where Q^s is the quantity of wheat produced in Canada (in billions of bushels) when *P* is the price of wheat (dollars per bushel).

(a) What is the quantity of wheat supplied when the price of wheat is $2? When the price is $3? When the price is $4?
(b) Sketch the supply curve for wheat. Does it obey the law of supply?

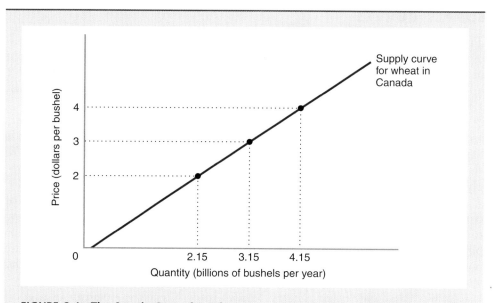

FIGURE 2.4   The Supply Curve for Wheat
The figure illustrates the supply curve for wheat in Canada derived in Learning-By-Doing Exercise 2.2. The law of supply holds in this market because the supply curve slopes upward.

Solution

(a) We can find the quantity of wheat supplied at these various prices with equation 2.2:

$$Q^s = 0.15 + 2 = 2.15$$
$$Q^s = 0.15 + 3 = 3.15$$
$$Q^s = 0.15 + 4 = 4.15$$

Thus, when the price is $2 per bushel, the quantity of wheat supplied is 2.15 billion bushels per year. When the price is $3 per bushel, the quantity of wheat supplied is 3.15 billion bushels per year. When the price is $4 per bushel, the quantity of wheat supplied is 4.15 billion bushels per year.

(b) Figure 2.4 shows the graph of this supply curve. We find it by plotting the prices and associated quantities from part (a) and connecting them with a line. The fact that the supply curve in Figure 2.4 slopes upward indicates that the law of supply holds. The fact that the coefficient on the price P in the supply curve is positive ($+1$) tells us the same thing.

Similar Problem: 2.2

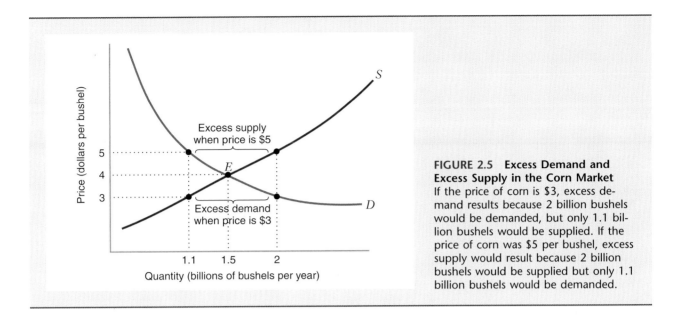

FIGURE 2.5 **Excess Demand and Excess Supply in the Corn Market**
If the price of corn is $3, excess demand results because 2 billion bushels would be demanded, but only 1.1 billion bushels would be supplied. If the price of corn was $5 per bushel, excess supply would result because 2 billion bushels would be supplied but only 1.1 billion bushels would be demanded.

MARKET EQUILIBRIUM

In Figure 2.2, the demand and supply curves intersect at point E, where the price is $4 per bushel and the quantity is 1.5 billion bushels. At this point, the market is in **equilibrium.** As we discussed in Chapter 1, an equilibrium is a point of stability—a point at which there is no tendency for the market price to change as long as exogenous conditions (e.g., rainfall, national income) remain unchanged. At any price other than the equilibrium price, pressures exist for the price to change. For example, as Figure 2.5 shows, if the price of corn is $5 per bushel, there is **excess supply**—the quantity supplied at that price (2 billion bushels) exceeds the quantity demanded (1.1 billion bushels). The fact that suppliers of corn cannot sell as much as they would like creates pressure for the price to go down. As the price falls, the quantity demanded goes up, the quantity supplied goes down, and the market moves toward the equilibrium price of $4 per bushel. If the price of corn is $3 per bushel, there is excess demand—the quantity demanded at that price (2 billion bushels) exceeds the quantity supplied (1.1 billion bushels). Buyers of corn cannot procure as much corn as they would like, and so there is pressure for the price to rise. As the price rises, the quantity supplied also rises, the quantity demanded falls, and the market moves toward the equilibrium price of $4 per bushel.

LEARNING-BY-DOING EXERCISE 2.3

Calculating Equilibrium Price and Quantity

Problem Suppose the market demand curve for cranberries in the United States is given by the equation $Q^d = 500 - 4P$, while the market supply curve for cranberries (when $P \geq 50$) is described by the equation $Q^s = -100 + 2P$,

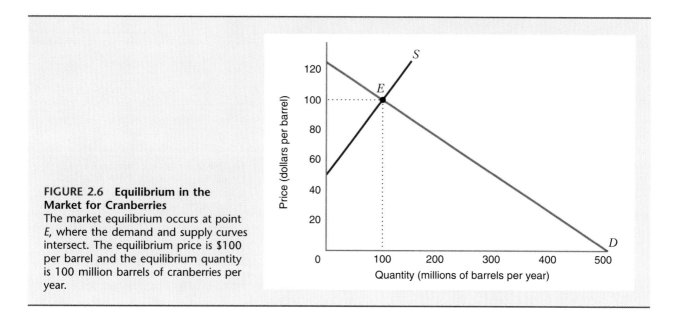

FIGURE 2.6   Equilibrium in the Market for Cranberries
The market equilibrium occurs at point E, where the demand and supply curves intersect. The equilibrium price is $100 per barrel and the equilibrium quantity is 100 million barrels of cranberries per year.

where P is the price of cranberries expressed in dollars per barrel, and quantity is in millions of barrels per year. What is the equilibrium price and quantity in the market for cranberries? Show this equilibrium price graphically.

Solution   We find the equilibrium price by equating the quantity supplied to the quantity demanded and solve for P:

$$Q^d = Q^s$$
$$500 - 4P = -100 + 2P$$

Rearranging terms,

$$6P = 600$$
$$P = 100$$

The equilibrium price is $100 per barrel. The equilibrium quantity is found by substituting the equilibrium price into either the demand or the supply curve:

$$Q^d = 500 - 4(100) = 100$$
$$Q^s = -100 + 2(100) = 100$$

Thus, the equilibrium quantity is 100 million barrels per year. Figure 2.6 illustrates this equilibrium graphically.

Similar Problem: 2.3

SHIFTS IN SUPPLY AND DEMAND

Shifts in Either Supply or Demand

Because demand and supply curves are drawn under the assumption that all other factors that influence the quantity demanded and quantity supplied are fixed, the position of the demand and supply curves and thus the position of the market equilibrium depends on the values of these other factors. Figure 2.7 and Figure 2.8 illustrate how we can enrich our analysis to account for the effects of these other variables on the market equilibrium. These figures illustrate comparative statics analysis, which we discussed in Chapter 1. In both cases, we can explore how a change in an exogenous variable (e.g., consumer income or wage rates) changes the equilibrium values of the endogenous variables (price and quantity).

To do a comparative statics analysis of the market equilibrium, you first must determine how a particular exogenous variable affects either demand or supply. You then represent changes in that variable by a shift in the demand curve, in the supply curve, or in both. For example, suppose that higher consumer incomes increase the demand for a particular good. The effect of higher disposable income on the market equilibrium is represented by a rightward shift in the demand curve (i.e., a shift away from the vertical axis), as shown in Figure 2.7.[5] This shift indicates that at any price the quantity demanded is greater than before. This shift moves the market equilibrium from point A to point B. The shift in demand due to higher income thus increases both the equilibrium price and the equilibrium quantity.

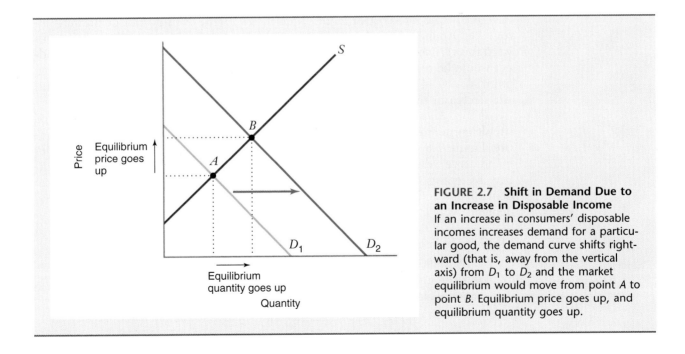

FIGURE 2.7 Shift in Demand Due to an Increase in Disposable Income
If an increase in consumers' disposable incomes increases demand for a particular good, the demand curve shifts rightward (that is, away from the vertical axis) from D_1 to D_2 and the market equilibrium would move from point A to point B. Equilibrium price goes up, and equilibrium quantity goes up.

[5]The shift does not necessarily have to be parallel, the way it is in Figure 2.7.

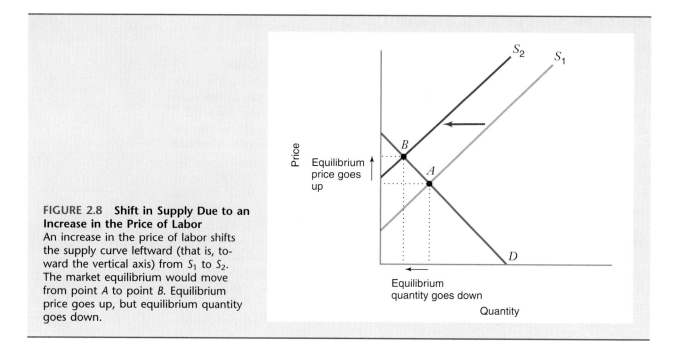

FIGURE 2.8   Shift in Supply Due to an Increase in the Price of Labor
An increase in the price of labor shifts the supply curve leftward (that is, toward the vertical axis) from S_1 to S_2. The market equilibrium would move from point *A* to point *B*. Equilibrium price goes up, but equilibrium quantity goes down.

For another example, suppose wage rates for workers in a particular industry go up. Some firms might then reduce production levels because their costs have risen with the cost of labor. Some firms might even go out of business altogether. An increase in labor costs would shift the supply curve leftward (i.e., toward the vertical axis), as shown in Figure 2.8. This shift indicates that less product would be supplied at any price and the market equilibrium would move from point *A* to *B*. The increase in the price of labor increases the equilibrium price and decreases the equilibrium quantity.

Figure 2.7 shows us that an increase in demand, coupled with an unchanged supply curve, results in a higher equilibrium price and a larger equilibrium quantity. Figure 2.8 shows that a decrease in supply, coupled with an unchanged demand curve, results in a higher equilibrium price and a smaller equilibrium quantity. By going through similar comparative statics analyses for a decrease in demand and an increase in supply, we can derive the four basic laws of supply and demand:

1. Increase in demand + unchanged supply curve = higher price and larger quantity (Figure 2.7).

2. Decrease in demand + unchanged supply curve = lower price and smaller quantity (Figure 2.9).

3. Increase in supply + unchanged demand curve = lower price and larger quantity (Figure 2.10).

4. Decrease in supply + unchanged demand curve = higher price and smaller quantity (Figure 2.8).

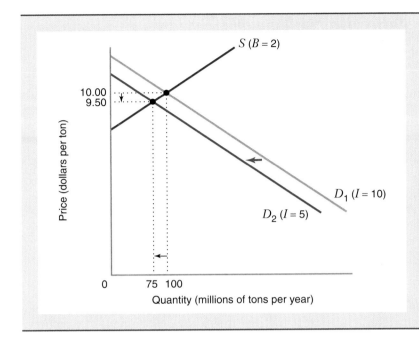

FIGURE 2.9 Equilibrium in the Market for Aluminum for Learning-By-Doing Exercise 2.4
The market equilibrium initially occurs at a price of $10 per ton and a quantity of 100 million tons. When average income goes down (that is, when we move from $I = 10$ to $I = 5$), the demand curve for aluminum shifts leftward. The new equilibrium price is $9.50 per ton, and the new equilibrium quantity is 75 million tons.

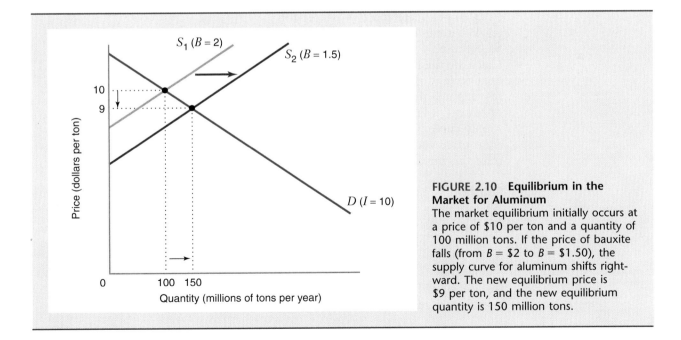

FIGURE 2.10 Equilibrium in the Market for Aluminum
The market equilibrium initially occurs at a price of $10 per ton and a quantity of 100 million tons. If the price of bauxite falls (from $B = 2 to $B = 1.50), the supply curve for aluminum shifts rightward. The new equilibrium price is $9 per ton, and the new equilibrium quantity is 150 million tons.

LEARNING-BY-DOING EXERCISE 2.4

Comparative Statics on the Market Equilibrium

Problem Suppose that the U.S. demand for aluminum is given by the equation

$$Q^d = 500 - 50P + 10I$$

where P is the price of aluminum expressed in dollars per ton and I is a measure of average income per person in the United States (in thousands of dollars per year). Average income is an important determinant of the demand for automobiles and other products that use aluminum, and hence is a determinant of the demand for aluminum itself. Suppose that the U.S. supply of aluminum is given by the equation

$$Q^s = 50P - 200B$$

where B is the average price of bauxite ore (in dollars per ton), the raw material from which aluminum is extracted, and thus a key determinant of the costs faced by aluminum producers. In both the demand and supply functions, quantity is measured in millions of tons of aluminum per year. In this problem assume that aluminum producers take the price of bauxite as given.

(a) What are the exogenous variables in this case? What are the endogenous variables?
(b) What is the market equilibrium price of aluminum when $I = 10$ (i.e., $10,000 per year) and $B = $2 per ton?
(c) What happens to the demand curve if average income per person was only $5,000 (i.e., $I = 5$ rather than $I = 10$). Sketch how the demand curve shifts. Calculate the impact of this demand shift on the market equilibrium price and quantity and then sketch supply and demand curves to illustrate this impact.
(d) Suppose that I remains at 10. What happens to the supply curve if the price of bauxite B falls from $2.00 per ton to $1.50 per ton? Sketch the shift in the supply curve. Calculate the impact of this supply shift on the market equilibrium price and quantity and then sketch supply and demand curves to illustrate this impact.

Solution

(a) The exogenous variables in this exercise are average income I and the price of bauxite B. They are exogenous because their values are determined outside the market we are analyzing. The price and quantity of aluminum are, by contrast, endogenous. Their values are determined within the market we are analyzing.
(b) We substitute $I = 10$ into the demand equation and $B = 2$ into the supply equation to get demand and supply curves for aluminum:

$$Q^d = 600 - 50P$$
$$Q^s = -400 + 50P$$

We then equate Q^d to Q^s to find the equilibrium price:

$$600 - 50P = -400 + 50P$$
$$1000 = 100P$$
$$10 = P$$

The equilibrium price is $10 per ton. The equilibrium quantity is

$$Q = 600 - 50(10)$$
$$= 100$$

Thus, the equilibrium quantity is 100 million tons per year.

(c) The change in I does not affect the supply curve, but it creates a new demand curve that we find by substituting $I = 5$ into the demand equation shown above:

$$Q^d = 550 - 50P$$

Figure 2.9 shows this demand curve as well as the demand curve for $I = 10$. As before, we equate Q^d to Q^s to find the equilibrium price:

$$550 - 50P = -400 + 50P$$
$$950 = 100P$$
$$9.5 = P$$

The equilibrium price thus decreases from $10 per ton to $9.50 per ton. The equilibrium quantity is

$$Q = 550 - 50(9.50)$$
$$= 75$$

Thus, the equilibrium quantity decreases from 100 million tons per year to 75 million tons. Figure 2.9 shows this impact. Note that it is consistent with the second law of supply and demand: A decrease in demand coupled with an unchanged supply curve results in a lower equilibrium price and a smaller equilibrium quantity.

(d) A decrease in B does not affect the demand curve, but it creates a new supply curve that we find by plugging $B = 1.50$ into the supply equation shown above:

$$Q^s = -300 + 50P$$

Figure 2.10 shows this new supply curve as compared to the initial supply curve. As before, we equate Q^d to Q^s to find the equilibrium price:

$$600 - 50P = -300 + 50P$$
$$900 = 100P$$
$$9 = P$$

The equilibrium price thus decreases from $10 per ton to $9 per ton. The equilibrium quantity is

$$Q = 600 - 50(9.00)$$
$$= 150$$

Thus, the equilibrium quantity increases from 100 million tons per year to 150 million tons. Figure 2.10 shows this impact. Note that it is consistent with the third law of supply and demand: An increase in supply coupled with an unchanged demand curve results in a lower equilibrium price and a larger equilibrium quantity.

Similar Problem: 2.6

EXAMPLE 2.1

The Market for Fresh-Cut Roses and the Valentine's Day Effect

If you have ever bought fresh-cut roses, you may have noticed that their price varies considerably during the year. In particular, the price you pay for fresh-cut roses—especially red roses—around Valentine's Day is usually three to five times higher than at other times during the year. Figure 2.11 illustrates this pattern by showing the prices and quantities of fresh-cut roses at two different times of the year: February and August in each of three years, 1991, 1992, and 1993.[6] Are the high prices of roses at Valentine's Day a result of a conspiracy among florists and rose growers to gouge romantic consumers? Probably not. This pricing behavior can best be understood as an application of comparative statics analysis.

Figure 2.12 depicts the market equilibrium in the U.S. market for fresh-cut roses in the early 1990s. During this period, wholesale prices for red hybrid tea roses were ordinarily about $0.20 per stem.[7] Every year, though, the market changes around Valentine's Day. During the days before Valentine's Day, demand for red roses increases dramatically, resulting in a rightward shift in the demand curve for roses from D_1 to D_2. This rightward shift occurs because around Valentine's Day, people who do not ordinarily purchase roses want to buy them for their spouses or sweethearts. The rightward shift in demand increases the equilibrium price to about $0.50 per stem. Even though the price is higher, the equilibrium quantity is also higher than it was before. This outcome does not contradict the law of demand. It reflects the fact that the Valentine's Day equilibrium occurs along a demand curve that is different from the demand curve before or after Valentine's Day.

Figure 2.12 explains why we would expect the prices of red roses to peak around Valentine's Day. The logic of Figure 2.12 also helps explain another aspect of the

---

[6]The data in Figure 2.11 are derived from Tables 12 and 17 of "Fresh Cut Roses from Colombia and Ecuador," Publication 2766, International Trade Commission (March 1994). The data for February actually consist of the last two weeks of January and the first two weeks of February.

[7]These are wholesale prices (i.e., the prices that retail florists pay their suppliers), not the retail prices paid by the final consumer.

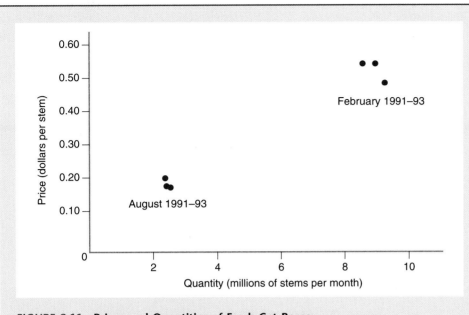

FIGURE 2.11 Prices and Quantities of Fresh-Cut Roses
Prices and quantities of roses during 1991–1993 for the months of August and February—both are much higher in February than they are in August.

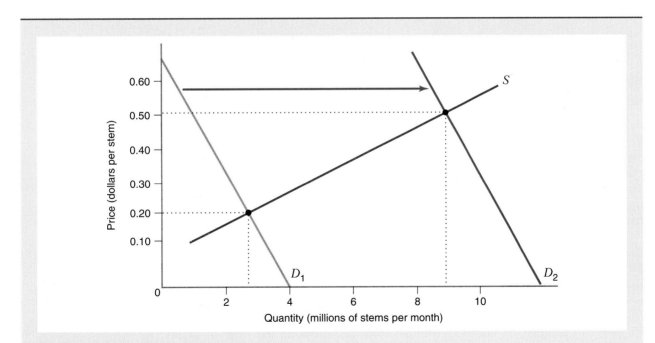

FIGURE 2.12 The Market for Fresh-Cut Roses
During "usual" months, the market for fresh-cut roses attains an equilibrium at a price of about $0.20 per stem. However, during the weeks around Valentine's Day, the demand curve for roses shifts rightward, from D_1 to D_2, and the equilibrium price and quantity go up.

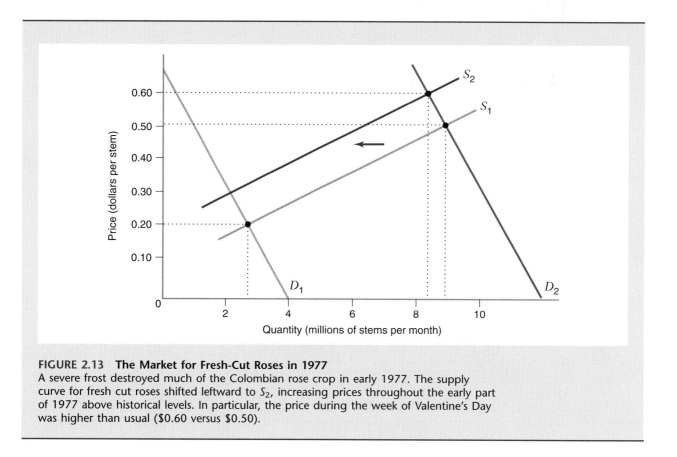

FIGURE 2.13   The Market for Fresh-Cut Roses in 1977
A severe frost destroyed much of the Colombian rose crop in early 1977. The supply
curve for fresh cut roses shifted leftward to S_2, increasing prices throughout the early part
of 1977 above historical levels. In particular, the price during the week of Valentine's Day
was higher than usual ($0.60 versus $0.50).

rose market: the prices of white and yellow roses. Their prices also go up around
Valentine's Day, but by less than the prices of red roses. Overall, their prices show
more stability than the prices of red roses because white and yellow roses are less
popular on Valentine's Day and are used more for weddings and other special events.
These events are spread more evenly throughout the year, so the demand curves
for white and yellow roses fluctuate less dramatically than the demand curve for
red roses. As a result, their equilibrium prices are more stable.

   Although the prices of red roses always go up around Valentine's Day, in some
years they rise to higher levels than others. This happened, for example, in early
1977, when a severe frost damaged the Colombian rose crop. Colombia was at
that time (and is still) the largest exporter of roses for sale in the United States. The
result was a leftward shift in the supply curve for roses sold in the United States,
from S_1 to S_2, and rose prices throughout early 1977 exceeded their historical levels. And in particular, as Figure 2.13 shows, rose prices during the week of Valentine's Day 1977 were higher than the usual inflated price ($0.60 per stem versus
$0.50 per stem).   ∎

Shifts in Both Supply and Demand

So far, we have focused on what happens when either the supply curve or the demand curve shifts. But sometimes we can better understand the dynamics of prices and quantities in markets by exploring what happens when both supply and demand shift.

We return to the example of the U.S. corn market in the 1990s to illustrate this point. Figure 2.14 shows the difference between the equilibrium in the corn market in 1996 when prices reached $4 per bushel (point *A*) and 1999 when prices fell below $2 per bushel (point *B*). As we discussed in the introduction, the decrease in the price of corn can be attributed to both a decrease in demand (e.g., due to the effects of a global currency crisis and China's move toward agricultural self-sufficiency) and an increase in supply (due to an improvement in harvests resulting from the good weather in 1996–1998.) The combined effect of both shifts was to decrease the equilibrium price. By contrast, the effect on the equilibrium quantity is more complicated. The decrease in demand tends to push the equilibrium quantity downward, while the increase in supply tends to push the equilibrium quantity upward. Figure 2.14 shows a net increase in equilibrium quantity from 1.5 billion bushels per year to 1.6 billion bushels per year.

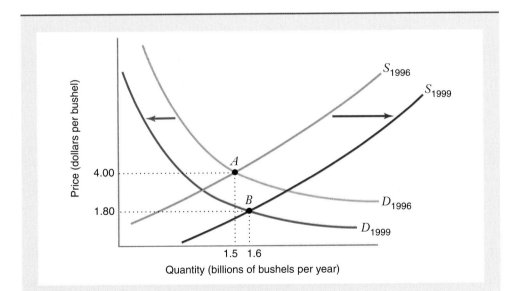

FIGURE 2.14   The U.S. Corn Market 1996–1999
The decrease in the U.S. corn price can be explained by the combined effect of a shift in supply and a shift in demand. In particular, the demand curve shifted leftward from D_{1996} to D_{1999}, while the supply curve shifted rightward from S_{1996} to S_{1999}, moving the equilibrium from point *A* to point *B*. The result is a decrease in the equilibrium price from $4 per bushel to $1.80 per bushel.

EXAMPLE 2.2

Using Supply and Demand Curves to Understand the Market for Broilers[8]

A *broiler* is a young chicken grown for its meat rather than for its eggs. Raising chickens for meat is, by the standards of U.S. agriculture, a relatively new industry. In the early 1900s, most farmers raised chickens for their eggs. Chicken was considered a luxury meat, one that was consumed on holidays or special days, such as the Sabbath. Herbert Hoover's 1928 promise, "A chicken in every pot," reflected the upscale status that chicken meat had in the United States at the time. But World War II was a boon for the chicken business. Beef was rationed, and consumers turned to chicken as a substitute. The demand created during World War II continued to grow after the war. In 1940, the per capita quantity of chicken consumed was just 2 pounds per year.[9] By 1945, it had grown to 5 pounds. From the 1960s through the 1980s, demand for chicken meat exploded. By 1990, with a per capita consumption of 70.1 pounds, chicken was the most consumed meat in the United States.

Figure 2.15 illustrates the real price[10] and the per-capita quantity of broilers over the period 1950–1990. The figure documents a dramatic decline in real broiler

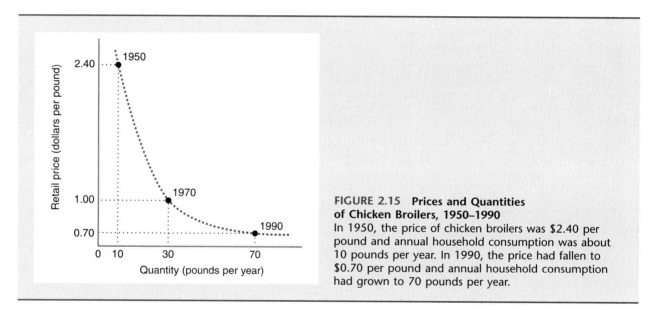

FIGURE 2.15   Prices and Quantities of Chicken Broilers, 1950–1990
In 1950, the price of chicken broilers was $2.40 per pound and annual household consumption was about 10 pounds per year. In 1990, the price had fallen to $0.70 per pound and annual household consumption had grown to 70 pounds per year.

[8]This example draws from Richard T. Rogers, "Broilers: Differentiating a Commodity," in Larry L. Deutsch (ed.), *Industry Studies* (Englewood Cliffs, NJ: Prentice Hall, 1993), pp. 3–32. In particular, the information in Figure 2.15 comes from Figure 1 in Rogers' article.

[9]*Per capita quantity* is an average quantity per person. Thus, if the total consumption for chicken broilers is 2 billion pounds per year and the total population is 200 million, the per capita consumption of chicken broilers would be 2,000,000,000/200,000,000 = 10 pounds per person.

[10]A *real price* is a price that is adjusted for the effects of inflation. For example, suppose the price of chicken broilers rose from $1.00 in 1985 to $1.20 in 1995, a 20 percent increase. Suppose, too, that the prices of all goods and services went up by 20 percent on average over this period (i.e., the rate of inflation was 20 percent.) Then, we would say that the real price of chicken broilers remained constant because the increase in the actual price of broilers matched the rate of inflation. When broiler prices increase by less than the rate of inflation, we say that real broiler prices have gone down. If broiler prices increase by more than the rate of inflation, we say that real broiler prices have gone up.

prices between 1950 and 1970, and a steady, though not as dramatic, decline in real prices from 1970 to 1990. Throughout this period, per capita consumption rose. What explains this pattern of prices and quantities?

Figure 2.16 illustrates what was happening. From 1950 to 1990, the demand curve for broilers shifted rightward. A combination of factors drove this rightward shift. In the early 1950s, when chicken was still a luxury meat, increases in consumer income drove the increase in chicken demand. Increased incomes continued to drive chicken demand beyond the 1950s as increasingly affluent consumers stepped up their purchases of premium chicken parts, such as chicken breasts. More recently, though, changes in consumption preferences have driven the rightward shift in demand for broilers. Many consumers believe that when its skin is removed and the meat is not fried, cooked chicken is healthier than beef and pork. Concerns over the health implications of high-fat diets have led American households to substitute chicken for beef and pork.

We know that an increase in demand, holding the supply curve fixed, should cause the equilibrium price to rise. That broiler prices fell between 1950 and 1990 indicates that something other than the demand curve must have shifted. Figure 2.16 shows that the pattern of observed broiler prices and quantities is consistent with a simultaneous rightward shift of both the demand and the supply curves. What has caused the increase in supply for broilers? In part, the rightward shift in the supply curve is due to technological advances that allow modern firms to producer leaner, higher-quality chickens at a lower cost than small family farms were

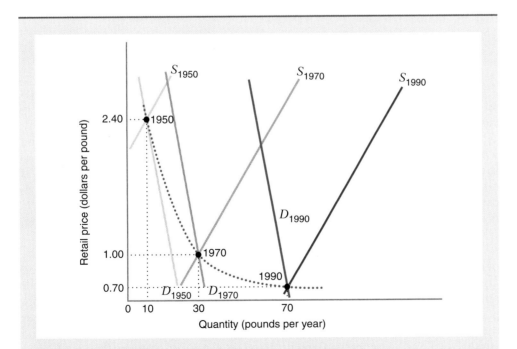

FIGURE 2.16 Supply and Demand for Broilers, 1950–1990
The pattern of prices and quantities in Figure 2.14 can be explained by rightward shifts over time in both the demand and supply curves for broilers. The supply curve has shifted from S_{1950} to S_{1970} to S_{1990}, while the demand curve has shifted from D_{1950} to D_{1970} to D_{1990}.

able to. It is also due to an increase in the number of broiler producers. For example, in 1947, 330 U.S. companies processed broilers for sale to final consumers. Just seven years later that number had more than tripled. The combined effect of technological advances and new entry pushed the supply curve for broilers rightward by an amount that equaled or exceeded the rightward shift in demand. The result is the long-term path for prices and quantities represented by the dashed line in Figure 2.16. ∎

2.2 PRICE ELASTICITY OF DEMAND

The **price elasticity of demand** measures the sensitivity of the quantity demanded to price. The price elasticity of demand (denoted by $\epsilon_{Q,P}$) is the percentage change of quantity demanded brought about by a 1 percent change in price:

$$\epsilon_{Q,P} = \frac{\frac{\Delta Q}{Q} \times 100\%}{\frac{\Delta P}{P} \times 100\%}$$

or rearranging terms and canceling the 100%s.

$$\epsilon_{Q,P} = \frac{\Delta Q}{\Delta P} \frac{P}{Q} \tag{2.3}$$

In equation (2.3), ΔP is the change in price, and ΔQ is the resulting change in quantity. The percentage change in price is thus $(\Delta P/P) \times 100\%$, and the percentage change in quantity is $(\Delta Q/Q) \times 100\%$.

Because a demand curve is downward sloping, the price elasticity of demand will be a negative number. If $\epsilon_{Q,P}$ is between 0 and -1, we say that demand is **inelastic.** In this case, the quantity demanded is relatively insensitive to price. If $\epsilon_{Q,P}$ is equal to -1, we say that demand is **unitary elastic,** meaning that the percentage increase in quantity demanded is equal to the percentage decrease in price. If $\epsilon_{Q,P}$ is between -1 and $-\infty$ (i.e., minus infinity), we say that demand is **elastic.** In this case, the quantity demanded is relatively sensitive to price.

To see the relationship between the price elasticity of demand and the shape of the demand curve, consider Figure 2.17. In this figure, demand curves D_1 and D_2 cross at point A, where the price is P and the quantity is Q. (For the moment ignore the line labeled D_3). For a given percentage increase in price $\Delta P/P$ from point A, the percentage decrease in quantity demand, $\Delta Q_2/Q$ along D_2 is larger than the percentage decrease in the quantity demanded, $\Delta Q_1/Q$, along demand curve D_1. Thus, at point A, demand is more elastic on demand curve D_2 than on demand curve D_1, i.e., the price elasticity of demand will be more negative for D_2 than for D_1. This shows that for any two demand curves that cross at a particular point, the flatter of the two demand curves is more elastic at the point at which the two curves cross.

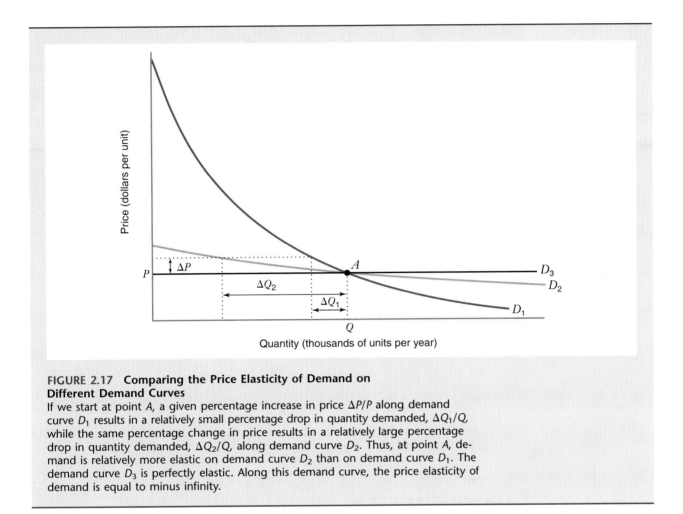

FIGURE 2.17   Comparing the Price Elasticity of Demand on Different Demand Curves
If we start at point A, a given percentage increase in price $\Delta P/P$ along demand curve D_1 results in a relatively small percentage drop in quantity demanded, $\Delta Q_1/Q$, while the same percentage change in price results in a relatively large percentage drop in quantity demanded, $\Delta Q_2/Q$, along demand curve D_2. Thus, at point A, demand is relatively more elastic on demand curve D_2 than on demand curve D_1. The demand curve D_3 is perfectly elastic. Along this demand curve, the price elasticity of demand is equal to minus infinity.

The demand curve D_3 in Figure 2.17 shows what happens in the extreme as the price elasticity of demand becomes increasingly negative. The demand curve D_3 illustrates **perfectly elastic demand.** When demand is perfectly elastic at a given price P, the price elasticity of demand equals minus infinity, i.e., $\epsilon_{Q,P} = -\infty$. This means that even the slightest increase in price above P results in the quantity demanded decreasing to 0, while just a slight decrease in price causes the quantity demanded to become infinite. Along the perfectly elastic demand curve D_3, any positive quantity can be sold at the price P, i.e., the demand curve is a horizontal line. The opposite of perfectly elastic demand is **perfectly inelastic demand.** When demand is perfectly inelastic, the price elasticity of demand is equal to 0 at every point along the demand curve, i.e., $\epsilon_{Q,P} = 0$, and the quantity demanded is completely insensitive to price.[11]

The price elasticity of demand can be an extremely useful piece of information for business firms, nonprofit institutions, and other organizations that are

[11]In Problem 2.7 at the end of the chapter, you will be asked to sketch the graph of a demand curve that is perfectly inelastic.

deciding how to price their products or services. It is also an important determinant of the structure and nature of competition within particular industries. Finally, the price elasticity of demand is important in determining the effect of various kinds of governmental interventions, such as price ceilings, tariffs, and import quotas. The analysis of these questions—which we explore in later chapters—involves the use of price elasticities of demand.

LEARNING-BY-DOING EXERCISE 2.5

Price Elasticity of Demand

Problem   Suppose price is initially $5, and the corresponding quantity demanded is 1000 units. Suppose, too, that if the price rises to $5.75, the quantity demanded will fall to 800 units. What is the price elasticity of demand over this region of the demand curve? Is demand elastic or inelastic?

Solution   In this case, $\Delta P = 5.75 - 5 = \$0.75$, and $\Delta Q = 800 - 1000 = -200$, so

$$\epsilon_{Q,P} = \frac{\Delta Q}{\Delta P}\frac{P}{Q} = -\frac{200}{\$0.75}\frac{\$5}{1000} = -1.33$$

Thus, over the range of prices between $5.00 and $5.75, quantity demanded falls at a rate of 1.33 percent for every 1 percent increase in price. Because the price elasticity of demand is between -1 and $-\infty$, demand is elastic (i.e., demand is relatively sensitive to price).

ELASTICITIES ALONG SPECIFIC DEMAND CURVES

Linear Demand Curves

A commonly used form of the demand curve is the **linear demand curve:**

$$Q = a - bP,$$

where a and b are positive constants. In this equation, the constant a embodies the effects of all the factors (e.g., income, prices of other goods) other than price that affect demand for the good. The coefficient b, which is the slope of the demand equation, reflects how the price of the good affects the quantity demanded.[12]

   Any downward-sloping demand curve has a corresponding **inverse demand curve** that expresses price as a function of quantity. We can find the inverse demand curve by taking the equation for the demand curve and solving it for P in terms of Q. The inverse demand curve for the linear demand curve is

$$P = \frac{a}{b} - \frac{1}{b}Q$$

---

[12]However, as you will see soon, the term $-b$ is not the price elasticity of demand.

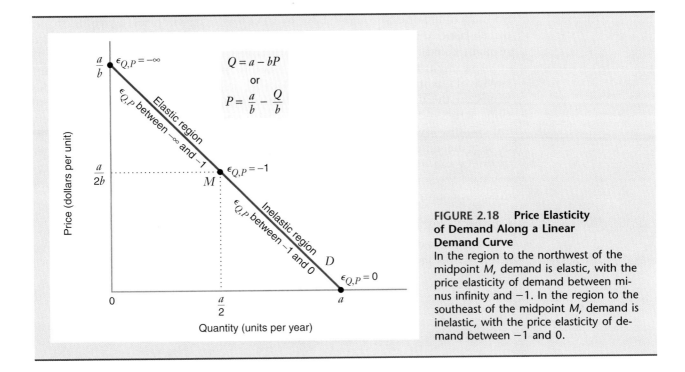

FIGURE 2.18 Price Elasticity of Demand Along a Linear Demand Curve
In the region to the northwest of the midpoint M, demand is elastic, with the price elasticity of demand between minus infinity and -1. In the region to the southeast of the midpoint M, demand is inelastic, with the price elasticity of demand between -1 and 0.

The term a/b is called the **choke price.** This is the price at which quantity demanded falls to 0.[13]

Figure 2.18 graphs a linear demand curve. Using equation 2.3 along a linear demand curve, the price elasticity of demand is given by the formula

$$\epsilon_{Q,P} = \frac{\Delta Q}{\Delta P} \frac{P}{Q} = -b\frac{P}{Q} \qquad (2.4)$$

This formula tells us that for prices close to the choke price a/b (where $Q = 0$) the price elasticity of demand approaches minus infinity. As price falls toward 0, the price elasticity of demand approaches 0. As Figure 2.18 illustrates, there is an elastic region of the demand curve where $\epsilon_{Q,P}$ is between -1 and $-\infty$. (These are the points on the demand curve to the northwest of the midpoint M.) There is also an inelastic region where $\epsilon_{Q,P}$ is between 0 and -1. (These are the points to the southeast of M.) At point M, the price elasticity of demand is exactly -1 (unitary elasticity).

The formula for the elasticity along a linear demand curve highlights the difference between the slope of the demand equation, $-b$, and the price elasticity of demand, $-b(P/Q)$. The slope measures the *absolute change* in quantity demanded

---

[13]You can verify that quantity demanded falls to 0 at the choke price by substituting $P = a/b$ into the equation of the demand curve:

$$Q = a - b\left(\frac{a}{b}\right)$$
$$= a - a$$
$$= 0 \cdot$$

(in units of quantity) brought about by a *one unit change* in price. By contrast, the price elasticity of demand measures the *percentage change* in quantity demanded brought about by a *one percent change* in price.

You might wonder why we do not simply use the slope to measure the sensitivity of quantity to price. The problem is that the slope of a demand curve depends on the units used to measure price and quantity. Thus, comparisons of slope across different goods (whose quantity units would differ) or across different countries (where prices are measured in different currency units) would not be very meaningful. By contrast, the price elasticity of demand expresses changes in prices and quantities in common terms (i.e., percentages). This allows us to compare the sensitivity of quantity demanded to price across different goods or different countries.

Constant Elasticity Demand Curves

Another commonly used demand curve is the **constant elasticity demand curve** given by this general formula:

$$Q = aP^{-b}, \tag{2.5}$$

where a and b are positive constants.

The corresponding inverse demand curve is[14]

$$P = a^{\frac{1}{b}}Q^{-\frac{1}{b}}$$

If we take natural logs of both sides of equation (2.5), we get an expression that is linear in the natural logs of Q and P:

$$\ln Q = \ln a - b \ln P$$

Because it is linear in the logs, the constant elasticity demand curve is sometimes called a **log-linear demand curve.**

For the constant elasticity demand curve, the price elasticity is always equal to the exponent $-b$.[15] For this reason, economists frequently use the constant elasticity demand curve to estimate price elasticities of demand using statistical techniques.

LEARNING-BY-DOING EXERCISE 2.6

Elasticities Along Special Demand Curves

Problem

(a) Suppose a demand curve is given by the formula $Q = 200P^{-\frac{1}{2}}$. What is the price elasticity of demand?

---

[14]This solution is obtained by first dividing each side of equation 2.5 by a. Then, we raise each side of the resulting expression to the power $-1/b$. In doing this, we note that the rules of exponents imply that $(P^{-b})^{-\frac{1}{b}} = P$ and $(1/a)^{-\frac{1}{b}} = a^{\frac{1}{b}}$.

[15]We prove this result in the Appendix to this chapter.

(b) Suppose a demand curve is given by the formula $Q = 400 - 10P$. What is the price elasticity of demand at $P = 30$? At $P = 10$?

(c) For the linear demand curve, $Q = 400 - 10P$, find the corresponding inverse demand curve. What is the choke price?

Solution

(a) This is a constant elasticity demand curve, so the price elasticity of demand is equal to $-1/2$ everywhere along the demand curve.

(b) This is a linear demand curve. For this demand curve, $\Delta Q/\Delta P$ equals the coefficient of price in the demand equation, i.e., $\Delta Q/\Delta P = -10$. Using equation 2.3 (or equivalently, equation 2.4) gives the price elasticity of demand at any price P for this particular linear demand curve:

$$\epsilon_{Q,P} = -10\frac{P}{Q}$$

Thus,

$$\epsilon_{Q,P} = -10\left(\frac{30}{400 - 10(30)}\right) = -3 \text{ when } P = 30.$$

$$\epsilon_{Q,P} = -10\left(\frac{10}{400 - 10(10)}\right) = -0.33 \text{ when } P = 10.$$

Note that demand is elastic at $P = 30$, but it is inelastic at $P = 10$. Thus, $P = 30$ is in the elastic region of the demand curve, while $P = 10$ in the inelastic region.

(c) The inverse demand curve is found by solving for P in terms of Q:

$$Q = 400 - 10P$$

$$10P = 400 - Q$$

$$P = 40 - 0.10Q$$

The choke price for the linear demand curve is the vertical intercept of the inverse demand curve. In this case, it is 40.

Similar Problem: 2.8

PRICE ELASTICITY OF DEMAND AND TOTAL REVENUE

Businesses, management consultants, and government bodies use price elasticities of demand a lot. To see why a business might care about the price elasticity of demand, let's consider how an increase in price might affect a business's **total revenue,** that is, the selling price times the quantity of product it sells, or PQ. You might think that when the price rises, so will the total revenue, but a higher price will generally reduce the quantity demanded. Thus, the "benefit" of the higher price is offset by the "cost" due to the reduction in quantity, so businesses generally face a revenue trade-off when they raise a price. If the demand is elastic (the quantity demanded is highly sensitive to price), the quantity reduction will outweigh the benefit of the higher price, and total revenue will fall. If the demand is inelastic (the quantity demanded is insensitive to price), the quantity reduction will not be too severe, and total revenue will go up. A knowledge of the price elasticity of demand can help a business predict the revenue impact of a price increase. We will discuss the implications of this relationship in Chapter 11, when we develop the theory of pricing in a profit-maximizing firm.

DETERMINANTS OF THE PRICE ELASTICITY OF DEMAND

Price elasticities have been estimated for many products using statistical techniques. Table 2.1 presents estimates of price elasticities of demand for a variety of food, liquor, and tobacco products in the United States, while Table 2.2 presents estimates of price elasticities of demand for various modes of transportation. For example, the estimated elasticity of -0.107 for cigarettes in Table 2.1 indicates that a 10 percent increase in the price of cigarettes would result in a 1.07 percent drop in the quantity of cigarettes demanded. This tells us that cigarettes have an inelastic demand: When the prices of all the individual brands of cigarettes go up (perhaps because of an increase in cigarette taxes), overall consumption of cigarettes is not likely to be affected very much. This conclusion makes sense. Even though consumers might want to cut back their consumption

TABLE 2.1
Estimates of the Price Elasticity of Demand for Selected Food, Tobacco, and Liquor Products*

Product	Estimated $\epsilon_{Q,P}$
Cigars	−0.756
Canned and cured seafood	−0.736
Fresh and frozen fish	−0.695
Cheese	−0.595
Ice cream	−0.349
Beer and malt beverages	−0.283
Bread and bakery products	−0.220
Wine and brandy	−0.198
Cookies and crackers	−0.188
Roasted coffee	−0.120
Cigarettes	−0.107
Chewing tobacco	−0.105
Pet food	−0.061
Breakfast cereal	−0.031

*Source: Pagoulatos, Emilio, and Robert Sorensen, "What Determines the Elasticity of Industry Demand," *International Journal of Industrial Organization*, 4 (1986): 237–250.

TABLE 2.2
Estimates of the Price Elasticity of Demand for Selected Modes of Transportation*

Category	Estimated $\epsilon_{Q,P}$
Airline travel, leisure	−1.52
Rail travel, leisure	−1.40
Airline travel, business	−1.15
Rail travel, business	−0.70
Urban transit	between −0.04 and −0.34

Source: Elasticities from the cross-sectional studies summarized in Tables 2, 3, 4 in Oum, Tae Hoon, W.G. Waters II, and Jong-Say Yong, "Concepts of Price Elasticities of Transport Demand and Recent Empirical Estimates," *Journal of Transport Economics and Policy* (May 1992): 139–154.

when cigarettes become more expensive, many would find it difficult to do so because cigarettes are habit forming.

In many circumstances, decision makers do not have precise numerical estimates of price elasticities of demand based on statistical techniques. Consequently, they have to rely on their knowledge of the product and the nature of the market to make educated conjectures about price sensitivity.

Here are some factors that determine the extent of a product's price elasticity—that is, the extent to which demand is relatively sensitive or insensitive to price.

- *Demand tends to be more price elastic when there are good substitutes for a product.* Demand tends to be less price elastic when the product has few or less satisfactory substitutes. One reason that the demand for airline travel by leisure travelers is price elastic (as Table 2.2 shows) is that leisure travelers usually perceive themselves as having reasonably good alternatives to traveling by air; for example, they can often travel by automobile instead. For business travelers, automobile travel is usually a less desirable substitute because of the time-sensitive nature of much business travel. This explains why, as Table 2.2 shows, the price elasticity of demand for business travel is smaller (in absolute magnitude) than that for leisure travel.

- *Demand tends to be more price elastic when a consumer's expenditure on the product is large (either in dollar terms or as a fraction of total expenditures).* For example, demand is more elastic for products such as refrigerators or automobiles. By contrast, demand tends to be less price elastic when a consumer's expenditure on the product is small, as is the case for many of the individual grocery items in Table 2.1. When a consumer must spend a lot of money to buy a product, the gain from carefully evaluating the purchase and paying close attention to price is greater than it is when the item does not entail a large outlay of money.

- *Demand tends to be less price elastic when, because of tax deductions or insurance, buyers pay only a fraction of the full price of the product.* Health care is an excellent example of this. Consumers with health insurance are thought to be insensitive to the prices of medical procedures because they do not bear the full cost of those procedures.

• *Demand tends to be less price elastic when the product is used in conjunction with another product that buyers have committed themselves to.* For example, an owner of a copying machine is likely to be fairly insensitive to the price of toner, because the toner is an essential input in running the copier.

MARKET-LEVEL VERSUS BRAND-LEVEL PRICE ELASTICITIES OF DEMAND

A common mistake in the use of price elasticities of demand is to suppose that just because the demand for a product is inelastic, the demand each seller of that product faces is also inelastic. Consider, for example, cigarettes. As already discussed, the demand for cigarettes is not especially sensitive to price: an increase in the price of all brands of cigarettes would only modestly affect overall cigarette demand. However, if the price of only a single brand of cigarettes (e.g., Salem) went up, the demand for that brand would probably drop substantially because consumers would switch to the now lower-priced brands whose prices did not change. Thus, while demand can be inelastic at the market level, it can be highly elastic at the individual brand level.

The distinction between market-level and brand-level elasticities reflects the impact of substitution possibilities on the degree to which consumers are sensitive to price. In the case of cigarettes, for example, a typical smoker *needs* cigarettes because there are no good alternatives. But that smoker doesn't necessarily *need* Salem cigarettes because, when the price of Salem goes up, switching to another brand will provide more or less the same degree of satisfaction.

What determines whether a firm should use market-level elasticity or a firm-level elasticity in assessing the effect of a price change? The answer depends on what the firm expects its competitors to do. If a firm expects its rivals to quickly match its price change, then the market-level elasticity will provide the appropriate measure of how the demand for the firm's product is likely to change with price. If, by contrast, a firm expects its rivals not to match its price change (or to do so only after a long time lag), then the brand-level elasticity is appropriate.

---

*E*XAMPLE 2.3   *Brand-Level Price Elasticities of Demand in the Automobile Market*

Using modern statistical techniques, Steven Berry, James Levinsohn, and Ariel Pakes recently estimated price elasticities of demand for numerous makes of automobiles.[16] Table 2.3 shows some of their estimates. These estimates illustrate that demands for individual models of automobiles are highly elastic (between −3.5 and −6.5). By contrast, estimates of the market-level price elasticity of demand for automobiles

---

[16]S. Berry, J. Levinsohn, and A. Pakes, "Automobile Prices in Market Equilibrium," *Econometrica*, 63 (July 1995): 841–890.

TABLE 2.3
Estimates of Price Elasticities of Demand for Selected Makes of Automobiles, 1990*

Model	Price	Estimated $\epsilon_{Q,P}$
Mazda 323	$ 5,039	−6.358
Nissan Sentra	$ 5,661	−6.528
Ford Escort	$ 5,663	−6.031
Chevrolet Cavalier	$ 5,797	−6.433
Honda Accord	$ 9,292	−4.798
Ford Taurus	$ 9,671	−4.220
Buick Century	$10,138	−6.755
Nissan Maxima	$13,695	−4.845
Acura Legend	$18,944	−4.134
Lincoln Town Car	$21,412	−4.320
Cadillac Seville	$24,544	−3.973
Lexus LS400	$27,544	−3.085
BMW 735i	$37,490	−3.515

Source: Table V in S. Berry, J. Levinsohn, and A. Pakes, "Automobile Prices in Market Equilibrium," *Econometrica* 63 (July 1995): 841–890.

generally fall between −1 and −1.5.[17] This highlights the distinction between brand-level price elasticity of demand and market-level price elasticity of demand.

Brand-level price elasticities of demand are more negative than market-level price elasticities of demand because consumers have greater substitution possibilities when only one firm raises its price. This suggests that the most negative brand-level elasticities for automobiles should be in those market segments in which consumers have the greatest substitution possibilities. The data in Table 2.3 bear this out. The most elastic demands are generally for automobiles in the compact and subcompact market segments (Mazda 323, Nissan Sentra), which are the most crowded. By contrast, demands for cars in the luxury segment (Lexus LS400, BMW 735i) are somewhat less price elastic because there are fewer substitutes for them. ◼

INCOME AND CROSS-PRICE ELASTICITIES OF DEMAND

2.3
OTHER ELASTICITIES

We can use elasticity to characterize the responsiveness of demand to any of the determinants of demand. Two of the more common elasticities in addition to the price elasticity of demand are the **income elasticity of demand** and the **cross-price elasticity of demand**.

[17]See, for example, Hymans, S. H., "Consumer Durable Spending: Explanation and Prediction," *Brookings Papers on Economic Activity*, 2 (1970): 173–199.

The income elasticity of demand measures the rate of percentage change of quantity demanded with respect to income, holding all prices and all other determinants of demand constant:

$$\epsilon_{Q,I} = \frac{\frac{\Delta Q}{Q} \times 100\%}{\frac{\Delta I}{I} \times 100\%}$$

or, after rearranging terms,

$$\epsilon_{Q,I} = \frac{\Delta Q}{\Delta I} \frac{I}{Q} \tag{2.6}$$

Table 2.4 shows estimated income elasticities of demand for a number of different food products. As the table shows, an income elasticity can be positive or negative. A positive income elasticity (e.g., apples, oranges, butter) indicates that demand for a good rises as consumer income goes up; a negative income elasticity (e.g., margarine, flour) indicates that demand for a good falls as consumer income goes up.

TABLE 2.4
Estimates of the Income Elasticity of Demand for Selected Food Products*

Product	Estimated $\epsilon_{Q,I}$
Cream	1.72
Peaches	1.43
Apples	1.32
Fresh peas	1.05
Oranges	0.83
Onions	0.58
Eggs	0.44
Milk	0.50
Butter	0.37
Potatoes	0.15
Margarine	−0.20
Flour	−0.36

**Sources:* The first ten entries in Table 2.4 come from Table 1-1 in Daniel B. Suits, "Agriculture," Chapter 1 in *The Structure of American Industry*, 9th edition, Walter Adams and James Brock, eds. (Englewood Cliffs, NJ: Prentice Hall), 1995; the last two entries come from H. S. Houthhakker and Lester D. Taylor, *Consumer Demand in the United States, 1929–1970* (Cambridge, MA: Harvard University Press), 1966.

The cross-price elasticity of demand for good i with respect to the price of good j measures the rate of percentage change of the quantity of good i demanded with respect to the price of good j:

$$\epsilon_{Q_i,P_j} = \frac{\frac{\Delta Q_i}{Q_i} \times 100\%}{\frac{\Delta P_j}{P_j} \times 100\%}$$

or, after rearranging terms,

$$\epsilon_{Q_i,P_j} = \frac{\Delta Q_i}{\Delta P_j}\frac{P_j}{Q_i} \tag{2.7}$$

where P_j denotes the initial price of good j, and Q_i denotes the initial quantity of good i demanded. Table 2.5 shows cross-price elasticities of demand for selected meat products.

Cross-price elasticities can be positive or negative. If $\epsilon_{Q_i,P_j} > 0$, a higher price for good j increases the demand for good i. In this case, goods i and j are **demand substitutes.** Table 2.5 shows examples of demand substitutes. For example, the fact that the cross-price elasticity of demand for chicken with respect to the price of beef is positive (0.12) indicates that as the price of beef goes up, the quantity of chicken demanded goes up. Evidently, as beef becomes more expensive, consumers purchase more chicken and less beef.

By contrast, if $\epsilon_{Q_i,P_j} < 0$, a higher price of good j decreases the demand for good i. This relationship indicates that goods i and j are **demand complements.** Breakfast cereal and milk are examples of demand complements. As the price of breakfast cereal goes up, consumers will buy less cereal and will thus need less milk to pour on top of their cereal. Consequently, the demand for milk will fall.

TABLE 2.5
Cross-Price Elasticities of Demand for Selected Meat Products*

	Price of Beef	Price of Pork	Price of Chicken
Demand for Beef	−0.65**	0.01***	0.20
Demand for Pork	0.25	−0.45	0.16
Demand for Chicken	0.12	0.20	−0.65

*Table 1-4 in Daniel B. Suits, "Agriculture," Chapter 1 in *The Structure of American Industry*, 8th edition, Walter Adams and James Brock, eds. (Englewood Cliffs, NJ: Prentice Hall, 1990).

**This is the price elasticity of demand for beef.

***This is the cross-price elasticity of demand for beef with respect to the price of pork.

TABLE 2.6
Cross-Price Elasticities of Demand for Selected Makes of Automobiles*

	Price of Sentra	Price of Escort	Price of LS400	Price of 735i
Demand for Sentra	−6.528**	0.078***	0.000	0.000
Demand for Escort	0.454	−6.031	0.001	0.000
Demand for LS400	0.000	0.001	−3.085	0.093
Demand for 735i	0.000	0.001	0.032	−3.515

*Adapted from Table VI in S. Berry, J. Levinsohn, and A. Pakes, "Automobile Prices in Market Equilibrium," *Econometrica* 63 (July 1995): 841–890.
**This is the price elasticity of demand for a Sentra.
***This is the cross-price elasticity of demand for a Sentra with respect to the price of an Escort.

EXAMPLE 2.4   *Cross-Price Elasticities of Demand in the Automobile Market*

Table 2.6 presents estimates of the cross-price elasticities of demand for the makes of automobiles shown in Table 2.3. (The table contains the price elasticities of demand for these makes as well.) The table shows, for example, that the cross-price elasticity of demand for Ford Escort with respect to the price of a Nissan Sentra is 0.454, indicating that the demand for Ford Escorts goes up at a rate of 0.454 percent for each 1 percent increase in the price of a Nissan Sentra. Although all of the cross-price elasticities are fairly small, note that the cross-price elasticities between compact cars (Sentra, Escort) and luxury cars (Lexus LS400, BMW 735i) are zero or close to zero. This makes sense: Compacts and luxury cars are distinct market segments. Different people buy BMWs than buy Ford Escorts, so the demand for one should not be much affected by the price of the other. By contrast, the cross-price elasticities within the compact segment are relatively higher. This suggests that consumers within this segment view Sentras and Escorts as substitutes for one another.   ■

EXAMPLE 2.5   *Price, Income, and Cross-Price Elasticities for Coke and Pepsi*[18]

If the price of Coke goes down, what is the effect on the demand for Pepsi? And if Pepsi's price goes down, how is Coke's demand affected? Farid Gasmi, Quang Vuong, and Jean-Jacques Laffont (GVL) studied competitive interactions in the U.S. soft drink market and estimated demand equations for Coca-Cola and Pepsi.[19] Their estimates are as follows:[20]

[18]This example is based on F. Gasmi, J.J. Laffont, and Q. Vuong, "Econometric Analysis of Collusive Behavior in a Soft Drink Market," *Journal of Economics and Management Strategy*, 1 (Summer 1992): 278–311. It was inspired by the classroom notes of our former colleague, Matthew Jackson.
[19]In Chapter 13, we will use these demand functions to study price competition between Coke and Pepsi.
[20]GVL estimated these demand functions under several different assumptions about market behavior. The ones reported here correspond to what the authors believe is the best model.

$$Q_C = 26.17 - 3.98P_C + 2.25P_P + 2.60A_C - 0.62A_P + 0.99I + 9.58S$$
$$Q_P = 17.48 - 5.48P_P + 1.40P_C + 2.83A_P - 4.81A_C + 1.92I + 11.98S$$

where:

Q_C = quantity demanded of Coca-Cola (ten million cases)
Q_P = quantity demanded of Pepsi (ten million cases)
P_C = price of Coca-Cola (dollars per ten cases, expressed in 1986 U.S. dollars)
P_P = price of Pepsi (dollars per ten cases, expressed in 1986 U.S. dollars)
A_C = square root of quarterly advertising expenditures on behalf of Coca-Cola (1986 dollars)
A_P = square root of quarterly advertising expenditures on behalf of Pepsi (1986 dollars)
I = disposable income in the United States (thousands of 1986 dollars)
S = a variable equal to 1 if we are in the spring and summer quarters (April–September), and 0, otherwise

We can use these estimated demand functions to calculate the price, cross-price, and income elasticities of demand for Coke and Pepsi. To do this, we need to choose values for each of the variables in the demand functions. We will use the average values observed by GVL in their study: $P_C = 12.96$, $P_P = 8.16$, $A_C = 5.89$, $A_P = 5.28$, $I = 20.63$, and we assume that $S = 1$ (i.e., we are considering the demand functions that prevail in the spring and summer quarters).

Table 2.7 shows the calculated elasticities. We will illustrate one of the calculations: the cross-price elasticity of demand of Coke with respect to the price of Pepsi. The formula for this cross-price elasticity is

$$\epsilon_{Q_C, P_P} = \frac{\Delta Q_C}{\Delta P_P} \frac{P_P}{Q_C}$$

We can determine the term $\Delta Q_C / \Delta P_P$ directly from the demand equation for Coke shown above: it equals the coefficient on the variable P_P in this equation, which is 2.25. We will compute the cross-price elasticity at the average value of Pepsi's price P_P which is 8.16. We can compute the quantity demanded for Coke by substituting the average values of the variables into Coke's demand equation; doing this gives us a value of Q_C equal to 34.99. Substituting these values for $\Delta Q_C / \Delta P_P$, P_P, and Q_C into the cross-elasticity formula yields:

$$\epsilon_{Q_C, P_P} = 2.25 \frac{8.16}{34.99} = 0.52$$

This tells us that a 1 percent increase in the price of Pepsi can be expected to increase the quarterly U.S. demand for Coca-Cola by 0.52 percent.

TABLE 2.7
Price, Cross-Price, and Income Elasticities of Demand for Coca-Cola and Pepsi

Elasticity	Coca-Cola	Pepsi
Price elasticity of demand	−1.47	−1.55
Cross-price elasticity of demand	0.52	0.64
Income elasticity of demand	0.58	1.38

As you can see in Table 2.7, the cross-price elasticities of demand are positive numbers (0.52 and 0.64). This tells us that a decrease in Coke's price will decrease the demand for Pepsi, and a decrease in Pepsi's price will decrease the demand for Coke. Thus, consumers view these products as substitutes, and a decrease in the price of one brand would hurt demand for the other. In addition, the demand for both products goes up when consumer income goes up, indicating that increases in consumer incomes benefit both brands. Finally, the price elasticity of demand for each brand falls in the range between -1 and $-\infty$. Thus, the brand-level demand for both Coke and Pepsi is elastic.   ■

PRICE ELASTICITY OF SUPPLY

The **price elasticity of supply** measures the sensitivity of quantity supplied Q^s to price. The price elasticity of supply—denoted by $\epsilon_{Q^s,P}$—tells us the percentage change in quantity supplied for each percent change in price:

$$\epsilon_{Q^s,P} = \frac{\frac{\Delta Q^s}{Q^s} \times 100\%}{\frac{\Delta P}{P} \times 100\%}$$

$$= \frac{\Delta Q^s}{\Delta P}\frac{P}{Q^s}$$

This formula applies to both the firm level and the market level. The firm-level price elasticity of supply tells us the sensitivity of an individual firm's supply to price, while the market-level price elasticity of supply tells us the sensitivity of market supply to price.

Just as we can have perfectly elastic and perfectly inelastic demand curves, we can also have perfectly elastic and perfectly inelastic supply curves. Along a perfectly elastic supply curve, the price elasticity of supply is equal to infinity. This means that the slightest increase in price will cause the quantity supplied to become infinitely large, while the slightest decrease in price would cause the quantity supplied to decrease to 0. For a perfectly inelastic supply curve, the price elasticity of supply is equal to 0. This means that the quantity supplied is completely insensitive to price.

2.4
LONG-RUN VERSUS SHORT-RUN DEMAND AND SUPPLY

GREATER ELASTICITY IN THE LONG RUN THAN IN THE SHORT RUN

Consumers cannot always adjust their purchasing decisions instantly in response to a change in price. For example, a consumer faced with an increase in the price of natural gas can, in the short run, turn down the thermostat, which will reduce consumption. But over time, this consumer can reduce natural gas consumption even more by replacing the old furnace with an energy-efficient model. Thus, it is useful to distinguish between the **long-run demand curve** for a product—the demand curve that pertains to the period of time in which consumers can *fully* adjust their purchase decisions to changes in price—and the **short-run demand curve**—the demand curve that pertains to the period of time in which consumers

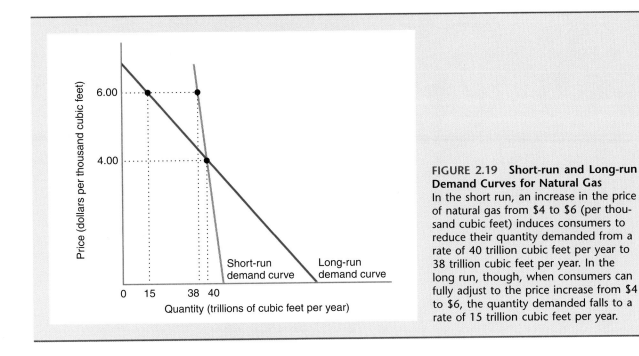

FIGURE 2.19 Short-run and Long-run Demand Curves for Natural Gas
In the short run, an increase in the price of natural gas from $4 to $6 (per thousand cubic feet) induces consumers to reduce their quantity demanded from a rate of 40 trillion cubic feet per year to 38 trillion cubic feet per year. In the long run, though, when consumers can fully adjust to the price increase from $4 to $6, the quantity demanded falls to a rate of 15 trillion cubic feet per year.

cannot fully adjust their purchasing decisions to changes in price. We would expect that for products, such as natural gas, for which consumption is tied to physical assets whose stocks change slowly, the long-run demand curve would be more price elastic than short-run demand. Figure 2.19 illustrates this possibility. The long-run demand curve is "flatter" than the short-run demand curve.

Similarly, firms sometimes cannot fully adjust their supply decisions in response to changes in price. For example, in the short run, a producer of semiconductors might not be able to increase its supply of chips in response to an increase in price by very much because it faces a capacity constraint—a fab[21] can only produce so many chips, even if extra workers are hired. However, if the price increase is expected to be permanent, then the firm can expand the capacity of its existing fabs or build new ones. The increase in the quantity supplied as a result of the price increase will thus be greater in the long run than in the short run. Figure 2.20 illustrates the distinction between the **long-run supply curve**— the supply curve that pertains to the period of time in which sellers can fully adjust their supply decisions in response to changes in price, and the **short-run supply curve**—the supply curve that pertains to the period of time in which sellers cannot fully adjust their supply decisions in response to a change in price. Figure 2.20 shows that for a good such as semiconductors the long-run supply curve is flatter than the short-run supply curve.

GREATER ELASTICITY IN THE SHORT RUN THAN IN THE LONG RUN

For certain goods, long-run market demand can be *less elastic* than short-run demand. This is particularly likely to be true for **durable goods**—goods such as automobiles or airplanes that provide valuable services over many years. To

---

[21]A fab is the term used for the facility in which semiconductor chips are manufactured.

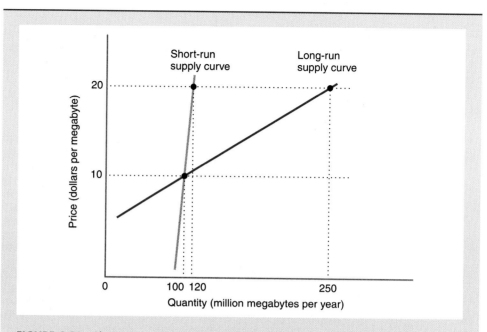

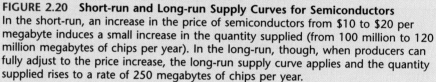

FIGURE 2.20   Short-run and Long-run Supply Curves for Semiconductors
In the short-run, an increase in the price of semiconductors from $10 to $20 per megabyte induces a small increase in the quantity supplied (from 100 million to 120 million megabytes of chips per year). In the long-run, though, when producers can fully adjust to the price increase, the long-run supply curve applies and the quantity supplied rises to a rate of 250 megabytes of chips per year.

illustrate this point, consider the demand for commercial airplanes. Suppose that Boeing and Airbus (the world's two producers of commercial aircraft) are able to raise the prices of new commercial aircraft. It seems unlikely that this would dramatically affect the demand for aircraft in the long run: Airlines, such as United and British Airways, need aircraft to do their business. There are no feasible substitutes.[22] But in the short run, the impact of higher aircraft prices might be dramatic. Airlines that might have operated an aircraft for 15 years might now try to get an extra 2 or 3 years out of it before replacing it. Thus, while demand for new commercial aircrafts in the long run might be relatively price inelastic, in the short run (within 2 or 3 years of the price change), demand would be relatively more elastic. Figure 2.21 shows this possibility. The steeper demand curve corresponds to the long-run effect of the price increase in the total size of aircraft fleets worldwide; the flatter demand curve shows the effect of the price increase on orders for new aircraft in the first year after the price increase.

For some goods, long-run market supply can be less elastic than short-run market supply. This is especially likely to be the case for goods that can be recycled and resold in the secondary market (i.e., the market for used or recycled goods). For example, in the short-run an increase in the price of aluminum would

[22]That is not to say there would be no impact on demand. Higher aircraft prices may raise the costs of entering the airline business sufficiently that some prospective operators of airlines would choose to stay out of the business.

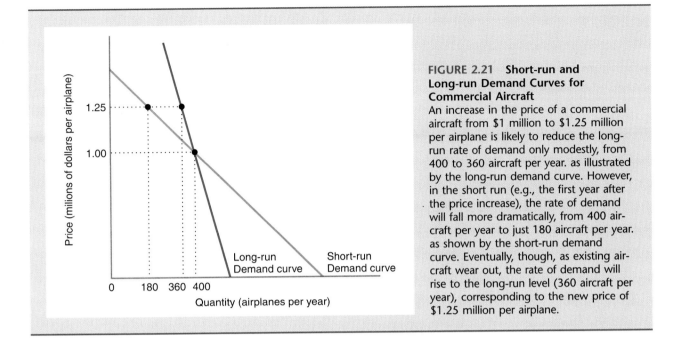

FIGURE 2.21 Short-run and Long-run Demand Curves for Commercial Aircraft
An increase in the price of a commercial aircraft from $1 million to $1.25 million per airplane is likely to reduce the long-run rate of demand only modestly, from 400 to 360 aircraft per year. as illustrated by the long-run demand curve. However, in the short run (e.g., the first year after the price increase), the rate of demand will fall more dramatically, from 400 aircraft per year to just 180 aircraft per year. as shown by the short-run demand curve. Eventually, though, as existing aircraft wear out, the rate of demand will rise to the long-run level (360 aircraft per year), corresponding to the new price of $1.25 million per airplane.

elicit increased supply from two sources: additional new aluminum and recycled aluminum made from scrap. However, in the long run, the stock of scrap aluminum will diminish, and the increase in quantity supplied induced by the increased price will mainly come from the production of new aluminum.

EXAMPLE 2.6

Using Long-Run and Short-Run Supply Curves to Understand the DRAM Price Collapse of 1996[23]

DRAM (dynamic random access memory) chips are semiconductor integrated circuits used for memory in personal computers. DRAM chips, produced by such companies, as Samsung, NEC, and Hitachi, are purchased by manufacturers of personal computers, such as Compaq and Apple, as well as by producers of cell phones, video games, and other digital electronic equipment.

Figure 2.22 shows that between 1993 and 1996, the world market for DRAM chips was stable. Prices held steady at about $30 per megabyte. But in 1996, prices suddenly collapsed. By the end of that year, they had fallen to $5 per megabyte. The collapse in DRAM prices was especially surprising because as late as the summer of 1995, analysts and industry observers were predicting that prices would go up! In fact, many analysts believed that the DRAM market was on the verge of an unprecented rise in prices.

What happened? The price collapse of 1996 came about as a result of several factors that can be depicted using supply and demand analysis. First, most of the

[23]This example draws from E. Capocchi, B. Firsov, and L. Pachano, "The DRAM Industry," unpublished term paper, Kellogg Graduate School of Management, (March 1997).

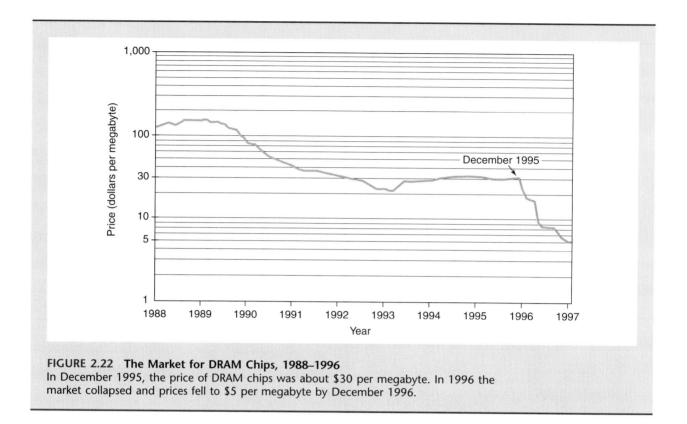

FIGURE 2.22   The Market for DRAM Chips, 1988–1996
In December 1995, the price of DRAM chips was about $30 per megabyte. In 1996 the market collapsed and prices fell to $5 per megabyte by December 1996.

major producers believed that the robust growth in demand for personal computers (PCs) from 1992 to 1995 (more than 20 percent a year) would not only continue, but also accelerate. In addition, it was widely believed that the introduction of Windows 95 in August 1995 would spur significant additional demand from PC owners needing memory upgrades. On the basis of these predictions, most producers expected that prices would increase by about $5 per megabyte over the 1995 level to $35 per megabyte. In light of these expectations, producers moved along the long-run market supply curve LS_{1996}, as shown in Figure 2.23, adding output to the industry by increasing production capacity. If forecasts about demand had been correct, the market equilibrium in 1996 would have occurred at point A.

But demand for DRAM chips did not grow. In the United States, PC demand stalled during the Christmas season of 1995, and it stayed flat throughout much of 1996. Moreover, adoption of Windows 95 occurred more slowly than most analysts had anticipated, so the expected flood of memory upgrades did not occur. As a result, computer producers that had stocked up on DRAM chips in the last six months of 1995, in anticipation of possible supply shortages, now had excessive inventories of DRAMs. Consequently, customers demanded even fewer chips than they had in 1995, so that the actual 1996 demand curve in Figure 2.23 was well to the left of the expected demand curve.

By the time new production capacity came on line in early 1996, producers were operating on the short-run market supply curve, shown as SS_{1996} in Figure 2.23. The steep short-run supply curve reflects the willingness of DRAM producers to operate existing fabs even at low DRAM prices. The resulting 1996 equilibrium occurred at a price of about $5 per megabyte, well below the 1995 price of $30 per megabyte.

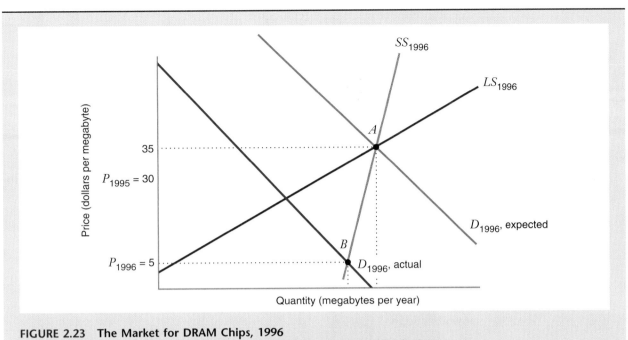

FIGURE 2.23 The Market for DRAM Chips, 1996
DRAM suppliers, anticipating a price of about $35 per megabyte in 1996, built new production capacity (new "fabs"), and effectively expanded output along the long-run supply curve LS_{1996}. Had forecasts of demand been correct, the market equilibrium would have occurred at point A. However, once the new capacity was built and prices fell in response to an unanticipated decline in demand in 1996, producers operated along their short-run supply curve SS_{1996}. By mid-1996, when the DRAM market reached a short-run equilibrium at point B, DRAM prices had fallen to $5 per megabyte.

Supply and demand analysis would predict that DRAM prices would eventually go up from their 1996 low. Semiconductor output would be reduced by not replacing existing fabs as they wore out, and supply would be more in line with the long-run market supply curve. This is what happened. Many of the major producers reduced output levels, and DRAM prices increased. ■

2.5 BACK-OF-THE-ENVELOPE CALCULATIONS

So where do demand curves come from, and how do you derive the equation of a demand function for a real product in a real market? One approach to determining demand curves involves collecting data on the quantity of a good purchased in a market, the prices of that good, and other possible determinants of that good's demand and then applying statistical methods to estimate an equation for the demand function that best fits the data. This broad approach is data-intensive: the analyst has to collect enough data on quantities, prices, and other demand drivers, so that the resulting statistical estimates are sensible. However, analysts often lack the resources to perform a sophisticated statistical analysis, so they need some techniques that allow them, in a conceptually correct way, to infer the shape or the equation of a demand curve from fragmentary information about prices, quantities, and elasticities. These techniques are called *back-of-the-envelope calculations* because they are simple enough to do on the back of an envelope.

FITTING LINEAR DEMAND CURVES USING QUANTITY, PRICE, AND ELASTICITY INFORMATION

Often, you can obtain information on the prevailing or typical prices and quantities within a particular market as well as estimates of the price elasticity of demand in that market. These estimates might come from statistical studies (this is where the elasticities in Tables 2.1, 2.2, and 2.3 came from) or the judgments of informed observers (e.g. industry participants, investment analysts, consultants). If you assume as a rough approximation that the equation of the demand curve is linear (i.e., $Q = a - bP$), you can then derive the equation of this linear demand (i.e., the values of a and b) from these three pieces of information (prevailing price, prevailing quantity, and estimated elasticity).

The approach to fitting a linear demand curve to quantity, price, and elasticity data proceeds as follows. Suppose Q^* and P^* are the known values of quantity and price in this market, and let $\epsilon_{Q,P}$ be the known value of the price elasticity of demand. Recall the formula for the price elasticity of demand for a linear demand function.

$$\epsilon_{Q,P} = -b \frac{P^*}{Q^*} \tag{2.8}$$

Solving equation 2.8 for b yields

$$b = -\epsilon_{Q,P} \frac{Q^*}{P^*} \tag{2.9}$$

To solve for the intercept a, we note that Q^* and P^* must be on the demand curve. Thus, it must be that

$$Q^* = a - bP^*$$

or

$$a = Q^* + bP^* = (1 - \epsilon_{Q,P})Q^* \tag{2.10}$$

The second equality in equation (2.10) comes from substituting our derived expression in equation (2.9) for b. Taken together, equations (2.9) and (2.10) provide a set of formulas for generating the equation of a linear demand curve.

We can illustrate the fitting process with the chicken broiler market discussed in Example 2.2. In 1990, the per capita consumption of chicken in the United States was about 70 pounds per person, while the average inflation-adjusted retail price was about $0.70 per pound. Demand for broilers is relatively price inelastic, with estimates in the range of -0.5 to -0.6.[24] Thus,

---

[24]All data are from Richard T. Rogers (1993). "Broilers: Differentiating a Commodity," in Duetsch, Larry (ed.), *Industry Studies* (Englewood Cliffs, NJ: Prentice Hall), pp. 3–32. See especially the data summarized on pp. 4–6.

$$Q^* = 70$$

$$P^* = 0.70$$

$$\epsilon_{Q,P} = -0.55 \text{ (splitting the difference)}$$

Applying formulas 2.9 and 2.10, we get

$$b = -(-0.55)\frac{70}{0.70} = 55$$

$$a = [1 - (-0.55)]70 = 108.5$$

Thus, the equation of our demand curve for chicken broilers in 1990 is

$$Q = 108.5 - 55P$$

This curve is the straight line depicted in Figure 2.24.

You might wonder whether we could fit the observed market and elasticity data to other possible functional forms or "shapes" of the demand curve. The answer is that we can. Suppose, for example, we had postulated that demand has the constant elasticity form, or

$$Q = aP^{-b}$$

In this case, the fitting is particularly simple because we know that the exponent $-b$ is the price elasticity of demand. Thus, starting with an observed quantity and

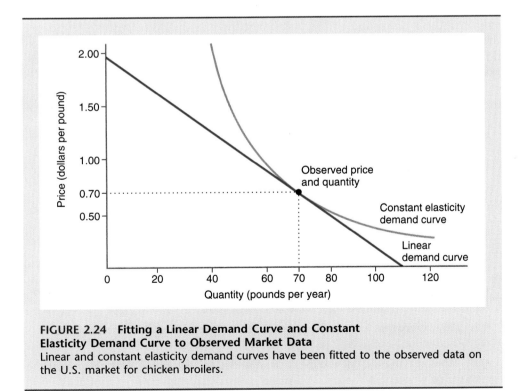

FIGURE 2.24 Fitting a Linear Demand Curve and Constant Elasticity Demand Curve to Observed Market Data
Linear and constant elasticity demand curves have been fitted to the observed data on the U.S. market for chicken broilers.

price, Q^* and P^*, and an estimate $\epsilon_{Q,P}$ of the price elasticity of demand, the fitted values of a and b are as follows:

$$b = -\epsilon_{Q,P}$$
$$a = Q^*(P^*)^b$$

Applying these formulas to the broiler example, we have

$$b = -(-0.55) = 0.55$$
$$a = 70(0.70)^{0.55} = 57.53$$

Thus, the equation of the constant elasticity demand curve that fits the observed market data is

$$Q = 57.53P^{-0.55}$$

This demand curve is also depicted in Figure 2.24. Note that both the linear demand curve and the constant elasticity demand curve go through the same point ($Q^* = 70$, $P^* = \$0.70$) because they have been constructed to fit the existing market data.

IDENTIFYING SUPPLY AND DEMAND CURVES FROM PRICE AND QUANTITY MOVEMENTS

Earlier in this chapter, we discussed how exogenous shifts in demand and supply will alter the equilibrium prices and quantities in a market. In this section, we show how information about shifts in demand and supply curves and observations of the resulting market prices can be used to do back-of-the-envelope derivations of supply and demand curves.

We will use a specific example to illustrate the logic of the analysis. Consider the market for crushed stone in the United States in the late 1990s. Let's suppose that the market demand and supply curves for crushed stone are linear:

$$Q^d = a - bP$$
$$Q^s = f + hP$$

Since we expect the demand curve to slope downward and the supply curve to slope upward, we expect that $b > 0$ and $h > 0$.

Now, suppose that we have the following information about the market for crushed stone between 1995 and 1999:

- Between 1995 and 1997, the market was uneventful. The market price was $9 per ton, and 30 million tons were sold each year.
- In 1998, there was a one year burst of highway building. The market price of crushed stone rose to $10 per ton, and 33 million tons were sold.
- By 1999, the burst of new construction ended. A new union contract raised the wages of workers in the crushed stone industry. The market price of crushed stone was $10 per ton, and 28 million tons were sold.

Let's now put this information to work. The one year burst of highway building in 1998 most likely resulted in a rightward shift in the demand curve for
crushed stone, as shown in Figure 2.25. On the assumption that there was no reason for any appreciable shift in the supply curve during this period, the rightward
shift in demand allows us to compute the slope of the supply curve because the
1995–97 and the 1998 market equilibria both fall along the initial supply curve,
labeled S_{1997} in Figure 2.25.

$$b = \text{Slope of } S_{1997} = \frac{\Delta Q^*}{\Delta P^*} = \frac{33 \text{ million} - 30 \text{ million}}{10 - 9} = 3 \text{ million}$$

Therefore, the shift in demand *identifies* the slope of the supply curve. It may
seem curious that it takes a shift in demand to provide information about the supply curve, but on reflection, it really isn't that surprising. The shift in demand
moves the market along a particular supply curve and thus tells us how sensitive
the quantity supplied is to the price. Similarly, the shift in the market supply of
crushed stone caused by the rise in wage rates identifies the slope of the demand
curve, labeled D_{1997} in Figure 2.25. Note that the burst of highway construction
subsided in 1999, so in that year the demand curve for crushed stone reverted to

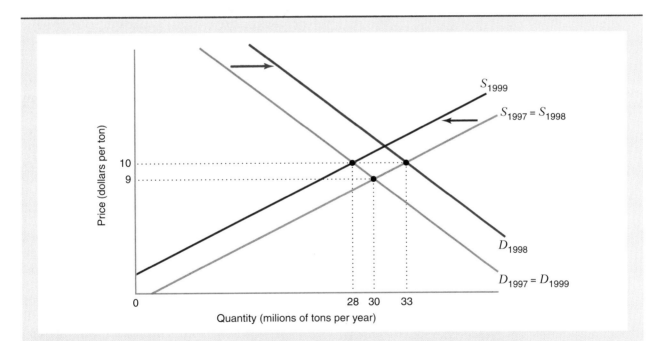

**FIGURE 2.25 Identifying Demand and Supply
Curves from Observed Price and Quantity Changes**
The market for crushed stone is in equilibrium during the years 1995 through 1997. This
is the point at which the initial demand curve D_{1997} and the initial supply curve S_{1997} intersect. In 1998, the one-year burst of highway construction activity shifts the demand
curve rightward to D_{1998}. The market moves along the supply curve S_{1997}, so the change
in equilibrium price and quantity identifies the slope of the supply curve S_{1997}. In 1999,
the demand curve shifts back to D_{1997}, but the supply curve shifts leftward to S_{1999} due
to an increase in the wages of workers in the crushed stone industry. The market thus
moves along the demand curve D_{1997}, so the change in the equilibrium price and quantity identifies the slope of the demand curve D_{1997}.

its initial position, and the shift in supply thus moved the market along the demand curve D_{1997}.

$$-b = \text{Slope of } D_{1997} = \frac{\Delta Q^*}{\Delta P^*} = \frac{28 \text{ million} - 30 \text{ million}}{10 - 9} = -2 \text{ million}$$

Note the unifying logic that was used in both calculations. Knowing that one curve shifted while the other did not allowed us to calculate the slope of the curve that did not shift.

Having now calculated the slopes of the demand and supply curves, we can now work backward to calculate the intercepts a and f of the demand and supply curves for 1999. Since we know that 28 million tons were sold at $10 per ton during those years, the following equations must hold:

$$28 = a - (2 \times 10) \qquad \text{(demand)}$$
$$28 = f + (3 \times 10) \qquad \text{(supply)}$$

Solving these equations implies $a = 48$ and $d = -2$. Thus, the demand and supply curves for this market in 1997 were

$$Q^d = 48 - 2P$$
$$Q^s = -2 + 3P$$

Having identified equations for the demand and supply curves, we can now use them to forecast how changes in demand or supply will affect the equilibrium price and quantity. For example, suppose we expected that in the year 2000 another burst of new road construction would increase the demand for crushed stone by 15 million tons per year no matter what the price. Suppose, further, that supply conditions were expected to resemble those in 1999. We could forecast the equilibrium price by solving the equation

$$48 - 2P + 15 = -2 + 3P$$

which implies $P = \$13$ per ton. The equilibrium quantity in the year 2000 would be expected to equal $-2 + 3(13) = 37$ million tons. Our back-of-the-envelope analysis provides us with a "quick and dirty" way to forecast future price and quantity movements in this market.

There is an important limitation to this analysis. We can identify the slope of the demand curve by a shift in supply only if the demand curve remains fixed, and we can identify the slope of the supply curve by a shift in demand only if the supply curve stays fixed. If both curves shift at the same time, then we are neither moving along a given demand curve nor a given supply curve, so changes in the equilibrium quantity and the equilibrium price cannot identify the slope of either curve.

IDENTIFYING THE PRICE ELASTICITY OF DEMAND FROM SHIFTS IN SUPPLY

In the preceding section, we used actual changes in prices and quantities to identify the equations of supply or demand curves. In some instances, however, we might not know the change in the equilibrium quantity for a product, but we might have a good idea about the extent to which its supply curve has shifted. (Business-

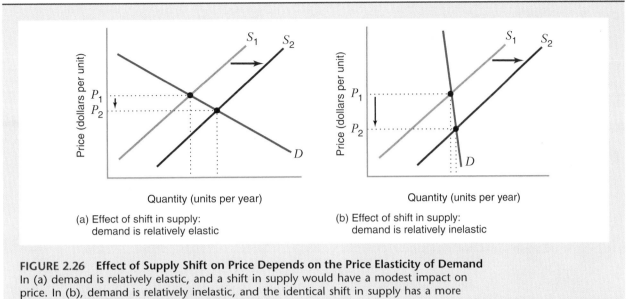

FIGURE 2.26 Effect of Supply Shift on Price Depends on the Price Elasticity of Demand
In (a) demand is relatively elastic, and a shift in supply would have a modest impact on price. In (b), demand is relatively inelastic, and the identical shift in supply has a more dramatic impact on the equilibrium price.

oriented newspapers such as the *Wall Street Journal* or the *Financial Times* often carry reports about supply conditions in markets for agricultural products, metals, and energy products.) If we also know the extent to which the market price has changed (which is also widely reported for many markets), we can use this information to assess the degree to which the demand for the product is price elastic or inelastic.

Figure 2.26 illustrates this point. Panel (a) in Figure 2.26 shows that when demand is relatively elastic, a given shift in supply (from S_1 to S_2) would have a modest impact on the equilibrium price. But when demand is relatively inelastic, panel (b) in Figure 2.26 shows that the same shift in supply would have a more pronounced impact on the equilibrium price. Figure 2.26 teaches us that when a modest change in supply has a large impact on the market price of a product, the demand for that product is most likely price inelastic. By contrast, when a large shift in supply for a product has a relatively small impact on the market price, demand for the product is likely to be relatively elastic.

EXAMPLE 2.7

Using Supply Shifts to Identify the Price Elasticity of Demand for Pepper on the Back of an Envelope

In early 1999, observers of the pepper market predicted that the world pepper crop would increase by 6 percent, primarily because of large increases in supply in India and Vietnam. Observers also expected that this increase in supply would drive prices down by as much as 40 or 50 percent, a remarkably large impact.[25] But large

---

[25]These forecasts were reported in "Big Fall Expected This Year in World Pepper Prices," *Financial Times* (February 19, 1999). It turns out that the experts' forecasts were wrong. Unexpectedly high rainfall in 1999 caused a shortfall in the Indonesian pepper crop of nearly 40 percent, and a shortfall in the Indian crop of nearly 30 percent. As a result, pepper prices increased rather than decreased in 1999. See "Rains Bring Pepper Shortfall," *Financial Times* (August 18, 1999), p. 28.

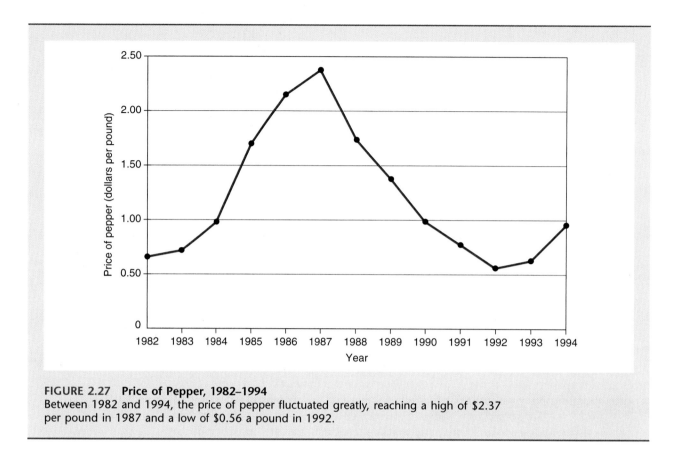

FIGURE 2.27   Price of Pepper, 1982–1994
Between 1982 and 1994, the price of pepper fluctuated greatly, reaching a high of $2.37 per pound in 1987 and a low of $0.56 a pound in 1992.

swings in pepper prices are not unusual. Figure 2.27 shows that between 1982 and 1994, the price of pepper fluctuated dramatically.[26] In particular, between 1987 and 1994, the price of pepper fell from $2.37 per pound to $0.56 per pound. Since the U.S. demand for pepper (the world's largest importer of pepper) probably does not change much from year to year, most of the fluctuations in the price of pepper are probably attributable to shifts in supply rather than to shifts in demand.[27] This was almost certainly true for the drop in pepper price between 1987 and 1994. By the early 1990s, new pepper plantings in countries such as Indonesia in the mid 1980s (when prices were high) had reached an age at which they yielded their most bountiful supply of pepper.

Why do changes in supply have such a large impact on the price of pepper? The logic of the preceding section tells us that the demand for pepper is probably quite inelastic. In fact, if we assume for the sake of illustration that the experts' forecasts for 1999 were correct, we can determine just how inelastic the demand for pepper must be. Figure 2.28 shows how.

[26]These data come from Peter J. Buzzanell and Fred Gray, "The Spice Market in the United States: Recent Developments and Prospects," *Agricultural Information Bulletin*, Number 709, Foreign Agriculture Service, U.S. Department of Agriculture, July 1995.

[27]This is not to say that the demand curve for pepper did not shift at all, only that the shifts in demand were probably much less pronounced than the shifts in supply.

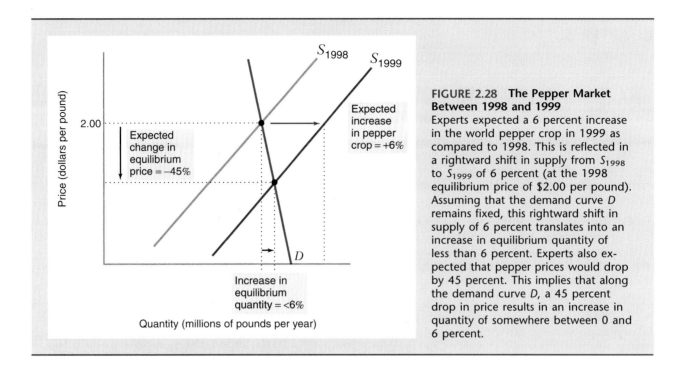

FIGURE 2.28 The Pepper Market Between 1998 and 1999
Experts expected a 6 percent increase in the world pepper crop in 1999 as compared to 1998. This is reflected in a rightward shift in supply from S_{1998} to S_{1999} of 6 percent (at the 1998 equilibrium price of $2.00 per pound). Assuming that the demand curve D remains fixed, this rightward shift in supply of 6 percent translates into an increase in equilibrium quantity of less than 6 percent. Experts also expected that pepper prices would drop by 45 percent. This implies that along the demand curve D, a 45 percent drop in price results in an increase in quantity of somewhere between 0 and 6 percent.

The increase in the supply of pepper by 6 percent is depicted as a rightward shift in the supply curve, from S_{1998} to S_{1999}. If the supply curve shifts outward by a given amount (6 percent), the equilibrium quantity demanded must increase, but by less than the amount of the supply shift, as Figure 2.28 shows. Thus, taking the experts' forecasts at face value, we can conclude the following:

- Percent change in equilibrium price of pepper ($\%\Delta P$) = −45 percent (the average of the experts' predictions).
- Percent change in the equilibrium quantity of pepper demanded ($\%\Delta Q$) is *no more* than 6 percent and *no less* than 0 percent.

Taken together, these forecasts imply that the price elasticity of demand ($\%\Delta Q$)/($\%\Delta P$) is between 0/(−45) and 6/(−45); that is, between 0 and −0.133. This tells us that the demand for pepper is quite inelastic. The conclusion that the demand for pepper is relatively price inelastic makes sense. Pepper is just a small fraction of a consumer's grocery budget or a restaurant's supply budget, and most of us who use pepper to season our food would be hard pressed to find a close substitute for it, so when the price of pepper goes up, the quantity of pepper demanded by households and by eating establishments probably does not change very much. ∎

CHAPTER SUMMARY

• The market demand curve shows the quantity that consumers are willing to purchase at different prices. The market supply curve shows the quantity that producers are willing to sell at different prices. **(LBD Exercises 2.1 and 2.2)**

• Market equilibrium occurs at the price at which quantity supplied equals quantity demanded. At this price, the supply curve and the demand curve intersect. **(LBD Exercise 2.3)**

• Comparative statics analysis on the market equilibrium involves tracing through the effect of a change in exogenous variables, such as consumer income, the prices of other goods, or the prices of factors of production, on the market equilibrium price and quantity. **(LBD Exercise 2.4)**

• The price elasticity of demand measures the sensitivity of quantity demanded to price. It is the rate of percentage change in quantity demanded per percentage change in price. **(LBD Exercise 2.5)**

• Commonly used demand curves include the constant elasticity demand curve and the linear demand curve. The price elasticity of demand is constant along a constant elasticity demand curve, while it varies along a linear demand curve. **(LBD Exercise 2.6)**

• A product's demand tends to be more price elastic when good substitutes are available and when the product represents a significant fraction of buyers' total expenditures. A product's demand tends to be less price elastic when it has few good substitutes, when it represents a small fraction of buyers' total expenditures, when

buyers (because of tax deductions or insurance) pay only a fraction of the full price of the product, or when the product is used in conjunction with another product that buyers have committed themselves to.

• It is important to distinguish between market-level price elasticities of demand and brand-level price elasticities of demand. Demand can be price inelastic at the market level but highly price elastic at the brand level.

• Other key elasticities include the income elasticity of demand and the cross-price elasticity of demand.

• For many products, long-run demand is likely to be more price elastic than short-run demand. However, for durable goods, such as commercial airframes, long-run demand is likely to be less price elastic than short-run demand.

• Similarly, long-run supply for many goods is likely to be more price elastic than short-run supply. However, for products that can be recycled, long-run supply can be less price elastic than short-run supply.

• Several back-of-the-envelope techniques can be used to fit demand and supply curves to observed market data. If you have price, quantity, and price elasticity of demand data, you can fit a linear or log-linear demand curve to observed data. Information on price movements, coupled with knowledge that the demand curve has shifted, can be used to identify a stationary supply curve. Knowledge that the supply curve has shifted can be used to identify a stationary demand curve.

REVIEW QUESTIONS

1. Explain why a situation of excess demand will result in an increase in the market price. Why will a situation of excess supply result in a decrease in the market price?

2. Use supply and demand curves to illustrate the impact of the following events on the market for coffee:
a) The price of tea goes up by 100 percent.
b) A study is released that links consumption of caffeine to the incidence of cancer.
c) A frost kills half of the Colombian coffee bean crop.
d) The price of styrofoam coffee cups goes up by 300 percent.

3. Suppose we observe that the price of soybeans goes up, while the quantity of soybeans sold goes up as well. Use supply and demand curves to illustrate two possible explanations for this pattern of price and quantity changes.

4. A 10 percent increase in the price of automobiles reduces the quantity of automobiles demanded by 8 percent. What is the price elasticity of demand for automobiles?

5. A linear demand curve has the equation $Q = 50 - 100P$. What is the choke price?

6. Explain why we might expect the price elasticity of demand for speedboats to be more negative than the price elasticity of demand for light bulbs.

7. Many business travelers receive reimbursement from their companies when they travel by air, whereas vacation travelers typically pay for their trips out of their own pockets. How would this affect the comparison between the price elasticity of demand for air travel for business travelers versus vacation travelers?

8. Explain why the price elasticity of demand for an entire product category (such as yogurt) is likely to be greater (i.e., less negative) than the price elasticity of demand for a typical brand (such as Dannon) within that product category.

9. What does the sign of the cross-price elasticity of demand between two goods tell us about the nature of the relationship between those goods?

10. Explain why a shift in the demand curve identifies the supply curve and not the demand curve.

PROBLEMS

2.1. The demand for beer in Japan is given by the following equation:

$$Q^d = 700 - 2P - P_N + 0.1I$$

where P is the price of beer, P_N is the price of nuts, and I is average consumer income.
a) What happens to the demand for beer when the price of nuts goes up? Are beer and nuts demand substitutes or demand complements?
b) What happens to the demand for beer when average consumer income rises?
c) Graph the demand curve for beer when $P_N = 100$ and $I = 10,000$.

2.2. Suppose the supply of steel is given by the following equation:

$$Q^s = 300P^2w^{-0.5}$$

where P is the price of steel, and w is the wage rate of steel workers.
a) What happens to the supply of steel when the wage rate of steel workers goes up?
b) Graph the supply curve for steel when $w = 16$. (Remember, $w^{-0.5} = 1/\sqrt{w}$)

2.3. The demand and supply curves for coffee are given by

$$Q^d = 600 - 2P$$

$$Q^s = 300 + 4P$$

a) Plot the supply and demand curves on a graph and show where the equilibrium occurs.

b) Using algebra, determine the market equilibrium price and quantity of coffee.

2.4. Every year there is a shortage of Super Bowl tickets at the official prices P_0. Generally, a black market (known as scalping) develops in which tickets are sold for much more than the official price. Use supply and demand analysis to answer these questions:
a) What does the existence of scalping imply about the relationship between the official price P_0 and the equilibrium price?
b) If the official price P_0 were lowered, how would the average black market price be affected?
c) If stiff penalties were imposed for scalping, how would the average black market price be affected?

2.5. You have decided to study the market for fresh-picked cherries. You learn that over the last 10 years, cherry prices have risen, while the quantity of cherries purchased has also risen. This seems puzzling because you learned in microeconomics that an increase in price usually decreases the quantity demanded. What might explain this seemingly strange pattern of prices and consumption levels?

2.6. Suppose that the quantity of corn supplied depends on the price of corn (P) and the amount of rainfall (R). The demand for corn depends on the price of corn and the level of disposable income (I). The equations describing the supply and demand relationships are as follows:

$$Q^s = 20R + 100P$$

$$Q^d = 4000 - 100P + 10I$$

a) Sketch a graph of demand and supply curves that shows the effect of an *increase* in rainfall on the equilibrium price and quantity of corn.

b) Sketch a graph of demand and supply curves that shows the effect of a *decrease* in disposable income on the equilibrium price and quantity of corn.

2.7.   Recall that when demand is perfectly inelastic, $\epsilon_{Q,P} = 0$ at every point on the demand curve.

a) Sketch a graph of a perfectly inelastic demand curve.

b) Suppose the supply of 1961 Roger Maris baseball cards is perfectly inelastic. Suppose, too, that renewed interest in Maris's career caused by Mark McGwire and Sammy Sosa's quest to break his home run record in 1998 caused the demand for 1961 Maris cards to go up. What will happen to the equilibrium price? What will happen to the equilibrium quantity of Maris baseball cards bought and sold?

2.8.   Consider a linear demand curve, $Q = 350 - 7P$.

a) Derive the inverse demand curve corresponding to this demand curve.

b) What is the choke price?

c) What is the price elasticity of demand at $P = 50$?

2.9.   Suppose that the market for air travel between Chicago and Dallas is served by just two airlines, United and American. An economist has studied this market and has estimated that the demand curves for round-trip tickets for each airline are as follows:

$$Q_U^d = 10000 - 100P_U + 99P_A \quad \text{(United's demand)}$$

$$Q_A^d = 10000 - 100P_A + 99P_U \quad \text{(American's demand)}$$

where P_U is the price charged by United, and P_A is the price charged by American.

a) Suppose that both American and United charge a price of $300 each for a round-trip ticket between Chicago and Dallas. What is the price elasticity of demand for United flights between Chicago and Dallas?

b) What is the market-level price elasticity of demand for air travel between Chicago and Dallas when both air-

lines charge a price of $300? (*Hint:* Because United and American are the only two airlines serving the Chicago-Dallas market, what is the equation for the total demand for air travel between Chicago and Dallas, assuming that the airlines charge the same price?)

2.10.   You are given the following information:

- Price elasticity of demand for cigarettes at current prices is -0.5.

- Current price of cigarettes is $0.05 per cigarette.

- Cigarettes are being purchased at a rate of 10 million per year.

a) Find a linear demand that fits this information, and graph that demand curve.

b) Find a constant elasticity demand curve that fits this information, and graph that demand curve.

2.11.   Consider the following sequence of events in the U.S. market for strawberries during the years 1998–2000:

- 1998: Uneventful. The market price was $5.00 per bushel, and 4 million bushels were sold.

- 1999: There was a scare over the possibility of contaminated strawberries from Michigan. The market price was $4.50 per bushel, and 2.5 million bushels were sold.

- 2000: By the beginning of the year, the scare over contaminated strawberries ended when the media reported that the initial reports about the contamination were a hoax. A series of floods in the Midwest, however, destroyed significant portions of the strawberry fields in Iowa, Illinois, and Missouri. The market price was $8.00 per bushel, and 3.5 million bushels were sold.

Find linear demand and supply curves that are consistent with this information.

APPENDIX A: Structural versus Reduced-Form Equations

The graphical analysis in Figures 2.7 to 2.10 illustrates how the market equilibrium price and quantity would be influenced by factors other than price that influence quantity demanded or quantity supplied. Instead of using graphs, we could have undertaken this analysis mathematically using demand and supply functions, as we did in Learning-By-Doing Exercise 2.4.

To illustrate, suppose a study of a particular market revealed that

$$Q^d = 100 - 4P + 5I \qquad\qquad \textbf{(A.1)}$$

$$Q^s = 20 + P - 10W \qquad\qquad \textbf{(A.2)}$$

where I is average consumer income and W is the price of labor. Equations (A.1) and (A.2) are called *structural equations* of the model. The structural equations describe the key economic relationships in the model, i.e., they describe its structure. Equation (A.1) indicates that an increase in income increases the quantity demanded, while equation (A.2) indicates that an increase in the price of labor decreases the quantity supplied. Equating Q^d and Q^s in equations (A.1) and (A.2) and solving for the equilibrium price P^* and equilibrium quantity Q^* results in the following expressions for the equilibrium price and quantity:

$$P^* = 16 + I + 2W \qquad\qquad \textbf{(A.3)}$$

$$Q^* = 36 + I - 8W \qquad\qquad \textbf{(A.4)}$$

Equations (A.3) and (A.4) are the *reduced-form equations* of the model. Reduced-form equations show how the equilibrium values of the endogenous variables change as a function of the exogenous variables. In this particular example, equation (A.3) tells us that the equilibrium price increases as income increases and as the price of labor increases. The equilibrium quantity increases as income goes up, but decreases as the price of labor increases.

The reduced-form equations are useful if you want to forecast how changes in exogenous variable affect the market price or quantity. You could collect data on variables, such as income or labor prices, that are likely to shift demand or supply, as well as on the historical pattern of price and quantity. Then, using statistical methods such as multiple regression analysis, you could estimate the reduced-form equations for the market. These equations could then be used to forecast future market prices or quantities.

APPENDIX B: More on Elasticity

Point versus Arc Price Elasticity

The formula for elasticity in equation (2.3) is defined in terms of finite changes in price ΔP and quantity ΔQ. It is therefore measured over a finite region, or "arc" of the demand schedule. For this reason, the formula in (2.3) is often called an **arc price elasticity of demand.** Notice, though, that the arc price elasticity of demand will, in general, differ, depending on the magnitude of the price change. Table A.1 shows a number of arc elasticity calculations from an initial price of $10, assuming that the quantity demanded is determined by the demand curve

$$Q = 1000P^{-2}$$

TABLE B.1
Arc Elasticities for Price Changes of Various Magnitudes

$P_0 = 10$	$Q_0 = 10$	$\%\Delta P = \dfrac{\Delta P}{P_0} \times 100\%$	$\%\Delta Q = \dfrac{\Delta Q}{Q_0} \times 100\%$	$\epsilon_{Q,P} = \dfrac{\%\Delta Q}{\%\Delta P}$
$P_1 = 30$	$Q_1 = 1.11$	200%	-88.89%	-0.444
$P_1 = 15$	$Q_1 = 4.44$	50%	-55.56%	-1.111
$P_1 = 11$	$Q_1 = 8.26$	10%	-17.36%	-1.736
$P_1 = 10.50$	$Q_1 = 9.07$	5%	-9.30%	-1.859
$P_1 = 10.10$	$Q_1 = 9.80$	1%	-1.97%	-1.970
$P_1 = 10.05$	$Q_1 = 9.90$	0.5%	-0.9925%	-1.985
$P_1 = 10.01$	$Q_1 = 9.98$	0.1%	-0.1997%	-1.997

From our discussion of constant elasticity demand curves (see equation (2.5)), we know that this demand curve has an elasticity of demand equal to -2 at every point on the curve. The calculations in Table A.1 give us approximate measures of the elasticity over various regions or arcs of the demand curve.

In the table, P_0 and Q_0 are the initial price and quantity, and P_1 and Q_1 are the new price and quantity. In this example, as the size of the price change becomes smaller, the calculated arc price elasticity approaches the true value of -2. If we were to let the size of the price change become smaller and smaller, the formula for the price elasticity of demand in equation 2.5 would approach

$$\epsilon_{Q,P} = -\frac{dQ}{dP}\frac{P}{Q} \tag{A.5}$$

where dQ/dP is the derivative of the demand function with respect to price. Equation (A.5) is called the *point price elasticity of demand*. The point price elasticity of demand measures the responsiveness of quantity demanded to price for "small" changes in price around a particular point. For the example, in Table A.1,

$$\frac{dQ}{dP} = (-2)1000P^{-3}$$

$$\frac{dQ}{dP}\frac{P_0}{Q_0} = (-2)1000(10)^{-3}\frac{10}{10} = -2$$

This calculation indicates that for "small" changes in price, quantity demanded changes at a rate of 2 percent for every 1 percent change in price. Thus, a 3 percent drop in price would be expected to increase quantity by approximately 6 percent. How small is "small" in order for the point price elasticity of demand to provide a reasonable approximation of the demand impact of a "small" price change? Table A.1 suggests that in this example for price changes of 5 percent or less, the point price elasticity of demand provides a good approximation to the actual rate of change of quantity with respect to price. This raises the question of whether, in practice, the point price elasticity of demand is ever useful for decision making or for economic analysis. As shown below, determining the arc price elasticity of demand requires "global" information about the shape of the demand curve. Sometimes this information is available, but sometimes it is not. By contrast, the point price elasticity of demand requires only "local" information about the shape of the demand curve. In many applications, this information is far easier to come by.

Price Elasticity of Demand Along a Constant Elasticity Demand Curve

In this section, we show that the point price elasticity of demand is the same along a constant elasticity demand curve of the form

$$Q = aP^{-b}.$$

For this demand curve

$$\frac{dQ}{dP} = -baP^{-(b+1)}$$

Forming the expression for the point elasticity of demand, we have:

$$\epsilon_{Q,P} = \frac{dQ}{dP}\frac{P}{Q}$$

$$= -baP^{-(b+1)} \cdot \frac{P}{aP^{-b}} \text{ (substituting in the expression for } Q)$$

$$= -b \text{ (after canceling terms)}$$

This shows that the price elasticity of demand for the constant elasticity demand curve is simply the exponent in the equation of the demand curve, $-b$. For more on the use of derivatives, see the Mathematical Appendix at the end of the book.

3

Consumer Preferences and the Concept of Utility

If you are thinking about buying a car, your choices can be overwhelming: Should you buy or lease? New car or used? A sport utility vehicle, a sedan, a sports car, or a minivan? Should you get a sunroof or four-wheel drive? How much extra would you pay for a vehicle that will have a high resale value in the future? What are the expected operating expenses for each model—insurance, repairs, gasoline, and so on? Finally, what opportunities will you forgo if you buy a car? How else could you spend your money, either today or in the future?

Making decisions about a product with many options is not easy. Before buying a car, for example, you might draw on the experiences of friends and family, read advertisements, visit dealers, and test-drive vehicles. You might also research different models and financing options on the Web, read *Consumer Reports*, price insurance rates for favorite models, or even visit chat rooms frequented by car buffs.

As a consumer, you make choices every day of your life. Besides choosing among automobiles, you must decide what kind of housing to rent or purchase, what food and clothing to buy, how much education to acquire, and so on. Consumer choice provides an excellent example of constrained optimization, one of the key tools discussed in Chapter 1. People have unlimited desires, but limited resources. The theory of consumer choice focuses on how consumers choose goods and services with limited resources.

In the next three chapters, we will learn about consumer choice. In this chapter we will examine **consumer preferences**. We study consumer preferences to understand how a consumer compares (or, *ranks*) the desirability of different sets of goods. For this discussion, we ignore the costs of purchasing the goods. Thus, consumer preferences indicate whether the consumer likes one particular set of goods better than another, assuming that all goods can be "purchased" at no cost.

Of course, in the real world it does cost the consumer something to purchase goods and a consumer has limited income. This reality leads us to the second part of our discussion of consumer choice, discussed in Chapter 4. When goods are costly, a consumer's income limits the sets of goods she can purchase. In Chapter 4 we will show how to describe the set of goods that is affordable given a consumer's income and the prices of goods. Then we will use consumer preferences to answer the following question: Which goods among those that are affordable will the consumer choose?

Why should we study consumer choice in such depth? Consumers are not the only parties interested in consumer choice, and in Chapter 5 we will use the theory of consumer choice to derive a consumer's demand curve for any good or service. Businesses care about consumer demand curves because they reveal how much a consumer is willing to pay for a product. Governments also care about consumer preferences and demands. For example, if a government is interested in helping low-income families buy food, policy makers must decide how to do it. Should the government simply give the families a cash supplement and let them spend the money in any way they wish? Or should the aid be in the form of certificates, such as food stamps, which can only be used to buy food? As we will see, the effectiveness and costliness of a program depends on consumers' preferences. ∎

3.1
REPRESENTA-TIONS OF PREFERENCES

In a modern economy, consumers can purchase a vast array of goods and services. We begin by considering a market **basket** (sometimes called a *bundle*), defined as a collection of goods and services that an individual might consume. For example, one basket of goods might include a pair of jeans, two pairs of shoes, and five pounds of chocolate candy. A second basket might contain two pairs of jeans, one pair of shoes, and two pounds of chocolate candy. More generally, a basket may contain specified amounts of not only jeans, shoes, and chocolate candy, but also housing, electronic goods, tickets for theatrical and sporting events, and many other items.

To illustrate the idea of a basket, consider a simplified example in which a consumer can purchase only two goods, food and clothing. Seven possible consumption baskets are illustrated in Figure 3.1. For example, if the consumer buys basket *E*, she consumes 20 units of food and 30 units of clothing per week. If she chooses basket *B* instead, her weekly consumption would include 60 units of food and 10 units of clothing. A basket might contain only one good, such as basket *J* (only food) or basket *H* (only clothing).

Consumer preferences tell us how an individual would rank (that is, compare the desirability of) any two baskets, *assuming the baskets were available at no cost.* Of course, a consumer's actual choice will ultimately depend on a number of factors, including preferences, income, and what the baskets cost. But for now we will consider only consumer preferences among different baskets.

ASSUMPTIONS ABOUT CONSUMER PREFERENCES

Our study of consumer preferences begins with three basic assumptions that underlie the theory of consumer choice. In making these assumptions, we take it for granted that consumers behave rationally under most circumstances. Later we will discuss situations in which these assumptions might not be valid.

1. *Preferences are complete.* That is, the consumer is able to rank any two baskets. For baskets *A* and *B*, for example, the consumer can state her preferences about the baskets according to one of the following possibilities:

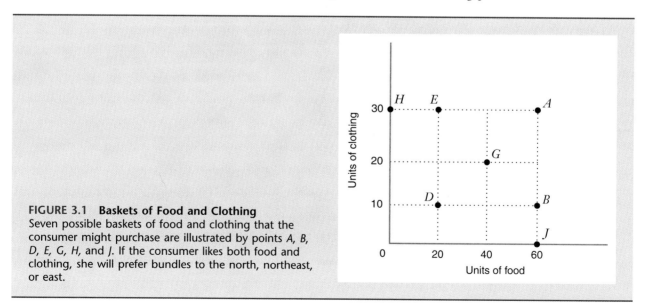

FIGURE 3.1 Baskets of Food and Clothing
Seven possible baskets of food and clothing that the consumer might purchase are illustrated by points *A, B, D, E, G, H,* and *J.* If the consumer likes both food and clothing, she will prefer bundles to the north, northeast, or east.

She prefers basket A to basket B (written $A > B$).

She prefers basket B to basket A (written $B > A$).

She is indifferent between, or equally happy with, baskets A and B (written $A \approx B$).

2. *Preferences are transitive.* By this we mean that the consumer makes choices that are consistent with each other. Suppose that a consumer tells us that she prefers basket A to basket B, and basket B to basket E. We can then expect her to prefer basket A to basket E. Using the notation we have just introduced to describe preferences, we can represent transitivity as follows: If $A > B$ and if $B > E$, then $A > E$.

   Why do we make the assumption that preferences are transitive? If, after telling us that $A > B$ and $B > E$, she also states that $E > A$, then her preferences would be inconsistent. The assumption of transitivity rules out such inconsistent behavior in our study of consumer choice.

3. *More is better.* In other words, having more of a good is better for the consumer. Suppose the consumer is considering the baskets in Figure 3.1. If more is better, she likes more food better than less food, and prefers to have more clothing rather than less clothing. In that case, she would prefer basket A to E or H because she receives the same amount of clothing with these three baskets, but more food at A. She would prefer basket A to B or J because she receives the same amount of food in these three baskets, but more clothing at A. She will also prefer A to G or D because she receives more food and more clothing at A than at either of the other two baskets. Therefore, among the seven baskets, her most preferred basket is A. However, without further information about the consumer's preferences, we do not know how she would rank every pair of baskets. For example, without further information we do not know whether she prefers E to G because she would receive more food but less clothing at G.

ORDINAL AND CARDINAL RANKING

In this book we will refer to two types of rankings, ordinal and cardinal rankings. **Ordinal rankings** give us information about the *order* in which a consumer ranks baskets. For example, for basket A in Figure 3.1 the consumer buys three times as much food and three times as much clothing as she does for basket D. We know that the consumer prefers basket A to D because more is better. However, an ordinal ranking would not tell us *how much more* she likes A than D.

Cardinal rankings give us information about the *intensity* of a consumer's preferences. With a cardinal ranking, we not only know that she prefers basket A to basket D, but we can also measure the strength of her preference for A over D. We can make a quantitative statement, such as "The consumer likes basket A twice as much as basket D."[1] A cardinal ranking therefore contains more information than an ordinal ranking.

It is usually easy for consumers to answer a question about an ordinal ranking, such as "Would you prefer a basket with a hamburger and french fries or an-

---

[1]As noted in the text, the consumer buys three times as much food and clothing at basket A as at D. However, this does not necessarily mean that the consumer likes basket A exactly three times more than basket D. Would your own satisfaction triple if you bought three times as much of all goods as you now do? For most consumers satisfaction would rise, but by less than three times.

other basket with a hot dog and onion rings?" However, consumers often have more difficulty describing how much more they prefer one bundle to another because they have no natural measure of the amount of pleasure they derive from different baskets. Fortunately, as we develop the theory of consumer behavior, you will see that it is not important for us to measure the amount of pleasure a consumer receives from a basket. Although we often use a cardinal ranking to facilitate exposition, an ordinal ranking will normally give us enough information to explain a consumer's decisions.

3.2
UTILITY FUNCTIONS

The three assumptions—preferences are complete, they are transitive, and more is better—allow us to represent preferences with a **utility function.** A utility function measures the level of satisfaction that a consumer receives from any basket of goods. We can represent the utility function with algebra or a graph.

PREFERENCES WITH A SINGLE GOOD

To illustrate the concept of a utility function, let's begin with a simple scenario in which a consumer purchases only one good, hamburgers. Let y denote the number of hamburgers she purchases each week, and let $U(y)$ measure the level of satisfaction (or utility) that she derives from purchasing y hamburgers. If we have enough information to write down the utility function, we can compare the intensities of her preference for various baskets of hamburgers. Therefore, if we know $U(y)$, then we will know her cardinal ranking over all baskets.

Suppose the consumer's preferences can be represented by the utility function $U(y) = 10\sqrt{y}$. We observe that her preferences satisfy the three assumptions just described. They are complete because she can assign a level of satisfaction to each value of y. The assumption that more is better is also satisfied because the more hamburgers consumed, the higher her utility. For example, suppose the number of hamburgers in basket A is y_1, the number in basket B is y_2, and the number in basket C is y_3, with $y_1 > y_2 > y_3$. Then the consumer ranks the baskets as follows: $A > B$ and $B > C$. Finally, the preferences are transitive: $A > B$ and $B > C$ implies that $A > C$.[2]

The levels of utility associated with various levels of consumption are illustrated for the utility function $U(y) = 10\sqrt{y}$ in Table 3.1. Given any level of consumption y (column 1), the corresponding level of utility is shown in column 2. Table 3.1 illustrates that more is better when preferences are described by this utility function.

---

[2]The utility function $U(y) = 10\sqrt{y}$ gives us both a cardinal and an ordinal ranking of all baskets. We could write down many other utility functions that give us the same ordinal ranking. Consider the utility function $R(y) = c_1 + c_2 U(y)$, where c_1 is a nonnegative constant and c_2 is a positive constant. The ordinal ranking of any two baskets will be the same with $U(y)$ and $R(y)$. In other words, if $A > B$ when utility is measured by $U(y)$, then $A > B$ when utility is measured by $R(y)$.

$R(y)$ is said to be "a positive monotonic transformation" of $U(y)$ because we multiplied $U(y)$ by a positive constant (c_2) and added a nonnegative constant (c_1) to get $R(y)$. In other words, any positive monotonic tranformation of one utility function gives us the same ordinal ranking of all baskets as the original utility function.

TABLE 3.1
Total and Marginal Utilities with a Single Good

Quantity Consumed (y)	Total Utility $U(y) = 10\sqrt{y}$	Marginal Utility $MU_y = 5/\sqrt{y}$
1	10.00	5.00
2	14.14	3.54
3	17.32	2.89
4	20.00	2.50
5	22.36	2.24
6	24.49	2.04

Marginal Utility

While studying consumer behavior, we will often want to know how the level of satisfaction will *change* (ΔU) in response to a *change* in the level of consumption (Δy where Δ is read as "the change in"). Economists refer to the ratio $\Delta U/\Delta y$ as the **marginal utility** (MU), the rate at which total utility changes as the level of consumption rises. We will denote the marginal utility of good y as MU_y.

Suppose y measures the number of hamburgers a consumer has eaten this week. If she is like most people, the *additional* satisfaction she receives from eating another hamburger (the marginal utility) will depend on how many hamburgers she has already consumed. The following equations express this relationship, where Δy is understood to be a small change in consumption.

$$MU_y = \frac{\Delta U}{\Delta y}$$

$$MU_y = \frac{U(y + \Delta y) - U(y)}{\Delta y} \tag{3.1}$$

When the total utility from consuming y hamburgers is $U(y) = 10\sqrt{y}$, the marginal utility will be $MU_y = 5/\sqrt{y}$. We could use equation (3.1) to derive the expression for MU_y given $U(y)$.[3] To eliminate the need for doing the algebra, we will normally just give you the expressions for the total and marginal utility.

The value of the marginal utility of hamburgers is shown in column 3 of Table 3.1. For example, when $y = 4$, the marginal utility is $MU_y = 5/\sqrt{4}$, or 2.5. Let's verify the value of the marginal utility numerically. Suppose consumption increases from $y = 4$ to $y = 4.01$, so that $\Delta y = 0.01$. Then the level of utility increases from $U(4) = 10\sqrt{4} = 20$ to $U(4.01) = 10\sqrt{4.01}$, or about 20.025. Therefore, utility has increased by $\Delta U \approx 0.025$. So the marginal utility is $\Delta U/\Delta y \approx$

[3]For example, if the total utility is $U(y) = 10\sqrt{y}$, equation (3.1) tells us that $MU_y = (U(y + \Delta y) - U(y))/\Delta y = (10\sqrt{(y + \Delta y)} - 10\sqrt{y})/\Delta y = 10(\sqrt{y + \Delta y} - \sqrt{y})(\sqrt{y + \Delta y} + \sqrt{y})/(\Delta y(\sqrt{y + \Delta y} + \sqrt{y})) = 10(y + \Delta y - y)/(\Delta y(\sqrt{y + \Delta y} + \sqrt{y})) = 10/(\sqrt{y + \Delta y} + \sqrt{y})$. For small values of Δy, it then follows that $MU_y = 10/(2\sqrt{y}) = 5/\sqrt{y}$. Therefore, the expression for marginal utility is $MU_y = 5/\sqrt{y}$.

0.025/0.01 $\approx$ 2.5. Thus, if the consumer is buying 4 units of the good, the marginal utility should be close to 2.5 for small changes in the level of consumption.

We can also verify that the value of the consumer's marginal utility depends on the amount of the good already purchased. For example, if she is buying five hamburgers per week ($y = 5$), the value of the marginal utility will be $MU_y = 5/\sqrt{5}$, or approximately 2.24.

Principle of Diminishing Marginal Utility

We can depict the total and marginal utilities graphically. Panel (a) of Figure 3.2 shows how total utility U depends on the number of hamburgers consumed per week, y. Panel (b) shows how the marginal utility MU_y depends on y.

When drawing total utility and marginal utility curves, you should keep the following points in mind:

- *Total utility and marginal utility should not be plotted on the same graph.* Although the horizontal axes in the two panels of Figure 3.2 are the same (both representing the number of hamburgers consumed each week, y), the vertical axes in the two graphs are *not* the same. Total utility has the dimensions of U (whatever that may be), while marginal utility has the dimensions of utility per hamburger (ΔU divided by Δy). Therefore, the curves representing total utility and marginal utility must be drawn on two different graphs.

- *The marginal utility is the slope of the (total) utility function.* The slope of the total utility curve in panel (a) of Figure 3.2 is $\Delta U/\Delta y$. The slope tells us the rate of change in total utility as consumption rises, and this rate of change is what marginal utility measures. At point B in panel (a), the slope of the utility function is 2.5, the value of $\Delta U/\Delta y$ when $y = 4$. The marginal utility is therefore 2.5, the vertical coordinate of point B' in panel (b). The slope of the utility curve at point B is the same as the slope of the line segment RS, which is tangent to the utility function.

- *The relationship between total and marginal functions holds for other measures in economics.* The concept of a *marginal* function is often simply the slope of the corresponding *total* function. We will explore this relationship for other functions throughout this book.

In the example in Table 3.1 and Figure 3.2, marginal utility declines as the consumer eats more hamburgers. This trend illustrates the **principle of diminishing marginal utility:** After some point, as consumption of a good increases, the marginal utility of that good will begin to fall. Diminishing marginal utility reflects a common human trait. The more of something we consume, whether it be hamburgers, candy bars, shoes, or baseball games, the less *additional* satisfaction we get from additional consumption. Marginal utility may not decline after the first unit, the second unit, or even the third unit. But it will normally fall after some level of consumption.

To understand the principle of diminishing marginal utility, think about the additional satisfaction you get from consuming another hamburger. Suppose you have already eaten one hamburger this week. If you eat a second hamburger, your utility will go up by some amount. This is the marginal utility of the second hamburger. If you have already consumed five hamburgers this week, and are about

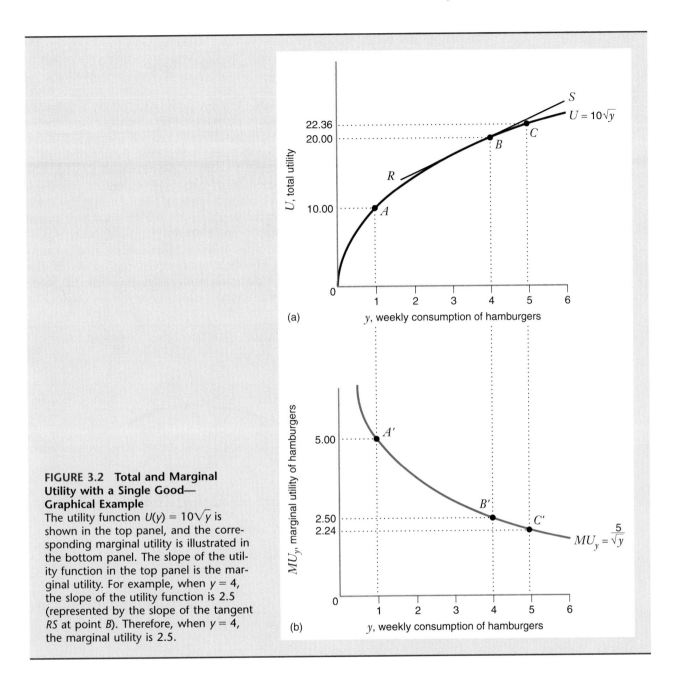

FIGURE 3.2 Total and Marginal Utility with a Single Good— Graphical Example
The utility function $U(y) = 10\sqrt{y}$ is shown in the top panel, and the corresponding marginal utility is illustrated in the bottom panel. The slope of the utility function in the top panel is the marginal utility. For example, when $y = 4$, the slope of the utility function is 2.5 (represented by the slope of the tangent RS at point B). Therefore, when $y = 4$, the marginal utility is 2.5.

to eat a sixth hamburger, the increase in your utility will be the marginal utility of the sixth hamburger. If you are like most people, the marginal utility of your sixth hamburger will be less than the marginal utility of the second hamburger. In that case, your marginal utility of hamburgers is diminishing.

Is More Always Better?

What does the assumption that *more is better* imply about marginal utility? If more of a good is better, then total utility must increase as consumption of the good increases. In other words, the marginal utility of that good must be positive.

In reality this assumption need not always be satisfied. Let's return to the example of consuming hamburgers. You may find that your total utility increases as you eat the first, second, and third hamburgers each week. For these hamburgers, your marginal utility is positive, even though it may be diminishing with each additional hamburger you eat. But presumably at some point you will say that an additional hamburger will bring you no more satisfaction. For example, you might find that the marginal utility of the seventh hamburger per week is zero, and the marginal utility of the eighth or ninth hamburgers might even be negative.

Figure 3.3 depicts the total and marginal utility curves for such a good. Initially (for values of $y < 7$ hamburgers), total utility rises as consumption increases. For example, when the consumer is purchasing her second hamburger, the slope of the utility curve is positive (note that the segment RS, which is tangent to the utility curve at point A, has a positive slope), and thus the marginal utility is positive (as depicted at point A'). The marginal utility is diminishing as consumption increases. At a consumption level of seven hamburgers, the consumer has purchased so much of the good that the marginal utility is zero (point B'). Since the marginal utility is zero, the slope of the total utility curve will be zero. (The

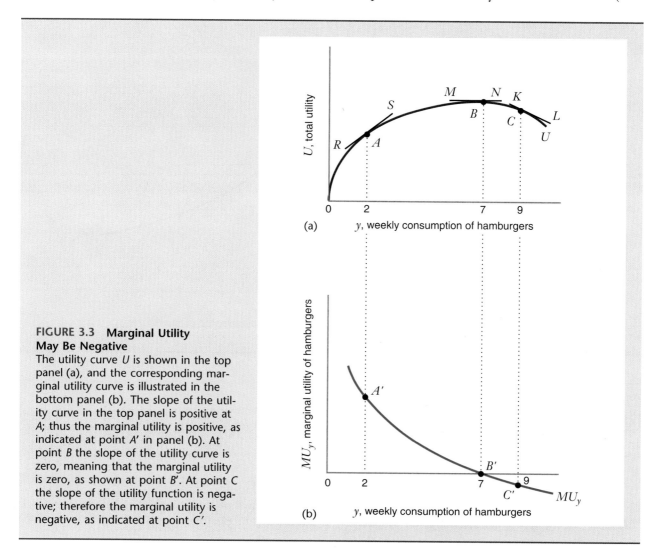

FIGURE 3.3 Marginal Utility May Be Negative
The utility curve U is shown in the top panel (a), and the corresponding marginal utility curve is illustrated in the bottom panel (b). The slope of the utility curve in the top panel is positive at A; thus the marginal utility is positive, as indicated at point A' in panel (b). At point B the slope of the utility curve is zero, meaning that the marginal utility is zero, as shown at point B'. At point C the slope of the utility function is negative; therefore the marginal utility is negative, as indicated at point C'.

segment *MN*, which is tangent to the utility curve at point *B*, has a slope of zero.) If the consumer were to buy more than seven hamburgers, her total satisfaction would decline. The slope of the total utility curve at point *C* is negative (and thus the marginal utility is negative, as indicated at point *C′*).

Although more may not *always* be better, it is nevertheless reasonable to assume that more is better for amounts of a good that a consumer might actually purchase. For example, in Figure 3.3 we would normally only need to draw the utility function for the first seven hamburgers. The consumer would never consider buying more than seven hamburgers because it would make no sense for her to spend money on hamburgers that reduce her satisfaction.

PREFERENCES WITH MULTIPLE GOODS

Let's look at how the concepts of total utility and marginal utility might apply to a more realistic scenario. In real life, consumers can choose among myriad goods and services. To study the trade-offs a consumer must make in choosing his optimal basket, we must examine the nature of consumer utility with multiple products.

We can illustrate many of the most important aspects of consumer choice among multiple products with a relatively simple scenario in which the consumer faces a choice between just two types of commodities, such as food and clothing. Let *x* measure the number of units of food and *y* measure the number of units of clothing purchased each month. Further, suppose that the consumer's utility for any basket (x, y) is measured by $U = \sqrt{xy}$. A graph of this consumer's utility function is shown in Figure 3.4. Because we now have two goods, a graph of the utility function must have three axes. In Figure 3.4 the number of units of food con-

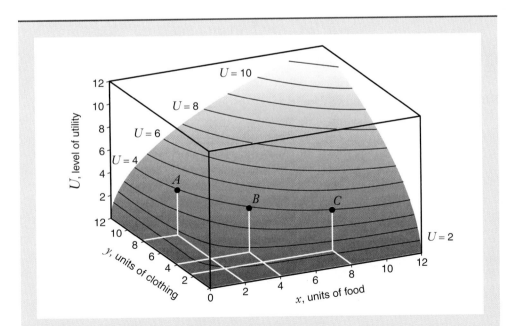

FIGURE 3.4 Graph of the Utility Function $U = \sqrt{xy}$
The level of utility is shown on the vertical axis and the amounts of food (*x*) and clothing (*y*) are shown, respectively, on the right and left axes. Contours representing lines of constant utility are also shown. For example, the consumer is indifferent between baskets *A*, *B*, and *C* because they all yield the same level of utility ($U = 4$).

sumed, x, is shown on the right axis, and the number of units of clothing consumed, y, is represented on the left axis. The vertical axis measures the consumer's level of satisfaction from purchasing any basket of goods. For example, basket A contains two units of food ($x = 2$) and eight units of clothing ($y = 8$). Thus, the consumer realizes a level of utility of $U = \sqrt{(2)(8)} = 4$ with basket A. As the graph indicates, the consumer can achieve the same level of utility ($U = 4$) by choosing other baskets, such as basket B (with $x = 4$ and $y = 4$) and basket C (with $x = 8$ and $y = 2$).

The concept of marginal utility is easily extended to the case of multiple goods. The marginal utility of any one good is the rate at which total utility changes as the level of consumption of that good rises, *holding constant the levels of consumption of all other goods.* For example, in the case in which only two goods are consumed and the utility function is $U(x, y)$, the marginal utility of food (MU_x) measures how the level of satisfaction will *change* (ΔU) in response to a *change* in the consumption of food (Δx), holding the level of y constant:

$$MU_x = \left. \frac{\Delta U}{\Delta x} \right|_{y \text{ is held constant}}$$

$$MU_x = \frac{U(x + \Delta x, y) - U(x, y)}{\Delta x} \tag{3.2}$$

Similarly, the marginal utility of clothing (MU_y) measures how the level of satisfaction will *change* (ΔU) in response to a small *change* in the consumption of clothing (Δy), holding constant the level of food (x).

$$MU_y = \left. \frac{\Delta U}{\Delta y} \right|_{x \text{ is held constant}}$$

$$MU_y = \frac{U(x, y + \Delta y) - U(x, y)}{\Delta y} \tag{3.3}$$

One could use equations (3.2) and (3.3) to derive the algebraic expressions for MU_x and MU_y from $U(x, y)$. When the total utility from consuming a bundle (x, y) is $U = \sqrt{xy}$, the marginal utilities are[4]

$$MU_x = \frac{1}{2}\sqrt{\frac{y}{x}}$$

$$MU_y = \frac{1}{2}\sqrt{\frac{x}{y}}$$

So, at basket A (with $x = 2$ and $y = 8$),

---

[4]For example, if the total utility is $U(y) = \sqrt{xy}$, equation 3.2 tells us that

$$MU_x = \frac{U(x + \Delta x, y) - U(x, y)}{\Delta x} = \frac{\sqrt{(x + \Delta x)y} - \sqrt{xy}}{\Delta x} =$$

$$\frac{\left(\sqrt{(x + \Delta x)y} - xy\right)\left(\sqrt{(x + \Delta x)y} + \sqrt{xy}\right)}{\Delta x\left(\sqrt{(x + \Delta x)y} + \sqrt{xy}\right)} = \frac{y\Delta x}{\Delta x\left(\sqrt{(x + \Delta x)y} + \sqrt{xy}\right)} = \frac{y}{(x + \Delta x)y + \sqrt{xy}}$$

For small values of Δx, it then follows that $MU_x = (1/2)\sqrt{y/x}$.

$$MU_x = \frac{1}{2}\sqrt{\frac{8}{2}} = 1$$

$$MU_y = \frac{1}{2}\sqrt{\frac{2}{8}} = \frac{1}{4}$$

The following exercises will help you see how to work with a utility function to verify whether it satisfies the assumption that more is better and whether the marginal utility for a particular good is diminishing.

LEARNING-BY-DOING EXERCISE 3.1

Marginal Utility

Let's look at a utility function that satisfies the assumptions that more is better and that marginal utilities are diminishing. Suppose a consumer's preferences between food and clothing can be represented by the utility function $U = \sqrt{xy}$ where x measures the number of units of food and y the number of units of clothing and the marginal utilities for x and y are expressed by the following equations:

$$MU_x = \frac{\sqrt{y}}{2\sqrt{x}}$$

$$MU_y = \frac{\sqrt{x}}{2\sqrt{y}}$$

Problem

(a) Show that a consumer with this utility function believes that more is better for each good.
(b) Show that the marginal utility of food is diminishing. Show also that the marginal utility of clothing is diminishing.

Solution

(a) By examining the utility function, we can see that U increases whenever x or y increases. This means that the consumer likes more of each good. "More is better" simply means that the marginal utility is positive. Therefore, we can also see that more is better for each good by looking at the marginal utilities MU_x and MU_y. When the consumer is buying positive amounts of food and clothing, both of the marginal utilities are positive, and so the consumer's utility does increase when he purchases more food and clothing.
(b) First examine $MU_x = \sqrt{y}/(2\sqrt{x})$. As x increases (holding y constant), MU_x falls. Therefore the consumer's marginal utility of food is diminishing. Now examine $MU_y = \sqrt{x}/(2\sqrt{y})$. As y increases, MU_y falls. Therefore the marginal utility of clothing is diminishing.

Similar Problem: 3.1

Learning-By-Doing Exercise 3.1 shows that the utility function $U = \sqrt{xy}$ satisfies the assumptions that more is better and that marginal utilities are diminishing. Because these are widely regarded as reasonable characteristics of consumer preferences, we will often use this utility function to illustrate concepts in the theory of consumer choice.

LEARNING-BY-DOING EXERCISE 3.2

Marginal Utility

Now let us consider utility functions that satisfy the assumption that more is better, but with a marginal utility that is not diminishing. Suppose a consumer's preferences for hamburgers and root beer can be represented by the utility function $U = \sqrt{H} + R$, where H measures the number of hamburgers and R the number of root beers. The marginal utilities are

$$MU_H = \frac{1}{2\sqrt{H}}$$

$$MU_R = 1$$

Problem

(a) Does the consumer believe that more is better for each good?
(b) Does the consumer have a diminishing marginal utility of hamburgers? Is the marginal utility of root beer diminishing?

Solution

(a) Observe that U increases whenever H or R increases. Therefore, more must be better for each good. Also, we can see that MU_H and MU_R are both positive, and thus the preferences do satisfy the assumption that more is better.
(b) As H increases (holding R constant), MU_H falls. Therefore the consumer's marginal utility of hamburgers is diminishing. However $MU_R = 1$. As R increases, MU_R remains constant. Therefore, the consumer has a *constant* (rather than a diminishing) marginal utility of R. This means that the consumer's utility always increases by the same amount when he purchases another root beer.

Learning-By-Doing Exercise 3.2 shows that there are two ways to determine whether the marginal utility of a good is positive. First, you can look at the total utility function. If it increases when more of the good is consumed, marginal utility is positive. Second, you can look at the marginal utility of the good to see if it is a positive number. When the marginal utility is a positive number, the total utility will increase when more of the good is consumed.

Indifference Curves

To illustrate the trade-offs involved in consumer choice, we can reduce the three-dimensional graph of a utility function, such as the one in Figure 3.4, to a two-dimensional graph like the one in Figure 3.5. Both graphs illustrate the same util-

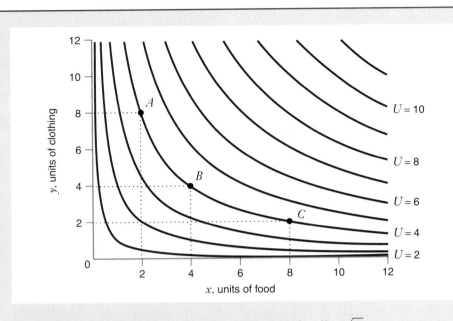

FIGURE 3.5 Indifference Curves for the Utility Function $U = \sqrt{xy}$
The figure illustrates indifference curves, that is, curves along which utility is constant. The utility is the same for all baskets on a given indifference curve. For example, the consumer is indifferent between baskets A, B, and C in the graph because they all yield the same level of utility ($U = 4$).

ity function $U = \sqrt{xy}$. In Figure 3.5 each contour represents baskets yielding the same level of utility to the consumer. Each contour is called an **indifference curve** because the consumer would be equally satisfied with (or *indifferent* in choosing among) all baskets on that indifference curve. For example, the consumer would be equally satisfied with baskets A, B, and C because they all lie on the indifference curve with the value $U = 4$. (Compare Figures 3.4 and 3.5 to see how the indifference curve $U = 4$ looks in a three-dimensional and a two-dimensional graph of the same utility function.) A graph like Figure 3.5 is sometimes referred to as an *indifference map* because it shows a set of indifference curves.

Indifference curves on an indifference map share the following four properties.

1. When the consumer likes both goods (MU_x and MU_y are both positive), the indifference curves will have a negative slope.
2. Indifference curves cannot intersect.
3. Every consumption basket lies on one and only one indifference curve.
4. Indifference curves are not "thick."

We will now explore these in further detail.

- *When the consumer likes both goods (MU_x and MU_y are both positive), the indifference curves will have a negative slope.* For example, consider the graph in Figure 3.6. Suppose the consumer currently has basket A. Since the consumer has positive marginal utility for both goods, she will prefer any baskets to the north, east, or northeast of A. We indicate this in the graph by drawing arrows to indicate

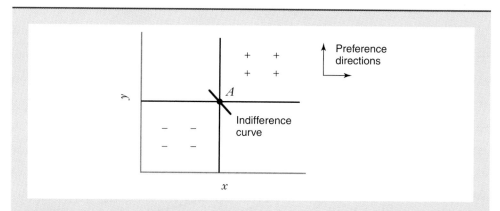

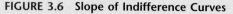

FIGURE 3.6   Slope of Indifference Curves
Suppose that goods x and y are both liked by the consumer ($MU_x > 0$ and $MU_y > 0$). In this case the consumer prefers more of y and more of x. Then indifference curves will have a negative slope. Points to the "northeast" of A cannot be on the same indifference curve as A since they will be preferred to A. The " + " signs denote that baskets in this region are preferred to basket A. Points to the "southwest" of A cannot be on the same indifference curve as A since they will be less preferred than A. The " − " signs denote that baskets in this region are less preferred than basket A. Thus points on the same indifference curve as basket A must lie to the "northwest" or "southeast" of A, and the slope of the indifference curve running through A must be negative.

preference directions. The arrow pointing to the east reflects the fact that $MU_x > 0$. The arrow pointing to the north reflects the fact that $MU_y > 0$.

Points to the northeast of A cannot be on the same indifference curve as A because they will be preferred to A. The plus signs in this region indicate that these points are preferred to A. Points to the southwest of A cannot be on the same indifference curve as A because they will be less preferred than A. The minus signs in this region indicate that these points are less preferred than A. Thus points on the same indifference curve as A must lie either to the northwest or southeast of A. This means that indifference curves will have a negative slope when both goods have positive marginal utilities.

• *Indifference curves cannot intersect.* To understand why, consider Figure 3.7. If we draw two indifference curves (with levels of utility U_1 and U_2) that cross, we

FIGURE 3.7   Indifference Curves Cannot Intersect
If we draw two indifference curves (with different levels of utility U_1 and U_2) that intersect each other, then we create a logical inconsistency in the graph. Since S lies to the northeast of T, then $U_1 > U_2$. But since R lies to the northeast of Q, then $U_2 > U_1$. This logical inconsistency (that $U_1 > U_2$ and $U_2 > U_1$) arises because the indifference curves intersect one another.

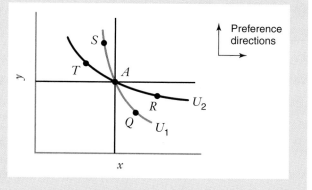

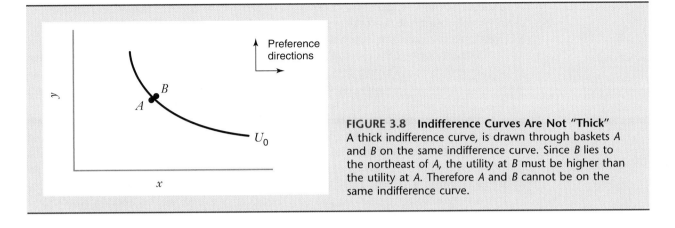

FIGURE 3.8 Indifference Curves Are Not "Thick"
A thick indifference curve, is drawn through baskets A and B on the same indifference curve. Since B lies to the northeast of A, the utility at B must be higher than the utility at A. Therefore A and B cannot be on the same indifference curve.

create a logical inconsistency, as shown in Figure 3.7. Because basket S lies to the northeast of T, $U_1 > U_2$. In other words, the consumer must prefer any basket on U_1 to any basket on U_2. But at the same time, because R lies to the northeast of Q, $U_2 > U_1$. This means that the consumer must prefer any basket on U_2 to any basket on U_1. Obviously it cannot be true that both $U_1 > U_2$ and $U_2 > U_1$. Indifference curves therefore must not intersect if the preferences are to satisfy the assumption of transitivity.

- *Every consumption basket lies on one and only one indifference curve.* Every point in the positive quadrant represents a possible consumption basket. Our assumption that the consumer is capable of ranking all baskets means that each basket has a unique level of utility. Other baskets with that level of utility will be on the same indifference curve.

- *Indifference curves are not "thick."* To see why, consider Figure 3.8, which shows a thick indifference curve, passing through distinct baskets A and B. Since B lies to the northeast of A, the utility at B must be higher than the utility at A. Therefore A and B cannot be on the same indifference curve.

Influencing Preferences

EXAMPLE 3.1

The theory of consumer behavior assumes that the indifference map for a consumer is given exogenously and remains fixed during the analysis. However, we must also recognize that a consumer's preferences may change over time. A consumer's tastes may change with age, education, or experience. Preferences may also change as a result of actions designed to influence consumer attitudes about goods and services.

Firms often pay great sums of money for the opportunity to influence your preferences by advertising. For example, for the telecast of the 1998 Super Bowl, NBC was able to sell commercial time for an average of $1.3 million for each 30-second commercial. Why would an advertiser pay so much? Super Bowl ratings are always high, regardless of how close the game is. When ratings are high, advertisers know their messages will reach millions of households. In 1998, the Denver Broncos upset the Green Bay Packers for the championship of the National Football League in a close game. The excitement of this contest led to a huge television viewing audience throughout the telecast. More than 44 million households on average were watching the game at any given time.

The amounts firms are willing to pay for advertising during the Super Bowl have continued to rise. During the 1999 Super Bowl, Fox broadcasting received an average price of $1.6 million for a 30-second commercial. For the Super Bowl in 2001, CBS sold its 30-second slots for an average of about $2.4 million.

The government and interest groups can also influence consumer preferences. For example, a government may require a producer to place a label on a product warning consumers about the potential dangers of consuming that product. Or a private organization may issue its own warning, as the American Cancer Society did in 1953 when it issued a report linking cigarette smoking with cancer. A government may also ban certain types of product promotion, as the Federal Communications Commission did between 1968 and 1970, when it required that one anti-smoking commercial be broadcast for every four prosmoking commercials. One study of the impact of government policy on the cigarette industry in the United States indicates that both of these events had significant negative impacts on consumer demand for cigarettes.[6]

The Marginal Rate of Substitution

When two goods have positive marginal utilities, the downward slope of an indifference curve illustrates an important economic trade-off in consumption. Start with any given basket, such as basket A in Figure 3.9. If the consumer is to remain at the same level of utility when she consumes more of one good, then she must give up some of the other good. When she moves from basket A to an equally preferred basket B, she receives more of good x, but she must also give up some of good y.

The slope of the indifference curve tells us something about the consumer's willingness to substitute one good for another. In economics, the term that describes this willingness to substitute is the **marginal rate of substitution.** Specifically, the marginal rate of substitution of x for y (denoted by $MRS_{x,y}$), is the rate at which the consumer will give up y to get more x, holding the level of utility constant.

The marginal rate of substitution is illustrated in Figure 3.9. Suppose a consumer is currently consuming basket A on the indifference curve U_0. The slope of the indifference curve at basket A is -5. (The slope of the indifference curve at basket A is the same as the slope of the line that is tangent to the indifference curve at that basket.) The slope tells us that the consumer would be willing to trade off y for x at the rate of 5 units of y for each additional unit of x. Her marginal rate of substitution of x for y is therefore 5.

Similarly, at basket D, the slope of the indifference curve is -2. Again, the slope of the indifference curve at basket D is the same as the slope of the line

[6]See R. Porter, "The Impact of Government Policy on the U.S. Cigarette Industry," in Ippolito, P. and Scheffman, D., eds., *Empirical Approaches to Consumer Protection Economics* (Federal Trade Commission, Washington, D.C., 1984).

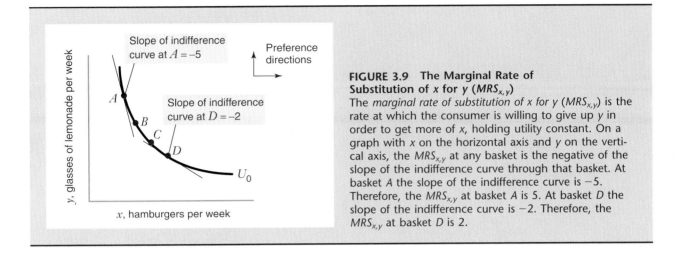

FIGURE 3.9 The Marginal Rate of Substitution of x for y ($MRS_{x,y}$)
The *marginal rate of substitution of x for y ($MRS_{x,y}$)* is the rate at which the consumer is willing to give up y in order to get more of x, holding utility constant. On a graph with x on the horizontal axis and y on the vertical axis, the $MRS_{x,y}$ at any basket is the negative of the slope of the indifference curve through that basket. At basket A the slope of the indifference curve is -5. Therefore, the $MRS_{x,y}$ at basket A is 5. At basket D the slope of the indifference curve is -2. Therefore, the $MRS_{x,y}$ at basket D is 2.

that is tangent to the indifference curve at that basket. Therefore, the consumer would be willing to forgo y for x at a rate of 2 units of y for each additional unit of x, and her $MRS_{x,y}$ at basket D is 2.

This discussion suggests a clear relationship between the $MRS_{x,y}$ and the slope of the indifference curve. On a graph with x on the horizontal axis and y on the vertical axis, the $MRS_{x,y}$ at any basket is the *negative* of the slope of the indifference curve through that basket. (As a memory tool, note that the first subscript, x, matches the coordinate on the horizontal (x) axis and the second subscript, y, matches the coordinate on the vertical (y) axis.) The $MRS_{x,y}$, then, is just the negative of the slope of a line that is tangent to the indifference curve at that basket.

We can express the marginal rate of substitution for any basket as a ratio of the marginal utilities of the goods in that basket. To illustrate, let us start with a particular basket on the indifference curve U_0. Now suppose the consumer changed the level of consumption of x and y by Δx and Δy, respectively. The corresponding impact on utility ΔU would be

$$\Delta U = MU_x(\Delta x) + MU_y(\Delta y)^7 \qquad (3.4)$$

Changes in x and y that move us along the indifference curve U_0 must keep utility unchanged, so that $\Delta U = 0$:

$$0 = MU_x(\Delta x) + MU_y(\Delta y)$$

which can be rewritten

$$MU_y(\Delta y) = -MU_x(\Delta x)$$

---

[7]You may recognize that this equation is an *approximation* of the change in utility that results from changing x and y by Δx and Δy, respectively. The approximation becomes more accurate when Δx and Δy are small because the marginal utilities will be approximately constant for small changes in x and y.

We can now solve for the slope of the indifference curve $\Delta y/\Delta x$:

$$\frac{\Delta y}{\Delta x}\bigg|_{\text{holding utility constant}} = -\frac{MU_x}{MU_y}$$

Finally, since the $MRS_{x,y}$ is the negative of the slope of the indifference curve $(-\Delta y/\Delta x)$, we observe that

$$-\frac{\Delta y}{\Delta x}\bigg|_{\text{holding utility constant}} = \frac{MU_x}{MU_y} = MRS_{x,y} \qquad (3.5)$$

Diminishing Marginal Rate of Substitution

For many (but not all) goods, the $MRS_{x,y}$ will diminish as the amount of x increases along an indifference curve. To see why, refer to Figure 3.9. At basket A, to get one more hamburger, the consumer would be willing to forgo as many as 5 glasses of lemonade. After all, at basket A the consumer is drinking much lemonade and eating only a few hamburgers. So the $MRS_{x,y}$ might be large. However, if she were to move to basket D, where she has more hamburgers and less lemonade, she might not be willing to give up as many glasses of lemonade to get still another hamburger. Thus, her $MRS_{x,y}$ will be lower at D than at A. We have already shown that her $MRS_{x,y}$ at basket D is 2, which is lower than her $MRS_{x,y}$ at basket A. In this case the consumer's preferences exhibit a **diminishing marginal rate of substitution of x for y.** In other words, the marginal rate of substitution of x for y declines as the consumer increases her consumption of x along an indifference curve.

What does a diminishing marginal rate of substitution of x for y imply about the shape of the indifference curves? Remember that the marginal rate of substitution of x for y is just the negative of the slope of the indifference curve on a graph with x on the horizontal axis and y on the vertical axis. If the $MRS_{x,y}$ diminishes as the consumer increases x along an indifference curve, then the slope of the indifference curve must be getting flatter (less negative) as x increases. Therefore, with diminishing $MRS_{x,y}$, the indifference curves must be bowed in toward the origin, as in Figure 3.9.

LEARNING-BY-DOING EXERCISE 3.3

Graphing Indifference Curves

To see how you can use information about the total and marginal utilities to understand the shape of a consumer's indifference curves, suppose a consumer has preferences between two goods that can be represented by the utility function $U = xy$. For this utility function, $MU_x = y$ and $MU_y = x$.[8]

---

[8]Once again, to omit the algebra, we give you the marginal utilities that go with the utility function $U(y) = xy$. If the marginal utilities had not been given, we could have derived the marginal utilities from the utility function. For example, equation (3.2) tells us that $MU_x = (U(x + \Delta x, y) - U(x, y))/\Delta x = ((x + \Delta x)y - xy)/\Delta x = (y\Delta x)/\Delta x = y$. Similarly, equation (3.3) gives us $MU_y = (U(x, y + \Delta y) - U(x, y))/\Delta y = (x(y + \Delta y) - xy)/\Delta y = (x\Delta y)/\Delta y = x$.

Problem

(a) On a graph illustrate the shape of the indifference curve, $U_1 = 128$. Then answer the following questions:

1. Does the indifference curve intersect either axis?
2. Does the shape of the indifference curve indicate that the $MRS_{x,y}$ is diminishing?

On the same graph draw a second indifference curve, $U_2 = 200$.
(b) Show how $MRS_{x,y}$ depends on x and y, and use this information to determine if there is diminishing $MRS_{x,y}$ for this utility function.

Solution

(a) First note that both MU_x and MU_y are positive whenever the consumer has positive amounts of x and y. Therefore, indifference curves will be negatively sloped. This means that as the consumer increases x along an indifference curve, y must decrease.

Can the indifference curve U_1 intersect either axis? If so, it must be possible to achieve a positive level of utility when one of the goods is not consumed. Since $U = xy$, to achieve a positive level of utility, such as U_1, the consumer must buy positive amounts of both goods. If either $x = 0$ or $y = 0$, then $U = 0$. So indifference curves for this utility function do not intersect either axis.

To draw the indifference curve $U_1 = 128$, we look for combinations of x and y that give $xy = 128$. One such basket is $(x, y) = (8, 16)$, labeled as basket G on the graph. Two other baskets on the indifference curve are basket H, with $(x, y) = (16, 8)$, and basket I, with $(x, y) = (32, 4)$. Figure 3.10 illustrates that this indifference curve is bowed in toward the origin, and therefore there is a diminishing $MRS_{x,y}$. The indifference curve corresponding to $U_2 = 200$ lies up and to the right of $U_1 = 128$, confirming that the consumer likes more of both goods.

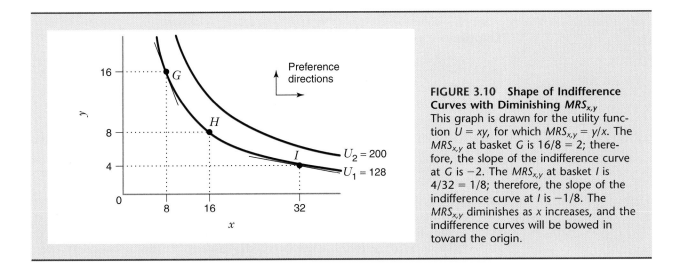

FIGURE 3.10   Shape of Indifference Curves with Diminishing $MRS_{x,y}$
This graph is drawn for the utility function $U = xy$, for which $MRS_{x,y} = y/x$. The $MRS_{x,y}$ at basket G is $16/8 = 2$; therefore, the slope of the indifference curve at G is -2. The $MRS_{x,y}$ at basket I is $4/32 = 1/8$; therefore, the slope of the indifference curve at I is $-1/8$. The $MRS_{x,y}$ diminishes as x increases, and the indifference curves will be bowed in toward the origin.

(b) We know that $MRS_{x,y} = MU_x/MU_y = y/x$. As we move along the indifference curve by increasing x and decreasing y, then $MRS_{x,y} = y/x$ will decrease. So we have diminishing marginal rate of substitution of x for y. We can numerically verify that there is a diminishing $MRS_{x,y}$. At basket G, $MRS_{x,y} = MU_x/MU_y = 16/8 = 2$. So the slope of the indifference curve through basket G is -2. If we move along the indifference curve to basket I, the marginal rate of substitution diminishes to $MRS_{x,y} = MU_x/MU_y = 4/32 = 1/8$. The slope of the indifference curve through basket H is $-1/8$.

Similar Problem: 3.5

As Exercise 3.3 shows, you can learn about the shape of indifference curves by plotting several baskets that give the consumer the same level of utility. You can also learn about the shape by studying the marginal rate of substitution.

LEARNING-BY-DOING EXERCISE 3.4

Graphing Indifference Curves

In this exercise we consider what happens when a utility function has an *increasing* marginal rate of substitution.

Problem
Suppose a consumer has preferences between two goods that can be represented by the utility function $U = Ax^2 + By^2$, where A and B are positive constants. For this utility function $MU_x = 2Ax$ and $MU_y = 2By$.

(a) Show that the $MRS_{x,y}$ is increasing.
(b) On a graph illustrate the shape of a typical indifference curve for $U = Ax^2 + By^2$. Label the curve U_1. Does the indifference curve intersect either axis? On the same graph draw a second indifference curve U_2, with $U_2 > U_1$.

Solution

(a) As before, since both MU_x and MU_y are positive, indifference curves will be negatively sloped. This means that as x increases along an indifference curve, y must decrease. We know that $MRS_{x,y} = MU_x/MU_y = 2Ax/(2By) = Ax/(By)$. As we move along the indifference curve by increasing x and decreasing y, $MRS_{x,y}$ will increase. So we have an increasing marginal rate of substitution of x for y.
(b) Since we have an increasing $MRS_{x,y}$, the indifference curves will be bowed out from the origin. Consider two baskets, G and H, on the same indifference curve U_1, shown in Figure 3.11.

At basket G, the value of y is higher and the value of x is lower than at basket H. Thus, the $MRS_{x,y}$ is higher at H than at G. Since the $MRS_{x,y}$ is the negative of the slope of the indifference curve, the slope at H must be steeper (more

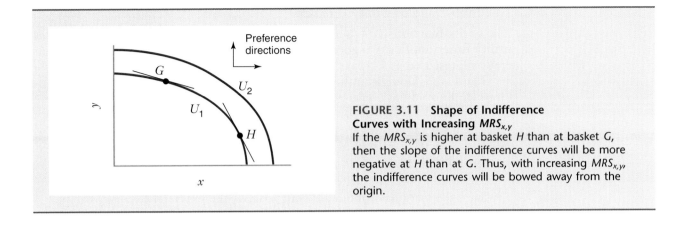

FIGURE 3.11 Shape of Indifference Curves with Increasing $MRS_{x,y}$
If the $MRS_{x,y}$ is higher at basket H than at basket G, then the slope of the indifference curves will be more negative at H than at G. Thus, with increasing $MRS_{x,y}$, the indifference curves will be bowed away from the origin.

negative) than the slope of the indifference curve at G. This means that the indifference curve must be bowed out from the origin, as shown in Figure 3.11.

Can indifference curve U_1 intersect either axis? Since $U = Ax^2 + By^2$, it is possible to achieve a positive level of utility if one of the goods is not consumed. For example, if $y = 0$, the consumer can still realize some satisfaction from consuming only x. Similarly, if $x = 0$, the consumer can still realize some satisfaction from consuming only y. Thus, the indifference curve U_1 intersects both axes, as shown in Figure 3.11.

Finally, since the marginal utilities are both positive, the preference directions are up and to the right, as shown in Figure 3.11. We can draw a second indifference curve U_2 containing baskets that are preferred to those on the indifference curve U_1. The indifference curve U_2 lies above and to the right of the indifference curve U_1.

Although this exercise suggests that it is theoretically possible to have indifference curves that are bowed out from the origin, we would not normally expect to encounter such curves.

Similar Problem: 3.7

SPECIAL UTILITY FUNCTIONS

Although the marginal rate of substitution is normally diminishing, this need not always be the case. A consumer's willingness to substitute one good for another will depend on the commodities in question. For example, one consumer may view Coke and Pepsi as perfect substitutes and always be willing to substitute a glass of one for a glass of the other. If so, the marginal rate of substitution of Coke for Pepsi will be constant and equal to 1, rather than diminishing. Sometimes a consumer may simply be unwilling to substitute one commodity for another. For example, a consumer might always want exactly one ounce of peanut butter for each ounce of jelly on his sandwiches and be unwilling to consume peanut butter and jelly in any other proportions. To cover cases such as these, there are several special utility functions. Here we discuss four: the Cobb–Douglas utility function, the case of perfect substitutes, the case of perfect complements, and quasi-linear preferences.

The Cobb–Douglas Utility Function

The utility functions $U = \sqrt{xy}$ and $U = xy$ are examples of the **Cobb–Douglas utility function.** For two goods, the Cobb–Douglas utility function is more generally represented as $U = Ax^\alpha y^\beta$, where A, α, and β are positive constants.[9]

The Cobb–Douglas utility function has three properties that make it of interest in the study of consumer choice.

- The marginal utilities are positive for both goods. The marginal utilities are $MU_x = \alpha Ax^{\alpha-1}y^\beta$ and $MU_y = \beta Ax^\alpha y^{\beta-1}$, and both MU_x and MU_y are positive when A, α, and β are positive constants. This means that "the more is better" assumption is satisfied.
- Since the marginal utilities are both positive, the indifference curves will be downward sloping.
- The Cobb–Douglas utility function also exhibits a diminishing marginal rate of substitution. The indifference curves will therefore be bowed in toward the origin, as in Figures 3.5 and 3.10. Problem 3.14 at the end of the chapter asks you to verify that the marginal rate of substitution is diminishing.

Perfect Substitutes

In some cases, a consumer might view two commodities as **perfect substitutes** for one another. Two goods are perfect substitutes when the marginal rate of substitution of one for the other is a constant. For example, suppose a consumer likes both butter (B) and margarine (M) and that he is always willing to substitute a pound of either commodity for a pound of the other. Then $MRS_{B,M} = MRS_{M,B} = 1$. We can use a utility function, such as $U = aB + aM$, where a is any positive constant, to describe these preferences. With this utility function, $MU_B = a$ and $MU_M = a$. It also follows that $MRS_{B,M} = MU_B/MU_M = a/a = 1$. So the marginal rate of substitution is a constant (*not* diminishing) in this case, indicating that the consumer is always willing to give up 1 unit of margarine to get another unit of butter. (Since the $MRS_{M,B}$ is also 1, the consumer is always willing to give up 1 unit of butter to get another unit of margarine.) Because $MRS_{B,M}$ is the slope of the indifference curves on a graph with butter on the horizontal axis and margarine on the vertical axis, the slope of the indifference curves will be constant and equal to -1.

More generally, indifference curves for perfect substitutes are straight lines, and the marginal rate of substitution will be constant, though not necessarily equal to 1. For example, suppose the consumer likes both pancakes and waffles, and he is always willing to substitute two pancakes for one waffle. One utility function that would describe his preferences is

$$U = P + 2W$$

[9]This type of function is named for Charles Cobb, a mathematician at Amherst College, and Paul Douglas, a professor of economics at the University of Chicago (and later a U.S. senator from Illinois). It has often been used to characterize production functions, as we shall see in Chapter 6 when we study the theory of production. The Cobb-Douglas utility function can easily be extended to cover more than two goods. For example, with three goods the utility function might be represented as $U = Ax^\alpha y^\beta z^\gamma$, where z measures the quantity of the third commodity, and A, α, β, and γ are all positive constants.

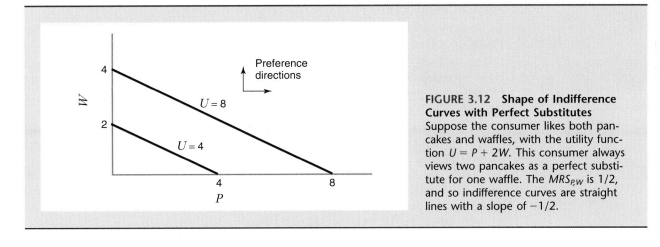

FIGURE 3.12 Shape of Indifference Curves with Perfect Substitutes Suppose the consumer likes both pancakes and waffles, with the utility function $U = P + 2W$. This consumer always views two pancakes as a perfect substitute for one waffle. The $MRS_{P,W}$ is 1/2, and so indifference curves are straight lines with a slope of $-1/2$.

where P is the number of pancakes and W the number of waffles. With these preferences, $MU_P = 1$ and $MU_W = 2$, so each waffle yields twice the marginal utility of a single pancake. We also observe that $MRS_{P,W} = MU_P/MU_W = 1/2$. How would we draw an indifference curve for these preferences? Two indifference curves are shown in Figure 3.12. Since $MRS_{P,W} = 1/2$, on a graph with P on the horizontal axis and W on the vertical axis, the slope of the indifference curves will be $-1/2$.

Taste Tests and Consumer Preferences

EXAMPLE 3.2

If you listen to advertisements on television, you might believe that beer is a highly differentiated product and that most consumers have strong preferences for one beer over another. To be sure, there are differences among beers, and not all brands are sold at the same price. But are brands so different that one brewer could raise the price of its product without losing a significant portion of its sales?

In looking at the U.S. beer industry, Kenneth Elzinga observed, "Several studies indicate that, at least under blindfold test conditions, most beer drinkers cannot distinguish between brands of beer." He also noted that brewers have devoted "considerable talent and resources ... to publicizing real or imagined differences in beers, with the hope of producing product differentiation." In the end, Elzinga suggested that, despite brewers' efforts to differentiate their products from those of their competitors, most consumers are quite willing to substitute one brand of beer for another, especially if one brand were to raise its price significantly.[10]

Elzinga's analysis does not suggest that all consumers regard brands of beer as perfect substitutes. However, when a consumer does not have a strong preference for one beer over another, then the marginal rate of substitution of brand A for brand B might be nearly constant, and probably near 1, since a consumer would give up one glass of brand A for one glass of brand B. ■

[10]K. Elzinga, "The Beer Industry," in Adams, W., *The Structure of American Industry,* 8th ed. (New York: MacMillan Publishing Company, 1990).

Perfect Complements

In some cases, consumers might be unwilling to substitute one good for another. Consider a typical consumer's preferences for left shoes and right shoes, depicted in Figure 3.13. The consumer wants shoes to come in pairs, with exactly one left shoe for every right shoe. The consumer derives satisfaction from complete pairs of shoes, but gets no added utility from extra right shoes or extra left shoes. For example, the consumer's utility at basket G, with 2 left shoes and 2 right shoes, is not increased by moving to basket H, where the consumer has 2 left shoes and 3 right shoes. The indifference curves in this case comprise straight line segments at right angles, as shown in Figure 3.13.

The consumer with the preferences illustrated in Figure 3.13 regards left shoes and right shoes as **perfect complements** in consumption. Perfect complements are goods the consumer always wants to consume in fixed proportion to each other; in this case, the desired proportion of left shoes to right shoes is $1:1$.[11]

To illustrate the consumer's utility for perfect complements algebraically, suppose that $U_1 = 10$, $U_2 = 20$, and $U_3 = 30$, as in Figure 3.13. The utility function can be expressed as

$$U(R, L) = 10 \min(R, L)$$

where U is the utility achieved from R right shoes and L left shoes. The notation "min" means "take the minimum value of the two numbers in parentheses." For example, at basket G, $R = 2$ and $L = 2$. So the minimum of R and L is 2, and $U = 10(2) = 20$. Similarly, at basket H, $R = 3$ and $L = 2$. So the minimum of R and L is still 2, and $U = 10(2) = 20$. This solution verifies that baskets G and H are on the same indifference curve.

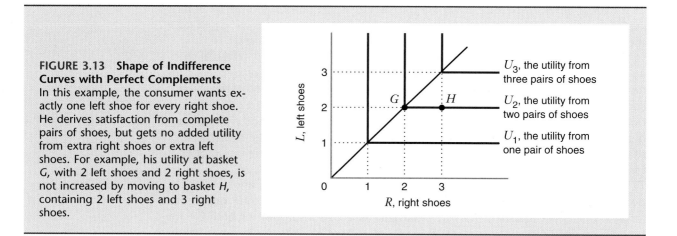

FIGURE 3.13 Shape of Indifference Curves with Perfect Complements
In this example, the consumer wants exactly one left shoe for every right shoe. He derives satisfaction from complete pairs of shoes, but gets no added utility from extra right shoes or extra left shoes. For example, his utility at basket G, with 2 left shoes and 2 right shoes, is not increased by moving to basket H, containing 2 left shoes and 3 right shoes.

[11]The fixed-proportions utility function is sometimes called a *Leontief utility function*, after the economist Wassily Leontief, who employed fixed-proportion production functions to model relationships between sectors in a national economy. We shall examine Leontief production functions in Chapter 6.

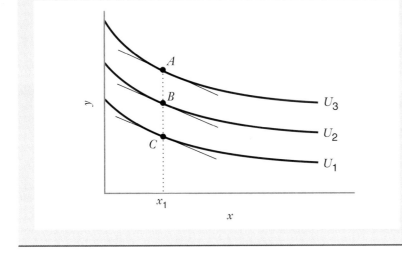

FIGURE 3.14 Quasi-Linear Utility Function
A quasi-linear utility function has the form $U(x, y) = v(x) + by$, where $v(x)$ is a function that increases in x and b is a positive constant. The indifference curves are parallel as we move directly to the north on the graph. For any value of x (such as x_1), the slope of the indifference curves will be the same. Thus, baskets A, B, and C all contain the same amount of x, and the slopes of the indifference curves are identical at these baskets.

Quasi-Linear Preferences

Figure 3.14 shows the indifference curves for a **quasi-linear utility function.** The distinguishing characteristic of a quasi-linear utility function is that as we move due north on the indifference map, the marginal rate of substitution of x for y remains the same. Put another way, the indifference curves are parallel to each other as we move vertically. At any value of x, the slopes of all of the indifference curves will be the same.

The equation for a utility function that is quasi-linear in y is

$$U(x, y) = v(x) + by$$

where $v(x)$ is an increasing function (e.g., $v(x) = \sqrt{x}$, $v(x) = x^2$, or $v(x) = 3x$) and b is a positive constant. This utility function is linear in y, but generally not linear in x. That is why it is called quasi-linear.

The properties of a quasi-linear utility function often simplify analysis. Further, economic studies suggest that they may reasonably approximate consumer preferences in many settings. As we shall see in Chapter 5, a quasi-linear utility function can describe preferences for a consumer who purchases the same amount of a commodity (such as toothpaste or coffee) regardless of his income.

Consumer Preferences and Fads

EXAMPLE 3.3

The preferences of individual consumers are often influenced by fads, typically short-lived episodes during which the consumption of a good or service enjoys widespread popularity. One of the greatest fads of the past century was the Hula Hoop, a light plastic cylindrical tube developed in 1957 by Wham-O. The Hula Hoop was a patterned after bamboo hoops that children in Australia twirled around their waists in physical education classes, and was named after the Hawaiian dance involving similar movements.

Although children have always played with wooden or metal hoops by rolling, tossing, or spinning them, Wham-O found the durable, light, plastic version of the hoop to be especially popular. When Wham-O test-marketed a prototype of the Hula Hoop in California, interest in the new toy spread quickly. In its first few months on the market in 1958, an astonishing 25 million Hula Hoops were sold. Orders for an additional 100 million units followed as the fad spread to Europe and Japan. By the end of 1958, the fad had subsided, and Wham-O moved on to its next major product, the Frisbee.

Of course, there have been many other fads over time. In 1975, Gary Dahl created Pet Rocks as an alternative to traditional pets, such as dogs, cats, and goldfish. Initially, Pet Rocks were just plain rocks, sometimes painted with faces. Dahl suggested that his creations were perfect pets because they made no mess, were well behaved, were inexpensive to feed, and required little care. The Pet Rock captured consumers' imaginations. Dahl appeared on *The Tonight Show* twice, and articles about Pet Rocks appeared in many newspapers and magazines. Before the fad ran its course, several million had been sold. More recent fads have included the wildly successful Cabbage Patch Dolls in the 1980s and Beanie Babies in the 1990s.

Fads change consumer preferences. To keep matters simple, suppose that a typical consumer purchases only two goods, Pet Rocks and food. Suppose the consumer is currently buying basket *A* in Figure 3.15(a). During the fad, the consumer would increase his utility significantly if he purchases more Pet Rocks (moving up from basket *A* to basket *B* in the figure). After the fad has ended and his interest in pet rocks has diminished, he receives relatively little satisfaction from increasing his consumption of the rocks from basket *A* to basket *B*.

As the consumer's interest in Pet Rocks diminishes, the indifference curves will become steeper, i.e., the marginal rate of substitution of food for Pet Rocks increases. As the graph in Figure 3.15(b) is drawn, the consumer still has some interest in Pet Rocks when the fad is over. If he stops caring about Pet Rocks altogether, then the indifference curves will become vertical, with higher indifference curves located further to the right.[12]

In this chapter we have kept the discussion of preferences (including the graphs) simple by analyzing cases in which the consumer buys two goods. But the principles presented here also apply to much more complicated consumer choice problems, including choices among many different goods. For example, as observed in the introduction to this chapter, a consumer typically considers many factors when buying an automobile, including the dimensions of the car, the size of the engine, the fuel used, fuel efficiency, reliability, the availability of options, and safety features. Using the framework developed in this chapter, we would say that the utility a consumer derives from an automobile depends on the characteristics of that vehicle. The fact that there are cross elasticities of demand for various makes of automobiles (as shown in Table 2.6 in Chapter 2) shows that consumers are often willing to trade off one attribute for another.

[12]For more on fads, see J. Stern and M. Stern, *Jane & Michael Stern's Encyclopedia of Pop Culture: an A to Z Guide of Who's Who and What's What, from Aerobics and Bubble Gum to Valley of the Dolls and Moon Unit Zappa* (New York: Harper Collins Publishers, 1992).

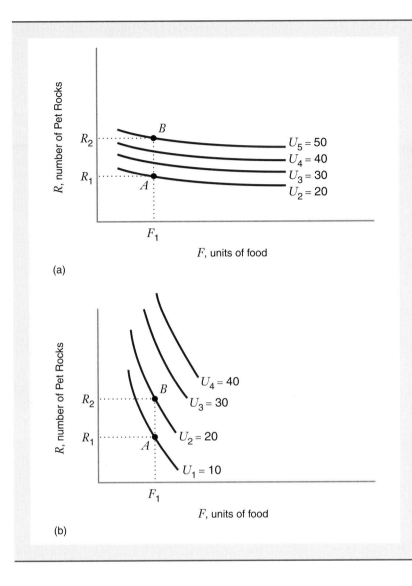

(a)

(b)

FIGURE 3.15 Fads and Preferences
During the Pet Rock fad, the consumer can achieve much added satisfaction (moving from indifference curve U_2 to U_5) by purchasing more Pet Rocks (moving from basket A to basket B), as shown in panel (a). When the fad is over, the move from basket A to basket B generates much less additional satisfaction (the utility increases from U_1 to only U_2); as shown in panel (b), the consumer now has less interest in Pet Rocks. The indifference curves will become steeper as his interest in Pet Rocks fades.

CHAPTER SUMMARY

- Consumer preferences tell us how a consumer ranks (compares the desirability of) any two baskets, assuming the baskets are available at no cost. In most situations, it is reasonable to make three assumptions about consumer preferences:

1. They are complete, so that the consumer is able to rank all baskets.

2. They are transitive, meaning that if $A > B$ and if $B > E$, then $A > E$.

3. They satisfy the property that more is better, so that having more of either good increases the consumer's satisfaction.

- A utility function measures the level of satisfaction that a consumer receives from any basket of goods. The assumptions that preferences are complete, transitive, and that more is better imply that preferences can be represented by a utility function.

- The marginal utility of good x (MU_x) is the rate at which total utility changes as the consumption of x rises. **(LBD Exercises 3.1 and 3.2)**

- An indifference curve shows a set of consumption baskets that yield the same level of satisfaction to the consumer. Indifference curves cannot intersect. If goods x and y are both liked by the consumer (MU_x and MU_y are both positive), then indifference curves will have a negative slope.

- The marginal rate of substitution of x for y ($MRS_{x,y}$) at any basket is the rate at which the consumer will give up y to get more x, holding the level of utility constant. On a graph with x on the horizontal axis and y on the vertical axis, the $MRS_{x,y}$ at any basket is the negative of the slope of the indifference curve at that basket.   **(LBD Exercises 3.3 and 3.4)**

- For most goods we would expect to observe a diminishing $MRS_{x,y}$. In this case the indifference curves will be bowed in toward the origin.

- If two goods are perfect substitutes in consumption, the marginal rate of substitution of one good for the other will be constant, and the indifference curves will be straight lines.

- If two goods are perfect complements in consumption, the consumer wants to purchase the two goods in a fixed proportion. The indifference curves in this case will be L-shaped.

- If a consumer's utility function is quasi-linear (for example, linear in y, but generally not linear in x), the indifference curves will be parallel. At any value of x, the slopes of all of the indifference curves (and the $MRS_{x,y}$) will be the same.

REVIEW QUESTIONS

1. What is a basket (or a bundle) of goods?

2. What does the assumption that preferences are complete require of the consumer's ability to rank any two baskets?

3. Consider Figure 3.1. If the *more is better* assumption is satisfied, is it possible to say which of the seven baskets is *least* preferred by the consumer?

4. Give an example of preferences (i.e., a ranking of baskets) that do not satisfy the assumption that preferences are transitive.

5. What does the assumption that more is better imply about the marginal utility of a good?

6. What is the difference between an ordinal ranking and a cardinal ranking?

7. Suppose a consumer purchases only hamburgers. Assume that her marginal utility is always positive and diminishing. Draw a graph with total utility on the vertical axis and the number of hamburgers on the horizontal axis. Explain how you would determine marginal utility at any given point on your graph.

8. Why should the total utility and marginal utility curves not be plotted on the same graph?

9. Adam consumes two goods: housing and food.
a) Suppose we are given Adam's marginal utility of housing and his marginal utility of food at the basket he currently consumes. Can we determine his marginal rate of substitution of housing for food at that basket?

b) Suppose we are given Adam's marginal rate of substitution of housing for food at the basket he currently consumes. Can we determine his marginal utility of housing and his marginal utility of food at that basket?

10. Suppose a consumer purchases only two goods, hamburgers (H) and Cokes (C).
a) What is the relationship between $MRS_{H,C}$ and the marginal utilities MU_H and MU_C?
b) Draw a typical indifference curve for the case in which the marginal utilities of both goods are positive and the marginal rate of substitution of hamburgers for Cokes is diminishing. Using your graph, explain the relationship between the indifference curve and the marginal rate of substitution of hamburgers for Cokes.
c) Suppose the marginal rate of substitution of hamburgers for Cokes is constant. In this case, are hamburgers and Cokes perfect substitutes or perfect complements?
d) Suppose that the consumer always wants two hamburgers for every Coke. Draw a typical indifference curve. In this case, are hamburgers and Cokes perfect substitutes or perfect complements?

11. Suppose a consumer is currently purchasing 47 different goods, one of which is housing. The quantity of housing is measured by H. Explain why, if you wanted to measure the consumer's marginal utility of housing (MU_H) at the current basket, the levels of the other 46 goods consumed would be held fixed.

PROBLEMS

3.1. Consider the utility function $U(x,y) = y\sqrt{x}$ with the marginal utilities $MU_x = y/(2\sqrt{x})$ and $MU_y = \sqrt{x}$.
a) Does the consumer believe that more is better for each good?
b) Do the consumer's preferences exhibit a diminishing marginal utility of x? Is the marginal utility of y diminishing?

3.2. For the following sets of goods draw two indifference curves, U_1 and U_2, with $U_2 > U_1$. Draw each graph placing the amount of the first good on the horizontal axis.
a) Hot dogs and chili (the consumer likes both and has a diminishing marginal rate of substitution of hot dogs for chili)
b) Sugar and Sweet'N Low (the consumer likes both and will accept an ounce of Sweet'N Low or an ounce of sugar with equal satisfaction)
c) Peanut butter and jelly (the consumer likes exactly 2 ounces of peanut butter for every ounce of jelly)
d) Nuts (which the consumer neither likes nor dislikes) and ice cream (which the consumer likes)
e) Apples (which the consumer likes) and liver (which the consumer dislikes)

3.3. The utility that Julie receives by consuming food F and clothing C is given by $U(F,C) = FC$. For this utility function, the marginal utilities are $MU_F = C$ and $MU_C = F$.
a) On a graph with F on the horizontal axis and C on the vertical axis, draw indifference curves for $U = 12$, $U = 18$, and $U = 24$.
b) Do the shapes of these indifference curves suggest that Julie has a diminishing marginal rate of substitution of food for clothing? Explain.
c) Using the marginal utilities, show that the $MRS_{F,C} = C/F$. What is the slope of the indifference curve $U = 12$ at the basket with 2 units of food and 6 units of clothing? What is the slope at the basket with 4 units of food and 3 units of clothing? Do the slopes of the indifference curves indicate that Julie has a diminishing marginal rate of substitution of food for clothing? (Make sure your answers to parts (b) and (c) are consistent!)

3.4. Sandy consumes only hamburgers (H) and milkshakes (M). At basket A, containing 2 hamburgers and 10 milkshakes, his $MRS_{H,M}$ is 8. At basket B, containing 6 hamburgers and 4 milkshakes, his $MRS_{H,M}$ is 1/2. Both baskets A and B are on the same indifference curve. Draw the indifference curve, using information about the $MRS_{H,M}$ to make sure that the curvature of the indifference curve is accurately depicted.

3.5. James Bond likes his vodka martinis to contain exactly 10 parts of vodka for every 1 part of vermouth. On a graph with the amount of vodka on one axis and the amount of vermouth on the other axis, draw two of his indifference curves, U_1 and U_2, with $U_2 > U_1$.

3.6. Draw indifference curves to represent the following types of consumer preferences.
a) I like both peanut butter and jelly, and always get the same additional satisfaction from an ounce of peanut butter as I do from 2 ounces of jelly.
b) I like peanut butter, but neither like nor dislike jelly.
c) I like peanut butter, but dislike jelly.
d) I like peanut butter and jelly, but I only want 2 ounces of peanut butter for every ounce of jelly.

3.7. Dr. Strangetaste buys only food (F) and clothing (C) out of his income. He has positive marginal utilities for both goods, and his $MRS_{F,C}$ is *increasing*. Draw two of Dr. Strangetaste's indifference curves, U_1 and U_2, with $U_2 > U_1$.

The following exercises will give you practice in working with a variety of utility functions and marginal utilities, and to help you understand how to graph indifference curves.

3.8. Consider the utility function $U(x, y) = 3x + y$, with $MU_x = 3$ and $MU_y = 1$.
a) Is the assumption that more is better satisfied for both goods?
b) Does the marginal utility of x diminish, remain constant, or increase as the consumer buys more x? Explain.
c) What is the $MRS_{x,y}$?
d) Is the $MRS_{x,y}$ diminishing, constant, or increasing as the consumer substitutes x for y along an indifference curve?
e) On a graph with x on the horizontal axis and y on the vertical axis, draw a typical indifference curve (it need not be exactly to scale, but it needs to reflect accurately whether there is a diminishing $MRS_{x,y}$). Also indicate on your graph whether the indifference curve will intersect either or both axes. Label the curve U_1.
f) On the same graph draw a second indifference curve U_2, with $U_2 > U_1$.

3.9. Answer all parts of Problem 3.8 for the utility function $U(x,y) = \sqrt{xy}$. The marginal utilities are $MU_x = \sqrt{y}/(2\sqrt{x})$ and $MU_y = \sqrt{x}/(2\sqrt{y})$.

3.10. Answer all parts of Problem 3.8 for the utility function $U(x,y) = xy + x$. The marginal utilities are $MU_x = y + 1$ and $MU_y = x$.

3.11.   Answer all parts of Problem 3.8 for the utility function $U(x, y) = x^{0.4}y^{0.6}$. The marginal utilities are $MU_x = 0.4\,(y^{0.6}/\,x^{0.6})$ and $MU_y = 0.6(x^{0.4}/y^{0.4})$.

3.12.   Answer all parts of Problem 3.8 for the utility function $U = \sqrt{x} + 2\sqrt{y}$. The marginal utilities for x and y are, respectively, $MU_x = 1/(2\sqrt{x})$ and $MU_y = 1/\sqrt{y}$.

3.13.   Answer all parts of Problem 3.8 for the utility function $U(x, y) = x^2 + y^2$. The marginal utilities are $MU_x = 2x$ and $MU_y = 2y$.

3.14.   Suppose a consumer's preferences for two goods can be represented by the Cobb–Douglas utility function $U = Ax^{\alpha}y^{\beta}$, where A, α, and β are positive constants. The marginal utilities are $MU_x = \alpha Ax^{\alpha-1}y^{\beta}$ and $MU_y = \beta Ax^{\alpha}y^{\beta-1}$. Answer all parts of Problem 3.8 for this utility function.

3.15.   Suppose a consumer has preferences over two goods that can be represented by the quasi-linear utility function $U(x, y) = 2\sqrt{x} + y$. The marginal utilities are $MU_x = 1/\sqrt{x}$ and $MU_y = 1$.

a) Is the assumption that more is better satisfied for both goods?

b) Does the marginal utility of x diminish, remain constant, or increase as the consumer buys more x? Explain.

c) What is the expression for $MRS_{x,y}$?

d) Is the $MRS_{x,y}$ diminishing, constant, or increasing as the consumer substitutes more x for y along an indifference curve?

e) On a graph with x on the horizontal axis and y on the vertical axis, draw a typical indifference curve (it need not be exactly to scale, but it should accurately reflect whether there is a diminishing $MRS_{x,y}$). Indicate on your graph whether the indifference curve will intersect either or both axes.

f) Show that the slope of every indifference curve will be the same when $x = 4$. What is the value of that slope?

CHAPTER 4

Consumer Choice

According to the United States Bureau of Labor Statistics, in 1999 there were about 107 million households in the United States. The average household in the United States had an after-tax annual income just over $39,000. Consumers in these households faced many decisions.

How much should they spend out of their income, and how much should they save? On average, they spent just over $36,000. They also had to decide how much to spend on various types of goods and services, including food, housing, clothing, transportation, health care, entertainment, and other items.

Of course, the average values of statistics reported for all households mask the great variation in consumption patterns by age, location, income level, marital status, and family composition. Table 4.1 compares expenditure patterns for all households and for selected levels of income.

A casual examination of the table reveals some interesting patterns in consumption. Consumers with lower income tend to spend more than their current after-tax income, electing to borrow today and repay their loans in the future. For example, households with incomes in the $20,000 − $30,000 range spend about $5,000 per year more than their after-tax income. By contrast, households with incomes in excess of $90,000 save nearly a third of their after-tax income. The table also indicates that consumers who attend college can expect to earn substantially higher incomes, a fact that influences the choice to attend college.

Consumer decisions have a profound impact on the economy as a whole and on the fortunes of individual firms and institutions. For example, consumer expenditures on transportation affect the financial viability of the airline and automobile sectors of the economy, as well as the demand for related items such as fuel and insurance. The level of spending on health care will affect not only providers of health care services in the private sector, but also the need for public sector programs such as Medicare and Medicaid.

This chapter develops the theory of consumer choice, explaining how consumers allocate their limited incomes among available goods and services. It begins where Chapter 3 left off. In that chapter, we developed the first building block in the study of consumer choice: consumer preferences. However, preferences alone do not explain why consumers make the choices they do. Consumer preferences tell us whether a consumer likes one particular basket of goods and services better than another, assuming that all baskets could be "purchased" at no cost. But it *does* cost the consumer something to purchase baskets of goods and services, and a consumer has limited resources with which to make these purchases.

In this chapter we will study how the consumer chooses goods and services to maximize satisfaction while living within a budget constraint. We will learn how a consumer's purchase decisions depend not only on the consumer's preferences and income, but also on the prices of goods and services.

TABLE 4.1
U.S. Average Expenditures by Consumer Unit, 1999

	All Households	Households with Income $20,000–$29,999	Households with Income $40,000–$49,999	Households with Income Over $90,000
Number of Households	107,824,000	12,091,000	7,518,000	7,870,000
Average number of people in unit	2.5	2.4	2.7	3.1
Age of the reference person[a]	47.8	48.6	44.5	46.2
Percent (reference person) having attended college	54	47	64	85
Income (before taxes)	$42,770	$24,561	$44,304	$139,168
Income (after taxes)	$39,346	$23,544	$41,143	$123,165
Average annual expenditures	$36,267	$28,394	$40,379	$87,623
Expenditure on Selected Categories				
Food	$4,921	$4,196	$5,671	$9,415
Housing (including shelter, utilities, supplies, furnishings, and equipment)	$11,843	$9,293	$12,268	$26,693
Apparel and services	$1,708	$1,441	$1,872	$4,236
Transportation	$6,815	$5,404	$7,911	$14,768
Health Care	$1,931	$1,930	$2,051	$3,121
Entertainment	$1,844	$1,277	$1,944	$4,690

Source: Bureau of Labor Statistics. Table 7050. *Income Before Taxes: Average Annual Expenditures and Characteristics,* Consumer Expenditure Survey, 1998–1999.

Notes:

[a]Reference Person: The first member mentioned by the respondent when asked to "Start with the name of the person or one of the persons who owns or rents the home." It is with respect to this person that the relationships of the other household members are determined.

4.1
THE BUDGET CONSTRAINT

The **budget constraint** defines the set of baskets that a consumer can purchase with a limited amount of income. Suppose a consumer, Eric, purchases only two types of goods, food and clothing. Let x be the number of units of food he purchases each month and y the number of units of clothing. The price of a unit of food is P_x, and the price of a unit of clothing is P_y. Finally, to keep matters simple, let's assume that Eric has a fixed income of I dollars per month.

Eric's total monthly expenditure on food will be $P_x x$ (the price of a unit of food times the amount of food purchased). Similarly, his total monthly expenditure on clothing will be $P_y y$ (the price of a unit of clothing times the number of units of clothing purchased).

The **budget line** indicates all of the combinations of food and clothing that Eric can purchase if he spends *all* of his available income on the two goods. In other words, the budget line shows what baskets (combinations of x and y) he can purchase if his total expenditures on food and clothing equal his income:

$$P_x x + P_y y = I \tag{4.1}$$

Let's look at the graph of the budget line in Figure 4.1. Eric has an income of $I = \$800$ per month. The price of food is $P_x = \$20$ per unit and the price of clothing is $P_y = \$40$ per unit. If he spends all $800 on food, he will be able to buy, at most, $I/P_x = 800/20 = 40$ units of food. So the horizontal intercept of the budget line will be at $x = 40$. Similarly, if Eric buys only clothing, he will be able to buy at most $I/P_y = 800/40 = 20$ units of clothing. So the vertical intercept of the budget line will be at $y = 20$.

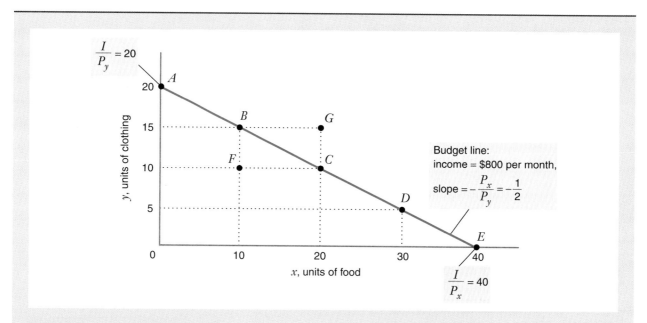

FIGURE 4.1 Example of Budget Line
The line connecting baskets A and E is Eric's budget line when he has an income of $I = $800 per month, the price of food is $P_x = $20 per unit, and the price of clothing is $P_y = $40 per unit. The equation of the budget line is $P_x x + P_y y = I$, that is, $20x + 40y = 800$. Eric can buy any basket on or inside the budget line. All of the baskets A, B, C, D, and E are on the budget line because they can be purchased if Eric spends all his income. He can also purchase any basket inside the budget line, such as basket F, which he could purchase for only $600. However, he cannot buy a basket outside the budget line, such as basket G. To buy G he would need $1000, requiring more than his monthly income.

Using equation (4.1), we can plot the whole budget line. If $I = \$800$, $P_x = \$20$, and $P_y = \$40$:

$$\$20x + \$40y = \$800$$

Eric's income permits him to buy any basket on or inside the budget line. For example, he could purchase any of the following baskets lying on the budget line by spending *all* the available income:

- Basket A, with $x = 0$ and $y = 20$. This is the vertical intercept of the budget line. He buys only clothing (no food).
- Basket B, with $x = 10$ and $y = 15$.
- Basket C, with $x = 20$ and $y = 10$.
- Basket D, with $x = 30$ and $y = 5$.
- Basket E, with $x = 40$ and $y = 0$. This is the horizontal intercept of the budget line. He buys only food (no clothing).

The budget constraint tells us that the consumer could also buy any basket inside the budget line. For example, Eric could buy F ($x = 10$ and $y = 10$). For this basket he would need to spend only $P_x x + P_y y = 20(10) + 40(10) = \$600$, an amount well below his income of $\$800$.[1] Eric cannot buy a basket outside the budget line, such as G. To buy G he would need to spend $\$1000$, which is more than his monthly income.

What does the *slope* of the budget line tell us? Suppose Eric is at basket B, spending all his income. If he wants more food, he must give up some clothing. In fact, since food is half as expensive as clothing, Eric must give up 1/2 unit of clothing for every additional unit of food he buys. *The slope of the budget line therefore tells us how many units of clothing (the good on the vertical axis) he must give up to obtain an additional unit of food (the good on the horizontal axis).* If he moves from basket B to basket C, he gives up 5 units of clothing ($\Delta y = -5$) to purchase 10 more units of food ($\Delta x = +10$). The slope of the budget line is therefore $\Delta y / \Delta x = -1/2$.

Note that on a graph with x on the horizontal axis and y on the vertical axis, the slope of the budget line is $\Delta y / \Delta x = -P_x / P_y$. If the price of good x is three times the price of good y, the consumer must give up 3 units of y to get 1 more unit of x, and the slope is -3. If the prices are equal, the slope of the budget line is -1 because the consumer can always get 1 more unit of x by giving up 1 unit of y.[2]

---

[1]The distinction between the budget line and the budget constraint can be further explained in the following way. The budget line can be written as $P_x x + P_y y = I$, whereas the budget constraint requires that $P_x x + P_y y \leq I$. A consumer may spend all of his income (and choose a basket *on* the budget line) or less than his income (and choose a basket *inside* the budget line); either choice will satisfy the budget constraint.

[2]We can solve the budget line in equation (4.1) for y in terms of x. We find that $y = (I/P_y) - (P_x/P_y)x$. It may help to recall the equation of a straight line from algebra: $y = mx + b$, where m is the slope of the graph ($\Delta y / \Delta x$), and b is the intercept on the y axis. For our budget line, the y intercept b is I/P_y, and the slope m is $-P_x/P_y$.

HOW DOES A CHANGE IN INCOME AFFECT THE BUDGET LINE?

As we have shown, the location of the budget line depends on the level of income and on the prices of the goods the consumer purchases. As you might expect, when income rises, the set of choices available to the consumer will increase. Let's see how the budget line changes as income varies.

In the example just discussed, suppose income rises from I_1 = $800 per month to I_2 = $1000 per month, with the prices P_x = $20 and P_y = $40 unchanged. If Eric buys only clothing, he can now purchase I_2/P_y = 1000/40 = 25 units of clothing, the vertical intercept of the new budget line. The extra $200 of income allows him to buy an extra 5 units of y, since P_y = $40.

If he buys only food, he could purchase I_2/P_x = 1000/20 = 50 units, the horizontal intercept on the new budget line. With the extra $200 of income he can buy an extra 10 units of x, since P_x = $20. The consumer can also buy baskets such as G with an income of $1000.

The initial budget line with an income of $800 ($BL_1$) and the new budget line with income of $1000 ($BL_2$) are shown in Figure 4.2. The slopes of the two budget

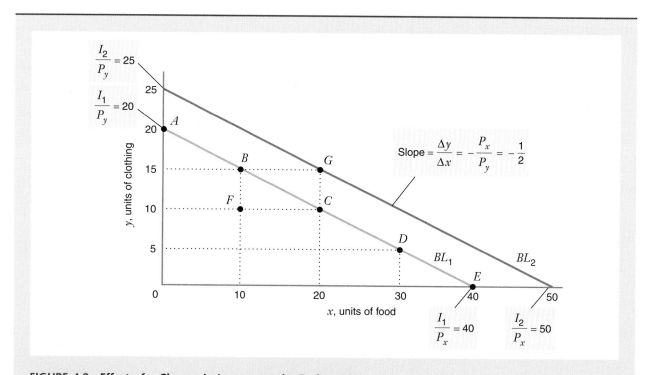

FIGURE 4.2   Effect of a Change in Income on the Budget Line
If the consumer initially has an income of I_1 = $800 per month, the price of food is P_x = $20 per unit, and the price of clothing is P_y = $40 per unit. Then the budget line will be BL_1 in the graph, with a vertical intercept of y = 20, a horizontal intercept of x = 40, and a slope of −1/2. If income grows to I_2 = $1000 per month, then the budget line will be BL_2, with a vertical intercept of y = 25, a horizontal intercept of x = 50, and a slope of −1/2. Although the consumer cannot buy basket G with an income of $800, he can afford it if income rises to $1000.

lines are the same, because the prices of food and clothing are unchanged. The slope of each budget lines is $\Delta y/\Delta x = (P_x/P_y) = -1/2$.

In summary, an increase in income shifts the budget line out in a parallel fashion. It expands the set of possible baskets from which a consumer may choose. Similarly, a decrease in income will shift the budget line in towards the origin, reducing the set of choices available to the consumer.

HOW DOES A CHANGE IN PRICE AFFECT THE BUDGET LINE?

How does Eric's budget line change if the price of food rises from $P_{x_1} = \$20$ to $P_{x_2} = \$25$ per unit, while income and the price of clothing are unchanged? The vertical intercept of the budget line will remain unchanged since I and P_y do not change. However, the horizontal intercept will decrease from $I/P_{x_1} = 800/20 = 40$ units to $I/P_{x_2} = 800/25 = 32$ units. The higher price of food means that if Eric spends all \$800 on food, he can purchase only 32 units of food. The slope of the budget line has changed from $-(P_{x_1}/P_y) = -(20/40) = -1/2$ to $-(P_{x_2}/P_y) = -(25/40) = -5/8$. The initial budget line (BL_1) and the new budget line (BL_2) are shown in Figure 4.3. BL_2 has a steeper slope than BL_1. The steeper slope tells us that, to purchase one more unit of food, the consumer must give up more units of clothing than before. When the price of food was \$20, the consumer needed to give up only 1/2 unit of clothing. At the higher price of food (\$25), the consumer is required to give up 5/8 of a unit of clothing.

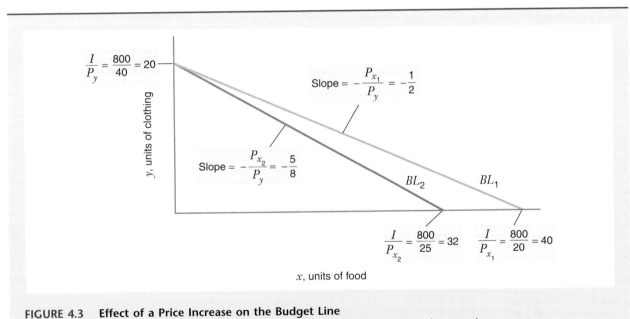

FIGURE 4.3   Effect of a Price Increase on the Budget Line
When the price of food rises from \$20 to \$25 per unit, the budget line rotates in toward the origin, from BL_1 to BL_2. If he buys only food out of his income of \$800, the horizontal intercept shifts in from 40 to 32 units. The vertical intercept does not change because income and the price of clothing are unchanged. The new budget line BL_2 has a steeper slope because the price of food has risen.

In summary, an increase in the price of one good will move the intercept on that good's axis toward the origin. A decrease in the price of one good will move the intercept on that good's axis away from the origin. On a graph drawn with x on the horizontal axis and y on the vertical axis, the slope of the budget line is $-(P_x/P_y)$. The slope of the budget line will change as this ratio changes.

When the budget line rotates in, the consumer's purchasing power declines because the set of baskets from which he can choose is reduced. When the consumer is able to buy more baskets than before, we say that the consumer's purchasing power has increased. An increase in income will expand the set of baskets the consumer can buy, thereby increasing purchasing power. A decrease in one of the prices will also increase the set of baskets available to the consumer. Consumer purchasing power decreases when there is an increase in a price or a decrease in income, because such changes reduce the number of baskets available to the consumer.

LEARNING-BY-DOING EXERCISE 4.1

Graphing a Budget Line

Problem   What will happen to the number of baskets available to the consumer if the prices of both goods and income double? The consumer views the doubling of income as good news because it increases his purchasing power. However, the doubling of prices is bad news because it decreases his purchasing power. What is the net effect of the good and bad news?

Solution   You can answer this question by observing how the budget line changes as prices and income double. Initially, the intercept on the y axis is I/P_y. If both I and P_y double, then the vertical intercept will be unchanged. Similarly, if both I and P_x double, then the intercept along the x axis (I/P_x) will be unchanged. And the slope of the budget line $-(P_x/P_y)$ will also be unaffected because both prices double. In short, the location of the budget line will be unaffected if all (in this case, both) prices and income double. The consumer's purchasing power is unaffected because the set of baskets available to him does not change.

We have learned that the consumer can choose any basket on or inside the budget line. Which basket will he choose? We are now ready to answer this question.

4.2
OPTIMAL CHOICE

If we know a consumer's preferences and budget constraint, we can determine the optimal amount of each good to purchase. We will assume that a consumer makes these choices rationally. More precisely, **optimal choice** means that the consumer chooses a basket of goods that (1) maximizes his satisfaction (utility) while (2) allowing him to live within his budget constraint.

Suppose that Eric buys only two goods (say, food and clothing) and that he likes more of both goods. Then an optimal consumption basket must be located on the budget line. A basket such as F in Figure 4.1 cannot be optimal, because there are baskets to the north and east of F that are both affordable and preferred to F. If Eric purchases basket F, he will not spend all his income. The unspent income could be used to increase satisfaction with the purchase of additional food or clothing.[3] In fact, no point inside the budget line can be optimal for exactly this reason.

Of course, consumers do not always spend all of their available income at any given time. They often save part of their income for future consumption. The introduction of time into the analysis of consumer choice really means that the consumer is making choices over more than just two goods, including for instance the consumption of food today, clothing today, food tomorrow, and clothing tomorrow. For now, let us keep matters simple and assume that there is no tomorrow. Later we will introduce time (with the possibility of borrowing and saving) into the discussion.

To state the problem of optimal consumer choice, let $U(x, y)$ represent the consumer's utility from purchasing x units of food and y units of clothing. The consumer chooses x and y, but must do so while satisfying the budget constraint $P_x x + P_y y \leq I$. The optimal choice problem for the consumer is expressed like this:

$$\max_{(x,y)} U(x, y) \qquad\qquad (4.2)$$
$$\text{subject to } P_x x + P_y y \leq I$$

where the notation "$\max_{(x,y)} U(x, y)$" means "choose x and y to maximize utility," and the notation "subject to $P_x x + P_y y \leq I$" means "the expenditures on x and y must not exceed the consumer's income." If the consumer likes more of both goods, the marginal utilities of food and clothing are both positive. At an optimal basket all income will be spent (that is, the consumer will choose a basket *on* the budget line $P_x x + P_y y = I$).

In Chapter 1 we pointed out the importance of distinguishing between endogenous and exogenous variables in any economic analysis. Since the consumer faces a given set of prices for the goods, the prices P_x and P_y are exogenous. So is the level of the monthly income I, which we assume here to be fixed. The endogenous variables are the amounts of food x and clothing y purchased by the consumer. The amounts purchased are determined by the consumer.

Figure 4.4 represents Eric's optimal choice problem graphically. He has an income of $I = \$800$ per month, the price of food is $P_x = \$20$ per unit, and the price of clothing is $P_y = \$40$ per unit. The budget line has a vertical intercept at $y = 20$, indicating that if he were to spend all his income on clothing, he could buy up to 20 units of clothing each month. Similarly, the horizontal intercept at $x = 40$ shows that Eric could buy up to 40 units of food each month if he were to spend all his income on food. The slope of the budget line is $-P_x/P_y = -1/2$. Three of Eric's indifference curves are shown as U_1, U_2, and U_3.

---

[3]This observation can be generalized to the case in which the consumer is considering purchases of more than two goods, say N goods, all of which yield positive marginal utility to the consumer. At an optimal consumption basket, all income must be exhausted.

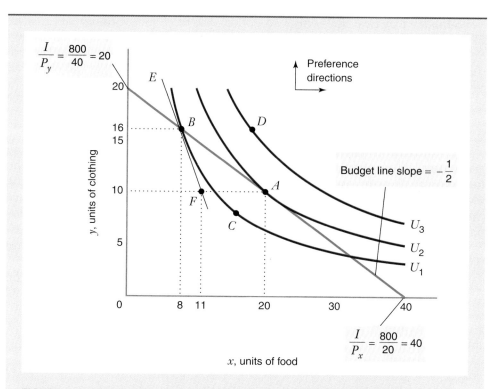

FIGURE 4.4 Optimal Choice: Maximizing Utility with a Given Budget
Which basket should the consumer choose if he wants to maximize utility while living
within a budget constraint limiting his expenditures to $800 per month? He should
select basket *A*, achieving a level of utility U_2. Any other basket on or inside the budget
line (such as *B*, *F*, or *C*) is affordable, but leads to less satisfaction. A point outside the
budget line (such as *D*) is not affordable.
    At the optimal basket *A* the budget line is tangent to an indifference curve. The
slopes of the budget line and the indifference curve U_2 are both −1/2.

If Eric maximizes utility while satisfying the budget constraint, he will choose
the basket that allows him to reach the highest indifference curve while being
on or inside the budget line. In Figure 4.4 that optimal basket is *A*, where Eric
achieves a level of utility U_2. Any other point on or inside the budget line will
leave him with a lower level of utility.

    To understand why basket *A* is the optimal choice, let's explore why other
baskets are *not* optimal. First, baskets outside (i.e., to the northeast of) the budget
line, such as *D*, cannot be optimal because Eric cannot afford them. We can therefore restrict our attention to baskets on or inside the budget line. Any basket inside the budget line, such as *F* or *C*, will also not be optimal. As indicated by the
preference directions on the graph, the consumer likes more of both goods (the
marginal utilities are both positive). Since there are affordable baskets to the
northeast of baskets such as *F* and *C*, *F* and *C* cannot be optimal. Thus, an optimal basket must lie on the budget line.

    If Eric were to move along the budget line away from *A*, even by a small
amount, his utility would fall because the indifference curves are bowed in toward the origin or, in economic terms, because there is diminishing marginal rate

of substitution of x for y ($MRS_{x,y}$). At the optimal basket A, the budget line is just tangent to the indifference curve U_2. This means that the slope of the budget line ($-P_x/P_y$) and the slope of the indifference curve are equal. Recall from equation (3.5) that the slope of the indifference curve is $-MU_x/MU_y$ (that is, $-MRS_{x,y}$). Thus, at the optimal basket A, the tangency condition requires that

$$\frac{MU_x}{MU_y} = \frac{P_x}{P_y} \tag{4.3}$$

or, equivalently, that

$$MRS_{x,y} = \frac{P_x}{P_y}$$

In Figure 4.4 the optimal basket A is said to be an **interior optimum**, that is, an optimum at which the consumer will be purchasing both commodities ($x > 0$ and $y > 0$). The optimum occurs at a point of tangency between the budget line and the indifference curve. In other words, at an interior optimal basket, the consumer will choose the commodities so that the ratio of the marginal utilities (that is, the marginal rate of substitution) will equal the ratio of the prices of the goods.

We can also express the tangency condition by rewriting equation (4.3) as follows:

$$\frac{MU_x}{P_x} = \frac{MU_y}{P_y} \tag{4.4}$$

This form of the tangency condition states that, at an interior optimal basket, Eric will choose commodities so that the marginal utility per dollar spent on each commodity will be the same. Put another way, at an interior optimum, the extra utility per dollar spent on good x is equal to the extra utility per dollar spent on good y. Thus, at the optimal basket, each good gives Eric the same "bang for the buck."

Although we have focused on the case in which the consumer purchases only two goods, such as food and clothing, the consumer's optimal choice problem can also be analyzed when the consumer buys more than two goods. For example, suppose the consumer chooses among baskets of three commodities (x, y, z) to maximize utility $U(x, y, z)$ while living within the budget constraint $P_x x + P_y y + P_z z \leq I$. If all of the goods have positive marginal utilities, then an optimal basket will be on the budget line. At an interior optimal basket, the consumer will choose the goods so that the marginal utility per dollar spent on all three goods will be the same, that is, so that $MU_x/P_x = MU_y/P_y = MU_z/P_z$. The same principles apply to the case in which the consumer buys any larger number of goods.

USING THE TANGENCY CONDITIONS TO UNDERSTAND WHEN A BASKET IS *NOT* OPTIMAL

Let's use the tangency conditions represented in equations (4.3) and (4.4) to explore why an interior basket such as B in Figure 4.4 is *not* optimal. In the figure we are given an indifference map, which comes from the utility function $U(x, y) = xy$. As we showed in Learning-By-Doing Exercise 3.3, the marginal utilities for this utility function are $MU_x = y$ and $MU_y = x$. For example, at basket B (where $y = 16$ and $x = 8$), the marginal utilities are $MU_x = 16$ and $MU_y = 8$. We also are given that $P_x = \$20$ and $P_y = \$40$.

Why is *B* not an optimal choice? Consider equation (4.3). The left-hand side of that equation tells us that $MU_x/MU_y = 16/8 = 2$ at *B*. Eric's marginal rate of substitution of *x* for *y* is 2. At *B* he would be *willing* to give up 2 units of clothing (*y*) to get one more unit of food (*x*).[4] But, given the prices of the goods, will Eric have to give up 2 units of clothing to get one more unit of food? The right-hand side of equation (4.4) tells us that $P_x/P_y = 20/40 = 1/2$ because clothing is twice as expensive as food. However, to buy one more unit of food, he needs to give up only 1/2 unit of clothing. To summarize, to get one more unit of food, he is *willing* to give up two units of clothing, but he is only *required* to give up 1/2 units of clothing. Therefore, he will surely want to give up some clothing to obtain more food. This is why basket *B* cannot be his optimal choice.

So far we have used one form of the tangency condition to illustrate why *B* cannot be optimal. We will show how to find an optimal basket shortly. First, let's examine the other form of the tangency condition in equation (4.4) to see why the marginal utility per dollar spent must be equal for all goods at an interior optimum.

If we compare the marginal utility per dollar spent on the two commodities at *B*, we find that $MU_x/P_x = 16/20 = 0.8$ and that $MU_y/P_y = 8/40 = 0.2$. Eric's marginal utility per dollar spent on food (MU_x/P_x) is higher than his marginal utility per dollar spent on clothing (MU_y/P_y). He should therefore take the last dollar he spent on clothing and instead spend it on food. How would this reallocation of income affect his utility? Decreasing clothing expenditures by a dollar would decrease utility by about 0.2, but increasing food expenditures by that dollar would increase utility by about 0.8; the net effect on utility is the difference, a gain of about 0.6.[5] So if Eric is currently purchasing basket *B*, he is not choosing his optimal basket. We know that if he spends a dollar more on food and a dollar less on clothing, he will be able to increase his total utility while continuing to live within his budget.

FINDING AN OPTIMAL CONSUMPTION BASKET

We have seen that basket *B* is not optimal, and we even know which way the consumer should move along the budget line to improve his satisfaction. However, we cannot yet say where the optimal basket is. How can we determine the location of the optimal basket? As our discussion to this point suggests, when both marginal utilities are positive, an optimal consumption basket will be on the budget line. Further, when there is a diminishing marginal rate of substitution, then an interior optimal consumption basket will occur at the tangency between an indifference curve and the budget line. This is the case illustrated at basket *A* in Figure 4.4.

[4]Remember, $MRS_{x,y} = MU_x/MU_y = -$(slope of the indifference curve). In Figure 4.4, the slope of the indifference curve at *B* is -2. The slope of the indifference curve at *B* is the same as the slope of *EF*, the line tangent to the indifference curve at *B*.

[5]Since $P_x = \$20$, the increased spending of a dollar on food means that the consumer will buy an additional 1/20 unit of food, so that $\Delta x = +1/20$. Similarly, since $P_y = \$40$, a decreased expenditure of one dollar on clothing will mean that the consumer reduces consumption of clothing by 1/40, so that $\Delta y = -1/40$. Recall from equation (3.4) that the effect of changes in consumption on total utility can be approximated by $\Delta U = (MU_x \times \Delta x) + (MU_y \times \Delta y)$. If Δx and Δy are small, then MU_x and MU_y will not change by much. Then the reallocation of one dollar of expenditures from clothing to food will affect utility by approximately $\Delta U = (16) \times (+1/20) + (8) \times (-1/40) = 0.6$.

The following exercise illustrates how to use information about the consumer's budget line and preferences to find a consumer's optimal consumption basket.

LEARNING-BY-DOING EXERCISE 4.2

Finding an Interior Optimum

Problem   Eric purchases food (measured by x) and clothing (measured by y) and has the utility function $U(x,y) = xy$. His marginal utilities are $MU_x = y$ and $MU_y = x$. He has a monthly income of $800. The price of food is $P_x = \$20$, and the price of clothing is $P_y = \$40$. Find his optimal consumption bundle.

Solution   In Learning-By-Doing Exercise 3.3, we learned that the indifference curves for this utility function are bowed in toward the origin and do not intersect the axes. So the optimal basket must be interior, with positive amounts of food and clothing being consumed.

How do we find an optimal basket? We know two conditions that must be satisfied at an optimum:

- An optimal basket will be on the budget line. This means that $P_x x + P_y y = I$, or, with the given information,

$$20x + 40y = 800$$

- Since the optimum is interior, the indifference curve must be tangent to the budget line. From equation (4.3), we know that a tangency requires that $MU_x/MU_y = P_x/P_y$, or, with the given information,

$$\frac{y}{x} = \frac{20}{40}$$

or, more simply,

$$x = 2y$$

So we have two equations with two unknowns: $20x + 40y = 800$ (coming from the budget line) and $x = 2y$ (coming from the tangency condition). If we substitute $x = 2y$ into the equation for the budget line, we get $20(2y) + 40y = 800$. So $y = 10$ and $x = 20$. Eric's optimal basket involves the purchase of 20 units of food and 10 units of clothing each month, as is indicated at basket A in Figure 4.4.

You should make sure that you understand *both* the algebraic and graphical approaches to finding an optimal consumption basket.

Similar Problems: Problems 4.1 and 4.2

TWO WAYS OF THINKING ABOUT OPTIMALITY

We have shown that basket A in Figure 4.4 is optimal for the consumer because it answers this question: *What basket should the consumer choose to maximize utility, given a budget constraint limiting expenditures to $800 per month?* In this case, since the consumer chooses the basket of x and y to maximize utility while spending no more than $800 on the two goods, optimality can be described as follows:

$$\max_{(x,y)} \text{Utility} = U(x, y) \tag{4.5}$$
$$\text{subject to } P_x x + P_y y \leq I = 800$$

In this example, the endogenous variables are x and y (the consumer chooses the basket). The exogenous variables are the prices P_x, P_y, and income (i.e., the level of expenditures). The graphical approach solves the consumer choice problem by locating the basket on the budget line that allows the consumer to reach the highest indifference curve. That indifference curve is U_2 in Figure 4.4.

There is another way to see the optimality of basket A. Let's ask a different question: *What basket should the consumer choose to minimize her expenditure (i.e., the income she needs) and also achieve a given level of utility U_2?* Here the consumer chooses the basket of goods x and y that will minimize the total spending (income) necessary to purchase the two goods ($P_x x + P_y y$), while achieving a given level of utility (U_2). Equation (4.6) expresses this algebraically:

$$\min_{(x,y)} \text{Expenditure} = P_x x + P_y y \tag{4.6}$$
$$\text{subject to } U(x, y) = U_2$$

This is called the **expenditure minimization problem.** In this problem the endogenous variables are still x and y, but the exogenous variables are the prices P_x, P_y, and the required level of utility U_2. Basket A in Figure 4.5 is optimal because it solves the expenditure minimization problem. Let's see why.

Using Figure 4.5, let's look for a basket that would require the lowest expenditure to reach indifference curve U_2. (In this figure, U_2 corresponds to a utility level of 200.)

In the figure, we have drawn three different budget lines. All baskets on the budget line BL_1 can be purchased if the consumer spends $640 per month. Unfortunately, none of the baskets on BL_1 allows him to reach the indifference curve U_2, so he will need an income higher than $640 to achieve the required utility. Could he reach the indifference curve U_2 with a monthly income of $1000? All baskets on budget line BL_3 can be purchased with a monthly income of $1000. It is true that baskets such as R and S will indeed allow him to reach the indifference curve U_2. But there are other baskets on U_2 that would cost the consumer less than $1000. To find the basket that minimizes expenditure, we have to find the budget line that is just tangent to the indifference curve U_2. That budget line is BL_2, which would enable the consumer to reach U_2 by purchasing basket A, which costs only $800. And any income less than $800 will not give the consumer enough money to purchase a basket on indifference curve U_2.

The utility maximization problem of equation (4.5) and the expenditure minimizing problem of equation (4.6) are said to be *dual* to one another. The basket that maximizes utility with a given level of income I (expenditure) leads the con-

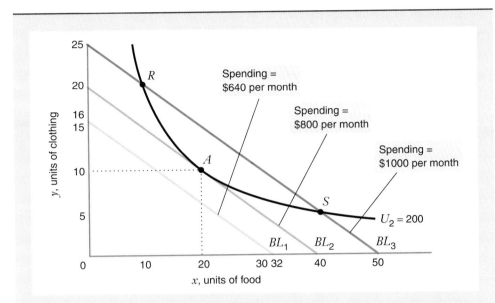

FIGURE 4.5 Optimal Choice: Minimizing Expenditure to Achieve a Given Utility
Which basket should the consumer choose if he wants to minimize the expenditure
(the required income) necessary to achieve a level of utility U_2? He should select basket
A, which can be purchased at a monthly expenditure of $800. Other baskets on U_2 will
cost the consumer more than $800. For example, to purchase R or S (also on U_2), the
consumer would need to spend $1000 per month (since R and S are on budget line
3). Any total expenditure less than $800 (for example, $640, represented by budget
line 1) will not enable the consumer to reach the indifference curve U_2.

sumer to a level of utility U_2. That *same* basket minimizes the level of expenditure I (income) necessary for the consumer to achieve a level of utility U_2.

We can use these two ways of thinking about optimality to understand why a basket such as B in Figure 4.6 is not optimal. If the consumer is at B, he is spending $800 and realizing a level of utility U_1. We have already discovered that B is not an optimum because the budget line is not tangent to the indifference curve at that basket.

How might the consumer improve his choice if he is at basket B? He may ask, "If I spend $800 per month, what basket will maximize my satisfaction? He will choose basket A and realize a higher level of utility U_2. Alternatively, if the consumer starts at B on the indifference curve U_1, he may ask, "If I am content with a level of utility U_1, what is the least amount of money I will need to spend to stay on that indifference curve?" As the graph shows, the answer to this question is basket C, where he needs to spend only $640 per month.

Thus, the nonoptimality of B is demonstrated in two ways. The consumer can increase utility if he continues to spend $800 monthly, or he can spend less money to stay at the same level of utility he is currently realizing at B.

CORNER POINTS

In all the examples considered so far, the optimal consumer basket has been interior, meaning that the consumer purchases positive amounts of both goods. In

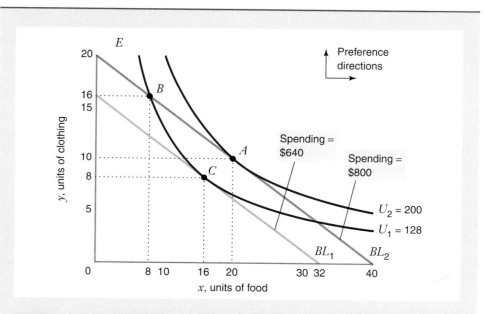

FIGURE 4.6 Nonoptimal Choice
At basket *B* the consumer spends $800 monthly and realizes a level of utility U_1. There are two ways to see that basket *B* is not an optimal choice. First, if the consumer continues to spend $800 per month, he can maximize utility by choosing basket *A*, reaching indifference curve U_2. Second, he can continue to achieve U_1 spending less than $800 per month. Basket *C* is on U_1, but the consumer needs to spend only $640 per month to purchase this basket.

reality, though, a consumer might not purchase positive amounts of all available goods. For example, not all consumers own an automobile or a house. Some consumers may not spend money on tobacco or alcohol. If the consumer cannot find an interior basket at which the budget line will be tangent to an indifference curve, then the consumer might find an optimal basket at a **corner point,** that is, at a basket along an axis, where one of the goods is not purchased at all. If an optimum occurs at a corner point, the budget line may not be tangent to an indifference curve at the optimal basket.

Let's consider again our consumer who chooses between just two goods, food and clothing. If his indifference map is like the one shown in Figure 4.7, no indifference curve is tangent to his budget line. At any interior basket on the budget line, such as basket *S*, the slope of the indifference curve is steeper (more negative) than the slope of the budget line. This means that $-MU_x/MU_y < -P_x/P_y$. If we remove the minus signs from both sides of this inequality, the inequality sign reverses, so that $MU_x/MU_y > P_x/P_y$. Then, by cross multiplying, we get $MU_x/P_x > MU_y/P_y$, which tells us the marginal utility per dollar spent is higher for food than for clothing and so the consumer would like to purchase more food and less clothing. This is true not only at basket *S*, but at all baskets on the budget line. The consumer would continue to substitute food for clothing, moving along the budget line until he reaches the corner point basket *R*. At basket *R* the slope

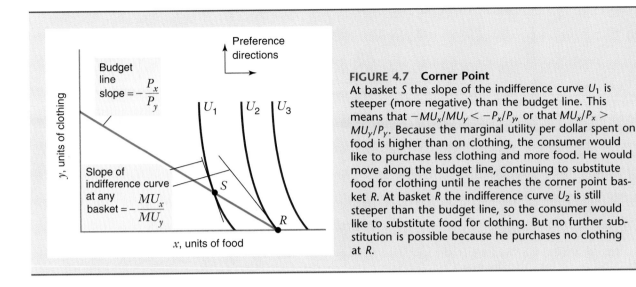

FIGURE 4.7   Corner Point
At basket S the slope of the indifference curve U_1 is steeper (more negative) than the budget line. This means that $-MU_x/MU_y < -P_x/P_y$, or that $MU_x/P_x > MU_y/P_y$. Because the marginal utility per dollar spent on food is higher than on clothing, the consumer would like to purchase less clothing and more food. He would move along the budget line, continuing to substitute food for clothing until he reaches the corner point basket R. At basket R the indifference curve U_2 is still steeper than the budget line, so the consumer would like to substitute food for clothing. But no further substitution is possible because he purchases no clothing at R.

of the indifference curve U_2 is still steeper than the slope of the budget line. He would like to substitute more food for clothing if that were possible. But no further substitution is possible because no clothing is purchased at basket R. Therefore the optimal choice for this consumer is basket R, because that basket gives the consumer the highest utility possible (U_2) on the budget line.

LEARNING-BY-DOING EXERCISE 4.3

Finding a Corner-Point Solution

Problem   David is considering his purchases of food and clothing. The number of units of food and clothing he purchases are measured respectively by x and y. He has the utility function $U(x, y) = xy + 10x$, with marginal utilities $MU_x = y + 10$ and $MU_y = x$. His income is $I = 10$. He faces a price of food $P_x = \$1$ and a price of clothing $P_y = \$2$. Find David's optimal basket.

Solution   The budget line, shown in Figure 4.8, has a slope of $-(P_x/P_y) = -1/2$. The equation of the budget line is $P_x x + P_y y = I$, or $x + 2y = 10$. To find an optimum, we must make sure that we understand what the indifference curves look like. Both marginal utilities are positive, so the indifference curves are negatively sloped. The marginal rate of substitution of x for y [$MRS_{x,y} = MU_x/MU_y = (y + 10)/x$] diminishes as we increase x and decrease y along an indifference curve. The indifference curves are therefore bowed in toward the origin. Finally, the indifference curves do intersect the x axis because it is possible to achieve a positive level of utility with purchases of food ($x > 0$) but no purchases of clothing ($y = 0$). This means that the consumer's optimal basket *may* be at a corner point along the x axis. We have plotted three of David's indifference curves in the figure.

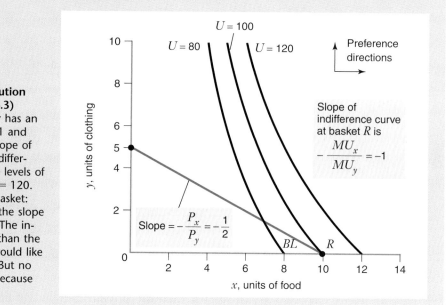

FIGURE 4.8 Corner Point Solution (Learning By Doing Exercise 4.3)
The Budget Line: The consumer has an income of 10, with prices $P_x = 1$ and $P_y = 2$. The budget line has a slope of $-1/2$. The Indifference Map: Indifference curves are drawn for three levels of utility, $U = 80$, $U = 100$, and $U = 120$.

The Optimal Consumption Basket: The optimal basket is R, where the slope of the indifference curve is -1. The indifference curve at R is steeper than the budget line, so the consumer would like to substitute food for clothing. But no further substitution is possible because no clothing is purchased at R.

Suppose we (mistakenly) assume that David's optimal basket is interior, on the budget line at a tangency between the budget line and an indifference curve. If the optimal basket is on the budget line, then it must satisfy $x + 2y = 10$. If the basket is at a point of tangency, then $MU_x/MU_y = P_x/P_y$, or $(y + 10)/x = 1/2$, which simplifies to $x = 2y + 20$. Together the budget line and tangency conditions would be satisfied only if $x = 15$ and $y = -2.5$. The algebraic "solution" suggests that David would buy a *negative* amount of clothing. But this does not make sense because x and y cannot be negative. The algebraic approach tells us that there is no basket on the budget line where the budget line is tangent to an indifference curve. The optimal basket is therefore *not* interior, and the optimum will be at a corner point.

Where is the optimal basket? As we can see in the figure, the optimum will be at basket R (a corner point), where $x = 10$ and $y = 0$. At this basket $MU_x = y + 10 = 10$ and $MU_y = x = 10$. So at R the marginal utility per dollar spent on x is $MU_x/P_x = 10/1 = 10$, while the marginal utility per dollar spent on y is $MU_y/P_y = 10/2 = 5$. David would *like* to purchase more food (x) and less clothing (y), but he cannot because basket R is at a corner point on the x axis. At R, David reaches the highest indifference curve possible while choosing a basket on the budget line.

You can also see that the tangency condition cannot be satisfied at basket R by comparing the slope of the budget line with the slope of the indifference curve through R. The slope of the indifference curve through R is $-MU_x/MU_y = -10/10 = -1$. This is steeper than the slope of the budget line, which is $-P_x/P_y = -1/2$. Thus both the algebraic and graphical approaches show that the budget line is not tangent to the indifference curve at R.

Learning By Doing Exercise 4.3 illustrates that a corner point may exist when the consumer has a diminishing marginal rate of substitution (the indifference curves are bowed in toward the origin). A corner point is often optimal when a consumer is quite willing to substitute one commodity for another. For example, if you view butter and margarine as perfect substitutes and are always willing to substitute an ounce of one for an ounce of the other, you would buy only the product that has a lower price per ounce.

LEARNING-BY-DOING EXERCISE 4.4

Corner Point Solution with Perfect Substitutes

Problem   Sara is a consumer who views chocolate and vanilla ice cream as perfect substitutes. She likes both, and is always willing to trade one scoop of chocolate for two scoops of vanilla ice cream. In other words, her marginal utility for chocolate is twice as large as her marginal utility for vanilla. Thus, $MRS_{C,V} = MU_C/MU_V = 2$.

(a) If the price of a scoop of chocolate ice cream (P_C) is three times the price of vanilla (P_V), will Sara buy both types of ice cream? If not, which will she buy?
(b) If the price of a scoop of chocolate ice cream (P_C) is twice the price of vanilla (P_V), will she buy both types of ice cream? If not, which will she buy?

Solution

(a) If Sara does buy both types of ice cream, then there is an interior optimum and the tangency condition must be satisfied. But we know that $MU_C/MU_V = 2 < P_C/P_V = 3$. The slopes of the indifference curves are all -2, and the slope of the budget line is -3. As Figure 4.9(a) shows, the indifference curves are straight lines and less steeply sloped (flatter) than the budget line. Thus, the optimal basket will be at a corner point (basket A), at which Sara buys only vanilla ice cream.

Another way of seeing this is to observe that $MU_C/MU_V = 2$, while $P_C/P_V = 3$. Therefore $MU_C/MU_V < P_C/P_V$, or $MU_C/P_C < MU_V/P_V$. Since the marginal utility per dollar spent on chocolate ice cream is less than the marginal utility per dollar spent on vanilla ice cream, Sara will always try to substitute more vanilla for chocolate. This will lead her to a corner point such as basket A in Figure 4.9(a).

(b) Now we know that $MRS_{C,V} = P_C/P_V = 2$. The slopes of the indifference curves are all -2 and the slope of the budget line is -2, so the indifference curves are straight lines parallel to the budget line. As Figure 4.9(b) shows, the optimal basket will thus be at any point along the budget line, since the consumer is equally satisfied with any of these baskets.

Note that $MU_C/MU_V = 2$, while $P_C/P_V = 2$. Therefore $MU_C/MU_V = P_C/P_V$, or $MU_C/P_C = MU_V/P_V$. Since the marginal utility per dollar spent on chocolate ice cream is always equal to the marginal utility per dollar spent on vanilla, Sara will be equally happy with any basket on the budget line.

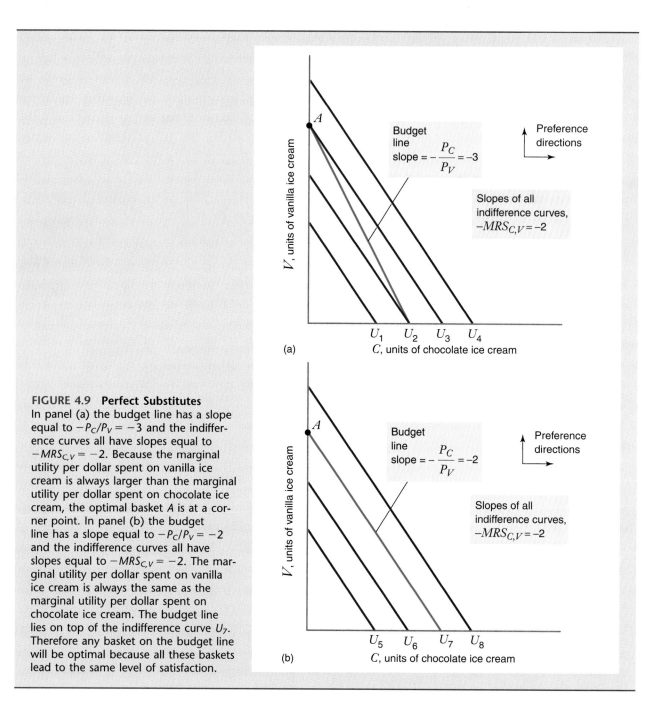

FIGURE 4.9 Perfect Substitutes
In panel (a) the budget line has a slope equal to $-P_C/P_V = -3$ and the indifference curves all have slopes equal to $-MRS_{C,V} = -2$. Because the marginal utility per dollar spent on vanilla ice cream is always larger than the marginal utility per dollar spent on chocolate ice cream, the optimal basket A is at a corner point. In panel (b) the budget line has a slope equal to $-P_C/P_V = -2$ and the indifference curves all have slopes equal to $-MRS_{C,V} = -2$. The marginal utility per dollar spent on vanilla ice cream is always the same as the marginal utility per dollar spent on chocolate ice cream. The budget line lies on top of the indifference curve U_7. Therefore any basket on the budget line will be optimal because all these baskets lead to the same level of satisfaction.

Sara would buy only vanilla if chocolate costs more than twice as much as vanilla. If chocolate costs less than twice as much as vanilla, she would buy only chocolate. The only case in which she might choose both occurs when chocolate costs exactly twice as much as vanilla. This exercise illustrates why a corner point is highly likely when two goods are perfect substitutes.

Although consumers typically purchase many goods and services, economists often want to focus on the consumer's selection of a *particular* good or service, such as the consumer's choice of housing or level of education. In that case, it is useful to present the consumer choice problem using a two-dimensional graph with the amount of the commodity of interest (say, housing) on the horizontal axis, and the amount of expenditures on all other goods on the vertical axis. The good represented on the vertical axis is called a **composite good** because it represents the collective expenditures on all other goods. The vertical axis represents the number of units of the composite good (measured by y), with the price of a unit of the composite good being $P_y = \$1$.

In this section we will use composite goods to illustrate four applications of the theory of consumer choice. Let's begin by considering Figure 4.10. Here we are interested in the consumer's choice of housing. On the horizontal axis are the units of housing h (measured, for example, in square feet). The price of housing is P_h. On the vertical axis is the composite good, measured in units by y, and with a price $P_y = \$1$. If the consumer spends all his income on housing, he could purchase at most I/P_h units of housing, the intercept of the budget line on the horizontal axis. If he spends all of his income on other goods, he could purchase at most I units of the composite good, the intercept of the budget line on the vertical axis. The optimal basket will be A in the graph.

APPLICATION: COUPONS AND CASH SUBSIDIES

Governments often have programs aimed at helping low-income consumers purchase more of an essential good, such as food, housing, or education. For exam-

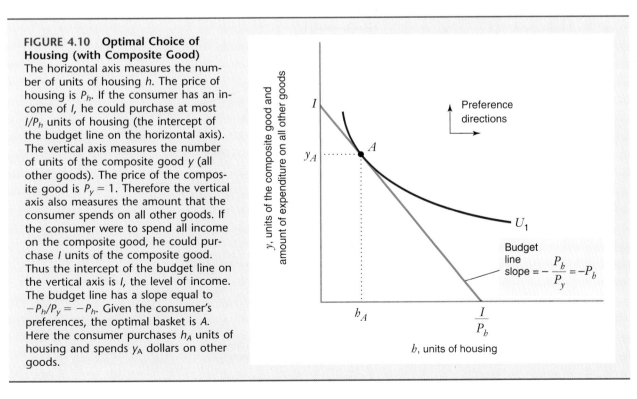

FIGURE 4.10 Optimal Choice of Housing (with Composite Good)
The horizontal axis measures the number of units of housing h. The price of housing is P_h. If the consumer has an income of I, he could purchase at most I/P_h units of housing (the intercept of the budget line on the horizontal axis). The vertical axis measures the number of units of the composite good y (all other goods). The price of the composite good is $P_y = 1$. Therefore the vertical axis also measures the amount that the consumer spends on all other goods. If the consumer were to spend all income on the composite good, he could purchase I units of the composite good. Thus the intercept of the budget line on the vertical axis is I, the level of income. The budget line has a slope equal to $-P_h/P_y = -P_h$. Given the consumer's preferences, the optimal basket is A. Here the consumer purchases h_A units of housing and spends y_A dollars on other goods.

ple, as will be discussed below, the United States government administers a food stamp program that subsidizes purchases of food and beverages. The U.S. government also provides assistance to help low-income consumers purchase housing. Let's use the theory of consumer choice to examine how a government program might increase the amount of housing chosen by a consumer.

Suppose the consumer has preferences for housing and other goods as shown by the indifference curves in Figure 4.11. The consumer has an income I and must pay a price P_b for each "unit" (e.g., square foot) of housing he rents and $P_y = 1$ for each unit of the composite "other goods" he buys. The budget line is the segment KJ. If he spends all his income on housing, he could rent I/P_b units of housing. If he spends all his income on other goods, he could buy $I/P_y = I$ units of the composite good. With his preferences and the budget line KJ, he chooses bundle A with h_A units of housing.

Now suppose that the government concludes that an amount of housing such as h_A does not provide an adequate standard of living and mandates that every consumer should have at least h_B units of housing, where $h_B > h_A$. How might

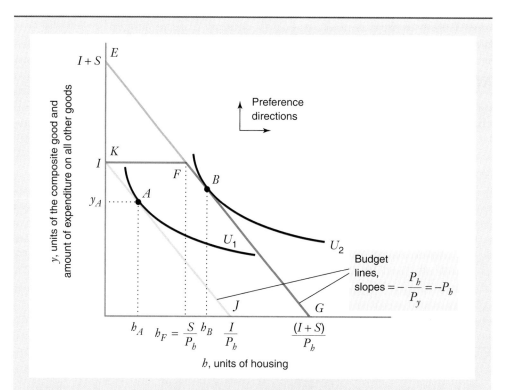

FIGURE 4.11   Optimal Choice of Housing: Subsidy and Voucher
Consider two types of programs that might be implemented to increase the consumer's purchases of housing. *Income Subsidy:* If the consumer receives an income subsidy of S dollars from the government, the budget line moves from *KJ* to *EG*. *Housing Voucher:* If the government gives the consumer a voucher of S dollars that can only be spent on housing, the budget line moves from *KJ* to *KFG*. If the consumer has the indifference map shown in the graph, he is indifferent between receiving an income subsidy of S dollars and a housing voucher worth S dollars. He will select basket *B*.

the government induce the consumer to increase his consumption of housing from h_A to h_B?

One possible way of doing this is to give the consumer an income subsidy of S dollars in cash. This increase in income shifts the budget line out from KJ to EG in Figure 4.11. If the consumer spent all his income of I and the S cash subsidy on other goods, he would be able to purchase basket E, which contains $(I + S)/P_y$ (i.e., $(I + S)/1$) units of the composite good and no housing. If he were to spend all of his income and the cash subsidy on housing, he would be able to buy basket G. At basket G he could rent $(I + S)/P_h$ units of housing if he bought none of the composite good.

With the budget line EG and the indifference curves in the figure, his optimal choice will be basket B, and he will reach the indifference curve U_2. Note that the cash subsidy S is just large enough to induce the consumer to rent h_B units of housing, satisfying the government standard for housing.

Another way to stimulate the housing consumption would be to give the consumer a housing coupon (sometimes called a voucher), that is, a certificate worth some amount of money that can be redeemed only for housing. Such a housing voucher could not be applied toward the purchase of food, clothing, or any items other than housing.

To compare the effects of an income subsidy with the effects of a housing voucher, suppose the housing voucher were also worth S dollars. With the voucher the budget line for the consumer would become KFG. Because the consumer cannot apply the voucher to purchase other goods, the maximum amount he could spend on other goods is his cash income I. The consumer could not purchase baskets to the north of the segment KF under the voucher program.

If he spends all his cash income (I) on other goods, using only the voucher to purchase housing, he will be able to consume basket F. At basket F he could purchase I units of the composite good while renting S/P_h units of housing. If he were to spend all his cash income and the voucher on housing, he would be able to acquire basket G, renting $(I + S)/P_h$ units of housing and purchasing none of the composite good.

Would it matter to the consumer or to the government whether the consumer receives an income subsidy of S dollars or a housing voucher that can be redeemed for S dollars worth of housing? If the indifference map is as depicted in Figure 4.11, the consumer will be equally happy under either program. In either case he would choose basket B and reach the indifference curve U_2.

However, if the indifference map is as depicted in Figure 4.12, then the type of program *does* matter. With no government program, the budget line is again KJ, and the consumer chooses basket A, with a level of housing h_A. To induce the consumer to rent h_B units of housing with a cash subsidy, the size of the subsidy must be S. With that subsidy the consumer will choose basket T and reach the indifference curve U_4. However, the government can induce the consumer to rent h_B units of housing with a voucher that can be redeemed for V dollars. With such a voucher the budget line will be KRG. The consumer will purchase R and reach the indifference curve U_2.[6] At basket R the consumer purchases h_B units of housing, and $h_B = V/P_h$.

---

[6]While the slope of the indifference curve U_2 is defined at basket R, the slope of the budget line is not defined because the budget "line" has a corner at R. Thus one cannot apply a tangency condition to find an optimum such as R.

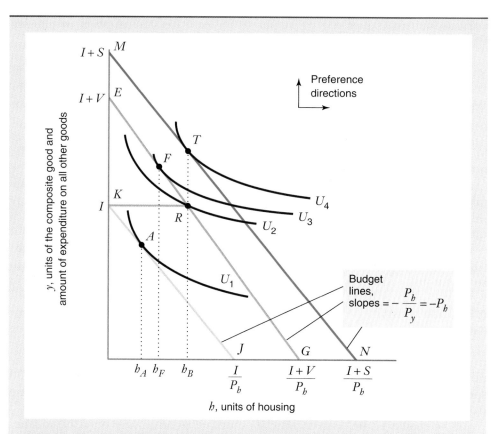

FIGURE 4.12   Optimal Choice of Housing: Subsidy and Voucher
If a consumer has an income I, he will choose h_A units of housing. The government could induce him to choose h_B units of housing with either of the following two programs:

1. Give him an income subsidy of S dollars, moving the budget line to MN. The consumer chooses basket T.
2. Give him a housing voucher worth V dollars that can be spent only on housing, moving the budget line to KRG. The consumer chooses basket R.

Since basket T lies on a higher indifference curve than basket R, a consumer with the preferences in the graph would prefer an income subsidy of S dollars over a housing voucher worth V dollars. However, the government might choose the voucher program because it would cost less. To induce the consumer to choose h_B units of housing, the government must spend $(S - V)$ dollars more if it chooses the cash subsidy program instead of the voucher program.

With the indifference map illustrated in Figure 4.12, the consumer is worse off with the voucher worth V dollars than with an income subsidy of S dollars. Why, then, might the government implement a voucher scheme instead of a direct income subsidy? If the government's primary goal is to increase the consumption of housing to h_B, the voucher will cost the government less than an income subsidy would. The government can save $(S - V)$ dollars if it uses the voucher program instead of an income subsidy.

One can also ask how the consumer would act if given a cash subsidy of V dollars. Then the budget line would be EG. The consumer would choose basket F and reach the indifference curve U_3. The consumer would prefer the cash subsidy of V dollars (allowing him to choose basket F and reach indifference curve U_3) to the voucher worth V dollars (allowing him to choose basket R and reach indifference curve U_2). However, with a voucher for V dollars, the consumer's choice of housing (h_F) is below the government's target level (h_B).

EXAMPLE 4.1

The Food Stamp Program

The Food Stamp Program is the largest food assistance program in the United States. It began in 1964, when Congress passed the Food Stamp Act. The program is designed to improve the nutrition and food purchasing power of people with low incomes.

Food stamps are paper or electronic coupons issued by the government. The coupons can be redeemed at authorized stores to buy food, beverages, and food-producing seeds or plants. However, the coupons cannot be used to buy nonfood items such as alcohol, tobacco, pet food, and nonprescription drugs.

Federal expenditures under the program were nearly $17 billion in 1998, when the program provided an average monthly benefit of $71 per person to about 19.8 million people. The federal government provides the funds used to pay for the coupons. The administrative costs of the program are shared by federal, state, and local governments.

To be eligible for food stamps, a household must have assets and income below government-specified levels. Since 1979, recipients have not had to pay for food stamps. However, the number of food stamps an individual or household receives depends on the household size, composition, and location. In 1998 the average monthly gross income of households receiving food stamps was $584. The maximum food stamp benefit for a family of four living in the contiguous United States was $408 per month.

The effect of the food stamp program on the consumer can be illustrated on graphs like the ones in Figure 4.11 and 4.12, with the composite good on the vertical axis and the amount of food consumed on the horizontal axis. As the analysis in Figure 4.11 suggests, some consumers will be equally happy with food stamp coupons or cash. However, other consumers will prefer to have cash instead of coupons, as suggested in Figure 4.12.[7]

Many people believe that the government should help low-income households with cash supplements instead of in-kind supplements such as coupons. Proponents

[7]Some of the data in this example were drawn from "Characteristics of Food Stamp Households: Fiscal Year 1998," United States Department of Agriculture, Office of Analysis, Nutrition, and Evaluation, July 1999.

of cash supplements argue that coupon programs are very expensive to administer, and that it is inappropriate for the government to place requirements on individuals' consumption decisions. Proponents of in-kind supplements argue that in-kind programs are often significantly less costly to taxpayers than cash supplements.[8]   ■

APPLICATION: JOINING A CLUB

Consumers can often join clubs that let them purchase goods and services at a discount. Consider the following example. Suppose a music-loving college student spends his income of $300 per month on compact discs (CDs) and other goods. The consumer has positive marginal utilities of CDs and other goods, and his marginal rate of substitution is diminishing. He currently must pay $20 per CD, and given this price, he buys 10 CDs per month and spends $100 on other goods.

He has just received an advertisement announcing that he can join a CD club. He would have to pay a membership fee of $100 per month, but then he would be able to buy as many CDs as he wishes at $10 each. The theory of consumer choice explains why he might want to join the club and how joining the club would affect the basket he would choose.

This consumer's choice problem is illustrated in Figure 4.13. The number of CDs consumed per month is measured on the horizontal axis, and the number of units of the composite other good (y) appears on the vertical axis. The price of a CD is P_{CD}, and the price of the composite good is $P_y = \$1$. Before the consumer joins the club, the budget line is BL_1 in the graph. He could spend all his money on other goods (and buy $y = 300$) or all of it on CDs (and buy $CD = 15$). The slope of BL_1 is $-P_{CD}/P_y = -20$. With BL_1 the consumer chooses basket A, where BL_1 is tangent to the indifference curve U_1. The tangency at basket A tells us that $MRS_{CD,y} = 20 = P_{CD}/P_y$.

The budget line he would face if he were to join the music club is BL_2 in the figure. If he joins the club, he must pay the fee of $100 per month. That means he has only $200 remaining from which he purchases other goods and CDs. He could buy as many as 20 CDs if he spends all of his remaining income on CDs; this would place him at the horizontal intercept of BL_2. If he spends all of the remaining $200 on other goods, he could purchase $y = 200$, the vertical intercept of BL_2. The slope of BL_2 is $-P_{CD}/P_y = -10$.

As the figure indicates, the budget lines BL_1 and BL_2 happen to intersect at basket A. This means that the consumer could continue to choose basket A after joining the club. To see this, observe that his total expenditures will still be $300 if he joins the club and chooses basket A. In that case he would spend $100 for the membership, $100 on CDs (buying 10 CDs at the club price of $10 each), and $100 on other goods. This tells us that the consumer can be no worse off after joining the club, because he can still purchase the basket he chose when he was not in the club.

[8]For more on this debate, and for an analysis of the Food Stamp Program, see Joseph Stiglitz, *Economics of the Public Sector* (New York: W. W. Norton & Company, 1986).

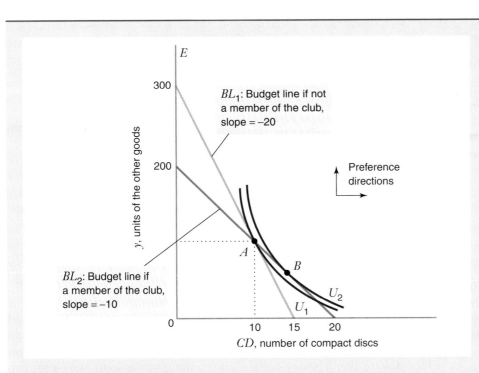

FIGURE 4.13 Joining a Club
If the consumer does not belong to the CD club, he faces budget line BL_1. He could spend his entire income of $300 on "other goods" (the vertical intercept of BL_1), or buy up to 15 compact discs if he spends all his income on CDs (the horizontal intercept of BL_1). When he is not in the club, he chooses basket A, and reaches the indifference curve U_1. If he joins the club, he faces budget line BL_2. After paying the $100 membership fee, he could spend his remaining $200 on other goods and buy no CDs (the vertical intercept of BL_2), or buy up to 20 CDs (the horizontal intercept of BL_2). He is still able to buy basket A, but it is not optimal for him to do so. The indifference curve through A is not tangent to the new budget line BL_2. If indifference curves are bowed in toward the origin (as assumed in this example), the consumer would choose basket B, at a point of tangency between BL_2 and an indifference curve U_2. The consumer will be better off joining the club, and will buy more CDs.

However, basket *A* will *not* continue to be optimal for the consumer if he joins the club. We already know that at *A*, $MRS_{CD,y} = 20$; with the new price of CDs, $P_{CD}/P_y = 10$. So the budget line BL_2 will not be tangent to the indifference curve passing through basket *A*. The consumer will seek a new basket, *B*, at which the budget line BL_2 will be tangent to the indifference curve (and $MRS_{CD,y} = 10 = P_{CD}/P_y$). The consumer will be better off in the club at basket *B* (achieving a level of utility U_2) and will purchase more CDs if he joins the club.

Consumers make similar decisions when deciding on many other types of purchases. For example, when customers subscribe to cellular telephone service, they can pay a smaller monthly subscription charge and a higher price per minute of telephone usage, or a larger monthly subscription charge and a smaller price per minute of telephone usage. Similarly, a consumer who joins a country club pays a membership fee, but can also pay less for each round of golf than someone who does not join the club.

EXAMPLE 4.2   *Pricing of Sprint's "Free and Clear" PCS Calling Plan*

Companies providing cellular telephone and other wireless communications services often offer customers a menu of pricing and service options. Consumers choose a plan from the menu and are billed accordingly. For example, here are the calling plans available for Sprint's "Free and Clear" PCS service as of early 1999:[9]

- For $50 per month, you can call up to 400 minutes per month. Each additional minute beyond 400 costs $0.35 per minute. Let's call this Plan A.[10]
- For $100 per month, you can call up to 1000 minutes per month. Each additional minute beyond 1000 costs $0.25 per minute. Let's call this Plan B.

Which plan would a utility-maximizing consumer choose? A *first* step in answering this question is to draw the budget line that corresponds to each plan. In Figure 4.14, the horizontal axis measures the number of minutes of telephone calls. The vertical axis measures the number of units of a composite good whose price is $1. The consumer has a monthly income of $400. If he spent all of his income on the composite good, he would be able to buy 400 units (basket E).

Suppose the consumer subscribes to Plan A. After paying the $50 subscription fee, he will be able to buy 350 units of the composite good as long as he uses cellular service for less than 400 minutes during the month. Until he reaches 400 minutes, his budget line is flat. Once the monthly fee is paid, the consumer, in effect, gets the first 400 minutes of PCS service at a price of zero dollars. Indeed, this is how these plans are often advertised: "Pay $50 and your first 400 minutes are free." Since he must pay an extra $0.35 per minute for calls exceeding the 400 minute limit on Plan A, the slope of the budget line to the right of basket R is −0.35. If the consumer were to use the network for 500 minutes under Plan A, his total cellular telephone bill would be $85 [i.e., $50 + $0.35(500 − 400)]. The budget line under Plan A is *MRT*. If he spends his entire budget on PCS calling, he will be able to consume 1400 minutes per month (basket T).

Figure 4.14 also shows the budget line for Plan B. The budget line is *NSV*.

The figure helps us understand why some consumers might choose one plan, while others choose another plan. If a consumer needs 400 minutes of service per month, he will choose Plan A and consume basket R. His cellular telephone bill will be $50. He could choose Plan B, but it would be more costly for the level of service he needs. (If he uses only 400 minutes of cellular service, Plan B will cost him $100.)

Similarly, if the consumer needs 1000 minutes of service per month, he will choose Plan B and consume basket S. His cellular bill under Plan B will be $100. He could choose Plan A, but it would be more expensive ($260), given the level of service he needs.

If the consumer has an indifference map like the one drawn in Figure 4.14, he will choose Plan B and consume basket S, using 1000 minutes of service each month.

---

[9]The example is drawn from an advertisement on page A28 of the *New York Times*, March 11, 1999.

[10]The plan actually had a monthly fee of $49.99. We have rounded up by a penny to simplify the numbers. Also, Sprint offered two other options on its menu. We consider a modified version of the plan (with only two options) to simplify the exposition.

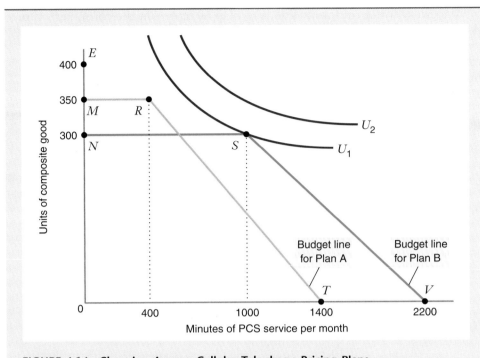

FIGURE 4.14 Choosing Among Cellular Telephone Pricing Plans
Under Plan A, the consumer pays $50 and can use the telephone up to 400 minutes per month at no extra charge. If he makes more calls, he must pay $0.35 for the extra minutes he uses. His budget line is therefore *MRT*. With Plan B, he pays $100 and can use the telephone up to 1000 minutes per month at no extra charge. If he makes more calls, he must pay $0.25 for each extra minute. His budget line is therefore *NSV*. In this example the consumer chooses Plan B. The actual choice of a plan by a consumer will depend not only on the budget lines but also on the indifference map.

We observe similar pricing options in many other consumer markets. For example, companies such as America Online, CompuServe, and MSN provide access to the Internet as well as software that enables consumers to browse the Internet. These companies recognize that some consumers will be heavy users of Internet services, while others will need less frequent service. They therefore offer consumers a variety of options for subscribing to their services. ■

APPLICATION: BORROWING AND LENDING

Up to this point, we have simplified the discussion by assuming that the consumer has a given amount of income, and can neither borrow nor lend. Using composite goods we can modify the model of consumer choice to allow for borrowing and lending.

Suppose the consumer lives for two periods (call them *years*), this year and next year. The consumer's income this year is I_1. He will have an income of I_2 next year. If the consumer cannot borrow or lend, he will spend I_1 this year and I_2 next year on goods and services.

We can now use composite goods to help us represent the consumer's choice of consumption in each of the two periods. To do this graphically, we will measure the amount of the composite good purchased in period 1 (this year) on the horizontal axis. The price of the composite good is $1, so the consumer's spending during period 1 is depicted on the horizontal axis in Figure 4.15.

Similarly, we will measure the amount of the composite good purchased in period 2 (next year) on the vertical axis. The price of this composite good is also $1, so the consumer's spending during period 2 is depicted on the vertical axis in Figure 4.15. With no borrowing or lending, the consumer can purchase basket A.

Now suppose the consumer can put money in the bank and earn an interest rate r this year. For example, suppose the interest rate is 10 percent per year ($r = 0.1$). If he saves $100 in period 1, he will receive the $100 plus the interest of $10 ($0.1 \times \$100$), for a total of $110 next year. So, if he starts at A, every time

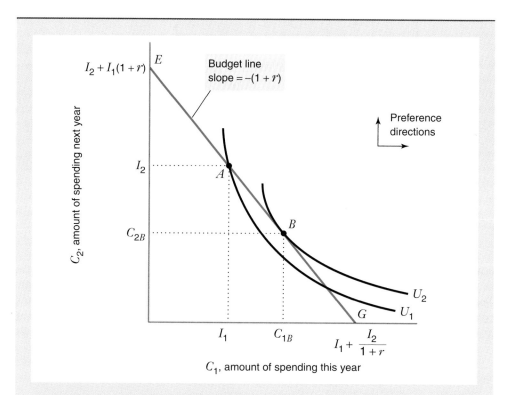

FIGURE 4.15   Borrowing and Lending
A consumer receives income I_1 this year and I_2 next year. If he neither borrows nor lends, he will be at basket A. Suppose he can borrow or lend at an interest rate r. If he chooses to save (and thus put money in the bank) this year, every dollar he saves will give him an additional $(1 + r)$ dollars (the principal plus the interest on the money he has put in the bank) next year. The slope of the budget line is therefore $-(1 + r)$, since a movement of 1 to the left (saving a dollar this year) allows him to increase consumption by $(1 + r)$ dollars next year. The consumer with the indifference map in the graph would choose basket B, borrowing ($C_{1B} - I_1$) from the bank this year and repaying the loan next year. Borrowing has increased his utility from U_1 to U_2.

he decreases consumption this year (moves to the left on the budget line) by $1, he will also be able to increase consumption next year (move up on the budget line) by $(1 + r)$ dollars. The slope of the budget line is therefore $-(1 + r)$.

Suppose, also, that the consumer can borrow money at an interest rate r this year. If the interest rate is 10 percent per period ($r = 0.1$) and he borrows $100 in period 1, he will have to pay back the $100 plus the interest of $10 (0.1 × $100), for a total of $110 in period 2. If he starts at A, every time he increases consumption this year (moves to the right on the budget line) by 1 dollar, he will need to decrease consumption next year (move down on the budget line) by $(1 + r)$ dollars. Again, this implies that the slope of the budget line is $-(1 + r)$.

If the consumer spends nothing this year, and instead puts I_1 in the bank, next year he will be able to spend $I_2 + I_1(1 + r)$; this is the vertical intercept of the budget line. Similarly, if he borrows the maximum amount possible this year, he will be able to spend up to $I_1 + I_2/(1 + r)$ this year; this is the horizontal intercept of the budget line.

The consumer with the indifference map shown in Figure 4.15 would choose basket B, borrowing some money ($C_{1B} - I_1$) from the bank this year and repaying the loan in period 2. Next year he will be able to consume only C_{2B}. Borrowing has increased his utility from U_1 to U_2.

The analysis shows how consumer preferences and the interest rates determine why some people are borrowers and others are savers. Can you draw an indifference map for a consumer who would like to save money in the first period?

Consumer Choice When Borrowing and Lending Rates Differ   **E**XAMPLE 4.3

Thus far in our discussion of borrowing and lending, we have assumed that the interest rate the consumer receives if he saves money (lends it to the bank) is the same as the rate that the consumer must pay if he borrows money. However, you might have observed that the interest rate you pay when you borrow is higher than the rate you earn when you save. For example, the interest rate you receive when you save may be 5 percent, but you may have to pay an interest rate of 10 percent when you borrow. Financial institutions rely on the difference between borrowing and lending rates to make money. When you deposit money in the bank, the bank loans some of that money to another consumer. During the year the bank will receive an interest payment of 10 cents for each dollar it loans out, and it will pay you 5 cents in interest on each dollar in your savings account.

Let's consider how different interest rates for borrowing and lending affect the shape of a consumer's budget line. Suppose Mark receives an income of $10,000 in year 1, and income of $13,200 in year 2. If he neither borrows nor lends, he can purchase basket A in Figure 4.16.

Let's find the corner point of the budget line along the vertical axis, at basket E in the figure. This basket is the one Mark can choose if he consumes nothing in the first year and saves his income to spend in the second year. He can save his income (lend it to the bank) at an interest rate of 5 percent ($r_L = 0.05$). If he saves all his $10,000 income in year 1, he will have $23,700 available next year (the $10,000 income in year 1, plus the interest payment of $500, plus the income of

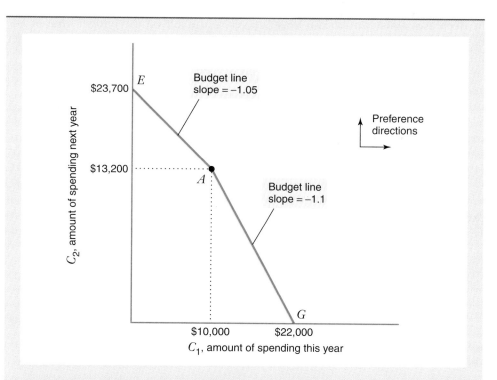

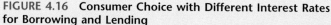

FIGURE 4.16   Consumer Choice with Different Interest Rates for Borrowing and Lending
A consumer receives an income of $10,000 this year and $13,200 next year. If he neither borrows nor lends, he will be at basket A. Suppose he can save (lend money to the bank) at an interest rate of 5 percent. Every dollar he saves this year will give him an additional $1.05 to spend next year. The slope of the budget line between E and A is therefore −1.05. Similarly, if he elects to borrow a dollar from the bank this year, he will have to pay back $1.10 next year. The slope of the budget line between A and G is therefore −1.1.

$13,200 in year 2). Using Figure 4.16, you can verify that the slope of the budget line between baskets A and E is $-(1 + r_L) = -1.05$. This slope reflects the fact that when Mark saves $1 this year, he has available an extra $1.05 to spend next year.

Let's consider the other corner of the budget line, at basket G along the horizontal axis. This is the basket Mark could choose if he buys as much as possible in year 1, and nothing in year 2. In the first year he would borrow as much as he can from the bank and pay it back with his income in year 2. He can borrow up to $12,000 in year 1. If the interest rate for borrowing is 10 percent per period ($r_B = 0.1$) and he borrows $12,000 in year 1, he will pay back a total of $13,200 in year 2, including the $12,000 he borrows plus the interest of $1,200 ($0.1 \times \$12,000$). Therefore, the maximum amount of money he could spend in the first year is $22,000 (his first year income of $10,000, plus the $12,000 he could borrow). If he starts at A, every time he increases consumption this year (moves to the right on the budget line) by 1 dollar, he will need to decrease consumption next year (move down on the budget line) by $(1 + r_B)$ dollars. Using Figure 4.16, you can verify that the slope of the budget line between baskets A and G is -1.1.

The borrowing and saving interest rates determine the slopes of the two parts of the budget line. To determine whether the consumer is a borrower or a lender, we would need to draw the consumer's indifference map. Can you draw an indifference map for a consumer who will save money in year 1? The highest indifference curve he can attain must be on the budget line between baskets *A* and *E*.

Can you draw an indifference map for a consumer who will borrow in year 1? The highest indifference curve he can reach must intersect the budget line between baskets *A* and *G*.

APPLICATION: QUANTITY DISCOUNTS

In many product markets sellers offer consumers quantity discounts. We can use the theory of consumer choice to understand how such discounts affect consumer behavior.

Firms offer many kinds of quantity discounts. Here we consider an example that is commonly observed in the electric power industry. In Figure 4.17 the horizontal axis measures the number of units of electricity a consumer buys each

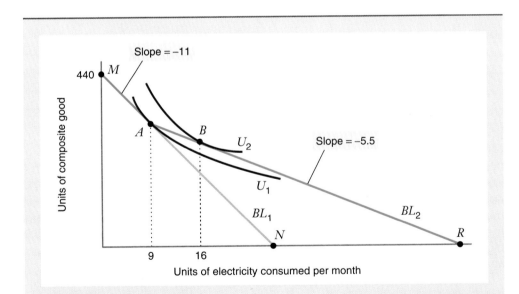

FIGURE 4.17   Quantity Discount
If the electric power company sells electricity at a price of $11 per unit, the budget line facing the consumer is *MN* and the slope of the budget line is −11. The consumer would choose basket *A*, with 9 units of electricity. Suppose the supplier offers a quantity discount, charging $11 for each of the first 9 units the consumer buys, and $5.50 for any *additional* units. The budget line is now composed of two segments, *MA* and *AR*. The slope of *AR* is −5.5. The consumer will buy a total of 16 units of electricity (at basket *B*) when she is offered the quantity discount. In other words, the quantity discount has induced her to buy 7 extra units of electricity. The figure illustrates that a quantity discount may enable the consumer to achieve a higher level of satisfaction than would be possible without the quantity discount.

month. The vertical axis measures the number of units of a composite good, whose price is $1. The consumer has a monthly income of $440.

Suppose the power company sells electricity at a price of $11 per unit, with no quantity discount. The budget line facing the consumer would be *MN*, and the slope of the budget line would be -11. With the indifference map shown in Figure 4.17, she would choose basket *A*, with 9 units of electricity.

Now suppose the supplier offers the following quantity discount: The seller continues to charge a price $P_1 = \$11$ for the first 9 units the consumer buys, and then offers *additional* units for sale at a price $P_2 = \$5.50$. The budget line is now composed of two segments. The first segment is *MA*. The second segment is *AR*, having a slope of -5.5 because the consumer pays a price of $5.50 for any additional units of electricity purchased beyond 9 units. Given the indifference map in the figure, the consumer will buy a total of 16 units (at basket *B*) when she is offered the quantity discount. The discount has induced her to buy 7 extra units of electricity.

Quantity discounts expand the set of baskets a consumer can purchase. In Figure 4.17, the additional baskets available to the consumer under the discount are the ones in the area bounded by *RAN*. Because the discount increases the set of baskets available to the consumer, she may choose a basket different from the one she would choose with no discount. As the figure illustrates, a discount may also enable the consumer to achieve a higher level of satisfaction than would otherwise be possible.

EXAMPLE 4.4   *Frequent Flyer Programs*

In 1981 American Airlines launched the industry's first frequent flyer program, AAdvantage Travel Awards. Later the same year, United Airlines created its own frequent flyer program, United Airlines Mileage Plus. Many other airlines around the world now offer such programs. These programs provide a number of rewards to travelers who repeatedly give their business to a particular airline. Members may accumulate credit for miles they have flown and redeem these miles for upgrades and free tickets. They also receive other benefits, including priority for upgrades to a higher class of service, preferred seating, and special treatment at ticket counters and in airport lounges.

Frequent flyer programs typically have different levels of membership, depending on the number of miles a consumer flies with the airline during the year. For example, under the AAdvantage Program, a consumer traveling less than 25,000 miles per year receives credit in a mileage account for each mile flown. A member traveling between 25,000 and 50,000 miles in a year attains AAdvantage Gold status for the next year. A holder of a Gold card receives credit for miles flown plus a 25 percent mileage bonus.

A consumer flying between 50,000 and 100,000 miles in a year attains AAdvantage Platinum status for the next year. Among other benefits, a Platinum member receives credit for miles flown plus a 100 percent mileage bonus. There is also a higher level of membership (Executive Platinum) with additional benefits for members who travel more than 100,000 miles per year.

The provisions of frequent flyer programs are often quite complicated, with a number of special rules and rewards not discussed here. The important idea is this: The more you travel, the less expensive additional travel becomes, so that you receive a quantity discount. That is why frequent flyer programs are so popular today. As of 2001, American's AAdvantage Program had enrolled more than 43 million members worldwide. ∎

4.4
REVEALED
PREFERENCE

You have now learned how to find a consumer's optimal basket *given* preferences (an indifference map) and *given* a budget line. In other words, if you know how the consumer ranks baskets, you can determine the optimal basket for any budget constraint the consumer faces.

But suppose you do *not* know the consumer's indifference map. Can you infer how he ranks baskets by observing his behavior as his budget line changes? In other words, do the consumer's choices of baskets reveal information about his preferences?

The main idea behind **revealed preference** is simple: If the consumer chooses basket A when basket B costs just as much, then we know that A is at least as preferred as B. (We write this as $A \succeq B$, meaning that either $A \succ B$ or $A \approx B$. When $A \succeq B$, we say that A is weakly preferred to B.) When he chooses basket C, which is more expensive than basket D, then we know that he must strongly prefer C to D ($C \succ D$). Given enough observations about his choices as prices and incomes vary, we can learn much about how he ranks baskets, even though we may not be able to determine the exact shape of his indifference map. Revealed preference analysis assumes that the consumer always chooses an optimal basket, and that, although prices and income may vary, his underlying preferences do *not* change.

Figure 4.18 illustrates how consumer behavior can reveal information about preferences. Given an initial level of income and prices for two goods, the consumer faces BL_1. When he faces BL_1, he chooses basket A. Suppose prices and income change so that the budget line becomes BL_2. When he faces BL_2, he chooses basket B. What does the consumer's behavior reveal about his preferences?

First, the consumer chooses basket A when he could afford any other basket on or inside BL_1. His behavior therefore reveals that A is at least as preferred as B ($A \succeq B$). But he has revealed even more about how he ranks A and B. Consider basket C, on BL_1 to the "northeast" of B. Since the consumer chooses A when he can afford C, we know that $A \succeq C$. Moreover, since C lies to the northeast of B, C must be strongly preferred to B ($C \succ B$). Then, by transitivity, A must be strongly preferred to B ($A \succ B$).

The consumer's behavior also helps us to learn about the shape of the indifference curve through A. All baskets to the north, east, or northeast of A are strongly preferred to A (including baskets in the darkly shaded area). A is strongly preferred to all baskets in the lightly shaded region, and at least as preferred as any other basket between F and E. We also know that A is strongly preferred to any basket on the segment EH because A is strongly preferred to B, and B is weakly preferred as any basket on BL_2. Therefore, although we do not know

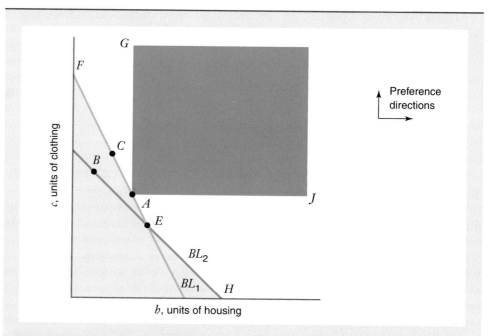

FIGURE 4.18   Revealed Preference
Suppose we do *not* know the indifference map. But we *do* have observations about consumer choice with two different budget lines.

1. When the budget line is BL_1, the consumer chooses basket *A*.

2. When the budget line is BL_2, the consumer chooses basket *B*. What does the consumer's behavior reveal about his preferences? First, the consumer chooses *A* when he could afford any other basket on or inside BL_1. Therefore, *A* is at least as preferred as *B* ($A \succeq B$). But we can make an even stronger statement about how the consumer ranks *A* and *B*. Consider bundle *C*, on BL_1 to the "northeast" of *B*. The consumer chooses *A* when he can afford *C*; therefore $A \succeq C$. Moreover, since *C* lies to the "northeast" of *B*, *C* must be strongly preferred to *B* ($C \succ B$). Then by transitivity *A* must be *strongly* preferred to *B* ($A \succ B$). All baskets to the north, east, or northeast of *A* are *strongly* preferred to *A* (including baskets in the dark shaded area). *A* is strongly preferred to all baskets in the light shaded region, strongly preferred to any basket on the segment *EH*, and at least as preferred as any other basket between *F* and *E*. Therefore, although we do not know exactly where the indifference curve through *A* lies, it must pass somewhere through the white area between *GAJ* and *FEH*, perhaps including baskets on *EF*.

exactly where the indifference curve through *A* lies, it must pass somewhere through the white area between *GAJ* and *FEH*, perhaps including baskets on *EF* other than *E*.

ARE OBSERVED CHOICES CONSISTENT WITH UTILITY MAXIMIZATION?

In our discussion of revealed preference, we have assumed that the consumer always chooses the best basket he can, given his budget constraint. Yet the consumer could be choosing his basket in some other way. Can revealed preference analysis tell us if a consumer is choosing baskets in a manner consistent with utility maximization? Or, to pose the question differently, what observations about consumer choice would lead us to conclude that the consumer is *not* always maximizing utility?

Using observed choices, we can infer whether a consumer's behavior is inconsistent with utility maximization. Consider a case in which a utility maximizing consumer buys only two goods. In any basket (x, y), x denotes the number of units of the first good and y the number of units of the second good. Suppose that when the prices of the goods are initially (P_x, P_y), the consumer chooses basket 1, containing (x_1, y_1). At a second set of prices $(\tilde{P}_x, \tilde{P}_y)$, he purchases basket 2, containing (x_2, y_2).

At the initial prices, basket 1 will cost the consumer $P_x x_1 + P_y y_1$. Let's suppose that basket 2 is also affordable at the initial prices, so that

$$P_x x_1 + P_y y_1 \geq P_x x_2 + P_y y_2 \tag{4.7}$$

The left-hand side of equation (4.7) tells us how much the consumer would need to spend to buy basket 1 at the initial prices. The right-hand side measures the expenditure necessary to buy basket 2 at the initial prices.

Since at the initial prices he chose basket 1 (and basket 2 was also affordable), he has revealed that he likes basket 1 at least as much as basket 2.

We also know that at the second set of prices, he chose basket 2 instead of basket 1. Since he has already revealed that he prefers basket 1 at least as much as basket 2, it must *also* be true that at the new prices basket 2 is no more expensive than basket 1. Otherwise, he would have chosen basket 1 at the new prices. Equation (4.8) states that basket 2 costs no more than basket 1 at the new prices.

$$\tilde{P}_x x_2 + \tilde{P}_y y_2 \leq \tilde{P}_x x_1 + \tilde{P}_y y_1. \tag{4.8}$$

Why *must* equation (4.8) be satisfied if the consumer's choices are consistent with utility maximization? If it is *not* satisfied, then

$$\tilde{P}_x x_2 + \tilde{P}_y y_2 > \tilde{P}_x x_1 + \tilde{P}_y y_1. \tag{4.9}$$

If equation (4.9) were true, it would tell us that basket 2 is more expensive than basket 1 at the second set of prices. Since the consumer chooses basket 2 at the second set of prices (when basket 1 is also affordable), he would then have to strongly prefer basket 2 to basket 1. But this would be inconsistent with the earlier conclusion that he likes basket 1 at least as much as basket 2. To eliminate this inconsistency, equation (4.8) *must* be satisfied (and, equivalently, equation (4.9) must not be satisfied).

The following exercise illustrates the use of revealed preference analysis to detect behavior that fails to maximize utility.

LEARNING-BY-DOING EXERCISE 4.5

Consumer Choice that Fails to Maximize Utility

Problem A consumer has an income of $24 per week and buys two goods in quantities measured by x and y. Initially he faces prices $(P_x, P_y) = (\$4, \$2)$ and chooses basket 1 containing $(x_1, y_1) = (5, 2)$. Later the prices change so that

$(\tilde{P}_x, \tilde{P}_y) = (\$3, \$3)$. He then chooses basket 2, containing $(x_2, y_2) = (2, 6)$. His income remains at $24 per week. These choices and budget lines are illustrated in Figure 4.19. Given his choices, show that he cannot be choosing baskets that maximize his utility in both periods.

Solution   There are two ways to demonstrate that the consumer is failing to maximize utility. First, let's use a graphical approach. Observe that with BL_1, he chose basket 1 when he could afford basket 3. Thus basket 1 is at least as preferred as basket 3. Further, since basket 3 lies to the northeast of basket 2, he must strongly prefer basket 3 to basket 2. Using transitivity, we can conclude that basket 1 is strongly preferred to basket 2.

Let's apply similar reasoning to the consumer's choice of basket 2 when given BL_2. Here the consumer chose basket 2 when he could afford basket 4. Thus basket 2 is at least as preferred as basket 4. Further, since basket 4 lies to the northeast of basket 1, he must strongly prefer basket 4 to basket 1. By transitivity we conclude that basket 2 is strongly preferred to basket 1.

It cannot simultaneously be true that basket 1 is strongly preferred to basket 2 and that basket 2 is strongly preferred to basket 1. Therefore, the consumer must not be choosing the best basket with each budget line.

We can also reach this conclusion by applying the test suggested by equations (4.7) and (4.8). At the initial prices he chose basket 1 when basket 2 was affordable. We can see this using equation (4.7). At the *initial* prices $(P_x, P_y) = (\$4, \$2)$:

Basket 1 costs \$24 $(P_x x_1 + P_y y_1 = \$4(5) + \$2(2) = \$24)$.
Basket 2 costs \$20 $(P_x x_2 + P_y y_2 = \$4(2) + \$2(6) = \$20)$.

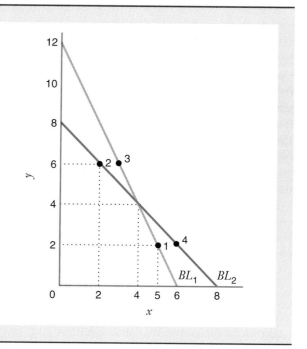

FIGURE 4.19 Consumer Choice that Fails to Maximize Utility
When the budget line is BL_1, the consumer selects basket 1. When the budget line is BL_2, the consumer selects basket 2.

The consumer's choices of baskets 1 and 2 are *inconsistent* with utility maximizing behavior. With BL_1, the consumer chose basket 1 when he could afford basket 3. Thus basket 1 is at least as preferred as basket 3. Further, since basket 3 lies to the "northeast" of basket 2, he must strongly prefer basket 3 to basket 2. By transitivity we conclude that basket 1 is strongly preferred to basket 2.

With BL_2, the consumer chooses basket 2 when he could afford basket 4. Thus basket 2 is at least as preferred as basket 4. Further, since basket 4 lies to the "northeast" of basket 1, he must strongly prefer basket 4 to basket 1. By transitivity we conclude that basket 2 is strongly preferred to basket 1.

Since it cannot simultaneously be true that basket 1 is strongly preferred to basket 2 and that basket 2 is strongly preferred to basket 1, the consumer must not always be choosing the optimal basket.

At the *initial* prices he chose basket 1 rather than basket 2, and basket 1 was more costly than basket 2. From this behavior we would infer that he strongly prefers basket 1 to basket 2. (Observe that equation (4.7) is satisfied.)

However, at the *new* prices, he chose basket 2 rather than basket 1. If this behavior is consistent with utility maximization, then basket 2 must cost no more than basket 1 at the new prices. Otherwise he would have chosen basket 1. Is equation (4.8) satisfied? At the *new* prices $(\tilde{P}_x, \tilde{P}_y) = (\$3,\$3)$:

Basket 1 costs $21 $(\tilde{P}_x x_1 + \tilde{P}_y y_1 = \$3(5) + \$3(2) = \$21)$.
Basket 2 costs $24 $(\tilde{P}_x x_2 + \tilde{P}_y y_2 = \$3(2) + \$3(6) = \$24)$.

So, at the new prices, the consumer bought basket 2, which cost more than basket 1. (Equation (4.8) is not satisfied.) This choice tells us he must prefer basket 2 to basket 1. This ranking is inconsistent with the ranking we inferred based on his choice at the initial prices.

This exercise demonstrates one of the potentially powerful applications of revealed preference analysis. Even though we do not know the consumer's indifference map, we have used evidence from the consumer's choices to infer that he is not always maximizing utility.

Similar Problem: 4.10

We conclude this section with an exercise that will help you see some of the types of inferences that can be drawn from revealed preference analysis.

LEARNING-BY-DOING EXERCISE 4.6

Revealed Preference

Problem Each of the graphs in Figure 4.20 depicts choices by an individual consuming two commodities, x and y. The consumer likes x and y (more of x is better and more of y is better). In each case when the budget line is BL_1, the consumer selects basket A. When the budget line is BL_2, the consumer selects basket B. What can be said about the way the consumer ranks the two baskets in each case?

Solution *Case 1:* With BL_2 the consumer chose basket B when he could have afforded A. Thus we know that the $B \succcurlyeq A$. In fact, we can make an even stronger statement about the way the consumer ranks the baskets since A is *inside* BL_2. Consider a basket C, on BL_2 to the northeast of A. Since the consumer chose B when he could afford C, we know that $B \succcurlyeq C$. Moreover, since C lies to the northeast of A, C must be strongly preferred to A ($C \succ A$). Then by transitivity, B must be strongly preferred to A ($B \succ A$). This case shows that when the consumer chooses a basket on a budget line, it will be strongly preferred to any basket inside that budget line.

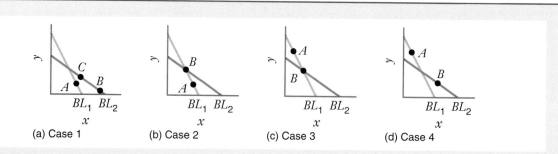

FIGURE 4.20   Revealed Preference

In each case, when the budget line is BL_1, the consumer selects basket A. When the budget line is BL_2, the consumer selects basket B. What can be said about the way the consumer ranks the two baskets in each case? In *Case 1* we conclude that B is strongly preferred to A, since B is weakly preferred to C and C is strongly preferred to A. In *Case 2* the consumer's choices are inconsistent with utility maximizing behavior. The graph simultaneously implies that B is strongly preferred to A and that A is weakly preferred to B. These rankings cannot both be true at the same time. In *Case 3* we infer that A is weakly preferred to B. In *Case 4* we cannot infer any ranking. Given BL_1 the consumer cannot afford B and given BL_2 he cannot afford A. Thus, we cannot tell how he ranks the baskets since he cannot afford both with either budget line.

Case 2: This case may surprise you. First, what do we learn about the consumer's preferences from his choice given BL_2? The consumer chose basket B, while he could have afforded basket A (A is *inside* BL_2). By the reasoning in Case 1, we know that $B \succ A$.

What do we learn from his choice given BL_1? Baskets A and B are both on BL_1, and given BL_1, the consumer chose A when he could have afforded B. Thus $A \succcurlyeq B$.

This consumer's behavior is inconsistent with utility maximization! His choice given BL_2 suggests that $B \succ A$, while his choice given BL_1 suggests that $A \succcurlyeq B$. These rankings are not consistent with one another. The consumer is apparently not always purchasing the best basket he can afford, given each budget line.

Case 3: Given BL_1, the consumer chose A when he could have afforded B; therefore $A \succcurlyeq B$. We do not learn anything new from his observed behavior given BL_2. He bought basket B but could not afford A. Thus, his behavior given BL_2 does not enable us to infer anything more about the ranking of A and B.

Case 4: Given BL_1, the consumer chose A but could not afford B; therefore, we learn nothing about the ranking from this choice. Similarly, given BL_2, the consumer chose B but could not afford A; therefore, we learn nothing about the ranking from this choice. To learn anything about a consumer's ranking of two baskets, we must have at least one observation in which he chooses one basket when he can afford both.

Similar Problems: 4.9 and 4.10

The theory of revealed preference contains a surprisingly powerful idea. It allows us to use information about consumer choices to infer how the consumer must rank bundles if he is maximizing utility with a budget constraint. It also allows us to discover when a consumer is failing to choose his optimal basket given a budget constraint. We can draw these inferences without knowing the consumer's utility function or indifference map.

In the analysis of revealed preference, we are assuming that a consumer *has* preferences, that the preferences do not change, and that the consumer chooses baskets optimally as income and prices vary. As we gather more observations about optimal choices, we may be able to be more precise about our description of the region within which a particular indifference curve must lie.

CHAPTER SUMMARY

• A budget line represents the set of all baskets that a consumer can buy if she spends all of her income. A budget line shifts out in a parallel fashion if the consumer receives more income. A budget line will rotate about its intercept on the vertical axis if the price of the good on the horizontal axis changes (holding constant the consumer's income and the price of the good on the vertical axis). **(LBD Exercise 4.1)**

• If the consumer maximizes utility while living within her budget constraint (that is, choosing a basket on or inside the budget line), and if there are positive marginal utilities for all goods, the optimal basket will be on the budget line. **(LBD Exercise 4.2)**

• When a utility-maximizing consumer buys positive amounts of two goods, she will choose the amounts of those goods so that the ratio of the marginal utilities of the two goods (which is the marginal rate of substitution) is equal to the ratio of the prices of the goods. **(LBD Exercise 4.2)**

• When a utility-maximizing consumer buys positive amounts of two goods, she will choose the amounts of those goods so that the marginal utility per dollar spent will be equal for the two goods. **(LBD Exercises 4.3 and 4.4)**

• It may not be possible for a utility-maximizing consumer to buy two goods so that the marginal utility per dollar spent is equal for the two goods. An optimal basket would then be at a corner point. **(LBD Exercises 4.3 and 4.4)**

• The analysis of revealed preference may help us to infer how an individual ranks baskets without knowing the individual's indifference map. We learn about preferences by observing which baskets the consumer chooses as prices and income vary. When the consumer chooses basket *A* over an equally costly basket *B*, then we know that *A* is at least as preferred as *B*. When she chooses basket *C*, which costs her more than basket *D*, then we know that *C* is strictly preferred to *D*. Revealed preference analysis may also help us identify cases in which observed consumer behavior is inconsistent with the assumptions of optimal consumer choice. **(LBD Exercises 4.5 and 4.6)**

REVIEW QUESTIONS

1. If the consumer has a positive marginal utility for each of two goods, why will the consumer always choose a basket on the budget line?

2. How will a change in income affect the location of the budget line?

3. How will an increase in the price of one of the goods purchased by a consumer affect the location of the budget line?

4. What is the difference between an interior optimum and a corner point optimum in the theory of consumer choice?

5. At an optimal interior basket, why must the slope of the budget line be equal to the slope of the indifference curve?

6. At an optimal interior basket, why must the marginal utility per dollar spent on all goods be the same?

7. Why will the marginal utility per dollar spent not necessarily be equal for all goods at a corner point?

8. Suppose that a consumer with an income of $1000 finds that basket A maximizes utility subject to his budget constraint, and realizes a level of utility U_1. Why will this basket also minimize the consumer's expenditures necessary to realize a level of utility U_1?

9. What is a composite good?

10. How can revealed preference analysis help us learn about a consumer's preferences without knowing the consumer's utility function?

PROBLEMS

4.1. In problem 3 of Chapter 3, we considered Julie's preferences for food F and clothing C. Her utility function was $U(F, C) = FC$. Her marginal utilities were $MU_F = C$ and $MU_C = F$. You were asked to draw the indifference curves $U = 12$, $U = 18$, and $U = 24$, and to show that she had a diminishing marginal rate of substitution of food for clothing. Suppose that food costs $1 a unit and that clothing costs $2 a unit. Julie has $12 to spend on food and clothing.
a) Using a graph (and no algebra), find the optimal (utility-maximizing) choice of food and clothing. Let the amount of food be on the horizontal axis and the amount of clothing be on the vertical axis.
b) Using algebra (the tangency condition and the budget line), find the optimal choice of food and clothing.
c) What is the marginal rate of substitution of food for clothing at her optimal basket? Show this graphically and algebraically.
d) Suppose Julie decides to buy 4 units of food and 4 units of clothing with her $12 budget (instead of the optimal basket). Would her marginal utility per dollar spent on food be greater than or less than her marginal utility per dollar spent on clothing? What does this tell you about how she should substitute food for clothing if she wants to increase her utility without spending any more money?

4.2. The utility that Ann receives by consuming food F and clothing C is given by $U(F,C) = FC + F$. The marginal utilities of food and clothing are $MU_F = C + 1$ and $MU_C = F$. Food costs $1 a unit, and clothing costs $2 a unit. Ann's income is $22.

a) Ann is currently spending all of her income. She is buying 8 units of food. How many units of clothing is she consuming?
b) Graph her budget line. Place the number of units of clothing on the vertical axis and the number of units of food on the horizontal axis. Plot her current consumption basket.
c) Draw the indifference curve associated with a utility level of 36, and another indifference curve associated with a utility level of 72. Are the indifference curves bowed in toward the origin?
d) Using a graph (and no algebra), find the utility-maximizing choice of food and clothing.
e) Using algebra, find the utility-maximizing choice of food and clothing.
f) What is the marginal rate of substitution of food for clothing when utility is maximized? Show this graphically and algebraically.
g) Does Ann have a diminishing marginal rate of substitution of food for clothing? Show this graphically and algebraically.

4.3. Jane likes hamburgers (H) and milkshakes (M). Her indifference curves are bowed in toward the origin and do not intersect the axes. The price of a milkshake is $1 and the price of a hamburger is $3. She is spending all her income at the basket she is currently consuming, and her marginal rate of substitution of hamburgers for milkshakes is 2. Is she at an optimum? If so, show why. If not, should she buy fewer hamburgers and more milkshakes, or the reverse?

4.4. This problem will help you understand what happens if the marginal rate of substitution is not diminishing. Dr. Strangetaste buys only french fries (F) and hot dogs (H) out of his income. He has positive marginal utilities for both goods, and his $MRS_{H,F}$ is *increasing*. The price of hot dogs is P_H, and the price of french fries is P_F.

a) Draw several of Dr. Strangetaste's indifference curves, including one that is tangent to his budget line.

b) Show that the point of tangency does *not* represent a basket at which utility is maximized, given the budget constraint. Indicate on your graph where the optimal basket is located.

4.5. Toni likes to purchase round trips between the cities of Pulmonia and Castoria and other goods out of her income of $10,000. Fortunately, Pulmonian Airways provides air service and has a frequent-flyer program. A round trip between the two cities normally costs $500, but any customer who makes more than ten trips a year gets to make additional trips during the year for only $200 per round trip.

a) On a graph with round trips on the horizontal axis and "other goods" on the vertical axis, draw Toni's budget line. (*Hint:* This problem demonstrates that a budget line need not always be a straight line.)

b) On the graph you drew in part (a), draw a set of indifference curves that illustrates why Toni may be better off with the frequent flyer program.

c) On a new graph draw the same budget line you found in part (a). Now draw a set of indifference curves that illustrates why Toni might *not* be better off with the frequent flyer program.

4.6. A consumer has preferences between two goods, hamburgers (measured by H) and milkshakes (measured by M). His preferences over the two goods are represented by the utility function $U = \sqrt{H} + \sqrt{M}$. For this utility function $MU_H = 1/(2\sqrt{H})$ and $MU_C = 1/(2\sqrt{M})$.

a) Determine if there is a diminishing $MRS_{H,M}$ for this utility function.

b) Draw a graph to illustrate the shape of a typical indifference curve. Label the curve U_1. Does the indifference curve intersect either axis? On the same graph, draw a second indifference curve U_2, with $U_2 > U_1$.

c) A consumer has an income of $24 per week. The price of a hamburger is $2 and the price of a milkshake is $1. How many milkshakes and hamburgers will he buy each week if he maximizes utility? Illustrate your answer on a graph.

4.7. A student consumes root beer and a composite good whose price is $1. Currently the government imposes an excise tax of $0.50 per six pack of root beer. The student now purchases 20 six packs of root beer per

month. (Think of the excise tax as increasing the price of root beer by $0.50 per six pack over what the price would be without the tax.) The government is considering eliminating the excise tax on root beer and, instead, requiring consumers to pay $10.00 per month as a lump sum tax (i.e., the student pays a tax of $10.00 per month, regardless of how much root beer is consumed). If the new proposal is adopted, how will the student's consumption pattern (in particular, the amount of root beer consumed) and welfare be affected? (Assume that the student's marginal rate of substitution of root beer for other goods is diminishing.)

4.8. When the price of gasoline is $2.00 per gallon, Joe consumes 1000 gallons per year. The price increases to $2.50, and to offset the harm to Joe, the government gives him a cash transfer of $500 per year. Will Joe be better off or worse off after the price increase and cash transfer than he was before? What will happen to his gasoline consumption? (Assume that Joe's marginal rate of substitution of gasoline for other goods is diminishing.)

4.9. Sally consumes housing (denote the number of units of housing by h) and other goods (a composite good whose units are measured by y), both of which she likes. Initially she has an income of $100, and the price of a unit of housing (P_h) is $10. At her "initial" choice basket she consumes 2 units of housing. A few months later her income rises to $120; unfortunately, the price of housing in her city also rises to $15. The price of the composite good does not change. At her "final" choice basket she consumes 1 unit of housing. Using revealed preference analysis (without drawing indifference curves), what can you say about how she ranks her initial and final baskets?

4.10. A consumer buys two goods, food and housing, and likes both goods. When she has budget line BL_1, her optimal choice is A. Given budget line BL_2, she chooses B, and with BL_3, she chooses C (see Figure 4.21).

a) What can you infer about how the consumer ranks baskets A, B, and C? If you can infer a ranking, explain how. If you cannot infer a ranking, explain why not.

b) On the graph, shade in (and clearly label) the areas that are revealed to be less preferred to basket B, and explain why you indicated these areas.

c) On the graph, shade in (and clearly label) the areas that are revealed to be (more) preferred to basket B, and explain why you indicated these areas.

4.11. Figure 4.17 illustrates the case in which a consumer is better off with a quantity discount. Can you draw an indifference map for a consumer who would *not* be better off with the quantity discount?

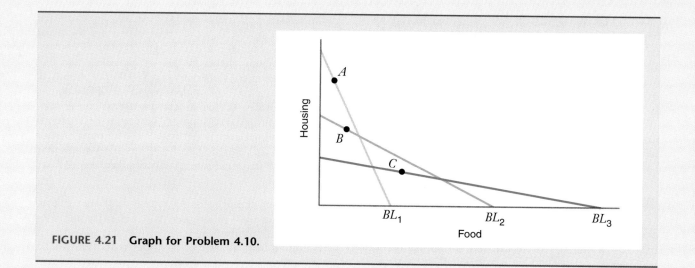

FIGURE 4.21   Graph for Problem 4.10.

APPENDIX: The Mathematics of Consumer Choice

In this section we solve the consumer choice problem using the calculus technique of Lagrange multipliers. Suppose the consumer buys two goods, where x measures the amount of the first good and y the amount of the second good he buys. The price of the first good is P_x and the price of the second is P_y. The consumer has an income I.

Let's assume that the marginal utilities of both goods are positive, so we know that he will expend all of his income at his optimal basket. The consumer choice problem is then

$$\max_{(x,y)} U(x, y) \tag{A4.1}$$
$$\text{subject to } P_x x + P_y y = I$$

We define the Lagrangian (Λ) as

$$\Lambda(x, y, \lambda) = U(x, y) + \lambda(I - P_x x - P_y y)$$

where λ is a Lagrange multiplier. The first order necessary conditions for an interior optimum (with $x > 0$ and $y > 0$) are

$$\frac{\partial \Lambda}{\partial x} = 0 \Rightarrow \frac{\partial U(x, y)}{\partial x} = \lambda P_x \tag{A4.2}$$

$$\frac{\partial \Lambda}{\partial y} = 0 \Rightarrow \frac{\partial U(x, y)}{\partial y} = \lambda P_y \tag{A4.3}$$

$$\frac{\partial \Lambda}{\partial \lambda} = 0 \Rightarrow I - P_x x - P_y y = 0 \tag{A4.4}$$

The partial derivative $\partial U(x,y)/\partial x$ is the mathematical expression for the marginal utility of x (MU_x). It measures how much utility increases as x increases, holding y constant. Similarly, the partial derivative $\partial U(x,y)/\partial y$ is the mathematical expression for the marginal utility of y (MU_y). It measures how much utility increases as y increases, holding x constant.

We can combine equations (A4.2) and (A4.3) to eliminate the Lagrange multiplier, so our first order conditions reduce to

$$\frac{MU_x}{MU_y} = \frac{P_x}{P_y} \tag{A4.5}$$

$$P_x x + P_y y = I \tag{A4.6}$$

Equation (A4.5) is just the condition requiring that the marginal utility per dollar spent be equal at an optimum ($MU_x/P_x = MU_y/P_y$), or equivalently, that the indifference curve and the budget line be tangent to one another ($MU_x/MU_y = P_x/P_y$). Equation (A4.6) is the equation for the budget line. So the mathematical solution to the consumer choice problem tells us that an optimal interior basket will satisfy the tangency condition and be on the budget line. This verifies the conditions for an optimum we developed in the text, using a graphical approach.

For a further discussion of the use of Lagrange Multipliers, see the Mathematical Appendix in this text.

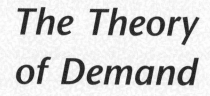

The Theory of Demand

During the 1990s and early 2000s the tobacco industry became increasingly embroiled in litigation over the damages caused by cigarette smoking. Many states sued tobacco companies to recover health care costs related to smoking. Several tobacco companies agreed to pay billions of dollars to Minnesota, Florida, Mississippi, Texas, New York, and other states. The tobacco companies then faced a difficult question. How would they pay for these legal settlements? Their response was to raise cigarette prices repeatedly.

Why did cigarette producers believe that they could collect more revenues if they raised cigarette prices? And what information would they need to estimate the size of the increase in their revenues from an increase of, say, five cents per pack? As we saw in Chapter 2, firms can predict the effects of a price increase if they know the shape of the market demand curve. An article in the *The Wall Street Journal* summarizes some of the extensive research on the market demand curve for cigarettes. "The average price for a pack of cigarettes is about $2. Prices vary by state because of taxes. Analysts say that for every 10 percent price increase, sales volumes drop between 3.5 percent and 4.5 percent. They say that small price increases generally don't cause most consumers to try to give up smoking, but that they smoke fewer cigarettes each day."[1]

Based on this information, we would conclude that the price elasticity of demand for cigarettes is approximately −0.35 to −0.45. Thus the demand for cigarettes is relatively price inelastic. As we learned in Chapter 2, when the demand is relatively inelastic, a small price increase will lead to an increase in sales revenues. In the cigarette market, if the price rises by 10 percent, the sales volumes will fall by about 4 percent. This means that with a 10 percent price increase, the revenues from cigarette sales would increase by about 6 percent. This explains why cigarette producers believed sales revenues would rise if they increased cigarette prices.

We begin this chapter by using graphical and algebraic approaches to study how a consumer's demand for a good (such as cigarettes) depends on the prices of all goods and income. We will learn how to use preferences and budget lines to find a consumer's demand curve.

We will then further examine how a change in the price of a good affects the consumer through an *income effect* and a *substitution effect*. The income and substitution effects will help us understand three measures used to assess how much better off or worse off a consumer is when a price changes: consumer surplus, compensating variation, and equivalent variation.

After we understand how to find an individual's demand curve, we ask: Where do *market* demand curves come from? For many goods the market demand curve is obtained by adding up the demand curves of all of the consumers in the market. However, in some cases a consumer's demand for a good depends on the number of other people purchasing that good. In that case, we say that there are *network externalities* that must be taken into account in determining the market demand.

We end this chapter with an application describing how a consumer allocates his time between work and leisure. You might normally expect that a consumer will be willing to work more hours if he is offered a higher wage rate. However, this may not always be true. We will use income and substitution effects to illustrate why a consumer may actually work *less* when the wage rate rises. ■

[1]Tara Parker-Pope, "Major Tobacco Companies Increase Cigarette Prices by Five Cents a Pack," *The Wall Street Journal* (May 12, 1998), page B15.

5.1

OPTIMAL CHOICE AND DEMAND

Where do demand curves come from? In Chapter 4, we showed how to determine a consumer's optimal basket. Given the consumer's preferences, income, and the prices of all goods, we could ask how much ice cream a consumer will buy each month if the price of a gallon of ice cream is $5. This will be a point on the consumer's demand curve for ice cream. We can find more points on his demand curve by repeating the exercise for different prices of ice cream, asking what his monthly consumption of ice cream will be if the price is $4, $3, or $2 per gallon. Let's see how to do this, using a simplified setting in which our consumer buys only two goods, food and clothing.

THE EFFECTS OF A CHANGE IN PRICE

What happens to the consumer's choice of food when the price of food changes while the price of clothing and the amount of income remain constant? We have two ways to answer this question, one using the optimal choice diagram in Figure 5.1(a), and the second using the demand curve in Figure 5.1(b). Let's first look at the optimal choice diagram. The graph in Figure 5.1(a) measures the quantity of food consumed (x) on the horizontal axis and the quantity of clothing (y) on the vertical axis. Suppose the consumer's weekly income is $40 and the price of clothing is $P_y = \$4$ per unit.

Consider the consumer's choices of food and clothing for three different prices of food. First, suppose the price of food is $P_x = \$4$. The budget line that the consumer faces when $P_x = \$4$, $P_y = \$4$, and $I = \$40$ is labeled BL_1 in the figure. The slope of her budget line is $-P_x/P_y = -4/4 = -1$. Her optimal basket is A, indicating that her weekly consumption of food is 2 units and her optimal consumption of clothing is 8 units.

What happens when the price of food falls to $P_x = \$2$? As we learned in Chapter 4, when the price of food falls, the budget line rotates out to BL_2. The vertical intercept is the same because income and the price of clothing are unchanged. However, the horizontal intercept of the budget line moves to the right as the price of food falls. The slope of the budget line BL_2 is $-P_x/P_y = -2/4 = -1/2$. Her optimal basket is B, with a weekly consumption of 10 units of food and 5 units of clothing.

Finally, suppose the price of food falls to $P_x = \$1$. The budget line rotates to BL_3 in the figure. The slope of the budget line BL_3 is $-P_x/P_y = -1/4$. The consumer's optimal basket is C, with a weekly consumption of 16 units of food and 6 units of clothing.

One way to describe how changes in the price of food affect the consumer's purchases of both goods is to draw a curve connecting all of the baskets that are optimal as the price of food changes (holding the price of clothing and income constant). This curve is called the **price consumption curve**.[2] Note that the optimal baskets A, B, and C all lie on the price consumption curve in Figure 5.1(a).

Observe that the consumer is better off as the price of food falls. When the price of food is $4 (and she chooses basket A), she reaches the indifference curve U_1. When the price of food is $2 (and she chooses basket B), her utility rises to U_2. If the price of food falls to $1, her utility rises even farther to U_3.

---

[2]In some textbooks the price consumption curve is called the "price expansion path."

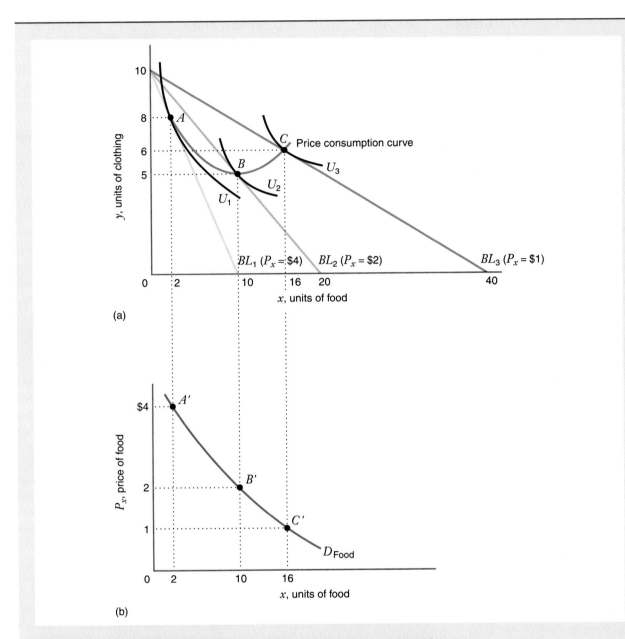

FIGURE 5.1 The Effects of Changes in the Price of a Good on Consumption
The consumer has a weekly income of $40. The price of clothing P_y is $4 per
unit. (a) When the price of food is $4, the budget line is BL_1. The slope of BL_1
is $-(P_x/P_y) = -4/4 = -1$. BL_2 and BL_3 are the budget lines when the price of food is
$2 and $1, respectively. The optimal baskets are A, B, and C. The curve connecting the
optimal baskets is called the price consumption curve.
(b) We can use the optimal choice diagram (a) to draw the demand curve for food. Note
that the consumer buys more food as its price falls, so the demand curve for food is
downward sloping.

Changing Price: Moving along a Demand Curve

We can use the optimal choice diagram of Figure 5.1(a) to trace out the demand schedule for food in Figure 5.1(b). In Figure 5.1(b) the *price* of food appears on the vertical axis, and the *quantity* of food on the horizontal axis.

Let's see how the two graphs are related to each other. When the price of food is $4, the consumer chooses basket *A* in Figure 5.1(a), containing 2 units of food. This tells us that point *A'* lies on her demand curve for food in Figure 5.1(b). Similarly, at basket *B* in Figure 5.1(a), the consumer purchases 10 units of food when the price of food is $2. Therefore, point *B'* must lie on her demand curve in Figure 5.1(b). Finally, if the price of food falls to $1, the consumer buys 16 units of food, as basket *C* in Figure 5.1(a) indicates. Therefore point *C'* must also be on the demand curve. In sum, a decrease in the price of food leads the consumer to move down and to the right *along* her demand curve for food.

The Demand Curve Is also a "Willingness to Pay" Curve

As you study economics, you will sometimes find it useful to think of a demand curve as a curve that represents a consumer's "willingness to pay" for a good. To see why this is true, let's ask how much the consumer would be willing to pay for another unit of food when she is currently at the optimal basket *A* (purchasing 2 units of food) in Figure 5.1(a). Her answer is that she would be willing to pay $4 for another unit of food. Why? At basket *A* her marginal rate of substitution of food for clothing is 1.[3] Thus, at basket *A* one more unit of food is worth the same amount to her as one more unit of clothing. Since the price of clothing is $4, the value of an additional unit of food will also be $4. This reasoning helps us to understand why point *A'* on the demand curve in Figure 5.1(b) is located at a price of $4. When the consumer is purchasing 2 units of food, the value of another unit of food to her (that is, her "willingness to pay" for another unit of food) is $4.

Note that her $MRS_{x,y}$ falls to 1/2 at basket *B*, and falls even farther to 1/4 at basket *C*. The value of an additional unit of food is therefore $2 at *B* (when she consumes 10 units of food) and only $1 at basket *C* (when she consumes 16 units of food). In other words, her willingness to pay for an additional unit of food falls as she buys more and more food.

THE EFFECTS OF A CHANGE IN INCOME

What happens to the consumer's choices of food and clothing as *income* changes? Let's look at the optimal choice diagram in Figure 5.2(a). The graph measures the quantity of food consumed (x) on the horizontal axis and the quantity of clothing (y) on the vertical axis. Suppose the price of food is $P_x = \$2$ and the price of clothing is $P_y = \$4$ per unit. Let's hold the prices of food and clothing constant. With the prices given, the slope of her budget line is $-P_x/P_y = -1/2$.

The figure illustrates the consumer's budget lines and optimal choices of food and clothing for three different levels of income. In Chapter 4 we saw that an increase in income results in an outward, parallel shift of the budget line. Initially,

---

[3]At *A* the indifference curve U_1 and the budget line BL_1 are tangent to one another, so their slopes are equal. The slope of the budget line is $-P_x/P_y = -1$. Recall that the $MRS_{x,y}$ at *A* is the negative of the slope of the indifference curve (and the budget line) at that basket. Therefore, $MRS_{x,y} = 1$.

EXAMPLE 5.1

Elasticity of Demand for Cable Television Subscriptions

The cable television industry is one of the most important sources of programming for households in the United States. Competitors include traditional broadcast stations, direct broadcast satellites, wireless cable, and video cassettes. However, about two-thirds of all households subscribe to cable television.

Public policy toward the cable television industry has changed repeatedly during the last two decades. In 1984 the industry was deregulated, and cable systems rapidly expanded the services they offered. However, by the early 1990s, Congress was concerned that local cable operators were charging unacceptably high prices, and that many homeowners lacked adequate access to alternative programming. In 1992, over President Bush's veto, Congress passed a sweeping set of regulations for the industry. However, in 1996 Congress again removed regulation from much of the cable television industry, recognizing that competition to provide programming had increased.

Public policy debates on this subject often focus on the nature of the demand for cable television. How much will consumers pay for basic cable television services? How sensitive are consumers to changes in the prices charged? In a study of the demand for cable television with data from 1992, Robert Crandall and Harold Furchtgott–Roth found the price elasticity of demand to be about -0.8 for the basic service offered by a typical cable television system.[4] Thus, a 10 percent increase in the price of a basic subscription would lead to a loss of 8 percent of the subscribers. Some of those who drop their subscriptions might opt for other forms of programming, while others might choose no programming at all. As competition from other sources of programming (including the Internet) intensifies over time, the demand for cable television will become more elastic. ∎

---

when the consumer's weekly income is $I_1 = \$40$, her budget line is BL_1. She chooses basket A, consuming 10 units of food and 5 units of clothing per week. As her income rises to $I_2 = \$68$, the budget line shifts out to BL_2. She then chooses basket B, with a weekly consumption of 18 units of food and 8 units of clothing. If her income increases to $I_3 = \$92$, she faces budget line BL_3. Her optimal basket is C, with 24 units of food and 11 units of clothing.

One way we can describe how changes in income affect the consumer's purchases is by drawing a curve that connects all the baskets that are optimal as income changes (keeping prices constant). This curve is called the **income consumption curve.**[5] Note that the optimal baskets A, B, and C all lie on the income consumption curve in Figure 5.2(a).

---

[4]See R. Crandall, and H. Furchtgott–Roth, *Cable TV: Regulation or Competition?* (The Brookings Institution, Washington D.C. 1996), especially Chapter 3.

[5]Some textbooks call the income consumption curve the *income expansion path*.

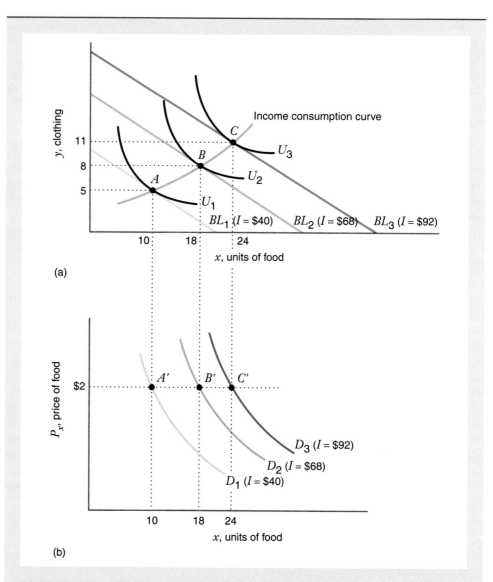

FIGURE 5.2   The Effects of Changes in Income on Consumption
The consumer buys food at $P_x = \$2$ per unit and clothing at $P_y = \$4$ per unit. Both prices are held constant as income varies. (a) The budget lines reflect three different levels of income. The slope of all budget lines is $-(P_x/P_y) = -1/2$. BL_1 is the budget line when the weekly income is $40. BL_2 and BL_3 are the budget lines when income is $68 and $92, respectively. As income changes, we can draw a curve connecting the baskets that are optimal (A, B, and C). This curve is called the income consumption curve. (b) The consumer's demand curve for food shifts out as income rises.

Changing Income: Shifting *a Demand Curve*

We can also use a second way to describe how changes in income affect the consumer's purchases. In Figure 5.2(a) the consumer purchases more of both goods as her income rises. In other words, an increase in income results in a rightward shift in her demand schedule for each good. In Figure 5.2(b) we can see how a change in income affects her demand curve for food. The *price* of food appears on the vertical axis, and the *quantity* of food on the horizontal axis. When the consumer's weekly income is $40 and the price of food is $2, she purchases 10 units of food each week. Thus, point A' must be on her demand curve for food [labeled D_1 in Figure 5.2(b)] when her income is $40.

If her income rises to $68, she will purchase 18 units of food when $P_x = \$2$ per unit. Therefore, her demand for food shifts out to D_2. This demand curve must go through point B', because she buys 18 units of food when the price of food is $2. Finally, if her income rises to $92, her demand for food shifts out to D_3, which must go through point C' because she buys 24 units of food when the price of food remains at $2.

Using a similar approach, you can also show how the demand curves for clothing shift as income changes. You can do this exercise on your own (see Problem 1 at the end of this chapter).

Engel Curves

We have a third way of showing how a consumer's choice of a particular good varies with income: We can draw a graph relating the amount of the good consumed to the level of income. We call this graph an **Engel curve.** We can use the information contained in an income consumption curve to construct an Engel curve. In Figure 5.3 we draw the Engel curve relating the amount of food consumed to the consumer's income. Here the amount of food (x) is on the horizontal axis and the level of income (I) is on the vertical axis. Point A'' on the Engel curve shows that the consumer buys 10 units of food when her weekly income is $40. Point B'' indicates that she buys 18 units of food when her income is $68. If her weekly income rises to $92, she will buy 24 units of food (point C''). Note that we draw the Engel curve holding constant the prices of all goods (the price of food is $2 and the price of clothing is $4). For a different set of prices we would draw a different Engel curve.

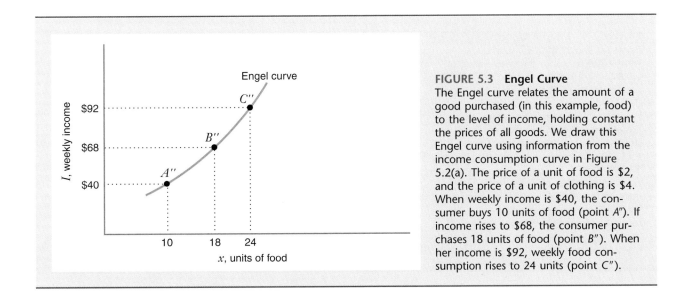

FIGURE 5.3 Engel Curve
The Engel curve relates the amount of a good purchased (in this example, food) to the level of income, holding constant the prices of all goods. We draw this Engel curve using information from the income consumption curve in Figure 5.2(a). The price of a unit of food is $2, and the price of a unit of clothing is $4. When weekly income is $40, the consumer buys 10 units of food (point A''). If income rises to $68, the consumer purchases 18 units of food (point B''). When her income is $92, weekly food consumption rises to 24 units (point C'').

If you look at the income consumption curve in Figure 5.2(a), you will see that the consumer purchases more food when her income rises. When this happens, food is said to be a **normal good**. A good is normal if a consumer wants to buy more of it when income rises. For a normal good the Engel curve will have a positive slope, as in Figure 5.3.

From Figure 5.2(a) you can also see that *clothing* is a normal good. Therefore, if you were to draw an Engel curve for clothing, with income on the vertical axis and the amount of clothing on the horizontal axis, the slope of the Engel curve would be positive.

As you might suspect, a consumer may not purchase more of *every* good as income rises. In fact, a consumer may buy *less* of some good when income rises.

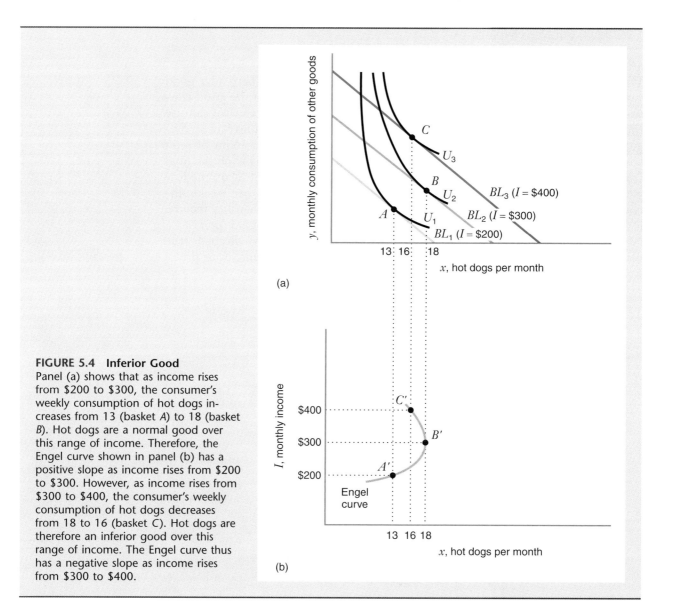

FIGURE 5.4   Inferior Good
Panel (a) shows that as income rises from $200 to $300, the consumer's weekly consumption of hot dogs increases from 13 (basket *A*) to 18 (basket *B*). Hot dogs are a normal good over this range of income. Therefore, the Engel curve shown in panel (b) has a positive slope as income rises from $200 to $300. However, as income rises from $300 to $400, the consumer's weekly consumption of hot dogs decreases from 18 to 16 (basket *C*). Hot dogs are therefore an inferior good over this range of income. The Engel curve thus has a negative slope as income rises from $300 to $400.

Consider a consumer with the preferences for hot dogs and a composite good ("other goods") depicted in Figure 5.4(a). For low levels of income, this consumer views hot dogs as a normal good. For example, as monthly income rises from $200 to $300, the consumer would change his optimal basket from A to B, buying more hot dogs. However, if income continues to rise, the consumer might prefer to buy fewer hot dogs and use his increased income instead to buy more of the other goods (such as steak or seafood). The income consumption curve in Figure 5.4(a) illustrates this possibility between baskets B and C. Over this range of the income consumption curve, hot dogs would be an **inferior good.** A good is inferior if a consumer wants to purchase *less* of that good when income rises.

Using the information from the optimal choice diagram in Figure 5.4(a), we can draw the Engel curve for hot dogs in Figure 5.4(b). Note that the Engel curve has a positive slope over the range of incomes for which hot dogs are a normal good, and a negative slope over the range of incomes for which hot dogs are an inferior good.

LEARNING-BY-DOING EXERCISE 5.1

A Normal Good Has a Positive Income Elasticity of Demand

Problem   A consumer likes to attend rock concerts and consume other goods. Suppose x measures the number of rock concerts he attends each year, and I denotes his annual income. Show that the following statement is true: If he views rock concerts as a normal good, then his income elasticity of demand for rock concerts must be positive.

Solution   In Chapter 2 we learned that the income elasticity of demand is defined as $\epsilon_{x,I} = (\Delta x/\Delta I)(I/x)$, where all prices are held constant. If rock concerts are a normal good, then x increases as income I rises. Therefore $(\Delta x/\Delta I) > 0$. [This just tells us that the Engel curve for rock concerts has a positive slope.] Since income I and the number of rock concerts attended x are positive, $\epsilon_{x,I} > 0$.

Similar Problem: 5.3

This exercise demonstrates a general proposition: If a good is normal, its income elasticity of demand is positive. The converse is also true: Any good whose income elasticity of demand is positive will be a normal good.

Using similar reasoning you can demonstrate that the following statements are also true: Any inferior good has a negative income elasticity of demand. Further, any good with a negative income elasticity of demand will be an inferior good.

EXAMPLE 5.2   *The Irish Potato Famine*

During the early nineteenth century, Ireland's population grew rapidly. Nearly half of the Irish people lived on small farms that produced little income. Many others who were unable to afford their own farms leased land from owners of big estates. But these landlords charged such high rents that leased farms also were not profitable.

Because they were poor, many Irish people depended on potatoes as an inexpensive source of nourishment. In *Why Ireland Starved*, noted economic historian Joel Mokyr described the increasing importance of the potato in the Irish diet by the 1840s:

> It is quite unmistakable that the Irish diet was undergoing changes in the first half of the nineteenth century. Eighteenth-century diets, the evergrowing importance of potatoes notwithstanding, seem to have been supplemented by a variety of vegetables, dairy products, and even pork and fish. … Although glowing reports of the Irish cuisine in the eighteenth century must be deemed unrepresentative since they pertain to the shrinking class of well-to-do farmers, things were clearly worsening in the nineteenth. There was some across-the-board deterioration of diets, due to the reduction of certain supplies, such as dairy products, fish, and vegetables, but the main reason was the relative decline of the number of people who could afford to purchase decent food. The dependency on the potato, while it cut across all classes, was most absolute among the lower two-thirds of the income distribution.[6]

Mokyr's account suggests that the income consumption curve for a typical Irish consumer might have looked like the one in Figure 5.4 (with potatoes on the horizontal axis instead of hot dogs). For people with a low income, potatoes might well have been a normal good. But consumers with higher incomes could afford other types of food, and therefore consumed fewer potatoes.

Given the heavy reliance on potatoes as food and as a source of income, it is not surprising that a crisis occurred between 1845 and 1847, when a plant disease caused the potato crop to fail. During the Irish potato famine, about 750,000 people died of starvation or disease, and hundreds of thousands of others emigrated from Ireland to escape poverty and famine.   ■

So far in this chapter, we have used a *graphical* approach to show how the amount of a good consumed depends on the levels of prices and income. We have shown how to find the shape of the demand curve when the consumer has a given level of income (as in Figure 5.1), and how the demand curve shifts as the level of income changes (as in Figure 5.2).

We can also describe the demand curve *algebraically*. In other words, given a utility function and a budget constraint, we can show how the amount of a good that is consumed depends on prices and income. The next two exercises show how we can find the equation of the consumer's demand curve.

[6]Joel Mokyr, *Why Ireland Starved: A Quantitative and Analytical History of the Irish Economy, 1800–1850,* George Allen and Unwin (London: 1983), pages 11 and 12.

LEARNING-BY-DOING EXERCISE 5.2

Finding a Demand Curve (No Corner Points)

A consumer purchases two goods, food and clothing. The utility function is $U(x, y) = xy$, where x denotes the amount of food consumed and y the amount of clothing. The marginal utilities are $MU_x = y$ and $MU_y = x$. The price of food is P_x, the price of clothing is P_y, and income is I.

Problem

(a) Show that the equation for the demand curve for food is $x = I/(2P_x)$.
(b) Is food a normal good? Draw the consumer's demand curve for food when the level of income is $I = 120$. Label this demand curve D_1. Draw the demand curve when $I = 200$, and label this demand curve D_2.

Solution

(a) We have already encountered the utility function $U(x, y) = xy$ in previous chapters. In Learning-By-Doing Exercise 3.3, we learned that the indifference curves for this utility function are bowed in toward the origin and do not intersect the axes. So any optimal basket must be interior, that is, the consumer buys positive amounts of both food and clothing.

How do we determine the optimal choice of food? We know that an interior optimum must satisfy two conditions:

- An optimal basket will be on the budget line. This means that

$$P_x x + P_y y = I$$

- Since the optimum is interior, the tangency condition must hold.

From equation (4.3), we know that at a tangency, $MU_x/MU_y = P_x/P_y$, or with the marginal utilities given,

$$\frac{y}{x} = \frac{P_x}{P_y}$$

or more simply $y = (P_x/P_y)x$.

So far the solution looks very much like the solution to Learning-By-Doing Exercise 4.2. In that exercise we were interested in finding the optimal consumption of food and clothing given a *specific* set of prices and income. Now we want to know how much food the consumer buys for *any* set of prices and income. That is why we are using the exogenous variables (P_x, P_y, and I) instead of actual numbers for the prices and income. So we have two equations with two unknowns (the endogenous variables x and y). Let's substitute $y = (P_x/P_y)x$ (coming from the tangency condition) into the budget line $P_x x + P_y y = I$. This gives us

$$P_x x + P_y \left(\frac{P_x}{P_y} x \right) = I$$

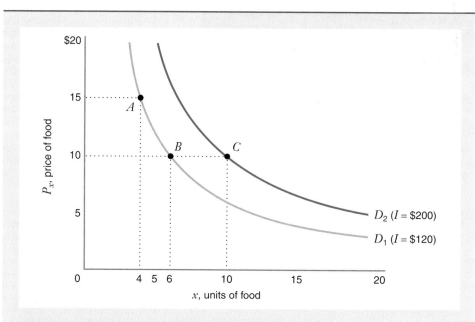

FIGURE 5.5   Demand Curves for Food at Different Income Levels
The quantity of food demanded, x, depends on the price of food, P_x, and on the level of income, I. The equation representing the demand for food is $x = I/(2P_x)$. When income is 120, the demand curve is D_1 in the graph. If the price of food is $15, the consumer buys 4 units of food (point A). If the price of food drops to $10, she buys 6 units of food (point B). If income rises to $200, the demand curve shifts to the right, to D_2. For example, if income is $200 and the price of food is $10, the consumer buys 10 units of food (point C).

When we solve for the amount of food demanded, x, we find that $x = I/(2P_x)$. This is the equation of the demand curve for food. Given any numerical values of income and the price of food, we can easily find the quantity of food the consumer will purchase.

(b) If income is 120, the amount of food demanded will be $x = 120/(2P_x) = 60/P_x$. We can plot points on the demand curve, as we have done in Figure 5.5. When the price of food is 15, the consumer buys 4 units of food (point A in the graph). At a price of 10, she buys 6 units of food (point B in the graph).

An increase in income shifts the demand schedule to the right. Thus, food is a normal good. At a price of 10 and an income of 200, the consumer buys 10 units of food (point C in the graph).

Note that the consumer always buys some food (x is always positive), no matter how high the price. This is what we expected to see, since there will be no corner-point solution at which she buys no food.

Similar Problem: 5.5

Why would we want to go through the exercise of finding the equation of a demand curve, as we have done in this exercise? If we only want to know the optimal amount of food consumed at a specific set of prices and income, we could just use the approach of Learning-By-Doing Exercise 4.2. But if we want to find out how much food would be purchased for many different prices of food, it would be tedious to repeat that exercise using new numbers. Instead, once we have the equation for the demand curve, we can easily find the quantity of food demanded for any price and income.

LEARNING-BY-DOING EXERCISE 5.3

Finding a Demand Curve (With a Corner-Point Solution)

A consumer purchases two goods, food and clothing. He has the utility function $U(x,y) = xy + 10x$, where x denotes the amount of food consumed and y the amount of clothing. The marginal utilities are $MU_x = y + 10$ and $MU_y = x$. The price of food is P_x, the price of clothing is P_y, and his income is I.

Problem

(a) Show that the equation for the consumer's demand curve for clothing is

$$y = \begin{cases} \dfrac{I - 10P_y}{2P_y}, & \text{when } P_y \le \dfrac{I}{10} \\[2ex] 0, & \text{when } P_y > \dfrac{I}{10} \end{cases}$$

(b) Suppose his income is $I = 100$. Fill in the following table to show how much clothing he will purchase at each price of clothing (these are points on his demand curve):

P_y	2	4	5	10	12
y					

Solution

(a) We have already examined optimal choice with the utility function $U(x, y) = xy + 10x$ in Learning-By-Doing Exercise 4.3. There we learned that the indifference curves for this utility function are bowed in toward the origin. They also intersect the x axis, since the consumer could have a positive level of utility with purchases of food ($x > 0$) but no purchases of clothing ($y = 0$). So he might not buy any clothing (and choose a corner point) if the price of clothing is too high.

How do we determine the consumer's optimal choice of clothing? If he is at an interior optimum, we know that his optimal basket will be on the budget line. This means that

$$P_x x + P_y y = I$$

At an interior optimum, the tangency condition must hold. From equation (4.4), we know that at a tangency, $MU_x/MU_y = P_x/P_y$, or with the marginal utilities given,

$$\frac{y + 10}{x} = \frac{P_x}{P_y}$$

or more simply $P_x x = P_y y + 10P_y$.

So far the solution looks like the one for Learning-By-Doing Exercise 4.3. Now we want to know how much clothing the consumer buys for *any* set of prices and income. We therefore use the exogenous variables (P_x, P_y, and I) instead of actual numbers for the prices and income. So we have two equations with two unknowns (the endogenous variables x and y). Let's substitute $P_x x = P_y y + 10P_y$ (coming from the tangency condition) into the budget line $P_x x + P_y y = I$. This gives us $2P_y y + 10P_y = I$. When we solve for the amount of clothing demanded, y, we find that $y = (I - 10P_y)/(2P_y)$. This is the equation of the consumer's demand curve for clothing. Note that the consumer will demand a positive amount of clothing when $I - 10P_y > 0$, or when $P_y < I/10$. When $P_y = I/10$, the consumer buys no clothing.

What happens if $P_y > I/10$? Then the consumer will be at a corner point. To see this, let's compare the marginal utilities per dollar spent on each good. At a corner point at which the consumer buys only food, she will have $x = I/P_x$ units of food and zero units of clothing ($y = 0$). In that case, $MU_x/P_x = (y + 10)/P_x = 10/P_x$. For clothing, $MU_y/P_y = x/P_y = (I/P_x)/P_y$. Note that he will buy only food when $MU_x/P_x > MU_y/P_y$, that is, when $10/P_x > (I/P_x)/P_y$, which simplifies to $P_y > I/10$. So if $P_y > I/10$, he will choose a corner point and buy the basket ($x = I/P_x$, $y = 0$).

(b) Using the equation for the demand curve we found in (a), the table can be completed as follows:

P_y	2	4	5	10	12
y	20	7.5	5	0	0

Note that the equation for the demand curve helps us easily determine the quantity of clothing that the consumer will demand at any price. That is why we did this exercise. We could have repeated Learning-By-Doing Exercise 4.3 five times (once for each price of clothing) to fill in the table, but that would have required a lot of repetitious work. It is much simpler just to find the equation of the demand curve (as we have done in this exercise), and then use that equation to fill in the table.

Similar Problem: 5.10

A decrease in the price of a good affects the consumer in two ways. First, as the price of a good falls, that good becomes cheaper relative to other goods, leading to a *substitution effect*. For example, if the price of food falls, the consumer may decide to buy more food and less of other goods, because food is now less expensive relative to other goods. Second, as the price goes down, purchasing power increases, since the consumer could buy the same basket of goods with money left over to buy still more goods. This increase in purchasing power affects the consumer much the way it would if income increased, giving rise to an *income effect*.

These two effects occur at the same time when the price of a good falls. However, we need to distinguish between the two effects to understand better how a price change affects a consumer.

SUBSTITUTION EFFECT

Let's consider what happens when the price of food changes. The **substitution effect** is the change in the amount of food consumed as the price of food changes, *holding constant the level of utility*. The substitution effect tells us how much more food the consumer would buy now that food is cheaper relative to clothing.

You can find the substitution effect associated with a price change by following the three steps illustrated in the three optimal choice diagrams in Figure 5.6. Here the consumer buys two goods, food and clothing, both of which have positive marginal utilities. We have drawn the diagrams assuming the price of food *decreases*.

Step 1: Find the *initial* basket, that is, the basket the consumer chooses at the initial price of food. Figure 5.6(a) illustrates Step 1. Initially, when the price of food is P_{x_1}, the consumer faces the budget line BL_1. When she maximizes utility, she chooses basket A on the indifference curve U_1. The *initial* quantity of food purchased is x_A.

Step 2: Find the *final* basket, that is, the basket the consumer would optimally choose at the final price of food. Figure 5.6(b) illustrates Step 2. When the price of food falls to P_{x_2}, the budget line rotates outward to BL_2. The consumer is surely going to be better off as a result of the decrease in the price of food, because the initial basket A lies inside the new budget line BL_2. The consumer now chooses basket C and realizes the higher level of utility that the indifference curve U_2 represents. The *final* quantity of food consumed is x_C. When the price of food falls, food consumption increases by $x_C - x_A$.

Step 3: Find the *decomposition* basket. Figure 5.6(c) illustrates Step 3. We can find the decomposition basket by drawing a budget line parallel to the *new* budget line BL_2 (to reflect the fall in the price of food), but tangent to the *initial* indifference curve U_1 (to keep the initial level of utility unchanged). You can think of this tangent line as the budget line that will help us separate (or decompose) the effect of the price change on the consumption of food ($x_C - x_A$) into the substitution and income effects. We will therefore call it the *decomposition budget line* and label it BL_d in Figure 5.6(c). The decomposition budget line BL_d is tangent to the indifference curve U_1. At that point of tangency, basket B, she purchases x_B units of food.

Since we are holding the level of utility constant, a movement along the initial indifference curve U_1 determines the substitution effect. In Figure 5.6(c), the substitution effect is $x_B - x_A$.

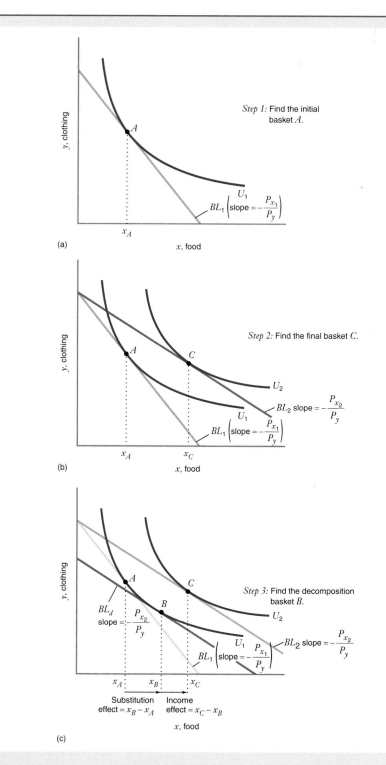

FIGURE 5.6 Income and Substitution Effects Case 1: x Is a Normal Good
As the price of food drops from P_{x_1} to P_{x_2}, the substitution effect leads to an increase in the amount of food consumed from x_A to x_B (so the substitution effect is $x_B - x_A$). Since food is a normal good, the income effect also leads to an increase in food consumption, from x_B to x_C (so the income effect is $x_C - x_B$). When a good is normal, the income and substitution effects reinforce each other. In this case the demand curve for food will be downward sloping. As the price of food decreases from P_{x_1} to P_{x_2}, the quantity of food will increase from x_A to x_C.

As the price of food falls, the substitution effect will lead to an increase in the amount of food purchased. This is true because the consumer has a diminishing marginal rate of substitution of food for clothing, and therefore the indifference curves are bowed in toward the origin. When the price of food falls, the slope of the decomposition budget line is less steep than the original budget line. The decomposition basket B will therefore be to the southeast of the original basket A.

The consumer has income I, and this income enables her to choose any basket on BL_1 when the price of food is P_{x_1}, and any basket along BL_2 when the price of food is P_{x_2}. Note that the decomposition budget line BL_d lies inside the final budget line BL_2. This means that the level of income necessary to choose a basket along BL_d is lower than the income necessary to choose a basket on BL_2. Suppose I_d is the level of income along BL_d.

Since baskets A and B are on the same indifference curve, either basket equally satisfies the consumer. She is therefore indifferent between the following two situations: (1) having an income I and paying the price for food P_{x_1}, and (2) having a lower income I_d and paying the lower price for food P_{x_2}. In other words, she would be indifferent between forgoing an amount of income $(I - I_d)$ and purchasing food at the lower price. At basket B she would maximize her utility if she were given the lower income I_d and could purchase food at the lower price. She would be just as well off as she was initially at A, when she had more income but had to pay the higher price for food.

INCOME EFFECT

Now let's find the income effect. The **income effect** is the change in the amount of a good consumed as the consumer's utility changes, *holding price constant*. In this example, the movement from A to B does not involve any change in utility because some income is "taken away" as the price of food falls. However, in reality, the consumer does not have to forgo any income when the price of food is lowered. The income effect measures the change in food consumption when the level of income is *restored*—that is, increased from I_d back to I, moving the budget line from BL_d to BL_2. In Figure 5.6(c), note what happens when the level of income is increased from I_d to I (and the budget line therefore shifts from BL_d to BL_2). The optimal basket would change from B to C. The income effect is the corresponding change in the consumption of food, that is, $(x_C - x_B)$.

What is going on here? Initially, the consumer pays a price P_{x_1} and chooses basket A. In the final situation the consumer pays a price P_{x_2} and chooses basket C. Income does not change. When the price of food falls from P_{x_1} to P_{x_2}, the *total* change on food consumption is $(x_C - x_A)$. In reality the consumer moves directly from basket A to basket C and never actually chooses basket B.

However, we have introduced basket B to decompose the total change on food consumption into an income and a substitution effect. The movement from A to B holds utility constant. As the price of food drops, just enough income is "taken away" to make the consumer indifferent between the two baskets. The difference in food consumption as the consumer moves from A to B is the substitution effect.

To find the income effect, the income that is "taken away" in the movement from A to B is then "restored." The price of food is held constant. As income is restored, the optimal choice changes from B to C.

In sum, when the price of food falls from P_{x_1} to P_{x_2}, the *total* change on food consumption is $(x_C - x_A)$. This can be decomposed into the substitution effect $(x_B - x_A)$ and the income effect $(x_C - x_B)$. When we add the substitution effect and the income effect, we get the total change in consumption.

The graphs in Figure 5.6 are drawn for the case (we call it Case 1) in which food is a normal good. As the price of food falls, the income effect leads to an increase in food consumption. As we noted earlier, because the marginal rate of substitution is diminishing, the substitution effect will also lead to increased food consumption. Thus, the income and substitution effects work in the same direction. If the price of food falls, both effects will be positive. The demand curve for food will be downward sloping because the quantity of food purchased will clearly increase when the price of food falls. Similarly, if the price of food were to rise, both effects would be negative. At a higher price of food, the consumer would buy less food.

However, the income and substitution effects do not always have to work in the same direction. Consider Case 2, in Figure 5.7. Instead of drawing three more graphs like those in Figure 5.6, we have only drawn the final graph [like Figure 5.6(c)] with the initial, final, and decomposition baskets. Note that basket C, the final basket, lies directly above basket B, the decomposition basket. As the budget

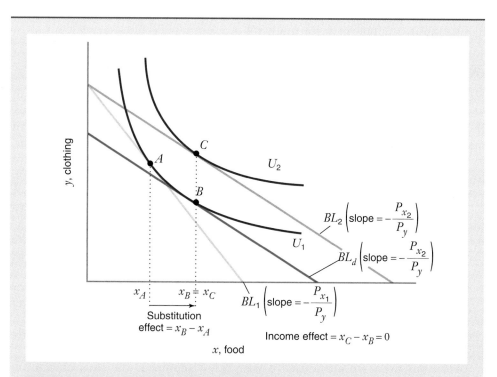

FIGURE 5.7   Income and Substitution Effects Case 2:
***x* is Neither a Normal Good nor an Inferior Good**
As the price of food drops from P_{x_1} to P_{x_2}, the substitution effect leads to an increase from x_A to x_B in the amount of food consumed. But food is neither a normal good nor an inferior good. The income effect on food consumption is zero because x_B is the same as x_C. In this case the demand curve for food will be downward sloping. As the price of food decreases from P_{x_1} to P_{x_2}, the quantity of food will increase from x_A to x_C.

line shifts out from BL_d to BL_2, the quantity of food consumed does not change. The income effect is therefore zero because $x_C - x_B = 0$. Here a decrease in the price of food leads to a positive substitution effect on food consumption (since x_B is greater than x_A) and a zero income effect. The demand curve for food will be downward sloping because more food is purchased at the lower price.

The income and substitution effects might even work in opposite directions. This happens when a good is inferior. Consider Case 3, in Figure 5.8. In this figure we draw the indifference curves so that the income effect is negative. In other words, for this consumer, food is an inferior good. Note that basket C, the final basket, lies to the left of basket B, the decomposition basket. As the budget line shifts out from BL_d to BL_2, the quantity of food consumed decreases. The income effect is therefore negative because $x_C - x_B < 0$. Here a decrease in the price of food leads to a *positive* substitution effect on food consumption (because x_B is greater than x_A), and a *negative* income effect.

Will the demand curve for food be downward sloping for the preferences in Figure 5.8? Yes. The final basket C lies to the right of the initial basket A. When

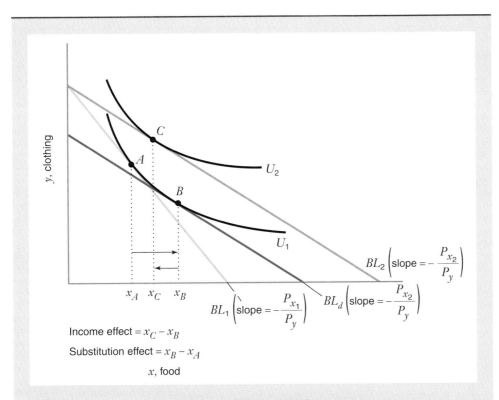

FIGURE 5.8   Income and Substitution Effects Case 3:
x is an Inferior Good with a Downward-Sloping Demand Curve
As the price of food drops from P_{x_1} to P_{x_2}, the substitution effect leads to an increase from x_A to x_B in the amount of food consumed. But food is an inferior good. The income effect on food consumption is negative because x_C is less than x_B. When a good is inferior, the income and substitution effects work in opposite directions. Because the substitution effect is larger than the income effect, the demand curve for food will still be downward sloping. As the price of food decreases from P_{x_1} to P_{x_2}, the quantity of food will increase from x_A to x_C.

the price of food drops from P_{x_1} to P_{x_2}, the quantity of food does increase from x_A to x_C. The demand curve for food will therefore be downward sloping.

The final case is the rather strange Case 4, in Figure 5.9. Note that we draw the indifference curves for the case in which food is strongly inferior. Basket C, the final basket, lies not only to the left of the decomposition basket B, but also to the left of the initial basket A. The income effect is so strongly negative that it more than cancels out the positive substitution effect.

Will the demand curve for food be downward sloping for the preferences in Figure 5.9? No. When the price of food drops from P_{x_1} to P_{x_2}, the quantity of food actually *decreases* from x_A to x_C. The demand curve for food will therefore be *upward* sloping over the range of prices between P_{x_1} and P_{x_2}. Case 4 illustrates the famous case of the **Giffen good.** A Giffen good is a good that has a demand curve that has a positive slope over part of the curve.

As we have already noted, some goods are inferior for some consumers. As we suggested earlier, your consumption of hot dogs may fall if your income rises, as you decide to eat more steaks and fewer hot dogs. But expenditures on inferior goods typically represent only a small part of a consumer's income. Income effects for individual goods are usually not large, and the largest income effects

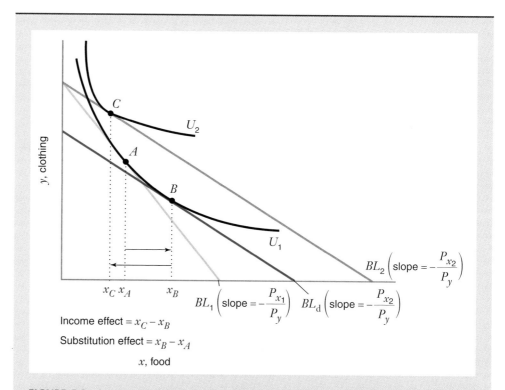

FIGURE 5.9   Income and Substitution Effects Case 4: x is a Giffen Good
As the price of food drops from P_{x_1} to P_{x_2}, the substitution effect leads to an increase from x_A to x_B in the amount of food consumed. But food is a strongly inferior good. The income effect on food consumption is negative, since x_C is less than x_B. When a good is inferior, the income and substitution effects work in opposite directions. For a Giffen good, when the income effect is larger than the substitution effect, the demand curve for food will be positive sloping. As the price of food decreases from P_{x_1} to P_{x_2}, the quantity of food purchased will decrease from x_A to x_C.

are usually associated with goods that are normal rather than inferior, such as food and housing. For an inferior good to have an income effect large enough to offset the substitution effect, the income elasticity of demand would have to be negative and the expenditures on the good would need to represent a large part of the consumer's budget. Thus, while the Giffen good is intriguing as a theoretical possibility, it is not of much practical concern.

How Do Rats Respond to Changes in Prices?

EXAMPLE 5.3

In Chapter 2 we cited studies showing that people have negatively sloped demand curves for goods and services, and that many goods are adequate substitutes for one another. In the early 1980s several economists conducted experiments designed to ask how rats would respond to changes in relative prices. In one famous experiment, white rats were offered root beer and collins mix in different containers. To extract a unit of the beverage, a rat had to "pay a price" by pushing a lever a certain number of times. The researchers allowed the rat a specified number of pushes per day. This was the rat's income.

Each rat was then able to choose its initial basket of the beverages. Then the experimenters altered the relative prices of the beverages by changing the number of times the rat needed to push the lever to extract a unit of each beverage. The rat's income was adjusted so that it would allow a rat to consume its initial basket. The researchers found that the rats altered their consumption patterns to choose more of the beverage with the lower relative price. The choices the rats made indicated that they were willing to substitute one beverage for the other when the relative prices of the beverages changed.

In another experiment, rats were offered a similar set of choices between food and water. When relative prices were changed, the rats were willing to engage in some limited substitution toward the good with the lower relative price. But the cross-price elasticities of demand were much lower in this experiment because food and water are not good substitutes for one another.

In a third study, researchers designed an experiment to see if they could confirm the existence of a Giffen good for rats. When the rats were offered a choice between quinine water and root beer, researchers discovered that quinine water was an inferior good. They reduced the rats' incomes to low levels, and set prices so that the rats spent most of their budget on quinine water. This was the right environment for the potential discovery of a Giffen good. Theory predicts that we are most likely to observe a Giffen good when an inferior good (quinine water) also comprises a large part of a consumer's expenditures. When researchers lowered the price of quinine water, they found that the rats did in fact extract less quinine water, using their increased wealth to choose more root beer. The researchers concluded that for rats, quinine water was a Giffen good.[7] ■

[7]See J. Kagel, R. Battalio, H. Rachlin, L. Green, R. Basmann, and W. Klemm, "Experimental Studies of Consumer Demand Behavior," *Economic Inquiry* (March, 1975); and J. Kagel, R. Battalio, H. Rachlin, and L. Green, "Demand Curves for Animal Consumers," *Quarterly Journal of Economics* (February 1981); and R. Battalio, J. Kagel, and C. Kogut, "Experimental Confirmation of the Existence of a Giffen Good," *American Economic Review* (September 1991).

While researchers have not yet confirmed the existence of a Giffen good for human beings, some economists have suggested that the Irish potato famine (see Example 5.2) came close to creating the right environment. However, as Joel Mokyr observed, "For people with a very low income, potatoes might have well been a normal good. But consumers with higher levels of income could afford other types of food, and therefore consumed fewer potatoes." Thus, while expenditures on potatoes did constitute a large part of consumer expenditures, they may not have been inferior at low incomes. This may explain why researchers have not shown the potato to have been a Giffen good at that time.

LEARNING-BY-DOING EXERCISE 5.4

Numerical Example of Income and Substitution Effects

In Learning-By-Doing Exercises 4.2 and 5.2, we met a consumer who purchases two goods, food and clothing. She has the utility function $U(x, y) = xy$, where x denotes the amount of food consumed and y the amount of clothing. Her marginal utilities are $MU_x = y$ and $MU_y = x$. Now suppose that she has an income of $72 per week and that the price of clothing is $P_y = \$1$ per unit. Suppose that the price of food is initially $P_{x_1} = \$9$ per unit, and that the price subsequently falls to $P_{x_2} = \$4$ per unit.

Problem Find the numerical values of the income and substitution effects on food consumption, and graph the results.

Solution To find the income and substitution effects, we follow the three steps we identified earlier in this section.

Step 1: Find the initial consumption basket A when the price of food is $9. To find the amount of food and clothing consumed, we know that two conditions must be satisfied at an optimum. First, an optimal basket will be on the budget line. This means that $P_x x + P_y y = I$, or with the given information

$$9x + y = 72$$

Second, since the optimum is interior, the tangency condition must hold. From equation (4.3), we know that at a tangency, $MU_x/MU_y = P_x/P_y$, or with the given information,

$$\frac{y}{x} = \frac{9}{1}$$

or more simply $y = 9x$.

So we have two equations with two unknowns: $9x + y = 72$ (coming from the budget line) and $y = 9x$ (coming from the tangency condition). Together these imply that $x = 4$ and $y = 36$. So the consumer's optimal basket involves the purchase of 4 units of food and 36 units of clothing each month, as basket A in Figure 5.10 indicates.

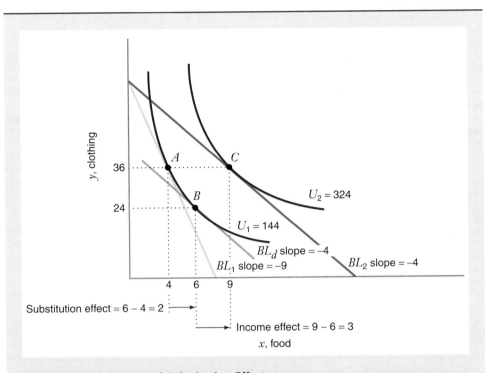

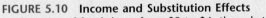

FIGURE 5.10 Income and Substitution Effects
As the price of food drops from $9 to $4, the substitution effect leads to an increase in food consumption from 4 (at the initial basket *A*) to 6 (at the decomposition basket *B*). The substitution effect is therefore 2. We measure the income effect by the change in food consumption as the consumer moves from the decomposition basket *B* (where 6 units of food are purchased) to the final basket *C* (where 9 units of food are bought). The income effect is therefore 3.

Now, suppose you had already worked out the equation for the demand curve for food from Learning-By-Doing Example 5.2. There we found that the demand curve for food $x = I/(2P_x)$. When the income is $I = 72$ and the price of a unit of food is $9, the equation for demand tells us that the consumer will buy 4 units of food. This food costs her $P_x x$ = ($9 per unit of food)(4 units of food) = $36. She spends the rest of her income ($72 total income − $36 spent on food) on clothing. So she spends $36 on clothing, and each unit of clothing costs her $1. She therefore buys 36 units of clothing.

We summarize the information about the initial basket *A* in Table 5.1. The initial level of utility is $U_1 = xy = (4)(36) = 144$. So the indifference curve passing through the initial basket *A* has a value of 144. The slopes of the indifference curve and budget line at basket *A* are −9, and she will need to spend $72 to purchase basket *A* when the price of a unit of food is $9 and the price of a unit of clothing is $1.

Step 2: Find the final consumption basket *C* when the price of food is $4. We repeat part (a) of this exercise, now with the price of a unit of food of $4.

So we have two equations with two unknowns:

$$4x + y = 72 \text{ (coming from the budget line)}$$
$$y = 4x \text{ (coming from the tangency condition)}$$

Solving the two equations together yields the following:

$$4x + 4x = 72$$
$$8x = 72$$

Then $x = 9$ and $y = 4x$, or 36.

So the consumer's optimal basket involves the purchase of 9 units of food and 36 units of clothing each month, as basket C in Figure 5.10 indicates.

The last row of Table 5.1 summarizes the information about the final basket C. The final level of utility is $U_2 = xy = (9)(36) = 324$. So the indifference curve passing through the final basket C has a utility value of 324. The slopes of the indifference curve and budget line at basket C are -4, and the consumer will need to spend \$72 to purchase basket C when the price of a unit of food is \$4 and the price of a unit of clothing is \$1.

Step 3: Find the decomposition basket B. The decomposition basket must satisfy two conditions. First, it must lie on the *original* indifference curve. Therefore, the amounts of food and clothing must yield a level of utility equal to U_1, which is 144. At basket B the amounts of food and clothing must therefore satisfy $xy = 144$. Second, at basket B the indifference curve and decomposition budget line must be tangent to one another. The *final* price of food determines the slope of the decomposition budget line. The tangency will occur when $MU_x/MU_y = P_x/P_y$, or when $y/x = 4/1$. The tangency condition requires that $y = 4x$.

We now have all of the information we need to find the decomposition basket. We know that the purchases of food and clothing at B must allow the consumer to reach the *initial* level of utility ($xy = 144$) and that the tangency condition with the *new* price of food will be satisfied ($y = 4x$). These two equations tell us that the decomposition basket B will contain 6 units of food and 24 units of clothing ($x = 6$ and $y = 24$).

We summarize the information about the decomposition basket in Table 5.1. At basket B the level of utility is 144, and the slopes of the indifference curve and decomposition budget lines are both -4. The last column indicates

TABLE 5.1
Optimal Baskets for Learning-By-Doing Exercise 5.4

Basket	x	y	$U = xy$	$\dfrac{MU_x}{MU_y} = \dfrac{P_x}{P_y}$	Expenditure $P_x x + P_y y$
A	4	36	144	$\dfrac{9}{1} = \dfrac{9}{1}$	$(9)(4) + (1)(36) = 72$
B	6	24	144	$\dfrac{4}{1} = \dfrac{4}{1}$	$(4)(6) + (1)(24) = 48$
C	9	36	324	$\dfrac{4}{1} = \dfrac{4}{1}$	$(4)(9) + (1)(36) = 72$

that if the consumer were to buy basket B when the price of food is 4 and the price of clothing is 1, she would need to spend only $48. Because the decomposition budget line is tangent to the initial indifference curve U_1, basket B represents the choice she would make if she wants to minimize her total expenditure when (1) she faces the new price of food of $4 and (2) she wants to remain on the indifference curve U_1.

Baskets A and B both lie on the same indifference curve. Therefore, the consumer would be equally happy with either of the following two situations: (1) having an income of $72 and paying $9 per unit of food (and buying basket A), or (2) having an income of $48 and paying $4 per unit of food (and buying basket B).

Now we can measure the income and substitution effects. The substitution effect is the increase in food purchased as the consumer slides around the initial indifference curve, moving from basket A (at which she purchases 4 units of food) to basket B (at which she purchases 6 units of food). The substitution effect is therefore $+2$ units of food.

The income effect is the increase in food purchased as she moves from basket B (at which she purchases 6 units of food) to basket C (at which she purchases 9 units of food). The income effect is therefore $+3$ units of food.

Figure 5.10 graphs the income and substitution effects. In this exercise food is a normal good. As expected, the income and substitution effects have the same sign. The consumer's demand curve for food is downward sloping because the quantity of food she purchases increases when the price of food falls.

LEARNING-BY-DOING EXERCISE 5.5

Income and Substitution Effects with a Price Increase

Problem   The family of indifference curves in Figure 5.11 depicts a consumer's preferences for housing and "other goods." x measures the number of square feet of housing. y is the number of units of a composite good representing other goods. The consumer's marginal utilities for both goods are positive. At current prices and income he could purchase at most y^* units of the composite good or x^* units of housing. On the graph illustrate and clearly label the income and substitution effects on housing if the current price of housing were to double.

Solution   Figure 5.11 shows the income and substitution effects. At the initial price of housing the consumer could purchase x^* units of housing if he spent all of his money on housing. If he bought no housing, he could buy y^* units of the composite good. The initial budget line is therefore BL_1. His optimal basket is A, and he reaches the indifference curve U_1. When the price of housing doubles, the final budget line BL_2 has the same vertical intercept as BL_1 but twice the slope. The horizontal intercept of BL_2 is $x^*/2$. The consumer purchases basket C and reaches the indifference curve U_2.

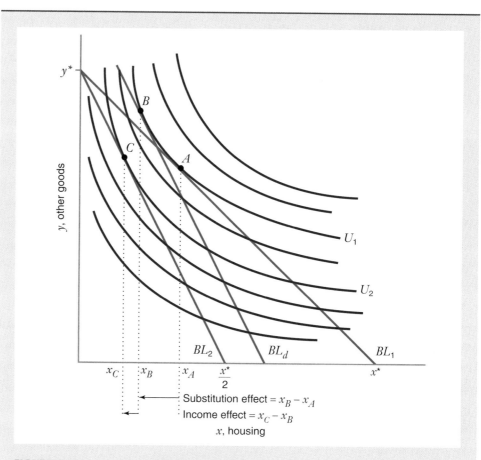

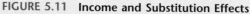

FIGURE 5.11 **Income and Substitution Effects**
At the initial price of housing the budget line is BL_1, and the consumer buys basket A and receives a level of utility U_1. When the price of housing doubles, the budget line becomes BL_2, and the consumer purchases basket C, reaching the indifference curve U_2. The decomposition budget line BL_d is parallel to BL_2, and the decomposition basket B is located where BL_d is tangent to the initial indifference curve U_1. The substitution effect is $x_B - x_A$, because housing consumption decreases from x_A (at the initial basket A) to x_B (at the decomposition basket B). The income effect ($x_C - x_B$) is measured by the change in housing consumption as the consumer moves from the decomposition basket B to the final basket C.

To draw the decomposition budget line BL_d, remember that BL_d is parallel to the final budget line BL_2. The decomposition basket B is located where BL_d is tangent to the *initial* indifference curve U_1. (Students often err by placing the decomposition basket on the final indifference curve instead of on the initial indifference curve.) As we move from the initial basket A to the decomposition basket B, housing consumption decreases from x_A to x_B. The substitution effect is therefore ($x_B - x_A$). The income effect is measured by the change in housing consumption as the consumer moves from the decomposition basket B to the final basket C. The income effect is therefore ($x_C - x_B$).

Similar Problem: 5.6

LEARNING-BY-DOING EXERCISE 5.6

Income and Substitution Effects with a Quasi-Linear Utility Function

A college student who loves chocolate has a budget of $10 per day, and out of that income she purchases chocolate and other goods. The variable x measures the number of ounces of chocolate she purchases, while y measures the number of units of the composite good that she buys. The price of the composite good is 1.

The utility function $U(x, y) = 2\sqrt{x} + y$ represents the student's preferences. You may recall from Chapter 3 that this is a quasi-linear utility function of two goods because it is a linear function of one of its arguments (the composite good, y), but not a linear function of the amount of chocolate she buys. For this utility function, $MU_x = 1/\sqrt{x}$ and $MU_y = 1$.

Problem

(a) Suppose the price of chocolate is initially $0.50 per ounce. How many ounces of chocolate and how many units of the composite good are in the student's optimal consumption basket?

(b) Suppose the price of chocolate drops to $0.20 per ounce. How many ounces of chocolate and how many units of the composite good are in the optimal consumption basket?

(c) What are the substitution and income effects that result from the decline in the price of chocolate? Illustrate these effects on a clearly labeled graph.

Solution

(a) At an interior optimum, $MU_x/MU_y = P_x/P_y$, which tells us that $1/\sqrt{x} = P_x$. The student's demand for x is therefore $x = 1/(P_x)^2$. When the price of x is $0.50 per ounce, she buys $1/(0.5)^2 = 4$ ounces of chocolate per day.

We can find the number of units of the composite good from the budget line, $P_x x + P_y y = I$. With the information given, the budget line is $(0.5)(4) + (1)y = 10$, so the student buys $y = 8$ units of the composite good.

(b) We use the demand curve for chocolate from part (a) to find her demand for chocolate when the price falls to $0.20 per ounce. She buys $1/(0.2)^2 = 25$ ounces of chocolate at the lower price. Her budget constraint is now $(0.2)(25) + (1)y = 10$, so she buys 5 units of the composite good.

(c) In the first two parts of this problem we already found all we need to know about the initial basket A and the final basket C. Figure 5.12 shows these baskets. Table 5.2 summarizes the information about these baskets.

To find the income and substitution effects, we need to find the decomposition basket B. We know two things about the tangency at basket B:

1. The utility at B must be the same as at the initial basket A. Therefore we know that $2\sqrt{x} + y = 12$.

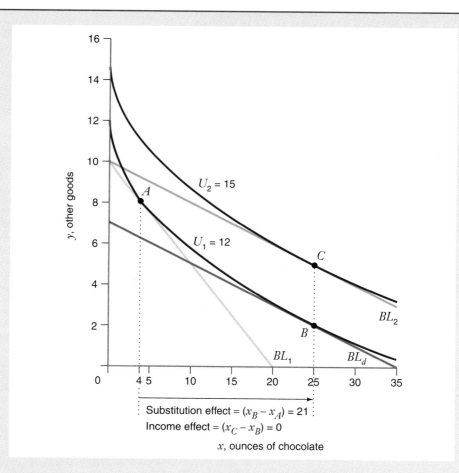

FIGURE 5.12   Income and Substitution Effects
At the initial price of chocolate ($P_x = \$0.50$ per ounce) the budget line is BL_1. The consumer buys basket A, containing 4 ounces of chocolate, and receives a level of utility $U_1 = 12$. When the price of chocolate falls to $0.20 per ounce, the budget line becomes BL_2. The consumer purchases basket C, containing 25 ounces of chocolate, and has the utility $U_2 = 15$. The decomposition budget line BL_d is parallel to BL_2, and the decomposition basket B is located where BL_d is tangent to the initial indifference curve U_1. The substitution effect is +21 ounces because chocolate consumption increases from 4 ounces (at the initial basket A) to 25 ounces (at the decomposition basket B). The income effect is measured by the change in chocolate bought as the consumer moves from the decomposition basket B (where 25 ounces of chocolate are purchased) to the final basket C (where she still buys 25 ounces of chocolate). The income effect is therefore zero.

2. The decomposition budget line must have the same slope as the final budget line at the point of tangency. Therefore $MU_x/MU_y = P_x/P_y$, or $(1/\sqrt{x})/1 = 0.20/1$. These two conditions tell us that $x = 25$ and $y = 2$ at the decomposition basket B. Figure 5.12 also plots this basket.

In the graph we can measure the size of the substitution effect by the change in chocolate purchased as the consumer moves from the initial basket A (where

TABLE 5.2
Optimal Baskets for Learning-By-Doing Exercise 5.6

Basket	x	y	$U = 2\sqrt{x} + y$	$\dfrac{MU_x}{MU_y} = \dfrac{P_x}{P_y}$	Expenditure $P_x x + P_y y$
A	4	8	12	$\dfrac{1/\sqrt{4}}{1} = \dfrac{0.50}{1}$	$(0.50)(4) + (1)(8) = 10$
B	25	2	12	$\dfrac{1/\sqrt{25}}{1} = \dfrac{0.20}{1}$	$(0.20)(25) + (1)(2) = 7$
C	25	5	15	$\dfrac{1/\sqrt{25}}{1} = \dfrac{0.20}{1}$	$(0.20)(25) + (1)(5) = 10$

she consumes 4 ounces of chocolate) to the decomposition basket B (where she consumes 25 ounces of chocolate). The substitution effect on chocolate is therefore +21 ounces. The income effect is zero because she consumes the same amount of chocolate at B and C.

Similar Problem: 5.6

Learning-By-Doing Exercise 5.6 illustrates one of the properties of a quasi-linear utility function with a constant marginal utility of y and indifference curves that are bowed in toward the origin. When prices are constant, at an interior optimum the consumer will purchase the same amount of x as income varies. In other words, the income consumption curve will be a vertical line in the graph. This means that the income effect associated with a price change on x will be zero, as in Case 2 in Figure 5.7.[8]

5.3

CONSUMER SURPLUS

We've seen how changes in prices affect consumer decision making and utility. But how might we measure the effect of a price change on consumer well-being if we do not know the utility function? If all we know is the demand curve, the concept of consumer surplus can be a useful tool for approximating the impact of a price change on consumer well-being.

Consumer surplus is the difference between the maximum amount a consumer is willing to pay for a good and the amount he must acutally pay to purchase the good in the marketplace. It therefore measures how much better off the consumer will be when he purchases the good.

[8]You can see this more formally as follows: If the utility function is quasi-linear, then $U(x, y) = f(x) + ky$, where k is a constant. For this utility function, $MU_y = k$. Let MU_x be the marginal utility of x. At an interior optimum, $MU_x/MU_y = P_x/P_y$, which tells us that $MU_x/k = P_x/P_y$. If income changes (and prices are constant), then MU_x must remain constant. This can happen only if x remains constant because MU_x would change if x were to change. Therefore, as long as the optimal basket is interior as income varies, the optimal choice of x will remain constant. This means that $\Delta x/\Delta I = 0$, and also that the income elasticity is zero.

Let's begin with an example. Suppose you are considering buying an automobile and that you will either buy one automobile or no automobile at all. You are willing to pay up to $15,000 for it. But you can buy that automobile for $12,000 in the marketplace. Because your willingness to pay exceeds the amount you will actually have to pay for it, you will buy it. When you do, you will walk away from the marketplace with a consumer surplus of $3,000 from that purchase. Your consumer surplus is your net economic benefit from making the purchase, that is, the maximum amount you would be willing to pay ($15,000) less the amount you actually have to pay ($12,000).

Of course, for many types of commodities you might want to consume more than one unit. You will have a demand curve for such a commodity, and, as we have already pointed out, it represents your willingness to pay for the good. For example, suppose you like to play tennis, and that you must rent the tennis court for an hour each time you play. Your demand curve for court time appears in Figure 5.13. It shows that you would be willing to pay up to $25 for the first hour of court time each month. For the second hour in the month, you are willing to pay $23, and for the third hour $21. Your demand schedule is downward sloping because you have a diminishing marginal utility for playing tennis.

Suppose you must pay $10 per hour to rent the court. At that price your demand curve indicates that you will play tennis for 8 hours during the month. You are willing to pay $11 for the eighth hour, but only $9 for the ninth hour, and even less for additional hours. You are therefore not willing to play more than 8 hours when court time costs $10 per hour.

How much consumer surplus do you get from playing tennis each month? To find out, you add the surpluses from each of the units you consume. Your consumer surplus from the first hour is $15, that is, the $25 you are willing to pay minus the $10 you actually must pay. The consumer surplus from the second hour is $13. The consumer surplus from using the court for the 8 hours during the

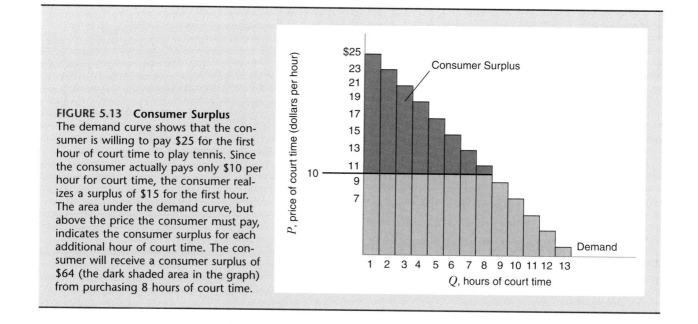

FIGURE 5.13 Consumer Surplus
The demand curve shows that the consumer is willing to pay $25 for the first hour of court time to play tennis. Since the consumer actually pays only $10 per hour for court time, the consumer realizes a surplus of $15 for the first hour. The area under the demand curve, but above the price the consumer must pay, indicates the consumer surplus for each additional hour of court time. The consumer will receive a consumer surplus of $64 (the dark shaded area in the graph) from purchasing 8 hours of court time.

month is then $64 (the sum of the consumer surpluses for each of the 8 hours, or $15 + $13 + $11 + $9 + $7 + $5 + $3 + $1).

As the example illustrates, the consumer surplus is the area below the demand schedule and above the price that the consumer must pay for the good. We represented the demand schedule here as a series of "steps" to help us illustrate the consumer surplus from each unit purchased. Of course, more generally, a demand function may be a smooth curve, often represented as an algebraic equation. The concept of consumer surplus is the same for a smooth demand curve.

As we shall show, the area under a demand curve exactly measures net benefits for a consumer only if the consumer experiences no income effect over the range of price change. This may often be a reasonable assumption. However, if the assumption is not satisfied, then the area under the demand curve will not measure the consumer's net benefits exactly. For the moment, let's not worry about this complication. We assume that there is no income effect.

LEARNING-BY-DOING EXERCISE 5.7

Consumer Surplus

Suppose the following equation represents a consumer's monthly demand schedule for milk: $Q = 40 - 4P$, where Q is the number of gallons of milk purchased when the price is P dollars per gallon. Note that the income effect here is zero because the level of income does not appear in the demand function.

Problem

(a) What is the consumer surplus per month if the price of milk is $3 per gallon?
(b) What is the *increase* in consumer surplus if the price falls to $2 per gallon?

Solution

(a) Figure 5.14 shows the demand curve for milk. When the price is $3, the consumer will buy 28 gallons of milk. The consumer surplus is the area under the demand curve and above the price of $3. Since the demand curve given in the exercise is a straight line, the area representing the consumer surplus is triangle G. The area of G is $(1/2)(10 - 3)(28) = \$98$.
(b) If the price drops from $3 to $2, the consumer will buy 32 gallons of milk. Consumer surplus will *increase* by the areas H and I. The increase will therefore be $28 + $2 = $30. The total consumer surplus will now be $128, that is, the sum of areas G, H, and I.

If we have a demand curve, we can calculate the consumer surplus for any price we might choose. Let's do this using the demand curve for milk in Learning-By-Doing Exercise 5.7. If the price is P, the consumer will buy $(40 - 4P)$ gallons of milk. The consumer surplus will be area F in Figure 5.15. The height of the consumer surplus triangle is $10 - P$, and the base of the triangle (the

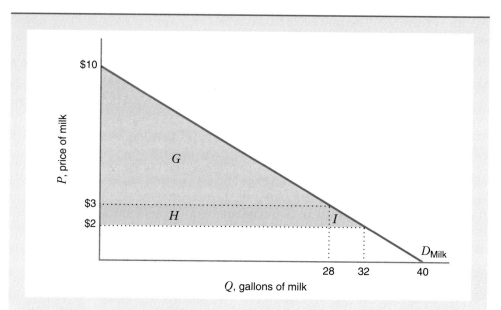

FIGURE 5.14 Consumer Surplus
The consumer surplus when the price is $3 per gallon is the area of triangle *G*. This area is (0.5)(10 − 3)(28) = $98. If the price drops from $3 to $2 per gallon, the *increase* in consumer surplus is the sum of areas *H* ($28) and *I* ($2), or $30. When the price is $2, the total consumer surplus is therefore $128.

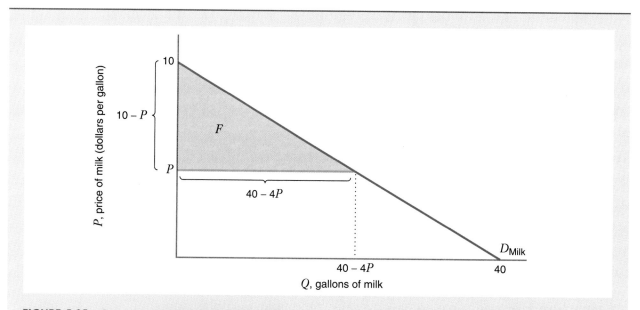

FIGURE 5.15 Consumer Surplus Varies with Price
The consumer surplus when the price per gallon is *P* is the area of triangle *F*. The height of the triangle is (10 − *P*). The base of the triangle is the quantity demanded (40 − 4*P*). The consumer surplus is therefore $S = 0.5(10 - P)(40 - 4P)$, which simplifies to $S = 200 - 40P + 2P^2$.

quantity demanded) is $40 - 4P$. The consumer surplus is therefore $CS(P) = (1/2)(10 - P)(40 - 4P)$, which simplifies to $CS(P) = 200 - 40P + 2P^2$.

We can verify that this formula gives us the consumer surplus when the price of milk is $3 per gallon. Then $CS(3) = 200 - 40(3) + 2(3)^2 = 98$, which is that same answer we calculated in part (a). Similarly, when the price is $2, $CS(2) = 200 - 40(2) + 2(2)^2 = 128$, which is the same value of consumer surplus we determined in (b).

Note, too, that the consumer surplus will be zero if the price is $10 because none of the demand curve lies above that price. Our formula also confirms this because $CS(10) = 200 - 40(10) + 2(10)^2 = 0$.

UNDERSTANDING CONSUMER SURPLUS FROM THE OPTIMAL CHOICE DIAGRAM

We have now learned how to understand consumer surplus as the area under a demand curve and above the price paid. But we also need to see how to measure the net benefits to a consumer using the diagram of optimal choice.

Compensating Variation and Equivalent Variation

How can we estimate the monetary value that a consumer would assign to a change in the price of a good, for example, if the price of a good falls from P_1 to P_2? Here, we study two ways to answer this question. First, one could ask: How much money would the consumer be willing to give up *after* the price reduction to make her just as well off as she was *before* the price change? We call the change in income necessary to restore the consumer to the initial level of utility the **compensating variation.** It is the change (*variation*) in income that would just *compensate* her for the price change.[9]

In an optimal choice diagram, such as Figure 5.16, the compensating variation is the difference between the consumer's income (the amount of income necessary to buy A at the old price or C at the new price) and the amount she would have to spend to purchase the decomposition basket B at the *new* price. Recall that basket B is determined by finding where a line parallel to the *final* budget line is tangent to the *initial* indifference curve.

We could also measure the monetary effect of a price change in a different way. We could ask how much money we would have to give the consumer *before* a price reduction to keep her as well off as she would be *after* the price change. We call the change in income necessary to hold the consumer at the final level of utility as price changes the **equivalent variation.**[10] To see the equivalent variation on the optimal choice diagram, we need to introduce another basket (call it E) on the *final* indifference curve. To determine basket E, we need to find where a line parallel to the *initial* budget line is tangent to the *final* indifference curve. In an optimal consumption diagram, the equivalent variation is the difference between the consumer's income (again, the amount of income necessary to buy A

---

[9]If the price of the good were to *rise* from P_1 to P_2, we would have to answer the following question to find out the size of the compensating variation: How much money (i.e., additional income) would we have to give the consumer *after* the price increase to make her just as well off as she was *before* the price change?

[10]Suppose the price were to increase (instead of decrease). The equivalent variation would tell us how much money the consumer would be willing to give up *before* the price increase to keep her as well off as she would be *after* the price change.

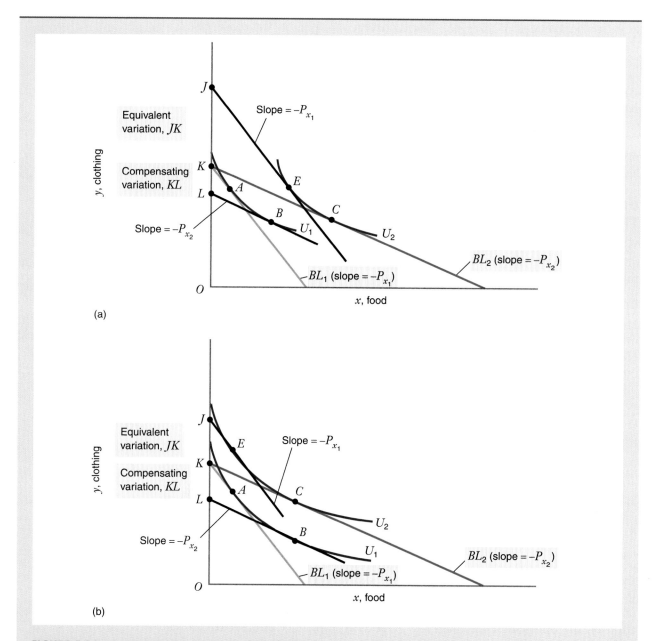

FIGURE 5.16   Compensating and Equivalent Variations
In panel (a), there are positive income effects (C lies to the right of B, and E lies to the
right of A). In this case the equivalent variation (the length of the segment JK) is larger
than the compensating variation (KL). In panel (b), the utility function is quasi-linear.
Therefore, the indifference curves are parallel as y increases, and there is no income effect
(C lies directly above B, and E lies directly above A). The compensating variation (JK) and
equivalent variations (KL) are equal. The price of y is $1 in both graphs.

at the old price or C at the new price) and the expenditure needed to purchase basket E at the *old* price.

In graphical terms, the compensating and equivalent variations are simply two different ways of measuring the *distance* between the initial and final indifference curves [see Figure 5.16(a)]. If the price of clothing (the good the y axis measures) is 1, the compensating variation will be the length of the segment KL. If the price of y is \$1, then the segment OK measures the consumer's income. The segment OL measures the expenditures she would need to buy basket B at the *new* price of food. The difference (the segment KL) is the compensating variation. Because baskets B and A are on the same indifference curve, the consumer would accept a reduction in income of KL if she can buy food at a lower price.

The equivalent variation will be the length of the segment KJ. As before, the segment OK measures the consumer's income. The segment OJ measures the expenditures she would need to buy basket E at the *old* price of food. The difference (the segment KJ) is the equivalent variation. Because baskets E and C are on the same indifference curve, she would require an extra income of KJ if she is asked to buy food at the initial higher price instead of at the lower final price.

In general the sizes of the compensating variation (the segment KL) and the equivalent variation (the segment KJ) will not be the same. That is why one must be careful when trying to measure the monetary value that a consumer associates with a price change.

However, if the utility function is quasi-linear, the equivalent and compensating variations *will* always be the same. For a quasi-linear utility function, the vertical distance between any two indifference curves will be the same, regardless of the amount of food consumed.[11] With a quasi-linear utility function [illustrated in Figure 5.16(b)], there is no income effect on x as the price of x changes. Basket C will always lie directly above (or below) basket B. Basket E will always lie directly above (or below) basket A. The vertical distance between the indifference curves will always be the same, whether measured as the length of the segment AE or the length of the segment BC. The length of BC is the same as the length of KL, the compensating variation. The length of AE is the same as the length of KJ, the equivalent variation. That is why the equivalent and compensating variations will be identical when the utility function is quasi-linear.

We now work through an exercise that illustrates the following important point: If there is *no* income effect, the compensating variation and equivalent variation will give us the *same* measure of the monetary value that a consumer would assign to the reduction in price of the good. Further, the change in the area under the demand curve (i.e., the change in the consumer surplus) as a result of the price change will be the same as the compensating variation and equivalent variation. Therefore, *with no income effect the change in the area under the demand curve exactly measures both the compensating and equivalent variations.*

---

[11]Suppose the utility function $U(x, y)$ is quasi-linear, so that $U(x, y) = f(x) + ky$, where k is some positive constant. Since U always increases by k units whenever y increases by 1 unit, we know that $MU_y = k$. Therefore, the marginal utility of y is constant. For any given level of x, $\Delta U = k\Delta y$. So the vertical distance between indifference curves will be $y_2 - y_1 = (U_2 - U_1)/k$. Note that this vertical distance between indifference curves is the same for all values of x. That is why the indifference curves are *parallel* as we increase y.

LEARNING-BY-DOING EXERCISE 5.8

Compensating and Equivalent Variations with No Income Effect

In Learning-By-Doing Exercise 5.6, a student consumed chocolate and "other goods" with the quasi-linear utility function $U(x, y) = 2\sqrt{x} + y$. She had an income of $10 per day, and the price of the composite good y was $1 per unit.

Problem

(a) What is the compensating variation of the reduction in the price of chocolate?
(b) What is the equivalent variation of the reduction in the price of chocolate?

Solution

(a) Consider the optimal choice diagram in Figure 5.17. The compensating variation answers the following question: How much money would the consumer be willing to give up *after* the price reduction to make her just as well off as she was *before* the price change? The compensating variation is the difference between her income ($10) and what she would have to spend to purchase the decomposition basket B at the *new* price of chocolate of $0.20. How much money would she need to spend to purchase basket B at the new price? The answer is $P_x x + P_y y = (\$0.20)(25) + (\$1)(2) = \$7$. She would be willing to have her income reduced from $10 to $7 (a change of $3) if the price of chocolate falls from $0.50 to $0.20 per ounce.

(b) How can we find the basket E in Figure 5.17? We know two things about the location of basket E. First, E lies on the final indifference curve ($U_2 = 15$). Therefore, we know that $2\sqrt{x} + y = 15$. Second, the tangency condition tells us that at E, the slope of the final indifference curve $-MU_x/MU_y$ must equal the slope of the initial budget line $-P_x/P_y$, or that $(1/\sqrt{x})/1 = 0.5/1$. So the tangency condition tells us that $x = 4$. This means that $y = 11$.

To purchase basket E at the *old* price (with $P_x = \$0.50$), the consumer would need to spend $13 [$P_x x + P_y y = \$0.50(4) + \$1(11) = \$13$]. The equivalent variation is therefore the difference between $13 and her income ($10), or $3. In other words, we would have to give her $3 *before* the price change (when the price of chocolate is $0.50) to make her as well off as she is after the price is reduced to $0.20.

Similar Problem: 5.13

In Learning-By-Doing Exercise 5.8 the compensating and equivalent variations are the same (both $3). We expected to find this because there is no income effect.

Now let's see what happens if we try to measure the change in the consumer surplus by looking at the change in the area under her demand curve for chocolate. In Learning-By-Doing Exercise 5.6, we showed that her daily demand for chocolate is $x = 1/(P_x)^2$. Figure 5.18 shows the demand curve for chocolate. As the price of chocolate falls from $0.50 per ounce to $0.20 per ounce, her daily

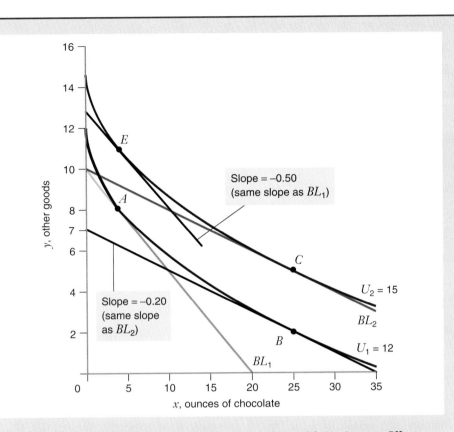

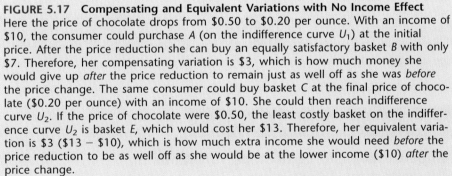

FIGURE 5.17 Compensating and Equivalent Variations with No Income Effect
Here the price of chocolate drops from $0.50 to $0.20 per ounce. With an income of
$10, the consumer could purchase A (on the indifference curve U_1) at the initial
price. After the price reduction she can buy an equally satisfactory basket B with only
$7. Therefore, her compensating variation is $3, which is how much money she
would give up *after* the price reduction to remain just as well off as she was *before*
the price change. The same consumer could buy basket C at the final price of chocolate ($0.20 per ounce) with an income of $10. She could then reach indifference
curve U_2. If the price of chocolate were $0.50, the least costly basket on the indiffer-
ence curve U_2 is basket E, which would cost her $13. Therefore, her equivalent varia-
tion is $3 ($13 − $10), which is how much extra income she would need *before* the
price reduction to be as well off as she would be at the lower income ($10) *after* the
price change.

consumption of chocolate rises from 4 ounces to 25 ounces. The shaded area in
the figure illustrates the increase in consumer surplus as the price of chocolate
falls. The size of that shaded area is $3, exactly the same as both the compensat-
ing and equivalent variations.

This exercise has illustrated that the change in the area under the demand
curve exactly measures the monetary value of a price change when the utility function is quasi-linear (there is no income effect).

As we have already noted, if there *is* an income effect, the compensating variation and equivalent variation will give us the *different* measures of the monetary
value that a consumer would assign to the reduction in price of the good. These

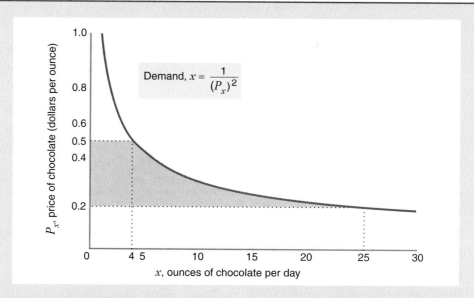

FIGURE 5.18   Consumer Surplus
When the price of chocolate falls from $0.50 per ounce to $0.20 per ounce, the consumer increases consumption from 4 ounces to 25 ounces per day. Her consumer surplus increases by the shaded area, that is, by $3 per day.

measures will generally be different from the change in the area under the demand curve. If the income effect is small, the equivalent and compensating variations may be close to one another, and then the area under the demand curve will be a good approximation (although not an exact measure) of the compensating and equivalent variations.

LEARNING-BY-DOING EXERCISE 5.9

Compensating and Equivalent Variations with an Income Effect

In Learning-By-Doing Exercise 5.4, the consumer had the utility function $U(x, y) = xy$. She had an income of $72 per day, and the price of clothing (measured by y) was $1 per unit. Suppose the price of food falls from $9 to $4 per unit.

Problem

(a) What is the compensating variation of the reduction in the price of food?
(b) What is the equivalent variation of the reduction in the price of food?

Solution

(a) Consider the optimal choice diagram in Figure 5.19. The compensating variation answers the following question: How much money would the consumer be willing to give up *after* the price reduction to make her just as well off as she was *before* the price change? The compensating variation is the difference between her income ($72) and what she would have to spend to purchase the decomposition basket B at the *new* price of food of $4. How much money would she need to spend to purchase basket B at the new price? The answer is $P_x x + P_y y = \$4(6) + \$1(24) = \$48$. The consumer would be willing to have her income reduced from $72 to $48 (a change of $24) if the price of food falls from $9 to $4. Therefore, the compensating variation associated with the price reduction is $24.

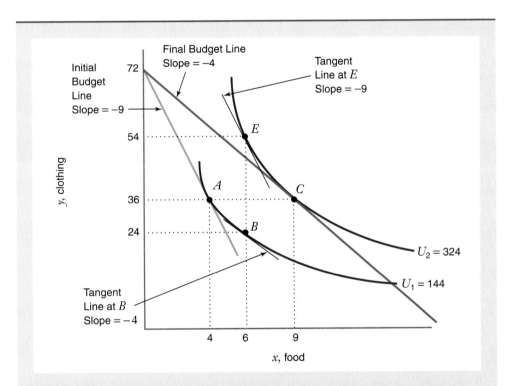

FIGURE 5.19   Compensating and Equivalent Variation with an Income Effect
In this example, the price of food drops from $9 to $4. With an income of $72, the consumer could purchase A (on the indifference curve U_1) at the initial price ($9 per unit). After the price reduction, she can buy an equally satisfactory basket B with only $48. Therefore, her compensating variation is $24, the amount of money she would give up *after* the price reduction to make her just as well off as she was *before* the price change. The same consumer could buy basket C at the final price of food ($4 per unit) with an income of $72. She could then reach indifference curve U_2. If the price of food were $9, the least costly basket on the indifference curve U_2 is basket E, which would cost her $108. Therefore, her equivalent variation is $36 ($108 − $72), the amount of money we would have to give her *before* the price reduction to keep her as well off as she would be *after* the price change.

(b) Now we need to determine the equivalent variation. How can we find the basket E in Figure 5.19? We know two things. First, basket E lies on the final indifference curve. Therefore, we know that $U = xy = 324$. Second, the tangency condition tells us that at E, the slope of the indifference curve $-MU_x/MU_y$ must equal the slope of the initial budget line $-P_x/P_y$, or that $y/x = 9/1$. The tangency condition thus tells us that $y = 9x$. So we have two equations with two unknowns: (1) $xy = 324$, and (2) $y = 9x$. These two conditions tell us that $x = 6$ and $y = 54$.

How much would the consumer need to spend to purchase basket E at the *old* price (with $P_x = 9$)? The answer is $P_x x + P_y y = \$9(6) + \$1(54) = \$108$. So she would have needed an expenditure of $108 to buy basket E at the initial price. The equivalent variation is therefore the difference between $108 and her income ($72), or $36. The equivalent variation tells us that we would have to give her $36 *before* the price change (when the price of chocolate is $9) to make her as well off as she is after the price is reduced to $4.

Now let's see what happens if we measure consumer surplus using the area under the demand curve for chocolate. In Learning-By-Doing Exercise 5.4, we showed that her demand for chocolate is $x = I/(2P_x)$. Figure 5.20 shows her demand curve when her income is $72. As the price of chocolate falls from $9 to $4 per unit, her consumption rises from 4 units to 9 units. If we use the shaded area in Figure 5.20 to measure the increase in consumer surplus, we would conclude that her consumer surplus increases by $29.20. Note that the size of the shaded area ($29.20) is different from both the compensating variation ($24) and the equivalent variation ($36).

This exercise illustrates that the change in the area under the demand curve will *not* measure exactly either the compensating variation or the equivalent variation when the income effect is not zero. Generally speaking, the compensating variation and equivalent variation will become closer to each other (and to the area under the demand curve) when the income effect is small.

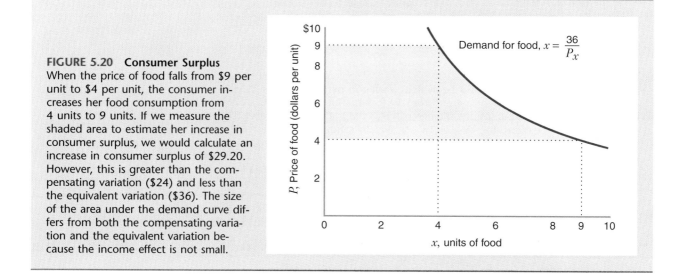

FIGURE 5.20   Consumer Surplus
When the price of food falls from $9 per unit to $4 per unit, the consumer increases her food consumption from 4 units to 9 units. If we measure the shaded area to estimate her increase in consumer surplus, we would calculate an increase in consumer surplus of $29.20. However, this is greater than the compensating variation ($24) and less than the equivalent variation ($36). The size of the area under the demand curve differs from both the compensating variation and the equivalent variation because the income effect is not small.

Demand for food, $x = \dfrac{36}{P_x}$

Businesses often have information about the demands for their products in different market "segments." For example, a seller of computer software may know that there are academic users of software and business customers. If the seller wants to know the market demand curve for its software, it can add up the demands for the two segments to find the market demand. Similarly, a rental car agency may be aware that there are two types of customers in its market, business travelers and vacation travelers. If the agency knows the demand curves for the two segments, it can add their demands to determine the market demand for rental cars.

Where do *market* demand curves come from? We illustrate an important principle in this section: The market demand curve is the horizontal sum of the demands of the individual consumers. This principal holds whether two consumers, three consumers, or a million consumers are in the market.

Let's work through an example how to derive a market demand from individual consumer demands. To keep it simple, suppose only two consumers are in the market for orange juice. The first is "health conscious" and likes orange juice because of its nutritional value and its taste. The second column of Table 5.3 tells us how many liters of orange juice he would buy each month at the prices listed in the first column. The second user (a "casual consumer" of orange juice) also likes its taste, but is less concerned about its nutritional value. The third column of Table 5.3 tell us how many liters of orange juice she would buy each month at the prices listed in the first column.

To find the total amount consumed in the market at any price, we simply add the quantities that each consumer would purchase at that price. For example, if the market price is $5 per liter, neither consumer will buy orange juice. If the price is between $3 and $5, only the health-conscious consumer will buy it. Thus, if the price in the market is $4 per liter, he will buy 3 liters, and the market demand will also be 3 liters. If the price in the market is $3 per liter, the market demand will be 6 liters.

Finally, if the market price is below $3, both consumers will purchase orange juice. If the price is $2 per liter, the market demand will be 11 liters. At a price of $1 the market demand will be 16 liters.

In Figure 5.21 we show both the demand curve for each consumer and the market demand. The thick line is the market demand curve for orange juice.

TABLE 5.3
Market Demand for Orange Juice

Price ($/liter)	Health Conscious (Liters/Month)	Casual (Liters/Month)	Market Demand (Liters/Month)
5	0	0	0
4	3	0	3
3	6	0	6
2	9	2	11
1	12	4	16

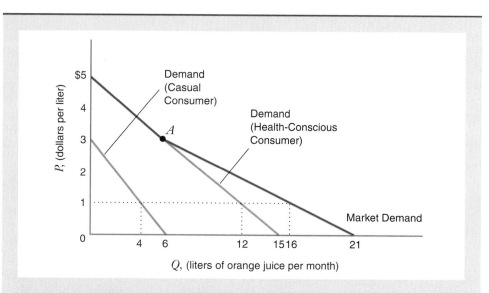

FIGURE 5.21   Market and Segment Demand Curves
In this example, only two consumers of orange juice are in the market, a casual consumer and a health-conscious consumer. The market demand curve (the dark curve) is found by adding the demand curves for the individual consumers horizontally. For example, if the price is $1 per liter, the casual consumer will buy 4 liters per month and the health conscious buyer will purchase 12 liters; the total monthly demand for orange juice will be 16 liters.

Finally, we can describe the three demand curves algebraically. Let Q_b be the quantity demanded by the health-conscious consumer, Q_c be the quantity demanded by the casual consumer, and Q_m be the quantity demanded in the whole market (which contains only the two consumers in this exercise). See if you can write down the three demand functions $Q_b(P)$, $Q_c(P)$, and $Q_m(P)$.

As you can see in Figure 5.21, the demand curve for the health-conscious consumer is a straight line; he buys orange juice only when the price is below $5 per liter. You can verify that the equation of the demand curve for this segment is

$$Q_b(P) = \begin{cases} 15 - 3P, & \text{when } P \le 5 \\ 0, & \text{when } P > 5 \end{cases}$$

The demand curve for the casual consumer is also a straight line; she buys orange juice only when the price is below $3 per liter. The equation of the demand curve for this segment is

$$Q_c(P) = \begin{cases} 6 - 2P, & \text{when } P \le 3 \\ 0, & \text{when } P > 3 \end{cases}$$

As the graph shows, the market demand curve is *kinked* at point A, with connecting straight lines. When the price is higher than $5, neither consumer buys orange juice. When the price is between $3 and $5, only the health-conscious consumer buys it. Therefore, over this range of prices, the market demand curve is the same as the demand curve for the health-conscious consumer. Finally, when the price is below $3, both consumers buy orange juice. So the market demand $Q_m(P)$ is just the sum of the segment demands $Q_h(P) + Q_c(P) = (15 - 3P) + (6 - 2P) = 21 - 5P$. Therefore, the market demand $Q_m(P)$ is

$$Q_m(P) = \begin{cases} 21 - 5P, & \text{when} & P \leq 3 \\ 15 - 3P, & \text{when} & 3 \leq P \leq 5 \\ 0, & \text{when} & P > 5 \end{cases}$$

You can verify that the descriptions of the demand curves in the table, in the graph, and with algebra are all consistent with one another.

The exercise demonstrates that you must be careful when you add segment demands to get a market demand curve. First, since the construction of a market demand curve involves adding *quantities*, you must write the demand curves in the normal form (with Q expressed as a function of P) before adding them, rather than using the inverse form of the demand (with P written as a function of Q).

Second, you must pay attention to the range of prices for which the underlying segment demands are positive when you add the segment demands algebraically. If you simply added the equations for the segment demands to get the market demand $Q_m = Q_h(P) + Q_c(P) = 21 - 5P$, this expression would *not* be valid for a price above $3. For example, if the price is $4, the expression $Q_m = 21 - 5P$ would tell you that the quantity demanded in the market would be 1 liter. Yet this is incorrect, because according to Table 5.3, the correct quantity demanded in the market at that price is 3 liters. See if you can figure out why this approach leads to an error. (If you give up, look at the footnote.)[12]

Thus far we have been assuming that one person's demand for a good is independent of everyone else's demand. For example, the amount of chocolate a consumer wants to purchase depends on that consumer's income, the price of chocolate, and possibly other prices, but not on anyone else's demand for chocolate. This assumption enables us to find the market demand curve for a good by adding up the demand curves of all of the consumers in the market.

Yet, for some goods, a consumer's demand does depend on how many other people purchase the good. In that case, there are **network externalities.** If one consumer's demand for a good increases with the number of other consumers who buy the good, the externality is *positive.* If the amount a consumer demands

---

[12]The error arises because we derived the market demand equation $Q_m = 21 - 5P$ by adding $Q_h(P) = 15 - 3P$ and $Q_c(P) = 6 - 2P$. According to these segment demand equations, when $P = 4$, $Q_h(P) = 3$ and $Q_c(P) = -2$. Sure enough, the sum is 1. But you are assuming that the casual consumer demands a negative quantity of orange juice (-2 liters) when the price is $4, and this is economic nonsense! The expression for the demand of the casual consumer $Q_c(P) = 6 - 2P$ is not valid at a price of $4. At this price, $Q_c(P) = 0$, not -2.

increases when fewer other consumers have the good, the externality is *negative*. Many goods or services have network externalities.

Although we can often find network externalities in physical networks (as in Example 5.4), we may also see them in other settings (sometimes called *virtual* networks because there is no physical connection among consumers). For example, a piece of computer software (such as Microsoft Word) has some value to prepare written documents even if that software had only one user. However, the product becomes more valuable to any one user when it has many other users. A virtual network of users makes it possible to exchange and process documents with the software.

A virtual network may also be present if a good or service requires two complementary components to have value. For example, a computer operating system, such as Microsoft Windows 2000, only has value if software applications exist that can run on the operating system. The operating system is more valuable when many applications can be used with the operating system. A software application also has a higher value if it runs on a widely accepted operating system.

Finally, positive network externalities can occur if a good or service is a fad. We often see fads for goods and services that affect lifestyles, such as fashions of clothing, children's toys, or beer. Advertisers and marketers often try to highlight the popularity of a product as part of its image.

EXAMPLE 5.4   *Network Externalities in Physical Networks*

We can easily understand why products like telephones or fax machines have positive network externalities. A telephone is useless unless at least one other telephone exists to communicate with. For most people, a telephone becomes more useful as the number of other people with telephones increases.

Imagine a telephone network with only two subscribers. Each person on the network would be able to call only one other person. Thus, it would be possible to make two calls on that network. If we add a third subscriber to the network, each person can call two other people. It will now be possible to make a total of six calls because each of the three subscribers can call the other two subscribers. More generally, in a telephone network with N subscribers, the addition of another subscriber allows for $2N$ additional calls to be made. If consumers value being able to call (and be called by) more people, then the value of telephone service to an individual rises as the number of the subscribers increases.

Many settings beyond telephone and fax networks have positive network externalities. Positive network externalities are perhaps nowhere more pronounced than in the case of the Internet. In the 1990s, the number of sites on the Internet and the number of individuals and firms with access to it grew rapidly. For most people, the value of access to the Internet increases as the number of sites and other people with Internet access grows. These strong positive network externalities have surely helped Internet traffic snowball. Some estimates suggest that the amount of traffic on the Internet in the late 1990s doubled every 120 days. ∎

Figure 5.22 illustrates the effects of a positive network externality. The graph shows a set of market demand curves for connections to the Internet. For this example, let's assume that a connection to the Internet refers to a subscription to a provider of access to the Internet, such as the connections America Online or Microsoft Network provide. The curve D_{30} represents the demand if consumers believe that 30 million subscribers have access to the Internet. The curve D_{60} represents the demand if consumers believe that 60 million subscribers have access. Suppose initially that access costs $20 per month and that there are 30 million subscribers (point A in the graph).

What happens if the monthly price of access drops to $10? If there were *no* positive network externality, the quantity demanded will simply change as we move *along* D_{30}. The quantity of subscriptions will grow to 38 million lines (point B in the graph). However, there *is* a positive network externality; as more people use e-mail and other Internet features, more people will want to sign up. Therefore, at the lower price, the number of consumers wanting access will be even greater than a movement along D_{30} to point B would indicate. The total number of subscriptions actually demanded at a price of $10 per month will grow to 60 million (point C in the graph). The total effect of the price decrease is an increase of 30 million subscribers. The total effect is the pure price effect of 8 million new subscribers (moving from point A to point B) plus a *bandwagon effect* of 22 million new subscribers (moving from point B to point C). A **bandwagon effect** refers to the increased quantity demanded as more consumers are connected

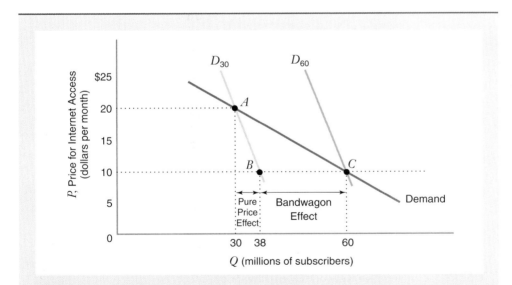

FIGURE 5.22 Positive Network Externality: Bandwagon Effect
The bandwagon effect is a positive network externality that refers to the increase in the quantity of a good demanded as more consumers buy it. What happens to the demand for access to the Internet if the monthly charge for access falls from $20 to $10? Without network externalities, the quantity demanded would increase from 30 to 38 million subscribers because of the pure price effect. But this increase in subscribers leads even more people to want access because they can reach more people with services such as e-mail. The positive network externality (a bandwagon effect) adds another 22 million subscribers to the Internet.

to the Internet. Thus, a demand curve observed with positive network externalities (such as the heavy demand curve in Figure 5.22) is more elastic than a demand curve with no network externalities (such as D_{30}).

For some goods, the quantity demanded may *decrease* when more people have the good. Then there is a *negative* network externality. Rare items, such as Stradivarius violins, Babe Ruth baseball cards, and expensive automobiles are examples of such goods. These goods enjoy a **snob effect.** The snob effect is a negative network externality that refers to the decrease in the quantity of a good that is demanded as more consumers buy it. A snob effect may arise because consumers value being one of the few to own a particular type of good. We might also see the snob effect if the value of a good or service diminishes because congestion increases when more people purchase that good or service.

Figure 5.23 shows the effects of a snob effect. The graph illustrates a set of market demand curves for memberships to a health and fitness club. The curve D_{1000} represents the demand if consumers believe the club has 1,000 members. Similarly, the curve D_{1300} shows the demand if consumers believe it has 1,300 members. Suppose initially a membership costs \$1,200 per year, and that the club has 1,000 members (point A in the graph).

What happens if the membership price decreases to \$900? If consumers believe that the number of members will stay at 1,000, 1,800 would actually want

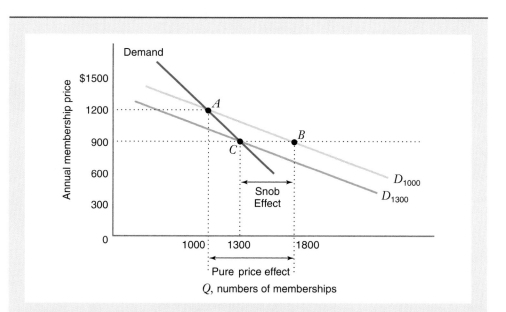

FIGURE 5.23   Negative Network Externality: Snob Effect
The snob effect is a negative network externality that refers to the decrease in the quantity of a good demanded as more consumers buy it. What happens to the demand for memberships in a fitness club if the annual membership charge falls from \$1,200 to \$900? Without network externalities, the pure price effect would increase the membership by 800 (from 1,000 to 1,800). But this increase in membership would cause congestion in the club, discouraging some people from joining. The negative externality (a snob effect) leads to a reduction of 500 members (from 1,800 to 1,300). The net effect of the price reduction is therefore an increase of 300 members.

to join the club (point B in the graph). However, the fitness club will become more congested as more members join, and would shift the demand curve inward. The total number of memberships actually demanded at a price of $900 per month will grow only to 1,300 (point C in the graph). The total effect of the price decrease is an increase of 300 members. The total effect is the pure price effect of 800 new members (moving from point A to point B) plus a *snob effect* of −500 members (moving from point B to point C). A demand curve observed with negative network externalities (such as the demand curve connecting points A and C in Figure 5.23) is less elastic than a demand curve without network externalities (such as D_{1000}).

5.6 THE CHOICE OF LABOR AND LEISURE

As we have already seen, the model of optimal consumer choice has many everyday applications. Let's examine a consumer's choice of how much to work.

Let's divide the day into two parts, the hours when an individual works and the hours when he pursues leisure. Why does the consumer work at all? Because he works, he earns an income, and he uses the income to pay for the activities he enjoys in his leisure time. The term *leisure* includes all nonwork activities, such as eating, sleeping, recreation, and entertainment. We assume that the consumer likes leisure activities.

Let's suppose the consumer chooses to work L hours per day. Since a day has 24 hours, the time available for leisure will be the time that remains after work, that is, $24 - L$ hours.

The consumer is paid an hourly wage rate w. Thus, his total daily income will be wL. He uses the income to purchase units of a composite good measured by y. The price of each unit of the composite good is $1.

The consumer's utility U depends on the amount of leisure time and the number of units of the composite good he can buy. We can represent the consumer's decision on the optimal choice diagram in Figure 5.24. On the horizontal axis, we plot the number of hours of leisure each day, which must be no greater than 24 hours. On the vertical axis we represent the number of units of the composite good that he may purchase from his income. Since the price of the composite good is $1, the vertical axis also measures the consumer's income.

To find an optimal choice of leisure and other goods, we need a set of indifference curves and a budget constraint. The figure shows a set indifference curves for which the marginal utility of leisure and the composite good are both positive. Thus $U_5 > U_4 > U_3 > U_2 > U_1$. The indifference curves are bowed in toward the origin, so there is also a diminishing marginal rate of substitution.

The consumer's budget line for this problem will tell us all the combinations of the composite good y and hours of leisure $(24 - L)$ that the consumer can choose. If the consumer does no work, he will have 24 hours of leisure, but no income to spend on the composite good. This corresponds to point A on the budget line in the graph.

The location of the rest of the budget line depends on the wage rate w. Suppose the wage rate is $5 per hour. This means that for every unit of leisure the consumer gives up to work, he can buy 5 units of the composite good. The budget

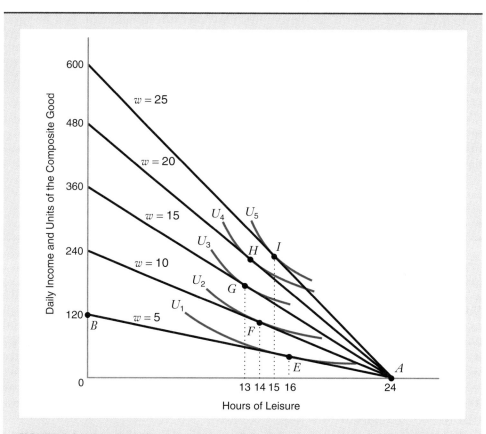

FIGURE 5.24   Optimal Choice of Labor and Leisure
The graph shows a series of budget lines and optimal baskets for different wages rates. When the wage rate is $5 per hour, the consumer chooses 16 hours of leisure (and therefore 8 hours of work). As the wage rate rises to $15, the amount of leisure decreases to 13 hours, and the consumer works more (11 hours). But when the wage rate rises above $15, he chooses more leisure (and less labor). For example, if the wage rate rises from $15 to $25, the consumer increases leisure time from 13 to 15 hours per day, and decreases work time from 11 hours to 9 hours.

line will have a slope of −5. If the consumer works 24 hours per day, his income would be $120 and could buy 120 units of the composite good. This is B on the budget line. The consumer's optimal choice will then be at basket E. The diagram tells us that when the wage rate is $5, the consumer will work 8 hours.

For any wage rate, the slope of the budget line is $-w$. In the figure, budget lines are drawn for five different values of the wage rate ($5, $10, $15, $20, and $25). The graph shows the optimal choice for each wage rate. As the wage rate rises from $5 to $15, the number of hours of leisure falls. However, as the wage rate continues to rise, the consumer begins to increase his choice of leisure time.

THE BACKWARD-BENDING SUPPLY OF LABOR

Since a day has only 24 hours, the consumer's choice about the amount of leisure time is also a choice about the amount of labor he will supply. The optimal choice diagram in Figure 5.24 contains enough information to enable us to construct a curve showing how much labor the consumer will supply at any wage rate. In other words, we can draw the consumer's supply of labor curve. Figure 5.25 shows this curve.

The points E', F', G', H', and I' in Figure 5.25 correspond, respectively, to points E, F, G, H, and I in Figure 5.24. For example, when the wage rate is $5, the consumer will work 8 hours. The supply of labor rises for wage rates up to $15. When the wage rate reaches $15, the consumer works 11 hours.

However, look what happens when wage rates exceed $15. While we normally think that a higher price (remember, the wage rate is the price of labor) stimulates supply for most goods and services, here a higher wage rate *decreases* the quantity of labor the consumer supplies. The supply of labor curve is *backward bending* for wage rates above $15. For example, if the wage rate rises from $15 to $25, the consumer decreases work time from 11 hours to 9 hours.

Why might there be a backward bending region on the supply of labor curve? To understand this, think about the income and substitution effects associated with a change in the wage rate.

Look at the optimal choice diagram in Figure 5.24. Instead of having a fixed income, our consumer has a fixed amount of time in the day, 24 hours. That is why the horizontal intercept of the budget line stays at 24 hours, regardless of the wage rate. An hour of work always "costs" the consumer an hour of leisure, no matter what the wage rate is.

However, an increase in the wage rate makes a unit of the composite good look less expensive to the consumer. If the wage rate doubles, the consumer needs to work only half as long to buy as much of the composite good as before. That

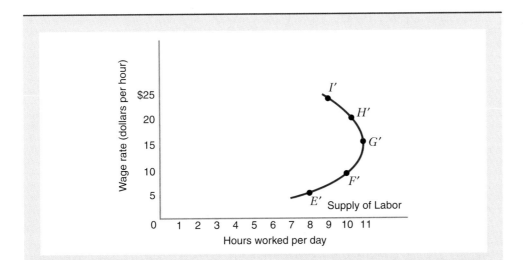

FIGURE 5.25 Backward-Bending Supply of Labor
We can use the optimal choice diagram in Figure 5.24 to show how many hours of labor the consumer will supply at any wage rate. The points E', F', G', H', and I' correspond, respectively, to points E, F, G, H, and I in Figure 5.24. The supply of labor curve is backward bending for wage rates above $15. For example, if the wage rate rises from $15 to $25, the consumer decreases work time from 11 hours to 9 hours.

is why the vertical intercept of the budget line moves up as the wage rate rises. The increase in the wage rate therefore leads to an upward rotation of the budget line, as Figure 5.24 shows.

Two kinds of effects are associated with a wage increase. First, the amount of work required to buy a unit of the composite good falls. This effect alone would induce the consumer to substitute more of the composite good for leisure. The substitution effect leads to less leisure, and therefore more labor.

Second, the consumer feels as though he has more income, again because it takes less work to buy a unit of the composite good. So an income effect will be associated with the wage increase. Since leisure is a normal good for most people, the income effect on the amount of leisure will be positive. This means that the income effect on the amount of *labor* will be negative.

Now let's examine the income and substitution effects of a wage increase from $15 to $25. In Figure 5.26, we have drawn the initial budget line (with the wage

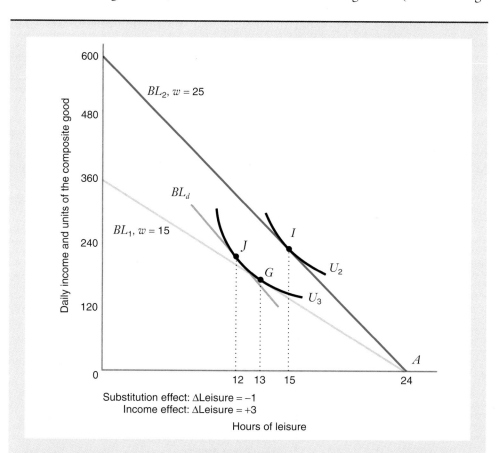

FIGURE 5.26   Optimal Choice of Labor and Leisure
This figure helps us understand why the supply of labor curve in Figure 5.25 is backward bending for wage rates above $15. Suppose the wage rate rises from $15 to $25. The substitution effect reduces the amount of leisure (and increases the amount of work) by 1 hour. But the income effect increases the amount of leisure (and decreases the amount of work) by 3 hours. Thus, although the substitution effect would induce the consumer to work more at higher wages, he will actually work less because the income effect outweighs the substitution effect.

rate of \$15) and shown the optimal consumption of leisure (13 hours) at point G. The number of hours worked is therefore 11 hours.

Next we draw the final budget line (with the wage rate of \$25). The optimal consumption of leisure is 15 hours at point I. Therefore, the consumer works 9 hours.

Finally, we draw the decomposition budget line BL_d. This line will be tangent to the initial indifference curve (U_3) and parallel to the final budget line. At the decomposition basket (point J), the number of hours of leisure is 12 hours, and the number of hours worked is therefore also 12 hours.

The substitution effect on leisure is thus -1 hour (the change in leisure as we move from G to J). The income effect on leisure is $+3$ hours (the change in leisure as we move from J to I). Since the income effect outweighs the substitution effect, the net effect of the change in the wage rate on the amount of leisure is $+2$ hours. Put another way, the net effect of the increase in the wage rate on the amount of *labor* is -2 hours.

The Supply of Nursing Services

EXAMPLE 5.5

Medical groups and hospitals have long had difficulty attracting enough workers. They have often increased pay to stimulate the supply of medical workers. Yet raising wage rates may not always increase the amount of labor supplied.

In 1991 the *The Wall Street Journal* described some of these difficulties in an article titled "Medical Groups Use Pay Boosts, Other Means to Find More Workers." According to the article, the American Hospital Association concluded, "Pay rises may have worsened the nursing shortage in Massachusetts by enabling nurses to work fewer hours."[13]

Why might this have happened? We can use Figure 5.26, which we have already seen, to depict an optimal choice diagram for an individual nurse who is deciding how much to work. A higher wage may induce a consumer to pursue more leisure, and thus fewer hours worked. In other words, many nurses may be on the backward-bending region of their supply curve for labor.

Since wage increases alone do not always attract more workers, employers have resorted to other strategies. For example, the article in *The Wall Street Journal* states that the M.D. Anderson Cancer Center at the University of Texas gave employees a \$500 bonus if they referred new applicants who took "hard-to-fill" jobs. The Texas Heart Institute in Houston recruited nurses partly by showcasing prospects for promotion. The University of Pittsburgh Medical Center started an "adopt-a-high-school" program to encourage students to enter the health care sector, and reimbursed employees' tuition fees when they enrolled in programs to increase their skills. ∎

[13] *The Wall Street Journal* (August 27, 1991), page 1.

In sum, we will see the backward-bending region of the labor supply curve when the income effect associated with a wage increase outweighs the substitution effect. We will observe the upward-sloping region of the labor supply curve when the substitution effect outweighs the income effect.

5.7
CONSUMER PRICE INDICES

The Consumer Price Index (CPI) is one of the most important sources of information about trends in consumer prices and inflation in the United States. It is often viewed as a measure of the change in the cost of living and is used extensively for economic analysis in both the private and public sectors. For example, in contracts among individuals and firms, the prices at which goods are exchanged are often adjusted over time to reflect changes in the CPI. In negotiations between labor unions and employers, adjustments in wage rates often reflect past or expected future changes in the CPI.

The CPI also has an important impact on the budget of the federal government. On the expenditure side, the government uses the CPI to adjust payments to Social Security recipients, to retired government workers, and for many entitlement programs such as food stamps and school lunches. As the CPI rises, the government's payments increase. And changes in the CPI also affect how much money the government collects through taxes. For example, individual income tax brackets are adjusted for inflation using the CPI. As the CPI increases, tax revenues decrease.

Measuring the CPI is not easy. Let's construct a simple example to see what factors might be desirable in designing a CPI. Suppose we have only one consumer, who buys only two goods, food and clothing. In the year 1, a unit of food costs $P_{F_1} = \$3$ and a unit of clothing costs $P_{C_1} = \$8$. The consumer had an income of $480 and faced the budget line BL_1. He purchased basket A, containing 80 units of food and 30 units of clothing. Figure 5.27 depicts the optimal basket A, located on indifference curve U_1.

Now suppose that in year 2 the prices of food and clothing increase to $P_{F_2} = \$6$ and $P_{C_2} = \$9$. How much income will the consumer need in year 2 to be as well off as in year 1, that is, to reach the indifference curve U_1? The new budget line he requires (BL_2) will be tangent to U_1 and have a slope reflecting the new prices, $-P_{F_2}/P_{C_2} = -2/3$. At the new prices, the least costly combination of food and clothing on the indifference curve is at basket B, with 60 units of food and 40 units of clothing. The total expenditure necessary to buy basket B at the new prices is $P_{F_2}F + P_{C_2}C = (\$6)(60) + (\$9)(40) = \$720$.

In principle, the CPI should measure the percentage increase in expenditures that would be necessary for the consumer to remain as well off in year 2 as he was in year 1. In the example, the expenditures increased from $480 in year 1 to $720 in year 2. The "ideal" CPI would be the ratio of the new expenses to the old expenses, that is $720/$480 = 1.5. In other words, at the higher prices, it would take 50 percent more expenditure in year 2 to make the consumer as well off as he was in year 1. In this sense the "cost of living" in year 2 is 50 percent greater than it was in year 1. In calculating this ideal CPI, we would need to recognize that the consumer would substitute more clothing for food when

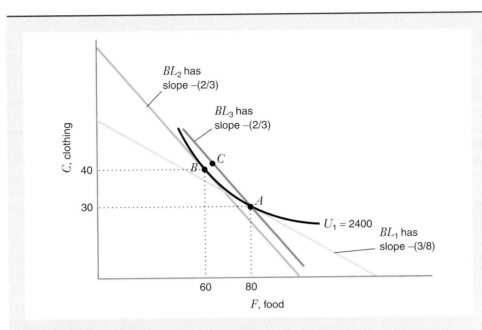

FIGURE 5.27 Substitution Bias in the Consumer Price Index
In year 1 the consumer has an income of $480, the price of food is $3, and the price of clothing is $8. The consumer chooses basket A. In year 2 the price of food rises to $6, and the price of clothing rises to $9. The consumer could maintain his initial level of utility at the new prices by purchasing basket B, costing $720. An ideal cost of living index would be 1.5 (= $720/$480), telling us that the cost of living has increased by 50 percent. By contrast, the CPI assumes the consumer does not substitute clothing for food as relative prices change. If the consumer continues to buy basket A at the new prices, he would need an income of $750. The CPI ($750/$480 = 1.56) suggests that the consumer's cost of living has increased by about 56 percent, which overstates the actual increase in the cost of living.

the price of food rises relative to the price of clothing, moving from the initial basket A to basket B.

Note that to determine the ideal CPI, the government would need to collect data on the old prices and the new prices *and* on changes in the composition of the basket (how much food and clothing are consumed). But, considering the huge number of goods and services in the economy, this is an enormous amount of data to collect! It is hard enough to collect data on the way so many prices change over time, and even more difficult to collect information on the changes in the baskets that consumers actually purchase.

In practice, to simplify the measurement of the CPI, the government has historically calculated the change in expenditures necessary to buy a *fixed* basket as prices change, where the fixed basket is the amount of food and clothing purchased in year 1. In our example, the fixed basket is A. The income necessary to buy basket A at the new prices is $P_{F_2}F + P_{C_2}C = (\$6)(80) + (\$9)(30) = \$750$. If he were given $750 with the new prices, he would face the budget line BL_3. If we were to calculate a CPI using the fixed basket A, the ratio of the new expenses to the old expenses is $750/$480 = 1.5625$. This index tells us that the consumer's expenditures would need to increase by 56.25 percent to buy the fixed basket (that is, the basket purchased in year 1) at the new prices.[14]

As the example shows, the index based on the fixed basket overcompensates the consumer for the higher prices. Economists refer to the overstatement of the increase in the cost of living as the "substitution bias." By assuming that the consumer's basket is fixed at the initial levels of consumption, the index ignores the possible substitution that consumers will make toward goods that are relatively less expensive in a later year. In fact, if the consumer were given an income of $750 instead of $720 in year 2, he could choose a basket such as C on BL_3 and make himself better off than he was at A.

EXAMPLE 5.6   *The Substitution Bias in the Consumer Price Index*

While economists have long argued that the Consumer Price Index overstates changes in the cost of living, the bias in the CPI took center stage in the 1990s when Congress tried to balance the budget. In 1995 Alan Greenspan, the Chairman of the Federal Reserve, brought this controversy to the fore when he told Congress that the official CPI may be overstating the increase in the true cost of living by perhaps 0.5 to 1.5 percent. The Senate Finance Committee appointed a panel to study the magnitude of the bias. The panel concluded that the CPI overstates the cost of living by about 1.1 percent.

While estimates of the impact of the substitution bias are necessarily imprecise, they are potentially very important. Greenspan estimated that if the annual level of inflation adjustments to indexed programs and taxes were reduced by 1 percentage point, the annual level of the deficit would be lowered by as much as $55 billion after five years. The Office of Management and Budget estimated that in fiscal year 1996, a 1 percent increase in the index led to an increase in government expenditures of about $5.7 billion, as well as a decrease in tax revenues of about $2.5 billion.

The government has long been aware of the need to periodically update the "fixed basket" used in the CPI calculation. In fact, the basket has been revised approximately every ten years.[15] At the dawn of the new millennium the government continues to investigate ways to improve how it calculates the Consumer Price Index. ∎

---

[14]An index that measures the expenditure necessary to buy the fixed basket at the prices in year 2 divided by the expenditure necessary to purchase the same basket at the prices in year 1 is called a Laspeyers index. Let's see how to calculate this index with the example in the text. Denote the prices of food in years 1 and 2 as P_{F_1} and P_{F_2}, and the prices of clothing in years 1 and 2 P_{C_1} and P_{C_2}. The fixed basket is the quantity of food and clothing consumed in year 1; F and C denote these quantities. Then the Laspeyers index L is

$$L = \frac{P_{F_2}F + P_{C_2}C}{P_{F_1}F + P_{C_1}C}$$

[15]See, for example, John S. Greenless and Charles C. Mason, "Overview of the 1998 Revision of the Consumer Price Index," *Monthly Labor Review*, December 1996, pages 3–9, and Moulton, Brent R. "Bias in the Consumer Price Index: What is the Evidence?" *Journal of Economic Perspectives*, Fall 1996.

CHAPTER SUMMARY

• We can derive an individual's demand curve for a good from her preferences and the budget constraint. A consumer's demand curve shows how the optimal choice of a commodity changes as the price of the good varies. We can also think of a demand curve as a schedule of the consumer's "willingness to pay" for a good. **(LBD Exercises 5.2, 5.3)**

• A good is normal if the consumer purchases *more* of that good as income rises. A good is inferior if he purchases *less* of that good as income increases. **(LBD Exercise 5.1)**

• We can separate the effect of a price change on the quantity of a good into two parts, a substitution effect and an income effect. The substitution effect is the change in the amount of a good that would be consumed as the price of that good changes, holding constant the level of utility. When the indifference curves are bowed in toward the origin (because of diminishing marginal rate of substitution), the substitution effect will move in the *opposite* direction from the price change. If the price of the good decreases, its substitution effect will be positive. If the price of the good increases, its substitution effect will be negative. **(LBD Exercises 5.4, 5.5, 5.6)**

• The income effect for a good is the change in the amount of that good that a consumer would buy as her purchasing power changes, holding price constant. If the good is normal, the income effect will reinforce (move in the same direction) as the substitution effect. If the good is inferior, the income effect will move in the direction opposite from the substitution effect.

• If the good is so strongly inferior that the income effect outweighs the substitution effect, the demand curve would have an upward slope over some range of prices. Such a good is called a Giffen good. Although the Giffen good is of theoretical interest, it is not of much practical importance.

• Consumer surplus is the difference between what a consumer is willing to pay for a good and what he must pay for it. Without income effects, consumer surplus provides a monetary measure of how much better off

the consumer will be when he purchases a good. On a graph the consumer surplus will be the area under an ordinary demand curve and above the price of the good. Changes in consumer surplus can also measure how much better off or worse off a consumer is if the price changes. **(LBD Exercise 5.7)**

• The compensating variation measures how much money the consumer would be willing to give up *after* a reduction in the price of a good to make her just as well of as she was *before* the price change.

• The equivalent variation measures how much money we would have to give the consumer *before* a price reduction to keep her as well off as she would be *after* the price change.

• If there is an income effect, the compensating variation and equivalent variation will differ, and these measures will also be different from the area under the ordinary demand curve. **(LBD Exercise 5.9)**

• If the income effect is small, the equivalent and compensating variations may be close to one another, and the area under an ordinary demand curve will be a good approximation (although not an exact measure) of consumer surplus. **(LBD Exercise 5.8)**

• Without an income effect, the compensating variation and equivalent variation will give us the same measure of the monetary value that a consumer would assign to a change in the price of the good. The change in the area under an ordinary demand curve will be the same as the compensating variation and equivalent variation. **(LBD Exercise 5.8)**

• The market demand curve for a good is the horizontal sum of the demands of all of the individual consumers in the market (assuming there are no network externalities).

• The bandwagon effect is a positive network externality. With a bandwagon effect, the quantity of a good that is demanded increases as more consumers buy it. The snob effect is a negative network externality. With a snob effect the quantity of a good that is demanded decreases as more consumers buy it.

REVIEW QUESTIONS

1. What is a price consumption curve for a good?

2. How does a price consumption curve differ from an income consumption curve?

3. What can you say about the income elasticity of demand of a normal good? Of an inferior good?

4. If indifference curves are bowed in toward the origin and the price of a good drops, can the substitution effect ever lead to less consumption of the good?

5. Suppose a consumer purchases only three goods, food, clothing and shelter. Could all three goods be normal? Could all three goods be inferior? Explain.

6. Does economic theory require that a demand curve always be downward sloping? If not, under what circumstances might the demand curve have an upward slope over some region of prices?

7. What is consumer surplus?

8. Two different ways of measuring the monetary value that a consumer would assign to the change in price of the good are (1) the compensating variation and (2) the equivalent variation. What is the difference between the two measures, and when would these measures be equal?

9. Consider the following four statements. Which might be an example of a positive network externality? Which might be an example of a negative network externality?
(i) People eat hot dogs because they like the taste, and hot dogs are filling.
(ii) As soon as Zack discovered that everybody else was eating hot dogs, he stopped buying them.
(iii) Sally wouldn't think of buying hot dogs until she realized that all her friends were eating them.
(iv) When personal income grew by 10 percent, hot dog sales fell.

10. Why might an individual supply less labor (demand more leisure) as the wage rate rises?

PROBLEMS

5.1. Figure 5.2(a) shows a consumer's optimal choices of food and clothing for three values of weekly income: $I_1 = \$40$, $I_2 = \$68$, and $I_3 = \$92$. Figure 5.2(b) illustrates how the consumer's demand curves for *food* shift as income changes. Draw three demand curves for *clothing* (one for each level of income) to illustrate how changes in income affect the consumer's purchases of clothing.

5.2. Use the income consumption curve in Figure 5.2(a) to draw the Engel curve for clothing, assuming the price of food is $2 and the price of clothing is $4.

5.3. Show that the following statements are true:
a) An inferior good has a negative income elasticity of demand.
b) A good whose income elasticity of demand is negative will be an inferior good.

5.4. If the demand for a product is perfectly price inelastic, what does the corresponding price consumption curve look like? Draw a graph to show the price consumption curve.

5.5. Suzie purchases two goods, food and clothing. She has the utility function $U(x, y) = xy$, where x denotes the amount of food consumed and y the amount of clothing. The marginal utilities for this utility function are $MU_x = y$ and $MU_y = x$.
a) Show that the equation for her demand curve for clothing is $y = I/(2P_y)$.
b) Is clothing a normal good? Draw her demand curve for clothing when the level of income is $I = 200$. Label this demand curve D_1. Draw the demand curve when $I = 300$ and label this demand curve D_2.
c) What can be said about the cross-price elasticity of demand of food with respect to the price of clothing?

5.6. Rick purchases two goods, food and clothing. He has a diminishing marginal rate of substitution of food for clothing. Let x denote the amount of food consumed, and y the amount of clothing. Suppose the price of food *increases* from P_{x_1} to P_{x_2}. On a clearly labeled graph, illustrate the income and substitution effects of the price change on the consumption of food. Do so for each of the following cases:

a) Case 1: Food is a normal good.
b) Case 2: The income elasticity of demand for food is zero.
c) Case 3: Food is an inferior good, but not a Giffen good.
d) Case 4: Food is a Giffen good.

5.7. Some texts define a "luxury good" as a good for which the income elasticity of demand is greater than 1. Suppose that a consumer purchases only two goods. Can both goods be luxury goods? Explain.

5.8. Scott consumes only two goods, steak and ale. When the price of steak falls, he buys more steak and more ale. On an optimal choice diagram (with budget lines and indifference curves), illustrate this pattern of consumption.

5.9. Dave consumes only two goods, coffee and doughnuts. When the price of coffee falls, he buys the same amount of coffee and more doughnuts.
a) On an optimal choice diagram (with budget lines and indifference curves), illustrate this pattern of consumption.
b) Is this purchasing behavior consistent with a quasilinear utility function? Explain.

5.10. Suppose that a consumer's utility function is $U(x, y) = xy + 10y$. The marginal utilities for this utility function are $MU_x = y$ and $MU_y = x + 10$. The price of x is P_x and the price of y is P_y, with both prices positive. The consumer has income I. (This problem shows that an optimal consumption choice need not be interior, and may be at a corner point.)
a) Assume first that we are at an interior optimum. Show that the demand schedule for x can be written as $x = I/(2P_x) - 5$.
b) Suppose now that $I = 100$. Since x must never be negative, what is the maximum value of P_x for which this consumer would ever purchase any x?
c) Suppose $P_y = 20$ and $P_x = 20$. On a graph illustrating the optimal consumption bundle of x and y, show that since P_x exceeds the value you calculated in part (b), this corresponds to a corner point at which the consumer purchases only y. (In fact, the consumer would purchase $y = I/P_y = 5$ units of y and no units of x.)
d) Compare the marginal rate of substitution of x for y with the ratio (P_x/P_y) at the optimum in part (c). Does this verify that the consumer would reduce utility if she purchased a positive amount of x?
e) Assuming income remains at 100, draw the demand schedule for x for all values of P_x. Does its location depend on the value of P_y?

5.11. Suppose rental cars have two market segments, business travelers and vacation travelers. The demand curve for rental cars by business travelers is $Q_b = 35 - 0.25P$, where Q_b is the quantity demanded by business travelers (in thousands of cars) when the rental price is P dollars per day. No business customers will rent cars if the price exceeds $140 per day.

The demand curve for rental cars by vacation is $Q_v = 120 - 1.5P$, where Q_v is the quantity demanded by vacation travelers (in thousands of cars) when the rental price is P dollars per day. No vacation customers will rent cars if the price exceeds $80 per day.
a) Fill in the table to find the quantities demanded in the market at each price in the table.

Price ($/day)	Business (000 cars/ day)	Vacation (000 cars/ day)	Market Demand (000 cars/ day)
100			
90			
80			
70			
60			
50			

b) Graph the demand curves for each segment, and draw the market demand curve for rental cars.
c) Describe the market demand curve algebraically. In other words, show how the quantity demanded in the market Q_m depends on P. Make sure that your algebraic equation for the market demand is consistent with your answers to parts (a) and (b).
d) If the price of a rental car is $60, what is the consumer surplus in each market segment?

5.12. One million consumers like to rent movie videos in Pulmonia. Each has an identical demand curve for movies. The price of a rental is P. At a given price, will the market demand be more elastic or less elastic than the demand curve for any individual. (Assume there are no network externalities.)

5.13. Joe's income consumption curve for tea is a vertical line on an optimal choice diagram, with tea on the horizontal axis and other goods on the vertical axis.
a) Show that Joe's demand curve for tea must be downward sloping.
b) When the price of tea drops from $9 to $8 per pound, the change in Joe's consumer surplus (i.e., the change in

the area under the demand curve) is $30 per month. Would you expect the compensating variation and the equivalent variation resulting from the price decrease to be near $30? Explain.

5.14. Consider the optimal choice of labor and leisure discussed in the text. Suppose the consumer can work the first 8 hours of the day at a wage rate of $10 per hour, but receives an overtime wage rate of $20 for additional time worked.

a) On an optimal choice diagram, draw the budget constraint. [*Hint:* It is not a straight line.]

b) Draw a set of indifference curves that would make it optimal for him to work four hours of overtime each day.

6

Inputs and Production Functions

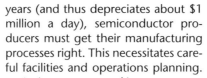

The production of semiconductor chips—thin, glass-like wafers that are used to store information in digital equipment—is costly, complex, and delicate.[1] Production involves hundreds of steps and takes place in facilities called fabs, expensive factories that can cost $1 billion to $2 billion to construct. To avoid contaminating chips, fabs must be 1000 times cleaner than a hospital operating room. Because the manufacturing process is so expensive and because a typical fab is obsolete in three to five years (and thus depreciates about $1 million a day), semiconductor producers must get their manufacturing processes right. This necessitates careful facilities and operations planning.

An important trend in recent years in semiconductor manufacturing has been the substitution of robots for humans to perform certain repetitive processing tasks. Despite protective clothing, footwear, and headgear used by workers, robots are cleaner than human workers and thus offer the prospect of higher chip yields (the fraction of good chips per total chips produced). This is vital because an invisible speck of dust can ruin a $20,000 wafer of chips.

Since robots are not cheap, semiconductor manufacturers face an important tradeoff: Are the cost savings from better chip yields and less labor worth the investments in state-of-the-art robotics? Some chip manufacturers have decided that they are, others that they are not.

This chapter lays the foundations for studying this type of economic tradeoff. It covers factors of production, or inputs, and explains the production process using a concept known as the production function. We use the production function to characterize the productivity of inputs and to describe how production volume or output depends on the mix of inputs the firm employs. ■

[1]This example draws from John Teresko, "Robot Renaissance," *Industry Week* (September 16, 1996), pp. 38–41.

Production of goods and services involves transforming resources—such as labor power, raw materials, and the services provided by facilities and machines—into finished products. Semiconductor producers, for example, combine the labor services provided by their employees and the capital services provided by fabs, robots, and processing equipment with raw materials, such as silicon, to produce finished chips. The productive resources, such as labor and capital equipment, that firms use to manufacture goods and services are called **inputs** or **factors of production,** and the amount of goods and services produced is the firm's **output.**

As our semiconductor example suggests, real firms can often choose one of several combinations of inputs to produce a given volume of output. A semiconductor firm can produce a given number of chips using workers and no robots or using fewer workers and many robots. The **production function** is a mathematical representation of the various technological recipes from which a firm can choose to configure its production process. In particular, the production function tells us the *maximum* quantity of output the firm can produce given the quantities of the inputs that it might employ. We will write the production function this way:

$$Q = f(L, K) \qquad (6.1)$$

where Q is the quantity of output, L is the amount of labor used, and K is the quantity of capital employed. This expression tells us that the maximum quantity of output the firm can get depends on the quantities of labor and capital it employs. We could have listed more categories of inputs, but many of the important tradeoffs that real firms face involve choices between labor and capital (e.g., robots and workers for semiconductor firms). Moreover, we can develop the main ideas of production theory using just these two categories of inputs.

The production function in equation (6.1) is analogous to the utility function in consumer theory. Just as the utility function depends on exogenous consumer tastes, the production function depends on exogenous technological conditions. Over time, these technological conditions may change, an occurrence known as technological progress, and the production function may then shift. We discuss technological progress in Section 6. Until then, we will view the firm's production function as fixed and unchangeable.

The production function in equation (6.1) tells us the *maximum* volume of output a firm could get from a given combination of labor and capital. Of course, inefficient management could reduce output from what is technologically possible. Figure 6.1 depicts this possibility by showing the production function for a single input, labor; $Q = f(L)$. Points on or below the production function make up the firm's **production set,** the set of technically *feasible* combinations of inputs and outputs. Points, such as A and B, in the production set are **technically inefficient** (i.e., at these points the firm gets less output from its labor than it should). Points, such as C and D, on the boundary of the production set are **technically efficient.** At these points, the firm produces as much output as it possibly can given the amount of labor it employs.

If we invert the production function, we get a function $L = g(Q)$, which tells us the *minimum* amount of labor that is required to produce a given amount of output Q. This function is the **labor requirements function.** If, for example, $Q = \sqrt{L}$ is the production function, then $L = Q^2$ is the labor requirements function. Thus, to produce a flow of output of 7 units, a firm will need a flow of at least $7^2 = 49$ units of labor.

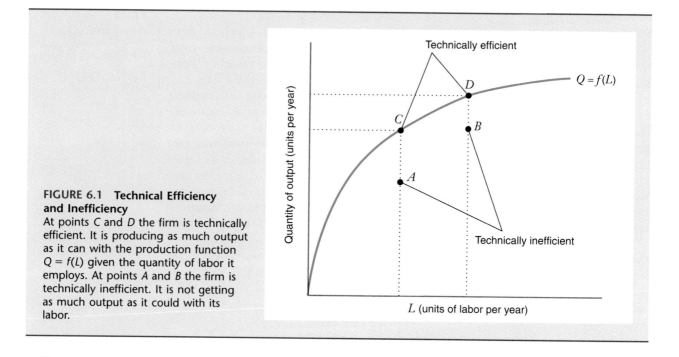

FIGURE 6.1   Technical Efficiency and Inefficiency
At points C and D the firm is technically efficient. It is producing as much output as it can with the production function $Q = f(L)$ given the quantity of labor it employs. At points A and B the firm is technically inefficient. It is not getting as much output as it could with its labor.

EXAMPLE 6.1

Technical Inefficiency Among U.S. Manufacturers

Using data from the U.S. Census of Manufacturing (a government survey that takes place every five years to track manufacturing activity in the United States), Richard Caves and David Barton studied the extent of technical inefficiency among U.S. manufacturers.[2] For the typical manufacturer in Caves and Barton's study, the ratio of actual output to the maximum output that would be attainable given the firm's labor and capital employment was 63 percent. (If we express this result in the notation in the text, we would say that $Q/f(L, K) = 0.63$ for the typical firm.) This finding implies that the typical U.S. manufacturer was technically inefficient.

According to Caves and Barton, an important determinant of technical efficiency is the extent to which a firm faces competition from other firms. Caves and Barton found that manufacturing firms in industries that did not face much competition from foreign imports tended to be more technically inefficient than firms in industries that were subject to significant import competition. They also found that firms in industries with high levels of concentration (sales concentrated in relatively few firms) tended to be more technically inefficient than firms in industries containing a large number of smaller competitors. These findings suggest that the pressure of competition—whether from imports or other firms in the industry—tends to induce firms to search for ways to get as much output as they can from their existing combinations of inputs, thus moving them closer to the boundaries of their production sets. ∎

[2]Richard Caves and David Barton, *Efficiency in U.S. Manufacturing Industries* (Cambridge, MA: MIT Press, 1990).

Because the production function tells us the maximum attainable volume from a given combination of inputs, we will sometimes write $Q \leq f(L, K)$ to emphasize that the firm could, in theory, produce a quantity of output that is less than the maximum level attainable given the quantities of inputs it employs.

The business press is full of discussions of productivity, which broadly refers to the amount of output a firm can get from the resources it employs. We can use the production function to illustrate a number of important ways in which the productivity of inputs can be characterized. To illustrate these concepts most clearly, we will start our study of production functions with the simple case in which the quantity of output depends on a single input, labor.

6.2
PRODUCTION FUNCTIONS WITH A SINGLE INPUT

TOTAL PRODUCT FUNCTIONS

Single-input production functions are sometimes called **total product functions.** Table 6.1 shows a total product function for a semiconductor producer. It shows the quantity of semiconductors Q the firm can produce in a year when it employs various quantities L of labor within a fab of a given size with a given set of machines.

Figure 6.2 shows a graph of the total product function in Table 6.1. This graph has four noteworthy properties. First, when $L = 0$, $Q = 0$. That is, no semiconductors can be produced without using some labor. Second, between $L = 0$ and $L = 12$, output rises with additional labor at an increasing rate, i.e., the total product function is convex. Over this range, we have **increasing marginal returns to labor.** When there are increasing marginal returns to labor, an increase in the quantity of labor increases total output at an increasing rate. Increasing marginal returns are usually thought to occur because of the gains from specialization of labor. In a plant with a small work force, workers may have to

TABLE 6.1
Total Product Function

L	Q
0	0
6	30
12	96
18	162
24	192
30	150

(L is expressed in thousands of man-hours per day, and Q is expressed in thousands of semiconductor chips per day)

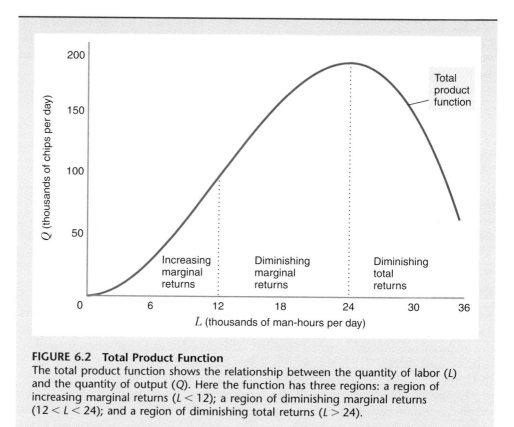

FIGURE 6.2   Total Product Function
The total product function shows the relationship between the quantity of labor (L)
and the quantity of output (Q). Here the function has three regions: a region of
increasing marginal returns (L < 12); a region of diminishing marginal returns
(12 < L < 24); and a region of diminishing total returns (L > 24).

perform multiple tasks. For example, a worker might be responsible for moving raw materials within the plant, operating the machines, and inspecting the finished goods once they are produced. As additional workers are added, workers can specialize—some will be responsible only for moving raw materials in the plant; others will be responsible only for operating the machines, while still others would specialize in inspection and quality control. Specialization enhances the marginal productivity of workers because it allows them to concentrate on tasks for which they are most productive.

Third, between $L = 12$ and $L = 24$, output rises with additional labor but at a decreasing rate (i.e., the total product function is concave). Over this range we have **diminishing marginal returns to labor.** When there are diminishing marginal returns to labor, an increase in the quantity of labor increases total output at a decreasing rate. Diminishing marginal returns set in when the firm exhausts its ability to increase labor productivity through the specialization of workers.

Finally, when the quantity of labor exceeds $L = 24$, an increase in the quantity of labor results in a decrease in total output. In this region, we have **diminishing total returns to labor.** When there are diminishing total returns to labor, an increase in the quantity of labor decreases total output. Diminishing total returns occur because of the fixed size of the fabricating plant: if the quantity of labor used becomes too large, workers don't have enough space to work effectively. Also, as the number of workers employed in the plant grows, their efforts become increasingly difficult to coordinate.[3]

MARGINAL AND AVERAGE PRODUCT

We are now ready to characterize the productivity of the firm's labor input. There are two related, but distinct, notions of productivity that we can derive from the production function. The first is the **average product of labor,** which we write as AP_L. The average product of labor is the average amount of output per unit of labor.[4] This is usually what commentators mean when they write about, say, the productivity of U.S. workers as compared to their foreign counterparts. Mathematically, the average product of labor is equal to

$$AP_L = \frac{\text{total product}}{\text{quantity of labor}} = \frac{Q}{L}.$$

Table 6.2 shows the average product of labor for the total product function in Table 6.1, and Figure 6.3 shows average product graphically. It shows that the average product varies with the amount of labor the firm uses. In our example, it increases for quantities of labor less than $L = 18$ and falls thereafter.

Figure 6.4 shows the graphs of the total product and average product curves simultaneously. The average product of labor at any arbitrary quantity L_0 corresponds to the slope of a ray drawn from the origin to the point along the total product function corresponding to L_0. For example, the height of the total product function at point A is Q_0, and the amount of labor is L_0. The slope of the line segment connecting the origin to point A is Q_0/L_0. But this is just the average product. At $L = 18$, the slope of a ray from the origin attains its maximal value, which is why AP_L reaches its peak at this quantity of labor.

TABLE 6.2
Average Product of Labor in Table Form

L	Q	$AP_L = \dfrac{Q}{L}$
6	30	5
12	96	8
18	162	9
24	192	8
30	150	5

[3]We could also have diminishing total returns to other inputs, such as materials. For example, adding fertilizer to an unfertilized field will increase crop yields. But too much fertilizer will burn out the crop, and output will be zero.

[4]The average product of labor is also sometimes called the average physical product of labor and is written APP_L.

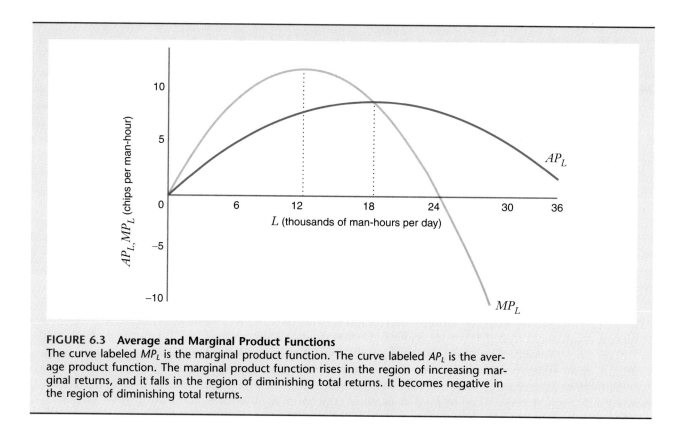

FIGURE 6.3 Average and Marginal Product Functions
The curve labeled MP_L is the marginal product function. The curve labeled AP_L is the average product function. The marginal product function rises in the region of increasing marginal returns, and it falls in the region of diminishing total returns. It becomes negative in the region of diminishing total returns.

The other concept of productivity is the **marginal product of labor,** which we write as MP_L. The marginal product of labor is the rate at which total output changes as the firm changes its quantity of labor:

$$MP_L = \frac{\textit{change in total product}}{\textit{change in quantity of labor}} = \frac{\Delta Q}{\Delta L}$$

The marginal product of labor is analogous to the concept of marginal utility from consumer theory, and just as we could represent that curve graphically, we can also represent the marginal product curve graphically. Figure 6.3 shows the marginal product curve. Marginal product, like average product, is not a single number but varies with the quantity of labor. In the region of increasing marginal returns, $0 \leq L < 12$, the marginal product function is increasing. When diminishing marginal returns set in, $L > 12$, the marginal product function is decreasing. When diminishing total returns set in, $L > 24$, the marginal product function cuts through the horizontal axis and becomes negative. As shown in the upper panel in Figure 6.4, the marginal product corresponding to any particular amount of labor L_1 is the slope of the line that is tangent to the total product function at L_1 (line BC in the figure). Since the slopes of these tangent lines vary as we move along the production function, the marginal product of labor must also change.

LAW OF DIMINISHING MARGINAL RETURNS

Economists believe that in most real-world production processes the marginal product of an input eventually declines when the quantities of all other inputs are

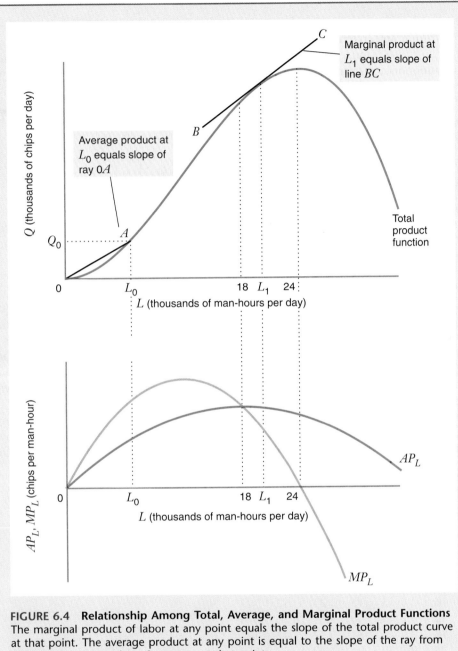

FIGURE 6.4 Relationship Among Total, Average, and Marginal Product Functions
The marginal product of labor at any point equals the slope of the total product curve at that point. The average product at any point is equal to the slope of the ray from the origin to the total product curve at that point.

held constant. Indeed, this phenomenon seems so pervasive that economists call it **the law of diminishing marginal returns.** This says that as the use of one input (e.g., labor) increases and the quantities of other inputs (such as capital or land) are held fixed, a point will be reached beyond which the marginal product of that input will decrease. This law is derived from the actual experience of real-world firms and seems true in most circumstances.

6.3
PRODUCTION FUNCTIONS WITH MORE THAN ONE INPUT

The single-input production function is useful for developing key concepts, such as marginal and average product, and building intuition about the relationships between these concepts. However, to study the tradeoffs facing real firms, such as semiconductor companies thinking about substituting robots for humans, we need to study multiple-input production functions. In this section, we will see how to describe a multiple-input production function graphically, and we will explore how to characterize the ease with which a firm can substitute among the inputs within its production function.

TOTAL PRODUCT AND MARGINAL PRODUCT WITH TWO INPUTS

To illustrate a production function with more than one input, let's consider a situation in which the production of output requires two inputs: labor and capital. This might broadly illustrate the technological possibilities facing a semiconductor manufacturer contemplating the use of robots (capital) or humans (labor).

Table 6.3 shows a production function (or, equivalently, the total product function) for semiconductors, where the quantity of output Q depends on the quantity of labor, L, and the quantity of capital, K, employed by the semiconductor firm. Figure 6.5 shows this production function as a three-dimensional graph. The graph in Figure 6.5 is a **total product hill.** A total product hill is a three-dimensional graph that shows the relationship between the quantity of output and the quantity of the two inputs employed by the firm.[5]

The height of the hill at any point is equal to the amount of output the firm gets from the quantities of inputs it employs. We could move along the hill in various directions, but it is easiest to imagine moving in one of two directions. Starting from the lower left corner of the graph at which $L = 0$ and $K = 0$, we could move eastward by increasing the quantity of labor, or we could move north-

TABLE 6.3
Production Function for Semiconductors

		\(K\) 0	6	12	18	24	30
	0	0	0	0	0	0	0
	6	0	5	15	25	30	23
L	**12**	0	15	48	81	96	75
	18	0	25	81	137	162	127
	24	0	30	96	162	192	150
	30	0	23	75	127	150	117

L is expressed in thousands of man-hours per day; *K* is expressed in thousands of machine-hours per day, and *Q* is expressed in thousands of semiconductor chips per day.

[5]In Figure 6.5, we show the "skeleton" or frame of the total product hill, so that we can draw various lines underneath it. Figure 6.6 shows the same total product hill as a solid surface.

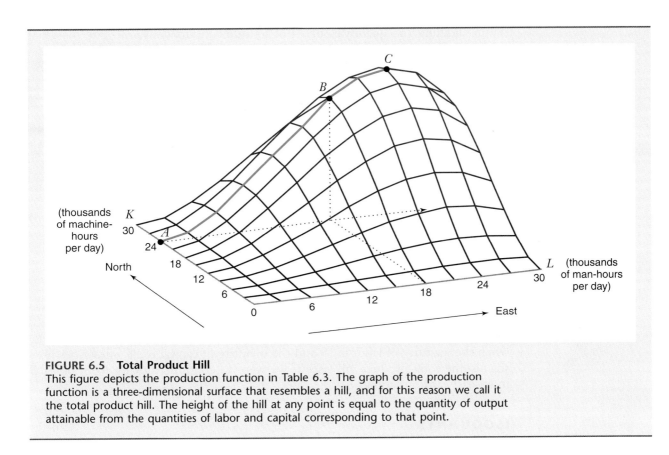

FIGURE 6.5 Total Product Hill
This figure depicts the production function in Table 6.3. The graph of the production function is a three-dimensional surface that resembles a hill, and for this reason we call it the total product hill. The height of the hill at any point is equal to the quantity of output attainable from the quantities of labor and capital corresponding to that point.

ward by increasing the quantity of capital. As we move either eastward or northward, we move to different elevations along the total product hill, where each elevation corresponds to the particular quantity of output.

Let's now see what happens when we fix the quantity of capital at a particular level, say $K = 24$, and increase the quantity of labor. Table 6.3 shows that when we do this, we initially increase the quantity of output, but output eventually begins to decrease. In fact, notice that the quantities in the column of Table 6.3 corresponding to $K = 24$ are identical to the total product function in Table 6.1. This shows that total product function for labor can be derived from a two-input production function by holding the quantity of capital fixed at a particular level and varying the quantity of labor.

We can make the same point with Figure 6.5. Let's fix the quantity of capital at $K = 24$ and move eastward up the total product hill by changing the quantity of labor. As we do so, we trace out the path ABC, with point C being at the peak of the hill. This path looks like the graph of the total product function in Figure 6.2. Or, put differently, if we move eastward up the total product hill and chart our elevation at various quantities of labor, the resulting chart would correspond exactly to Figure 6.2, just as the $K = 24$ column in Table 6.3 corresponds exactly to Table 6.1.

Just as the concept of total product extends directly to the multiple input case, so too does the concept of marginal product. The marginal product of an input is the rate at which output changes as the firm changes its use of *one* of its inputs, holding the quantities of all of its other inputs constant. The marginal product of labor is given by

$$MP_L = \frac{change \text{ in quantity of output}}{change \text{ in quantity of labor}}\bigg|_{K \text{ is held constant}} \quad \text{(6.2)}$$

$$= \frac{\Delta Q}{\Delta L}\bigg|_{K \text{ is held constant}}$$

Similarly, the marginal product of capital is given by

$$MP_K = \frac{change \text{ in quantity of output}}{change \text{ in quantity of capital}}\bigg|_{L \text{ is held constant}} \quad \text{(6.3)}$$

$$= \frac{\Delta Q}{\Delta K}\bigg|_{L \text{ is held constant}}$$

The marginal product tells us how steeply the total product hill rises as we change the quantity of an input, holding the quantities of all other inputs fixed. For example, in Figure 6.5, the marginal product of labor at point B—that is, when the quantity of labor is 18 and the quantity of capital is 24—describes how steeply the total product hill rises if we were to continue moving from point B in an eastward direction.

ISOQUANTS

To illustrate economic tradeoffs, it helps to reduce the three-dimensional production function to a two-dimensional graph. Therefore, just as we used a contour plot of indifference curves to represent utility functions in consumer theory, we can also use a contour plot to represent the production function. However, instead of calling the contour lines indifference curves, we are going to call them **isoquants.** *Isoquant* means "same quantity," because any combination of labor and capital along a given isoquant allows the firm to produce the same quantity of output.

To illustrate, let's once again consider the production function described in Table 6.3 (reproduced here for convenience). From this table we see that two different combinations of labor and capital—($L = 6$, $K = 18$), ($L = 18$, $K = 6$)—result in an output of $Q = 25$ units (where each "unit" of output represents a thousand semiconductors). Thus, each of these input combinations is on the $Q = 25$ isoquant.

We can also illustrate an isoquant with Figure 6.6. Figure 6.6 once again shows the total product hill for the production function in Table 6.3. Suppose that you started walking along the total product hill from point A with the goal of maintaining a constant elevation. Line segment $ABCDE$ is the path you should follow. At each input combination along this path, the height of the total product hill is the same, and thus each of these input combinations produces the same quantity of output, $Q = 25$. All of these input combinations are on the $Q = 25$ isoquant.

When we think about an isoquant as a path along the total product hill in Figure 6.6 that holds our elevation constant, we see that an isoquant is like a line on a topographical map such as the one of Mt. Hood in Oregon in Figure 6.7.

TABLE 6.3
Production Function for Semiconductors

				K		
		0	**6**	**12**	**18**	**24**	**30**
	0	0	0	0	0	0	0
	6	0	5	15	25	30	23
L	**12**	0	15	48	81	96	75
	18	0	25	81	137	162	127
	24	0	30	96	162	192	150
	30	0	23	75	127	150	117

L is expressed in thousands of man-hours per day; K is expressed in thousands of machine-hours per day, and Q is expressed in thousands of semiconductor chips per day.

A line on the topographical map shows points in geographic space at which the elevation of the land is constant. The total product hill in Figure 6.6 is analogous to the three-dimensional map of Mt. Hood in the upper part of Figure 6.7, and the isoquants of the total product hill are analogous to the topographical map of Mt. Hood in the lower part of Figure 6.7.

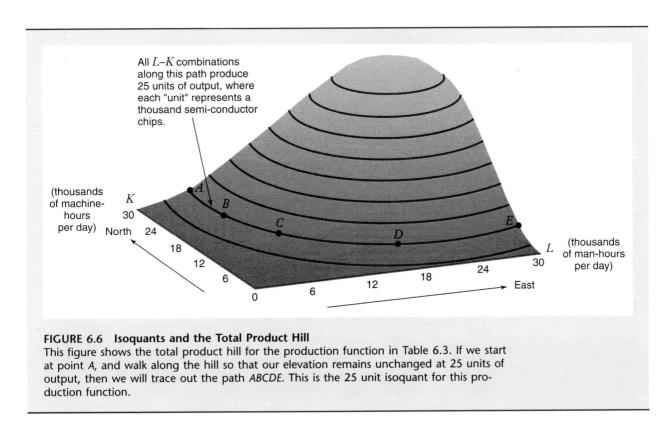

FIGURE 6.6 Isoquants and the Total Product Hill
This figure shows the total product hill for the production function in Table 6.3. If we start at point *A*, and walk along the hill so that our elevation remains unchanged at 25 units of output, then we will trace out the path *ABCDE*. This is the 25 unit isoquant for this production function.

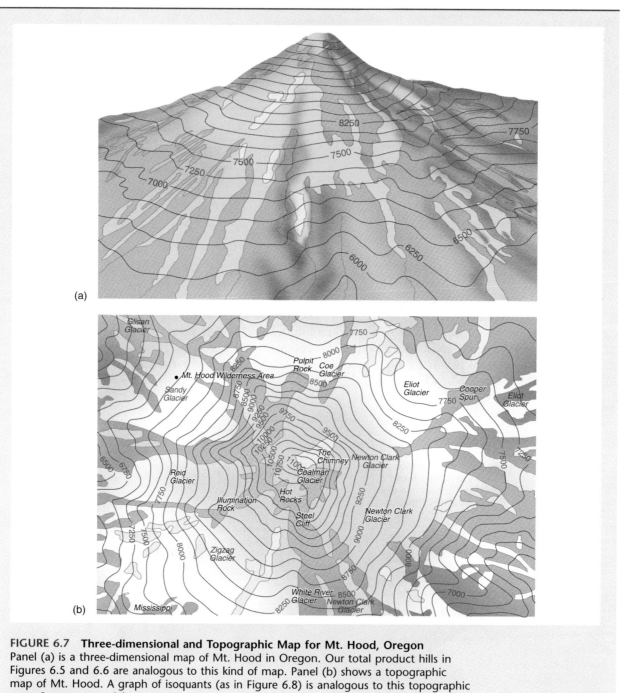

FIGURE 6.7 **Three-dimensional and Topographic Map for Mt. Hood, Oregon**
Panel (a) is a three-dimensional map of Mt. Hood in Oregon. Our total product hills in
Figures 6.5 and 6.6 are analogous to this kind of map. Panel (b) shows a topographic
map of Mt. Hood. A graph of isoquants (as in Figure 6.8) is analogous to this topographic
map. Source: www.delorme.com.

Figure 6.8 shows isoquants for the production function in Table 6.3 and Figure 6.6. The isoquants are downward sloping. A downward-sloping isoquant
illustrates an important economic tradeoff: A firm can substitute capital for labor
and keep its output unchanged. If we apply this idea to a semiconductor firm, it
would tell us that the firm could produce a given quantity of semiconductors

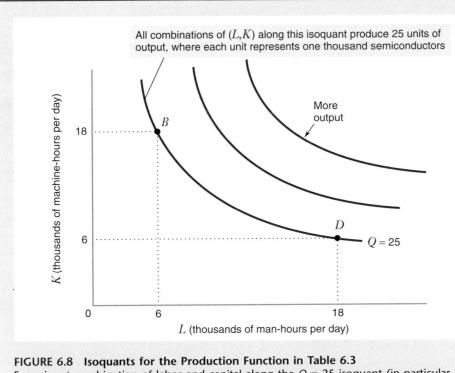

All combinations of (L,K) along this isoquant produce 25 units of output, where each unit represents one thousand semiconductors

FIGURE 6.8 Isoquants for the Production Function in Table 6.3
Every input combination of labor and capital along the $Q = 25$ isoquant (in particular, combinations B and D) produces the same output, 25,000 semiconductor chips per day. As we move to the northeast, the isoquants correspond to higher and higher outputs.

using, say, lots of workers but a small number of robots, or it could produce that same quantity using fewer workers but more robots. Such substitution is always possible whenever both labor and capital (e.g., robots) have positive marginal products.

Any production function has an infinite number of isoquants, each one corresponding to a particular level of output. In Figure 6.8, we have labeled the isoquant corresponding to 25 units of output. The other (unlabeled) isoquants correspond to different levels of output. Notice that points B and D along the $Q = 25$ isoquant in Figure 6.8 correspond to the input combinations in Table 6.3 that we have highlighted. When both inputs have positive marginal products, using more of each input increases the amount of output attainable. Hence, as we move to the northeast in Figure 6.8, we reach isoquants corresponding to larger and larger quantities of output.

LEARNING-BY-DOING EXERCISE 6.1

Deriving the Equation of an Isoquant

Problem

(a) Consider the production function whose equation is given by the formula $Q = K^{1/2} L^{1/2}$. What is the equation of the isoquant corresponding to $Q = 20$?

(b) For the same production function, what is the equation of the isoquant corresponding to an arbitrary level of output Q?

Solution

(a) The $Q = 20$ isoquant shows all of the combinations of labor and capital that allow the firm to produce 20 units of output. Given our production function, the combinations of labor and capital on this isoquant satisfy the following equation:

$$20 = K^{\frac{1}{2}}L^{\frac{1}{2}}. \tag{6.4}$$

To find the equation of the 20-unit isoquant, we solve this equation for K in terms of L. The easiest way to do this is to square each side of equation (6.4) and then solve for K in terms of L. Doing this yields

$$K = \frac{400}{L}$$

This is the equation of the 20-unit isoquant.
(b) We will use the same logic that we used in part (a). The combinations of labor and capital that give rise to Q units of output are

$$Q = K^{\frac{1}{2}}L^{\frac{1}{2}}$$

To find the equation of the isoquant, square each side and solve for K in terms of L and Q. Doing this yields

$$K = \frac{Q^2}{L}$$

If you substitute $Q = 20$ into this equation, you will see that you get the equation of the 20-unit isoquant that we solved for in part (a).

Similar Problem: 6.5

ECONOMIC AND UNECONOMIC REGIONS OF PRODUCTION

The isoquants in Figure 6.8 are downward sloping: As we increase the amount of labor we use, we can hold output constant by reducing the amount of capital. But Figure 6.9 shows the same isoquants when we expand the scale of Figure 6.8 to include quantities of labor and capital greater than 24,000 man-hours and machine-hours per day. The isoquants now have upward-sloping and backward-bending regions. What does this mean?

The upward-sloping and backward-bending regions correspond to a situation in which one input has a negative marginal product, or what we earlier called diminishing total returns. For example, the upward-sloping region in Figure 6.8 occurs when we have diminishing total returns to labor, while the backward-bending region occurs when we have diminishing total returns to capital. If we have

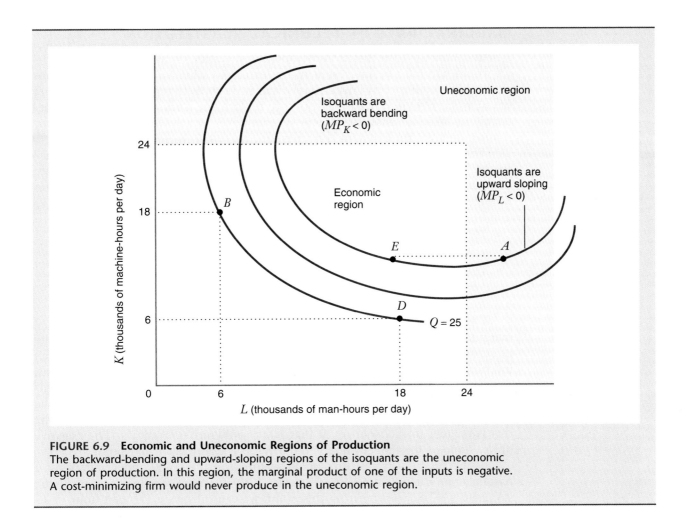

FIGURE 6.9 Economic and Uneconomic Regions of Production
The backward-bending and upward-sloping regions of the isoquants are the uneconomic region of production. In this region, the marginal product of one of the inputs is negative. A cost-minimizing firm would never produce in the uneconomic region.

diminishing total returns to labor, then as we increase the quantity of labor, holding the quantity of capital fixed, total output would go down. Thus, to keep output constant (remember, this is what we do when we move along an isoquant), we must also increase the amount of capital to compensate for the diminished total return to labor.

A firm that wants to minimize its production costs should *never* operate in the region of upward-sloping or backward-bending isoquants. For example, a semiconductor producer should not operate at a point like *A* in Figure 6.8 where there are diminishing total returns to labor. The reason is that it could produce the same output but at a lower cost by producing at point *E*. By producing in the range where the marginal product of labor is negative, the firm would be wasting money by spending it on unproductive labor. For this reason, we refer to the range in which isoquants slope upward as the **uneconomic region of production.** By contrast, the **economic region of production** is the region of downward-sloping isoquants. From now on, we will show only the economic region of production in our pictures.

MARGINAL RATE OF TECHNICAL SUBSTITUTION

A semiconductor firm that is contemplating investments in sophisticated robotics would naturally be interested in the extent to which it can replace humans with robots. Will the firm need to invest in two robots to replace the labor power of one worker? Will it need five robots to replace one worker? Ten? Twenty? Determining whether that investment in robotics is worthwhile requires that the semiconductor firm confront this question.

The "steepness" of an isoquant determines the rate at which the firm can substitute between labor and capital in its production process. The **marginal rate of technical substitution of labor for capital,** denoted by $MRTS_{L,K}$, measures how steep an isoquant is. The $MRTS_{L,K}$ tells us the following:

- The rate at which the quantity of capital can be *decreased* for every one unit *increase* in the quantity of labor, holding the quantity of output constant, *or*
- The rate at which the quantity of capital must be *increased* for every one unit *decrease* in the quantity of labor, holding the quantity of output constant.

The marginal rate of technical substitution is analogous to the concept of marginal rate of substitution from consumer theory. Just as the marginal rate of substitution of good X for good Y corresponded to minus the slope of an indifference curve drawn with X on the horizontal axis and Y on the vertical axis, the marginal rate of technical substitution of labor for capital corresponds to minus the slope of an isoquant drawn with L on the horizontal axis and K on the vertical axis. The slope of an isoquant at a particular point is the slope of the line that is tangent to the isoquant at that point, as Figure 6.10 shows. The negative of the slope of the tangent line is the $MRTS_{L,K}$ at any particular point.

Figure 6.10 illustrates the $MRTS_{L,K}$ along the $Q = 1000$ unit isoquant for a particular production function. At point A, the slope of the line tangent to the isoquant is -2.5. Starting from this point, we can substitute 1.0 man-hour of labor for 2.5 machine-hours of capital, and output will remain unchanged at 1000 units. Thus, $MRTS_{L,K} = 2.5$ at point A. At point B, the slope of the isoquant is -0.4. Thus, starting from this point, we can substitute 1.0 man-hour of labor for 0.4 machine-hours of capital without changing our output. Thus, $MRTS_{L,K} = 0.4$ at point B.

Notice that as we move down along the isoquant in Figure 6.10, the $MRTS_{L,K}$ gets smaller and smaller. This property is known as **diminishing marginal rate of technical substitution.** When a production function exhibits diminishing marginal rate of technical substitution, the $MRTS_{L,K}$ along an isoquant decreases as the quantity of labor, L, increases. Or, equivalently, the isoquants are convex to (that is, bowed in toward) the origin.

Diminishing marginal rate of technical substitution is related to the law of diminishing marginal returns discussed in the previous section. Diminishing $MRTS_{L,K}$ arises because, as we increase the amount of labor employed, the diminishing marginal productivity of labor implies that subsequent increments of labor are less and less productive. To understand this point, imagine a semiconductor firm that has invested in robotics but is now considering a return to a more traditional production approach by replacing some of its robots (i.e., capital) with labor. To maintain the same quantity of output as before, the first additional worker it hires—let's call him Ron—might be able to replace three robots. But because of the law of diminishing marginal returns, the marginal product of

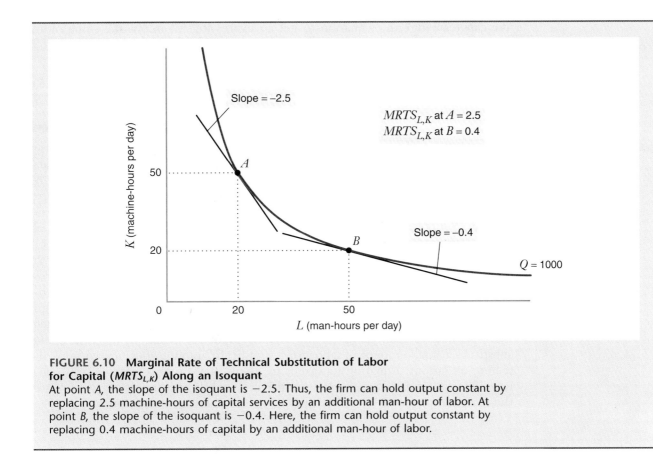

FIGURE 6.10 Marginal Rate of Technical Substitution of Labor for Capital ($MRTS_{L,K}$) Along an Isoquant
At point *A*, the slope of the isoquant is −2.5. Thus, the firm can hold output constant by replacing 2.5 machine-hours of capital services by an additional man-hour of labor. At point *B*, the slope of the isoquant is −0.4. Here, the firm can hold output constant by replacing 0.4 machine-hours of capital by an additional man-hour of labor.

the labor of the second additional worker—let's call him David—will be less than the first. By adding this worker, the firm might be able to replace just two robots, not as many as it did by hiring the first additional worker. This is not because David is necessarily less talented or skillful than Ron. Rather, it is because Ron and David working together produce less than twice as much additional output as Ron does by himself. Because of this, the $MRTS_{L,K}$ for the first unit of labor is bigger than the $MRTS_{L,K}$ for the second unit, which implies that the firm's isoquants become flatter the more labor it uses.

To draw a more precise connection between $MRTS_{L,K}$ and diminishing marginal returns, we need to develop mathematical arguments. We begin by noting that when we change the quantity of labor by ΔL units and the quantity of capital by ΔK units of capital, the change in output that results from this substitution would be as follows:

$$\Delta Q = \text{change in output from change in quantity of capital}$$
$$+ \text{ change in output from change in quantity of labor}$$
$$= (\Delta K \times MP_K) + (\Delta L \times MP_L).$$

Changes in K and L that move us along a given isoquant keep output unchanged, *so along a given isoquant*, $\Delta Q = 0$, and thus

$$0 = (\Delta K \times MP_K) + (\Delta L \times MP_L).$$

We can rearrange this equation to get an expression for minus the slope of an isoquant:

$$-\frac{\Delta K}{\Delta L} = \frac{MP_L}{MP_K} \tag{6.5}$$

$$= MRTS_{L,K}$$

This equation tells us that the marginal rate of technical substitution of labor for capital is equal to the ratio of the marginal product of labor (MP_L) to the marginal product of capital (MP_K). This is analogous to the relationship between marginal rate of substitution and marginal utility that we saw in consumer theory.

To illustrate why this relationship is significant, consider semiconductor production. Suppose that, at the existing input combination, an additional unit of labor would increase output by 10 units, while an additional unit of capital (robots) would increase output by just 2 units, i.e., $MP_L = 10$, while $MP_K = 2$. Thus, at our current input combination, labor has a much higher marginal productivity than capital. Equation (6.5) then tells us that the marginal rate of technical substitution of labor for capital is 10/2 = 5. The firm can substitute 1 unit of labor for 5 units of capital without affecting output. Because labor is much more productive than capital at the existing input combination, the firm could substitute a small amount of labor for a significant amount of capital without affecting its output. Equation (6.5) tells us, then, that a semiconductor firm contemplating the mix between robots and human workers would want to compare the marginal productivity of both inputs before making its decision.

***E*XAMPLE 6.2**   *The Marginal Rate of Technical Substitution Between High-Tech and Low-Tech Workers*

Over the last twenty years computers have become a ubiquitous part of the business landscape. As this has happened, firms have changed the composition of their work force, replacing "low-tech" workers with "high-tech" workers with greater knowledge and experience in using computers.

Using data on employment and computer usage over the period 1988–1991, Frank Lichtenberg has estimated the extent to which computer equipment and computer-oriented personnel have contributed to output in U.S. businesses.[6] As part of this study, Lichtenberg estimated the marginal rate of technical substitution of high-tech labor—computer and information systems personnel—for low-tech labor—workers employed in activities other than information systems and technology. If we hold a typical U.S. firm's output fixed, and also assume that its stock of computer equipment remains fixed, then the *MRTS* of high-tech labor for low-tech labor is about 6. That is, once the firm has determined its stock of computers, one high-tech worker can be substituted for six low-tech workers and output will remain unchanged. The reason that this *MRTS* is so large is that once the firm has invested in the acquisition of computer equipment, the marginal product of high-

---

[6]F. Lichtenberg, "The Output Contributions of Computer Equipment and Personnel: A Firm-Level Analysis," *Economics of Innovation and New Technology*, 3 (3–4, 1995), pp. 201–17.

tech, computer-literate workers is much higher than the marginal product of low-tech workers with fewer computer skills.

Lichtenberg notes that his estimate of the *MRTS* of low-tech and high-tech workers is consistent with the experience of real firms. He notes, for example, that when a large U.S. telecommunications company decided to automate and computerize its responses to customer service inquiries, it hired nine new computer programmers and information systems workers. These new workers displace seventy five low-tech service workers who had handled customer inquiries under the old system. For every additional high-tech worker the firm hired, it was able to replace more than eight low-tech workers ($75/9 \approx 8.3$). ■

6.4 SUBSTITUTABILITY AMONG INPUTS

A semiconductor manufacturer that is considering the choice between robots and workers would want to know how easily it can substitute between these inputs. Are there many potential combinations of robot and labor employment from which it could choose to produce a given level of output, or are its substitution opportunities more limited? The answer to this question will determine, in part, a firm's ability to shift from one mode of production (e.g., a high ratio of labor to capital) to another (e.g., a low ratio of capital to labor) as the relative prices of labor and capital change. In this section, we explore how to describe the ease or difficulty with which a firm can substitute between different inputs.

DESCRIBING A FIRM'S INPUT SUBSTITUTION OPPORTUNITIES GRAPHICALLY

Let's consider two possible production functions for the manufacture of semiconductors. Figure 6.11(a) shows the 1-million-chip-per-month isoquant for the first production function, while Figure 6.11(b) shows the 1-million-chip-per-month isoquant for the second production function.

These two production functions differ in terms of how easy it is for the firm to substitute between labor and capital. In Figure 6.11(a), suppose the firm operates at point *A*, with 100 man-hours of labor and 50 machine-hours of capital. At this point, the firm's ability to substitute labor for capital is limited. Even if the firm quadruples its use of labor, from 100 to 400 man-hours per month, it can only reduce its quantity of capital by a small amount—from 50 to 45 machine-hours—to keep monthly output at 1 million chips. A firm facing the production function of Figure 6.11(a) will find it difficult to substitute between labor and capital. If it wants to produce 1 million chips per month, there is really just one input combination it probably needs to consider: $L = 100$, $K = 50$.

By contrast, in Figure 6.11(b), the firm's substitution opportunities are more abundant. Starting from input combination *A*, the firm can reduce its employment of capital significantly—from 50 to 20 machine-hours—if it increases the quantity of labor from 100 to 400 man-hours per month. Of course, whether it would want to do either would depend on the relative cost of labor versus capital (an issue we will study in the next chapter), but the point is that the firm can potentially make substantial labor-for-capital (or capital-for-labor) substitutions. In contrast to Figure 6.11(a), the production function in Figure 6.11(b) gives the firm more opportunities to substitute labor for capital.

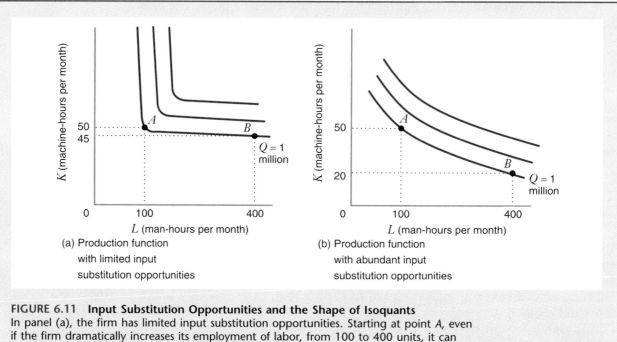

FIGURE 6.11   Input Substitution Opportunities and the Shape of Isoquants
In panel (a), the firm has limited input substitution opportunities. Starting at point *A*, even if the firm dramatically increases its employment of labor, from 100 to 400 units, it can only decrease its employment of capital by a small amount, from 50 to 45 units. By contrast, in panel (b) the firm has more abundant substitution opportunities. If it increases its employment of labor by a large amount, it can decrease its capital by a large amount without changing its output.

A semiconductor firm would probably want to know whether its opportunities to substitute labor for capital are limited or abundant. But what distinguishes one situation from the other? To answer this question, note that in Figure 6.11(a), the $MRTS_{L,K}$ changes dramatically as we move down the 1-million-unit isoquant toward point *A* and then beyond. Just above point *A* on the isoquant, $MRTS_{L,K}$ is quite large, almost infinitely so, but just beyond point *A*, the $MRTS_{L,K}$ abruptly shifts and becomes practically equal to 0. By contrast, in the isoquants of Figure 6.11(b), the $MRTS_{L,K}$ changes gradually.

This suggests that a firm's ability to substitute among inputs depends on the curvature of its isoquants. Specifically,

- When the production function offers limited input substitution opportunities, the $MRTS_{L,K}$ changes substantially as we move along an isoquant. The isoquants are nearly L-shaped, as in Figure 6.11(a).

- When the production function offers abundant input substitution opportunities, the $MRTS_{L,K}$ changes gradually as we move along an isoquant. The isoquants are nearly straight lines, as in Figure 6.11(b).

ELASTICITY OF SUBSTITUTION

The concept of **elasticity of substitution** is a numerical measure that can help us describe the firm's input substitution opportunities based on the relationships we just derived in the previous section. Specifically, the elasticity of substitution measures how quickly the marginal rate of technical substitution of labor for capital changes as we move along an isoquant. Figure 6.12 illustrates elasticity of substitution. As labor is substituted for capital, the ratio of the quantity of capital to the quantity of labor, known as the **capital–labor ratio**, K/L, must fall. The marginal rate of substitution of capital for labor, $MRTS_{L,K}$, also falls, as we saw in the previous section. The elasticity of substitution, often denoted by σ, measures the percentage change in the capital–labor ratio for each 1 percent change in $MRTS_{L,K}$ as we move along an isoquant. Mathematically, the elasticity of substitution is defined as

$$\sigma = \frac{\textit{percentage change} \text{ in capital–labor ratio}}{\textit{percentage change} \text{ in } MRTS_{L,K}}$$

$$= \frac{\%\Delta\left(\dfrac{K}{L}\right)}{\%\Delta MRTS_{L,K}} \tag{6.6}$$

In general, the elasticity of substitution could be any number greater than or equal to 0. Here is how to interpret the elasticity of substitution:

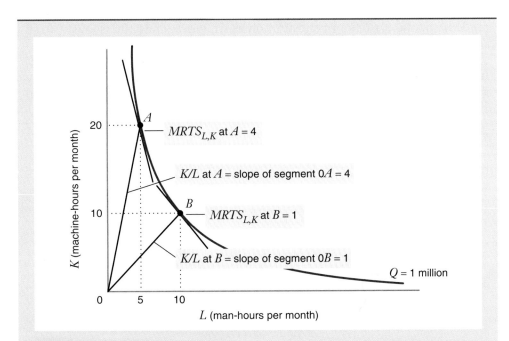

FIGURE 6.12 Elasticity of Substitution
The elasticity of substitution σ is the percentage change in the capital–labor ratio for each 1 percent change in $MRTS_{L,K}$. The $MRTS_{L,K}$ is equal to minus the slope of the isoquant, while the capital–labor ratio is equal to the slope of a ray from the origin to the input combination on the isoquant. In this case, the capital–labor ratio in moving from A to B changes from 4 to 1, as does the $MRTS_{L,K}$. Thus, the percentage change in $MRTS_{L,K}$ is -75 percent, and the percentage change in K/L is also -75 percent. The elasticity of substitution σ over the interval A to B equals 1.

- If the percentage change in $MRTS_{L,K}$ is large as we move along an isoquant, as it would be when substitution between labor and capital is hard [as in Figure 6.11(a)], the elasticity of substitution will be close to 0. There is little substitutability between capital and labor.

- If the percentage change in $MRTS_{L,K}$ is small as we move along an isoquant, as it would be when substitution between labor and capital is easy [Figure 6.11(b)], the elasticity of substitution will be large. There is significant substitutability between capital and labor.

LEARNING-BY-DOING EXERCISE 6.2

Calculating the Elasticity of Substitution

Problem Suppose that for the two input combinations shown in Figure 6.12,

$$MRTS_{L,K}^A = 4, \quad \frac{K^A}{L^A} = 4$$

$$MRTS_{L,K}^B = 1, \quad \frac{K^B}{L^B} = 1$$

(a) What is the elasticity of substitution as we move along the isoquant from A to B?

(b) Judging by the curvature of the isoquants shown in Figures 6.11 and 6.12, how do the elasticities of substitution for the production functions in Figure 6.11 compare to the elasticities of substitution for the production function in Figure 6.12?

Solution

(a) The change in the marginal rate of technical substitution, $\Delta MRTS_{L,K}$, as we move from A to B is

$$
\begin{aligned}
\Delta MRTS_{L,K} &= MRTS_{L,K}^B - MRTS_{L,K}^A \\
&= 1 - 4 \\
&= -3
\end{aligned}
$$

The percentage change in $MRTS_{L,K}$ is

$$\%\Delta MRTS_{L,K} = \frac{\Delta MRTS_{L,K}}{MRTS_{L,K}^A} \times 100\%$$

which in this case is $(-3/4) \times 100 = -75$ percent.

The change $\Delta(K/L)$ in the capital–labor ratio as we move from A to B is

$$
\begin{aligned}
\Delta \frac{K}{L} &= \frac{K^B}{L^B} - \frac{K^A}{L^A} \\
&= 1 - 4 \\
&= -3
\end{aligned}
$$

The percentage change in the capital–labor ratio is $\Delta(K/L)/(K^A/L^A) \times 100\% = -75$ percent.

Thus, using the formula from equation (6.6),

$$\sigma = \frac{\%\Delta\left(\frac{K}{L}\right)}{\%\Delta MRTS_{L,K}}$$

$$= \frac{-75}{-75} = 1$$

This calculation implies that starting at point A, a 1 percent decrease in the capital–labor ratio results in a 1 percent decrease in the marginal rate of technical substitution of labor for capital.

(b) The production function in Figure 6.12 seems to imply a greater degree of input substitutability than the production function in Figure 6.11(a), but a lesser degree of input substitutability than the production function in Figure 6.11(b). We would therefore expect that the elasticity of substitution for the production function in Figure 6.11(a) would be less than 1, while the elasticity of substitution for the production function in Figure 6.11(b) would be greater than 1.

Similar Problem: 6.10, part (a)

EXAMPLE 6.3

Elasticities of Substitution In German Industries[7]

Using data on output and input quantities over the period 1970–1988, Claudia Kemfert has estimated the elasticity of substitution between capital and labor in a number of manufacturing industries in Germany. Table 6.4 shows the estimated elasticities:

TABLE 6.4
Elasticities of Substitution in German Manufacturing Industries

Industry	Elasticity of Substitution
Chemicals	0.37
Stone and earth	0.21
Iron	0.50
Motor vehicles	0.10
Paper	0.35
Food	0.66

[7]This example is based on "Estimated Substitution Elasticities of a Nested CES Production Function Approach for Germany," *Energy Economics* 20 (1998), pp. 249–264.

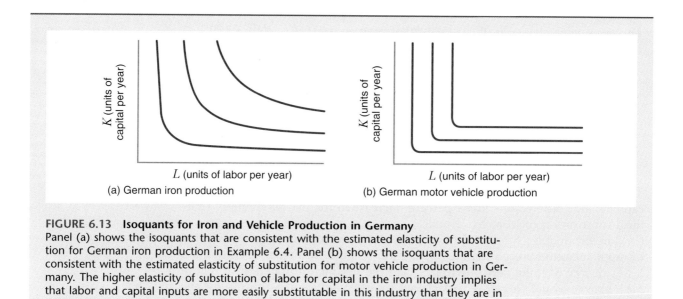

FIGURE 6.13 Isoquants for Iron and Vehicle Production in Germany
Panel (a) shows the isoquants that are consistent with the estimated elasticity of substitution for German iron production in Example 6.4. Panel (b) shows the isoquants that are consistent with the estimated elasticity of substitution for motor vehicle production in Germany. The higher elasticity of substitution of labor for capital in the iron industry implies that labor and capital inputs are more easily substitutable in this industry than they are in the production of motor vehicles.

The results in Table 6.4 show two things. First, the fact that the estimated elasticity of substitution is less than 1 in all industries tells us that, generally speaking, labor and capital inputs are not especially substitutable in these industries. Second, Table 6.4 shows that the ease of substitutability of capital for labor is higher in some industries than in others. For example, in the production of iron (elasticity of substitution equal to 0.50), labor and capital can be substituted to a much greater extent than they can in the production of motor vehicles (elasticity of substitution 0.10). Figure 6.13 shows this graphically. Isoquants in iron production would have the shape of Figure 6.13(a), while the isoquants in vehicles production would have the shape of Figure 6.13(b). ■

SPECIAL PRODUCTION FUNCTIONS

The relationship between the curvature of isoquants, input substitutability, and the elasticity of substitution is most apparent when we compare and contrast a number of special production functions that are frequently used in microeconomic analysis. In this section, we will consider four special production functions: the linear production function, the fixed-proportions production, the Cobb–Douglas production function, and the constant elasticity of substitution production function.

Linear Production Function

Suppose that a firm is choosing between two types of computers to store company data. One has a high-capacity hard drive that can store 20 gigabytes of data, while the other has a low-capacity hard drive that can store 10 gigabytes of data. If the firm needs to store 200 gigabytes of data, it could either purchase

10 high-capacity computers and no low-capacity computers (point A in Figure 6.14), or it could purchase no high-capacity computers and 20 low-capacity computers (point B in Figure 6.14). Or it could purchase 5 high-capacity computers and 10 low-capacity computers (point C in Figure 6.14), because $(5 \times 20) + (10 \times 10) = 200$.

In this example, the firm has a **linear production function** whose equation would be

$$Q = 20H + 10L$$

where H is the number of high-capacity computers the firm employs, L is the number of low-capacity computers the firm employs, and Q is the total gigabytes of data the firm can store. A linear production function is a production function whose isoquants are straight lines. Figure 6.14 shows that for a linear production function, the slope is constant and the marginal rate of technical substitution does not change as we move along the isoquant (i.e., $\Delta MRTS_{L,H} = 0$).

Because $MRTS_{L,H}$ is constant along an isoquant, the elasticity of substitution for a linear production function is infinite ($\sigma = \infty$). In other words, the inputs in a linear production function are infinitely or perfectly substitutable for each other. Thus, when we have a linear production function, we say that the inputs are **perfect substitutes.** In our computer example, the fact that low-capacity and high-capacity

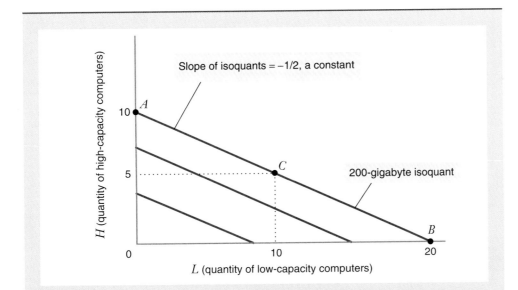

FIGURE 6.14 Isoquants for a Linear Production Function
When the firm can choose between two types of computers that differ only in the capacity of their hard drives, it faces a linear production function. To store 200 gigabytes of data, the firm could use 10 high-capacity machines and 0 low-capacity machines (point A). Or it could employ 0 high-capacity machines and 20 low-capacity machines (point B). Or the firm could employ any combination of machines (e.g., point C) on the straight line connecting points A and B. The isoquants for a linear production function are straight lines. The $MRTS_{L,K}$ at any point is thus a constant.

computers are perfect substitutes means that in terms of data storage capabilities, two low-capacity computers are just as good as one high-capacity computer. Or, put another way, the firm can perfectly replicate the productivity of one high-capacity computer by employing two low-capacity computers.

Fixed-Proportions Production Function

Figure 6.15 illustrates a dramatically different case. These are isoquants for the production of water, where the inputs are atoms of hydrogen (H) and atoms of oxygen (O). Since each molecule of water takes two hydrogen atoms and one oxygen atom, the inputs must be combined in fixed proportions. A production function where the inputs must be combined in fixed proportions is called a **fixed-proportions production function,** and the inputs in a fixed proportions production function are called **perfect complements.**[8] Adding more hydrogen to a fixed number of oxygen atoms gives us no additional water molecules; neither does adding more oxygen to a fixed number of hydrogen atoms. Thus, the quantity Q of water molecules that we get is given by

$$Q = \min\left(\frac{H}{2}, O\right)$$

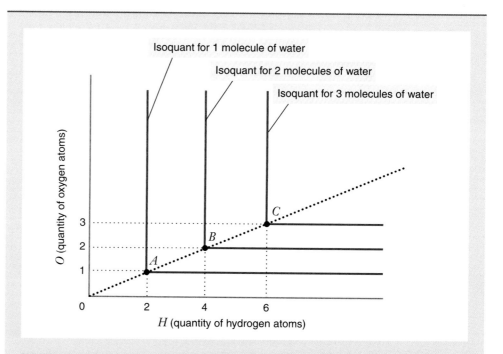

FIGURE 6.15   Isoquants for a Fixed-Proportions Production Function
The production of water molecules is characterized by fixed proportions: two atoms of hydrogen (H) and one atom of oxygen (O) are needed to make one molecule of water. The isoquants for this production function are L-shaped, which indicates that adding additional atoms of oxygen produces no additional water unless additional atoms of hydrogen are also added in a two-to-one proportion.

---

[8]The fixed-proportions production function is also called the Leontief production function, after the economist Wassily Leontief, who used it to model relationships between sectors in a national economy.

where the notation *min* means "take the minimum value of the two numbers in the parentheses."

When inputs are combined in fixed proportions, the elasticity of substitution is zero (i.e., $\sigma = 0$). This is because the marginal rate of technical substitution along the isoquant of a fixed-proportions production function changes drastically from ∞ to 0 when we pass through the corner of an isoquant (e.g., points, A, B, or C). The fact that the elasticity of substitution is zero tells us that when a firm faces a fixed-proportions production function it has no flexibility in its ability to substitute among inputs. We can see this in the example in Figure 6.15. To produce a single molecule of water, there is only one sensible input combination: two atoms of hydrogen and one atom of oxygen.

Cobb–Douglas Production Function

Figure 6.16 illustrates a case that is intermediate between a linear production function and a fixed proportions production function. This production function is known as the **Cobb–Douglas production function,** and it is given by the formula

$$Q = AL^{\alpha}K^{\beta}$$

where A, α, and β are positive constants (in Figure 6.16, these values are 100, 0.4, and 0.6, respectively). With the Cobb–Douglas production function, capital and labor can be substituted for each other. Unlike a fixed proportions production function, capital and labor can be used in variable proportions. Unlike a linear production function, though, the rate at which labor can be substituted for capital is not constant as you move along an isoquant. This suggests that the elasticity of substitution for a Cobb–Douglas production function falls somewhere

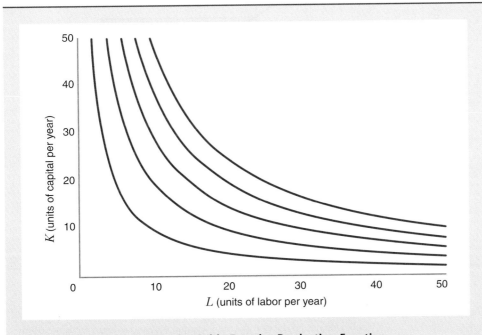

FIGURE 6.16 Isoquants for the Cobb–Douglas Production Function
The isoquants for a Cobb–Douglas production function are nonlinear downward-sloping curves.

in between 0 and ∞. In fact, it turns out that the elasticity of substitution along a Cobb–Douglas production function is exactly equal to 1. (This result is derived in the appendix to this chapter.)

CES Production Function

One production function includes all of the above production functions as special cases. It is called the **constant elasticity of substitution (CES) production function.** It is given by the equation

$$Q = \left[aL^{\frac{\sigma-1}{\sigma}} + bK^{\frac{\sigma-1}{\sigma}} \right]^{\frac{\sigma}{\sigma-1}}$$

where a, b, and σ are positive constants. Although it is not obvious, the constant σ in this production function is the elasticity of substitution. Figure 6.17 shows that as σ varies between 0 and ∞, the isoquants of the CES production function move from the fixed proportions to the Cobb–Douglas to the linear production function.[9]

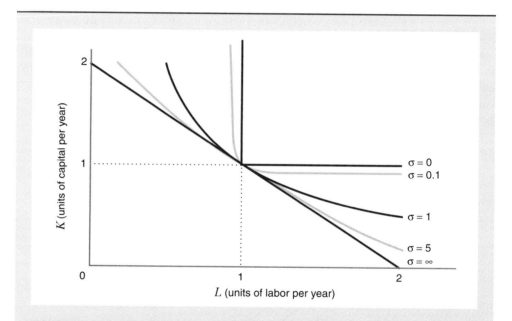

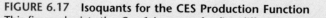

FIGURE 6.17   Isoquants for the CES Production Function
This figure depicts the $Q = 1$ isoquant for five different CES production functions, each corresponding to a different value of the elasticity of substitution σ. As σ increases from 0, we move from the fixed-proportions production function ($\sigma = 0$) to the Cobb–Douglas production function ($\sigma = 1$), and eventually approach the linear production function ($\sigma = \infty$).

[9]In the text, we observe that the CES production function describes a fixed-proportions production function when $\sigma = 0$, a Cobb–Douglas production function when $\sigma = 1$, and a linear production function when $\sigma = \infty$. It is *not* possible to see that these are special cases just by substituting values of σ equal to 0, 1, or ∞. Instead, to prove this we would need to use advanced mathematical techniques that are beyond the scope of this text.

To summarize, we have just seen four specific production functions, each distinguished by their elasticity of substitution:

- Linear production function (perfect substitutes): $\sigma = \infty$.
- Fixed proportions production function (perfect complements): $\sigma = 0$.
- Cobb–Douglas production function: $\sigma = 1$.
- CES production function: σ is constant, and ranges between 0 and ∞. Linear, Cobb–Douglas, and fixed proportions production functions are all particular examples of the CES production function.

In the previous section, we explored the extent to which inputs could be substituted for each other to produce a given level of output. In this section, we study how increases in all input quantities affect the quantity of output the firm can produce.

DEFINITION OF RETURNS TO SCALE

When inputs have positive marginal products, a firm's total output must increase when the quantities of all inputs are increased simultaneously—that is, when a firm's *scale* of operations increases. Often, though, we might want to know by *how much* output will increase when all inputs are increased by a given percentage amount. For example, by how much would a semiconductor firm be able to increase its output if it doubled its man-hours of labor and its machine-hours of robots? The concept of **returns to scale** tells us the percentage increase in output when a firm increases all of its input quantities by a given percentage amount:

$$\text{Returns to scale} = \frac{\%\Delta \text{ (quantity of output)}}{\%\Delta \text{ (quantity of } \textit{all} \text{ inputs)}}$$

To illustrate returns to scale, suppose that a firm uses two inputs, labor, L, and capital, K, to produce its quantity of output Q. Now suppose that all inputs are "scaled up" by the same proportionate amount $\lambda > 1$ (i.e., the quantity of labor increases from L to λL, and the quantity of capital increases from K to λK.[10] Let ϕ represent the resulting proportionate increase in the quantity of output Q (i.e., the quantity of output increases from Q to ϕQ). Then:

- If $\phi > \lambda$, we have **increasing returns to scale.** In this case, a proportionate increase in all input quantities results in a greater-than-proportionate increase in output.

---

[10]Therefore, the percentage change in all input quantities is $(\lambda - 1) \times 100$ percent.

- If $\phi = \lambda$, we have **constant returns to scale.** In this case, a proportionate increase in all input quantities results in the same proportionate increase in output.

- If $\phi < \lambda$, we have **decreasing returns to scale.** In this case, a proportionate increase in all input quantities results in a less-than-proportionate increase in output.

Figure 6.18(a) illustrates increasing returns to scale: if we double the quantities of labor and capital, output more than doubles. Figure 6.18(b) illustrates constant returns to scale: doubling the quantities of labor and capital doubles the quantity of output. Figure 6.18(c) illustrates decreasing returns to scale. Doubling the quantities of labor and capital less than doubles the quantity of output.

Why are returns to scale important? When a production process exhibits increasing returns to scale, there are cost advantages from large-scale operation. In particular, a single firm will be able to produce a given amount of output at *a lower cost per unit* than could two equal-size firms, each producing exactly half as much output. For example, if two semiconductor firms can each produce 1 million chips at $0.10 per chip, one large semiconductor firm could produce 2 million chips for less than $0.10 per chip. This is because, with increasing returns to scale, the large firm needs to employ less than twice as many units of labor and capital as the smaller firms to produce twice as much output. If a large firm did have such a cost advantage over smaller firms, a market would be most efficiently served by one large firm rather than several smaller firms.

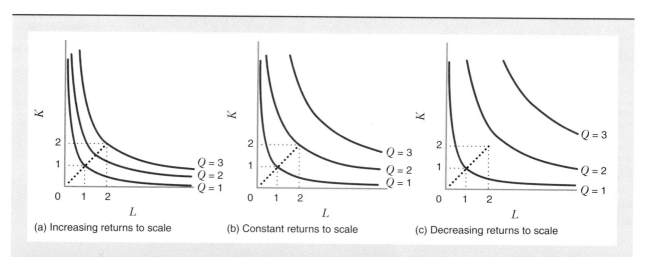

FIGURE 6.18   Increasing, Constant, and Decreasing Returns to Scale
In panel (a), we have increasing returns to scale; doubling the quantities of capital and labor more than doubling output. In panel (b), we have constant returns to scale; doubling the quantities of capital and labor, exactly doubling output. In panel (c), we have decreasing returns to scales; doubling the quantities of capital and labor less than doubles output.

This cost advantage of large-scale operation has been the traditional justification for allowing firms to operate as regulated monopolists in markets such as electric power and oil pipeline transportation.

LEARNING-BY-DOING EXERCISE 6.3

Returns to Scale for a Cobb–Douglas Production Function

Problem Does a Cobb–Douglas production function, $Q = AL^{\alpha}K^{\beta}$, exhibit increasing, decreasing, or constant returns to scale?

Solution Let L_1, K_1 denote the initial quantities of labor and capital and let Q_1 denote the initial quantity, so

$$Q_1 = AL_1^{\alpha}K_1^{\beta}$$

Now, let's increase all input quantities by the same proportional amount λ, $\lambda > 1$, and let Q_2 denote the resulting volume of output:

$$\begin{aligned} Q_2 &= A(\lambda L_1)^{\alpha}(\lambda K_1)^{\beta} \\ &= A\lambda^{\alpha}L_1^{\alpha}\lambda^{\beta}K_1^{\beta} \\ &= \lambda^{\alpha+\beta}AL_1^{\alpha}K_1^{\beta} \\ &= \lambda^{\alpha+\beta}Q_1 \end{aligned}$$

Now, whether we have increasing, constant, or decreasing returns to scale depends on whether the term $\lambda^{\alpha+\beta}$ is bigger than, the same as, or less than λ. From the properties of exponents, we know that $\lambda^{\alpha+\beta}$ will be greater than, equal to, or less than λ depending on whether the exponent $\alpha + \beta$ is bigger than, equal to, or less than one. Specifically, if

- $\alpha + \beta > 1$, then $\lambda^{\alpha+\beta} > \lambda$, and so $Q_2 > \lambda Q_1$. We thus have increasing returns to scale.
- $\alpha + \beta = 1$, then $\lambda^{\alpha+\beta} = \lambda$, and so $Q_2 = \lambda Q_1$. We thus have constant returns to scale.
- $\alpha + \beta < 1$, then $\lambda^{\alpha+\beta} < \lambda$, and so $Q_2 < \lambda Q_1$. We thus have decreasing returns to scale.

This shows that the Cobb–Douglas production function can exhibit increasing or decreasing returns to scale. In particular, this analysis shows that the sum of the exponents $\alpha + \beta$ in the Cobb–Douglas production function determines the degree to which returns to scale are increasing, constant, or decreasing. For this reason, economists have paid considerable attention to estimating this sum when studying production functions in specific industries.

EXAMPLE 6.4   *Returns to Scale In Electric Power Generation*

Returns to scale have been thoroughly studied in electric power generation. The pioneering work on returns to scale in electricity generation was done by economist Marc Nerlove.[11] Using data from 145 electric utilities in the United States during the year 1955, Nerlove estimated the exponents of a Cobb–Douglas production function and found that their sum was greater than 1. As illustrated in Learning-By-Doing Exercise 6.3, this implies that electricity generation is subject to increasing returns to scale. Other studies in this same industry using data from the 1950s and 1960s also found evidence of increasing returns to scale. However, studies using more recent data (and functional forms for the production function other than Cobb–Douglas) have found that electricity generation in large plants is probably now characterized by constant returns to scale.[12]

Is it possible that both conclusions could be right? Perhaps. If both conclusions are correct—that is, if generation was characterized by increasing returns to scale in the 1950s and 1960s but constant returns to scale thereafter—we should expect to see a growth in the scale of generating units throughout the 1950s and 1960s followed by smaller growth in later years. This is exactly what we observe. The average capacity of all units installed between 1960 and 1964 was 151.7 megawatts. By the period 1970–1974, the average capacity of new units had grown to 400.3 megawatts. Over the next 10 years, the average capacity of new units continued to grow, but more slowly: Of all units installed between 1980 and 1982, the average capacity was 490.3 megawatts.[13]   ∎

RETURNS TO SCALE VERSUS DIMINISHING MARGINAL RETURNS

It is important to understand the distinction between the concepts of returns to scale and diminishing marginal returns discussed in Section 6.2. Returns to scale pertains to the impact of an increase in *all input quantities* simultaneously, while diminishing marginal returns pertains to the impact of an increase in the *quantity of a single input,* such as labor, holding the quantities of all of the other inputs fixed.

Figure 6.19 illustrates this distinction. If we double the quantity of labor, from 10 to 20 units per year, holding the quantity of capital fixed at 10 units per year, we move from point *A* to *B*, and output goes up from 100 to 140. If we then in-

[11]Marc Nerlove, "Returns to Scale in Electricity Supply," Chapter 7 in Carl F. Christ, ed., *Measurement in Economics: Studies in Honor of Yehuda Grunfeld* (Stanford, CA: Stanford University Press, 1963), pp. 167–198.

[12]See T. G. Cowing, and V. K. Smith, "The Estimation of a Production Technology: A Survey of Econometric Analyses of Steam Electric Generation," *Land Economics* (May 1978), pp. 157–170, and L. R. Christensen and W. Greene, "Economies of Scale in U. S. Electric Power Generation," *Journal of Political Economy* (August 1976), pp. 655–676.

[13]These data come from Table 5.3 (p. 50) in P. L. Joskow and R. Schmalensee, *Markets for Power: An Analysis of Electric Utility Deregulation* (Cambridge, MA: MIT Press, 1983).

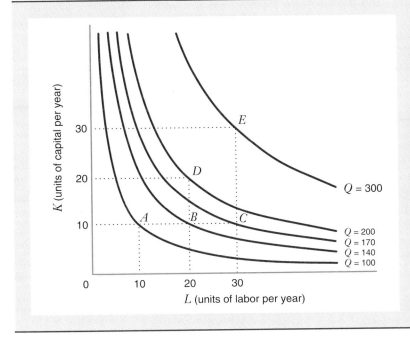

FIGURE 6.19 Diminishing Marginal Returns versus Returns to Scale
If we hold capital fixed at 10 units and increase labor from 10 to 20 to 30 units, we move from point *A* to *B* to *C*. The increase in output from *A* to *B* is 40 units, while the increase in output from *B* to *C* is just 30 units. Thus, the increase in output brought about by a 10-unit increase in labor goes down as we employ more labor. But this production function also exhibits constant returns to scale. Starting at point *A*, if we double the quantities of both capital and labor, output exactly doubles (i.e., we move from point *A* to *D*), and if we triple the quantities of capital and labor, output exactly triples (i.e., we move from point *A* to *E*). This figure thus illustrates that diminishing marginal returns and returns to scale are distinct concepts.

crease the quantity of labor from 20 to 30, we move from point *B* to *C*. Output goes up some more, but only to 170. In this case, we have diminishing marginal returns to labor: The increase in output brought about by a 10-unit increase in the quantity of labor goes down as we employ more and more labor.

By contrast, if we double the quantity of both labor and capital from 10 to 20 units per year, we move from point *A* to *D*, and output doubles from 100 to 200 units per year. If we triple the quantity of labor and capital from 10 to 30, we move from point *A* to *E*, and output triples from 100 to 300 units. For the production function in Figure 6.19 we have constant returns to scale but diminishing marginal returns to labor.

EXAMPLE 6.5

Returns to Scale in Oil Pipelines

Another industry in which returns to scale have been extensively studied is the transportation of oil through pipelines. The product of an oil pipeline is the volume of oil transported through the pipeline during a given period—usually called *throughput*. It is often measured in barrels of oil per day. The throughput of an oil pipeline of a given length depends primarily on two factors: pipe size (i.e., its diameter) and amount of power (hydraulic horsepower) that is applied to the oil as it travels through the pipeline. For a fixed amount of horsepower, a larger oil pipeline will result in a greater throughput. For a pipe of a given size, the more horsepower, the more throughput. In planning a pipeline, a company controls both of these factors. It can influence the horsepower by the number of pumping stations it installs along the pipeline. And, of course, it can choose the diameter of the pipeline itself. Pumping stations are costly, and pipe is more expensive as its diameter increases, so in planning a pipeline, a company must trade off the benefits of a larger throughput against the expense of generating that throughput.

Unlike electric power generation in which returns to scale have been estimated using statistical methods, returns to scale for oil pipelines can be deduced using engineering principles. Applying such principles yields a Cobb–Douglas production function[14]

$$Q = AH^{0.37}K^{1.73}$$

where H denotes hydraulic horsepower, K denotes the size of the pipe, Q denotes throughput, and A is a constant that depends on a variety of factors including the length of the pipeline, the variation in the terrain over which the pipeline travels, and the viscosity of the oil. Because the exponents of H and K add up to a number greater than 1, this production function exhibits increasing returns to scale. That is, if we double the diameter of the pipe and double the horsepower used to pump the oil, the throughput of oil more than doubles. This implies that there are significant cost advantages to building pipelines with large pipes and powerful pumping stations. ■

6.6
TECHNOLOG-
ICAL
PROGRESS

So far, we have treated the firm's production function as fixed; that is, it remains stationary over time. But as knowledge in the economy evolves and as firms acquire know-how through experience and investment in research and development, a firm's production function will change. The notion of **technological progress** captures the idea that production functions can shift over time. In particular, technological progress refers to a situation in which a firm can achieve more output from a given combination of inputs, or equivalently, the same amount of output from less inputs.

We can classify technological progress into three categories: neutral technological progress, labor-saving technological progress, and capital-saving technological progress.[15] Figure 6.20 illustrates **neutral technological progress.** In this case, an isoquant corresponding to a given level of output (100 units in the figure) shifts inward (indicating that lesser amounts of labor and capital are needed to produce a given output), but the isoquants shift so as to leave $MRTS_{L,K}$, the marginal rate of technical substitution of labor for capital, unchanged along any ray (e.g., OA) from the origin. Under neutral technological progress, in effect, the firm's entire map of isoquants is simply relabeled, each one now corresponding to a higher level of output, but the isoquants themselves retain the same shape.

Figure 6.21 illustrates **labor-saving technological progress.** As before, the isoquant corresponding to a given level of output shifts inward, but now along

---

[14]This is an approximation of a formula presented in L. Cockenboo, *Crude Oil Pipe Lines and Competition in the Oil Industry* (Cambridge, MA: Harvard University Press, 1955).

[15]J. R. Hicks, *The Theory of Wages* (London: Macmillan, 1932).

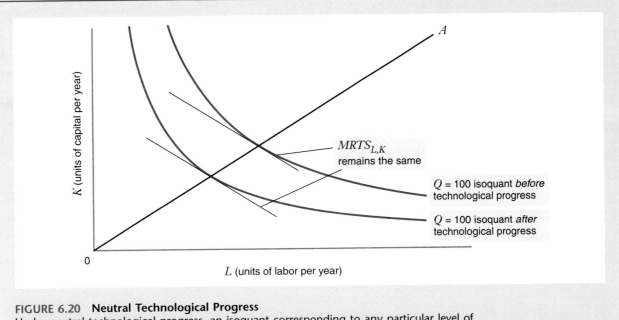

FIGURE 6.20 Neutral Technological Progress
Under neutral technological progress, an isoquant corresponding to any particular level of output shifts inward, but the $MRTS_{L,K}$ along any ray from the origin, such as OA, remains the same.

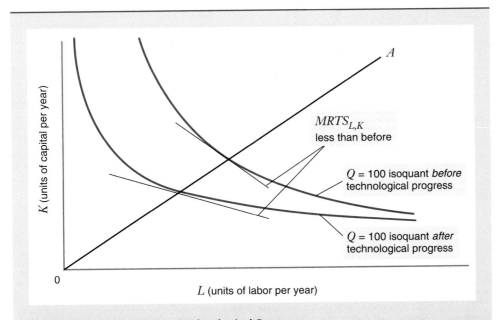

FIGURE 6.21 Labor-Saving Technological Progress
Under labor-saving technological progress, an isoquant corresponding to any particular level of output shifts inward, but the $MRTS_{L,K}$ along any ray from the origin, such as OA, goes down.

any ray from the origin, the isoquant becomes flatter, indicating that the $MRTS_{L,K}$ is now less than it was before. You should recall from Section 6.3 that $MRTS_{L,K} = MP_L/MP_K$, so the fact that the $MRTS_{L,K}$ decreases implies that under this form of technological progress the marginal product of capital increases more rapidly than the marginal product of labor. This form of technological progress would arise when technical advances in capital equipment, robotics, or computers increase the marginal productivity of capital relative to the marginal productivity of labor.

Figure 6.22 depicts **capital-saving technological progress.** Here, as an isoquant shifts inward, $MRTS_{L,K}$ increases, indicating that the marginal product of labor is increasing more rapidly than the marginal product of capital. This form of technological progress would arise if, for example, the education or skill level of the firm's actual (and potential) work force rose, increasing the marginal productivity of labor relative to the marginal product of capital.

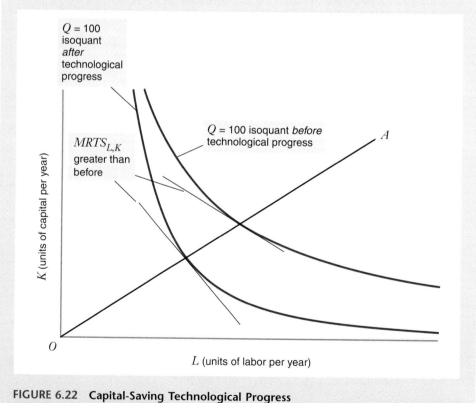

FIGURE 6.22 Capital-Saving Technological Progress
Under capital-saving technological progress, an isoquant corresponding to any particular level of output shifts inward, but the $MRTS_{L,K}$ along any ray from the origin, such as *OA,* goes up.

EXAMPLE 6.6

Technological Progress and Productivity Growth in U.K. Manufacturing Industries

Banu Suer has estimated the magnitude and nature of technological progress in a number of manufacturing industries in the United Kingdom.[16] Among the industries included in this study were: general chemicals, pharmaceuticals, paint, soap, detergents, synthetic rubber, synthetic plastics and resins, dyes and pigments, and fertilizers. In the United Kingdom, these industries have traditionally been characterized by high profit margins, above-average rates of spending on research and development as compared to U.K. manufacturing firms generally, and higher-than-average rates of patent activity. These industries have generally had a good productivity record, but their growth rate of labor productivity declined considerably after the oil crisis of 1973. Since 1981, however, labor productivity in these industries has improved. This coincides with a period in which firms in these industries aggressively reduced the sizes of their work forces through layoffs.

Suer found evidence of significant technological progress in the manufacturing industries he studied. This technological progress was not neutral. Instead, it resulted in an increase in the marginal product of capital relative to the marginal product of labor (i.e., it was labor-saving technological progress). The steep reduction in labor employment in the industries that Suer studied is a sign that this type of technological progress was occurring. ∎

CHAPTER SUMMARY

• The production function represents the various technological recipes a firm can choose from in configuring its production process. It tells us the *maximum* quantity of output the firm can get as a function of the quantities of various inputs that it might employ.

• Single-input production functions are called total product functions. A total product function typically has three regions: a region of increasing marginal returns, a region of decreasing marginal returns, and a region of decreasing total returns.

• The average product of labor is the average amount of output per unit of labor. The marginal product of labor is the rate at which total output changes as the quantity of labor the firm uses changes.

• The law of diminishing marginal returns says that as the usage of one input (e.g., labor) increases—the quantities of other inputs, such as capital or land, being held fixed—then at some point the marginal product of that input will decrease.

• Isoquants depict with multiple inputs production functions in a two-dimensional graph. An isoquant shows all combinations of labor and capital that produce the same quantity of output. Each isoquant corresponds to a particular level of output, and as we move to the northeast on a graph, we reach isoquants corresponding to higher and higher levels of output.

• For some production functions, the isoquants have an upward-sloping and backward-bending region. This region is called the uneconomic region of production. Here, one of the inputs has a negative marginal product. The economic region of production is the region of downward-sloping isoquants.

[16]Banu Suer, "Total Factor Productivity Growth and Characteristics of the Production Technology in the UK Chemicals and Allied Industries," *Applied Economics*, 27 (1995), pp. 277–285.

- The marginal rate of technical substitution of labor for capital tells us the rate at which the quantity of capital can be reduced for every one unit increase in the quantity of labor, holding the quantity of output constant. Mathematically, the marginal rate of technical substitution of labor for capital is equal to the ratio of the marginal product of labor to the marginal product of capital.

- Isoquants that are convex to the origin (bowed in toward the origin) exhibit diminishing marginal rate of technical substitution (i.e., the marginal rate of substitution falls as we move downward along an isoquant). When the marginal rate of technical substitution of labor for capital diminishes, fewer and fewer units of capital can be sacrificed as additional labor is added.

- The elasticity of substitution is a measure of the curvature of an isoquant. Specifically, it measures the percentage rate of change K/L for each 1 percent change in $MRTS_{L,K}$.

- Three important special production functions are the linear production function, the fixed-proportions production function, and the Cobb–Douglas production function. Each of these is a member of a class of production functions known as constant elasticity of substitution production functions.

- Returns to scale tell us how much output will increase when all inputs are increased by a given percentage. If a given percentage increase in the quantities of all inputs increases output by more than that percentage, we have increasing returns to scale. If a given percentage increase in the quantities of all inputs increases output by less than that percentage, we have decreasing returns to scale. If a given percentage increase in the quantities of all inputs increases output by the same percentage, we have constant returns to scale.

- Technological progress refers to a situation in which a firm can achieve more output from a given combination of inputs, or equivalently, the same amount of output from smaller quantities of inputs. Technological progress can be neutral, labor saving, or capital saving.

REVIEW QUESTIONS

1. We said that the production function tells us the *maximum* output that the firm can produce with its quantities of inputs. Why do we include the word *maximum* in this definition?

2. What is the labor requirements function? Suppose the total product function has the "traditional shape" shown in Figure 6.2. Sketch the shape of the labor requirements function (with quantity of output on the horizontal axis and quantity of labor on the vertical axis).

3. What is the difference between average product and marginal product? Can you sketch a total product function such that the average and marginal product functions coincide with each other?

4. What is the difference between *diminishing total returns* to an input and *diminishing marginal returns to an input*? Can a total product function exhibit diminishing marginal returns but not diminishing total returns?

5. Why must an isoquant be downward sloping when both labor and capital have positive marginal products?

6. Could the isoquants corresponding to two different levels of output ever cross?

7. Why would a firm that seeks to minimize its expenditures on inputs not want to operate on the uneconomic portion of an isoquant?

8. What is the elasticity of substitution? What does it tell us?

9. Suppose the production of electricity requires just two inputs, capital and labor, and that the production function is Cobb–Douglas. Now consider the isoquants corresponding to three different levels of output: $Q = 100,000$ kilowatt-hours, $Q = 200,000$ kilowatt-hours, and $Q = 400,000$ kilowatt-hours. Sketch these isoquants under three different assumptions about returns to scale: constant returns to scale, increasing returns to scale, and decreasing returns to scale.

PROBLEMS

6.1. A firm uses the inputs of fertilizer, labor, and hothouses to produce roses. Suppose that when the quantity of labor and hothouses is fixed, the relationship between the quantity of fertilizer and the number of roses produced is given by the following table:

Tons of Fertilizer Per Month	Number of Roses Per Month
0	0
1	500
2	1000
3	1700
4	2200
5	2500
6	2600
7	2500
8	2000

a) What is the average product of fertilizer when 4 tons are used?
b) What is the marginal product of the sixth ton of fertilizer?
c) Does this total product function exhibit diminishing marginal returns? If so, over what quantity of fertilizer do they occur?
d) Does this total product function exhibit diminishing total returns? If so, over what quantity of fertilizer do they occur?

6.2. Suppose that the production function for floppy disks is given by

$$Q = KL^2 - L^3$$

where Q is the number of disks produced per year, K is machine-hours of capital, and L is man-hours of labor flow of capital services.
a) Suppose $K = 600$. Find the total product function and graph it over the range $L = 0$ to $L = 500$. Then sketch the graphs of the average and marginal product functions. At what level of labor L does the average product curve appear to reach its maximum? At what level does the marginal product curve appear to reach its maximum?
b) Replicate the analysis in (a) for the case in which $K = 1200$.
c) When either $K = 600$ or $K = 1200$, does the total product function have a range of increasing marginal returns?

6.3. Are the following statements correct or incorrect?
a) If average product is increasing, marginal product must be less than average product.
b) If marginal product is negative, average product must be negative.
c) If average product is positive, total product must be rising.
d) If total product is increasing, marginal product must also be increasing.

6.4. Economists sometimes "prove" the law of diminishing marginal returns with the following exercise: Suppose that production of steel requires two inputs, labor and capital, and suppose that the production function is characterized by constant returns to scale. Then, if there were increasing marginal returns to labor, you or I could produce all the steel in the world in a backyard blast furnace. Using numerical arguments based on the production function shown in the following table, show that this (logically absurd) conclusion is correct. The fact that it is correct shows that marginal returns to labor cannot be everywhere increasing when the production function exhibits constant returns to scale.

L	K	Q
0	100	0
1	100	1
2	100	4
4	100	16
8	100	64
16	100	256
32	100	1024

6.5. Suppose the production function is given by the equation

$$Q = L\sqrt{K}$$

Graph the equation of the isoquant corresponding to $Q = 10$, $Q = 20$, and $Q = 50$. Do these isoquants exhibit diminishing marginal rate of technical substitution?

6.6. Consider again the production function for floppy disks

$$Q = KL^2 - L^3$$

a) Sketch a graph of the isoquants for this production function.
b) Does this production function have an uneconomic region? Why?

6.7. Suppose the production function is given by the equation (where a and b are positive constants)

$$Q = aL + bK$$

What is the marginal rate of technical substitution of labor for capital ($MRTS_{L,K}$) at any point along an isoquant?

6.8. Let B be the number of bicycles produced from F bicycle frames and T tires. Every bicycle needs exactly two tires and one frame.

a) Draw the isoquants for bicycle production.

b) Write a mathematical expression for the production function for bicycles.

6.9. A firm produces a quantity Q of breakfast cereal using labor L and material M with the production function

$$Q = 50\sqrt{ML} + M + L$$

The marginal product functions for this production function are

$$MP_L = 25\sqrt{\frac{M}{L}} + 1$$

$$MP_M = 25\sqrt{\frac{L}{M}} + 1$$

a) What is the nature of returns to scale (increasing, constant, or decreasing) for this production function?

b) Is the marginal product of labor ever diminishing for this production function? If so, when? Is it ever negative, and if so, when?

6.10. Consider a CES production function given by

$$Q = [K^{0.5} + L^{0.5}]^2$$

a) What is the elasticity of substitution for this production function?
b) Does this production function exhibit increasing, decreasing, or constant returns to scale?
c) Suppose that the production function took the form

$$Q = [100 + K^{0.5} + L^{0.5}]^2$$

Does this production function exhibit increasing, decreasing, or constant returns to scale?

6.11. Suppose initially a firm's production function took the form

$$Q = 500[L + 3K]$$

However, as a result of a manufacturing innovation, its production function is now

$$Q = 1000[0.5L + 10K]$$

a) Show that the innovation has resulted in technological progress in the sense defined in the text.
b) Is the technological progress neutral, labor saving, or capital saving?

APPENDIX: The Elasticity of Substitution for a Cobb–Douglas Production Function

In this appendix we derive the elasticity of substitution for a Cobb–Douglas production function, $f(L,K) = AL^\alpha K^\beta$. The marginal product of labor and capital are found by taking the partial derivatives of the production function with respect to labor and capital respectively (for a discussion of partial derivatives, see the Mathematical Appendix in this book):

$$MP_L = \frac{\partial f}{\partial L} = \alpha AL^{\alpha-1}K^\beta$$

$$MP_K = \frac{\partial f}{\partial K} = \beta AL^\alpha K^{\beta-1}$$

Now, recall that, in general,

$$MRTS_{L,K} = \frac{MP_L}{MP_K}$$

Using the above expressions for the marginal products of labor and capital for a Cobb–Douglas production function, the marginal rate of technical substitution for a Cobb–Douglas production function can be derived by forming the following ratio:

$$MRTS_{L,K} = \frac{\alpha AL^{\alpha-1}K^{\beta}}{\beta AL^{\alpha}K^{\beta-1}}$$
$$= \frac{\alpha K}{\beta L}$$

Rearranging terms yields

$$\frac{K}{L} = \frac{\beta}{\alpha} MRTS_{L,K} \tag{A6.1}$$

Therefore, $\Delta(K/L) = (\beta/\alpha) \Delta MRTS_{L,K}$ or :

$$\frac{\Delta\left(\frac{K}{L}\right)}{\Delta MRTS_{L,K}} = \frac{\beta}{\alpha}. \tag{A6.2}$$

Also, from (A6.1),

$$\frac{MRTS_{L,K}}{\left(\frac{K}{L}\right)} = \frac{\alpha}{\beta} \tag{A6.3}$$

Now, using the definition of the elasticity of substitution in (6.6)

$$\sigma = \frac{\%\Delta\left(\frac{K}{L}\right)}{\%\Delta MRTS_{L,K}} = \frac{\Delta\left(\frac{K}{L}\right)/\frac{K}{L}}{\left(\frac{\Delta MRTS_{L,K}}{MRTS_{L,K}}\right)}$$

$$= \left(\frac{\Delta\left(\frac{K}{L}\right)}{\Delta MRTS_{L,K}}\right)\left(\frac{\Delta MRTS_{L,K}}{\frac{K}{L}}\right) \tag{A6.4}$$

Substituting (A6.2) and (A6.3) into (A6.4) yields

$$\sigma = \frac{\beta}{\alpha} \cdot \frac{\alpha}{\beta} = 1$$

That is, the elasticity of substitution along a Cobb–Douglas production function is equal to 1 for all values of K and L.

7

Costs and Cost Minimization

In the mid-1990s, Burke Mills, a textile producer located in Burke County in western North Carolina, had a problem.[1] Burke County had one of the lowest unemployment rates in the United States, and wage rates in the county had increased as local manufacturers competed to fill jobs. Burke Mills was trying to expand its sales in a highly competitive international market, and given the high wage rates in Burke County, Burke Mills' management believed that it would be at a disadvantage compared to its competitors. So to improve its cost competitiveness, Burke Mills launched a multimillion-dollar project to automate its production. The project allowed Burke Mills to double the capacity of its production facility without significantly increasing its work force. By 1997, Burke Mills's textile plant was one of the most heavily automated in the business, and Burke Mills was poised to become a significant international player in its portion of the textile business.

How do prices of inputs affect a firm's input decisions and how do those decisions affect its costs of production? Burke Mills was faced with an increase in the price of labor, and it responded by increasing the capital–labor ratio in its production process. By moving to a more cost efficient combination of labor and capital for the input prices it faced, Burke Mills was able to lower its total production costs, which allowed it to compete more effectively in a global market.

In this chapter we will look at costs of production. In the first part of the chapter, we will explore how economists define costs so that costs can be a useful concept for decision making. In the second part of the chapter, we explore how firms should choose their input quantities to minimize their costs of production. With this analysis we can better understand the trade-offs faced by a firm such as Burke Mills as it contemplates how to respond to an increase in the price of a key input. ■

[1]This example draws from John McCurry, "Burke Mills Robotizes its Dyehouse," *Textile World* 146 (January 1996), 78–79.

7.1
COST CONCEPTS FOR DECISION MAKING

Managers are most experienced with cost presented as monetary expenses in an income statement. Politicians and policy analysts are more familiar with costs as an expense item in a budget statement. Consumers think of costs as their monthly bills and other expenses.

But economists use a broader concept of cost. To an economist, cost is the value of sacrificed opportunities. What is the cost to you of devoting 20 hours every week to studying microeconomics? It is the value of whatever you would have done instead with that 20 hours (leisure activities, perhaps). What is the cost to an airline of flying its fleet of jets? In addition to the direct costs (fuel, flight-crew salaries, maintenance, and so forth), it also includes the income the airline sacrifices by not renting out its jets to other airlines that would be willing to lease them. What are the costs involved in repairing an expressway in Chicago? Besides the costs of construction workers and materials, they would include the value of the time that drivers sacrifice as they sit immobilized in traffic jams.

Viewed this way, costs are not necessarily synonymous with monetary outlays. When the airline flies the planes that it owns, it does pay for the fuel, flight-crew salaries, maintenance, and so forth. However, it does not spend money for the use of the airplane itself (i.e., it does not need to lease it from someone else). Still, in most cases, the airline incurs a cost when it uses the plane because it sacrifices the opportunity to lease that airplane to others who could use it.

Although the idea that cost is a sacrifice may be clear, it is often difficult to apply to a particular situation, especially if you need to put a monetary value on a sacrificed opportunity. How would you go about placing a value on the leisure time that you sacrifice while reading this book? How would an airline assign a dollar value to the cost of airplane services it "consumes" each time one of its airplanes takes off? How would the government assess the cost of traffic congestion when evaluating the net social benefits of a highway renovation project?

In practice, cost is a useful concept only when applied in specific contexts. In fact, you will see that the meaning of "cost" usually depends on the issue being analyzed. To prepare you for the context-specific nature of cost, we need to introduce you to a number of important cost concepts that economists use: opportunity costs, implicit costs, economic costs, and sunk costs.

OPPORTUNITY COST

Consider a decision maker who has to choose from a set of mutually exclusive alternatives, each of which entails a particular monetary payoff. The **opportunity cost** of a particular alternative is the payoff associated with the *best of the alternatives that are not chosen*.

To understand opportunity costs more concretely, consider two examples:

- You own and manage your own business. The business requires an average of 80 hours of your time every week. Suppose instead of working in your own business, your best alternative is to work the same amount of hours in a large corporation for an income of $75,000 per year. The opportunity cost of the time you devote to your business would therefore be $75,000.

- An automobile firm has an inventory of sheet steel that it purchased for $1,000,000. It is planning to use the sheet steel to manufacture 2,000 automobiles. As an alternative, it can resell the steel to other firms. Suppose that the price of sheet steel has gone up since the firm made its purchase, so if it resells its steel the firm would get $1,200,000. The opportunity cost of using the steel to produce the 2,000 automobiles is thus $1,200,000, or $600 per automobile. Note the opportunity cost differs from the original expense incurred by the firm.

After reading this last example, students sometimes ask, "Why isn't the opportunity cost of the steel $200,000: the difference between the market value of the steel ($1,200,000) and its original cost ($1,000,000)?" After all, the firm has already spent $1,000,000 to buy the steel. Why isn't the opportunity cost the amount above and beyond that original cost ($200,000 in this example)? The way to answer this question is to remember that the notion of opportunity cost is forward looking, not backward looking. That is, opportunity cost measures what the decision maker sacrifices *at the time the decision is made and beyond*. When the automobile company uses the steel to produce cars, it gives up more than just $200,000. It forecloses the opportunity to receive a payment of $1,200,000 from reselling the steel. The opportunity cost of $1,200,000 measures the full amount the firm sacrifices at the moment it makes the decision to use the steel to produce cars rather than to resell it in the open market.

Opportunity Costs Depend on the Decision Being Made

The forward-looking nature of opportunity costs implies that opportunity costs can change as time passes and circumstances change. To illustrate this point, let's return to our example of the automobile firm that purchased $1,000,000 worth of sheet steel. When the firm first confronted the decision to "buy the steel" or "don't buy the steel," the relevant opportunity cost was the purchase price of $1,000,000. This is because the firm would save $1,000,000 if it did not buy the steel.

But—moving ahead in time—once the firm purchases the steel and the market price of steel changes, the firm faces a *different decision*: "use the steel to produce cars" or "resell it in the open market." The opportunity cost of *using the steel* is the $1,200,000 payment that the firm sacrifices by not selling the steel in the open market. Same steel, same firm, but different opportunity cost! The opportunity costs differ because *there are different opportunity costs for different decisions under different circumstances*.

Opportunity Costs and Market Prices

Note that the unifying feature of this example is that the relevant opportunity cost was, in both cases, the current market price of the sheet steel. This is no coincidence. *From the firm's perspective*, the opportunity cost of using the productive services of an input is the current market price of the input. The opportunity cost of using the services of an input is what the firm's owners would save or gain by *not* using those services. A firm can "not use" the services of an input in two ways. It can refrain from buying those services in the first place, in which case the firm saves an amount equal to the market price of the input. Or it can resell unused services of the input in the open market, in which case it gains an amount equal to the market price of the input. In both cases, the opportunity cost of the input services is the current market price of those services.

EXAMPLE 7.1   *Economic Value Added*

G. Bennett Stewart, co-founder of the financial consulting firm of Stern–Stewart, is a proponent of using opportunity costs in business decision making.[2] Stewart has developed a comprehensive approach to measuring the performance of business firms built around the concept of economic value added (EVA): In its simplest form:

$$EVA = \text{operating profit} - \text{opportunity cost of capital}$$

EVA is a method of measuring a firm's true economic profitability, taking into account the opportunity cost that investors in the firm incur by having their capital tied up inside the firm's assets. Stern–Stewart keeps track of EVAs for hundreds of companies. For example, in 1998 General Motors had a negative EVA of more than $5 billion. By contrast, General Electric had a positive EVA of approximately $4.3 billion.

Stewart likens a company with a high operating profit but a negative EVA to a basketball player who scores a lot of baskets (has high accounting earnings) only because he takes lots of shots (invests lots of capital). Just as the team might do better if the player passed the ball to other teammates whose scoring efficiency is higher, a negative EVA company would make its investors better off by forgoing investments in marginal projects and returning funds to shareholders whose alternative investment opportunities are better than the company's.

The concept of EVA has been embraced by both investors and senior managers. Eugene Vesell, a senior vice president of Oppenheimer Capital, which manages $26 billion in funds, has stated "We like to invest in companies that use EVA and similar measures. Making higher returns than the cost of capital is how we look at the world." Roberto Goizueta, the late CEO of Coca Cola, was an enthusiastic believer in EVA: "When I played golf regularly," he said, "my average score was 90, so every hole was a par 5. I look at EVA like I look at breaking par. At Coca-Cola we are way under par and adding a lot of value."[3] During Goizueta's tenure, Coca-Cola adopted EVA techniques for company-wide financial planning and used EVA as a basis for managerial compensation and bonuses.   ■

EXPLICIT VERSUS IMPLICIT COSTS

Opportunity costs do not necessarily involve direct outlays of cash by the firm. For example, the opportunity cost of the time that an owner devotes to his or her business does not entail a cash outlay. For this reason, economists distinguish between **explicit costs** and **implicit costs.** Explicit costs involve a direct monetary outlay. Purchases of labor or materials entail explicit costs. Implicit costs do not involve outlays of cash. The opportunity costs associated with the use of a firm's capital assets are often implicit costs.

[2]This example draws from Stewart's book, *The Quest for Value: A Guide for Senior Managers* (New York: Harper Business, 1991).

[3]Both quotes come from "The Real Key to Creating Wealth," *Fortune* (September 23, 1993), pp. 38–50.

ECONOMIC VERSUS ACCOUNTING COSTS

Closely related to the distinction between explicit and implicit costs is the distinction between **economic costs** and **accounting costs.** Accounting statements typically show historical expenses: How much did the firm spend on labor or on materials in a particular year? Accounting statements are designed to serve an audience outside the firm, such as lenders and equity investors. Because accounting numbers must be objective and verifiable, historical costs serve the purpose best. By contrast, economists emphasize the use of costs for decision making. To economists, decision-relevant costs are opportunity costs.

Economic costs are therefore the sum of explicit and implicit costs. By contrast, accounting costs include explicit costs but do not include implicit costs. For example, the income statement for a typical manufacturing firm would not include the opportunity costs associated with the use of the firm's factories. This omission is not because accountants do not understand opportunity costs, but rather because opportunity costs of capital are often hard to measure in an objectively verifiable way. An income statement for an owner-operated small business would also not include the opportunity cost of the owner's time. And because accounting statements use historical costs, not current market prices, to compute costs, the costs on the profit-and-loss statement of the automobile firm that purchased that sheet steel would reflect the $1,000,000 purchase price of that steel, but it would not reflect the $1,200,000 opportunity cost that it incurs when the firm actually uses that steel to manufacture automobiles.

*E*XAMPLE 7.2

DRAM Chips, Opportunity Costs, and the Difference Between Accounting Costs and Economic Costs[4]

DRAM stands for dynamic random access memory. DRAM chips are silicon semiconductor integrated circuits used to create memory in personal computers. DRAM chips are produced by companies such as Samsung, NEC, and Hitachi, and they are purchased by manufacturers of personal computers, such as Compaq and Apple.

Firms that buy memory chips typically do so at prices set by contracts covering three to six months. For example, a firm such as Compaq, might contract to obtain chips from a DRAM supplier, such as Hitachi, at a price of $25 per megabyte over a three-month period. But there is also an active spot market for DRAM chips, and prices in this market can fluctuate a lot. For example, between December 1995 and January 1997, prices of DRAM chips fell from over $35 per megabyte to just over $5 per megabyte.[5]

Because the spot market price fluctuates so much, the opportunity cost of using DRAM chips in production will not necessarily equal the historical contract price that a firm paid for its chips. Instead, that opportunity cost will equal the current spot market price, which represents what the firm could get if it resold its inventory of DRAM chips in the open market. This opportunity cost is a real one. It is not at all difficult for a firm to liquidate its inventory of DRAM chips, a phenome-

[4]This example draws from "The DRAM Industry," a term paper prepared by E. Cappochi, B. Firsov, and L. Pachano, 1997 graduates at the Kellogg Graduate School of Management.

[5]Example 2.6 uses supply and demand analysis to explain why this happened.

non known as *backflush*. Intel, for example, was part of the backflush in November 1995 when it liquidated a huge inventory of chips that it had purchased in the expectation of producing its own personal computers.

In mid-1996, with chip prices collapsing, DRAM buyers (e.g., Compaq) that had overestimated demand for Windows 95 and stocked up on higher-priced DRAM chips found themselves facing an opportunity cost for DRAM chips that was far lower than the historical cost they incurred to buy them in the first place.[6] This created a situation in which the accounting costs of the DRAM chips were greater than the economic costs. Thus, from this example we see that accounting costs can sometimes be greater than economic costs. In other words, just because accounting costs exclude implicit costs, while economic costs include implicit costs, it does not follow that accounting costs are always less than economic costs. Sometimes accounting costs can be greater than economic costs. ∎

SUNK VERSUS NONSUNK COSTS

To analyze costs we also need to distinguish between sunk and nonsunk costs. When assessing the costs of a decision, the decision maker should consider only those costs that the decision actually affects. Some costs must be incurred no matter what decision is made. They are costs that have already been incurred and cannot be avoided. These are called **sunk costs.** By contrast, **nonsunk costs** are costs that are incurred only if a particular decision is made and are thus avoided if the decision is not made (For this reason nonsunk costs are also called *avoidable costs*). When evaluating alternative decisions, the decision maker should ignore sunk costs and consider only nonsunk costs.

Here is an example: You pay $7.50 to go see a movie. Ten minutes into the movie, it is clear that the movie is awful. You face a choice: Should you leave or stay? The relevant cost of staying is that you could more valuably spend your time doing just about anything else. The relevant cost of leaving is the enjoyment that you might forgo if the movie proves to be better than the first ten minutes suggest. The relevant cost of leaving *does not* include the $7.50 price of admission. That cost is sunk. No matter what you decide to do, you've already paid the admission fee, and its amount should be irrelevant to your decision to leave.

To illustrate the distinction between sunk costs and nonsunk costs, consider a sporting goods firm that manufactures bowling balls. Let's assume that a bowling ball factory costs $5 million to build. Once it is built, suppose that the factory is so highly specialized that it has no alternative uses. Thus, if the sporting goods firm shuts the factory down and produces nothing, it cannot "recover" any of the $5 million it spent to build the factory in the first place.

---

[6]Based on this observation, you might be asking, "If the opportunity cost is the spot price, and the spot price is less than the contract price, why would a firm ever buy chips in advance under contract?" If PC makers had known for certain that the spot price of DRAM chips was going to fall, they would not have bought under contract at a higher price. But in reality these firms did not know for certain what the spot price would be three or six months from the time they signed their contracts. Indeed, an important reason for buying on contract is to eliminate the uncertainty about input prices that the firm would otherwise face if it always purchased in the spot market. In Chapter 15, we discuss reasons why risk reduction might be desirable.

- *To decide whether to build the factory*, the $5 million is a *nonsunk cost*. It is a cost the sporting goods firm incurs only if it builds the factory. At the time the decision is being considered, the decision maker can avoid spending the $5 million.

- After the factory is built, the $5 million is a *sunk cost*. It is a cost the sporting goods firm incurs no matter what it chooses to do when confronted with this decision, so this cost is unavoidable. *When deciding whether to operate the factory or shut it down*, the sporting goods firm therefore should ignore this cost.

This example illustrates an important point: *Whether a cost is sunk or nonsunk depends on the decision that is being contemplated.* To identify what costs are sunk and what costs are nonsunk in a particular decision, you should always ask which costs would change as a result of making one choice as opposed to another. These are the nonsunk costs. The costs that do not change no matter what choice we make are the sunk costs.

EXAMPLE 7.3

Sparky Anderson, Mike Moore, and Sunk Costs When Managing a Major League Baseball Team[7]

Sparky Anderson was one of the greatest managers in the history of major league baseball. He managed the Cincinnati Reds from 1970 to 1978 and the Detroit Tigers from 1979 to 1995. His teams won the World Series three different times (the Reds in 1975 and 1976 and the Tigers in 1984), and he is still the only manager in baseball history who has won the World Series in both the National and American Leagues.

Despite his greatness, though, late in his career, Sparky Anderson made a critical "sunk cost" mistake in deciding who should pitch for the Detroit Tigers. In late 1992, the Tigers signed a pitcher named Mike Moore to a guaranteed contract of $5 million per year, an enormous amount for a pitcher whose career until then had been less than spectacular. No matter how poorly Moore performed, no matter how little he pitched, the Tigers would have to pay his $5 million annual salary. A bad decision? Probably. For the next three seasons, Moore pitched very ineffectively. He lost more games than he won, and each season his earned run average (ERA) was over 5.00, a poor performance by major league baseball standards of that period. Still, between 1993 and 1995, Sparky used Moore regularly. He explained to reporters that the Tigers were paying this guy a huge salary, so they had to pitch him regularly.

This is a sunk cost fallacy. Sparky should have realized that the Tigers had to pay Moore whether he pitched or not. In deciding whether to let Moore pitch a game, Moore's salary was a sunk cost. It should not have affected Sparky's decisions.

Why did Sparky do this? It's hard to say. He was a shrewd manager throughout his career who rarely made decisions that hurt his teams (like this one did). Maybe he was doing what he felt top Tiger management wanted him to do, reasoning that it would make them look bad to pay a pitcher who doesn't play on a

---

[7]This example draws from *The Bill James Guide to Baseball Managers From 1870 to Today* (New York: Scribner, 1997).

regular basis such a large salary. Or maybe he felt that Moore would eventually break out of his slump if he continued to pitch regularly. (He didn't.) But if he really did continue to pitch Moore because of Moore's salary, then there is an important lesson here, even for those of you who don't aspire to be baseball managers. Don't be like Sparky and let sunk costs influence your decisions.   ∎

LEARNING-BY-DOING EXERCISE 7.1

Using the Cost Concepts for an Internet Business

Imagine that you have started an Internet-based snack food delivery business on your college campus. Students send you orders for snacks, such as potato chips and candy bars. You shop at local grocery stores to fill these orders and then deliver the orders. To operate this business, you pay $500 a month to a local Web-hosting company to use their server to host and maintain your Web site. You also own a sports utility vehicle (SUV) in which to make deliveries. Your monthly car payment is $300, and you pay $100 a month in insurance costs. Each order that you fill takes, on average, a half hour and consumes $0.50 worth of gasoline.[8] When you fill an order, you pay the grocer for the merchandise. You then collect a payment, along with a delivery fee, from the students to whom you sell. If you did not operate this business, you could work at the campus dining hall, earning $6 an hour. Right now, you operate your business five days a week, Monday through Friday. On weekends, your business is idle, and you work in the campus dining hall.

Problem

(a) What are your explicit costs and what are your implicit costs? What are your accounting costs and what are your economic costs? How would they differ?

(b) Last week you purchased five large cases of Fritos for a customer who, as it turned out, did not accept delivery. You paid $100 for these cases. You have a deal with your grocers that they will pay you $0.25 for each dollar of returned merchandise. Just this week, you found a fraternity on campus that will buy the five cartons for $55 (and will pick them up from your apartment, relieving you of the need to deliver them to the frat house). What is the opportunity cost of filling this order, i.e. selling the cartons to the fraternity? Should you sell the Fritos to the fraternity?

(c) Suppose you are thinking of cutting back your operation from five days to four days a week? (You will not operate on Monday and instead will work in the campus dining hall.) What costs are sunk with respect to this decision? What costs are nonsunk?

(d) Suppose you contemplate going out of business altogether. What costs are sunk with respect to this decision? What costs are nonsunk?

---

[8]For simplicity, let's ignore other costs such as wear and tear on your vehicle.

Solution

(a) Your explicit costs are those that involve direct monetary outlays. These include your car payment, insurance, leasing computer time, gasoline, and the cost you pay the grocer for the merchandise you deliver to your customers. Your main implicit cost is the opportunity cost of your time. This is $6 per hour.

Your economic costs are the sum total of your explicit and implicit costs. They would thus be the sum of your car payment, insurance, computer time, gasoline, and merchandise costs, plus the opportunity cost of your time. If your accountant were to prepare a profit-and-loss statement for your business, he or she would include all of the explicit costs that we just mentioned but would not include the opportunity cost of your time. Moreover, the accounting statement would be a historical record of the costs you incurred last year. If, for example, gasoline prices have gone down since then, your current gasoline costs would not equal those on your accounting statement.

(b) The opportunity cost of filling this order is $25. This is what you could have gotten for the Fritos if you had resold them to your grocer. Because you can sell the Fritos at a price that exceeds this opportunity cost, you should fill the order. By filling the order, your firm's profit is $55 − $25 = $30 higher than it would have been if you returned the merchandise to the grocery store.

Some students might ask: Why isn't the opportunity cost $100, the original cost? The opportunity cost is $25 because opportunity cost is a forward-looking concept: It measures what you sacrifice by filling this order at the time you make your decision. Had you assessed the opportunity cost of the order to be $100, you might have been misled into not making a decision (selling the week-old Fritos to the fraternity) that benefits your company by offsetting some of the loss that you incurred by buying the Fritos in the first place.

What, then, does the difference between your $100 original cost and the $25 opportunity cost represent? It must represent something, right? In fact, it does. This $75 difference is, in retrospect, the net cost you incurred in trying to satisfy a customer who proved to be unreliable. It is a sunk (unavoidable) cost of doing business. But it does not represent the forward-looking opportunity cost of satisfying the fraternity's order.

(c) Your nonsunk costs with respect to this decision are those costs that you will avoid if you make this decision. Among your nonsunk costs are the costs of gasoline and the costs of purchased merchandise. (Of course, you also "avoid" receiving the revenue from this merchandise, as well as delivery fees.) In addition, though, you also avoid one day of the implicit opportunity cost of your time. That is, by not operating on Monday, you no longer sacrifice the opportunity to work in the dining hall on Mondays.

Your sunk costs are those that you cannot avoid by making this decision. Because you still need your SUV for deliveries, your car and insurance payments are sunk with respect to this one-day cutback decision. Your leasing of computer time is also sunk since you still need to maintain your Web site.

(d) You certainly will avoid your merchandising costs and gasoline costs if you cease operations. These costs are thus nonsunk with respect to the shut-down decision. You also avoid the opportunity cost of your time, so this too is a nonsunk cost. Since shutting down your business implies that you will no longer maintain a Web site, you also avoid the cost of leasing computer time from the local Internet service provider. Thus, while the computer leasing cost was sunk with respect to the decision to scale back operations by one day, it is non-sunk with respect to the decision to cease operations altogether.

What about the costs of your SUV? Suppose that you plan to get rid of it, which means that you can avoid your $100 a month insurance bill. Your insurance costs are therefore nonsunk. But also suppose that you customized the SUV, for example by painting your logo on it. Because of this and because of the general wariness that the public has about buying used vehicles, you can recover only 30 percent of the cost you paid for it. Thus, by exiting the business, you can offset 30 percent of your car payment. This means that 70 percent of your car payment is sunk (it can't be avoided if you go out of business), while 30 percent is nonsunk (it is avoided when you go out of business and sell your SUV). Thus, to summarize, when you contemplate exiting the business, your merchandising, gasoline, leasing, and insurance expenses are nonsunk (i.e., avoidable). Moreover, 30 percent of your car payment is avoidable. The remaining 70 percent of it is a sunk cost.

Similar Problem: 7.1

7.2
THE COST-MINIMIZA-TION PROBLEM

Now that we have introduced a variety of different cost concepts, let's apply them to analyze an important decision problem for a firm: How to choose a combination of inputs to minimize the cost of producing a given quantity of output. We saw in Chapter 6 that firms can typically produce a given amount of output using many different input combinations. Of all the input combinations that can be chosen, a firm that wants to make its owners as wealthy as possible should choose the one that minimizes its costs of production. The problem of finding the input combination that minimizes a firm's costs of production is called the **cost-minimization problem,** and a firm that seeks to minimize the cost of producing a given amount of output is called a **cost-minimizing firm.**

LONG RUN VERSUS SHORT RUN

We will study the firm's cost-minimization problem in the long run and in the short run. Although the terms *long run* and *short run* seem to connote a length of time, it is more useful to think of them as pertaining to the degree to which the firm faces constraints in its decision-making flexibility. A firm that makes a **long-run** decision faces a blank slate: It is free to vary the quantities of all its inputs as much as it desires. When our sporting goods firm in the previous section decides whether to build a new bowling ball factory, it faces a long-run decision. It is free to choose whether to build the factory, and if so, how large to make it. As it does this, it can simultaneously choose other input quantities such as the size of the work force to employ and the amount of land that will surround the factory. Because the firm can, in principle, avoid the costs of all inputs by choosing not to produce, the costs associated with long-run decisions are necessarily nonsunk.

By contrast, a firm facing a **short-run** decision is subject to constraints. It is unable to adjust the quantities of some of its inputs, and/or it is unable to reverse the consequences of initial decisions that it has made regarding those inputs. For example, once our bowling ball firm builds a factory, it will, at least for a while, face short-run decisions, such as how many workers it should employ given the physical constraints of its capacity.

In microeconomics, the concept of short run and long run are convenient analytical simplifications to help us focus our attention on the interesting features of the problem at hand. In reality, firms face a continuum of "runs"; some decisions involve "blanker slates" than others. In this section, we first focus on long-run cost minimization in order to study carefully the trade-offs that firms can make in input choices when they start with a blank slate. In the next section, we turn to short-run cost minimization to highlight how constraints on input usage can limit the firm's ability to make its costs as low as possible.

THE LONG-RUN COST-MINIMIZATION PROBLEM

The cost-minimization problem is another example of constrained optimization that we discussed in Chapter 1. We want to minimize the firm's total costs, subject to the requirement that the firm produce a given amount of output. We have encountered two other examples of constrained optimization problems so far: The problem of maximizing utility subject to a budget constraint (utility maximization) in Chapter 4 and the problem of minimizing consumption expenditures, subject to achieving a minimum level of utility (expenditure minimization), also discussed in Chapter 4. You will see that the cost-minimization problem closely resembles the expenditure-minimization problem from consumer choice theory.

Let's study the long-run cost-minimization problem for a firm that uses two inputs: labor and capital. Each input has a price. The price of a unit of labor services—also called the wage rate—is w. This price per unit of capital services is r. The price of labor could either be an explicit cost or implicit cost. It would be an explicit cost if the firm (as most firms do) hires workers in the open market. It could be an implicit cost if the firm's owner is providing his or her own labor to run the firm and in so doing, sacrifices outside employment opportunities. Similarly, the price of capital could either be an explicit cost or an implicit cost. It would be an explicit cost if the firm leased capital services from another firm (e.g., an e-commerce firm that leases computer time on a server to host its Web site). It would be an implicit cost if the firm owned the physical capital and, by using it in its own business, sacrificed the opportunity to sell capital services to other firms.

The firm has decided to produce Q_0 units of output during the next year. In later chapters we will study how the firm makes output decisions. For now, the quantity Q_0 is exogenous. To understand this, you might imagine that the manufacturing manager of the firm has been told how much to produce. The problem is to figure out how to produce that amount in the cost-minimizing way. Thus, the manager must choose a quantity of capital, K, and a quantity of labor, L, to minimize the total cost $TC = wL + rK$ of producing Q_0 units of output. This total cost is the sum of all the economic costs the firm incurs when it hires labor and capital services to produce output.

ISOCOST LINES

Let's now try to solve the firm's cost-minimization problem graphically. Our first step is to draw **isocost lines.** An isocost line is a set of combinations of labor and capital that have the same total cost (*TC*) for the firm. An isocost line is analogous to a budget line from the theory of consumer choice.

Consider, for example, a case in which $w = \$10$ per labor hour, $r = \$20$ per machine hour, and $TC = \$1$ million per year. The $1 million isocost line is described by the equation

$$1,000,000 = 10L + 20K.$$

This can be rewritten as

$$K = \frac{1,000,000}{20} - \frac{1}{2}L.$$

The $2 million and $3 million isocost lines have similar equations:

$$K = \frac{2,000,000}{20} - \frac{1}{2}L$$

$$K = \frac{3,000,000}{20} - \frac{1}{2}L$$

More generally, for an arbitrary level of total cost TC_0, and input prices w and r, the equation of the isocost line is

$$K = \frac{TC_0}{r} - \frac{w}{r}L.$$

Figure 7.1 shows graphs of these isocost lines for a variety of different total cost levels, TC_0, TC_1, TC_2 where $TC_2 > TC_1 > TC_0$. In general, there are an infinite number of isocost lines, one corresponding to every possible level of total cost. Figure 7.1 illustrates that the slope of every isocost line is the same: With K on the vertical axis and L on the horizontal axis, that slope is $-w/r$, or minus the ratio of the price of labor to the price of capital. The K-axis intercept of any particular isocost line is the cost level for that isocost line divided by the price of capital. Thus, for the TC_0 isocost line, the K-axis intercept is TC_0/r. Similarly, the L-axis intercept of the TC_0 isocost line is TC_0/w. Notice that as we move to the northeast in the isocost map in Figure 7.1, isocost lines correspond to higher levels of cost.

GRAPHICAL CHARACTERIZATION OF THE SOLUTION TO THE LONG-RUN COST-MINIMIZATION PROBLEM

Figure 7.2 shows isocost lines and the isoquant corresponding to Q_0 units of output. The solution to the firm's cost-minimization problem occurs at point A, where the isoquant is just tangent to an isocost line. That is, of all the input

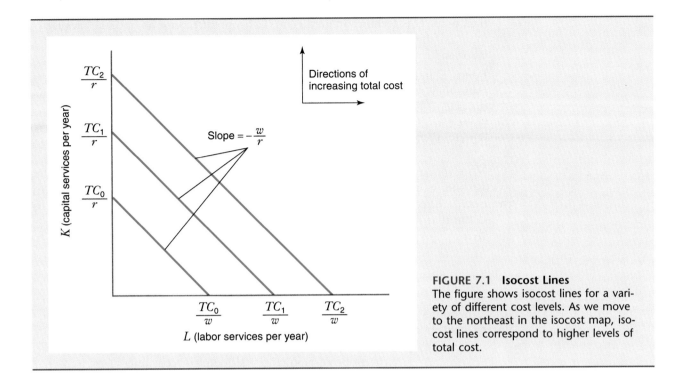

FIGURE 7.1   Isocost Lines
The figure shows isocost lines for a variety of different cost levels. As we move to the northeast in the isocost map, isocost lines correspond to higher levels of total cost.

combinations along the isoquant, point A provides the firm with the lowest level of cost.

To verify this, consider several other points in Figure 7.2, such as E, F, and G:

- Point G is "off" the Q_0 isoquant altogether. Although this input combination *could* produce Q_0 units of output, in using it the firm would be wasting inputs

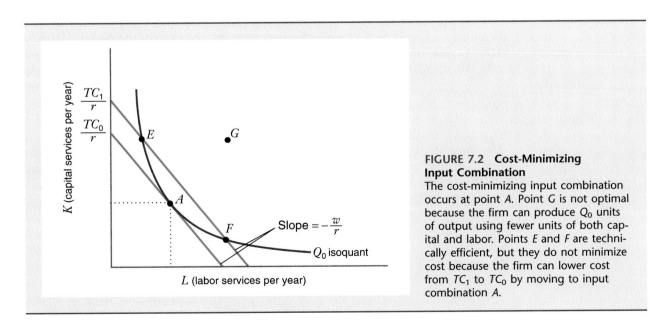

FIGURE 7.2   Cost-Minimizing Input Combination
The cost-minimizing input combination occurs at point A. Point G is not optimal because the firm can produce Q_0 units of output using fewer units of both capital and labor. Points E and F are technically efficient, but they do not minimize cost because the firm can lower cost from TC_1 to TC_0 by moving to input combination A.

(i.e., point G is technically inefficient). This point cannot be optimal because input combination A also produces Q_0 units of output but uses fewer units of labor and capital.

- Points E and F are technically efficient, but they are not cost-minimizing because they are on an isocost line that correspond to a higher level of cost than the isocost line passing through the cost-minimizing point A. By moving from point E to A or from F to A, the firm can produce the same amount of output, but at a lower total cost.

Note that at the cost-minimizing point A, the isoquant is just tangent to an isocost line, which means that the slope of the isoquant is equal to the slope of the isocost line. In Chapter 6, we saw that minus the slope of the isoquant is called the marginal rate of technical substitution of labor for capital, $MRTS_{L,K}$, and that

$$MRTS_{L,K} = \frac{MP_L}{MP_K},$$

As we just illustrated, the slope of an isocost line is $-w/r$. Thus, the cost-minimizing condition is

$$\text{slope of isoquant} = \text{slope of isocost line,}$$

$$-MRTS_{L,K} = -\frac{w}{r},$$

$$\frac{MP_L}{MP_K} = \frac{w}{r}, \tag{7.1}$$

$$\text{ratio of marginal products} = \text{ratio of input prices}$$

In Figure 7.2, the optimal input combination A is an interior optimum. An interior optimum involves positive amounts of both inputs ($L > 0$ and $K > 0$), and the optimum occurs at a tangency between the isoquant and an isocost line. Equation (7.1) tells us that at an interior optimum, the ratio of the marginal products of labor and capital equals the ratio of the price of labor to the price of capital. We could also rewrite (7.1) to state the optimality condition in this form:

$$\frac{MP_L}{w} = \frac{MP_K}{r}, \tag{7.2}$$

This condition tells us that at a cost-minimizing input combination, the additional output per dollar spent on labor services equals the additional output per dollar spent on capital services. Thus, if we are minimizing costs, we get equal "bang for the buck" from each input. Recall that we obtained a similar condition at the solution to a consumer's utility-maximization problem in Chapter 4.

To see why equation (7.2) must hold, consider a noncost-minimizing point such as E. At point E, the slope of the isoquant is more negative than the slope of the isocost line. Therefore,

$$-\frac{MP_L}{MP_K} < -\frac{w}{r},$$

or

$$\frac{MP_L}{MP_K} > \frac{w}{r},$$

or

$$\frac{MP_L}{w} > \frac{MP_K}{r}.$$

This condition implies that a firm operating at E could spend an additional dollar on labor and save *more than one dollar* by reducing its employment of capital services in a manner that keeps output constant. Since this would reduce total costs, it follows that an interior input combination, such as E, at which (7.2) *does not hold* cannot be optimal.

LEARNING-BY-DOING EXERCISE 7.2

Finding an Interior Cost-Minimization Optimum for a Cobb–Douglas Production Function

Problem The optimal input combination satisfies equation (7.1) [or, equivalently, (7.2)]. But how would you calculate it? To see how, let's consider a specific example. Suppose that the firm's production function is a Cobb–Douglas production function of the form $Q = 50L^{\frac{1}{2}}K^{\frac{1}{2}}$. For this production function, the equations of the marginal products of labor and capital are

$$MP_L = 25L^{-\frac{1}{2}}K^{\frac{1}{2}}.$$
$$MP_K = 25L^{\frac{1}{2}}K^{-\frac{1}{2}},$$

Suppose, too, that the price of labor w is $5 per unit and the price of capital r is $20 per unit. What is the cost-minimizing input combination if the firm wants to produce 1,000 units per year?

Solution Using the expressions for the marginal products of labor and capital, we have

$$\frac{MP_L}{MP_K} = \frac{K}{L}.$$

Thus, our tangency condition (7.1) is

$$\frac{K}{L} = \frac{5}{20},$$

which simplifies to $L = 4K$. In addition, the input combination must lie on the 1,000 unit isoquant, i.e., the input combination must allow the firm to produce exactly 1,000 units of output. This means that

$$1,000 = 50L^{\frac{1}{2}}K^{\frac{1}{2}}.$$

Simplifying this implies $L = 400/K$. Thus, we have two equations in two unknowns: $L = 4K$ and $L = 400/K$. Solving this system of equations yields $K = 10$ and $L = 40$. The optimal input combination is to use 10 units of capital and 40 units of labor.

Similar Problems: 7.7, 7.8

CORNER-POINT SOLUTIONS

In discussing the theory of consumer behavior in Chapter 4, we studied corner-point solutions: optimal solutions at which we did not have a tangency between a budget line and an indifference curve. We can also have corner-point solutions to the cost-minimization problem. Figure 7.3 illustrates this case. The cost-minimizing input combination for producing Q_0 units of output occurs at point A where the firm uses no capital.

At this corner point, the isocost line is flatter than the isoquant. Mathematically, this says

$$-\frac{MP_L}{MP_K} < -\frac{w}{r},$$

or equivalently

$$\frac{MP_L}{MP_K} > \frac{w}{r}.$$

Another way to write this would be

$$\frac{MP_L}{w} > \frac{MP_K}{r}. \tag{7.3}$$

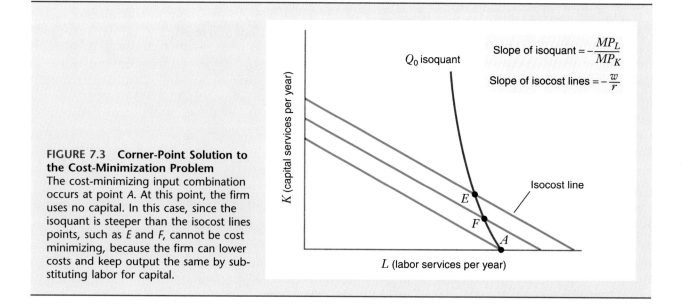

FIGURE 7.3   Corner-Point Solution to the Cost-Minimization Problem
The cost-minimizing input combination occurs at point A. At this point, the firm uses no capital. In this case, since the isoquant is steeper than the isocost lines points, such as E and F, cannot be cost minimizing, because the firm can lower costs and keep output the same by substituting labor for capital.

Thus, at the corner solution at point A, the marginal product per dollar spent on labor exceeds the marginal product per dollar spent on capital services. If you look closely at other points along the Q_0 unit isoquant, you see that isocost lines are always flatter than the isoquant. Hence, condition (7.3) holds for all input combinations along the Q_0 isoquant. A corner solution at which no capital is used can be thought of as a response to a situation in which every additional dollar spent on labor yields more output than every additional dollar spent on capital. In this situation, the firm should substitute labor for capital until it uses no capital at all. This is because for every additional dollar the firm spends on labor, the firm can save more than one dollar by reducing its employment of capital services so as to keep output fixed.

LEARNING-BY-DOING EXERCISE 7.3

Finding a Corner-Point Solution with Perfect Substitutes

Problem In Chapter 6 we saw that a production function that is linear in input quantities implies that the inputs are perfect substitutes. Suppose that we have a linear production function $Q = 10L + 2K$. For this production function $MP_L = 10$ and $MP_K = 2$. Suppose, too, that the price of labor w is \$5 per unit, and the price of capital services r is \$2 per unit. Find the optimal input combination given that the firm wishes to produce 200 units of output.

Solution Figure 7.4 shows that the optimal input combination is a corner solution at which $K = 0$. The following argument tells us that we must have a corner-point solution. We know that when inputs are perfect substitutes, $MRTS_{L,K} = MP_L/MP_K$ is constant along an isoquant; in this particular example, it is equal to 5. But $w/r = 2.5$, so there is no point that can satisfy $MP_L/MP_K = w/r$. This tells us that we cannot have an interior solution.

But what corner point will we end up at? In this case, $MP_L/w = 10/5 = 2$, and $MP_K/r = 2/2 = 1$, so the marginal product per dollar of labor exceeds the marginal product per dollar of capital. This implies that the firm will substitute labor for capital until it uses no capital. Hence the optimal input combination involves $K = 0$. Since the firm is going to produce 200 units of output, the quantity of labor satisfies $200 = 10L + 2(0)$ or $L = 20$.

Similar Problem: 7.9

ANALOGY TO CONSUMER THEORY

The cost-minimization problem we have been studying in this chapter should strike you as familiar because it is analogous to the expenditure-minimization problem that we studied in Chapter 4. In the expenditure-minimization problem, a consumer seeks to minimize his or her total expenditures, subject to attaining a given level of utility. In the cost-minimization problem, a firm seeks to minimize its expenditures on goods and services, subject to producing a given level of output. Both the graphical analysis and the mathematics of the two problems are identical. The key difference is that in the expenditure-minimization problem we used notation x and y to denote quantities, P_x and P_y to denote prices, and

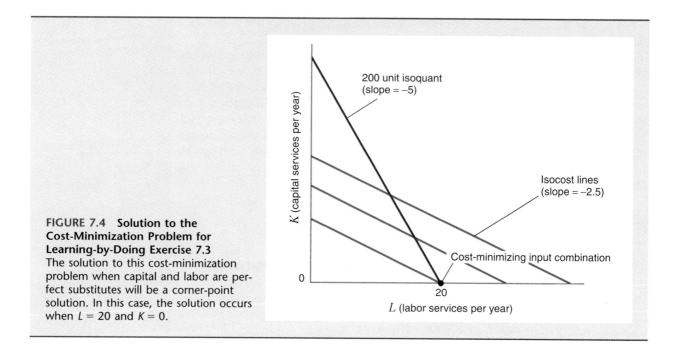

FIGURE 7.4 Solution to the Cost-Minimization Problem for Learning-by-Doing Exercise 7.3
The solution to this cost-minimization problem when capital and labor are perfect substitutes will be a corner-point solution. In this case, the solution occurs when $L = 20$ and $K = 0$.

$U(x, y)$ to denote the utility function. In the cost-minimization problem, we use L and K to denote input quantities, w and r to denote input prices, and $f(L, K)$ to denote the production function.

7.3
COMPARATIVE STATICS ANALYSIS OF THE COST-MINIMIZA-TION PROBLEM

We have now characterized the solution to the firm's cost-minimization problem. Let's now explore how changes in input prices and output affect the solution to this problem.

COMPARATIVE STATICS ANALYSIS OF CHANGES IN INPUT PRICES

Figure 7.5 shows a comparative statics analysis of the cost-minimization problem as the price of labor w changes. It shows how the optimal input combination changes when the price of labor increases from $w = 1$ to $w = 2$, holding the price of capital fixed at $r = 1$ and holding output fixed. The cost-minimizing quantity of labor goes down as w goes up, while the cost-minimizing quantity of capital goes up. That is, the increase in the price of labor causes the firm to substitute capital for labor in its production process.

Why does this happen? Figure 7.5 shows that the increase in the price of labor makes the isocost lines steeper. With diminishing $MRTS_{L,K}$, the tangency between an isocost line and the isoquant occurs "farther up" the isoquant (i.e., the cost-minimizing quantity of labor falls while the cost-minimizing quantity of capital rises). By similar logic, an increase in the price r of capital services (holding w and Q fixed) must decrease the cost-minimizing quantity of capital and increase the cost minimizing quantity of labor.

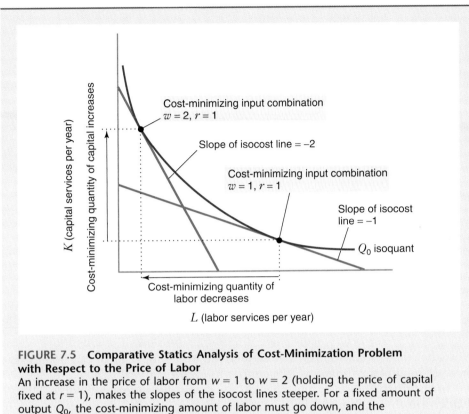

FIGURE 7.5 Comparative Statics Analysis of Cost-Minimization Problem with Respect to the Price of Labor
An increase in the price of labor from $w = 1$ to $w = 2$ (holding the price of capital fixed at $r = 1$), makes the slopes of the isocost lines steeper. For a fixed amount of output Q_0, the cost-minimizing amount of labor must go down, and the cost-minimizing quantity of capital must go up.

This relationship relies on two important assumptions. First, at the initial input prices, the firm must be using a positive quantity of both inputs. That is, we do not start from a corner-point solution. If this did not hold—if the the firm was initially using a zero quantity of an input—and the price of that input went up, the firm would continue to use a zero quantity of the input. Thus, the cost-minimizing input quantity would not go down as in Figure 7.5 but instead would stay the same. Second, the analysis in Figure 7.5 applies when the firm has "smooth" isoquants (i.e., the isoquants do not have kinks in them). Figure 7.6 shows what happens when the firm has a fixed-proportions production function and thus has isoquants with a kink in them. As in the case where we start with a corner point, an increase in the price of labor leaves the cost-minimizing quantity of labor unchanged.

Let's summarize the results of our comparative statics analysis:

- When the firm has smooth isoquants and the firm is initially using positive quantities of an input, an increase in the price of that input (holding output and other input prices fixed) will cause the cost-minimizing quantity of that input to go down.

- When the firm is using a zero quantity of the input or the firm has a fixed-proportions production function as in Figure 7.6, an increase in the price of the input will leave the cost-minimizing input quantity unchanged.

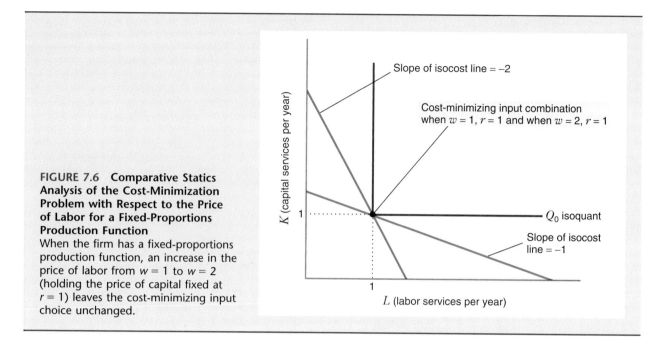

FIGURE 7.6 Comparative Statics Analysis of the Cost-Minimization Problem with Respect to the Price of Labor for a Fixed-Proportions Production Function
When the firm has a fixed-proportions production function, an increase in the price of labor from $w = 1$ to $w = 2$ (holding the price of capital fixed at $r = 1$) leaves the cost-minimizing input choice unchanged.

Note that these results imply that an increase in the input price can never cause the cost-minimizing quantity of the input to go up.

In the introduction to this chapter, we discussed the case of Burke Mills, a textile firm that automated its production process in response to an increase in the price of labor. Figure 7.5 explains why this move made sense for Burke Mills. Faced with an increase in the price of labor, Burke Mills responded in a way consistent with cost-minimizing behavior: it increased the ratio of capital to labor it employed in its production process.

EXAMPLE 7.4   *Oil Tankers[9]*

The transportation of oil by tanker is a volatile and risky business that has been described as "the world's largest poker game." Massive fortunes have been made and lost in the tanker business. For example, Aristotle Onassis, the second husband of Jacqueline Kennedy Onassis, amassed his immense wealth by owning oil tankers. Tankers themselves are enormous steel vessels that, if turned on their ends, would be taller than the world's highest skyscrapers. They are also *very* expensive: In the early 1990s, a single tanker cost upwards of $50 million.

The major participants in the oil tanker business are oil companies, independent shipowners, and governments. Independent shipowners come from all over the world, but have historically been concentrated in Norway, Greece, and Hong Kong. In the 1970s, the Norwegians were among the first shipowners to invest in supertankers, large oil tankers with capacities over 200,000 deadweight tons (DWT).[10]

---

[9]This example draws heavily from "The Oil Tanker Shipping Industry in 1983," Harvard Business School case 9-384-034.

[10]A deadweight ton of capacity is approximately 7 barrels of oil.

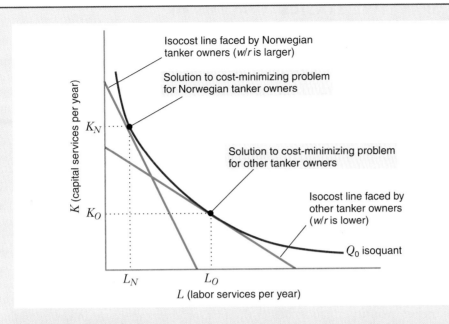

FIGURE 7.7 Oil Tankers
The Norwegians faced a higher price of labor and a lower price of capital than tanker owners from other countries. They thus face more steeply sloped isocost lines. The solution to their cost minimization problem for a given output of transported oil, Q_0, is to operate at a higher capital–labor ratio, K_N/L_N, as compared to the capital–labor ratio K_O/L_O used by other shipowners.

Until then, conventional tankers had capacities that were under 100,000 DWT. Thus, in the early 1980s, the Norwegians owned 15 percent of the world's tankers but accounted for nearly 50 percent of the tonnage.

Supertankers require proportionately less labor to operate and maintain than conventional tankers. For example, in the early 1980s, crew costs accounted for 28 percent of the costs of operating a 50,000 DWT tanker, but only 14 percent of the costs of operating a 250,000 DWT tanker. Thus, supertankers embody a higher ratio of capital to labor than conventional tankers do.

Was it a coincidence that the Norwegians were the most aggressive adopters of the supertanker technology? Probably not. The Norwegians had strong economic incentives to substitute capital for labor in the operation of their tankers. Norwegian law requires Norwegian tankers to operate under the Norwegian flag, which meant that they had to pay their crews higher wage rates than did owners who operated under so-called "flags of convenience" (usually Liberian or Panamanian). In addition, the Norwegian government allowed shipowners liberal depreciation and reinvestment allowances, which reduced the owners' effective price of capital. On balance, then, Norwegian tanker operators probably faced a higher price of labor and a lower price of capital than did operators from other countries. As Figure 7.7 shows, a cost-minimizing firm faced with this situation has an incentive to operate with a higher capital–labor ratio than does a firm facing a lower price of labor and a higher price of capital. The early adoption of supertankers by the Norwegians was consistent with these economic incentives. ∎

COMPARATIVE STATICS ANALYSIS OF CHANGES IN OUTPUT

Figure 7.8 shows a different comparative statics analysis: How does the cost-minimizing combination of labor and capital vary with Q, holding the input prices w and r fixed? For the technology represented by the isoquants on the graph, an increase in Q moves the firm to isoquants farther to the northeast. Holding input prices fixed, the cost-minimizing solution moves from point A (when $Q = 100$) to point B (when $Q = 200$) to point C (when $Q = 300$). The line in Figure 7.8 that connects the cost-minimizing input combinations as Q varies is called the **expansion path.** It summarizes the comparative statics analysis as Q changes. In this case, as the firm produces more output, the cost-minimizing quantities of labor and capital go up. Here, labor and capital are **normal inputs.** An input is normal if the firm uses more of it when producing more output. If both inputs are normal, the expansion path is an upward-sloping line.

Figure 7.9 shows a different possibility. In this case, the cost-minimizing quantity of capital rises as output goes up but the cost-minimizing quantity of labor falls. Figure 7.9 would represent the situation of a firm that drastically automates its production process as it increases the scale of its operation. When the cost-minimizing quantity of labor falls as the firm produces more output, we say that labor is an **inferior input.** When one of the inputs is inferior, the expansion path is downward sloping, as Figure 7.9 shows.

When the firm uses just two inputs to produce its output, both inputs can be normal or one can be normal and the other can be inferior. However, both inputs could never be inferior. Can you see why not? If both inputs were inferior, the firm would reduce the quantities of both as it produced more output. But if

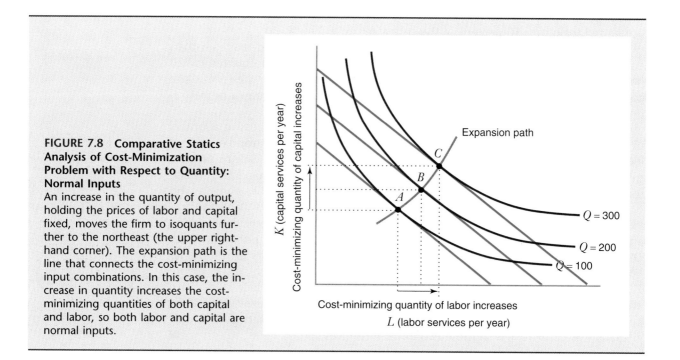

FIGURE 7.8 Comparative Statics Analysis of Cost-Minimization Problem with Respect to Quantity: Normal Inputs
An increase in the quantity of output, holding the prices of labor and capital fixed, moves the firm to isoquants further to the northeast (the upper right-hand corner). The expansion path is the line that connects the cost-minimizing input combinations. In this case, the increase in quantity increases the cost-minimizing quantities of both capital and labor, so both labor and capital are normal inputs.

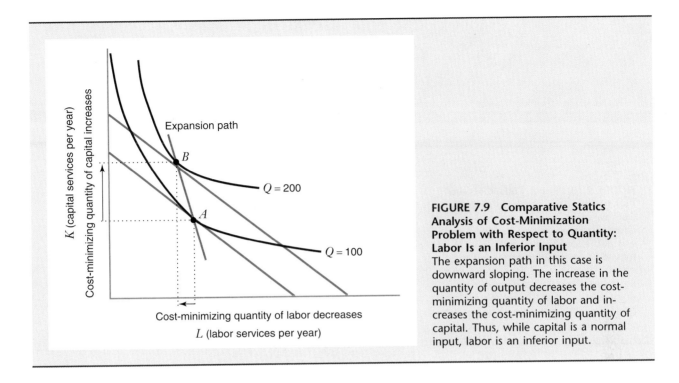

FIGURE 7.9 Comparative Statics Analysis of Cost-Minimization Problem with Respect to Quantity: Labor Is an Inferior Input
The expansion path in this case is downward sloping. The increase in the quantity of output decreases the cost-minimizing quantity of labor and increases the cost-minimizing quantity of capital. Thus, while capital is a normal input, labor is an inferior input.

the firm is technically efficient, as it must be if it is minimizing its costs, a simultaneous reduction in both input quantities would reduce output, not increase it. Inferiority of both inputs would thus be inconsistent with the notion that the firm is getting the most output it can get from the inputs it uses.

EXAMPLE 7.5

Burke Mills Revisited

Let's return to the example of Burke Mills that we discussed in the introduction. Even though Burke Mills automated its production process, it did not significantly change the size of its work force. This seems to run counter to the comparative statics analysis in Figure 7.5, which says that Burke Mills's labor usage should have gone down. What explains this apparent contradiction?

It turns out that two elements of Burke Mills's cost-minimization problem were changing at the same time. In the mid-1990s it was faced with an increase in the price of labor. But it was also expanding into overseas markets, so it was increasing its output. Figure 7.10 shows two comparative statics analyses at the same time: an increase in the price of labor and an increase in output. The increase in the price of labor causes a cost-minimizing firm to increase its capital–labor ratio, which is exactly what occurred at Burke Mills. Assuming that labor and capital are both normal inputs, an increase in output causes a cost-minimizing firm to increase the quantities of all inputs. What probably was happening at Burke Mills is that the *increase* in the quantity of labor that occurred as it expanded output offset the *decrease* in

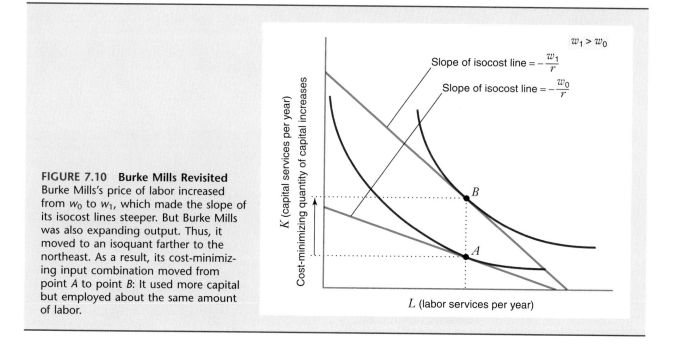

FIGURE 7.10 Burke Mills Revisited
Burke Mills's price of labor increased from w_0 to w_1, which made the slope of its isocost lines steeper. But Burke Mills was also expanding output. Thus, it moved to an isoquant farther to the northeast. As a result, its cost-minimizing input combination moved from point A to point B: It used more capital but employed about the same amount of labor.

the quantity of labor that would have occurred if Burke Mills had substituted capital for labor while holding the volume of output fixed. In other words, Burke Mills would have probably laid off some workers if its strategy had been to remain the same size. The fact that it was in the midst of an overseas expansion prevented it from reducing its work force, even in the face of automation. ∎

SUMMARIZING THE COMPARATIVE STATICS ANALYSIS: THE INPUT DEMAND CURVES

We've seen that the solution to the cost-minimization problem is an optimal input combination: a quantity of capital and a quantity of labor. We've also seen that this input combination depends on how much output the firm wants to produce, Q, and the prices of labor and capital, w and r. Figure 7.11 shows one way to summarize how the cost-minimizing quantity of labor varies with the price of labor. The graph in Figure 7.11 is the firm's **labor demand curve.** The labor demand curve shows how the firm's cost-minimizing quantity of labor varies with the price of labor. This curve will, as Figure 7.11 shows, generally be downward sloping.[11] Similarly, the firm's capital demand curve (not pictured in Figure 7.11) shows how the firm's cost-minimizing quantity of capital varies with the price of capital.

Figure 7.11 also shows how an increase in output affects the firm's demand for labor. Although a change in the price of labor moves the firm *along* its

---

[11]As noted above, exceptions to this occur when the firm has a fixed-proportions production function or when we are in the range when the cost-minimizing quantity of labor is zero. In these cases, as we saw, the quantity of labor demanded does not change as the price of labor goes up.

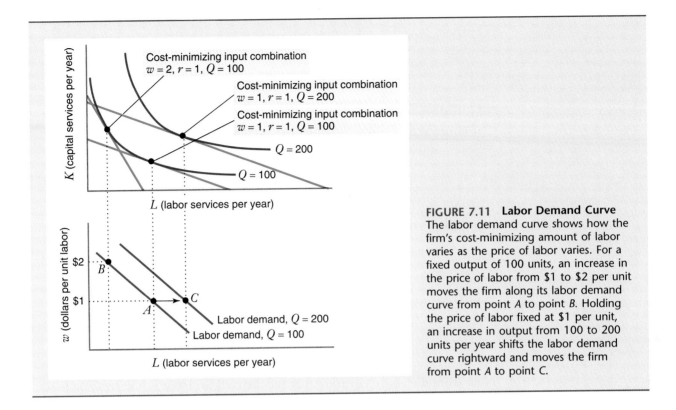

FIGURE 7.11 **Labor Demand Curve**
The labor demand curve shows how the firm's cost-minimizing amount of labor varies as the price of labor varies. For a fixed output of 100 units, an increase in the price of labor from $1 to $2 per unit moves the firm along its labor demand curve from point A to point B. Holding the price of labor fixed at $1 per unit, an increase in output from 100 to 200 units per year shifts the labor demand curve rightward and moves the firm from point A to point C.

labor demand curve, a change in output shifts the labor demand curve itself. Figure 7.11 illustrates the case when labor is a normal input. In this case, an increase in output shifts the labor demand curve rightward. Had labor been an inferior input, the increase in output would have shifted the labor demand curve leftward.

LEARNING-BY-DOING EXERCISE 7.4

The Input Demand Curves for a Cobb–Douglas Production Function

Problem To see how the input demand curves are derived, suppose that the production function is $Q = 50L^{\frac{1}{2}}K^{\frac{1}{2}}$. What are the demand curves for labor and capital?

Solution We begin with our tangency condition $MP_L/MP_K = w/r$. As shown in Learning-By-Doing Exercise 7.2,

$$\frac{MP_L}{MP_K} = \frac{K}{L}.$$

Thus, our tangency condition is

$$\frac{K}{L} = \frac{w}{r}, \text{ or } L = \frac{r}{w}K.$$

This is the equation of the expansion path.

Let's now substitute this into the production function and solve for K in terms of Q, w, and r:

$$Q = 50\left(\frac{r}{w}K\right)^{\frac{1}{2}}K^{\frac{1}{2}},$$

which yields the demand curve for capital:

$$K = \frac{Q}{50}\left(\frac{w}{r}\right)^{\frac{1}{2}}.$$

Since $L = (r/w)K$, it follows that the demand curve for labor is

$$L = \frac{Q}{50}\left(\frac{r}{w}\right)^{\frac{1}{2}}.$$

Note from the above equation that the demand for labor is a decreasing function of w and an increasing function of r. This is consistent with the graphical analysis in Figures 7.5 and 7.11. Note also that both K and L increase when Q increases. Therefore, both capital and labor are normal inputs.

Similar Problem: 7.10

THE PRICE ELASTICITY OF DEMAND FOR INPUTS

We have just seen how we can summarize the solution to the cost-minimization problem with input demand curves. In Chapter 2, we learned that we can describe the sensitivity of the demand for any product to its price using the concept of price elasticity of demand. We can apply this concept to input demand curves. The **price elasticity of demand for labor** $\epsilon_{L,w}$ is the percentage change in the cost-minimizing quantity of labor with respect to a 1 percent change in the price of labor:

$$\epsilon_{L,w} = \frac{\dfrac{\Delta L}{L} \times 100\%}{\dfrac{\Delta w}{w} \times 100\%} \text{ or, rearranging terms and cancelling the 100\%s,}$$

$$\epsilon_{L,w} = \frac{\Delta L}{\Delta w}\frac{w}{L}.$$

Similarly, the **price elasticity of demand for capital** $\epsilon_{K,r}$ is the percentage change in the cost-minimizing quantity of capital with respect to a 1 percent change in the price of capital:

$$\epsilon_{K,r} = \frac{\dfrac{\Delta K}{K} \times 100\%}{\dfrac{\Delta r}{r} \times 100\%}$$ or, rearranging terms and cancelling the 100%s,

$$\epsilon_{K,r} = \frac{\Delta K}{\Delta r} \frac{r}{K}.$$

An important determinant of the price elasticity of demand for inputs is the elasticity of substitution that we discussed in Chapter 6. The two left-hand diagrams in Figure 7.12 show that when the elasticity of substitution is small—that is, when the firm faces limited opportunities to substitute among inputs—large changes in the price of labor result in small changes in the cost-minimizing quantity of labor. For example, in the upper-left-hand diagram, we see a firm that faces a constant elasticity of substitution (CES) production function whose elasticity of substitution is 0.25. With this production function, the firm's opportunities to substitute between labor and capital are limited. As a result, a 50 percent decrease in the price of labor, from $w = 2$ to $w = 1$ (holding the price of capital fixed at

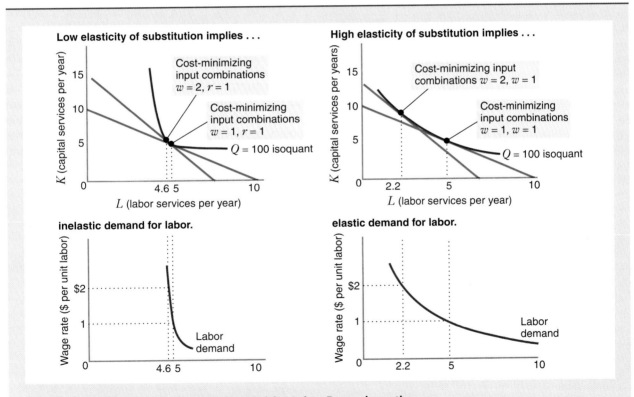

FIGURE 7.12   The Price Elasticity of Demand for Labor Depends on the Elasticity of Substitution Between Labor and Capital
The diagrams on the left-hand side of this figure show that when the elasticity of substitution between capital and labor is low, labor demand will be price inelastic. The diagrams on the right-hand side show that when the elasticity of substitution between labor and capital is high, labor demand will be price elastic.

$r = 1$) results in an 8 percent increase in the cost-minimizing quantity of labor, from 4.6 to 5, shown in the lower left-hand diagram. In this case, the price elasticity of demand for labor is quite small, i.e., the demand for labor is relatively insensitive to the price of labor.

By contrast, in the upper right-hand diagram in Figure 7.12, a firm faces a CES production function whose elasticity of substitution is 2. With this production function, the firm has relatively abundant opportunities to substitute capital for labor. As a result, a 50 percent decrease in the price of labor, from $w = 2$ to $w = 1$, increases the firm's cost-minimizing quantity of labor from 2.2 to 5, an increase of 127 percent. With a greater flexibility to substitute between capital and labor, the firm's demand for labor is relatively more sensitive to the price of labor.

EXAMPLE 7.6

The Price Elasticity of Demand for Inputs in Manufacturing Industries

How elastic or inelastic are input demands in real industries? Research by A. H. Barnett, Keith Reutter, and Henry Thompson suggests that input demands in manufacturing industries might be relatively inelastic.[12] Using data on input quantities, input prices, and outputs over the period 1971–1991, they estimated how the cost-minimizing quantities of capital, labor, and electricity varied with the prices of these inputs in four industries in the state of Alabama: textiles, paper, chemicals, and metals.

Table 7.1 shows their findings. To interpret these numbers, consider the textile industry. Table 7.1 tells us that the price elasticity of demand for production labor in the textile industry is −0.50. This means that faced with a 1 percent increase in the wage rate for production workers, a typical Alabama textile firm will reduce the cost-minimizing quantity of labor by 0.50 percent. This implies that the demand for production labor in Alabama's textile industry is price inelastic, which means

TABLE 7.1
Price Elasticities of Input Demand for Manufacturing Industries in Alabama

Input Industry	Capital	Production Labor	Nonproduction Labor	Electricity
Textiles	−0.41	−0.50	−1.04	−0.11
Paper	−0.29	−0.62	−0.97	−0.16
Chemicals	−0.12	−0.75	−0.69	−0.25
Metals	−0.91	−0.41	−0.44	−0.69

From Table 1 in A.H. Barnett, K. Reutter, and H. Thompson, "Electricity Substitution: Some Local Industrial Evidence," *Energy Economics* 20 (1998), 411–419.

[12]A. H. Barnett, K. Reutter, and H. Thompson, "Electricity Substitution: Some Local Industrial Evidence," *Energy Economics* 20 (1998), 411–419.

that the cost-minimizing quantity of labor is not that sensitive to changes in the price of labor. All but one of the price elasticities of input demand in Table 7.1 are between 0 and −1, which suggests that in the four industries studied, firms do not aggressively substitute among inputs as input prices change. That is, firms in these industries face situations more akin to the left-hand diagrams in Figure 7.12 than the right-hand diagrams.

7.4

SHORT-RUN COST MINIMI-ZATION

So far, we have only studied long-run cost minimization. When one or more of the firm's factors of production cannot be changed, however, the firm operates in the short run. This section studies the firm's costs and its cost-minimization problem in the short run. For simplicity, we will continue to focus on the case in which the firm uses just two inputs, capital and labor. In contrast to the previous section, though, we now assume that because of past decisions, the firm is unable to alter the quantity of capital and thus faces the constraint that its quantity of capital is fixed at a level $\overline{K}$, even when the firm produces zero output. You might imagine, for example, that the firm cannot vary the size of its plant, in which case $\overline{K}$ would represent the firm's fixed plant size. By contrast, we assume that the firm can still vary the quantity of labor. Given its fixed quantity of capital and a variable quantity of labor, the firm's total costs are $wL + r\overline{K}$.

CHARACTERIZING COSTS IN THE SHORT RUN

Fixed versus Variable Costs; Sunk versus Nonsunk Costs

The two components of the firm's total cost, wL and $r\overline{K}$, differ from each other in important ways. One way in which these two components of cost differ is in the extent to which they are sensitive to output. As we will see, the firm's expenditures on labor will go up or down as the firm produces more or less output. The firm's labor cost thus constitutes its **total variable cost.** A firm's total variable cost is the component of the firm's total cost that goes up or down as the firm produces more or less output. That is, the firm's total variable cost is the output-sensitive component of its costs. By contrast, the firm's capital cost, $r\overline{K}$, will not go up or down as the firm produces more or less output. The firm's capital cost might be the payment that it makes to lease factory space from another firm, or it might be a mortgage payment if the firm borrowed money to build its own plant. These costs would not change if the firm varies the amount of output it produces within its plant. The capital cost thus constitutes the firm's **total fixed cost.** The total fixed cost is the component of the firm's cost that remains fixed as the firm varies its output (i.e., it is the component that is output insensitive).

Another way in which the firm's two categories of costs differ is in the extent to which they are sunk or nonsunk with respect to the decision to cease operations by producing zero output. This decision can be couched in terms of the question: Should we produce no output, or should we produce some positive level of output? With respect to the shut-down decision, the firm's total expenditure on labor, wL, is a nonsunk cost. If the firm produces no output, it can avoid its labor costs altogether. By contrast, the firm's capital cost $r\overline{K}$ is a sunk cost. Because the firm cannot adjust the quantity of its capital in the short run, the firm cannot avoid the cost associated with this capital, even if it were to produce no output. For example, if the firm has borrowed money to build its plant, it must still make its mortgage payments, even if it does not operate the plant to produce output.[13]

Are Fixed Costs and Sunk Costs the Same?

At this point you might be asking yourself: Aren't all variable costs nonsunk? Aren't all fixed costs sunk? From everything we've said so far, it certainly appears that the answer to both questions is yes: labor costs are both variable and non-sunk, while capital costs, in the short run, are both fixed and sunk. And, in fact, the answer to the first question *is* definitely yes. Variable costs are, by their nature, avoidable if the firm produces no output. They must therefore be nonsunk. The trickier question is the second one. Are all fixed costs also sunk costs? The answer is: not necessarily.

It is possible, to imagine inputs whose costs do not go up or down as the firm produces more or less output, but that would go away if the firm produced no output. Managers sometimes refer to these costs as *overhead costs*. An example would be heating in a factory. As long as the firm operates, the heating bill will probably be the same no matter how much the firm produces, but if the firm shuts down, it can turn the heat off, and this cost would go away.[14,15] It is even possible that under some circumstances capital costs might be fixed but not sunk. For example, while a firm might not be able to vary the size $\overline{K}$ of its plant as it changes from one positive output level to another, it might be able to avoid its capital costs if it produces zero output. This would happen if, when the firm shuts down, it is able to find someone else that wants its plant and is willing to assume the capital costs $r\overline{K}$ associated with it.

Thus, to summarize, all fixed costs need not be sunk. As Figure 7.13 indicates, the costs associated with inputs whose quantity is fixed in the short run, even if the firm produces zero output, will be both fixed and sunk. But inputs whose usage could be avoided if the firm produced no output entail fixed but nonsunk costs. We will not encounter such inputs in the rest of this chapter, but we will revisit them—and explore them in more detail—in Chapter 9 where we will explicitly consider the impact that fixed but nonsunk costs have on the decision of a firm to shut down.

COST MINIMIZATION IN THE SHORT RUN

Let's now consider the firm's cost-minimization decision in the short run. Figure 7.14 shows the firm's decision problem when it seeks to produce a quantity of output Q_0 but is unable to change the quantity of capital from its fixed level $\overline{K}$. The firm's only technically efficient alternative is to operate at point F. This

[13]This illustration helps us identify what the length of the short run might be. It would be the shorter of the following two time frames: the period of time over which the firm is obligated to make its mortgage payments or the period of time it takes the firm to sell the plant (thus allowing the firm to repay its lender and relieve itself of the mortgage payment).

[14]Of course, this might not be the case if, by eliminating a shift from the plant, the firm could turn down the heat during the period in which workers are not in the plant. But in many real-world factories, heating costs will not change much as the volume of output changes, either because of the need to keep the plant at a constant temperature in order to maintain equipment in optimal operating condition or because of the time it takes to adjust temperature up and down.

[15]We saw another example of fixed but nonsunk costs in Learning-By-Doing Exercise 7.1. Our Internet-based grocery delivery service needed to rent computer time in order to maintain its Web site. This cost did not go up or down as the firm increased or decreased the number of days it operated. But it did go away if the firm ceased operations.

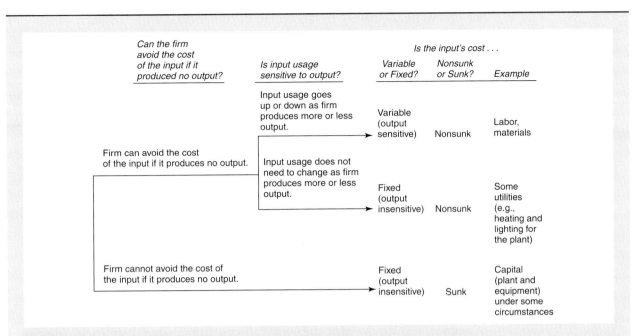

		Is the input's cost . . .		
Can the firm avoid the cost of the input if it produced no output?	Is input usage sensitive to output?	Variable or Fixed?	Nonsunk or Sunk?	Example
Firm can avoid the cost of the input if it produces no output.	Input usage goes up or down as firm produces more or less output.	Variable (output sensitive)	Nonsunk	Labor, materials
	Input usage does not need to change as firm produces more or less output.	Fixed (output insensitive)	Nonsunk	Some utilities (e.g., heating and lighting for the plant)
Firm cannot avoid the cost of the input if it produces no output.		Fixed (output insensitive)	Sunk	Capital (plant and equipment) under some circumstances

FIGURE 7.13 Classifying Inputs and Costs in the Short Run
Inputs are classified according to whether the firm can, in theory, vary the quantity of the input in the short run if it wanted to or must regard the input's quantity as fixed. For those inputs whose cost *can* be avoided if the firm produces no output, there are two possibilities. The firm might need to vary the quantity of the input as it produces more or less output. Those inputs give rise to variable and nonsunk costs. Alternatively, the firm might *not* need to vary an input's usage as it produces more or less output. These inputs give rise to fixed but nonsunk costs. If the firm cannot avoid the cost of the input when it produces no output, then the input gives rise to fixed and sunk costs.

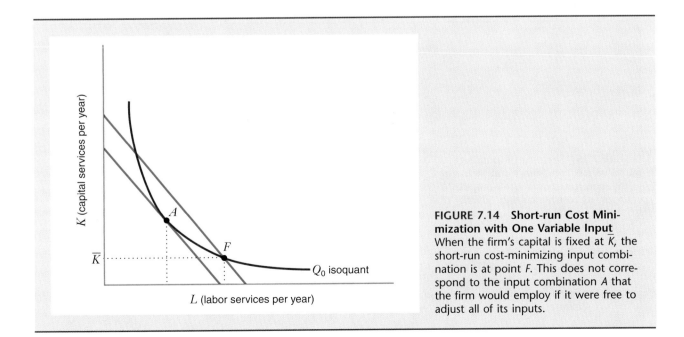

FIGURE 7.14 Short-run Cost Minimization with One Variable Input
When the firm's capital is fixed at $\overline{K}$, the short-run cost-minimizing input combination is at point F. This does not correspond to the input combination A that the firm would employ if it were free to adjust all of its inputs.

involves using a quantity of labor that, in conjunction with the fixed quantity of $\overline{K}$, allows the firm to produce exactly the desired output Q_0.

Note that the short-run cost-minimizing input combination does not involve a tangency condition, as was the case in the long run. The short-run optimal input combination F would not be the combination the firm would use in the long run. In the long run, when the firm can freely adjust all input quantities, it will operate at point A. Figure 7.14 thus illustrates that cost minimization in the short-run will not, in general, coincide with cost minimization in the long run, which means that in the short run the firm will operate with higher total costs than it would if it could adjust all of its inputs in a cost minimizing fashion.

There is, however, one exception to this rule. If the firm wants to produce the level of output for which $\overline{K}$ is long-run cost-minimizing, then the quantity of labor that solves the short-run cost-minimization problem must also solve the long-run cost-minimization problem. This occurs at point B in Figure 7.15. In this case, the total cost the firm incurs in the short run coincides with the total cost the firm incurs in the long run.

COMPARATIVE STATICS: SHORT-RUN INPUT DEMAND VERSUS LONG-RUN INPUT DEMAND

In Section 7.3, we saw that the long-run cost-minimizing quantity of labor varied with input prices and the quantity of output. In the short run, when the firm has just one variable input, the firm's demand for its variable input is independent of changes in input prices (assuming that output remains fixed). This is because, as we saw in Figure 7.14, the firm's fixed quantity of capital constrains its choice of labor. The tangency condition that, in the long run, makes the firm's input demand depend on the input prices is not applicable when the firm operates in the short run with just one variable input.

The firm's demand for labor will, however, vary with the quantity of output in the short-run. Figure 7.15 shows this relationship using the concept of an expansion path introduced in Section 7.3. As the firm varies its output from Q_0 to

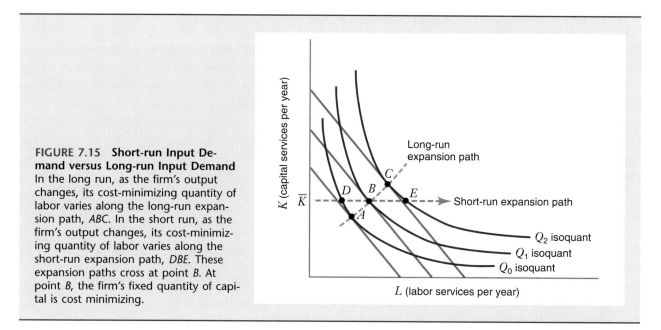

FIGURE 7.15 Short-run Input Demand versus Long-run Input Demand
In the long run, as the firm's output changes, its cost-minimizing quantity of labor varies along the long-run expansion path, *ABC*. In the short run, as the firm's output changes, its cost-minimizing quantity of labor varies along the short-run expansion path, *DBE*. These expansion paths cross at point *B*. At point *B*, the firm's fixed quantity of capital is cost minimizing.

Q_1 to Q_2, the expansion path ABC shows the long-run cost-minimizing input combinations for the firm. By contrast, segment DBE is the expansion path for the firm operating in the short run. For output level Q_2, the firm's fixed capital $\overline{K}$ is cost minimizing in the long run. This is represented by the intersection of the two expansion paths at point B.

LEARNING-BY-DOING EXERCISE 7.5

Short-Run Cost Minimization with One Variable Input

Problem   Suppose that the firm's production function is given by

$$Q = K^{\frac{1}{2}}L^{\frac{1}{2}}.$$

The firm's capital is fixed at $\overline{K}$. What amount of labor will the firm hire to minimize cost in the short run?

Solution   With just two inputs, there is no tangency condition to worry about in the short run. To find the short-run cost-minimizing quantity of labor, we need only solve the production function for L in terms of Q and $\overline{K}$:

$$Q = \overline{K}^{\frac{1}{2}}L^{\frac{1}{2}}.$$

This gives us

$$L = \frac{Q^2}{\overline{K}}.$$

This is the cost-minimizing quantity of labor in the short run.

Similar Problem: 7.10

MORE THAN ONE VARIABLE INPUT

When the firm has more than one variable input, the analysis of cost minimization in the short run is very similar to the analysis of long-run cost-minimization. To illustrate, suppose that the firm uses three inputs: labor, capital, and raw materials. The firm's production function is $f(L, K, M)$, where M denotes the quantity of raw materials. The price of raw materials per unit will be denoted by m. Again suppose that the firm's capital is fixed at a level $\overline{K}$. The firm's short-run cost-minimization problem is to choose quantities of labor and materials to minimize total cost, $wL + mM + r\overline{K}$, given that the firm wants to produce an output level Q_0.

From a graphical point of view, the approach that we would take to analyze the short-run cost-minimization problem with two variable inputs differs little from the approach that we took to analyze the long-run cost-minimization problem when the firm had only two inputs. As Figure 7.16 shows, using a graph with L on the horizontal axis and M on the vertical axis, we identify the isoquant corresponding to the level of output the firm wishes to produce, and we then find the point on that isoquant that lies on the lowest cost isocost line. If the short-run cost

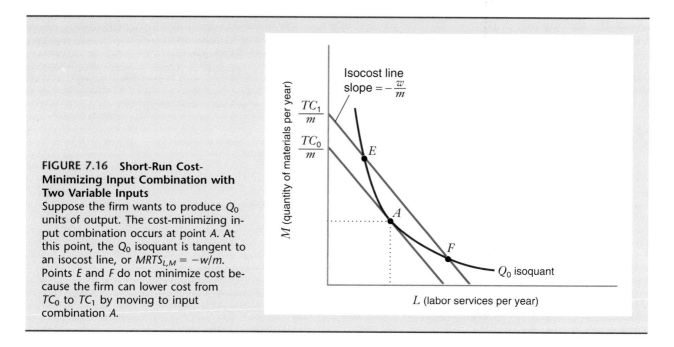

FIGURE 7.16 Short-Run Cost-Minimizing Input Combination with Two Variable Inputs
Suppose the firm wants to produce Q_0 units of output. The cost-minimizing input combination occurs at point A. At this point, the Q_0 isoquant is tangent to an isocost line, or $MRTS_{L,M} = -w/m$. Points E and F do not minimize cost because the firm can lower cost from TC_0 to TC_1 by moving to input combination A.

minimization problem has an interior solution, the cost-minimizing input combination will involve a tangency between the isoquant and an isocost line. At this tangency point, we have

$$MRTS_{L,M} = -\frac{MP_L}{MP_M} = -\frac{w}{m},$$

or, rearranging terms

$$\frac{MP_L}{w} = \frac{MP_M}{m}.$$

Thus, just like in the long run, the firm minimizes its total costs by equating the marginal product per dollar that it spends on the variable inputs it uses in positive amounts.

LEARNING-BY-DOING EXERCISE 7.6

Short-Run Cost Minimization and Input Demand Functions with Two Variable Inputs

Suppose that the firm's production function is given by

$$Q = K^{\frac{1}{2}}L^{\frac{1}{4}}M^{\frac{1}{4}}.$$

For this production function, the marginal products of capital, labor, and materials are:

$$MP_K = \frac{1}{2}K^{-\frac{1}{2}}L^{\frac{1}{4}}M^{\frac{1}{4}}.$$

$$MP_L = \frac{1}{4}K^{\frac{1}{2}}L^{-\frac{3}{4}}M^{\frac{1}{4}}.$$

$$MP_M = \frac{1}{4}K^{\frac{1}{2}}L^{\frac{1}{4}}M^{-\frac{3}{4}}.$$

The input prices of capital, labor, and materials are $r = 2$, $w = 16$, $m = 1$, respectively.

Problem

(a) What is the solution to the firm's long-run cost-minimization problem given that the firm wants to produce Q units of output?

(b) What is the solution to the firm's short-run cost-minimization problem when the firm wants to produce Q units of output and capital is fixed at $\overline{K}$?

(c) Verify that when $Q = 16$ and $\overline{K} = 32$, which is the long-run cost-minimizing quantity of capital when $Q = 16$, the short-run and long-run quantities of labor and materials are the same.

Solution

(a) Here we have two tangency conditions and the requirement that L, K, and M produce Q units of output:

$$\frac{MP_L}{MP_M} = \frac{\frac{1}{4}K^{\frac{1}{2}}L^{-\frac{3}{4}}M^{\frac{1}{4}}}{\frac{1}{4}K^{\frac{1}{2}}L^{\frac{1}{4}}M^{-\frac{3}{4}}} = \frac{16}{1} \Rightarrow M = 16L.$$

$$\frac{MP_L}{MP_K} = \frac{\frac{1}{4}K^{\frac{1}{2}}L^{-\frac{3}{4}}M^{\frac{1}{4}}}{\frac{1}{2}K^{-\frac{1}{2}}L^{\frac{1}{4}}M^{\frac{1}{4}}} = \frac{16}{2} \Rightarrow K = 16L.$$

$$Q = K^{\frac{1}{2}}L^{\frac{1}{4}}M^{\frac{1}{4}}.$$

This is a system of three equations in three unknowns. The solution to this system gives us the long-run cost-minimizing input combination:

$$L = \frac{Q}{8}.$$

$$M = 2Q.$$

$$K = 2Q.$$

(b) The tangency condition $MP_L/MP_M = w/m$ is

$$\frac{\frac{1}{4}\overline{K}^{\frac{1}{2}}L^{-\frac{3}{4}}M^{\frac{1}{4}}}{\frac{1}{4}\overline{K}^{\frac{1}{2}}L^{-\frac{1}{4}}M^{-\frac{3}{4}}} = \frac{16}{1},$$

which implies

$$M = 16L.$$

To find the short-run cost-minimizing quantity of labor, we substitute this back into the production function and solve for L in terms of Q and $\overline{K}$:

$$Q = \overline{K}^{\frac{1}{2}}L^{\frac{1}{4}}(16L)^{\frac{1}{4}},$$

which, when we solve for L, gives us the short-run cost-minimizing quantity of labor:

$$L = \frac{Q^2}{4\overline{K}}.$$

Since $M = 16L$, the short-run cost-minimizing quantity of materials:

$$M = \frac{4Q^2}{\overline{K}}.$$

(c) Substituting $Q = 16$ into the expressions for the long-run cost-minimizing quantities of labor and materials gives us:

$$L = 2$$
$$M = 32.$$

Substituting $Q = 16$ and $\overline{K} = 32$ into the expressions for the short-run cost-minimizing quantities of labor and materials gives us:

$$L = \frac{16^2}{4(32)} = 2.$$

$$M = \frac{4(16)^2}{32} = 32.$$

Similar Problem: 7.11

CHAPTER SUMMARY

• The opportunity cost of a decision is the payoff associated with the best of the alternatives that are not chosen.

• Opportunity costs are forward looking. When evaluating the opportunity cost of a particular decision, you need to identify the value of the alternatives that the decision forecloses in the future.

• From a firm's perspective, the opportunity cost of using the productive services of an input is the current market price of the input.

• Explicit costs involve a direct monetary outlay. Implicit costs do not involve an outlay of cash.

• Accounting costs include explicit costs. Economic costs include explicit and implicit costs.

• Sunk costs are costs that have already been incurred and cannot be recovered. Nonsunk cost are costs that can be avoided if certain choices are made.

• The long run is that period of time that is long enough for the firm to vary the quantities of all its inputs. The short run is the period of time in which at least one of the firm's input quantities cannot be changed.

• An isocost line shows all combinations of inputs that entail the same total cost. When graphed with quantity of labor on the horizontal axis and quantity of capital on the vertical axis, the slope of an isocost line is minus the ratio of the price of labor to the price of capital.

• At an interior solution to the long-run cost-minimization problem, the firm adjusts input quantities so that the marginal rate of technical substitution equals the ratio of the input prices. Equivalently, the additional output per dollar spent on each input is equalized.

• At corner-point solutions to the cost-minimization problem, the additional output per dollar spent on each input may not be equal.

• An increase in the price of an input causes the cost-minimizing quantity of that input to go down or stay the same. It can never cause the cost-minimizing quantity to go up.

• An increase in the quantity of output will cause the cost-minimizing quantity of an input to go up if the input is a normal input and will cause the cost-minimizing quantity of the input to go down if the input is an inferior input.

• The expansion path summarizes how the cost-minimizing quantity of inputs varies as quantity of output varies.

• An input demand curve shows how the cost-minimizing quantity of the input varies with its input price.

• The short-run cost-minimization problem involves a choice of inputs when at least one input quantity is held fixed.

REVIEW QUESTIONS

1. A biotechnology firm purchased an inventory of test tubes at a price of $0.50 per tube at some point in the past. It plans to use these tubes to clone snake cells. Explain why the opportunity cost of using these test tubes might not equal the price at which they were acquired.

2. You decide to start a business that provides computer consulting advice for students in your dormitory. What would be an example of an explicit cost you would incur in operating this business? What would be an example of an implicit cost you would incur in operating this business?

3. Why does the "sunkness" or "nonsunkness" of a cost depend on the decision being made?

4. How does an increase in the price of an input affect the slope of the isocost line?

5. Could the solution to the firm's cost-minimization problem ever occur off the isoquant representing the required level of output?

6. Explain why, at an interior optimal solution to the firm's cost-minimization problem, the additional output that the firm gets from a dollar spent on labor equals the additional output from a dollar spent on capital. Why would this condition not necessarily hold at a corner-point optimal solution?

7. What is the difference between the *expansion path* and *input demand curve*?

8. In Chapter 5 you learned that, under certain conditions, a good could be a Giffen good: An increase in the price of the good could lead to an increase, rather than a decrease, in the quantity demanded. In the theory of cost minimization, however, we learned that, an increase in the price of an input will never lead to an increase in the quantity of the input used. Explain why there cannot be "Giffen inputs."

9. For a given quantity of output, under what conditions would the short-run quantity demanded for a variable input (such as labor) equal the quantity demanded in the long run?

PROBLEMS

7.1. In 2000, a computer-products retailer purchased laser printers from a manufacturer at a price of $500 per printer. During the year the retailer will try to sell the printers at a price higher than $500 but may not be able to sell all of the printers. At the end of the year, the manufacturer would pay the retailer 30 percent of the original price *for any unsold laser printers*. No one other than the manufacturer would be willing to buy these unsold printers at the end of the year.
a) At the beginning of the year, before the retailer has purchased any printers, what is the opportunity cost of laser printers?
b) After the retailer has purchased the laser printers, what is the opportunity cost associated with selling a laser printer to a prospective customer? (Assume that if this customer does not buy the printer, it will be unsold at the end of the year.)
c) Suppose that at the end of the year, the retailer still has a large inventory of unsold printers. The retailer has set a retail price of $1,200 per printer. A new line of printers is due out soon, and it is unlikely that many more old printers will be sold at this price. The marketing manager of the retail chain argues that the chain should cut the retail price by $1,000 and sell the laser printers at $200 each. The general manager of the chain strongly disagrees, pointing out that at $200 each, the retailer would "lose" $300 on each printer it sells. Is the general manager's argument correct?

7.2. A consulting firm has just finished a study for a manufacturer of wine. It has determined that an additional man-hour of labor would increase wine output by 1,000 gallons per day. Adding an additional machine hour of fermentation capacity would increase output by 200 gallons per day. The price of a man-hour of labor is $10 per hour. The price of a machine-hour of fermentation capacity is $0.25 per hour. Is there a way for the wine manufacturer to lower its total costs of production and yet keep its output constant? If so, what is it?

7.3. A firm uses two inputs, capital and labor, to produce output. Its production function exhibits diminishing marginal rate of technical substitution.
a) If the price of capital and labor services both increase by the same percentage amount (e.g., 20 percent), what will happen to the cost-minimizing input quantities for a given output level?
b) If the price of capital increases by 20 percent while the price of labor increases by 10 percent, what will happen to the cost-minimizing input quantities for a given output level?

7.4. The text discussed the expansion path as a graph that summarizes the cost-minimizing input quantities, holding fixed the prices of inputs. What the text didn't say is that there is a *different* expansion path for each pair of input prices the firm might face. In other words, how the inputs vary with output depends, in part, on the input prices. Consider, now, the expansion paths associated with two distinct pairs of input prices, (w_1, r_1) and (w_2, r_2) and assume that at both pairs of input prices, we have an interior solution to the cost-minimization problem for any positive level of output. Assuming that the firm's isoquants have no kinks in them and exhibit diminishing marginal rate of technical substitution, could these expansion paths ever cross each other at a point other than the origin ($L = 0$, $K = 0$)?

7.5. A researcher claims to have estimated input demand curves in an industry in which the production technology involves two inputs, capital and labor. The input demand curves he claims to have estimated are

$$L = wr^2 Q.$$
$$K = w^2 r Q.$$

Are these valid input demand curves? In other words, could they have come from a firm that minimizes its costs?

7.6. Suppose the production of airframes is characterized by a CES production function

$$Q = (L^{\frac{1}{2}} + K^{\frac{1}{2}})^2.$$

The marginal products for this production function are:

$$MP_L = (L^{\frac{1}{2}} + K^{\frac{1}{2}})L^{-\frac{1}{2}}.$$
$$MP_K = (L^{\frac{1}{2}} + K^{\frac{1}{2}})K^{-\frac{1}{2}}.$$

Suppose that the price of labor is $10 per unit and the price of capital is $1 per unit. Find the cost-minimizing combination of labor and capital for an airframe manufacturer that wants to produce 121,000 airframes.

7.7. Suppose the production of airframes is characterized by a Cobb–Douglas production function

$$Q = LK.$$

The marginal products for this production function are:

$$MP_L = K.$$
$$MP_K = L.$$

Suppose the price of labor is $10 per unit and the price of capital is $1 per unit. Find the cost-minimizing combination of labor and capital if the manufacturer wants to produce 121,000 airframes.

7.8. The processing of payroll for 10,000 workers in the department of a large firm can either be done using one hour of computer time (denoted by K) and no clerks or with ten hours of clerical time (denoted by L) and no computer time. Computers and clerks are perfect substitutes so that, for example, the firm could also process its payroll using 1/2 hour of computer time and 5 hours of clerical time.
a) Sketch the isoquant that shows all combinations of clerical time and computer time that allows the firm to process the payroll for 10,000 workers.
b) Suppose computer time costs $5 per hour and clerical time costs $7.50 per hour. What are the cost-minimizing choices of L and K? What is the minimized total cost of processing the payroll?
c) How high would the price of an hour of computer have to be before the firm would find it worthwhile to use only clerks to process the payroll?

7.9. Consider, again, the production function

$$Q = LK.$$

The marginal products for this production function are:

$$MP_L = K.$$
$$MP_K = L.$$

Suppose that the price of labor equals w, and the price of capital equals r. Derive expressions for the input demand curves.

7.10. Suppose that the firm's production function is given by

$$Q = 10KL^{\frac{1}{3}}.$$

The firm's capital is fixed at $\overline{K}$. What amount of labor will the firm hire to solve its short-run cost minimization problem?

7.11. Suppose that the firm uses three inputs to produce its output: capital, K, labor, L, and materials, M. The firm's production function is given by

$$Q = K^{\frac{1}{3}}L^{\frac{1}{3}}M^{\frac{1}{3}}.$$

For this production function, the marginal products of capital, labor, and materials are:

$$MP_K = \frac{1}{3}K^{-\frac{2}{3}}L^{\frac{1}{3}}M^{\frac{1}{3}}.$$

$$MP_L = \frac{1}{3}K^{\frac{1}{3}}L^{-\frac{2}{3}}M^{\frac{1}{3}}.$$

$$MP_M = \frac{1}{3}K^{\frac{1}{3}}L^{\frac{1}{3}}M^{-\frac{2}{3}}.$$

The prices of capital, labor, and materials are $r = 1$, $w = 1$, and $m = 1$, respectively.
a) What is the solution to the firm's long-run cost-minimization problem given that the firm wants to produce Q units of output?
b) What is the solution to the firm's short-run cost-minimization problem when the firm wants to produce Q units of output and capital is fixed at $\overline{K}$?
c) Verify that when $Q = 4$ and $\overline{K} = 4$, which is the long-run cost-minimizing quantity of capital when $Q = 4$, the short-run and long-run quantities of labor and materials are the same.

APPENDIX: Advanced Topics in Cost Minimization

SOLVING THE COST-MINIMIZATION PROBLEM USING THE MATHEMATICS OF CONSTRAINED OPTIMIZATION

In this section, we set up the long-run cost-minimization problem as a constrained optimization problem, and solve it using Lagrange multipliers.

With two inputs, labor and capital, the cost-minimization problem can be stated as

$$\min_{(L,\,K)} wL + rK \qquad\qquad \textbf{(A7.1)}$$

$$\text{subject to: } f(L, K) = Q \qquad\qquad \textbf{(A7.2)}$$

We proceed by defining a Lagrangian function

$$\Lambda(L, K, \lambda) = wL + rK - \lambda[f(L, K) - Q],$$

where λ is a Lagrange multiplier. The conditions for an interior optimal solution ($L > 0$, $K > 0$) to this problem are

$$\frac{\partial \Lambda}{\partial L} = 0 \Rightarrow w = \lambda \frac{\partial f(L, K)}{\partial L}. \tag{A7.3}$$

$$\frac{\partial \Lambda}{\partial K} = 0 \Rightarrow r = \lambda \frac{\partial f(L, K)}{\partial K}. \tag{A7.4}$$

$$\frac{\partial \Lambda}{\partial \lambda} = 0 \Rightarrow f(L, K) = Q. \tag{A7.5}$$

Recalling from Chapter 6 that

$$MP_L = \frac{\partial f(L, K)}{\partial L}$$

$$MP_K = \frac{\partial f(L, K)}{\partial K}$$

we can combine (A7.3) and (A7.4) to eliminate the Lagrange multiplier, so our first-order conditions reduce to

$$\frac{MP_L}{MP_K} = \frac{w}{r}. \tag{A7.6}$$

$$f(L, K) = Q. \tag{A7.7}$$

Conditions (A7.6) and (A7.7) are two equations in two unknowns, L and K. They are identical to the conditions that we derived for an interior solution to the cost-minimization problem using graphical arguments. The solution to these conditions are the long-run input demand functions, $L^*(Q, w, r)$ and $K^*(Q, w, r)$.

For more on the use of Lagrange multipliers to solve problems of constrained optimization, see the Mathematical Appendix in this book.

DUALITY: "BACKING OUT" THE PRODUCTION FUNCTION FROM THE INPUT DEMAND FUNCTIONS

The above analysis shows how we can start with a production function and derive the input demand functions. But we can also reverse directions: If we start with input demand functions, we can "back out" the production function. **Duality** refers to this link between the production function and the input demand functions. For every production function, we can derive a corresponding set of input demand functions by solving the cost-minimization problem.

And if we know the input demand functions, we can back out the production function.

We will illustrate duality by *reverse engineering* the production function from the input demand curves that we derived in Learning-By-Doing Exercise 7.4. We use that example because we already know what the underlying production function is, and we can thus confirm whether the production function we derive is correct. We will proceed in three steps.

- **Step 1:** Start with the labor demand function and "solve" for w in terms of Q, r, and L:

$$L = \frac{Q}{50}\left(\frac{r}{w}\right)^{\frac{1}{2}}$$

so solving for w in terms of the other variables gives us

$$w = \left(\frac{Q}{50L}\right)^2 r.$$

- **Step 2:** Substitute the solution for w into the capital demand function $K = (Q/50)(w/r)^{\frac{1}{2}}$:

$$K = \frac{Q}{50}\left(\frac{\left(\frac{Q}{50L}\right)^2 r}{r}\right)^{\frac{1}{2}}$$

which simplifies to

$$K = \frac{Q^2}{2,500L}.$$

- **Step 3:** Solve the resulting expression for Q in terms of L and K:

$$K = \frac{Q^2}{2,500L} \Rightarrow Q = 50K^{\frac{1}{2}}L^{\frac{1}{2}}.$$

If you go back to Learning-By-Doing Exercise 7.4, you will see that this is indeed the production function from which we derived the input demand functions. Thus, we have shown that it is possible to start with a set of input demand functions and back out the underlying production function. That is, we have illustrated the duality between the production function and the input demand functions.

You might wonder why duality is important. Why would we care about deriving production functions from input demand functions? We will discuss the significance of duality in Chapter 8, after we have introduced the concept of a long-run total cost function.

CHAPTER

8

Cost Curves

The Chinese economy in the 1990s underwent an unprecedented boom. As part of that boom, enterprises such as HiSense Group grew rapidly.[1] HiSense, one of China's largest television producers, increased its rate of production by 50 percent per year during the mid-1990s. Its goal was to transform itself from a sleepy domestic producer of television sets into a consumer electronics giant whose brand name was recognized throughout Asia.

Of vital concern to HiSense and the thousands of other Chinese enterprises that were plotting similar growth strategies in the late 1990s was how production costs would change as its volume of output increased. There is little doubt that HiSense's production costs would go up as it produced more television sets. But *how fast* would they go up? HiSense's executives hoped that as it produced more television sets, the cost of *each television set* would go down, that is, its unit costs will fall as its annual rate of output goes up.

HiSense's executives also needed to know how input prices would affect its production costs. For example, HiSense competes with other large Chinese television manufacturers to buy up smaller factories. This competition bids up the price of capital. HiSense had to reckon with the impact of this price increase on its total production costs.

This chapter is about cost curves—relationships between costs and the volume of output. It picks up where Chapter 7 left off: with the comparative statics of the cost-minimization problem. The cost-minimization-problem—both in the long run and the short run—gives rise to total, average, and marginal cost curves. This chapter studies these curves. ◼

[1]This example is based on "Latest Merger Boom Is Happening in China and Bears Watching," *Wall Street Journal* (July 30, 1997), pp. A1 and A9.

LONG-RUN TOTAL COST CURVES

In Chapter 7, we studied the firm's long-run cost-minimization problem and saw how the cost-minimizing combination of labor and capital depended on the quantity of output Q and the prices of labor and capital, w and r. Figure 8.1(a) shows how the optimal input combination for a television firm, such as HiSense, changes as we vary output, holding input prices fixed. For example, when the firm produces 1 million televisions per year, the cost-minimizing input combination occurs at point A, with L_1 units of labor and K_1 units of capital. At this input combination, the firm is on an isocost line corresponding to TC_1 dollars of total cost,

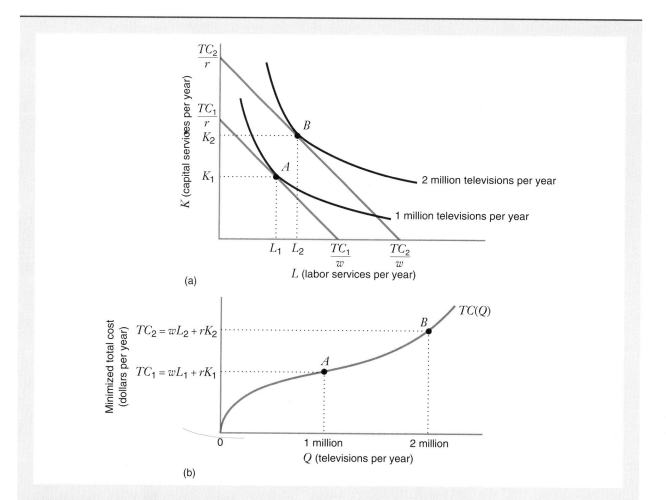

(a)

(b)

FIGURE 8.1   Cost Minimization and the Long-Run Total Cost Curve for a Producer of Television Sets
Panel (a) shows how the solution to the cost-minimization problem for a television producer changes as output changes from 1 million televisions per year to 2 million televisions per year. When output increases, the minimized total cost increases from TC_1 to TC_2. Panel (b) shows the long-run total cost curve. This curve shows the relationship between the volume of output and the minimum level of total cost the firm can attain when it produces that output.

where $TC_1 = wL_1 + rK_1$. TC_1 is thus the minimized total cost when the firm produces 1 million units of output. As the firm increases output from 1 million to 2 million televisions per year, it ends up on an isocost line farther out to the northeast at point B, with L_2 units of labor and K_2 units of capital. Thus, its minimized total cost goes up (i.e., $TC_2 > TC_1$). It cannot be otherwise, because if the firm could decrease total cost by producing more output, it couldn't have been using a cost-minimizing combination of inputs in the first place.

Figure 8.1(b) shows the **long-run total cost curve,** denoted by $TC(Q)$. The long-run total cost curve shows how minimized total cost varies with output, holding input prices fixed. Because the cost-minimizing input combination moves us to higher isocost lines, the long-run total cost curve must be increasing in Q. We also know that when $Q = 0$, long-run total cost is 0. This is because, in the long run, the firm is free to vary all its inputs, and if it produces a zero quantity, the cost-minimizing input combination is zero labor and zero capital. Thus, comparative statics analysis of the cost-minimization problem implies that the *long-run total cost curve must be increasing and must equal 0, when $Q = 0$.*

LEARNING-BY-DOING EXERCISE 8.1

The Long-Run Total Cost Curve for a Cobb–Douglas Production Function

Let's return again to the production function $Q = 50L^{\frac{1}{2}}K^{\frac{1}{2}}$ that we analyzed in the Learning-By-Doing Exercises in Chapter 7.

Problem

(a) How does minimized total cost depend on the output Q and the input prices w and r for this production function?
(b) What is the graph of the long-run total cost curve when $w = 25$ and $r = 100$?

Solution

(a) In Learning-By-Doing Exercise 7.4 in Chapter 7, we saw that the following equations described the cost-minimizing quantities of labor and capital:

$$L = \frac{Q}{50}\left(\frac{r}{w}\right)^{\frac{1}{2}} \tag{8.1}$$

$$K = \frac{Q}{50}\left(\frac{w}{r}\right)^{\frac{1}{2}} \tag{8.2}$$

To find the minimized total cost, we calculate the total cost the firm incurs when it uses this cost-minimizing input combination:

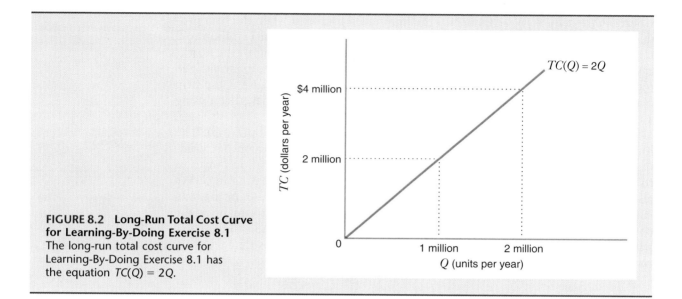

FIGURE 8.2   Long-Run Total Cost Curve for Learning-By-Doing Exercise 8.1
The long-run total cost curve for Learning-By-Doing Exercise 8.1 has the equation $TC(Q) = 2Q$.

$$TC = wL + rK$$
$$= w\frac{Q}{50}\left(\frac{r}{w}\right)^{\frac{1}{2}} + r\frac{Q}{50}\left(\frac{w}{r}\right)^{\frac{1}{2}},$$
$$= \frac{Q}{50}w^{\frac{1}{2}}r^{\frac{1}{2}} + \frac{Q}{50}w^{\frac{1}{2}}r^{\frac{1}{2}}$$
$$= \frac{w^{\frac{1}{2}}r^{\frac{1}{2}}}{25}Q. \tag{8.3}$$

(b) Figure 8.2 shows that the graph of the long-run total cost curve is a straight line. We derive it by substituting $w = 25$ and $r = 100$ into expression (8.3) to get

$$TC(Q) = 2Q.$$

Similar Problems: 8.1, 8.3, 8.4

HOW DOES THE LONG-RUN TOTAL COST CURVE SHIFT WHEN INPUT PRICES CHANGE?

What Happens When Just One Input Price Changes?

In the introduction, we discussed how HiSense faced the prospect of higher prices for certain inputs, such as capital. To illustrate how an increase in an input price affects a firm's total cost curve, let's return to the cost-minimization problem for our hypothetical television producer. Figure 8.3 shows what happens when the price of capital increases, holding output and the price of labor constant. Suppose that at the initial situation, the optimal input combination for an annual output of 1 million television sets occurs at point A, and the minimized total cost is $50 million per year. The figure shows that after the increase in the price of cap-

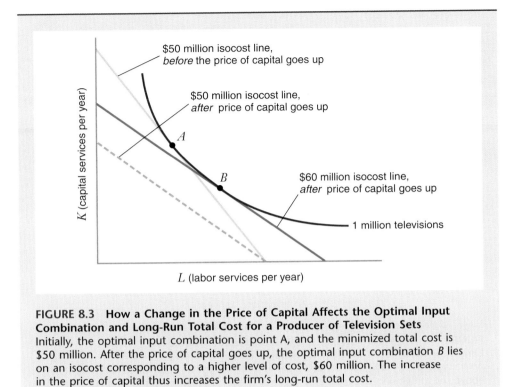

FIGURE 8.3 How a Change in the Price of Capital Affects the Optimal Input Combination and Long-Run Total Cost for a Producer of Television Sets
Initially, the optimal input combination is point A, and the minimized total cost is $50 million. After the price of capital goes up, the optimal input combination B lies on an isocost corresponding to a higher level of cost, $60 million. The increase in the price of capital thus increases the firm's long-run total cost.

ital, the optimal input combination, point *B*, must lie along an isocost line corresponding to a total cost that is *greater* than $50 million. To see why, note that the $50 million isocost line *at the new input prices* intersects the horizontal axis in the same place as the $50 million isocost line *at the old input prices*. However, the new $50 million isocost line is flatter because the price of capital has gone up. You can see from Figure 8.3 that the firm could not operate on the $50 million isocost line because it would be unable to produce the desired quantity of 1 million television sets. To produce 1 million television sets, the firm must operate on an isocost line that is farther to the northeast and thus corresponds to a higher level of cost ($60 million perhaps). Thus, holding output fixed, the minimized total cost goes up when the price of capital goes up.[2]

This analysis then implies that an increase in the price of capital results in a new total cost curve that lies above the original total cost curve at every $Q > 0$. At $Q = 0$, long-run total cost is still zero. Thus, as Figure 8.4 shows, an increase in an input price rotates the long-run total cost curve upward.[3]

---

[2]An analogous argument would show that minimized total cost would go down when the price of capital goes down.

[3]There is one case in which an increase in an input price would not affect the long-run total cost curve. If the firm is initially at a corner-point solution using a zero quantity of the input, an increase in the price of the input will leave the firm's cost-minimizing input combination—and thus its minimized total cost—unchanged. In this case, the increase in the input price would not shift the long-run total cost curve.

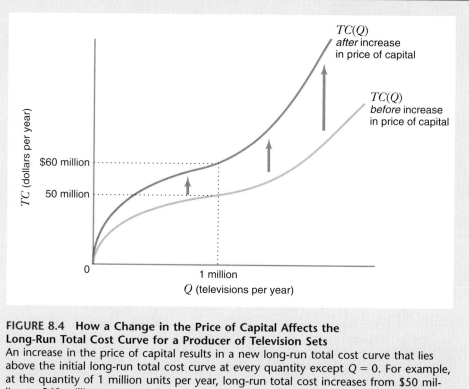

FIGURE 8.4   How a Change in the Price of Capital Affects the Long-Run Total Cost Curve for a Producer of Television Sets
An increase in the price of capital results in a new long-run total cost curve that lies above the initial long-run total cost curve at every quantity except $Q = 0$. For example, at the quantity of 1 million units per year, long-run total cost increases from $50 million to $60 million per year. Thus, the increase in the price of capital rotates the long-run total cost curve upward.

What Happens to Long-Run Total Cost When All Input Prices Change Proportionately?

What if the price of capital and the price of labor both go up by the same percentage amount, say 10 percent? Returning once again to the cost-minimization problem, we see from Figure 8.5 that *a proportionate increase in both input prices leaves the optimal input combination unchanged*. The slope of the isocost line stays the same because it equals the ratio of the price of labor to the price of capital. Because both input prices increased by the same percentage amount, this ratio remains unchanged.

However, the total cost curve must shift in a special way. Since the optimal input combination remains the same, a 10 percent increase in the prices of all inputs must increase the minimized total cost by exactly 10 percent! More generally, any given percentage increase in *all* input prices will do the following:

- Leave the optimal input combination unchanged, *and*
- Shift up the total cost curve by exactly the same percentage as the common increase in input prices.

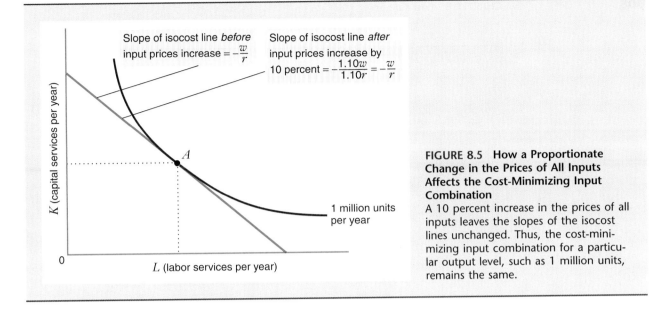

Slope of isocost line *before* input prices increase $= -\dfrac{w}{r}$

Slope of isocost line *after* input prices increase by 10 percent $= -\dfrac{1.10w}{1.10r} = -\dfrac{w}{r}$

A

1 million units per year

K (capital services per year)

L (labor services per year)

0

FIGURE 8.5 How a Proportionate Change in the Prices of All Inputs Affects the Cost-Minimizing Input Combination
A 10 percent increase in the prices of all inputs leaves the slopes of the isocost lines unchanged. Thus, the cost-minimizing input combination for a particular output level, such as 1 million units, remains the same.

EXAMPLE 8.1

How Would Input Prices Affect the Long-Run Total Costs for a Trucking Firm?[4]

The intercity trucking business is a good setting in which to study the behavior of long-run total costs because when input prices or output changes, trucking firms can adjust their input mixes without too much difficulty. Drivers can be hired or laid off relatively easily, and trucks can be bought or sold as circumstances dictate. There are also considerable data on output, expenditures on inputs, and input quantities, so we can use statistical techniques to estimate how total cost varies with input prices and output. Utilizing such data, Ann Friedlaender and Richard Spady estimated long-run total cost curves for trucking firms that carry general merchandise. Many semis fall into this category.

Trucking firms use three major inputs: labor, capital (e.g., trucks), and diesel fuel. Their output is transportation services, usually measured as ton-miles per year. One ton-mile is one ton of freight carried one mile. A trucking company that hauls 50,000 tons of freight 100,000 miles during a given year would thus have a total output of $50,000 \times 100,000$, or 5,000,000,000 ton-miles per year.

Figure 8.6 illustrates an example of the cost curve estimated by Friedlaender and Spady. Note that total cost increases with the quantity of output, as the theory we just discussed implies. Total cost also increases in the prices of inputs. Figure 8.6 shows how doubling the price of labor (holding all other input prices fixed) affects the total cost curve. The increase in the input price shifts the total cost curve upward at every point except $Q = 0$. Figure 8.6 also shows the effects of doubling the price of capital and doubling the price of fuel, respectively. These increases also shift the total cost curve upward, though this shift is not as much as when the price of labor goes up. Friedlaender and Spady's analysis shows that the total cost of a trucking firm is most sensitive to changes in the price of labor and least sensitive to changes in the price of diesel fuel. ■

---

[4]This example draws from A. F. Friedlaender, and R. H. Spady, *Freight Transport Regulation: Equity, Efficiency, and Competition in the Rail and Trucking Industries* (Cambridge, MA: MIT Press, 1981).

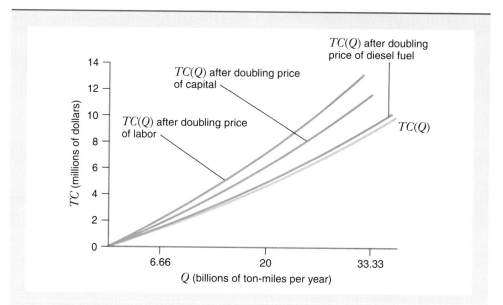

FIGURE 8.6 Long-Run Total Cost Curve for a Trucking Firm
The curve $TC(Q)$ is a graph of the long-run total cost function for a typical trucking firm. Doubling the price of labor shifts the long-run total cost function upward, as does a doubling in the price of capital or diesel fuel. However, an increase in the price of labor has a bigger impact on total cost than either an increase in the price of capital or diesel fuel.

8.2

LONG-RUN AVERAGE AND MARGINAL COST

WHAT ARE LONG-RUN AVERAGE AND MARGINAL COSTS?

Two other types of cost play an important role in microeconomics: long-run average cost and long-run marginal cost. **Long-run average cost** is the firm's cost per unit of output. It equals long-run total cost divided by Q:

$$AC(Q) = \frac{TC(Q)}{Q}.$$

Long-run marginal cost is the rate of change at which long-run total cost changes with respect to output:

$$MC(Q) = \frac{TC(Q + \Delta Q) - TC(Q)}{\Delta Q}$$

$$= \frac{\Delta TC}{\Delta Q}.$$

Although long-run average and marginal cost are both derived from the firm's long-run total cost curve, the two costs are generally different. Average cost is the cost per unit that the firm incurs in producing all of its output. Marginal cost, by contrast, is the increase in cost from producing an additional unit of output.

Figure 8.7 illustrates the difference between marginal and average cost. At a particular output level, such as 50 units per year, average cost is equal to the slope of ray 0A. This slope is equal to $1,500/50 units, so the firm's average cost when it produces 50 units per year is $30 per unit. By contrast, the marginal cost when the firm produces 50 units per year is the slope of the total cost curve at a quantity of 50. In Figure 8.7 this is represented by the slope of the line BAC that is tangent to the total cost curve at a quantity of 50 units. The slope of this tangent line is 10, so the firm's marginal cost at a quantity of 50 units is $10 per unit. As we vary total output, we can trace out the long-run average cost curve by imagining how the slope of rays such as 0A change as we move along the long-run total cost curve. Similarly, we can trace out the long-run marginal cost curve by imagining how the slope of tangent lines such as BAC change as we move along the total cost curve. As Figure 8.7 shows, these two "thought processes" will generate two different curves.

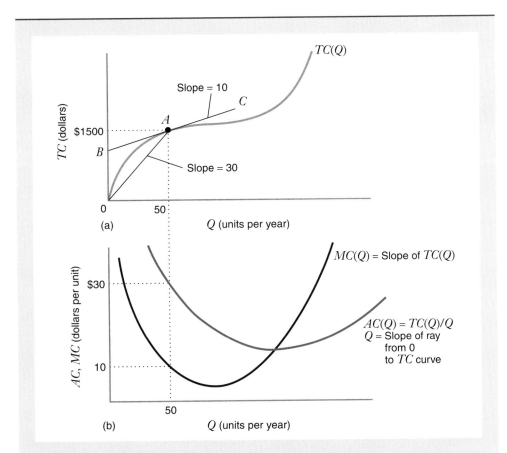

FIGURE 8.7 Deriving Average and Marginal Cost from the Total Cost Curve
The top panel shows the firm's total cost curve. The average cost at a quantity of 50 units is the slope of the ray from 0A, or $30 per unit. The marginal cost at a quantity of 50 units is the slope of the total cost curve at this quantity, which equals the slope of tangent line BAC. This tangent line's slope is 10, so marginal cost at 50 units is $10 per unit. More generally, we can trace out the average cost curve by imagining how the slope of rays from 0 to the total cost curve (such as 0A) change as we move along the total cost curve. We can trace out the marginal cost curve by imagining how the slope of tangent lines (such as BAC) change as we move along the total cost curve.

LEARNING-BY-DOING EXERCISE 8.2

Deriving Long-Run Average and Marginal Costs from a Long-Run Total Cost Curve

Average cost and marginal cost are often different. However, there is one special case in which they are the same.

Problem   In Learning-By-Doing Exercise 8.1 we derived the long-run total cost curve for a Cobb–Douglas production function. For particular input prices ($w = 25$ and $r = 100$), the long-run total cost curve was described by the equation $TC(Q) = 2Q$. What are the long-run average and marginal cost curves associated with the long-run total cost curves?

Solution   Long-run average cost is

$$AC(Q) = \frac{2Q}{Q} = 2.$$

Note that average cost does not depend on Q. Its graph would be a horizontal line, as Figure 8.8 shows.
  Long-run marginal cost is

$$MC(Q) = \frac{2(Q + \Delta Q) - 2Q}{\Delta Q} = \frac{2\Delta Q}{\Delta Q} = 2.$$

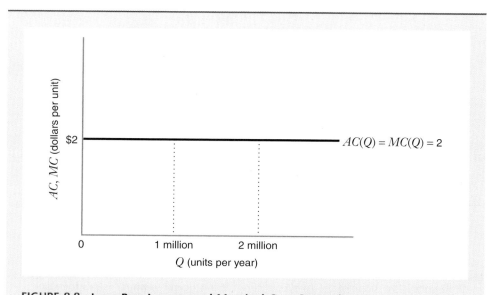

FIGURE 8.8   Long-Run Average and Marginal Cost Curves for Learning-By-Doing Exercise 8.2
The long-run average and marginal cost curves in Learning-By-Doing Exercise 8.2 are identical horizontal lines.

Long-run marginal cost also does not depend on Q. In fact, it is identical to the long-run average cost curve, so its graph is also a horizontal line.

This exercise illustrates a general point. Whenever the long-run total cost is a straight line (as in Figure 8.2), long-run average and long-run marginal cost will be the same, and their common graph will be a horizontal line.

Similar Problem: 8.2

RELATIONSHIP BETWEEN LONG-RUN MARGINAL AND AVERAGE COST CURVES

As with other average and marginal concepts you will study in this book (e.g., average product versus marginal product), there is a systematic relationship between the long-run average and long-run marginal cost curves. Figure 8.9 illustrates this relationship:

- When average cost is *decreasing in quantity*, marginal cost is *less than* average cost. That is, if $AC(Q)$ decreases in Q, $MC(Q) < AC(Q)$.

- When average cost is *increasing in quantity*, marginal cost is *greater than* average cost. That is, if $AC(Q)$ increases in Q, $MC(Q) > AC(Q)$.

- When average cost *neither increases nor decreases in quantity*, either because its graph is flat or we are at a point at which $AC(Q)$ is at a minimum, then marginal cost is *equal to* average cost.

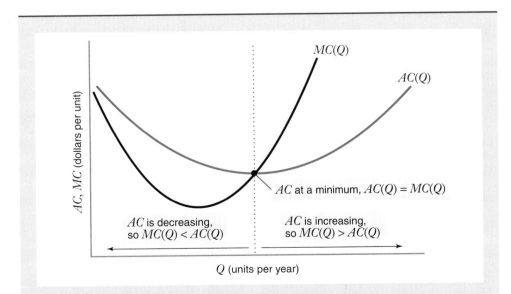

FIGURE 8.9   Relationship Between the Average and Marginal Cost Curves
When average cost is decreasing, marginal cost is less than average cost. When average cost is increasing, marginal cost is greater than average cost. When average cost attains its minimum, marginal cost equals average cost.

The relationship between marginal cost and average cost is the same as the relationship between the marginal of anything and the average of anything. To illustrate this point, suppose that the average height of students in your class is 160 cm. Now, a new student, Mike Margin, joins the class, and the average height rises to 161 cm. What do we know about his height? Since the average height is increasing, the "marginal height" (Mike Margin's height) must be above the average. If the average height had fallen to 159 cm, it would have been because his height was below the average. Finally, if the average height had remained the same when Mr. Margin joined the class, his height had to exactly equal the average height in the class.

The relationship between average and marginal height in your class is the same as the relationship between average and marginal product that we observed in Chapter 6. It is also the relationship between average and marginal cost that we just described. And it is the relationship between average and marginal revenue that we will study in Chapter 11.

EXAMPLE 8.2

The Relationship Between Average and Marginal Cost in Higher Education

How big is your college or university? Is it a large school, such as Ohio State, or a smaller university, such as Northwestern? At which school is the cost per student likely to be lower? Does university size affect the average and marginal cost of "producing" education?

Rajindar and Manjulika Koshal have studied how size affects the average and marginal cost of education.[5] They collected data on the average cost per student from 195 U.S. universities from 1990 to 1991 and estimated an average cost curve for these universities.[6] To control for differences in cost that stem from differences among universities in terms of their commitment to graduate programs, the Koshals estimated average cost curves for four groups of universities, primarily distinguished by the number of Ph.Ds awarded per year and the amount of government funding for Ph.D. students these universities received. For simplicity, we discuss the cost curves for the category that includes the 66 universities nationwide with the largest graduate programs (e.g., schools like Harvard, Northwestern, and the University of California at Berkeley).

Figure 8.10 shows the estimated average and marginal cost curves for this category of schools. It shows that the average cost per student declines until about

---

[5]R. Koshal and M. Koshal, "Quality and Economies of Scale in Higher Education," *Applied Economics 27* (1995): 773–778.

[6]To control for variations in cost that might be due to differences in academic quality, their analysis also allowed average cost to depend on the student-faculty ratio and the academic reputation of the school, as measured by factors such as average SAT scores of entering freshmen. In the graph in Figure 8.10, these variables are assumed to be equal to their national averages.

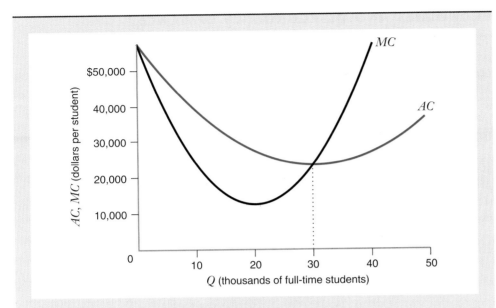

**FIGURE 8.10   The Average and Marginal Cost Curves for
University Education at U.S. Universities**
The marginal cost of an additional student is less than the average cost per student until enrollment reaches about 30,000 students. Until that point, average cost per student falls with the number of students. Beyond that point, the marginal cost of an additional student exceeds the average cost per student, and average cost increases with the number of students.

30,000 full-time undergraduate students (about the size of Indiana University, for example). Because few universities are this large, the Koshals' research suggests that for most universities in the United States with large graduate programs, the marginal cost of an additional undergraduate student is less than the average cost per student, and thus an increase in the size of the undergraduate student body would reduce the cost per student.

This finding seems to make sense. Think about your university. It already has a library and buildings for classrooms. It already has a president and a staff to run the school. These costs will probably not go up much if more students are added. Adding students is, of course, not costless. For example, more classes might have to be added. But it is not *that* difficult to find people who are able and willing to teach university classes (e.g., graduate students). Until the point is reached at which more dormitories or additional classrooms are needed, the extra costs of more students are not likely to be that large. Thus, for the typical university, while the *average* cost per student might be fairly high, the *marginal* cost of matriculating an additional student is often fairly low. If so, average cost will decrease with the number of students. ∎

ECONOMIES AND DISECONOMIES OF SCALE

The term **economies of scale** describes a situation in which average cost decreases as output goes up, and **diseconomies of scale** describes the opposite: average cost increases as output goes up. Economies and diseconomies of scale are important concepts. The extent of economies of scale can affect the structure of an industry. Economies of scale can also explain why some firms are more profitable than others in the same industry. Claims of economies of scale are often used to justify mergers between two firms producing the same product.[7]

Figure 8.11 illustrates economies and diseconomies of scale by showing an average cost curve that many economists believe typifies real-world production processes. For this average cost curve, there is an initial range of economies of scale (0 to Q'), followed by a range over which average cost is flat (Q' to Q''), and eventually a range of diseconomies of scale ($Q > Q''$).

Economies of scale have various causes. They may result from the physical properties of processing units that give rise to increasing returns to scale in inputs (e.g., as in the case of oil pipelines as discussed in Example 6.5 of Chapter 6). Economies of scale can also arise due to specialization of labor. As the number of workers increases with the output of the firm, workers can specialize on tasks, which often increases their productivity. Specialization can also eliminate time-consuming changeovers of workers and equipment. This, too, would increase worker productivity and lower unit costs.

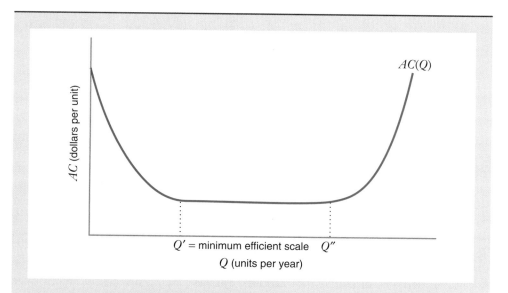

FIGURE 8.11   Real-World Average Cost Curve
This average cost curve typifies many real-world production processes. There are economies of scale for outputs less than Q'. Average costs are flat between Q' and Q'', and there are diseconomies of scale thereafter. The output level Q' at which the economies of scale are exhausted is called the minimum efficient scale.

[7]See Chapter 4 of F. M. Scherer and D. Ross, *Industrial Market Structure and Economic Performance* (Boston: Houghton Mifflin, 1990) for a detailed discussion of the implications of economies of scale for market structure and firm performance.

Economies of scale may also result from the need to employ **indivisible inputs.** An indivisible input is an input that is available only in a certain minimum size; its quantity cannot be scaled down as the firm's output goes to zero. An example of an indivisible input is a high-speed packaging line for breakfast cereal. Even the smallest such lines have huge capacity, 14 million pounds of cereal per year. A firm that might only want to produce 5 million pounds of cereal a year would still have to purchase the services of this indivisible piece of equipment.

Indivisible inputs lead to decreasing average costs (at least over a certain range of output) because when a firm purchases the services of an indivisible input, it can "spread" the cost of the indivisible input over more units of output as output goes up. For example, a firm that purchases the services of a minimum-scale packaging line to produce 5 million pounds of cereal per year will incur the same total cost on this input when it increases production to 10 million pounds of cereal per year.[8] This will drive the firm's average costs down.

The region of diseconomies of scale in Figure 8.11 is usually thought to occur because of **managerial diseconomies.** Managerial diseconomies arise when a given percentage increase in output forces the firm to increase its spending on the services of managers by more than this percentage. To see why managerial diseconomies of scale can arise, imagine an enterprise whose success depends on the talents or insight of one key individual (e.g., the entrepreneur who started the business). As the enterprise grows, that key individual cannot be replicated. To compensate, the firm may have to employ enough additional managers that total costs increase at a faster rate than output, which then pushes average costs up. Viewed this way, managerial diseconomies are another example of diminishing marginal returns to variable inputs that arise when certain other inputs (specialized managerial talent) are in fixed supply.

The smallest quantity at which the long-run average cost curve attains its minimum point is called the **minimum efficient scale,** or **MES.** The MES occurs at output Q' in Figure 8.11. The magnitude of MES relative to the size of the market often indicates the magnitude of economies of scale in particular industries. The larger MES is in comparison to overall market sales, the greater the magnitude of economies of scale. Table 8.1 shows MES as a percentage of total industry output, for a selected group of U.S. food and beverage industries.[9] The industries with the largest MES-market size ratios are breakfast cereal and cane sugar refining. These industries have significant economies of scale. The industries with the lowest MES-market size ratios are mineral water and bread. Economies of scale in manufacturing in these industries appear to be weak.

---

[8]Of course, it may spend more on other inputs, such as raw materials, that are not indivisible.

[9]In this table, MES is measured as the capacity of the median plant in an industry. The median plant is the plant whose capacity lies exactly in the middle of the range of capacities of plants in an industry. That is, 50 percent of all plants in a particular industry have capacities that are smaller than the median plant in that industry, and 50 percent have capacities that are larger. Estimates of MES based on the capacity of the median plant correlate highly with "engineering estimates" of MES that are obtained by asking well-informed manufacturing and engineering personnel to provide educated estimates of minimum efficient scale plant sizes. Data on median plant size in U.S. industries are available from the U.S. Census of Manufacturing.

TABLE 8.1
MES as a Percentage of Industry Output for Selected U.S. Food and Beverage Industries

Industry	MES as % of Output	Industry	MES as % of Output
Beet sugar	1.87	Breakfast cereal	9.47
Cane sugar	12.01	Mineral water	0.08
Flour	0.68	Roasted coffee	5.82
Bread	0.12	Pet food	3.02
Canned vegetables	0.17	Baby food	2.59
Frozen food	0.92	Beer	1.37
Margarine	1.75		

Source: Table 4.2 in J. Sutton, *Sunk Costs and Market Structure: Price Competition, Advertising, and the Evolution of Concentration* (Cambridge, MA: MIT Press, 1991).

EXAMPLE 8.3   *Economies of Scale in Alumina Refining*[10]

Manufacturing aluminum involves several steps, one of which is alumina refining. Alumina is a chemical compound consisting of aluminum and oxygen atoms (Al_2O_3). Alumina is created when bauxite ore—the basic raw material used to produce aluminum—is transformed using a technology known as the Bayer process.

There are substantial economies of scale in the refining of alumina. Table 8.2—drawn from John Stuckey's study of the aluminum industry—shows estimated long-run average costs as a function of the capacity of an alumina refinery. As plant capacity doubles from 150,000 tons per year to 300,000 tons per year, long-run average cost declines by about 12 percent. Stuckey reports that average costs in alumina refining may continue to fall up to capacities of 500,000. If so, then the minimum efficient scale of an alumina refinery would occur at an output of 500,000 tons per year.

If firms understand this, we would expect most alumina plants to have capacities of at least 500,000 tons per year. In fact, this is true. In 1979, the average capacity of the 10 alumina refineries in North America was 800,000 tons per year, and only two were under 500,000 tons per year. No alumina refinery's capacity exceeded 1.3 million tons per year. This suggests that diseconomies of scale set in at about this level of output. ■

---

[10]The information in this example draws from J. Stuckey, *Vertical Integration and Joint Ventures in the Aluminum Industry* (Cambridge, MA: Harvard University Press, 1983), especially pp. 12–14.

TABLE 8.2
Plant Capacity and Average Cost in Alumina Refining

Plant Capacity (tons)	Index of Average Cost (equals 100 at 300,000 tons)
55,000	139
90,000	124
150,000	114
300,000	100

Source: Table 1-1 in Stuckey, *Vertical Integration and Joint Ventures in the Aluminum Industry* (Cambridge, MA: Harvard University Press, 1983).

Economies of Scale for "Backoffice" Activities in a Hospital

EXAMPLE 8.4

The business of health care was in the news a lot during the 1990s. One of the most interesting trends was the consolidation of hospitals through mergers. In the Chicago area, for example, Northwestern Memorial Hospital merged with several suburban hospitals, such as Evanston Hospital, to form a large multi-hospital system covering the North Side of Chicago and the North Shore.

Proponents of hospital mergers argue that mergers enable hospitals to achieve cost savings through economies of scale in "backoffice" operations—activities, such as laundry, housekeeping, cafeterias, printing and duplicating services, and data processing that do not generate revenue for a hospital directly, but that the hospital cannot function without. Opponents argue that such cost savings are illusory and that hospital mergers mainly reduce competition in local hospital markets. The U.S. antitrust authorities have blocked several hospital mergers on this basis.

David Dranove has studied the extent to which backoffice activities within a hospital are subject to economies of scale.[11] Figure 8.12 summarizes some of his findings. The figure shows the average cost curves for three different activities: cafeterias, printing and duplicating, and data processing. Output is measured as the annual number of patients who are discharged by the hospital. (For each activity, average cost is normalized to equal an index of 1.0, at an output of 10,000 patients per year.) These figures show that economies of scale vary from activity to activity. Cafeterias are characterized by significant economies of scale. For printing and duplicating, the average cost curve is essentially flat. And for data processing, diseconomies of scale arise at a fairly low level of output. Overall, averaging the 14 backoffice activities that he studied, Dranove found that there are economies of scale in these activities, but they are largely exhausted at an output of about 7,500 patient discharges per year. This would correspond to a hospital with 200 beds, which is medium-sized by today's standards.

Dranove's analysis shows that a merger of two large hospitals would be unlikely to achieve additional economies of scale in backoffice operations. This suggests that claims that hospital mergers generally reduce costs per patient should be viewed with skepticism, unless both merging hospitals are small. ∎

[11]"Economies of Scale in Non-revenue Producing Cost Centers: Implications for Hospital Mergers," *Journal of Health Economics* 17 (1998): 69–83.

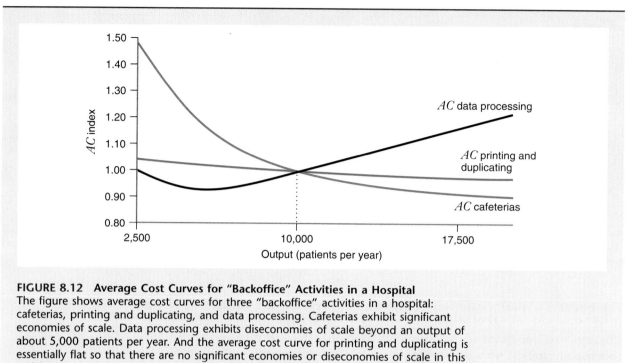

FIGURE 8.12   Average Cost Curves for "Backoffice" Activities in a Hospital
The figure shows average cost curves for three "backoffice" activities in a hospital: cafeterias, printing and duplicating, and data processing. Cafeterias exhibit significant economies of scale. Data processing exhibits diseconomies of scale beyond an output of about 5,000 patients per year. And the average cost curve for printing and duplicating is essentially flat so that there are no significant economies or diseconomies of scale in this activity.

RETURNS TO SCALE VERSUS ECONOMIES OF SCALE

The concept of economies of scale is closely related to the concept of returns to scale introduced in Chapter 6. The returns to scale of the production function will determine how average cost varies with output and thus the existence of economies or diseconomies of scale.

We can illustrate this point most clearly with a single-input production function. Table 8.3 shows three different production functions in which output Q is a function of the quantity of labor L. The first exhibits constant returns to scale (CRTS); the second exhibits increasing returns to scale (IRTS), and the third

TABLE 8.3
Relationship Between Returns to Scale and the Long-Run Average Cost Curve

	CRTS	IRTS	DRTS
Production function	$Q = L$	$Q = L^2$	$Q = \sqrt{L}$
Labor requirements function	$L = Q$	$L = \sqrt{Q}$	$L = Q^2$
Total cost	$TC = wQ$	$TC = w\sqrt{Q}$	$TC = wQ^2$
Average cost	$AC = w$	$AC = \dfrac{w}{\sqrt{Q}}$	$AC = wQ$
How does AC vary with Q?	Constant	Decreasing	Increasing

exhibits decreasing returns to scale (DRTS). Table 8.3 also shows the labor-requirements functions for these three production functions.[12] It also shows expressions for total cost and average cost, given a price of labor w. For the production function exhibiting constant returns to scale, the average cost function is independent of the quantity of output (i.e., it equals w no matter what Q is). For the production function exhibiting increasing returns to scale, average cost is a decreasing function of the quantity of output Q (i.e., as Q goes up, AC goes down). And for the production function exhibiting decreasing returns to scale, the average cost is an increasing function of output (i.e., as Q goes up, AC also goes up).

This can be summarized in three general relationships:

- When the production function exhibits *increasing returns to scale*, the long-run average cost curve exhibits *economies of scale* (i.e., $AC(Q)$ must decrease in Q).
- When the production function exhibits *decreasing returns to scale*, the long-run average cost curve exhibits *diseconomies of scale* (i.e., $AC(Q)$ must increase in Q).
- When the production function exhibits *constant returns to scale*, the long-run average cost curve is flat: It neither increases nor decreases in output.

MEASURING THE EXTENT OF ECONOMIES OF SCALE: THE OUTPUT ELASTICITY OF TOTAL COST

In Chapter 2 you learned that elasticities of demand, such as the price elasticity of demand or income elasticity of demand, tell us how sensitive demand is to the various factors that drive demand, such as price or income. We can also use elasticities to tell us how sensitive total cost is to the factors that influence it. An important cost elasticity is the **output elasticity of total cost,** denoted by $\epsilon_{TC,Q}$. It is defined as the percentage change in total cost per 1 percent change in output:

$$\epsilon_{TC,Q} = \frac{\frac{\Delta TC}{TC}}{\frac{\Delta Q}{Q}}.$$

We can rewrite this as follows:

$$\epsilon_{TC,Q} = \frac{\Delta TC}{\Delta Q} \div \frac{TC}{Q} = \frac{MC}{AC}.$$

Because the output elasticity of total cost is equal to the ratio of marginal to average cost, it tells us whether there are economies of scale or diseconomies of scale. This is because the following conditions hold:

- If $\epsilon_{TC,Q} < 1$, $MC < AC$, so AC decreases in Q, and we have *economies of scale*.
- If $\epsilon_{TC,Q} > 1$, $MC > AC$, so AC increases in Q, and we have *diseconomies of scale*.
- If $\epsilon_{TC,Q} = 1$, $MC = AC$, so AC neither increases nor decreases in Q.

The output elasticity is often used to characterize the nature of economies of scale in different industries. Table 8.4, for example, shows the results of a study that estimated the output elasticity of total cost for several manufacturing industries

---

[12]Recall from Chapter 6 that the labor requirements function tells us the quantity of labor needed to produce a given amount of output.

TABLE 8.4
Estimates of the Output Elasticities for Selected Manufacturing Industries in India

Industry	Output Elasticity of Total Cost
Iron and steel	0.553
Cotton textiles	1.211
Cement	1.162
Electricity and gas	0.3823

in India.[13] Iron and steel industries and electricity and gas industries have output elasticities significantly less than 1, indicating the presence of economies of scale. By contrast, textile and cement firms' output elasticities are a little higher than 1, indicating slight diseconomies of scale.[14]

8.3
SHORT-RUN COST CURVES

The long-run total cost curve shows how the firm's minimized total cost varies with output when the firm is free to adjust all its inputs. The **short-run total cost curve**, $STC(Q)$, tells us the minimized total cost of producing Q units of output when at least one input is fixed at a particular level. In the following discussion we assume that the amount of capital used by the firm is fixed at $\overline{K}$. The short-run total cost curve is the sum of two components: the **total variable cost curve**, $TVC(Q)$, and the **total fixed cost curve**, TFC (i.e., $STC(Q) = TVC(Q) + TFC$). The total variable cost curve, $TVC(Q)$, is the sum of expenditures on variable inputs, such as labor and materials, at the short-run cost-minimizing input combination. Total fixed cost is equal to the cost of the fixed capital services (i.e., $TFC = r\overline{K}$) and thus does not vary with output. Figure 8.13 shows a graph of the short-run total cost curve, the total variable cost curve, and the total fixed cost curve.

LEARNING-BY-DOING EXERCISE 8.3

Deriving the Short-Run Total Cost Curve

Let us return to the production function in Learning-By-Doing Exercise 7.6 in Chapter 7. For that production function, the firm uses three inputs: capital, labor, and materials:

$$Q = K^{\frac{1}{2}}L^{\frac{1}{4}}M^{\frac{1}{4}}$$

[13]R. Jha, M.N. Murty, S. Paul, and B. Bhaskara Rao, "An Analysis of Technological Change, Factor Substitution, and Economies of Scale in Manufacturing Industries in India," *Applied Economics 25* (October 1993): 1337–1343. The estimated output elasticities are reported in Table 5.

[14]The estimated output elasticities for textiles and cement are not *statistically* different from 1. Thus, these industries might be characterized by constant returns to scale.

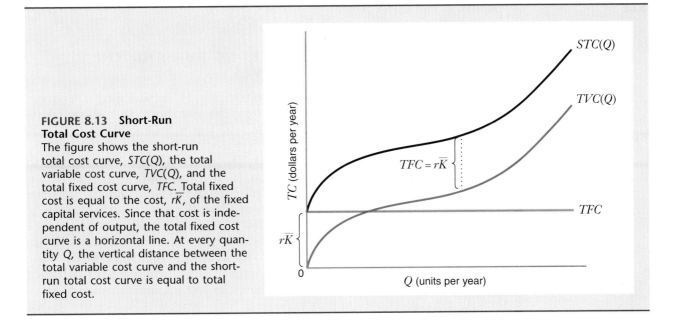

FIGURE 8.13 Short-Run Total Cost Curve
The figure shows the short-run total cost curve, STC(Q), the total variable cost curve, TVC(Q), and the total fixed cost curve, TFC. Total fixed cost is equal to the cost, $r\overline{K}$, of the fixed capital services. Since that cost is independent of output, the total fixed cost curve is a horizontal line. At every quantity Q, the vertical distance between the total variable cost curve and the short-run total cost curve is equal to total fixed cost.

Problem What is the short-run total cost curve for this production function when capital is fixed at a level $\overline{K}$ and input prices are $w = 16$, $m = 1$, and $r = 2$? What are total variable cost and total fixed cost?

Solution In Learning-By-Doing Exercise 7.6, we derived the short-run cost-minimizing quantities for labor and materials for this production function:

$$L = \frac{Q^2}{4\overline{K}}$$

$$M = \frac{4Q^2}{\overline{K}}$$

We can obtain the short-run total cost curve directly from this solution:

$$STC(Q) = wL + mM + r\overline{K}$$
$$= \left(\frac{16}{4\overline{K}} Q^2 \right) + 1 \left(\frac{4Q^2}{\overline{K}} \right) + 2\overline{K} = \frac{8Q^2}{\overline{K}} + 2\overline{K}$$

The total variable and total fixed cost curves follow:

$$TVC(Q) = \frac{8Q^2}{\overline{K}}$$

$$TFC = 2\overline{K}$$

Note that, holding Q constant, total variable cost is decreasing in the quantity of capital $\overline{K}$. This is because for a given amount of output, a firm that uses more capital can typically reduce the amount of labor and raw materials it employs. Since TVC is the sum of expenditures on labor and materials, it follows that TVC should decrease in $\overline{K}$. We will see a real-world illustration of this phenomenon in Example 8.5.

Similar Problem: 8.4.

RELATIONSHIP BETWEEN THE LONG-RUN AND THE SHORT-RUN TOTAL COST CURVES

To develop the relationship between the long-run and short-run total cost curves, let's return to a graphical analysis of the long-run and short-run cost-minimization problems for a producer of television sets. Figure 8.14 shows the relationship between the two problems when the firm uses just two inputs: labor and capital. It illustrates a point that we made in Chapter 7: When the firm is free to vary the quantity of capital in the long run, it can attain lower total costs than it can when its capital is fixed. This makes sense: the firm is more constrained when it operates in the short run because it cannot adjust the quantity of capital freely. Specifically, suppose initially the firm wants to produce 1 million television sets, and it is free to vary both capital and labor. It would minimize total costs by operating at point A, using L_1 units of labor and K_1 units of capital. However, if the firm's desired output goes up to 2 million units but its capital remains fixed at K_1, it would operate at point B. By contrast, long-run cost minimization would move the firm along its expansion path to point C. Since point B is on a higher isocost line than point C, the firm incurs higher costs in the short run to produce an output of 2 million televisions than it would in the long run if it were free to vary the quantity of its capital.

Figure 8.15 shows the corresponding relationship between the long-run and short-run total cost curves. The short-run total cost curve when capital is fixed at K_1 lies everywhere above the long-run total cost curve, except at point A. This

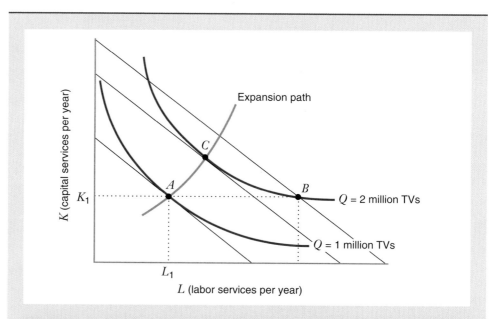

FIGURE 8.14 Why Total Costs Are Higher in the Short Run than in the Long Run
Initially, the firm produces 1 million TV sets, and it minimizes long-run costs by operating at point A. If the firm's desired output then goes up to 2 million TV sets but it cannot increase the quantity of capital, it must operate at point B. In the long run, when it can adjust the quantity of its capital, it will move from point B to point C. Since point C lies on a lower isocost line than B, the long-run total cost of producing 2 million TVs is less than the short-run total cost.

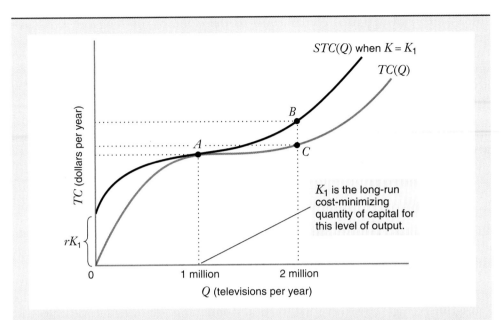

FIGURE 8.15 Relationship Between Short-Run and Long-Run Total Cost Curves
The short-run total cost curve when the quantity of capital is fixed at K_1 lies above the long-run total cost curve at every level of output, except point A. At this point, short-run total cost equals long-run total cost. For example, as we saw in Figure 8.14, at an output of 2 million TVs per year, the short-run total cost exceeds the long-run total cost. At point A, the quantity of capital K_1 is the long-run cost-minimizing quantity of capital for the output of 1 million units per year.

illustrates the point we just made: The firm cannot attain as low a level of total cost as it can in the long run when it is free to vary all its inputs. At point A, the short-run total cost is equal to the long-run total cost. What is special about point A? At point A, the firm produces 1 million televisions per year, the quantity of output for which the fixed capital K_1 is cost minimizing in the long run. That is, at a quantity of 1 million units, the solution to the short-run cost-minimization problem when $K = K_1$ coincides with the solution to the long-run cost-minimization problem (see Figure 8.14). Therefore, at a quantity of 1 million units, short-run total cost STC must equal the long-run total cost TC.

SHORT-RUN MARGINAL AND AVERAGE COSTS

Just as we can define long-run average and long-run marginal costs, we can also define **short-run average cost** (SAC) and **short-run marginal cost** (SMC):

$$SAC(Q) = \frac{STC(Q)}{Q}$$

$$SMC(Q) = \frac{STC(Q + \Delta Q) - STC(Q)}{\Delta Q}$$

$$= \frac{\Delta STC}{\Delta Q}$$

Just as long-run marginal cost is equal to the slope of the long-run total cost curve, short-run marginal cost is equal to the slope of the short-run total cost curve. Note that in Figure 8.15 at point A (i.e., when output equals 1 million units per year), the slopes of the long-run total cost and short-run total cost curves are equal. It therefore follows that at this level of output, not only does $STC = TC$, but $SMC = MC$.

Because we can break short-run total cost into two pieces (total variable cost and total fixed cost), we can also break short-run average cost into two pieces: **average variable cost** (AVC) and **average fixed cost** (AFC):

$$STC = TVC + TFC, \text{ so}$$

$$SAC = AVC + AFC.$$

Put another way, average fixed cost is total fixed cost per unit of output, i.e. $AFC = TFC/Q$. Average variable cost is total variable cost per unit of output, that is, $AVC = TVC/Q$.

Figure 8.16 illustrates typical graphs of the short-run marginal, short-run average cost, average variable cost, and average fixed cost curves. We obtain the short-run average cost curve by "vertically summing" the average variable cost curve and the average fixed cost curve.[15] The average fixed cost curve decreases everywhere and approaches the horizontal axis as Q becomes very large. This reflects the fact that as output increases, fixed capital costs are "spread out" over an increasingly large volume of output, driving fixed costs per unit downward toward zero. Because AFC becomes smaller and smaller as Q increases, the AVC and SAC curves get closer and closer together. The short-run marginal cost curve SMC intersects the short-run average cost curve and the average variable cost curve at the minimum point of each curve. This property mirrors the relationship

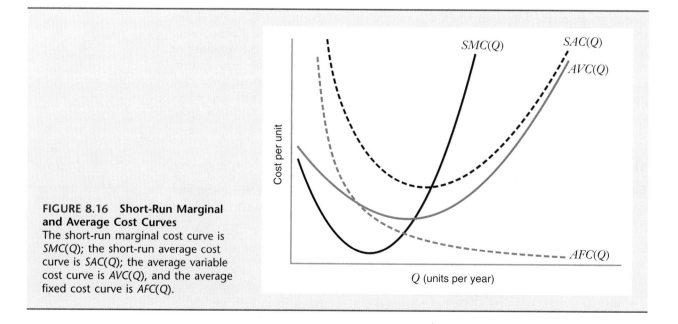

FIGURE 8.16 Short-Run Marginal and Average Cost Curves
The short-run marginal cost curve is $SMC(Q)$; the short-run average cost curve is $SAC(Q)$; the average variable cost curve is $AVC(Q)$, and the average fixed cost curve is $AFC(Q)$.

[15]*Vertically summing* means that, for any Q, we find the height of the SAC curve by adding together the heights of the AVC and AFC curves at that quantity.

between the long-run marginal and long-run average cost curves (and again reflects the relationship between the average and marginal measures of anything).

THE LONG-RUN AVERAGE COST CURVE AS AN ENVELOPE CURVE

Figure 8.17 illustrates the relationship between the long-run average cost curve and short-run average cost curves for a U-shaped long-run average cost curve $AC(Q)$. The figure shows different short-run average cost curves: $SAC_1(Q)$, $SAC_2(Q)$, and $SAC_3(Q)$. These curves are also U-shaped. Each corresponds to a different level of fixed capital, or *plant size*, K_1, K_2, and K_3 where $K_1 < K_2 < K_3$. Thinking of a television producer, such as HiSense, K_3 might either be a larger factory than K_1 or K_2, or it might entail a greater degree of automation.

A short-run average cost curve for a particular plant size lies above the long-run average cost curve except at the level of output for which that plant size is optimal. For example, a television producer, such as HiSense, that planned to produce 1 million televisions per year would minimize its long-run total cost by building a small plant of size K_1. If it built a plant of this size and in fact produced 1 million television sets, its short-run average cost would equal the long-run average cost of $50 per television. But if HiSense expanded its output in this small plant to, say, 2 million units, its short-run average cost would be $110 per television, even though its long-run average cost at 2 million units is only $35 per television.

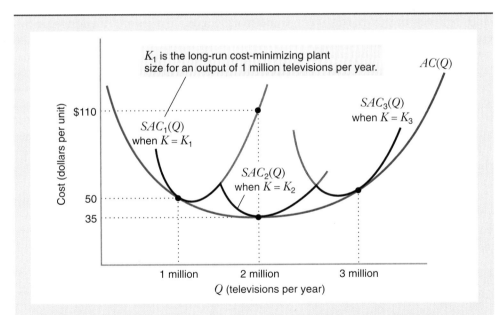

FIGURE 8.17 The Long-Run Average Cost Curve as an Envelope Curve
The figure shows three different short-run average cost curves: $SAC_1(Q)$, $SAC_2(Q)$, and $SAC_3(Q)$. Each corresponds to a different level of fixed capital, or plant size. Each short-run average cost curve lies above the long-run average cost curve except at the level of output for which that plant size is cost minimizing in the long run. If we trace out the lower boundary of the three short-run average cost curves, we obtain a scalloped-shaped curve. This curve tells us the minimum attainable average cost if the firm could choose among just three plant sizes: K_1, K_2, and K_3. This scalloped curve approximates the long-run average cost curve. If we drew more short-run average cost curves and traced the lower boundary including these additional curves, we would more closely approximate the long-run average cost curve.

This difference between the short-run average cost and the long-run average cost illustrates a point we made in our earlier discussion of the relationship between the short-run total cost and long-run total cost curves: you can never do better (i.e., have lower total costs) in the short run than in the long run because in the long run you can set *all* of your inputs to the levels that minimize total cost. (In practice, the high unit cost that HiSense would incur from producing a relatively large output in a small plant might reflect reductions in the marginal product of labor that arise from crowding a large work force into a small plant.) In order to attain the long-run average cost of $35 per television when producing 2 million televisions, HiSense would need to expand the size of its plant from K_1 to K_2.

If we traced the lower boundary of the three short-run average cost curves, we would obtain the dark "scalloped" curve in Figure 8.17. This curve tells us the minimum attainable average cost if the firm could choose only one of three plant sizes: K_1, K_2, and K_3. The scalloped curve approximates the actual long-run average cost curve when the firm can choose any plant size it desires. If we drew more short-run average cost curves and traced the lower boundary including these additional curves, the resulting scalloped curve would be an even better approximation to the long-run average cost curve. This argument tells us that you can think of the long-run average cost curve as the "lower envelope" of an infinite number of short-run average cost curves. The long-run average cost curve is thus sometimes referred to as the *envelope curve*.

Figure 8.18 takes Figure 8.17 one step further and shows the special relationships between the short-run average and marginal cost curves and the long-run average and marginal cost curves. At an output of 1 million units, short-run average cost when plant size equals K_1 equals long-run average cost. Short-run marginal cost when plant size equals K_1 also equals long-run marginal cost at 1 million units. These relationships reflect our earlier discussions of those between the short-run and long-run cost curves. Note, too, that since long-run average cost and long-run marginal cost are *not equal* at this particular level of output, short-run average cost and short-run marginal cost are also not equal here. (They are equal at a higher level of output.) At an output level of 3 million units, the relationships between the short-run and long-run average and marginal cost curves are analogous to those at an output of 1 million units per year.

An output of 2 million units corresponds to the point at which long-run average cost attains its minimum level—the MES. At MES, long-run marginal cost equals long-run average cost, and short-run marginal cost equals short-run average cost; that is, $AC = MC = SAC_2 = SMC_2$.

LEARNING-BY-DOING EXERCISE 8.4

The Relationship Between Short-Run and Long-Run Average Cost Curves

Problem

Let us return to the production function in Learning-By-Doing Exercises 7.6 and 8.3:

$$Q = K^{\frac{1}{2}}L^{\frac{1}{4}}M^{\frac{1}{4}}$$

As in that exercise, we assume that the input prices are $w = 16$, $m = 1$, and $r = 2$.

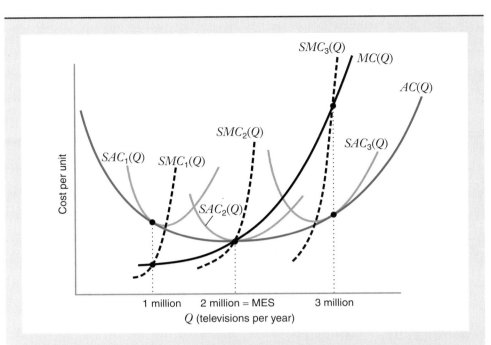

FIGURE 8.18 The Relationship Between the Long-Run Average and Marginal Cost Curves and the Short-Run Average and Marginal Cost Curves
At an output level of 1 million TVs per year (the output level for which plant size K_1 solves the long-run cost-minimization problem), short-run average cost (SAC_1) equals long-run average cost ($AC(Q)$). Short-run marginal cost (SMC_1) also equals long-run marginal cost ($MC(Q)$) at 1 million units. Since $AC(Q)$ and $MC(Q)$ are not equal at this level of output, SAC_1 and SMC_1 are also not equal here. At an output level of 3 million TVs per year, the relationships between the short-run and long-run average and marginal cost functions are analogous to those at 1 million units. An output of 2 million units is where $AC(Q)$ attains its minimum level; that is, it is the MES. At the MES, $MC(Q)$ equals $AC(Q)$, and thus $SMC_2 = SAC_2$.

(a) What is the long-run average cost curve for this production function?
(b) What is the short-run average cost curve for a fixed level of capital $\overline{K}$?
(c) Graph the long-run average cost curve and the short-run average cost curves corresponding to $\overline{K} = 10$, $\overline{K} = 20$, and $\overline{K} = 40$.

Solution

(a) Recall from Learning-By-Doing Exercise 7.6 that the solution to the long-run cost-minimization problem at the given input prices is

$$L = \frac{Q}{8}.$$

$$M = 2Q.$$

$$K = 2Q.$$

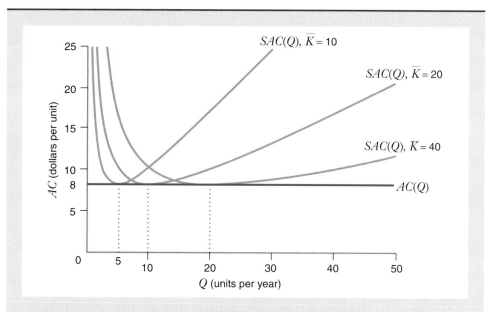

FIGURE 8.19 Long-Run and Short-Run Average Cost Curves for Learning-By-Doing Exercise 8.4
Each short-run average cost curve corresponds to a particular plant size: $\overline{K} = 10$, 20, and 40. These curves are U-shaped. The long-run average cost curve is the lower envelope of the short-run average cost curves and is a horizontal line.

Because the input prices are $w = 16$, $m = 1$, and $r = 2$, the long-run total cost curve is

$$TC(Q) = 16\left(\frac{Q}{8}\right) + 1(2Q) + 2(2Q) = 8Q.$$

The long-run average cost curve is thus

$$AC(Q) = \frac{TC(Q)}{Q} = \frac{8Q}{Q} = 8.$$

(b) We derived the short-run total cost curve for this production function in Learning-By-Doing Exercise 8.3: $STC(Q) = (8Q^2/\overline{K}) + 2\overline{K}$. Thus, the short-run average cost curve is

$$SAC(Q) = \frac{8Q}{\overline{K}} + \frac{2\overline{K}}{Q}.$$

(c) The long-run average cost curve is a horizontal line, as Figure 8.19 shows. This makes sense because the production function exhibits constant returns to scale. The short-run average cost curves are U-shaped and attain their minimum point at $Q = 5$, $Q = 10$, and $Q = 20$, respectively.

Similar Problem: 8.4

EXAMPLE 8.5

The Short-Run and Long-Run Cost Curves for an American Railroad Firm[16]

The 1990s were an interesting time for U.S. railroads. On the positive side, the railroad industry was healthier than it had been in years, and the bankruptcies that had plagued the industry in the 1960s and 1970s were over. Some railroads, such as the Norfolk Southern, had become so optimistic about the future that they had begun ambitious investments in new track. On the negative side, however, U.S. railroads had developed a generally poor reputation for service, particularly speed of delivery. On some routes, shipping freight by train in the late 1990s took longer than it did thirty years earlier. Service became so bad that in 1997 Lionel, a company that makes toy trains, began shipping by truck rather than by rail. "We feel a little guilty forsaking our big brothers," said Lionel President Gary Moreau, "but we have no choice." Part of the problem, according to industry observers, arose because the railroad industry downsized too much. During the 1980s and 1990s, U.S. railroads sold or abandoned 55,000 miles of track. According to one expert, the railroads ". . . have too much freight trying to go over too little track."

These concerns over the quality of rail service and how they relate to the amount of track a railroad employs might make you wonder how a railroad's production costs depend on these factors. For example, would a railroad's total variable costs go down as it adds track? If so, at what rate? Would a faster service increase or decrease a railroad's cost of operation?

One way to study these questions would be to estimate the short-run and long-run cost curves for a railroad. In the 1980s, Ronald Braeutigam, Andrew Daughety, and Mark Turnquist (hereafter BDT) undertook such a study.[17] With the cooperation of the management of a large American railroad firm, BDT obtained data on costs of shipment, input prices (price of fuel, price of labor service), volume of output, and speed of service for this railroad.[18] Using statistical techniques, they estimated a short-run total variable cost curve for the railroad. In the study, total variable cost is the sum of the railroad's monthly costs for labor, fuel, maintenance, rail cars, locomotives, and supplies.

Table 8.5 shows the impact on total variable costs of a hypothetical 10 percent increase in (1) traffic volume (car-loads of freight per month); (2) the quantity of the railroad's track (in miles); (3) speed of service (miles per day of loaded cars); and (4) the prices of labor, fuel, and equipment.[19] You should think of track miles as a fixed input, analogous to capital in our previous discussion. A railroad cannot instantly vary the quantity or quality of its track to adjust to month-to-month variations in shipment volumes in the system and thus must regard track as a fixed input.

Table 8.5 contains several interesting findings. First, total variable cost increases with total output and with the prices of the railroad's inputs. This is consistent with the predictions of the theory you have been learning in this chapter and Chapter

---

[16]The first part of this example box draws from "A Long Haul: America's Railroads Struggle to Capture Their Former Glory," *Wall Street Journal* (December 5, 1997), pp. A1 and A6.

[17]R. R. Braeutigam, A. F. Daughety, and M. A. Turnquist, "A Firm-Specific Analysis of Economies of Density in the U. S. Railroad Industry," *Journal of Industrial Economics 33* (September 1984); 3–20.

[18]The identity of the firm remained anonymous to ensure the confidentiality of its data.

[19]In this study, the railroad's track mileage was adjusted to reflect changes in the quality of its track over time.

TABLE 8.5
What Affects Total Variable Costs for a Railroad?

A 10 Percent Increase In . . .	Changes Total Variable Cost By . . .
Volume of output	+3.98%
Track mileage	−2.71%
Speed of service	−0.66%
Price of fuel	+1.90%
Price of labor	+5.25%
Price of equipment	+2.85%

Adapted from Table 1 of R. R. Braeutigam, A. F. Daughety, and M. A. Turnquist, "A Firm-Specific Analysis of Economies of Density in the U.S. Railroad Industry," *Journal of Industrial Economics, 33* (September 1984): 3–20. The percentage changes in the various factors are changes away from the average values of these factors over the period studied by BDT.

7. Second, as we discussed in Learning-By-Doing Exercise 8.3, we would expect that total variable costs would go down as the volume of the fixed input is increased. Table 8.5 shows that this is true for BDT's railroad. Holding traffic volume and speed of service fixed, an increase in track mileage (or an increase in the quality of track, holding mileage fixed) would be expected to decrease the amount the railroad spends on variable inputs, such as labor and fuel. For example, with more track (holding output and speed fixed), the railroad would reduce the congestion of trains on its mainlines and in its train yards. As a result, it would probably need fewer dispatchers to control the movement of trains. Third, Table 8.5 tells us that improvements in average speed may also reduce costs. Although this impact is not large, it does suggest that improvements in service not only can benefit the railroad's consumers, they might also benefit the railroad itself through lower variable costs. For this railroad, higher speeds might reduce the use of labor (e.g., fewer train crews would be needed to haul a given amount of freight) and increase the fuel efficiency of the railroad's locomotives.

Having estimated the total variable cost function, BDT go on to estimate the long-run total and average cost curves for this railroad. They do so by finding the track mileage that, for each quantity Q, minimizes the sum of total variable costs and total fixed costs, where total fixed cost is the monthly opportunity cost to the firm's owners of a given amount of track mileage. Figure 8.20 shows the long-run average cost function estimated by BDT using this approach. It also shows two short-run average cost curves, each corresponding to a different level of track mileage. (Track mileage is stated in relation to the average track mileage observed in BDT's data.) The units of output in Figure 8.20 are expressed as a percentage of MES, and the average level of output produced by the railroad at the time of the study was about 40 percent of MES. This study thus suggests that increases in traffic volume, accompanied by cost-minimizing adjustments in track mileage, would reduce this railroad's average production costs over a wide range of output. ■

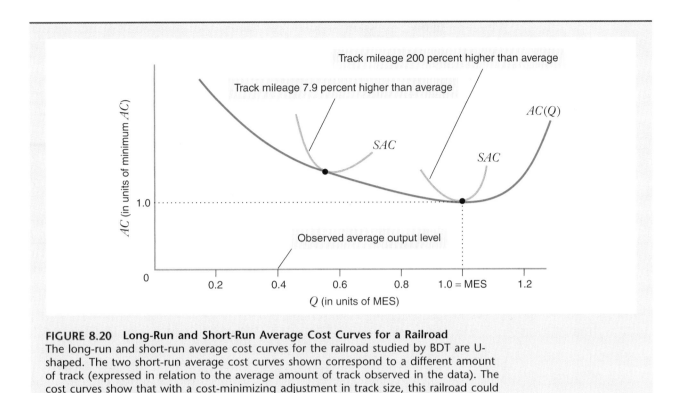

FIGURE 8.20 Long-Run and Short-Run Average Cost Curves for a Railroad
The long-run and short-run average cost curves for the railroad studied by BDT are U-shaped. The two short-run average cost curves shown correspond to a different amount of track (expressed in relation to the average amount of track observed in the data). The cost curves show that with a cost-minimizing adjustment in track size, this railroad could decrease its unit costs over a wide range of output above its current output level.

ECONOMIES OF SCOPE

This chapter has concentrated on cost curves for firms that produce just one product or service. In reality, though, many firms produce more than one product. For a firm that produces two products, total costs would depend on the quantity Q_1 of the first product the firm makes and the quantity Q_2 of the second product it makes. We will use the expression $TC(Q_1, Q_2)$ to denote how the firm's costs vary with Q_1 and Q_2. The total cost TC would be the minimized total cost of producing given quantities of the firm's two products and would come from a cost-minimization problem that is analogous to the cost-minimization problem for a single-product firm.

In some situations, efficiencies arise when a firm produces more than one product. That is, a two-product firm may be able to manufacture and market its products at a lower total cost than two single-product firms would incur when producing on a stand-alone basis. These efficiencies are called **economies of scope.**

Specifically, economies of scope exist when the total cost of producing given quantities of two goods in the same firm is less than the total cost of producing those quantities in two single-product firms. Mathematically, this definition says

$$TC(Q_1, Q_2) < TC(Q_1, 0) + TC(0, Q_2). \qquad \textbf{(8.4)}$$

The zeros in the expressions on the right-hand side of equation (8.4) indicate that the single-product firms produce positive amounts of one good but none of the other. These are sometimes called the **stand-alone costs** of producing goods 1 and 2.

Intuitively, the existence of economies of scope tells us that "variety" is more efficient than "specialization." We can develop an intuitive interpretation of the definition in 8.4 by rearranging terms as follows:

$$TC(Q_1, Q_2) - TC(Q_1, 0) < TC(0, Q_2) - TC(0, 0),$$

where $TC(0, 0) = 0$. That is, the total cost of producing zero quantities of both products is zero. The left-hand side of this equation is the *additional cost* of producing Q_2 units of product 2 *when the firm is already producing Q_1 units of product 1*. The right-hand side of this equation is the *additional cost of producing Q_2 when the firm does not produce Q_1*. Economies of scope exist if it is less costly for a firm to add a product to its product line given that it already produces another product. Economies of scope would exist, for example, if it is less costly for Coca-Cola to add a cherry-flavored soft drink to its product line than it would be for a new company starting from scratch.

Why would economies of scope arise? An important reason is a firm's ability to use a common input to make and sell more than one product. For example, BSkyB, the British satellite television company, can use the same satellite to broadcast a news channel, several movie channels, several sports channels, and several general entertainment channels.[20] Companies specializing in the broadcast of a single channel would each need to have a satellite orbiting the Earth. BSkyB's channels save hundreds of millions of dollars as compared to stand-alone channels by sharing a common satellite. Another example is Eurotunnel, the 31-mile tunnel that runs underneath the English Channel between Calais, France, and Dover, Great Britain. The Eurotunnel accommodates both highway and rail traffic. Two separate tunnels, one for highway traffic and one for rail traffic, would have been more expensive to construct and operate than a single tunnel that accommodates both forms of traffic.

---

*E*XAMPLE 8.6   *Nike Enters the Market for Sports Equipment*[21]

An important source of economies of scope is marketing. A company with a well-established brand name in one product line can sometimes introduce additional products at a lower cost than a stand-alone company would be able to. This is because when consumers are unsure about a product's quality they often make inferences about its quality from the product's brand name. This can give a firm with an established brand reputation an advantage over a stand-alone firm in introduc-

---

[20]BSkyB is a subsidiary of Rupert Murdoch's News Corporation.

[21]This example is based on "Just Doing It: Nike Plans to Swoosh Into Sports Equipment But It's a Tough Game," *Wall Street Journal* (January 6, 1998), pp. A1 and A10.

ing new products. Because of its brand reputation, an established firm would not have to spend as much on advertising as the stand-alone firm to persuade consumers to try its product. This is an example of an economy of scope based on the ability of all products in a firm's product line to "share" the benefits of its established brand reputation.

A company with an extraordinary brand reputation is Nike. Nike's "swoosh," the symbol that appears on its athletic shoes and sports apparel, is one of the most recognizable marketing symbols of the modern age, and its slogan, "Just Do It," has become ingrained in American popular culture. Nike's slogan and swoosh are so recognizable that Nike can run television commercials that never mention its name and be confident that consumers will know whose products are being advertised.

In the late 1990s, Nike turned its attention to the sports equipment market, introducing products such as hockey sticks and golf balls. Nike's goal was to become the dominant firm in the $40 billion per year sports equipment market by 2005. This is a bold ambition. The sports equipment market is highly fragmented, and no single company has ever dominated the entire range of product categories that Nike intends to enter. In addition, while no one can deny Nike's past success in the athletic shoe and sports apparel markets, producing a high-quality hockey stick or an innovative golf ball has little in common with making sneakers or jogging clothes. It therefore seems unlikely that Nike could attain economies of scope in manufacturing or product design.

Nike hopes to achieve economies of scope in marketing. These economies of scope would be based on its incredibly strong brand reputation, its close ties to sports equipment retailers, and its special relationships with professional athletes such as Tiger Woods and Ken Griffey, Jr. Nike's plan is to develop sports equipment that it can claim is innovative and then use its established brand reputation and its ties with the retail trade to convince consumers that its products are technically superior to existing products. If this plan works, Nike will be able to introduce its new products at far lower costs than a stand-alone company would incur to introduce otherwise identical products.

It will be interesting to see whether Nike succeeds. Economies of scope in marketing can be powerful, but they also have their limits. A strong brand reputation can induce consumers to try a product once, but if it does not perform as expected or if its quality is inferior, it may be difficult to penetrate the market or get repeat business. Nike's preliminary forays into the sports equipment market illustrate this risk. In July 1997, Nike "rolled out" a new line of roller skates at the annual sports equipment trade show in Chicago. But when a group of skaters equipped with Nike skates rolled into the parking lot, the wheels on the skates began to disintegrate! Quality problems have also arisen with a line of ice skates that Nike introduced several years ago. Jeremy Roenick, a star with the Phoenix Coyote's NHL hockey team, turned down a six-figure endorsement deal with Nike because he felt the skates were poorly designed and did not fit properly. Rumor has it that other hockey players who do have equipment deals with Nike use the products of competitors. According to one NHL equipment manager, "They're still wearing the stuff they've been wearing for years. They just slap the swoosh on it." ◾

ECONOMIES OF EXPERIENCE: THE EXPERIENCE CURVE

Learning-by-Doing and the Experience Curve

Economies of scale refer to the cost advantages that flow from producing a larger output at a given point in time. **Economies of experience** refer to cost advantages that result from accumulated experience over an extended period of time or as it is sometimes called, *learning-by-doing*. This is the reason we gave that title to the exercises in this book—they are designed to help you *learn* microeconomics *by doing* microeconomics problems.

Economies of experience arise for several reasons. Workers often improve their performance of specific tasks by performing them over and over again. Engineers often perfect product designs as they accumulate know-how about the manufacturing process. Firms often become more adept at handling and processing materials as they deepen their production experience. The benefits of learning are usually greater labor productivity (more output per unit of labor input), fewer defects, and higher material yields (more output per unit of raw material input).

Economies of experience are described by the **experience curve,** a relationship between average variable cost and cumulative production volume.[22] A firm's cumulative production volume at any given time is the total amount of output that it has produced over the history of the product until that time. For example, if Boeing's output of 777 jet aircraft was 30 in 1997, 45 in 1998, 50 in 1999, 70 in 2000, and 60 in 2001, its cumulative output as of the beginning of 2002 would be 30 + 45 + 50 + 70 + 60, or 255 aircraft. A typical relationship between average variable cost and cumulative output is

$$AVC(N) = AN^B,$$

where AVC is the average variable cost of production and N denotes cumulative production volume. In this formulation, A and B are constants, where $A > 0$ and B is a negative number between -1 and 0. The constant A represents the average variable cost of the first unit produced, and B represents the **experience elasticity:** the percentage change in average variable cost for every 1 percent increase in cumulative volume.

The magnitude of cost reductions that are achieved through experience is often expressed in terms of a concept known as the **slope of the experience curve.**[23] The slope of the experience curve tells us how much average variable costs go down as a percentage of an initial level when cumulative output doubles.[24] For example, if doubling a firm's cumulative output of semiconductors results in average variable cost falling from $10 per megabyte to $8.50 per megabyte, we would say that the slope of the experience curve for semiconductors is 85 percent, since average variable costs fell to 85 percent of their initial level. In terms of an equation,

$$\text{slope} = \frac{AVC(2N)}{AVC(N)}.$$

[22]The experience curve is also known as the learning curve.
[23]The slope of the experience curve is also known as the progress ratio.
[24]Note that the term "slope" as used here is *not* the usual notion of the slope of a straight line.

The slope and the experience elasticity are systematically related. If the experience elasticity is equal to B, the slope turns out to equal 2^B. Figure 8.21 shows experience curves with three different slopes: 90 percent, 80 percent, and 70 percent. The smaller the slope, the "steeper" the experience curve, (i.e., the more rapidly average variable costs fall as the firm accumulates experience). Note, though, that all three curves eventually flatten out. For example, beyond a volume of $N = 40$, increments in cumulative experience have a small impact on average variable costs, no matter what the slope of the experience curve is. At this point, most of the economies of experience are exhausted.

Experience curve slopes have been estimated for many different products. The median slope appears to be about 80 percent, implying that for the typical firm, each doubling of cumulative output reduces average variable costs to 80 percent of what they were before. Slopes vary from firm to firm and industry to industry, however, so that the slope enjoyed by any one firm for any given production process generally falls between 70 and 90 percent and may be as low as 60 percent or as high as 100 percent (i.e., no economies of experience).

Economies of Experience versus Economies of Scale

Economies of experience differ from economies of scale. Economies of scale refer to the ability to perform activities at a lower unit cost when those activities are performed on a larger scale at a given point in time. Economies of experience refer to reductions in unit costs due to accumulating experience overtime. Economies of scale may be substantial even when learning economies are minimal. This is likely to be the case in mature, capital-intensive production processes, such as aluminum can manufacturing. Likewise, economies of experience may be substantial even when economies of scale are minimal, as in complex labor-intensive activities such as the production of handmade watches.

Firms that do not correctly distinguish between economies of scale and experience might draw incorrect inferences about the benefits of size in a market. For example, if a firm has low average costs because of economies of scale,

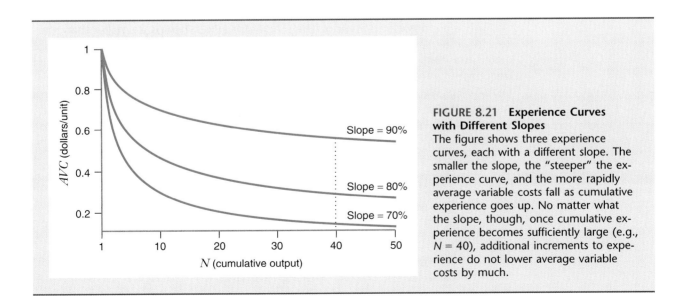

FIGURE 8.21   Experience Curves with Different Slopes
The figure shows three experience curves, each with a different slope. The smaller the slope, the "steeper" the experience curve, and the more rapidly average variable costs fall as cumulative experience goes up. No matter what the slope, though, once cumulative experience becomes sufficiently large (e.g., $N = 40$), additional increments to experience do not lower average variable costs by much.

reductions in the current volume of production will increase unit costs. If the low average costs are the result of cumulative experience, the firm may be able to cut back current production volumes without necessarily raising its average costs.

EXAMPLE 8.7

The Experience Curve in the Production of EPROM Chips[25]

An interesting example of economies of experience occurs in the production of semiconductors, the memory chips that are used in personal computers, cellular telephones, and electronic games. It is widely believed that the "yield" of semiconductor chips—the ratio of usable chips to total chips on a silicon wafer—goes up as a firm gains production experience.[26] Silicon is an expensive raw material, and the cost of a chip is primarily determined by how much silicon it uses. The rate at which yields go up with experience is thus important for a semiconductor manufacturer to know.

Harald Gruber estimated the experience curve for a particular type of semiconductor: erasable programmable read only memory (EPROM) chips. EPROM chips are used to store program code for cellular phones, pagers, modems, video games, printers, and hard disk drives. An EPROM chip differs from the more common DRAM in that it is *nonvolatile*, which means that unlike a DRAM chip it retains its stored data when the power is turned off. And in contrast to DRAM chips, which are produced by large semiconductor firms such as Samsung and NEC, EPROM chips are generally produced by smaller firms, such as the Taiwanese firm Macronix.

Gruber recognized that other factors, such as economies of scale and memory capacity, could influence the average cost of producing an EPROM chip. After controlling for these factors, Gruber found evidence of economies of experience in the production of EPROM chips. His estimate of the slope of the EPROM experience curve was 78 percent. Thus, by doubling its cumulative volume of chips, an EPROM producer would expect its average variable costs to fall to 78 percent of their initial level.

This is an interesting finding. The market for EPROM chips is smaller than markets for other semiconductors, such as DRAMs, and as mentioned, most firms operate on a small scale. Moreover, new generations of EPROM chips are introduced frequently, typically about once every 18 months. By contrast, new generations of DRAM chips were introduced about every 3 years during the 1980s and 1990s. This suggests that it is unlikely that an EPROM manufacturer will operate on the "flat" portion of the experience curve for long. By the time a firm starts to "move down" the experience curve, a new generation of chip will have come along. This, then, implies that a firm, such as Macronix, that can achieve a head start in bringing a new generation of EPROM chips to market, may achieve a significant cost advantage over slower competitors.   ∎

---

[25]This example draws from H. Gruber, "The Learning Curve in the Production of Semiconductor Memory Chips," *Applied Economics*, 24 (August 1992): 885–894.

[26]A *wafer* is a slice of polycrystalline silicon. A chip producer will etch hundreds of circuits onto a single wafer.

Suppose you wanted to estimate how the total costs for a television producer, such as HiSense, varied with the quantity of its output or the magnitude of its input prices. To do this, you might want to estimate what economists call a **total cost function**. A total cost function is a mathematical relationship that shows how total costs vary with the factors that influence total costs. These factors are sometimes called **cost drivers.** We've spent much of this chapter analyzing two key cost drivers: input prices and scale (volume of output). Our discussion in the previous section suggests two other cost drivers that could also influence total costs: scope (variety of other goods produced by the firm) and cumulative experience.

How would you estimate a cost function? You would first need to gather data. When estimating cost functions, many economists use data from a cross-section of firms or plants at a particular point in time. A cross-section of television producers would consist of a sample of manufacturers or manufacturing facilities in a particular year, such as 2001. For each observation in your cross-section, you would need information about total costs and cost drivers. The set of *cost drivers* that you include in your analysis is usually specific to what you are studying. In television manufacturing, scale, cumulative experience, labor wages, materials prices, and costs of capital would probably be important drivers for explaining the behavior of average costs in the long run.

Having gathered data on total costs and cost drivers, you would then use statistical techniques to construct an estimated total cost function. The most common technique used by economists is multiple regression. The basic idea behind this technique is to find a function that best fits our available data.

CONSTANT ELASTICITY COST FUNCTION

An important issue when you use multiple regression to estimate a cost function is the functional form that relates the dependent variable of interest—in this case, total cost—to the independent variables of interest, such as output and input prices. One common functional form is the **constant elasticity cost function.** A constant elasticity cost function specifies a multiplicative relationship between total cost, output, and input prices.

For a production process that involves two inputs, capital and labor, the constant elasticity long-run total cost function is

$$TC = aQ^b w^c r^d,$$

where a, b, c, and d are positive constants. It is common to convert this into a relationship that is linear in the logs:

$$\log TC = \log a + b \log Q + c \log w + d \log r,$$

and in this form, the positive constants a, b, c, and d can be estimated using multiple regression.

A useful feature of the constant elasticity specification is that the constant b is the output elasticity of total cost, discussed earlier. Analogously, the constants c and d are the elasticities of long-run total cost with respect to the prices of labor and capital. These elasticities must be positive since, as we saw earlier, an increase in an input price will increase long-run total cost. We also learned earlier that a given percentage increase in w and r would have to increase long-run total cost by the same percentage amount. This implies that the constants c and d must add up to 1 (i.e., $c + d = 1$). Thus, for the estimated long-run total cost function to be consistent with long-run cost minimization, this restriction would have to hold. This restriction can be readily incorporated into the multiple regression analysis.

TRANSLOG COST FUNCTION

The constant elasticity cost function does not allow for the possibility of average costs that first decrease in Q and then increase in Q (i.e., economies of scale, followed by diseconomies of scale). A cost function that allows for this possibility is the **translog cost function.** A translog cost function postulates a quadratic relationship between the log of total cost and the logs of input prices and output. The equation of the translog cost function is

$$\log TC = b_0 + b_1\log Q + b_2\log w + b_3\log r + b_4(\log Q)^2 \qquad (8.5)$$
$$+ b_5(\log w)^2 + b_6(\log r)^2 + b_7(\log w)(\log r)$$
$$+ b_8(\log w)(\log Q) + b_9(\log r)(\log Q).$$

This formidable-looking expression turns out to have a lot of useful properties. For one thing, it is often a good approximation of the cost functions that come from just about *any* production function. Thus, if (as is often the case) we don't know the exact functional form of the production function, the translog might be a good choice for the functional form of the cost function. In addition, the average cost function for the translog total cost function can be U-shaped. Thus, it allows for both economies of scale and diseconomies of scale. Note, too, that if $b_4 = b_5 = b_6 = b_7 = b_8 = b_9 = 0$, the translog cost function reduces to the constant elasticity cost function. Thus, the constant elasticity cost function is a special case of the translog cost function. Finally, the restrictions on the constants that make a percentage increase in all input prices lead to the same percentage increase in long-run total cost (so that the cost function is consistent with long-run cost minimization) are not difficult to state. For the cost function in (8.5) they are as follows:

$$b_2 + b_3 = 1$$
$$b_5 + b_6 + b_7 = 0$$
$$b_8 + b_9 = 0.$$

CHAPTER SUMMARY

• The long-run total cost curve shows how the minimized level of total cost varies with the quantity of output.   **(LBD Exercise 8.1)**

• An increase in factor prices rotates the long-run total cost curve upward through the point $Q = 0$.

• Long-run average cost is the firm's cost per unit of output. It equals total cost divided by output.   **(LBD Exercise 8.2)**

• Long-run marginal cost is the rate of change of long-run total cost with respect to output.   **(LBD Exercise 8.2)**

• Economies of scale describe a situation in which long-run average cost decreases in output. Economies of scale arise because of the physical properties of processing units, specialization of labor, and indivisibilities of inputs.

• Diseconomies of scale describe a situation in which long-run average cost increases in output. A key source of diseconomies of scale is managerial diseconomies.

• The minimum efficient scale (MES) is the smallest quantity at which the long-run average cost curve attains its minimum.

• The output elasticity of total cost is the percentage change in total cost per 1 percent change in output.

• The short-run total cost curve tells us the minimized total cost as a function of output, input prices, and the level of the fixed input(s). **(LBD Exercise 8.3)**

• Short-run total cost is the sum of two components: total variable cost and total fixed cost.

• Corresponding to the short-run total cost curve are the short-run average cost and short-run marginal cost curves. Short-run average cost is the sum of average variable cost and average fixed cost.

• The long-run average cost curve is the lower envelope of short-run average cost curves. **(LBD Exercise 8.4)**

• Economies of scope exist when it is less costly to produce given quantities of two products with one firm than it is with two firms, each specializing in the production of a single product.

• Economies of experience exist when average variable cost decreases with cumulative production volume. The experience curve tells us how average variable costs are affected by changes in cumulative production volume.

• Cost drivers are factors such as output or the prices of inputs that influence the level of costs.

• Two common functional forms that are used for real-world estimation of cost functions are the constant elasticity cost function and the translog cost function.

REVIEW QUESTIONS

1. What is the relationship between the solution to the firm's long-run cost-minimization problem and the long-run total cost curve?

2. Explain why an increase in the price of an input must typically cause an increase in the long-run total cost of producing any particular level of output.

3. If the price of labor increases by 20 percent, but all other input prices remain the same, would the long-run total cost at a particular output level go up by more than 20 percent, less than 20 percent, or exactly 20 percent? If the prices of all inputs went up by 20 percent, would long-run total cost go up by more than 20 percent, less than 20 percent, or exactly 20 percent?

4. How would an increase in the price of labor shift the long-run *average* cost curve?

5. a) If the *average* cost curve is increasing, must the marginal cost curve lie above the average cost curve? Why or why not?
b) If the *marginal* cost curve is increasing, must the marginal cost curve lie above the average cost curve? Why or why not?

6. Sketch the long-run marginal cost curve for the "flat-bottomed" long-run average cost curve shown in Figure 8.11.

7. Could the output elasticity of total cost ever be negative?

8. Explain why the short-run marginal cost curve must intersect the average variable cost curve at the minimum point of the average variable cost curve.

9. Suppose the graph of the average variable cost curve is flat. What shape would the short-run marginal cost curve be? What shape would the short-run average cost curve be?

10. Suppose that the minimum level of short-run average cost was the same for every possible plant size. What would that tell you about the shapes of the long-run average and long-run marginal cost curves?

11. What is the difference between economies of scope and economies of scale? Is it possible for a two-product firm to enjoy economies of scope but not economies of scale? Is it possible for a firm to have economies of scale but not economies of scope?

12. What is an experience curve? What is the difference between economies of experience and economies of scale?

PROBLEMS

8.1. A firm produces a product with labor and capital, and its production function is described by

$$Q = LK.$$

The marginal products associated with this production function are

$$MP_L = K.$$
$$MP_K = L.$$

Suppose that the price of labor equals 2 and the price of capital equals 1. Derive the equations for the long-run total cost curve and the long-run average cost curve.

8.2. A firm's long-run total cost curve is

$$TC(Q) = 1000Q - 30Q^2 + Q^3.$$

Derive the expression for the corresponding long-run average cost curve and then sketch it. At what quantity is minimum efficient scale?

8.3. Consider a production function of two inputs, labor and capital, given by

$$Q = [L^{\frac{1}{2}} + K^{\frac{1}{2}}]^2.$$

The marginal products associated with this production function are as follows:

$$MP_L = [L^{\frac{1}{2}} + K^{\frac{1}{2}}] L^{-\frac{1}{2}}.$$
$$MP_K = [L^{\frac{1}{2}} + K^{\frac{1}{2}}] K^{-\frac{1}{2}}.$$

Let $w = 2$ and $r = 1$.

a) Suppose the firm is required to produce Q units of output. Show how the cost-minimizing quantity of labor depends on the quantity Q. Show how the cost-minimizing quantity of capital depends on the quantity Q.
b) Find the equation of the firm's long-run total cost curve.
c) Find the equation of the firm's long-run average cost curve.
d) Find the solution to the firm's short-run cost-minimization problem when capital is fixed at a quantity of 9 units (i.e., $\overline{K} = 9$).
e) Find the short-run total cost curve, and graph it along with the long-run total cost curve.
f) Find the associated short-run average cost curve.

8.4. Consider a production function of three inputs, labor, capital, and materials, given by

$$Q = LKM$$

The marginal products associated with this production function are as follows:

$$MP_L = KM$$
$$MP_K = LM$$
$$MP_M = LK$$

Let $w = 5$, $r = 1$, and $m = 2$, where m is the price per unit of materials.

a) Suppose that the firm is required to produce Q units of output. Show how the cost-minimizing quantity of labor depends on the quantity Q. Show how the cost-minimizing quantity of capital depends on the quantity Q. Show how the cost-minimizing quantity of materials depends on the quantity Q.
b) Find the equation of the firm's long-run total cost curve.
c) Find the equation of the firm's long-run average cost curve.
d) Suppose that the firm is required to produce Q units of output, but that its capital is fixed at a quantity of 50 units (i.e., $\overline{K} = 50$). Show how the cost-minimizing quantity of labor depends on the quantity Q. Show how the cost-minimizing quantity of materials depends on the quantity Q.
e) Find the equation of the short-run total cost curve when capital is fixed at a quantity of 50 units (i.e., $\overline{K} = 50$) and graph it along with the long-run total cost curve.
f) Find the equation of the associated short-run average cost curve.

8.5. A short-run total cost curve is given by the equation

$$STC(Q) = 1000 + 50Q^2.$$

Derive expressions for, and then sketch, the corresponding short-run average cost, average variable cost, and average fixed cost curve.

8.6. A producer of hard disk drives has a short-run total cost curve given by

$$STC(Q) = \overline{K} + \frac{Q^2}{\overline{K}}.$$

Within the same set of axes, sketch a graph of the short-run average cost curves for three different plant sizes: $\overline{K} = 10$, $\overline{K} = 20$, and $\overline{K} = 30$. Based on this graph, what is the shape of the long-run average cost curve?

8.7. Figure 8.17 shows that the short-run marginal cost curve may lie above the long-run marginal cost curve. Yet, in the long run, the quantities of all inputs are variable, whereas in the short run, the quantities of just some of the inputs are variable. Given that, why isn't short-run marginal cost less than long-run marginal cost for all output levels?

8.8. Suppose that the total cost of providing satellite television services is as follows

$$TC(Q_1, Q_2) = \begin{cases} 0 & \text{if } Q_1 = 0 \text{ and } Q_2 = 0. \\ 1000 + 2Q_1 + 3Q_2 & \text{otherwise,} \end{cases}$$

where Q_1 and Q_2 are the number of households that subscribe to a sports and movie channel, respectively. Does the provision of satellite television services exhibit economies of scope?

8.9. A researcher has claimed to have estimated a long-run total cost function for the production of automobiles. His estimate is that

$$TC(Q, w, r) = 100w^{-\frac{1}{2}}r^{\frac{1}{2}}Q^3,$$

where w and r are the prices of labor and capital. Is this a valid cost function—that is, is it consistent with long-run cost minimization by the firm? Why or why not?

APPENDIX: Shephard's Lemma and Duality

WHAT IS SHEPHARD'S LEMMA?

Let's compare our calculations in Learning-By-Doing Exercise 7.4 in Chapter 7 and Learning-By-Doing Exercise 8.1 in this chapter. Both pertain to the production function $Q = 50K^{\frac{1}{2}}L^{\frac{1}{2}}$. Our input demand functions were

$$K^*(Q, w, r) = \frac{Q}{50}\left(\frac{w}{r}\right)^{\frac{1}{2}}.$$

$$L^*(Q, w, r) = \frac{Q}{50}\left(\frac{r}{w}\right)^{\frac{1}{2}}.$$

Our long-run total cost function was

$$TC(Q, w, r) = \frac{w^{\frac{1}{2}}r^{\frac{1}{2}}}{25}Q.$$

Let's see how the long-run total cost function varies with respect to the price of labor w, holding Q and r fixed.

$$\frac{\partial TC(Q, w, r)}{\partial w} = \frac{Q}{50}\left(\frac{r}{w}\right)^{\frac{1}{2}} = L^*(Q, w, r). \tag{A8.1}$$

The rate of change of long-run total cost with respect to the price of labor is equal to the labor demand function. Similarly,

$$\frac{\partial TC(Q, w, r)}{\partial r} = \frac{Q}{50}\left(\frac{w}{r}\right)^{\frac{1}{2}} = K^*(Q, w, r). \tag{A8.2}$$

The rate of change of long-run total cost with respect to the price of capital is equal to the capital demand function.

The relationships summarized in equations (A8.1) and (A8.2) are no coincidence. They reflect a general relationship between the long-run total cost function and the input demand functions. This relationship is known as **Shephard's Lemma.** Shephard's Lemma states that the *rate of change of long-run total cost function with respect to an input price is equal to the corresponding input demand function.*[27] Mathematically,

$$\frac{\partial TC(Q, w, r)}{\partial w} = L^*(Q, w, r).$$

$$\frac{\partial TC(Q, w, r)}{\partial r} = K^*(Q, w, r).$$

Shephard's Lemma makes intuitive sense: If a firm experienced an increase in its wage rate by \$1 per hour, then its total costs should go up (approximately) by the \$1 increase in wages multiplied by the amount of labor it is currently using; that is, the rate of increase in total costs should be approximately equal to its labor demand function. We say "approximately" because if the firm minimizes its total costs, the increase in w should cause the firm to decrease the quantity of labor and increase the quantity of capital it uses. Shephard's Lemma tells us that for small enough changes in w (i.e., Δw sufficiently close to 0), we can use the firm's current usage of labor as a good approximation for how much a firm's costs will rise.

DUALITY

What is the significance of Shephard's Lemma? It provides a key link between the production function and the cost function, a link that in the Appendix to Chapter 7 we called duality. Duality works like this:

- Shephard's Lemma tells us that if we know the total cost function, we can derive the input demand functions.

- In turn, as we saw in the Appendix to Chapter 7, if we know the input demand functions, we can "back out" the production function.

Thus, if we know the total cost function, we can always "back out" the production function from which it must have been derived. In this sense, the cost function is *dual* (i.e., linked) to the production function. For any production function, there is a unique total cost function that can be derived from it via the cost-minimization problem. And if we know that total cost function, we can recover the production function that is "dual" to it.

This is a valuable insight. Estimating a firm's production function by statistical methods is often difficult. For one thing, among the many choices of "specific" functional forms for a production function, how would you know which one is most appropriate for a particular industry or firm? In addition, data on input prices and total costs are often more readily available than data on the quantities of inputs. An example of research that took advantage of Shephard's Lemma

---

[27]Shephard's Lemma also applies to the relationship between short-run total cost functions and the short-run input demand functions. For that reason, we will generally not specify whether we are in the short run or long run in the remainder of this section. However, to maintain a consistent notation, we will use the "long-run" notation used in this chapter and Chapter 7.

are the studies of economies of scale in electricity power generation discussed in Example 6.4. In these studies, the researchers estimated cost functions using statistical methods. They then applied Shephard's Lemma and the logic of duality to infer the nature of returns to scale in the production function.

HOW DO TOTAL, AVERAGE, AND MARGINAL COST VARY WITH INPUT PRICES?

We can use Shepard's Lemma to determine how the total, average, and marginal cost functions vary with input prices. Total and average cost are easy. For any $Q > 0$, Shephard's Lemma tells us that total cost $TC(Q, w, r)$ must go up as an input price goes up, provided that the firm uses a positive amount of the input. Using the price of labor w as an example, this is because:

$$\frac{\partial TC(Q, w, r)}{\partial w} = L^*(Q, w, r) > 0.$$

And because average cost is total cost divided by quantity, it follows that

$$\frac{\partial AC(Q, w, r)}{\partial w} = \frac{L^*(Q, w, r)}{Q} > 0.$$

Thus, average cost must also increase as an input price goes up.

The impact of an input price on marginal cost is trickier. Recall that marginal cost is the rate of change of total cost with respect to Q, or:

$$MC(Q, w, r) = \frac{\partial TC(Q, w, r)}{\partial Q}.$$

Thus, we express the rate of change of marginal cost with respect to an input price, such as w, this way:

$$\frac{\partial MC(Q, w, r)}{\partial w} = \frac{\partial^2 TC(Q, w, r)}{\partial w \partial Q}$$

$$= \frac{\partial \left(\frac{\partial TC(Q, w, r)}{\partial w} \right)}{\partial Q}$$

$$= \frac{\partial L^*(Q, w, r)}{\partial Q}.$$

The last line in the above expression is a consequence of Shephard's Lemma since

$$\frac{\partial TC(Q, w, r)}{\partial w} = L^*(Q, w, r).$$

Thus, Shephard's Lemma implies that the *rate of change of marginal cost with respect to the price of an input (e.g., labor) is equal to the rate of change of the demand for that input (e.g., labor) with respect to output*. It then follows that

- An increase in the price of a *normal input* (input demand increases in output Q) will *increase* marginal cost.[28]
- An increase in the price of an *inferior input* (input demand decreases in output Q) will *decrease* marginal cost.

We can now summarize what Shephard's Lemma tells us about the relationship between input prices and the cost functions:

- An increase in an input price will increase total cost TC as long as quantity Q is positive and the firm uses a positive quantity of the input.
- An increase in an input price will increase average cost AC as long as quantity Q is positive and the firm uses a positive quantity of the input.
- An increase in an input price will increase marginal cost MC if the input is normal input, and it will decrease marginal cost if the input is inferior.

A decrease in the price of an input will affect total, average, and marginal cost in an analogous manner.

PROOF OF SHEPHARD'S LEMMA

For a fixed Q, let L_0 and K_0 be the cost-minimizing input combination for any arbitrary combination of input prices (w_0, r_0),

$$L_0 = L^*(Q, w_0, r_0).$$
$$K_0 = K^*(Q, w_0, r_0).$$

Now define a function of w and r, $g(w, r)$ equal to

$$g(w, r) = TC(Q, w, r) - wL_0 - rK_0.$$

What is special about this function? Well, we know that since L_0, K_0 is the cost-minimizing input combination when $w = w_0$ and $r = r_0$, it must be the case that

$$g(w_0, r_0) = 0. \tag{A8.3}$$

Moreover, since (L_0, K_0) is a feasible (but possibly nonoptimal) input combination to produce output Q at other input prices (w, r) besides (w_0, r_0), it must be the case that

$$g(w, r) \leq 0 \text{ for } (w, r) \neq (w_0, r_0). \tag{A8.4}$$

---

[28]See Chapter 7 to review the concepts of normal and inferior inputs.

Conditions (A8.3) and (A8.4) imply that the function $g(w, r)$ attains its maximum when $w = w_0$ and $r = r_0$. Hence, at these points, its partial derivatives with respect to w and r must be zero:[29]

$$\frac{\partial g(w_0, r_0)}{\partial w} = 0 \Rightarrow \frac{\partial TC(Q, w_0, r_0)}{\partial w} = L_0. \qquad \textbf{(A8.5)}$$

$$\frac{\partial g(w_0, r_0)}{\partial r} = 0 \Rightarrow \frac{\partial TC(Q, w_0, r_0)}{\partial r} = K_0. \qquad \textbf{(A8.6)}$$

But since $L_0 = L^*(Q, w_0, r_0)$ and $K_0 = K^*(Q, w_0, r_0)$, (A8.5) and (A8.6) imply

$$\frac{\partial TC(Q, w_0, r_0)}{\partial w} = L^*(Q, w_0, r_0). \qquad \textbf{(A8.7)}$$

$$\frac{\partial TC(Q, w_0, r_0)}{\partial r} = K^*(Q, w_0, r_0). \qquad \textbf{(A8.8)}$$

Since (w_0, r_0) is an arbitrary combination of input prices, conditions (A8.7) and (A8.8) hold for any pair of input prices, and this is exactly what we wanted to show to prove Shephard's Lemma.

---

[29]For more on the use of partial derivatives to find the optimum of a function depending on more than one variable, see the Mathematical Appendix in this book.

9

Perfectly Competitive Markets

Nakao Growers, Inc. is one of the largest rose growers in the United States.[1] The company was started in Pomona, California, by two Japanese-American brothers in 1948. As U.S. demand for fresh-cut roses grew, Nakao Growers, Inc. grew as well, adding rose-growing locations in Santa Cruz, California, and Tucson, Arizona.

Even though Nakao Growers is one of the largest of the 250 U.S. rose-growing firms, it accounts for less than 5 percent of rose production in the United States. In fact, all producers in the major rose-growing countries around the world (Colombia, Ecuador, and the United States) are small companies. For example, the typical U.S. rose grower accounts for less than 1 percent of U.S. output.

Because an individual rose producer, such as Nakao, is so small compared to the overall size of the market, its production decisions have virtually no impact on the market price of roses. The key decision Nakao faces is not what price to charge, but how many rose stems it should produce given the market price. Nakao Growers is an example of a firm operating in a perfectly competitive market. A perfectly competitive market consists of firms that produce identical products that sell at the same price. Each firm's volume of output is so small in comparison to overall market demand that no single firm has an impact on the market price.

Perfect competition is worth studying for two reasons. First, a number of important real-world markets—including most agricultural products, many minerals (e.g., copper and gold), metal fabrication, commodity semiconductors, and oil tanker shipping—are like the fresh-cut rose indus-

try: They consist of many small firms, each producing nearly identical products, each with approximately equal access to the resources needed to participate in the industry. The theory of perfect competition developed in this chapter will help us understand the determination of prices and the dynamics of entry and exit in these markets. Second, the theory of perfect competition forms an important foundation for the rest of microeconomics. Many of the key concepts that we develop in this chapter, such as the vital roles of marginal revenue and marginal cost in output decisions, will apply when we study other market structures, such as monopoly and oligopoly, in later chapters.

[1]This example is based on a real company, but its name has been disguised.

9.1
WHAT IS PERFECT COMPETITION?

The market for fresh-cut roses is an example of a perfectly competitive market, and Nakao Growers is an example of a perfectly competitive firm. But what is it, exactly, that makes a market perfectly competitive? And what, if anything, is special about a perfectly competitive firm?

Perfectly competitive industries have four characteristics:

1. The industry is **fragmented.** It consists of many buyers and sellers. Each buyer's purchases are so small that they have an imperceptible effect on market price. Each seller's output is so small in comparison to market demand that it has an imperceptible impact on the market price. In addition, each seller's *input* purchases are so small that it has an imperceptible impact on *input prices.* The market for fresh-cut roses is an excellent example of a fragmented market. Even the largest producers, such as Nakao Growers, are very small in comparison to the overall scale of the market. Buyers that purchase fresh-cut roses from the producers—wholesalers, brokers, and florists—are also small and numerous.

2. Firms produce **undifferentiated products.** That is, consumers perceive the products to be identical no matter who produces them. When you buy fresh-cut roses from a local flower shop, it probably does not matter to you that they were produced by Nakao Growers or one of its competitors. As far as you are concerned, the roses from one grower are just as good as the roses from another grower. And because this is true for you, it is also true for the flower shops and the wholesalers who buy the roses directly from the growers. If the final consumer sees no difference in the roses grown by the different growers, then florists and wholesalers don't care who they buy roses from either, as long as they get the best price. Roses are thus an example of an undifferentiated product.

3. Consumers have **perfect information about prices** all sellers in the market charge. This is certainly true in the rose market. The wholesalers and florists that buy roses from the growers are keenly aware of the prevailing prices. In fact, as just noted, these consumers need to be deeply knowledgeable about prices because the price is the main thing they care about when deciding which growers to buy roses from.

4. The industry is characterized by **equal access to resources.** All firms—those currently in the industry, as well as prospective entrants—have access to the same technology and inputs. Firms can hire inputs, such as labor, capital, and materials, as they need them, and they can release them from their employment when they do not need them. This characteristic is generally true of the fresh-cut rose industry: the technology for growing roses is well understood, and the key inputs necessary to operate a rose growing firm (land, greenhouses, rose bushes, and labor) are readily available in well-functioning markets.

These characteristics have three implications for how perfectly competitive markets work:

- The first characteristic—the market is fragmented—implies that sellers and buyers act as **price takers.** That is, a firm takes the market price of the product as given when making an output decision, and a buyer takes the market price as given when making purchase decisions. Condition 1 also implies that a firm takes input prices as fixed when making decisions about input quantities.[2]

- The second and third characteristics—firms produce undifferentiated products and consumers have perfect information about prices—implies a **law of one price:** that is, transactions between buyers and sellers occur at a single market price. Because the products of all firms are perceived to be identical and the prices of all sellers are known, a consumer will purchase at the lowest price available in the market. No sales can be made at any higher price.

- The fourth characteristic—equal access to resources—implies that the industry is characterized by **free entry.** That is, if it is profitable for new firms to enter the industry, they will eventually do so. Free entry does not mean that a new firm incurs no cost when it enters the industry but that it has access to the same technology and inputs that existing firms have.

In this chapter, we will develop a theory of perfect competition that includes each of these three implications: price-taking behavior by firms, a common market price charged by each firm in the industry, and free entry. To keep the development of this theory manageable, we will organize our study of perfect competition in three steps:

1. In the next section, we study profit maximization by a price-taking firm.

2. Then, we will study how the common market price is determined when the industry consists of a fixed number of firms (a number which is assumed to be large, as in the case of the rose industry which consists of hundreds of firms). This is called the analysis of the short-run equilibrium of a perfectly competitive market.

3. Finally, we will study how the market price is affected by free entry. This is called the analysis of the long-run equilibrium of a perfectly competitive market.

Once we go through all of these steps, we will have built a coherent theory of perfect competition. In Chapter 10, we will then employ this theory to explore how perfectly competitive markets facilitate the allocation of resources and the creation of economic value.

9.2 PROFIT MAXIMIZATION BY A PRICE-TAKING FIRM

We begin our analysis of perfect competition by studying decision making by a price-taking firm that maximizes economic profit. To do this, though, we need to explore briefly what we mean by economic profit.

ECONOMIC PROFIT VERSUS ACCOUNTING PROFIT

In Chapter 7, we distinguished between accounting cost and economic cost. The key difference between the two cost concepts is that economic cost measures the opportunity cost of the resources that the firm uses to produce and sell

---

[2]This is the assumption that we maintained throughout our analysis of input choices and cost functions in Chapters 7 and 8.

its products, whereas accounting cost measures the historical expenses the firm incurred to produce and sell its output.

We will now make a similar distinction between accounting profit and **economic profit:**

$$\text{accounting profit} = \text{sales revenue} - \text{accounting costs}$$

$$\text{economic profit} = \text{sales revenue} - \text{economic costs}$$

That is, economic profit is the difference between a firm's sales revenue and the totality of its economic costs, including all relevant opportunity costs. To illustrate, consider a small dot-com firm operated by its owner. In 2001, the firm earned revenues of $1,000,000 and incurred expenses on supplies and hired labor of $850,000. The owner's best outside employment opportunity would be to work for AOL Time Warner for $200,000 a year. The firm's accounting profit is

$$\$1,000,000 - \$850,000 = \$150,000.$$

The firm's economic profit deducts the opportunity cost of the owner's labor and is thus

$$\$1,000,000 - \$850,000 - \$200,000 = -\$50,000.$$

The fact that this firm earns a *negative* economic profit of $50,000 means that the owner made $50,000 less in income by operating this business than could have been made in the best outside alternative. We might say that the business "destroyed" $50,000 of the owner's wealth: by operating the dot-com business, the owner earned $50,000 less income than he or she might have otherwise.

A key cost omitted from the determination of accounting profit in modern firms is the opportunity cost of the firm's capital assets, such as its plant and equipment.[3] Recall from Chapter 7 that the cost of the productive services of the physical capital the firm owns are often implicit costs. That is, they do not involve explicit payments of cash and are thus not included in the firm's accounting statements. Still, these capital services entail an opportunity cost to the firm's owners. By providing the funds that allow the firm to purchase physical capital, the firm's owners forgo the opportunity of investing these funds in alternative investments that yield returns over time. The firm's accounting costs do not include a provision for this opportunity cost of funds.

When a firm's accounting profit does not cover this opportunity cost, it will earn a positive accounting profit but a negative economic profit. For example, in 1995 IBM had a positive accounting profit of more than $10 billion, but (according to one investment analyst's calculations) had a negative economic profit of $252 million.[4] As in the example of the dot-com firm, a negative economic profit indicates that IBM's assets, when liquidated and deployed elsewhere, would have earned

[3]In addition to physical capital, such as plant and equipment, the firm's capital assets also include "working capital," such as its cash and inventories.

[4]These estimates come from S. Milunovich and A. Tsuei, "EVA in the Computer Industry," Morgan Stanley U.S. Investment Research (April 23, 1996). The specific measure of accounting profit used is operating profit before taxes. The specific measure of economic profit used is economic value added (EVA), a concept discussed in Example 7.1 in Chapter 7. The reference above provides a detailed example showing how EVA was calculated for firms in the computer industry.

$252 million more income than IBM earned in the computer business. In this sense, in 1995 IBM "destroyed" $252 million in wealth in that its owners would have been that much better off if they had invested their money elsewhere.

Not all firms, of course, make a negative economic profit. In 1995, Hewlett–Packard (HP) earned an accounting profit of slightly over $4 billion and an economic profit of $1.3 billion. This positive economic profit means that HP created $1.3 billion more in income for its owners than would have been created had HP's assets been liquidated and invested in the best alternative use. In this sense, in 1995 HP "created" an additional $1.3 billion in wealth for its owners that they could not have gotten elsewhere.

Whenever we discuss profit maximization, we are talking about economic profit maximization. Economic profit is the appropriate objective for a firm, whether it is Nakao Growers, IBM, or Hewlett–Packard that is acting on its owners' behalf.

Wealth Creators and Wealth Destroyers in the United States

EXAMPLE 9.1

In the 1990s, financial analysts, mutual fund managers, and business executives began studying economic profit as an indicator of firm performance. Financial analysts began computing measures of economic profit, such as economic value added (EVA), which we discussed in Example 7.1. Some firms (e.g., Coca-Cola) tied the pay of their top executives to measures of economic profit, while other firms, such as the cereal manufacturer Kellogg, began reporting their economic profit in their annual reports to shareholders.[5]

The financial consulting firm Stern Stewart regularly tracks EVA for a broad range of U.S. firms over many years. Tables 9.1 and 9.2 show EVA for a few well known U.S. firms in 1998. Philip Morris, the cigarette company that produces Marlboro and that also owns Kraft Food and Miller Brewing Company, had positive economic profit of more than $5 billion in a single year! Microsoft had positive economic profit of over $3.7 billion in 1998 and, in fact, has had positive economic profit every year since 1986. Philip Morris and Microsoft earned returns that exceeded their opportunity cost of capital, thus creating wealth for their owners.

TABLE 9.1 **Top Wealth Creators, 1998**	
Company	**EVA (millions)**
Philip Morris	$5,180
General Electric	$4,370
Intel	$4,280
Merck Co.	$4,175
Microsoft	$3,776
Coca Cola	$2,194
Source: Stern Stewart Performance 1000 Database.	

TABLE 9.2 **Top Wealth Destroyers, 1998**	
Company	**EVA (millions)**
General Motors	−$5,525
Time Warner	−$2,779
Exxon	−$2,262
CBS	−$1,621
Nabisco	−$1,449
Boeing	−$1,065
Source: Stern Stewart Performance 1000 Database.	

[5]EVA is the version of economic profit developed by Stern Stewart & Company.

By contrast, some well known firms had negative economic profit in 1998. For example, General Motors had negative economic profit of about $5.5 billion that year. Its returns did not exceed the cost of capital, and as a result it destroyed shareholder wealth.   ■

THE PROFIT-MAXIMIZING OUTPUT CHOICE FOR A PRICE-TAKING FIRM

Having defined economic profit, we can now study the problem of a price-taking firm that seeks to maximize its economic profit. We denote profit by the Greek letter π, and it equals the difference between total revenue, TR, and total cost, TC:[6]

$$\max \pi = TR(Q) - TC(Q).$$

Total revenue, in turn, equals the market price P multiplied by the quantity of output Q produced by the firm: $TR(Q) = P \times Q$. Total cost $TC(Q)$ is the total cost curve that we discussed in Chapter 8 and tells us the total cost of producing Q units of output, assuming that the firm chooses the input combination to produce that output at minimum cost.

Because the firm is a price taker, it perceives that its volume decision has a negligible impact on market price. Thus, it takes the market price P as given. Its goal is to choose a quantity of output Q to maximize its total profit.

To illustrate the firm's problem, suppose that Nakao anticipates that the market price for fresh-cut roses will be $P = \$1.00$ per rose. Table 9.3 shows total rev-

TABLE 9.3
Total Revenue, Cost, and Profit for a Price-taking Rose Producer

Q (thousands of roses per month)	TR (thousands of $ per month)	TC (thousands of $ per month)	π (thousands of $ per month)
0	0	0	0
60	60	95	−35
120	120	140	−20
180	180	155	25
240	240	170	70
300	**300**	**210**	**90**
360	360	300	60
420	420	460	−40

[6]Economists commonly use the Greek letter π to denote profit. In this book, π *does not* refer to the number 3.14.

enue, total cost, and total profit for various output levels, and the top diagram in Figure 9.1 graphs these numbers.

Figure 9.1 shows that profit is maximized at $Q = 300$ (i.e., 300,000 roses per month). It also shows that the graph of total revenue is a straight line with a slope of 1. Thus, as we increase Q, the firm's total revenue goes up at a constant rate equal to the market price, $1.00.

For any firm (price taker or not), the rate at which total revenue changes with respect to output is called **marginal revenue.** It is defined by

$$MR = \frac{TR(Q + \Delta Q) - TR(Q)}{\Delta Q} = \frac{\Delta TR}{\Delta Q}.$$

For a price-taking firm, each additional unit sold increases total revenue by an amount equal to the market price, or $(\Delta TR/\Delta Q) = P$. Thus, *for a price-taking firm*, marginal revenue is equal to the market price, $MR = P$.

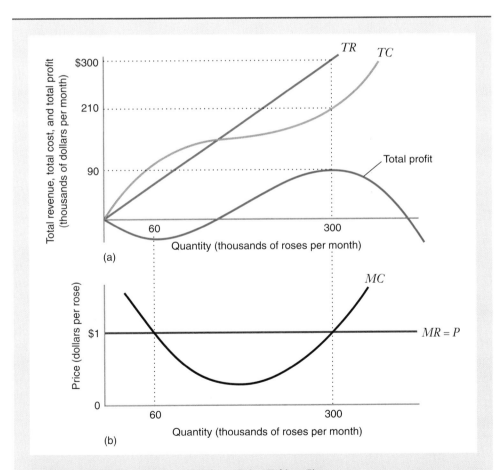

(a)

(b)

FIGURE 9.1 Profit Maximization by a Price-Taking Firm
Panel (a) shows that the firm's profits are maximized when $Q = 300{,}000$ roses per year. Panel (b) shows that at this point $MC = P$. Marginal cost also equals price when $Q = 60{,}000$ roses per year, but this point is a profit minimum.

Figure 9.1 shows that for quantities between $Q = 60$ and the profit-maximizing quantity $Q = 300$, producing *more* roses *increases* profit. Increasing the quantity in this range increases total revenue faster than total cost:

$$\frac{\Delta TR}{\Delta Q} > \frac{\Delta TC}{\Delta Q}, \text{ or}$$

$$P > MC.$$

When $P > MC$, each time Nakao increases its output by one rose, its profit will go up by $P - MC$, the difference between the marginal revenue and the marginal cost of that extra rose.

Figure 9.1 shows that for quantities greater than $Q = 300$, producing *fewer* roses *increases* profit. Decreasing quantity in this range decreases total cost faster than it decreases total revenue:

$$\frac{\Delta TR}{\Delta Q} < \frac{\Delta TC}{\Delta Q}, \text{ or}$$

$$P < MC.$$

When $P < MC$, each time Nakao reduces its output by one rose, its profit will go up by $MC - P$, the difference between the marginal cost and the marginal revenue of that extra rose.[7]

If Nakao can increase its profit when either $P > MC$ or $P < MC$, quantities at which these inequalities hold cannot maximize Nakao's profit. It must be the case, then, that at the profit-maximizing output,

$$P = MC. \tag{9.1}$$

Equation (9.1) tells us that in order for a *price-taking firm to maximize its profit, it must produce at a quantity Q^* at which marginal cost equals the market price.*

Figure 9.1(b) illustrates this condition. Nakao's marginal revenue curve is a horizontal line at the market price of \$1.00. The profit-maximizing quantity occurs at $Q = 300$, where this MR curve intersects the MC curve. This tells us that when Nakao faces a market price of \$1.00 per fresh-cut rose, its profit-maximizing decision is to produce and sell 300,000 fresh-cut roses per month.

Figure 9.1 also illustrates that there is another quantity, $Q = 60$, at which $MR = MC$. The difference between $Q = 60$ and $Q = 300$ is that at $Q = 300$, the marginal cost curve is rising, while at $Q = 60$ the marginal cost curve is falling. Is $Q = 60$ also a profit-maximizing quantity? The answer is no. Figure 9.1(a) shows us that $Q = 60$ represents the point at which profit is *minimized* (i.e., it is as small as possible) rather than maximized. This illustrates that at a profit-maximizing quantity, two conditions must hold:

- $P = MC$
- MC must be increasing

---

[7]Or, equivalently, each extra rose produced decreases profit by $P - MC$.

These are the **profit-maximization conditions for a price-taking firm.** If either of these conditions does not hold, the firm cannot be maximizing its profit. It would be able to increase profit either by increasing its output or decreasing it.

The previous section showed that a price-taking firm such as Nakao Growers would maximize its profit by producing an output level at which the market price equals marginal cost. But how does the market price get determined in the first place? In this section, we study how the market price is determined in the short run. The short run is the period of time in which (1) the number of firms in the industry is fixed, and (2) at least one input, such as the plant size (i.e., quantity of capital or land) of each firm, is fixed. For example, in the market for fresh-cut roses, short-run swings in the market price from one month to the next are determined by the interaction of a fixed number of firms (several hundred very small firms!), each of which operates with a fixed amount of land, a fixed quantity of greenhouses, and a fixed quantity of rose bushes. With land, greenhouses, and rose plants fixed, rose producers control their output through pinching and pruning decisions, as well as through the amounts of fertilizer and pesticide they apply to the rose plants. These decisions determine how many fresh-cut roses stems will be available to meet demand throughout the year.

We will see that the profit-maximizing output decisions of individual producers such as Nakao will give rise to short-run supply curves for these firms. If we then add together the short-run supply curves for all of the producers currently in the industry, we will obtain a market supply curve. The market price is then determined by the interaction of this market supply curve and the market demand curve.

THE FIRM'S SHORT-RUN COST STRUCTURE

Our goal in the next several sections is to learn how to construct an individual firm's short-run supply curve. To do this, we need to explore the cost structure of a typical firm in the industry.

The firm's short-run total cost is

$$STC(Q) = \begin{cases} SFC + NSFC + TVC(Q) & \text{if } Q > 0, \\ SFC & \text{if } Q = 0. \end{cases}$$

This equation identifies three categories of costs for this firm.

- *TVC(Q)* are total variable costs. These are **output-sensitive costs.** That is, they go up or down as the firm increases or decreases its output. This category includes materials costs and the costs of certain kinds of labor (e.g., factory labor). For Nakao, the costs of fertilizer and pesticide would be included in *TVC* because they go up as the grower produces more roses, and they go down as the grower produces fewer roses. Total variable costs are zero if the firm produces zero output and thus are examples of *nonsunk costs.* That is, they can be avoided if the firm shuts down, (i.e., produces zero output). If Nakao decided to shut down its rose-growing operations, it would avoid the need to spend money on fertilizer and pesticide. These costs would thus be nonsunk.

- *SFC* is the firm's **sunk fixed cost** (hence the notation *SFC*). A sunk fixed cost is a fixed cost that the firm cannot avoid if it shuts down and produces zero output. To illustrate *SFC*, imagine that a grower such as Nakao has signed a long-term lease (e.g., for 5 years) to rent land on which to grow roses and that the lease prevents Nakao from subletting the land to anyone else. The lease cost is *fixed* because it does not vary with the quantity of roses that Nakao produces. It is **output insensitive.** It is also *sunk* because Nakao cannot avoid its rental payments even if it produces zero output.[8]

- *NSFC* is the firm's **nonsunk fixed cost.** A nonsunk fixed cost is a fixed cost that must be incurred if the firm is to produce any output, but it does not have to be incurred if the firm produces no output. For Nakao, an example of *NSFC* would be the cost of heating the greenhouses. Nakao's greenhouses must be maintained at a constant temperature whether Nakao grows 10 or 10,000 roses within the greenhouse, so the cost of heating the greenhouses is *fixed* (i.e., it is insensitive to the number of rose stems produced). But the heating costs are *nonsunk* because they can be avoided if Nakao chooses to produce no roses in the greenhouse (i.e., $Q = 0$).

The firm's total fixed (or output-insensitive) cost, *TFC*, is thus given by

$$TFC = NSFC + SFC.$$

If $NSFC = 0$, there are no fixed costs that are nonsunk. In that case, $TFC = SFC$. This is the case that we consider in the next section.

SHORT-RUN SUPPLY CURVE FOR A FIRM: ALL FIXED COSTS ARE SUNK

In this section, we derive the supply curve for a firm. To simplify, we begin with the easiest case: all fixed costs are sunk. That is, $NFSC = 0$, and thus $TFC = SFC$. Figure 9.2 depicts the short-run marginal cost curve, *SMC*, short-run average cost curve, *SAC*, and average variable cost curve, *AVC*, for this firm, which we will imagine is in the fresh-cut rose industry.

Consider three possible market prices for fresh-cut roses: $0.25 per rose, $0.30 per rose, and $0.35 per rose. If we apply the $P = MC$ profit-maximization condition from the previous section, the firm's profit-maximizing output level when the price is $0.25 is 50,000 roses per month. Similarly, when the market price is $0.30 and $0.35 per rose, the profit-maximizing output levels are 55,000 and 60,000 roses per month, respectively. Each of these quantities represents the point at which the firm's short-run marginal cost equals the relevant market price, or $P = SMC$.

The firm's **short-run supply curve** tells us how its profit-maximizing output decision changes as the market price changes. Graphically, for the prices $0.25,

---

[8]Of course, Nakao eventually avoids having to make payments on the lease, but not because it decides to shut down its operations today. Rather, the lease payments would go away once the five-year term of the lease expires.

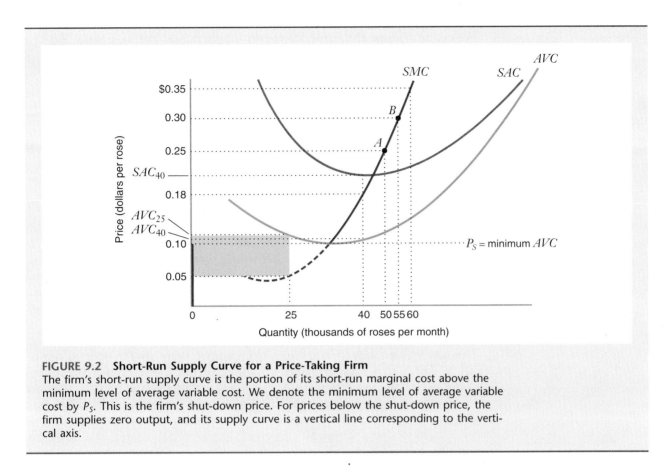

FIGURE 9.2 Short-Run Supply Curve for a Price-Taking Firm
The firm's short-run supply curve is the portion of its short-run marginal cost above the minimum level of average variable cost. We denote the minimum level of average variable cost by P_S. This is the firm's shut-down price. For prices below the shut-down price, the firm supplies zero output, and its supply curve is a vertical line corresponding to the vertical axis.

$0.30, and $0.35, the firm's short-run supply curve coincides with the short-run marginal cost curve *SMC*. For instance, point *A*, ($0.25, 50,000), is one point on the firm's short-run supply curve, and point *B*, ($0.30, 55,000) is another.

However, the firm's short-run marginal cost curve is not necessarily the firm's supply curve at *all* possible prices. To see why, suppose the price of roses is $0.05. If the firm maximized its profits at this price, it would produce at the point at which price equals marginal cost, an output of 25,000 roses per month. But at this price, the firm would earn a loss: It would incur its total fixed cost *TFC* and, on top of that, it would lose the difference between the price of $0.05 and the average variable cost, AVC_{25}, on each of the 25,000 roses it produces. If it produces, the firm's total loss is thus *TFC* plus the shaded region in Figure 9.2. If the firm did not produce, its loss would only be its (sunk) total fixed cost *TFC*. At a price of $0.05, then, the firm cuts its loss by shutting down and not producing. By doing so, it avoids incurring the additional losses given by the shaded region.

More generally, the firm is better off cutting its short-run losses by shutting down if the market price *P* is less than the average variable cost $AVC(Q^*)$ at the output level Q^*, at which *P* equals short-run marginal cost. Or mathematically, the firm is better off shutting down if

$$P < AVC(Q^*).$$

We can now draw the firm's short-run supply curve. We have seen that

- A profit-maximizing price-taking firm, if it produces positive output, produces where $P = SMC$, and SMC slopes upward.
- A profit-maximizing price-taking firm *never* produces where $P < AVC$.

Thus: the firm would *never* produce on the portion of the SMC curve where $SMC < AVC$. This is the portion below the minimum level of the AVC curve. It then follows that if price is below the minimum level of AVC, the firm will produce $Q = 0$.

In light of this, the firm's supply curve has two parts:

- For prices that are *less than* the minimum level of AVC—a level we denote by P_S in Figure 9.2—the firm will supply zero output (i.e., $Q = 0$). In Figure 9.2, P_S is \$0.10 per rose. As Figure 9.2 shows, this portion of the firm's supply curve is a vertical "spike" that coincides with the vertical axis. We call P_S the firm's **shut-down price:** the price below which it produces a quantity of zero.
- For prices that are greater than P_S, the firm will produce a positive amount of output, and its supply curve coincides with its short-run marginal cost curve.

This analysis implies that perfectly competitive firms might operate during periods in which they earn negative economic profit. For example, Figure 9.2 shows that when the price is \$0.18 per rose, the firm produces 40,000 roses per month. It earns a loss because at this level of output, the price \$0.18 is less than the short-run average cost corresponding to 40,000 roses per month, SAC_{40}. However, because the price of \$0.18 exceeds the average variable cost at 40,000 roses per month, AVC_{40}, the firm's total revenue exceeds its total variable cost. Thus, by continuing to produce, the firm offsets some of the loss it would incur if it produced nothing. Of course, if the rose grower expects the price of \$0.18 per rose to persist, then given enough time, it would reduce its plant size (i.e., devote less land to growing roses), or it might even exit the industry altogether.

LEARNING-BY-DOING EXERCISE 9.1

Deriving the Short-Run Supply Curve for a Firm

Suppose that a firm has a short-run total cost curve given by

$$STC = 100 + 20Q + Q^2,$$

where the total fixed cost is 100, and the total variable cost is $20Q + Q^2$. The corresponding short-run marginal cost curve is $SMC = 20 + 2Q$.

Problem

(a) What is the equation for average variable cost (AVC)?
(b) What is the minimum level of average variable cost?
(c) What is the firm's short-run supply curve?

Solution

(a) Average variable cost is total variable cost divided by output. Thus,

$$AVC = \frac{20Q + Q^2}{Q}$$

$$= 20 + Q.$$

(b) We know that the minimum level of average variable cost occurs at the point at which AVC and SMC are equal. Thus, this occurs where $20 + Q = 20 + 2Q$, or $Q = 0$. The minimum level of AVC is found by substituting $Q = 0$ into the equation of the AVC curve $20 + Q$, giving us a minimum level of AVC equal to 20.

(c) For prices below the minimum level of average variable cost of 20, the firm will not produce. For prices above 20, we can find the supply curve by equating price to marginal cost and solving for Q:

$$P = 20 + 2Q,$$

which implies

$$Q = -10 + \frac{1}{2}P.$$

The firm's short-run supply curve, which we denote by $s(P)$, is thus:

$$s(P) = \begin{cases} 0 & \text{if } P < 20 \\ -10 + \frac{1}{2}P & \text{if } P \geq 20. \end{cases}$$

Similar Problems: 9.1, 9.2

SHORT-RUN SUPPLY CURVE FOR A FIRM: *SOME* FIXED COSTS SUNK, SOME NONSUNK

Let's now consider the possibility that the firm has some nonsunk fixed costs. That is, $TFC = SFC + NSFC$, where $NSFC > 0$. As before, the firm maximizes its profit by equating price to marginal cost. The thing that changes in comparison to the previous section is the rule that defines when the firm produces zero, as opposed to positive, output.

To show why, we first need to define a new cost curve. The firm's **average nonsunk cost**, $ANSC$, is equal to the sum of its average variable cost and its average nonsunk fixed cost:

$$ANSC = AVC + \frac{NSFC}{Q}.$$

Figure 9.3 shows that the average nonsunk cost curve is U-shaped and lies between the short-run average cost curve SAC and the average variable cost curve AVC. At its minimum point, $MC = ANSC$. In this sense, the $ANSC$ curve behaves much like the SAC curve.

To illustrate how we modify the price-taking firm's shut-down rule when it has nonsunk fixed costs, suppose, as shown in Figure 9.3, that the price of roses is $0.15. If the firm maximized its profits at this price, it would produce at the point at which price equals marginal cost, an output of 35,000 roses per month. But at this price, the firm would earn a loss: it would incur its sunk fixed cost SFC and, on top of that, for every rose it produced, it would lose the difference between the price of $0.15 and its average nonsunk costs, $ANSC_{35}$. By contrast, if the firm did not produce, its loss would only be its sunk fixed cost SFC. This is because by shutting down the firm would avoid both its variable costs and its nonsunk fixed costs. At a price of $0.15, then, the firm cuts its loss by shutting down and not producing. By doing so, it avoids the additional loss given by the shaded region.

More generally, the firm is better off cutting its short-run losses by shutting down if the market price P is less than the average nonsunk cost $ANSC(Q^*)$ at the output Q^* at which P equals short-run marginal cost. Or mathematically, the firm is better off shutting down if

$$P < ANSC(Q^*).$$

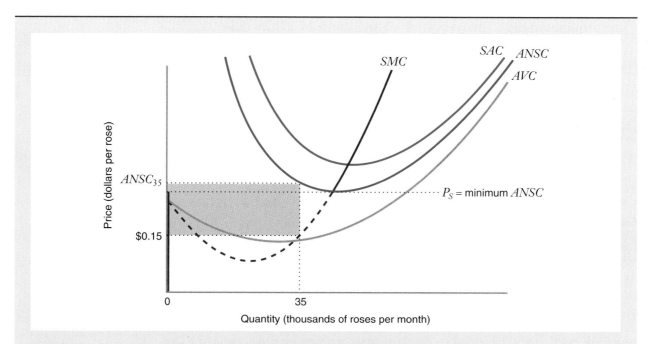

FIGURE 9.3   Short-Run Supply Curve for a Firm with Nonsunk Fixed Costs
The shut-down price P_S is the minimum level of average nonsunk cost. The firm's supply curve coincides with the short-run marginal cost curve for prices above P_S. For prices below P_S, it is a vertical spike that coincides with the vertical axis.

We can now draw the firm's short-run supply curve. We have seen that

- A profit-maximizing price-taking firm, if it produces positive output, produces where $P = SMC$, and SMC slopes upward.
- A profit-maximizing price-taking firm with nonsunk fixed costs would not produce where $P < ANSC$.

Thus: the firm would *never* produce on the portion of the SMC curve where $SMC < ANSC$. This is the portion below the minimum level of the $ANSC$ curve. It then follows that if price is below the minimum level of $ANSC$—denoted by P_S in Figure 9.3—the firm will produce $Q = 0$.

Figure 9.3 shows the short-run supply curve for a rose-growing firm when there are nonsunk fixed costs. It is a vertical spike for prices below the minimum level of average nonsunk cost, and it corresponds to the short-run marginal cost curve for prices above this level.

The concept of average nonsunk cost is sufficiently flexible that we can identify the firm's supply curve and shut-down price for three special cases:

- *All fixed costs are sunk.* This is the case we studied in the previous section. When all fixed costs are sunk, $ANSC = AVC$, and our shut-down rule, $P < ANSC$, becomes

$$P < AVC.$$

  The firm's short-run supply curve is thus the portion of SMC above the minimum point of the average variable cost curve. *This is identical to the conclusion of the previous section.*

- *All fixed costs are nonsunk.* In this case, $ANSC = SAC$.[9] Our shut-down rule, $P < ANSC$, now becomes

$$P < SAC.$$

  When all fixed costs are nonsunk, the firm's short-run supply curve is the portion of SMC above the minimum point of the short-run average cost curve.

- *Some fixed costs are sunk and some are nonsunk.* This is the case we studied in this section. As we have seen, the firm's short-run supply curve is the portion of SMC above the minimum point of the average nonsunk cost curve. As Figure 9.3 shows, the shut-down price P_S when some, but not all, fixed costs are sunk, is above the minimum level of AVC but below the minimum level of SAC.

LEARNING-BY-DOING EXERCISE 9.2

Deriving the Short-Run Supply Curve for a Firm When There Are Nonsunk Fixed Costs

The firm's short-run total cost curve is $STC = 100 + 20Q + Q^2$. The corresponding short-run marginal cost curve is $SMC = 20 + 2Q$.

---

[9]This is because $SFC = 0$, and thus $TNSC = TVC + TFC$. As a result $ANSC = (TVC + TFC)/Q$, which equals SAC.

Problem

(a) Suppose that $SFC = 36$, while $NSFC = 64$. What is the firm's average non-sunk cost curve?
(b) What is the minimum level of average nonsunk cost?
(c) What is the firm's short-run supply curve?
(d) How does the firm's economic profit depend on the market price P?

Solution

(a) The average nonsunk cost curve is

$$ANSC = AVC + \frac{NSFC}{Q}$$

$$= 20 + Q + \frac{64}{Q}.$$

(b) As Figure 9.3 shows, the average nonsunk cost curve reaches its minimum when average nonsunk cost equals short-run marginal cost. This occurs at a quantity level that solves the following equation:

$$20 + 2Q = 20 + Q + \frac{64}{Q},$$

or after rearranging terms:

$$Q^2 = 64,$$

which implies $Q = 8$. Thus, the average nonsunk cost curve attains its minimum value at $Q = 8$. Substituting $Q = 8$ back into the average nonsunk cost curve will tell us the minimum level of average nonsunk cost:

$$ANSC = 20 + 8 + \frac{64}{8} = 36.$$

Thus, as Figure 9.4 shows, the minimum level of average nonsunk cost is $36 per unit.
(c) As Figure 9.4 shows, for prices below the minimum level of $ANSC$ (i.e., for $P < 36$), the firm does not produce. For prices above this level, the firm's profit-maximizing quantity is given by equating price to marginal cost, i.e.,

$$P = 20 + 2Q,$$

which implies that $Q = -10 + (1/2)P$. The firm's short-run supply curve $s(P)$ is thus:

$$s(P) = \begin{cases} 0 & \text{if } P < 36 \\ -10 + \frac{1}{2}P & \text{if } P \geq 36. \end{cases}$$

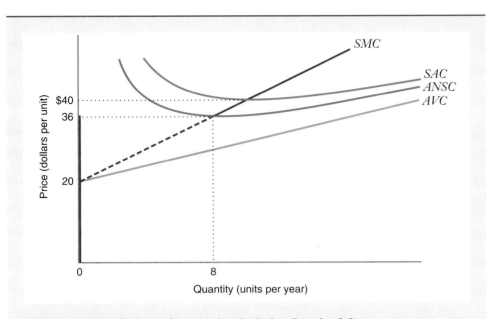

FIGURE 9.4 Supply Curve for Learning-By-Doing Exercise 9.2
The firm's shut-down price is the minimum level of average nonsunk cost. This is $36.
The firm's supply curve coincides with the short-run marginal cost for prices above
$36, and it is a vertical spike for prices below $36. For prices between $36 and $40,
the firm produces but earns negative economic profit.

(d) As Figure 9.4 shows, the minimum level of short-run average cost is $40
per unit. When the price is equal to $40, we can see from Figure 9.4 that the
firm earns zero economic profit. For prices above $40, the firm earns positive
economic profit. When the price is between $36 and $40 per unit, the firm
produces, but earns negative economic profit. For prices below $36, the firm
does not produce, and incurs an economic loss equal to the sunk portion of its
fixed costs. We summarize the firm's supply decisions and profit in Table 9.4.

Similar Problem: 9.3

TABLE 9.4
Economic Profit in Learning-By-Doing Exercise 9.2

Price	Produce or Not?	Supply Curve?	Economic Profit?
$P > 40$	Produce	SMC curve	Positive
$P = 40$	Produce	SMC curve	Zero
$36 \leq P < 40$	Produce	SMC curve	Negative
$P < 36$	Do not produce	Vertical axis	Negative

EXAMPLE 9.2

The Supply Curve for an American Corn Producer[10]

Agricultural markets are often cited as the classic example of perfect competition. An individual farmer's output of a product, such as corn, soybeans, or cotton, is small in comparison to the overall market for such products. Therefore, it is reasonable to view an individual farm as a price taker in the markets in which it participates.

Figure 9.5 illustrates a supply curve for a typical Iowa corn farmer. The figure shows the farmer's short-run marginal cost curve, as well as its short-run average cost curve and its average variable cost curve. Economist Daniel Suits constructed these cost curves based on data collected by the U.S. Department of Agriculture.[11]

If we assume that all fixed costs are sunk, the corn farmer's supply curve is the portion of the short-run marginal cost curve above the minimum level of average variable cost. In Figure 9.5, the minimum level of average variable cost occurs at about $1.36 per bushel. In fact, marginal and thus average variable costs are constant at this level until output reaches about 36,000 bushels per year. This implies that for a price below $1.36 per bushel, the farm would not produce, but at a price of $1.36 per bushel, it would be willing to produce any amount of corn between 0 and 36,000 bushels per year. Thus, at prices below $1.36, the farmer's supply curve is a vertical spike, while at $1.36 per year it is a horizontal line extending to 36,000 bushels per year.

For prices above $1.36 per bushel, the supply curve coincides with the short-run marginal cost curve. This curve rises rapidly. For example, at an output of 52,000 bushels, short-run marginal cost is about $3.50 per bushel. At this output, the farm is close to the effective capacity of its land, and the incremental cost of additional bushels of corn is very high.

When the price of corn is greater than $1.36, the farm may produce even though economic profit might be negative. For example, at a price of $1.75, the profit-maximizing output for the farm would be 46,000 bushels. The difference between price and average cost at this point is about $0.81, so the farm would lose about $37,260 for the year by producing corn at this price. Nevertheless, the farmer is better off producing 46,000 bushels of corn than producing nothing. If it produced nothing, it would earn a loss equal to its annual fixed cost of about $47,250. The farm cuts its annual loss by $9,990 by producing the profit-maximizing quantity. ∎

SHORT-RUN MARKET SUPPLY CURVE

We have just derived the short-run supply curve for an individual price-taking firm. Let's now see how to go from the firm's supply curve to the supply curve for the entire industry.

Because the number of producers in the industry is fixed in the short run, market supply at any price is equal to the sum of the quantities that each estab-

---

[10]This example draws from Suits, D. B., "Agriculture," Chapter 1 in *The Structure of American Industry*, 9th edition (Adams, W. and Brock, J. W., eds.) (Englewood Cliffs, NJ: Prentice Hall), 1995.

[11]Updated to 1991 dollars.

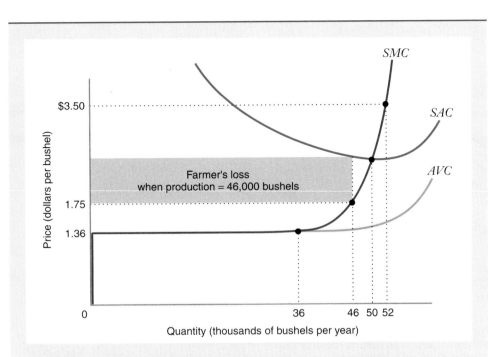

FIGURE 9.5 Supply Curve for a U.S. Corn Farmer
Short-run marginal cost, average variable cost, and short-run average cost curves for a typical Iowa corn farmer in 1991. Short-run marginal cost is constant at $1.36 until output of about 36,000 bushels and increases sharply thereafter. The farmer's supply curve coincides with the short-run marginal cost curve for prices above $1.36 and is a vertical spike for lower prices. At a price of $1.75, for example, the farmer would produce about 46,000 bushels, even though that price is less than the short-run average cost at that quantity. The farmer would lose about $37,000 producing this quantity. This loss equals the area of the shaded region in the figure.

lished firm supplies at that price. To illustrate, suppose that the market for fresh-cut roses consists of three types of firms illustrated in Figure 9.6(a): 100 firms with short-run marginal cost function SMC_1, 100 firms with short-run marginal cost function SMC_2, and 100 firms with short-run marginal cost function SMC_3. Suppose that the shut-down prices for these firms are $0.20, $0.22, and $0.24 per rose, respectively.

Figure 9.6(a) shows that when the price is, say, $0.30 per rose, each type 1 firm supplies 50,000 roses per month, each type 2 firm supplies 40,000 roses per month, and each type 3 firm supplies 30,000 roses per month. Thus, the total market supply at a price of $0.30 would be $(100 \times 50{,}000) + (100 \times 40{,}000) + (100 \times 30{,}000) = 12$ million roses per month. Figure 9.6(b) shows this market supply. Similarly, when the price is $0.23 per rose, each type 1 firm supplies 20,000 roses, each type 2 firm supplies 10,000 roses, and the type 3 firms do not produce. Total market supply at a price of $0.23 would thus be $(100 \times 20{,}000) + (100 \times 10{,}000) + 100(0) = 3$ million roses per month.

This process of horizontally summing the individual firm supply curves generates the **short-run market supply curve** in Figure 9.6. The short-run market supply curve tells us the quantity supplied in the aggregate by all firms in the market. Note that while the scales of the vertical axes of the two parts of

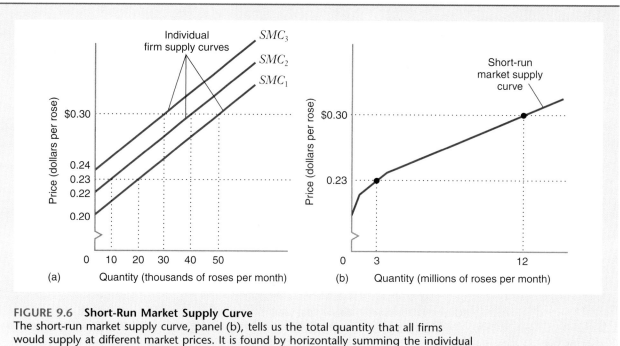

FIGURE 9.6 Short-Run Market Supply Curve
The short-run market supply curve, panel (b), tells us the total quantity that all firms would supply at different market prices. It is found by horizontally summing the individual firm supply curves, shown in panel (a).

Figure 9.6 are the same, the scales of the horizontal axes differ because total market output is much larger than the output of any individual firm.

Because each firm's supply curve coincides with its marginal cost curve (over the range of prices for which the firm is willing to produce positive output), the market supply curve tells us the marginal cost of producing the last unit supplied in the market. For example, in Figure 9.6, when the quantity of roses supplied in the market is 12 million, the marginal cost of supplying the twelve-millionth rose is $0.30. We can see this from Figure 9.6(a): At a market price of $0.30, the marginal cost of the last rose produced by any active producer is $0.30. This must be the case because, as we have seen, profit-maximizing behavior induces each rose producer to expand production to the point at which its marginal cost of the last unit produced equals the market price.

EXAMPLE 9.3   *Short-Run Supply Curves for Copper*

Copper is produced all over the world, in countries ranging from Chile to the United States to Portugal. In the year 2000, there were more than 70 copper mines worldwide, operated by 29 different companies. Analysts following the copper industry collect detailed data on the production capacities and costs of production of these mines. Because so many copper producers compete in the world market and because each one is small in comparison to the scale of that market, it is reasonable to view them as price-taking firms. Given this, we can describe their behavior with supply curves. Figure 9.7 shows supply curves for an individual copper mine, for all producers in the United States, and for the overall world market constructed from actual data on the costs and capacities of copper mines around the world.[12]

The curve in the far left of Figure 9.7 is the supply curve for a single copper mine, the Bingham Canyon mine located in Utah and owned by copper producer Rio Tinto. The supply curve is approximately constant at the mine's marginal cost of 47 cents per pound until we reach the mine's capacity of 285 kilotons of copper per year. Beyond that point, marginal costs rise rapidly and the supply curve becomes virtually vertical.

If we horizontally sum the individual supply curves for the 17 copper mines in the United States, we obtain the supply curve for U.S. copper producers shown in Figure 9.7.[13] The fact that the U.S. supply curve is upward sloping tells us that different mines have different marginal costs of production. The lower the price, the fewer the number of mines that would supply copper. For example, at a price below 45 cents per pound, only four U.S. mines would find it profitable to produce (Bingham Canyon would not be one of these). The overall capacity of the 17 U.S. copper mines is about 1,560 kilotons of copper per year. At this quantity, the U.S. supply curve rises sharply and becomes virtually vertical.

If we construct the supply curve for each of the countries that produce copper—e.g., United States, Chile, Canada, Australia—and add these curves horizontally, we would obtain the world supply curve for copper. This curve is upward sloping for the same reason the U.S. supply curve slopes upward: different mines have different marginal costs, so at different prices different quantities of copper will be supplied. The overall capacity of the copper producers around the world is nearly 9,000 kilotons of copper per year. At this quantity, the world supply curve rises sharply, reflecting that in the short run, the supply of copper cannot be easily expanded beyond this capacity level.

If the price of copper was 70 cents per pound (the price that prevailed in early 1999), the supply of copper from the Bingham Canyon mine would be 285 kilotons per year, indicated by point *A* on the mine's supply curve. At this price, this mine would operate at its full capacity. The supply of copper of all U.S. producers would be about 1,320 kilotons per year, indicated by point *B* on the U.S. supply curve. This is less than the total U.S. mining capacity, indicating that not all mines would supply copper at this price. The world supply of copper at a price of 70 cents per pound would be about 8,518 kilotons per year. This is less than the total worldwide copper-mining capacity, illustrating that not all mines would operate at this price. ■

[12]We constructed these curves using data from the Mine Cost Data Exchange (www.minecost.com), a firm that specializes in the analysis of mining operations in a variety of mineral industries, including copper.

[13]Strictly speaking, the horizontal summation of the supply curves of individual mines with different vertical intercepts will result in a supply curve that has kinks in it, as in Figure 9.6. But when we add together so many supply curves (seventeen of them), this kinked curve will very nearly be smooth. The U.S. supply curve shown here is the best linear approximation to the kinked curve that results from summing the supply curves of the seventeen U.S. mines. Likewise, the world supply curve is a smooth approximation of the kinked supply curve that results from summing the supply curve of all seventy mines worldwide.

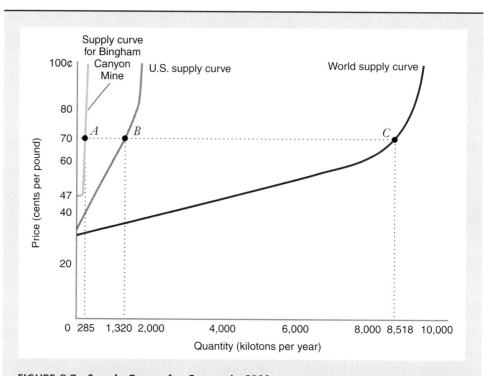

FIGURE 9.7 Supply Curves for Copper in 2000
This figure shows the supply curve of an individual copper mine, Bingham Canyon, in the year 2000. It also shows the supply curve for all U.S. producers, which we obtain by horizontally summing the supply curves of all U.S. copper mines. Finally, it shows the supply curve for the overall world market, which we get by horizontally summing the supply curves of all countries in which copper is produced.

The process of obtaining the market supply curve by summing the individual firm supply curves is subject to one important qualification: this approach is valid only if the prices that firms pay for their inputs are constant as the market output varies. The assumption that input prices are constant may be valid in many markets. Suppose, for example, firms in a particular industry hire unskilled labor. If the industry's demand for the services of unskilled labor is but a small fraction of the overall demand for unskilled labor throughout the economy, then changes in the industry's output would have a negligible effect on the going wage rate for unskilled workers.

However, in some markets the prices of certain kinds of inputs may vary as market output changes. For example, if an industry employs a particular kind of skilled labor that no other industry employs and the supply curve for this skilled labor is upward sloping, then as producers in the industry expand the quantity supplied in response to an increase in the price of their product, demand for the skilled labor would raise, pushing up its wage rate. A higher price of an input such as skilled labor would be expected to shift each producer's marginal cost curve upward. The higher marginal cost means that a producer in this industry would supply less output at any market price than it woiuld have had the wage rate of skilled labor not increased. This implies that the market supply for this product would be less responsive to a change in the price of this product than it would have if the wage rate for skilled workers were constant.

We will further discuss the effects of changing input prices on market supply in the section below that deals with long-run market supply curves. In what follows, unless otherwise explicitly stated, we will assume that input prices do not change as industry output varies.

THE PRICE ELASTICITY OF SUPPLY

The short-run supply curve tells us how changes in the market price translate into changes to the quantity of a good that is offered for sale in a perfectly competitive market. In Chapter 2 we introduced a concept, the **price elasticity of supply,** that measures the sensitivity of the relationship between price and the quantity supplied. Specifically, the price elasticity of supply, denoted by $\epsilon_{Q^s,P}$, tells us the percentage change in quantity supplied, Q^s, for each 1 percent change in price:

$$\epsilon_{Q^s,P} = \frac{\dfrac{\Delta Q^s}{Q^s} \times 100\%}{\dfrac{\Delta P}{P} \times 100\%}$$

$$= \frac{\Delta Q^s}{\Delta P} \frac{P}{Q^s}.$$

This formula applies to both firms and markets. The firm-level price elasticity of supply tells us the sensitivity of an individual firm's supply to price, while the market-level price elasticity of supply tells us the sensitivity of market supply to price.

There are two important special cases of the price elasticity of supply, and both are illustrated in Figure 9.8:

- Figure 9.8(a) shows the case of **perfectly inelastic supply.** When supply is perfectly inelastic, the price elasticity of supply is zero (i.e., $\epsilon_{Q^s,P} = 0$). In this case, changes in the market price have no impact on the quantity of the good supplied, and the supply curve is thus vertical. One-of-a-kind or rare items (paintings, sculptures, rare baseball cards) are examples of objects that have perfectly inelastic supply curves.

- Figure 9.8(b) shows the case of **perfectly elastic supply.** When supply is perfectly elastic, the price elasticity of supply is infinite (i.e., $\epsilon_{Q^s,P} = \infty$). In this case, firms are willing to supply any quantity of output at the price P_0.

Since the supply curve of an individual firm corresponds to the portion of the firm's marginal cost curve above the shut-down price, an important determinant of the price elasticity of supply is the extent to which the marginal cost curve rises rapidly or modestly as the firm produces more output. Typically, as a firm approaches the limits of its fixed plant (e.g., as a rose producer utilizes its land and greenhouses more intensively or a corn farmer tries to grow more corn on a fixed plot of land), the law of diminishing marginal returns sets in, and marginal costs rise rapidly.[14] In such cases, the price elasticity of supply will typically

---

[14]We discussed the law of diminishing marginal returns in Chapter 6.

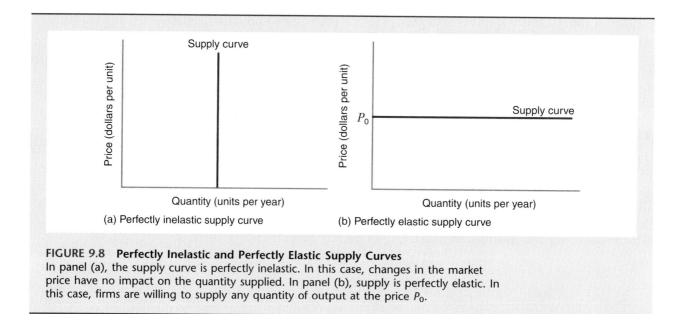

FIGURE 9.8   Perfectly Inelastic and Perfectly Elastic Supply Curves
In panel (a), the supply curve is perfectly inelastic. In this case, changes in the market price have no impact on the quantity supplied. In panel (b), supply is perfectly elastic. In this case, firms are willing to supply any quantity of output at the price P_0.

be small because, as the firm approaches the limits of its fixed plant, even large increases in the market price will elicit just modest increases in the quantity supplied.

SHORT-RUN PERFECTLY COMPETITIVE EQUILIBRIUM

The goal of this section was to explore how the market price is determined in a competitive market. We are now prepared to do that. The key concept that we will now explore is the notion of a market equilibrium, a concept that you encountered in Chapters 1 and 2 and that we will reintroduce here.

A **short-run perfectly competitive equilibrium** occurs when quantity demanded equals quantity supplied. Figure 9.9 illustrates the short-run equilibrium for a perfectly competitive market. Figure 9.9(b) shows the market demand curve D and the short-run market supply curve SS. The equilibrium price is P^*, where quantity supplied is equal to quantity demanded. Figure 9.9(a) shows that a typical firm will produce output Q^*, at which its marginal cost equals the market price P^*.

Mathematically, let $D(P)$ denote the market demand curve, and suppose that the industry consists of 100 firms, each with its own supply curve. If input prices do not change as market output varies, the market supply is the sum of the amounts supplied by the firms in the market. If $s_1(P)$ denotes the supply curve of firm 1, $s_2(P)$ the supply curve of firm 2, and so on, then the short-run equilibrium condition that supply equals demand can be described as follows:

$$s_1(P^*) + s_2(P^*) + \ldots + s_{100}(P^*) = D(P^*).$$

Knowing $D(P)$ and having derived the individual supply curves from a firm's profit-maximization problem, we can determine the equilibrium by solving a single equation in a single unknown, P.

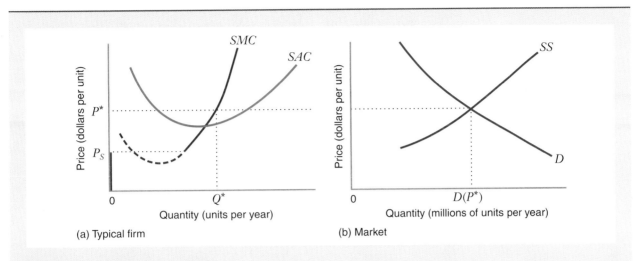

FIGURE 9.9 Short-Run Equilibrium
The short-run equilibrium price is P^*. At this price, market supply equals market demand. The total quantity demanded at P^* is $D(P^*)$. At P^*, a typical firm produces Q^*, where short-run marginal cost equals price.

LEARNING-BY-DOING EXERCISE 9.3

Deriving a Short-Run Market Equilibrium

The market consists of 300 identical firms, and the market demand curve is given by $D(P) = 60 - P$. Each firm has a short-run total cost curve $STC = 0.1 + 150Q^2$, and all fixed costs are sunk. The corresponding short-run marginal cost curve is $SMC = 300Q$. The corresponding average variable cost curve is $AVC = 150Q$. You should verify (e.g., by sketching the SMC and AVC curves) that the minimum level of AVC is 0. Thus, a firm will continue to produce as long as price is positive.

Problem

(a) Find the short-run equilibrium in this market.
(b) At the market equilibrium, do firms make positive economic profit?

Solution

(a) We first derive the supply curve $s(P)$ of an individual firm. Each firm's profit-maximizing quantity is given by equating marginal cost and price

$$300Q = P,$$

which implies

$$s(P) = \frac{P}{300}.$$

The short-run equilibrium thus occurs where market supply ($300s(P)$) equals market demand or

$$300\frac{P}{300} = 60 - P,$$

$$P = 30.$$

At a market price of $30 per unit, each firm produces $30/300 = 0.1$ units per year. Total market demand and supply is $300 \times 0.1 = 30$ units per year.
(b) A firm's short-run average cost function is given by

$$SAC = \frac{STC}{Q} = \frac{0.1}{Q} + 150Q.$$

When each firm produces $Q = 0.1$, short-run average cost is

$$SAC = \frac{0.1}{0.1} + (150 \times 0.1) = 16.$$

Each firm's cost per unit is $16, while the market price is $30, so $P > SAC$. Each firm thus makes a positive economic profit.

Similar Problems: 9.2, 9.4

COMPARATIVE STATICS ANALYSIS OF THE SHORT-RUN EQUILIBRIUM

The competitive equilibrium shown in Figure 9.9 should look familiar. We introduced it in Chapter 1 and studied it extensively in Chapter 2. As in those chapters, it is useful to perform comparative statics analysis on the competitive equilibrium so that we can better understand the factors that determine the market equilibrium price.

Figure 9.10 shows one example of a comparative statics analysis. In particular, it shows what happens when the number of firms in the market goes up. Adding more firms to the market moves the short-run market supply curve rightward, from SS_0 to SS_1. The rightward movement indicates that at a given market price such as $10 per unit, the quantity supplied goes up as more firms are in the market. As a result of the increase in the number of firms, the market price falls, and the equilibrium quantity supplied and demanded goes up.

Figure 9.11 shows another example of a comparative statics analysis. Both diagrams in Figure 9.11 show what happens when the market demand increases, a shift that might be due to an increase in the price of a substitute good or (if the product is a normal good) an increase in consumer income. The increase in market demand shifts the market demand curve rightward, indicating that at a given market price the quantity demanded is now higher than before. As a result of the increase in market demand, the market price goes up and the equilibrium quantity supplied and demanded goes up as well.

Figure 9.11 shows that the price elasticity of supply is an important determinant of the extent to which the market equilibrium price fluctuates in response

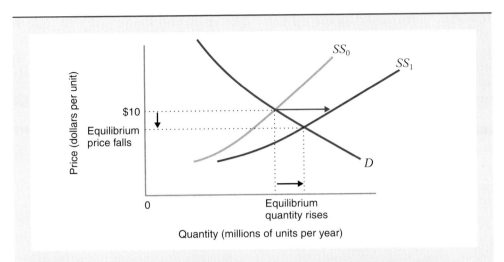

FIGURE 9.10 Comparative Statics Analysis: Increase in the Number of Firms
An increase in the number of firms shifts the short-run supply curve rightward, from SS_0 to SS_1. This indicates that at any given market price, such as $10, the quantity supplied in the market goes up. The rightward shift in the number of firms drives the market price down, while the equilibrium quantity demanded and supplied goes up.

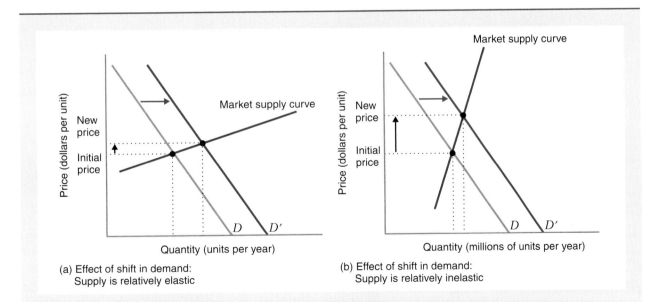

FIGURE 9.11 The Impact of a Shift in Demand on Price Depends on the Price Elasticity of Supply
In panel (a), supply is relatively elastic, and a shift in demand would have a modest impact on price. In panel (b), supply is relatively inelastic, and the identical shift in demand has a more dramatic impact on the equilibrium price.

to a shift in demand. Comparing panel (a) to panel (b) shows that a given shift in demand in a market with relatively inelastic supply will have a more dramatic impact on the market price than the same shift in demand in a market with relatively elastic supply. We would therefore expect that in markets in which market supply is relatively price inelastic, small fluctuations in demand could be expected to lead to dramatic fluctuations in price. The boom-and-bust cycles experienced in industries such as oil tankers can be explained, at least in part, by the inelasticity of short-run market supply.[15]

EXAMPLE 9.4   *Using Comparative Statics to Derive the Short-Run Price Elasticity for Fresh-Cut Roses on the "Back of an Envelope"*

Figure 9.12 shows wholesale prices and quantities of long-stem red roses in the United States in 1991, 1992, and 1993 in four distinct one-month periods: May, August, November, and the last two weeks of January and first two weeks of February.[16] These are the prices that Nakao Growers and its counterparts faced as they contemplated supply decisions during the early 1990s.

Demand conditions in the U.S. rose market vary in a predictable way within a year. Monthly demand for fresh-cut roses is lowest in the third and fourth quarters of the year (July through December) because there are no major holidays during this period for which gifts of roses are customary. We represent demand during August and November by D_{AN}. Because of Valentine's Day, U.S. rose demand is highest during the last two weeks of January and the first two weeks of February. We represent monthly demand in this period by D_{JF}. Monthly demand during the second quarter (April through June) is less than it is before Valentine's Day but greater than the third and fourth quarters. This is because roses are often given as gifts for Mother's Day (mid-May) and because May and June are the busiest months for weddings. We represent the monthly demand curve during May by D_M.

Because supply conditions were stable during 1991–1993, we can employ back-of-the-envelope techniques to identify the short-run market supply curve for fresh-cut red roses. That is, we use the month-to-month shifts in demand during the year to trace out the supply curve. In the early 1990s, the supply curve for fresh-cut roses was perfectly elastic at a price of about $0.22 per rose for quantities up to 4.5 million roses per month. Rose growers were willing to supply any quantity of red roses at $0.22 per rose. However, price must increase above $0.22 per stem to elicit additional supply from growers for Valentine's Day. In particular, the price and quantity during the month before Valentine's Day is (on average) $0.55 and 8.9

---

[15]We discuss the example of oil tankers in detail in the next section on long-run competitive equilibrium.

[16]The data are derived from Tables 12 and 17 of "Fresh Cut Roses from Colombia and Ecuador," Publication 2766, International Trade Commission (March 1994). Figure 9.12 shows a weighted average of prices of U.S. and Colombian growers. These prices have been adjusted for decreases in the value of the Colombian peso relative to the U.S. dollar and to reflect the normal "quality premium" that U.S. roses commanded vis-à-vis Colombian roses during 1991–93. The reference cited above reports quarterly quantities. The monthly quantities in Figure 9.12 are estimated based on the seasonal pattern of roses imported from Colombia.

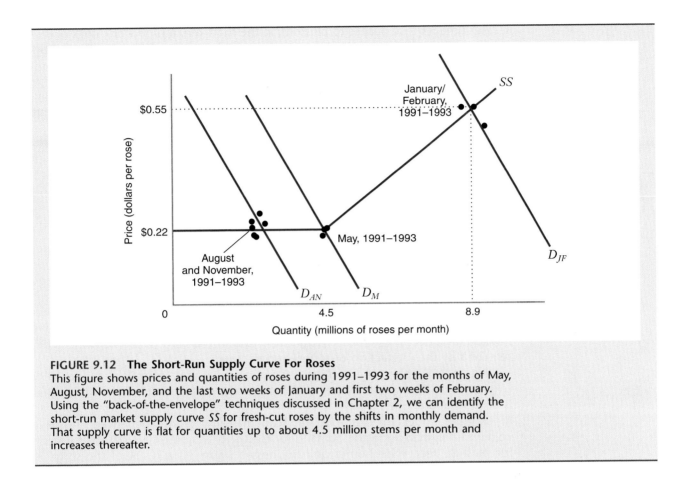

FIGURE 9.12   The Short-Run Supply Curve For Roses
This figure shows prices and quantities of roses during 1991–1993 for the months of May,
August, November, and the last two weeks of January and first two weeks of February.
Using the "back-of-the-envelope" techniques discussed in Chapter 2, we can identify the
short-run market supply curve SS for fresh-cut roses by the shifts in monthly demand.
That supply curve is flat for quantities up to about 4.5 million stems per month and
increases thereafter.

million roses per month. We estimate the slope of the supply curve over the range
between 4.5 and 8.9 million roses as

$$\frac{\Delta Q^s}{\Delta P} = \frac{(8.9 - 4.5)}{(55 - 22)} = 0.1333$$

That is, supply increases at a rate of .1317 million roses for every 1 cent increase
in price. We can use this calculation to determine the price elasticity of supply for
fresh-cut roses in the month before Valentine's Day:

$$\epsilon_{Q^s,P} = 0.1333 \times \frac{55}{8.9}$$

$$= 0.82$$

The supply of roses around Valentine's Day increases at a rate of 0.82 percent for
every 1 percent increase in price. The short-run market supply of roses is thus relatively inelastic.

In light of our discussion of the determinants of the price elasticity of supply,
this finding makes sense. It is not easy for a producer such as Nakao Growers to
increase the supply of roses dramatically without planting more rose bushes. Since

it takes time for rose bushes to blossom, in the short-run, a producer's stock of rose bushes is fixed. Moreover, fresh-cut roses can only be stored for a short time before they must be sold, so producers cannot prepare for Valentine's Day by producing roses ahead of time. It thus takes a relatively large increase in price to induce rose growers to expand their supplies of roses to meet the Valentine's Day rush. ∎

EXAMPLE 9.5   *The Price of Electricity on Nord Pool*[17]

One of the byproducts of the deregulation of electricity markets in the United States and Western Europe has been the establishment of regional power exchanges, free markets in which electric power is bought and sold. Nord Pool is a power exchange that includes four countries: Norway, Sweden, Finland, and Denmark. In fact, it is the world's only multinational electric power exchange, and is viewed as a model for how a competitive market in electric power can operate. As in any competitive market, the price of electricity bought and sold in the Nord Pool exchange is determined by the interaction of supply and demand.

Figure 9.13 shows the average price of electricity on Nord Pool during 1999 [expressed as Norwegian Krone (NKr) per megawatt hour of electricity]. What is striking about this figure is the volatility of electricity prices during the year. In early December, for example, the Scandinavian region experienced unusually cold weather, increasing the demand for electricity as consumers ran their heaters full blast to keep their homes and businesses warm. As a result of the surge in demand, electricity prices, which usually range between 100 and 150 NKr per megawatt-hour (about $12.50 to $18.50 per megawatt-hour), shot up to over 200 NKr per megawatt-hour.

The reason that electricity prices on Nord Pool shot up so much in early December 1999 is that the short-run price elasticity of supply for electricity is very low. With normal capacity already being fully utilized, firms that produce electric power were forced to start their back-up power stations, which normally are much more costly to operate. As Thor Lien, vice president of Euron Nordic Energy (an electricity producer), explains: "Starting up a station for two to four hours on a single day to cover an extreme period is very expensive." Although he didn't express it this way, what Mr. Lien is saying is that the short-run marginal cost curve for an electricity producer becomes very steep once the producer's normal capacity is fully utilized. As we have just discussed, a steeply rising short-run marginal curve for producers translates into a short-run market supply curve that is relatively inelastic. And as we have seen, when market supply is relatively inelastic, even a modest change in demand can cause a dramatic shift in the market price. The prices on Nord Pool in December 1999 illustrate well the comparative statics of supply and demand in a competitive market. ∎

---

[17]This example is based on "Nordic Electricity Embraces the Power of the Market," *Financial Times* (January 18, 2000), p. 24.

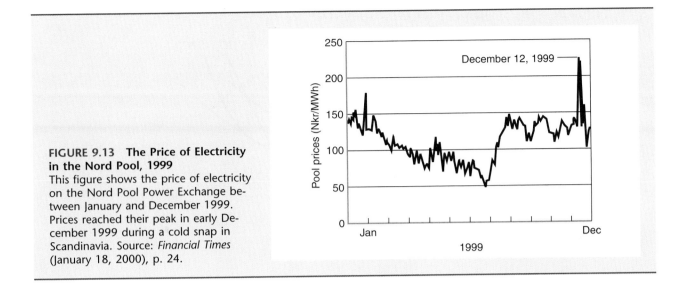

FIGURE 9.13 The Price of Electricity in the Nord Pool, 1999
This figure shows the price of electricity on the Nord Pool Power Exchange between January and December 1999. Prices reached their peak in early December 1999 during a cold snap in Scandinavia. Source: *Financial Times* (January 18, 2000), p. 24.

9.4
HOW THE MARKET PRICE IS DETERMINED: LONG-RUN MARKET EQUILIBRIUM

In the short run, firms operate within a given plant size, and the number of firms in the industry does not change. As a result, at the short-run perfectly competitive equilibrium, firms might earn positive or negative economic profits. By contrast, in the long run, established firms can adjust their plant sizes, and can even leave the industry altogether. In addition, new firms can enter the industry. You will learn that in the long run, these forces drive a firm's economic profits to zero.

LONG-RUN OUTPUT AND PLANT-SIZE ADJUSTMENTS BY ESTABLISHED FIRMS

In the long run, an established firm can adjust both its plant size and its rate of output to maximize its profit. Thus, as the firm looks out over the long-run horizon and contemplates the possible output levels it *might* produce, it should evaluate the cost of those outputs using its long-run cost functions.

Long-run and short-run profit maximization both involve equating marginal cost to price. The key difference between the long run and the short run is that

- In the long run, the firm contemplates its output options under the assumption that it can adjust the amounts of all of inputs, including its plant size. It thus evaluates its marginal costs using its long-run marginal cost function.

- In the short run, by contrast, the firm contemplates its output options under the assumption that at least one input, such as its plant size, is fixed. It thus evaluates its marginal costs using the short-run marginal cost function corresponding to its fixed input.

To illustrate, Figure 9.14 shows a rose producer that faces a price of $0.40 per rose. With its current plant size—its current stock of land and greenhouses—the firm's short-run marginal and average cost curves are SAC_0 and SMC_0,

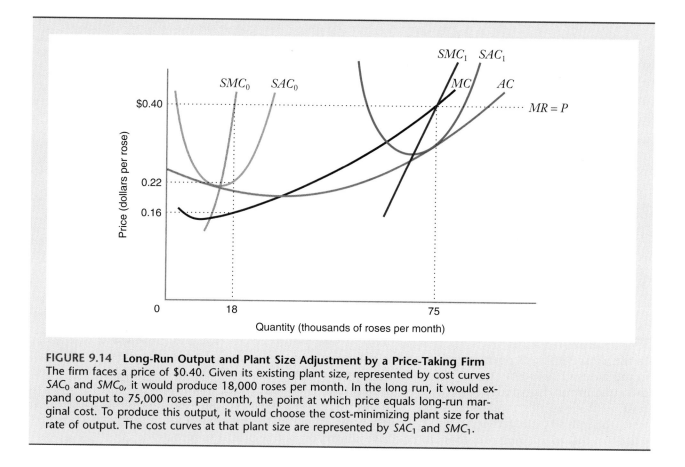

FIGURE 9.14   Long-Run Output and Plant Size Adjustment by a Price-Taking Firm
The firm faces a price of $0.40. Given its existing plant size, represented by cost curves
SAC_0 and SMC_0, it would produce 18,000 roses per month. In the long run, it would expand output to 75,000 roses per month, the point at which price equals long-run marginal cost. To produce this output, it would choose the cost-minimizing plant size for that
rate of output. The cost curves at that plant size are represented by SAC_1 and SMC_1.

respectively. Its short-run profit-maximizing output is 18,000 roses per month.
At this quantity and the price of $0.40, the firm earns a positive economic profit
because the price exceeds the firm's short-run average cost of about $0.22 per
rose.

If the grower expects that, over the foreseeable future, the market price will
remain at $0.40 per rose, it would want to increase its output above 18,000 roses
per month.[18] Even though the price of $0.40 equals its *short-run* marginal cost
at an output of 18,000 roses, it exceeds its *long-run* marginal cost at 18,000
units (about $0.16). By expanding its stock of land and greenhouses—and grow-
ing more roses within this expanded plant size—the rose producer can increase
its profit.

Long-run profit maximization involves producing a quantity of output at
which long-run marginal cost equals the market price, $P = MC$. To produce this
quantity of output, the firm chooses a plant size that is cost-minimizing for that

[18]For the case of the rose market, you might wonder whether it would make sense for a rose grower to
expect that the price would remain constant (e.g., at $0.40 per stem) over the long term. As Example
9.4 showed, rose prices do not remain constant from one month to the next; they fluctuate in a predictable fashion during the year. As we study the long-run problem of a price-taking firm and talk about
the firm "taking the market price as given," you can imagine that the firm is reacting to what it believes
the *average* market price will be over the foreseeable future, taking into account the predictable fluctuations in price that are due to anticipated seasonal changes in demand.

rate of output. In Figure 9.14, at a price of $0.40, the firm would expand its rate of output to 75,000 roses per month, and it would choose the plant size (amount of land and greenhouses) that is cost minimizing for producing 75,000 roses per month. The firm's short-run cost curves for this plant size are SAC_1 and SMC_1.

THE FIRM'S LONG-RUN SUPPLY CURVE

The preceding analysis suggests that a firm's long-run supply curve is its long-run marginal cost curve. This is almost correct. Remember that in the long run a firm can avoid all input costs. In other words, a firm has no sunk costs in the long run. Thus, as Figure 9.15 shows, a firm would not participate in this industry if price were less than the minimum level of long-run average cost, AC (about $0.20 per unit in the figure). At prices below this level, the firm earns negative economic profits, even after making all available adjustments in its input mix to minimize its total costs.

Thus, a firm's long-run supply curve is the portion of its long-run marginal cost curve above the minimum level of long-run average cost. This is because:

- For prices *above* the minimum level of average cost, the firm produces an output at which $P = MC$. For example, if a rose producer expected that the price would be $0.40 per rose over the foreseeable future, it would produce at a rate of 75,000

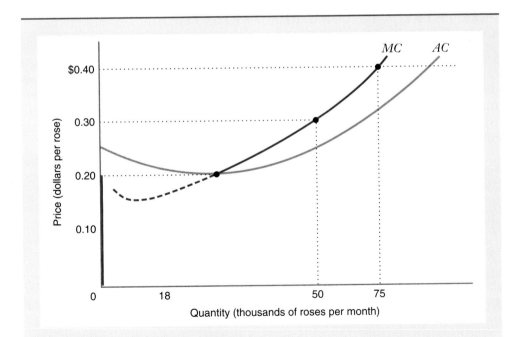

FIGURE 9.15 The Firm's Long-Run Supply Curve
For prices greater than the minimum level of long-run average cost (about $0.20 here), the firm's long-run supply curve coincides with its long-run marginal cost curve. For prices below the minimum level of long-run average cost, the firm's supply curve is a vertical spike that coincides with the vertical axis.

roses per month. If it expected a price of $0.30 per rose, it would produce 50,000 roses per month. The long-run marginal cost curve thus identifies the firm's profit-maximizing supply for prices above the minimum level of average cost.

- For prices *below* the minimum level of average cost, a firm would not participate in this industry. A prospective rose grower that anticipated a market price of, say, $0.10 per rose would earn a negative economic profit if it entered the industry at this price: It would choose not to enter in the first place. An existing firm would not find it worthwhile to renew the lease on its land and replace its capital (e.g., greenhouses) if it expected that the prevailing price would be $0.10 per rose. (In reality, in the mid-1990s, decreases in the market price of roses led Nakao to contemplate this very action.) Over the long run, a firm (existing or new entrant) would supply no output under these circumstances.

The logic underlying the construction of the firm's long-run supply curve is analogous to the logic we used to construct the firm's short-run supply curve. In both cases, we considered the relationship between price and marginal cost to determine the optimal level of output if indeed the firm produced positive output. And in both cases, we asked whether the firm would be better off not producing in light of the costs it avoids if it does not produce. The difference is that in the long run, all costs are avoidable (i.e., they are nonsunk), whereas in the short run, some costs might not be avoidable (i.e., they are sunk) if the firm produces a quantity of zero.

FREE ENTRY AND LONG-RUN PERFECTLY COMPETITIVE EQUILIBRIUM

In our short-run analysis of the perfectly competitive equilibrium, we assumed that the number of firms in the industry was fixed. But in the long run, new firms can enter the industry. A firm will enter the industry if, given the market price, it can earn positive economic profits. Positive economic profit indicates that there is an opportunity for an entrant to create wealth for its owners by participating in the industry.

A **long-run perfectly competitive equilibrium** occurs at a price at which supply equals demand and firms have no incentive to enter or exit the industry. More specifically, a long-run perfectly competitive equilibrium is characterized by a market price P^*, a number of firms n^*, and a quantity of output Q^* per firm that satisfies three conditions:

1. *Long-run profit is maximized with respect to output and plant size.* Given the price P^*, each active firm chooses a level of output that maximizes its profit, and selects a plant size that minimizes the cost of producing that output. This condition implies that a firm's long-run marginal cost equals the market price:

$$P^* = MC(Q^*). \tag{9.2}$$

2. *Economic profit is zero.* Given the price P^*, a prospective entrant cannot earn positive economic profit by entering this industry. Moreover, an active firm cannot earn negative economic profit by participating in this industry.

This condition implies that a firm's long-run average cost equals the market price:

$$P^* = AC(Q^*). \tag{9.3}$$

3. *Demand equals supply.* At the price P^*, market demand equals market supply, given the number of firms n^* and individual firm supply decisions Q^*. This implies that

$$D(P^*) = n^*Q^*, \tag{9.4}$$

or equivalently

$$n^* = \frac{D(P^*)}{Q^*}.$$

Figure 9.16 shows these conditions graphically. (The numbers in the figure correspond to Learning-By-Doing Exercise 9.4.) Because the equilibrium price simultaneously equals long-run marginal cost and long-run average cost, each firm produces at a minimum point on its long-run average cost curve. If the minimum of the average cost occurs at a single level of output such as Q^* in Figure 9.16, the firm produces at minimum efficient scale. The condition that supply equals demand then implies that the equilibrium number of firms equals market demand divided by minimum efficient scale output.

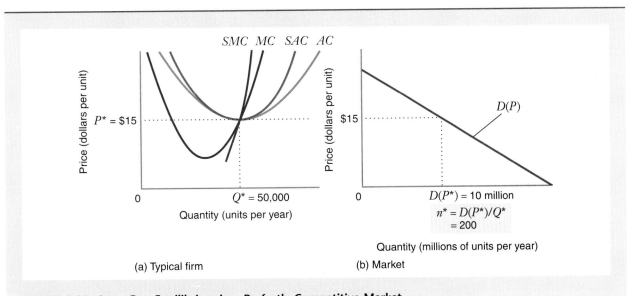

(a) Typical firm

(b) Market

FIGURE 9.16 Long-Run Equilibrium in a Perfectly Competitive Market
The long-run equilibrium price P^* equals the minimum level of long-run average cost, which in this case is $15 per unit. Each firm produces a quantity Q^* equal to its minimum efficient scale, which in this case is 50,000 units. The equilibrium quantity demanded is 10 million units. The equilibrium number of firms is this amount divided by the output per firm of 50,000. In this case, the equilibrium number of firms is 200.

LEARNING-BY-DOING EXERCISE 9.4

Calculating a Long-Run Equilibrium

Problem   In this market, each firm and potential entrant has a long-run average cost curve

$$AC(Q) = 40 - Q + 0.01Q^2$$

and a corresponding long-run marginal cost curve

$$MC(Q) = 40 - 2Q + .03Q^2,$$

where Q is thousands of units per year. The market demand curve is

$$D(P) = 25,000 - 1,000P,$$

where $D(P)$ is also measured in thousands of units. Find the long-run equilibrium price, quantity per firm, and number of firms.

Solution   Let asterisks denote equilibrium values. The long-run competitive equilibrium satisfies the following three equations.

$$P^* = 40 - 2Q^* + .03(Q^*)^2 \text{ (profit maximization)}$$
$$P^* = 40 - Q^* + .01(Q^*)^2 \text{ (zero profit)}$$
$$n^* = \left(\frac{25,000 - 1,000P^*}{Q^*} \right) \text{ (supply equals demand).}$$

By combining the first two equations, we can solve for the quantity per firm:

$$40 - 2Q^* + .03(Q^*)^2 = 40 - Q^* + .01(Q^*)^2$$
$$.03(Q^*)^2 - .01(Q^*)^2 = 2Q^* - Q^*$$
$$.02(Q^*)^2 = Q^*.$$

Thus, $Q^* = 50$, so each firm in equilibrium produces 50,000 units per year. Note that this quantity is a firm's minimum efficient scale. Substituting $Q^* = 50$ back into the average or marginal cost function gives us the minimum level of average cost and thus the equilibrium price:

$$P^* = 40 - 50 + .01(50)^2 = 15.$$

The equilibrium price of $15 per unit corresponds to a firm's minimum level of average cost. By substituting P^* into the demand function we can find the market demand at $15. It is given by

$$25,000 - 1,000(15) = 10,000,$$

or 10 million units per year. The equilibrium number of firms is equilibrium market demand divided by minimum efficient scale:

$$n^* = \frac{10,000}{50} = 200.$$

To summarize, the long-run equilibrium price is $15 per unit. The quantity supplied by an individual firm is 50 thousand units per year. The equilibrium number of firms is 200. Market demand and market supply in equilibrium equal 10 million units per year.

Similar Problem: 9.7

EXAMPLE 9.6

Free Entry into the Internet Access Market[19]

How do you access the Internet? You might do it through the computer lab at your school. Or, like millions of Americans, you might rely on an Internet Service Provider or ISP. An ISP is a company that allows you to access the Internet by making a local phone call. Large companies, such as AT&T, IBM, and MCI-WorldCom, provide Internet access. But so do companies you probably have never heard of, such as New Visions, Inc. and Whole Earth 'Lectronic Link.

The theory of perfect competition teaches us that when there is free entry, the number of firms in a market will be determined by the relationship between market demand and minimum efficient scale. For a given minimum efficient scale, the greater the market demand, the greater the number of firms in a long-run equilibrium.

The market for ISPs illustrates this point. The ISP market is characterized by free entry. To become an ISP provider, all a firm needs is a bank of modems, one or more servers, and a connection to the Internet. In 1994, with the Internet and the World Wide Web just about to hit the public consciousness, there were virtually no ISPs. By the spring of 1998, over 6,000 ISPs provided Internet access in the United States.

Because most individuals prefer to make local rather than long distance phone calls to access the Internet and because many ISPs operate locally rather than nationally, the relevant market for Internet access is probably a county or metropolitan area. As a general tendency, we would expect that the greater the population in a local market, the greater the demand for Internet access.[20] If the structure of the ISP market is consistent with the theory of perfect competition depicted in Figure 9.16, we should expect a positive relationship between the population of a local market and the number of ISPs operating in that market.

---

[19]This example is based on Thomas A. Downes and Shane M. Greenstein, "Do Commercial ISPs Provide Universal Access?" in S. E. Gillett and I. Vogelsang, eds., *Competition, Regulation, and Convergence: Current Trends in Telecommunications Policy Research* (Mahwah, NJ: Lawrence Erlbaum Associates, 1999).

[20]There are exceptions to this rule, of course. A small university town such as Champaign, Illinois (home of the University of Illinois) with an Internet-savvy population might have greater demand for Internet access than a larger town with less Internet sophistication.

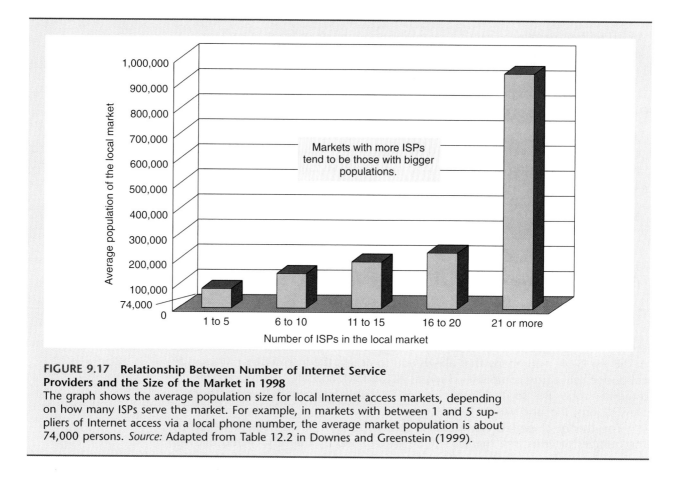

**FIGURE 9.17   Relationship Between Number of Internet Service
Providers and the Size of the Market in 1998**
The graph shows the average population size for local Internet access markets, depending
on how many ISPs serve the market. For example, in markets with between 1 and 5 suppliers of Internet access via a local phone number, the average market population is about
74,000 persons. *Source:* Adapted from Table 12.2 in Downes and Greenstein (1999).

As Figure 9.17 illustrates, this is what we see. Of 3,110 local Internet access
markets in the continental United States, about 700 had between one and five
ISPs.[21] These markets were generally located far outside major metropolitan areas
(e.g., in states such as Montana and Nevada). By contrast, 1,293 local markets were
served by 21 or more ISPs. These markets had an average population of about
943,000 persons and included all of the major U.S. cities such as New York, Los
Angeles, and Chicago. More generally, Figure 9.17 shows a positive relationship between market size and the number of ISPs, which is exactly what the model of perfect competition predicts. ∎

THE LONG-RUN MARKET SUPPLY CURVE

In our analysis of the short-run competitive equilibrium, we depicted the equilibrium price by the intersection of the market demand curve and the short-run
market supply curve. In this section, we will see that the long-run equilibrium
can be depicted in a similar way: by the intersection of the market demand curve
and the **long-run market supply curve.**

[21]In Downes and Greenstein's study, a local market is defined to be an area within 30 miles from the
geographic center of each of the 3,110 counties in the continental United States.

The long-run market supply curve tells us the total quantity of output that will be supplied at various market prices, assuming that all long-run adjustments (plant size, new entry) take place. However, we cannot obtain the long-run market supply curve in the same way we derived the short-run market supply curve (i.e., by horizontally summing the short-run supply curves of individual firms).[22] This is because in the long run, there are two sources for long-run changes in the supply of output: (1) established firms can expand or contract output; (2) new firms can enter or established firms can exit the industry. Horizontally summing the long-run supply curves of established firms would miss this second source for changes in output.

Figure 9.18 shows how to construct the long-run market supply curve. (For consistency, we focus on the market we originally depicted in Figure 9.16.) We assume that the market is initially in long-run equilibrium at a price of $15. At this price, each firm produces at its minimum efficient scale of 50,000 units per year. The equilibrium number of firms is 200. Given this number, market supply equals 10 million units. This supply equals market demand at the $15 equilibrium price.

Now suppose that market demand shifts from D_0 to D_1. We assume that this demand shift is expected to persist long enough for the market to reach a new

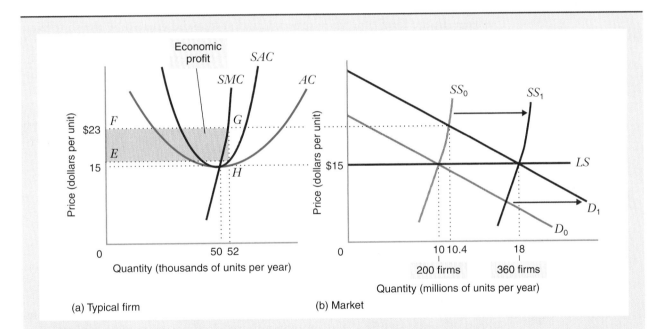

(a) Typical firm   (b) Market

FIGURE 9.18   Long-Run Industry Supply Curve
The industry is initially at a long-run equilibrium price of $15. Each of 200 firms produces its minimum efficient scale output, 50,000. Demand then shifts rightward from D_0 to D_1. The short-run equilibrium price is $23, where short-run supply SS_0 intersects demand. Each firm supplies 52,000 units and earns a positive economic profit equal to the area of rectangle $EFGH$. This induces a new entry, which shifts the short-run supply curve rightward, eventually becoming SS_1. At the new long-run equilibrium, the industry now has 360 firms, each supplying 50,000 units. The long-run equilibrium price is once again $15. The long-run industry supply curve is thus a horizontal line at $15. In the long run, all market supply occurs at this price.

[22]As already discussed, obtaining the short-run market supply curve by "horizontally summing" assumes that changes in industry output do not affect input prices.

long-run equilibrium. The initial adjustment to the demand shift occurs in the short run through establishment of a new short-run equilibrium. That equilibrium occurs at the intersection of D_1 and the short-run supply curve SS_0, corresponding to a market of 200 firms. The short-run equilibrium price is $23. At this price, each firm maximizes profits by producing 52,000 units per year, and the total market supply and demand is $200 \times 52,000 = 10.4$ million units.

At a price of $23, existing firms earn a positive economic profit equal to the area of the shaded rectangle *EFGH*. The positive economic profit attracts new entrants. The addition of new firms to the industry shifts the short-run supply curve rightward, and as this occurs, short-run equilibrium price falls, as do the profits of established firms. In this sense, free entry "competes away" industry profit.

At what point does the erosion of price and profitability due to new entry stop? Once the entry process fully unfolds, the short-run supply curve will have shifted to SS_1, and the market price falls back to $15 per unit. At this point, 160 new firms have entered the industry, and each firm (new and old) maximizes its profit by producing at its minimum efficient scale of 50,000 units per year. Once price falls to $15, there is no incentive for additional entry or exit because each firm earns zero economic profit. Moreover, the market clears because market demand at $15 equals the total market supply of $360 \times 50,000 = 18$ million units per year. In the long run, the additional market demand created by the shift from D_0 to D_1 is satisfied by new entrants.

This analysis shows that in the long run, output expansion or contraction in this industry occurs along the horizontal line *LS* corresponding to the minimum level of long-run average cost of $15. *LS* is the long-run market supply curve. It tells us that in the long run, industry output is only supplied at a price of $15. At a lower price, firms would earn negative economic profit, and would supply no output. At a higher price, entry would occur, which, as we just showed, will drive the price back to $15 in the long run.

EXAMPLE 9.7   *The Collapse of the Supertanker Market*[23]

Supertankers are enormous ships that transport crude oil around the world. The tanker business has been called the "world's largest poker game," a reference not only to the high risks and large stakes involved in entering the business—a single tanker can cost more than $100 million—but also to the colorful figures, such as Aristotle Onassis and Sir Y. K. Pao, who amassed fortunes by owning tankers.

No episode underscores how quickly fortunes in the tanker business can shift than the collapse of the supertanker market in the 1970s. Figure 9.19 shows the spot price for supertanker services—the price to charter a supertanker for a single voyage—between 1973 and 1976.[24] In September 1973, the spot rate for supertanker voy-

---

[23]This example draws from a variety of sources, including "The Oil Tanker Shipping Industry," Harvard Business School Case 9-379-086; "The Oil Tanker Shipping Industry in 1983," Harvard Business School Case 9-384-034; R. Thomas, "Perfect Competition Among Supertankers: Free Enterprise's Greatest Mistake," Chapter 14 in *Microeconomic Applications* (Cincinnati, OH: South-Western, 1981); and *Market Conditions and Tanker Economics* (London: H. P. Drewry, July 1976).

[24]This price is measured in units called Worldscale (abbreviated W), a price index for tanker services based on a standard-sized ship operating under standard conditions.

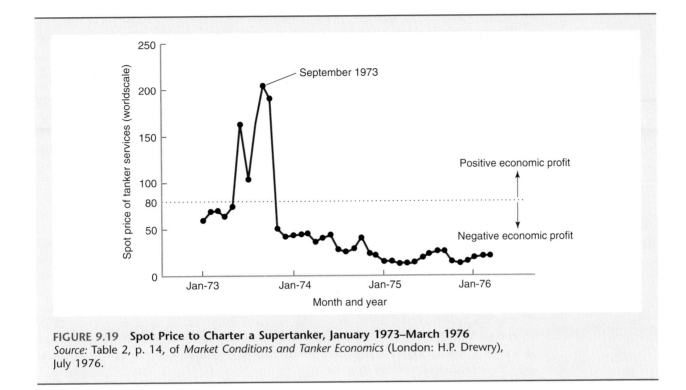

FIGURE 9.19   Spot Price to Charter a Supertanker, January 1973–March 1976
Source: Table 2, p. 14, of *Market Conditions and Tanker Economics* (London: H.P. Drewry), July 1976.

ages averaged W205. A month later, it fell to W95, and by the end of the year, it was W68. By 1975, the spot rate had fallen even further and was far below the level (approximately W80) that would allow supertankers to earn a positive economic profit.

What happened? To answer this question, we first need to understand what determines tanker demand. The demand for tanker services depends on the world demand for oil and on the distance between producers and consumers of oil. In the 1960s and early 1970s, the demand for oil grew briskly, and more oil came from the Middle East. Oil sales from the Persian Gulf grew at close to 10 percent each year in the early 1970s, and most industry observers expected that growth to continue. Demand growth was especially strong in the first nine months of 1973 because oil exports from the Persian Gulf increased faster than anyone expected. This accounted for the big increase in prices during the summer of 1973. Figure 9.20 depicts this increase in price as a short-run equilibrium response to a shift in demand, with the industry operating on a given short-run supply curve SS_0.

Expectations of continued high prices led owners to invest in new tanker capacity in the late 1960s and early 1970s. By 1973, just six years after the first supertanker was launched, there were nearly 400 supertankers worldwide, and 500 more were on order. Had the demand side of the market unfolded as expected, this increase in tanker capacity would have driven the market price toward the long-run equilibrium price P^* at which supertankers earn zero economic profit.

But demand conditions did not unfold as expected. In October 1973, the Yom Kippur War between Israel and the Arab states broke out, and shortly thereafter, the Organization of Petroleum Exporting Countries (OPEC) imposed its oil embargo on the United States. Oil prices skyrocketed, and OPEC exports to the United States dropped substantially. Oil tankers, whose services were desperately needed in

September 1973, floated empty in December 1973. Figure 9.20 depicts this as a leftward shift in demand to D_1. Given the supply curve SS_0, the price of tanker services fell far below the long-run equilibrium level P^*.

The increase in price in 1973 and the subsequent drop in price later that year were especially dramatic because the short-run supply of supertankers is inelastic. This is because tanker operators have limited options for adjusting output in the short run. They can steam their tankers faster or slower to increase or decrease supply, but such tactics have only a modest effect. Operators can also deactivate tankers, either by "mothballing" them with the option of activating them later, or selling them for scrap. Mothballing is costly, and sale for scrap is irreversible, so neither is done unless low prices are expected to persist. Moreover, supertankers have no alternative uses. In particular, an owner cannot easily convert a tanker from shipping oil to, say, shipping grain. All of this implies that short-run supply curves, such as SS_0, are nearly vertical over a wide range of prices.

The oil embargo eventually ended, but the demand for tanker services remained low throughout 1974 and 1975. Prices of OPEC-produced oil stayed high, and demand fell as Western nations, such as the United States, cut back their oil consumption. Oil tankers last for a long time (typically 20 years), so it takes capacity a long time to leave the industry. In fact, in 1974 and 1975, the short-run supply curve actually shifted rightward to SS_1 as new supertankers that were ordered in the early 1970s were commissioned for service. For example, in 1974 worldwide tanker capacity increased 18 percent despite record-low prices for tanker services. This accentuated the fall in price.

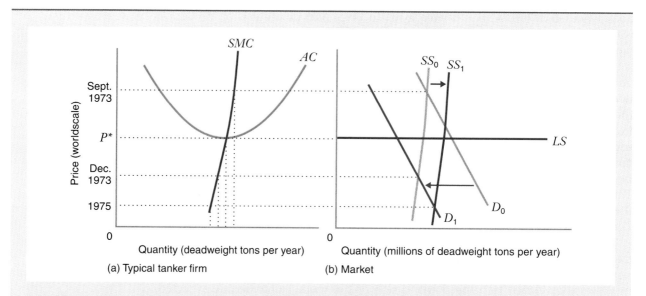

FIGURE 9.20   The Collapse of the Oil Tanker Market, 1973–1975
Demand in the early fall of 1973 is D_0. This results in a short-run equilibrium price that is significantly above the long-run equilibrium price P^*. As a result of the Arab oil embargo later that Fall, the demand for tanker services shifted leftward to D_1, and remained at that level through 1974 and 1975. The price of tanker services decreased sharply in the Fall of 1973. It decreased even further in 1974 and 1975 as new supertankers that were ordered in the early 1970s came into service.

Eventually, tanker supply did adjust. In 1977 and 1978, over 20 million tons worth of tanker capacity was sold for scrap. In addition, almost half of the orders for unfinished tankers were cancelled, costing owners millions of dollars in lost down payments and cancellation fees. The decrease in tanker capacity, coupled with gradual increase in demand for oil, caused tanker prices to creep upward in the late 1970s. Still, it took more than 10 years for the industry to recover from the collapse in prices that began in the autumn of 1973. ∎

CONSTANT-COST, INCREASING-COST, AND DECREASING-COST INDUSTRIES

Constant-Cost Industry

When constructing the long-run supply curve in the previous section, we assumed that the expansion of industry output that occurs as a result of new entry does not affect the prices of inputs (e.g., labor, raw materials, capital) used by firms in the industry. As a result, when new firms enter the industry, the cost curves of incumbent producers do not shift. By making this assumption, we are assuming that the industry's demand for an input is a small part of the total demand from all industries in the economy. If so, increases or decreases in the industry's use of that input would not affect its market price. For example, firms in the rose industry use a significant amount of natural gas, distillates, and other fuels to heat greenhouses. But many other industries also use these fuels. Because of this, an increase or decrease in the amount of rose production—and a corresponding increase in the demand for heating fuels by rose growers—would be unlikely to have much impact on overall demand for heating fuels and would probably not significantly change the free-market prices of such fuels.

When changes in industry output have no effect on input prices, we have a **constant-cost industry.** The industry depicted in Figure 9.18 is a constant-cost industry. "Constant cost" is not the same as "constant returns to scale," which, as you learned in Chapter 8, implies a horizontal long-run average cost function. Figure 9.18 shows that we can have a constant-cost industry even though firms do not have constant returns to scale. Conversely, firms in an industry can have constant returns to scale, but the industry need not be constant cost.

Increasing-Cost Industry

When an expansion of industry output increases the price of an input, we have an **increasing-cost industry.** An industry is likely to be increasing cost if firms use **industry-specific inputs**—scarce inputs that only firms in that industry use. For example, a rose producer, such as Nakao Growers, employs a master grower who is responsible for planting rose bushes, determining fertilizer and pesticide levels, scheduling harvesting, and creating hybrids. Good master growers are hard to find, and those with a track record of success are highly sought after.

Figure 9.21 illustrates the equilibrium adjustment process in an increasing cost industry. As in Figure 9.18, the industry is initially in long-run equilibrium at a price of $15. There are 200 firms in the industry, each producing 50,000 units per year. Market demand now shifts rightward, from D_0 to D_1. The short-run equilibrium is, as before, established at a price of $23, at the intersection of

D_1 and SS_0. That price attracts entry, which shifts the short-run market supply curve rightward.

So far, the analysis parallels that in Figure 9.18. But now, as industry output expands through new entry, the prices of industry-specific inputs begin to rise. For example, additional entry of rose producers in the United States would be expected to increase the demand for highly skilled master growers. As new entrants sought to lure master growers away from their current employers with offers of better salaries, their salaries would go up. The increase in input prices causes a firm's long-run and short-run cost functions to shift upward.[25] (Figure 9.21 depicts an upward shift that leaves the minimum efficient scale unchanged.)

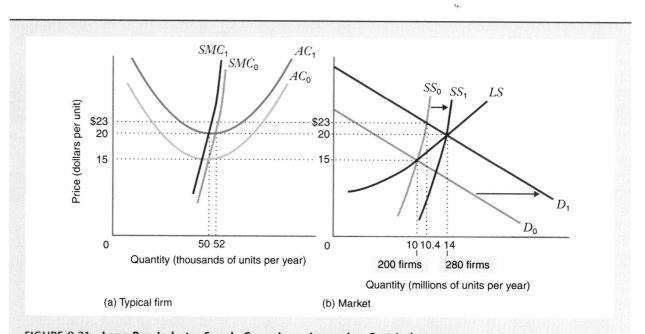

(a) Typical firm

(b) Market

FIGURE 9.21   Long-Run Industry Supply Curve in an Increasing-Cost Industry
The industry is initially at a long-run equilibrium price of $15. Each of 200 firms produces its minimum efficient scale output, 50,000. Demand then shifts rightward from D_0 to D_1. The short-run equilibrium price is $23, where short-run supply SS_0 intersects demand. Each firm supplies 52,000 units and earns a positive economic profit. This induces new entry, which shifts the short-run supply curve rightward, eventually becoming SS_1. As new firms enter, the prices of industry-specific inputs go up, shifting the long-run and short-run cost curves upward. In particular, the minimum level of long-run average cost increases from $15 to $20. At the new long-run equilibrium, 280 firms are now in the industry, each supplying 50,000 units. The long-run equilibrium price is $20. The long-run industry supply curve is the upward sloping line, LS.

---

[25]For the case of a rose-growing firm that employs a single master grower, the salary of the master grower would be a *fixed* cost. An increase in the salaries of master growers would thus affect the AC curve but not the SMC curve. Figure 9.21 shows the case of an increase in the price of an input that firms use in variable amounts. Increases in the price of a variable input would shift the SMC curve as shown in the figure.

The adjustment process stops when price falls to a point at which firms earn zero profits. This occurs at a price of $20. That price equals the minimum level of the *new* long-run average curve AC_1 that results from the increase in input prices. Industry output expands from 10 million to 14 million units per year. Since each firm produces the minimum efficient scale output of 50,000 units, the equilibrium number of firms is now 14,000,000/50,000 = 280. Thus, an additional 80 firms have entered the industry.

The long-run market supply curve in an increasing cost industry is described by the upward-sloping line *LS* in Figure 9.21(b). The upward-sloping market supply curve tells us that increases in price are needed to elicit additional industry output in the long run. The increases in price compensate for the increases in the minimum level of long-run average cost that are driven by the expansion of industry output.

Decreasing-Cost Industry

In some situations an increase in industry output can lead to a *decrease* in the price of an input. We then have a **decreasing-cost industry.** To illustrate, suppose an industry relies heavily on a special kind of computer chip as an input. The industry may be able to acquire computer chips more inexpensively as the industry's demand for chips rises, perhaps because manufacturers of computer chips can employ cost-reducing techniques of production at higher volumes. Similarly, a larger industry may be able to better organize transportation activities to take advantage of lower transport prices when shipping larger volumes. In a decreasing-cost industry, each firm's average and marginal cost curves may fall, not because the firms produce with economies of scale, but because input prices fall when the industry produces more. The supply curves of the individual firms are upward sloping because each firm is so small that it believes its own production decisions will have no effect on factor prices. However, in a decreasing-cost industry, the long-run market supply curve is downward sloping because, at the market level, input prices do fall as output increases. As the market demand shifts to the right, the equilibrium market quantity increases and the long-run equilibrium price falls.

WHAT DOES PERFECT COMPETITION TEACH US?

In this section, we have studied how free entry affects how the long-run market price in a perfectly competitive market is determined. In doing so, we have seen a key implication of the theory of perfect competition: Free entry will eventually drive economic profit to zero. This is one of the most important ideas in microeconomics. It tells us that when profit opportunities are freely available to all firms, economic profits will not last. This confirms the business wisdom: "If anyone can do it, you can't make money at it." The lesson of the theory of perfect competition for managers is that if you base your firm's strategy on skills that can easily be imitated or resources that can easily be acquired, you put yourself at risk to the forces that are highlighted by the theory of perfect competition. In the long run, your economic profit will be competed away.

EXAMPLE 9.8

Free Entry into an Increasing-Cost Industry:
The Solvent Extraction Business in India[26]

Are you familiar with the solvent extraction business? Probably not. It is the kind of industry that rarely attracts headlines. Yet, as events in the early 1990s illustrate, the solvent extraction business in India provides an excellent example of an increasing-cost industry.

Firms in the solvent extraction business purchase oil cakes—ground-up sunflower, sesame, or mustard seeds—and, using a solvent called hexane, they extract the oil that remains in the cakes. The extracted oil is then sold to other firms who refine it into edible products, such as sunflower oil or sesame seed oil. The remains of the oil cakes—called de-oiled cakes—are sold for cattle feed.

Until 1990, firms in India's solvent extraction business operated in a protected market. The Indian government regulated entry into this business, and it restricted the number of firms that could participate in it. As a result, most firms in this business earned positive economic profits.

But in 1990, the Indian government changed its policy and began to allow unlimited entry into the solvent extraction business. Attracted by the high profits earned by incumbent producers, numerous firms entered the industry. Within three years, the industry's total capacity had increased by 60 percent.

As entry occurred, industry profits fell. This occurred for two reasons. First, as more producers entered the market, the prices of the industry's finished products (extracted oils and de-oiled cakes) fell. Second, new entry increased the prices of important inputs. As new firms entered the market, the demand for oil cakes—the key raw material used by solvent extraction firms—went up. Firms competed with one another to secure scarce supplies of oil cakes. Competition was so fierce that it was not uncommon in this period for oil cake suppliers to break existing contracts with incumbent solvent extraction firms so that they could get higher prices from new entrants who were eager to obtain their own supplies. Oil cakes weren't the only input whose price went up. As more firms entered the market, the price of hexane, another important raw material, also rose.

By 1993, most firms in the solvent extraction business—established firms as well as new entrants—were losing money. Some companies stuck it out, while others, facing better opportunities elsewhere, shut down their plants and exited the industry. This example illustrates that in an increasing-cost industry, such as the solvent extraction business in India, unrestricted entry can squeeze firms' profits in two ways: new entry drives down the price of the finished product, but it also drives up the price of industry-specific inputs whose supply is scarce. Many firms that entered the solvent extraction business underestimated this second effect.

As the 1990s ended, the solvent extraction market had begun to recover. This recovery was helped by a fall in the value of the rupee (the Indian currency), which made de-oiled cakes that were exported for cattle feed relatively cheap in the rest of the world, thus increasing industry demand. But even now, it is doubtful whether many firms make positive economic profits in this industry. Free entry took its toll. ∎

[26]We would like to thank Amol Patel for suggesting and researching this example.

In the preceding sections, we studied how price-taking firms adjust their production decisions in light of the market price. We also explored how the market price is determined. We now explore how we can describe the extent to which firms and input owners (e.g., providers of labor services or owners of land or capital) profit from their activities in perfectly competitive markets. We will introduce two concepts to describe the profitability of firms and input owners in perfectly competitive markets: economic rent and producer surplus.

ECONOMIC RENT

In the theory we have developed so far, we have assumed that all firms that operate in a perfectly competitive market have access to identical resources. This was reflected in our assumption that all active firms and potential entrants had the same long-run cost curves.

But in many industries some firms gain access to extraordinarily productive resources, while others do not. For example, in the rose industry, several thousand individuals might be good enough to be master growers, but only a handful are truly extraordinary master growers. The rose producers lucky enough to hire this handful will be more productive than firms that hire the merely good growers.

Economic rent measures the economic surplus that is attributable to an extraordinarily productive input whose supply is limited. Specifically, economic rent is equal to the difference between the maximum amount a firm is willing to pay for the services of the input and the input's **reservation value.** The input's reservation value, in turn, is the return that the input owner could get by deploying the input in its best alternative use outside the industry. Putting the pieces of this definition together we thus have:

$$\text{economic rent} = A - B,$$

where:

> A = maximum amount firm is willing to pay for services of input
>
> B = return that input owner gets by deploying the input
>   in its best alternative use outside the industry.

To illustrate this definition, suppose that the maximum amount that a rose firm would be willing to pay to hire an extraordinary master grower—the A term in our definition of economic rent—is equal to $105,000.[27] Suppose further that the grower's best available employment opportunity outside the rose industry is to work as a grower in the tulip industry for an annual salary of $70,000. This is the B term in our definition. The economic rent attributable to the extraordinary master grower is thus $105,000 − $70,000 = $35,000 per year.

Economic rent is frequently confused with economic profit. These concepts are related but distinct. To illustrate the difference between economic profit and economic rent, let's develop our rose growing example further. Suppose that every rose-producing firm needs one and only one master grower. Also suppose that

---

[27]Later in this section, we will see how we would determine this maximum willingness to pay.

there are two types of master growers: extraordinary and run of the mill. There is a limited number—let's say 20—of the former, but a virtually unlimited supply of the latter. Imagine that the reservation value of either type of master grower is $70,000 dollar per year, and for now, let's suppose that all master growers are paid an annual salary that equals this reservation value.

An extraordinary master grower can grow more roses with the same inputs (labor, capital, land, materials) than a run-of-the-mill master grower. Thus, as Figure 9.22 shows, when all master growers are paid the same annual salary of $70,000, a rose firm that employs an extraordinary master grower has lower average and marginal cost curves than a firm that employs a run-of-the-mill master grower [AC' and MC' in panel (a) versus AC and MC in panel (b)]. Note that the average cost curves, AC and AC', are the sum of two parts: the cost per unit for all of the expenses incurred by a rose firm *other* than the salary of the master grower (e.g., labor, materials, land, capital), and the master grower's salary per unit of output, which equals $70,000 divided by the number of roses produced. It is the "other expenses" that the firm economizes on if it employs an extraordinary master grower. Also note that because the master grower's salary is independent of the quantity of roses produced (i.e., the grower's salary is a fixed cost), the magnitude of the grower's salary does not influence the position of a rose

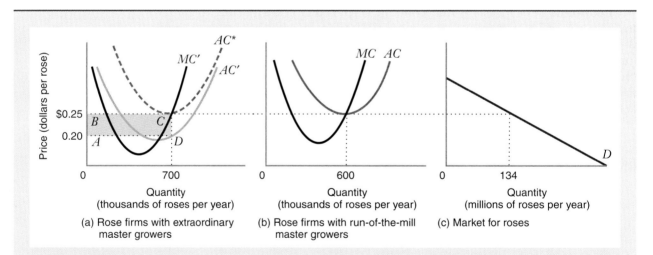

FIGURE 9.22   Economic Rent
Rose firms that employ extraordinary master growers have lower marginal cost curves (MC' versus MC) than firms that employ run-of-the-mill master growers. When all master growers are paid the same salary per year, they also have lower average cost curves (AC' versus AC). The equilibrium price of $0.25 per rose occurs at the minimum level of the long-run average cost of firms with run-of-the-mill master growers. At this price, firms with run-of-the-mill master growers produce 600,000 roses per year, while firms with extraordinary master growers produce 700,000 roses per year. The economic rent for extraordinary master growers is the area of rectangle ABCD. When all master growers are paid the same salary, this area is also the economic profit of firms that employ extraordinary master growers. However, with competition for extraordinary master growers, the salary for such growers would rise to a point at which the economic profit of firms with extraordinary master growers is zero. At this salary, firms that employ extraordinary master growers operate on average cost curve AC* and marginal cost curve MC'.

firm's *marginal* cost curve.[28] The difference between MC and MC' is attributable solely to the extra productivity that the firm gains from hiring a master grower.

Figure 9.22 shows the market equilibrium when all master growers are paid the same salary. A firm with a run-of-the-mill master grower produces 600,000 roses per year, its minimum efficient scale. A firm with an extraordinary master grower produces 700,000 roses per year, the point at which its marginal cost curve MC' intersects the equilibrium market price of $0.25 per rose. Total market demand for roses at $0.25 is 134 million roses. Of that, $20 \times 700,000 = 14$ million roses are supplied by the 20 firms that hire the 20 extraordinary master growers; the remaining 120 million roses are supplied by firms with run-of-the-mill master growers. Notice from Figure 9.22 that when a firm hires an extraordinary master grower at a salary of $70,000, its average cost is equal to $0.20 per rose. By contrast, a firm that hires a run-of-the-mill master grower at the same $70,000 annual salary has an average cost equal to the equilibrium price of $0.25 per rose. Thus, by employing an extraordinary master grower, a rose firm attains a cost savings of $0.05 per rose produced.

Now, let's identify the *economic rent* generated by an extraordinary master grower. In light of our definition above, we must first ask: What is the *maximum* salary that a firm would be willing to pay to hire an extraordinary master grower? The *most* that a firm would be willing to pay a master grower would be that salary—call it S^*—that makes this firm's economic profit equal to zero. At any higher salary, the firm would be better off dropping out of the industry. From Figure 9.22, we can see that paying this maximum salary of S^* would have to push a firm's average cost upward, from AC' to AC^*, so that at a quantity of 700,000, average cost just equals the market price of $0.25 per rose.[29] That is, a salary of S^* rather than $70,000 is just enough to offset the $0.05 per rose cost advantage created by the extraordinary grower's talent. The upward shift in the average cost curve is equal to the difference between the salary per unit at S^*, $S^*/700,000$, and the salary per unit at $70,000, or $70,000/700,000$, and this upward shift must be exactly equal to $0.05. Thus:

$$\frac{S^*}{700,000} - \frac{70,000}{700,000} = 0.05$$
$$S^* = \$105,000.$$

That is, the highest salary a rose firm would be willing to pay an extraordinary master grower is $105,000 per year. The economic rent is the difference between this maximum willingness to pay and a master grower's reservation value of $70,000:

$$\text{Economic rent} = \$105,000 - \$70,000 = \$35,000.$$

Notice that this economic rent of $35,000 corresponds to the shaded area $ABCD$ in Figure 9.22(a).[30]

---

[28]The grower's salary is an another example of a nonsunk fixed cost that we discussed earlier in the chapter and in Chapter 7. It is nonsunk because if a rose firm goes out of business, it can lay off its employees, including the master grower.

[29]Remember, the magnitude of the grower's salary does not affect the position of the rose firm's marginal cost curve, so a firm that hires an extraordinary master grower would still produce 700,000 roses per year, the point at which its (unshifting) MC' curve equals the market price of $0.25.

[30]This is because area $ABCD = (0.25 - 0.20) \times 700,000 = \$35,000$.

Now let's compute a rose firm's economic profit. Firms with run-of-the-mill master growers earn zero economic profit. By contrast, the 20 firms with the extraordinary master growers earn positive economic profit equal to their $0.05 per rose cost advantage times the number of roses they produce. This product equals the area of rectangle *ABCD*. When an extraordinary master grower is paid the same as a run-of-the-mill master grower, economic profit equals economic rent. That is, each of the 20 firms that employs an extraordinary master grower captures all of the economic rent for itself as positive economic profit. An extraordinary grower, by contrast, captures none of the economic rent that his or her talent generates. This is clearly a great outcome for a firm that is lucky enough to hire an extraordinary master grower.

But suppose that rose firms had to compete to hire the extraordinary master growers. This would be a market not unlike the market for free agents in major league baseball or professional basketball. The competition among rose firms to hire the best master growers would bid up the salaries of the extraordinary ones. If competition is sufficiently intense, the salaries of extraordinary master growers would be bid up to $105,000, the maximum a firm would be willing to pay. Firms with such master growers would then, in fact, operate on long-run average cost curve *AC**.[31] In a long-run equilibrium, these firms, like their run-of-the-mill counterparts, earn zero economic profit. The cost advantage due to employing an extra productive master grower is just offset by the higher salary that must be paid to lure the grower from other rose firms that also want to employ his or her services. The economic rent of the scarce input is still the area *ABCD*. In this case, though, the rent is captured by an extraordinary master grower as a "salary premium" above the reservation value of $70,000, rather than by rose firms as positive economic profit. If you like, you can think of this $35,000 salary premium ($105,000 − $70,000) as the economic profit earned by an extraordinary master grower.

In general, the salary of an extraordinary master grower could fall anywhere between $70,000 per year and $105,000. Depending on this salary, the economic profit of a rose firm that hires an extraordinary master grower would range between $35,000 and $0. Table 9.5 illustrates this point. The table shows that the economic rent is a *pie*, or a surplus that gets divided between firms and input owners. The economic rent is always $35,000, but economic profit depends on how the "rent pie" gets divided.

TABLE 9.5
Relationship Between Economic Rent and Economic Profit

Master Grower's Salary	Economic Profit of Firm that Employs Extraordinary Master Grower	"Salary Premium" (Part of Rent Captured by Extraordinary Master Grower)	Economic Rent Generated by Extraordinary Master Grower
$70,000	$35,000 (area *ABCD*)	$0	$35,000 (area *ABCD*)
$105,000	$0	$35,000	$35,000
Between $70,000 and $105,000	Between $35,000 and $0	Between $0 and $35,000	$35,000

[31]Recall that the marginal cost curves would be unaffected since a master grower's salary is a fixed cost.

The division of the economic rent between firms and master growers ultimately depends on resource mobility. If master growers can easily move from firm to firm, we would expect intense bidding for their services and master grower salaries close to firms' maximum willingness to pay $105,000. In this case, the economic profits of rose growers are dissipated through competition in the market to hire master growers (just as the profits of baseball teams are dissipated as they compete for talented free agents). If, by contrast, master growers cannot easily move from firm to firm, or if a master grower's extraordinary talent is specialized to a particular firm (i.e., the master grower is extraordinary for one particular firm but run-of-the-mill for all others), master grower salaries might not be bid up. If not, the economic rents would be captured by firms as positive economic profits.

PRODUCER SURPLUS

In Chapter 5, we introduced the concept of consumer surplus. Consumer surplus, as you might recall, was a monetary measure of the net benefit enjoyed by price-taking consumers from being able to purchase a product at the going market price. In Chapter 5, we saw that consumer surplus was the area between the demand curve and the market price.

In this section we show that there is an analogous concept for price-taking firms: **producer surplus.** Producer surplus is the area between the supply curve and the market price. Figure 9.23 shows the producer surplus for an individual

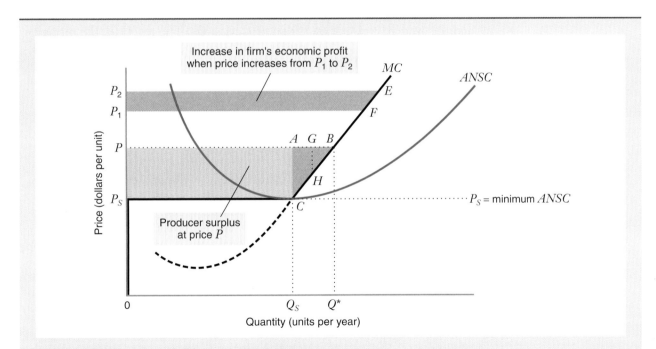

FIGURE 9.23 Producer Surplus for a Price-Taking Firm
The producer surplus at price P is equal to the area between the price and the supply curve, area $P_S PABC$. This area is equal to the difference between the firm's total revenue and its total nonsunk cost when it produces Q^* units of output. The change in producer surplus when the market price moves from P_1 to P_2 is equal to the shaded region $P_1 P_2 EF$. This is the change in the firm's economic profit that results when the market price increases from P_1 to P_2.

firm, and Figure 9.24 shows the producer surplus for the entire market. Just as consumer surplus provides a measure of the net benefit enjoyed by price-taking consumers from buying a product at a given market price, producer surplus provides a measure of the net benefit enjoyed by price-taking firms from supplying a product at a given market price.

Producer Surplus for an Individual Firm

To explain why this is so, let's begin by computing the producer surplus for an individual firm that faces a marginal cost curve MC and an average nonsunk cost curve $ANSC$ as shown in Figure 9.23. For the purpose of this discussion, it does not matter whether this firm operates in the short run or the long run. Recall that in the long run, all the firm's costs are nonsunk, and thus the $ANSC$ curve would correspond to the firm's long-run average cost curve.

Figure 9.23 shows the firm's supply curve. The supply curve is a vertical spike up to the shut-down price of P_S and the rising portion of MC beyond this price. If, for example, the market price is P, the firm would supply Q^* units.

The firm's producer surplus at the price P is the area between the supply curve and the market price, or the area of region $P_S PABC$. To show what this area equals, let's divide it into two parts: triangle ABC and the rectangle $P_S PAC$ and interpret the area of each part.

- Rectangle $P_S PAC$: Notice that P_S is equal to the average nonsunk cost at Q_S. The height of this rectangle is thus the difference between the market price P and the average nonsunk cost from producing Q_S. The length of the rectangle is equal to output Q_S. Therefore, the entire rectangle must correspond to the difference between the firm's total revenue and its total nonsunk cost if it produced Q_S units of output. Recalling that total nonsunk cost is the sum of total variable cost and the firm's nonsunk fixed costs:

$$\text{area of } P_S PAC = \text{total revenues} - \text{total variable cost} - \text{nonsunk fixed}$$
$$\text{cost if firm produces } Q_S.$$

- Triangle ABC: To determine what this area means, suppose the firm expands its output from Q_S units (the point at which the average nonsunk cost curve reaches its minimum) to Q^*. For each additional unit of output the firm produces in this range, its profit goes up by the difference between the price P and the marginal cost MC of that additional unit. At any quantity, this difference is the height of a line segment (such as GH) that connects the top and the bottom of triangle ABC. The total area of ABC is the sum of the heights of each of these line segments. This means that the area of triangle ABC corresponds to the increase in profit that the firm enjoys when it expands its output from Q_S to Q^*, or equivalently,

$$\text{Area of } ABC = \text{increase in total revenues} - \text{increase in total variable cost}$$
$$\text{if firm expands output from } Q_S \text{ to } Q^*.$$

Let's now add together these two areas.

$$P_S PAC + ABC =$$

(total revenue − total variable cost − nonsunk fixed cost if firm produces Q_S) + (increase in total revenue − increase in total variable cost if firm expands output from Q_S to Q^*)

Thus, producer surplus = total revenues − total variable cost − nonsunk fixed cost if firm produces Q^*. That is, the producer surplus for an individual firm is equal to the difference between its total revenue and its total nonsunk costs. We can take this a step further and distinguish between the producer surplus of a firm that operates in the short run and the long run:

- In the short run, when some of the firm's fixed costs might be sunk, a firm's producer surplus and its economic profit are not equal. They differ by the extent of the firm's sunk fixed costs. In particular:

$$producer\ surplus = economic\ profit + sunk\ fixed\ costs$$

- In the long run, when all of the firm's costs are nonsunk (i.e., avoidable), producer surplus and economic profit are identical:

$$producer\ surplus = economic\ profit$$

Notice that in both cases the *difference* in producer surplus at one market price and producer surplus at another price is equal to the difference in the firm's economic profits at these two prices. Thus, for example, in Figure 9.23, area P_1P_2EF is the increase in economic profit that the firm enjoys when the price increases from P_1 to P_2.

Producer Surplus for the Entire Market: Fixed Number of Firms

Let's now move from the producer surplus of an individual firm to the producer surplus for the entire industry when the number of producers in the industry is fixed and input prices do not change as industry output expands. In this case, the market supply curve is the horizontal summation of the supply curves of individual producers, as is shown in Figure 9.24. When this is so, the area below the market price and above the market supply curve—the producer surplus from the entire market—must equal the sum of the producer surpluses of the individual firms in the market.

Figure 9.24 illustrates this point for a market that consists of 1,000 identical firms, each with a supply curve *ss*. The market supply curve in Figure 9.24(b), *SS*, is the horizontal summation of these individual supply curves. The area between this supply curve and the price—the producer surplus for the entire market— equals total market revenue minus the total nonsunk costs of all firms in the industry. For example, when the price is $10 per unit, each individual firm in Figure 9.24 produces 200 units per year and has a producer surplus equal to area *ABCD*, which in this case equals $350.[32] Total market supply at $10 is equal to 200,000 units per year, and the area between the market supply curve and price, area *EFGH*, is equal to $350,000. This is the combined producer surplus of 1,000 individual firms, each with a producer surplus of $350 ($350,000 = $350 × 1,000). The market-level producer surplus of $350,000 is thus the difference between the total revenue of all 1,000 firms and their total nonsunk costs.

---

[32]The area of *ABCD* equals (10 − 8) × 150 plus (1/2) × (10 − 8) × (200 − 150), which equals 350.

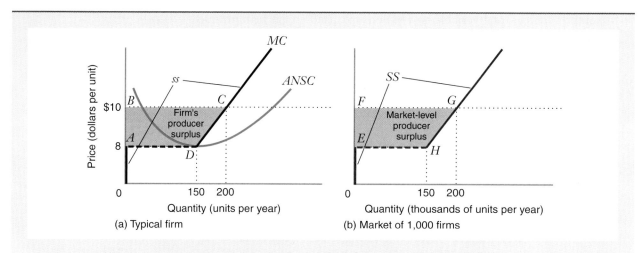

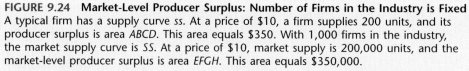

FIGURE 9.24   Market-Level Producer Surplus: Number of Firms in the Industry is Fixed
A typical firm has a supply curve *ss*. At a price of $10, a firm supplies 200 units, and its producer surplus is area *ABCD*. This area equals $350. With 1,000 firms in the industry, the market supply curve is *SS*. At a price of $10, market supply is 200,000 units, and the market-level producer surplus is area *EFGH*. This area equals $350,000.

EXAMPLE 9.9   *Producer Surplus in the World Copper Market*

In the late 1990s, the world copper market was rocked by declining demand and falling prices. Not surprisingly, the profits of most major copper producers fell. We can use the concept of producer surplus in the previous section, along with the world supply curve for copper that we presented in Example 9.3, to illustrate the impact of falling copper prices on industry producer surplus.

In early 1998, the price of copper was about 90 cents a pound. By early 1999, the price had fallen to about 70 cents a pound, a drop of about 22 percent. Figure 9.25 shows the resultant decrease in market-level producer surplus: the shaded region *ABCD* in Figure 9.25(b). This is roughly equal to $1,774 million.[33] This is a significant decrease. The producer surplus at a price of 90 cents per pound—the area between the supply curve and a price of 90 cents—is approximately $3,573 million. The 22 percent drop in copper prices during 1999 reduced industry producer surplus by almost 50 percent.

Part of the drop in industry producer surplus was because some high-cost mines that were profitable at a price of 90 cents were no longer profitable at a price of 70 cents. These high-cost mines significantly reduced their operations or shut down altogether. But much of the drop in producer surplus is due to the fact that many lower-cost mines—such as the Bingham Canyon mine described

---

[33]We computed this figure using calculus. Area *ABCD* is total industry revenue (industry price times quantity supplied) minus the area underneath the supply curve. The equation of the supply curve shown in panel (b) of Figure 9.25 is $P = 32.54 + .00378Q + 14.01(Q/8926)^{20.73}$, and the area underneath the supply curve is the integral of this expression between 0 and the quantity supplied.

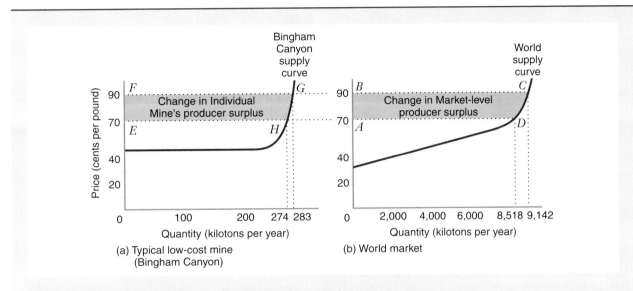

FIGURE 9.25 Producer Surplus in the World Copper Market
Area *ABCD* in panel (b) shows the reduction in industry-wide producer surplus when the price of copper dropped from 90 cents per pound to 70 cents per pound. This area is approximately equal to $1,774 million. Area *EFGH* in panel (a) shows the reduction in producer surplus for a particular mine, the Bingham Canyon mine in Utah, with medium to low costs, that continues to produce at close to full capacity despite the drop in price.

in Example 9.3 and whose supply curve is reproduced in Figure 9.25(a)[34]—continued to operate at near full capacity but at lower profits margins. These mines were less profitable to operate when copper sold at 70 cents a pound rather than 90 cents a pound, as indicated by the shaded region *EFGH*. But their owners still earned higher profits by keeping them open rather than shutting them down. ∎

Producer Surplus for the Entire Market: Long Run with Free Entry

The concept of producer surplus becomes more subtle when we consider the long-run perfectly competitive equilibrium with free entry. This is because, as we discussed in the previous section, the long-run industry supply curve no longer corresponds to the horizontal summation of the supply curves of individual firms.

To illustrate, consider Figure 9.26. Panel (a) shows a typical price-taking firm in an increasing-cost industry (i.e., an industry with an upward-sloping long-run industry supply curve). At the equilibrium price P^*, this firm earns zero economic profit, as do all other firms in the industry. Yet, according to Figure 9.26(b), industry producer surplus is positive (area FP^*E). But if all firms earn zero profit, area FP^*E cannot represent the economic profit of the firms in the industry. What is it then?

[34]This is a close-up picture of the graph of Bingham Canyon's supply curve in Figure 9.7.

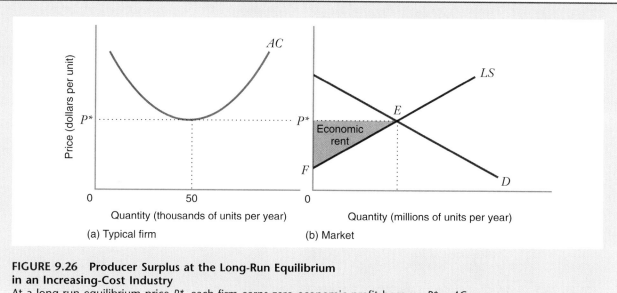

FIGURE 9.26   Producer Surplus at the Long-Run Equilibrium in an Increasing-Cost Industry
At a long-run equilibrium price P^*, each firm earns zero economic profit because $P^* = AC$. The area between the supply curve and the market price, area FP^*E, equals the economic rent that goes to the inputs whose supply is scarce.

We can clear up this mystery when we recall that a perfectly competitive industry has an upward-sloping long-run supply curve because firms must compete for the services of a scarce input (e.g., extra talented master growers in the rose industry). As we discussed in the previous section on economic rent, the result of such competition is that the economic rents are fully captured by the owners of the input. Thus, area FP^*E is not the economic profit of firms (that is equal to zero). Rather it is the economic rent that is captured by owners of scarce industry-specific inputs. For example, if the market in Figure 9.26 is the rose market, then area FP^*E is the salary earned by the master growers above and beyond the minimum salary that would be necessary to induce them to supply their services to a rose firm.

ECONOMIC PROFIT, PRODUCER SURPLUS, ECONOMIC RENT

Let's conclude this section by summarizing the relationship between the three measures of performance that we have discussed in this chapter: economic profit, producer surplus, and economic rent.

Let's start by summarizing what we know about the relationship between economic profit and producer surplus for an *individual firm*:

For an individual firm operating in the short run (i.e., a firm that has sunk fixed costs):

$$\text{Economic profit} = \text{total revenues} - \text{total costs.}$$

$$\text{Producer surplus} = \text{total revenues} - \text{total nonsunk costs.}$$

In this case, producer surplus is bigger than economic profit, but the difference between producer surplus at two market prices will equal the difference in the firm's economic profit at these prices.

For an individual firm operating in the long run (and thus facing no sunk costs):

$$\text{Economic profit} = \text{total revenues} - \text{total costs.}$$

$$\text{Producer surplus} = \text{total revenues} - \text{total costs.}$$

In this case, producer surplus and economic profit are identical.

Let's next summarize the relationship between economic profit and producer surplus for a *market with a fixed number of firms* (i.e., there is no entry or exit):

$$\text{Economic profit for industry} = \text{total revenues} - \text{total costs.}$$

$$\text{Producer surplus for industry} = \text{total revenues} - \text{total nonsunk costs.}$$

Thus, the market-level producer surplus exceeds the total economic profit in the market by the extent of sunk fixed costs. However, the difference between producer surplus at two different prices equals the difference in industry economic profit at these prices.

Finally, let's summarize the relationship between economic profit, economic rent, and the area between the supply curve and the long-run equilibrium price in an industry with an upward-sloping long-run supply curve (i.e., an increasing-cost industry):

$$\text{Economic profit for industry} = 0.$$

$$\text{Economic rent} > 0.$$

In an increasing-cost industry, the area between the long-run supply curve and the long-run equilibrium price does not measure the economic profits of firms in the industry; rather, it tells us the economic rents captured by owners of scarce industry-specific inputs.

CHAPTER SUMMARY

- Perfectly competitive markets have four characteristics: firms produce undifferentiated products, consumers have perfect information about prices, the industry is fragmented, and all firms have equal access to resources. These characteristics imply that output sells at a single price, firms act as price takers, and the industry is characterized by free entry.

- Marginal revenue is the additional revenue a firm generates by selling one additional unit or the revenue it sacrifices by producing one fewer unit.

- A price-taking firm's marginal revenue curve is a horizontal line equal to market price.

- A price-taking firm maximizes its profit by producing an output level at which marginal cost equals the market price, and marginal cost is upward sloping.

- If all fixed costs are sunk, a perfectly competitive firm will produce positive output in the short-run only if the market price for its output exceeds average variable cost. The shut-down price—the price below which the firm produces zero output—is the minimum level of average variable cost. **(LBD Exercise 9.1)**

- If some fixed costs are nonsunk, the firm produces positive output only if price exceeds average nonsunk costs. The shut-down price is the minimum level of average nonsunk cost. **(LBD Exercise 9.2)**

- If input prices do not change as market output varies, the short-run market supply is the sum of the short-run supplies of individual firms.

- The short-run equilibrium price equates market demand to short-run market supply. **(LBD Exercise 9.3)**

- The price elasticity of supply measures the percentage change in quantity supplied for each percent change in price.

- In the long run, perfectly competitive firms can adjust their plant sizes and thus maximize profit by producing a quantity at which long-run marginal cost equals price.

- In the long run, free entry drives the market price to the minimum level of long-run average cost. If firms have identical U-shaped long-run average cost curves, each firm supplies a quantity equal to its minimum efficient scale. The equilibrium number of firms is such that total market supply equals the quantity demanded at the equilibrium price.   **(LBD Exercise 9.4)**

- In a constant-cost industry, the expansion of industry output that occurs as firms enter the industry does not affect market price. The long-run market supply curve is horizontal.

- In an increasing-cost industry, the expansion of industry output that occurs as firms enter the industry increases the prices of industry-specific inputs. The long-run market supply curve is upward sloping.

- The economic rent of a scarce input is the difference between a firm's maximum willingness to pay for a scarce input and the input's reservation value. When a firm captures the scarce input's economic rent, it earns positive economic profits. Competition for the scarce input, however, will dissipate these profits. In this case, economic rent is positive while economic profit is zero.

- Producer surplus is the area above the supply curve below the market price.

- For a firm with sunk fixed costs, producer surplus differs from economic profit. In particular, producer surplus equals the difference between total revenues and total non-sunk costs, while economic profit equals the difference between total revenues and all total costs. If the firm has no sunk fixed costs, producer surplus equals economic profit.

- For a market consisting of a fixed number of firms, the market-level producer surplus is the area between the short-run supply curve and the market price. It equals the sum of the producer surpluses of individual firms in the market.

- In a market in which the long-run industry supply curve is upward sloping, the area between the price and the long-run supply curve measures the economic rents of inputs that are in scarce supply and whose price is bid up as more firms enter the industry.

REVIEW QUESTIONS

1. What is the difference between accounting profit and economic profit? How could a firm earn positive accounting profit but negative economic profit?

2. Why is the marginal revenue of a perfectly competitive firm equal to the market price?

3. Would a perfectly competitive firm produce if price is less than the minimum level of average variable cost? Would it produce if price is less than the minimum level of short-run average cost?

4. What is the shut-down price when all fixed costs are sunk? What is the shut-down price when all fixed costs are nonsunk?

5. How does the price elasticity of supply affect changes in the short-run equilibrium price that results from an exogenous shift in the market demand curve?

6. Consider two perfectly competitive industries— Industry 1 and Industry 2. Each faces identical demand and cost conditions except that the minimum efficient scale output in Industry 1 is twice that of Industry 2. In a long-run perfectly competitive equilibrium, which industry will have more firms?

7. What is economic rent? How does it differ from economic profit?

8. What is the producer surplus for an individual firm? What is the producer surplus for a market when the number of firms in the industry is fixed and input prices do not vary as industry output changes? When is producer surplus equal to economic profit (for either a firm or industry)? When producer surplus and economic profit are not equal, which is bigger?

9. In the long-run equilibrium in an increasing-cost industry, each firm earns zero economic profits. Yet, there is a positive area between the long-run industry supply curve and the long-run equilibrium price. What is this area?

10. Explain the difference between the following concepts: producer surplus, economic profit, and economic rent.

9.1. Ron's Window Washing Service is a small business that operates in the perfectly competitive residential window washing industry in Evanston, Illinois. The short-run total cost of production is

$$STC(Q) = 40 + 10Q + 0.1Q^2,$$

where Q is the number of windows washed per day. The corresponding short-run marginal cost function is

$$SMC(Q) = 10 + 0.2Q.$$

The prevailing market price is $20 per window.
a) How many windows should Ron wash to maximize profit?
b) What is Ron's maximum daily profit?
c) Graph SMC, SAC, and the profit-maximizing quantity. On this graph, indicate the maximum daily profit.
d) What is Ron's short-run supply curve, assuming that all of the $40 per day fixed costs are sunk?
e) What is Ron's short-run supply curve, assuming that if he produces zero output, he can rent or sell his fixed assets and therefore avoid all his fixed costs?

9.2. The bolt industry currently consists of 20 producers, all of whom operate with identical short-run total cost functions

$$STC(Q) = 16 + Q^2,$$

where Q is the annual output of a firm. The corresponding short-run marginal cost curve is

$$SMC(Q) = 2Q.$$

The market demand curve for bolts is

$$D(P) = 110 - P,$$

where P is the market price.

a) Assuming that all of the firm's $16 fixed cost is sunk, what is a firm's short-run supply curve?
b) What is the short-run market supply curve?
c) Determine the short-run equilibrium price and quantity in this industry.

9.3. A market contains a group of identical firms. Each firm acts as a price taker and has a short-run total cost function

$$STC(Q) = 250 + Q^2,$$

where Q is the annual output of each firm. The corresponding marginal cost curve is

$$SMC(Q) = 2Q.$$

A study reveals that part of the $250 fixed cost is sunk, and each firm will produce if the price exceeds $20 per unit and will shut down if price is less than $20 per unit. The market demand curve for the industry is

$$D(P) = 240 - \frac{1}{2}P,$$

where P is the market price.
a) How much of the fixed cost is sunk for each firm?
b) At the current market price, each firm produces 20 units. What is the market price and how many firms are in this industry?

9.4. The wood-pallet market contains many identical firms, each with a short-run total cost function

$$STC(Q) = 400 + 5Q + Q^2,$$

where Q is a firm's annual output (and all of a firm's $400 fixed cost is sunk). The corresponding marginal cost function is

$$SMC(Q) = 5 + 2Q.$$

The market demand curve for this industry is

$$D(P) = 262.5 - \frac{1}{2}P,$$

where P is the market price. Each firm in the industry is currently earning zero economic profit. How many firms are in this industry, and what is the market equilibrium price?

9.5. The semiconductor market consists of 100 identical firms, each with short-run total cost curve

$$STC(Q) = TFC + 2Q^2$$

where Q is a firm's annual output in thousands of semiconductors per year and TFC is the firm's total fixed cost. The corresponding short-run marginal cost curve is

$$SMC(Q) = 4Q.$$

The current market price is $P = \$200$.
a) Assuming that all of the firm's fixed costs are sunk, what is the producer surplus of an individual firm?
b) What is the overall producer surplus for the market?
c) What is the maximum level of fixed costs such that firms in this market make positive economic profit?

9.6. During the week of February 9–15, 2001, the U.S. rose market cleared at a price of $1.00 per stem, and 4,000,000 stems were sold that week. During the week of June 5–11, 2001, the U.S. rose market cleared at a price of $0.20 per stem, and 3,800,000 stems were sold that week. From this information, what would you conclude about the price elasticity of supply in the U.S. rose market?

9.7. Propylene is used to make plastic. The propylene industry is perfectly competitive, and each producer has a long-run marginal cost function given by

$$MC(Q) = 40 - 12Q + Q^2.$$

The corresponding long-run average cost function is

$$AC(Q) = 40 - 6Q + \frac{1}{3}Q^2.$$

The market demand curve for propylene is

$$D(P) = 2200 - 100P.$$

a) What is the long-run equilibrium price in this industry?
b) At this price, how much would an individual firm produce?
c) How many firms are in the propylene market in a long-run competitive equilibrium?
d) Suppose the demand curve shifted so that it is now

$$D(P) = A - 100P.$$

How large would A have to be so that in the new long-run competitive equilibrium, the number of propylene firms was twice what it was in the initial long-run equilibrium?

9.8. The long-run total cost function for producers of mineral water is

$$TC(Q) = cQ,$$

where Q is the output of an individual firm expressed as thousands of liters per year. The market demand curve is

$$D(P) = a - bP.$$

Find the long-run equilibrium price and quantity in terms of a, b, and c. Can you determine the equilibrium number of firms? If so, what is it? If not, why not?

9.9. In a constant-cost industry in which firms have U-shaped average cost curves, the long-run market supply curve is a horizontal line. This market supply curve is not the horizontal summation of firms' long-run supply curves. In this respect, the long-run market supply curve

differs from the short-run market supply curve which, in a constant-cost industry, will equal the horizontal summation of firms' short-run supply curves. Why does the derivation of the long-run market supply curve differ from the derivation of the short-run market supply curve?

9.10. The long-run average cost for production of hard-disk drives is given by

$$AC(Q) = \sqrt{wr}(120 - 20Q + Q^2)$$

where Q is the annual output of a firm, w is the wage rate for skilled assembly labor, and r is the price of capital services. The corresponding long-run marginal cost curve is

$$MC(Q) = \sqrt{wr}(120 - 40Q + 3Q^2).$$

Suppose, further, that the demand for labor for an individual firm is

$$L(Q, w, r) = \frac{\sqrt{r}[120Q - 20Q^2 + Q^3]}{2\sqrt{w}}.$$

Let's suppose throughout this problem that the price of capital services is fixed at $r = 1$.

a) In a long-run competitive equilibrium, how much output will each firm produce?
b) In a long-run competitive equilibrium, what will be the market price? Note that your answer will be expressed as a function of w.
c) At a long-run competitive equilibrium, how much skilled labor will each firm demand? Again, your answer will depend on w.
d) Now, suppose that the market demand curve is given by

$$D(P) = \frac{10,000}{P}.$$

What is the market equilibrium quantity as a function of w?

e) What is the long-run equilibrium number of firms as a function of w?
f) Using your answers to parts (c) and (e), what is the overall demand for skilled labor in this industry as a function of w?
g) Suppose that the supply curve for the skilled labor used in this industry is given by

$$\Gamma(w) = 50w.$$

At what value of w does the supply of skilled labor equal the demand for skilled labor?

h) Using your answer from part g, go back through parts b, d, and e to determine the long-run equilibrium price, market demand, and number of firms in this industry.

i) Repeat the analysis in this problem, now assuming that the market demand curve is given by

$$D(P) = \frac{20,000}{P}$$

9.11. Consider an industry in which chief executive officers (CEOs) run firms. There are two types of CEOs: exceptional and average. There is a fixed supply of 100 exceptional CEOs and an unlimited supply of average CEOs. Any individual capable of being a CEO in this industry is willing to work for a salary of $144,000 per year. The long-run total cost of a firm that hires an exceptional CEO at this salary is

$$TC_E(Q) = \begin{cases} 144 + \dfrac{1}{2}Q^2, & \text{if } Q > 0. \\ 0 & \text{if } Q = 0. \end{cases}$$

where Q is annual output in thousands of units, and total cost is expressed in thousands of dollars per year. The corresponding long-run marginal cost curve is

$$MC_E(Q) = Q,$$

where marginal cost is expressed as dollars per unit. The long-run total cost for a firm that hires an average CEO for $144,000 per year is

$$TC_A(Q) = 144 + Q^2.$$

The corresponding marginal cost curve is

$$MC_A(Q) = 2Q.$$

The market demand curve in this market is

$$D(P) = 7200 - 100P,$$

where P is the market price and $D(P)$ is the market quantity, expressed in thousands of units per year.

a) What is the minimum efficient scale for a firm run by an average CEO? What is the minimum level of long-run average cost for such firms?

b) What is the long-run equilibrium price in this industry, assuming that it consists of firms with both exceptional and average CEOs?

c) At this price, how much output will a firm with an average CEO produce? How much output will a firm with an exceptional CEO produce?

d) At this price, how much output will be demanded?

e) Using your answers to parts (c) and (d), how many firms with average CEOs will there be in this industry at a long-run equilibrium?

f) What is the economic rent attributable to an exceptional CEO?

g) If firms with exceptional CEOs hire them at the reservation wage of $144,000 per year, how much economic profit do these firms make?

h) Assuming that firms bid against each other for the services of exceptional CEOs, what would you expect their salaries to be in a long-run competitive equilibrium?

APPENDIX: Profit Maximization Implies Cost Minimization

In Chapters 7 and 8, we studied decision making by firms that chose an input combination to minimize the total cost of producing a given level of output. In this chapter, we studied the output choice of a price-taking firm seeking to maximize profit. How are these analyses related?

Intimately. In particular, *profit-maximizing output choice implies cost-minimizing input choices,* or in short, *profit maximization implies cost minimization.* To develop this point, note that we could study the profit-maximization problem of a price-taking firm in two ways:

- *The input choice method:* We could view the firm as choosing *inputs* (e.g., quantities of capital and labor) to maximize profits, recognizing that these input choices determine the firm's output through the production function.

- *The input choice method:* We could view the firm as choosing *inputs* (e.g., quantities of capital and labor) to maximize profits, recognizing that these input choices determine the firm's output through the production function.
- *The output choice method:* We could view the firm as first choosing *output* and then choosing input quantities to minimize total costs, given the selected output level.

We used the output choice method in this chapter. To persuade you that profit maximization implies cost minimization, we will show you here that the input choice method implies that a profit-maximizing firm *must* produce its output with a cost-minimizing input combination. That, in turn, implies that the output choice method and the input choice method, though analytically different, are equivalent approaches to analyzing the behavior of a profit-maximizing firm.

Suppose that a firm uses two inputs, capital and labor. Input prices are w and r, respectively. The firm's production function is $Q = f(L, K)$. This firm is a price-taker in the output and input markets (i.e., it takes as given the market price P and the input prices, w and r). The firm chooses quantities of its inputs, L and K, recognizing that output is determined through the production function $f(L, K)$. We can thus state the firm's profit maximization problem this way:

$$\max_{(L,K)} \pi(L, K) = Pf(L, K) - wL - rK.$$

The first term $pf(L, K)$ is the firm's total revenue (i.e., market price multiplied by the volume of output). The last two terms are the total labor costs and total capital costs, respectively. The expression $\pi(L, K)$ denotes the firm's total profit as a function of its choices of labor and capital.

Profit maximization implies two conditions:

$$\frac{\partial \pi}{\partial L} = P\frac{\partial f}{\partial L} - w = 0 \Rightarrow P = \frac{MP_L}{w}. \tag{A9.1}$$

$$\frac{\partial \pi}{\partial K} = P\frac{\partial f}{\partial K} - r = 0 \Rightarrow P = \frac{MP_K}{r}. \tag{A9.2}$$

In writing these expressions, we have used the notation for marginal product that we introduced in Chapter 6 and used frequently in Chapter 7.

These two conditions say that a profit-maximizing firm will choose its inputs so that the additional output that the firm gets from every additional dollar spent on labor (i.e., MP_L/w) equals the market price and the additional output that the firm gets from every additional dollar spent on capital (i.e., MP_K/r) also equals the market price. This implies that, given the profit maximizing input choices,

$$\frac{MP_L}{w} = \frac{MP_K}{r}. \tag{A9.3}$$

But this is the condition for cost minimization derived in Chapter 7. Thus, of the many input combinations that the firm might use to produce its output, condition (A9.3) tells us that the profit maximizing firm employs the cost-minimizing one. Thus, *profit maximization implies cost minimization*.

10

Competitive Markets: Applications

Price and income support programs are commonplace in the world. In the United States, major agricultural programs have been around since the 1930s. Government expenditures on these programs have ranged in the billions of dollars annually, especially prior to 1996, when Congress passed a major farm bill that eliminated or reduced many of the program benefits. Historically, Congress has required the Department of Agriculture to support the prices of about twenty commodities, including sugar (sugar cane and beets), cotton, rice, feed grains (including corn, barley oats, rye, and sorghum), peanuts, wheat, tobacco, milk, soybeans and various types of oil seeds (such as sunflower seed, mustard seed). During the fiscal years between 1983 and 1992, govern-

ment expenditures on agricultural programs like the ones described here were more than $140 billion.

Price support programs can take many forms. For example, under "acreage limitation programs" wheat or feed grain farmers agree to restrict the number of acres they plant. In exchange, the government gives the farmers an option to sell their crops to the government at a guaranteed price. Farmers are not required to sell their crops to the government, and would not do so if the market price exceeds the guaranteed price. But a farmer will take the option to sell to the government if the market price is lower than the guaranteed price. Further, because an acreage limitation program reduces the amount of the crop on the market, the market price is higher than it otherwise would be.

Other programs have supported prices for other commodities. For example, the government has supported the price of peanuts by establishing "poundage quotas," limiting the quantity of edible peanuts that a farmer could sell. For many years domestic sugar producers have relied on restrictive import quotas to raise sugar prices in the United States. The government has also supported tobacco prices by restricting production to certain farms and by limiting the amounts that those farms could produce.

Acreage limitation programs, subsidies, and import and production quotas are all forms of government intervention. In this chapter we will learn how to analyze the consequences of government intervention in *perfectly competitive* markets. Since there are many small consumers and producers of agricultural commodities, agricultural markets have the structural features of perfect competition. Absent price supports, the forces of supply and demand would lead to a competitive equilibrium and an economically efficient allocation of agricultural resources.

We will learn how programs of government intervention move the market away from a competitive equilibrium, creating "distortions" in the market as economic resources are reallocated. We will also find that intervention typically makes some people better off, while leaving others worse off, helping us to understand how the lines for debates over public policy are drawn. For example, farmers who benefit from price supports often organize themselves into a tightly focused interest group that fights hard to retain the

government programs, while some consumer groups and taxpayers may oppose the programs.

In this chapter we will analyze several forms of government intervention:

- Imposing excise taxes
- Granting subsidies to producers
- Regulating the maximum price producers may charge
- Regulating the minimum price producers may charge
- Setting quotas limiting the amount that may be produced in a market
- Imposing tariffs or quotas on imports

Before we begin, note some important points as we study the effects of government intervention. In this chapter, we will use a **partial equilibrium** approach, usually focusing on only a single market. For example, we may examine the effect of rent controls on the market for housing. A partial equilibrium approach will not allow us to ask how rent controls affect prices in other markets, including the market for housing that is not rented, and the markets for furniture, automobiles, and computers. To examine how a change in one market affects all markets simultaneously, we would need to employ a **general equilibrium** model. A general equilibrium analysis determines the equilibrium prices and quantities in all markets simultaneously. We will introduce you to this more complex form of analysis in Chapter 16. The

conclusions we draw from a partial equilibrium analysis may not be the same as those found with a general equilibrium approach. Nevertheless, a partial equilibrium framework can often be used to provide important insights about the primary effects of government intervention.

In this chapter we examine markets that would be perfectly competitive absent government intervention. As we observed in Chapter 9, in a competitive market all producers and consumers are fragmented; that is, they are so small in the market that they behave as price takers. If decision makers have the ability to influence the price in the market, we cannot use supply and demand analysis. Instead, we would need to apply an appropriate model of market power, such as the ones discussed in Chapters 11–14.

As we also learned in Chapter 9, in a perfectly competitive market consumers have perfect information about the nature of the product being provided, as well as the price of the product. Sometimes governments intervene in markets because consumers are unable to gather enough information about the products in the market. For example, the health care sector would seem to have a competitive structure, with many providers and consumers of health care services. Yet health care products, including medication and medical procedures, can be so complex that the average consumer finds it difficult to make informed choices. Government intervention in this sector is often designed to protect

consumers in such a complicated market.

In perfectly competitive markets there are no **externalities.** Externalities are present in a market if the actions of either consumers or producers lead to costs or benefits that are not reflected in the price of the product in that market. For example, a production externality will be present if a producer pollutes the environment. Pollution creates a social cost that might be ignored by a producer absent government intervention. A consumption externality exists when the action of an individual consumer imposes costs on, or leads to benefits for, other consumers. For example, zoning ordinances in housing markets are often intended to ensure that consumers of housing do not undertake activities that reduce the value of property owned by others in a neighborhood. In this chapter we do not consider the effects of externalities; instead, we will address them in Chapter 17.

Finally, throughout this chapter we use consumer surplus to measure how much better off or worse off a consumer is when intervention affects the price in the market. As we showed in Chapter 5, consumer surplus may not always be a good way to measure the impact of a price change on a consumer. For some goods (for example, for goods with large income effects), it may be important to measure the effects of price changes on consumers by examining compensating or equivalent variations instead of using changes in consumer surplus. ◼

10.1

THE INVISIBLE HAND

One of the main lessons from the study of perfectly competitive markets is the following: In a long-run equilibrium, a competitive market allocates resources efficiently. Figure 10.1 illustrates the economically efficient allocation of resources in a partial equilibrium model of a single market. In a competitive equilibrium, the market price is $8, with 6 million units per year exchanged in the market.

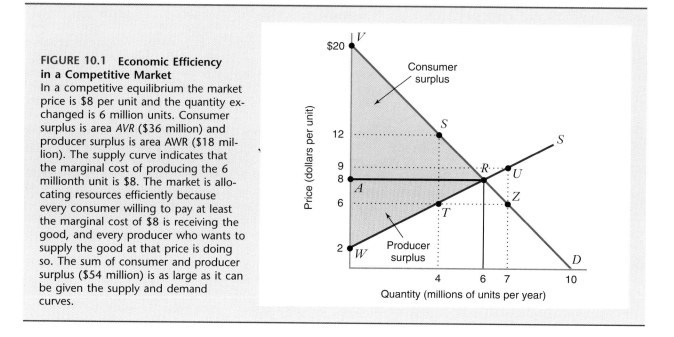

FIGURE 10.1   Economic Efficiency in a Competitive Market
In a competitive equilibrium the market price is $8 per unit and the quantity exchanged is 6 million units. Consumer surplus is area *AVR* ($36 million) and producer surplus is area *AWR* ($18 million). The supply curve indicates that the marginal cost of producing the 6 millionth unit is $8. The market is allocating resources efficiently because every consumer willing to pay at least the marginal cost of $8 is receiving the good, and every producer who wants to supply the good at that price is doing so. The sum of consumer and producer surplus ($54 million) is as large as it can be given the supply and demand curves.

The sum of consumer and producer surplus will be *VRW,* the area below the demand curve and above the supply curve, or $54 million per year.

Why it is economically efficient for the market to produce 6 million units? Let's answer this by asking why it is *not* efficient to produce some other level of output. For example, why is it not efficient for the market to produce only 4 million units? The demand curve tells us that some consumer is willing to pay $12 for the 4 millionth unit. Yet the supply curve reveals that it only costs society $6 to produce that unit. (Remember, the supply curve indicates the marginal cost of producing the next unit in the market.) Thus, total surplus would be increased by $6 (that is, $12 − $6) if the 4 millionth unit is produced. When the demand curve lies above the supply curve, total surplus will increase if another unit is produced. If output is expanded from 4 to 6 million units, total surplus will increase by area *RST,* or $6 million.

Is it efficient for the market to produce 7 million units? The demand curve indicates that the consumer of the last unit is willing to pay $6. But the supply curve shows that it costs $9 to produce that unit. Thus, total surplus would be *decreased* by $3 (that is, $6 − $9) if the 7 millionth unit is produced. When the demand curve lies below the supply curve, total surplus will decrease if the next unit is produced. In other words, net benefits can be increased by *cutting back* production when the demand curve lies below the supply curve. If output is cut back from 7 to 6 million units, total surplus will increase by area *RUZ,* or $1.5 million.

To sum up, the efficient (surplus-maximizing) level of output is the one determined by the intersection of the supply and demand curves. Any production level other than 6 million units per year will lead to net benefits smaller than $54 million per year in total surplus.

This brings us to a second major lesson. In a perfectly competitive market each producer acts in its own self interest, deciding whether to be in the market, and, if so, how much to produce to maximize its own producer surplus. Further, each consumer also acts in his or her own self interest, maximizing utility to determine how many units of the good to buy. There is no grand social planner telling producers and consumers how to behave so that the efficient level of output is produced. Nevertheless, *the output in the competitive market is the one that maximizes net economic benefits* (as measured by the sum of the surpluses). As Adam Smith described it in his classic treatise in 1776 (*An Inquiry into the Nature and Causes of the Wealth of Nations*), it is as though there is an "Invisible Hand" guiding a competitive market to the efficient level of production and consumption.[1]

10.2
IMPACT OF AN EXCISE TAX

Economists often use a partial equilibrium model to study the effects of a tax on a competitive market. For example, we might ask how a gasoline tax will affect the market for gasoline. As we have already observed, a partial equilibrium approach is limited to capturing the effects of a tax on the particular market being studied. A gasoline tax will change the price consumers pay for gasoline, as well as the price producers receive. A partial equilibrium analysis of the gasoline market will treat the prices of other goods (such as automobiles, tires, and even ice cream) as constant. However, if a gasoline tax is imposed, the prices of other goods may change, and the partial equilibrium framework will not capture the effects of those changes.

When there is no tax, the equilibrium in a competitive market will be like the one depicted in Figure 10.1. Since the market clears in equilibrium, the quantity supplied (Q^s) equals the quantity demand, (Q^d). In Figure 10.1 we observe that in equilibrium $Q^s = Q^d = 6$ million units. With no tax, the price that consumers pay (call this P^d) equals the price producers receive (P^s). In the equilibrium illustrated in Figure 10.1, $P^s = P^d = \$8$ per unit.

An excise tax is a tax on a specific commodity, such as gasoline, alcohol, tobacco, or airline tickets. Suppose the government imposes an excise tax of $6 per unit. The tax creates a "tax wedge" because the price consumers pay will be $6 more than the price producers receive. Thus, in equilibrium $P^d = P^s + \$6$. More generally, with a tax of T per unit ($T = \$6$ in this example), the price consumers pay (P^d) will equal the price producers receive (P^s) *plus* the tax T. In a market with an upward-sloping supply curve and a downward-sloping demand curve, the effects of an excise tax are as follows:

- The market will *under*produce relative to the efficient level.
- Consumer surplus will be *lower* than with no tax.
- Producer surplus will be *lower* than with no tax.
- The impact on the government budget will be *positive* because tax receipts are collected. The tax receipts are part of the net benefit to society because they will be distributed to people in the economy.
- The tax receipts are *less* than the decrease in consumer and producer surplus. Thus, the tax causes a reduction in net economic benefits.

[1]Adam Smith, *An Inquiry into the Nature and Causes of the Wealth of Nations*, printed for W. Strahan and T. Cadell, London, 1776.

One way to see the effect of the tax is to draw a new curve that adds the amount of the tax vertically to the supply curve, as shown in Figure 10.2 (see the curve labeled $S + \$6$). This new curve tells us how much producers will offer for sale when the price charged to consumers covers the marginal cost of production on the supply curve *plus* the $6 tax. For example, if price including tax is $10, producers offer 2 million units for sale (see point E on the curve labeled $S + \$6$). When consumers pay $10, producers receive only $4 after the tax is deducted from the sales price ($P^s = \$4$). Point F on the supply curve indicates that 2 million units will be offered for sale when the producer receives the after-tax price of $4.

Figure 10.2 indicates that the market will not clear if consumers pay a price $P^d = \$10$. At that price consumers want to buy 5 million units (at point $\mathcal{J}$). But producers want to sell only 2 million units, as point E on the $S + \$6$ curve shows. There would be an excess demand of 3 million units (the horizontal distance between points E and $\mathcal{J}$).

The equilibrium with the tax is determined at the intersection of the demand curve and the $S + \$6$ curve. Figure 10.2 shows that the market-clearing quantity is 4 million units. Consumers pay $P^d = \$12$ (at point M on the graph), the government collects its $6 tax on each unit produced, and producers receive a price $P^s = \$6$ (at point N).

Now we can compare the equilibria with and without the excise tax.[2] Using Figure 10.3, we can calculate the consumer surplus, producer surplus, and tax receipts in the two cases. The areas of various portions of the graph are labeled,

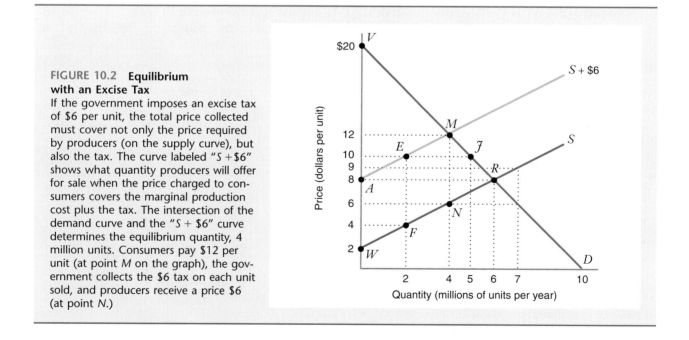

FIGURE 10.2 Equilibrium with an Excise Tax
If the government imposes an excise tax of $6 per unit, the total price collected must cover not only the price required by producers (on the supply curve), but also the tax. The curve labeled "$S + \$6$" shows what quantity producers will offer for sale when the price charged to consumers covers the marginal production cost plus the tax. The intersection of the demand curve and the "$S + \$6$" curve determines the equilibrium quantity, 4 million units. Consumers pay $12 per unit (at point M on the graph), the government collects the $6 tax on each unit sold, and producers receive a price $6 (at point N.)

[2]The comparison of the market with and without the tax is an exercise in comparative statics, as described in Chapter 1. The exogenous variable is the size of the tax, which changes from zero to $6 per unit. We can ask how various endogenous variables (such as the quantity exchanged, the price producers receive, and the price consumers pay) change as the size of the tax varies.

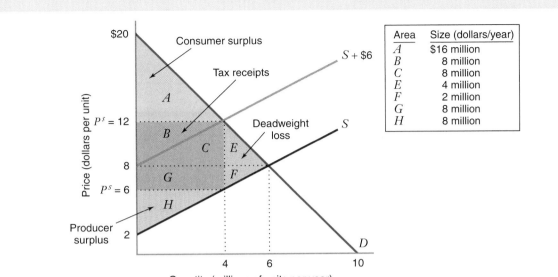

Area	Size (dollars/year)
A	$16 million
B	8 million
C	8 million
E	4 million
F	2 million
G	8 million
H	8 million

	No Tax	**With Tax**	**Impact of Tax**
Consumer surplus	$A + B + C + E$ ($36 million)	A ($16 million)	$-B - C - E$ (−$20 million)
Producer surplus	$F + G + H$ ($18 million)	H ($8 million)	$-F - G$ (−$10 million)
Government receipts from tax	zero	$B + C + G$ ($24 million)	$B + C + G$ ($24 million)
Net benefits (Consumer + Producer surplus + Government receipts)	$A + B + C + E +$ $F + G + H$ ($54 million)	$A + B + C + G + H$ ($48 million)	$-E - F$ (−$6 million)
Deadweight loss	zero	$E + F$ ($6 million)	

FIGURE 10.3   Impact of a $6 Excise Tax
With no tax, the sum of consumer and producer surplus is $54 million, the maximum net benefit possible in this market. The excise tax of $6 reduces consumer surplus by $20 million, reduces producer surplus by $10 million, and generates government tax receipts of $24 million. The tax receipts are a part of the net economic benefit because these receipts are distributed to society.

and the legend at the right side of the figure shows the size of each area, measured in dollars per year. With no tax, the consumer surplus will be areas $A + B + C + E$. This is the area below the demand curve and above the price consumers pay ($8). The consumer surplus is $36 million dollars per year. The producer surplus is area $F + G + H$, the area above the supply curve and below the price producers receive. The producer surplus is $18 million per year. There are no tax receipts. The net benefits are therefore $54 million per year.

With the tax, the consumer surplus is $16 million, the size of area A. This is the area under the demand curve and above the price consumers pay ($P^d = \$12$). Producer surplus is $8 million, the size of area H. This is the area above the supply curve and below the price producers receive ($P^s = \$6$). As noted earlier, the tax receipts are a net benefit to society because they will be distributed over the economy. The tax receipts will be $24 million per year, the size of the rectangle $B + C + G$, reflecting the collection of the tax of $6 on each unit sold (the height of the rectangle) times the 4 million units produced (the length of the rectangle). Thus, with the tax the annual net benefit is $48 million per year.

Finally, consider the row of the table labeled *Net Benefits*. It shows that the annual net benefit with the tax ($48 million) is smaller than the net benefit without the tax ($54 million). This loss in net benefits ($6 million per year) is called the **deadweight loss** resulting from the tax. The deadweight loss represents potential net economic benefits that no one (producers, consumers, or the government) captures when the tax is imposed.

We can also understand how the deadweight loss arises by examining the last column in the table. It shows that the tax reduces consumer surplus by $20 million, reduces producer surplus by $10 million, and generates government tax receipts of $24 million. When we add these changes ($-\$20$ million $- \$10$ million $+ \$24$ million), we find that net benefits decrease by $6 million, the size of the deadweight loss.

The deadweight loss is the area $E + F$ in Figure 10.3. This area is part of the net benefit when there is no tax. E was a part of the consumer surplus with no tax. The benefits in E disappeared because consumers reduced their purchases from 6 to 4 million units with the tax. Similarly, F was a part of the producer surplus. But producers only supply 4 million units with the tax, and they therefore no longer receive F.

LEARNING-BY-DOING EXERCISE 10.1

Excise Tax

In this exercise we reproduce the results illustrated in Figure 10.3, using algebra. The exercise will reinforce your understanding of how an excise tax works in a competitive market.

The demand and supply curves in Figure 10.3 are as follows:

$$Q^d = 10 - 0.5P^d,$$

$$Q^s = \begin{cases} -2 + P^s, & \text{when } P^s \geq 2 \\ 0, & \text{when } P^s \leq 2, \end{cases}$$

where Q^d is the quantity demanded when the price consumers pay is P^d, and Q^s is the quantity supplied when the price producers receive is P^s. The last line of the supply equation simply indicates that nothing will be supplied if the price producers receive is less than $2 per unit. Thus, for prices between zero and $2, the supply curve lies on the vertical axis.

Problem

(a) With no tax, what are the equilibrium price and quantity?

(b) At the equilibrium in part (a), what is consumer surplus? Producer surplus? Deadweight loss? Show all of these graphically.

(c) Suppose the government imposes an excise tax of $6 per unit. What will the new equilibrium quantity be? What price will the buyers pay? What price will the sellers receive?

(d) At the equilibrium with the tax in part (c), what is consumer surplus? Producer surplus? The impact on the government budget (here a positive number, the government tax receipts)? Deadweight loss?

(e) Verify for your answers to parts (b) and (d) that the following sum is identical:

Consumer surplus + Producer surplus + Tax receipts + Deadweight loss

Explain why the sum must be equal in both parts.

Solution

(a) With no tax, two conditions must be satisfied:

(i) $P^d = P^s$ (there is no tax wedge). Since there is only one price in the market, let's call it P^*.

(ii) Also, the market clears, so that $Q^d = Q^s$.

Together these conditions require that $10 - 0.5P^* = -2 + P^*$, so the equilibrium price is $P^* = \$8$ per unit. The equilibrium quantity can be found by substituting $P = \$8$ into either the supply or demand equation. If we use the demand equation, we find that the equilibrium quantity is $Q^d = 10 - 0.5(8) = 6$ million units.

(b) The consumer surplus is the triangle $A + B + C + E$ in Figure 10.3. The area of this triangle is $(1/2)[\$(20 - 8)(6 \text{ million})]$, or $36 million. The producer surplus is the triangle $G + H + F$. The area of this triangle is $(1/2)[\$(8 - 2)(6 \text{ million})]$, or $18 million. There is zero deadweight loss at the competitive equilibrium.

(c) With a $6 excise tax, there are two conditions that must be satisfied:

(i) $P^d = P^s + 6$ (there is a tax wedge of $6).

(ii) Also, the market clears, so that $Q^d = Q^s$, or $10 - 0.5P^d = -2 + P^s$.

Thus $10 - 0.5(P^s + 6) = -2 + P^s$. The price producers receive is $P^s = \$6$ per unit. The price consumers pay is $P^d = P^s + \$6 = \$12$. The equilibrium quantity can be found by substituting $P^d = \$12$ into the demand equation, that is, $Q^d = 10 - 0.5P^d = 10 - 0.5(12) = 4$ million units. (Alternatively, we could have substituted $P^s = \$6$ into the supply equation.)

(d) The consumer surplus is area A in Figure 10.3. The area of this triangle is $(1/2)[\$(20 - 12)(4 \text{ million})] = \$16$ million. The producer surplus is area H. The area of this triangle is $(1/2)[\$(6 - 2)(4 \text{ million})] = \$8$ million. The government collects $6 on each of the 4 million units sold. The tax receipts are thus $24 million per year (area $B + C + G$). The size of the deadweight loss is the area of triangle $(E + F)$, or $(1/2)[\$(12 - 6)(6 - 4 \text{ million})] = \$6$ million.

(e) With no tax:

Consumer surplus ($36 million) + Producer surplus ($18 million) +
Tax receipts (zero) + Deadweight loss (zero) = $54 million

With a $6 tax:

Consumer surplus ($16 million) + Producer surplus
($8 million) + Tax receipts ($24 million) + Deadweight loss
($6 million) = $54 million

The potential net benefit in the market is always $54 million. Consumers and producers capture all of the potential net benefits when there is no tax; there is no deadweight loss. With the tax, only $48 million of the potential net benefits are captured, so $6 million in potential benefits have disappeared, becoming a deadweight loss. *When the deadweight loss grows by a dollar, the net benefits obtained by the economy must shrink by that dollar.*

Similar Problems: 10.4, 10.6, 10.7

INCIDENCE OF A TAX

In a market with an upward-sloping supply curve and a downward-sloping demand curve, an excise tax will cause the price consumers pay to rise, and the price producers receive to fall. Which price change will change more as a result of the tax? In Learning-By-Doing Exercise 10.1, the price the consumers pay increases by $4 (rising from $8 to $12). The price the producers receive falls by $2 (decreasing from $8 to $6). The **incidence of the tax** is the effect that the tax has on the prices consumers pay and sellers receive in a market. The incidence, or burden of the tax, is shared by both consumers and producers, although in the exercise the larger share is borne by the consumers.

The incidence of the tax will depend on the shapes of the supply and demand curves. Figure 10.4 illustrates two cases. In both cases the equilibrium price with no tax is $30 per unit. However, the effects of a tax of $10 are quite different in the two markets.

In Case 1 the demand curve is relatively inelastic, and the supply curve is quite elastic. The tax causes consumers to pay $8 more than they would with no tax. The tax also reduces the amount producers receive by $2. The price change resulting from the tax is larger for consumers because the demand is comparatively inelastic.

In Case 2 the tax has a larger impact on producers because the supply curve is relatively inelastic, while the demand curve is comparatively elastic. The tax decreases the price producers receive by $8, while it increases the price consumers pay by only $2.

As the two cases suggest, the tax will have a larger impact on consumers if the demand is less elastic than the supply curve at the competitive equilibrium, and a larger impact on producers if the reverse is true. At least for small price changes, it is reasonable to assume that the demand and supply curves have approximately constant own-price elasticities, $\epsilon_{Q^d,P}$ and $\epsilon_{Q^s,P}$. We can summarize

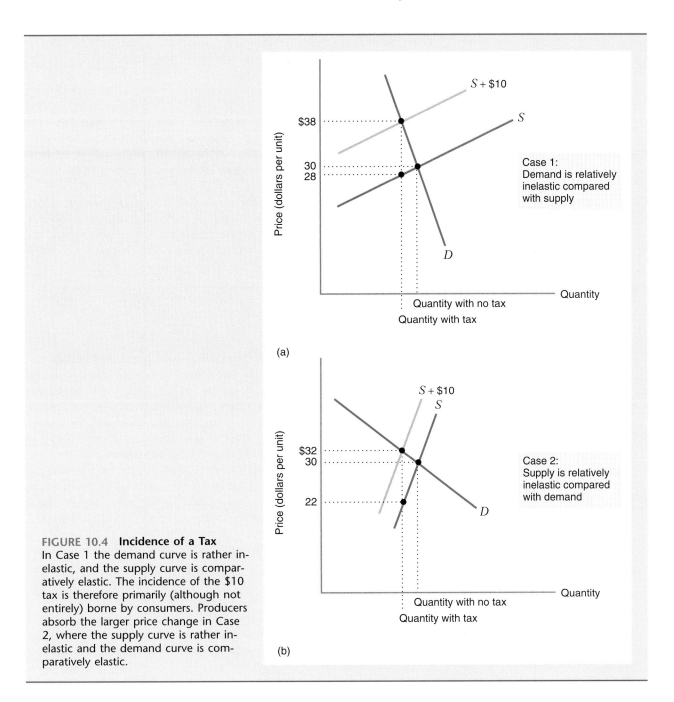

FIGURE 10.4 Incidence of a Tax
In Case 1 the demand curve is rather inelastic, and the supply curve is comparatively elastic. The incidence of the $10 tax is therefore primarily (although not entirely) borne by consumers. Producers absorb the larger price change in Case 2, where the supply curve is rather inelastic and the demand curve is comparatively elastic.

the quantitative relationship between the incidence of a tax and the elasticities of demand as follows:

$$\frac{\Delta P^d}{\Delta P^s} = \frac{\epsilon_{Q^s,P}}{\epsilon_{Q^d,P}} \qquad (10.1)$$

Equation (10.1) tells us that the impact of the price change on consumers and producers will be equal when the absolute values of the price elasticities are the same (remember that the demand elasticity is negative and the supply elasticity is positive). For example, if $\epsilon_{Q^d,P} = -0.5$ and $\epsilon_{Q^s,P} = +0.5$, then $\Delta P^d/\Delta P^s = -1$. In other words, if a tax of \$1 is imposed, the price consumers pay would rise by \$0.50, while the price producers would receive would fall by \$0.50.

As another example, suppose the supply is relatively elastic compared with demand (for example, $\epsilon_{Q^d,P} = -0.5$ and $\epsilon_{Q^s,P} = 2.0$). Then $\Delta P^d/\Delta P^s = 2.0/(-0.5) = -4$. In this case the increase in the price consumers pay will be four times as much as the decrease in the price producers receive. Thus, if an excise tax of \$1 is imposed, the price consumers pay would rise by \$0.80, while the price producers receive would fall by \$0.20. The impact of the tax is therefore primarily borne by consumers.[3]

Equation (10.1) explains much about the impact of federal and state taxes on many markets. For example, the demands for goods such as alcohol and tobacco are quite inelastic, while their supply curves are comparatively elastic. Thus, the greater incidence of an excise tax falls on consumers in these markets.

---

*E*XAMPLE 10.1   *Gasoline Taxes*

In the late 1990s about 110 billion gallons of gasoline were purchased annually in the United States. Although consumer prices fluctuate a great deal over time and vary by region, the price consumers paid at the pump (P^d) was about \$1.10 per gallon at that time. Taxes on gasoline are often imposed not only at the federal level, but also by state and local governments. Thus, the taxes paid vary by region. In most areas of the country, the total tax on gas was about \$0.30 to \$0.40 per gallon, although in some areas taxes were close to \$0.50 per gallon.

In a "back of the envelope" exercise, let's assume that the tax on gasoline (*T*) was \$0.30 per gallon. This means that the price producers received (P^s) was about \$0.80 per gallon. In the intermediate run of, say, two to five years, studies have shown that the own-price elasticities of demand and supply are about $\epsilon_{Q^d,P} = -0.5$ and $\epsilon_{Q^s,P} = +0.4$.

Using the information about the current equilibrium, let's examine two questions.

1. What quantities and prices would we anticipate if the taxes were removed?

2. Discussions of gasoline taxes sometimes suggest that for every increase of one cent in the gasoline tax, the tax revenues collected will increase by about \$1 billion per year. Is this reasonable, at least for levels of taxes near the current \$0.30 per gallon?

In this exercise we assume that the demand and supply curves are both linear, and that the elasticities are correct at the equilibrium with the excise tax of

---

[3]To see why equation (10.1) is true, consider the effect of a small tax in a market. Suppose that the equilibrium price and quantity in the market with no tax are respectively P^* and Q^*. For a small tax, $\epsilon_{Q^d,P} = (\Delta Q/Q^*)/(\Delta P^d/P^*)$, which can be written as $\Delta Q/Q^* = (\Delta P^d/P^*)\epsilon_{Q^d,P}$. Similarly, $\epsilon_{Q^s,P} = (\Delta Q/Q^*)/(\Delta P^s/P^*)$, which means that $\Delta Q/Q^* = (\Delta P^s/P^*)\epsilon_{Q^s,P}$. Because the market will clear, a tax will reduce the quantity demanded and supplied by the same amount ($\Delta Q/Q^*$). This requires that $(\Delta P^d/P^*)\epsilon_{Q^d,P} = (\Delta P^s/P^*)\epsilon_{Q^s,P}$, which can be simplified to equation (10.1).

$0.30 per gallon. Let's begin by determining the equation of the demand curve, which must pass through point R in Figure 10.5, where the price is $1.10 and the quantity (measured in billions of gallons) is 110. If the demand curve is linear, it has the form

$$Q^d = a - bP^d. \tag{10.2}$$

Using the data, let us find the constants a and b in equation (10.2). By definition, the own-price elasticity of demand is $\epsilon_{Q^d,P} = (\Delta Q / \Delta P)(P^d / Q^d)$. In the linear demand curve, $\Delta Q / \Delta P = -b$. Thus, $-0.5 = -b\,(1.10/110)$, which implies that $b = 50$. Now we know that $Q^d = a - 50P^d$. We can calculate a by using the price and quantity data at point R. Thus, $110 = a - 50(1.10)$, so $a = 165$. The equation of the demand curve is

$$Q^d = 165 - 50P^d \tag{10.3}$$

The equation of a linear supply curve (where e and f are constants) is

$$Q^s = e + fP^s \tag{10.4}$$

The own-price elasticity of supply is $\epsilon_{Q^s,P} = (\Delta Q / \Delta P)(P^s / Q^s)$. In equation (10.4), $\Delta Q / \Delta P = f$. Thus, at point W in Figure 10.5, $0.4 = f(0.8/110)$, or $f = 55$. Therefore, $Q^s = e + 55P^s$. We can calculate e by using the price and quantity data at point W.

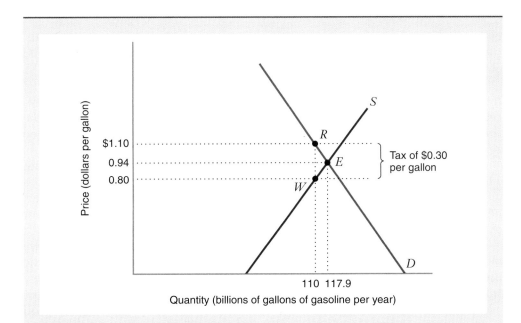

FIGURE 10.5 Effects of Gasoline Tax
With an excise tax of $0.30 per gallon, consumers pay about $1.10 per gallon (at point R), and producers receive about $0.80 per gallon (at point W). If there were no tax, the equilibrium price would be about $0.94 per gallon (at point E). The incidence of the tax is shared nearly equally by consumers and producers.

TABLE 10.1

Tax per gallon	Quantity (billions of gallons of gasoline per year)	Price Producers Receive (P^s)	Price Consumers Pay (P^d)	Tax Revenues (billions of dollars per year)
$0.00	117.9	$0.94	$0.94	$0.00
$0.10	115.2	$0.90	$1.00	$11.52
$0.20	112.6	$0.85	$1.05	$22.52
$0.30	110.0	$0.80	$1.10	$33.00
$0.40	107.4	$0.75	$1.15	$42.95
$0.50	104.8	$0.70	$1.20	$52.38
$0.60	102.1	$0.66	$1.26	$61.29

Thus, $110 = e + 55(0.8)$, which means that $e = 66$. So the equation of the supply curve is

$$Q^s = 66 + 55P^s. \tag{10.5}$$

The supply and demand curves are drawn in Figure 10.5. If there were no taxes, the equilibrium price P^* would be at point E, where $P^* = P^s = P^d$ (there is no tax wedge). Using the market clearing condition ($Q^s = Q^d$), we find that $165 - 50P^* = 66 + 55P^*$. The equilibrium price is $P^* \approx \$0.94$ per gallon. With no tax, about 118 billion gallons of gas would be sold.

Note that the incidence of the current tax ($T = \$0.30$ per gallon) is rather evenly shared by consumers and producers. This is not surprising because the elasticities of supply and demand are about the same. With the tax consumers pay $1.10 instead of $0.94 per gallon. Similarly, producers receive $0.80 with the tax instead of $0.94 without it.

We can repeat Learning-By-Doing Exercise 10.1 to find how different levels of the gasoline tax will affect the quantity sold, the prices paid by consumers and received by producers, and the revenues from gasoline taxes. Table 10.1 shows the results of this exercise (the calculations are not shown) for taxes varying between zero and $0.60 per gallon.

Table 10.1 indicates that revenues from gasoline taxes will increase by about $10 billion (from $33 billion to about $43 billion per year) if the gasoline tax is raised from its current level of $0.30 per gallon to $0.40 per gallon. Thus, at least near the current equilibrium, the tax receipts do rise about $1 billion for each cent of increase in the tax.

While this example helps us to understand the effects of gasoline taxes, we must remember that there are a number of strong assumptions that may limit the usefulness of the model, especially if we try to use it to predict the effects of very large tax changes. First, the supply and demand curves are assumed to be linear, even for large variations in price. While linear approximations are often quite good for relatively small movements around the current equilibrium, they may not be accurate for large movements. Second, large changes in gasoline taxes may have significant impacts on the prices in other markets. To study how other markets are affected by changes in the gasoline tax, we would need more than a partial equilibrium analysis of a single market.   ∎

Instead of taxing a market, a government might decide to subsidize it. We can think of a subsidy as a *negative tax*. With a subsidy of T per unit, the price producers receive (P^s) will be the price consumers pay (P^d) *plus* the subsidy T. As you might suspect, many of the effects of a subsidy are opposite those of a tax.

- The market will *over*produce relative to the efficient level.
- Consumer surplus will be *higher* than with no subsidy.
- Producer surplus will be *higher* than with no subsidy.
- The impact on the government budget will be *negative*. Government expenditures on the subsidy are a negative net benefit since the money to pay for the subsidy must be collected elsewhere in the economy.
- Government expenditures on the subsidy will be *larger* than the increase in consumer and producer surplus. Thus, there will be a deadweight loss from overproduction.

Figure 10.6 shows how a subsidy of $3 per unit affects the competitive market with the supply and demand curves in Learning-By-Doing Example 10.1. The figure shows a new curve (labeled $S - \$3$) which subtracts the amount of the subsidy vertically from the supply curve. This curve tells us how much producers will offer for sale when the price received by producers includes the price consumers pay *plus* the subsidy.

We can find the equilibrium with the subsidy by looking at the intersection of the demand curve and the $S - \$3$ curve. In Figure 10.6 the market-clearing quantity is $Q_1 = 7$ million units per year. Producers receive a price $P^s = \$9$ per unit, including the price consumers pay $P^d = \$6$, and the subsidy the government pays $3 per unit.

We can compare the equilibria with and without the subsidy. From Exercise 10.1 we know that the consumer surplus with no subsidy is $36 million per year. Using the labels in Figure 10.6, the consumer surplus is areas $A + B$. The producer surplus is $18 million per year ($E + F$). There are no government expenditures. The net benefit is therefore $54 million ($A + B + E + F$).

With the subsidy the consumer surplus is $49 million, which is the area $A + B + E + G + K$, below the demand curve and above the $6 price consumers pay. Annual producer surplus is $24.5 million, which is the area $B + C + E + F$, above the supply curve and below the $9 price producers receive. The subsidy costs the government $21 million per year, the area of rectangle $B + C + E + G + K + \mathcal{J}$, reflecting the subsidy of $3 on each unit produced (the height of the rectangle) times the 7 million units produced per year (the length of the rectangle). The expenditures are shown as a negative benefit in the table because they must be financed by taxes collected elsewhere in the economy.

Finally, consider the row of the table labeled "Net benefits." It shows that the annual net benefit with the subsidy is $52.5 million, smaller than the net benefit without the subsidy by area $\mathcal{J}$, which measures $1.5 million. This is the deadweight loss resulting from the subsidy.

We can also find the deadweight loss by examining the right column in the table. It shows that the subsidy increases consumer surplus by $13 million ($E + G + K$), increases producer surplus by $6.5 million ($B + C$), and costs the government $21 million ($-B - C - E - G - K - \mathcal{J}$). As before, when we add these changes, we find that net benefits decrease by $1.5 million, the deadweight loss represented by area

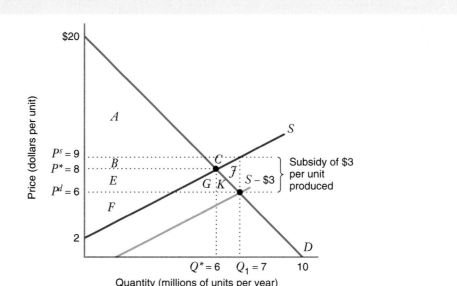

FIGURE 10.6   Subsidy on Each Unit Produced
With a subsidy of $3 per unit, the price producers receive ($P^s = \$9$) is the price consumers pay ($P^d = \$6$) *plus* the subsidy of $3. The market clears at 7 million units, above the efficient level of 6 million units. For each unit produced between Q^* and Q_1, the supply curve lies above the demand curve, indicating that the marginal cost exceeds the value consumers place on those units. The deadweight loss J occurs because of the overproduction relative to the efficient level Q^*.

	No Subsidy	With Subsidy	Impact of Subsidy
Consumer surplus	$A + B$ ($36 million)	$A + B + E + G + K$ ($49 million)	$E + G + K$ ($13 million)
Producer surplus	$E + F$ ($18 million)	$B + C + E + F$ ($24.5 million)	$B + C$ ($6.5 million)
Impact on government budget	zero	$-B - C - E - G - K - J$ (−$21 million)	$-B - C - E - G - K - J$ (−$21 million)
Net benefits (Consumer + Producer surplus − Government expenditures)	$A + B + E + F$ ($54 million)	$A + B + E + F - J$ ($52.5 million)	$-J$ (−$1.5 million)
Deadweight loss	zero	J ($1.5 million)	

J. The deadweight loss arises because the quantity produced rises from 6 million units with no subsidy, to 7 million with the subsidy. Over that range of output the supply curve lies above the demand curve, so net benefits are reduced as each of these units is produced. Thus, net economic benefits are reduced because the subsidy causes market to overproduce relative to the efficient level.

LEARNING-BY-DOING EXERCISE 10.2

Subsidy

Problem

(a) Using the supply and demand curves in Learning-By-Doing Example 10.1, use algebra to find the equilibrium for a subsidy of $3 per unit. Find the equilibrium quantity, the price the buyers pay, and the price the sellers receive.
(b) In Learning-By-Doing Exercise 10.1, we found that the potential net benefits in the market are Consumer surplus + Producer surplus + Tax receipts + Deadweight loss = $54 million. For the case of the subsidy, show that the potential net benefits [Consumer surplus + producer surplus + Expenditures on subsidy (a negative number) + deadweight loss] are still $54 million.

Solution

(a) With a $3 subsidy, two conditions must be satisfied in equilibrium:
  (i) $P^d = P^s - 3$ (there is a subsidy wedge of $3).
  (ii) Also, the market clears, so that $Q^d = Q^s$, or $10 - 0.5P^d = -2 + P^s$.
  These conditions require that $10 - 0.5(P^s - 3) = -2 + P^s$, which means that producers receive a price of $9 ($P^s = \$9$) in equilibrium. The equilibrium price consumers pay is $P^d = P^s - \$3 = \$6$ per unit. The equilibrium quantity can be found by substituting $P^d = \$6$ into the demand equation, that is $Q^d = 10 - 0.5P^d = 10 - 0.5(6) = 7$ million units. (Alternatively, we could have substituted $P^s = \$9$ into the supply equation.)
(b) With the $3 subsidy:

Consumer surplus ($49 million) + Producer surplus ($24.5 million) +
Expenditures on subsidy (−$21 million) + Deadweight loss ($1.5 million) =
$54 million

This part is similar to part (e) of Learning-By-Doing Exercise 10.1. It reminds us that the potential net benefits are the same, whether the market is efficient or not. With no subsidy, we know there is no deadweight loss and the net benefit is $54 million. With the subsidy, the net benefits to society are $52.5 million, so $1.5 million in potential benefits have disappeared. Again, the important point is that if the deadweight loss grows by a dollar, the net benefits going to the economy must shrink by that dollar.

Similar Problem: 10.6

Sometimes a government may set a maximum allowable price in a market, such as the price of food, gasoline, crude oil, or the rental price for housing. If the price ceiling is below the equilibrium price in a market with an upward-sloping supply curve and a downward-sloping demand curve, the ceiling has the following effects:

- The market will not clear. There will be an excess demand for the good.

10.4

PRICE CEILINGS (MAXIMUM PRICE REGULATION)

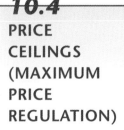

- The market will *under*produce relative to the efficient level (that is, the amount that would be supplied in an unregulated market).
- Producer surplus will be *lower* than with no price ceiling.
- Some (but not all) of the lost producer surplus will be transferred to consumers.
- Because there is excess demand with a price ceiling, the size of the consumer surplus depends on which of the consumers who want the good are able to purchase it. Consumer surplus may either increase or decrease with a price ceiling.
- There will be a deadweight loss.

Let's examine the effects of a price ceiling with rent controls. For decades rent controls have been in force in many cities around the world. Rent controls are legally imposed ceilings on the rents that landlords may charge their tenants. They often originated as temporary ceilings imposed in the inflationary time of war, as was the case in London and Paris during World War I, in New York during World War II, and in Boston and several nearby suburbs during the Vietnam conflict in the late 1960s and early 1970s.

In 1971 President Nixon imposed wage and price controls throughout the United States, freezing all rents. After the federal controls expired, many city governments continued to place ceilings on rents. In 1997 William Tucker noted, "During the 1970s it appeared that rent control might be the wave of the future... By the mid-1980s, more than 200 separate municipalities nationwide, encompassing about 20 percent of the nation's population, were living under rent control. However, this proved to be the high tide of the movement. As inflationary pressures eased, the agitation for rent control subsided."[4]

Figure 10.7 illustrates the supply and demand curves in the market for a particular type of housing, such as the market for studio apartments in New York City. For various rental prices the supply curve shows how many units landlords would be willing to make available, and the demand curve indicates how many units consumers would like to rent. If there were no rent controls, the market for studio apartments would clear at a rental price of $1,600 per month and 80,000 units being rented.

If there is no rent control, the market clears. Every consumer who is willing to pay the equilibrium price of $1,600 (consumers between points *Y* and *V* on the demand curve) will find housing. Further, every landlord willing to supply housing at that price (those at between point *Z* and *V* on the supply curve) will serve the market. Consumer surplus will be area *A* + *B* + *E*, and producer surplus will be area *C* + *F* + *G*. The sum of consumer and producer surplus will therefore be *A* + *B* + *C* + *E* + *F* + *G*.

Suppose the government imposes rent control by setting a maximum rental price of $1,000 per month. At that price landlords will be willing to supply 50,000 units (point *W* on the supply curve). The rent control has moved landlords from point *V* to point *W* on the supply curve, reducing the supply of housing by 30,000 units.

When a price ceiling is set below the unregulated market price, the market does not clear. When the price ceiling is $1,000, consumers would like to rent 140,000 units (point *X* on the demand curve). But, as we have already noted, landlords offer only 50,000 units for rent. There is therefore an excess demand

[4]William Tucker, "How Rent Control Drives Out Affordable Housing," Cato Policy Analysis, paper no. 274 (Washington, D.C.: The Cato Institute, May 21, 1997).

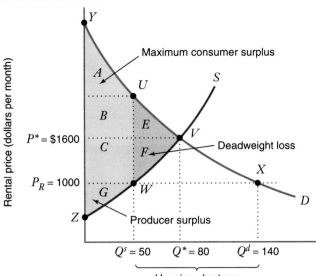

	Free Market	**With Rent Control**	**Impact of Rent Control**
Consumer surplus	A + B + E	A + B + C	C − E
Producer surplus	C + F + G	G	− C − F
Net benefits (Consumer + Producer surplus)	A + B + C + E + F + G	A + B + C + G	− E − F
Deadweight loss	zero	E + F	

FIGURE 10.7   Rent Controls Case 1: Maximum Consumer Surplus
Rent controls require that landlords charge no more than $1,000 per month for a type of housing that would rent for $1,600 without controls. At the price of $1,000, consumers would like to purchase 140,000 units, but suppliers make only 50,000 units available. Thus, rent control induces an excess demand for housing (a shortage of 90,000 units). Because there is excess demand, it is not clear which consumers will actually get the housing. If consumers with the highest willingness to pay (those located between points Y and U on the demand curve) purchase the 50,000 units available, the deadweight loss from rent controls is area E + F.

of 90,000 units (the horizontal distance between X and W). The excess demand in the housing market is more commonly referred to as a *housing shortage*.

With rent control, the landlords serving the market are the producers between points Z and W on the supply curve. The producer surplus they receive is area G. Thus, producer surplus falls (by areas C and F). This decline in producer surplus explains why landlords often strongly oppose rent controls.

Consumers who are lucky enough to get the 50,000 units available with the rent control will pay only $1,000 per unit instead of $1,600. The savings to consumers is measured by area C. This area is often referred to as an *income transfer* because it represents money transferred away from producers and saved by consumers who are lucky enough to get the housing available under rent controls. Observe that area *F is* part of the lost producer surplus, but *not* part of the income transfer. The units of housing between *W* and *V* on the supply curve are not produced at all under rent control. The potential benefits in area *F* disappear with rent control, becoming part of the deadweight loss.

How will consumer surplus be affected by rent controls? To answer this question, we must recognize that all of the consumers between *Y* and *X* on the demand curve want housing at a price of $1,000, but only some of them will find it. Since only 50,000 units are available, we need to know which of the 140,000 consumers who want the housing at $1,000 will be able to find housing. Let's consider two possible answers to this question.

- *Case 1. Consumers with the highest willingness to pay receive the housing.* One possibility is that the consumers with the highest willingness to pay receive the housing. Here consumers between *Y* and *U* on the demand curve would be the ones lucky enough to find housing. The other consumers between *U* and *X* would be unable to do so, even though they are willing to pay $1,000.

  With this allocation of housing, the consumer surplus is area *A* + *B* + *C* (the area below the demand curve and above the rental price of $1,000). This is the maximum possible consumer surplus with rent control. As Figure 10.7 indicates, the sum of consumer and producer surplus is *A* + *B* + *C* + *G*. The rent control creates a deadweight loss of *E* + *F*, the amount of the reduction in the sum of consumer and producer surplus. The deadweight loss arises because the amount of housing available in the market has been reduced from 80,000 units in the unregulated market to 50,000 with rent control. With rent control the potential net benefits represented by the area *E* + *F* are lost to society.

- *Case 2. Consumers with the lowest willingness to pay receive the housing.* The other extreme possibility is that the 50,000 available units are rented by those consumers with the lowest willingness to pay. In Figure 10.8 these consumers are the ones between *T* and *X* on the demand curve.[5] The other consumers between *Y* and *T* are unable to find housing, even though they are willing to pay more than $1,000.

With this allocation of housing, the consumer surplus is area *H* (again, for those consumers who get the housing, this is the area below the demand curve and above the rental price of $1,000). This is the minimum possible consumer surplus with rent control. As Figure 10.8 indicates, the sum of consumer and producer surplus is *G* + *H*. Rent control now creates a deadweight loss of *E* + *F* + *A* + *B* + *C* − *H*. The deadweight loss is larger in Case 2 than in Case 1 because the consumer surplus is smaller in Case 2.

The two cases just considered define upper and lower limits on the consumer surplus and deadweight loss from rent controls. The producer surplus will be area *G* in either case. The maximum consumer surplus and the minimum deadweight loss are shown in Case 1. The minimum consumer surplus and the maximum deadweight loss are shown in Case 2. The actual consumer surplus and deadweight loss may be in between the levels in these two polar cases. To find the exact consumer surplus and the deadweight loss, we would need to know more about how the available housing is actually allocated.

---

[5] We do not consider consumers to the right of point *X* on the demand curve because they would not be willing to rent housing at $1,000 even if they could find it.

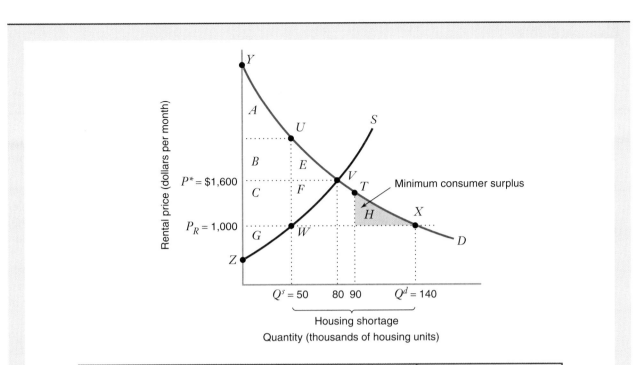

FIGURE 10.8 Rent Controls Case 2: Minimum Consumer Surplus
The market does not clear with rent controls. Because there is excess demand, it is not obvious which consumers will actually get the housing. If consumers with the *lowest* willingness to pay (those located between points *T* and *X* on the demand curve) purchase the 50,000 units available, the consumer surplus with rent controls will be area *H*. Producer surplus with rent controls is still area *G*, as in Figure 10.7. The welfare loss from rent controls will be much larger than in Figure 10.7 because consumer surplus is lower when consumers with the lowest willingness to pay obtain the housing.

Most textbooks depict the effects of a price ceiling with a graph like the one in Figure 10.7, assuming that the good ends up in the hands of consumers with the highest willingness to pay. This assumption is reasonable when consumers can easily resell the good to other consumers with a higher willingness to pay. The following example illustrates how resale enables consumers toward the upper end of the demand curve to buy the good in a resale market, even though they might not be able to obtain the good when it is initially sold.

EXAMPLE 10.2   *Scalping Super Bowl Tickets on the Internet*

When the National Football League (NFL) sells tickets to the Super Bowl, it establishes face values (the prices printed on the tickets) that are far below the market prices. The NFL understands that there will be a large excess demand for tickets sold at face value. It therefore accepts requests for tickets a year in advance of the event, and then chooses the recipients of the tickets in a random drawing.

Face prices for tickets to Super Bowl XXXIV in Atlanta in 2000 ranged from $325 to $400, depending on the location of the seats. Because of the excess demand, there was an active resale market for tickets. In the month before the game, several sites on the Internet offered box seats at prices around $4,500, more than ten times the face value of the ticket.

The winners of the random drawing are indeed lucky. They can use the tickets themselves, or resell the tickets at a handsome profit. The existence of an easily accessible, active resale market helps move the tickets ultimately into the hands of people who most highly value the opportunity to see the game in person.

Beyond the face value of the ticket and the attractiveness of the event, two types of transactions costs affect the possibility of resale. First, in some states resale ("scalping") is illegal. A law prohibiting resale is likely to be more effective when the penalty for a violation is high and when the probability of being caught reselling is high. Even though resale is illegal in many areas, it may nevertheless be common where penalties are low or there is little risk of being caught. Second, resellers incur transactions costs in searching out supplies of tickets and locating buyers.

In recent years the Internet has lowered both types of transactions costs considerably. Buyers and sellers can conduct business from the comfort of home or the office. With a Web site, scalpers can widely advertise tickets at a very low cost and with less risk of being caught than would be the case if the transactions took place in the shadow of the stadium.

If resale involves low transactions costs, total surplus will be close to the maximum possible, as assumed in Case 1 (Figure 10.7) in the discussion of price ceilings. Part of the surplus may go to middlemen (scalpers and brokers) instead of the final holders of the tickets, but the net benefits do not disappear from the economy.

Of course, scalping typically involves a certain amount of risk, including the possibility that the tickets are not as desirable as advertised, or perhaps are not valid at all. Those supporting laws against scalping often cite examples of fraud. If the original sellers of tickets or governing authorities are willing to impose very strict conditions, it may be possible to reduce resale greatly. For example, the seller could put the buyer's picture on the ticket (as is often done with monthly passes on urban transport systems), or write the buyer's name on the ticket and require the buyer to produce a picture I.D. when she uses the ticket (as the airlines often do). However, these measures add significant costs to businesses and to law enforcement efforts, and are often difficult to implement. ∎

Before leaving rent controls, we note that government attempts to regulate the price of a commodity rarely work in a straightforward fashion. For example, when a shortage develops in the rental market for housing, some landlords may demand *key money*—that is, an extra payment from a prospective renter—before agreeing to lease an apartment. Although such payments are illegal, they are difficult to monitor, and renters who are willing to pay more than the rent controlled price may willingly (though not happily) pay the key money. Landlords may also recognize that with excess demand, they will be able to find renters even if they allow the quality of the apartments to deteriorate. Rent control laws often attempt to specify that the quality should be maintained, but it is quite difficult to write the laws to enforce this intent effectively. Further, landlords may recognize that they would be better off in the long run if they can convert apartments under rent control to other uses not subject to price controls, such as condominiums or even parking lots. Critics of rent controls often observe that the amounts of housing available have been reduced over time as owners of controlled housing convert to alternative uses of land.[6]

We must remember that there are limitations in a partial equilibrium analysis of the effect of a price ceiling, such as the one in Figures 10.7 and 10.8. If a rent control is imposed in the market for studio apartments, people who cannot find a studio apartment will seek another type of housing, such as a larger apartment, a condominium, or even a house. This will affect the demand for other types of housing, and thus the equilibrium prices in those markets. As the prices of other types of housing change, the demand for studio apartments may shift, resulting in additional consequences on the size of the shortage of studio apartments, as well as consumer and produce surplus and deadweight loss. Calculating these additional effects is beyond the scope of a simple partial equilibrium analysis, but you should recognize that they may be important.

The unintended consequences of price ceilings are present in many markets other than housing. For example, in an effort to fight inflation in the 1970s, the Nixon administration imposed price ceilings on domestic suppliers of oil, creating a shortage of domestic oil. The excess demand for oil led to increased imports of oil. When the price controls were imposed in 1971, imports constituted only 25 percent of the nation's supply. As time passed, the shortage grew substantially. By 1973, imports made up nearly 33 percent of the total oil consumed in the United States. OPEC countries recognized the growing dependence on imports in the United States, and they responded by quadrupling the price of imported oil. In the end the domestic price controls contributed to still higher inflation in the United States, working against the intent of the original price controls.[7]

[6]See, for example, Denton Marks, "The Effects of Partial-Coverage Rent Control on the Price and Quantity of Rental Housing," *Journal of Urban Economics, 16* (1984): 360–369.

[7]See George Horwich and David Weimer, "Oil Price Shocks, Market Response, and Contingency Planning," The American Enterprise Institute, Washington, D.C., 1984.

EXAMPLE 10.3   *Price Ceilings in the Market for Natural Gas*

Following a decision of the U.S. Supreme Court in 1954 (*Phillips Petroleum Company v. Wisconsin, et. al.*), the federal government regulated the price of natural gas sold in interstate commerce, that is, gas produced in one state (such as Texas) and sold to consumers or industries in another state (such as Ohio). By contrast, prices in intrastate markets (for example, gas produced and sold in Texas) were not regulated.

For several years following this historic decision, the Federal Power Commission imposed price ceiling regulations on natural gas at the wellhead, the point at which natural gas leaves the ground. Prior to 1962 the ceiling price was above the price that cleared the interstate market for natural gas. Thus, before 1962 the price ceiling constraints were not binding, and the market cleared.

Figure 10.9(a) illustrates a market with price ceiling P_R *higher* than the equilibrium price P^*. At the equilibrium price all buyers and sellers were satisfied, and the price ceiling was not violated. Thus, the price ceiling had no effect on the market.

After 1962 the price ceiling did become binding, and excess demand began to develop in the industry. The shortage of natural gas became severe as the price of oil rose in the world market and many consumers wanted to switch to natural gas for heating. Absent a price ceiling, the market-clearing price of natural gas in the interstate market would have been about $2 per MCF (thousand cubic feet) in the mid-1970s.[8] However, federal regulations imposed a price ceiling of about $1 per MCF, as Figure 10.9(b) illustrates. At the price ceiling the quantity of gas supplied (Q^s) was about two-thirds of the quantity demanded (Q^d), creating a severe shortage of natural gas in interstate markets.

At a minimum, the deadweight loss was the area bounded by the points *UVW*. Since resale of natural gas at higher prices was illegal, some consumers between *U* and *X* may have received gas, displacing consumers with higher willingnesses to pay. The deadweight loss was therefore probably greater than *UVW*.

The widespread shortages of natural gas caused national concern, especially because many people in the Midwest and Northeast could not purchase natural gas to heat their homes. In some states, such as Ohio, many schools were forced to close because there was not enough natural gas. The shortages, along with the difficulty of administering a complex set of price controls for thousands of producers, led to the deregulation of natural gas prices starting in 1978.   ∎

---

[8]Natural gas was selling for about $2 per MCF in unregulated intrastate markets, leading analysts to believe that the equilibrium price in the interstate market would have also been about $2 if the price ceiling were removed.

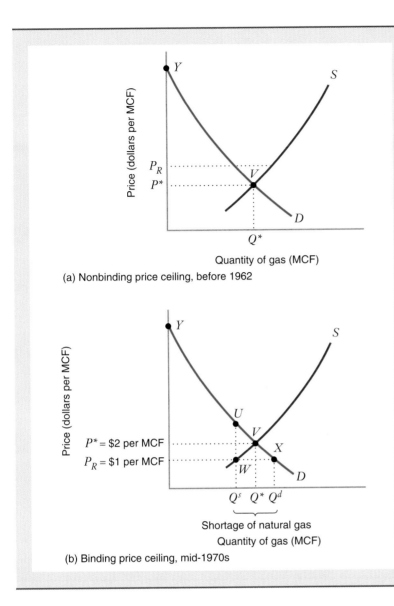

(a) Nonbinding price ceiling, before 1962

(b) Binding price ceiling, mid-1970s

FIGURE 10.9 Price Ceilings for Natural Gas
Before 1962, the price ceiling on natural gas sold in interstate markets (P_R) was higher than the equilibrium price (P^*). The ceiling had no effect on the market because the market cleared at a price below the ceiling.

By the mid-1970s, the maximum allowed price was lower than the equilibrium price. The ceiling induced a severe shortage, with the quantity supplied being only about two-thirds of the quantity demanded. The deadweight loss was at least the area bounded by the points UVW (assuming that the consumers between Y and U on the demand curve were the ones who received the gas). Resale in this market was illegal. Some consumers between U and X may have received gas, displacing consumers with higher willingnesses to pay. The deadweight loss was probably greater than UVW.

LEARNING-BY-DOING EXERCISE 10.3

Effect of a Price Ceiling

The supply and demand curves illustrated in Figure 10.10 are the same ones we have used in the previous two Learning-By-Doing Exercises. Suppose the government imposes a price ceiling of $6 in the market.

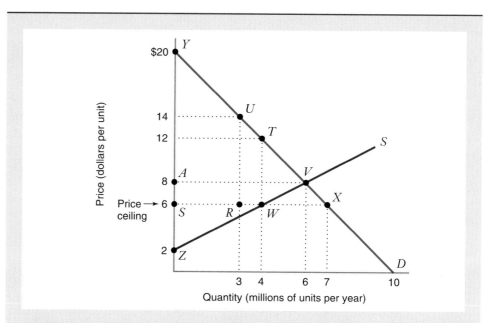

FIGURE 10.10   Price Ceiling: Learning-By-Doing Exercise 10.3
With no regulation, the equilibrium price would be $8, and the sum of consumer and producer surplus is the area *YVZ* ($54 million). With a price ceiling of $6, producers supply 4 million units and consumers demand 7 million units. There is an excess demand of 3 million units. Producer surplus is the area *SWZ* ($8 million). The size of the consumer surplus depends on which consumers are able to purchase the good:
     Case 1. Maximum Consumer Surplus: If consumers with the highest willingness to pay (those between *Y* and *T* on the demand curve) purchase the 4 million units supplied, consumer surplus will be the area *YTWS* ($40 million). The sum of consumer surplus ($40 million) and producer surplus ($8 million) is $48 million, or $6 million short of the total surplus possible in an unregulated market. This $6 million deadweight loss is area *TWV*.
     Case 2. Minimum Consumer Surplus: If the consumers with the lowest willingness to pay (those between *U* and *X* on the demand curve) purchase the 4 million units supplied, consumer surplus will be the area *URX* ($16 million). Now the sum of consumer surplus ($16 million) and producer surplus ($8 million) is only $24 million, or $30 million short of the total surplus possible in an unregulated market. The deadweight loss in Case 2 is therefore $30 million.

Problem

(a) What is the size of the shortage in the market with the price ceiling? What is the producer surplus?
(b) What is the maximum consumer surplus, assuming the good is purchased by consumers with the highest willingness to pay? What is the deadweight loss in this case?
(c) What is the minimum consumer surplus, assuming the good is purchased by consumers with the lowest willingness to pay? What is the deadweight loss in this case?

Solution

(a) If the price ceiling is $6, consumers demand 7 million units, but producers supply only 4 million. The excess demand (shortage) is 3 million units, the horizontal distance between W and X in the figure.

The producer surplus is the area of the triangle below the price ceiling of $6 and above the supply curve. Producer surplus will be the area SWZ ($8 million).

(b) Suppose consumers with the highest willingness to pay (those between Y and T on the demand curve) purchase the 4 million units available. Consumer surplus will be the area $YTWS$ ($40 million). The sum of consumer surplus ($40 million) and producer surplus ($8 million) is $48 million.

How much is the deadweight loss? With the price ceiling the consumer and producer surplus is only $48 million, or $6 million short of the total surplus possible in an unregulated market. This $6 million deadweight loss is area TWV.

(c) If consumers with the *lowest* willingness to pay (those between U and X on the demand curve) purchase the 4 million units available, consumer surplus will be the area URX ($16 million). The sum of consumer surplus ($16 million) and producer surplus ($8 million) is only $24 million, or $30 million short of the total surplus possible in an unregulated market ($54 million). The deadweight loss in Case 2 is $30 million.

Governments sometimes set minimum prices for goods or services. For example, in many countries there are minimum wage laws. Before 1978 in the United States, the federal government set airline fares that were higher than those that would have been observed without regulation.

When the government imposes a price floor higher than the free market price, we observe the following effects in a market with an upward-sloping supply curve and a downward-sloping demand curve:

10.5
PRICE FLOORS (MINIMUM PRICE REGULATION)

- The market will not clear. There will be an excess supply of the good or service in the market.
- Consumers will buy less of the good than they would in a free market.
- Consumer surplus will be *lower* than with no price floor.
- Some (but not all) of the lost consumer surplus will be transferred to producers.
- Because there is excess supply with a price floor, the size of the producer surplus depends on which of the producers actually supply the good.
- Producer surplus may either increase or decrease with a price floor.
- There will be a deadweight loss.

Let's begin by studying the effects of a minimum wage law. There are many types of labor in an economy. Some workers are unskilled, while others are highly skilled. For most types of skilled labor, the minimum wage set by the government will be well below the equilibrium wage rate in a free market. A minimum wage law will have no effect in such a market. We therefore focus on the market for unskilled labor, where the minimum wage requirement may be above the wage level in a free market.

Figure 10.11 illustrates the supply and demand curves in the market for unskilled labor. The vertical axis shows the price of labor, that is, the wage rate, w. The horizontal axis measures the number of hours of labor, L. The supply curve shows how many hours workers will supply at any wage rate. The demand curve indicates how many hours of labor employers will hire.

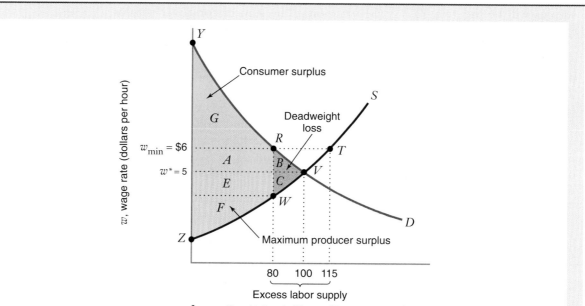

	Free Market	With Minimum Wage	Impact of Minimum Wage
Consumer surplus	$A + B + G$	G	$-A - B$
Producer surplus	$C + E + F$	$A + E + F$	$A - C$
Net benefits (Consumer + Producer surplus)	$A + B + C + E + F + G$	$A + E + F + G$	$-B - C$
Deadweight loss	zero	$B + C$	

FIGURE 10.11 Minimum Wage Law Case 1: Maximum Producer Surplus
A minimum wage law requires employers to pay at least $6 per hour. At that wage rate workers would like to supply 115 million hours, but employers will only hire workers for 80 million hours. The minimum wage law causes an excess supply of labor of 35 million hours. Because there is an excess supply of labor, it is not clear which workers who want jobs will be hired. If the most efficient workers (those located between points Z and W on the supply curve) supply the 80 million hours, the deadweight loss from the minimum wage law is $B + C$.

Suppose a minimum wage law requires employers to pay at least $6 per hour. With no minimum wage law, the market would clear. At the equilibrium wage rate of $5 per hour, workers would supply 100 million hours, exactly the amount employers want to hire. With the minimum wage law, employers wish to hire only 80 million hours at $6 per hour (point R), reducing the quantity of labor demanded by 20 million hours.

But the full measure of unemployment is more than 20 million hours. Unemployment measures the amount of labor that workers would like to supply but cannot supply because labor is in excess supply. At the minimum wage of $6 per hour, workers would like to supply 115 million hours, but employers will only hire workers for 80 million hours. Thus, the minimum wage law causes an excess supply of labor (unemployed labor) of 35 million hours (the horizontal distance between R and T).

With the minimum wage law the employers who hire labor are the ones between points Y and R on the demand curve. The consumer surplus they receive (remember, employers are the consumers of labor) is area G. Thus, consumer surplus falls (by areas A and B) with the minimum wage. This explains why businesses often strongly lobby policy makers to keep the minimum wage from being raised.

Workers who are lucky enough to get jobs with the minimum wage will receive $6 instead of $5 per hour. The extra income to these workers is measured by area A. This is an income transfer because it represents money transferred away from employers to workers. Observe that area B is *not* part of the income transfer. Because the minimum wage reduces the number of jobs, the benefits in area B simply disappear, becoming part of the deadweight loss.

How will producer surplus be affected by a minimum wage law? To answer this question, we must recognize that all of the suppliers of labor between Z and T on the supply curve want to work at the minimum wage, but only some of them will find jobs. Since there is an excess supply of labor, we need to know who finds a job. Let's consider two possible scenarios.

- *Case 1. The most efficient workers find jobs.* Suppose the workers between Z and W on the supply curve are the ones who find jobs. The other workers between W and T are unable to do so, even though they are willing to work at $6 per hour.

   The producer surplus is area $A + E + F$. This is the maximum possible producer surplus under the minimum wage. As Figure 10.11 indicates, the sum of consumer and producer surplus is $A + E + F + G$. The deadweight loss is $B + C$.

- *Case 2. The least efficient workers find jobs.* A second possibility is that the 80 million hours are supplied by those workers between points X and T on the supply curve in Figure 10.12.[9] The other potential workers between Z and X would be unable to find jobs, even though they are willing to work at a wage of $6 per hour and could do so more efficiently.

Now the producer surplus is area $M + N + \mathcal{J}$. This is the minimum possible producer surplus. As Figure 10.12 indicates, the sum of consumer and producer surplus is $G + \mathcal{J} + L + M + N$. The minimum wage law creates a deadweight loss of

---

[9]We do not consider workers to the right of point T on the supply curve because they would not be willing to take jobs at a wage of $6 per hour.

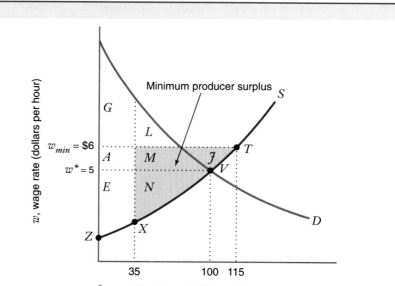

FIGURE 10.12   Minimum Wage Law Case 2: Minimum Producer Surplus
Since minimum wage law creates an excess supply of labor, it is not obvious which workers will find jobs. If the least efficient workers (those located between points X and T on the supply curve) find jobs, the deadweight loss from the minimum wage law is $A + E - J$. The welfare loss from the minimum wage law will be larger than in Figure 10.11 because producer surplus is smaller when inefficient workers displace more efficient workers.

	Free Market	With Minimum Wage	Impact of Minimum Wage Law
Consumer surplus	$A + G + L + M$	$G + L$	$-A - M$
Producer surplus	$E + N$	$M + N + J$	$M + J - E$
Net benefits (Consumer + Producer surplus)	$A + E + G + L + M + N$	$G + J + L + M + N$	$J - A - E$
Deadweight loss	zero	$A + E - J$	

$A + E - J$. The deadweight loss is larger in Case 2 than in Case 1 because the producer surplus is smaller when inefficient workers displace more efficient workers.

The two cases define upper and lower limits on the producer surplus and deadweight loss from a minimum wage law. The actual producer surplus and deadweight loss typically falls in between the levels in these two polar cases, depending on which workers find the available jobs.

There are several simplifying assumptions that are important in the analysis of minimum wage laws. First, we assume that the quality of labor does not change as the minimum wage rises. It is sometimes suggested that employers are able to hire better workers at high wages. If this is the case, the analysis would need to be modified to recognize that the quality of labor changes as the wage rate rises. Also, a minimum wage control in one market may affect wage rates in other markets, ultimately affecting the prices of many goods and services. A study of these additional effects is beyond the scope of the analysis here, but you should recognize that these effects may be important.

Unintended Consequences of Price Regulation in Airline Markets

Between 1938 and 1978, the Civil Aeronautics Board (CAB) controlled many key features of the interstate airline market, including air fares and the number of carriers in city-pair markets. Regulators required all carriers serving a given interstate city-pair market (e.g., the route between Chicago and Los Angeles) to charge the same fare. The CAB also made it difficult for new firms to enter the market.

Although the CAB closely regulated service in interstate markets, it did not have the authority to regulate airline service in intrastate markets. In unregulated intrastate markets (for example, on the route between San Francisco and Los Angeles), the fares were as much as 45 percent lower than on a route of comparable distance in a regulated interstate market.

Figure 10.13(a) illustrates the cost difference for two carriers in comparable markets (e.g., in two routes of 400 miles with similar demand curves). The fare in the interstate market is P_{REG}, while the fare in the unregulated intrastate route is P_{UNREG}. There was little producer surplus in interstate and intrastate markets. Unregulated price competition and relatively easy entry dissipated profits in intrastate markets.

Profits were also low in interstate markets, but for different reasons. Because of CAB regulation, interstate carriers were not able to engage in price competition. They were also unable to restructure their routes to reduce costs. Without strong price competition, labor unions were often able to win large wage increases. Although prices were regulated, carriers competed away almost all of their profits with *nonprice competition,* attempting to attract more passengers by serving expensive meals, having more flight attendants, and providing other amenities to passengers. Airlines also competed by offering more frequent flights, often leading to low "load factors," meaning that planes typically departed with a high percentage of empty seats. The ultimate effect of regulation was to raise costs in interstate markets.

As Figure 10.13(b) suggests, the consumer surplus for a comparable route was much higher in an intrastate market (area $A + B + G$) than in an interstate market (area G). If the costs for interstate carriers had been as low as the costs in intrastate markets, airlines would have earned a producer surplus equal to area A, and the deadweight loss from regulation would have been area B. However, because of nonprice competition, interstate airlines did not capture A as producer surplus. Labor unions did capture part of area A with higher wages, and the rest of the potential economic benefit disappeared because of inefficiencies in airline operations.

After deregulation occurred in interstate markets, real (deflated) airline fares dropped significantly, and performance in interstate markets more closely resembled that already observed in intrastate markets.[10]   ∎

[10]For more on airline deregulation see E. Bailey, D. Graham, and D. Sibley, *Deregulating the Airlines* (Cambridge, Mass., MIT Press, 1985), and S. Borenstein, "The Evolution of U.S. Airline Competition," *Journal of Economic Perspectives*, 6 (2) (Spring 1992).

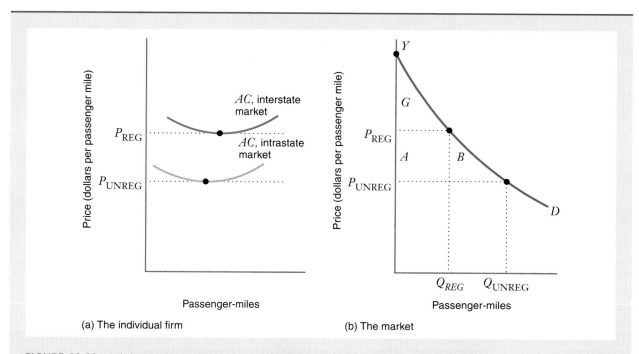

(a) The individual firm

(b) The market

FIGURE 10.13   Minimum Price Regulation for Airlines
Before 1978, the Civil Aeronautics Board controlled many key features of the interstate airline market, including airline fares (P_{REG}). Intrastate airline markets were unregulated (P_{UNREG}), with costs and fares as much as 45 percent lower than fares in comparable regulated markets. The consumer surplus for a comparable route was much higher in an intrastate market (area $A + B + G$) than in an interstate market (area G). If the costs for interstate carriers had been as low as the costs in intrastate markets, airlines would have earned a producer surplus equal to area A, and the deadweight loss from regulation would have been area B. However, because of nonprice competition, interstate airlines did not capture A as producer surplus. Labor unions captured part of area A with higher wages, and the rest of the potential economic benefit disappeared because of inefficiencies in airline operations.

LEARNING-BY-DOING EXERCISE 10.4

Price Floor

The supply and demand curves illustrated in Figure 10.14 are the same ones we have used in the previous three Learning-By-Doing Exercises. With no price floor, the sum of consumer and producer surplus would be area YVZ ($54 million). Suppose the government sets a price floor of $12 in the market.

Problem

(a) What is the size of the excess supply in the market with the price floor? What is the consumer surplus?

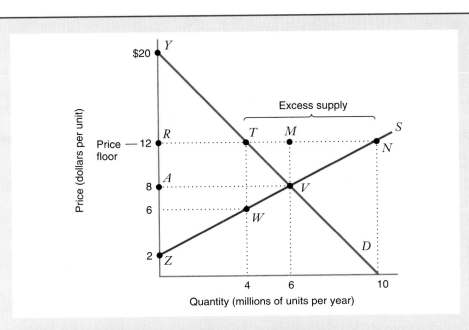

FIGURE 10.14 Price Floor: Learning-By-Doing Exercise 10.4
With a price floor of $12, producers would like to supply 10 million units, but consumers demand only 4 million units. There is an excess supply of 6 million units. Consumer surplus is the area *RTY* ($16 million). The size of the producer surplus depends on which suppliers are in the market.

Case 1. Maximum Producer Surplus: If producers with the lowest costs (those between *Z* and *W* on the supply curve) supply the 4 million units consumers desire, producer surplus will be the area *ZWTR* ($32 million). The sum of consumer surplus ($16 million) and producer surplus ($32 million) is $48 million, or $6 million short of the total surplus possible in an unregulated market. This $6 million deadweight loss is area *TWV*.

Case 2. Minimum Producer Surplus: If producers with the highest costs (those between *V* and *N* on the supply curve) supply the 4 million units, producer surplus will be the area *MNV* ($8 million). The sum of consumer surplus ($16 million) and producer surplus ($8 million) is only $24 million, or $30 million short of the total surplus possible in an unregulated market. The deadweight loss in Case 2 is therefore $30 million.

(b) What is the maximum producer surplus, assuming producers with the lowest costs sell the good? What is the deadweight loss in this case?
(c) What is the minimum producer surplus, assuming producers with the highest costs sell the good? What is the deadweight loss in this case?

Solution

(a) If the price floor is $12, consumers will demand 4 million units, but producers will want to supply 10 million. The excess supply is 6 million units, the distance between *T* and *N*.

The consumer surplus is the area of the triangle above the price floor of $12 and below the demand curve. Consumer surplus will be the area *RTY* ($16 million).

(b) Suppose that the most efficient producers (those between Z and W on the supply curve) supply the 4 million units consumers desire. Producer surplus will be the area $ZWTR$ ($32 million). The sum of consumer surplus ($16 million) and producer surplus ($32 million) is $48 million.

How much is the deadweight loss? With the price floor, the consumer and producer surplus is only $48 million, or $6 million short of the total surplus possible in an unregulated market. This $6 million deadweight loss is area TWV.

(c) If the least efficient suppliers (those between V and N on the supply curve) sell the 4 million units, producer surplus will be the area MNV ($8 million). Now the sum of consumer surplus ($16 million) and producer surplus ($8 million) is only $24 million, or $30 million short of the total surplus possible in an unregulated market ($54 million). The deadweight loss in Case 2 is $30 million.

Similar Problem: 10.7

10.6
PRODUCTION QUOTAS

If the government wants to support the price at a level above the equilibrium price in a free market, it may restrict the quantity produced. To limit the quantity produced, the government may place a quota, or a limit, on the number of producers in the market, or on the amount that each producer can sell. A quota attempts to place a ceiling on the *quantity* that producers can supply.

We have historically observed quotas in many agricultural markets. For example, the government may limit the number of acres a farmer can plant. Quotas are used in other industries, too. In many cities governments limit the number of taxis that may be operated, often leading to fares higher than those that would be observed in unregulated markets.

When the government imposes a quota in a market with an upward-sloping supply curve and a downward sloping demand curve, it results in the following:

- The market will not clear. There will be an excess supply of the good or service in the market.
- Consumers will buy less of the good than they would in a free market.
- Consumer surplus will be *lower* than would be the case with no quota.
- Some (but not all) of the lost consumer surplus will be transferred to producers.
- Because there is excess supply with a quota, the size of the producer surplus depends on which of the producers who want to supply the good are able to do so. If the most efficient suppliers serve the market, a quota may increase producer surplus.[11]
- There will be a deadweight loss.

Figure 10.15 illustrates the effects of a production quota. With no quota, the equilibrium price is $8, and the sum of consumer and producer surplus is area $A + B + C + E + F$ ($54 million).

---

[11]We say that producer surplus *may* increase. If the most efficient producers serve the market, producer surplus *will* increase for some levels of the quota. However, if the quota is too low (for example, close to zero), producer surplus could actually decrease.

The demand curve indicates that consumers will pay $12 per unit when a quota limits production to 4 million units. At that price producers would like to supply 10 million units. There will be an excess supply of 6 million units.

With a quota, consumer surplus (area F, $16 million) is lower than the amount in the competitive market (areas $A + B + F$, $36 million). The reduction in consumer surplus occurs because the quota supports the price at $12, well above the $8 equilibrium price in a competitive market.

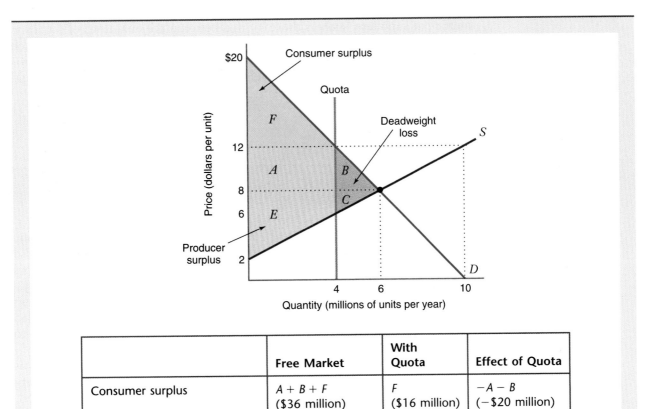

	Free Market	With Quota	Effect of Quota
Consumer surplus	$A + B + F$ ($36 million)	F ($16 million)	$-A - B$ ($-20 million)
Producer surplus	$C + E$ ($18 million)	$A + E$ ($32 million)	$-A - C$ ($14 million)
Net benefits (Consumer + Producer surplus)	$A + B + C + E + F$ ($54 million)	$A + E + F$ ($48 million)	$-B - C$ ($-6 million)
Deadweight loss	zero	$B + C$ ($6 million)	

FIGURE 10.15 Production Quota
If a quota limits production to 4 million units, consumers pay a price of $12. Producers would like to supply 10 million units at that price. There is therefore an excess supply of 6 million units. Consumer surplus is the area F ($16 million). The size of the producer surplus depends on which suppliers are in the market. In this example we assume producers with the lowest costs supply the 4 million units consumers desire. Producer surplus is the area $A + E$ ($32 million). The sum of consumer surplus ($16 million) and producer surplus ($32 million) is $48 million, or $6 million short of the total surplus possible in an unregulated market. This $6 million deadweight loss is area $B + C$.

The size of the producer surplus depends on which suppliers are in the market. If producers with the lowest costs serve the market, producer surplus is the area $A + E$ ($32 million). In this case, the quota leads to an increase in producer surplus. The sum of consumer surplus ($16 million) and producer surplus ($32 million) is $48 million, $6 million short of the total surplus possible in an unregulated market. This $6 million deadweight loss is area $B + C$.

Finally, because producers would like to supply 10 million units when the price is $12, there is no guarantee that the most efficient producers will supply the 4 million units allowed by the quota. The 4 million units might be supplied by inefficient suppliers, such as those located between the quantities of 6 million and 10 million units on the supply curve. Then producer surplus will be much lower ($8 million). Note that in this case, the quota leads to a decrease in producer surplus. You should verify this, and also show that the deadweight loss could be as high as $30 million.

EXAMPLE 10.5   *Quotas for Taxi Cabs*

The taxi cab industry has the features of a competitive market. There are many small consumers of taxi service, and, if entry were unregulated, there would also be many firms providing service. However, in many cities around the world, taxis are regulated. Sometimes government control takes the form of direct price regulation. More often, cities restrict the number of licenses authorizing a taxi to operate on the street. Historically, the licenses have often been metallic objects (called *medallions*) issued by the government to certify that the driver has permission to provide taxi service. These days, a medallion is often just a paper document.

It is not surprising that taxi fares are substantially higher in cities with quotas than in cities that allow free entry because the number of medallions limits the supply of taxis. For example, in Washington, D.C., it is quite easy to enter the market, and fares are low, often half as high as they are in cities with quotas.

There are usually active markets that enable the owner of a medallion to sell it to other prospective drivers. If you want to operate a taxi in a market with a quota, you must buy an existing medallion from someone who has one. Because the quotas support the price above the equilibrium level, the medallions can be quite valuable. For example, in New York City a taxi medallion was worth about $230,000 in 1999.

When medallions can be sold, a more efficient supplier will be willing to pay more for a medallion than a less efficient supplier. The suppliers of taxi service are likely to be those with the lowest costs. This suggests that the deadweight loss from the quota system will be at the lower end of the theoretically possible range. If the supply and demand curves are similar to those in Figure 10.15, the deadweight loss should be near the area $B + C$.

In recent years many cities have been increasing the number of medallions over time, making the market more competitive. For example, early in the 1980s, the City of Chicago had a restrictive quota system with only two major suppliers of taxi service (Yellow and Checker). The city government initiated a program to increase the number of medallions gradually over a number of years.

The political reasons for the move toward competition are interesting. As the number of medallions increases, the value of medallions will fall. Owners of medallions often form a powerful interest group, strenuously objecting to increasing the number of medallions. However, there are also strong interests in favor of entry. People with low incomes frequently use taxi service, and they are strongly in favor of the program to increase competition. Politicians understand that customers of taxi service will benefit from lower fares, and these taxi customers are voters. In the end, in Chicago the voters carried the day, sending the move toward more competition on its way.

One might ask why the City of Chicago did not deregulate taxis all at once by simply eliminating the need for medallions. Out of fairness to existing holders of medallions, the government phased in increased entry over time. Anyone who bought a medallion just before the program of increased entry was announced paid a handsome price for it. By phasing in the program over a number of years, the program allowed existing holders to recover much of their investment in medallions. ■

LEARNING-BY-DOING EXERCISE 10.5

Comparing a Tax, a Price Floor, and a Quota

Before going further, let's compare three types of government intervention that lead consumers to pay a price higher than the free market price. Throughout this chapter we have used the supply and demand curves in Figure 10.1 to study the effects of government intervention. We have found that the price consumers pay will be $12 per unit for each of the following forms of intervention:

1. An excise tax of $6 (Learning-By-Doing Exercise 10.1)
2. A price floor of $12 (Learning-By-Doing Exercise 10.4)
3. A production quota of 4 million units (Figure 10.15)

To review and compare the results of these examples, answer the following questions:

Problem

(a) How will consumer surplus differ in each of the three cases?
(b) For which of the forms of intervention will we expect the producers in the market to be the efficient suppliers (the ones at the lower end of the supply curve)?
(c) Which type (or types) of government intervention might producers prefer?
(d) Which type (or types) of government intervention lead to the lowest deadweight loss?

Solution

(a) Since the price charged to consumers is $12 with each type of intervention, consumer surplus is the same.

(b) Since the market clears with an excise tax, the suppliers in the market will be the efficient ones. The market does not clear with a price floor or a quota. Inefficient suppliers may serve the market. However, if the quota is implemented with a certificate that authorizes production (as with taxi medallions in Example 10.5), and if the certificates can be resold in a competitive market, then we would expect the suppliers who ultimately acquire the certificates to be efficient.

(c) Producers would prefer the price floor or the quota, both of which may increase producer surplus. Producers will least prefer the excise tax because the tax will reduce producer surplus.

(d) Since the price and output levels are the same with all three forms of intervention, the deadweight loss will be smallest when there are efficient producers in the market (and the conditions under which efficient producers will serve the market are summarized in part (b)).

This exercise helps us to appreciate why programs that have a common consequence (here, the price consumers pay) may still differ substantially in other ways. For example, a higher consumer price does not necessarily mean that producers are better off, or that alternative programs are equally efficient. Furthermore, people who do not consume the good may benefit if tax revenues collected in this market can be used to reduce tax burdens elsewhere.

10.7
OTHER PRICE SUPPORTS

As noted in the introduction to this chapter, price support programs are common in the agricultural sector. These programs typically increase producer surplus for the farmers. In the United States, supports for products such as soybeans, corn, and peanuts often hold prices above their free market levels. Because price support programs are expensive to taxpayers, many governments have reduced price support programs over the last decade. However, many programs remain in place, and sometimes enjoy a resurgence in years when low prices threaten farming incomes.

In this section we describe two price support programs that have been used in the agricultural sector: acreage limitation programs and government purchase programs.

With an acreage limitation program, the government gives farmers an incentive to hold production below the free market level by paying farmers not to plant. Figure 10.16 illustrates how such a program works, using supply and demand curves similar to those in Figure 10.1. (We have labeled the horizontal axis in billions of bushels because agricultural support programs often involve billions instead of millions of dollars.) In equilibrium, farmers produce 6 billion bushels per year.

Suppose the government wants to support a price of $10 per bushel. Instead of imposing a quota, it provides farmers with an incentive to reduce output to 5 billion bushels, the level that would lead consumers to pay a price of $10. At a price of $10, farmers would like to produce 8 billion bushels. They would be willing to

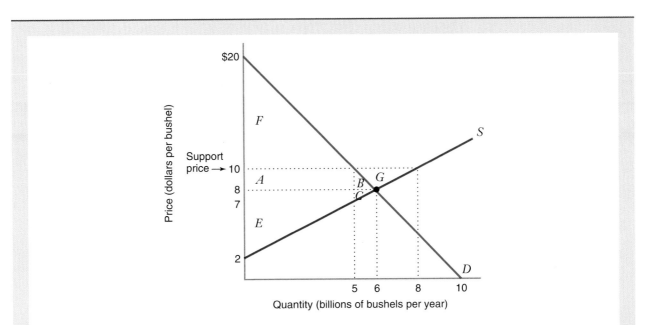

FIGURE 10.16 Acreage Limitation Program
The government could support a price of $10 per bushel by offering farmers cash for planting less acreage, reducing output to 5 billion bushels. The program costs the government $4.5 billion, increases producer surplus by $14 billion, and causes a deadweight loss of $1.5 billion (area $B + C$).

restrict production to 5 billion bushels only if the government compensates them for not producing the additional 3 billion bushels they would like to supply. The amount of producer surplus farmers would forgo to limit production to 5 billion bushels is equal to area $B + C + G$. This is the payment they will require to participate in the program.

The program increases producer surplus by $14 billion ($A + B + G$). It costs the government $4.5 billion ($B + C + G$). The net benefit to society is the sum of consumer surplus ($25 billion) and producer surplus ($32 billion), *less* the cost to the government ($4.5 billion), or $52.5 billion. The deadweight loss is $1.5 billion ($B + C$).

Since the program introduces a deadweight loss, one might ask why the government does not simply give farmers a cash transfer of $14 billion, and then let the market function without intervention to produce 6 billion bushels at a price of $8. This might seem attractive because the deadweight loss would then be zero. The government would collect the money to pay for the program from taxes imposed elsewhere. Although such a program would be efficient, the public may find it more palatable to pay farmers $4.5 billion to reduce output (and forgo a profit opportunity) than to give farmers $14 billion to do nothing at all.[12]

As an alternative to an acreage limitation program, the government can support the price with a government purchase program. Figure 10.17 illustrates how such a program might work. At a price of $10 per bushel farmers would like to produce 8 billion bushels. The market demand would be only 5 billion bushels at that price. There would be an excess supply of 3 billion bushels.

To maintain a price of $10 per bushel, the government could buy the extra 3 billion bushels to eliminate the excess supply. Producer surplus increases by $14 billion ($A + B + G$) the same amount as under the acreage limitation program.

How much would the program cost the government? The government must purchase the excess supply (3 billion bushels) at a price of $10 per bushel. The cost to the government is thus $30 billion (area $B + C + G + H + I + J$). The government could reduce the cost of the program if it were to sell some of the commodity somewhere in the world, even at a low price to help countries in need. However, if it releases some of the commodity into the market, it must recognize that it could drive the price down, lowering farmers' producer surplus, thereby working against the original goal of the support program.

The net benefit to society is the sum of consumer surplus ($25 billion, area F) and producer surplus ($32 billion, area $A + B + C + E + G$), less the cost to the government ($30 billion). The program results in a net benefit of $27 billion and a deadweight loss of $27 billion (area $B + C + H + I + J$).

LEARNING-BY-DOING EXERCISE 10.6

Comparing Price Support Programs: Government Purchases and Acreage Limitations

This exercise will help you compare the two price support programs we have just discussed, the acreage limitation program illustrated in Figure 10.16 and the government purchase program depicted in Figure 10.17. The labels in the areas in the two figures correspond to one another (for example, area B is the

---

[12]Of course, we must recognize that the government may create deadweight losses in other markets when it imposes taxes to raise the $14 billion to pay for the acreage limitation program.

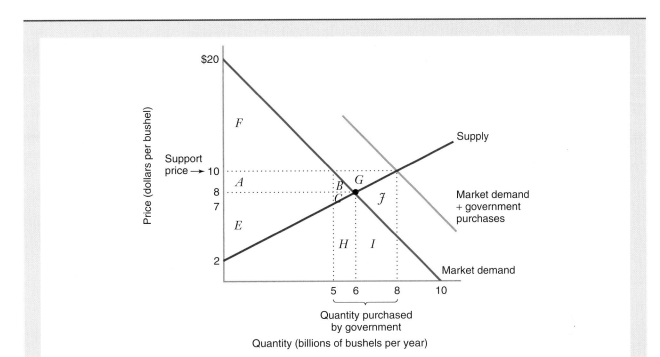

FIGURE 10.17   Government Purchase Program
At a price of $10 per bushel there would be an excess supply of 3 billion bushels. The government buys 3 billion bushels to eliminate the excess supply and maintain the support price. The program costs the government $30 billion, since it must buy 3 billion bushels at $10 per bushel. Producer surplus increases by $14 billion. The net benefit to society is the sum of consumer surplus ($25 billion) and producer surplus ($32 billion), less the cost to the government ($30 billion), resulting in a net benefit of $27 billion and a deadweight loss of $27 billion (area $B + C + H + I + J$).

same in both figures). Use the labels in the areas in the two figures to answer the following questions:

Problem

(a) If the two programs support the same price in a market, which program will cost the government more?
(b) Which program will create a larger deadweight loss?
(c) Which program would farmers prefer?

Solution

(a) The cost to the government with an acreage limitation program is area $B + C + G$. The cost with the government purchase program is $B + C + G + H + I + J$. Thus, the government purchase program is more costly.
(b) The deadweight loss with an acreage limitation program is area $B + C$. The deadweight loss with the government purchase program is $B + C + G + H + I + J$. Thus, the deadweight loss is greater with the government purchase program.
(c) Farmers are indifferent since they receive the same addition to producer surplus $(A + B + G)$ under either program.

   Government purchase programs are therefore more costly and less efficient than acreage limitation programs.[13] Often a government must spend much more than one dollar to increase farmers' producer surplus by a dollar. Nevertheless, many countries resort to government purchase programs, and they are generally more palatable politically than direct cash payments to farmers.

10.8

IMPORT TARIFFS AND QUOTAS

Many countries impose tariffs and quotas on imports to help support the price of a good in the domestic market, especially when the price in the world market is quite low and unrestricted imports would hurt domestic producers. Tariffs and quotas lead to higher domestic prices, enabling domestic producers to expand production and earn higher levels of producer surplus. In this section we will see that tariffs and quotas help domestic producers and reduce domestic consumer surplus. We will also show that these forms of intervention lead to deadweight losses by diminishing the level of total domestic surplus.

   Consumers in a country will import a good when the world price of the good is below the equilibrium price that would be observed in the domestic market if there were no imports. In Figure 10.18 the domestic supply and demand curves indicate that the equilibrium price in the market would be $8 if there were no international trade. At that price 6 million units would be produced and sold in

---

[13]If we think in terms of general equilibrium, the government purchase program in one sector is likely to create even more deadweight loss in other sectors of the economy because larger taxes will have to be collected elsewhere to finance the program.

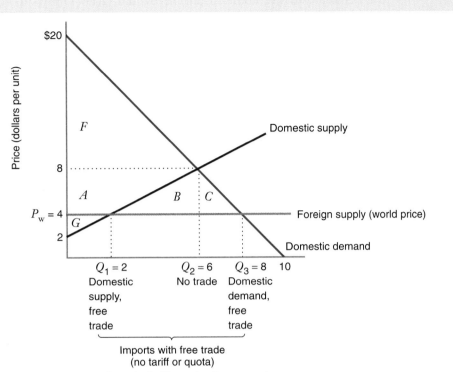

FIGURE 10.18 Imports with Free Trade

If trade were not allowed, the intersection of the domestic supply and demand curves would determine the equilibrium in the domestic market, leading to a price of $8 and a quantity of 6 million units. If the trade prohibition is removed (free trade is allowed), the good can be imported at a price of $4. The domestic price will be $4 because no domestic consumer need pay more than that price. Domestic production will fall to Q_1, but the total amount consumed domestically is Q_3. Imports are the difference between domestic consumption (Q_3) and domestic production (Q_1). Domestic consumers benefit from free trade (their consumer surplus increases by $A + B + C$). But domestic producers find their producer surplus reduced by area A when there is free trade. A prohibition on trade reduces total domestic surplus by $B + C$, the deadweight loss.

Table from the figure:

	Free Trade	No Trade	Effect of Trade Prohibition
Consumer surplus	$A + B + C + F$	F	$-A - B - C$
Domestic producer surplus	G	$A + G$	A
Net benefits (Domestic) (Consumer + Producer surplus)	$A + B + C + F + G$	$A + F + G$	$-B - C$
Deadweight loss	zero	$B + C$	

the market, and the domestic market would clear. Domestic consumer surplus would be area F, and domestic producer surplus would be $A + G$. Thus, the sum of domestic consumer and producer surplus would be area $A + F + G$.

Now suppose that foreign suppliers are willing to sell any amount of the good at a price of $4, which just covers their average cost of producing and delivering the good to the domestic market. Since this price is below the equilibrium price in the domestic market with no trade, domestic consumers will want to import the good. With free trade, the equilibrium price in the domestic market will become $4 because no domestic consumer ever needs to pay more than that price to purchase the good.

What are the consequences of free trade in the domestic market? At a price of $4, domestic consumers would purchase Q_3 (8 million units per year). At that price domestic producers would only be willing to supply Q_1 (2 million units). The amount imported would therefore be the difference between the quantity demanded and the quantity supplied domestically, or $(Q_3 - Q_1)$, that is, 6 million units per year. Consumer surplus with free trade will be $A + B + C + F$. Because domestic production has fallen with free trade, domestic producers will have a surplus of G.

As the graph indicates, domestic producers in this industry will be unhappy about free trade. Because domestic production falls with free trade, domestic producers will benefit from a prohibition on free trade, gaining the additional producer surplus A.

Since domestic producers stand to lose with free trade, they often attempt to restrict or even eliminate imports. Let's suppose that they succeed in lobbying Congress to eliminate free trade altogether. The consequences of this policy are summarized in the table below the graph in Figure 10.18. As already noted, domestic producers would increase their surplus by A. Consumers would lose $A + B + C$ because the price would increase to $8. As a whole, net benefits to society would decrease by $B + C$, the deadweight loss from prohibition.

A government may also eliminate imports if it imposes a large enough tariff on the good. A tariff is a tax on an imported good. If the world price is $4 and the government charges a tariff of $5, a domestic consumer would have to pay $9 to buy the imported good. But no consumer would buy an imported good because it would be available for $8 in the domestic market if there were no trade. In other words, if the tariff is at least as large as the difference between the domestic price with no trade and the world price, nothing will be imported. In the example in Figure 10.18, no imports will occur if the tariff is larger than $4.

What happens if a tariff less than $4 is imposed? For example, suppose a tariff of $2 is levied on the good. Figure 10.19 illustrates the equilibrium with the tariff. Domestic consumers will now be able to buy the imported good for $6, the payment required to cover the world price of $4 *plus* the $2 tariff. Thus, $6 will be the price in the domestic market. Since the $6 price is below the $8 price with no trade, some imports will occur.

How much will be imported? When the price is $6, consumers will demand Q_3 (7 million units). At that price domestic suppliers will produce Q_2 (4 million units). The difference $(Q_3 - Q_2)$, or 3 million units, will be imported.

How will the imposition of a tariff affect the domestic market? As the table in Figure 10.19 shows, domestic producers stand to gain from the tariff. Their producer surplus increases by the area A. This gain to domestic producers explains why producers often lobby for tariffs.

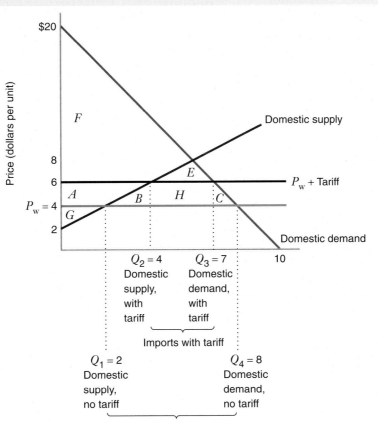

	Free Trade	**With Tariff**	**Effect of Tariff**
Consumer surplus	$A + B + C + E + F + H$	$E + F$	$-A - B - C - H$
Domestic producer surplus	G	$A + G$	A
Impact on Treasury	zero	H	H
Net benefits (domestic) (Consumer + producer surplus + impact on Treasury)	$A + B + C + E + F + G + H$	$A + E + F + G + H$	$-B - C$
Deadweight loss	zero	$B + C$	
Producer surplus, foreign	zero	zero	zero

FIGURE 10.19 Import Tariff

With free trade the price in the domestic market will be $4, the price at which the good can be imported. At that price the amount imported will be the difference between Q_4 (the quantity demanded domestically) and Q_1 (the quantity supplied by domestic producers). If the government imposes a tariff of $2 per unit, domestic consumers will have to pay $6 per unit. The amount imported will be ($Q_3 - Q_2$), or 3 million units. The tariff increases producer surplus for domestic suppliers by the area A. However, consumers lose $A + B + C + H$. The government collects revenues from the tariff equal to area H. Thus, the domestic deadweight loss is $B + C$. Producer surplus for foreign suppliers is zero with free trade and with the tariff because these suppliers receive a price of $4, which exactly covers their average cost.

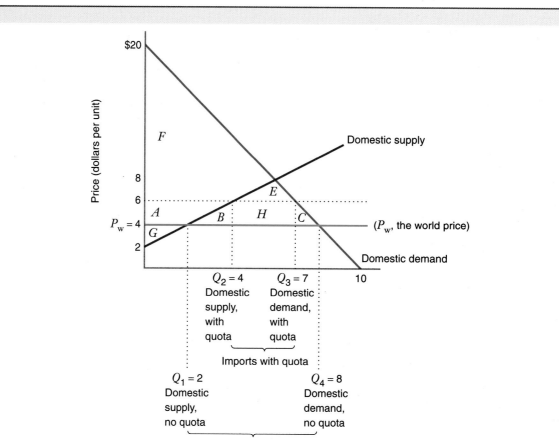

	No Quota	With Quota	Effect of Quota
Consumer surplus	$A + B + C + E + F + H$	$E + F$	$-A - B - C - H$
Producer surplus	G	$A + G$	A
Impact on Treasury	zero	zero	zero
Net benefits (domestic) (Consumer + producer surplus + impact on Treasury)	$A + B + C + E + F + G + H$	$A + E + F + G$	$-B - C - H$
Domestic deadweight loss	zero	$B + C + H$	
Producer surplus, foreign	zero	H	H

FIGURE 10.20   Import Quota
When the government restricts imports, the price in domestic markets will rise. Suppose a quota limits imports to be no larger than 3 million units ($Q_3 - Q_2$). The price in the domestic market will be $6. At that price the quantity imported plus the quantity supplied domestically will equal the quantity demanded by domestic consumers. The quota increases producer surplus for domestic suppliers by the area A. However, consumers lose $A + B + C + H$. The government collects no revenues from a quota, so the area H becomes producer surplus for *foreign* suppliers because the price they receive ($6) is higher than their average cost ($4). Thus, the *domestic* deadweight loss is $B + C + H$.

However, benefits to domestic consumers are reduced. Consumer surplus falls by $A + B + C + H$ as a result of the tariff.

There is one further impact of the tariff on the domestic economy. The government is collecting revenues from the tariff. The size of that revenue is obtained by multiplying the tariff ($2 per unit) by the number of units imported ($Q_3 - Q_2$), or 3 million units. In the example, revenues from the tariff would be $6 million per year, the amount represented by area H in the figure. The area H is a net benefit because it can be redistributed to people in the domestic economy.

When we add all of the net benefits from the tariff, we find that domestic benefits have fallen by $B + C$, the deadweight loss resulting from the tariff. Area B is a deadweight loss arising from the overproduction by domestic producers with the tariff. Area C is a deadweight loss because consumers are purchasing fewer units than they would have at the free market price.

The tariff has reduced imports from 6 million units to 3 million units per year and in the process raised the price from $4 to $6. As Figure 10.20 illustrates, the government could also raise the domestic price from $4 to $6 by imposing a quota. A quota sets a maximum limit on the amount of a good that may be imported.

Suppose the government sets a quota of 3 million units per year in this market. The equilibrium price in the domestic market is the one that clears the market, that is, makes total supply (domestic and imports) equal to domestic demand. As the graph shows, the equilibrium price will be $6. At that price domestic suppliers will produce 4 million units and imports will be 3 million units. This is the amount necessary to satisfy domestic consumers, who want to purchase 7 million units at a price of $6.

How will the imposition of the quota affect the domestic market? As the table in Figure 10.20 shows, domestic producer surplus increases by the area A. And, as before, the quota reduces domestic consumer surplus by $A + B + C + H$.

The tariff in Figure 10.19 and the quota in Figure 10.20 lead to the same equilibrium price and level of imports. As the figures show, the impacts of the tariff and quota are the same for consumers and producers. However, there is one important difference between the tariff and the quota. With the tariff, the government collects area H as revenue from the tariff. As noted earlier, this is a benefit to the economy because these revenues can be redistributed to members of society. With the quota no revenues are collected by the government. Area H becomes a part of producer surplus for foreign suppliers who are able to sell their goods at a price of $6 when they would have been willing to supply at a price of $4. Thus, area H is lost to the domestic economy and becomes part of the domestic deadweight loss. When we add all of the net benefits from the quota, we find that domestic benefits have fallen by $B + C + H$, the deadweight loss resulting from the tariff.

EXAMPLE 10.6

Dumping

In the past decade some countries have complained that foreign countries have subsidized their own industries to help them gain a larger share of the world market. For example, it has often been alleged that Japanese producers of steel are selling in foreign markets at a price below their cost, in part because of subsidies from the Japanese government. In this example we study the effects of dumping.

Suppose that the world price of steel delivered to the United States is P_W, set in a competitive world market in which price, average cost, and marginal cost are

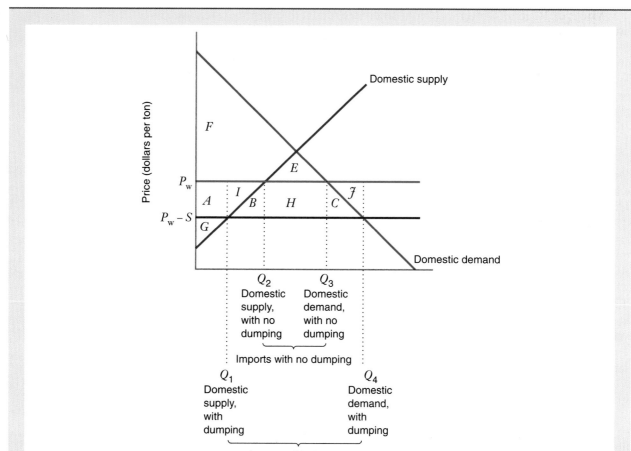

	Free Trade (No Dumping)	With Dumping	Effect of Dumping
Consumer surplus	$E + F$	$A + B + C + E + F + H + I$	$A + B + C + H + I$
Producer surplus	$A + G + I$	G	$-A - I$
Net benefits (Domestic) (Consumer + Producer surplus)	$A + E + F + G + I$	$A + B + C + E + F + G + H + I$	$B + C + H$
Impact on treasury of foreign government	zero	$-B - C - H - I - J$	$-B - C - H - I - J$

FIGURE 10.21   Dumping

Suppose steel can be produced in the rest of the world and delivered to the United States at the price P_W. If a foreign government engages in dumping, it is subsidizing its steel industry to help it gain a larger share of the world market. Suppose a foreign government gives its steel producers a subsidy of $\$S$ per ton. The price to domestic consumers in the United States is then $P_W - S$. Imports will expand from $(Q_3 - Q_2)$ to $(Q_4 - Q_1)$. Domestic consumers will benefit as their surplus increases by $A + B + C + H + I$. However, domestic producers will be unhappy with the dumping because their surplus falls by $A + I$. Net domestic benefits rise by $B + C + H$. Part of the increase in domestic benefit results from the subsidy the foreign government is paying to its producers, $B + C + H + I + J$.

equal. If a foreign government provides a subsidy of $\$S$ per unit, the domestic consumers would be able to import steel at a price $P_W - S$, as Figure 10.21 illustrates. Under free trade (with no dumping) imports would be $Q_3 - Q_2$. However, with the new, lower domestic price with dumping, imports will expand to $Q_4 - Q_1$.

How will dumping affect the domestic market? Domestic consumers will benefit as their surplus increases by $A + B + C + H + I$. However, domestic producers will be quite unhappy with the dumping because their surplus falls by $A + I$. Among other things, they will note that dumping keeps workers on the job in the country engaging in dumping, while unemployment is likely to rise among steel workers at home. That is why it is often said that dumping leads to an export of jobs from the domestic country to the country subsidizing its industry.

In practice, it is not easy to establish that dumping is occurring because one needs proof that firms are selling at a price below cost. It may be especially difficult to gather data on the costs of production for foreign firms. ■

CHAPTER SUMMARY

• In a competitive market each producer acts in its own self interest, deciding whether to be in the market, and, if so, how much to produce to maximize its own producer surplus. Similarly, each consumer also acts in his or her own self interest, maximizing utility to determine how many units of the good to buy. Even though there is no social planner telling producers and consumers how to behave, the output in a competitive market maximizes net economic benefits (as measured by the sum of the surpluses). It is as though there is an "invisible hand" guiding a competitive market to the efficient level of production and consumption.

• Government intervention can take many forms, including taxes and subsidies, minimum and maximum price regulation, production quotas, price support programs, and tariffs on imports and exports. For some kinds of government intervention (such as taxes and subsidies) the market will clear. For other types of intervention (such as price ceilings, price floors, and production quotas) the market will not clear. When the market does not clear, we must understand who is participating in the market when we measure consumer and producer surplus.

• When a tax is imposed in a market, the price consumers pay usually rises by less than the amount of the tax, and the price producers receive usually falls by less than the amount of the tax. The incidence of a tax measures the impact of the tax on the price consumers pay versus the price that sellers receive. When demand is rather inelastic and supply is relatively elastic, the incidence of an excise tax will be larger for consumers than for producers. When the relative magnitudes of the elasticities are reversed, the incidence of an excise tax will be larger for producers than for consumers.

• Government intervention in competitive markets usually leads to a deadweight loss. Deadweight loss is an economic inefficiency that arises when consumers and producers do not capture potential net benefits.

• Government intervention in competitive markets often redistributes income from one part of the economy to another. If the government collects revenues through taxes or tariffs, the receipts are part of the net benefit to the economy because the revenues can be redistributed. Similarly, net flows away from the government are a part of the cost of a program.

• An excise tax leads to a deadweight loss because the market produces less than the efficient level. A tax also reduces both consumer and producer surplus. **(LBD Exercise 10.1)**

• When the government pays a subsidy for each unit produced, the market produces more than the efficient level, leading to a deadweight loss. A subsidy increases both consumer and producer surplus, but these gains are less than the government's cost to pay for the subsidy. **(LBD Exercise 10.2)**

• With a binding price ceiling (i.e., a ceiling below the free market price), the amount exchanged in the market will be less than the efficient level because producers restrict supply. There will be excess demand in the market, and consumers who value the good the most may not be able to purchase the good. **(LBD Exercise 10.3)**

• With a binding price floor (i.e., a floor above the free market price), the amount exchanged in the market will be less than the efficient level because consumers buy less. There will be excess supply in the market, and the lowest-cost producers may not be those who supply the good.   **(LBD Exercise 10.4)**

• A production quota raises the price consumers pay by limiting the output in the market. Although one would normally expect producer surplus to rise with such a quota, this need not always occur. Because the market does not clear with a production quota, there is no guar-

antee that the suppliers serving the market are the ones with the lowest cost.   **(LBD Exercise 10.5)**

• Acreage limitation and government purchase programs have often been used to support prices in the agricultural sector. These programs can be quite costly to the government and also may introduce large deadweight losses.   **(LBD Exercise 10.6)**

• Governments may resort to import tariffs and quotas to enhance producer surplus for domestic suppliers. These forms of intervention reduce consumer surplus and create deadweight loss for the domestic economy.

REVIEW QUESTIONS

1. What is the significance of the "invisible hand" in a competitive market?

2. What is the size of the deadweight loss in a competitive market with no government intervention?

3. What is meant by the incidence of a tax? How is the incidence of an excise tax related to the elasticities of supply and demand in a market?

4. In the competitive market for hard liquor, the demand is relatively inelastic and the supply is relatively elastic. Will the incidence of an excise tax of $T be greater for consumers or producers?

5. Gizmos are produced and sold in a competitive market. When there is no tax, the equilibrium price is $100 per gizmo. The own-price elasticity of demand for gizmos is known to be about −0.9 and the own-price elasticity of supply is about 1.2. In commenting on a proposed excise tax of $10 per gizmo, a newspaper article states that "the tax will probably drive the price of gizmos up by about $10." Is this a reasonable conclusion?

6. The cheese-making industry in Castoria is competitive, with an upward-sloping supply curve and a downward-sloping demand curve. The government gives cheese

producers a subsidy of $T for each kilogram of cheese they make. Will consumer surplus increase? Will producer surplus increase? Will there be a deadweight loss?

7. Will a price ceiling always increase consumer surplus? Will a price floor always increase producer surplus?

8. Will a production quota in a competitive market always increase producer surplus?

9. Why are agricultural price support programs, such as acreage limitation and government purchase programs, often very costly to implement?

10. If an import tariff and an import quota lead to the same price in a competitive market, which one will lead to a larger domestic deadweight loss?

11. Why does a market clear when the government imposes an excise tax of $T per unit?

12. Why does a market clear when the government gives producers a subsidy of $S per unit?

13. Why does the market not clear with a production quota?

14. With a price floor, will the most efficient producers necessarily be the ones supplying the market?

PROBLEMS

10.1. In a competitive market with no government intervention, the equilibrium price is $10 and the equilibrium quantity is 10,000 units. Explain whether the market will clear under each of the following forms of government intervention:

a) The government imposes an excise tax of $1 per unit.
b) The government pays a subsidy of $5 per unit produced.

c) The government sets a price floor of $12.
d) The government sets a price ceiling of $8.
e) The government sets a production quota, allowing only 5,000 units to be produced.

10.2. In Learning-By-Doing Exercise 10.1 we examined the effects of an excise tax of $6 per unit. Repeat that exercise for an excise tax of $3.

10.3. Gadgets are produced and sold in a competitive market. When there is no tax, the equilibrium price is $20 per gadget. The own price elasticity of demand for gadgets is −0.5. If an excise tax of $4 leads to an increase in the price of gadgets to $24, what must be true about the own price elasticity of supply for gadgets?

10.4. Table 10.1 indicates that revenues from gasoline taxes will increase by about $10 billion (from $33 billion to about $43 billion per year) if the gasoline tax is raised from $0.30 to $0.40 per gallon. Using the supply and demand curves in Example 10.1, show that the equilibrium quantity, price consumers pay, price producers receive, and tax receipts are as indicated in the table when the tax is $0.40 per gallon. Draw a graph illustrating the equilibrium when the tax is $0.40 per gallon.

10.5. Assume that a competitive market has an upward-sloping supply curve and a downward-sloping demand curve, both of which are linear. A tax of size T is currently imposed in the market. Suppose the tax is doubled. By what multiple will the deadweight loss increase? (You may assume that at the new tax, the equilibrium quantity is positive.)

10.6. Suppose the market for corn in Pulmonia is competitive. No imports and exports are possible. The demand curve is:

$$Q^d = 10 - P^d,$$

where Q^d is the quantity demanded (in millions of bushels) when the price consumers pay is P^d. The supply curve is:

$$Q^s = \begin{cases} -4 + P^s, & \text{when } P^s \geq 4 \\ 0, & \text{when } P^s \leq 4 \end{cases}$$

where Q^s is the quantity supplied (in millions of bushels) when the price producers receive is P^s.

a) What are the equilibrium price and quantity?
b) At the equilibrium in part (a), what is consumer surplus? Producer surplus? Deadweight loss? Show all of these graphically.
c) Suppose the government imposes an excise tax of $2 per unit to raise government revenues. What will the new equilibrium quantity be? What price will buyers pay? What price will sellers receive?
d) At the equilibrium in part (c), what is consumer surplus? Producer surplus? The impact on the government budget (here a positive number, the government tax receipts)? Deadweight loss? Show all of these graphically.
e) Suppose the government has a change of heart about the importance of corn revenues to the happiness of the

Pulmonian farmers. The tax is removed, and a subsidy of $1 per unit is granted to corn producers. What will the equilibrium quantity be? What price will the buyer pay? What amount (including the subsidy) will corn farmers receive?
f) At the equilibrium in part (e), what is consumer surplus? Producer surplus? What will be the total cost to the government? Deadweight loss? Show all of these graphically.
g) Verify that for your answers to parts (b), (d), and (f) the following sum is identical:

Consumer surplus + Producer surplus +
Budgetary impact + Deadweight loss

Why is the sum equal in all three cases?

10.7. Figure 10.22 on the next page shows the supply schedule and the demand schedule for cigarettes. The equilibrium price in the market is $2.00 per pack if the government does not intervene, and the quantity exchanged in the market would be 1,000 units. Suppose the government has decided to discourage smoking, and is considering two possible policies that would reduce the quantity sold to 600. The two policies are (i) a tax on cigarettes, (ii) a law setting a minimum price for cigarettes. Analyze each of the policies using the graph and fill in the table.

10.8. Suppose that in the domestic market for computer chips the demand is $P^d = 110 - Q^d$, where Q^d is the number of units of chips demanded domestically when the price is P^d. The domestic supply is $P^s = 10 + Q^s$, where Q^s is the number of units of chips supplied domestically when domestic suppliers receive a price P^s. Foreign suppliers would be willing to supply any number of chips at a price of $30. The government is contemplating three possible policies:

Policy I: The government decides to ban imports of chips.
Policy II: Foreign suppliers are allowed to import chips (with no tariff).
Policy III: The government allows imports, but imposes a tariff of 10 per unit.

Fill in the table in Figure 10.23 (page 461). (Give a numerical answer for each part.)

10.9. The domestic demand for portable radios is given by $Q^d = 5,000 - 100P$, where Q^d is the number of radios that would be purchased when the price is P. The domestic supply schedule for radios is given by $Q^s = 150P$, where Q^s is the quantity of radios that would be produced domestically if the price were P. Suppose radios can be obtained in the world market at a price of $10 per radio. Domestic radio producers have successfully lobbied Congress to impose a tariff of $5 per radio.

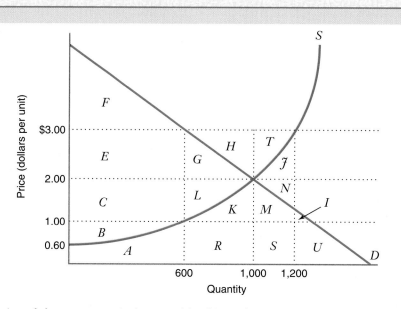

a) What is the size of the tax per unit that would achieve the government's target of 600 units sold in the market? Explain.

b) Using areas in the graph, answer the following.

	Tax	Minimum Price
What price per unit would consumers pay?		
What price per unit would producers receive?		
What area represents consumer surplus?		
What area represents the largest producer surplus possible under the policy?		
What area represents the smallest producer surplus possible under the policy?		
What area represents government receipts?		
What area represents smallest deadweight loss possible under the policy?		

FIGURE 10.22   Graph and Table for Problem 10.7

Policy	Policy I Ban Imports	Policy II No Tariff	Policy III Import Tariff
How many units of chips would be consumed domestically?			
How many units of chips would be produced domestically?			
What is the size of domestic producer surplus?			
What is the size of consumer surplus?			
What is the size of government receipts?			

FIGURE 10.23   **Table for Problem 10.8**

a) Draw a graph illustrating the free trade equilibrium (with no tariff). Clearly illustrate the equilibrium price.
b) By how much would the tariff increase producer surplus for domestic radio suppliers?
c) How much would the government collect in tariff revenues?
d) What is the deadweight loss from the tariff?

10.10. Suppose the supply curve in a market is upward-sloping, and that the demand curve is totally inelastic. In a free market the price is $30 per ton. If an excise tax of $2 per ton is imposed in the market, what will be the resulting deadweight loss?

CHAPTER 11

Monopoly and Monopsony

What do golf clubs, oil field instruments, appliances, and semiconductor packages have in common?[1] They are all products that are manufactured using beryllium. Beryllium is a light metal distinguished by its high rigidity, its resistance to corrosion, and its stability when heated. In nature, beryllium ore—called bertrandite—is found in mineral rocks, coal, and volcanic dust. In the United States, beryllium ore is concentrated in one place: central Utah.

Why talk about beryllium in a microeconomics textbook? Because the market for beryllium has just one seller: Brush Wellman. Brush Wellman is a U.S. firm whose proven ore reserves are large enough to supply the world's beryllium needs for the next sixty years. A company that uses beryllium to manufacture its products, such as Kyocera America (a producer of semiconductor packages) or Dynacraft Golf (a maker of golf clubs), has only one place to go for its beryllium needs: Brush Wellman. Brush Wellman is, in short, a *monopolist* in the market for beryllium.

This chapter studies the production and pricing decision in a **monopoly market**. A monopoly market consists of a single seller facing many buyers. While pure monopolies, such as Brush Wellman, are not widespread, many markets operate under near-monopoly conditions in which a single firm accounts for an overwhelming share of sales. For example, the German firm Hauni Maschinen-

bau has a global market share of over 90 percent for cigarette-making machines. Another German company, Konig and Bauer, produces 90 percent of the worldwide supply of money printing presses. Within the United States, Gillette sells over 80 percent of cartridge razor products (razors and blades), and Microsoft's Windows accounts for over 90 percent of the market for operating systems for personal computers.

Unlike a perfectly competitive market in which each firm has an imperceptible impact on the market price, a monopolist must recognize that its output decision critically affects the market price for its product. If, for example, Brush Wellman cut its rate of production, the price of beryllium would probably rise. Of course, Brush Wellman, by itself, can only

raise the price of beryllium so much. After all, at some point, it might make sense for a buyer of beryllium to switch to other substitute materials (e.g., copper-tungsten or aluminum). Thus, a monopolist, such as Brush Wellman, must recognize that the properties of the market demand curve—in particular the price elasticity of market demand—will affect the price it can set in the market.

When an individual agent can affect the price that prevails in the market, we say the agent has market power. In a monopoly market, the seller has market power. However, buyers can also have market power. A **monopsony market** consists of a single *buyer* purchasing a product from many suppliers. Monopsonies most frequently arise in markets for inputs, such as raw materials or industrial

---

[1]A semiconductor package protects the semiconductor from exposure to the air and allows it to be attached to a larger piece of equipment, such as a circuitboard. The package also allows the semiconductor to dissipate heat and can enhance the semiconductor's performance.

components. They also arise in industries, such as aerospace, where the buyer is often a government agency, such as the U.S. Department of Defense or NASA. In this chapter, we will use the tools that we develop to study monopoly markets to examine the price-setting decisions by a buyer in a monopsony market. ∎

11.1
PROFIT MAXIMIZATION BY A MONOPOLIST

THE PROFIT MAXIMIZATION CONDITION

A firm in a perfectly competitive market has an inconsequential impact on the market price and thus takes it as given. By contrast, a monopolist like Brush Wellman in the beryllium market *sets* the market price for its product. So what would stop the monopolist from setting an infinitely-high price? The answer is that the monopolist must take account of the market demand curve: the higher the price it sets, the fewer units of its product it will sell. The lower the price it sets, the more units it will sell. The profit-maximizing monopolist's problem is finding the optimal trade-off between volume (the number of units it sells) and margin (the differential between price and marginal cost on the units it sells). The logic we develop to analyze this volume–margin trade-off will apply in the nonmonopoly market settings (oligopoly and monopolistic competition) that we study in later chapters.

To analyze the monopolist's price-setting problem, it is easiest to imagine the monopolist first choosing a quantity Q of output to sell and then, from the market demand curve, determining the price $P(Q)$ it would need to charge to sell that amount of output from the market demand curve. To illustrate, suppose a monopolist in the market for beryllium faces the market demand curve in Figure 11.1. The equation of this demand curve is $P(Q) = 12 - Q$. (Q is expressed in millions of ounces per year, and P is expressed in dollars per ounce.) To sell 2 million ounces, the monopolist would charge a price of $10 per ounce. But to sell a higher quantity such as 5 million ounces, the monopolist would have to lower its price to $7 per ounce.

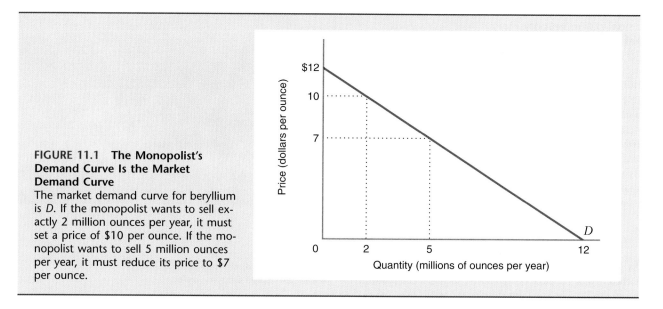

FIGURE 11.1 The Monopolist's Demand Curve Is the Market Demand Curve
The market demand curve for beryllium is *D*. If the monopolist wants to sell exactly 2 million ounces per year, it must set a price of $10 per ounce. If the monopolist wants to sell 5 million ounces per year, it must reduce its price to $7 per ounce.

As we move along the monopolist's demand curve, different quantities and their associated prices generate different amounts of total revenue for the monopolist. Total revenue is price times quantity, so in this case the monopolist's total revenue is $TR(Q) = P(Q) \times Q = 12Q - Q^2$. Let's further suppose that the monopolist's total cost of production is given by the equation $TC(Q) = (1/2)Q^2$. Table 11.1 shows numerical calculations for price, total revenue, total cost, and profit for the monopolist, and the top panel of Figure 11.2 illustrates total revenue, total cost, and total profit graphically.

Figure 11.2 reveals that total cost TC increases as Q increases. Total revenue TR, by contrast, first rises as Q increases but then falls. Similarly, total profit first rises and then falls. The monopolist's profit is maximized at the peak of the profit hill, which occurs at $Q = 4$ million ounces. For quantities less than $Q = 4$ million, increasing the output increases total revenues more than it increases total cost, which moves the firm up its profit hill in Figure 11.2. As the bottom panel of Figure 11.2 shows, over this range of output, the monopolist's *marginal revenue* exceeds its *marginal cost*:

$$MR > MC$$

For quantities greater than $Q = 4$ million, producing *less output* increases profit. Over this range, decreasing quantity decreases total cost faster than it decreases total revenue, which also moves the firm up its profit hill. Over this range of output, the monopolist's *marginal revenue* is less than its *marginal cost*:

$$MR < MC$$

Let's summarize what this discussion implies:

- If the firm produced a quantity at which $MR > MC$, the firm cannot be maximizing its profit. Why? Because it could *increase* its output and its profit would go up.

TABLE 11.1
Total Revenue, Cost, and Profit for the Beryllium Monopolist

Q (million ounces)	P ($/oz.)	TR ($ million)	TC ($ million)	Profit ($ million)
0	12	0	0	0
1	11	11.00	0.50	10.50
2	10	20.00	2.00	18.00
3	9	27.00	4.50	22.50
4	8	32.00	8.00	24.00
5	7	35.00	12.50	22.50
6	6	36.00	18.00	18.00
7	5	35.00	24.50	10.50
8	4	32.00	32.00	0
9	3	27.00	40.50	13.50
10	2	20.00	50.00	−30.00

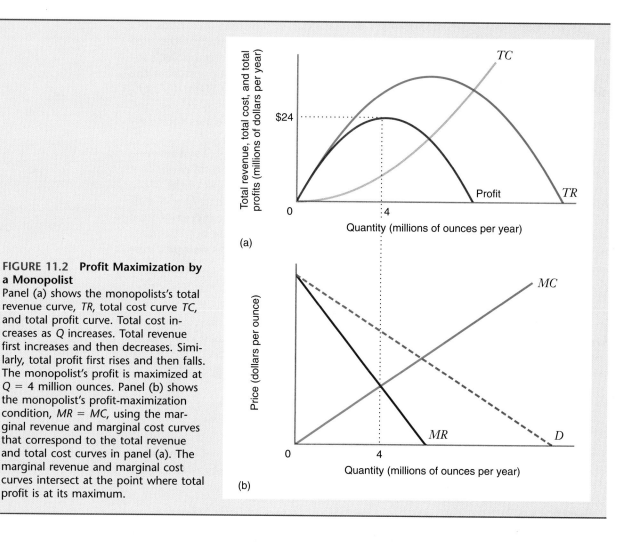

FIGURE 11.2   Profit Maximization by a Monopolist
Panel (a) shows the monopolists's total revenue curve, *TR*, total cost curve *TC*, and total profit curve. Total cost increases as *Q* increases. Total revenue first increases and then decreases. Similarly, total profit first rises and then falls. The monopolist's profit is maximized at *Q* = 4 million ounces. Panel (b) shows the monopolist's profit-maximization condition, *MR* = *MC*, using the marginal revenue and marginal cost curves that correspond to the total revenue and total cost curves in panel (a). The marginal revenue and marginal cost curves intersect at the point where total profit is at its maximum.

- If the firm produced a quantity at which *MR* < *MC*, the firm cannot be maximizing its profit. Why? Because it could decrease its output and its profit would go up.

- The only situation at which the monopolist *cannot* improve its profit by increasing or decreasing output is where *MR* = *MC*.

- Therefore, we conclude that at the monopolist's profit-maximizing output, marginal revenue must equal marginal cost. That is, if *Q** denotes the profit-maximizing output, then

$$MR(Q^*) = MC(Q^*). \tag{11.1}$$

Equation (11.1) is the **profit-maximization condition for a monopolist.** In words: *A monopolist maximizes profit by producing quantity Q* where marginal revenue equals marginal cost.* The lower panel of Figure 11.2 shows this condition graphically. The quantity at which marginal revenue equals marginal cost occurs where the two curves, *MR* and *MC*, cross.

The profit-maximization condition in equation (11.1) is a general one. It applies both to a monopolist and a perfectly competitive firm. In Chapter 9, we saw that the marginal revenue for a perfectly competitive firm is equal to the market price P. Thus, equation (11.1) reduces to the condition for profit maximization in a competitive market: Produce at the point at which price equals marginal cost.

A CLOSER LOOK AT MARGINAL REVENUE

As we discussed in Chapter 9, for a price-taking firm, marginal revenue equals the market price. For a monopolist, however, *marginal revenue is not equal to market price*. To see why, let's take another look at the demand curve for our beryllium monopolist, labeled as D in Figure 11.3. Suppose the monopolist initially contemplates producing 2 million ounces and charging a price of $10 per ounce. The total revenue it gets at this price is 2 million $\times$ $10, which corresponds to the area of rectangle *0EFG*. Now suppose the monopolist contemplates producing a larger output, 5 million ounces. To sell this quantity, it must lower its price to $7 per ounce, as dictated by the market demand curve. The monopolist's total revenue is now equal to area *0HJK*. The change in the monopolist's revenue when it increases output from 2 million ounces to 4 million ounces is area *0HJK* minus *0EFG*, which is area *II* minus area *I*.

Let's interpret what each of these areas means:

- Area *II* represents the additional revenue the monopolist gets from the additional 3 million ounces it sells: $7 $\times$ (5 − 2) million = $21 million. The extra 3 million ounces of beryllium the monopolist sells when it lowers its price are called the marginal units. By lowering price, the monopolist *gains* revenue from the increase in the volume of its sales—that is, the marginal units it sells. In this case, the gain is $21 million dollars in total.

- Area *I* represents the revenue the monopolist sacrifices on the 2 million ounces it could have sold at the higher price of $10: ($10 − $7) $\times$ 2 million = $6 million.

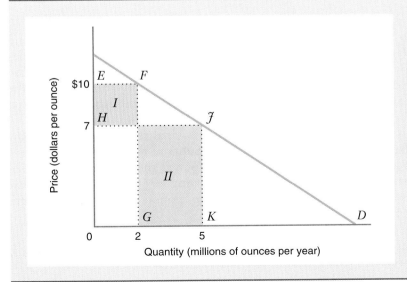

FIGURE 11.3   The Change in Total Revenue When the Monopolist Increases Output
When the monopolist charges $10 per ounce, it sells 2 million ounces and earns a total revenue equal to *0EFG*. If the monopolist increases the amount it sells to 5 million ounces, it must drop price to $7 per ounce. The monopolist's total revenue is now equal to *0HJK*. The change in the monopolist's total revenue is thus equal to area *II* minus area *I*. Area *II* represents the additional revenue the monopolist gets from the additional or marginal units it sells. Area *I* represents the revenue the monopolist sacrifices on the 2 million inframarginal units it could have sold at the higher price of $10 per ounce.

The 2 million ounces of beryllium that the monopolist could have sold at the higher price of $10 per ounce are called the monopolist's *inframarginal* units. When the monopolist lowers its price, it *sacrifices* revenue on these inframarginal units. In this case, it sacrifices $6 million in revenue on the inframarginal units.

The change in total revenue, ΔTR, is the sum of the revenue gain on the marginal units minus the revenue sacrificed on the inframarginal units:

$$\Delta TR = \text{area } II - \text{area } I$$
$$= \$7 \times (5 - 2) \text{ million} - (\$10 - \$7) \times 2 \text{ million} = \$15 \text{ million.}$$

In this case, by increasing output by 3 million ounces per year, the monopolist's total revenue goes up by $15 million. Or, put another way, for each additional ounce the monopolist produces, total revenues go up at a rate of $15 million/3 million = $5 per ounce.

To derive a general expression for marginal revenue, note that in Figure 11.3:[2]

$$\text{Area } II = \text{price} \times \text{change in quantity} = P\Delta Q$$
$$\text{Area } I = -\text{quantity} \times \text{change in price} = Q\Delta P.$$

Thus, the change in the monopolist's total revenue is equal to

$$\Delta TR = \text{area } II - \text{area } I$$
$$= P\Delta Q + Q\Delta P.$$

If we divide this change in total revenue by the change in quantity, we get the rate of change in total revenue with respect to quantity, or marginal revenue:

$$MR = \frac{\Delta TR}{\Delta Q} = P + Q\frac{\Delta P}{\Delta Q}. \qquad (11.2)$$

Marginal revenue consists of two parts. The first part, P, corresponds to the increase in revenue due to higher volume—the *marginal* units. The second part, $Q(\Delta P/\Delta Q)$ (which is negative, since $\Delta P/\Delta Q < 0$), corresponds to the decrease in revenue for the monopolist due to the reduced price of the *inframarginal* units. Because $\Delta P/\Delta Q < 0$, $MR < P$. That is, for any quantity greater than 0, the marginal revenue is less than the price the monopolist can charge to sell that quantity.

When $Q = 0$, equation (11.2) implies that marginal revenue and price coincide. This makes sense in light of Figure 11.3. Suppose the monopolist charges a price of $12 per ounce and thus sells zero output. If the monopolist increases its output, it still has to lower its price, but starting at $Q = 0$, it has no inframarginal units. Therefore, the rate at which the monopolist's revenue changes will equal the market price.

---

[2]We put a minus sign in front of this expression for area I because if price goes down, as in Figure 11.2, the change in price will be negative. The minus sign ensures that the calculated area is a positive number.

Note that marginal revenue can either be positive or negative. It can be negative because the increased revenue the firm gets from selling additional volume is more than offset by the reduction in price on units that it could have sold at a higher price. In fact, the greater the quantity, the more likely it is that marginal revenue will be negative. This is because the impact of the reduced price (needed to sell more output) affects more inframarginal units.

AVERAGE REVENUE AND MARGINAL REVENUE

In previous chapters, we usually contrasted the average of something with the marginal of the same thing (e.g., average product versus marginal product, average cost versus marginal cost). For a monopolist, it is important to contrast **average revenue** with marginal revenue because this will help explain why the monopolist's marginal revenue curve in Figure 11.4 is not the same as its demand curve.

The monopolist's average revenue is the ratio of total revenue to quantity:

$$AR = \frac{TR}{Q}.$$

Since we know that total revenue is price times quantity, it follows that

$$AR = \frac{P \times Q}{Q} = P.$$

Thus, average revenue is equal to price. Now, for any quantity of output Q, the price $P(Q)$ the monopolist can charge to sell that output is determined by the market demand curve. Thus, the monopolist's average revenue curve coincides with the market demand curve:

$$AR(Q) = P(Q).$$

Let's now see what we can learn from this:

- In the preceding section, we saw that marginal revenue is less than price when output is positive.
- Because average revenue is equal to price, it therefore follows that for a monopolist, marginal revenue is less than average revenue for positive quantities of output.
- Since the average revenue curve coincides with the demand curve, this in turn tells us that the marginal revenue curve must lie below the demand curve whenever the quantity Q is greater than 0.

Figure 11.4 shows the relationship among total revenue, average revenue, and marginal revenue.

The relationship between average revenue and marginal revenue is consistent with other average–marginal relationships we have seen elsewhere in the book. Do you remember the height example from Chapter 8? If the average height of students in your class is initially 160 cm, and the addition of a new student to

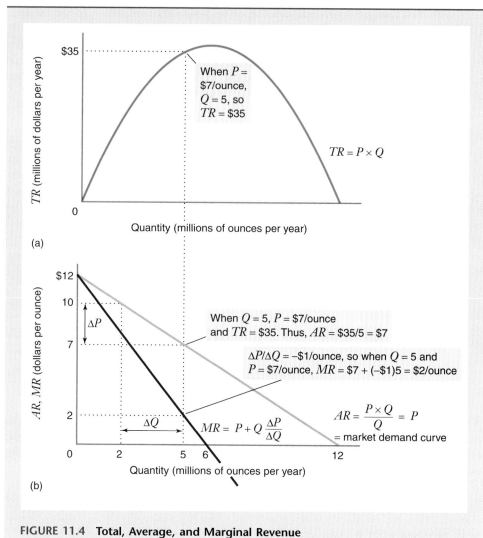

FIGURE 11.4 Total, Average, and Marginal Revenue
Panel (a) shows the monopolists's total revenue curve, TR. Total revenue is price times quantity, or $P \times Q$. Panel (b) shows the monopolist's average and marginal revenue curves, AR and MR. Average revenue is total revenue divided by price, or $(P \times Q)/Q = P$. The average revenue curve thus coincides with the demand curve. For positive quantities, the marginal revenue curve lies below the average revenue curve.

your class lowers the classes average height to 159 cm, we can conclude that the height of the new student—the marginal height—must be below the average. More generally, when the average of something (e.g., average product, average cost) is falling, the marginal of that thing (marginal product, marginal cost) must be below the average. This relationship holds for a monopolist's revenue, too. Because market demand slopes downward and the average revenue curve corresponds to the demand curve, the marginal revenue curve must be below the average revenue curve. Of course, we already deduced this insight, but it is reassuring to see that our general relationship between averages and marginals applies here.

LEARNING-BY-DOING EXERCISE 11.1

Marginal and Average Revenue for a Linear Demand Curve

Suppose that the equation of the market demand curve is

$$P = a - bQ.$$

Problem What are the expressions for the average and marginal revenues curves?

Solution Average revenue coincides with the demand curve. Thus,

$$AR = a - bQ.$$

As a first step to derive marginal revenue, note that

$$\frac{\Delta P}{\Delta Q} = -b.$$

Now, use formula (11.2):

$$
\begin{aligned}
MR(Q) &= P + Q\frac{\Delta P}{\Delta Q} \\
&= a - bQ + Q(-b) \\
&= a - 2bQ.
\end{aligned}
$$

Thus, the marginal revenue curve for a linear demand curve is also linear. In fact, it has the same P-intercept as the demand curve, with twice the slope. This implies that the marginal revenue curve intersects the Q-axis halfway between the origin and the horizontal intercept of the demand curve (which occurs at $Q = a/(2b)$). For quantities greater than this halfway point, marginal revenue not only lies below the demand curve, it is also negative. Notice that the shape of the marginal curve in the lower panel of Figure 11.4 is consistent with these properties.

Similar Problem: 11.1

THE MONOPOLIST'S PROFIT-MAXIMIZATION CONDITION SHOWN GRAPHICALLY

Figure 11.5 illustrates the profit-maximization condition $MR = MC$ for our beryllium monopolist. The marginal revenue curve MR is a decreasing line that lies below the demand curve (which is also the average revenue curve) for all positive output levels. The firm's marginal cost curve MC is a straight line from the origin. Figure 11.5 also shows the monopolist's average cost curve, AC. For all positive output levels, the firm's marginal cost curve lies above this average cost curve.

FIGURE 11.5 The Monopolist's Profit-Maximization Condition

The profit-maximizing output is 4 million ounces per year, the point at which $MC = MR$. We find the monopolist's price by asking: At what price will the monopolist sell exactly 4 million units? This occurs at a price of $8 per ounce. At the optimal monopoly output, the monopolist's total revenue is $P \times Q$, which equals areas $B + E + F$. The monopolist's total cost is $AC \times Q$, which equals area F. The monopolist's profit is thus area $B + E + F - F = B + E$. Consumer surplus at the optimal monopoly solution is area A, the area beneath the demand curve but above the price of $8.

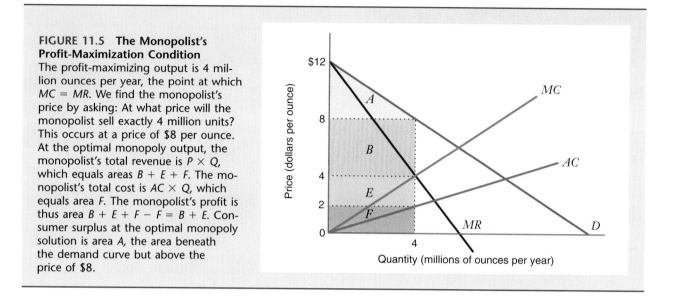

The profit-maximizing quantity is where the marginal revenue curve intersects the marginal cost curve. This occurs at a quantity of 4 million ounces per year. We find the monopolist's profit-maximizing price by referring back to the market demand curve. In Figure 11.5 this price is $8 per ounce, the price at which quantity demanded is equal to 4 million ounces.

The monopolist's profit is the difference between total revenue and total cost. Total revenue is price (or average revenue) times quantity, which corresponds to area $B + E + F$ in Figure 11.5. Total cost is average cost times quantity, which corresponds to area F. Total profit is thus $B + E + F - F = B + E$. This area equals $24 million, a calculation consistent with Table 11.1.

Figure 11.5 illustrates three important points about the equilibrium in a monopoly market:

- First, the monopolist's profit-maximizing price ($8) exceeds the marginal cost of the last unit supplied ($4). This differs from the outcome in a perfectly competitive market, in which price equals the marginal cost of the last unit supplied.

- Second, in contrast to a perfectly competitive firm in a long-run equilibrium, the monopolist's economic profits can be positive. This is because the monopolist does not face the threat of free entry that drives economic profits to zero in competitive markets.

- Third, even though the monopolist raises price above marginal cost and earns positive economic profits, consumers still enjoy some benefits at the monopoly equilibrium. The consumer surplus at the equilibrium in Figure 11.5 is area A, the area between price and the demand curve. In this example, consumer surplus equals $8 million. The total economic benefit at the monopoly equilibrium is thus the sum of consumer surplus and the monopolist's profit, which is equal to $A + B + E$, or $32 million per year.

LEARNING-BY-DOING EXERCISE 11.2

Computing a Monopoly Equilibrium by Equating Marginal Revenue to Marginal Cost

Recall that the equation of the monopolist's demand curve is $P = 12 - Q$, while the equation of marginal cost is given by $MC = Q$, where Q is expressed in millions of ounces.

Problem What is the profit-maximizing quantity and price for the monopolist?

Solution Our approach to solve this problem proceeds in three steps: First, we find the marginal revenue curve. Second, we equate marginal revenue to marginal cost to find the profit-maximizing quantity. Third, we substitute this quantity back into the demand curve to find the profit-maximizing monopoly price.

Using the formula we derived in Learning-By-Doing Exercise 11.1 for the marginal revenue curve associated with a linear demand curve, our marginal revenue curve has the same intercept as our demand curve but twice the slope. Thus:

$$MR = 12 - 2Q.$$

If we now equate this to marginal cost, we can solve for the profit-maximizing quantity of output:

$$MR = MC$$
$$12 - 2Q = Q, \text{ which implies}$$
$$Q = 4.$$

We can now substitute this back into the market demand curve to determine the monopolist's optimal price:

$$P = 12 - 4 = 8.$$

The monopolist's profit-maximizing price is thus $8 per ounce, and its profit-maximizing quantity is 4 million ounces, just as we found when we solved the monopolist's problem graphically in Figure 11.5.

Similar Problem: 11.4

A MONOPOLIST DOES NOT HAVE A SUPPLY CURVE

A perfectly competitive firm takes the market price as given and chooses a profit-maximizing quantity. The fact that the perfect competitor views price as exogenous allows us to construct a supply schedule for that firm. This schedule takes each possible market price and associates it with the corresponding profit-maximizing quantity.

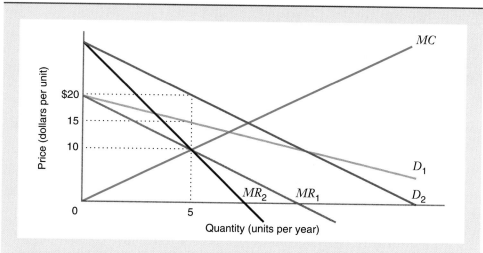

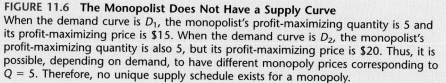

FIGURE 11.6   The Monopolist Does Not Have a Supply Curve
When the demand curve is D_1, the monopolist's profit-maximizing quantity is 5 and its profit-maximizing price is \$15. When the demand curve is D_2, the monopolist's profit-maximizing quantity is also 5, but its profit-maximizing price is \$20. Thus, it is possible, depending on demand, to have different monopoly prices corresponding to $Q = 5$. Therefore, no unique supply schedule exists for a monopoly.

For the monopolist, however, price is *endogenous*, not *exogenous*. That is, the monopolist determines both quantity and price. Depending on the shape of the demand curve, the monopolist might supply the same quantity at two different prices or different quantities at the same price. The unique association between price and quantity that exists for a perfectly competitive firm does not exist for a monopolist. Thus, a monopolist does not have a supply curve.

Figure 11.6 illustrates this point. For demand curve D_1, the profit-maximizing quantity is 5 million units per year, and the profit-maximizing price is \$15 per unit. If the monopolist's demand curve shifts to D_2, the profit-maximizing quantity continues to be 5 million units per year but the profit-maximizing price is now \$20 per unit. It is thus possible, depending on market demand, to have different (nonunique) prices corresponding to a given profit-maximizing quantity (e.g., $Q^* = 5$ million units). Therefore, no unique supply curve exists for a monopolist.

11.2

THE INVERSE ELASTICITY PRICING RULE

We have just seen that the monopolist uses the market demand curve to set price. We have also seen that the monopolist's profit-maximizing price exceeds the marginal cost of the last unit supplied. In this section, we explore in more detail how the nature of the demand curve affects the gap between the monopolist's profit-maximizing price and its marginal cost. In particular, we will see that this gap is influenced in a very important way by the price elasticity of demand.

PRICE ELASTICITY OF DEMAND AND THE PROFIT-MAXIMIZING PRICE

Figure 11.7 shows why the price elasticity of demand plays such an important role in the monopolist's profit-maximization condition. Figure 11.7(a) shows the profit-maximizing price, P_A, and quantity, Q_A, in a particular monopoly market, A. Figure 11.7(b) shows another monopoly market, B, in which demand is less sensitive to price. In particular, we constructed the demand curve in market B by pivoting the demand curve in market A through the profit-maximizing price and quantity in market A. That is, demand curve D_B is less price elastic than demand curve D_A at the profit-maximizing price P_A for market A. Comparing the two markets, we see that the gap between the profit-maximizing price and marginal cost is much less in monopoly market A, in which demand is relatively more price elastic, than it is in market B, where demand is relatively less price elastic. This shows us that the price elasticity of demand plays an important role in determining the extent to which the monopolist can raise price above its marginal costs.

The insight that the price elasticity of demand plays a key role in determining the monopolist's profit-maximizing price suggests an important point about the role of indirect competition from outside an industry. Any real-world monopolist will typically face some sort of competition from outside its industry. For example, the beryllium monopolist Brush Wellman faces competition from substitute metals, such as titanium and aluminum. If there are especially close substitutes for the monopolist's product, consumers are likely to be relatively price sensitive, and the monopolist will be unable to mark up its price very much above its marginal cost. The firm will be a monopoly, but the threat of substitute prod-

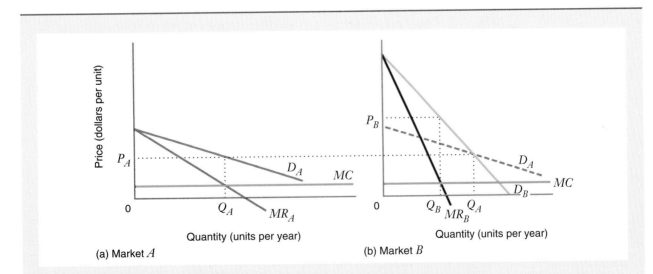

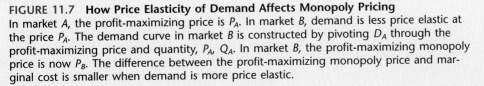

FIGURE 11.7 How Price Elasticity of Demand Affects Monopoly Pricing
In market A, the profit-maximizing price is P_A. In market B, demand is less price elastic at the price P_A. The demand curve in market B is constructed by pivoting D_A through the profit-maximizing price and quantity, P_A, Q_A. In market B, the profit-maximizing monopoly price is now P_B. The difference between the profit-maximizing monopoly price and marginal cost is smaller when demand is more price elastic.

ucts will not allow it to translate that monopoly into a large markup of price over marginal cost. This would explain why Brush Wellman, despite having the beryllium market to itself, does not set outrageously high prices for beryllium. For example, in sales of beryllium oxide to producers of semiconductor packages, such as Kyocera America, Brush Wellman keeps its price close to the level of competing materials, such as alumina and copper-tungsten. This reflects a recognition of price elasticity of demand: by setting too high a price, Brush Wellman will lose customers to competing materials.

MARGINAL REVENUE AND THE PRICE ELASTICITY OF DEMAND

Let's now formalize the relationship between the price elasticity of demand and the monopolist's markup of price over marginal cost by deriving an equation that shows how they are related. As a first step, we need to restate the formula for marginal revenue that we just derived above:

$$MR = P + Q\frac{\Delta P}{\Delta Q}.$$

By rearranging terms in this formula, we can write marginal revenue in terms of the price elasticity of demand, $\epsilon_{Q,P}$:[3]

$$MR = P\left(1 + \frac{1}{\epsilon_{Q,P}}\right).$$

This formula shows us that marginal revenue depends on the price elasticity of demand. Since $\epsilon_{Q,P} < 0$, this formula confirms our earlier conclusion that $MR < P$. But the formula reveals another important set of relationships:

- When demand is elastic, that is, when $\epsilon_{Q,P}$ is between -1 and $-\infty$, marginal revenue is positive. This is because when $\epsilon_{Q,P}$ is between -1 and $-\infty$, the expression $1 + (1/\epsilon_{Q,P})$ is greater than zero. Thus, when the monopolist operates on the *elastic* region of the demand curve, it can increase total revenue by *increasing quantity* through a *lower price*.
- When demand is inelastic, that is, when $\epsilon_{Q,P}$ is between 0 and -1, marginal revenue is negative. This is because when $\epsilon_{Q,P}$ is between 0 and -1, the

---

[3] To see how we derived this expression, start with our initial formula:

$$MR = P + Q\frac{\Delta P}{\Delta Q}.$$

If we factor out P, we get

$$MR = P\left(1 + \frac{Q}{P}\frac{\Delta P}{\Delta Q}\right).$$

Now recall that the price elasticity of demand $\epsilon_{Q,P}$ is given by the formula $(\Delta Q/\Delta P)(P/Q)$. Thus, the term $(Q/P)(\Delta P/\Delta Q)$ is equal to $1/\epsilon_{Q,P}$, that is, the reciprocal of the price elasticity of demand. Making this substitution gives us

$$MR = P\left(1 + \frac{1}{\epsilon_{Q,P}}\right).$$

expression $1 + (1/\epsilon_{Q,P})$ is less than zero. Thus, when the monopolist operates on the *inelastic* region of the demand curve, it can increase total revenue by *decreasing quantity* through a *higher price*.

- When demand is unitary elastic, that is, when $\epsilon_{Q,P} = -1$, marginal revenue is zero. This is because $\epsilon_{Q,P} = -1$ implies $1 + (1/\epsilon_{Q,P}) = 0$.

If these relationships between total revenue and price sound familiar, it is because you have already read about them in Chapter 2. There we discussed how the price elasticity of demand determined how a firm's total revenue would respond to a price change.

Figure 11.8 summarizes the relationship between price elasticity of demand and marginal revenue for a linear demand curve, whose equation is given by $P = a - bQ$. The range of quantities over which marginal revenue is positive corresponds to the elastic region of the demand curve. The quantities for which marginal revenue is negative corresponds to the inelastic region of the demand curve. Marginal revenue is zero (i.e., it crosses the horizontal axis) at the quantity at which demand is unitary elastic ($Q = a/(2b)$).

THE INVERSE ELASTICITY PRICING RULE

The relationship between marginal revenue and the price elasticity of demand gives us another way to express the monopolist's profit-maximization condition.

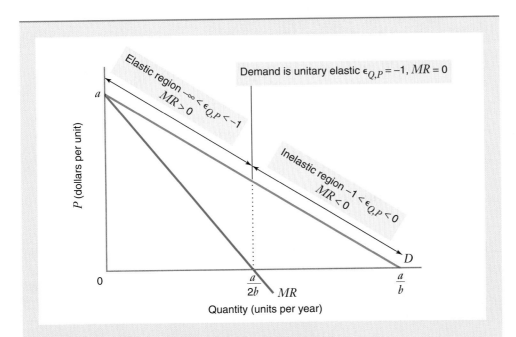

FIGURE 11.8 Marginal Revenue and Price Elasticity of Demand for a Linear Demand Curve
Over the range where demand is elastic ($Q < a/(2b)$), marginal revenue is positive. Over the range where demand is inelastic $a/(2b) < Q < a/b$, marginal revenue is negative. When demand is unitary elastic, marginal revenue is 0.

The equality between marginal revenue and marginal cost implies that the profit-maximizing price P^* and quantity Q^* satisfies the following condition:

$$P^*\left(1 + \frac{1}{\epsilon_{Q,P}}\right) = MC(Q^*). \qquad (11.3)$$

If we rearrange this expression algebraically, we get

$$\frac{P^* - MC^*}{P^*} = -\frac{1}{\epsilon_{Q,P}}, \qquad (11.4)$$

where $MC^* = MC(Q^*)$ denotes the marginal cost at the profit-maximizing output level. The left-hand side of equation (11.4) is the monopolist's optimal markup of price over marginal cost, expressed as a percentage of the price. Condition (11.4) is called the **inverse elasticity pricing rule (IEPR).** The IEPR states that the monopolist's optimal markup of price above marginal cost is equal to minus the inverse of the price elasticity of demand. Why is it important? The IEPR tells us that the price elasticity of demand plays a vital role in determining what price a monopolist should charge to maximize profits. Specifically, the IEPR summarizes the relationship between price elasticity of demand and the monopoly price that we saw in Figure 11.7: The more price elastic the monopolist's demand, the smaller will be the optimal markup of price over marginal cost.

LEARNING-BY-DOING EXERCISE 11.3

Using the IEPR to Compute the Optimal Monopoly Price for a Constant Elasticity Demand Curve

If we know the price elasticity of demand, we can directly apply the IEPR to compute the profit-maximizing monopoly price.

Problem

(a) Consider a market demand curve given by the equation

$$Q = 100P^{-2}.$$

This is a particular example of a constant elasticity demand curve in which the price elasticity of demand is equal to -2 at every point along the demand curve.[4] Suppose that a monopolist has a constant marginal cost given by $MC = \$50$. What is the monopolist's optimal price?

(b) Now suppose that the market demand curve is given by the equation

$$Q = 100P^{-5}.$$

What is the monopolist's optimal price?

---

[4]Review Section 2.2 of Chapter 2 if you have forgotten what a constant elasticity demand curve is.

Solution

(a) Because we know that the price elasticity of demand is always equal to -2, we can use the IEPR to directly determine the monopolist's profit-maximizing price. The IEPR implies that the monopolist's mark-up is given by

$$\frac{P - 50}{P} = -\frac{1}{-2}.$$

Solving this equation for P we get

$$P = \$100.$$

(b) Again we employ IEPR, this time using a price elasticity of demand of -5:

$$\frac{P - 50}{P} = -\frac{1}{-5}.$$

Solving this equation for P we get

$$P = \$62.50.$$

Notice that by making demand more elastic, the monopolist's profit-maximizing price goes down (holding marginal cost constant). This is a concrete illustration of how the price elasticity of demand affects the monopoly price.

LEARNING-BY-DOING EXERCISE 11.4

Using the IEPR to Compute the Optimal Monopoly Price for a Linear Demand Curve

In the previous exercise, we saw that for a constant elasticity demand curve, we could directly apply the IEPR to compute the profit-maximizing monopoly price. Can we do the same for a linear demand curve? This exercise shows that we can, but we have to be careful to recognize that along a linear demand curve, the price elasticity of demand does not remain constant. This makes the application of the IEPR a little trickier. This exercise also shows that the profit-maximizing price and quantity that we get from applying the IEPR coincides with the price and quantity we get if we directly apply the $MR = MC$ rule. This will show that these two routes to finding the monopoly solution get us to the same answer.

Let's suppose that the monopolist has a constant marginal cost MC equal to $50 and faces a demand curve given by the equation

$$P = 100 - \frac{1}{2}Q.$$

Notice that by solving this equation for Q in terms of P, we can rewrite the demand curve as

$$Q = 200 - 2P,$$

Problem

(a) Find the profit-maximizing price and quantity for the monopolist using the IEPR.
(b) Find the profit-maximizing price and quantity for the monopolist by equating MR to MC.

Solution

(a) This demand curve is linear, so unlike the constant elasticity curve in Learning-By-Doing Exercise 11.3, the price elasticity of demand is not a single number.[5] Rather, it is given by a formula which we need to derive from the general expression for elasticity, $\epsilon_{Q,P} = (\Delta Q/\Delta P)(P/Q)$ In this particular example, $\Delta Q/\Delta P = -2$, so the price elasticity of demand along the curve is

$$\epsilon_{Q,P} = -2\frac{P}{Q} = -\frac{2P}{200 - 2P}$$

(substituting in the equation for Q in terms of P).

Let's now apply the IEPR, $(P - MC)/P = -1/\epsilon_{Q,P}$. In this case, the IEPR can be expressed as

$$\frac{P - 50}{P} = \frac{200 - 2P}{2P}$$

(substituting in the above expression for $\epsilon_{Q,P}$).

If we multiply each side of this expression by $2P$, we get a simple linear equation:

$$2P - 100 = 200 - 2P,$$

whose solution is $P = 75$. This is the profit-maximizing monopoly price. We find the profit-maximizing monopoly quantity by substituting this price into the demand curve: $Q = 200 - 2(75) = 50$.
(b) For our demand curve, $P = 100 - (1/2)Q$, marginal revenue is

$$MR = 100 - Q.$$

Equating this to our marginal cost of 50 gives us

$$100 - Q = 50$$

---

[5]If this point seems unfamiliar to you, go back to Chapter 2 and review the section that discusses how the price elasticity of demand varies along a linear demand curve.

whose solution is $Q = 50$, the same answer as before. We find the optimal price by plugging this quantity back into the demand curve: $P = 100 - (1/2)(50) = 75$, also the same answer as before!

What have we learned from this exercise? We've just seen that both the IEPR and the $MR = MC$ condition can be used to solve for the optimal monopoly price and quantity. This is as it should be, since the IEPR was derived from the $MR = MC$ condition. We have also seen that for a linear demand curve, on which elasticity is not a single number, we have to be careful to use the formula for the price elasticity of demand $\epsilon_{Q,P}$ when we apply the IEPR.

Similar Problem: 11.9

Chewing Gum, Baby Food, and the IEPR

EXAMPLE 11.1

Supermarkets are not monopolists, but many consumers often shop at the same supermarket week after week.[6] This suggests that supermarkets have the ability to mark up prices above marginal costs, an ability that they evidently take advantage of. For most grocery products, the difference between the retail price that the shopper pays to the supermarket and the wholesale price that the supermarket pays to its suppliers (manufacturers or distributors) ranges between 10 and 40 percent. Interestingly, though, these markups differ systematically across product categories in most every grocery store, and markups within a particular product category remain fairly stable over time. For example, the retail markup on candy and chewing gum in most grocery stores is usually between 30 and 40 percent, while the markup on baby food and disposable diapers is usually less than 10 percent.

The IEPR can help us understand why the markups for chewing gum and candy are so different from the markups for baby food and disposable diapers. Retailers believe that chewing gum and candy are impulse purchase items. That is, consumers often decide to purchase these products on the basis of whims or momentary urges once they are inside the store, usually without thinking much about their prices. By contrast, retailers believe that baby food and disposable diapers are not purchased impulsively. They believe that most consumers of these products put considerable thought into their purchase decisions and pay close attention to price when deciding how much to buy. This suggests that the demand for chewing gum and candy is less price elastic than the demand for baby food and

---

[6]Margaret Slade reports that grocery-store marketing managers believe that fewer than 10 percent of households engage in comparison shopping among local grocery stores to find the lowest priced items. For the 90 percent of consumers who frequent the same store each week, their choice of store is thought to be determined by location (proximity to home or work) and by the quality of the store (e.g., product variety, freshness of produce). See M. Slade, "Product Rivalry with Multiple Strategic Weapons: An Analysis of Price and Advertising Competition, *Journal of Economics and Management Strategy* (Fall 1995): 445–476.

disposable diapers. If so, the IEPR implies that we should see precisely what we do see: higher markups for chewing gum and candy than for baby food and disposable diapers. For these products, at least, grocery stores seem to set retail prices in a manner that is broadly consistent with the IEPR. ∎

THE MONOPOLIST ALWAYS PRODUCES ON THE ELASTIC REGION OF THE MARKET DEMAND CURVE

Although a monopolist could, in theory, set its price anywhere along the market demand curve, a profit-maximizing monopolist will only want to operate on the *elastic region* of the market demand curve (i.e., the region in which the price elasticity of demand $\epsilon_{Q,P}$ is between -1 and $-\infty$). Figure 11.9 illustrates why. If you were a monopolist and you contemplated operating at a point such as A at which

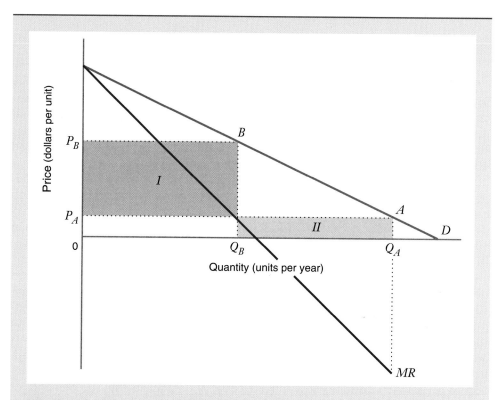

FIGURE 11.9   Why a Profit-Maximizing Monopolist Will Not Operate on the Inelastic Region of the Market Demand Curve
Suppose the monopolist is initially at point A (charging price P_A and selling quantity Q_A). It is on the inelastic region of the demand curve, and marginal revenue is thus negative. By decreasing quantity and raising price, the monopolist can increase total revenue. For example, if the monopolist moves to point B (raising price to P_B and reducing quantity to Q_B), its total revenue increases by an amount equal to the area of rectangle *I* minus the area of rectangle *II*. This amount is positive. Also, the monopolist's total costs go down because it produces less than before. With a higher total revenue and a lower total cost, the monopolist's profit must go up.

demand was inelastic, you could always increase profit by raising your price, reducing your quantity, and moving to point *B*. By moving from point *B* to point *A*, your total revenue goes up by the difference between the area of region *I* and region *II*. Moreover, your total costs must go down because you are producing less. If your total revenue goes up and your total costs go down, your profit will go up. Thus, at any point on the inelastic region of the market demand curve, the monopolist can always find a point on the elastic region that gives it a higher profit.

We can use the IEPR to reach the same conclusion. To see why, we start with the (perhaps obvious) observation that marginal cost is positive. In equation (11.3) this then implies that the term $1 + (1/\epsilon_{Q,P})$ must also be positive. But the only way this term can be positive is if $\epsilon_{Q,P}$ is between -1 and $-\infty$, that is, if demand is price elastic. Thus, the IEPR implies that the monopolist's profit-maximizing price and quantity occur along the elastic region of the market demand curve.

IEPR DOES NOT ONLY APPLY TO MONOPOLISTS

The IEPR applies to any firm that faces a downward-sloping demand for its product. Consider, for example, the pricing problem Coca-Cola faces. Coca-Cola does not have a monopoly in the U.S. cola market: Pepsi is an important competitor. Still, Coca-Cola and Pepsi are not perfectly competitive firms. In other words, if Coca-Cola raised its price, it would not lose all its sales to Pepsi, and if it lowered its price, it would not steal all of Pepsi's business. This is because the two colas exhibit **product differentiation.** Product differentiation between two or more products exists when the products possess attributes that, in the minds of consumers, set the products apart from one another and make them less than perfect substitutes. Some people prefer the sweeter taste of Pepsi to the less sweet taste of Coke, and would continue to buy Pepsi even if it cost more than Coke. You might prefer the taste of Coke. Or you might be indifferent about the taste but prefer Coca-Cola's packaging or advertisements.

When products are differentiated, they will have downward-sloping demand curves, even though the sellers of the products are not monopolies. The optimal pricing decision for a seller of a differentiated product can thus be characterized by an IEPR. For example, the optimal prices for Coca-Cola and Pepsi (denoted by P^A and P^I, respectively) would be described by

$$\frac{P^A - MC^A}{P^A} = -\frac{1}{\epsilon_{Q_A,P_A}}.$$

$$\frac{P^I - MC^I}{P^I} = -\frac{1}{\epsilon_{Q_I,P_I}}.$$

In the formulas, ϵ_{Q_A,P_A} is not a market-level price elasticity of demand. Rather, it is the brand-level price elasticity of demand for Coca-Cola. It tells us the sensitivity of Coca-Cola's demand to Coca-Cola's price, holding all other factors affecting Coke's demand (including Pepsi's price) fixed.[7] Similarly, ϵ_{Q_I,P_I} is the brand-level price elasticity of demand for Pepsi.

---

[7]Chapter 2 presents a detailed discussion of the difference between the brand-level price elasticity of demand and the market-level price elasticity of demand.

QUANTIFYING MARKET POWER: THE LERNER INDEX

When a firm faces a downward-sloping demand curve, either because (like Brush Wellman) it is a monopolist or (like Coca-Cola) it produces a differentiated product, the firm will have some control over the market price it sets. For a monopoly, the ability to set the market price is constrained by competition from substitute products outside the industry. For example, titanium prices constrain Brush Wellman's ability to set the price of beryllium. In the case of differentiated products, a firm's direct competitors constrain its pricing freedom. For example, Pepsi's price limits the price Coca-Cola can charge and vice versa.

When a firm can control its price in the market, we say that it has **market power.**[8] Note that perfectly competitive firms *do not have* market power. Because perfectly competitive firms produce at the point where price equals marginal cost, while monopolists or producers of differentiated products will, in general, charge prices that exceed marginal cost, a natural measure of market power is the percentage markup of price over marginal cost, $(P - MC)/P$. This measure of monopoly power was suggested by the economist Abba Lerner and is called the **Lerner Index of market power.**

The Lerner index ranges from 0 to 1 (or from 0 percent to 100 percent). It is zero for a perfectly competitive industry. It is positive for any industry that departs from perfect competition. The IEPR tells us that in the equilibrium in a monopoly market, the Lerner Index will be inversely related to the market price elasticity of demand. As we've discussed, an important driver of the price elasticity of demand is the threat of substitute products outside the industry. If a monopoly market faces strong competition from substitute products, the Lerner Index can still be low. In other words, a firm might have a monopoly, but its market power might still be weak.

EXAMPLE 11.2   *The Lerner Index of Market Power in the Breakfast Cereal Industry*

In the spring of 1995, two U.S. Congressmen, Charles Schumer of New York (later a senator from New York) and Sam Gejdenson of Connecticut, accused the four largest cereal companies—Kellogg, General Mills, Post, and Quaker Oats—of collusion to keep prices high. Citing evidence that cereal prices increased at twice the rate of other food prices between 1983 and 1990, Schumer urged Attorney General Janet Reno to investigate cereal industry pricing. "There is no real competition in this industry," said Schumer. "We are paying caviar prices for corn flakes quality." Asked if there was evidence that the cereal producers were colluding, Gejdenson responded: "Price is the prima facie evidence."[9]

---

[8]Monopolists and differentiated products oligopolists are not the only kinds of firms with market power. As you will learn in Chapter 13, a firm in an oligopolistic industry in which firms' products are identical can also have market power.

[9]These quotes are taken from "Congressmen Point to Collusion in Cereal Pricing," *Reuters Limited* (March 7, 1995).

Why are cereal prices so high? Is it because Kellogg, General Mills, Post, and Quaker collectively act as a monopolist? Or are the high prices a natural outcome of competition in a market in which there is significant product differentiation?

Economist Aviv Nevo has studied this question.[10] Using data on cereal prices, product characteristics, and consumer demographics (e.g., household income), he estimated price elasticities of demand for each brand of cereal. Nevo then used these estimated elasticities to compute the hypothetical Lerner Indices, $(P - MC)/P$, that would be expected to prevail under two scenarios: one in which cereal producers collectively act as a profit-maximizing monopolist and the other in which the producers compete as independent firms in a market with differentiated products.[11] Given his estimated demand elasticities, Nevo concludes that in a collusive cereal industry, the median Lerner Index of an individual brand would be approximately 65 to 75 percent. In an industry with competition, the median Lerner Index of an individual brand would have been 40 to 44 percent.

How do these hypothetical calculations compare to the actual Lerner Index in the cereal industry? According to Nevo, the actual Lerner Index for the cereal industry overall in the mid-1990s was approximately 45 percent. This is far below the hypothetical Lerner Index you would expect to see if Kellogg's, Post, General Mills, and Quaker Oats had colluded to fix prices. There is no denying that the Lerner Index in the cereal industry is positive, indicating that cereal firms enjoy market power. But the market power in the cereal industry seems to arise because brands of cereal are differentiated products, not because of collusion among manufacturers. ∎

11.3
MONOPOLY COMPARATIVE STATICS

Now that we have explored how the monopolist determines its profit-maximizing quantity and price and the role that the price elasticity of demand plays in that determination, we are ready to examine how shifts in demand or cost affect the monopolist's decisions.

SHIFTS IN MARKET DEMAND

Figure 11.10 illustrates how a rightward in market demand affects the monopoly equilibrium. In both panels, we assume that quantity demanded increases at *all* market prices. In Figure 11.10(a), in which marginal cost is increasing in output, the increase in demand increases both the equilibrium quantity and the equilibrium price. In Figure 11.10(b), in which marginal cost is decreasing in output, the increase in demand again increases the equilibrium quantity but decreases the equilibrium price. The equilibrium price goes down even though the monopolist can charge a higher price for any given quantity than it could have before demand increased. However, because marginal cost is decreasing in output, the monopolist ends up producing a lot more output than it did before. As a result, the drop

[10]A. Nevo, "Measuring Market Power in the Ready-to-Eat Breakfast Cereal Industry," *Econometrica*, 69 (March 2001): 307–342.

[11]Computation of cereal markups under this scenario requires using oligopoly theory. You will study oligopoly theory in Chapter 13.

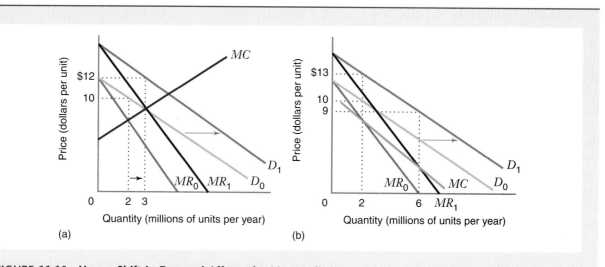

FIGURE 11.10 How a Shift in Demand Affects the Monopolist's Profit-Maximizing Quantity and Price
In panel (a), a rightward shift in demand from D_0 to D_1 results in an increase in the profit-maximizing quantity from 2 to 3 million units. As a result, the profit-maximizing price goes up from $10 per unit to $12 per unit. In panel (b), the same shift in market demand increases the profit-maximizing quantity from 2 to 6 million units, but the profit-maximizing price goes down from $10 to $9. This happens even though the firm could have sold its initial quantity at a higher price, i.e., $13 per unit.

in price from increasing quantity along the new demand curve more than offsets the increase in price that the shift in the demand curve would otherwise induce.

In general, as long as the rightward shift in the demand curve results in a rightward shift in the marginal revenue curve, the increase in demand will increase the monopolist's equilibrium quantity. The rightward shift in marginal revenue guarantees that the intersection of marginal revenue and marginal cost will occur at a quantity that is higher than the initial one. Similarly, a decrease in demand accompanied by a corresponding leftward shift in the marginal revenue curve will always decrease the monopolist's equilibrium quantity. As you just saw, however, a shift in demand will (in general) have an ambiguous impact on the equilibrium market price.

LEARNING-BY-DOING EXERCISE 11.5

The Comparative Statics of a Shift in a Linear Demand Curve for a Monopolist with a Constant Marginal Cost: The Monopoly Midpoint Rule

In this exercise you will learn a convenient formula for the profit-maximizing monopoly price for a monopolist that faces a linear demand curve and has a constant marginal cost: the monopoly midpoint rule.

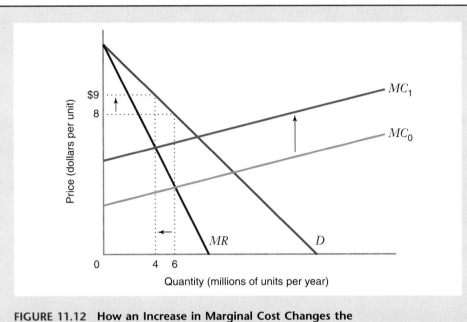

FIGURE 11.12 How an Increase in Marginal Cost Changes the Monopoly Equilibrium
When the monopolist's marginal cost curve shifts from MC_0 to MC_1, the profit-maximizing quantity falls from 6 million units per year to 4 million units per year and price goes up from $8 per unit to $9 per unit.

CHANGES IN MARGINAL COST

Comparative Statics

The IEPR suggests that an increase in marginal cost will increase the profit-maximizing price and decrease the profit-maximizing quantity. Figure 11.12 confirms this intuition. An upward shift in the monopolist's marginal cost curve must necessarily decrease the monopolist's total output. The increase in the marginal cost implies that the point of intersection between the marginal revenue curve and the marginal cost curve moves leftward. Thus, in Figure 11.12, the profit-maximizing quantity decreases. This moves the firm leftward along its demand curve, resulting in an increase in the profit-maximizing price. Although not illustrated, a downward shift in marginal cost will induce an increase in the monopolist's profit-maximizing quantity and a decrease in the profit-maximizing price.

How the Revenue Impact of a Shift in Marginal Cost Can Tell Us Whether Firms are Behaving as a Profit-Maximizing Monopolist

As Example 11.2 illustrates, firms in an oligopoly industry (an industry with just a few producers) are occasionally accused of acting collusively, i.e., collectively acting as a profit-maximizing monopolist. Apart from documentary evidence that firms acted in concert to fix prices, is there any way to tell whether such an accusation is true? The answer is yes. By looking at the impact of a shift in marginal cost on the industry's total revenue, we might be able to refute the claim that firms in the industry are colluding. Figure 11.13 shows why.

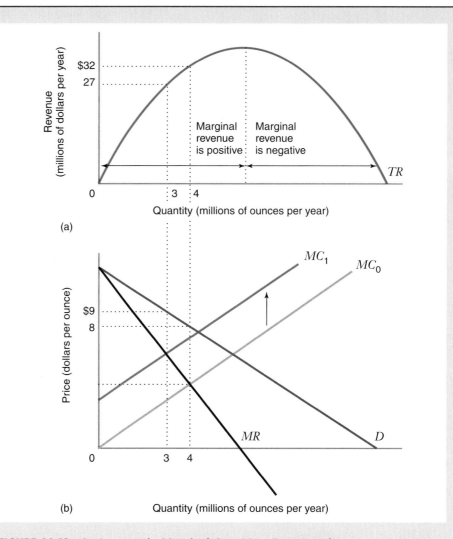

(a)

(b)

FIGURE 11.13   An Increase in Marginal Cost Must Decrease the Monopolist's Total Revenue
Panel (b) shows that an upward shift in the marginal cost decreases the monopolist's optimal quantity from 4 million to 3 million ounces per year. Because the monopolist always operates on the elastic region of market demand, the monopolist operates in the region in which total revenue goes down as output goes down. The decrease in the profit-maximizing output thus decreases total revenue from $32 million to $27 million.

Figure 11.13 illustrates what happens when our beryllium monopolist, Brush Wellman, faces an increase in its marginal cost. When marginal cost shifts upward, the monopolist reduces its output. Now recall from our earlier discussion that the monopolist operates on the elastic range of the demand curve. This implies that the monopolist operates where marginal revenue is positive, which in turn means that it must be on the upward-sloping part of its total revenue hill, as shown in Figure 11.13(a). As the monopolist reduces its output in response to the upward shift in marginal cost, it moves down the total revenue hill, and its total revenues thus decrease. This illustrates the following comparative statics results:[14]

[14]See J. Panzar and J. Rosse, "Testing for Monopoly Equilibrium," *Journal of Industrial Economics* (1987) for further exploration of the implications of these comparative statics results.

- An upward shift in marginal cost reduces the profit-maximizing monopolist's total revenue.
- A downward shift in marginal cost increases the profit-maximizing monopolist's total revenue.

We could use these comparative statics results to potentially refute the hypothesis that firms in a non–monopoly industry are collectively acting as a profit-maximizing monopolist. Suppose, for example, that we discovered that an increase in the federal excise tax on beer resulted in an increase in overall total revenue in the brewing industry. Because our comparative statics analysis tells us that industry revenue *could not have increased* if beer firms were collectively acting as a monopolist, the fact that industry revenue *did increase* suggests that beer firms *were not* acting collusively.

Do Cigarette Producers Act as a Profit-Maximizing Monopolist? EXAMPLE 11.4

The cigarette industry is one of the most highly concentrated in the U.S. economy. In the 1990s, the four largest firms accounted for more than 92 percent of industry sales. Throughout most of the twentieth century, firms in the cigarette industry displayed remarkable pricing discipline. Twice a year (generally in June and December), one of the dominant firms announced its intention to raise the list prices of its cigarettes, and within days the other cigarette manufacturers followed with increases of their own. Since the 1970s, either Philip Morris or RJR has generally been the price leader. Such discipline has made cigarettes one of the most profitable businesses in the American economy. The success of such pricing coordination naturally raises the question of whether the big tobacco companies have collectively acted as a profit-maximizing monopolist.

Daniel Sullivan explored this question using the comparative statics analysis that we just described.[15] Using statistical methods, Sullivan studied how prices, quantities, and revenues over the period 1955–1982 changed in response to changes in state excise taxes. His research led him to conclude that observed industry outcomes during this period were *inconsistent* with the hypothesis that cigarette firms were jointly acting as a profit-maximizing monopolist.

If cigarette producers do not act as a profit-maximizing cartel, why do they appear to be so profitable? One answer is that firms in an oligopoly industry can still be highly profitable, even if they do not replicate the outcome that a profit-maximizing monopolist would attain. You will learn in Chapter 13 that, under some circumstances, the equilibrium in an oligopoly market can entail prices that exceed marginal cost. This will be another reminder that market power and monopoly are not synonymous. ∎

---

[15]D. Sullivan, "Testing Hypotheses About Firm Behavior in the Cigarette Industry," *Journal of Political Economy* (June 1985): 586–597.

11.4
MULTIPLANT MONOPOLY

Many firms operate more than one production facility. For example, an electric utility, such as Chicago's Commonwealth Edison, often uses several power plants for generating electricity. The theory of monopoly can be easily extended to cover the case of a multiplant firm. We first consider the choice of output by a monopolist with two plants. We then consider the optimal number of plants for the monopolist to employ.

OUTPUT CHOICE WITH TWO PLANTS

Consider a monopolist with two plants: One has a marginal cost function $MC_1(Q)$, the other a marginal cost function $MC_2(Q)$. The monopolist's output choice problem consists of two parts: How much should it produce overall, and how should it divide its production between its two plants?

It's easiest to answer the second question first. Suppose the firm plans to produce 6 million units, and it initially divides up the output equally between plants 1 and 2. Figure 11.14 shows that at an output of 3 million units, plant 1 has a higher marginal cost than plant 2: $6 per unit versus $3 per unit (point B versus point A). Under these circumstances, there is a simple way for the firm to reduce its total costs (while holding revenues fixed): Increase output at plant 2 and decrease output at plant 1 by the same amount. Increasing output at plant 2 increases costs at a rate of $3 per unit, but decreasing output at plant 2 saves costs

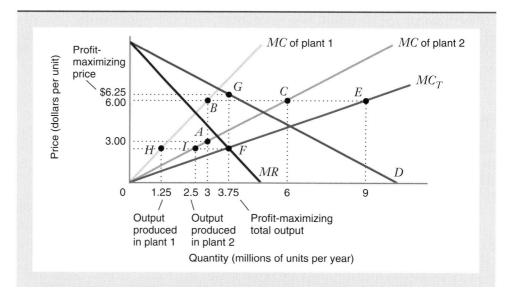

FIGURE 11.14 **Profit Maximization by a Multiplant Monopolist**
The monopolist's multiplant marginal cost curve is MC_T. This curve is the horizontal summation of the marginal cost curves of the monopolist's individual plants. For example, to attain a marginal cost of $6, the monopolist can produce 3 million units in plant 1 and 6 million units in plant 2, for a total of 9 million units. Thus, ($6, 9 million) is one point on the multiplant marginal cost curve MC_T. The monopolist's optimal total output is where $MC_T = MR$, or 3.75 million units. Of this total, 2.5 million should be produced in plant 1 and 1.25 million should be produced in plant 2. The monopolist's profit-maximizing price is $6.25.

at a rate of $6 per unit. Reallocating production away from plant 1 toward plant 2 reduces the firm's total production costs. Since reallocation is always profitable whenever the firm operates at a point at which the marginal costs of the plants differ, we conclude that a profit-maximizing firm will always allocate output among the plants so as to keep their marginal costs equal.

This insight allows us to construct a marginal cost schedule for a multiplant firm. Consider, again, Figure 11.14, and pick any possible level of marginal cost, such as $6. To attain this level of marginal cost, the firm would produce 3 million units in plant 1 and 6 million units in plant 2 (points B and C). Thus, it can attain a marginal cost of $6 when it produces a total output of 9 million units (point E). The curve MC_T—**the multiplant marginal cost curve**—traces out the set of points we generate when we horizontally sum the marginal cost curves of the individual plants.

Having derived the multiplant marginal cost curve, the answer to the first question—how much should the monopolist produce in total—is relatively easy to find. The monopolist equates marginal revenue to its multiplant marginal cost curve, $MR = MC_T$. In Figure 11.14, this occurs at a total output of 3.75 million units (point F). The optimal price corresponding to this output is $6.25 (point G). Given this output, the monopolist produces 1.25 million units in plant 1 and 2.5 million units in plant 2 (points H and I).

LEARNING-BY-DOING EXERCISE 11.6

Optimal Price and Output for a Multiplant Monopolist

In this exercise, you will learn how to solve the profit-maximization problem for a multiplant monopolist. Let's consider a monopolist that faces a demand curve given by

$$P = 120 - 3Q.$$

The monopolist has two plants. The first has a marginal cost curve given by

$$MC_1 = 10 + 20Q_1.$$

The second plant's marginal cost curve is given by

$$MC_2 = 60 + 5Q_2.$$

Problem   Find the monopolist's optimal total quantity and price. Also find the optimal division of the monopolist's quantity between its two plants.

Solution   As a first step in solving this problem, let's construct the monopolist's multiplant marginal cost curve MC_T. As you just learned, this curve is the horizontal summation of the marginal cost curves of the individual plants, as shown graphically in Figure 11.14. To find the equation of MC_T, you have to be careful. You might be tempted to just add together the two marginal cost equations as follows: $10 + 20Q + 60 + 5Q = 70 + 25Q$. This is incorrect. Adding the two marginal cost curves would give us the *vertical* summation of the marginal cost curves. To get the horizontal summation of the curves, we first must invert each marginal cost curve by expressing Q as a function of MC:

$$Q_1 = -\frac{1}{2} + \frac{1}{20} MC_1.$$

Similarly:

$$Q_2 = -12 + \frac{1}{5} MC_2.$$

You just learned that the marginal cost allocates output across plants to equate marginal production costs in the two plants. Thus, let MC_T be an arbitrary common marginal cost level. The horizontal summation of the two marginal cost curves is the total output in the two plants that we get when both plants have a marginal cost MC_T. We find this by adding the inverted marginal cost curves.

$$Q_1 + Q_2 = -\frac{1}{2} + \frac{1}{20} MC_T + -12 + \frac{1}{5} MC_T$$
$$= -12.5 + 0.25 MC_T.$$

If we let $Q = Q_1 + Q_2$ denote the monopolist's total output, we now just invert this sum to get overall marginal cost as a function of total output:

$$Q = -12.5 + 0.25 MC_T \Rightarrow$$
$$MC_T = 50 + 4Q.$$

This is the monopolist's multiplant marginal cost curve.

Now we can find the monopolist's profit-maximizing quantity and price. We proceed as always by equating marginal revenue to marginal cost:

$$MR = MC_T$$
$$120 - 6Q = 50 + 4Q.$$

The solution to this equation is $Q = 7$. We can find the optimal price by substituting this quantity back into the demand curve:

$$P = 120 - 3(7) = 99.$$

To find the division of output across the monopolist's plants, we first determine the monopolist's marginal cost at the optimal quantity. Since the optimal quantity is $Q = 7$, the marginal cost of the monopolist is

$$MC_T = 50 + 4(7) = 78.$$

To find the output at each individual plant, we can use the inverted marginal cost curves we derived above. These curves tell us how much we must produce at an individual plant, so that we attain a marginal cost of 78 at each plant:

$$Q_1 = -\frac{1}{2} + \frac{1}{20}(78) = 3.4$$

$$Q_2 = -12 + \frac{1}{5}(78) = 3.6.$$

Thus, of the total quantity of 7, plant 1 produces 3.4 units, while plant 2 produces 3.6 units.

Similar Problem: 11.10

PROFIT MAXIMIZATION BY A CARTEL

A **cartel** is a group of producers that collusively determines the price and output in a market. One of history's most famous (or notorious) cartels is the Organization of Petroleum Exporting Countries, or OPEC, whose members include some of the world's largest oil producers such as Saudi Arabia, Kuwait, Iran, and Venezuela. Sometimes cartels are even sanctioned by government. For example, in the early 1980s, the seventeen firms in Japan's electric cable industry received permission from Japan's Ministry of International Trade and Industry to act as a cartel. The cartel's stated goal was to reduce industry output in order to raise price and increase industry profits.

When a cartel works as its members intend, it acts as a single monopoly firm that maximizes total industry profit. The problem a cartel faces in allocating output levels across individual producers is identical to the problem faced by a multiplant monopolist in allocating output across its individual plants. Thus, the conditions for profit maximization by a cartel are identical to those for a multiplant monopolist. To illustrate, suppose the cartel consists of two firms, with marginal cost functions $MC_1(Q_1)$ and $MC_2(Q_2)$. At the profit-maximizing solution, the cartel allocates production between the two firms, so that marginal costs are equalized and the common marginal cost equals the industrywide marginal revenue. Mathematically, letting Q^* and P^* be the optimal total output and price for the cartel as a whole, and letting Q_1^* and Q_2^* be the outputs of the individual cartel members, we can express the profit-maximization condition of the cartel as follows:[16]

$$MR(Q^*) = MC_1(Q_1^*).$$

$$MR(Q^*) = MC_2(Q_2^*).$$

Figure 11.15 illustrates the solution to the cartel's profit-maximization problem. In this example, the profit-maximizing cartel output occurs at 3.75 million

[16]We can also express the cartel's profit-maximization condition as an IEPR:

$$\frac{P^* - MC_1(Q_1^*)}{P^*} = \frac{P^* - MC_2(Q_2^*)}{P^*} = -\frac{1}{\epsilon_{Q,P}}.$$

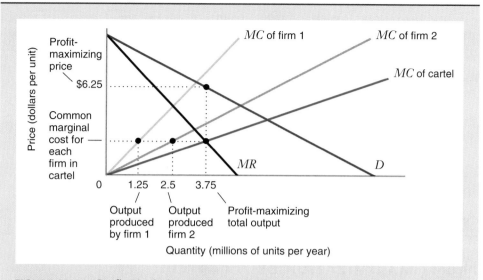

FIGURE 11.15   Profit Maximization by a Cartel
The cartel's marginal cost curve is MC_T, which is the horizontal summation of the marginal cost curves of the individual firms in the cartel. The cartel's profit-maximizing output is where $MC_T = MR$, or 3.75 million units. To equalize the marginal costs of individual producers, firm 2 should produce 2.5 million units and firm 1 should produce 1.25 million units. The cartel's profit-maximizing price is $6.25.

units per year, and the profit-maximizing price is $6.25 per unit.[17] The cartel then allocates production across its members to equalize marginal costs across firms. Notice that the firm with the higher marginal cost schedule (firm 1) is allocated the smaller share of total cartel output (1.25 million units versus 2.5 million units for firm 2). Thus, the cartel does not necessarily divide up the market equally among its members. The low-marginal cost firms supply a bigger share of total cartel output than do the high-marginal cost firms.

EXAMPLE 11.5   *Allocating Production Quotas in a Cartel: The Case of OPEC*

To increase the world price of oil, OPEC members must restrict their outputs, or else they will produce more oil than the world will demand. Each member nation must therefore agree to an output quota. For example, in 1982, OPEC set an overall output limit of 18 million barrels per day, down from 31 million barrels per day in 1979. Prices were to be maintained at $34 per barrel. Each member nation had an individual production quota, except for Saudi Arabia (the largest OPEC producer), which adjusted its output as necessary to maintain prices.

---

[17]Careful readers will notice that Figure 11.15 is identical to Figure 11.14 which depicted profit maximzation for a multiplant monopolist. We do this to illustrate that the cartel's profit-maximization problem is identical to that of a multiplant monopolist.

The marginal cost of oil depends on where the oil is produced. For example, Saudi Arabian oil is generally thought to have a lower marginal cost than Nigerian or Indonesian oil. In light of these cost differences, an interesting question is whether OPEC production quotas generally correspond to profit-maximizing output levels predicted by the cartel theory described above. It is difficult to answer this question definitively because precise estimates of marginal cost by location are not available. However, we can group oil-producing locations according to their average cost per barrel. Stephen Martin recounts evidence that indicates that, in the mid-1980s, a greater share of OPEC output came from locations with average cost per barrel of $2 to $4 than from locations with average costs less than $2 per barrel.[18] This suggests that OPEC did not allocate production quotas consistent with the way that a profit-maximizing cartel would. In Martin's view, "Despite the immense economic profit earned by OPEC from 1973 through (say) 1986, a monopolist could have done better." ∎

11.5
THE WELFARE ECONOMICS OF MONOPOLY

Chapter 10 showed that the perfectly competitive equilibrium maximizes social welfare. It also showed that departures from the perfectly competitive equilibrium create deadweight losses. As we will see, the monopoly equilibrium does not, in general, correspond to the perfectly competitive equilibrium. For that reason, the monopoly equilibrium entails a deadweight loss as well.

THE MONOPOLY EQUILIBRIUM DIFFERS FROM THE PERFECTLY COMPETITIVE EQUILIBRIUM

Figure 11.16 shows the equilibrium in a perfectly competitive market. The competitive equilibrium price occurs at a price of $5.00 per unit, where the industry supply curve S intersects the demand curve D. The equilibrium quantity in this market is 1000 units.

Suppose now this industry was monopolized. We might imagine a single firm acquiring all of the perfect competitive firms, keeping some in operation and shutting down the rest. Now recall from Chapters 9 and 10 that the industry supply curve in a competitive market tells us the marginal cost of supplying units to the market. For example, if a perfectly competitive industry supplied 600 units, the supply curve tells us the marginal cost of the 600th unit: $3. When the industry is monopolized, the supply curve S now becomes the monopolist's marginal cost curve, MC. Given this, the profit-maximizing monopoly equilibrium occurs at a quantity of 600 units and price of $9 per unit. We can see from Figure 11.16 how the monopoly equilibrium and the competitive equilibrium differ: The monopoly price is higher than the perfectly competitive price, and the monopolist supplies less output than the perfectly competitive industry does.

---

[18]S. Martin, *Industrial Economics: Economic Analysis and Public Policy* (New York: Macmillan, 1988) pp. 137–138.

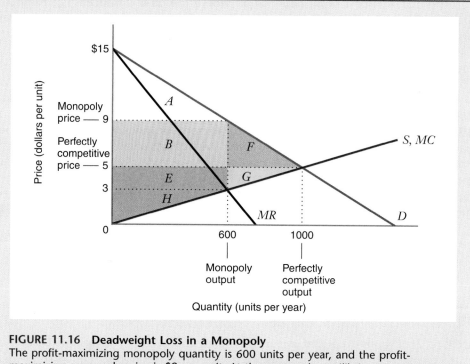

FIGURE 11.16   Deadweight Loss in a Monopoly
The profit-maximizing monopoly quantity is 600 units per year, and the profit-maximizing monopoly price is $9 per unit. At the monopoly equilibrium, consumer surplus is *A* and producer surplus is *B + E + H*. In a perfectly competitive market, the equilibrium quantity is 1,000 units and the equilibrium price is $5 per unit. Consumer surplus in the competitive market is *A + B + F* while producer surplus is *E + G + H*. The deadweight loss due to monopoly is thus *F + G*.

MONOPOLY DEADWEIGHT LOSS

How does the difference between the monopoly and competitive outcomes affect economic benefits in this market? At the monopoly equilibrium the consumer surplus is area *A*. The monopolist's producer surplus—its total revenue minus total cost—is the accumulation of the difference between the monopolist's price and the marginal cost of each unit it produces. This corresponds to the sum of areas *B*, *E*, and *H* in Figure 11.16. Thus, the net economic benefit at the monopoly equilibrium is *A + B + E + H*.

We know from Chapter 10 that the competitive market outcome maximizes the net economic benefit in this market. In the perfectly competitive market, consumer surplus is *A + B + F* and producer surplus is *E + G + H*. Net economic benefit under perfect competition is thus *A + B + E + F + G + H*.[19]

Table 11.2 compares the net benefits under monopoly and perfect competition. It shows that the net economic benefit under perfect competition exceeds the net economic benefit under monopoly by an amount equal to *F + G*. This

[19]We should be slightly more careful here. Area *A + B + E + H* is total economic benefit before deducting the monopolist's fixed costs. Similarly *A + B + E + F + G + H* is the total economic benefit under perfect competition before deducting the fixed costs of the competitive firms. Since the magnitude of the fixed costs does not affect the *comparison* of total economic benefits between monopoly and perfect competition, we can ignore them.

TABLE 11.2
Deadweight Loss at the Monopoly Equilibrium in a Natural Monopoly Market

	Perfect Competition	Monopoly	Difference
Consumer surplus	$A + B + F$	A	$-B - F$
Producer surplus	$E + G + H$	$B + E + H$	$B - G$
Net economic benefit	$A + B + E + F + G + H$	$A + B + E + H$	$-F - G$

difference is the **deadweight loss due to monopoly.** This deadweight loss is analogous to the deadweight losses you saw in Chapter 10. It represents the difference between the net economic benefit that would arise if the market were perfectly competitive and the net benefit attained at the monopoly equilibrium. In Figure 11.16, the monopoly deadweight loss arises because the monopolist does not produce units of output between 600 and 1,000 for which consumers' marginal willingness to pay (represented by the demand curve) exceeds marginal cost. Production of these units enhances total economic benefit, but they reduce the monopolist's profit, and therefore the monopolist does not produce them.

RENT-SEEKING ACTIVITIES

Table 11.2 could understate the monopoly deadweight loss. Because a monopolist often earns positive economic profits, you might expect that firms would have an incentive to acquire monopoly power. For example, during the 1990s, cable television companies spent millions lobbying Congress to preserve regulations that limit the ability of satellite broadcasters to compete with traditional cable service. Activities aimed at creating or preserving monopoly power are called **rent-seeking activities.** Expenditures on rent-seeking activities can represent an important social cost of monopoly that Table 11.2 does not measure.

The incentive to engage in rent-seeking activities gets stronger the greater the potential monopoly profit (area $B + E + H$ in Figure 11.16). Indeed, the monopoly profit represents the maximum a firm would be willing to spend on rent-seeking activities to protect its monopoly. If a firm spent this maximum amount, the deadweight loss from monopoly would be the sum of monopoly profit $B + E + H$ and the traditional deadweight loss $F + G$. If the monopolist engages in rent-seeking activities to acquire or preserve its monopoly position, $F + G$ represents a lower bound on the deadweight loss from monopoly, while $B + E + F + G + H$ represents an upper bound.

11.6
WHY DO MONOPOLY MARKETS EXIST?

We have studied how a profit-maximizing monopolist determines its quantity and price. And because quantity and price differ from the perfectly competitive equilibrium, we have seen that the monopoly equilibrium creates a deadweight loss. But how do monopolies arise in the first place. Why, for example, does BSkyB have a monopoly on satellite broadcasting in the United Kingdom? Why does Microsoft Windows have nearly 100 percent of the market for personal computer operating systems? In this section we explore why monopoly markets might arise. To do so, we first study the concept of a natural monopoly. Then, we explore the notion of barriers to entry.

NATURAL MONOPOLY

A market is a **natural monopoly** if, for any relevant level of industry output, the total cost a single firm producing that output incurs is less than the combined total cost that two or more firms would incur if they divided that output among them. A good example of a natural monopoly is satellite television broadcasting. If, for example, two firms split a market consisting of 50 million subscribers, each must incur the cost of buying, launching, and maintaining a satellite to provide service to its 25 million subscribers. But if a single firm serves the entire market, the satellite that served 25 million subscribers can just as well serve 50 million subscribers. That is, the cost of the satellite is fixed: It does not go up as the number of subscribers goes up. A single firm needs just one satellite to serve the market, while two independent firms need would need two satellites to serve the same number of subscribers overall.

Figure 11.17 shows a natural monopoly market. The market demand curve is D, and each firm has access to a technology that generates a long-run average cost curve AC. For any output less than 10,000 units per year, a single firm can produce output more cheaply than two or more firms could. To illustrate

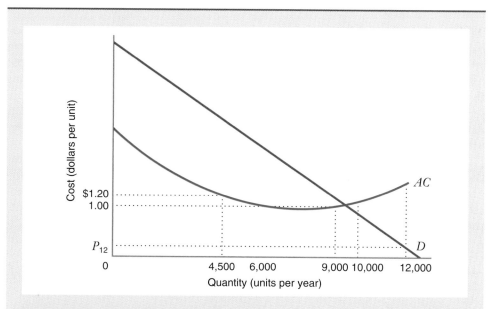

FIGURE 11.17   Natural Monopoly Market
Suppose the figure shows a natural monopoly market. Any output level less than 10,000 units per year can be produced most cheaply by a single firm. For example, a single firm can produce an output of 9,000 units for an average cost of $1 per unit. Two firms, each producing 4,500 units, would incur an average cost of $1.20 per unit. Two firms could produce 12,000 units at a lower total cost than one firm could. However, this level of output would not be profitable because the price P_{12} at which 12,000 units would be demanded is less than the minimum level of average cost.

why, consider an output level, such as $Q = 9,000$ units per year. A single firm's total cost of producing 9,000 units per year is $TC(9,000) = 9,000 \times AC(9,000) = \$9,000$, since $AC(9,000) = \$1$. Suppose we divided this output equally between, say, two firms, each with the cost functions shown in Figure 11.17. The total cost of production would be $9,000 \times AC(4,500) = \$11,800$, since $AC(4,500) = \$1.2$. Thus, it is more expensive to split production of 9,000 units of output among two firms than it is to produce all 9,000 units in a single firm. Now, in Figure 11.17 some levels of output along the demand curve can be produced more cheaply by two firms than one (e.g., $Q = 12,000$). However, such output levels would only be demanded at prices less than the minimum level of average cost. Thus, they would not be profitable. At all relevant levels of market demand—that is, all levels of market demand that could be profitably produced—the total cost of production is minimized when one firm serves the entire market.

If one firm can serve a market at lower total cost than two or more firms, we would expect that the market would eventually become monopolized. This is what happened in the satellite broadcasting market in the United Kingdom. Two firms entered that market in the early 1990s: British Satellite Broadcasting and Sky Television. But with both firms in the market, neither could make a profit. In fact, at one point both companies were losing more than \$1 million a day. Eventually, the two firms merged, forming the satellite television monopolist BSkyB, which, since the merger, has become profitable.

The analysis in Figure 11.17 implies two important points about natural monopoly markets. First, a necessary condition for natural monopoly is that the average cost curve must decrease with output over some range. That is, natural monopoly markets must involve economies of scale. In the previous example of satellite broadcasting, earlier, the fixed cost of the satellite and its associated infrastructure gives rise to significant economies of scale. Second, whether a market is a natural monopoly depends not only on technological conditions (the shape of the AC curve) but also on demand conditions. A market might be a natural monopoly when demand is low but not when demand is high. This would explain why the satellite broadcasting market in the United Kingdom contains just one firm (BSkyB), while the much larger U.S. market can accommodate several competitors.

BARRIERS TO ENTRY

A natural monopoly is an example of a more general phenomenon known as **barriers to entry.** Barriers to entry are factors that allow an incumbent firm to earn positive economic profits, while at the same time making it unprofitable for newcomers to enter the industry. Perfectly competitive markets have no barriers to entry: When incumbent firms earn positive profits, new firms enter the industry, driving profits to zero. But barriers to entry are essential for a firm to remain a monopolist. Without the protection of barriers to entry, a monopoly or cartel that earned positive economic profits would attract new market entry, and competition would then dissipate industry profit.

Barriers to entry can be structural, legal, or strategic. **Structural barriers to entry** exist when incumbent firms have cost or marketing advantages that would make it unattractive for a new firm to enter the industry and compete against it. The interaction of economies of scale and market demand that gives rise to a natural monopoly market is an example of a structural barrier to entry. The Internet auction market provides an example of another type of structural entry barrier, this one based on positive network externalities. As noted in Chapter 5, positive network externalities arise when a firm's product is more attractive to a given consumer the more the product is used by other consumers. The auction site of market leader eBay is attractive to auction buyers because there are so many items offered for sale and there are often several sellers of the same item. Auction sellers like eBay because there are so many buyers. The sheer volume of transactions on eBay, in and of itself, is an important part of eBay's appeal. This network externality creates a significant barrier to entry. A newcomer seeking to establish its own Internet auction site (to make money, as eBay does, through commissions on transactions) would face an enormous challenge: Lacking the critical mass that eBay possesses, it would simply not be as attractive a site. This barrier to entry explains why some very savvy Internet companies, including Amazon.com and Yahoo, have found it difficult to establish their own auction sites to compete against eBay.

Legal barriers to entry exist when an incumbent firm is legally protected against competition. Patents are an important legal barrier to entry. Government regulations can also create legal barriers to entry. Between 1994 and 1999, the company Network Solutions had a government-sanctioned monopoly in the business of registering domain names on the Internet.

Strategic barriers to entry result when the incumbent firm takes explicit steps to deter entry. An example of a strategic barriers to entry would be the development of a reputation over time as a firm that will aggressively defend its market against encroachment by new entrants (e.g., by starting a price war if a new firm chooses to come into the market). Polaroid's aggressive response to Kodak's entry into the instant photography market in the 1970s is an illustration of this strategy.

EXAMPLE 11.6

United States of America versus Microsoft: The Applications Barrier to Entry

Between October 1998 and June 1999, one of America's best known and most successful companies, Microsoft, went on trial for violating the U.S. antitrust statutes. The U.S. government accused Microsoft of employing tactics aimed at monopolizing the market for operating systems for personal computers (PCs). In the opinion of the U.S. District Court, "Microsoft . . . engaged in a concerted series of actions designed to protect the applications barrier to entry, and hence its monopoly power, from a variety of . . . threats, including Netscape's Web browser and Sun's implementation of Java. Many of these actions have harmed consumers in ways that are immediate and easily discernible."[20]

What does the Court mean by the term *applications barrier to entry?* This phrase appears repeatedly in the Court's opinion in this case. The Court uses the term *applications barrier to entry* to describe a barrier to entry in the market for PC

---

[20]This quote comes from p. 204 of the *United States of America v. Microsoft*, United States District Court for the District of Columbia, Findings of Fact.

operating systems based on positive network externalities. This barrier, in the Court's opinion, allowed Microsoft Windows to monopolize the market for operating systems for Intel-compatible PCs. The Court described the applications barrier to entry this way:

> The fact that there is a multitude of people using Windows makes the product more attractive to consumers. The large installed base attracts corporate customers who want to use an operating system that new employees are already likely to know how to use, and it attracts academic consumers who want to use software that will allow them to share files easily with colleagues at other institutions. The main reason that demand for Windows experiences positive network effects, however, is that the size of Windows' installed base impels ISVs [companies that write software applications] to write applications first and foremost to Windows . . . The large body of applications thus reinforces the demand for Windows, augmenting Microsoft's dominant position and thereby perpetuating ISV incentives to write applications principally for Windows. This self-reinforcing cycle is often referred to as a "positive feedback loop."
>
> What for Microsoft is a positive feedback loop is for would-be competitors a vicious cycle. For just as Microsoft's large market share creates incentives for ISVs to develop applications first and foremost for Windows, the small or non-existent market share of an aspiring competitor makes it prohibitively expensive for the aspirant to develop its PC operating system into an acceptable substitute for Windows (pp. 18–19).

In the Court's opinion—an opinion that Microsoft strongly disputes—many of Microsoft's actions toward competitors, such as Netscape and Sun, were attempts to preserve this applications barrier to entry. For example, in the summer of 1995, Microsoft attempted to convince Netscape to drop efforts to develop a Web browser that could have served as a platform for Internet-based software applications. The Court believed that Microsoft did this in order to remove a threat to the applications barrier to entry that sustained Windows' dominance. ■

11.7 MONOPSONY

A **monopsony market** is a market consisting of a single buyer that can purchase from many sellers. We call this single buyer a *monopsonist*. For example, until 1976, major league baseball players were not allowed to bargain with more than one team simultaneously. Thus, each baseball team was a monopsonist in the baseball players market. As in this case, a monopsonist could be a firm that constitutes the only potential buyer of an input. Or a monopsonist can be an individual or organization that is the only buyer of a finished product. For example, the U.S. government is the monopsonist in the market for U.S. military uniforms. In this section, we study a firm that is a monopsonist in the market for one of its inputs.

MONOPSONY EQUILIBRIUM

Let's imagine a firm whose production function depends on a single input L. The firm's total output is $Q = f(L)$. You might, for example, imagine that L is the quantity of labor a coal mine employs. If the mine size is fixed, the amount Q of coal produced per month depends only on the amount L of labor hired. Imagine that this firm is a perfect competitor in the market for coal (e.g., it sells its coal in a national or global market) and thus takes the market price P as given. The coal company's total revenue is thus $Pf(L)$. The **marginal revenue product of labor**—denoted by MRP_L—is the additional revenue that the firm gets when it employs an additional unit of labor. Since the firm is a price taker, marginal revenue product is the market price times the marginal product of labor:

$$MRP_L = P \times MP_L$$
$$= P \frac{\Delta Q}{\Delta L}.$$

Let's imagine that our coal mine is the only employer of labor in its region. Hence, it acts as a monopsonist in the labor market. The supply of labor in the coal company's region of operation is described by the labor supply curve shown in Figure 11.18. For any wage, this curve tells us the quantity of labor that will be supplied at that wage. This curve can also be interpreted in inverse form: It tells us the wage that is necessary to induce a given amount of labor to be offered in the market.

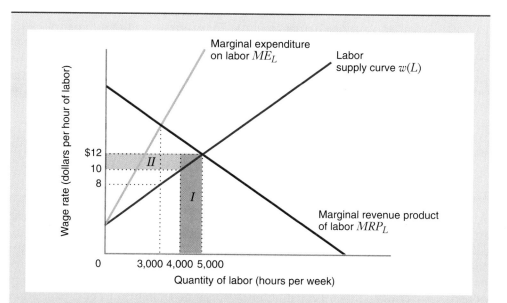

FIGURE 11.18   The Monopsony Equilibrium
Suppose the monopsonist initially employs 4,000 hours of labor per week. To increase the quantity of labor it employs to 5,000 hours per week, it must raise the wage it pays from $10 per hour to $12 per hour. The additional labor cost to the monopsonist has two components: area *I* is the extra cost that comes from employing more workers at the new wage rate; area *II* is the extra cost that comes from having to raise the wage for all hours of labor that would have been supplied at the initial wage of $10 per hour. The monopsonist maximizes profit by choosing a quantity of labor at which its marginal revenue product equals the marginal expenditure on labor. This is 3,000 hours of labor a week. The wage it must pay to elicit this supply of labor is $8 per hour.

The inverse supply curve $w(L)$ shows the wage–labor combinations available to our coal monopsonist. For example if the monopsonist desires to hire 1,000 more hours of labor per week above an initial level of 4,000 hours per week, it will have to increase the wage from $10 per hour to $12 per hour to do so. The firm's total cost is the firm's total expenditure on labor: $TC = wL$. The firm's **marginal expenditure on labor** is the rate at which the firm's total cost goes up, per unit of labor, as it hires more labor. Figure 11.18 reveals that this additional cost has two components: areas I and II. Area I ($w\Delta L$) represents the extra cost that comes from employing more workers. Area II (($\Delta w)L$) is the extra cost that comes from having to raise the wage for all units of labor that would have been supplied at the initial wage rate of $10. The marginal expenditure on labor is thus:

$$ME_L = \frac{\Delta TC}{\Delta L} = \frac{\text{area } I + \text{area } II}{\Delta L}$$
$$= \frac{w\Delta L + (\Delta w)L}{\Delta L}$$
$$= w + L\frac{\Delta w}{\Delta L}.$$

Since the supply curve for labor is upward sloping $\Delta w/\Delta L > 0$. The marginal expenditure curve therefore lies above the labor supply curve, as Figure 11.18 shows.

The coal mine's profit-maximization problem is to choose a quantity of labor L to maximize total profit, π, which is the difference between total revenue and total cost:

$$\pi = Pf(L) - w(L)L.$$

The firm will maximize profit at the point at which marginal revenue product of labor equals marginal expenditure on labor:

$$MRP_L = ME_L.$$

The profit maximum occurs in Figure 11.18 at a quantity of labor equal to 3,000 hours per week. The wage rate needed to induce this supply of labor is $8 per hour, which is less than the marginal expenditure on labor at $L = 3,000$.

LEARNING-BY-DOING EXERCISE 11.7

Calculating the Equilibrium in a Monopsony Market

Let's consider a firm that acts as monopsonist in the market for labor. Suppose this firm's only input is labor, and it has a production function (or equivalently, a total product function) described by the equation:

$$Q = 5L,$$

where L is the quantity of labor (expressed in thousands of person-hours per week).

Problem   Suppose the monopsonist can sell all the output it wants at a market price of $10 per unit. Suppose, too, that the supply curve for labor is described by the equation

$$w(L) = 2 + 2L.$$

This curve tells us the wage rate w (expressed in dollars per hour) needed to induce a labor supply of L. Find the monopsony equilibrium in this market.

Solution   Let's begin by finding the marginal expenditure function. You just learned that the marginal expenditure on labor is given by the equation

$$ME_L = w + L\,\frac{\Delta w}{\Delta L},$$

where $\Delta w/\Delta L$ is the slope of the supply curve. To apply this formula to the supply function above, note that $w = 2 + 2L$ while $\Delta w/\Delta L = 2$. Thus,

$$ME_L = 2 + 2L + 2L$$
$$= 2 + 4L.$$

Now, let's identify the firm's marginal revenue product curve. Recall that MRP_L is found by multiplying the marginal product of labor, MP_L by the market price—in this case, $10. Thus:

$$MP_L = \frac{\Delta Q}{\Delta L} = 5$$

$$MRP_L = 10(5) = 50.$$

We find the monopsonist's optimal quantity of labor by equating marginal revenue product to the marginal expenditure:

$$MRP_L = ME_L$$
$$50 = 2 + 4L$$
$$12 = L.$$

The monopsonist optimally employs 12,000 hours of labor per week. The wage needed to induce this supply of labor is found from the labor supply curve:

$$w = 2 + 2(12) = \$26 \text{ per hour.}$$

Similar Problem: 11.12

AN INVERSE ELASTICITY PRICING RULE FOR MONOPSONY

The monopoly equilibrium condition, $MR = MC$, gave rise to an inverse elasticity pricing rule (IEPR), as we saw above. The monopsony equilibrium condition, $MRP_L = ME_L$, also gives rise to an inverse elasticity pricing rule. The key elasticity in this rule is the elasticity of labor supply, $\epsilon_{L,w}$ which indicates the percentage change in labor supplied per 1 percent change in the labor wage.[21]

The IEPR in a monopsony market is

$$\frac{MRP_L - w}{w} = \frac{1}{\epsilon_{L,w}}.$$

In words, this condition says that the percentage deviation between the marginal revenue product and the wage is equal to the inverse of the elasticity of labor supply.

Why is this IEPR significant? One important reason is that this condition distinguishes monopsony labor markets from perfectly competitive labor markets. In a perfectly competitive labor market in which many firms purchase labor services, each firm would take the price of labor w as given. Each firm would thus maximize its profits by choosing a quantity of labor that equates the marginal revenue product of labor with the wage rate:

$$MRP_L = w.$$

In a monopsony labor market, by contrast, the monopsony firm pays a wage that is *less than* the marginal revenue product. The IEPR tells us that the amount by which the wage falls short of the marginal revenue product is determined by the inverse elasticity of labor supply.

Monopsony Power in the Market for Nurses[22]

EXAMPLE 11.7

Every so often, one encounters news stories about the shortage of nurses. This shortage has, in the past, led hospitals to institute some creative programs for recruiting nurses. For example, in the early 1990s, the M.D. Anderson Cancer Center at the University of Texas gave employees $500 for every nursing applicant they successfully recruited.[23]

The shortage of nurses is often cited as evidence that nursing markets are monopsonistic. The idea is that since the marginal revenue product exceeds the wage in a monopsony equilibrium, a monopsonistic hospital might want to hire more nurses at the *existing* wage. However, it would not want to *increase the wage* to attract more nurses because the gain from hiring additional nurses would be

---

[21] This is analogous to the price elasticity of supply that we discussed in Chapters 2 and 9.

[22] This example draws from D. Sullivan, "Monopsony Power in the Market for Nurses," *Journal of Law and Economics*, 32 (October 1989): S135–S178.

[23] This figure comes from the Work Week column on page 1 of the *Wall Street Journal* (August 27, 1991).

outweighed by the higher wage bill it would face for the nurses it already employs.

Are nursing markets monopsonistic? In local markets with only one hospital (Bloomington, Indiana, for example), the local hospital might literally be the only nursing-employment option for nurses in the local community, so it might make sense that the local hospital would act as a monopsonist. In larger cities with more than one hospital, metropolitan hospital associations often have wage standardization programs that allow hospitals to coordinate the establishment of nursing wages. Some have argued that these programs allow hospitals to act as a "buyers cartel" in the market for nurses and thus replicate the profit-maximizing monopsony outcome.

Daniel Sullivan, whose work on the cigarette industry you read about in Example 11.5, has estimated the extent to which hospitals exert monopsony power in the market for nurses. Based on data on nurses' salaries and employment for U.S. hospitals in the early 1980s, Sullivan estimates the gap between nurses' marginal revenue products and wages. He finds that this gap was significantly different from zero, even within major metropolitan areas. This gap exists in both the short run and the long run. This evidence is consistent with a monopsony equilibrium in which differences between wages and marginal revenue products are governed by an inverse elasticity pricing rule. ■

DEADWEIGHT LOSS UNDER MONOPSONY

Just as monopoly results in a deadweight loss, so does monopsony. To see why, consider the monopsony equilibrium in Figure 11.19: a wage rate of $8 per hour and a total quantity of labor of 3,000 hours per week. In our monopsonistic market, the coal mining firm is a "consumer" of labor services, while the workers are the "producers" of labor services. The coal firm's profit equals total revenue less total expenditures on labor. Total revenue is the area under the marginal revenue product curve up to the monopsony labor supply of 3,000, or $A + B + C + D + E$ in Figure 11.19. The firm's total cost of labor is $D + E$, so the coal firm's profit, or equivalently, the input buyer's *consumer surplus*, is $A + B + C$.

The labor suppliers' *producer surplus* is the difference between total wages received and the total opportunity cost of the labor supplied. Total wage payments equal $D + E$ in Figure 11.19. The opportunity cost of labor supply is reflected in the labor supply curve. The area underneath the supply curve up to the quantity of 3,000—or area E in Figure 11.19—represents the total compensation needed to elicit that supply of labor, which corresponds to the economic value workers receive in their best outside opportunity. That outside opportunity might be the value of the leisure a worker enjoys by not working, or it might be the wage he or she would get if he or she migrated from the region to another labor market. Thus, in Figure 11.19, producer surplus is $D + E - E = D$. The sum of producer and consumer surplus thus equals $A + B + C + D$.

If the market for labor had been competitive, not monopsonistic, the market clearing price of labor would equal $12 per hour, and the corresponding quantity of labor would be 5,000 hours per week. Thus, a monopsony market results in an underemployment of the input—in this case, labor—relative to the com-

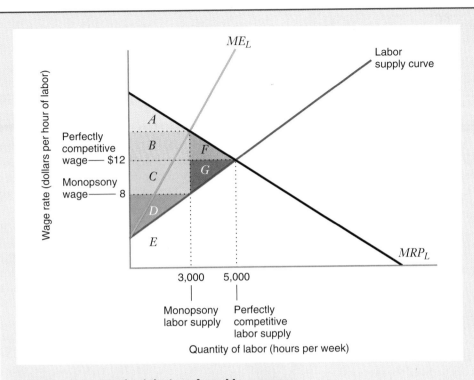

FIGURE 11.19 Deadweight Loss from Monopsony
The monopsony equilibrium occurs at a quantity of labor equal to 3,000 hours per week and a wage of $8 per hour. Consumer surplus at this equilibrium is $A + B + C$, while producer surplus is D. In a perfectly competitive labor market, by contrast, the equilibrium quantity of labor would be 5,000 hours per week, and the wage would be $12 per hour. Consumer surplus would be $A + B + F$, while producer surplus would be $C + D + G$. The deadweight loss due to monopsony is thus $F + G$.

petitive market outcome. In a competitive market, consumer surplus equals $A + B + F$, while producer surplus equals $C + D + G$. As Table 11.3 reveals, monopsony transfers surplus from the owners of the input to buyers of the input—in this case from workers to the coal mining firm. Since the monopsonist uses fewer units of the input than a competitive market would use, there is also a deadweight loss. Table 11.3 shows that this deadweight loss is the familiar triangular shape: area F plus area G.

TABLE 11.3
Deadweight Loss Under Monopsony

	Perfect Competition	Monopsony	Difference
Consumer surplus	$A + B + F$	$A + B + C$	$C - F$
Producer surplus	$C + D + G$	D	$-C - G$
Net economic benefit	$A + B + C + D + F + G$	$A + B + C + D$	$-F - G$

CHAPTER SUMMARY

• A monopoly market consists of a single seller facing many buyers. In setting its price, the monopolist must take account of the market demand curve: the higher the price it sets, the fewer units of product it will sell. The lower the price it sets, the more units it will sell.

• The monopolist's demand curve is downward sloping, and it lies above the marginal revenue curve at all positive quantities.   (LBD Exercise 11.1)

• A monopolist maximizes profit by producing at that quantity of output at which marginal cost equals marginal revenue.   (LBD Exercise 11.2)

• The monopolist's marginal revenue is the sum of two parts. The first part, which is equal to the market price, corresponds to the increase in revenue the monopolist gets when it sells marginal units. The second part, which is negative, corresponds to the decrease in revenue on inframarginal units the monopolist absorbs when it lowers its price to sell additional units. This decrease in revenue occurs because the monopolist lowers the price on units that it could have sold at a higher price.

• A monopolist does not have a supply curve.

• The inverse elasticity pricing rule (IEPR) states that the difference between the profit-maximizing price and marginal cost, as a percentage of price, is equal to minus the inverse of the price elasticity of market demand. (LBD Exercises 11.3, 11.4)

• The IEPR implies that a profit-maximizing monopolist facing positive marginal cost produces only on the elastic portion of the market demand curve.

• When a firm can control its price in the market, we say that it has market power. The IEPR applies not only to a monopolist but to any firm that has market power, such as a firm that competes in an industry with differentiated products.

• If an increase (i.e., rightward shift) in demand results in a rightward shift in the marginal revenue curve, the increase in demand will also increase the monopolist's equilibrium quantity. The monopolist's price might go up or down.   (LBD Exercise 11.5)

• A profit-maximizing firm with multiple plants will always allocate output among the plants so as to keep their marginal costs equal. The multiplant monopolist equates marginal revenue with an overall marginal cost curve, which is found by horizontally summing the marginal cost curves of the monopolist's individual plants. (LBD Exercise 11.6)

• The monopolist produces less output than a perfectly competitive industry would produce in equilibrium. This implies that the monopoly equilibrium entails a deadweight loss.

• A monopsonist is the sole buyer of a particular product or input that is sold by many sellers.

• A profit-maximizing monopsonist will hire a quantity of the input (e.g., labor) at which the marginal revenue product of the input equals the marginal expenditure on the input. The price that the monopsonist then pays for the input is determined from the supply curve of the input.   (LBD Exercise 11.7)

• Like monopoly, the monopsony equilibrium entails a deadweight loss compared to the perfectly competitive market outcome.

REVIEW QUESTIONS

1. Why is the demand curve facing a monopolist the market demand curve?

2. The marginal revenue for a perfectly competitive firm is equal to the market price. Why is the marginal revenue for a monopolist less than the market price for positive quantities of output?

3. Why can a monopolist's marginal revenue be negative for some levels of output? Why is marginal revenue negative when market demand is price inelastic?

4. Assume that the monopolist's marginal cost is positive at all levels of output.

a) *True or false*: When the monopolist operates on the inelastic region of the market demand curve, it can always increase profit by producing less output.

b) *True or false*: When the monopolist operates on the elastic region of the market demand curve, it can always increase profit by producing more output.

5. At the quantity of output at which the monopolist maximizes total profit, is the monopolist's total revenue *TR* maximized? Explain.

6. What is the IEPR? How does it relate to the monopolist's profit-maximizing condition, $MR = MC$?

7. Evaluate the following statement: Toyota faces competition from many other firms in the world market for automobiles; therefore, Toyota cannot have market power.

8. What rule does a multiplant monopolist use to allocate output among its plants? Would a multiplant perfect competitor use the same rule?

9. Why does the monopoly equilibrium give rise to a deadweight loss?

10. How does a monopsonist differ from a monopolist? Could a firm be both a monopsonist and a monopolist?

11. What is a monopsonist's marginal expenditure function? Why does a monopsonist's marginal expenditure exceed the input price at positive quantities of the input?

12. Why does the monopsony equilibrium give rise to a deadweight loss?

PROBLEMS

11.1. Suppose that the market demand curve is given by $Q = 100 - 5P$.
a) What is the inverse market demand curve?
b) What is the average revenue function for a monopolist in this market?
c) What is the marginal revenue function that corresponds to this demand curve?

11.2. Suppose that Intel has a monopoly in the market for microprocessors in Brazil. During the year 2001, it faces a market demand curve given by

$$P = 9 - Q,$$

where Q is millions of microprocessors sold per year. Suppose you do not know anything about Intel's costs of production. Assuming that Intel acts as a profit-maximizing monopolist, would it ever sell 7 million microprocessors in Brazil in 2001?

11.3. Suppose that United Airlines has a monopoly on the route between Chicago and Omaha, Nebraska. During the winter (December–March), the monthly demand on this route is given by $P = a_1 - bQ$. During the summer (June–August), the monthly demand is given by $P = a_2 - bQ$, where $a_2 > a_1$. Assuming that United's marginal cost function is the same in both the summer and the winter, and assuming that the marginal cost function is independent of the quantity Q of passengers served, will United charge a higher price in the summer or in the winter?

11.4. Assume that a monopolist sells a product with a total cost function

$$TC = 1,200 + 0.5Q^2$$

and a corresponding marginal cost function

$$MC = Q.$$

The market demand curve is given by the equation $P(Q) = 300 - Q$.
a) Find the profit-maximizing output and price for this monopolist. Is the monopolist profitable?
b) Calculate the price elasticity of demand at the monopolist's profit-maximizing price. Also calculate the marginal cost at the monopolist's profit-maximizing output. Verify that the IEPR holds.

11.5. A monopolist faces a demand curve $P = 210 - 4Q$, and initially faces a constant marginal cost $MC = 10$.
a) Calculate the profit-maximizing monopoly quantity and price and compute the monopolist's total revenue at the optimal price.
b) Suppose that the monopolist's marginal cost increases to $MC = 20$. Verify that the monopolist's total revenue goes down.
c) Suppose that all firms in a perfectly competitive equilibrium had marginal cost $MC = 10$. Find the long-run perfectly competitive industry price and quantity.

d) Suppose that all firms' marginal costs increased to $MC = 20$. Verify that the increase in marginal cost causes total industry revenue to go up.

11.6. A monopolist faces a demand function given by $P(Q) = 100 - Q + I$, where I is average consumer income in the monopolist's market. Suppose we know that the monopolist's marginal cost function is not downward sloping. If consumer income goes up, will the monopolist charge a higher price, a lower price, or will its price remain the same?

11.7. Two monopolists in different markets have identical marginal cost functions that are constant in output.
a) Suppose both face linear demand curves that are parallel to one another. Which monopolist will have the higher markup (ratio of P to MC): the one whose demand curve is closer to the origin or the one whose demand curve is farther from the origin?
b) Suppose both face linear demand curves with identical vertical intercepts but with different slopes. Which monopolist will have a higher markup: the one with the flatter demand curve or the one with the steeper demand curve?
c) Suppose both face linear demand curves with identical horizontal intercepts but with different slopes. Which monopolist will have a higher markup: the one with the flatter demand curve or the one with the steeper demand curve?

11.8. Suppose a monopolist faces a market demand function given by $P = a - bQ$. Its marginal cost is given by $MC(Q) = c + eQ$. We will assume that $a > c$ and $2b + e > 0$.
a) Derive an expression for the monopolist's optimal quantity and price in terms of the parameters a, b, c, and e.
b) Show that an increase in c (which corresponds to an upward parallel shift in marginal cost) or a decrease in a (which corresponds to a leftward parallel shift in demand) must decrease the equilibrium quantity of output.
c) Show that when $e \geq 0$, an increase in a must increase the equilibrium price.

11.9. Suppose a monopolist has a demand function given by

$$Q = 1,000P^{-3}.$$

What is the monopolist's optimal markup of price above marginal cost?

11.10. Imagine that Gillette has a monopoly in the market for razor blades in Mexico. The market demand curve for blades in Mexico is

$$P = 968 - 20Q$$

where P is the price of blades in cents and Q is annual demand for blades expressed in millions. Gillette has two plants in which it can produce razor blades for the Mexican market: one in Los Angeles, California, and one in Mexico City. In its L.A. plant, Gillette can produce any quantity of razors it wants at a marginal cost of 8 cents per blade. Letting Q_1 and MC_1 denote the output and marginal cost at the L.A. plant, we have

$$MC_1(Q_1) = 8.$$

The Mexican plant has a marginal cost function given by

$$MC_2(Q_2) = 1 + 0.5Q_2.$$

a) Find Gillette's profit-maximizing price and quantity of output for the Mexican market overall. How will Gillette allocate production between its Mexican plant and its U.S. plant?
b) Suppose Gillette's L.A. plant had a marginal cost of 10 cents rather than 8 cents per blade. How would your answer to part (a) change?

11.11. Suppose that market demand is given by

$$P = 100 - 2Q$$

and a monopolist's marginal cost is given by

$$MC = \frac{1}{2}Q.$$

a) Calculate the profit-maximizing monopoly price and quantity.
b) Calculate the price and quantity that arise under perfect competition with a supply curve $P = (1/2)Q$.
c) Compare consumer and producer surplus under monopoly versus marginal cost pricing. What is the deadweight loss due to monopoly?
d) Suppose market demand is given by

$$P = 180 - 4Q.$$

What is the deadweight loss due to monopoly now? What explains why this deadweight loss differs from that in part (c).

11.12. A coal mine operates with a production function

$$Q = \frac{1}{2}L$$

where L is the quantity of labor it employs and Q is total output. The firm is a price taker in the output market, where the price is currently 32. The firm is a monopsonist in the labor market, where the supply curve for labor is

$$w(L) = 4L.$$

a) What is the monopsonist's marginal expenditure function, ME_L?
b) Calculate the monopsonist's optimal quantity of labor. What wage rate must the monopsonist pay to attract this quantity of labor?
c) What is the deadweight loss due to monopsony in this market?

C H A P T E R

12

Capturing Surplus

On October 15, 1997, United Airlines Flight 815 departed from Chicago to Los Angeles. On board the Boeing 757 aircraft were 204 passengers, paying an average fare of $775. However, the actual price for an airline ticket typically varies widely on any given flight. As Table 12.1 shows, Flight 815 was no exception.[1] Some passengers paid more than $2,000 for their tickets. Others paid no money, using tickets obtained with frequent flyer miles.

Why are there so many different prices for tickets on most flights? Part of the reason is that some travelers fly in first class, while others fly in coach class. But that is not the whole story. Ticket prices vary widely even within each class, where passengers sit in similar seats and receive the same service. For example, on Flight 815, 34 passengers in coach class paid less than $199, 23 paid between $200 and $399, and 23 more paid between $400 and $599.

Airlines recognize that any given flight has different types of travelers. Some are business travelers, who often must fly to a specific destination at a particular time, even if the fares are high. Other travelers, such as families going on vacation, will be much more sensitive to the prices they pay for tickets. To avoid high fares, they may be willing to alter the timing of their vacation or even their destination. To take advantage of attractive fares, they may also be willing to purchase their tickets weeks or even months in advance.

When an airline knows that it can influence the number of travelers on a given flight by changing its

TABLE 12.1
Prices for United Airlines Flight 815

Ticket Price	Number of Passengers	Average Advance Purchase
$2000 or more	18	12 days
$1000–$1999	15	14 days
$800–$999	23	32 days
$600–$799	49	46 days
$400–$599	23	65 days
$200–$399	23	35 days
Less than $199	34	26 days
$0	19	—

fares, it has market power. It employs a system of *yield management* to fill the plane with travelers in the most profitable way. Yield management helps the airline determine how many seats it should allocate to each class of service. It is a balancing act. On the one hand, the airline wants to fill the plane because empty seats yield no revenue. It could do so by selling many seats well in advance of the flight at low discount fares. However, this could mean that the flight has no seats left to accommodate last-minute business travelers who would pay a high price for a ticket. A yield

[1]"IBM's Deep Blue Takes to the Skies," *The Chicago Tribune*, Section N, November 17, 1997.

management system will estimate the number of seats that should be made available at discount fares as well as the number that should be reserved for last-minute travelers who might pay high fares.

In Chapter 11 we saw that managing a firm with market power is more complex than managing a perfectly competitive firm. In a perfectly competitive market, managers cannot control the prices of inputs or outputs. All they can decide are the amounts of inputs they will purchase and outputs they will produce. However, a firm with market power in its product market must take into account the nature of demand. For example, to choose an optimal price, an airline must know something about the relationship between the quantity demanded and the price it sets. This

enables it to capture more surplus than a competitive firm can.

In Chapter 11 the monopolist charged a single, uniform price to all its customers. With a uniform price every unit of output is sold at the same price. In this chapter we will show how a firm with market power can capture even more surplus by engaging in price discrimination—that is, by charging consumers different prices for the same good. We will study three basic types or degrees of price discrimination, and show how price discrimination affects profits and the sum of consumer and producer surplus.

We will also examine how firms can capture more surplus if they bundle two related products together and sell them as a package. Firms often use bundling as a marketing strategy.

For example, computer firms may offer bundles that include not only a central processing unit (the computer itself), but also monitors, keyboards, and software, at a "special" price for the whole package. Photographic suppliers frequently offer bargains on bundles that include a camera, lenses, a case, and other accessories. Cable television suppliers usually sell basic service packages consisting of news, sports, and movie channels.

Finally, we will examine the use of advertising, a form of nonprice competition, to create and capture surplus. Advertising can increase the demand for a product. However, advertising is also costly. We will show how the decisions about the level of advertising and pricing should be made if a firm is to capture more surplus. ∎

12.1
CAPTURING SURPLUS

In Chapter 11 we saw how a monopolist will choose its quantity (and its uniform price) to maximize its profit. When the monopolist faces a downward-sloping demand curve, as in Figure 12.1, it wants to produce and sell the quantity Q_m because at this quantity marginal revenue and marginal cost are equal. The monopolist charges the price P_m because that price leads consumers to buy the Q_m units it produces. The monopolist captures the producer surplus indicated by the area $G + H + K + L$ in the graph. This is the maximum amount of producer surplus that the monopolist can capture when it charges the same uniform price for every unit it sells.

However, the monopolist does not capture all the potential economic benefits when it charges the price P_m. It does not receive the consumer surplus indicated by the area $E + F$ in Figure 12.1 because consumers capture those benefits. Furthermore, the deadweight loss indicated by area $J + N$ represents still other potential net economic benefits that neither producers nor consumers capture. The deadweight loss arises because there are potential consumers between points A and B on the demand curve who do not buy the good even though they are willing to pay a price at least as high as the marginal cost.

How can the monopolist capture even more surplus by charging more than one price for its product, which is the essential feature of price discrimination? The firm might do this by charging different prices to different consumers. It might also offer an individual consumer a quantity discount, so that the price paid for a good depends on the number of units the consumer purchases.

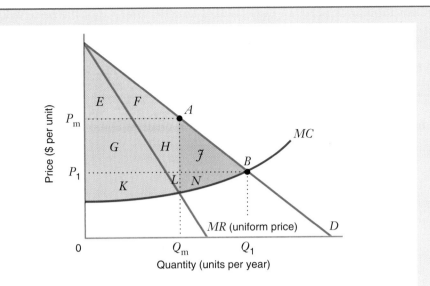

	Monopoly	Monopoly
	Uniform Price	First-Degree Price Discrimination
Consumer surplus	E + F	zero
Producer surplus	G + H + K + L	E + F + G + H + J + K + L + N
Total surplus	E + F + G + H + K + L	E + F + G + H + J + K + L + N
Deadweight loss	J + N	zero

FIGURE 12.1   Monopoly with Uniform Pricing and First-Degree Price Discrimination
A profit-maximizing monopolist charging a uniform price would choose the price P_m and sell Q_m. Its producer surplus would be the area $G + H + K + L$. However, some consumer surplus (area $E + F$) escapes the producer. In addition, the deadweight loss (area $J + N$) represents potential surplus that neither producers nor consumers are capturing. With first-degree price discrimination the firm charges each customer a price equal to the consumer's maximum willingness to pay, and therefore captures all of the surplus. The producer surplus is area $E + F + G + H + J + K + L + N$. The firm sells Q_1 units because for each of those units, the price it charges exceeds marginal cost. There is no deadweight loss and no consumer surplus.

There are three basic types (traditionally called *degrees*) of price discrimination. We will describe the three types briefly here, and then treat each of them in more detail.

FIRST-DEGREE PRICE DISCRIMINATION

With first-degree price discrimination, the firm tries to price each unit at the consumer's reservation price (i.e. the consumer's maximum willingness to pay) for that unit. For example, when a firm sells a product at an auction, it is attempting to get consumers to bid up the price so that the consumer with the highest reservation price purchases the good. The seller hopes that the price will be close to the maximum amount the consumer is willing to pay for the good.

SECOND-DEGREE PRICE DISCRIMINATION

Under second-degree price discrimination, the firm offers consumers a quantity discount. The amount you pay per unit depends on the number of units you purchase. For example, the price you pay for a piece of computer software often depends on the number of copies you buy. A firm may offer you a computer game for $50 if you buy only one copy. But it may also offer you 10 copies for $400, or only $40 per copy.

With second-degree price discrimination, the amount you pay for a good or service actually depends on two or more prices. For example, many consumers buy their telephone service under a *multipart tariff*. You may pay $20 per month to be hooked up to the telephone system, even if you never make a telephone call. The $20 fee is often called a subscriber charge. You may also pay a *usage charge*—that is, an additional amount (say, five cents) for each local call you make. If you make only one call, your monthly total telephone bill will be $20.05. If you make 100 calls, your total bill will be $25.00. Note that your average expenditure per telephone call falls when you make more calls. The average price you pay is $20.05 if you make only one call per month, but the average price falls to $0.25 if you make 100 calls.

THIRD-DEGREE PRICE DISCRIMINATION

With third-degree price discrimination, the firm identifies different consumer groups or segments in a market. The profit-maximizing firm then sets a price for each segment of the market by setting marginal revenue equal to marginal cost, or equivalently, by using the inverse elasticity rule.[2] For example, an airline knows that both business and vacation travelers fly between two cities. If it knows the demand in the business segment, it can maximize profits by setting marginal revenue equal to marginal cost in that segment. It can do the same thing in the vacation segment if it knows the demand for seats among vacation travelers. Within each segment the firm charges a uniform price, but the uniform prices may differ between the two segments. For example, the airline might charge business customers $500 per ticket, but charge vacation travelers only $200.

Certain market features must be present for a firm to capture more surplus with price discrimination:

- *A firm must have some market power to price discriminate.* In other words, the demand curve the firm faces must be downward sloping. If the firm has no market power, it is a price taker, and thus has no ability to set different prices for different units of output. As we suggested in Chapter 11, market power is present in many markets. In many industries there are only a few producers, and each producer may have some control over the price of its output. For

---

[2]We saw the inverse elasticity rule in Chapter 11: $(P_i - MC_i)/P_i = -1/\epsilon_{Q_i,P_i}$, where P_i is the price of product i, MC_i is the marginal cost, and ϵ_{Q_i,P_i} is the firm's own price elasticity of demand for the product. The inverse elasticity rule is another way of expressing the optimal quantity choice rule (marginal revenue equals marginal cost) for a firm facing a downward-sloping demand schedule.

example, in the airline industry, each company knows that it can attract more customers if it lowers its price. Even though an airline is not a monopolist, it may still have market power.

- *The firm must have some information about the different amounts people will pay for its product.* The firm would like to know how reservation prices or elasticities of demand differ across consumers.

- *A firm must be able to prevent resale, or arbitrage.* If the firm cannot prevent resale, then a customer who buys at a low price can act as a middleman, buying at a low price and reselling the good to other customers who are willing to pay more for it. In that case, the middleman, not the firm who sells the good initially, captures the surplus. Resale defeats price discrimination.

12.2 FIRST-DEGREE PRICE DISCRIMINATION

To understand first-degree price discrimination, it helps to think of the demand schedule for a product as a *willingness-to-pay schedule.* After all, a demand curve represents the amounts consumers are willing to pay for the units they purchase. Since the demand curve slopes downward, the person buying the first unit is willing to pay a higher price than the consumer buying the second unit. The maximum willingness to pay declines with each successive unit purchased.

First-degree price discrimination is ideal from the seller's viewpoint. If the seller can perfectly implement first-degree price discrimination, it will price each unit at the maximum amount the consumer of that unit is willing to pay.[3]

To illustrate how first-degree price discrimination works, suppose that you own a particular line of designer jeans and that all of the customers in the market walk in to your store. When each customer enters, you can see indelibly and truthfully stamped on her forehead the number that tells you the maximum amount she is willing to pay for a pair of your jeans. Once all of the customers are in your store, you will know the demand curve for your jeans. Suppose Figure 12.1 shows this demand curve.

How would you price your jeans to maximize your profits? You would charge the customer with the highest reservation price (the one at the top of the demand curve) a price just equal to her reservation price. For example, suppose she is willing to pay up to $100 for a pair of your jeans. You would then charge her $100, and capture all of the surplus for yourself.[4] Similarly, if the person with the second highest reservation price is willing to pay $99, you would charge that person $99 and capture all of the surplus for that pair of jeans as well. If you can perfectly price discriminate, you would be able to sell every unit at the reservation price for the consumer buying that unit.

How many jeans would you sell? If your marginal cost and demand schedules are as in Figure 12.1, you will sell Q_1 units. The price you receive exceeds

---

[3]Some texts call first-degree price discrimination *perfect price discrimination.*

[4]As a finer point, you might note that a customer with a reservation price of $100 is just indifferent between buying the jeans and not buying if you charge her $100. To make sure that she buys the jeans, you might therefore charge her $99.99. She will have a consumer surplus of $0.01, but you, the producer, will capture essentially all of the surplus. As a practical matter, we will assume that she buys the jeans if you charge her $100.

the marginal cost of production for each unit sold up to Q_1, so you will sell Q_1 units. You will not sell any more units because the marginal cost exceeds the price received for any additional units. Your producer surplus will then be represented by the area between the demand curve and the marginal cost curve (that is, area $E + F + G + H + \mathcal{J} + K + L + N$).[5] Consumers will receive no surplus because you, the producer, have captured all of it.

This example illustrates some of the important features of price discrimination that we have already described. First, the seller must have market power—that is, the demand curve for its designer jeans must be downward sloping. The seller need not be a monopolist in the designer jeans market, because other stores may sell other brands of designer jeans.

Second, the seller must know something about how willingness to pay varies across consumers. In this example, we assume that we can observe willingness to pay just by looking at the number on the customer's forehead. In the real world, it is harder to learn about willingness to pay. If you ask a customer about her willingness to pay, she will not want to tell you the truth if she thinks you will charge her a price equal to her willingness to pay. A consumer would like to tell you that she has a low willingness to pay, so that she can capture some consumer surplus herself. Often sellers can learn something about willingness to pay based on knowledge of where a person lives and works, how she dresses or speaks, the kind of car she drives, or how much money she makes. The information may not perfectly reveal a consumer's willingness to pay, but it can help the seller to capture more surplus than it could without such information.

Third, the seller must prevent resale. In this example, suppose the only people who walk into your store have reservation prices of $50 or less. Those with a higher willingness to pay wait outside the store. If you sell jeans for $50 or less, the customers who buy the jeans can become middlemen. They can walk out the door and resell jeans to those with a higher willingness to pay. Because of resale, you will fail to capture some of the surplus. Instead, middlemen will capture some of the surplus.

As we observed in Figure 12.1, there is a deadweight loss when a monopolist charges a uniform price. What can we say about the deadweight loss with first-degree price discrimination? In Figure 12.1, note that every customer who is receiving the good (those to the left of Q_1) has a willingness to pay exceeding or equal to the marginal cost of production. And every customer who does not purchase the good (those to the right of Q_1) has a willingness to pay below marginal cost. Perfect first-degree price discrimination therefore leads to an economically efficient level of output. In other words, there is no deadweight loss with perfect first-degree price discrimination![6]

---

[5] As we saw in Chapter 9, producer surplus is the difference between revenue and nonsunk cost. Here we are assuming that any fixed costs are sunk.

[6] Although perfect first-degree price discrimination leads to an efficient market (with zero deadweight loss), not everyone would be happy with this outcome. In particular, consumers may not be happy with the distribution of income because all of the surplus goes to producers. What is efficient may not always be viewed as "fair" or "equitable" by participants in a market. For more on the potential conflicts between the two, see Edward E. Zajac, *Political Economy of Fairness* (Cambridge, Mass.: MIT Press, 1995).

LEARNING-BY-DOING EXERCISE 12.1

Capturing Surplus with First-Degree Price Discrimination

In this exercise we will see how a monopolist can capture more surplus with first-degree price discrimination than with a uniform price. Suppose a monopolist has a constant marginal cost $MC = 2$. The firm faces the demand curve $P = 20 - Q$. Figure 12.2 shows the demand and marginal cost curves. There are no fixed costs.

Problem

(a) Suppose price discrimination is not allowed (or is not possible). How large will the producer surplus be?

(b) Suppose the firm can engage in perfect first-degree price discrimination. How large will the producer surplus be?

Solution

(a) Since the inverse demand is $P = 20 - Q$, we know that the marginal revenue curve is $MR = P + (\Delta P/\Delta Q)Q = (20 - Q) + (-1)Q = 20 - 2Q$. To find the optimal quantity, we set marginal revenue equal to marginal cost. Thus, $20 - 2Q = 2$, which tells us that $Q = 9$. From the demand curve, we learn that the optimal uniform price is $P = 20 - 9 = 11$.

Since there are no fixed costs, producer surplus (PS) is revenue less total variable cost which is equal to $2Q$. Therefore $PS = PQ - 2Q = (11)(9) - 2(9) = 81$. On the graph, producer surplus is the revenue (area $ORTN$) less the vari-

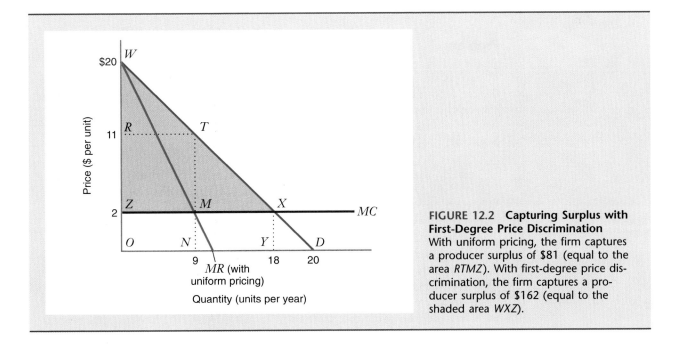

FIGURE 12.2 Capturing Surplus with First-Degree Price Discrimination
With uniform pricing, the firm captures a producer surplus of $81 (equal to the area *RTMZ*). With first-degree price discrimination, the firm captures a producer surplus of $162 (equal to the shaded area *WXZ*).

able cost (the area under the marginal cost curve *OZMN*). Producer surplus is thus area *RTMZ*.

(b) With first-degree price discrimination the firm will produce output until the demand and marginal cost curves intersect. As shown in Figure 12.2, this means that $Q = 18$. (Using algebra, we determine this value of Q by equating the demand equal to marginal cost. Thus $20 - Q = 2$, which tells us that $Q = 18$.) The monopolist's total revenue with perfect first-degree price discrimination will be the area below the demand curve for all units produced. The revenue is area *OWXY* in the graph. The numerical value of this area is 198.

The producer surplus is once again total revenue less variable cost. Thus $PS = \text{Revenue} - 2Q = 198 - 2(18) = 162$. On the graph, producer surplus is the revenue (area *OWXY*) less the variable cost (the area under the marginal cost curve *OZXY*). Producer surplus is thus area *WXZ*.

Note that the producer surplus for the firm increases by 81 when the firm moves from the uniform price in (a) to the first-degree price discrimination in (b).

Similar Problem: 12.2

LEARNING-BY-DOING EXERCISE 12.2

Where Is the Marginal Revenue Curve with First-Degree Price Discrimination?

In Chapter 11 we saw that, with uniform pricing, the marginal revenue curve is $MR = P + (\Delta P/\Delta Q)Q$.

Problem

Where is the marginal revenue curve when the firm engages in perfect first-degree price discrimination? Does marginal revenue equal marginal cost at the output the firm chooses?

Solution

In words, the expression for the marginal revenue with *uniform* pricing $MR = P + (\Delta P/\Delta Q)Q$ tells us that marginal revenue is the sum of two effects. When the firm sells one more unit, (1) revenues go up because the firm receives the price P for that next unit, and (2) revenues are reduced because the price falls by $\Delta P/\Delta Q$ for all of the Q units the firm is already selling.

With perfect first-degree price discrimination, only the first effect is present. When the firm sells one more unit, it receives the price P for that unit. However, when the firm sells the additional unit, it does *not* have to reduce its price on all the other units it is already selling. So the marginal revenue curve with first-degree price discrimination is just $MR = P$. The marginal revenue curve is the same as the demand curve.

With first-degree price discrimination, the seller in Figure 12.2 is choosing output so that marginal revenue equals marginal cost. But now the seller chooses the level of output at which the marginal cost and demand curves intersect ($Q = 18$). At this level of output, the marginal revenue from the last unit sold is the price of the unit ($2). The producer is maximizing profit because the marginal revenue just covers the marginal cost of that unit. The producer would not want to sell any fewer units than 18 because marginal revenue would be greater than marginal cost. Similarly, the seller would not want to sell any more units than 18 because marginal revenue would be less than marginal cost.

Examples of first-degree price discrimination are plentiful. Consider what happens when you walk through a flea market, or try to buy a car or a house. Sellers often try to assess your willingness to pay based on what they observe about you. A seller may ask more than you are willing to pay initially, but adjust the price as he bargains with you and learns more about you. (Of course, you are simultaneously trying to increase your consumer surplus by trying to find out how low the seller will go!) Auctions are also designed to push sales prices closer to a buyer's willingness to pay. While the highest bidder for an object of art or a tract of land may not have to pay as much as the bidder is willing to pay, the seller hopes to capture as much of the surplus as possible by making potential buyers compete for the good being sold.

Undergraduate Financial Aid at American Universities

EXAMPLE 12.1

A college education in the United States can be expensive. It costs more than $100,000 for four years at many private colleges and universities, and often more than $50,000 at state-supported colleges. Colleges are naturally concerned about whether families of prospective students can afford such large expenses.

Some types of financial aid are based on *merit,* recognizing a student's academic performance. More often, at the undergraduate level, financial aid is based on a family's *financial need.* The amount a student's family will be required to contribute toward college expenses will be based on how much money the family has saved and expects to earn, as well as on the cost of the education at a particular institution.

How do colleges determine how much you should be willing to pay for a college education? Before being considered for many types of aid, students must supply information about their family finances on forms such as the Free Application for Federal Student Aid (FAFSA). Colleges then use a government-approved formula to calculate the amount the family is expected to contribute toward college expenses. This is called the Expected Family Contribution (EFC). If the EFC is equal to or more than the cost at a particular college, then the student will probably be ineligible for much financial aid. However, if the projected cost of an education at a college exceeds the EFC, then the student will probably qualify for assistance, maybe even enough to meet the full costs.

When colleges base the amount of financial aid they give you on your ability to pay, they are engaging in first-degree price discrimination. Although no college is a monopolist, each knows that the demand for the education it offers is downward sloping. The number of students who would like to attend a college rises as the price the college charges (for room, board, and tuition, less any financial aid) falls. To price discriminate, colleges must have information on willingness to pay. Although colleges may not be able to get an exact measure of the amount a family will be willing to expend, that amount is probably highly related to the calculated EFC. Finally, colleges can easily prevent "resale" because you cannot sell your college education to someone else.   ■

12.3

SECOND-DEGREE PRICE DISCRIMINA-TION

In many markets each consumer buys more than one unit of the good or service in a given time period. For example, each month consumers buy many units of electricity and water. People who commute to work on mass transit systems make many trips a month. And many airline travelers are frequent flyers.

Sellers know that each customer's demand curve for a good is typically downward sloping. In other words, the customer's willingness to pay decreases as successive units are purchased. A seller may use this information to capture extra surplus by offering quantity discounts to consumers.

While we observe quantity discounts in everyday life, not every form of quantity discounting is the result of price discrimination. Often sellers offer quantity discounts because it costs them less to sell a larger quantity. For example, a pizza that serves four people usually sells for less than twice the price of a pizza for two people. Labor, cooking, and packaging costs are not very sensitive to the size of the pizza. The pricing reflects the fact that the cost per ounce is lower for a large pizza.

How are the quantity discounts implemented with second-degree price discrimination? In this section we will consider two examples of discounts: block pricing and pricing with subscription and usage charges.

BLOCK PRICING

Let's see how a seller might use second-degree price discrimination to capture surplus. To keep matters simple, suppose only one consumer is in the market for electricity. Figure 12.3 shows the consumer's demand and the marginal cost for electricity. The consumer has the demand $P = 20 - Q$, where the consumer demands Q units of electricity if the price is P. The marginal cost of electricity is $MC = 2$. As we saw in Learning-By-Doing Exercise 12.1, the uniform price that maximizes profit is $P = 11$.

Now suppose the seller offers a quantity discount. Using Figure 12.3, we can see immediately that the seller can capture extra surplus. For example, suppose the seller continues to charge a price $P_1 = 11$ for the first 9 units the consumer buys, and then offers any *additional* units for sale at a price $P_2 = 8$. Now the consumer will buy a total of 12 units. In other words, the quantity discount has induced the consumer to buy 3 extra units of electricity. Producer surplus will rise by 18, the area $JKLM$ in Figure 12.3.

The pricing schedule in Figure 12.3 is an example of what is often called a **block tariff.** With the block tariff, the consumer pays a price (tariff) of $11 for

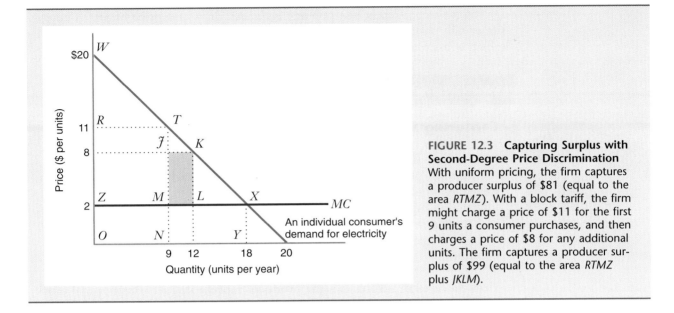

FIGURE 12.3 Capturing Surplus with Second-Degree Price Discrimination
With uniform pricing, the firm captures a producer surplus of $81 (equal to the area *RTMZ*). With a block tariff, the firm might charge a price of $11 for the first 9 units a consumer purchases, and then charges a price of $8 for any additional units. The firm captures a producer surplus of $99 (equal to the area *RTMZ* plus *JKLM*).

the first 9 units and then pays $8 for any additional units. Even though we have made no attempt to calculate the most profitable block prices, we have shown how a seller can capture more surplus with a block tariff. The firm is charging different block prices, even though the marginal cost of producing the electricity is constant.

How much better can the producer do if it chooses an optimal block tariff? Let's assume the electricity company offers a tariff with only two blocks. The block tariff that maximizes producer surplus is the one illustrated in Figure 12.4. The consumer can buy the first 6 units at a price of $14 (i.e., $P_1 = \$14$ and

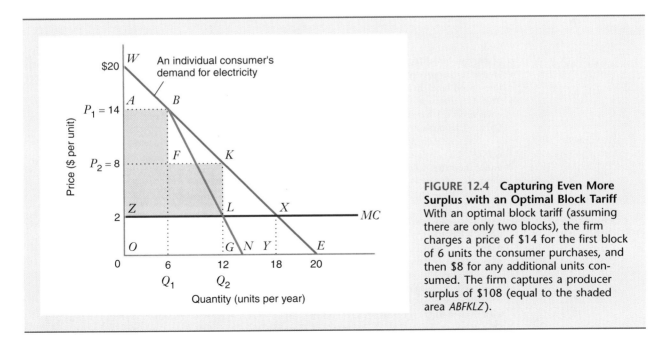

FIGURE 12.4 Capturing Even More Surplus with an Optimal Block Tariff
With an optimal block tariff (assuming there are only two blocks), the firm charges a price of $14 for the first block of 6 units the consumer purchases, and then $8 for any additional units consumed. The firm captures a producer surplus of $108 (equal to the shaded area *ABFKLZ*).

$Q_1 = 6$). The consumer can buy any *additional* units at a price of $8.[7] The consumer will purchase a total of 12 units with this tariff ($Q_2 = 12$). The producer sells the last 6 units ($Q_2 - Q_1$) at $P_2 = \$8$.

LEARNING-BY-DOING EXERCISE 12.3

Capturing Surplus with a Block Tariff

In Learning-By-Doing Exercise 12.1 (a) we learned that the profit-maximizing uniform price would be $P = \$11$. The firm would sell 9 units of output. Revenues would be $99, and producer surplus would be 81. In the example illustrated in Figure 12.4, the optimal block tariff involves selling the first block of 6 units at a price of $14 and additional units at a price of $8.

Problem

How much extra surplus can the producer capture if it sets this optimal block tariff instead of a uniform price that maximizes producer surplus?

Solution

With the optimal block tariff, the total revenue collected by the seller is $132, the area *ABFKGO*. The variable cost is the area under the marginal cost curve *ZLGO*, or (12)$2 = \$24$. The producer surplus will be revenue less variable cost, or $132 - \$24 = \$108$ (the shaded area *ABFKLZ* in Figure 12.4). The optimal block tariff has increased producer surplus by $27 (the difference between $108 with the block tariff in Figure 12.4 and $81 with the profit-maximizing uniform price).

---

[7] We can determine the optimal block prices as follows. Let's begin by supposing we know the optimal price and quantity (P_1 and Q_1) for the first block. In Figure 12.4 the segment *BE* represents what's left of the consumer's demand curve after he has purchased the first block Q_1. The marginal revenue associated with this part of the demand curve is the segment *BN*. We can determine the optimal quantity for the second block by the intersection of the marginal revenue curve *BN* with the marginal cost curve *MC*. The intersection occurs at Q_2. Since the demand curve is linear in the example, the marginal revenue curve *BN* has twice the slope of the demand curve. Thus the optimal quantity in the second block, Q_2, must be halfway between Q_1 and 18, that is, $Q_2 = (Q_1 + 18)/2$.

We can then calculate the producer surplus from block pricing. The revenue from the first block is P_1Q_1. The revenue from the second block is $P_2(Q_2 - Q_1)$. Finally, the variable costs will be the area under the marginal cost curve, $2Q_2$. The producer surplus is then $PS = P_1Q_1 + P_2(Q_2 - Q_1) - 2Q_2$. From the demand equation we know that $P_1 = 20 - Q_1$ and $P_2 = 20 - Q_2$. Thus, $PS = (20 - Q_1)Q_1 + (20 - Q_2)(Q_2 - Q_1) - 2Q_2$. Finally, we substitute into PS the optimal $Q_2 = (Q_1 + 18)/2$. After some algebra we find that $PS = -(3/4)(Q_1 - 6)^2 + 108$.

The producer surplus is maximized at a level of 108 when $Q_1 = 6$. Thus, the optimal quantity for the first block is $Q_1 = 6$. The optimal price for the first block is then $P_1 = 20 - Q_1 = 14$. The optimal quantity for the second block is then $Q_2 = (Q_1 + 18)/2 = (6 + 18)/2 = 12$. The optimal price for the second block is then $P_2 = 20 - Q_2 = 8$.

One can also find the optimal block tariffs using calculus. The firm chooses Q_1 and Q_2 to maximize producer surplus, $PS = (20 - Q_1)Q_1 + (20 - Q_2)(Q_2 - Q_1) - 2Q_2$. It sets the partial derivative of PS with respect to Q_1 equal to zero to find that (i) $Q_2 = 2Q_1$. It also sets the partial derivative of PS with respect to Q_2 equal to zero to find that (ii) $18 - 2Q_2 + Q_1 = 0$. Together (i) and (ii) tell us that $Q_1 = 6$ and $Q_2 = 12$. The block prices are therefore $P_1 = 14$ and $P_2 = 8$. For more on the use of derivatives to find a maximum, see the Mathematical Appendix at the end of the book.

These block tariff examples illustrate how second-degree price discrimination can enhance producer surplus. With a quantity discount, the average expenditure per unit (sometimes called the *average outlay*) falls as more units are purchased. Let's see how average expenditure per unit falls in Learning-By-Doing Exercise 12.3. First, let's examine the consumer's *total* expenditure (or the total outlay), E. As long as the consumer purchases 6 or fewer units, the price of each unit is $14. In that case the consumer's total outlay will just be $14Q$. For purchases of more than 6 units, the total outlay will just be $14(6) + \$8(Q - 6)$. We can summarize the consumer's total outlay schedule as follows:

$$E = \begin{cases} \$14Q & \text{if } Q \le 6 \\ \$84 + \$8(Q - 6) & \text{if } Q > 6 \end{cases}.$$

The average outlay (average expenditure) schedule is just E/Q, or

$$\frac{E}{Q} = \begin{cases} \$14 & \text{if } Q \le 6 \\ \dfrac{\$84 + \$8(Q - 6)}{Q} & \text{if } Q > 6. \end{cases}$$

An outlay schedule like the one in this example is said to be *nonlinear*. A **nonlinear outlay schedule** is an expenditure schedule in which the average outlay (i.e., the average expenditure) changes as the number of units purchased varies. Second-degree price discrimination involves the use of nonlinear outlay schedules because the firm charges different prices for different quantities purchased. With the block tariff in Learning-By-Doing Exercise 12.3, the average outlay schedule falls when the consumer buys more than 6 units. Figure 12.5 illustrates the quantity discount. As long as the consumer purchases 6 or less units, the

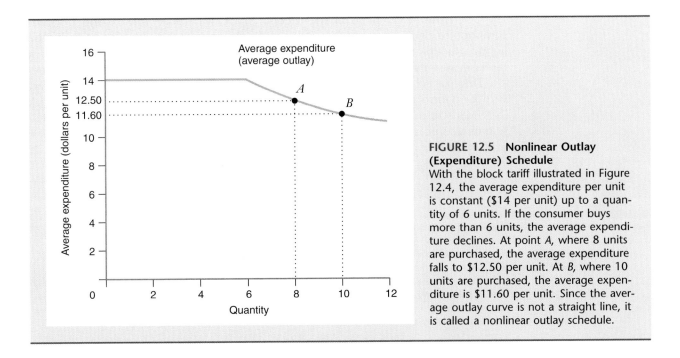

FIGURE 12.5 Nonlinear Outlay (Expenditure) Schedule
With the block tariff illustrated in Figure 12.4, the average expenditure per unit is constant ($14 per unit) up to a quantity of 6 units. If the consumer buys more than 6 units, the average expenditure declines. At point *A*, where 8 units are purchased, the average expenditure falls to $12.50 per unit. At *B*, where 10 units are purchased, the average expenditure is $11.60 per unit. Since the average outlay curve is not a straight line, it is called a nonlinear outlay schedule.

average expenditure is $14 per unit. After 6 units, the average expenditure falls. For example, if the consumer buys 8 units (point A), the average expenditure is $12.50 per unit. If the consumer buys 10 units (point B), the average expenditure falls to $11.60 per unit.

Although economists regard block pricing as a form of second-degree pricing discrimination, it is not "illegal" because the same block pricing schedule is offered to all consumers.

EXAMPLE 12.2   *Declining Block Tariffs for Electricity*

When a power company sells electricity with a block tariff, it does not know each individual's demand schedule. However, it does know that some customers have larger demands for electricity than others. It also knows that each consumer's demand curve is downward sloping, so that a lower price will stimulate that consumer to purchase more electricity.

Suppose the market has two customers in the market, Mr. Large and Mr. Small. Figure 12.6 shows their demand curves for electricity D_{Large} and D_{Small}. If the company charges a uniform price P_1 for all units of electricity sold, Mr. Small will buy Q_{1S} units of electricity, and Mr. Large will purchase Q_{1L} units.

Now let the company introduce a block tariff. It announces that it will sell up to Q_{1L} units (the first block) at a price of P_1. Any customer who buys more than Q_{1L} units can purchase the additional units at a lower block price P_2.

How will the block pricing affect Mr. Small, Mr. Large, and the electric power company? Mr. Small's purchases are unchanged because he does not purchase enough electricity to take advantage of the lower block price P_2. He still buys Q_{1S} units at a price P_1, and his consumer surplus is therefore the same as it was under the uniform price.

Given the lower price of the second block, Mr. Large will expand his consumption of electricity from Q_{1L} to Q_{2L} units. His consumer surplus increases by the lightly shaded area in the figure. Finally, the company is better off with the block tariff because its producer surplus increases by the darkly shaded box in the figure.

This example illustrates an important potential benefit of block tariffs. If we start with a uniform tariff that is different from marginal cost, then introducing a block tariff leads to a **Pareto superior** allocation of resources. A Pareto superior allocation of resources makes at least one participant in the market better off and no one else worse off.[8]   ∎

[8]For more on this topic, see R.D. Willig, "Pareto Superior Nonlinear Outlay Schedules," *Bell Journal of Economics*, 9 (1978): 56–69. The argument for the Pareto superiority of nonlinear outlay schedules is clearest when the consumers are end users of electricity (for example, households). The argument is a bit more complex when the purchasers of the electricity are firms that compete with one another in some market. One of the complications arises because quantity discounts from block pricing could conceivably allow a large, less efficient firm to produce with lower costs than a smaller, more efficient firm, because the larger firm can purchase electricity at a lower average price. Pareto superiority is named for the Italian economist Vilfredo Pareto (1848–1923).

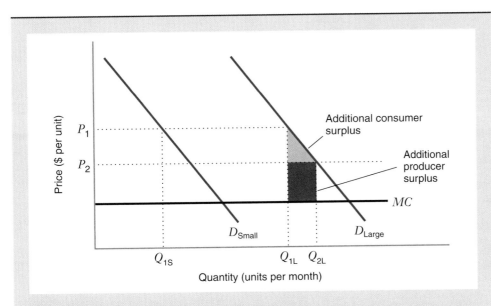

FIGURE 12.6   Declining Block Pricing for Electricity
The electric power firm announces that it will sell up to Q_{1L} units (the first block) at a price of P_1. Any customer who buys more than Q_{1L} units can purchase additional units at a lower block price P_2. Given the lower price of the second block, Mr. Large will expand his consumption of electricity from Q_{1L} to Q_{2L} units. His consumer surplus increases by the lightly shaded area. The firm is better off with the block tariff because its producer surplus increases by the darkly shaded area. Mr. Small does not consume enough electricity to buy any electricity in the second block at P_2.

SUBSCRIPTION AND USAGE CHARGES

We also see other applications of second-degree price discrimination every day. When you buy telephone service, you often pay a fixed amount (for example, $20 per month) just to be hooked up to the telephone company, even if you do not make a single telephone call. This fixed fee is sometimes called a *subscriber charge* or an *access charge*. You may also pay a *usage charge* (for example, 5 cents per call) every time you make a local telephone call.

The combination of subscription and usage charges allows the firm to give consumers quantity discounts. The consumer's *total* monthly expenditure is $E = \$20 + \$0.05Q$, that is, the $20 monthly subscription charge plus $0.05 per call times the number of calls made in the month. The average expenditure is just $E/Q = (\$20/Q) + \$0.05$. The average expenditure per call will fall as the consumer makes more calls in a month. For example, if the consumer makes 10 calls per month, the average expenditure per call is $2.05. But at 100 calls, the average expenditure per call falls to $0.25.

How might a firm use subscription and usage charges to capture more surplus? Let's consider a simple example in which all consumers are alike. Each consumer has a demand for telephone service like the one shown in Figure 12.7. Assume the telephone company incurs a marginal cost of $0.05 for each call. The company could make sure that there is no deadweight loss if it sets a usage charge of $0.05 for each call the consumer makes. The consumer will make Q_1 calls each month, and his consumer surplus will be S_1, the shaded area in the figure. The

FIGURE 12.7   Subscriber and Usage Charges
Each consumer has the demand curve D for telephone service, and the telephone company incurs a marginal cost of $0.05 for each call. If the company sets a usage charge of $0.05 for each call, the consumer would make Q_1 calls each month and realize a consumer surplus of S_1. The telephone company could then capture consumer surplus by implementing a monthly subscription charge. As long as the subscription charge is less than S_1 dollars, the consumer will continue to buy telephone service.

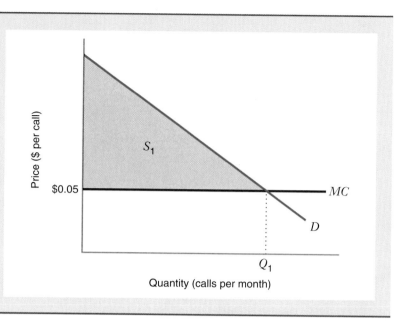

telephone company could then capture consumer surplus by implementing a monthly subscription charge. As long as the subscription charge is less than S_1 dollars, the consumer will continue to buy telephone service.

In this example, the consumer would just be indifferent between subscribing and not subscribing if the firm sets a subscription charge equal to S_1. To ensure that each consumer subscribes, the firm might set the subscription charge to be slightly less than S_1. The firm would then capture virtually all the surplus by setting a subscription charge of S_1.[9]

Where else have you encountered subscription and user charges? Often the subscription charge is just a fee charged for a membership in a club. The usage charges are the fees you pay when you use the club. For example, when you join a music club, you often pay a membership fee and then pay a certain amount for every CD or cassette you buy. Members of a country club pay a membership fee and then pay usage fees to use the golf course or the tennis courts. Some computer networks charge you a subscription fee to have access to a service, and then a user charge for every minute you actually use the network.

[9] In the real world the firm cannot easily capture all the surplus for two reasons. First, demands will differ from one consumer to the next. If the firm increases its subscription and usage charges to capture more surplus from customers with large demands, some consumers with small demands will not buy the service at all. The firm therefore needs to know how many consumers have large demands and how many have small demands.

In addition, although the firm may know that there are different types of consumers, it may not know *which* consumers are large and which are small users of telephone service. Firms therefore often offer customers a menu of subscription and usage charges, and then allow each consumer to select the combination of subscription and usage charges that is best for himself. For example, a cellular telephone company may offer one package with a monthly subscription charge of $20 and a usage charge of $0.25 per call. It may also offer another package with a subscription charge of $30 and a usage charge of $0.20 per call. A consumer who expects to make fewer than 200 calls per month will prefer the first package, while a consumer who expects to make more than 200 calls per month will prefer the second.

For more on second-degree price discrimination, see Robert B. Wilson, *Nonlinear Pricing* (New York: Oxford University Press, 1992), and S. J. Brown and D. S. Sibley, *The Theory of Public Utility Pricing* (New York: Cambridge University Press, 1986).

12.4
**THIRD-
DEGREE
PRICE
DISCRIMINA-
TION**

Sometimes a firm can identify different consumer groups or segments in a market. With third-degree price discrimination, the firm may use the demand curve for each consumer group to set a profit-maximizing price for that segment. In each segment the firm may choose the price to equate marginal revenue and marginal cost or, equivalently, to satisfy the inverse elasticity pricing rule.

Let's begin with an example of third-degree price discrimination. In the United States, railroad transportation rates were largely deregulated in the 1980s.[10] Since that time, railroads have used third-degree price discrimination to charge different prices for the movements of different kinds of goods.

Let's consider the prices railroads charge for movements of coal and grain. Coal and grain are both bulk commodities because they are loaded into cars with no special handling or packaging. Because a car loaded with grain weighs about the same amount as a car loaded with coal (typically around 100 tons), the marginal cost of moving a ton of either commodity over a given distance is about the same. Yet railroads charge two or three times as much to move coal as they do to move grain. Why is this the case?

The answer lies in the differences in the demands for moving coal and grain. Railroads face more competition from barges and trucks when they carry grain. For example, grain shipped from Iowa to port facilities in New Orleans can be moved by barges along the Mississippi River or along highways by trucks. Therefore, the demand for rail transport services by shippers of grain is sensitive to the price a railroad charges. The demand curve faced by a railroad firm illustrating this price sensitivity appears in the right graph of Figure 12.8. If the railroad charges a high price for moving grain, many shippers will not use rail service.

On the other hand, coal is often shipped over much longer distances, such as from coal-producing regions in Wyoming to electric power companies in Arkansas and Louisiana. Railroads have a cost advantage over trucks for such long shipments. Furthermore, there are few options for moving the coal by water because most coal mines are not located near canals or navigable rivers. Competition from barge transport is therefore limited. Figure 12.8(a) illustrates the demand curve for rail transport services by shippers of coal. Coal shippers are more dependent on rail transport than are grain shippers, and they are therefore willing to pay more for rail service.

In Figure 12.8 we have assumed that the marginal cost is the same ($10) for moving a ton of either commodity over a given distance.[11] The profit-maximizing price for moving a ton-mile of coal is $24, reflecting the lack of price sensitivity in the demand for coal transport. However, when the railroad equates the marginal revenue and marginal cost of grain transport, it finds that the profit-maximizing transport rate for moving a ton-mile of grain is only half as much ($12). The lower price of grain movements reflects the greater price sensitivity of the demand for grain shipments.

---

[10]For a good discussion of regulatory reform in the railroad industry, see Ted Keeler, *Railroads, Freight, and Public Policy* (Washington, D.C.: The Brookings Institution, 1983), and Tony Gomez-Ibanez and Cliff Winston (editors), *Transportation Economics and Policy: A Handbook in Honor of John Meyer* (Washington, D.C., The Brookings Institution: 1999).

[11]One can measure the output of a freight transportation company in more than one way. One measure commonly used in the United States is the "ton-mile," which refers to the movement of one ton of the commodity over one mile. In other parts of the world, output is often measured by "ton-kilometers."

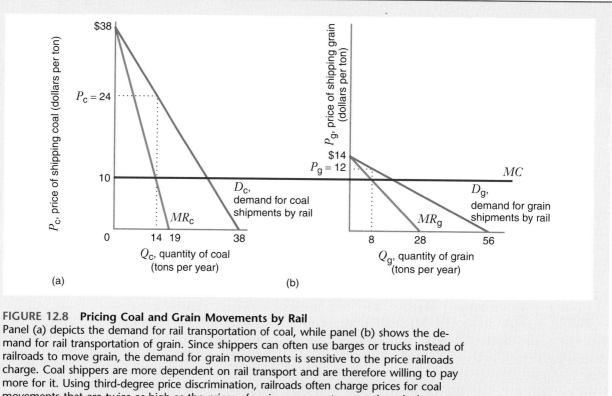

FIGURE 12.8   Pricing Coal and Grain Movements by Rail
Panel (a) depicts the demand for rail transportation of coal, while panel (b) shows the demand for rail transportation of grain. Since shippers can often use barges or trucks instead of railroads to move grain, the demand for grain movements is sensitive to the price railroads charge. Coal shippers are more dependent on rail transport and are therefore willing to pay more for it. Using third-degree price discrimination, railroads often charge prices for coal movements that are twice as high as the prices of grain movements, even though the marginal costs of transporting grain and coal are approximately equal. In this example, the profit-maximizing coal transport rate is $24 and the profit-maximizing grain transport rate is $12.

Railroads have little trouble implementing price discrimination in the movement of coal and grain. Once they have an idea about the nature of the demands for the rail services, they can price discriminate without having to worry about resale. They know who buys coal transport services (e.g., electric utilities) and who buys grain transport. An electric utility wanting to buy coal is not likely to find ways of transporting coal at a price lower than the railroad charges.

LEARNING-BY-DOING EXERCISE 12.4

Third-Degree Price Discrimination in Railroad Service

This exercise shows you how to determine the optimal rail transport rates for coal and grain movements illustrated in Figure 12.8. Suppose a railroad faces the following demand for coal movements: $P_c = 38 - Q_c$, where Q_c is the amount of coal moved when the transport price for coal is P_c. The railroad's demand for grain movement is $P_g = 14 - 0.25Q_g$, where Q_g is the amount of grain shipped when the transport price for grain is P_g. The marginal cost for moving either commodity is 10.

Problem

What are the profit-maximizing rates for coal and grain movements?

Solution

Since the demand for coal movements is $P_c = 38 - Q_c$, we know that the marginal revenue curve is

$$MR_c = P_c + \frac{\Delta P_c}{\Delta Q_c} Q_c = (38 - Q_c) + (-1)Q_c = 38 - 2Q_c.$$

To find the optimal quantity, we set marginal revenue equal to marginal cost. Thus $38 - 2Q_c = 10$, which tells us that $Q_c = 14$. From the demand curve, we learn that the optimal coal transport rate is then $P_c = 38 - 14 = 24$.

Similarly, the demand for grain movements is $P_g = 14 - 0.25Q_g$. The marginal revenue curve is

$$MR_g = P_g + \frac{\Delta P_g}{\Delta Q_g} Q_g = (14 - 0.25Q_g) + (-0.25)Q_g = 14 - 0.5Q_g.$$

When we set marginal revenue equal to marginal cost ($14 - 0.5Q_g = 10$), we find that $Q_g = 8$. From the demand curve, we find that the optimal grain transport rate is then $P_g = 14 - 0.25(8) = 12$.

In summary, in each segment the railroad determines the optimal quantity it wants customers to buy by equating marginal revenue and marginal cost. It then charges the price that leads consumers to buy the optimal quantity.

Similar Problems: 12.4, 12.6

EXAMPLE 12.3

Forward Integration to Implement Price Discrimination

At the beginning of this chapter, we pointed out that a firm needs to be able to prevent resale if it is to price discriminate successfully. One interesting strategy for implementing price discrimination is forward integration. Forward integration is a strategy whereby a firm moves into the same business that its customers are in. An example of forward integration would be if Intel, a manufacturer of microprocessors, began making personal computers (manufacturers of which purchase microprocessors from Intel). Let's see how Alcoa, which was a monopolistic producer of primary aluminum ingot until the 1930s, used forward integration to prevent resale.[12]

Aluminum can be used in making many kinds of products. To keep matters simple, let's suppose there are two types of products, depicted in Figure 12.9.

[12]See Martin Perry, "Forward Integration by Alcoa: 1888–1930," *The Journal of Industrial Economics*, 29 (1980):37–53.

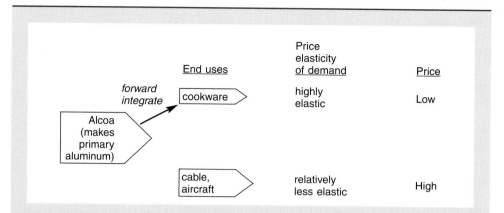

FIGURE 12.9   Alcoa: Forward Integration to Achieve Price Discrimination
Alcoa knew that the demand for primary aluminum was relatively inelastic for its sales to manufacturers of airplane wings and cable for bridges. No other materials could be substituted for aluminum in making these products. However, Alcoa's demand for primary aluminum in making cookware was relatively elastic because other materials could be used to make pots and pans. Alcoa wanted to sell aluminum at high prices to cable and aircraft manufacturers, and at low prices to makers of cookware. But Alcoa knew it would have to worry about resale if it sold aluminum externally at two prices. To prevent resale, Alcoa decided to make pots and pans itself (that is, it integrated forward into the cookware business). It did not sell any primary aluminum externally at the low price. Its only external sales were at high prices.

Alcoa knew that aluminum was particularly valuable in some uses because of its metallurgical properties. For example, it is a light metal, making it desirable in the manufacturing of airplane wings. It also has special "tensile" properties (relating to how it stretches when it bears a load), making it especially useful in cables for bridges. Since other materials could not be substituted for aluminum in these uses, Alcoa knew that the demand for primary aluminum was relatively inelastic for its sales to manufacturers of airplane wings and bridge cable.

In the manufacturing of other products the advantages of aluminum over other materials are less important. For example, aluminum can be used to make pots and pans. But so can copper, steel, or cast iron. Given these substitutes for aluminum, Alcoa's demand for primary aluminum in making cookware was relatively elastic.

Alcoa wanted to use third-degree price discrimination by selling aluminum at a high price to cable and aircraft manufacturers, and at a low price to makers of cookware. However, Alcoa knew it would have to worry about resale if it sold aluminum externally at two prices. If it announced that cookware buyers could purchase primary aluminum at a low price, every buyer (including makers of airplane wings and cable) would claim to be a cookware manufacturer. Even if Alcoa knew that a buyer made cookware, what would prevent that buyer from reselling the aluminum at a higher price to a maker of airplane wings?

To prevent resale, Alcoa decided to make aluminum pots and pans itself (that is, it integrated forward into the cookware business). It did not sell primary aluminum to any external buyers at the low price. Its only external sales were at high prices. By vertically integrating, Alcoa could price discriminate and prevent resale.   ∎

SCREENING

Have you ever wondered why businesses, such as movie theaters, airlines, urban mass transit authorities, and restaurants, often give discounts to senior citizens and students? One possible answer to this question is that this form of price discrimination helps businesses capture more surplus.[13] Older people, particularly those who are retired, often live on limited incomes. Most students also have limited incomes. Both students and senior citizens typically have more free time to shop around than many people who work full time. Consequently, senior citizens and students often have relatively elastic demands for goods and services. The inverse elasticity pricing rule therefore suggests that businesses ought to set prices lower for these consumers.

Businesses often use observable characteristics, such as age and student status as **screening** mechanisms. Screening sorts consumers based on a consumer characteristic that (1) the firm can observe (such as age or student status), and (2) that is strongly related to another consumer characteristic that the firm cannot observe but would like to observe (such as willingness to pay or elasticity of demand). For example, the movie theater manager would like to see the consumer's elasticity of demand or willingness to pay when he walks up to the ticket counter, but she cannot observe that information directly. If she were to ask the consumer how much he would be willing to pay, he might lie, knowing that the manager might charge a higher price if he reveals that he has a high willingness to pay.

However, the manager *can* observe characteristics such as the consumer's age or student status. Most students and senior citizens have more elastic demands, so the manager can set prices that are lower for these consumer segments. To prevent arbitrage, the manager can require the consumer to present an identity card to verify the age or student status when the consumer enters the theater.

EXAMPLE 12.4

Pricing Airline Tickets

Airlines typically sell tickets at a variety of fares. At the beginning of the chapter we observed the many different prices that United charged passengers on Flight 815 from Chicago to Los Angeles. Third-degree price discrimination is one of the strategies airlines use to fill the plane with travelers in the most profitable way. Airlines often charge different prices for seats in the same class of service, such as coach class, even though the marginal cost of serving a passenger is about the same for all coach passengers. The reason for this is that different customers are willing to pay different amounts for tickets. For example, people traveling on vacation often can book their tickets weeks or months in advance of the flight, and they are willing to shop around for the best price. Vacation travelers often choose their destinations based on the availability of relatively inexpensive airline tickets. They are usually sensitive to price, especially if the vacation involves buying tickets for a whole family.

On the other hand, passengers traveling on business are often less sensitive to the price of the ticket. When business requires that a passenger be in London for

---

[13]There are surely other reasons to offer discounts to senior citizens and students. For example, regulators of urban mass transit systems may view a lower price for these consumers as a socially noble objective, perhaps as a means of creating more purchasing power for deserving sets of consumers.

an important meeting on Monday morning at 8:00 A.M., the traveler will make the trip even if the fare is expensive.

An airline knows that markets have different segments. It knows that business customers typically have relatively inelastic demands, and that most vacation travelers have relatively elastic demands. Using the inverse elasticity pricing rule, an airline would like to charge a higher price for business travelers.

How does the airline implement price discrimination? It often imposes restrictions on tickets sold at lower prices. For example, an airline knows that business travelers often do not know about the meeting in London far in advance, whereas the excursion traveler schedules a vacation months in advance. Business travelers often cannot stay at the destination over Saturday night, whereas vacation travelers will be willing to stay over Saturday night, especially if they can get a cheaper ticket by doing so. The airlines therefore use these restrictions to screen passengers. ■

LEARNING-BY-DOING EXERCISE 12.5

Pricing Airline Tickets

In this exercise you will learn how to use the inverse elasticity pricing rule to set different prices with third-degree price discrimination. In Table 2.2 we showed estimates of the price elasticity of demand for regular full fare tickets often purchased by business travelers ($\epsilon_{Q_R, P_R} = -1.15$). The table also shows that the price elasticity of demand for leisure (vacation) travelers to be -1.52.[14]

Problem

Suppose an airline facing these demand elasticities were to set P_R (the price of a regular ticket) and P_V (the price of a ticket to vacation travelers) to maximize profit. What would the ratio P_R/P_V be? For this exercise assume that the price elasticity of demand for full fare tickets is always -1.15 regardless of the price, and that the price elasticity of demand for excursion tickets is always -1.52. Since both are coach fares, you may also assume that the marginal cost of service (MC) is about the same for business and vacation travelers.

Solution

The inverse elasticity pricing rule tells us that $(P_V - MC)/P_V = -1/\epsilon_{Q_V, P_V}$. Therefore $(MC/P_V) = 0.342$. Similarly, the inverse elasticity pricing rule requires that $(P_R - MC)/P_R = -1/\epsilon_{Q_R, P_R}$. Thus $MC/P_R = 0.130$. Therefore, $P_R/P_V = 0.342/0.130 = 2.63$. To maximize profits, the airline should set the price for regular economy travel two or three times higher than the price charged to excursion (vacation) travelers. The exact levels of the fares will depend on the marginal cost.

Similar Problem: 12.8

---

[14] Since there is no business class service for most domestic flights, most business travelers fly in the coach section of the airplane.

There are many other examples of screening that we see in everyday life. Consider the following:

Intertemporal price discrimination. Many services are sold at different prices depending on the season, the time of day, or year. For example, telephone companies often set higher prices during the day, when they know consumers and enterprises must conduct business. Similarly, electricity prices often vary by the time of day, generally being set higher when the demand is at its peak.

In addition, many consumers want to be "the first one on the block" to own a new computer product, to purchase a new home sound system, or to see a new movie. Sellers know that these people will pay more to get the product early, and often use time (early sales) as a screening mechanism. As a result, sellers price many goods higher when they are first introduced. For example, buyers often paid several hundred dollars for a four-function calculator (a hand calculator that could add, subtract, multiply, and divide) when they were first introduced in the 1960s. A few years later, such simple calculators were often available for a few dollars.[15] We can observe similar trends today with much more complex computers. Often the price of a new model may fall by fifty percent within a year of its introduction.

Of course, price discrimination is not the *only* reason for setting a higher price early in the life of a product. The price of a product may fall over time because manufacturing costs fall. As the price of a type of computer chip falls over time, the price of a model of computer using that chip can also be expected to fall. Also, as newer, faster computers become available, the demand for an older model will fall, leading to a lower price for the older model.

Coupons and rebates. Almost any Sunday newspaper carries coupons that you may redeem at a store for discounts on items. Brand managers often offer coupons on new products, food products, pet food, toilet paper, and toothpaste. If you have a coupon, you pay a lower net price (the retail price less the value of the coupon) than you would without a coupon. A rebate is similar to a coupon, but is typically offered on the package containing the product you purchase. For example, you may buy a package of batteries for $5.00. On the package is a printed form that you may fill out and send in to the manufacturer to receive a $1.50 rebate in the mail.

Researchers have suggested that coupons and rebates are often used to price discriminate in consumer product markets. The basic idea is this: Brand managers know that people who are willing to take the time to collect and redeem coupons or redeem rebate certificates are likely to be more sensitive to price than consumers who do not.[16] In other words, coupons and rebates are screening mechanisms. They offer a lower net price to those consumers who are likely to have more price elastic demands for the product.

Once again, price discrimination is not the *only* possible reason for offering coupons or rebates. For example, firms may offer them to induce consumers to try a product, hoping that an initial purchase will lead to more sales.

---

[15]See N. Stokey, "Intertemporal Price Discrimination," *Quarterly Journal of Economics*, 94(1979): 355–371.

[16]Marketing studies show that consumers who use coupons to buy products typically have a more elastic demand than consumers who do not use coupons. See, for example, Narasimhan, C., "A Price Discrimination Theory of Coupons," *Marketing Science*, Spring 1984, pp. 128–147.

12.5

TYING (TIE-IN SALES)

Another technique that firms use to capture surplus is tying. **Tying** (also called **tie-in sales**) refers to a sales practice that allows a customer to buy one product (the "tying" product) only if she agrees to buy another product (the "tied" product) as well.

Often tying is used when customers differ by the frequency with which they wish to use a product. For example, suppose a firm has a patent on a copy machine with some distinctive features or a unique copying process. Such a patent may give the firm some market power because the patent prevents other firms from selling the same kind of machine. If it could price discriminate, the firm would like to charge more to a customer who makes 15,000 copies per month than to a customer making only 4,000 copies. However, it may be difficult for a firm making only copy machines to implement price discrimination. The firm might like to charge more to customers who are likely to produce more copies each month, but it may be impossible for the firm to know how many copies a customer will make.

How, then, can the firm use its market power in copying machines to capture surplus? The firm might tie the sale of the machine to the purchase of materials used to make copies, such as copying paper. The firm might sell its copier under a "requirements contract," that is, a contract that requires a purchaser of a copy machine to buy all copying paper from the firm. By setting a price for the paper that exceeds the cost of making it, the firm can generate higher profits.

As the example illustrates, tying often enables a firm to extend its market power from the tying product to the tied product. In the copier example, without the tie-in sale, the firm could probably not make any extranormal return in the market for copying paper. The market for copying paper would be competitive because no special technology is involved in making paper. If the firm wants to sell copying paper at a price higher than the competitive price, it must make sure that its customers do not buy the paper from other companies. For example, it might try to enforce tying by informing users of the copy machine that the warranty on the machine remains valid only if customers use the firm's copying paper.[17]

Tying arrangements often lead to disputes. The manufacturer of a computer printer may want to require users to buy its own ink. The printer manufacturer may argue that the tie-in is necessary to guarantee that the ink will not damage or jam the printer, and that such quality control is necessary to protect the reputation of the manufacturer. Other manufacturers who want to sell ink may feel that the tie-in violates antitrust laws by illegally foreclosing them from the market. With large profits at stake, the battle over tying arrangements often ends up in court.

In the United States the primary law addressing tying arrangements is the Clayton Act, Section 3. The law has been interpreted in a series of cases over the years. In practice the courts often try to determine what the relevant market is for the tied product, and to measure the seller's share of that market. Some requirements contracts have been found to be legal, usually when the seller of a tied product has

---

[17]The practice of charging more to customers who use a product more is often called *metering*. A copy machine typically has a device (a meter) that measures the number of copies made. With such a meter, when the seller of the machine performs maintenance, it can determine how many copies have been made.

only a small share of the market. As F. M. Scherer notes, "Requirements contracts negotiated by sellers possessing a very small share of the relevant market do stand a good chance of escaping challenge, and not all challenged contracts have been found illegal."[18] However, in other cases, tying is illegal. For example, when McDonald's sells a franchise, it cannot require its franchisee to buy supplies such as napkins and cups from McDonald's. The franchisees can buy cups from any supplier whose products meet standards set by McDonald's.

EXAMPLE 12.5

IBM (1936)

In the 1930s, computing revolved around the use of *punch cards,* thin cardboard cards that were used by a variety of machines. Key punch machines entered data on the cards, and tabulating and sorting machines processed the data and punched cards to record output.

IBM knew that some users had larger needs for numerical processing than others. It wanted to tie the use of the machinery to the punch cards. IBM did not sell its computing machinery. Instead, it leased the machinery to customers and required them to use IBM punch cards. IBM charged more for punch cards than the price other firms would have set. IBM made profits on the sale of punch cards. The tying arrangement enabled IBM to collect larger profits from heavy users of the cards, and these were the customers who typically had the highest willingness to pay for computing services.

IBM knew that the tying arrangement would fail if its customers could buy punch cards at lower prices from other suppliers. To prevent this, IBM leased machines with the stipulation that the lease would be cancelled if the customer used any punch cards other than those made by IBM.

In a famous antitrust case, IBM defended the practice of tying the use of its machines to its own punch cards to ensure that the cards were of sufficiently high quality.[19] It argued that faulty cards could damage the computing machines, lead to errors in computation, and damage IBM's reputation. The Supreme Court rejected IBM's argument. The Court found that other suppliers could make cards that met IBM's standards. The Court allowed IBM to set quality standards for cards, but ordered IBM to allow customers to buy cards from any supplier who satisfied those standards. ■

BUNDLING

Bundling refers to tie-in sales in which customers are required to purchase goods in a package. The customer cannot buy the goods separately. You have no doubt encountered bundling. For example, when you subscribe to cable television, you typically have to buy a "package" of channels together, rather than subscribing

---

[18]See F. M. Scherer, *Industrial Market Structure and Economic Performance,* Chicago: Rand McNally, 1980, pp. 585–586.

[19]*International Business Machines Corp. v. U.S.* 298 U.S. 131 (1936).

to each channel individually. When you go to Disney World, the ticket you buy at the park entrance gives you admission *and* entitles you to go on all the rides inside the park.[20] A computer manufacturer may offer you a bundle that includes both a computer (a central processing unit) and a monitor.

Why do firms sometimes sell two or more items as a package instead of separately? Bundling can increase profits when customers have different tastes (different willingnesses to pay) for the two products, and when the firm cannot price discriminate. To see how this practice can be used to increase producer surplus, let's consider a company that sells two different products, a computer and a computer monitor. The marginal cost of the computer is $1,000, and the marginal cost of the monitor is $300.

For simplicity, suppose only two customers are in the market, but the firm cannot price discriminate. Table 12.2 shows how much each customer is willing to pay for a computer and for a monitor. Both customers might like to buy a new computer and a new monitor. However, either customer might like to buy a new computer alone (perhaps already having an old monitor) or a new monitor alone (perhaps for use with an old computer). Customer 1 would pay up to $1,200 for a computer and $600 for a monitor. Customer 2 would pay up to $1,500 for a computer and $400 for a monitor.

First, let's see how much profit the firm can earn if it does *not* bundle the computer and the monitor. What price should it set for the computer (P_c)? If the firm sets $P_c = \$1,500$, it will sell only one computer (to customer 2) and earn a profit of $500 (equal to the price, $1,500, less the marginal cost of the computer, $1,000).[21] If it sets $P_c = \$1,200$, it will sell two computers (one to each customer) and earn a profit of $400 ($200 from each computer). So it should set the price of the computer at $1,500.

What price should it set for the monitor (P_m)? If the firm sets $P_m = \$600$, it will sell only one monitor (to customer 1) and earn a profit of $300 (equal to the

TABLE 12.2
Bundling Can Increase Profit When Customer Preferences are Negatively Correlated

	Reservation Price (Maximum Willingness to Pay)	
	Computer	**Monitor**
Customer 1	$1,200	$600
Customer 2	$1,500	$400
Marginal cost	$1,000	$300

[20]Bundling is a kind of tying, but not all tying involves bundling. For example, as described above, a tying arrangement might require a customer who buys a copy machine from a manufacturer also to buy all copying paper from the manufacturer. The machine and the paper are not bundled because a customer could buy paper without buying a machine. In contrast, in the Disney World bundling example, the customer cannot buy admission to the park without also buying entitlement to the rides. Nor can the customer buy entitlement to the rides without buying admission.

[21]The reservation price for customer 1 is $1,500. Strictly speaking, if the manufacturer sets a computer price $P_c = \$1,500$, customer 1 will be indifferent between buying and not buying. Here we will suppose that a customer buys when the price equals the maximum willingness to pay. (The firm could always cut the price by one cent to ensure that it makes the sale.)

price, $600, less the marginal cost of the monitor, $300). If it sets $P_m = \$400$, it will sell two monitors (one to each customer) and earn a profit of $200 ($100 from each monitor).

The best the firm can do without bundling is to set $P_c = \$1,500$ and $P_m = \$600$. It will then earn a total profit of $800, $500 from the computer sales and $300 from the monitor sales.

Now consider the option to bundle the computer and the monitor, selling the two components in a single package. What is the maximum profit it can earn? Customer 1 would be willing to pay up to $1,800 for the package, and customer 2 would pay up to $1,900. If the bundle is sold at $P_b = \$1,900$, only customer 2 will buy the bundle. The revenue would be $1,900, and the cost would be $1,300 ($1,000 for the computer and $300 for the monitor). Thus, the profit would be $600.

However, the firm can do better by setting the price of the bundle at $P_b = \$1,800$. For each package sold, the profit will be $500, equal to the revenue of $1,800, less the cost of $1,300. Both customers will buy the bundle, and the total profit will be $1,000. Thus, the manufacturer will maximize profit by selling a bundle at $P_b = \$1,800$. Bundling has increased profit from $800 (without bundling) to $1,000 (with bundling).

Why does bundling work to increase profit? The key is that the customers' demands are *negatively correlated*. The negative correlation means that customer 1 is willing to pay more than customer 2 for the computer, while customer 2 is willing to pay more than customer 1 for the monitor. By bundling the goods, the manufacturer is inducing the consumers to take both products when they might not otherwise do so.

To see why the negative correlation of customer demands is important, let's see what happens if the customer demands are *positively correlated*. Suppose the customer demands are as shown in Table 12.3. Here the customer preferences are positively correlated because customer 1 is willing to pay more for a monitor, and more for a computer, than customer 2.

If the manufacturer does not bundle, it maximizes profit by selling computers at $1,500, earning a profit of $500 from each computer sold. Only customer 2 buys a computer at this price. The most the firm can earn in the monitor market is a profit of $300, and it earns this by selling monitors at $600. Only customer 2 buys a monitor. Total profit will be $800. (You should verify that it would be less profitable for the firm to sell either a computer or a monitor at a price low enough to attract customer 1.)

TABLE 12.3
Bundling Does Not Increase Profit When Customer Preferences are Positively Correlated

	Reservation Price (Maximum Willingness to Pay)	
	Computer	Monitor
Customer 1	$1,200	$400
Customer 2	$1,500	$600
Marginal cost	$1,000	$300

If the manufacturer offers the computer and monitor as a bundle, the best the firm can do is to set the price at $2,100, earning a profit of $800. Therefore, bundling does not increase the firm's profits.

MIXED BUNDLING

In practice, firms often allow customers to purchase components individually, as well as offering a bundle. For example, you can purchase a computer from Dell with or without a monitor. This is called mixed bundling. To see why mixed bundling might be the most profitable strategy for a firm, consider the example illustrated in Table 12.4. In this example, each of the four customers is willing to pay $1,700 for a bundle. Their demands are negatively correlated because a customer who is willing to pay more for a computer is willing to pay less for a monitor. However, as we shall see, the manufacturer will not maximize profits by offering only a bundle at a price of $1,700.

To see what the optimal strategy will be, let's consider three options.

- *Option 1: No bundling.* If the manufacturer does not bundle, it maximizes profit by selling computers at $1,300 and monitors at $600. When the price of a computer is $1,300, customers 3 and 4 will buy computers. The firm's profit from computers will be $600 because two computers are sold, the price of each is $1,300, and the cost of each is $1,000. When the price of a monitor is $600 customers 1 and 2 will buy monitors. The firm's profit from monitors will also be $600 because two monitors are sold, the price of each is $600, and the marginal cost of each is $300. The total profit will be $1,200.

- *Option 2: Pure bundling (selling only a bundle).* If the manufacturer offers the computer and monitor as a bundle, priced at $1,700, all four customers buy the bundle. On each bundle the profit will be $400 (the revenue of $1,700 less the marginal cost of $1,300). The total profit will therefore be $1,600.

- *Option 3: Mixed bundling.* Here the manufacturer offers customers three options. It sells a computer separately at one price (P_c), sells a monitor separately at another price (P_m), and offers a package with a computer and a monitor at a bundled price (P_b).

Why is the firm's optimal strategy to offer mixed bundling in this example? This pricing strategy discourages any customer from buying a component when

TABLE 12.4
Mixed Bundling Can Increase Profit

	Reservation Price (Maximum Willingness to Pay)	
	Computer	Monitor
Customer 1	$900	$800
Customer 2	$1,100	$600
Customer 3	$1,300	$400
Customer 4	$1,500	$200
Marginal cost	$1,000	$300

the customer's willingness to pay is less than the marginal cost of that component.

Note that customer 1 is only willing to pay $900 for a computer, which is less than the marginal cost of the computer. It will therefore not be profitable for the firm to sell a computer to customer 1. If customer 1 buys a bundle at $1,700, the firm makes a profit of $400 (i.e., $1,700 revenue less $1,300 cost) from the sale of that bundle. If the customer buys the bundle, he earns a surplus of zero dollars.

However, the firm can make more profit from customer 1 by selling the monitor separately. The firm could induce customer 1 to buy the monitor separately by pricing it to give him more surplus than the customer would get from the bundle. If the manufacturer prices the monitor separately at $799, customer 1 will buy it, and the sale of that monitor generates a profit of $499 for the firm. The firm is better off (by $99) when the customer buys only the monitor instead of the bundle. And the customer is better off buying only the monitor, earning a consumer surplus of $1 (equal to her willingness to pay for a monitor, $800, less the price of the monitor, $799). So the firm should set $P_m = \$799$.

Similarly, customer 4 is only willing to pay $200 for a monitor, which is less than the marginal cost of the monitor. It will therefore not be profitable for the firm to sell a monitor to customer 4. Customer 4 will be happier purchasing only the computer at $1,499 (earning $1 of consumer surplus) instead of the bundle at $1,700 (earning a surplus of zero). The sale of the computer separately to customer 4 generates a profit of $499 for the firm, in contrast to the $400 profit it would have earned if customer 4 had bought the bundle. The firm should set $P_c = \$1,499$.

Finally, customers 2 and 3 have negatively correlated demands. Further, the amounts that they are willing to pay for each component exceed the marginal cost. The firm would therefore like to sell them a bundle. It should offer a package with a computer and a monitor at $P_b = \$1,700$.

In sum, with mixed bundling, customer 4 buys the computer separately, customer 1 takes the monitor alone, and customers 2 and 3 buy the bundle. Total profit is $1,798. The profit is higher with mixed bundling than it would be with no bundling ($1,200) or selling only a bundle ($1,600).

12.6 ADVERTISING

So far in this chapter, we have examined how a firm can capture surplus with *pricing* strategies. We now show how a firm with market power can also create and capture surplus with *nonprice* strategies, such as by choosing the amount of advertising for its product.

By advertising, a seller hopes to increase the demand for its product, shifting the demand curve rightward, and creating more surplus in the market. However, the firm must also recognize that advertising is costly. By correctly choosing the level of advertising, the firm can then capture as much surplus as possible.

Figure 12.10 illustrates the effects of advertising. In the figure we assume that the firm cannot price discriminate and that advertising expenditures affect the firm's fixed costs but does not shift its marginal cost curve. For example, it is reasonable to assume that the marginal cost curve for brewing beer is not affected by advertising.

Suppose first that the firm does not advertise at all. In that case the demand and marginal revenue curves for its product are D_0 and MR_0. The average and

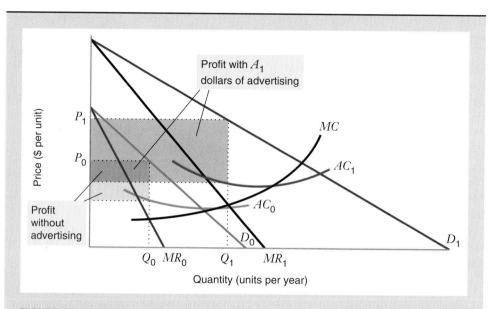

FIGURE 12.10   Effects of Advertising
When the firm does not advertise, the demand curve for its product is D_0 and the marginal revenue curve is MR_0. The average cost curve is AC_0. The firm produces Q_0 and sells at a price P_0. The graph indicates the maximum profit the firm can earn with no advertising. If the firm spends A_1 dollars on advertising, the demand curve for its product is D_1, the marginal revenue curve is MR_1, and the average cost curve is AC_1. The firm produces Q_1 and sells at a price P_1. When it spends A_1 on advertising, the maximum profit the firm can earn increases to the area shown on the graph.

marginal cost curves are AC_0 and MC. The firm produces Q_0 and sells at a price P_0. The graph indicates the maximum profit the firm can earn with no advertising.

If the firm spends A_1 dollars on advertising, the demand curve for its product shifts to the right, to D_1, and the marginal revenue curve becomes MR_1. Since advertising adds to the firm's total costs, the average cost curve rises to AC_1. To maximize profits, the firm produces Q_1 and sells at a price P_1. For the demand and cost curves depicted in the figure, it is clearly profitable for the firm to advertise. When it spends A_1 on advertising, the maximum profit the firm can earn increases, as shown in the graph.

If a firm maximizes profit by advertising $(A > 0)$ and producing a positive quantity $(Q > 0)$, two conditions must hold:

1. When output Q is chosen optimally, the change in total revenue from the last unit produced $\Delta TR/\Delta Q$, (i.e., the marginal revenue MR_Q), must equal the marginal cost of that last unit $\Delta TC/\Delta Q$ (denoted by MC_Q). The requirement that $MR_Q = MC_Q$ is the usual optimal quantity choice rule for a monopolist, as we saw in Chapter 11. We can write the optimal quantity choice equivalently as the inverse elasticity pricing rule

$$\frac{P - MC_Q}{P} = -\frac{1}{\epsilon_{Q,P}}, \qquad (12.1)$$

where P is the price of the product and $\epsilon_{Q,P}$ is the price elasticity of demand for the firm's product.

2. When the level of advertising A is chosen optimally, the marginal revenue from the last unit of advertising $\Delta TR/\Delta A$ (which we denote by MR_A) must equal the marginal cost that the firm incurs when it undertakes the last unit of advertising $\Delta TC/\Delta A$ (denoted by MC_A).

Why must $MR_A = MC_A$ at a profit maximum? If at the current level of advertising $MR_A > MC_A$, an additional unit of advertising would increase revenues by more than it would increase cost. Therefore, the firm could increase profit by advertising *more*. By similar reasoning, if $MR_A < MC_A$, the firm could increase profit by advertising *less*.

We can represent the condition that $MR_A = MC_A$ in another way. When we hold price constant, how does a change in the level of advertising affect the total revenue for the firm? If the demand for the product is $Q(P, A)$, i.e., the quantity demanded depends on both price and advertising, the firm's total revenue is $TR = PQ(P, A)$. When advertising goes up by a small amount (ΔA), the change in total revenue (ΔTR) will be equal to the price (P) times the change in quantity demanded as advertising increases (ΔQ). Thus, $\Delta TR = P\Delta Q$. When we divide both sides by ΔA, we get $\Delta TR/\Delta A = P(\Delta Q/\Delta A)$. So the marginal revenue from advertising is $MR_A = P(\Delta Q/\Delta A)$.

How does a change in the level of advertising affect the total cost for the firm? The total cost is $TC = C(Q(P, A)) + A$. The marginal cost from another unit of advertising is just $\Delta TC/\Delta A$, which we denote for convenience as MC_A. When advertising goes up by a small amount (ΔA), two things happen to costs. First, advertising expenditures go up by ΔA. But the quantity demanded also goes up, by ΔQ. When the firm produces this extra quantity, production costs will increase by $(MC_Q)(\Delta Q)$. Thus the impact of the extra advertising on total cost is $\Delta TC = (MC_Q)(\Delta Q) + \Delta A$. Dividing both sides by ΔA reveals that $MC_A = (MC_Q)(\Delta Q/\Delta A) + 1$.

When $MR_A = MC_A$, then $P(\Delta Q/\Delta A) = MC_Q(\Delta Q/\Delta A) + 1$. After some algebra[22] we can write this as

$$\frac{P - MC_Q}{P} = \frac{1}{\epsilon_{Q,A}} \frac{A}{PQ}, \qquad (12.2)$$

where $\epsilon_{Q,A}$ is the *advertising* elasticity of demand. The advertising elasticity of demand measures the percentage increase in sales that would result from a one percent increase in advertising. The left-hand sides of equations (12.1) and (12.2) are the same (the Lerner Index). When we equate the right-hand sides of these two equations, we learn that

$$\frac{A}{PQ} = -\frac{\epsilon_{Q,A}}{\epsilon_{Q,P}}. \qquad (12.3)$$

The left-hand side of equation (12.3) is the ratio of advertising expenditures A to the sales revenues PQ. The right-hand side is the negative ratio of the advertising elasticity of demand to the own price elasticity of demand. If you think

---

[22]Equation (12.2) can be rewritten as $[(P - MC_Q)/P](\epsilon_{Q,A})(PQ/A) = 1$. We can substitute the definition of the advertising elasticity of demand: $\epsilon_{Q,A} = (\Delta Q/\Delta A)(A/Q)$. This substitution results in $(P - MC_Q)(\Delta Q/\Delta A) = 1$. This is equivalent to the expression in the text: $P(\Delta Q/\Delta A) = MC_Q(\Delta Q/\Delta A) + 1$.

about it, this relationship simply makes good business sense. Suppose you examined two markets with approximately the same own price elasticity of demand, but greatly different advertising elasticities of demand. In the market in which demand is highly sensitive to the amount of advertising, you would expect the advertising-to-sales ratio to be higher compared to the market with a low elasticity of demand for advertising.

LEARNING-BY-DOING EXERCISE 12.6

Markup and Advertising-to-Sales Ratio

In this exercise we use information about the price elasticity and advertising elasticity of demand to determine the profit-maximizing ratio of advertising expenditures to sales revenues. Suppose you own a restaurant specializing in fine steak dinners, and you want to maximize your profits. Your marketing studies have revealed that your own price elasticity of demand is around -1.5, and that your advertising elasticity of demand is 0.1. In this exercise you may assume that these elasticities are approximately constant, even if you change your price and your level of advertising.

Problem

(a) Interpret the advertising elasticity of demand.
(b) How much should you mark up your price over marginal cost for your dinners? What should your advertising-to-sales ratio be?

Solution

(a) The advertising elasticity, $\epsilon_{Q,A} = 0.1$, implies that a one percent increase in advertising expenditures will stimulate demand by about one-tenth of 1 percent.
(b) The inverse elasticity pricing rule, equation (12.1), $(P - MC_Q)/P = -1/\epsilon_{Q,P} = (1/1.5)$. Thus $P - MC_Q = (2/3)P$, or $P = 3MC_Q$. The dinners should be priced at about three times marginal cost. According to equation (12.3), the optimal advertising-to-sales ratio should be $A/(PQ) = -\epsilon_{Q,A}/\epsilon_{Q,P} = (-0.1)/(-1.5) = 0.067$. Thus your advertising expenses should be about 6 or 7 percent of your sales revenues.

Similar Problem: 12.10

As we have already suggested, a firm may also improve its profits by carefully choosing the quality of the good. A higher quality may shift the demand curve to the right, but it is also costly to produce a better product. As with advertising, a firm may therefore choose quality so that the marginal revenue from improving quality equals the marginal cost of the improvement.[23]

---

[23] For important early work on advertising, including some of the main insights discussed in this section, see R. Dorfman, and P. Steiner, "Optimal Advertising and Optimal Quality," *American Economic Review*, 44 (December 1954).

CHAPTER SUMMARY

- A firm with market power can influence the price in the market. A firm need not be a monopolist to have market power. What is important is that the demand curve the firm faces be downward sloping.

- Many possible strategies may enable a producer with market power to capture more surplus (increase profit). A pricing strategy can be relatively simple, such as choosing a uniform price in a market. However, the success of this strategy will depend on how much the firm knows about the shape of the demand schedule.

- A firm may capture even more surplus if it can price discriminate, that is, charge more than one price for its product. A firm must have some market power to price discriminate. If the firm has no market power, it is a price taker and thus cannot set different prices for different units of output.

- To price discriminate, the firm must have more information than it requires to set a uniform price. It must have some idea about the different amounts people will pay for the product. The firm would like to know how reservation prices or elasticities of demand differ across consumers.

- Resale defeats price discrimination. To price discriminate, a firm has to prevent resale, or arbitrage.

- With first-degree price discrimination, the firm attempts to price each unit at the consumer's reservation price (that is, the consumer's maximum willingness to pay) for that unit. The marginal revenue curve is therefore the same as the demand curve. First-degree price discrimination allows the producer to capture all of the surplus. **(LBD Exercises 12.1 and 12.2)**

- Under second-degree price discrimination, the firm offers consumers a quantity discount, for example, with a block tariff. With a block tariff, the consumer pays one price for units consumed in the first block of output (up to a given quantity), and a different (usually lower) price for any additional units consumed in the second block.

- Second-degree price discrimination can also be implemented with a combination of subscription and usage charges. The subscription charge is an entry fee that enables the consumer to buy the good at specified price per unit (the usage charge). **(LBD Exercise 12.3)**

- With third-degree price discrimination, the firm identifies different consumer groups or segments in a market, and then charges a price for each segment by setting marginal revenue equal to marginal cost or, equivalently, by using the inverse elasticity pricing rule. The price within any segment is a uniform price, but the uniform price in one segment may differ from the uniform price in another segment. **(LBD Exercises 12.4 and 12.5)**

- Firms sometimes use screening to infer how reservation prices or elasticities of demand differ across consumers. Screening sorts consumers based on a consumer characteristic that (1) the firm can see (such as age or status), and (2) that is strongly related to a consumer characteristic that the firm cannot see but would like to observe (such as willingness to pay or elasticity of demand).

- Tying allows a customer to buy one product (the *tying product*) only if the customer agrees in a *requirements contract* to buy another product (the *tied product*). The consumer might buy the tied product without the tying product, but not the reverse. Tying often enables a firm to extend its market power from the tying product to the tied product.

- Bundling refers to tie-in sales that require customers to purchase goods in a package. The customer cannot buy the goods separately. Bundling may increase profits when customers have heterogeneous (different) demands. It may be profitable to offer consumers the option of "mixed bundling," so that consumers have a choice of buying goods in a bundle or separately.

- Advertising can help the firm capture more surplus when advertising increases the demand for a product. However, advertising is costly. When a firm simultaneously chooses its level of output and the level of advertising, it must attempt to (1) equate the marginal revenue from production to the marginal cost of production and (2) equate the marginal revenue from advertising to the marginal cost of advertising. When a firm maximizes profit, the advertising-to-sales ratio equals minus one times the ratio of the advertising and own price elasticities of demand. **(LBD Exercise 12.6)**

REVIEW QUESTIONS

1. Why must a firm have at least some market power to price discriminate?

2. Does a firm need to be a monopolist to price discriminate?

3. Why must a firm prevent resale if it is to price discriminate successfully?

4. What are the differences among first-degree, second-degree, and third-degree price discrimination?

5. With first-degree price discrimination, why is the marginal revenue curve the same as the demand curve?

6. How large will the deadweight loss be if a profit-maximizing firm engages in first-degree price discrimination?

7. What is the difference between a uniform price and a nonuniform (nonlinear) price? Give an example of a nonlinear price.

8. Suppose a company is currently charging a uniform price for its two products, creamy and crunchy peanut butter. Will third-degree price discrimination necessarily improve its profit? Would the firm ever be worse off with price discrimination?

9. How might screening help a firm price discriminate? Give an example of screening and explain how it works.

10. Why might a firm try to implement a tying arrangement? What is the difference between tying and bundling?

11. How might bundling increase a firm's profits? When is bundling *not* likely to increase profits?

12. Even if a monopolist knows that advertising shifts the demand curve for its product to the right, why might it decide not to advertise at all? If it does advertise, what factors determine how much advertising it will do?

PROBLEMS

12.1. Which of the following are examples of first-degree, second-degree, and third-degree price discrimination?

a) The publishers of the *Journal of Price Discrimination* charge a subscription price of $75 per year to individuals and $300 per year to libraries.
b) The U.S. government auctions off leases on tracts of land in the Gulf of Mexico. Oil companies bid for the right to explore each tract of land and to extract oil.
c) Ye Olde Country Club charges golfers $12 to play the first 9 holes of golf on a given day, $9 to play an additional 9 holes, and $6 to play 9 more holes.
d) The telephone company charges you $0.10 per minute to make a long-distance call from Monday through Saturday and $0.05 per minute on Sunday.
e) You can buy 1 computer disk for $10, a pack of three for $27, 10 for $75.
f) When you fly from New York to Chicago, the airline charges you $250 if you buy your ticket 14 days in advance, but $350 if you buy the ticket on the day of travel.

12.2. Suppose a profit-maximizing monopolist producing Q units of output faces the demand curve $P = 20 - Q$. Its total cost when producing Q units of output is $TC = 24 + Q^2$. The fixed cost is sunk and the marginal cost curve is $MC = 2Q$.

a) Suppose price discrimination is impossible. How large will the profit be? How large is the producer surplus?
b) Suppose the firm can engage in perfect first-degree price discrimination. How large will the profit be? How large is the producer surplus?
c) How much extra surplus does the producer capture when it can engage in first-degree price discrimination instead of charging a uniform price?

12.3. Suppose a monopolist producing Q units of output faces the demand curve $P = 20 - Q$. Its total cost when producing Q units of output is $TC = F + Q^2$, where F is a fixed cost. The marginal cost is $MC = 2Q$.

a) For what values of F can a profit-maximizing firm charging a uniform price earn at least zero economic profit?
b) For what values of F can a profit-maximizing firm engaging in perfect first-degree price discrimination earn at least zero economic profit?

12.4. Suppose that Acme Pharmaceutical Company discovers a drug that cures the common cold. Acme has plants in both the United States and Europe and can manufacture the drug on either continent at a marginal cost of 10. Assume there are no fixed costs. In Europe, the demand for the drug is $Q_E = 70 - P_E$, where Q_E is the quantity demanded when the price in Europe is P_E. In the United States, the demand for the drug is $Q_U = 110 - P_U$, where Q_U is the quantity demanded when the price in the United States is P_U.

a) If the firm can engage in third-degree price discrimination, what price should it set on each continent to maximize its profit?
b) Assume now that it is illegal for the firm to price discriminate, so that it can charge only a single price P on both continents. What price will it charge, and what profits will it earn?
c) Will the total consumer and producer surplus in the world be higher with price discrimination or without price discrimination? Will it sell the drug on both continents?

12.5. Consider Problem 12.4 with the following change. Suppose the demand for the drug in Europe declines to $Q_E = 30 - P_E$. If the firm cannot price discriminate, will it be in the firm's interest to sell on both continents?

12.6. Consider Problem 12.4 with the following change. Suppose the demand for the drug in Europe becomes $Q_E = 55 - 0.5P_E$. Will third-degree price discrimination increase the firm's profits?

12.7. Think about the problem that Acme faces in Problem 12.4. Consider *any* demands for the drug in Europe and in the Unites States. Will its profits ever be *lower* with third-degree price discrimination than they would be if price discrimination were impossible?

12.8. There is another way to solve Learning-By-Doing Exercise 12.5. Recall that marginal revenue can be written as $MR = P + (\Delta P/\Delta Q)Q$. By factoring out P, we can write the marginal revenue as $MR = P[1 + (\Delta P/\Delta Q)(Q/P)] = P[1 + (1/\epsilon_{Q,P})]$. Since third-degree price discrimination means that marginal cost equals marginal revenue in each market segment, the profit-maximizing regular and vacation fares will be determined by $MR_R = MR_V = MC$. (Remember the marginal cost of both classes of service is assumed to be the same in the exercise.) Thus $P_R[1 + (1/\epsilon_{Q_R,P_R})] = P_E[1 + (1/\epsilon_{Q_E,P_E})] = MC$. Use this relationship to verify the answer given in the exercise.

12.9. You are the only European firm selling vacation trips to the North Pole. You know only three customers are in the market. You offer two services, round-trip airfare and a stay at the Igloo Hotel. It costs you 300 euros to host a traveler at the Igloo and 300 euros for the airfare. If you do not bundle the services, a customer might buy your airfare but not stay at the hotel. A customer could also travel to the North Pole in some other way (by private plane), but still stay at the Igloo. The customers have the following reservation prices for these services:

Reservation Prices (in euros)

Customer	Airfare	Hotel
1	100	800
2	500	500
3	800	100

a) If you do not bundle the hotel and airfare, what are the optimal prices P_A and P_H, and what profits do you earn?
b) If you only sell the hotel and airfare in a bundle, what is the optimal price of the bundle P_B, and what profits do you earn?
c) If you follow a strategy of mixed bundling, what are the optimal prices of the separate hotel, the separate airfare, and the bundle (P_A, P_H and P_B, respectively) and what profits do you earn?

12.10. Suppose your company produces athletic footwear. Marketing studies indicate that your own price elasticity of demand is around -3 and that your advertising elasticity of demand is 0.5. You may assume these elasticities to be approximately constant over a wide range of prices and advertising expenses.

a) By how much should the company mark up price over marginal cost for its footwear?
b) What should the company's advertising-to-sales ratio be?

13

Market Structure and Competition

What brand of cola can you buy on your campus? If you are a student at Penn State or the University of Nebraska, you can buy Pepsi but not Coke. If you attend the University of Minnesota, Ohio State, or Indiana University, you can get Coca-Cola but not Pepsi. Your choice is limited because over the last ten years Coke and Pepsi have been competing to sign exclusive distribution deals with colleges throughout the United States. In 1992, for example, Pepsi paid Penn State $14 million to be the school's official drink. No other sodas can be sold anywhere on Penn State's twenty-one campuses. Not to be outdone, in 1994 Coke paid $28 million to the University of Minnesota to be that university's sole supplier of soft drinks and to place signs at sports venues and in campus food service areas. The $28 million was used for schol-

arships, student activities, and a women's hockey team.

This example highlights key ideas that we develop in this chapter. The "cola war" between Coke and Pepsi is an example of competition between a few firms whose fortunes are closely intertwined. Thus, neither the theory of perfect competition that we studied in Chapter 9 nor the theory of monopoly in Chapter 11 applies to the competitive battle between these two soft drink giants. Moreover, Coca-Cola and Pepsi sell differentiated products. Although most people view Coca-Cola and Pepsi Cola as *similar* products, few consider them *identical* products. Indeed, many consumers have long-standing loyalties to either Coke or Pepsi. It is the desire to develop these brand loyalties at an early age that has led Coke and Pepsi to place such strategic importance on gaining exclusive access to college campuses.

Our main objective in this chapter is to help you understand the forces that drive the outcome of competitive battles in markets that have only a few sellers or in which consumers see products as imperfect substitutes. The title of this chapter, "Market Structure and Competition," reflects the view among economists that the structure of a market—the number of firms that compete with each other, the ease with which firms can enter or leave the market, and the extent to which firms' products are differentiated from competitors' products—affects how firms compete with each other. To develop this point, we will study competition in the following different types of market structures: homogeneous product oligopoly, dominant firm, differentiated product oligopoly, and monopolistic competition. ■

13.1

TYPES OF MARKET STRUCTURES

Market structures differ on two important dimensions: the number of sellers and the nature of product differentiation.[1] Table 13.1 shows how different combinations of these characteristics give rise to different market structures. Going across the table, we move from competitive markets, in which there are many sellers, to oligopoly markets, in which there are just a few sellers, to monopoly markets, in which there is just one seller. Reading down the table, we move from markets in which firms sell identical or nearly identical products, to differentiated products markets in which firms sell products that consumers view as distinctive. The table indicates the economic theory that applies to each market structure and provides an example to which each of the theories might apply.

As we go through this chapter, we will move clockwise through Table 13.1 to study the four market structures that we have yet to encounter in this book. (Recall that we studied perfectly competitive markets in Chapters 9 and 10 and monopoly markets in Chapter 11.) We start in the top row of Table 13.1 by studying **homogeneous products oligopoly markets.** In these markets, a small number of firms sell products that have virtually the same attributes, performance characteristics, image, and (ultimately) price. For example, in the U.S. salt industry in which Morton Salt (now owned by Rohm and Haas), Cargill, and IMC Salt compete to sell an identical chemical compound (sodium chloride). In the global market for commodity semiconductor chips, such as DRAMs, several large firms such as Samsung, NEC, and Lucky Goldstar sell chips that are nearly identical in terms of product attributes and performance characteristics. We then move across the first row in Table 13.1 and turn our attention to **dominant firm markets.** In a dominant firm market, one firm possesses a large share of the market but competes against numerous small firms, each offering identical products. The German market for long-distance telephone service is a good example of a dom-

TABLE 13.1
Types of Market Structure

Product Differentiation	Number of Firms			
	Many	Few	One Dominant	One
Firms produce identical products	**Perfect competition** (Chapter 9) Example: fresh-cut rose market	**Homogeneous products oligopoly** Example: U.S. salt market	**Dominant firm** Example: German long-distance telephone market	**Monopoly** (Chapter 11) Example: Internet domain name registration*
Firms produce differentiated products	**Monopolistic competition** Example: local physicians markets	**Differentiated products oligopoly** Example: U.S. cola market	No applicable theory	

*until 1999

[1]Recall that Chapter 11 introduced and briefly discussed the concept of product differentiation.

inant firm market: Many small firms (e.g., Mobilcom and VIAG Interkom) compete in this market, but more than 60 percent of all sales are made by a single firm, Deutsche Telecom.

The chapter then moves to the bottom row of Table 13.1 and studies markets with differentiated products. In **differentiated products oligopoly markets,** a small number of firms sell products that are substitutes for each other but also differ from each other in significant ways, including attributes, performance, packaging, and image. Examples include the U.S. market for soft drinks where Coke and Pepsi are archrivals, the U.S. market for breakfast cereals in which Kellogg, General Mills, Post (owned by Philip Morris), and Quaker sell more than 85 percent of all cereal purchased in the United States, and the market for beer in Japan in which four firms, Asahi, Kirin, Sapporo, and Suntory account for nearly 100 percent of Japanese beer sales. We then move leftward in Table 13.1 to study monopolistic competition. **Monopolistic competition** refers to a market in which many firms produce differentiated products that are sold to many buyers. Local markets for video rentals, dry cleaning, and physician services are good examples of monopolistically competitive markets.

13.2 OLIGOPOLY WITH HOMO-GENEOUS PRODUCTS

In perfectly competitive and monopoly markets, firms do not have to worry about their rivals. In a monopoly market, this is because the monopolist has no rivals. In a perfectly competitive market, this is because each seller is so small that it has an imperceptible competitive impact on rival producers. A central feature of oligopoly markets, by contrast, is competitive interdependence: The decisions of every firm significantly affect the profits of competitors. For example, in the world market for memory chips, Samsung recognizes that the profit it gets from selling DRAM chips depends, in part, on the volume of chips that key competitors such as NEC and Lucky Goldstar will produce. If Samsung's competitors increase output, the market price for DRAM chips is likely to fall; if they decrease output, the market price will rise. In planning how many chips to produce within its current facilities, or in deciding whether to expand or build new facilities, Samsung's management must forecast how much output NEC, Lucky Goldstar, and other large semiconductor competitors are likely to produce. A central question of oligopoly theory, therefore, is how the close interdependence among firms in the market affects their behavior. Answering this question helps us understand the unique impact that an oligopoly market structure can have on prices, output levels, and profits.

THE COURNOT MODEL OF OLIGOPOLY

Microeconomics offers several models of oligopoly because oligopolists might interact with each other in a variety of plausible ways. Different theories highlight different assumptions about how oligopolists might interact.

Augustin Cournot developed the first theory of oligopoly in 1838 in his book *Researches into the Mathematical Principles of the Theory of Wealth*.[2] Although

---

[2] A. Cournot, "On the Competition of Producers," Chapter 7 in *Researches into the Mathematical Principles of the Theory of Wealth*, translated by N. T. Bacon (New York: Macmillan, 1897).

Cournot's model of oligopoly was part of a broader mathematical treatment of microeconomics, including demand, monopoly, and taxes. His theory of oligopoly was the most original part of his book and has had the greatest impact on the field of economics.

Profit Maximization by Cournot Firms

The Cournot model pertains to a homogeneous products oligopoly. Cournot initially considered a **duopoly market:** a market in which there are just two firms. In Cournot's duopoly, the two firms produced mineral water. To give Cournot's theory a more modern feel, let's imagine that these firms produce DRAM chips. One firm (Firm 1) might be Samsung, while the other (Firm 2) might be Lucky Goldstar (LG).

Because Samsung's and LG's DRAMs are identical, both firms charge the same price. In the Cournot model, the only decision a firm makes is how much to produce. Each firm selects its output simultaneously and noncooperatively—that is, without communicating or colluding with the other firm. Once each firm selects its output, the market price instantly adjusts to "clear the market." That is, given the firm's output choices, the price that each firm charges is equal to the price at which consumers are willing to buy their combined output. As Figure 13.1(a) shows, this market clearing price is determined from the market demand curve D_M. For example, if LG produces 50 units and Samsung produces 30 units, total market supply will be 80 units, and the market price will be $20.

How much will each firm produce? Because market price depends on the total production of both firms and because each firm will take into account the market price when it selects its production level, it follows that the amount that each firm produces depends on the amount it expects its rival to produce. In the Cournot model, each firm guesses how much output the other firm will produce and then chooses a profit-maximizing level of production in response to this guess. Thus, Samsung will choose the level of production that maximizes its profits, given what it thinks LG's output will be, and LG will choose the level of production that maximizes its profits, given what output it thinks Samsung will produce. In the Cournot model, firms thus act as *quantity takers*.

Figure 13.1(a) shows Samsung's output-choice problem. Suppose that Samsung expects LG to produce 50 units of output. Then, the relationship between the market price and Samsung's output is given by the **residual demand curve** D_{50}. A residual demand curve traces out the relationship between the market price and a firm's quantity when the other firm sells a fixed amount of output (50 units, in this case). The residual demand curve D_{50} is the market demand curve (D_M) shifted leftward by an amount equal to LG's output of 50. This ensures that when Samsung's output is added to LG's output of 50, the price along the residual demand curve D_{50} equals the price along the market demand curve D_M when we combine the two firms' outputs. For example, when LG produces 50 and Samsung produces 30, the price along the residual demand curve is $20, which is also the price along the market demand curve D_M when total output equals 80. MR_{50} is the marginal revenue curve associated with D_{50}. It bears the same relationship to the residual demand curve that a monopolist's marginal revenue curve bears to a market demand curve.

Samsung acts as a monopolist relative to its *residual* demand curve when it chooses its output. It thus equates MR_{50} to its marginal cost MC (which is assumed to be constant at $10 per unit). This occurs at an output of 20 units. An

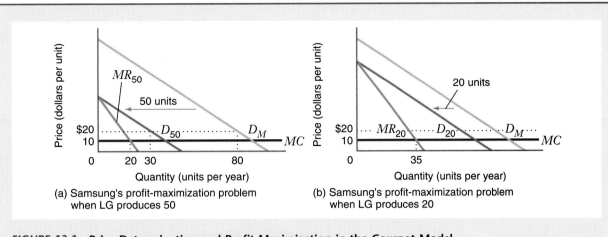

FIGURE 13.1   Price Determination and Profit Maximization in the Cournot Model
Panel (a) shows that when Samsung produces 30 units and LG produces 50, the market
price will be $20. When LG produces 50 units, Samsung's residual demand curve is D_{50},
which is the market demand curve shifted leftward by 50 units. The residual demand
curve traces out the quantity–price combinations that are available to Samsung when LG's
output is 50 units. Facing this residual demand curve, Samsung maximizes its profits by
producing 20 units, the point at which its marginal revenue, MR_{50}, equals its marginal
cost, MC. This output is Samsung's best response when LG produces 50 units. Panel (b)
shows that when LG produces 20 units, Samsung faces residual demand and marginal
revenue curves D_{20} and MR_{20}, respectively, and maximizes profit by producing 35 units,
where $MR_{20} = MC$.

output of 20 units is thus Samsung's **best response** to an output of 50 units from
LG. A Cournot firm's best response to a particular level of output by rival firms
is the firm's profit-maximizing choice of output given the rival's output. Figure
13.1(b) shows that when LG's output is 20 units, Samsung's best response is to
produce 35 units.

For every possible output that LG might choose, we could determine Samsung's profit-maximizing output as we did in Figure 13.1. The curve R_1 in Figure
13.2 summarizes Samsung's profit-maximizing output choices. The curve R_1 is a
reaction function. It tells us a firm's best response (i.e., profit-maximizing output choice) to the output level of a rival firm. Figure 13.2 also graphs LG's reaction function R_2. Note that both reaction functions are downward sloping.
Thus, each firm's profit maximizing output choice becomes smaller as its rival
produces more output.

Equilibrium in a Cournot Market

Under perfect competition, a key feature of the market equilibrium is that no
firm has an incentive to deviate from its profit-maximizing decision once the market equilibrium has been attained. The same is true of an equilibrium in a Cournot
market. Specifically, a **Cournot equilibrium** is a pair of outputs that simultaneously satisfies two conditions:[3]

[3] In Chapter 14, you will see that the Cournot equilibrium is a particular example of what is called a
Nash equilibrium. For this reason, some textbooks refer to the Cournot equilibrium as the Cournot-
Nash equilibrium or the Nash equilibrium in quantities.

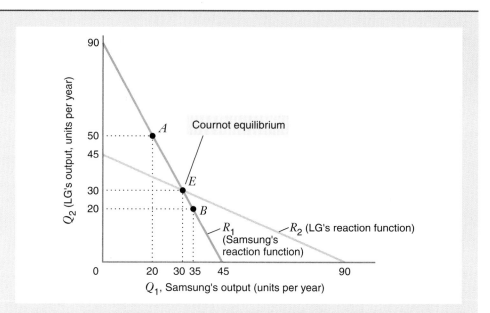

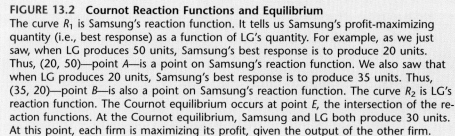

FIGURE 13.2 Cournot Reaction Functions and Equilibrium
The curve R_1 is Samsung's reaction function. It tells us Samsung's profit-maximizing quantity (i.e., best response) as a function of LG's quantity. For example, as we just saw, when LG produces 50 units, Samsung's best response is to produce 20 units. Thus, (20, 50)—point A—is a point on Samsung's reaction function. We also saw that when LG produces 20 units, Samsung's best response is to produce 35 units. Thus, (35, 20)—point B—is also a point on Samsung's reaction function. The curve R_2 is LG's reaction function. The Cournot equilibrium occurs at point E, the intersection of the re-action functions. At the Cournot equilibrium, Samsung and LG both produce 30 units. At this point, each firm is maximizing its profit, given the output of the other firm.

1. *Samsung's output is a best response to LG's output.* Samsung's output maximizes its profit given LG's output. Thus, in equilibrium, Samsung is doing as well as it can, given LG's output.

2. *LG's output is a best response to Samsung's output.* LG's output maximizes its profit given Samsung's output. Thus, in equilibrium, LG is doing as well as it can, given Samsung's output.

In Figure 13.2, the Cournot equilibrium occurs at the point at which the two reaction functions intersect—that is, when each firm produces 30 units. To verify that this is an equilibrium, we see from R_1 that when LG produces 30 units, Samsung's best response is to produce 30 units. And we see from R_2 that when Samsung produces 30 units, LG's best response is to produce 30 units. Thus, when each firm produces 30 units, neither firm has any after-the-fact regret about its output choice.

Figure 13.3 portrays each firm's profit-maximization problem at the Cournot equilibrium. Because each firm expects that its competitor will produce 30 units, each firm faces a residual demand curve D_{30}. Equating marginal cost to the marginal revenue curve MR_{30}, each firm's profit-maximizing output is, in fact, 30 units. Note that when each firm produces 30 units and expects the other to do so as well, both firms will end up setting a price of $40 per unit, which is the market-clearing price.

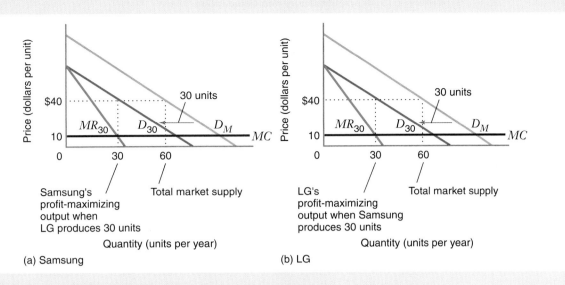

(a) Samsung

(b) LG

FIGURE 13.3 Profit Maximization at the Cournot Equilibrium
Panel (a) shows that when LG produces an output of 30, Samsung's profit-maximizing output (which occurs where $MR_{30} = MC$) is 30 units. Panel (b) shows that when Samsung produces 30 units, LG's profit-maximizing output is 30 units. Thus, each firm producing 30 units is a Cournot equilibrium. When each firm produces 30 units, the market price is $40. We can identify this price from either firm's residual demand curve or from the market demand curve (corresponding to the total market supply at the equilibrium).

LEARNING-BY-DOING EXERCISE 13.1

Computing a Cournot Equilibrium

The market demand curve in Figure 13.1 is given by

$$P = 100 - Q_1 - Q_2,$$

where Q_1 is the amount of output Samsung produces and Q_2 is LG's level of output. The marginal cost of each firm is $10.

Problem

(a) Given this market demand curve, what is Samsung's profit-maximizing quantity when LG produces 50 units?
(b) What is Samsung's profit-maximizing output when LG produces an arbitrary output Q_2 (i.e., what is the equation of Samsung's reaction function)?
(c) Compute the Cournot equilibrium quantities and price in this market.

Solution

(a) We can compute Samsung's best response using concepts from monopoly theory in Chapter 11. When LG produces $Q_2 = 50$, Samsung's residual demand curve is given by

$$P = 100 - Q_1 - 50 = 50 - Q_1.$$

557

This is a linear demand curve, so the associated marginal revenue (MR) is

$$MR = 50 - 2Q_1.$$

Equating this marginal revenue to Samsung's marginal cost yields

$$50 - 2Q_1 = 10, \text{ or } Q_1 = 20.$$

(b) Samsung now faces a residual demand curve given by

$$P = (100 - Q_2) - Q_1.$$

We use parentheses to highlight the terms that Samsung views as fixed. Samsung's residual demand curve is therefore linear, with a vertical intercept of $(100 - Q_2)$ and a slope of -1. As we learned in Chapter 11, the corresponding marginal revenue curve has the same vertical intercept and twice the slope of the demand curve. Therefore, Samsung's marginal revenue is

$$MR = (100 - Q_2) - 2Q_1.$$

Equating marginal revenue to marginal cost yields Samsung's best response:

$$(100 - Q_2) - 2Q_1 = 10, \text{ or } Q_1 = 45 - \frac{1}{2}Q_2.$$

This is Samsung's reaction function. Using symmetric logic, we can compute LG's best response to any arbitrary guess Q_1 about Samsung's output:

$$Q_2 = 45 - \frac{1}{2}Q_1.$$

(c) The Cournot equilibrium occurs where the two reaction functions intersect. This corresponds to the pair of outputs that simultaneously solve the two firm's reaction functions:

$$Q_1 + \frac{1}{2}Q_2 = 45 \text{ (Samsung's reaction function, rearranged).}$$

$$\frac{1}{2}Q_1 + Q_2 = 45 \text{ (LG's reaction function, rearranged).}$$

You should verify that the solution to this system of equations is $Q_1 = Q_2 = 30$. We find the equilibrium market price P^* by substituting these quantities into the market demand curve:

$$P^* = 100 - 30 - 30 = 40.$$

Similar Problem: 13.1

How Do Firms Achieve the Cournot Equilibrium?

The Cournot theory is a static model of oligopoly: It pertains to firms that make a single, once-and-for-all decision about output. It does not explain how the firms reach the equilibrium. All it tells us is that once each firm has chosen its equilibrium output, neither firm regrets its choice.

Does this require the two firms to be omniscient? Perhaps not. Let's think through how Samsung could anticipate how the Cournot equilibrium might arise. Consider Figure 13.4. Based on this figure, Samsung's managers could reason as follows:

> Putting ourselves in LG's shoes, LG would never produce a quantity greater than 45. This is because no matter what output we choose, a quantity greater than 45 never maximizes LG's profits. We can see this because LG's reaction function R_2 does not "extend" above $Q_2 = 45$.[4]

If they are clever, Samsung's managers would then conclude:

> Given that LG will not produce more than 45, we should produce at least 22.5. Why? Because we see from R_1 that any quantity less than 22.5 could never be profit maximizing for us given that LG will never produce more than 45.

But Samsung can go even deeper:

> We should assume that LG has reasoned the same way we have—after all, they are just as clever as we are. LG should realize that we will produce at least 22.5. But if LG believes this, we see from R_2 that LG would never produce more than 33.75.

But, of course, Samsung's managers can reason more deeply still:

> Given that LG will produce no more than 33.75, we should produce at least 28.125. Why? Because we see from R_1 that any quantity smaller than 28.125 could never be profit-maximizing for us given that LG will never produce more than 33.75.

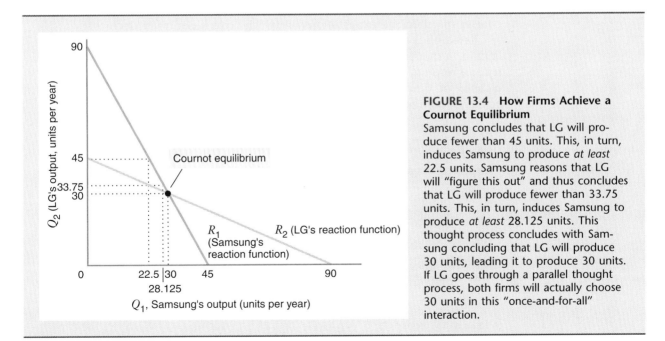

FIGURE 13.4 How Firms Achieve a Cournot Equilibrium
Samsung concludes that LG will produce fewer than 45 units. This, in turn, induces Samsung to produce *at least* 22.5 units. Samsung reasons that LG will "figure this out" and thus concludes that LG will produce fewer than 33.75 units. This, in turn, induces Samsung to produce *at least* 28.125 units. This thought process concludes with Samsung concluding that LG will produce 30 units, leading it to produce 30 units. If LG goes through a parallel thought process, both firms will actually choose 30 units in this "once-and-for-all" interaction.

---

[4] In the language of game theory that we will introduce in Chapter 14, we say that quantities greater than $Q_2 = 45$ are dominated strategies.

Do you see where this is headed? The more deeply Samsung's managers think through LG's and their own profit-maximization problems, they will keep eliminating output choices until they reach the Cournot equilibrium 30 units for each firm.[5] To be sure, this is complicated reasoning. But it is no more complicated than what a smart chess or bridge player uses against equally clever rivals. Seen this way, the Cournot equilibrium is a natural outcome when both firms fully understand their interdependence and have confidence in each other's rationality.

EXAMPLE 13.1   *Cournot Equilibrium in the Corn Wet-Milling Industry*

Michael Porter and Michael Spence's study of the corn wet-milling industry is an application of the Cournot model to a real-world market.[6] Firms in the corn wet-milling industry convert corn into corn starch and corn syrup. The industry had been a stable oligopoly until the early 1970s. But in 1972, a major development occurred: The production of high fructose corn syrup (HFCS) became commercially viable. HFCS can be used instead of sugar to sweeten products, such as soft drinks. With sugar prices expected to rise, a significant market for HFCS beckoned. Firms in the corn wet-milling industry had to decide whether to add capacity to meet the expected demand.

Porter and Spence studied this capacity expansion process by constructing a model of competitive behavior based on an in-depth study of the eleven major competitors in the industry. They then used this model to calculate a Cournot equilibrium for the corn wet-milling industry. In this equilibrium, each firm's capacity choice was an optimal response to its expectations about rival firms' capacity choices, and the total industry capacity expansion that resulted from these optimal choices matched the expectations on which firms based their decisions.

Based on their analysis, Porter and Spence concluded that at an industry equilibrium, a moderate amount of additional capacity would be added to the industry as a result of the commercialization of HFCS. Table 13.2 shows the specific predictions of their model compared with the pattern of capacity expansion that actually occurred.

TABLE 13.2
Capacity Expansion in the Corn Wet-Milling Industry

	1973	1974	1975	1976+	Total
Actual capacity expansion*	0.6	1.0	1.4	6.2	9.2
Predicted capacity expansion	0.6	1.5	3.5	3.5	9.1

*billions of pounds.

[5] In Chapter 14, we will learn that in game theory, this approach to solving a game is called elimination of dominated strategies.

[6] M. Porter and A. M. Spence, "The Capacity Expansion Decision in a Growing Oligopoly: The Case of Corn Wet Milling," in J. J. McCall (ed.), *The Economics of Information and Uncertainty* (Chicago, IL: University of Chicago Press, 1982), pp. 259–316.

Though not perfect, Porter and Spence's calculated equilibrium was close to the actual capacity expansion in the industry, particularly in 1973 and 1974. Their research suggests that the Cournot model, when adapted to specific industry conditions, can accurately describe the dynamics of capacity expansion in a homogeneous-product oligopoly. ■

The Cournot, Perfectly Competitive, and Monopoly Market Equilibria

In the Samsung-LG example above, the Cournot equilibrium price of \$40 exceeds each firm's marginal cost of \$10. Therefore, the Cournot outcome does not correspond to the perfectly competitive equilibrium. In general, then, Cournot firms exhibit market power.

But that does not imply that they can attain the monopoly or collusive equilibrium. Recall that industry output at the Cournot equilibrium is 60 units. This output *does not* maximize industry profit. The monopoly outcome in this market occurs where marginal revenue equals marginal cost, which occurs at a market output of 45 units, and the corresponding monopoly price is \$55.[7] If Samsung and LG were to act as a profit-maximizing cartel, they would charge this price and split the market evenly, each producing a quantity of 22.5. This is point M in Figure 13.5.

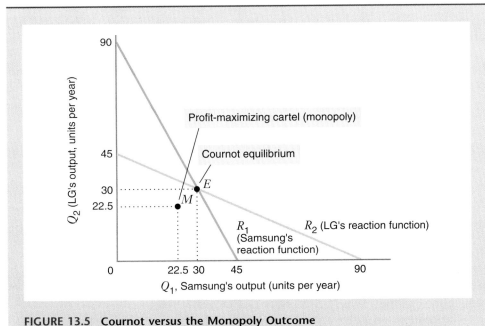

FIGURE 13.5 Cournot versus the Monopoly Outcome
If Samsung and LG behave as a profit-maximizing cartel, they will produce a total of 45 units. Splitting this equally gives each an output of 22.5. The cartel or monopoly outcome, point M, thus differs from the Cournot equilibrium, point E.

[7] You should verify this for yourself!

TABLE 13.3
Cournot Equilibrium for Various Numbers of Firms

Number of Firms	Price	Market Quantity	Per-Firm Profit	Total Profit
1 (monopoly)	$55.0	45.0		$2025
2	$40.0	60.0	$900	$1800
3	$32.5	67.5	$506	$1519
5	$25.0	75.0	$225	$1125
10	$18.2	81.8	$ 67	$ 669
100	$10.9	89.1	<$1	$ 79
∞ (perfect competition)	$10.0	90.0	0	0

By independently maximizing their own profits, firms produce more output than they would if they collusively maximized industry profits. This is an important characteristic of oligopolistic industries. The pursuit of individual self-interest does not typically maximize the well-being of the industry as a whole.

The inability of the two firms to attain the collusive outcome occurs for the following reason. When one firm, say Samsung, expands its output, it reduces the market price and thus lowers the sales revenues of rival chip producers. Samsung does not care about lowering its rival's revenue because it is seeking to maximize its own profit, not total industry profit. Thus, Samsung expands its production volume more aggressively than it would if it had sought to maximize industry profit. If all DRAM producers behave this way, the market price must be less than the monopoly price.

The smaller a firm's share of industry sales is, the greater the divergence will be between its private gain and the revenue destruction it causes by expanding its output. This suggests that when the number of firms in the industry increases, the Cournot equilibrium diverges further from the monopoly outcome. Table 13.3 illustrates this point by showing equilibrium prices, profits, and outputs in a Cournot oligopoly with the same demand and cost curves as in the Samsung-LG example.[8] The equilibrium price and profit per firm decline as the number of firms increases.

EXAMPLE 13.2   *Individual versus Group Rationality in the Copper Industry*[9]

In the late 1990s, the world copper industry experienced hard times. Industry analysts believed that firms would have to cut production to restore prices to levels that would allow the industry to make a profit. But most firms were reluctant to reduce their output. Why?

The head of Rio Tinto, one of the world's largest copper mining companies, explained it this way: "What makes sense for an individual company is lunacy for the

---

[8] In Learning-By-Doing Exercise 13.2, you will learn how to calculate a Cournot equilibrium with more than two firms.

[9] This example is based on "Rio Tinto May Hold Back on Production Cuts," *Financial Times* (Friday, February 26, 1999), p. 36.

industry as a whole." He meant that most companies are better off not reducing production, but that when no one reduces output, everyone in the industry is hurt. Even though a reduction in output by an individual company would reduce industry supply and cause copper prices to go up, the firm that reduces its output doesn't gain the full benefit from this price increase. Much of that benefit flows to competitors who keep their outputs the same but now can sell at a higher price. Cutting production could thus create additional revenue for the rest of the industry, but the firm that closes the mine might actually experience a drop in its profit because it is now selling less than before. This is the revenue destruction effect in reverse!

For its part, Rio Tinto held fast and kept its copper mines operating. As one of the low-cost producers in the market, Rio Tinto was profitable even at the low prices that prevailed in the late 1990s. Rio Tinto hoped that some of its competitors would eventually bite the bullet and cut their production first. The grim logic of the "reverse revenue destruction effect" suggests that this hope can often be in vain. ■

LEARNING-BY-DOING EXERCISE 13.2

Computing the Cournot Equilibrium for Two or More Firms with Linear Demand

Problem

(a) Suppose that inverse demand is given by $P = a - bQ$, and that firms have identical marginal cost given by c. Assume that $a > c$ so that part of the demand curve lies above the marginal cost curve (otherwise the industry would not produce any output). What is the monopoly equilibrium in this market?
(b) What is the perfectly competitive market outcome?
(c) What is the Cournot equilibrium in a market with two firms?
(d) Suppose the market consists of N identical firms. What is the Cournot equilibrium quantity per firm, market quantity, and price?

Solution

(a) The monopolist's marginal revenue curve is given by

$$MR = a - 2bQ.$$

Equating marginal revenue to marginal cost yields $a - 2bQ = c$, or

$$Q = \frac{a - c}{2b}.$$

We find the monopolist's price by substituting this expression back into the demand curve:

$$P = a - b\left(\frac{a - c}{2b}\right) = \frac{a}{2} + \frac{c}{2}.$$

(b) At the competitive market output, price equals marginal cost. Thus, $a - bQ = c$, or

$$Q = \frac{a - c}{b}.$$

With linear demand and constant marginal cost, the competitive equilibrium output is twice as large as the monopoly output.

(c) Consider Firm 1's profit-maximization problem first. Its residual demand curve is

$$P = (a - bQ_2) - bQ_1,$$

where we put parentheses around the terms that Firm 1 views as fixed. Again utilizing what we learned in Chapter 11 about marginal revenue curves, Firm 1's marginal revenue curve is

$$MR = (a - bQ_2) - 2bQ_1.$$

Equating Firm 1's marginal revenue to its marginal cost and solving for Q_1 yields Firm 1's reaction function: $a - bQ_2 - 2bQ_1 = c$, or

$$Q_1 = \frac{a - c}{2b} - \frac{1}{2}Q_2.$$

We can derive Firm 2's reaction function in a similar fashion:

$$Q_2 = \frac{a - c}{2b} - \frac{1}{2}Q_1.$$

We could find the equilibrium by solving these two equations simultaneously. But we can resort to a convenient trick. Because each firm has the same marginal cost, it stands to reason that in equilibrium all firms will choose the same quantity. That is, the equilibrium will be symmetric. By imposing symmetry we can quickly solve for the equilibrium quantity per firm Q^* by equating Q_1 to Q_2 along a firm's reaction function:

$$Q^* = \frac{a - c}{2b} - \frac{1}{2}Q^*,$$

or

$$Q^* = \frac{a - c}{3b}.$$

This is the equilibrium output per firm. The total market equilibrium output is twice this amount, or

$$\frac{2}{3}\left(\frac{a - c}{b}\right),$$

or two-thirds of the competitive equilibrium output. The Cournot equilibrium price with two firms is given by

$$a - b\left(\frac{2}{3}\left(\frac{a-c}{b}\right)\right) = \frac{1}{3}a + \frac{2}{3}c.$$

You should verify that this matches the equilibrium price we derived in the Samsung-LG example. Also note that it lies between the monopoly price $(1/2)a + (1/2)c$ and the perfectly competitive price c.

(d) Consider Firm 1. Its residual demand curve is now

$$P = (a - bX) - bQ_1,$$

where X now denotes the combined output of all the other $N - 1$ firms. Firm 1's marginal revenue curve is

$$MR = (a - bX) - 2bQ_1.$$

Equating its marginal revenue to marginal cost yields Firm 1's reaction function:

$$Q_1 = \frac{a-c}{2b} - \frac{1}{2}X.$$

Now, we again note that the equilibrium will be symmetric. Hence, each firm will produce the same amount, and thus Firm 1's $N - 1$ competitors will produce $(N - 1)$ times Firm 1's equilibrium output. Therefore, at a symmetric equilibrium, the equilibrium output per firm, Q^*, is as follows:

$$Q^* = \frac{a-c}{2b} - \left(\frac{N-1}{2}\right)Q^*,$$

which implies

$$Q^* = \frac{1}{(N+1)}\left(\frac{a-c}{b}\right).$$

The total industry output is N times this amount or

$$\frac{N}{N+1}\left(\frac{a-c}{b}\right).$$

Note that as N gets bigger and bigger, $N/(N + 1)$ gets closer to 1, and the Cournot equilibrium output thus approaches the perfectly competitive equilibrium output. We find the Cournot equilibrium price by substituting this quantity back into the demand curve:

$$P = a - b\left(\frac{N}{N+1}\right)\left(\frac{a-c}{b}\right) = \frac{a}{N+1} + \frac{N}{N+1}c.$$

Note that the numbers in Table 13.3 are consistent with this formula. Also note that as N gets big, the Cournot equilibrium price gets closer and closer to marginal cost c.

Similar Problems: 13.1, 13.2, and 13.3

TABLE 13.4
Computations for Learning-By-Doing Exercise 13.2

Market Structure	Price	Market Quantity	Per-Firm Quantity
Monopoly	$\frac{1}{2}a + \frac{1}{2}c$	$\frac{1}{2}\frac{a-c}{b}$	$\frac{1}{2}\frac{a-c}{b}$
Cournot duopoly	$\frac{1}{3}a + \frac{2}{3}c$	$\frac{2}{3}\frac{a-c}{b}$	$\frac{1}{3}\frac{a-c}{b}$
N-firm Cournot oligopoly	$\frac{1}{N+1}a + \frac{N}{N+1}c$	$\frac{N}{N+1}\frac{a-c}{b}$	$\frac{1}{N+1}\frac{a-c}{b}$
Perfect competition	c	$\frac{a-c}{b}$	virtually 0

Table 13.4 summarizes the results of this exercise.

Cournot Equilibrium and the IEPR

In Chapters 11 and 12, we saw how a monopolist's profit-maximization condition could be expressed as an inverse elasticity pricing rule (IEPR): When the monopolist maximizes profits, it will set its percentage contribution margin (PCM)—the difference between the monopolist's price and marginal cost expressed as a percentage of price—equal to minus one over the price elasticity of market demand. In the Appendix to this chapter, we show that a version of the IEPR arises in a Cournot equilibrium. In particular, suppose that all firms are the same, and let MC denote their common marginal cost. Then, percentage contribution margin (PCM) for each firm at the Cournot equilibrium is given by the following:

$$\frac{P^* - MC}{P^*} = -\frac{1}{N} \times \frac{1}{\epsilon_{Q,P}}$$

where $\epsilon_{Q,P}$ is the market price elasticity of demand and N is the number of firms in the market.

This modified inverse elasticity pricing rule provides a compelling link between market structure and how firms perform in an oligopoly market. It implies that the more firms there are in the industry, the smaller their percentage contribution margin will be. (This mirrors the relationship shown in Table 13.3.) Recall from Chapter 11 that the PCM (or Lerner Index) is commonly used to measure market power. The Cournot model thus implies that market power will go down as more firms compete in the market.

BERTRAND PRICE COMPETITION IN A HOMOGENEOUS PRODUCTS OLIGOPOLY

In the Cournot model, each firm selects a quantity to produce, and the resulting total output determines the market price. Alternatively, one might imagine a market in which each firm selects a price and stands ready to meet all the demand for its product at that price. This model of competition was first articulated by

French mathematician Joseph Bertrand in 1883 in a review of Cournot's book.[10] Bertrand criticized Cournot's assumption of quantity-taking behavior and argued that a more plausible model of oligopoly was one in which each firm chose a price, taking as given the prices of other firms. Once firms choose their prices, they would then adjust their production to satisfy all of the demand that comes their way.[11] Because firms produce identical products, the firm that sets the lowest price captures the entire market demand, and the other firms sell nothing.

To illustrate Bertrand price competition, let's return to our example of rival DRAM producers Samsung and LG. A **Bertrand equilibrium** occurs when each firm chooses a profit-maximizing price, given the price set by the other firm. Recall from Figures 13.2 and 13.3 that at the Cournot equilibrium each firm produced 30 units and sold them at a price of $40. Is this also the Bertrand equilibrium? The answer is no. To see why, consider Samsung's pricing problem in Figure 13.6. Taking LG's price as fixed at $40, Samsung's demand curve is a broken line that corresponds to the market demand curve D_M at prices below $40 and the vertical axis at prices above $40. If Samsung slightly undercut LG's price by charging $39, it would steal all of LG's business and would also stimulate one unit of additional demand as well. Thus, though Samsung's price is lower than before, it more than compensates for the lower price by more than doubling its volume. As a result, Samsung enjoys an increase in profit given by area B (the gain from the additional volume of output it sells) minus area A (the reduction in profit due to the fact that it could have sold 30 units at the higher price of $40).

But note that $P_1 = \$39$ and $P_2 = \$40$ cannot be an equilibrium either. At these prices, LG would gain by undercutting Samsung's price. Indeed, as long as

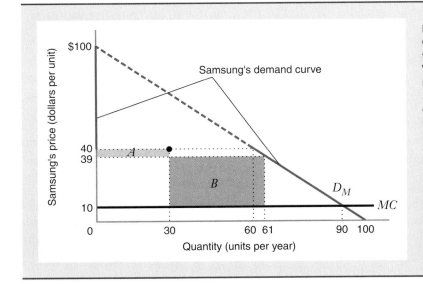

FIGURE 13.6 Samsung's Demand Curve under Bertrand Price Competition with Homogeneous Products
When LG's price is $40, Samsung's demand curve has two pieces. Above $40, Samsung sells nothing, and its demand curve corresponds to the verical axis. Below $40, Samsung captures the entire market demand, so its demand curve corresponds to the market demand curve D_M. (At a price equal to $40, Samsung splits the market demand with LG and sells 30 units.) If Samsung lowers its price to $39, it sacrifices profits by an amount equal to area A, but it gains profits by a larger amount equal to area B. Thus, a slight price cut will increase Samsung's profits.

[10]Bertrand, J., book reviews of Walras's *Theorie Mathematique de la Richese Sociale* and Cournot's *Researches sur les Principes Mathematique de la Theorie des Richesses*, reprinted as Chapter 2 in A. F. Daughety (ed.), *Cournot Oligopoly: Characterization and Applications* (Cambridge: Cambridge University Press, 1988).

[11]Bertrand writes: "By treating (the quantities) as independent variables, (Cournot) assumes that the one quantity happening to change by the will of the owner, the other would remain constant. The contrary is obviously true." *Ibid*, p. 77.

both firms set prices that exceed their common marginal cost of $10, one firm can always increase its profits by slightly undercutting its competitor. This implies that the only possible equilibrium in the Bertrand model is when each firm sets a price equal to its marginal cost of $10. At this point, neither firm can do better by changing its price. If either firm lowers price further, it would lose money on each unit it sells. If either firm raises price, it would sell nothing. Thus, in the Bertrand equilibrium, $P = MC = \$10$, and the resulting market demand is 90 units. Thus, unlike the Cournot equilibrium with two firms, the Bertrand equilibrium with two firms results in the same outcome as a perfectly competitive market with a large number of firms.

WHY ARE THE COURNOT AND BERTRAND EQUILIBRIA DIFFERENT?

The Cournot and Bertrand models make dramatically different predictions about the quantities, prices, and profits that will arise under oligopolistic competition. In the Cournot model, the equilibrium price is generally above marginal cost, and the Cournot equilibrium price approaches the perfectly competitive price only as the number of competitors in the market place becomes large. In the Bertrand model, by contrast, competition between even two firms is enough to replicate the perfectly competitive equilibrium. How can one reconcile these differences between the two models?

One way is to recognize that Cournot and Bertrand competition might take place over different time frames. Cournot competitors can be thought of as first choosing capacities and then competing as price setters given these capacities. The result of this "two-stage" competition (first choose capacities and then choose prices) can be shown to be identical to the Cournot equilibrium in quantities.[12] Viewed in these terms, the Bertrand model discussed above can be thought of as short-run price competition when both firms have more than enough capacity to satisfy market demand at any price greater than or equal to marginal cost.

Another way to understand the difference between the Cournot and Bertrand models is to recognize that they make different assumptions about how a firm expects its rivals to react to its competitive moves. One interpretation of the Cournot assumption that a firm takes its competitors' outputs as given is that a firm, in effect, believes that its competitors will instantly match any price change the firm makes so that they can keep their sales volumes constant. This expectation might make sense in industries, such as mining or chemical processing, in which firms can often adjust their prices more quickly than their rates of production. Thus, if a firm lowers its price in a Cournot market, it can not expect to "steal" customers from its rivals. Because business stealing is thus not an option, Cournot competitors behave less aggressively than Bertrand competitors. Thus, the Cournot equilibrium outcome, while not the monopoly one, nevertheless results in positive profits and a price that exceeds marginal cost.

By contrast, when firms' products are perfect substitutes, a Bertrand firm believes that it can lure customers from its competitors by small cuts in price, and

---

[12] The idea that the Cournot equilibrium can (under some circumstances) emerge as the outcome of a "two-stage game" in which firms first choose capacities and then choose prices is due to D. Kreps, and J. Scheinkman, "Quantity Precommitment and Bertrand Competition Yield Cournot Outcomes," *Bell Journal of Economics*, 14 (1983), pp. 326–337.

it knows that it has sufficient production capacity to be able to satisfy this additional demand. These beliefs might make sense in a market, such as the U.S. airline industry in the early 1990s, that had significant excess capacity. Many airlines at that time believed that they would fly their planes empty unless they cut their prices below their competitors. Of course, if all firms in the market think this way, each one will attempt to steal business from its competitors through price cutting. In equilibrium, prices drop to marginal cost, and each firm earns zero profit.

13.3 DOMINANT FIRM MARKETS

In some industries, a single company with an overwhelming share of the market, what economists call a dominant firm, competes against many small producers, each of whom has a small market share. For example, in Germany, Deutsche Telecom had 64 percent of the long distance telephone market in 1999. The next largest competitor, Mobilcom, had just 10 percent.[13] Taking a more historical view, U.S. Steel was once the dominant firm in the U.S. steel industry, and Alcoa was the dominant firm in the aluminum industry.

Figure 13.7 illustrates a model of price setting by a dominant firm. Market demand is D_M. The dominant firm sets the market price and splits the market demand with a group of small firms that constitute the industry's competitive fringe. Fringe firms produce identical products and act as perfect competitors: each chooses a quantity of output, taking the market price as given. The curve S_F is the competitive fringe's supply curve.[14]

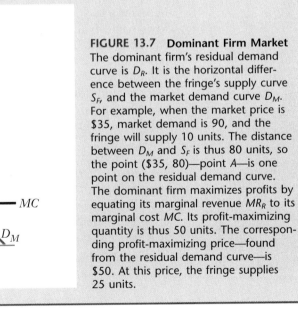

FIGURE 13.7 Dominant Firm Market
The dominant firm's residual demand curve is D_R. It is the horizontal difference between the fringe's supply curve S_F, and the market demand curve D_M. For example, when the market price is $35, market demand is 90, and the fringe will supply 10 units. The distance between D_M and S_F is thus 80 units, so the point ($35, 80)—point A—is one point on the residual demand curve. The dominant firm maximizes profits by equating its marginal revenue MR_R to its marginal cost MC. Its profit-maximizing quantity is thus 50 units. The corresponding profit-maximizing price—found from the residual demand curve—is $50. At this price, the fringe supplies 25 units.

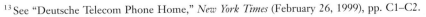

[13] See "Deutsche Telecom Phone Home," *New York Times* (February 26, 1999), pp. C1–C2.

[14] With a fixed number of fringe firms, S_F is the horizontal summation of fringe marginal cost curves. The vertical intercept of S_F thus shows the minimum price at which a fringe firm would supply output.

The dominant firm's problem is to find a price that maximizes its profits, taking into account how that price affects the competitive fringe's supply. To solve this problem, we need to identify the dominant firm's residual demand curve. This curve tells us how much the dominant firm can sell at different prices. We derive it by subtracting the fringe's supply from the market demand at each price. For example, at a price of $35, market demand is 90 units, and the price-taking fringe would supply 10 units. The dominant firm's residual demand at a price of $35 is thus 80 units. The point ($35, 80)—point A in Figure 13.7—is thus one point on the dominant firm's residual demand curve. By identifying the horizontal distance between D_M and S_F at every price, we can trace out the full residual demand curve D_R. At prices less than $25 per unit, fringe firms will not supply output, and the dominant firm's residual demand curve coincides with the market demand curve. At $75, the dominant firm's residual demand shrinks to zero, and fringe firms satisfy the entire market demand.

The dominant firm finds its optimal quantity and price by equating the marginal revenue MR_R associated with the residual demand curve to its marginal cost MC, which equals $25 in Figure 13.7. We see that the dominant firm's optimal quantity equals 50. Its profit-maximizing price—$50 per unit—is the price along the residual demand curve corresponding to the quantity of 50. We use the residual demand curve D_R, rather than the market demand curve D_M, to determine the price because it is the residual demand curve, not the market demand curve, that tells us how much the dominant firm can sell at various market prices. Given the supply behavior of the fringe, the dominant firm must set a price of $50 to sell 50 units per year.

At the profit-maximizing price of $50, market demand is 75 units per year and the competitive fringe supplies 25 units. By setting a price of $50, which is twice as high as the minimum price of $25 at which fringe firms would be willing to supply output, the dominant firm creates a price umbrella that allows some fringe firms to operate profitably. This price is also profitable for the dominant firm, which earns a profit equal to ($50 − $25) × 50, or $1,250 per year.

Figure 13.8 shows what happens when the size of the competitive fringe grows because additional fringe producers enter the market. The fringe's supply curve pivots rightward, from S_F to S'_F, which in turn pivots the dominant firm's residual demand curve leftward from D_R to D'_R. As a result, the dominant firm sets a lower price—$42 per unit rather than $50 per unit. Its optimal quantity continues to be 50 units, but the fringe's supply increases from 25 to 33.[15] The dominant firm's market share falls from 67 percent to 60 percent, and its profit falls from $1,250 to $833.

Given this, why doesn't the dominant firm do something to slow the rate of entry of fringe firms? The prices $50 and $42 maximize the dominant firm's profit at a particular point in time (e.g., in a given year). But if the rate of entry by fringe firms depends on the current market price, the dominant firm might want

---

[15] The dominant firm's profit-maximizing quantity stayed at 50 units per year because of the way we constructed the demand curve and fringe supply curve for this example. A shift in the fringe's supply curve could, in general, change the dominant firm's profit-maximizing output.

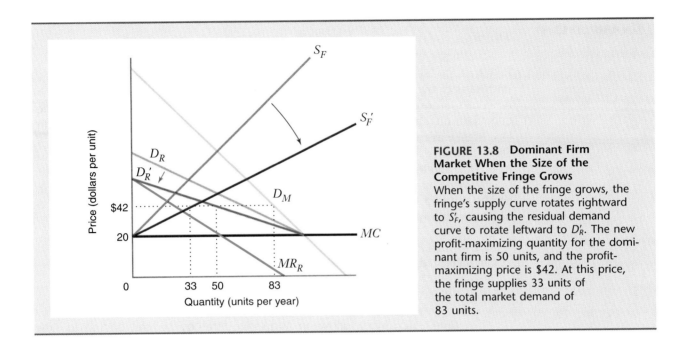

FIGURE 13.8 Dominant Firm Market When the Size of the Competitive Fringe Grows
When the size of the fringe grows, the fringe's supply curve rotates rightward to S_F', causing the residual demand curve to rotate leftward to D_R'. The new profit-maximizing quantity for the dominant firm is 50 units, and the profit-maximizing price is $42. At this price, the fringe supplies 33 units of the total market demand of 83 units.

to follow a strategy of **limit pricing.** Under a limit pricing strategy, the dominant firm keeps its price below the level that maximizes its current profit to reduce the rate of expansion by the fringe.[16] Under limit pricing, the dominant firm sacrifices profits today in order to keep future profits higher than they would otherwise be.

A limit pricing strategy is most appealing when high current price induces the competitive fringe to expand rapidly.[17] Limit pricing is also attractive when the dominant firm takes the "long view" and emphasizes future over current profits in making decisions. Finally, the limit pricing strategy tends to be attractive when a dominant firm has a significant cost advantage over its rivals. A cost advantage allows the dominant firm to keep its price low to slow the rate of entry without much sacrifice of current profit.

[16] It is an interesting question—beyond the scope of this book—why the rate of fringe expansion might depend on the current industry price. One possibility is that existing fringe firms rely on current profits to finance their expansion plans, and so a lower price will mean lower current profits and (for some) more difficulty expanding their capacity. This point, however, is subtle (e.g., if expansion is profitable, why can't fringe firms go to their bankers and get a loan to fund their expansion plans), and is best explored in advanced courses, such as industrial economics and finance.

[17] These insights about the limit pricing problem come from D. Gaskins, "Dynamic Limit Pricing: Optimal Pricing Under the Threat of Entry," *Journal of Economic Theory, 3* (September 1971): 306–322.

EXAMPLE 13.3   *Dominant Firm Pricing by U.S. Steel*[18]

With sales of over $6 billion, the U.S. Steel group of the USX Corporation is one of America's largest steel companies. But while large in absolute terms, U.S. Steel accounts for only about 11 percent of U.S. domestic steel sales. At one time, though, U.S. Steel was much bigger. In fact, when it was formed (by merger) in 1901, U.S. Steel produced 66 percent of the steel ingot sold in the United States. In those days, U.S. Steel was a classic dominant firm.

However, as Table 13.5 shows, U.S. Steel's market share soon began to decline, and by the mid-1930s, it had fallen to 33 percent of the market. According to economic historians Thomas K. McCraw and Forest Reinhardt:

> For three decades [1900–1930], U.S. Steel followed patterns of pricing and investment that guaranteed an erosion of its market share. Instead of raising barriers to entry into the steel industry, it lowered them. It neither tried vigorously to retain its existing markets nor to take advantage of new growth opportunities in structural and rolled markets.

Why didn't U.S. Steel follow an aggressive strategy of limit pricing to slow the expansion by rival firms? Our discussion of dominant firm pricing illuminates why. Scholars who have studied the history of U.S. Steel believe that before World War II (1941–1945), U.S. Steel probably did not have an appreciable cost advantage over its competitors. F. M. Scherer writes, "Although some of the Corporation's plants may have had lower costs, on average USS could pour and shape steel at costs no lower than those of its rivals, actual or potential."[19] In addition, as Scherer notes, entry into the steel industry in the early twentieth century took time. It required building an integrated steel mill, and it was not (in those days) easy to secure either financial capital or reliable sources of iron ore.

As a result, it probably made sense for U.S. Steel to eschew an aggressive limit pricing strategy and instead set prices at or close to the levels implied by the dom-

TABLE 13.5
U.S. Steel's Market Share 1901–1935

Year	Market Share	Year	Market Share
1901	66%	1920	46%
1905	60%	1925	42%
1910	54%	1930	41%
1915	51%	1935	33%

[18] This example was inspired by a fuller and more detailed discussion of U.S. Steel's history and dominant firm pricing behavior by F. M. Scherer in Chapter 5 of his book *Industry Structure, Strategy, and Public Policy* (New York: HarperCollins, 1996). The quotation below and the data in Table 13.5 come from McCraw, T. K. and F. Reinhardt, "Losing to Win: U.S. Steel's Pricing, Investment Decisions, and Market Share, 1901–1938," *Journal of Economic History* XLIX (September 1989), pp. 593–619.

[19] F. M. Scherer, *Structure, Strategy, and Public Policy* (New York; HarperCollins, 1996), p. 155.

inant firm model. And, as we saw from Figure 13.8, with an expanding fringe, this implied an erosion of the dominant firm's share over time. Hideki Yamawaki provides some statistical evidence that U.S. Steel actually behaved this way.[20] Using data on steel prices and production (by U.S. Steel and rival firms) from that era, Yamawaki shows that U.S. Steel's pricing decisions were influenced by the market share of fringe producers. He also shows that the price set by U.S. Steel significantly influenced the fringe's rate of production and the rate at which the fringe expanded over time. Based on this evidence, we can conclude that the logic of the dominant firm model nicely fits competitive dynamics in the U.S. steel industry from 1900 to 1940. ■

13.4
OLIGOPOLY
WITH
DIFFEREN-
TIATED
PRODUCTS

In many markets, such as beer, ready-to-eat breakfast cereals, automobiles, and soft drinks, firms sell products that consumers consider distinctive from each other. In these markets, we say that firms produce differentiated products. We briefly discussed product differentiation in Chapter 11. In this section, we take a deeper look at product differentiation and then explore how firms in a differentiated products oligopoly might compete against each other.

WHAT IS PRODUCT DIFFERENTIATION?

Economists distinguish between two types of product differentiation: vertical product differentiation and horizontal product differentiation. **Vertical differentiation** is about inferiority or superiority. Two products are vertically differentiated when consumers consider one product better or worse than the other. Duracell batteries are vertically differentiated from generic store-brand batteries because they last longer. This makes Duracell batteries unambiguously superior to store-brand batteries.

Horizontal differentiation is about substitutability. Two products, A and B, are horizontally differentiated when, at equal prices, some consumers view B as a poor substitute for A and thus will continue to buy A, even when A's price is higher than B's, while other consumers view A as a poor substitute for B and thus will continue to buy B, even when B's price is higher than A's. Diet Coke and Diet Pepsi are horizontally differentiated. Some consumers view Diet Pepsi as a poor substitute for Diet Coke, while other view Diet Coke as a poor substitute for Diet Pepsi.[21]

Horizontal differentiation and vertical differentiation are distinctive forms of product differentiation. For example, all consumers might agree that Duracell batteries are better than a store-brand battery because they last twice as long, but if all consumers also regard two store-brand batteries as equivalent to one Duracell battery, then the two products, though vertically differentiated, would not

---

[20] H. Yamawaki, "Dominant Firm Pricing and Fringe Expansion: The Case of the U.S. Iron and Steel Industry, 1907–1930," *The Review of Economics and Statistics*, 67 (August 1985): 429–437.

[21] We see this at our office at Northwestern in the fact that students and faculty continue to buy Diet Pepsi from a vending machine even though its price per ounce is higher than the Diet Coke that is sold less than 30 feet away at the student cafe.

be horizontally differentiated.[22] Once the store-brand price was less than half the price of Duracell, all consumers would switch to the store brand. By contrast, although few people could make a compelling case that Diet Coke has an unambiguously higher quality than Diet Pepsi, some consumers have loyalties toward one brand over the other, and thus do not regard the products as perfect substitutes. These brands are horizontally differentiated but not vertically differentiated.

Horizontal differentiation is an important concept for the theory of oligopoly and monopolistic competition that we study in this chapter. When firms sell horizontally differentiated products, they will have downward-sloping demand curves. Figure 13.9(a) shows that when horizontal differentiation is weak, a firm's demand is sensitive to changes in the price of its product. A small increase in price (holding competitors' prices fixed) will induce consumers to switch to the other products that consumers regard as close substitutes. Moreover, a decrease in a competitor's price (holding the firm's price fixed) will cause a significant drop in the demand for the firm's product—that is, it will result in a big leftward shift in the firm's demand curve. In short, weak horizontal differentiation implies that

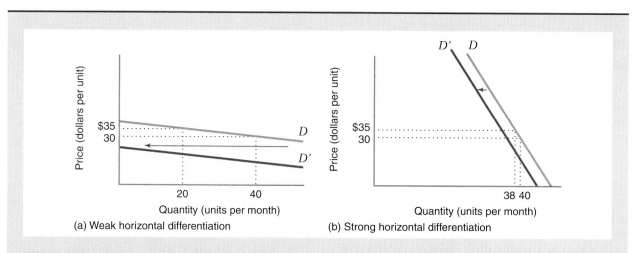

FIGURE 13.9   Horizontal Differentiation and the Firm's Demand Curve
In panel (a), horizontal differentiation is weak. The firm's demand curve D is downward sloping, but the quantity demanded is sensitive to changes in the firm's price. A given increase in price, say from $30 per unit to $35 per unit, holding competitors' prices fixed, leads to a large reduction in the quantity demanded. Moreover, when competitors reduce their prices, the firm's demand curve shifts leftward, from D to D', by a large amount. By contrast, in panel (b), horizontal differentiation is stronger. The firm's demand is not as sensitive to a change in its own price, and when competitors cut their prices, the firm's demand curve does not shift much.

[22] In the language of Chapters 4 and 5, consumer indifference curves for Duracell batteries and store-brand batteries would be linear. In reality, consumers might not equate two store-brand batteries with one Duracell battery because of the convenience factor. A battery that lasts longer takes up less space than two batteries and does not have to be changed as often. For simplicity, here we ignore the convenience factor.

firms face large own- and cross-price elasticities of demand. Figure 13.9(b) shows that when horizontal differentiation is strong, a firm's demand is less sensitive to its own price and to the prices of competitors. In that case, firms face relatively smaller own- and cross-price elasticities of demand.

EXAMPLE 13.4

Horizontal Product Differentiation—Apple versus Microsoft Windows[23]

In the late 1980s, Apple Computer was a symbol of the American economic renaissance. From 1986 to 1989, the company's return on investment exceeded its cost of capital by 27 percent. Wall Street loved Apple, and investors flocked to buy its stock. In the movie *Forrest Gump*, Lieutenant Dan invested Gump's shrimp-boat earnings in Apple stock—and Gump became a millionaire (from an orchard, he said).

But within a decade, Apple had fallen apart. Apple's CEO John Sculley was fired in 1993. His successor, Michael Spindler, was fired in 1996. His successor, Gil Amelio, was fired in 1997. In 1996, the company lost $816 million. In 1997, it lost $1.04 billion.

Apple's collapse is a complicated story that involves both economics and personalities. But one important factor in its demise in the early 1990s was the narrowing of product differentiation that existed between Macintosh computers and IBM-compatible personal computers (PCs) that ran on Intel microprocessors and the Microsoft operating system. In 1989, you could clearly see the difference between a Mac and a PC. Macs relied on an easy-to-use graphical-user-interface controlled by the click of a mouse. IBM-compatible PCs used the confusing and cumbersome DOS operating system. As one analyst said at the time, "The majority of IBM and compatible users 'put up' with their machines, but Apple customers 'love' their Macs."[24]

Until 1990, the personal computer market exhibited clear horizontal differentiation. Serious number-crunchers preferred Intel-based computers because of their power, and businesses often preferred them because of the availability of DOS-based "killer apps" such as Lotus 1-2-3 and Word Perfect. Home users, especially those with kids, loved Apples for their ease of use, while graphics designers loved the Mac because of its superior desktop publishing and multimedia capabilities. This strong horizontal differentiation allowed Apple to follow what John Sculley called the 50–50–50 rule: If Apple can sell 50,000 Macs per month with a gross margin of 50 percent, its stock price would be $50 per share.[25]

But the release of Windows 3.0 in 1990 eroded this horizontal differentiation. Windows 3.0 was still inferior to the Apple's operating system, but it was nevertheless a big improvement over DOS. Suddenly, IBM-compatible PCs became much more user-friendly. For many consumers, particularly home buyers that used IBM-compatible PCs at work, the user-friendliness was just "good enough."

---

[23] This example draws from *Apple Computer 1992*, Harvard Business School Case 9-792-081 and J. Carlton, *Apple: The Inside Story of Intrigue, Egomania, and Business Blunders* (New York: Times Business), 1997.

[24] *Apple Computer 1992*, p. 7.

[25] Gross margin is the difference between a firm's price and the average cost of making its product, expressed as a percentage of the selling price.

The narrowing of product differentiation hurt Apple. During the second half of the 1980s, prices of IBM-compatible PCs fell, as low-cost clone makers, such as Dell and Gateway, entered the market and used price to compete against established firms, such as IBM. Until the early 1990s, the horizontal differentiation between the Mac and DOS was so strong that Apple was largely immune from the effects of this price war. For many consumers, a cheap clone was a poor substitute for an elegant Mac, and so, as in Figure 13.9(b), Apple's demand curve was largely unaffected by falling PC prices. But with Windows installed, those cheap clones looked a lot better. By 1991 Apple found itself under severe pressure from the price war among the "Wintel" producers. It responded by cutting prices on all its Macs and rolling out a low-end Mac Classic for under $1,000. But with the highest marginal costs in the personal computer industry, Apple could not make much money by cutting prices. Moreover, despite lower-priced Macs, the Wintel side of the market enjoyed a huge momentum from the wide availability of business software and games.

Apple eventually abandoned its attempts to compete on price and is now a niche player in the personal computer industry. Its hugely successful (and colorful) iMacs have restored some of its former product differentiation. Apple has also dramatically improved its operating efficiency (e.g., its inventories are even leaner than Dell's, a company widely admired for its lean inventory management). But Apple remains strongest in a few segments (desktop publishing, education markets) that are small parts of the broader PC market. In 1998 Steve Jobs, one of the co-founders of Apple, returned as President. He has helped restore Apple's reputation for innovation with a series of sleekly designed computers. Still as long as the Windows operating system remains "good enough," Apple may find it difficult to increase its market share substantially. ∎

BERTRAND PRICE COMPETITION WITH HORIZONTALLY DIFFERENTIATED PRODUCTS

Let's now study how firms in a differentiated products market would set their prices. To do so, we return to the model of Bertrand price setting and adapt it to deal with horizontally differentiated products.[26] As a specific illustration of this model, let's consider a market in which product differentiation is significant: the U.S. cola market.

Farid Gasmi, Quang Vuong, and J. J. Laffont (GVL) have used statistical methods to estimate demand curves for Coke (Firm 1) and Pepsi (Firm 2):[27,28]

---

[26] We could also study a Cournot quantity-setting model of competition in a model of differentiated products. Just as the the Cournot model with no product differentiation leads to a different equilibrium than the Bertrand price model, the Cournot quantity-setting model with product differentiation leads to a different equilibrium price than the Bertrand model that we study in this section. You will get a chance to prove this point for yourself in Problem 13.10.

[27] The use of this example was inspired by our former colleague, Matt Jackson, who used it in teaching his microeconomics classes at the Kellogg Graduate School of Management.

[28] F. Gasmi, Q. Vuong, and J. Laffont, "Econometric Analysis of Collusive Behavior in a Soft-Drink Market," *Journal of Economics and Management Strategy* (Summer 1992): 277–311. To keep the numbers simple, we have rounded GVL's estimates (which come from Model 10 in the paper) to the nearest whole number. In their paper, prices are inflation-adjusted and are expressed in dollars per unit, while quantities are expressed in millions of units of cola; a unit is defined as 10 cases, with twelve 24-ounce cans in each case.

$$Q_1 = 64 - 4P_1 + 2P_2. \qquad (13.1)$$

$$Q_2 = 50 - 5P_2 + P_1. \qquad (13.2)$$

These demand functions imply that Coke and Pepsi are horizontally differentiated: When Coke raises its price, Coke's demand falls gradually. GVL also estimated that Coca-Cola and Pepsi had marginal costs of $5 and $4, respectively.[29] Given these demand curves and marginal costs, what price should each firm charge?

As in the Cournot model, an equilibrium occurs when each firm is doing the best it can given the actions of its rival. The logic of finding this equilibrium is similar to the logic of the Cournot model, so we begin by deriving each firm's price reaction function—that is, its profit-maximizing price as a function of its rival's price.

Consider Coca-Cola's problem. Figure 13.10(a) shows Coke's demand curve when Pepsi sets a price of $8. (We denote this curve D_8 to emphasize that Pepsi's price is $8.) This curve tells us how much Coke can sell at various prices, given that Pepsi's price remains fixed at $8. Note that D_8 satisfies equation (13.1). For example, when Pepsi sets a price of $8 and Coke sets a price of $7.50, Coke can sell 50 million units. Equating Coca-Cola's marginal revenue to its marginal cost tells us that its profit-maximizing output is 30. To sell this quantity, Coke must set a price of $12.50. Thus, $12.50 is Coke's best response to Pepsi's price of $8.

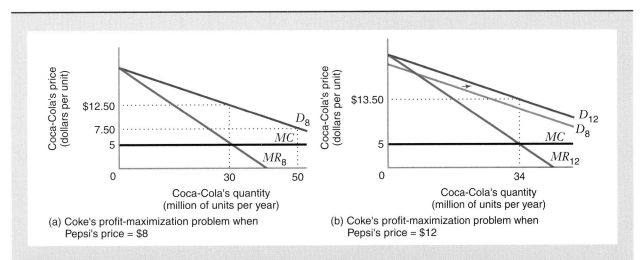

FIGURE 13.10 Profit-Maximizing Price Setting by Coca Cola
Panel (a) shows that when Pepsi sets a price of $8, Coca-Cola's demand curve is D_8. This demand curve tells us the quantity that Coke can sell at various prices, given that Pepsi's price is $8. For example, if Coca-Cola sets a price of $7.50, it can sell 50 million cases of Coke per year. Given this demand curve, Coca-Cola's profit-maximizing price is $12.50 and its profit-maximizing quantity is 30 million cases per year. Thus, $12.50 is Coke's best response to Pepsi's price of $8. Panel (b) shows that when Pepsi's price is $12, Coca-Cola's demand curve is D_{12}. Given this demand curve, Coca-Cola's profit-maximizing price is $13.50. Thus, $13.50 is Coke's best response to Pepsi's price of $12.

---

[29]These are also expressed in dollars per unit.

Figure 13.10(b) shows that when Pepsi sets a price of $12, Coca-Cola's best response is to charge $13.50.

Figure 13.11 depicts Coke's and Pepsi's reaction functions in a graph with P_1 on the horizontal axis and P_2 on the vertical axis. Coke's reaction function R_1 tells us how its profit-maximizing price varies with Pepsi's price, and Pepsi's reaction function R_2 tells us how its profit-maximizing price depends on the price Coke sets. Note that the profit-maximizing prices for Coke that are shown in Figure 13.9, ($P_1 = \$12.50$, $P_2 = 8$) and ($P_1 = \$13.50$, $P_2 = 12$), are points along R_1. Note, too, that the reaction functions are upward-sloping. Thus, the lower your rival's price is, the lower your price should be. In this sense, "aggressive" behavior by one firm (price cutting) is met by "aggressive" behavior by rivals. Note the contrast with the Cournot model, where "aggressive" behavior by one firm (output expansion) was met by "passive" behavior by rivals (output reduction).

At the Bertrand equilibrium, each firm chooses a price that maximizes its profit given the other firm's price.[30] In Figure 13.11, this occurs where the two reaction functions intersect, $P_1^* = \$12.56$ and $P_2^* = \$8.26$. By substituting these prices back into the demand functions, we can compute the equilibrium quanti-

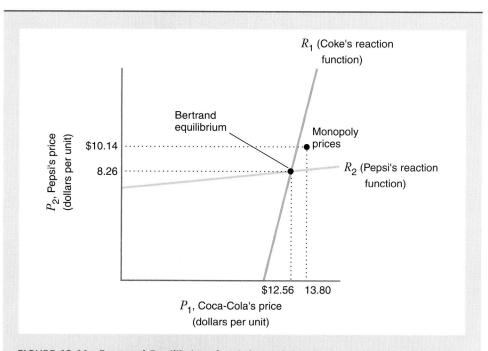

FIGURE 13.11 Bertrand Equilibrium for Coke and Pepsi
Coke's reaction function is R_1. This tells us Coke's profit-maximizing price given Pepsi's price. Pepsi's reaction function is R_2. It tells us Pepsi's profit-maximizing price given Coke's price. The Bertrand equilibrium occurs where the two reaction functions intersect. This occurs when Coke charges a price of $12.56 and Pepsi charges a price of $8.26.

[30]Like the Cournot equilibrium, you will see in Chapter 14 that the Bertrand equilibrium is a particular example of a Nash equilibrium. For this reason, some textbooks refer to the Bertrand equilibrium as the Nash equilibrium in prices.

ties for Coca-Cola and Pepsi: $Q_1^* = 30.28$ million units and $Q_2^* = 22.88$ million units. In fact, the average (inflation-adjusted) prices over the time period (1968–1986) of GVL's study were actually $12.96 for Coca-Cola and $8.16 for Pepsi. The corresponding quantities were 30.22 million units and 22.72 million units. Thus, the Bertrand model, when applied to the demand curves estimated by GVL, does a good job of matching the actual pricing behavior of these two firms in the U.S. market.

Why is Pepsi's equilibrium price so much lower than Coca-Cola's price? For two important reasons. First, Pepsi's marginal cost is lower than Coke's. Second, and more subtly, Pepsi's own price elasticity of demand is larger than Coke's. You can confirm this by computing each firm's own price elasticities of demand at the equilibrium prices. Or you can go back to Example 2.5 in Chapter 2 and review the own price elasticities of demand that GVL estimated for Coke and Pepsi.[31] Since we know (from Chapter 11) that profit maximization along a downward-sloping demand curve implies an inverse elasticity pricing rule (IEPR), applying the IEPR to Coke and Pepsi's pricing problem implies that Pepsi should have a smaller markup than Coke. A smaller markup applied to a smaller marginal cost makes Pepsi's price lower than Coca-Cola's.

Given the equilibrium prices, the percentage contribution margins (PCMs) for Coke and Pepsi are

$$\frac{P_1^* - MC_1}{P_1^*} = \frac{12.56 - 5}{12.56} = 0.60 \text{ or } 60 \text{ percent.}$$

$$\frac{P_2^* - MC_2}{P_2^*} = \frac{8.26 - 4}{8.26} = 0.52 \text{ or } 52 \text{ percent.}$$

To interpret these numbers, Coke's PCM implies that for every dollar's worth of Coke that Coca-Cola sells, it has 61 cents left over to cover marketing expenses, company overhead, interest, and taxes. This PCM is higher than the typical U.S. manufacturing firm.[32] This example thus illustrates how product differentiation softens price competition. When products are as strongly differentiated as Coke and Pepsi are, price cutting is less effective for stealing a rival's business than when products are perfect substitutes. Of course, Coke and Pepsi incur a heavy cost to achieve this product differentiation. Both companies spend hundreds of millions of dollars in the United States to advertise their colas. And, as discussed in the introduction to this chapter, the two companies compete intensely for exclusive distribution deals on college campuses to develop brand loyalties among young people.

---

[31]Since GVL computed their elasticities at the actual average prices, your calculations based on the computed equilibrium prices won't exactly match those in Example 2.5, but they will be close.

[32]A commonly used estimate of the PCM can be contructed from data from the U.S. Census of Manufacturing:

$$\frac{\text{Sales revenue} - \text{Materials cost} - \text{Factory payrolls}}{\text{Sales revenue}}$$

This measure uses material and labor costs as a proxy for marginal cost. Historically, this measure of PCM has been on the order of 23 to 25 percent for all U.S. manufacturing firms.

Even though horizontal differentiation softens price competition, the Bertrand equilibrium prices do not correspond to the monopoly prices (i.e., the prices that maximize the joint profit of Pepsi and Coca-Cola). As Figure 13.11 shows, these prices are about $13.80 for Coke and $10.14 for Pepsi. As in the Cournot model, independent profit-maximizing oligopolists will typically not attain the outcome that a profit-maximizing monopolist would. This is because in making its pricing decisions independently, neither firm takes into account the adverse affect that a price cut or the beneficial effect that a price increase would have on its rival.

LEARNING-BY-DOING EXERCISE 13.3

Computing a Bertrand Equilibrium with Differentiated Products

Problem

(a) What is Coca-Cola's profit-maximizing price, given that Pepsi sets a price of $8?
(b) What is Coca-Cola's profit-maximizing price when Pepsi sets an arbitrary price P_2 (i.e., what is the equation of Coca-Cola's reaction function)?
(c) What is Pepsi's best response to any arbitrary price P_1 for Coke?
(d) Compute the Bertrand equilibrium prices for Coke and Pepsi in this market.

Solution

(a) Substitute $P_2 = 8$ into equation (13.1) to get the perceived demand curve D_8 in Figure 13.10(a). $Q_1 = 64 - 4P_1 + 16 = 80 - 4P_1$. Expressing this in inverse form gives us $P_1 = 20 - 0.25Q_1$. (You should verify that this describes the graph of D_8 in Figure 13.10.) The associated marginal revenue curve is

$$MR = 20 - 0.5Q_1.$$

Equating this marginal revenue to Coke's marginal cost yields

$$20 - .5Q_1 = 5, \text{ or } Q_1 = 30.$$

We get Coke's profit-maximizing price by substituting this quantity back into the equation of Coke's perceived demand curve: $P_1 = 20 - 0.25(30) = 12.50$. This is Coke's best response when Pepsi charges a price of $8.
(b) Coca-Cola's perceived demand curve is given by $Q_1 = (64 + 2P_2) - 4P_1$, where we use parentheses to highlight the terms that Coke views as fixed. Let's express this curve in inverse form by solving for P_1 in terms of Q_1:

$$P_1 = \left(16 + \frac{1}{2}P_2\right) - \frac{1}{4}Q_1.$$

You should verify that when we substitute in $P_2 = 8$ and $P_2 = 12$, we get the equations of D_8 and D_{12} in Figure 13.10. Once again, using what we know about marginal revenue curves for linear demand curves, Coca-Cola's marginal revenue is

$$MR = \left(16 + \frac{1}{2}P_2\right) - \frac{1}{2}Q_1.$$

Equating marginal revenue to marginal cost yields Coke's profit-maximizing quantity:

$$\left(16 + \frac{1}{2}P_2\right) - \frac{1}{2}Q_1 = 5, \text{ or } Q_1 = 22 + P_2.$$

To find Coke's profit-maximizing price, substitute this back into Coke's perceived demand curve:

$$P_1 = \left(16 + \frac{1}{2}P_2\right) - \frac{1}{4}(22 + P_2), \text{ or } P_1 = 10.5 + \frac{1}{4}P_2.$$

This is Coca-Cola's reaction function.

(c) We use the same logic that we just used. Pepsi's perceived demand curve is given by $Q_2 = (50 + P_1) - 5P_2$. Expressing this in inverse form we get,

$$P_2 = \left(10 + \frac{1}{5}P_1\right) - \frac{1}{5}Q_2.$$

The corresponding marginal revenue curve is

$$MR = \left(10 + \frac{1}{5}P_1\right) - \frac{2}{5}Q_2.$$

Equating this to Pepsi's marginal cost of \$4 gives us Pepsi's profit-maximizing quantity:

$$\left(10 + \frac{1}{5}P_1\right) - \frac{2}{5}Q_2 = 4, \text{ or } Q_2 = 15 + \frac{1}{2}P_1.$$

To get Pepsi's profit-maximizing price, we substitute this back into Pepsi's perceived demand curve:

$$P_2 = \left(10 + \frac{1}{5}P_1\right) - \frac{1}{5}\left(15 + \frac{1}{2}P_1\right), \text{ or } P_2 = 7 + \frac{1}{10}P_1.$$

This is Pepsi's reaction function.

(d) The Bertrand equilibrium occurs where the two reaction functions intersect. This corresponds to the pair of prices that simultaneously solve the two firms' reaction functions:

$$P_1 - \frac{1}{4}P_2 = 10.5 \text{ (Coke's reaction function, rearranged)}.$$

$$-\frac{1}{10}P_1 + P_2 = 7 \text{ (Pepsi's reaction function, rearranged)}.$$

The solution to this system of equations yields the equilibrium prices: $P_1^* = \$12.56$, $P_2^* = \$8.26$. We find the equilibrium quantities by substituting these prices into each firm's demand curve:

$$Q_1^* = 64 - 4(12.56) + 2(8.26) = 30.28;$$

$$Q_2^* = 50 - 5(8.26) + 12.56 = 21.26.$$

Similar Problems: 13.3, 13.5

EXAMPLE 13.5 *Bertrand Price Competition: Eurotunnel versus the Channel Ferry Boats*

One of the most impressive feats of modern engineering is the 32-mile-long Channel Tunnel (Chunnel) that links Calais, France, to Dover, England. Eurotunnel (ET), the company that owns and operates the Chunnel, offers two main services: passenger service and freight service. Under ET's passenger service, called Le Shuttle, you drive your car aboard specially designed rail cars at a terminus of the tunnel, and a train then transports your car (with you inside) through the tunnel to the other end.[33] Under ET's freight services, trucks are driven aboard special rail cars, and the train transports the trucks through the tunnel. For both of these services, ET competes against cross-channel ferries. When the Chunnel opened, there were two major ferry companies: Britain's P&O and Sweden's Stena Line. Together, they carried about 80 percent of the cross-channel passenger and freight traffic. Since then, these two companies have merged their cross-channel operations and compete as a duopolist against ET.[34]

Before the Chunnel opened, John Kay, Alan Manning, and Stefan Szymmanski (KMS) used the Bertrand model of price competition to analyze the likely outcome of price competition between ET and the ferry operators (which they presciently treated as a single firm) in the market for freight service. Using information from ET's 1987 prospectus (a document prepared for investors and lenders discussing its plan for doing business) and some educated back-of-the-envelope conjectures, KMS estimated price reaction functions for both ET and the ferry operators. Figure 13.12 shows these reaction functions. The Bertrand equilibrium that they predicted occurred at a price of £87 for the tunnel and £150 for the ferry operators. At this price, KMS conjectured that the tunnel would capture about 75 percent of the freight business, while the ferries would get the remaining 25 percent.

Two factors account for the big difference between the estimated equilibrium prices of the tunnel and the ferries: the relatively high price sensitivity of freight shippers (i.e., ferries and the tunnel were characterized by relatively low levels of horizontal differentiation) and the significant difference between the marginal cost of the ferry operators and the marginal cost of the Chunnel. KMS estimated that

[33] This service is also offered for buses.
[34] The European Union Commission gave its final approval to this merger in January 1999. The joint venture is called P&O Stena Line.

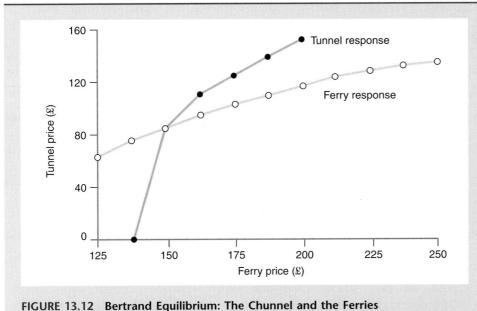

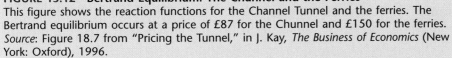

FIGURE 13.12 Bertrand Equilibrium: The Chunnel and the Ferries
This figure shows the reaction functions for the Channel Tunnel and the ferries. The Bertrand equilibrium occurs at a price of £87 for the Chunnel and £150 for the ferries. *Source*: Figure 18.7 from "Pricing the Tunnel," in J. Kay, *The Business of Economics* (New York: Oxford), 1996.

the Chunnel's marginal cost of carrying a car or a truck was one-tenth that of the ferries. This is mainly because to carry an extra truck or motor car, ET doesn't need to expand the size of the Chunnel. (Indeed, given the size of the Chunnel and ET's investment in equipment, ET's capacity was more than two times as big as the entire amount of cross-channel traffic that was expected in the mid-1990s.) By contrast, ferries have significantly smaller capacities, and so to carry more cars or trucks, a ferry operator would need to put more ferries into service, hire more crew members, spend more on fuel, and pay more port fees.

When KMS did their analysis, ET anticipated that ferry rates would fall modestly after the Chunnel opened and that ET's best response would be to match those rates. KMS painted a different competitive picture, illustrating that ET would be more profitable if it significantly undercut the prices charged by the ferries. Competitive dynamics between the ferries and the tunnel have more closely resembled those predicted by KMS than those predicted by ET's own managers in its 1987 prospectus. ET's prices are now significantly below the ferry prices that prevailed before the tunnel opened, and the Chunnel now claims a significant fraction of the cross-channel traffic. For example, in 1996, ET captured 44 percent of the cross-channel truck traffic versus 40 percent for the ferries. And ET's 41 percent of the passenger traffic equalled P&O and Stena's combined share.[35]

Given KMS's prediction that ET would capture almost 75 percent of the freight traffic at equilibrium prices, you might wonder why ET's share of the freight market is "only" 44 percent. Part of the reason is that the two ferry operators have

[35]"Channel Ferries Plan Merger to Fight Tunnel," *Reuters Business Report* (October 3, 1996).

matched ET's fares rather than keep them higher, as the Bertrand equilibrium model predicted they would. In light of what we know about the marginal cost differences between ET and the ferries, we have to question whether this is a viable long-run strategy for the ferry operators. Both ferry operators were clearly hurt by the opening of the Chunnel. Indeed, one of the factors behind the decision of Stena and P&O to merge their cross-channel ferry operations was the desire to coordinate their capacity and scheduling decisions to respond to the competitive threat the Chunnel created. Some observers of this market predict that this merger is likely to lead to an increase in prices, and this might be happening. In late 1998, P&O Stena raised its freight fares by 15 percent.[36]   ∎

13.5 MONOPOLISTIC COMPETITION

A monopolistically competitive market has three distinguishing features.[37] First, the market is fragmented. It consists of many buyers and sellers. Second, there is free entry and exit. Any firm can hire the inputs (labor, capital, and so forth) needed to compete in the market, and they can release these inputs from employment when they do not need them. Third, firms produce horizontally differentiated products. Consumers view firms' products as *imperfect* substitutes for each other.

Local retail and service markets often have these characteristics. Consider, for example, the restaurant market within the city of Evanston, Illinois. The market is highly fragmented—the Evanston Yellow Pages, for example, has nearly five pages of restaurant listings. The Evanston restaurant market also has free entry and exit. Prospective restaurateurs can easily rent space, acquire cooking equipment, and hire servers. A comparison of the Yellow Pages listings for 1994 with those for 1999 reveals a remarkable turnover of establishments. When times are good, new restaurants are opened. When a restaurant proves to be unprofitable, it is shut down.

Market fragmentation and free entry and exit are also characteristics of perfectly competitive markets. But unlike perfectly competitive firms, Evanston restaurants are characterized by significant product differentiation. There are many different types of restaurants (Chinese, Thai, Italian, vegetarian) that cater to the wide variety of buyer tastes that exist in Evanston. Some restaurants are formal, while others are casual. And each restaurant is conveniently located for people who live or work close to it but might be inconvenient for people who have to drive several miles to get to it.

SHORT-RUN AND LONG-RUN EQUILIBRIUM IN MONOPOLISTICALLY COMPETITIVE MARKETS

In choosing their prices, monopolistic competitors behave much like the differentiated products oligopolists that we studied in the previous section. Taking the

---

[36]"Strikes and Fares Blow on Chunnel," *Daily Telegraph* (November 14, 1998), p. 11.

[37]Monopolistic competition was developed by the economist Edward Chamberlin is his book *The Theory of Monopolistic Competition* (Cambridge, MA: Harvard University Press), 1933.

prices of other firms as given, each firm faces a downward-sloping demand curve. Even though the market is fragmented, a firm's demand curve will be downward sloping because of product differentiation. Each firm maximizes its profit at the point at which its marginal revenue equals marginal cost.

Figure 13.13 illustrates the profit-maximization problem facing a typical firm under monopolistic competition. Taking the prices of other firms as given, our firm faces a demand function D. When the firm maximizes its profit along this demand curve, it charges a price of $43 and produces an output of 57 units. The price of $43 is the firm's best response to the prices charged by other firms in the market. As in the Bertrand model of oligopoly with differentiated products, the market attains an equilibrium when *every* firm is charging a price that is a best response to the set of prices charged by *all other* firms in the market. Let's suppose this condition holds when each firm in the market sets a price of $43.

What, then, makes monopolistic competition different from a differentiated products oligopoly? The key difference is that monopolistically competitive markets are characterized by free entry. If profit opportunities in the market exist, new entrants will appear to seize these opportunities. In Figure 13.13, note that the price of $43 exceeds the firms' average cost. The typical firm in the market is thus earning positive economic profits. The situation in Figure 13.13 constitutes a short-run equilibrium—a typical firm is maximizing profits given the actions of rival firms—but it is not a long-run equilibrium. We expect that firms will enter this market to take advantage of the profit opportunity that currently exists.

What happens as more firms enter? As more firms come into the market, each firm's share of overall market demand will fall. This causes a leftward shift of a typical firm's demand curve. Entry and the resultant leftward shift in firms' demand curves will cease when firms make zero economic profit. In Figure 13.14, this occurs at a price of $20. When the average industry price is $20, each firm's demand curve D' is tangent to its average cost curve AC. Firms that are in the market make zero economic profit. Put another way, the margin between a firm's

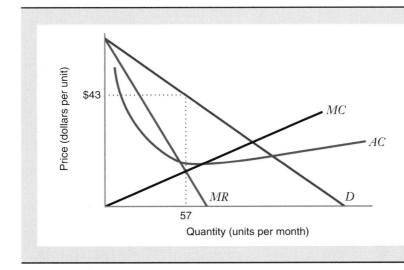

FIGURE 13.13 Profit Maximization and Short-Run Equilibrium Under Monopolistic Competition
A typical firm faces a demand curve D, and maximizes profit by producing at the point at which marginal revenue equals marginal cost. The profit-maximizing price is thus $43. If we suppose that each firm is maximizing its profits, given the prices of rival firms, the market will be in short-run equilibrium. It is not in long-run equilibrium, however, because the price of $43 exceeds the typical firm's average cost at the output of 57 units per month. This situation will attract new entrants to the industry.

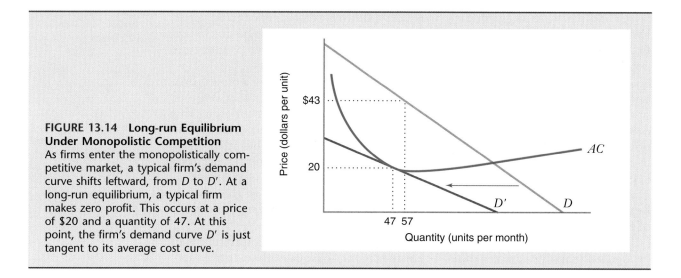

FIGURE 13.14   Long-run Equilibrium Under Monopolistic Competition
As firms enter the monopolistically competitive market, a typical firm's demand curve shifts leftward, from D to D'. At a long-run equilibrium, a typical firm makes zero profit. This occurs at a price of $20 and a quantity of 47. At this point, the firm's demand curve D' is just tangent to its average cost curve.

price and its variable costs is just sufficient to cover its fixed costs of operation and the up-front costs of entering the business. Given that this is so, entrants have no incentive to come into the market.

PRICE ELASTICITY OF DEMAND, MARGINS, AND MARKET STRUCTURE

In monopolistically competitive markets, free entry and exit of firms determines how many firms ultimately compete in the market. Figure 13.15 illustrates two possible outcomes that could emerge in a long-run equilibrium.

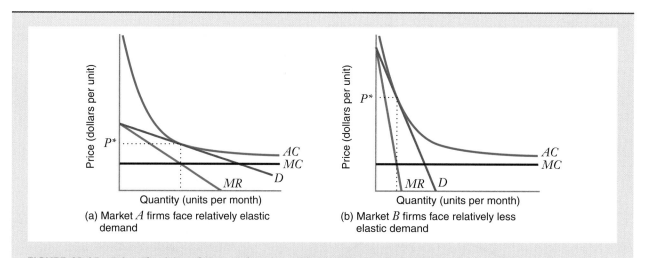

FIGURE 13.15   Price Elasticity of Demand and Equilibrium Market Structure
In Market A, firms face relatively elastic demand. At a long-run equilibrium, the margin $P* - MC$ between price and marginal cost is small, and each firm produces a large volume of output. In Market B, firms face relatively less elastic demand. At a long-run equilibrium, the margin between price and marginal cost is large, and each firm produces a small volume of output.

In Market *A*, consumers are sensitive to price differences when they choose among existing sellers. A seller in this market has a demand curve that is highly price elastic. In a long-run equilibrium, the margin ($P^* - MC$) between price and marginal cost is small, and firms produce a large volume of output. By contrast, in Market *B*, consumers are not especially sensitive to price differences among competing sellers. As a result, a firm's demand is not as sensitive to price as in Market *A*. In a long-run equilibrium, the margin between price and marginal cost is large and each firm produces a small volume of output. If the total number of units purchased in equilibrium is about the same in Markets *A* and *B*, Market *B* would have more firms than Market *A*. Because demand in Market *B* is relatively less price elastic, firms are able to operate at prices significantly above marginal cost, which in turn means that Market *B* can profitably support more firms than Market *A*, where price elastic demand conditions necessitate that firms operate with relatively thin margins.

Wine or Roses? The Structure of Local Retail Markets

EXAMPLE 13.6

If you look in your local *Yellow Pages*, you will probably see that there are a lot more florists than liquor stores. For example, the 1998 Evanston, Illinois, *Yellow Pages* (which covers Evanston and several other communities on the North Shore of Chicago) listed 124 flower shops but only 31 liquor stores. You see a similar pattern in the Bloomington, Indiana, *Yellow Pages*: it lists 26 florists but only 14 liquor stores.

Why is this? Do these numbers tell us that there is significantly more demand for roses than wine? Probably not. In fact, the typical U.S. household probably spends more per year on wine, beer, and spirits than it does on flowers. Instead, this pattern of local retail market structure probably reflects (at least in part) the logic of Figure 13.15.[38] The analysis in Figure 13.15 implies that when there is free entry, markets in which firms can attain high margins of price over marginal cost should contain numerous small firms, while markets in which firms have low margins of price over marginal cost should have bigger but fewer firms. In a high-margin market such as *B* in Figure 13.15, a firm does not need to attain a large volume of sales in order to cover the up-front costs of entry and the fixed costs of doing business. Lots of firms can fit into the market, and with free entry, lots of firms will enter. In low-margin markets such as *A* in Figure 13.15, a firm needs to attain a larger volume in order to cover its up-front costs of entry and its fixed costs of doing business. Fewer firms can fit into the market, and with free entry, fewer will enter.

In retailing, the margin between price and marginal cost is best approximated by what is called the *gross margin*. The gross margin represents the difference between a product's price and its cost to the retailer, expressed as a percentage of the price. Flower shops typically have gross margins that exceed 40 percent. By contrast, liquor stores have gross margins that are typically close to 20 percent. The logic of Figure 13.15 tells us that, all else equal, the typical local retail market should have

---

[38]It could also, of course, reflect other factors, such as differences in cost conditions across the two retail trades, differences in the extent of product variety available in flower shops versus liquor stores, and the fact that beer and wine (but not spirits) can also be purchased in grocery and convenience stores.

more flower shops than liquor stores, the pattern we observe in Evanston and Bloomington. It also suggests that we should see more jewelry stores (whose gross margins have historically been 50 percent) than bakeries (gross margins of 40 percent) and more bakeries than hardware stores (gross margins between 20 and 30 percent). In Evanston, Illinois, and Bloomington, Indiana, we do: Evanston's *Yellow Pages* listed 101 jewelry stores, 60 bakeries, and 26 hardware stores. Bloomington's *Yellow Pages* listed 36 jewelry stores, 16 bakeries, and 13 hardware stores. Page through your local *Yellow Pages* to see whether this pattern holds in your town.   ■

DO PRICES FALL WHEN MORE FIRMS ENTER?

When we studied the Cournot model earlier in this chapter, we saw that the equilibrium price went down as more firms competed in the market. Figure 13.14 portrays a similar phenomenon in a monopolistically competitive market. In that figure, the entry of more firms resulted in a reduction in the market price.

But will this always happen? Not necessarily. To see why, consider Figure 13.16, which shows a monopolistically competitive industry that has attained a long-run equilibrium at a price of $50. Suppose, now, that all firms experience a decrease in their average cost (represented by a shift from *AC* to *AC'* in the figure). At the current price of $50, firms now enjoy positive economic profit, which encourages the entry of additional firms. When long-run equilibrium is restored, a typical firm again earns zero profits. In Figure 13.16 this occurs at the higher price of $55 per unit. The entry of more firms drives the equilibrium price up!

Why could this happen? One reason is that the new entrants might lure away the less loyal customers of existing firms—those that are more or less indifferent among competing sellers—leaving each existing firm with a small core of loyal customers. In effect, the entry of additional firms into the market could push existing firms into narrow niches of the market. For example, in the video rental market in an urban area, the entry of new video stores might cause an existing store to lose customers located far away from the store, leaving the store to operate in

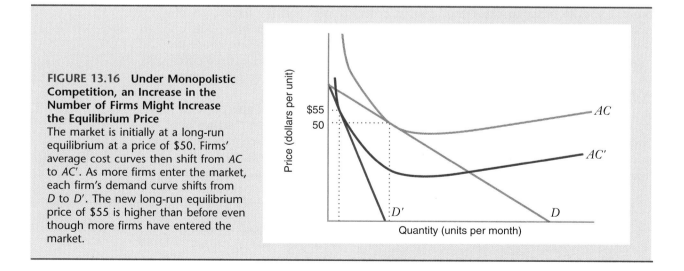

FIGURE 13.16 Under Monopolistic Competition, an Increase in the Number of Firms Might Increase the Equilibrium Price
The market is initially at a long-run equilibrium at a price of $50. Firms' average cost curves then shift from *AC* to *AC'*. As more firms enter the market, each firm's demand curve shifts from *D* to *D'*. The new long-run equilibrium price of $55 is higher than before even though more firms have entered the market.

a niche that consists of customers located in a few surrounding blocks of the store. These people remain loyal to the store because for them it is conveniently located. Another reason is that as more firms enter the market, consumers might find it more difficult to learn and compare the prices of all the sellers in the market. With less efficient comparison shopping, consumers could become less sensitive to price in choosing which seller to buy from. Under both of these explanations, a typical firm's demand curve would, as Figure 13.16 shows, become steeper as more firms enter. When demand shifts in this fashion due to new entry, each firm's output could fall by such a large amount that it moves to a higher point along its new average cost curve. At the new long-run equilibrium, more firms are in the market, but each firm is smaller than before and charges a higher price.

Can More Firms Lead to Higher Prices? The Case of Primary Care Physicians Markets

EXAMPLE 13.7

Local markets for doctors are a good example of monopolistic competition. Different doctors produce differentiated products, and entry and exit are not difficult. Mark Pauly and Mark Satterthwaite studied the relationship between price and the number of physicians in 92 metropolitan markets in the United States.[39] After controlling for demographic and market factors that might plausibly affect the average price of a patient's visit to a primary care doctor, Pauly and Satterthwaite found that an increase in the number of primary care physicians per square mile (a measure of the number of primary care doctors in the local market) was associated with an increase in the average price per office visit. In other words, markets with more firms also had higher prices.

What would explain this finding? Pauly and Satterthwaite observe that consumers search among physicians mainly by asking friends, relatives, or co-workers for recommendations. In local markets with a small number of doctors (three or four, for example), search is easy: Each doctor will probably have a well-known reputation throughout the market. Most consumers will probably have a pretty clear impression of each doctor and the prices he or she charges. However, in markets with many physicians, it is probably harder for consumers to keep straight the various pieces of information they might learn about different doctors in the market. As a result, consumer search tends to be much less efficient. Because it is harder for consumers to comparison shop, consumers might become less sensitive to price in markets in which there are many doctors. In such markets, an individual physician's demand curve would be more likely to resemble D' in Figure 13.16 than D.

To explore whether the efficiency of consumer search might have had something to do with the pattern of prices they observed, Pauly and Satterthwaite looked at whether physicians' prices in markets in which a large proportion of the population had recently moved (and thus had poorer information about local doctors) were higher than in markets in which households were more settled. They were. This and other evidence they collected suggests that the efficiency of the consumer search process is an important determinant of prices in local physicians markets. ∎

---

[39] M. Pauly and M. Satterthwaite, "The Pricing of Primary Care Physicians' Services: a Test of the Role of Consumer Information," *Bell Journal of Economics*, 12 (1982): 488–506.

CHAPTER SUMMARY

• In the Cournot model of oligopoly, each firm chooses a level of output, taking as given the level of output of its competitors.

• At the Cournot equilibrium, each firm chooses a level of output that maximizes its profit, given the output of the other firms. Thus, at a Cournot equilibrium, no firm has any after-the-fact regret about its output choice. **(LBD Exercises 13.1, 13.2)**

• The Cournot theory of oligopoly pertains to firms that make a single, once-and-for-all decision on output. The Cournot equilibrium outcome is a natural focal point for firms that fully understand that they are simultaneously choosing output on a once-and-for-all basis and have full confidence in the rationality of their rival.

• In a market in which firms produce perfect substitutes, the Cournot equilibrium price will be less than the monopoly price but greater than the perfectly competitive price. **(LBD Exercises 13.2)**

• With a larger number of firms in the industry, the Cournot equilibrium industry output goes up and the equilibrium market price goes down.

• We can characterize the Cournot equilibrium using a modified inverse elasticity pricing rule (IEPR).

• In the Bertrand model of oligopoly, each firm selects a price to maximize profits, given the prices other firms set.

• In a homogeneous products industry in which all firms have the same constant marginal cost, the Bertrand equilibrium price is equal to marginal cost.

• We can reconcile the different predictions made about industry equilibrium in the Cournot and Bertrand

models in two ways. First, the Cournot model can be thought of as pertaining to long-run capacity competition, while the Bertrand model can be thought of as pertaining to short-run price competition for firms with sufficient capacity to satisfy market demand. Second, the two models make different assumptions about the expectations each firm has about its rivals' reactions to its competitive moves.

• In a dominant firm market, the dominant firm takes the competitive fringe's supply curve into account in setting a price. If the fringe's supply is growing over time, the dominant firm's price will fall and its share of the market might also fall.

• Two products are vertically differentiated when consumers view one product as unambiguously better or worse than the other.

• Two products are horizontally differentiated when some consumers regard one as a poor substitute for the other, while other consumers have the opposite opinion.

• In a Bertrand equilibrium with differentiated products, equilibrium prices generally exceed marginal cost. When horizontal product differentiation between the firms is significant, the gap between prices and marginal costs can be substantial. **(LBD Exercise 13.3)**

• A monopolistically competitive market contains many firms, each facing a downward-sloping demand curve. A short-run equilibrium is attained when every firm chooses a profit-maximizing price, given the prices of all other firms.

• In a long-run equilibrium in a monopolistically competitive market, free entry drives firms' economic profits to zero.

REVIEW QUESTIONS

1. Explain why, at a Cournot equilibrium with two firms, neither firm would have any regret about its output choice after it observes the output choice of its rival.

2. What is a reaction function? Why does the Cournot equilibrium occur at the point at which the reaction functions intersect?

3. Why is the Cournot equilibrium price less than the monopoly price? Why is the Cournot equilibrium price greater than the perfectly competitive price?

4. Explain the difference between the Bertrand model of oligopoly and the Cournot model of oligopoly. In a homogeneous products oligopoly, what predictions do these models make about the equilibrium price relative to marginal cost?

5. What is the role played by the competitive fringe in the dominant firm model of oligopoly? Why does an increase in the size of the fringe result in a reduction in the dominant firm's profit-maximizing price?

6. What is the difference between vertical product differentiation and horizontal product differentiation?

7. Explain why, in the Bertrand model of oligopoly with differentiated products, a greater degree of product differentiation is likely to increase the markup between price and marginal cost.

8. What are the characteristics of a monopolistically competitive industry? Provide an example of a monopolistically competitive industry.

9. Why is it the case in a long-run monopolistically competitive equilibrium that the firm's demand curve is tangent to its average cost curve? Why could it not be a long-run equilibrium if the demand curve "cut through" the average cost curve?

PROBLEMS

13.1. A homogeneous products duopoly faces a market demand function given by $P = 300 - 3Q$, where $Q = Q_1 + Q_2$. Both firms have a constant marginal cost $MC = 100$.
a) What is Firm 1's profit-maximizing quantity, given that Firm 2 produces an output of 50 units per year? What is Firm 1's profit-maximizing quantity when Firm 2 produces 20 units per year?
b) Derive the equations of each firm's reaction curve and then graph these curves.
c) What is the Cournot equilibrium quantity per firm and price in this market?
d) What would the equilibrium price in this market be if it were perfectly competitive?
e) What would the equilibrium price in this market be if the two firms colluded to set the monopoly price?
f) What is the Bertrand equilibrium price in this market?
g) What are the Cournot equilibrium quantities and industry price when one firm has a marginal cost of 100 but the other firm has a marginal cost of 90?

13.2. A homogeneous products oligopoly consists of two firms, and each firm has a marginal cost curve, $MC = 10 + Q_i$, $i = 1, 2$. The market demand curve is $P = 50 - Q$, where $Q = Q_1 + Q_2$.
a) What are the Cournot equilibrium quantities and price in this market?
b) What would be the equilibrium price in this market if the two firms acted as a profit-maximizing cartel?
c) What would the equilibrium price in this market be if firms acted as price-taking firms?

13.3. A homogeneous products oligopoly consists of four firms, each of which has a constant marginal cost $MC = 5$. The market demand curve is given by $P = 15 - Q$.
a) What are the Cournot equilibrium quantities and price? Assuming that each firm has zero fixed costs, what is the profit earned by each firm in equilibrium?

b) Suppose Firms 1 and 2 merge but in so doing their marginal cost remains at 5. What are the new Cournot equilibrium quantities and price? Is the profit of the merged firm bigger or smaller than the combined profit of Firms 1 and 2 in the initial equilibrium in part a? Provide an explanation for the effect of the merger on profit in this market.

13.4. An industry is known to face market price elasticity of demand $\epsilon_{Q,P} = -3$. (Think of this elasticity as being approximately constant as the industry moves along its demand curve.) The marginal cost in this industry is $10 per unit, and there are 5 firms in the industry. What would the Lerner Index be at the Cournot equilibrium in this industry?

13.5. Suppose that the market demand for cobalt is given by $Q = 200 - P$. Suppose that the industry consists of 10 firms, each with a marginal cost of $40 per unit. What is the Cournot equilibrium quantity for each firm? What is the equilibrium market price?

13.6. Consider the same setting as in the previous problem, but now suppose that the industry consists of a dominant firm, Braeutigam Cobalt (BC), that has a constant marginal cost equal to $40 per unit. There are 9 other fringe producers, each of whom has a marginal cost curve $MC = 40 + 10q$, where q is the output of a typical fringe producer. Assume there are no fixed costs for any producer.
a) What is the supply curve of the competitive fringe?
b) What is BC's residual demand curve?
c) Find BC's profit-maximizing output and price. At this price, what is BC's market share?
d) Repeat parts (a) to (c) under the assumption that the competitive fringe consists of 18 firms.

13.7. Consider the Coke and Pepsi example discussed in the chapter.
a) Explain why each firm's reaction function slopes upward. That is, why does Coke's profit-maximizing price

go up the higher is Pepsi's price? Why does Pepsi's profit-maximizing price go up the higher Coke's price is?
b) Explain why Pepsi's profit-maximizing price seems to be relatively insensitive to Coke's price. That is, why is Pepsi's reaction function so *flat*?

13.8. Again, consider the Coke and Pepsi example discussed in the chapter. Use graphs of reaction functions to illustrate what would happen to equilibrium prices if:
a) Coca-Cola's marginal cost increased.
b) For any pair of prices for Coke and Pepsi, Pepsi's demand went up.

13.9. When firms choose *outputs*, as in the Cournot model, reaction functions slope downward. But when firms choose *prices*, as in the Bertrand model with differentiated products, reaction functions slope upward. Why do output reaction functions differ from price reaction functions in this way?

13.10. United Airlines and American Airlines both fly between Chicago and San Francisco. Their demand curves are given by

$$Q_A = 1000 - 2P_A + P_U$$
$$Q_U = 1000 - 2P_U + P_A.$$

Q_A and Q_U stand for the number of passengers per day for American and United, respectively, measured in terms of numbers of passengers per day. The marginal cost of each carrier is $10 per passenger.
a) If American sets a price of $200, what is the equation of United's perceived demand curve and its per-ceived marginal revenue curve? What is United's profit-maximizing price when American sets a price of $200?
b) Redo part a under the assumption that American sets a price of $400.
c) Derive the equations for American and United's price reaction curves.
d) What is the Bertrand equilibrium in this market?

13.11. (*advanced*) Suppose American and United take each others quantity as given rather than taking each others price as given. That is, assume that American and United act as Cournot competitors rather than Bertrand competitors. The inverse demand curves corresponding to the demand curves in the previous problem are[40]

$$P_A = 1000 - \frac{2}{3} Q_A - \frac{1}{3} Q_U$$
$$P_U = 1000 - \frac{2}{3} Q_U - \frac{1}{3} Q_A.$$

a) Suppose that American chooses to carry 660 passengers per day, i.e., $Q_A = 660$. What is United's profit-maximizing quantity of passengers? Suppose American carries 500 passengers per day. What is United's profit-maximizing quantity of passengers?
b) Derive the quantity reaction functions for each firm.
c) What is the Cournot equilibrium in quantities for both firms? What are the corresponding equilibrium prices for both firms?
d) Why does the Cournot equilibrium in this problem differ from the Bertrand equilibrium in the previous problem?

APPENDIX: The Cournot Equilibrium and the Inverse Elasticity Price Rule

At a Cournot equilibrium, each firm equates its marginal cost to the marginal revenue corresponding to its residual demand curve:

$$P^* + \frac{\Delta P}{\Delta Q}Q_i^* = MC, \text{ for } i = 1, 2, \ldots, N, \tag{A.1}$$

where Q_i^* is firm i's equilibrium output. Rearranging condition (A.1) gives us

$$\frac{P^* - MC}{P^*} = -\frac{\Delta P}{\Delta Q}\frac{Q_i^*}{P^*}. \tag{A.2}$$

[40]We derived the inverse demand curves by solving the two demand curves simultaneously for the prices, P_A and P_U, in terms of the quantities, Q_A and Q_U.

Multiplying the top and bottom of the right-hand side of (A.2) by overall market output Q^* gives us

$$\frac{P^* - MC}{P^*} = -\left(\frac{\Delta P}{\Delta Q} \frac{Q^*}{P^*}\right)\frac{Q_i^*}{Q^*}. \tag{A.3}$$

Now note that $(\Delta P/\Delta Q)(Q^*/P^*) = 1/\epsilon_{Q,P}$, i.e., the inverse of the price elasticity of demand. Moreover, note that Q_i^*/Q^* is firm i's equilibrium market share. If all firms are identical, then each firm will split the market evenly. Thus, $Q_i^*/Q^* = 1/N$. We can thus write the Cournot equilibrium condition in (A.3) as a modified inverse elasticity pricing rule:

$$\frac{P^* - MC}{P^*} = -\frac{1}{\epsilon_{Q,P}} \times \frac{1}{N}. \tag{A.4}$$

14

Game Theory and Strategic Behavior

In the late 1990s, both Honda and Toyota had to decide whether to build new auto assembly plants in North America.[1] By adding more production capacity, each firm would be able to sell more cars in the United States and Canada. On the face of it, the decision to add capacity seemed sound. Both Honda and Toyota were making money from the cars they sold in North America, and by selling more cars each company would make even more money.[2] But because demand in the North American automobile market was not growing that fast, a decision by both firms to build new plants and increase production would probably make prices on competing models (e.g., Honda Civics and Toyota Corollas; Honda Accords and Toyota Camrys) lower than they otherwise would be. It seemed possible that if *both firms* built new plants, both would be worse off than if *neither* built new plants. Each firm's decision making was thus complicated by the interdependence that existed between its decision and that of its rival. Because Toyota and Honda were making their decision at approximately the same time, each firm would need to take into account the probable behavior of the other.

Game theory is the branch of microeconomics concerned with the analysis of optimal decision making

in competitive situations, situations in which the actions of each decision maker have a significant impact on the fortunes of rival decision makers. Though the term *game* might sound frivolous, in fact there are many interesting situations that can be studied as games. The competitive interaction between Honda and Toyota is one example. Honda's decision to add capacity affects the profit that Toyota could expect to gain by building a new plant, and Toyota's decision to add capacity affects the additional profit that Honda could reap by con-

structing a new plant. A game theoretic analysis of this interaction can help us better understand the decision problem that each firm faced. Other social interactions in which game theory has been fruitfully applied include the competition among buyers in auctions, races by nations to accumulate nuclear weapons, and competition between candidates in elections.

Our goal in this chapter is to introduce you to the central ideas of game theory and to give you an appreciation for the wide variety of competitive situations to which game

[1] See, for example, "Detroit Challenge: Japanese Car Makers Plan Major Expansion of American Capacity," *Wall Street Journal* (September 24, 1997), p. A1.

[2] In addition, the Hondas and Toyotas built in the new plants in the United States would be exempt from U.S. tariffs. Also, by building U.S. plants, Honda and Toyota would also insulate Japan from criticism by U.S. politicians because the cars would be built by American workers.

theory can be applied. In many ways, you already began your study of game theory in Chapter 13. Most of the theories of oligopoly (e.g., Cournot, Bertrand) you studied in that chapter are particular examples of game theory models. Our hope is that this chapter will build on that foundation and equip you with basic game theory concepts and tools that will enable you to analyze competitive interactions, such as that between Honda and Toyota in the North American automobile market, that arise in real life. ∎

14.1
THE CONCEPT OF NASH EQUILIBRIUM

A SIMPLE GAME

To introduce the key ideas of game theory, we begin with the easiest kind of game to analyze: a one-shot, simultaneous-move game. In this type of game, two or more players make a single decision, at the same time. To illustrate, consider the competition between Honda and Toyota in the North American automobile market described in the introduction. Recall that in 1997 each firm faced the decision of whether to build a new auto assembly plant in North America. Table 14.1 describes the potential impact of each firm's capacity expansion decision. Each firm has two choices or **strategies**—build a new plant or do not build—which thus gives rise to four capacity expansion scenarios. A player's strategy in a game specifies the actions that each player might take under every conceivable circumstance that the player might face. In a one-shot, simultaneous-move game, strategies are simple: they consist of a single decision.

The first entry in each cell is Honda's annual economic profit (in millions of dollars) under a scenario; the second entry is Toyota's annual economic profit (in millions of dollars).[3] These profits represent the payoffs in the game: the amount that each player can expect to get under different combinations of strategy choices by the players. The payoffs in Table 14.1 show the extent to which the players in this game are interdependent: Toyota's payoff depends on what Honda does, and vice versa. In game theory, a player will very rarely control its own fate. The payoffs in Table 14.1 are fictitious but accurately reflect the dynamic that existed between these two firms at the time.

TABLE 14.1
Capacity Expansion Game Between Toyota and Honda

		Toyota	
		Build a New Plant	Do Not Build
Honda	Build a New Plant	16, 16	20, 15
	Do Not Build	15, 20	18, 18
	(payoffs are in millions of dollars)		

[3] In this, and in all subsequent tables in this chapter, we use the following convention. The first entry is the payoff of the player listed on the side of the table—the so-called *row player* because this player chooses among the different rows in the table. The second entry is the payoff of the player listed at the top of the table—the so-called *column player*, because this player chooses among the different columns in the table.

THE NASH EQUILIBRIUM

Game theory seeks to answer the question: What is the likely outcome of a game? To identify "likely outcomes" of games, game theorists use the concept of a **Nash equilibrium.** At a Nash equilibrium, each player chooses a strategy that gives it the highest payoff, given the strategies chosen by the other players in the game. Does this sound familiar? If you recently finished reading Chapter 13, it should. This is the same idea that we used to define a Cournot equilibrium (in a quantity-setting oligopoly) and a Bertrand equilibrium (in a price-setting oligopoly). In fact, both of these equilibrium "concepts" are particular examples of the Nash equilibrium.

In this game, the Nash equilibrium strategy for each firm is "Build a New Plant."

- Given that Toyota builds a new plant, Honda's best response is also to build a new plant: It gets a profit of $16 million if it builds but only $15 million if it does not build. (*Note:* For the "row" player Honda, we compare payoffs between the two rows.)

- Given that Honda builds a new plant, Toyota's best response is to build: It gets a profit of $16 million if it builds versus the $15 million it gets if it doesn't expand its capacity. (*Note:* For the "column" player, we compare payoffs between the two columns.)

Why does the Nash equilibrium represent a plausible outcome of a game? Probably its most compelling property is that the Nash equilibrium outcome is self-enforcing. If each party expects the other party to choose its Nash equilibrium strategy, then both parties will, in fact, choose their Nash equilibrium strategies. At the Nash equilibrium, then, expectation equals outcome—expected behavior and actual behavior converge. This would not be true at non–Nash equilibrium outcomes, as the game in Table 14.1 illustrates. If Toyota (perhaps foolishly) expects Honda not to build a new plant but builds a new plant of its own, then Honda—pursuing its own self-interest—would confound Toyota's expectations, build a new plant, and make Toyota worse off than it expected to be.

THE PRISONERS' DILEMMA

The capacity-expansion game between Toyota and Honda illustrates a noteworthy aspect of a Nash equilibrium. The Nash equilibrium does not necessarily correspond to the outcome that maximizes the aggregate profit of the players. Toyota and Honda would be collectively better off by not building new plants. However, the rational pursuit of self-interest leads each party to take an action that is ultimately detrimental to their collective interest.

This conflict between the collective interest and self-interest is often referred to as the **prisoners' dilemma.** The game in Table 14.1, as well as both the Cournot quantity-setting and Bertrand price-setting models from Chapter 13, are particular examples of prisoners' dilemma games—games in which the Nash equilibrium does not coincide with the outcome that maximizes the collective payoffs of the players in the game. The prisoners' dilemma is based on the following scenario: Two suspects in a crime, David and Ron, are arrested and placed in separate cells. The police, who have no real evidence to convict either, give each prisoner the chance to confess and implicate the other suspect for the crime. If neither confesses, both will be convicted on a minor charge and will serve just one year in jail. If both confess, both are convicted of the more serious crime, but they are treated somewhat leniently because they cooperated. Each goes to jail for five years. But if one suspect confesses and the other doesn't, the one that confesses goes free, while the other is convicted of the crime and spends ten years in jail. Table 14.2 shows the payoffs for this game, with jail terms corresponding to negative payoffs. (As in Table 14.1, the first payoff in each cell is that of the row player, Ron, and the second payoff is that of the column player, David.)

The Nash equilibrium in this game is for each player to confess. Given that David confesses, Ron gets a lighter jail term by confessing than by not confessing. And given that Ron confesses, David gets a lighter jail term by confessing than by not confessing. In equilibrium, both prisoners end up confessing and serving five years in jail, even though collectively they would be better off not confessing and spending only one year in jail.

The prisoners' dilemma is widely studied throughout the social sciences. Psychologists, political scientists, sociologists, and economists find the prisoners' dilemma a compelling idea because the tension it portrays between an individual player's self-interest and a group's collective interest shows up in many different ways in the world around us. For example, business firms start price wars, even though all firms in the industry get hurt as a result. Politicians run "attack ads" even though the bad will and distrust they engender makes it difficult for the winner of the election to govern effectively. The analysis of the prisoners' dilemma game can help us understand why these apparently counterproductive outcomes can occur.

DOMINANT AND DOMINATED STRATEGIES

Dominant Strategies

In the game between Toyota and Honda in Tables 14.1 finding the Nash equilibrium was easy because for each firm, the strategy "Build a New Plant" was better than "Do Not Build" no matter what strategy the other firm chose (e.g., if Toyota builds a new plant, Honda gets $16 million instead of $15 million by building a new plant, too; if Toyota doesn't build, Honda gets $20 million instead of $18 million by building a new plant). In this situation, we say that "Build a New Plant" is a **dominant strategy**. A dominant strategy is a strategy that is better than any other strategy a player might choose, no matter what strategy the other player follows. When a player has a dominant strategy, that strategy will be the player's Nash equilibrium strategy.

TABLE 14.2
Prisoners' Dilemma Game

		David	
		Confess	Do Not Confess
Ron	Confess	−5, −5	0, −10
	Do Not Confess	−10, 0	−1, −1

The Prisoners' Dilemma and the Law

Modern American society has been criticized for being excessively litigious. Individuals and firms seem increasingly willing to turn to lawyers to resolve their disputes. But if, as is commonly argued, this dependence on litigation has significant social costs, why would a free market system generate so much business for lawyers?

The research of two economists, Orley Ashenfelter and David Bloom, suggests a possible answer.[4] The decision to hire a lawyer to resolve a dispute is, they argue, the result of a prisoners' dilemma. Two parties in a dispute are collectively better off when they settle the dispute between themselves or hire a neutral arbitrator to resolve their differences. But if a party believes that by hiring a lawyer it will increase the odds of winning by a sufficiently large amount to make hiring a lawyer worthwhile, it will be a dominant strategy to hire a lawyer. But when both parties do this, the dispute is resolved no differently than if neither hired a lawyer, and each party is worse off by the amount it pays its attorney.

To test this theory, Ashenfelter and Bloom analyzed public employee wage disputes from 1981 to 1984 in New Jersey. They also studied union grievance proceedings involving the rights of discharged workers in Pennsylvania. In both cases, they found strong evidence that hiring a lawyer is a dominant strategy and that the decision to hire a lawyer leads to a prisoners' dilemma. Based on the New Jersey data, for example, they found that when one party hired a lawyer, the chances of successfully persuading the arbitrator to accept its wage proposal went up from roughly 50 percent to 75 percent. When both sides hired lawyers, though, the odds of winning remained roughly 50 percent, indicating that the benefit of hiring a lawyer is canceled out when the other party also hires a lawyer.

The possibility that hiring a lawyer is a prisoners' dilemma suggests that making society less litigious is likely to prove quite difficult. Lawyers clearly have no interest in curbing the demand for their services. And the logic of the prisoners' dilemma suggests that a party in a dispute has a strong individual incentive to hire a lawyer, even though society as a whole would be better off if he or she did not. ■

Dominant strategies are not inevitable. In many games some or all players do not have dominant strategies. Consider, for example, the capacity expansion game in Table 14.3 between Ambassador ("Amby") and Marutti in the automobile market in India. In this market, Marutti is much bigger than Amby and makes better cars. It thus gets far more profit than Amby does, no matter what capacity scenario occurs.

In this game, Marutti does not have a dominant strategy. It is better off not building a new plant if Amby builds one, but it prefers to build a new plant if Amby doesn't build. Despite the absence of dominant strategy for Marutti, there is still a Nash equilibrium: Amby builds a new plant, and Marutti doesn't. To see why, note that if Amby builds, Marutti's best response is not to build: Marutti gets 15 million rupees if it doesn't build and only 12 million rupees if it builds.

[4] O. Ashenfelter and D. Bloom, "Lawyers as Agents of the Devil," Princeton University, working paper, 1994.

TABLE 14.3
Capacity Expansion Game Between Marutti and Ambassador

		Amby Build a New Plant	Amby Do Not Build
Marutti	**Build a New Plant**	12, 4	20, 3
	Do Not Build	15, 6	18, 5

(payoffs are in millions of rupees)

And if Marutti does not build, Amby's best response is to build: it gets 6 million rupees if it builds but only 5 million rupees if it doesn't build.

It is interesting to see how Marutti might figure out which strategy to choose in this game. If it envisions this payoff matrix, it should realize that while it does not have a dominant strategy, Amby does ("Build"). Thus, Marutti should reason that Amby will choose this dominant strategy, and given this, Marutti should choose "Do Not Build." The Nash equilibrium is a natural outcome of this game because Marutti's executives—putting themselves "inside the mind" of their rival—figures that their rival will choose its dominant strategy, which then pins down what Marutti should do. Placing yourself inside the mind of rival players in the game—seeing the world from their perspective, not yours—is one of the most valuable lessons of game theory. Barry Nalebuff and Adam Brandenberger call this allocentric reasoning, which should be contrasted with egocentric reasoning that views the world exclusively from one's own perspective.[5]

Dominated Strategies

The opposite of a dominant strategy is a **dominated strategy.** A strategy is dominated when the player has another strategy that gives it a higher payoff no matter what the other player does. In Table 14.1, with just two strategies for each player, if one strategy is dominant then the other must be dominated. However, with more than two strategies available to each player, the player might have dominated strategies, but no dominant strategy.

Identifying dominated strategies can sometimes help us deduce the Nash equilibrium in a game where neither player has a dominant strategy. To illustrate, let's return to the Honda–Toyota game, but now let's suppose that each firm has three strategies: Do not build, build a small plant, or build a large plant. Table 14.4 shows the payoffs from each of these strategies.

Neither player in this game has a dominant strategy, and with three strategies rather than two, the task of finding a Nash equilibrium seems rather daunting. But notice that for each player "Large" is a dominated strategy: No matter what Toyota does, Honda is always better off by choosing "Small" rather than "Large." Similarly, no matter what Honda does, Toyota is always better off choosing "Small" rather than "Large." If each player thinks about the payoffs of the other—that is, if each employs allocentric reasoning—each should conclude that

[5]Nalebuff, B.J. and A.M. Brandenberger, *Coopetition*, (New York: Currency Doubleday), 1996.

TABLE 14.4
Modified Capacity Expansion Game Between Toyota and Honda

		Toyota		
		Large	Small	Do Not Build
Honda	Large	0, 0	12, 8	18, 9
	Small	8, 12	16, 16	20, 15
	Do Not Build	9, 18	15, 20	18, 18

(payoffs are in millions of dollars)

its rival will not choose "Large." If each player assumes that the other will *not* choose "Large" (and rules out choosing "Large" itself), then the 3 × 3 game in Table 14.4 reduces to the 2 × 2 game in Table 14.5.

Does this game look familiar? It should. It is the same game as in Table 14.1. As in Table 14.1, in this reduced game, each player now has a dominant strategy: "Small." By eliminating a dominated strategy, we were able to find a dominant strategy for each player that, in turn, enabled us to find the Nash equilibrium in the full game.[6] The Nash equilibrium in the game in Table 14.4 is for each firm to build a small plant. You can, by the way, verify this directly from Table 14.4: If Toyota chooses "Small," Honda's best response is to choose "Small," and if Honda chooses "Small," Toyota's best response is to choose "Small."

Summary: Finding a Nash Equilibrium by Identifying Dominant Strategies and Eliminating Dominated Strategies

We can summarize the main conclusions of this section as follows:

- Whenever both players have a dominant strategy, those strategies will constitute the Nash equilibrium in the game.

TABLE 14.5
Modified Capacity Expansion Game Between Toyota and Honda After Eliminating Dominated Strategies

		Toyota	
		Small	Do Not Build
Honda	Small	16, 16	20, 15
	Do Not Build	15, 20	18, 18

(payoffs are in millions of dollars)

---

[6] This is the same logic that we employed in Chapter 13 when we argued that the Cournot equilibrium was the natural outcome of the one-shot quantity game between Samsung and LG.

- If just one player has a dominant strategy, that strategy will be the player's Nash equilibrium strategy. We can find the other player's Nash equilibrium strategy by identifying that player's best response to the first player's dominant strategy.
- If neither player has a dominant strategy, but both have dominated strategies, we can often deduce the Nash equilibrium by eliminating the dominated strategies of one player, and then eliminating the dominated strategies of the other. The elimination of dominated strategies almost always simplifies the analysis of a game.

LEARNING-BY-DOING EXERCISE 14.1

Finding the Nash Equilibrium by Identifying Dominant Strategies: Coke versus Pepsi

Problem   In Chapter 13, we studied price competition between Coke and Pepsi. Table 14.6 illustrates this competition in table form. It shows Coke and Pepsi's profits for various combinations of prices that each firm might charge. Let's find the Nash equilibrium in this game.

Solution   With four strategies for each firm, this looks like a complicated game. But we can greatly simplify it by searching for dominant strategies. For Pepsi, a price of $8.25 is a dominant strategy. To see why, compare Pepsi's pay-offs among the four rows in the table. You will see that Pepsi's payoff is always higher in row 3—a price of $8.25—than in any other row. Thus, a price of $8.25 for Pepsi is a dominant strategy, and the other three prices ($6.25, $7.25, and $9.25) are dominated strategies for Pepsi. We note the elimination of these dominated strategies in Table 14.6a by drawing a line through them.

We are now practically done. If Coke assumes that Pepsi will follow its dominant strategy, Coke should expect that Pepsi will set a price of $8.25. Given this price, Coke's best response is to set a price of $12.50.

The Nash equilibrium in this game if for Pepsi to set a price of $8.25 and Coke to set a price of $12.50. This corresponds to the equilibrium we derived in Chapter 13.

Similar Problems: 14.1, 14.2

TABLE 14.6
Price Competition Between Coke and Pepsi

		Coke			
		$10.50	$11.50	$12.50	$13.50
	$6.25	66, 190	68, 199	70, 198	73, 191
Pepsi	$7.25	79, 201	82, 211	85, 214	89, 208
	$8.25	82, 212	86, 224	90, 229	95, 225
	$9.25	75, 223	80, 237	85, 244	91, 245
		(payoffs in millions of dollars)			

TABLE 14.6a
Price Competition Between Coke and Pepsi After Identifying Pepsi's Dominant Strategy and Dominated Strategies

		Coke			
		$10.50	$11.50	$12.50	$13.50
Pepsi	$6.25	~~66, 190~~	~~68, 199~~	~~70, 198~~	~~73, 191~~
	$7.25	~~79, 201~~	~~82, 211~~	~~85, 214~~	~~89, 208~~
	$8.25	82, 212	86, 224	90, 229	95, 225
	$9.25	~~75, 223~~	~~80, 237~~	~~85, 244~~	~~91, 245~~

GAMES WITH MORE THAN ONE NASH EQUILIBRIUM

All of the games we have just studied had a unique Nash equilibrium. But some games have more than one Nash equilibrium. A famous example of a game with more than one Nash equilibrium is Chicken. The Chicken game is based on the following fable: Two teenage boys are going to prove their manhood to their friends. They each get in their cars at opposite ends of a road and begin to drive toward each other at breakneck speed. If one car swerves before the other, the one that did not swerve (i.e., stays) proves his manhood and becomes a hero to his friends, while the other loses face (he is a "chicken"). If both swerve, nothing gets proven: Neither loses face, but neither gains status, either. If neither swerves, though, they crash into each other and are either injured or killed.

Table 14.7 shows the payoffs for the game of Chicken between two teenagers, Luke and Slick. There are two Nash equilibria in this game. The first is for Luke to swerve and for Slick to stay. The other is for Luke to stay and Slick to swerve. To verify that the first is a Nash equilibrium, note that if Slick swerves, Luke is better off not swerving (payoff of 10) than by swerving (payoff of 0). And if Luke follows the strategy "Stay," Slick is better off swerving (payoff of -10), than not swerving (payoff of -100).

Do Chicken games occur in real life? In the 1950s and 1960s, many felt that a Chicken game was a good description of how a nuclear showdown between the two atomic superpowers, the United States and the Soviet Union, would play out. The famous quote by John F. Kennedy's Secretary of State, Dean Rusk, following the Cuban Missile Crisis, "We're eyeball to eyeball and the other fellow just blinked," is an illustration of how one high-stakes game of Chicken during the

TABLE 14.7
The Game of Chicken

		Slick	
		Swerve	Stay
Luke	Swerve	0, 0	-10, 10
	Stay	10, -10	-100, -100

Cold War played out. Less dramatically, but perhaps more pervasively, games of Chicken arise in economics when two firms compete in a market that can profitably support only one firm. (In Chapter 11, we called these natural monopoly markets.) The Nash equilibrium in the Chicken game tells us that one firm will eventually exit the market and one firm will survive.

EXAMPLE 14.2

The Game of Chicken between Sky TV and British Satellite Broadcasting in the U.K. Satellite Television Market[7]

The satellite television market in the United Kingdom was the site of a high-stakes game of Chicken in the early 1990s. Two firms—Sky Television, owned by Rupert Murdoch's News Corporation, and British Satellite Broadcasting (BSB), owned by a consortium of four British firms—made plans to offer satellite television services in 1990. Murdoch's firm planned to lease space on an already-existing satellite. BSB planned to launch a satellite of its own.

The business of satellite television involves high fixed costs and low marginal costs. This is because once a company launches a satellite and acquires the rights to programs (e.g., movies), the marginal cost of adding one more household to its subscription base is relatively low. A key implication of this cost structure is that for a satellite TV company to break even, it would need to obtain a critical mass of subscribers. Although the market for satellite TV was thought to have great potential in the United Kingdom in the early 1990s, it was probably not large enough to allow more than one firm to make a profit. Making this problem even more severe for Sky and BSB was the fact that the two companies used incompatible technologies. The satellite dish and TV box that a household would need to receive Sky's programming could not be used to receive BSB's programming if at some point a household wanted to shift from one service to the other. Not knowing which service would ultimately succeed, consumers became reluctant to invest the £200 (about U.S. $400) required to buy a satellite dish. This made it all the more difficult for two firms to coexist profitably in this market.

Table 14.8 shows the estimates of the cumulative profit that investment analysts expected each firm to make between 1989 and 1999 if one or both were to commence operations in 1989.[8] These estimates reflect the costs of satellites, programming, advertising, and selling and administrative expenses. They also reflect estimates about how fast satellite broadcasting services would be able to penetrate the British market. If both firms enter the market, both would be expected to incur

---

[7] This example draws from *Sky Television versus British Satellite Broadcasting*, Harvard Business School Case 9-792-039.

[8] Technically, the payoffs in Table 14.8 are the present value of the profits (or losses) from 1989 into the future that analysts expected the firms would earn. A present value of a stream of profits involves adding up a stream of profits over a period of years with the twist that we discount profits received in later years to take into account the fact that a dollar of profit received ten years from now is worth less than a dollar of profit received today. You can find a good introduction to present value in a basic corporate finance textbook, such as R. A. Brealey and S. C. Myers, *Principles of Corporate Finance* (New York: McGraw-Hill, 1998).

TABLE 14.8
The Game of Chicken Between Sky and BSB

		BSB	
		In	Out
Sky	**In**	−118, −747	673, 0
	Out	0, 137	0, 0

(All payoffs are £ million)

significant losses. However, if only one firm entered the market, that firm would make a profit. Generally speaking, Sky's profit was expected to be bigger than BSB's (and its loss smaller) because of its decision to lease space on an already orbiting medium-powered satellite as opposed to BSB's decision to launch its own high-powered satellite and because Sky was thought to have lower administrative costs than BSB.

The game in Table 14.8 has two Nash equilibria: In one, Sky chooses "In" and BSB chooses "Out," while in the other equilibrium, Sky chooses "Out" and BSB chooses "In." Game theory, by itself, cannot tell us which of these two Nash equilibria is likely to arise. We need to know more details about the players and the particular circumstances that they face in order to make predictions about who will win. In satellite TV in the United Kingdom, Murdoch's Sky Television won the battle. An important reason for this is that Sky managed to get a jump on BSB in making its entry decision. By 1989, Sky was ready to commence operations, but because of technical problems with its satellite BSB was not. BSB was forced to delay its entry decision by almost a year, during which time Sky was able to establish a presence in the market and build awareness for its service. BSB did commence its operations, but faced with losses of almost £1 million per *day,* it did not stay in the market for long. It "swerved" when it discontinued its operations and sold its assets to Sky. The company that emerged, BSkyB, remains a monopolist in the U.K. satellite TV market and has been consistently profitable since 1993.   ■

Bank Runs

EXAMPLE 14.3

If you have ever seen the movie *It's a Wonderful Life*, you probably remember the scene just after George and Mary Bailey (Jimmy Stewart and Donna Reed) get married. They are about to catch their train for their honeymoon, when someone tells George: "There's a run on the bank!" In the ensuing scene, George goes to his family's business (The Bailey Brothers Building and Loan) and is confronted with a mob of anxious depositors who are demanding to withdraw their money. Rather than locking the doors as many real banks did during the Great Depression of the 1930s, George does his best to keep the Building and Loan open. He does so by pleading

TABLE 14.9
The Bank Run Game

		Depositor 2	
		Withdraw	Don't Withdraw
Depositor 1	Withdraw	25, 25	50, 0
	Don't Withdraw	0, 50	110, 110

with his depositors to not withdraw their money, or at least, to withdraw only as much as they need to pay their bills.

Bank runs seem to be a thing of the past in the United States, but they are nevertheless an intriguing phenomenon. Why do they occur? Are they the result of irrational fear and hysteria, a sort of dysfunctional mass psychology? It might seem so. After all, if all depositors remained clear-sighted and level-headed, they would realize that everyone would be better off if there was no run on the bank. The bank would remain open and depositors would eventually get their money. Or is something else going on? Could bank runs be consistent with rational maximizing behavior by depositors? Game theory suggests that the answer to the last question could be yes.

Table 14.9 presents a simple game theoretic analysis of a bank run. Two individuals have deposited $100 in the Bailey Building and Loan. The Building and Loan has taken this money and invested it (perhaps lending money for houses). If both depositors keep their money in the bank ("Don't Withdraw"), they will eventually get their deposit back with an interest payment of $10, for a total payoff of $110. If both withdraw their money at the same time (a bank run), though, the bank must liquidate its investment and then close its doors. In this case, each depositor gets 25 cents on the dollar. If one depositor withdraws it money but the other doesn't, the bank again must liquidate its investment and close. The depositor that withdraws its money gets $50 but the unlucky depositor who left his or her money in the bank loses everything.

Like the game of Chicken, the bank run game has two Nash equilibria. The first is that both depositors keep their money in the bank. If Depositor 2 chooses "Don't Withdraw," Depositor 1 is better off choosing "Don't Withdraw" as well (a payoff of 110 versus a payoff of 50). The same holds true for Depositor 1. The second Nash equilibrium is for both players to withdraw their money. If Depositor 2 chooses "Withdraw," Depositor 1's best response is to choose "Withdraw" as well.

As in the game of Chicken, game theory cannot tell us *which* equilibrium will occur, but it does teach us that bank runs *can* occur. This is so even though we assume that all depositors behave rationally and that a bank run makes all depositors worse off. Thus, as in the prisoners' dilemma game, purposeful utility maximizing behavior by individuals will not necessarily result in an outcome that maximizes the collective well being of the players in the game. ∎

LEARNING-BY-DOING EXERCISE 14.2

Finding All of the Nash Equilibria in a Game

Now that you have seen several games—some with a unique Nash equilibrium, some with more than one Nash equilibrium—you might be wondering if there is a systematic procedure for identifying the Nash equilibria in a game that is presented in tabular form. That is what you will learn to do in this exercise.

Problem   Consider the game in Table 14.10. What are the Nash equilibria in this game?

Solution   Generally speaking, the first step to finding the Nash equilibrium in a game should be to identify dominant or dominated strategies and attempt to simplify the game as we did in Learning-By-Doing Exercise 14.1. But in this game, neither player has a dominant strategy or dominated strategies. (You should verify this before going further.) Thus, we cannot use the approach we used in Learning-By-Doing Exercise 14.1.

Instead, to find all the Nash equilibria in this game, we proceed in three steps.

Step 1: Let's find Player 1's best response to each of the three possible strategies of Player 2. (Remember, Player 1's payoffs are listed first in Table 14.10)

- If Player 2 chooses *D*, Player 1's best response is *C*.
- If Player 2 choose *E*, Player 1's best response is *A*.
- If Player 2 chooses *F*, Player 1's best response is *B*.

To keep track of these, draw circles around the payoffs corresponding to each of Player 1's best responses. We show this in Table 14.10a.

Step 2: Let's find Player 2's best response to each of the three possible strategies of Player 1.

- If Player 1 chooses *A*, Player 2's best response is *E*.
- If Player 1 choose *B*, Player 2's best response is *D*.
- If Player 1 chooses *C*, Player 2's best response is *D*.

TABLE 14.10
Learning-By-Doing Exercise 14.2

		Player 2		
		Strategy *D*	Strategy *E*	Strategy *F*
	Strategy *A*	4, 2	13, 6	1, 3
Player 1	Strategy *B*	3, 10	0, 0	15, 2
	Strategy *C*	12, 14	4, 11	5, 4

TABLE 14.10a
Player 1's Best Responses

			Player 2	
		Strategy D	Strategy E	Strategy F
	Strategy A	4, 2	⑬ 6	1, 3
Player 1	Strategy B	3, 10	0, 0	⑮ 2
	Strategy C	⑫ 14	4, 11	5, 4

TABLE 14.10b
Player 1 and Player 2's Best Responses

			Player 2	
		Strategy D	Strategy E	Strategy F
	Strategy A	4, 2	⑬ 6̄	1, 3
Player 1	Strategy B	3, 10̄	0, 0	⑮ 2
	Strategy C	⑫ 14̄	4, 11	5, 4

To keep track of these, draw squares around the payoffs corresponding to each of Player 2's best responses. We show this in Table 14.10b.

Step 3: Let's identify the Nash equilibria. Recall that at a Nash equilibrium each player chooses a strategy that gives it the highest payoff, given the strategies chosen by the other players in the game. This occurs at points where each player is making a best response to the strategy of the other. In Table 14.10b, this occurs in cells with both a circle and a square. In this example, we have two Nash equilibria. One Nash equilibrium is where Player 1 chooses Strategy *A* and Player 2 chooses Strategy *E*. Another Nash equilibrium is where Player 1 chooses Strategy *C* and Player 2 chooses Strategy *D*. This game, like the games of Chicken we studied above, has two Nash equilibria.

The procedure we just used—first identifying Player 1's best responses to each of Player 2's strategies, then identifying Player 2's responses to each of Player 1's strategies—is a sure-fire way to identify all the Nash equilibria in a game.

MIXED STRATEGIES

In July 1999, the United States and the Chinese women's soccer teams fought to a 0–0 tie in the final match of the Women's World Cup. To decide the match, players on each team alternated in shooting penalty kicks, and the match eventually came down to a final penalty kick by the United States. If the U.S. player scored a goal, the United States would win the match; if the Chinese goalie blocked the kick, the game would continue, and the Chinese team would then have a chance to win the match with a penalty kick of its own. Both the U.S.

kicker and the Chinese goalie had to make split-second decisions. Should the kicker aim left or right? Should the goalie dive to the kicker's left or right? If the Chinese goalie dove in the direction in which the kicker aimed, the shot would be blocked, and the two teams would remain tied and would move on to another penalty kick. If the goalie guessed wrong, though, the U.S. team would score and win the match. (As you might remember, the final U.S. kicker, Brandi Chastain, did make the final kick, and the U.S. team won.)

Table 14.11 shows a payoff matrix that we might use to depict the final encounter between the U.S. and Chinese teams. Winning the match gives the U.S. team a payoff of 10, while losing the match would give the Chinese team a payoff of -10. If the two teams remain tied, each receives (from this encounter) a payoff of 0.

This game does not appear to have a Nash equilibrium. If the Chinese goalie believes the U.S. kicker will aim right, the goalie's best strategy is to dive to the kicker's right. But if the U.S. kicker believes the Chinese goalie will dive to the kicker's right, the kicker's best strategy is to aim left. And if the kicker aims left, the goalie's best response is to dive to the kicker's left.

This game illustrates the contrast between a **pure strategy** and a **mixed strategy.** A pure strategy is a specific choice among the possible moves in the game. The U.S. kicker has a choice between two pure strategies: "Aim Right" and "Aim Left." By contrast, under a mixed strategy, a player chooses among two or more pure strategies according to prespecified probabilities.[9] Even though some games might have no Nash equilibrium in pure strategies, every game has at least one Nash equilibrium in mixed strategies. The Women's World Cup game in Table 14.11 illustrates this point. We have seen that this game does not have a Nash equilibrium in pure strategies. However, there is a Nash equilibrium in mixed strategies. The U.S. kicker should "Aim Right" with probability 1/2 and "Aim Left" with probability 1/2. The Chinese goalie should "Dive Right" with probability 1/2 and "Dive Left" with probability 1/2. If the U.S. kicker believes that the Chinese goalie will dive right or left with probability 1/2, the U.S. kicker can do no better than to choose to aim left or right with probability 1/2. Similarly, if the Chinese goalie believes that the U.S. kicker will aim right or left with probability 1/2, the goalie can do no better than to choose to dive left or right with probability 1/2. Thus, when each player chooses these mixed strategies, each is doing the best it can given the actions of the other player.

The fact that games can have Nash equilibria in the form of mixed strategies illustrates that unpredictability can have strategic value. When your opponent can

TABLE 14.11
The U.S. versus the Chinese in the 1999 Women's World Cup

		U.S. Kicker	
		Aim Right	Aim Left
Chinese Goalie	Dive to Kicker's Right	0, 0	−10, 10
	Dive to Kicker's Left	−10, 10	0, 0

[9]For this reason, mixed strategies are sometimes referred to as randomized strategies.

predict what you will do, you can leave yourself vulnerable to being exploited by your opponent. Athletes in sports such as baseball, soccer, and tennis have long understood this point, and the World Cup game illustrates it nicely. If the kicker knew which way the goalie was going to dive, the kicker could simply aim the other way and score the goal. There is value in being unpredictable and mixed strategies illustrate how this value is present in game theory.

SUMMARY: HOW TO FIND ALL THE NASH EQUILIBRIA IN A SIMULTANEOUS-MOVE GAME WITH TWO PLAYERS

We can summarize the lessons of this section by outlining a five-step approach to identifying the Nash equilibria in simultaneous-move games involving two players.

1. If both players have a dominant strategy, these constitute their Nash equilibrium strategies.

2. If one player, say Player 1, has a dominant strategy, this is the player's Nash equilibrium strategy. We then find Player 2's best response to Player 1's dominant strategy to identify Player 2's Nash equilibrium strategy.

3. If neither player has dominant strategy, successively eliminate each player's dominated strategies in order to simplify the game and then search for Nash equilibrium strategies.

4. If neither player has dominated strategies, use the approach in Learning-By-Doing Exercise 14.2 to identify all of the pure-strategy Nash equilibria in the game. This approach is guaranteed to identify all of the pure-strategy Nash equilibria in a game.

5. If the approach in Learning-By-Doing Exercise 14.2 does not uncover any pure-strategy Nash equilibria—that is, if the game does not have a Nash equilibrium in pure strategies, as in the Womens' World Cup game—look for an equilibrium in mixed strategies.

14.2
THE REPEATED PRISONERS' DILEMMA

A key lesson of the prisoners' dilemma is that the individual pursuit of profit maximization does not necessarily result in the maximization of the collective profit of a group of a players. But the prisoners' dilemma is a one-shot game, and you might wonder if the game would turn out differently if it was played over and over again by the same players. When we allow the players to interact repeatedly, we open the possibility that each player can tie its current decisions to what its opponent has done in previous stages of the game. This expands the array of strategies that the players can follow, and as we will see, can dramatically alter the game's outcome.

To illustrate the impact of repeated play, consider the prisoners' dilemma game in Table 14.12. For each player, "Cheat" is a dominant strategy, but the players' collective profit is maximized when both play "Cooperate." In a one-shot game, the Nash equilibrium would be for both players to choose "Cheat."

TABLE 14.12
Prisoners' Dilemma Game

		Player 1	
		Cheat	Cooperate
Player 2	Cheat	5, 5	14, 1
	Cooperate	1, 14	10, 10

But let's now imagine that two players will be playing the game again and again, into the foreseeable future. In this case, it is possible that the players might achieve an equilibrium in which they play cooperatively. To see why, suppose that Player 1 believes that Player 2 will use the following strategy: "Start off choosing 'Cooperate' and continue to do so as long as Player 1 cooperates. The first time Player 1 chooses 'Cheat,' Player 2 will choose 'Cheat' in the next period and in all following periods." Of course, if Player 2 cheats in the ensuing periods, Player 1 might as well continue to cheat as well. Player 2's strategy is sometimes called the "Grim Trigger" strategy because one episode of cheating by one player triggers the grim prospect of a permanent breakdown in cooperation for the remainder of the game.

Figure 14.1 illustrates the payoffs that Player 1 would anticipate if he cooperated every period. By cooperating, Player 1 can ensure himself a stream of payoffs equal to 10 per period. By contrast, if Player 1 cheats, he receives a payoff

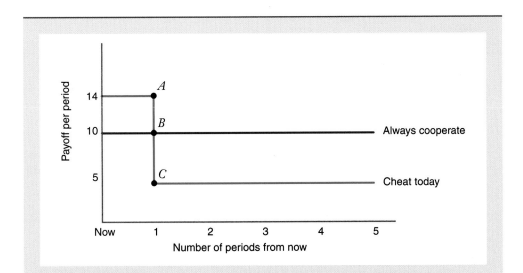

**FIGURE 14.1   Payoffs in the Repeated Prisoners' Dilemma under the
"Grim Trigger" Strategy**
If Player 1 cheats today, he receives a stream of payoffs given by the light line. If he cooperates today and in the future he can ensure himself a stream of payoffs given by the dark line. The distance of line segment *AB* is the one-time gain to Player 1 from cheating. The distance of line segment *AC* represents the reduction in Player 1's payoff because Player 2 retaliates against Player 1's cheating.

of 14 in the current period and a payoff of 5 in all subsequent periods. Which strategy is better? Without additional information about how Player 1 evaluates current versus future payoffs we cannot say for sure which strategy is better. But if Player 1 places sufficiently strong weight on future payoffs relative to current payoffs, Player 1 will prefer continued cooperation to cheating.[10] This illustrates that in the repeated prisoners' dilemma, cooperation can, under certain circumstances, result from self-interested behavior on the part of each player.

The Grim Trigger strategy is not the only strategy that can induce cooperative behavior in the repeated prisoners' dilemma. There are other strategies that can result in the same outcome (we discuss another one, tit-for-tat, in Example 14.3). The unifying feature of any cooperation-inducing strategy, however, is that it must punish the opposing player for cheating. A necessary condition for a player to voluntarily cooperate in the repeated prisoners' dilemma is that it anticipates that its rival will eventually retaliate if the player cheats. The prospect of eventual retaliation and the corresponding reduction in profit beyond the initial period (represented by the length of line segment *BC* in Figure 14.1) is what provides an incentive for a player to maintain cooperative behavior even though cheating is the dominant strategy in a one-shot game.

In light of this, it is possible to make some general statements about the likelihood that players will be able to sustain cooperative behavior when they interact in a repeated prisoners' dilemma game. Specifically, the likelihood of a cooperative outcome is enhanced under these conditions:

- *The players are patient.* That is, they value payoffs in future periods almost as much as payoffs in the current period. For patient players, the adverse consequences of punishment loom large in comparison to the short-term gains from cheating.

- *Interactions between the players are frequent.* This implies that the length of a "period" is short, and that the one-shot benefit to cheating accrues over a short period of time.

- *Cheating is easy to detect.* This has the same effect, roughly, as shortening the length of the period: A firm cannot get away with cheating for very long and thus finds that the short-term benefit from noncooperative behavior is fleeting.

- *The one-time gain from cheating is relatively small.* For example, the length of line segment *AB* in Figure 14.1 is *small* in comparison to the eventual cost of cheating, the length of line segment *BC*.

By contrast, the likelihood of a cooperative outcome diminishes under these conditions:

- *The players are impatient.* That is, they value current payoffs much more than future payoffs.

- *Interactions between the players are infrequent.* This implies that the length of a "period" is long, and that the one-shot benefit to cheating accrues over a relatively long period of time.

---

[10] We can formally represent the weight that players give to future versus current payoffs by the concept of present value mentioned in footnote 8.

- *Cheating is hard to detect.* When this is so, a firm can get away with cheating longer and can enjoy the benefit from cheating over a relatively longer period of time.

- *The one-time gain from cheating is large in comparison to the eventual cost of cheating.*

EXAMPLE 14.4

Trench Warfare in World War I and the Repeated Prisoners' Dilemma[11]

Trench warfare is ugly and brutal. This was certainly so along the Western front during World War I where the Allied army (France and Britain) faced the German army. Still, as Robert Axelrod has written, in the midst of these devastating circumstances, an unusual degree of cooperation emerged. Axelrod quotes a British staff officer who wrote that he was:

astonished to observe German soldiers walking about within rifle range behind their own line. Our men appeared to take no notice. I privately made up my mind to do away with that sort of thing when we took over; such things should not be allowed. These people evidently did not know there was a war on. Both sides apparently believed in the policy of 'live and let live.'

Axelrod goes on to point out that these circumstances were not isolated. "The live-and-let live system," he writes, "was endemic in trench warfare. It flourished despite the best efforts of senior officers to stop it, despite the passions aroused by combat, despite the military logic of kill or be killed, and despite the ease with which the high command was able to repress any local efforts to arrange a direct truce."

Axelrod interprets the "cooperative" trench warfare along the Western front as the outcome of a repeated prisoners' dilemma game. At any given point along the line, the two players were Allied and German battalions (military units consisting of roughly 1,000 men). On any given day, a battalion could "Shoot to Kill," a strategy corresponding to "Cheat" in Table 14.12. Or, it could "Live-and-Let-Live," a strategy that corresponds to "Cooperate" in Table 14.12. Axelrod argues that for each opposing battalion "Shoot to Kill" was a dominant strategy. This is because each battalion would occasionally be ordered by its army's high command into a major battle in its area of the line (e.g., a charge against the other side's trenches). By shooting to kill, a battalion would weaken its opponent, which would increase the likelihood of survival should a major engagement be ordered. At the same time, both sides are better off when both live-and-let-live than when both shoot to kill. The structure of the "game" between opposing battalions along the Western front was thus a prisoners' dilemma.

But if "Shoot to Kill" was a battalion's dominant strategy, why did cooperation emerge? The reason, Axelrod argues, is that the prisoners' dilemma game between enemy battalions was a repeated game. Trench warfare differs from other ways of fighting a war because each side's units face the same enemy units for months at a time. Although cooperation between Allied and German battalions usually evolved

---

[11]This example draws heavily from Chapter 4 of Robert Axelrod's book, *The Evolution of Cooperation* (New York: Basic Books, 1984).

by accident (e.g., during periods of unusually rainy weather during which fighting could not occur), the close interaction between the same battalions allowed them to follow strategies that tended to sustain the cooperation over time once it had emerged.

A particularly valuable strategy for sustaining cooperation between enemy battalions along the Western front was **tit-for-tat.** Under a tit-for-tat strategy, you do to your opponent what your opponent did to you last period. Along the Western front, it became well understood that if one side exercised restraint, the other would, too. If, by contrast, one side fired, the other side would shoot back in a proportional fashion. Wrote one soldier:

> It would be child's play to shell the road behind the enemy's trenches, crowded as it must be with ration wagons and water carts, into a bloodstained wilderness . . . but on the whole there is silence. After all, if you prevent your enemy from drawing his rations, his remedy is simple: he will prevent you from drawing yours.

The tit-for-tat strategy was carried to strong numerical extremes. One soldier noted:

> If the British shelled the Germans, the Germans replied, and the damage was equal: if the Germans bombed an advanced piece of trench and killed five Englishmen, an answering fusillade killed five Germans.

The use of tit-for-tat strategies meant that each side realized that an aggressive act would be met by an aggressive response. In choosing how to fight, battalions on each side weighed the trade-off between the short-term gain from shooting to kill against the long-term cost from a breakdown in restraint. Facing this trade-off, numerous battalions along the Western front chose cooperation over noncooperation.

Eventually, as World War I came to a close, the norm of cooperation along the Western front broke down. The reason is that the high commands of both the Allied and German armies took explicit steps to end the tacit truces that had broken out along much of the Western front. (In this sense, the high commands can be thought of as akin to antitrust enforcers that attempt to break up tacitly collusive behavior among business firms.) In particular, the armies' commanders began to organize much more frequent and larger raids in which the raiding parties were ordered to kill enemy soldiers in their own trenches. This changed the payoffs in the prisoners' dilemma game so that "Shooting to Kill" became a more attractive alternative compared to "Live-and-Let-Live." With larger and more frequent raids, the traditional wartime norm of "kill or be killed" took over, and by the time the war ended, both sides had returned to an incessantly aggressive posture. ■

LESSONS FROM THE REPEATED PRISONERS' DILEMMA

Our analysis of the repeated prisoners' dilemma game teaches an important lesson: In competitive settings you must anticipate the reactions of your competitors. If you are in a situation in which you will be interacting with the same group of competitors over time, it is important to anticipate the likely responses of competitors to the moves that you make in the game. In particular, you need to understand how your competitor is likely to respond when you engage in actions that could be construed as cheating. If, for example, you are a business firm in a market, and you cut price in order to increase your market share, you need to anticipate whether your price cut will be detected, whether your competitor will respond by matching the price, and if so, how long your competitor will take to match. By ignoring the possibility of competitive responses, you run the risk of overestimating the potential benefits that will accrue to you from various forms of noncooperative behavior. You also run the risk of plunging your market into a costly price war that will erase any temporary gains you might enjoy from having undercut the prices of your competitors.

EXAMPLE 14.5

The Price War in the Costa Rican Cigarette Market[12]

An excellent illustration of what can happen when one firm miscalculates competitor responses occurred in the cigarette industry in Costa Rica in 1993. The most famous cigarette price war of 1993 occurred in the United States, when Philip Morris initiated its "Marlboro Friday" price cuts. The lesser-known Costa Rican price war, also initiated by Philip Morris, began several months before and lasted a full year longer than the Marlboro Friday price war.

At the beginning of the 1990s, two firms dominated the Costa Rican cigarette market: Philip Morris, with 30 percent of the market, and B.A.T., with 70 percent of the market. The market consisted of three segments: premium, mid-priced, and value-for-money (VFM). Philip Morris had the leading brands in the premium and mid-priced segments (Marlboro and Derby, respectively). B.A.T., by contrast, dominated the VFM segment with its Delta brand.

Throughout the 1980s, a prosperous Costa Rican economy fueled steady growth in the demand for cigarettes. Both B.A.T. and Philip Morris were, as a result, able to sustain price increases that exceeded the rate of inflation. However, in the late 1980s, the market began to change. Health concerns slowed the demand for cigarettes in Costa Rica, a trend that hit the premium and mid-priced segments much harder than it did the VFM segment. In 1992, B.A.T. gained market share from Philip Morris for the first time since the early 1980s. Philip Morris faced the prospect of slow demand growth and a declining market share.

On Saturday, January 16, 1993, Philip Morris reduced the prices of Marlboro and Derby cigarettes by 40 percent. The timing of the price reduction was not by chance. Philip Morris reasoned that B.A.T.'s inventories would be low following the year-end holidays, and that B.A.T. would not have sufficient product to satisfy an immediate increase in demand should it match or undercut Philip Morris's price cut. Philip Morris also initiated its price cut on a Saturday morning, expecting that B.A.T.'s local management would be unable to respond without first undertaking lengthy consultations with the home office in London.

However, B.A.T. surprised Philip Morris with the speed of its response. Within hours, B.A.T. cut the price of its Delta brand by 50 percent, a price that industry observers estimated barely exceeded Delta's marginal cost. Having been alerted to Morris's move on Saturday morning, B.A.T. had salespeople out selling at the new price by Saturday afternoon.

---

[12] We would like to thank Andrew Cherry (MM 1998 Kellogg Graduate School of Management) for developing this example.

The ensuing price war lasted about two years. Cigarette sales increased 17 percent as a result of the lower prices, but market shares did not change. By the time the war ended in late 1994, Philip Morris's share of the Costa Rican market was unchanged, and it was $8 million worse off than it was before the war had started. B.A.T. lost even more—$20 million—but it had preserved the market share of its Delta brand and was able to maintain the same price gaps that had prevailed across market segments before the war.

Why did Philip Morris act as it did? In the early 1990s, Philip Morris had increased Marlboro's market share at B.A.T.'s expense in other Central American countries, such as Guatemala. Perhaps it expected that it could replicate that success in Costa Rica. Still, had it anticipated B.A.T.'s quick response, Philip Morris should have realized that its price cut would not result in an increase in market share. Whatever the motivation for Philip Morris's actions, this example highlights how quickly retaliation by competitors can nullify the advantages of a price cut. If firms understand that and take the long view, their incentive to use price as a competitive weapon to gain market share will be blunted.   ■

14.3 SEQUENTIAL-MOVE GAMES AND STRATEGIC MOVES

So far, we have studied games in which players make decisions simultaneously. In many interesting games, however, one player can move before other players do. These are called **sequential-move games.** In a sequential-move game, one player (the first mover) takes an action before another player (the second mover). The second mover observes the action taken by the first mover before it decides what action it should take. We shall see that the ability to move first in a sequential-move game can sometimes have significant strategic value.

ANALYZING SEQUENTIAL-MOVE GAMES

To learn how to analyze sequential-move games, let's return to the simultaneous-move capacity expansion game between Toyota and Honda in Table 14.4. (To refresh your memory of that game, Table 14.13 shows the payoff table.)

TABLE 14.13
Capacity Expansion Game Between Toyota and Honda

		Toyota		
		Large	Small	Do Not Build
Honda	Large	0, 0	12, 8	18, 9
	Small	8, 12	16, 16	20, 15
	Do Not Build	9, 18	15, 20	18, 18

Recall that the Nash equilibrium in this game was for Toyota and Honda to choose "Small."

But now suppose that Honda can make its capacity decision before Toyota decides what to do (perhaps because it has accelerated its decision-making process). We now have a sequential-move game in which Honda is the first mover and Toyota is the second mover. To analyze this sequential-move game, we use a **game tree.** A game tree shows the different strategies that each player can follow in the game and the order in which those strategies get chosen. Figure 14.2 shows the game tree for our capacity expansion game. In any game tree, the order of moves flows from left to right. Because Honda moves first, we represent its decisions by left-hand-most branches. For each of Honda's possible actions, we then show the possible decisions for Toyota.

To analyze the game tree in Figure 14.2, it is convenient to use a thought process called **backward induction.** When you solve a sequential-move game using backward induction, you start at the end of the game tree, and for each decision point (represented by the shaded squares), you find the optimal decision for the player at that point. You continue to do this until you reach the beginning of the game. The thought process of backward induction has the attractive property that it keeps the analysis manageable: It allows us to break a potentially complicated game into manageable pieces.

To apply backward induction in this example, we must find Toyota's optimal decision for each of the three choices Honda might make: "Do Not Build," "Small," and "Large":

• If Honda chooses "Do Not Build," Toyota's optimal choice is "Small."

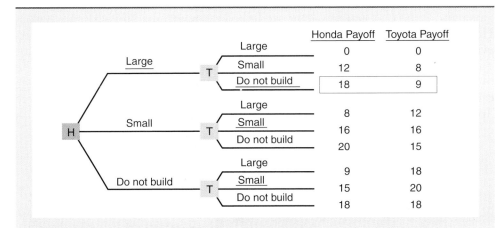

FIGURE 14.2 Game Tree for the Sequential-Move Capacity Expansion Game Between Toyota and Honda
Honda moves first and can choose among three strategies: "Large," "Small," and "Do Not Build." After observing Honda's choice, Toyota then moves. For any choice Honda makes, Toyota has three capacity expansion choices: "Large," "Small," and "Do Not Build." The shaded squares indicate the decision points for Honda and Toyota. The payoffs for each company are at the end of the tree. We underline Toyota's optimal capacity expansion decision for each of the three choices Honda might make. Taking into account these choices, Honda's best choice is "Large." The Nash equilibrium in the sequential-move game is for Honda to choose "Large" and Toyota to choose "Do Not Build."

- If Honda chooses "Small," Toyota's optimal choice is "Small."
- If Honda chooses "Large," Toyota's optimal choice is "Do Not Build."

(In Figure 14.2, Toyota's optimal choices are underlined.)

As we work backward in the tree, we assume that Honda anticipates that Toyota will choose its best response to each of the three actions Honda might take. Given these expectations, we can determine which of Honda's three strategies gives it the highest profit. We do so by identifying the profit that Honda gets from each option it might choose, given that Toyota responds optimally:

- If Honda chooses "Do Not Build," then given Toyota's optimal reaction, Honda's profit will be $15 million.
- If Honda chooses "Small," then given Toyota's optimal reaction, Honda's profit will be $16 million.
- If Honda chooses "Large," then given Toyota's optimal reaction, Honda's profit will be $18 million.

Honda attains the highest profit when it chooses "Large." The Nash equilibrium in this game is thus for Honda to choose "Large" and for Toyota to choose "Do Not Build." At this equilibrium, Honda's profit is $18 million and Toyota's profit is $9 million.

Notice that the Nash equilibrium of the sequential-move game differs significantly from that of the simultaneous-move game. Indeed, in the sequential-move game, Honda's equilibrium strategy ("Large") would be dominated if Toyota and Honda made their capacity choices simultaneously. Why is Honda's behavior so different when it can move first? Because in the sequential-move game, the firm's decision problems are linked through time: Toyota can see what Honda has done, and Honda counts on a rational response by Toyota to whatever action it chooses. This allows Honda to force Toyota into a corner. By committing to a large capacity expansion, Honda puts Toyota in a position where the best it can do is not build. By contrast, in the simultaneous-move game, Toyota cannot observe Honda's decision beforehand, and therefore Honda cannot force Toyota's hand. Because of this, the choice of "Large" by Honda is not nearly as compelling as it is in the sequential-move game.

LEARNING-BY-DOING EXERCISE 14.3 _____

An Entry Game

Avinash Dixit and Barry Nalebuff, authors of a delightful book on game theory, *Thinking Strategically*, have written, "It takes a clever carpenter to turn a tree into a table; a clever strategist knows how to turn a table into a tree."[13] In this exercise, we illustrate their point in the context of a simple entry game.

[13]A. Dixit and B. Nalebuff, *Thinking Strategically* (New York: Norton), 1991, p. 122.

TABLE 14.14
Entry into the Digital Camera Business

		Kodak	
		Accommodate	Launch Price War
You	Small	4, 20	1, 16
	Large	8, 10	2, 12
		(payoffs are in millions of dollars)	

Problem Suppose you own a firm that is considering entry into the digital camera business, where you will compete head to head with Kodak (who, let's say, currently has a monopoly). Kodak can react in one of two ways: Kodak can start a price war or it can be accommodating. You can enter this business at a large scale or a small scale. Table 14.14 shows the payoffs you and Kodak are likely to get under the various scenarios that can unfold in this market. In light of this and the payoffs in Table 14.14, how should you enter this business?

Solution If you and Kodak choose your strategies simultaneously, the Nash equilibrium is for you to enter at a large scale and for Kodak to launch a price war. You can see this most easily by noting that "Large" is your dominant strategy. Given that you choose this, Kodak will respond by launching a price war. At this Nash equilibrium, your profit is $2 million per year.

But you can do better if you turn this into a sequential-move game. Figure 14.3 shows the game tree if you can commit to your scale of operation in advance before Kodak decides what to do. If you choose "Large," Kodak's best

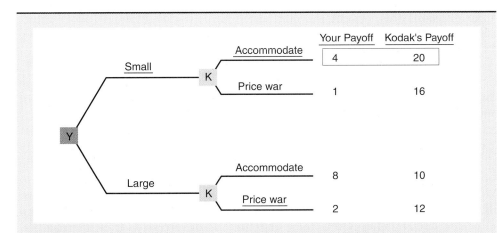

FIGURE 14.3 Game Tree for Learning-By-Doing Exercise 14.3
You move first by deciding whether to enter at a small scale or large scale. Kodak then responds by accommodating your entry or launching a price war. We underline Kodak's optimal decision for each of the two choices you can make. Taking into account these decisions, your best choice is to enter at a small scale. The Nash equilibrium in the sequential-move game is thus for you to choose "Small" and for Kodak to choose "Accommodate."

response, as we just saw, is to fight a price war, and you get a payoff of $2 million per year. But if you choose "Small," Kodak's best response is "Accommodate." In this case, you get a payoff of $4 million per year. If you can move first, your optimal strategy is "Small." The Nash equilibrium in the sequential-move game is for you to enter at a small scale and for Kodak to respond in an accommodating fashion.

How could you commit in advance to being small? One way would simply be to issue a public statement announcing that you have limited aspirations in this marketplace and have no plans to grow beyond your current small size. (This is the strategy Value-Jet followed when it competed with Delta Airlines in Atlanta in the mid-1990s.) Another way to commit to remaining small would be to tailor your product's attributes or your advertising messages to appeal to a niche market. This would make a strategy of "Small" very credible because it would constrain your ability to grow once you have entered the market. The key point is that even though you have a dominant strategy to be large in the simultaneous-move game, you can do better by moving first and turning your payoff table into a tree.

THE STRATEGIC VALUE OF LIMITING ONE'S OPTIONS

In the sequential-move capacity expansion game, Honda committed in advance to a particular course of action, whereas Toyota had the flexibility to respond to Honda. Yet, Honda's equilibrium profits were twice as large as Toyota's. The firm that tied its hands in advance fared better than the firm that maintained flexibility.

This illustrates a profound point. Strategic moves that seemingly limit options can actually make a player better off, or, put another way, inflexibility can have value. This is so because a firm's commitments can alter its competitors' expectations about how it will compete, and this, in turn, will lead competitors to make decisions that benefit the committed firm. In the Honda–Toyota game, when Honda commits itself in advance to an apparently inferior strategy ("Large"), it alters Toyota's expectations about what it will do. Had Honda not made the commitment, Toyota would understand that it would have been in Honda's interest to choose "Small," which in turn would have led Toyota to choose "Small" as well. By committing in advance to the more aggressive strategy of building a large plant, Honda makes it less appealing for Toyota to expand its capacity, moving the industry to an equilibrium that makes Honda better off than it would have been in the Nash equilibrium of the simultaneous-move game.

Generals throughout history have understood the value of inflexibility, as the famous example of Hernan Cortes' conquest of Montezuma's Aztec empire in Mexico illustrates. When he landed in Mexico, Cortes ordered his men to burn all but one of his ships. Rather than an act of lunacy, Cortes' move was purposeful and calculated: By eliminating their only method of retreat, Cortes' men had no choice but to fight hard to win. According to Bernal Diaz del Castillo, who chronicled Cortes' conquest of the Aztecs, "Cortes said that we could look for no help or assistance except from God for we now had no ships in which to return to Cuba. Therefore we must rely on our own good swords and stout hearts."[14]

---

[14]This quotation comes from Chapter 2 of Richard Luecke's book *Scuttle Your Ships Before Advancing: And Other Lessons from History on Leadership and Change for Today's Managers* (New York: Oxford University Press), 1994.

Honda's preemptive capacity expansion and Cortes' decision to scuttle his ships are examples of **strategic moves.** A strategic move is an action you take in an early stage of a game that alters your behavior and your competitors' behavior later in the game in a way that is favorable to you.[15] In business life, there are many examples of strategic moves. Decisions about how to position a product in the marketplace ("Do we aim at a mass market or at a high-end niche?"), about how to compensate executives ("Do we reward our executives based on profitability or based on market share?"), and about product compatibility ("Do we make our product compatible with those of our competitors?") are all examples of strategic moves because they can have an important impact on how competition in the marketplace unfolds later on.[16] For example, a firm's decision to position its product in a high-end niche might have strategic value by reducing the fierceness of price competition with other competitors. This is so even though the direct effect of a niche strategy would be to limit the size of the product's potential market.

Strategic moves are relevant in other domains besides business. For example, the Israeli government has for many years maintained a policy that it will not—under any circumstances—negotiate with terrorists. The objective of this commitment is to deter terrorist organizations from using hostage-taking as a strategy to induce Israel to make concessions, such as the release of prisoners. This policy ties Israel's hands, and it is possible to imagine particular circumstances in which an absolute stance against negotiation could be unwise. But if an unconditional refusal to negotiate alters the game by deterring terrorist acts, then this sort of inflexibility can have enormous strategic value.

In order for a strategic move to work, it must be visible, understandable, and hard to reverse. In our capacity expansion example, Toyota must observe and understand that Honda has made the commitment to the "Large" strategy. Otherwise, this move will not affect Toyota's decision making. Irreversibility is necessary in order for the strategic move to be credible. Toyota must believe that Honda will not back down from its commitment to build a large plant. This is important because in our simple example, Honda's ideal course of action is to bluff Toyota into believing that it intends to choose "Large," thereby causing Toyota to choose "Do Not Build," but then to actually choose "Small." For example, Honda might announce that it intends a large capacity expansion project in the hope that Toyota will then abandon its decision to expand. Once this happens, Honda would then scale back its own decision to expand. If Honda bluffs in this fashion and induces the outcome ("Small," "Do Not Build"), Honda enjoys a profit of $20 million, as opposed to the $18 million it would get if it carried out its "Large" strategy. Of course, Toyota should understand this, and discount as bluster any claims that Honda makes regarding its intention to choose the aggressive strategy unless those claims can be backed up with credible actions.

[15] This term was coined by Thomas Schelling in his book *The Strategy of Conflict* (Cambridge, Mass.: Harvard University Press, 1960).

[16] See J. Tirole, *Theory of Industrial Organization* (Cambridge, Mass.: MIT Press, 1988) for a careful analysis of these and many other strategic moves. Chapter 9 of D. Besanko, D. Dranove, and M. Shanley, *Economics of Strategy* (New York: Wiley, 1999) contains a less formal treatment of the economics of strategic moves in a business setting.

What makes a strategic move hard to reverse? One factor that contributes to irreversibility is the extent to which the strategic move involves the creation of specialized assets—assets that cannot be easily redeployed to alternative uses. To illustrate, suppose that Airbus, hoping to get a jump on arch-rival Boeing, decides to invest resources to build next-generation super-jumbo jets before Boeing decides whether it will offer a similar product.[17] The multibillion-dollar investment in tooling and equipment that Airbus must make to build super-jumbo jets is very specialized. Once these investments are made, the tooling and equipment have no good alternative uses. Given this, once Airbus has built its capacity for manufacturing super-jumbo jets, it will be unlikely to back down by shutting down its factory unless competitive circumstances become so bad that it cannot cover its average nonsunk costs. The specialized nature of the assets implies that most of Airbus's cost are sunk, so average non-sunk cost is small. This creates a strong economic incentive for Airbus not to reverse its strategic move. This irreversibility is especially important in Boeing and Airbus's race to develop super-jumbo jets because most observers believe that market demand is insufficient to profitably support more than one firm.

Contracts can also facilitate irreversibility. One example of this is a most favored customer clause (MFCC). Under a MFCC, if a seller includes such a clause in a sales contract with a buyer, the seller is required to extend the same price terms to the buyer that it extends to its other customers. For example, if the seller discounts below its list price to steal a customer from a competitor, the buyer with an MFCC in its contract is entitled to the same discount. The MFCC makes discounting "expensive," and for this reason it can create a credible commitment not to discount below the official list price.

Sometimes even public statements of intentions to take actions ("We plan to introduce a new and improved version of our existing product six months from now") make it hard for a firm to reverse course. For this to be true, however, the firm's competitors and customers must understand that the firm or its management are putting something at risk if it fails to match words with actions; otherwise, they will recognize that talk is cheap and discount the claims, promises, or threats the firm is making. The credibility of public announcements is enhanced when it is clear that the reputation of the firm or its senior management suffers when the firm fails to carry out what it has said it will do. In the computer software industry, it is more common for established firms, such as Microsoft, to make promises about new product performance and introduction dates than it is for smaller firms or industry newcomers to do so. This may, in part, be related to the fact that a newcomer has far more to lose in terms of credibility with consumers and opinion setters in the various personal computer magazines (an important forum for product reviews) than an established firm has. For this reason, smaller firms may be more reluctant to make exaggerated claims than established firms that have had a past track record of success. Failure to match actions to words will result in a significant loss of face or diminution of reputation for the firm and its senior management.

---

[17]Super-jumbo jets are ultra-large jets capable of carrying 500 or 600 passengers. The largest available commercial jet, Boeing's 747, can carry up to 400 passengers.

EXAMPLE 14.6

Irreversibility of Business Decisions in the Airline Industry

How irreversible are the business decisions that real companies actually make? Ming-Jer Chen and Ian MacMillan set out to answer this question in the airline industry.[18] They asked airline executives and industry analysts (e.g., financial analysts and academic experts) to rank the degree of irreversibility in various competitive moves that airlines often make. They learned that, in the opinion of industry participants and observers, mergers/acquisitions, investments in the creation of hub airports, and feeder alliances with commuter airlines had the highest degree of irreversibility. Decisions to abandon a route, increases in commission rates for travel agents, promotional advertising campaigns, and pricing decisions were seen by industry participants and experts as being the easiest moves to reverse.

Chen and MacMillan hypothesized that competitors are less likely to match an airline's competitive move when the original move is hard to reverse. Their logic is akin to the Honda–Toyota example in this chapter. The more credible is a firm's commitment to an aggressive strategic move, the more likely it is that its competitors will respond by choosing a less aggressive strategy. This logic would suggest that a preemptive move by one airline to expand its route system by acquiring another airline is less likely to provoke a matching response than is a decision to engage in a short-term promotional or advertising campaign. Chen and MacMillan test this hypothesis through an exhaustive study of competitive moves and countermoves reported over a eight-year period (1979–1986) in a leading trade publication of the airline industry, *Aviation Daily*. In general, their findings support their hypothesis: harder-to-reverse moves are less frequently matched than easier-to-reverse moves. The study suggests that price cuts are especially provocative and thus likely to be matched frequently and quickly. MacMillan and Chen find that rival airlines responded to price cuts more frequently than other moves they saw as having a similar, or even higher, degree of irreversibility. ■

CHAPTER SUMMARY

• Game theory is the branch of economics concerned with the analysis of optimal decision making when all decision makers are presumed to be rational, and each is attempting to anticipate the actions and reactions of its competitors.

• A Nash equilibrium in a game occurs when each player chooses a strategy that gives it the highest payoff, given the strategies chosen by the other players in the game. **(LBD Exercises 14.1, 14.2)**

• A prisoners' dilemma game illustrates the conflict between self interest and collective interest. In the Nash

equilibrium of a prisoners' dilemma game, each player chooses a "non-cooperative" action, even though it is in the players' collective interest to pursue a cooperative action.

• A dominant strategy is a strategy that is better than any other strategy the player might follow, no matter what the other player does. A player has a dominated strategy when it has other strategies that give it a higher payoff no matter what the other player does.

• A pure strategy is a specific choice among the possible moves in a game. Under a mixed strategy, a player

---

[18]M-J Chen and I.C. MacMillan, "Nonresponse and Delayed Response to Competitive Moves: The Role of Competitor Dependence and Action Irreversibility," *Academy of Management Journal*, 35, (1992): pp. 539–570.

chooses among two or more pure strategies according to prespecified probabilities. Every game has at least one Nash equilibrium in mixed strategies.

• In the repeated prisoners' dilemma game, the players might, in equilibrium, play cooperatively. The likelihood of a cooperative outcome is enhanced when the players are patient, their interactions are frequent, cheating is easy to detect, and the one-shot gain from cheating is small.

• An analysis of sequential-move games reveals that moving first in a game can have strategic value. **(LBD Exercise 14.3)**

• A strategic move is an action you take in an early stage of a game that alters your behavior and your competitors' behavior later in the game in a way that is favorable to you. Strategic moves can limit a player's flexibility and in so doing can have strategic value.

REVIEW QUESTIONS

1. What is a Nash equilibrium? Why would strategies that *do not* constitute a Nash equilibrium be an unlikely outcome of a game?

2. What is special about the prisoners' dilemma game? Is every game presented in this chapter a prisoners' dilemma?

3. What is the difference between a dominant strategy and a dominated strategy? Why would a player in a game be unlikely to choose a dominated strategy?

4. What is special about the game of Chicken? How does the game of Chicken differ from the prisoners' dilemma game?

5. Can a game have a Nash equilibrium even though neither player has a dominant strategy? Can a game have a Nash equilibrium even though neither player has a dominated strategy?

6. What is the difference between a pure strategy and a mixed strategy?

7. How can cooperation emerge in the infinitely-repeated prisoners' dilemma game even though in a single-shot prisoners' dilemma, non-cooperation is a dominant strategy?

8. What are the conditions that enhance the likelihood of a cooperative outcome in a repeated prisoners' dilemma game?

9. What is the difference between a simultaneous-move game and a sequential-move game?

10. What is a strategic move? Why must strategic moves be hard to reverse in order to have strategic value?

PROBLEMS

14.1. Coca-Cola and Pepsi are competing in the Brazilian soft-drink market. Each firm is deciding whether to follow an aggressive advertising strategy, in which the firm significantly increases its spending on media and billboard advertising over last year's level, or a restrained strategy, in which the firm keeps its advertising spending equal to last year's level. The profits associated with each strategy are as follows:

		Pepsi	
		Aggressive	Restrained
Coca-Cola	Aggressive	$100, $80	$170, $40
	Restrained	$80, $140	$120, $100

What is the Nash equilibrium in this game? Is this game an example of the prisoners' dilemma?

14.2. Asahi and Kirin are the two largest sellers of beer in Japan. These two firms compete head-to-head in the dry beer category in Japan. The following table shows the profit (in millions of yen) that each firm earns when it charges different prices for its beer:

		Kirin			
		¥630	¥660	¥690	¥720
Asahi	¥630	180, 180	184, 178	185, 175	186, 173
	¥660	178, 184	183, 183	192, 182	194, 180
	¥690	175, 185	182, 192	191, 191	198, 190
	¥720	173, 186	180, 194	190, 198	196, 196

a) Does Asahi have a dominant strategy? Does Kirin?
b) Both Asahi and Kirin have a dominated strategy: please find and identify it.

c) Let's now assume that Asahi and Kirin will not play the dominated strategy you identified in part (b). (You might cross out the dominated strategy for each firm.) Having eliminated the dominated strategy, show that Asahi and Kirin now have another dominated strategy.
d) Let's assume that Asahi and Kirin will not play the dominated strategy you identified in part (c). Having eliminated this dominated strategy, do Asahi and Kirin now have a dominant strategy?
e) What is the Nash equilibrium in this game?

14.3. Consider the game shown below:

		Player 2	
		Left	Right
Player 1	Up	1, 4	−100, 3
	Down	0, 3	0, 2

a) What is the Nash equilibrium in this game?
b) If you were Player 1, how would you play this game?

14.4. It is the year 2099, and the moon has finally become colonized by humans. Alcatel (the French telecom equipment company) and Nokia (the Finnish telecom equipment company) are trying to decide whether to invest in the first cellular telecommunications system on the moon. The market is big enough to support just one firm profitably. Both companies must make huge expenditures in order to construct a cellular network on the moon. The payoffs that each firm gets when it enters the moon market are as follows:

		Nokia	
		Enter	Do Not Enter
Alcatel	Enter	−1000, −1000	500, 0
	Do Not Enter	0, 500	0, 0

Find all of the Nash equilibria in this game.

14.5. In a World Series game Randy Johnson is pitching for the Arizona Diamondbacks, and Alex Rodriguez is the batter for the Texas Rangers. The count on Rodriguez is 3 balls and 2 strikes. Johnson has to decide whether to throw a fastball or a curveball. Rodriguez has to decide whether to swing or not swing. If Johnson throws a fastball, and Rodriguez doesn't swing, the pitch will almost certainly be a strike, and Rodriguez will be out. If Rodriguez does swing, however, there is a strong likelihood that he will get a hit. If Johnson throws a curve, and Rodriguez swings there is a strong likelihood that Rodriguez will strike out. But if Johnson throws a curve ball and Rodriguez doesn't swing, there is a good chance that it will be ball four and Rodriguez would walk (assume that a walk is as good as a hit in this instance).

The table below shows the payoffs from each pair of choices that the two players can make:

		Alex Rodriguez	
		Swing	Do Not Swing
Randy Johnson	Fastball	−100, 100	100, −100
	Curveball	100, −100	−100, 100

a) Is there a Nash equilibrium in pure strategies in this game?
b) Is there a mixed strategy Nash equilibrium in this game? If so, what is it?

14.6. Boeing and Airbus are competing to fill an order of jets for Singapore Airlines. Each firm can offer a price of $10 million per jet or $5 million per jet. If both firms offer the same price, the airline will split the order between the two firms, 50–50. If one firm offers a higher price than the other, the low-price competitor wins the entire order. Here is the profit that Boeing and Airbus expect they could earn from this transaction:

		Boeing	
		P = $5m	P = $10m
Airbus	P = $5m	30, 30	270, 0
	P = $10m	0, 270	50, 50

(payoffs are in millions of dollars)

a) What is the Nash equilibrium of this game?
b) Suppose, now, that Boeing and Airbus anticipate that they will be competing for orders like the one from Singapore Airlines every quarter, from now to the foreseeable future. Each quarter, each firm offers a price, and the payoffs are determined according to the table above. The prices offered by each airline are public information. Suppose that Airbus has made the following public statement:

To shore up profit margins, in the upcoming quarter we intend to be statesmanlike in the pricing of our aircraft, and will not cut price simply to win an order. However, if the competition takes advantage of our statesmanlike policy, we intend to abandon this policy and will compete all out for orders in every subsequent quarter.

Boeing is considering its pricing strategy for the upcoming quarter. What price would you recommend that Boeing charge? **Important Note:** to evaluate payoffs, imagine that each quarter, Boeing and Airbus receive their payoff right away. (Thus, if in the upcoming quarter, Boeing chooses $5 and Airbus chooses $10, Boeing will immediately receive its profit of $270 million.) Furthermore, assume that Boeing and Airbus evaluate future payoffs in the following way: a stream of payoffs of $1 starting *next* quarter and received in every quarter thereafter has exactly the same value as a one-time payoff of $40 received immediately *this* quarter.

c) Suppose that aircraft orders are received once a year rather than once a quarter. That is, Boeing and Airbus will compete with each other for an order this year (with payoffs given in the table above), but their next competitive encounter will not occur for another year. In terms of evaluating present and future payoffs, suppose that each firm views a stream of payoffs of $1 starting next year and received every year thereafter as equivalent to $10 received immediately this year. Again assuming that Airbus will follow the policy embodied in the passage quoted above, what price would you recommend that Boeing charge?

14.7. Two firms are competing in an oligopolistic industry. Firm 1, the larger of the two firms, is contemplating its capacity strategy, which we might broadly characterize as "aggressive" and "passive." The "aggressive" strategy involves a large increase in capacity aimed at increasing the firm's market share, while the passive strategy involves no change in the firm's capacity. Firm 2, the smaller competitor, is also pondering its capacity expansion strategy; it will also choose between an "aggressive strategy" or a "passive strategy." The table below shows the profits associated with each pair of choices made by the two firms:

		Firm 2	
		Aggressive	Passive
Firm 1	Aggressive	25, 9	33, 10
	Passive	30, 13	36, 12

a) If both firms decide their strategies simultaneously, what is the Nash equilibrium?
b) If Firm 1 could move first and credibly commit to its capacity expansion strategy, what is its optimal strategy? What will Firm 2 do?

15

Risk and Information

No company better symbolizes the emergence of the Internet as a vehicle for commerce than Amazon.com. Launched as "Earth's Biggest Bookstore" in July 1995 by 32-year-old Jeff Bezos, Amazon.com now offers CDs, videos, toys, consumer electronics, and even auctions. When some consumers use the Web to shop for a book, a CD, or a Palm hand-held computer, Amazon.com is their first and only destination.

But what would have happened if you had invested in Amazon.com? Suppose in August 1999 you had

bought $1,000 worth of Amazon's stock. Figure 15.1 shows how the market value of that $1,000 investment would have changed over the course of a year. By October 1999, the value of your investment would have grown to $1,800, and as you approached the holiday season in December 1999, that investment would have been worth close to $2,400, an increase in value of 140 percent in four months. In late January 2000, the value of your investment would have fallen to about $1,300, but it would have climbed back to about $1,700 by the end of February 2000. By early April 2000, the value of your investment would have slipped back below $1,000, although by late May it would have rebounded to about $1,200. But as the summer began, the value of that investment would have once again slipped below $1,000, and by August 2000 it would have fallen all the way to $600. Over the course of 12 months, your investment in Amazon.com would have lost about $400.

The fate of Amazon.com's stock between August 1999 and August 2000 is an excellent example of a risk. Investing in Amazon's stock is like riding a roller coaster in a fog bank. You suspect it will go up and down, but

you can't predict when the ups and downs will occur, nor how severe they will be. Although Amazon.com's stock is perhaps an extreme example, economic life is full of risky situations: entrepreneurs face a risk of failure when they launch new businesses; sports teams face a risk of sub-par performance when they sign a free agent to an expensive contract; owners of automobiles face the risk of accidents when they drive their cars; and bidders face the risk of overpaying for items of unknown value when participating in online auctions.

This chapter is about risk and imperfect information. It provides tools and concepts for describing risk; it discusses how we would describe the preferences of an individual who does not like to bear risk. And it provides a tool for analyzing decision making in the face of imperfect information and for assessing the economic value of steps you might take to improve that information. Our goal in introducing these tools and concepts is to help you better understand economic environments such as insurance and auction markets in which risk and imperfect information play a central role. We also hope that the use of some of the tools and concepts in this chapter will help you make better decisions in your own lives—decisions perhaps about what job to accept, whether to buy stock in an Internet-based company, such as Amazon, or how much to bid at an Internet auction site, such as eBay or Yahoo!. ∎

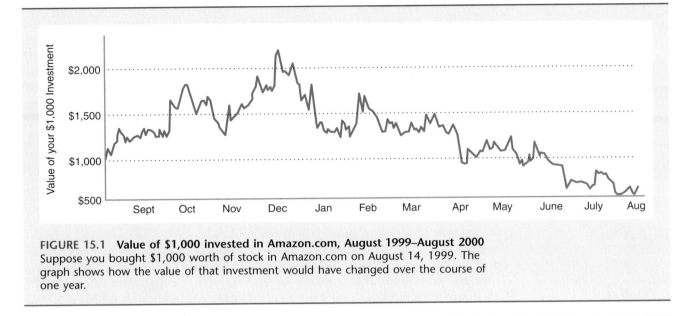

FIGURE 15.1 Value of $1,000 invested in Amazon.com, August 1999–August 2000
Suppose you bought $1,000 worth of stock in Amazon.com on August 14, 1999. The graph shows how the value of that investment would have changed over the course of one year.

15.1
DESCRIBING RISKY OUTCOMES

Suppose you have just bought $100 worth of stock in an Internet-based company such as Amazon.com. Because you don't know how the stock will perform over the next year—its value could go up or it could down—the stock is risky. But just how risky is it? How does the riskiness of this stock compare to the riskiness of other investments you might have made with this money? Answering this question involves describing a risky outcome. In this section, you will learn three concepts for describing risky outcomes: probability distributions, expected value, and variance.

LOTTERIES AND PROBABILITIES

Even though you don't know what the value of your Internet stock *will be* next year, you can still describe what it *might be*. In particular, suppose that over the next year, one of three things could happen to your $100 investment:

- Its value could go up by 20 percent to $120. Call this outcome *A*.
- Its value could remain the same. Call this outcome *B*.
- Its value could fall by 20 percent to $80. Call this outcome *C*.

Your investment in the Internet stock is an example of a **lottery.** In real life, a lottery is a game of chance. In microeconomics, the term has a similar meaning. We use the term *lottery* to describe any event—an investment in a stock, the outcome of a college football game, the spin of a roulette wheel—for which the outcome is uncertain.

The lottery described above has three outcomes: *A*, *B*, and *C*. The **probability** of a particular outcome of a lottery is the likelihood that this outcome occurs. If

629

there is a 3 in 10 chance that outcome *A* will occur, we say that the probability of *A* is 3/10, or 0.30. If outcome *B* has a 4 in 10 chance of occurring, we say that the probability of *B* is 4/10, or 0.40. And if there is a 3 in 10 chance that outcome *C* will occur, the probability of *C* is 0.30. The **probability distribution** of the lottery depicts all possible payoffs in the lottery and their associated probabilities. The bar graph in Figure 15.2 shows the probability distribution of our Internet company's stock price. Each bar represents a possible payoff from the lottery, and the height of each bar measures the probability of each payoff.

For any lottery, the probabilities of the possible outcomes have two important properties:

- The probability of any particular outcome is between 0 and 1.
- The sum of the probabilities of *all possible* outcomes is equal to 1.

In our example both of these properties hold.

Where do probabilities and probability distributions come from? Some probabilities result from predictable laws of nature. For example, if you toss a coin, the probability that it will come up heads will be 0.50. You can verify this by flipping a coin over and over again. With a large enough number of flips (100 or 200), you will see that the relative proportion of heads will be about 50 percent.

However, not all risky events are like coin flips. There are many risky events for which it might be difficult to deduce the probabilities of particular outcomes. For example, how would you really know whether the Internet stock has a 0.30 chance of going up by 20 percent? Your assessment reflects not immutable laws of nature but rather a subjective belief about how events might unfold. Probabilities that reflect subjective beliefs about risky events are called **subjective probabilities.** Subjective probabilities must also obey the two properties of probability just described. However, different decision makers might have different beliefs

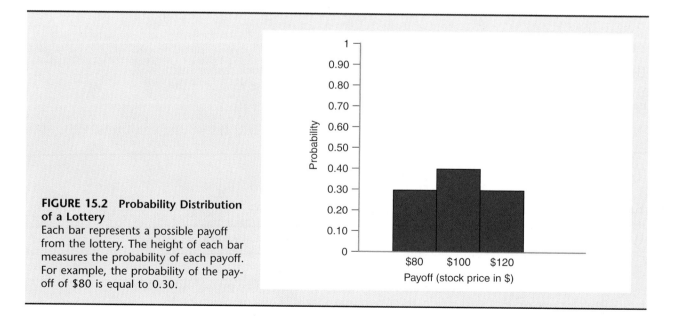

FIGURE 15.2   Probability Distribution of a Lottery
Each bar represents a possible payoff from the lottery. The height of each bar measures the probability of each payoff. For example, the probability of the payoff of $80 is equal to 0.30.

about the probabilities of possible outcomes of a given risky event. For example, an investor more optimistic than you might believe the following:

Probability of A = 0.50: there is a 5 in 10 chance that the stock will go up by 20 percent.

Probability of B = 0.30: there is a 3 in 10 chance that the stock's value will stay the same.

Probability of C = 0.20: there is a 2 in 10 chance that the stock will go down by 20 percent.

These subjective probabilities differ from yours, but they still obey the two basic laws of probability: Each probability is between 0 and 1, and the probabilities of all possible outcomes add up to 1.

EXPECTED VALUE

Given the probabilities associated with the possible outcomes of your risky investment, how much can you expect to make? The answer to this question is the **expected value.** The expected value of a lottery is a measure of the average payoff that the lottery will generate. We can illustrate this with our Internet stock example:

$$\text{Expected value} = \text{Probability of } A \times \text{Payoff if } A \text{ occurs}$$
$$+ \text{Probability of } B \times \text{Payoff if } B \text{ occurs}$$
$$+ \text{Probability of } C \times \text{Payoff if } C \text{ occurs.}$$

Applying this formula we get:

$$\text{Expected value} = (0.30 \times 120) + (0.40 \times 100) + (0.30 \times 80)$$
$$= 100$$

The expected value of your Internet stock is a weighted average of the possible payoffs that you believe might occur, where the weight associated with each payoff equals the probability that the payoff occurs. More generally, if A, B, . . . , Z denote a set of possible outcomes of a lottery, then the expected value of the lottery is as follows:

$$\text{Expected value} = \text{Probability of } A \times \text{Payoff if } A \text{ occurs}$$
$$+ \text{Probability of } B \times \text{Payoff if } B \text{ occurs} + \ldots$$
$$+ \text{Probability of } Z \times \text{Payoff if } Z \text{ occurs.}$$

The expected value of a lottery measures the average payoff you would get from the lottery if the lottery is repeated many times. If you made the same investment over and over again and took an average of the payoffs you made from this investment, that average would be nearly indistinguishable from the lottery's expected value of $100.

VARIANCE

Suppose you had a choice of two investments—$100 worth of stock in an Internet company or $100 worth of stock in a public utility (an electric company or local water works). Figure 15.3 depicts the probability distributions of the stock prices of these two companies. You should verify that the expected values of the two stocks are the same: $100. However, the Internet stock is riskier than the public utility stock because while the stock of the public utility will probably remain at its current value of $100, the Internet stock has a greater likelihood of going up or down. In other words, with the Internet stock, an investor stands to gain more or lose more than with a stock in a public utility.

We characterize the riskiness of a lottery by a measure known as the **variance.** The variance is a number that helps us distinguish between the two probability distributions in Figure 15.3. The variance of a lottery is the expected value of the squared deviations between the possible outcomes of the lottery and the expected value of the lottery. The probability distribution for the public utility stock in Figure 15.3 has a low variance: there is only a 2 in 10 chance that the actual value of the stock will deviate from its *expected* value of $100. By contrast, the probability distribution for the Internet stock has a high variance: There is a 6 in 10 chance that the actual stock price will differ from its expected value of $100.

How do we compute the variance? To find the variance of a lottery, we proceed in three steps:

1. Calculate the expected value of the lottery.
2. For each possible outcome of the lottery, take the difference between the lottery's payoff at that outcome and the lottery's expected value, and then square that result. This number is called the *squared deviation.*

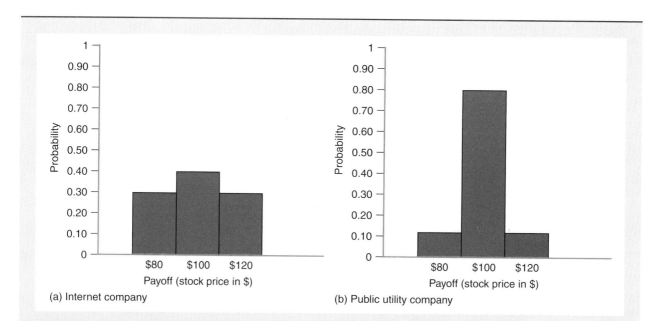

(a) Internet company   (b) Public utility company

FIGURE 15.3   Probability Distributions of the Stock Price of Two Companies
The diagram in panel (a) is the probability distribution of the stock price of the Internet company. (It is identical to the diagram in Figure 15.1.) The diagram in panel (b) is the probability distribution of the stock price of the public utility. In each diagram, a bar corresponds to a particular payoff (stock price). The height of a bar is the probability of that stock price. The probability distribution in (a) has greater variance than the one in (b).

3. For each possible outcome of the lottery, multiply the squared deviation by the associated probability and add up over all possible outcomes. The result is the *variance*.

When we do this calculation, we are, in effect, finding the average squared deviation between the actual payoff we get from the lottery and the expected value of the lottery if the lottery were repeated over and over.[1]

Table 15.1 illustrates how to calculate the variance for our two stocks. These calculations indicate that the variance of the Internet stock is greater than the variance of the public utility stock, which means that the average deviation away from expected value is greater for the Internet stock than for the public utility. It is in this sense that the Internet stock would be considered riskier than the public utility stock.

An alternative measure of the riskiness of a lottery is the **standard deviation.** The standard deviation is simply the square root of the variance. In our previous example, we would get the following:

- The standard deviation of the Internet stock is $\sqrt{240} = 15.5$.
- The standard deviation of the public utility stock is $\sqrt{80} = 8.9$.

TABLE 15.1
Variance of Two Different Stocks

Internet Company

Payoff	Probability	Squared Deviation	Multiplied by Probability
$80	0.30	$(80 - 100)^2 = 400$	$0.30 \times 400 = 120$
$100	0.40	$(100 - 100)^2 = 0$	$0.40 \times 0 = 0$
$120	0.30	$(120 - 100)^2 = 400$	$0.30 \times 400 = 120$
			Variance = 240

Public Utility

Payoff	Probability	Squared Deviation	Multiplied by Probability
$80	0.10	$(80 - 100)^2 = 400$	$0.10 \times 400 = 40$
$100	0.80	$(100 - 100)^2 = 0$	$0.80 \times 0 = 0$
$120	0.10	$(120 - 100)^2 = 400$	$0.10 \times 400 = 40$
			Variance = 80

[1] The reason that we define deviations as the *square* of the differences between actual payoffs and the expected payoff is because these differences could be either positive or negative numbers. This creates the following problem: Even though the deviations might be substantial, adding up positive and negative differences might result in the positive and negative differences canceling each other out. This could mislead us into believing that the average deviation is small. By squaring the differences between the possible payoffs and the expected value, all deviations become positive numbers, thus eliminating the "canceling-out" problem.

If the variance of one lottery is bigger than the variance of another lottery, it follows that the standard deviation of the first lottery will be bigger than the standard deviation of the second lottery. Thus, the standard deviation provides us with the same information about the relative riskiness of probability distributions as does the variance.

15.2
EVALUATING RISKY OUTCOMES

In the previous section, we saw how to describe risky outcomes using probability distributions, expected values, and variances. In this section, we explore how a decision maker might evaluate and compare alternatives whose payoffs have different probability distributions and thus different degrees of risk. In particular, we will show how we can use the concept of a utility function that we studied in Chapter 3 to evaluate the benefits that the decision maker would enjoy from alternatives with differing amounts of risk.

UTILITY FUNCTIONS AND RISK PREFERENCES

Imagine that you are about to graduate and that you have two job offers. One offer is to join a large, established company. At this company, you will earn an income of $54,000 per year. The second offer is from a small Internet company that has been started by your parents. Because this company has been operating at a loss, you are offered a token salary of $4,000 (i.e., you will work virtually for free). However, the company also promises you a bonus of $100,000 if the company manages to become profitable during the upcoming year. Based on your assessment of the company's prospects, there is a 0.50 probability that you will get the bonus and a 0.50 probability that you will not. Based on the salary offers of the two companies, which job would you accept?[2]

You face an interesting decision. Your salary at the established company is a sure thing. By contrast, your salary at the Internet start-up is a lottery: a 0.50 chance of $4,000 and a 0.50 chance of $104,000. But if you compare the offers according to their expected values, we see that the expected salary at the Internet company equals the certain salary at the established company: $54,000. We can determine this by employing the formula for expected value introduced in the previous section:

Expected salary at the Internet company:
$$(0.5 \times \$4,000) + (0.5 \times \$104,000) = \$54,000$$

Even so, it seems unlikely that you would view the offers as identical. After all, though you might get rich quick if you receive your bonus, you also face a significant risk of ending up with only $4,000. By contrast, the salary at the established company entails no risk.

[2] In real life, you would not only decide among the two jobs based on the current salary offers, but you would also consider your long-term earning prospects at each company. You would also, undoubtedly, consider various nonmonetary aspects of the two jobs, such as the nature of the work, working hours, location, and so forth.

How do we evaluate choices between alternatives that have different risks? One way is to use the concept of a utility function. We first encountered utility functions in Chapter 3, where we saw that utility is a measure of satisfaction from consuming a bundle of goods and services. Figure 15.4 depicts a possible relationship between your utility U and your income I. This utility function is increasing in income, implying that you prefer more income to less. It also exhibits diminishing marginal utility, a concept that we discussed in Chapter 3. Marginal utility is decreasing because the extra utility that you get from an increment to your income gets smaller as your income increases. For example, as Figure 15.4 shows, the increase in utility from an increment to your income when your income is low (say, $4,000) is greater than the increase in utility from the same increment to your income when your income is high (say, $104,000).

Figure 15.5 shows how we would use a utility function to evaluate your two job offers:

- Your utility at the established company corresponds to point B in Figure 15.5. At this point, you receive an income of $54,000. The utility associated with this level of income is 230, i.e., $U(54{,}000) = 230$.

- Your utility at the Internet company when you do not receive a bonus corresponds to point A in Figure 15.5. In this situation, you receive an income of $4,000, and the utility associated with this income is 60; i.e., $U(4{,}000) = 60$.

- Your utility at the Internet company when you receive a bonus corresponds to point C in Figure 15.5 In this situation, you receive an income of $104,000, and the utility associated with this income is 320; i.e., $U(104{,}000) = 320$.

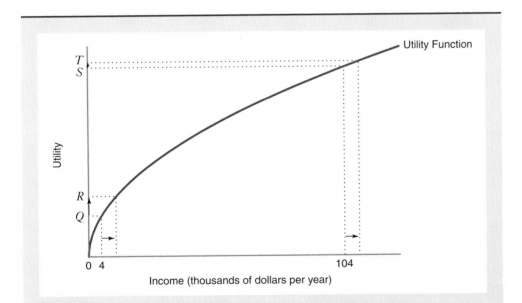

FIGURE 15.4 Relationship Between Utility and Income with Diminishing Marginal Utility
This utility function exhibits diminishing marginal utility. A given increment to income when income is low (say, $4,000 per year) increases utility by the length of segment *RQ*. The same increment to income when income is higher (say $104,000 per year) increases utility by a smaller amount, the length of segment *ST*.

• Your **expected utility** at the Internet company is the expected value of the utility levels you could receive if you worked for the Internet company. In this case, the expected utility is

$$0.5 \times U(4{,}000) + 0.5 \times U(104{,}000) = 0.5 \times 60 + 0.5 \times 320 = 190.$$

This corresponds to point D in Figure 15.5.

More generally, the expected utility of a lottery is the expected value of the utility levels that the decision maker receives from the payoffs in the lottery. In particular, if A, B, . . . , Z denote a set of possible payoffs of a lottery, then the expected utility of the lottery is as follows:

Expected utility = Probability of A × Utility of the Payoff if A occurs
$\qquad\qquad\qquad$ + Probability of B × Utility of the Payoff if B occurs + . . .
$\qquad\qquad\qquad$ + Probability of Z × Utility of the Payoff if Z occurs

$$(15.1)$$

The analysis in Figure 15.5 shows that although the Internet company offers the same expected salary as the established company, your expected utility at the Internet company is lower than the utility you get if you work for the established company. If you evaluate your prospects according to the utility function in Figure 15.5, you would strictly prefer the offer from the established company.

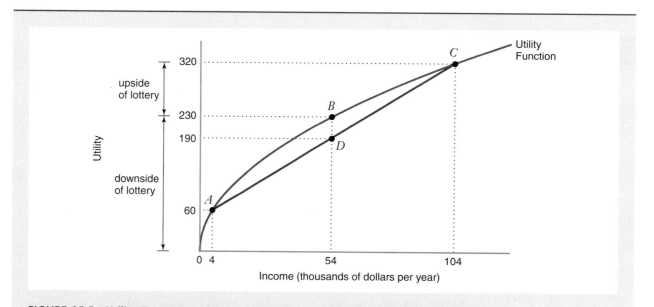

FIGURE 15.5   Utility Function and Expected Utility for a Risk-Averse Decision Maker
If you accept the job offer from the established company, you get a utility of 230, corresponding to point *B*. If you accept the job offer from the Internet company, there is a 0.50 probability that you get a utility of 60 (point *A*) and a 0.50 probability that you get a utility of 320 (point *C*). Your expected utility is 190, which corresponds to point *D*. The utility from the sure thing—the established company's offer—exceeds the expected utility of the lottery—the Internet company's offer—even though the offers have the same expected salary ($54,000). This indicates that you are risk averse.

The utility functions in Figures 15.4 and 15.5 depict the preferences of a decision maker who is **risk averse.** A risk-averse decision maker prefers a sure thing to a lottery of equal expected value. In the example above, the lottery (working for the Internet company) had the same expected value as the sure thing (working for the established company), but a risk-averse decision maker would prefer the certain salary of the established company to the risky salary of the Internet company, even though the expected salary of the Internet company equals the salary of the established company.

A utility function that exhibits diminishing marginal utility (like the one in Figure 15.5) implies that the utility of a sure thing will exceed the expected utility of a lottery with the same expected value. To see why this is the case, note that if you go to work for the Internet company, the upside of the lottery is that you have $104,000 − $54,000 = $50,000 more income than if you worked at the established company. The downside of that gamble is that if you don't get your bonus, you have $50,000 less income than you would have earned at the established company. Because of diminishing marginal utility, the reduction in utility from the downside is bigger than the gain in utility from the upside of the lottery, as Figure 15.5 shows. With diminishing marginal utility, the decision maker is thus hurt more by the downside of a lottery than he or she is helped by the lottery's upside. This tends to make the decision maker dislike bearing risk.

LEARNING-BY-DOING EXERCISE 15.1

Computing the Expected Utility for Two Lotteries for a Risk-Averse Decision Maker

Problem   Consider the two lotteries in Table 15.1. We saw that each lottery had the same expected value, but the first lottery (the Internet company's stock) had a larger variance than the second (the public utility company's stock). This tells us that the second lottery is riskier than the first lottery. Suppose that a risk-averse decision maker has a utility function described by the following equation:

$$U(I) = \sqrt{100I},$$

where I denotes the payoff of the lottery. Which lottery does the decision maker prefer? That is, which one has the bigger expected utility?

Solution   To compute the expected utility of each lottery, we will use the formula in equation (15.1). The expected utility from owning the stock of the Internet company can be computed as follows:

$$\text{Expected utility} = 0.30\sqrt{8,000} + 0.40\sqrt{10,000} + 0.30\sqrt{12,000}$$
$$= 0.30(89.4) + 0.40(100) + 0.30(109.5) = 99.7$$

The expected utility from owning the stock of the public utility company is computed in a similar fashion:

$$\text{Expected utility} = 0.10\sqrt{8,000} + 0.80\sqrt{10,000} + 0.10\sqrt{12,000}$$
$$= 0.10(89.4) + 0.80(100) + 0.10(109.5) = 99.9$$

Since the public utility company's stock has the higher expected utility, a risk-averse decision maker prefers it to the Internet company's stock. This illustrates a general point. If lotteries L and M have the same expected value, but lottery L has a lower variance than lottery M, a risk-averse decision maker will prefer L to M. We will use this property in some of our discussion.

Similar Problem: 15.3

RISK-NEUTRAL AND RISK-LOVING PREFERENCES

Risk aversion is one possible attitude that decision makers might have toward risk. But a decision maker might also be **risk neutral.** When a decision maker is risk neutral, he or she compares lotteries only according to their expected values and is therefore indifferent between a sure thing and a lottery with the same expected value.[3] Returning to our job offer example, if you were risk neutral, you would be indifferent between the sure $54,000 salary you would receive from the established company and the expected salary of $54,000 associated with the offer from the Internet company. Figure 15.6 shows the utility function of a risk-neutral individual. That utility function is a straight line, indicating that the marginal utility of income is constant. This is reflected in the fact that the change in utility from any given increment to income is the same, no matter what the decision maker's income level (i.e., the length of segment ST in Figure 15.6 is the same as the length of segment QR).

Still another possibility is that the decision maker is **risk loving.** A risk-loving decision maker prefers a lottery to a sure thing that is equal to the expected value of the lottery. If you are risk loving, your expected utility from accepting the offer from the Internet company would exceed the utility that you get from accepting the offer from the established company. Figure 15.7 shows the utility function of a risk-loving individual. A risk-loving decision maker has a utility function that exhibits increasing marginal utility. This is reflected by the fact that the change in utility from any given increment to income goes up as the decision maker's income goes up (i.e., the length of segment ST in Figure 15.7 is greater than the length of segment QR).

---

[3]To see why, note that a risk-neutral decision maker has a linear utility function, so $U = a + bI$, where a is a non-negative constant and b is a positive constant. Now, consider a lottery with payoffs I_1 and I_2, and associated probabilities p and $1 - p$. The expected utility EU of the lottery is

$$EU = p(a + bI_1) + (1 - p)(a + bI_2)$$
$$= a + b[pI_1 + (1 - p)I_2].$$

The term in the square brackets is the expected value EV of the lottery, so $EU = a + bEV$.

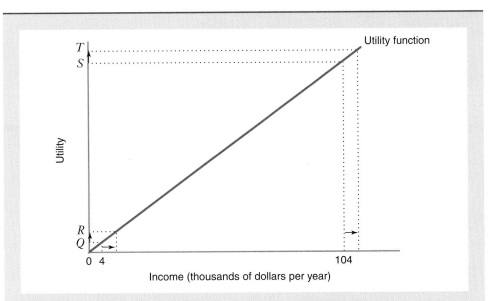

FIGURE 15.6   Utility Function for a Risk-Neutral Decision Maker
The graph of the utility function for a risk-neutral decision maker is a straight line. For
a risk-neutral decision maker, marginal utility is constant. The change in utility from
any given increment to income is the same, no matter what the decision maker's income level. The length of segment QR is the same as the length of segment ST.

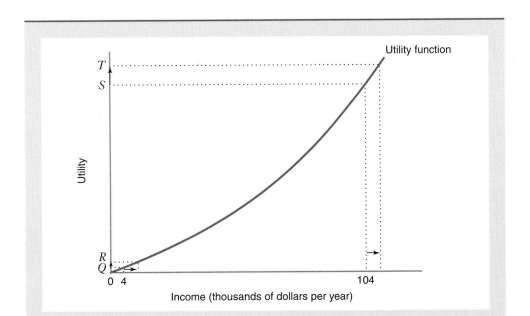

FIGURE 15.7   Utility Function for a Risk-Loving Decision Maker
The graph of the utility function for a risk-loving decision maker exhibits increasing
marginal utility. That is, the change in utility from any given increment to income goes
up as the decision maker's income goes up; the length of segment ST is larger than
the length of segment QR.

LEARNING-BY-DOING EXERCISE 15.2

Computing the Expected Utility for Two Lotteries: Risk-Neutral and Risk-Loving Decision Makers

Problem

(a) Consider the two lotteries whose variances we computed in Table 15.1. Suppose a decision maker is risk neutral and has a utility function described by the following equation:

$$U(I) = 100I,$$

where I denotes the payoff of the lottery. Which lottery does the decision maker prefer?

(b) Suppose a decision maker is risk loving and has a utility function described by the following equation:

$$U(I) = 100I^2.$$

Which lottery does the decision maker prefer?

Solution

(a) Let's compute the expected utility of each lottery to see which lottery has the highest expected utility. Using the formula for expected utility in (15.1) we have the following:

Internet Company

Expected utility = $0.30(8,000) + 0.40(10,000) + 0.30(12,000) = 10,000.$

Public Utility Company

Expected utility = $0.10(8,000) + 0.80(10,000) + 0.10(12,000) = 10,000.$

Both stocks have the same expected utility, so the decision maker is indifferent between the two. Notice that the expected utility of each lottery is equal to a hundred times the expected value of each lottery. This illustrates a general point: For a risk-neutral decision maker, the ranking of the expected utilities of lotteries will exactly correspond to the ranking of the expected payoffs of the lotteries.

(b) We again compute the expected utility of each lottery to see which lottery has the highest expected utility.

Internet Company

Expected utility = $0.30(100)(80^2) + 0.40(100)(100^2)$
$$+ 0.30(100)(120^2) = 1,024,000.$$

Public Utility Company

Expected utility $= 0.10(100)(80^2) + 0.80(100)(100^2)$
$$+ 0.10(100)(120^2) = 1,008,000.$$

In this case, the riskier stock (the Internet company) has the higher expected utility. This illustrates a general point. If lotteries L and M have the same expected value, but lottery L has a higher variance than lottery M, a risk-loving decision maker will prefer L to M.

Similar Problem: 15.4

15.3
BEARING
AND
ELIMINATING
RISK

We have now seen how to describe the riskiness of lotteries using the tools of expected value and variance. We have also seen how we can compute the expected utility of lotteries in order to determine an individual's preferences among them. Finally, we saw how we could use a utility function to characterize an individual's attitude toward risk (risk averse, risk neutral, or risk loving).

Although an individual could conceivably be risk neutral or risk loving, economists believe that for big, important decisions, such as whether to purchase insurance coverage for an automobile or how much of one's wealth to invest in the stock market, most individuals tend to act as if they were risk averse. For example, why would most car owners willingly pay monthly premiums for collision damage on their cars even though for most people the chances of having a costly automobile crash are relatively small (certainly less than 50–50 within any given year)? The answer is that when it comes to damage on our cars, most of us are risk averse. We believe that our insurance premiums are a small price to pay for the peace of mind that comes from knowing that if we ever did damage our vehicles, the cost of repairing or replacing the vehicle would be covered by our insurance policy. On the other hand, individuals do not strive to completely eliminate risk from their lives. Some motorists buy insurance policies with large deductibles (i.e., policies in which some damage is not covered), and many individuals invest at least a portion of their wealth in the stock market.

So when would risk-averse individuals choose to bear risk and when would they choose to eliminate it? In this section, we explore this question first by introducing the concept of a risk premium and then by examining a risk-averse individual's incentives to purchase insurance.

RISK PREMIUM

We have just seen that if you are risk averse, you prefer the certain income from the established company to the risky income from the Internet company. This example was special, though, because your expected salary from the Internet company was equal to your certain salary from the established company. If your expected salary from the Internet company had been sufficiently bigger than your salary at the established company, you might have preferred the risky salary at the Internet start-up to the sure salary at the established company. For example,

Figure 15.8 shows that when the expected salary of the Internet company is $54,000 and the established firm offers a certain salary of just $29,000, your expected utility at the Internet company (point *D* in the figure) exceeds your utility at the established firm (point *F*). This illustrates an important point: A risk-averse decision maker *might* prefer a gamble to a sure thing if the expected payoff from the gamble is sufficiently larger than the payoff from the sure thing. Put another way, a risk-averse decision maker will bear risk if there is additional reward to compensate for this risk.

How big this reward must be is indicated by the **risk premium** of the lottery. The risk premium of a lottery is the necessary difference between the expected value of a lottery and the payoff of a sure thing so that the decision maker is indifferent between the lottery and the sure thing. To explain the risk premium, imagine giving a risk-averse decision maker the choice between a lottery and a sure thing whose payoff equals the expected payoff of the lottery. From our earlier discussion of risk aversion, we know that the decision maker would choose the sure thing.

But now suppose that we reduced the payoff of the sure thing. If we reduced the payoff just a little, the decision maker would probably still prefer the sure thing to the risky lottery. But if we reduced the sure payoff a lot, the decision maker might actually prefer the lottery. The risk premium tells us at what point the decision maker's preferences switch. That is, the risk premium is the amount by which we must reduce the payoff from the sure thing so that a risk-averse decision maker is indifferent between the initial lottery and the sure thing with the reduced payoff. In terms of equations, if we have a lottery with two payoffs I_1 and I_2, with probabilities p and $1 - p$, respectively, the risk premium RP is found by solving the following equation:

$$pU(I_1) + (1 - p)\,U(I_2) = U(pI_1 + (1 - p)\,I_2 - RP). \tag{15.2}$$

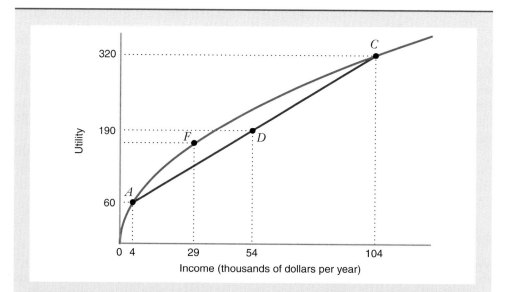

FIGURE 15.8   A Risk-Averse Decision Maker *Might* Prefer a Lottery to a Sure Thing
If the salary offer from the established company was only $29,000 per year, your expected utility from the Internet company's offer, point *D*, would exceed the utility from the established company's offer, point *F*. In this case, you would prefer the lottery to the sure thing.

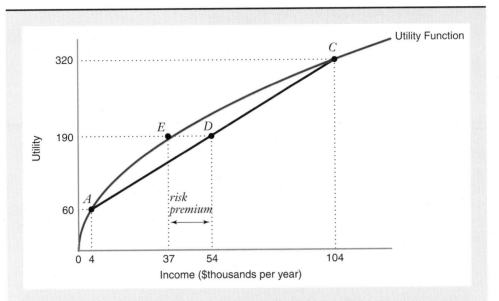

FIGURE 15.9 The Risk Premium for a Risk-Averse Decision Maker
If the salary offer from the established company was $37,000 per year, you would be indifferent between the Internet company's offer, whose expected salary is $54,000 and whose expected utility is given by point D, and the established company's offer, whose utility is given by point E. The risk premium is given by the length of line segment ED, which equals $17,000.

Figure 15.9 illustrates how we can graphically identify the risk premium for the Internet company's salary offer. Recall that the expected value of the Internet company's offer is $54,000. To find the risk premium of this lottery, we ask: What is the certain salary offer from the established company so that the utility of the established company's offer equals the expected utility of the Internet company's offer? In Figure 15.9, the expected utility of the Internet company's offer is given by point D. This expected utility is equal to the utility of a non-risky salary of about $37,000, point E in Figure 15.9. The risk premium of the Internet company's offer is thus $54,000 − $37,000 = $17,000, which is given by the length of line segment ED in Figure 15.9.

We can interpret this $17,000 risk premium as follows. If the established company had in fact offered you a salary of $37,000, then the Internet company would need to offer you an *expected* salary that is at least $17,000 larger before you would accept the Internet company's offer. This $17,000 is the minimum reward that you require in order to persuade you to give up the security of a sure thing and bear risk. This illustrates the general point of this section: a risk-averse decision maker will choose a risky lottery over a sure thing if the expected value of the lottery exceeds the payoff of the sure thing by more than the risk premium of the lottery.

An important determinant of the risk premium is the variance of the lottery. If we take two lotteries with the same expected value but different variances, the lottery with the bigger variance will entail a higher risk premium. This implies that the reward a risk-averse individual requires for bearing risk becomes larger the more risk the individual bears.

LEARNING-BY-DOING EXERCISE 15.3

Computing the Risk Premium from a Utility Function

Problem

(a) Let's return to the Internet salary lottery that we just discussed. The utility function in Figure 15.9 is given by $U = \sqrt{I}$. Using this utility function, show that the risk premium associated with the Internet company's salary offer is approximately $17,000.

(b) Suppose that the Internet company offered you a zero salary but a bonus of $108,000 if the company meets its growth targets. (Verify that this has the same expected value but a higher variance than the initial offer.) What is the risk premium associated with this offer?

Solution

(a) We can compute the risk premium by using the formula shown in equation (15.2). In particular, we need to set up the following equation and solve for *RP*:

$$0.50\sqrt{104,000} + 0.50\sqrt{4,000} = \sqrt{54,000 - RP}.$$

The value of *RP* that satisfies this equation is the necessary difference between the expected value of the lottery ($54,000) and the payoff from the sure thing ($54,000 − *RP*) that makes you indifferent between the lottery and the sure thing. The left-hand side of the equation is equal to 192.87, so to find *RP* we must solve $192.87 = \sqrt{54,000 - RP}$, which when we square both sides, becomes $37,199 = 54,000 - RP$, or

$$RP = 16,801.$$

The risk premium is thus $16,801, which is approximately $17,000.

(b) We compute the risk premium by setting up the following equation, and solving for *RP*:

$$0.50\sqrt{0} + 0.50\sqrt{108,000} = \sqrt{54,000 - RP}.$$

Solving this equation reveals that $RP = 27,000$. When the expected value of the lottery remains the same but the variance goes up, the risk premium also goes up. This calculation tells us that an offer from an established company of $27,000 per year is equivalent, from your point of view, to the offer from the Internet company to work for free and face a 50–50 chance of a year-end bonus of $108,000.

Similar Problem: 15.6

WHEN WOULD A RISK-AVERSE PERSON CHOOSE TO ELIMINATE RISK? THE DEMAND FOR INSURANCE

Our analysis of the risk premium tells us that a risk-averse individual will bear risk only if there is a sufficiently big reward for doing so. The logic of risk aversion also sheds light on the circumstances under which a risk-averse person would choose to eliminate risk by buying insurance.

To illustrate, let's imagine that you have just purchased a new car. If all goes well—if the car works as planned and if you don't have an accident—you will have $50,000 of income available for consumption on the goods and service that you would typically purchase over the course of a year. If, however, you have an accident and you are uninsured, you would expect to have to pay $10,000 in repairs. This would leave just $40,000 available for consumption of other goods and services. Let's suppose that your probability of an accident is 0.05, so the probability of not having an accident is thus 0.95. If you remain uninsured, you thus face a lottery: a 5 percent chance of $40,000 in disposable income and a 95 percent chance of $50,000 in disposable income.

Let's now suppose that you have the opportunity to buy $10,000 worth of annual insurance coverage at a total cost of $500 per year ($500 is called the insurance premium). Under this policy, the insurance company agrees to pay for the $10,000 worth of repairs on your automobile in the event that you have an automobile accident. This insurance policy has two notable features. First, it provides full coverage for any damage you might suffer if you have an accident.[4] Second, the insurance policy is **fairly priced.** A fairly priced insurance policy is one in which the insurance premium is equal to the expected value of the promised insurance payment. Because there is a 5 percent chance that the policy pays $10,000 and a 95 percent chance that it pays nothing, the expected value of the promised insurance payment is $(0.05 \times \$10,000) + (0.95 \times 0) = \$500$.[5] If the insurance company sold this policy to many individuals with an accident risk that is similar to yours, it would expect to break even on these policies.

We can use the logic of risk aversion to show that you should jump at the chance to buy this policy. If you buy the policy, you get

- $50,000 − $500 = $49,500, if you do not have an accident
- $50,000 − $500 − $10,000 + $10,000 = $49,500, if you have an accident

The insurance policy thus eliminates all of your risk and allows you to consume $49,500 worth of goods and services no matter what. If you do not buy the policy, you get

- $50,000 if you do not have an accident
- $40,000 if you have an accident

The expected value of your consumption in this case is $0.95 \times \$50,000 + 0.05 \times \$40,000 = \$49,500$. Thus, the expected value of consumption if you do not buy

[4]In the language of the insurance business, we would say that this policy fully *indemnifies* you against your loss.

[5]Another way to describe a fairly priced policy is that the insurance premium per dollar of insurance coverage, $500/$10,000, is equal to the probability of an accident.

insurance is equal to the certain value of your consumption if you do buy insurance. Because a risk-averse decision maker prefers a sure thing to a lottery with the same expected value, our analysis shows that a risk-averse individual will always prefer to buy a fair insurance policy that provides full coverage against a loss.

EXAMPLE 15.1

Why Does Anyone Supply Insurance? A Brief History of Insurance and the Sharing of Risk

We have just seen that a risk-averse consumer has an incentive to *demand* insurance. But why would anyone have an incentive to *supply* insurance? You might guess that if risk-aversion explains insurance demand, then risk-loving preferences explain insurance supply. After all, aren't insurance suppliers really taking a gamble that the insured party will not experience a loss? But the answer to why insurance gets supplied is more subtle than this. In particular, the supply of insurance does not require that insurance suppliers be risk lovers. A brief look at the history of insurance will help illustrate this point.

In his engaging history of the concept of risk, *Against the Gods,* Peter Bernstein points out that the insurance business had its roots in the ancient world.[6] In ancient Greece and Rome, for example, an early version of life insurance was provided by occupational guilds. These groups asked their members to contribute to a pool that would then be used to provide financial support to a family if the head of the family unexpectedly died. In medieval Italy, an early version of crop insurance arose when farmers created cooperative organizations that would insure one another against losses due to bad weather. Under this arrangement, farmers in one part of the country that experienced good weather would compensate farmers in another part of the country whose crops had been impaired by bad weather. And the most famous insurance company of all, Lloyds of London, started in 1771 when a group of individuals (the Society of Lloyds) who did business at Lloyds coffee house each agreed to commit their personal wealth to underwrite the losses incurred by each other and by other customers. The group that paid insurance premiums to the Society included ship owners, merchants, and building owners.

These historical examples illustrate the basic principle of insurance: A group of people that have not sustained losses provides money to pay off other people that have incurred losses. In modern economies, insurance companies such as Prudential or State Farm in effect serve as intermediaries in this process. For example, State Farm will use the cash that you paid last month for your automobile insurance policy to compensate some other car owner that had the misfortune to experience an automobile accident this month.

Viewed in this way, insurance is fundamentally about sharing risk among a group of individuals so that no party in the group bears an undue amount of risk. Because of this, insurance markets can arise even when all parties are risk averse. What is necessary for this to happen is that the risks the parties bear are, to some degree,

---

[6]See especially Chapter 5. Bernstein, P. L., *Against the Gods: The Remarkable Story of Risk,* (New York: John Wiley & Sons), 1996.

independent of each other. That is, when one individual (or group of individuals) suffers a loss, there are other individuals that do not suffer a loss. This is usually true of almost all risks for which standard forms of insurance exist—automobile accidents, fires, illnesses, and deaths. A notable example of when independence did not hold was Hurricane Andrew, which devastated the state of Florida in 1992. In that case, the damage to homes and businesses was so widespread throughout Florida that property insurance companies operating in the state had great difficulties paying off claims, and some, as a result, experienced serious financial difficulties. But Hurricane Andrew is the exception, not the norm. In most cases insurance markets work well because risk sharing is possible: when some parties suffer, other parties have, one way or another, put up the money to compensate for the losses. ◼

ASYMMETRIC INFORMATION IN INSURANCE MARKETS: MORAL HAZARD AND ADVERSE SELECTION

If you own a car and look over your own automobile insurance policy, you will probably notice that you have what is known as a deductible. In the context of the above example, a deductible would make the car owner responsible for a portion (e.g., the first $1,000 worth) of the damage from an accident, while the insurance company insures the rest. A deductible transforms an insurance policy from one of full insurance to one of partial insurance.[7]

Why do insurance policies have deductibles? An important reason is the presence of **asymmetric information.** Asymmetric information refers to situations in which one party knows more about its own actions or personal characteristics than another party. In insurance markets, there are two important forms of asymmetric information: moral hazard, which arises when the insured party can take hidden actions that affect the likelihood of an accident, and adverse selection, which arises when a party has hidden information about its risk of an accident or loss.

Hidden Action: Moral Hazard

Let's return to the automobile insurance example from the previous section. Suppose that you have just purchased a fairly priced insurance policy that completely reimburses you for any damage that your car suffers as a result of an automobile accident. Now that you know that you are fully insured, how careful will you be? Perhaps not as careful as you would have been had you not been fully insured. Perhaps you drive faster, or behave more recklessly under adverse weather conditions. Perhaps you take less care to protect your car against vandals or thieves (e.g., by parking it on the street rather than in a garage). The net effect of your exercising less care when you are fully insured is that your probability of suffering damage goes up. Perhaps instead of a 10 percent chance of a loss, it is now 15 or even 20 percent.

---

[7]Co-payments in health insurance policies do the same thing. A co-payment makes the insured party responsible for a pre-specified fraction (e.g., 10 percent) of his or her medical bills.

This example illustrates the concept of **moral hazard.** Moral hazard describes a phenomenon whereby an insured party exercises less care than he or she would in the absence of insurance. Since the insurance company cannot monitor the everyday actions of its policy holders—those actions are hidden from its view— once it sells you the policy it can't do much to affect your behavior. This is a problem for the insurance company because the possibility of moral hazard can directly affect its profits. Recall that the policy just described allowed the insurance company to just break even, assuming a probability of damage equal to 10 percent. But if fully insured individuals behave more recklessly because they are fully insured and the probability of damage rises to 20 percent, the insurance company will lose money.

One way that the insurance company might deal with the moral hazard problem would be to pay for damage only in cases in which the insured party could demonstrate that his or her recklessness or neglect was not the cause of the accident. But enforcing such contract provisions is often impractical. The insurance company would need to conduct detailed investigations of every accident, and even if it did so, getting at the truth in which it is easy for individuals to hide or shade the truth ("I really was obeying the speed limit!") would be very difficult.

A better solution is for the insurance company to provide incentives for careful driving. Deductibles are one way to provide such incentives. If you know that you will have to pay a portion of the repair bill in the event of an accident, there is a good chance that you will be more focused on driving carefully. In competing for the business of risk-averse customers, insurance companies face an interesting trade-off. The insurance has to be complete enough (i.e., it has to cover a large enough portion of the expected damage) so that the individual will buy insurance. At the same time, deductibles have to be significant enough to provide adequate incentives for insured parties to take care.

Hidden Information: Adverse Selection

Moral hazard provides one explanation for why insurance policies often do not provide full insurance. **Adverse selection** is another. While moral hazard refers to the effect of an insurance policy on the incentives of individual consumers to exercise care, adverse selection refers to how the magnitude of the insurance premium affects the types of individuals that buy insurance. In particular, adverse selection is a phenomenon whereby an increase in the insurance premium increases the overall riskiness of the pool of individuals who buy an insurance policy.

The population consists of all sorts of individuals. Some individuals are skillful or careful drivers, but some are not as skillful or careful and have a higher risk of an accident. Insurance companies understand this, of course, which is why some classes of drivers (young folks, for instance) face higher auto insurance premiums than other classes of drivers (those over 30 years old).

But insurance companies can go only so far in distinguishing good risks from bad risks. Even within broad risk classes, individuals might vary greatly in terms of their risk characteristics, and information about the inherent riskiness of a prospective policy holder is often hidden. The inability to distinguish among the riskiness of individuals that buy insurance creates a potential problem for an insurance company and gives rise to the adverse selection problem. Consider, for example, a company that sells health insurance. For a given insurance premium, a policy that fully insured the individual's medical bills would be more attractive to an individual who faces a high risk of illness (e.g., because of heredity or lifestyle) than one that faces a low risk of illness. This makes such a policy costly for the insurance company to offer. You might wonder whether raising the insurance premium would be a way for the insurance company to offset this high cost. But when the insurance company offers the same policy to all potential consumers and cannot distinguish among individuals according to their risk of illness, increasing the insurance premium makes matters even worse: high-risk individuals would continue to buy insurance (because it is so valuable to them), but some low-risk individuals might conceivably choose to go without health insurance.[8] The increase in the insurance premium that is needed to offset the expected cost of the insurance policy adversely affects the pool of individuals that are still willing to select the option of buying full insurance (hence the term, adverse selection).

How could an insurance company make money in the face of this adverse selection? One way would be to offer consumers an array of different policies and allow potential consumers to select the one they most prefer. A policy with a large deductible and low premium would appeal to an individual who is convinced that his chances of illness are low, whereas a policy with a smaller deductible but larger premium would be relatively more attractive to an individual that faces a more significant risk of illness. Another way insurance companies deal with the adverse selection problem is by selling insurance to groups of individuals. For example, if all employees in a particular company participate in a mandatory company-wide group health insurance plan, the insurance company offering the group plan will face a mix of high-and low-risk individuals. Had an identical insurance policy been offered on an individual-by-individual basis, low-risk individuals might opt not to purchase health insurance coverage, thus adversely affecting the mix of individuals covered by the insurance policy.

15.4 ANALYZING RISKY DECISIONS

So far, we have discussed how to describe risky outcomes (using concepts such as expected value and variance) and how to evaluate them (using expected utility). Let's now analyze how a decision maker might choose a plan of action in the face of risk. We do so by introducing you to the concept of a **decision tree**. A decision tree is a diagram that describes the options available to a decision maker, as well as the risky events that can occur at each point in time. It is a valuable tool for identifying the optimal plan of action when a decision maker faces risk.

DECISION TREE BASICS

To illustrate how a decision tree can be used to choose among risky alternatives, we begin with a simple example. Suppose an oil company has just discovered a new reserve of oil offshore in the North Sea. It can construct either of two types of offshore drilling platforms: A large capacity facility or a small capacity facility. The size of the facility the firm would want to construct depends on the amount of oil in the reservoir:

---

[8]Or, perhaps low-risk individuals might seek out less expensive alternatives, such as joining a health maintenance organization.

- If the reservoir is large, and the firm builds . . .
  —a large facility, the firm's profit is $50 million.
  —a small facility, the firm's profit is $30 million.
- If the reservoir is small, and the firm builds . . .
  —a large facility, the firm's profit is $10 million.
  —a small facility, the firm's profit is $20 million.

In this example, if the firm knew *for sure* that the reservoir was large, then it would build a large facility. If, by contrast, it knew for sure that the reservoir was small, it would build a small facility. What makes this a thorny problem for the oil company is that it doesn't know the size of the reservoir at the present time. It believes that the reservoir will be large with a probability of 0.50 and small with a probability of 0.50.

Figure 15.10 illustrates the oil company's decision tree. A decision tree has four basic parts:

- *Decision nodes.* A decision node, represented by a □ in the tree drawing, indicates a particular decision that the decision maker faces. Each branch from a decision node corresponds to a possible alternative that the decision maker might choose.
- *Chance nodes.* A chance node, represented by a ○ in the tree drawing, indicates a particular lottery that the decision maker faces. Each branch from a chance node corresponds to a possible outcome of the lottery.

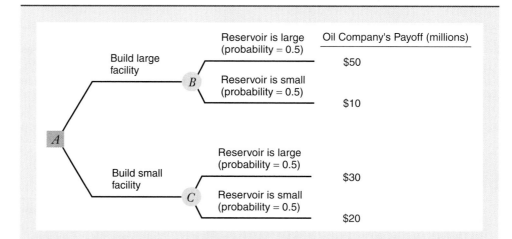

FIGURE 15.10   Decision Tree for Oil Company's Facility Size Decision
Node *A* is a decision node: It indicates that the oil company can choose a large or small facility. Node *B* depicts the lottery the company faces if it builds a large facility. Node *C* depicts the lottery the firm faces if it builds a small facility. Each of these lotteries has two possible outcomes: the reservoir will be large or small. The payoffs at the right end of the tree show the profit the oil company will get for each possible decision and lottery outcome.

- *Probabilities.* Each branch from a chance node has a probability. The sum of the probabilities along all branches from a chance node must add up to 1.

- *Payoffs.* Each branch at the right-hand end of the tree has a payoff associated with it. The payoff is the value of the outcome resulting from each possible combination of choices and risky outcomes. If the decision maker is risk neutral, payoffs are monetary values. If the decision maker is risk averse, payoffs are utilities of monetary values representing the options available to the company, the lotteries it faces, and the payoffs it can achieve.

To understand the decision tree in Figure 15.10, we begin at the left-hand side at the decision node labeled *A*. This node corresponds to the firm's facility-size decision. The two branches extending from this decision node show the firm's two choices: "Build a large facility" and "Build a small facility."

Moving to the right in the tree, we encounter chance node *B*. This is the lottery the firm faces if it builds a large facility. This lottery has two outcomes, each with probability 0.50, so two branches extend from chance node *B*. If the reservoir is large, the company's profit is $50 million; if the reservoir is small, the profit is $10 million. In this example, we will assume that the firm is risk neutral, so the firm's payoff is equal to its profit.[9] Below chance node *B* is chance node *C*. This is the lottery the firm faces if it builds a small facility. This lottery also has two outcomes. If the reservoir is large, the company's profit is $30 million; if the reservoir is small, the profit is $20 million.

To evaluate the tree, you might think that we should move from left to right, just as we have be doing in exploring the tree's constituent parts. But if you attempt to analyze a decision tree by working from left to right, you will encounter the inevitable frustration that arises when you encounter the chance nodes, which tell you that the value of either decision alternative is, "It all depends on uncertain events."

To deal with this, we start at the nodes at the right end of the tree and work backward from right to left. This is called *folding the tree back*. This is identical to the procedure that we used to analyze game trees in Chapter 14. Let's start at chance node *B*. How should it assign a value to the lottery that is represented by this node? Because our firm is risk neutral, it evaluates lotteries according to their expected values.[10] The expected value of chance node *B* is (0.5 × $50 million) + (0.5 × $10 million) = $30 million. This tells us that the firm's expected payoff from constructing the large facility is $30 million. From the firm's point of view as a risk-neutral decision maker, this is the value associated with being at chance node *B*. Similarly, we can calculate the expected value of chance node *C*, which would be (0.5 × $30 million) + (0.5 × $20 million) = $25 million.

We can now simplify the decision tree by replacing the chance nodes *B* and *C* by the expected values of their respective lotteries. Figure 15.11 shows the oil company's decision tree after we have folded it back. The firm is now in a position to work back to the decision node, and sees that the expected value of the large facility is greater than the expected value of the small facility. Its optimal decision would be to choose the large facility. The expected payoff from following this optimal decision is $30 million.

---

[9]If we had assumed that the firm was risk averse, we would need to specify a utility function for the firm and evaluate the utility of the profit of each outcome.

[10]If the firm was risk averse, we would evaluate the expected utility of the payoffs at chance node *B* using the firm's utility function.

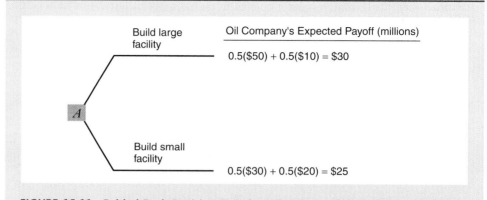

Build large
facility

Oil Company's Expected Payoff (millions)

$0.5(\$50) + 0.5(\$10) = \$30$

A

Build small
facility

$0.5(\$30) + 0.5(\$20) = \$25$

FIGURE 15.11 Folded Back Decision Tree for Oil Company's Facility Size Decision
This figure shows the oil company's decision tree when we replace chance nodes *B*
and *C* with the corresponding expected payoff that the firm gets at each of those
chance nodes. We can now see that the oil company's best decision is to build a large
facility.

DECISION TREES WITH A SEQUENCE OF DECISIONS

The preceding decision tree was easy to analyze because the decision maker faced just one decision. But sometimes decision makers face a sequence of decisions or must make a decision following the outcome of a chance event. To illustrate decision tree analysis in this more complicated setting, let's add an additional twist to our oil company example. The firm can still build a large facility or a small facility, but suppose that it can also conduct a seismic test to determine the size of the reservoir before it makes the decision about the size of the facility. Suppose, for a moment, that the test is costless.[11] Should the firm conduct the test, and if so, how much better off is the firm by doing so?

To answer these questions, consider the firm's decision tree in Figure 15.12. The top two decision branches coming out of decision node *A* are the same as in Figures 15.10 and 15.11. The third branch in the decision tree represents the new alternative: conduct a seismic test before building the facility. If the firm conducts the test, it will learn whether the reservoir is large or small, as depicted by chance node *D*. The outcome of the test is a chance node because, before the firm conducts the test, it does not know what its outcome will be.

In our example, the test has two possible outcomes, each with a probability of 0.50. The firm could learn that the reservoir is large. Given this, the firm faces another decision, represented by decision node *E*. If the firm chooses a large facility, it will earn a payoff of $50 million. If it chooses a small facility, it will earn a payoff of $30 million. Alternatively, the firm could learn that the reservoir is small. If so, the firm faces the decision represented by decision node *F*. In this case, if the firm chooses a large facility, it will earn a payoff of $10 million, while if it chooses a small facility, it will earn a payoff of $20 million.

As before, we analyze the decision problem by working backwards from the nodes at the right end of the tree. Decision node *E* is easy to analyze because

[11]In the next section, we will discuss what happens when (as is the case in reality) the test is costly.

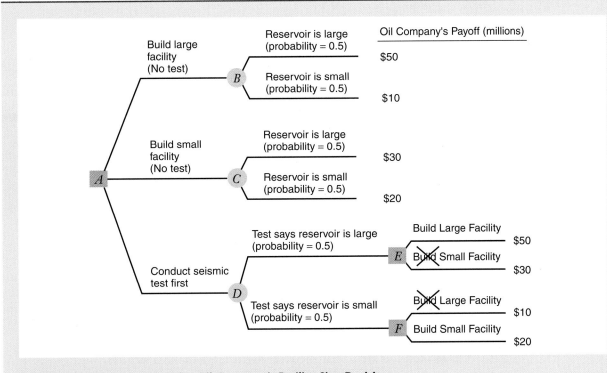

FIGURE 15.12 Decision Tree for Oil Company's Facility Size Decision with an Option to Test
This figure shows the oil company's decision tree when it has an option to conduct a seismic test at no cost. The option to conduct a seismic test adds an additional branch at node A. Chance node D indicates that there are two possible outcomes of the test: The test can say that the reservoir is either large or small. Given either outcome, the oil company has to decide whether to build a large or small facility. These decisions are represented by nodes E and F. The optimal decision at node E is to build a large facility. We place an X through the other choice at this node to indicate that it will not be chosen. Similarly the optimal decision at node F is to build a small facility.

once the firm learns that the reservoir is large, it should build a large facility. We place an "X" through the alternative to build a small facility, since it is the inferior choice at decision node E. Decision node F is also easy to resolve; if the firm learns that the reservoir is small, its best action is to build a small facility. We place an "X" through the alternative to build a large facility, since it is the inferior choice at decision node F.

Having identified the firm's optimal course of action at decision nodes E and F, we can now simplify the decision tree as represented in Figure 15.13. Once the tests are run, the firm will know what size facility to build, and we can calculate the expected payoff of the chance node D. That expected payoff is (0.5 × $50) million + (0.5 × $20 million) = $35 million.

We have now worked our way back to decision node A. We have already worked out the expected payoffs for the top two alternatives at that node ($30 million from constructing the large facility and $25 million from constructing the

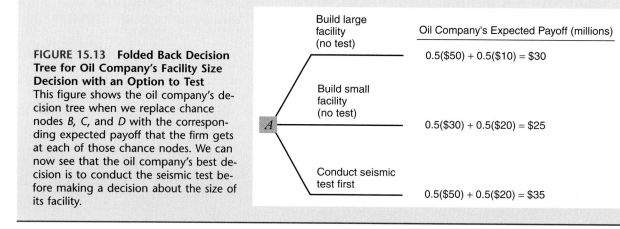

FIGURE 15.13   Folded Back Decision Tree for Oil Company's Facility Size Decision with an Option to Test
This figure shows the oil company's decision tree when we replace chance nodes *B, C,* and *D* with the corresponding expected payoff that the firm gets at each of those chance nodes. We can now see that the oil company's best decision is to conduct the seismic test before making a decision about the size of its facility.

small facility). The expected payoff from the third alternative of conducting a test is $35 million, which is bigger than the payoff from the other two alternatives. We can now summarize the firm's optimal plan of action:

- Conduct the seismic test.
- If the test identifies that the reservoir is large, build a large facility.
- If the test identifies that the reservoir is small, build a small facility.

This example illustrates the basic steps involved in constructing and analyzing a decision tree.

1. Begin by mapping out the sequence of decisions and risky events.
2. For each decision, identify the alternative choices the decision maker can make.
3. For each risky event, identify the possible outcomes.
4. Assign probabilities to the risky events.
5. Identify payoffs for all possible combinations of decision alternatives and risky outcomes.
6. Finally, find the optimal sequence of decisions by folding back the tree. In so doing, you identify the expected value of the lotteries at each chance node and determine the highest expected payoff option at each decision node. The payoff corresponding to that *highest expected payoff* option then becomes the value you assign to that decision node.

THE VALUE OF INFORMATION

When faced with risky decisions, it seems natural that decision makers would benefit from information that might help them reduce or even eliminate the risk. The value of information is reflected in the fact that oil companies spend money to perform seismic tests before drilling oil wells, that consumer products companies, such as Procter & Gamble and Unilever, spend money to test market new products before they roll them out on a national scale, and that prospective presidential candidates spend money taking polls and establishing exploratory committees before throwing their hats into the ring. The decision tree analysis that we just went through can help us identify the economic value of information.

Let's summarize the results of the decision tree analysis of the oil company example in the previous section:

- When the oil company could not conduct a seismic test, its optimal course of action is to build a large facility. Its expected payoff from this course of action is $30 million.
- When the oil company could conduct a seismic test at no cost, its optimal course of action is to conduct a test. If the test indicates a large reservoir, the company should build a large facility. If the test indicates a small reservoir, the company should build a small facility. Its expected payoff from this course of action is $35 million.
- Thus: When the firm can—at no cost—conduct a seismic test, its expected payoff is $5 million higher than when it cannot conduct the test.

This example illustrates the **value of perfect information** (VPI). The value of perfect information is the increase in a decision maker's expected payoff when the decision maker can—at no cost—conduct a test that will reveal the outcome of a risky event. In our oil-drilling example, the VPI is equal to $5 million, the difference between the expected payoff the decision maker enjoys when it can conduct a costless seismic test and the expected payoff the decision maker gets from making the optimal decision in the absence of the test.

Why does perfect information have value? It is not, as you might initially guess, because individuals are risk averse. We can see this in two ways. First, even though the seismic test revealed the true size of the oil reservoir, it did not eliminate the decision maker's risk: before the test is taken, its outcome is uncertain and thus represents a risk for the decision maker. Second, risk aversion by itself cannot account for the value of perfect information because, in the example above, there is a positive VPI even though we assumed that the firm is risk neutral.

Perfect information has value because it allows the decision maker to tailor its decisions to the underlying circumstances it faces. In our example, the oil company fares best when it could match the size of the drilling facility to the size of the oil reservoir (a small facility maximizes profits when it faces a small reservoir, but a large facility maximizes profits when it faces a large reservoir). The company could not match its decision to the reservoir size when it did not conduct a seismic test. In that case, it had to make an unconditional decision: "small" or "large." By contrast, when it conducted the test, it could look at the results of the test and make its decision accordingly.

The magnitude of VPI tells us the maximum amount of money the firm would be willing to pay for a test that revealed perfect information. It is, in short, the firm's willingness to pay for a crystal ball. In this case, if the seismic test costs $4 million, the firm should conduct it: It is paying $4 million for a test that is actually worth $5 million. If, by contrast, the test costs $7 million, it would not be worth doing. The firm is better off making a choice without the results of the seismic test.

EXAMPLE 15.2   *The Real Options Revolution and the VPI*[12]

Business Week magazine calls it a "revolutionary concept in corporate finance." The power of this approach, write two scholars, "is starting to change the economic 'equation' of many industries."[13] With this approach, says one consultant, "uncertainty has the potential to be your friend, not your enemy."

These quotes refer to the concept of a real option. A real option exists when a decision maker has the opportunity to tailor a decision to information that will be received in the future.[14] In the decision tree in Figure 15.12, undertaking a seismic test creates a real option for the oil company: It puts the oil company in the position of being able to make the decision about its new facility contingent on the outcome of the test. The VPI is the extra value of the real option, above and beyond the intrinsic value of the oil reservoir. That is, the VPI tells us the difference between the oil company's expected payoff if it can make a contingent decision (if it undertakes the test) and a noncontingent decision (if it doesn't take the test). More generally, determining the value of a real option closely parallels our analysis of VPI and can often involve the analysis of decision trees.[15]

In the world of business, firms are increasingly utilizing real options analysis to determine the benefits from creating opportunities to tailor decisions to future information:

- Oil companies Anadarko Petroleum and Chevron used real option analyses of seismic tests to make decisions about how to bid on Gulf of Mexico oil leases.

- Airbus and Boeing offer airline customers such as British Airways and United the option of cancelling or downsizing orders. Airlines use these options when the demand for airline services unexpectedly falls. Airbus recently began using real options analysis to determine the extra value that these options provide to customers.

- Hewlett–Packard (H–P) customizes some of its products (e.g., ink-jet printers) for particular foreign markets. Traditionally, it would customize the product at the factory (e.g., it would make ink-jet printers for France, ink-jet printers for Germany, and so forth) and ship them in finished form to the foreign market. But this was a risky strategy because demand in foreign markets was hard to predict, and H–P often guessed wrong and ended up shipping too few or too many printers. To reduce its risk, H–P decided to ship partially

---

[12]This example draws from "Exploiting Uncertainty: The Real-Options Revolution in Decision Making," *Business Week* (June 7, 1999).

[13]M. Amram, and N. Kulatilaka, *Real Options: Managing Strategic Investment in an Uncertain World* (Boston: Harvard Business School Press, 1999).

[14]The term *real* is used in order to distinguish this general notion of an option from the narrower notion of a financial option. There are many kinds of financial options. An example is a call option on a share of stock. The owner of a call option has the right, but not the obligation, to buy a share of stock at a pre-specified price.

[15]For sufficiently complex situations, there are other techniques that draw from the field of finance that are used to value real options. The book by Amram and Kulatilaka cited above presents a non-technical discussion of some of these techniques.

assembled printers to large overseas warehouses and then customize them once it had definite orders from particular markets. This increased H–P's production cost, but it allowed them to tailor the quantity of printers of a particular kind to demand conditions in foreign markets once demand became known. H–P used real option analysis to determine whether the benefits from this strategy were worth the increased production costs.

As the theory of real options becomes more popular in actual business firms, analysis of decision trees that incorporate a value of information will be an important tool for decision makers in actual firms to assess the value of the real options that their firms face. ■

15.5 AUCTIONS

Auctions are a prominent part of the economic landscape. Since the mid-1990s, several countries (e.g., the United States, the United Kingdom, and Germany) have used auctions to sell portions of the airwaves for communications services such as mobile telephones and wireless Internet access. (We discuss one such auction in more detail in Example 15.4.) Other countries, such as Mexico, have used auctions to privatize state-owned companies such as railroads and telephone companies. And now, of course, auctions are available to anyone with an Internet connection, as companies such as e-Bay, Yahoo, and Amazon.com have helped make online auctions one of the fastest growing areas of commerce on the World Wide Web.

Economists have been studying auctions for years, and a well-developed body of microeconomic theory pertains to them. Auctions typically involve relatively few players that make decisions under uncertainty. The analysis of auctions thus combines the game theory we discussed in Chapter 14 with concepts relating to information and decision making under uncertainty that we have discussed in this chapter. For this reason, a discussion of auctions provides a nice way of capping and integrating some of the ideas from both chapters.

TYPES OF AUCTIONS AND BIDDING ENVIRONMENTS

Auction Formats

There are a variety of different types of auctions. Perhaps the most familiar format (probably because it is often depicted in movies or on television) is the **English auction.** Under this format, participants cry out their bids, and each participant can increase his or her bid until the auction ends with the highest bidder winning the object. Another common auction type is the **first-price sealed-bid auction** in which each bidder submits one bid, not knowing the other bids. The highest bidder wins the object and pays a price equal to his or her bid. Many auctions in eBay are, in effect, sealed-bid auctions. Still another type of auction is the **second-price sealed-bid auction.** This format was used to sell airwave licenses in New Zealand. As in the first-price sealed-bid auction, each bidder submits a bid and the high bidder wins. However, the winning bidder pays an amount equal to the second-highest bid. A final common type of auction is the **Dutch**

descending auction, a format often used to sell agricultural commodities, such as tobacco and flowers (including tulips in Holland, which explains the name). Under a Dutch descending auction, the seller of the object announces a bid, which is then lowered until a buyer announces a desire to buy the item at that price.

Private Values versus Common Values

Auctions can also be classified as involving private values or common values. When buyers have **private values,** each bidder has his or her own personalized valuation of an object. You know how much the item is worth to you, but you are not sure how much it is worth to other potential bidders. A common setting in which bidders have private values is in the sale of antiques or art. For such items, individuals are likely to have idiosyncratic assessments of an item's value and are probably not going to change their minds if they find out that someone has a different value. In a private values setting your attitude would be, "I don't care what you think, I love that painting."

When buyers have **common values,** the item has the same intrinsic value to all buyers, but no buyer knows exactly what it is. To illustrate, imagine that your economics professor came to class with a briefcase full of dollar bills which he or she intended to auction. The monetary value of the dollars inside is the same to everyone, but no one knows how many bills are actually inside. The assumption of common values nicely characterizes the sale of items such as oil leases or U.S. treasury bills. In a common values setting, we usually assume that bidders have the opportunity to obtain estimates of the value of the object (e.g., you can look inside the briefcase for 30 seconds). Your estimate would be your best guess about the value of the object. In this situation, you might change your mind about the object's value if you knew the estimates of other bidders. In particular, if you later learned that every other bidder had a lower estimate of the object's true value than you did, you would probably revise your estimate of the object's value downward.

AUCTIONS WHEN BIDDERS HAVE PRIVATE VALUES

To illustrate bidding behavior in auctions, let's consider a setting in which bidders have private values. We will explore three different auction formats: the first-price sealed-bid auction, the English auction, and the second-price sealed-bid auction. Our goal is to see how the rules of the auction affect the behavior of bidders and the amount of revenue the auction raises for the seller.

First-Price Sealed-Bid Auctions with Private Values

Suppose you and a group of other bidders are competing to purchase an antique dining room table that is being offered for sale on eBay. Furthermore, suppose you have concluded that this table is worth $1,000 to you. That is, the most you are willing to spend to buy this table is $1,000. Because this is a private values auction, other individuals might attach a different value to this table. Let's suppose (realistically) that you do not know the valuations of other potential bidders. Let's also suppose, though, that you believe that some bidders could have valuations in excess or below your $1,000.

In deciding on a bidding strategy, it might seem natural to submit a bid of $1,000. After all, that is what the table is worth to you, and by bidding as high as possible, you maximize your chances of winning. However, this is generally not your best strategy. In a first-price sealed-bid auction, a bidder's optimal strategy is to submit a bid that is less than its maximum willingness to pay.

To see why, let's explore what happens when you reduce your bid from $1,000 to $900. Not knowing the valuations of the other bidders, you can't say for sure what the consequences of this move will be. However, it's likely that your probability of winning the auction will go down. Suppose that curve S in Figure 15.14 describes the relationship between your bid and the probability of winning. (In a moment, we'll talk about where S comes from.) If you bid $1,000, the expected value of your payment—your bid multiplied by the probability of winning—is area $A + B + C + D + E + F$. (Throughout this, and the rest of this section, we will assume that you are risk neutral and evaluate benefits and costs according to their expected value.) If, by contrast, you bid $900, your expected payment is area $E + F$. (Table 15.2 keeps track of these areas for you.) Your expected payment goes down by area $A + B + C + D$. It goes down for two reasons: First, you pay less if you win; second, your probability of winning is now lower. Reducing your expected payment is good, but when you lower your bid, you also reduce your expected benefit from winning the auction. Your expected benefit is your $1,000 value times the probability of winning. When you bid $1,000, your expected benefit is area $A + B + C + D + E + F$, but when you bid $900 your expected benefit is area $D + E + F$. Thus, your expected benefit goes *down* by

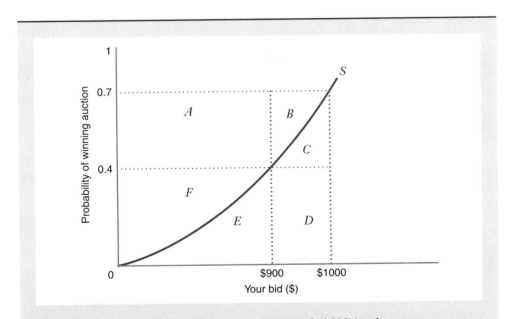

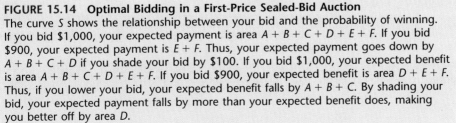

FIGURE 15.14 Optimal Bidding in a First-Price Sealed-Bid Auction
The curve S shows the relationship between your bid and the probability of winning. If you bid $1,000, your expected payment is area $A + B + C + D + E + F$. If you bid $900, your expected payment is $E + F$. Thus, your expected payment goes down by $A + B + C + D$ if you shade your bid by $100. If you bid $1,000, your expected benefit is area $A + B + C + D + E + F$. If you bid $900, your expected benefit is area $D + E + F$. Thus, if you lower your bid, your expected benefit falls by $A + B + C$. By shading your bid, your expected payment falls by more than your expected benefit does, making you better off by area D.

TABLE 15.2
Expected Benefits and Costs of Different Bids in First-Price Sealed-Bid Auction

	Bid	
	$1,000	**$900**
Expected benefit	$A + B + C + D + E + F$	$D + E + F$
Expected payment	$A + B + C + D + E + F$	$E + F$
Expected profit	0	D

area $A + B + C$. So is it worth shading your bid? The answer is yes. Table 15.2 tells us that when you shade your bid, your expected payment goes down by more than your expected benefit, and your net gain from shading your bid is area D. By shading your bid below your true valuation, you reduce your probability of winning, but you more than make up for it by saving money if you win the auction.

By how much should you shade your bid? This depends on the shape of S, which depends on your beliefs about the bidding strategies of the other bidders, and that, in turn, depends on your beliefs about their valuations. In the Nash equilibrium of the bidding game, each player forms an assessment of the relationship between a bid and the probability of winning—the S curve in Figure 15.14—by conjecturing a relationship between the valuations of each rival bidder and its equilibrium bidding behavior.[16] In equilibrium, these conjectures must be consistent with bidders' actual behavior. We illustrate Nash equilibrium bidding strategies for a first-price sealed-bid auction in Learning-By-Doing Exercise 15.4.

If there was a total of N bidders, the Nash equilibrium strategy for each bidder would be to submit a bid equal to $(N - 1)/N$ times the player's true valuation. Note that no matter how many bidders there are, the bidder with the highest valuation wins the auction and pays a price that is less than the bidder's maximum willingness to pay. Moreover, equilibrium bids go up as more bidders participate in the auction.

LEARNING-BY-DOING EXERCISE 15.4

Verifying the Nash Equilibrium in a First-Price Sealed-Bid Auction with Private Values

Problem Two bidders are competing to buy an object. Each bidder has a private valuation of the object. Each believes that the other bidder's valuation is equally likely to lie between $0 and $200. Let's verify that each player's Nash equilibrium bid is equal to one-half its true valuation.

---

[16]Remember from Chapter 14 that at a Nash equilibrium, each player in a game is doing the best it can given the strategies of the other players.

Solution We need to show that if Bidder 1 believes that Bidder 2 will submit a bid equal to half of Bidder 2's true valuation, then Bidder 1 will also submit a bid equal to half of its valuation.

If Bidder 2's bid is half of its true valuation, then Bidder 1 believes that Bidder 2's bid is equally likely to be between 0 and $100. Given this, if Bidder 1 submits a bid equal to Q, the probability that Bidder 1 wins the auction is equal to $Q/100$. Can you see why? If Bidder 1 submits a bid just a shade over $100, then given Bidder 2's anticipated behavior, Bidder 1 wins the auction for sure. If Bidder 1 submits a bid of $50, then there is a 0.50 probability that Bidder 2 will submit a higher bid, and a 0.50 probability that Bidder 2 will submit a lower bid. Note that the expression $Q/100$ corresponds to the S curve in Figure 15.14.

Suppose Bidder 1's true valuation of the object is $60. Bidder 1's total profit is its expected benefit from getting the object minus its expected payment:

$$\text{Expected benefit} - \text{Expected payment}$$

$$= (\text{Valuation} \times \text{Prob. of winning}) - (\text{Bid} \times \text{Prob. of winning})$$

$$= \left(60 \times \frac{Q}{100}\right) - \left(Q \times \frac{Q}{100}\right)$$

$$= (0.60 - 0.01Q)Q.$$

The formula for the bidder's total profit $(0.60 - 0.01Q)Q$ is analogous to the expression for total revenue along a linear demand curve.[17] The formula for the bidder's marginal profit will thus be analogous to the formula for marginal revenue for a linear demand curve. That expression will be $0.60 - 0.02Q$.[18] At the optimal bid, marginal profit equals 0, so the optimal bid must satisfy $0.60 - 0.02Q = 0$, or $Q = 30$. This equals half the bidder's valuation. Thus, if Bidder 1 believes that Bidder 2 will submit a bid equal to half of its valuation, Bidder 1's best response is to follow the same strategy.

What if this auction had more than two bidders? It is beyond the scope of this text to compute the Nash equilibrium in this case. It turns out that had there been N bidders, each of whose valuation was equally likely to fall between 0 and $200, the Nash equilibrium strategy for each bidder would be to submit a bid equal to $(N - 1)/N$ times the player's true valuation. Note that no matter how many bidders there are, the bidder with the highest valuation wins the auction and pays a price that is less than its maximum willingness to pay. Moreover, equilibrium bids go up the more bidders there are that participate in the auction.

Similar Problem: 15.10

English Auctions with Private Values

Let's now consider an English auction. Returning to the example in the previous setting, suppose that you and another bidder are competing to purchase the antique dining room table that is worth $1,000 to you. Unknown to you, your

---

[17]Remember from Chapter 11 that when demand is $P = a - bQ$, total revenue is $(a - bQ)Q$.

[18]Again recall from Chapter 11 that when total revenue is $(a - bQ)Q$, marginal revenue is $a - 2bQ$.

rival's valuation of the table is $800. Suppose that the auctioneer opens the bidding at $300. What should you do?

It turns out that when buyers have private values, your dominant strategy in an English auction is to continue bidding as long as the high bid is less than your maximum willingness to pay.[19] At that point you should stop. To see why, suppose that your rival has just shouted out a bid of, say, $450—and that the auctioneer is prepared to accept increases in bids in increments of $1. Should you bid $451 or should you drop out of the bidding? Clearly you should raise your bid to $451: The worst that can happen is that your bid will be topped by the other bidder, in which case you are no worse off than you are now. The best that can happen is that the other bidder will drop out, and you will get the table at a price ($451) that is below your willingness to pay.

If both players follow a strategy of bidding until the high bid reaches their maximum willingness to pay, it follows that the person who values the item the most (in this example, that's you) will win the item, and will pay a price that is just a shade higher than the valuation of the bidder with the *second-highest* valuation. In this example, your rival drops out when you raise the bid to $801. As a result, you are able to buy a table that is worth $1,000 to you for a price of $801.

Second-Price Sealed-Bid Auctions with Private Values

Let's now suppose that the seller uses a second-price sealed bid auction to sell the antique table. What bid should you submit? This auction seems much more complicated than the English auction or the first-price sealed-bid auction. Interestingly, though, game theory again yields a clear and powerful prediction about bidding behavior in second-price sealed-bid auctions: Each player's dominant strategy is to submit a bid equal to its maximum willingness to pay for the item. That is, if your valuation of the table is $1,000, then submitting a bid of $1,000 is at least as good as—and sometimes better than—any other bid you might consider submitting, *no matter what bids you think that rival bidders will submit*.

To see why bidding your valuation is a dominant strategy, let's consider your options:

- If you bid *less than* your maximum willingness to pay of $1,000, you might win or you might not. That depends on the valuation of the other player, which you don't know. But no matter what, you cannot hurt yourself by increasing your bid to $1,000 because you don't pay your own bid but instead pay a price equal to the second-highest bid. And by increasing your bid you might even help your chances of winning the object. Thus, any bid less than your maximum willingness to pay is dominated by a bid that is exactly equal to your maximum willingness to pay.

- What about bidding *more than* your maximum willingness to pay of $1,000, say $1,050? This might seem appealing because you don't actually pay your bid. The problem is that this strategy can never help you. If, for example, your rival bidder is planning to bid *more than $1,050* (remember, you can't rule out this possibility because you don't know that player's valuation), increasing your

---

[19]See Chapter 14 for a discussion of dominant strategies.

bid doesn't help you: you lose anyway. If, on the other hand, your rival plans to bid *less than $1,000*, you would have won had you kept your bid at $1000; the increase to $1,050 again doesn't help you. Finally, if the other bidder plans to bid between $1,000 and $1,050 (again, a possibility you can't rule out), you win the table, but you've paid a price more than it is worth to you. You would have been better off bidding $1,000 and not winning the table. Summing up, increasing your bid above your maximum willingness to pay of $1,000 can sometimes hurt you and can never help you. That is, any bid that is greater than your maximum willingness to pay is dominated by a bid exactly equal to your maximum willingness to pay.

If each player follows its dominant strategy to submit a bid equal to its maximum willingness to pay, you will submit a bid equal to $1,000, while your rival (whose valuation we have assumed to equal $800) submits a bid of $800. As in the English auction, you win the item. And the price that you pay—$800—is virtually identical to the $801 that you would have paid in an English auction. Remarkably, the second-price sealed-bid auction, even though it entails different rules than the English auction, generates virtually the same revenue for the seller of the object.[20]

Summing Up: Revenue Equivalence

Let's summarize our analysis of auctions when buyers have private values. If all players in the auction follow Nash equilibrium strategies (i.e., the strategies predicted by our game theory analysis), then the following is true:

- In a first-price sealed-bid auction, the buyer with the highest willingness to pay wins the auction but submits a bid that is less than his maximum willingness to pay for the object.
- In an English auction, the buyer with the highest willingness to pay wins the auction at a bid that is (virtually) equal to the second-highest valuation of all of the bidders in the auction.
- In a second-price sealed-bid auction, the buyer with the highest willingness to pay wins the auction. Each bidder submits a bid equal to its maximum willingness to pay, so the winning bidder pays a price equal to the second-highest valuation of all the bidders.

Notice what each auction format has in common. Each format successfully identifies the buyer with the highest valuation. But under each format the revenue that the seller collects—i.e., the winning bid—is less than the highest valuation. In particular, under the English and second-price auctions that revenue is identical: It equals the second-highest valuation of all bidders in the auction. Remarkably, the equivalence between English and second-price sealed-bid auctions extends to *all* auctions when buyers have private values. This amazing result is called the **revenue equivalence theorem.** The revenue equivalence theorem says that when buyers have private values, any auction format—including the three

---

[20]The difference arises because in the English auction we restricted the bid increment to $1. In general, the difference between the payment made by the winning bidder in the English auction and the second-price-sealed-bid auction is due entirely to the size of the bidding increment.

that we have considered—will, on average, generate the same revenue for the seller. In fact, on average, that revenue will equal the second-highest valuation of all the bidders participating in the auction.

AUCTIONS WHEN BIDDERS HAVE COMMON VALUES: THE WINNER'S CURSE

When bidders have common values, a complication arises that does not occur when bidders have private values: the **winner's curse.** The winner's curse refers to the phenomenon whereby the winning bidder in a common-values auction might bid an amount that exceeds the item's intrinsic value. To illustrate how this can happen, suppose your economics professor brings a briefcase full of dollar bills to class and auctions it off. Every student is given a peek inside the briefcase to estimate how much it contains. You estimate that it contains $150, which represents the most you would be willing to bid. Of course, your classmates develop their own estimates, and these might differ from yours. Let's suppose that these estimates are distributed according to the bell-shaped curve shown in Figure 15.15. The height of this curve indicates the relative frequency of different estimates. This curve is centered on the true intrinsic value of the item (i.e., the actual amount of money in the briefcase). Unknown to you and your classmates, this amount is $80.

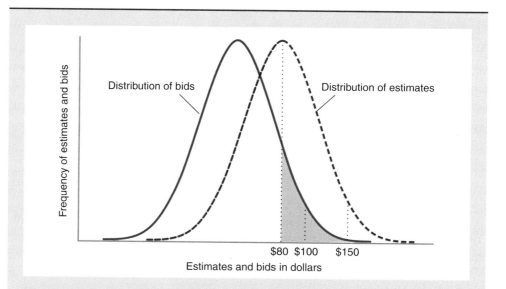

FIGURE 15.15   The Winner's Curse in an Auction with Common Values
The dashed bell-shaped curve shows the distribution of estimates of the amount of money in your professor's briefcase when the actual amount is $80. The solid bell-shaped curve shows the distribution of bids given that students shade their bids. Because your estimate is at the far right end of the bell-shaped curve of estimates, your bid will be at the far right end of the bell-shaped curve of bids, e.g., $100. If you win the auction, you will have bid $100 for an item worth only $80. This is the winner's curse. Any bidder located in the shaded region of the bell-shaped curve who wins the auction will suffer from the winner's curse.

Suppose, now, that your professor uses a first-price sealed-bid auction to sell the money in the briefcase. In the previous section you learned that when bidders have private values, you should shade your bid. If you and your classmates do this, the distribution of bids will be another bell-shaped curve, shifted to the left of the curve describing the distribution of estimates. Let's suppose that you submit a bid of $100, which is two-thirds of your estimate. To your initial delight, yours is the high bid and you win the briefcase. But when you count the money, you realize you have spent $100 to win a prize worth only $80. You've just experienced the winner's curse.

Figure 15.15 helps explain the winner's curse phenomenon.[21] The bid that wins the auction will be drawn from the right-hand tail of the distribution of bids. The winning bid will thus be based on the most optimistic estimate of the value of the object being auctioned. The winning bidder will almost surely have overestimated the value of the object being sold. Even if the bidder shades his or her bid, that winning bid could still fall within the shaded region of Figure 15.15 where winning bids exceed the true value of the object.

How can you avoid the winner's curse? A key lesson from our discussion of game theory in Chapter 14 is that you should think ahead. You should anticipate that if you win the auction, it is because you had the highest estimate of the object's value, and you should adjust your bidding behavior accordingly. Specifically, in the briefcase auction you should reason as follows:

- I estimate that the value of the money in the briefcase is $150.
- But if I win the auction, it means that my estimate was higher than everybody else's, which means that the true value of the item is probably less than $150.
- Because my goal is to win the auction but not pay more than the item is actually worth, I should act as if my estimate is not $150, but something less than $150, say, $a \times \$150$, where $a < 1$.

The amount by which you discount your estimate, a, depends on how many other bidders there are. Suppose the class has 29 other students. To determine how much to shade your bid, you should ask yourself: "If I knew that my estimate of $150 was the largest of 30 estimates, what would be my best guess about the intrinsic value of the item?" The answer: Significantly less than $150. Let's say it's $85.[22] This modified estimate of the value of the item ought to be your *starting point* in devising a bid strategy. We say starting point because you might want to scale down your bid even more (as you did in a private-values auction) as you consider the possible bidding behavior of other bidders in the game. The key point, though, is that the possibility of the winner's curse should make you even more conservative in your bidding behavior than you would have been in an auction in which bidders have private values.

The winner's curse implies that if bidders adjust their bidding strategies to avoid it, adding more bidders to the auction can actually make bidders behave more conservatively. This contrasts with the private-value case in which the addition of bidders tends to inflate the Nash equilibrium bids in the auction. Why

[21]This diagram is based on a similar diagram in M. Bazerman and W. F. Samuelson, "I Won the Auction But Don't Want the Prize," *Journal of Conflict Resolution*, 27, 4 (December 1983): 618–634.

[22]The exact answer to this question requires the application of advanced probability theory.

might you want to bid more conservatively when more bidders participate in the auction? Think about it this way: When are you more likely to have an overly optimistic estimate of the value of an object—when you are the winning bidder in an auction with three bidders or in an auction with 300 bidders? In the first case, if you win the auction, your estimate must have exceeded just two others. In the second case, your estimate must have exceeded 299 others. You are much more likely to have drawn an inflated estimate when yours is the highest of 300 than when it is the highest of just three.

If bidders respond to the possibility of the winner's curse by shading their bids in a sealed-bid auction, one might wonder whether a first-price sealed-bid auction is best from the auctioneer's perspective. It turns out that when bidders have common values, a better auction format for the seller is the English auction in which a bidder can see the bids of the other players. In an English auction, a bidder can revise his or her opinion of the item's value as the bidding progresses. In particular, if you are initially pessimistic about an item's value (because you have a low estimate), the fact that other players continue to bid aggressively on it will lead you to revise your beliefs about its actual value upwards. This, in turn, reduces your incentives and the incentives of other bidders to shade their bids downward in response to the winner's curse. Game theory analysis can show that the auctioneer's average revenue over many auctions will be higher under an English auction than under a first-price sealed-bid auction, a second-price sealed-bid auction, or a Dutch auction.[23] This might partly explain why English auctions are so prevalent in the real world: They allow bidders to learn from each other, which helps mitigate the winner's curse.

EXAMPLE 15.3

The Winner's Curse in the Classroom[24]

What do you think would happen if your economics professor really did bring in a briefcase of dollar bills? Do you think the class would suffer from the winner's curse? Two professors, Max Bazerman and William Samuelson, did this experiment in a number of MBA classes at Boston University. They used jars of pennies and nickels rather than a briefcase full of dollar bills. But the experiment was essentially the one we just described. Students were asked to guess the amount of money contained in a large jar that, unknown to the students, contained $8 worth of coins. (To motivate accurate guesses, a special prize was awarded to the student whose guess came closest to the actual amount of money in the jar.) Students then participated in a first-price sealed-bid auction in which they submitted an amount they were willing to pay for the money in the jar.

Bazerman and Samuelson found that students systematically succumbed to the winner's curse. In the 48 auctions they conducted, the average winning bid was $10.01, resulting in a loss of $2.01 for the winning bidder. This finding is even

---

[23]This is true when bidders are risk neutral and when they are risk averse.
[24]This example is based on M. Bazerman, and W. F. Samuelson, "I Won the Auction But Don't Want the Prize," *Journal of Conflict Resolution*, 27, 4 (December 1983): 618–634.

more remarkable because students' estimates of the amount of money in the jar tended to be on the low side. The average estimate was $5.13, $2.87 below the true value. Thus, the winner's curse in these auctions operated with special force. Despite underestimating the value of the item, students still overbid relative to its true value! Had subjects been unbiased in their estimates—that is, had the true value of the item been $5.13—the winning bidders' average loss would have been $4.88 ($10.01 − $5.13).

The lesson: Beware of the winner's curse! The temptation to bid aggressively in an auction is strong. If you fall prey to it, you may well regret you won. ∎

The "Greatest Auction of Them All": The FCC's Broadband Spectrum Auction[25]

EXAMPLE 15.4

It was, according to *New York Times* columnist William Safire, "The greatest auction of them all," and it involved the sale "of valuable thin air." Safire was talking about the auction that was held between December 1994 and March 1995 by the U.S. Federal Communications Commission (FCC) to sell licenses for portions of the electromagnetic spectrum across the United States.[26] This was the largest public auction ever held up to that time. When it was over, the FCC had raised more than $7.7 billion by selling licenses to companies such as AT&T, Sprint, GTE, and PacTel, so that they could offer an array of wireless telecommunications services, such as pagers, mobile telephones, and wireless data transmission.

The FCC's spectrum auction is especially interesting to economists because its rules were designed by three game theorists: Paul Milgrom and Robert Wilson of Stanford University, and Preston McAfee of the University of Texas. The FCC used a simultaneous ascending auction. In this auction, the FCC offered many licenses for sale at the same time. (In the auction that took place between December 1994 and March 1995, the FCC sold ninety-nine broadband licenses—two 30 MHz licenses in each of fifty-one major metropolitan areas, with the exception of New York, Washington, and Los Angeles, where just one license was sold.[27]) The bidding took place over multiple rounds, during which each bidder (firms such as AT&T, PacTel, and Airtouch) submitted simultaneous bids for any of the licenses in which they were interested. A firm might, for example, bid for licenses that covered New Orleans, El Paso, and Tulsa. The auction ended when there were no new bids on any of the licenses offered for sale. This particular auction took 112 rounds and lasted almost four months.

The simultaneous ascending auction format had several properties designed to help combat distortions in bidding behavior induced by fear of the winner's curse. Because the bids were ascending, firms could see how their competitors were

---

[25]This account draws heavily from P. Crampton, "The FCC Spectrum Auctions: An Early Assessment," *Journal of Economics and Management Strategy*, 6, 3 (Fall 1997): 431–495; R. P. McAfee and J. McMillan, "Analyzing the Airwaves Auction," working paper (1998); P. Milgrom, "Putting Auction Theory to Work: The Simultaneous Ascending Auction," working paper (1999).

[26]The formal name was the MTA broadband spectrum auction.

[27]In these markets, one of the two licenses was awarded to firms introducing pioneering communications technologies.

bidding and could respond to each other's bids. This made it akin to an English auction and helped alleviate bidders' fears of the winner's curse. Had the auction been a one-shot sealed-bid auction, buyers, seeking to avoid the winner's curse, might have been excessively cautious in their bidding strategies. Australia and New Zealand had sold spectrum licenses using single-round sealed-bid auctions and raised a disappointing amount of revenue. Because the licenses were auctioned simultaneously rather than one at a time, firms had the flexibility to seek the combinations of licenses they most desired. For example, Ameritech (a regional telecommunications company in the Midwest) entered the auction wanting to acquire several licenses in Midwestern metropolitan areas (Cleveland and Indianapolis, in particular) to build a regional network. Had the licenses been auctioned one at a time, Ameritech would have had to bid on one license (e.g., for the Cleveland market) without knowing whether it would win complementary licenses (e.g., the Indianapolis market) later on. This, too, can create fear of a winner's curse and lead to overly cautious bidding.

How did the auction unfold? The big winners were AT&T, which won twenty-one licenses, and WirelessCo, an alliance between Sprint and three large cable television companies, TCI (now owned by AT&T), ComCast, and Cox, which won twenty-nine licenses. The auctions were, in the view of most observers, remarkably successful. Peter Crampton, who has studied the FCC's auctions in detail, writes: "The assignment of licenses by auction is a huge improvement over allocation by lottery or comparative hearings. Market competition is putting the licenses in the hands of those companies best able to use them. Firms, consumers, and taxpayers all benefit." ∎

CHAPTER SUMMARY

- A lottery is any event whose outcome is uncertain. We describe this uncertainty by assigning a probability to each possible outcome of the lottery. These probabilities are between zero and one, and the probabilities of all possible outcomes add up to one.

- The expected value of a lottery is a measure of the average payoff the lottery will generate.

- The variance of the lottery characterizes the average deviation between the possible outcomes of the lottery and the expected value of the lottery.

- A risk-averse decision maker prefers a sure thing to a lottery of equal expected value.

- We can describe a risk-averse decision maker's preferences using a utility function that exhibits diminishing marginal utility. A risk-averse decision maker will evaluate lotteries according to their expected utility **(LBD Exercise 15.1).**

- A risk-neutral decision maker evaluates lotteries according to the expected value of their payoffs **(LBD Exercise 15.2).**

- A risk-loving decision maker evaluates lotteries according to their expected utility, using a utility function that exhibits increasing marginal utility **(LBD Exercise 15.2).**

- A risk premium is the necessary difference between the expected value of a lottery and the payoff from a sure thing so that the decision maker is indifferent between the lottery and the sure thing **(LBD Exercise 15.3).**

- A fair insurance policy is one in which the price of the insurance is equal to the expected value of the damage being covered. A risk-averse individual will always prefer to purchase a fair insurance policy that provides full insurance against a loss.

- A decision tree is a diagram that describes the options available to decision makers, as well as the uncertain events that can occur at each point in time. We analyze decision trees by starting at the right end of the tree and working backwards.

- The value of perfect information is the increase in the decision maker's expected payoff when the decision maker can—at no cost—conduct a test that will reveal the outcome of a risky event.

- There are a variety of different types of auction formats, including the English auction, the first-price sealed-bid auction, the second-price sealed-bid auction, and the Dutch descending auction. Auctions can also be classified according to whether bidders have private valuations of the item being sold or common valuations.

- In a first-price sealed-bid private-values auction, it is optimal for a participant to bid less than its maximum willingness to pay for the object **(LBD Exercise 15.4).**

- In an English auction, a bidder's dominant strategy is to continue bidding as long as the high bid is less than his maximim willingness to pay. If all bidders behave in

this way, the bidder with the highest valuation will win the auction and will pay a price that is (virtually) equal to the second-highest valuation of all bidders.

- In a second-price sealed-bid auction, a bidder's dominant strategy is to submit a bid equal to his maximum willingness to pay. If all bidders behave in this way, the bidder with the highest valuation will win the auction and will pay a price that is equal to the second-highest valuation of all bidders.

- The revenue equivalence theorem says that when buyers have private values, any auction format will, on average over many auctions, generate the same revenue for the seller. In fact, on average, that revenue will equal the second-highest valuation of all the bidders participating in the auction.

- In common-values auctions, bidders must worry about the winner's curse, the possibility that the winning bidder bids an amount that exceeds the item's intrinsic value. To avoid the winner's curse, a bidder in any auction format should discount its estimate of the value of the item when formulating its bidding strategy.

REVIEW QUESTIONS

1. Why must the probabilities of the possible outcomes of a lottery add up to 1?

2. What is the expected value of a lottery? What is the variance? What does each of these concepts measure?

3. What is the difference between the expected payoff of a lottery and the expected utility of a lottery?

4. Explain why diminishing marginal utility implies that a decision maker will be risk averse.

5. Suppose that a risk-averse decision maker faces a choice of two lotteries, 1 and 2. Lotteries 1 and 2 have the same expected value but Lottery 1 has a higher variance than Lottery 2. What lottery would a risk-averse decision maker prefer?

6. What is a risk premium? What determines the magnitude of the risk premium?

7. What is fair insurance? Why will a risk-averse consumer always be willing to buy full insurance that is fair?

8. What is the difference between a chance node and a decision node in a decision tree?

9. Why does perfect information have value, even for a risk-neutral decision maker?

10. What is the difference between an auction in which bidders have private values and one in which they have common values?

11. What is the winner's curse? Why can the winner's curse arise in a common-values auction but not in a private-values auction?

12. Why is it wise to bid conservatively in a common-values auction?

PROBLEMS

15.1. Consider a lottery with three possible outcomes: a payoff of -10, a payoff of 0, and a payoff of $+20$. The probability of each outcome is 0.2, 0.5, and 0.3 respectively.

a) Sketch the probability distribution of this lottery.
b) Compute the expected value of the lottery.
c) Compute the variance and the standard deviation of the lottery.

15.2.   Suppose that you flip a coin. If it comes up heads, you win $10; if it comes up tails, you lose $10.
a) Compute the expected value and variance of this lottery.
b) Now consider a modification of this lottery: You flip two fair coins. If both coins come up heads, you win $10. If one coin comes up heads and the other comes up tails, you neither win nor lose—your payoff is $0. If both coins come up tails, you lose $10. Verify that this lottery has the same expected value but a smaller variance than the lottery implied by a single coin flip. (*Hint:* The probability that two fair coins both come up heads is 0.25, and the probability that two fair coins both come up tails is 0.25.) Why does the second lottery have a smaller variance?

15.3.   Suppose that you have a utility function given by the equation $U = \sqrt{50I}$. Consider a lottery that provides a payoff of $0 with probability 0.75 and $200 with probability 0.25.
a) Sketch a graph of this utility function, letting I vary over the range 0 to 200.
b) Verify that the expected value of this lottery is $50.
c) What is the expected utility of this lottery?
d) What is your utility if you receive a sure payoff of $50? Is it bigger or smaller than your expected utility from the lottery? Based on your answers to these questions, are you risk averse?

15.4.   Consider two lotteries, A and B. With lottery A, there is a 0.90 chance that you receive a payoff of $0 and a 0.10 chance that you receive a payoff of $400. With lottery B, there is a 0.50 chance that you receive a payoff of $30 and a 0.50 chance that you receive a payoff of $50.
a) Verify that these two lotteries have the same expected value but that lottery A has a bigger variance than lottery B.
b) Suppose that your utility function is $U = \sqrt{I + 500}$. Compute the expected value from each lottery. Which lottery has the higher expected utility? Why?
c) Suppose that your utility function is $U = I + 500$. Compute the expected utility from each lottery. If you had this utility function, are you risk averse, risk neutral, or risk loving?
d) Suppose that your utility function is $U = (I + 500)^2$. Compute the expected utility from each lottery. If you had this utility function, are you risk averse, risk neutral, or risk loving?

15.5.   Sketch the graphs of the following utility functions as I varies over the range $0 to $100. Based on these graphs, indicate whether the decision maker is risk averse, risk neutral, or risk loving:
a) $U = 10I - (1/8)I^2$
b) $U = (1/8)I^2$

c) $U = \log(I + 1)$
d) $U = 5I$

15.6.   Suppose that your utility function is $U = \sqrt{I}$. Compute the risk premium of the two lotteries described in Problem 4.

15.7.   Consider a household that possesses $100,000 worth of valuables (computers, stereo equipment, jewelry, and so forth). This household faces a 0.10 probability of a burglary. If a burglary occurs, the household would have to spend $20,000 to replace the stolen items. Suppose it can buy an insurance policy for $500 that would fully reimburse it for the amount of the loss.
a) Should the household buy this insurance policy?
b) Should it buy the insurance policy if it cost $1,500? $3,000?
c) What is the most the household would be willing to pay for this insurance policy? How does your answer relate to the concept of risk premium discussed in the text?

15.8.   A small biotechnology company has developed a new burn treatment that has potential commercial applications. The company has to decide whether to produce the new compound itself or sell the rights to the compound to a large drug company. The payoffs from each of these courses of action depend on whether the treatment is approved by the Food and Drug Administration (FDA), the regulatory body in the United States that approves all new drug treatments. (The FDA bases its decision on the outcome of tests of the drug's effectiveness on human subjects.) The company must make its decision before the FDA. Here are the payoffs the drug company can expect to get under the two options it faces:

| | | Decision | |
| | | Sell the | Produce |
Outcome	Probability	Rights	Yourself
FDA approves	0.20	$10	$50
FDA does not approve	0.80	$2	−$10
(all payoffs are in millions of dollars)			

a) Draw a decision tree showing the decisions that the company can make and the payoffs from following those decisions. Carefully distinguish between chance nodes and decision nodes in the tree.
b) Assuming that the biotechnology company acts as a risk-neutral decision maker, what action should it choose? What is the expected payoff associated with this action?

15.9. Consider the same problem as in Problem 15.8, but suppose that the biotech company can conduct its own test—at no cost—that will reveal whether the new drug will be approved by the FDA. What is the biotech company's VPI?

15.10. You are bidding against one other bidder in a first-price sealed-bid auction. Your valuation and your competitor's valuation are completely idiosyncratic. That is, this is a private-values auction. You believe that the other bidder's valuation is equally likely to lie anywhere in the interval between 0 and $500. Your own valuation is $200. Suppose that you expect that your rival will submit a bid that is exactly one half of its valuation. Thus, you believe that your rival's bids are equally likely to fall between 0 and $250. Given this, if you submit a bid of Q, the probability that you win the auction is the probability that your bid Q will exceed your rival's bid. It turns out that this probability is equal to $Q/250$. (Don't worry about where this formula comes from, but you probably should plug in several different values of Q to convince yourself that this makes sense.) Your profit from winning the auction is as follows:

$$\text{Profit} = (200 - \text{Bid}) \times \text{Probability of winning.}$$

Show that a strategy of bidding half of your valuation is your profit-maximizing response.

16

General Equilibrium Theory

In the late spring of 2000, U.S. gasoline prices were front-page news. Shortfalls in supply resulting from miscalculations by oil refiners, pipeline accidents, and the onset of complicated new environmental regulations resulted in gasoline prices that averaged over $1.60 per gallon around the nation and over $2.00 per gallon in parts of the Midwestern United States. In response to these drastic rises in the price of gasoline, a number of states, including Illinois, began to consider reductions in gasoline sales taxes.

Federal, state, and local gasoline taxes represent a significant fraction of the price that the U.S. consumer pays at the pump. In the city of Chicago, Illinois, for example, taxes on gasoline account for 30 percent of the pump price of gasoline. (see Figure 16.1). Who do you think is hurt the most by gasoline taxes: lower-income households or higher-income households? Gasoline taxes make the price of gasoline higher than it would otherwise be, and lower-income households spend a higher fraction of their income on gasoline than higher-income households. Therefore, the most straightforward answer to this question is that lower-income households are hurt more than higher-income households by increases in gasoline excise taxes.

But this straightforward answer might not be correct. Governments use the proceeds of gasoline taxes to purchase goods and services. For ex-

ample, in the state of Illinois, the gasoline tax contributes $1.5 billion to the state's annual budget. How these proceeds get spent can have an important impact on economic activity in a variety of industries, which in turn can affect the prices of the finished goods produced in these industries and the prices of inputs employed by these industries. As we will see in this chapter, once we take into account the full effect of the tax as its impact ripples through the economy, it is possible that higher-income households might be hurt more by increases in gasoline excise taxes than lower-income households.

General equilibrium theory is the part of microeconomics that studies how finished goods and input prices are determined in many markets simultaneously. Because the gasoline tax affects several markets at the same time (e.g., the market for gasoline, the market for construction services, the market for manual labor employed in the construction trades), a general equilibrium analysis would be appropriate to analyze its impact on the wellbeing of different kinds of households in the economy.

This chapter gives you an overview of general equilibrium theory, and will

show how we can use it to explore the total impact of government policy interventions such as an excise tax. We will also use general equilibrium theory to explore the efficiency of resource allocation in an economy consisting of many competitive markets, all of which are interrelated and reach equilibrium at the same time. ■

	Dollars per gallon	Percentage of Total Price
Base Price	$1.52	70.21%
Federal motor fuel tax	$0.18	8.50%
Illinois motor fuel tax	$0.19	8.78%
Cook County motor fuel tax	$0.06	2.77%
City of Chicago motor fuel tax	$0.05	2.31%
Illinois environmental tax	$0.01	0.51%
Illinois and Chicago sales taxes	$0.15	6.93%
Total price	$2.17	100.00%

FIGURE 16.1 Gasoline Taxes in the City of Chicago, Illinois, June 2000
In June 2000, federal, state, and local gasoline taxes accounted for nearly 30 percent of the total price of gasoline paid by a typical consumer of gasoline in the city of Chicago, Illinois. The numbers in the table do not add exactly to totals because of rounding. *Source:* "State Mulls Gas Tax Cut," *Chicago Tribune* (June 22, 2000) pp. A1, A13.

16.1

GENERAL EQUILIBRIUM ANALYSIS: TWO MARKETS

When we studied supply and demand analysis in Chapters 2, 9, and 10, we used what is known as **partial equilibrium analysis.** A partial equilibrium analysis studies the determination of price and output in a single market, taking as given the prices in all other markets. This section illustrates **general equilibrium analysis.** In general equilibrium analysis, we study the determination of price and output in more than one market at the same time.

To see how general equilibrium analysis differs from partial equilibrium analysis, let's consider a simple example with two markets: coffee and tea. Figure 16.2 illustrates these two markets. Panel (a) shows supply and demand in the market for coffee, while panel (b) shows supply and demand in the market for tea.

In order for general equilibrium analysis to be useful, there must be something that links these two markets. In this example, we will assume (plausibly we think) that consumers view coffee and tea as substitute goods. Specifically, an increase in the price of coffee—holding the price of tea fixed—increases the demand for tea, while a decrease in the price of coffee decreases the demand for tea. Similarly, an increase in the price of tea—holding the price of coffee fixed—increases the demand for coffee, while a decrease in the price of tea decreases the demand for coffee.

Suppose, initially, that both markets are in equilibrium. The equilibrium price of coffee is $0.93 per pound, where the demand curve for coffee D_C intersects the supply curve for coffee S_C. The equilibrium price of tea is $0.63 per pound, where the demand curve for tea D_T intersects the supply curve for tea S_T.

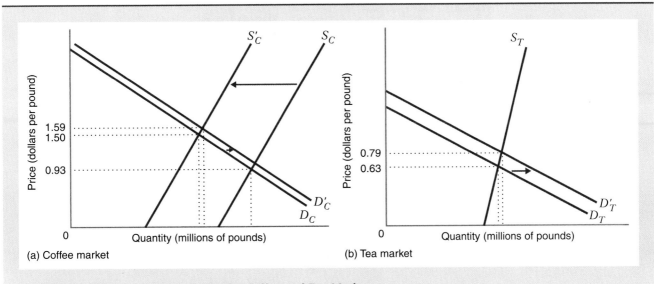

FIGURE 16.2   Supply and Demand in the Coffee and Tea Markets
The coffee market is initially in equilibrium at a price of $0.93 per pound, while the tea market is in equilibrium at a price of $0.63 per pound. A severe frost now destroys a large proportion of the coffee crop, which shifts the supply curve for coffee leftward, from S_C to S'_C. When we trace through the general equilibrium effects of this shift in supply, we find that the equilibrium price of tea rises from $0.63 per pound to $0.79, while the equilibrium price of coffee is now $1.59 per pound.

Now imagine that a severe frost in South America destroys a significant portion of the coffee crop. As a result, the coffee supply curve shifts leftward, from S_C to S'_C. The initial impact is to increase the price of coffee from $0.93 to $1.50 per pound. But because coffee and tea are demand substitutes, an increase in the price of coffee will increase the demand for tea. This shifts the demand curve for tea to the right. As a result, the equilibrium price of tea will go up. But things don't stop here. Because coffee and tea are substitutes, an increase in the price of tea will increase the demand for coffee, which shifts the demand curve for coffee to the right, which drives the price of coffee up some more. This in turn increases the demand for tea, shifting the demand curve for tea even further to the right. When all of these effects have played out, the demand curve for tea has shifted from D_T to D'_T, driving up the price of tea from $0.63 to $0.79 per pound. The demand curve for coffee is now D'_C, and the equilibrium price is $1.59.

We have just gone through a simple general equilibrium analysis. This analysis is significant for two reasons. First, we see that events in the coffee market cannot necessarily be viewed in isolation: The decrease in coffee supply had a significant impact on the price of tea. Second, because coffee and tea are substitutes, an exogenous event in the coffee market, for example, bad weather, that tends to increase the price of coffee, will also tend to increase the price of tea. Similarly, an exogenous event that tends to decrease the price of coffee will also tend to decrease the price of tea. This tells us that the prices of substitute goods will tend to be positively correlated.

LEARNING-BY-DOING EXERCISE 16.1

The Conditions for a General Equilibrium

In this exercise, you will see how to determine the equilibrium prices for coffee and tea for the market that is shown in Figure 16.2.

Problem   Suppose that the demand curves for coffee and tea are given by

$$Q_C^d = 120 - 50P_C + 40P_T$$
$$Q_T^d = 80 - 75P_T + 20P_C.$$

Similarly, suppose that the supply curves for coffee and tea are

$$Q_C^s = 80 + 20P_C$$
$$Q_T^s = 45 + 10P_T.$$

What are the equilibrium prices of coffee and tea? What happens to the equilibrium prices of coffee and tea when the supply curve for coffee is $Q_C^s = 40 + 20P_C$?

Solution   The general equilibrium in these two markets occurs at prices at which supply equals demand in both markets simultaneously, i.e.,

$$Q_C^d = Q_C^s$$
$$Q_T^d = Q_T^s.$$

Using the equations for the supply and demand curves, we can write these equilibrium conditions as:

$$120 - 50P_C + 40P_T = 80 + 20P_C$$
$$80 - 75P_T + 20P_C = 45 + 10P_T.$$

This is a system of two equations in two unknowns, P_C and P_T. Solving these equations simultaneously gives us

$$P_C = \$0.93$$
$$P_T = \$0.63.$$

When these prices prevail in the coffee and tea markets, supply equals demand in both markets simultaneously.

When the supply curve for coffee is $Q_C^s = 40 + 20P_C$, the equilibrium conditions are now

$$120 - 50P_C + 40P_T = 40 + 20P_C$$
$$80 - 75P_T + 20P_C = 45 + 10P_T.$$

Again, this is a system of two equations in the two unknown prices. Solving this system gives us the following:

$$P_C = \$1.59$$

$$P_T = \$0.79.$$

Similar Problems: 16.1, 16.2, and 16.3

Internet Sales Taxes[1]

The last time you purchased a product on the Internet—a book, CD, or even a personal computer—you probably did not pay a sales tax on the transaction. This is not because such transactions do not involve taxes; they usually do. Rather, the burden is on *you*, not the seller, to calculate and pay the state and local sales taxes on the items that you buy. (If you don't believe us, read the fine print on the invoice for your books or CDs: It will probably say something like, "The purchaser is responsible for remitting any additional taxes to the taxing authority.") This is in contrast to sales in traditional retail outlets. When you buy a CD at your local music store, for example, the store owner is responsible for paying the tax to the relevant tax authority, not you. Of course, with millions of individual consumer transactions on the Web every day, it is nearly impossible for state and local governments to force consumers to pay the sales taxes that they owe. The most straightforward way around this problem would be to treat Internet transactions like traditional retail transactions and require sellers to remit the sales taxes, not consumers. However, in 1998 the U.S. Congress imposed a moratorium on new Internet sales taxes, which rules out this solution. For now, consumers are able to shop on the Internet virtually tax free.

What would happen if the U.S. government were to change its policy and allow states to collect sales taxes directly from sellers? (A U.S. government commission is currently studying this proposal, which is strongly supported by state governments.) Let's use general equilibrium analysis to explore this question. In particular, we want to examine the impact of ending the Internet sales tax moratorium not only on the prices of products such as CDs and books that are purchased online, but also on the prices of services, such as the provision of Internet access—subscription to online services such as AOL or MSN that allow you to connect to the Web.[2]

Figure 16.3 analyzes what might happen. In a typical e-tail market such as CDs, the imposition of a requirement that sellers pay the sales tax would raise the marginal cost of a typical CD seller which, as shown in Figure 16.3(a), would shift the supply curve for online CD sales leftward, from S_{CD} to S'_{CD}. As a result, the price of

---

[1] This example is based on "States Chafe as Web Shoppers Ignore Sales Taxes," *Wall Street Journal* (January 26, 1999), p. B1.

[2] This is the service that allows you to connect to the Internet from your home via a phone line and a modem.

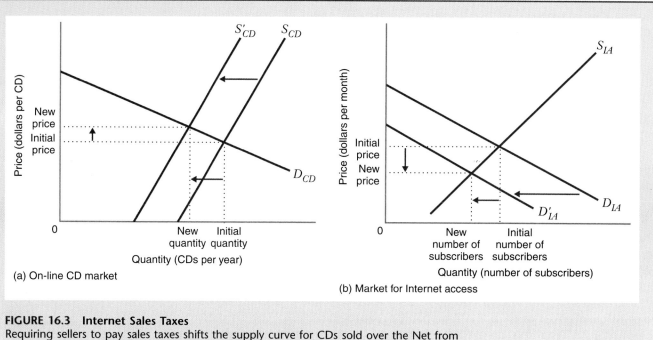

(a) On-line CD market

(b) Market for Internet access

FIGURE 16.3 Internet Sales Taxes
Requiring sellers to pay sales taxes shifts the supply curve for CDs sold over the Net from
S_{CD} to S'_{CD}. As a result, the prices of CDs sold online will rise, and the quantity purchased
online will fall. As this happens with CDs and other goods sold online, such as books,
toys, consumer electronics, and computers, the value of Internet access for consumers
goes down. As a result, fewer consumers will subscribe to Internet access services (e.g.,
AOL or MSN), shifting the demand for Internet access leftward from D_{IA} to D'_{IA}. This drives
the price of Internet access down and reduces the number of subscribers to Internet access services.

CDs sold online would go up. Similar price increases would occur in other online
retail markets such as books, toys, flowers, and personal computers, and the volume of online sales of these products would go down. In fact, research by economist Austan Goolsbee suggests that this impact would be quite dramatic.[3] He estimates that applying existing sales taxes to Internet commerce would reduce the
number of online buyers by 24 percent. This large impact is explained by the fact
that consumers have close available substitutes to buying a product like a CD online: They can get the same CD in a local music store or Wal-Mart.

But the effect of ending the sales tax moratorium would not stop here. As shopping on the Internet becomes more expensive and consumers do less of it, the benefits that consumers get from being connected to the Internet would go down. As
Figure 16.3(b) shows, the demand curve for Internet access services would shift
leftward, from D_{IA} to D'_{IA}. This leftward shift would result in a decrease in the price
of Internet access. Thus, by forcing online merchants to collect sales taxes, the price

[3] A. Goolsbee, "In a World Without Borders: The Impact of Taxes on Internet Commerce," working
paper (July 1999).

of online merchandise such as CDs would go up, but the price of Internet access would go down. This reduction in price benefits consumers but it would reduce the profitability of Internet providers such as AOL. This might explain why high-profile technology companies such as AOL have been vocal opponents of ending the Internet sales tax moratorium and have aggressively lobbied in favor of extending the ban.

Note the contrast between this analysis and our earlier analysis of the coffee and tea markets. In that analysis, the goods were demand substitutes, and as a result their prices were positively correlated. In this example, Internet access and online merchandise are demand complements. As a result, exogenous events in the online retailing market that tend to increase the prices of online merchandise will tend to decrease the price of the complementary good, Internet access services. ■

16.2 GENERAL EQUILIBRIUM ANALYSIS: MANY MARKETS

The previous section illustrated a simplified general equilibrium analysis focused on just two markets at the same time. However, we sometimes need to study more than two markets simultaneously. For example, to understand the effects of the gasoline excise tax on low and high income households, we need to explore several markets simultaneously, including markets for inputs. In this section, we see how to do this kind of analysis.

THE ORIGINS OF SUPPLY AND DEMAND IN A SIMPLE ECONOMY

Let's consider an economy consisting of two types of households, white-collar households and blue-collar households. Each type of household purchases two goods, energy (e.g., electricity, heating fuel, motor fuel) and food. And each of these goods is produced with two inputs, labor and capital.

Figure 16.4 outlines the interactions between households and business firms in our economy. Households, in their role as consumers of finished goods, purchase the energy and food that is supplied by firms. Firms, in their role as consumers of input services, purchase the services of labor and capital that are supplied by households. Households supply labor by offering to work as employees in business firms that need their services. Households supply capital by renting the land or the physical assets that they own to business firms, or by selling their intellectual capital to these firms.

As Figure 16.4 illustrates, this economy thus has four major components:

- Household demand for energy and food
- Firm demand for labor and capital
- Firm supply of energy and food
- Household supply of labor and capital

We will describe each component in turn.

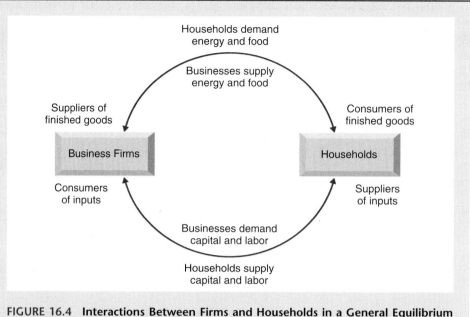

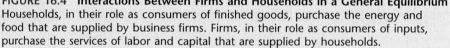

FIGURE 16.4   Interactions Between Firms and Households in a General Equilibrium
Households, in their role as consumers of finished goods, purchase the energy and
food that are supplied by business firms. Firms, in their role as consumers of inputs,
purchase the services of labor and capital that are supplied by households.

The Demand Curves for Energy and Food Come from Utility Maximization by Consumers

To derive the demand curves for energy and food, we need to consider the utility-maximization problems of individual households. The quantity of energy a household purchases is denoted by x, and the quantity of food a household purchases is denoted by y. To tell our two types of households apart, we will use the label W to denote white-collar households and B to denote blue-collar households. A white-collar household has a utility function $U_W(x, y)$, and a blue-collar household has a utility function $U_B(x, y)$ for these two goods.

Each household derives income from supplying labor and capital inputs to business firms. We'll assume that each household has a fixed endowment of labor and capital. Let's suppose that blue-collar households are the primary suppliers of labor in our economy, while white-collar households are the primary suppliers of capital, and that the aggregate supply of labor is greater than the aggregate supply of capital. This could be because there are more blue-collar households than white-collar households or because the amount of labor supplied by each blue-collar household is greater than the amount of capital supplied by each white-collar household. If the price received for a unit of labor is w and the price received for a unit of capital is r, then the incomes of each household, I_W and I_B, will depend on w and r.

Suppose, now, that the price of energy is P_x per unit, while the price of food is P_y. When a household maximizes its utility, it takes theses prices as well as input prices fixed. The utility-maximization problems for the households are thus:

$$\max_{(x,y)} U_W(x, y) \text{ subject to: } P_x x + P_y y = I_W(w, r)$$

$$\max_{(x,y)} U_B(x, y) \text{ subject to: } P_x x + P_y y = I_B(w, r),$$

where $I_W(w, r)$ and $I_B(w, r)$ signify that household incomes depend on the returns that households receive from selling their labor and their capital and that these returns depend on the prices of labor and capital, w and r.

The solution to these utility maximization problems yield the optimality conditions that we discussed in Chapter 4:

$$MRS_{x,y}^{W} = \frac{P_x}{P_y} \text{ and } MRS_{x,y}^{B} = \frac{P_x}{P_y}. \tag{16.1}$$

That is, each household equates its marginal rate of substitution of x for y with the ratio of the price of x to the price of y. These optimality conditions, along with the budget constraints, can be solved for the demand curves for each household, which depend on the prices and household income.

Figure 16.5 shows the aggregate demand curves for energy and food for each type of household. We find these demand curves by summing the demand curves of all the individual households. For example, D_x^W in panel (a) is the aggregate demand for energy by all white-collar households, while D_x^B is the demand for energy by all blue-collar households. (In this section and throughout the rest of this chapter, subscripts on demand and supply curves refer to the commodity being demanded or supplied and superscripts refer to the people or firms doing the demanding or supplying.) The overall market demand curve for energy, D_x, is

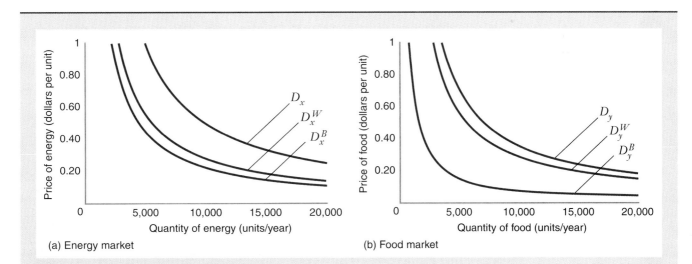

(a) Energy market   (b) Food market

FIGURE 16.5   Demand Curves for Energy and Food
Panel (a) shows the aggregate demand for energy from blue-collar households (D_x^B) and from white-collar households (D_x^W). If we sum these curves horizontally, we get the market demand curve for energy, D_x. Panel (b) shows the aggregate demand for food from blue-collar households (D_y^B) and from white-collar households (D_y^W). Summing these curves horizontally gives us the market demand curve for food, D_y.

the horizontal sum of D_x^W and D_x^B. The position of these demand curves will, in general, depend on the income levels of households, the price of good y, and the particular tastes of each household as embodied by its utility function. That is, changes in household income or in the price of good y will cause D_x^W, D_x^B, and D_x to shift.

To summarize, the demand curves for energy and food in our simple economy come from utility maximization by households. Summing the energy and food demand curves of all individual households generates the aggregate demand curves for energy and food.

The Demand Curves for Labor and Capital Come from Cost Minimization by Firms

To derive the demand curves for labor and capital in the economy, we need to consider the input choice decisions faced by individual firms. We imagine that some firms produce energy while others produce food and that each market is perfectly competitive. Each individual energy producer has a production function $x = f(l, k)$. The lower case l and k denote the amount of labor and capital used by an individual producer. Upper case L and K will refer to the aggregate amounts of labor and capital in the market. We assume that this production function is characterized by constant returns to scale. Recall from Chapter 6 that this means that doubling the amount of labor and capital exactly doubles the quantity of energy a typical producer can make. For a typical energy producer that produces x units of energy, the cost-minimization problem is as follows:

$$\min_{(l,k)} wl + rk, \text{ subject to } x = f(l, k).$$

Similarly, a typical food producer has a production function $y = g(l, k)$, which is also characterized by constant returns to scale. The cost-minimization problem for a typical food maker is given by:

$$\min_{(l,k)} wl + rk, \text{ subject to: } y = g(l, k).$$

These cost-minimization problems yield the optimality conditions that we discussed in Chapter 7:

$$MRTS_{l,k}^x = \frac{w}{r} \text{ and } MRTS_{l,k}^y = \frac{w}{r}. \qquad \textbf{(16.2)}$$

These expressions tell us that when each firm chooses a cost-minimizing input combination, it equates its marginal rate of technical substitution of labor for capital, $MRTS_{l,k}$, to the ratio of the price of labor to the price of capital services. These optimality conditions, along with the production constraints for energy and food, can be solved to determine the demand curves for labor and capital for typical energy and food producers. These demand curves for labor and capital depend on the input prices w and r and on the total amount of output produced by a firm.

Figure 16.6 shows the aggregate demand curves for labor and capital for each industry, energy and food. We find these demand curves by summing the demand curves of all the individual firms in each industry. For example, D_L^x in panel (a) is

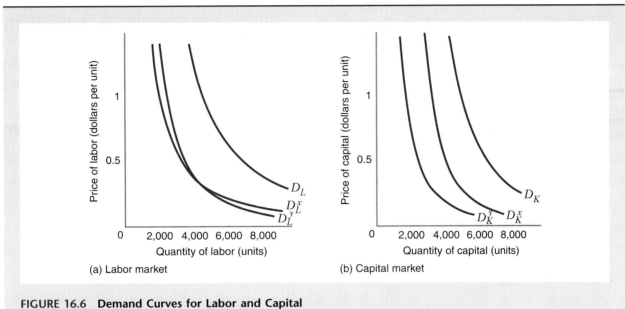

FIGURE 16.6   Demand Curves for Labor and Capital
Panel (a) shows the aggregate demand for labor from energy producers, D_L^x, and from food producers, D_L^y. If we sum these curves horizontally, we get the market demand curve for labor, D_L. Panel (b) shows the aggregate demand for capital from energy producers D_K^x, and from food producers D_K^y. Summing these curves horizontally gives us the market demand curve for capital, D_K.

the overall demand for labor by firms in the energy industry, while D_L^y is the overall demand for labor by firms in the food industry. The overall market demand curve for labor, D_L, is the horizontal sum of these demand curves. The positions of these input demand curves depends on the total amount of output produced in each industry, the price of the other input, and the nature of the technology embodied in the production functions. For example, an increase in the amount of output in the energy industry would increase the demand for labor in that industry and would thus shift D_L^x (and thus D_L) rightward. By contrast, a decrease in the price of capital, r, would encourage firms to substitute capital for labor and would shift both D_L^x and D_L^y (and thus D_L) to the left.

To summarize, the demand curves for labor and capital in each industry in our simple economy come from cost minimization by individual firms. Summing the labor and capital demand curves of all individual firms in both industries generates the aggregate demand curves for labor and capital.

The Supply Curves for Energy and Food Come from Profit Maximization by Firms

We saw in Chapter 8 that the cost-minimization problem of each firm yields a total cost curve and a marginal cost curve. Because each energy producer has an identical constant returns to scale technology, the marginal cost curve for a typical energy producer is a constant, MC_x, that is independent of output. Figure 16.7(a) shows this curve. The level of marginal cost (i.e., how high the curve is) depends on the input prices, w and r. Similarly, the cost-minimization problem for a typical food producer gives rise to the marginal cost curve MC_y shown in

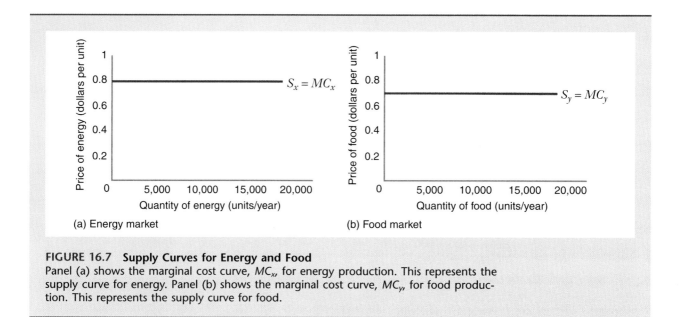

FIGURE 16.7   Supply Curves for Energy and Food
Panel (a) shows the marginal cost curve, MC_x, for energy production. This represents the supply curve for energy. Panel (b) shows the marginal cost curve, MC_y, for food production. This represents the supply curve for food.

Figure 16.7(b). The height of this curve depends on the input prices w and r as well. However, because the production function for food differs from the production function for energy, MC_y depends on w and r in a potentially different way than MC_x does. For example, if food production is labor-intensive—involves a high ratio of labor to capital—then MC_y might be more sensitive to the price w of labor than MC_x.

The energy and food industries are assumed to be perfectly competitive, and thus firms in these industries act as price takers. Because a firm in the energy industry faces a constant marginal cost, energy producers are willing to supply any positive amount of output at a price P_x equal to marginal cost MC_x. This means that the industry supply curve for energy is perfectly elastic at a price equal to MC_x. In other words, the industry supply curve for energy S_x coincides with the marginal cost curve for energy production, MC_x, as shown in Figure 16.7(a). Similarly, the industry supply curve for food S_y coincides with the marginal cost curve for food production, MC_y, as shown in Figure 16.7(b).

Because the industry supply curves coincide with the marginal cost curves, we can immediately see that the equilibrium price in the energy industry will equal the marginal cost of energy production and the equilibrium price in the food industry will equal the marginal cost of food production:

$$P_x = MC_x$$
$$P_y = MC_y. \tag{16.3}$$

Since we have constant returns to scale, marginal cost and average cost are equal, so at these prices each producer earns zero profit. At this point, we still cannot say what these equilibrium prices are, since the marginal costs in each market, MC_x and MC_y, depend on the input prices w and r. And these input prices, in turn, depend on supply and demand in the input markets. Thus, each of the markets in this economy are interdependent.

To summarize, the supply curves in each industry in our economy arise from profit maximization by households. Because production in both the energy and food industries is characterized by constant returns to scale, the supply curves in each industry are horizontal lines corresponding to the marginal cost of production in each industry.

The Supply Curves for Labor and Capital Come from Profit Maximization by Households

The final components of our economy are the supply curves for labor and capital. Labor and capital in this economy are provided by households. As already mentioned, each household can offer a fixed supply of labor and capital. We will assume that there is no opportunity cost to offering this supply of labor or capital. (This simplifies the presentation without affecting the main conclusions.) Profit maximization by individual households thus implies that a household will supply its labor and capital as long as those services can fetch a positive price in the marketplace. Moreover, we assume that households are indifferent between selling their labor to the energy or food industries as long as the wage w that they get from either industry is the same. Similarly, households will supply capital to either industry as long as the price of capital services, r, is the same in each industry.

Figure 16.8 shows the implications of these assumptions. The market supply curve for labor, S_L, is a vertical line corresponding to the overall supply

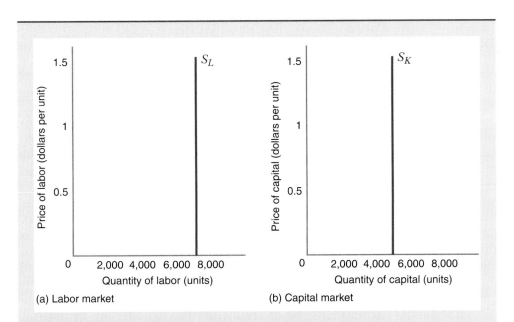

FIGURE 16.8 Supply Curves for Labor and Capital
Panel (a) shows the market supply curve for labor. It is a vertical line corresponding to the amount of labor households are willing to supply. Panel (b) shows the market supply curve for capital. It is a vertical line corresponding to the amount of capital households are willing to supply.

of labor, which is predominantly provided by blue-collar households. Similarly, the overall market supply curve for capital, S_K, is a vertical line corresponding to the overall supply of capital, which predominantly comes from white-collar households.

To summarize, the supply curves for labor and capital in our economy come from profit maximization by households. Because we have assumed that each household has a fixed supply of labor and capital that it can offer, these supply curves will be vertical lines.

THE GENERAL EQUILIBRIUM IN OUR SIMPLE ECONOMY

We are now ready to analyze the equilibrium in our simple economy. Four prices are simultaneously determined in a general equilibrium: a price P_x for energy, a price P_y for food, a price w for labor services, and a price r for capital services. These latter two prices, in turn, determine household income, which is derived from their sales of labor and capital services to firms. The four prices in our economy are interdependent. For example, the price of energy is determined by the marginal cost of energy, but the marginal cost of energy depends on the prices of labor and capital. These prices are pinned down by market clearing conditions in each of our four markets:

Household demand for energy = Industry supply of energy

Household demand for food = Industry supply of food

Industry demand for labor = Household supply of labor

Industry demand for capital = Household supply of capital.

Figure 16.9 illustrates our simple economy when it is in a general equilibrium. In particular, it illustrates that in light of the interdependence that exists among markets, supply equals demand in all four markets simultaneously. To see why, let's start with panels (a) and (b). They illustrate that when the prices of labor and capital are $0.50 and $1.00, respectively, the marginal costs of energy and food production are $0.80 and $0.70, respectively. The equilibrium input prices thus determine the height of the industry supply curves, S_x and S_y. These input prices also determine household incomes, $I_W(w, r)$ and $I_B(w, r)$, which determines the positions of the demand curves for energy and food. The intersection of demand and supply in the energy and food markets determines the total output in these industries: 6,300 units in the energy industry and 5,000 in the food industry. These outputs, in turn, determine the positions of the labor and capital demand curves in panels (c) and (d). And it is the intersection of these input demand curves with the input supply curves, S_L and S_K, that determines the equilibrium prices of labor and capital of $0.50 and $1.00.

Thus, to summarize, we have seen the following:

- The equilibrium input prices in the labor and capital markets determine the positions of the supply and demand curves in the energy and food markets.
- These supply and demand curves determine the equilibrium prices in the energy and food markets, and the equilibrium quantities in these markets.

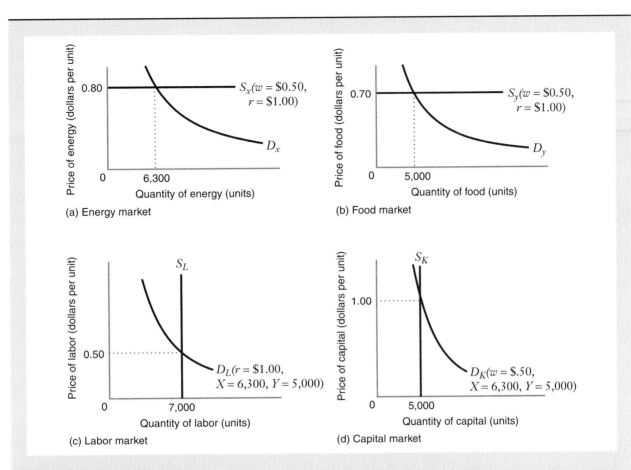

FIGURE 16.9 General Equilibrium
This figure shows the general equilibrium in our simple economy: all four markets (energy, food, labor, and capital) are simultaneously in equilibrium. Panels (a) and (b) illustrate that when the prices of labor and capital are $0.50 and $1.00, the equilibrium prices of energy and food are $0.80 and $0.70, and the equilibrium quantities of energy and food are 6,300 and 5,000 units. Panels (c) and (d) show that when the quantities of energy and food demanded are 6,300 and 5,000 units, the equilibrium prices of labor and capital are $0.50 and $1.00 per unit.

- The equilibrium quantities of energy and food determine the positions of the demand curves in the labor and capital markets, and the point where these curves cross the supply curves of labor and capital is what determines the equilibrium prices of labor and capital.

From this analysis we can see the extent to which the markets in our economy are intertwined. Thus, even in our simple economy, we cannot analyze events in one market without taking into account how those events affect the other markets.

One important lesson that comes from the general equilibrium analysis in Figure 16.9 is the relationship between the scarcity of factors of production, the relative prices of those factors, and the distribution of income in the economy. In the economy in Figure 16.9, the aggregate supply of capital is much less than the aggregate supply of labor (i.e., S_K is closer to its vertical axis than is S_L). As a result, the price of capital services exceeds the price of labor, i.e., capital services trade at a price premium as compared to labor services. This, in turn, allows the providers of capital inputs—the white-collar households in our economy—to earn higher incomes than the providers of labor inputs—primarily blue-collar households.

LEARNING-BY-DOING EXERCISE 16.2

The Conditions for a General Equilibrium

In this exercise, you will learn how to write the supply-equals-demand conditions that determine a general equilibrium for our simple economy.

Problem

(a) Suppose that the market supply curves for energy and food are:[4]

$$P_x = w^{\frac{1}{3}}r^{\frac{2}{3}} \text{ (supply curve for energy)}$$
$$P_y = w^{\frac{1}{2}}r^{\frac{1}{2}} \text{ (supply curve for food)}.$$

Also suppose that the market demand curves for energy and food are[5]

$$P_x = \frac{50I_W + 75I_B}{X} \text{ (demand curve for energy)}$$

$$P_y = \frac{50I_W + 25I_B}{Y} \text{ (demand curve for food)},$$

where X is the overall quantity of energy demanded, and Y is the overall quantity of food. Finally, suppose that each white-collar household supplies 10 units of labor and 50 units of capital, while each blue-collar household supplies 60 units of labor and 0 units of capital. Given this information, what are the supply-equals-demand conditions for the energy and product markets?

(b) Suppose that the market demand curves for labor and capital are:[6]

$$L = \frac{X}{3}\left(\frac{r}{w}\right)^{\frac{2}{3}} + \frac{Y}{2}\left(\frac{r}{w}\right)^{\frac{1}{2}} \text{ (demand curve for labor)}$$

$$K = \frac{2X}{3}\left(\frac{w}{r}\right)^{\frac{1}{3}} + \frac{Y}{2}\left(\frac{w}{r}\right)^{\frac{1}{2}} \text{ (demand curve for capital)}.$$

---

[4]In the Appendix, we show how these are determined from cost-minimizing input decisions by firms.

[5]In the Appendix, we show how to derive these demand curves from the utility-maximization problems of households.

[6]In the Appendix, we show how these demand curves are derived from the cost-minimization problems of individual firms.

Suppose further that there are 100 white-collar households and 100 blue-collar households. Given this information, what are the supply-equals-demand conditions for the labor and capital markets?

(c) How do we find the general equilibrium for the economy?

Solution

(a) Notice that the demand curves for energy and food depend on household incomes. But household incomes depend on the amount of labor and capital that households sell. Thus, before we can state the supply-equals-demand conditions for the energy and product markets, we need to write an expression for the amount of income of each household. In light of the amount of labor and capital each household supplies, household incomes are given by

$$I_W(w, r) = 10w + 50r. \tag{16.4}$$

$$I_B(w, r) = 60w. \tag{16.5}$$

The supply-equals-demand conditions for the energy and product markets are then

$$w^{\frac{1}{3}}r^{\frac{2}{3}} = \frac{5{,}000w + 2{,}500r}{X} \text{ (energy market)} \tag{16.6}$$

$$w^{\frac{1}{2}}r^{\frac{1}{2}} = \frac{2{,}000w + 2{,}500r}{Y} \text{ (food market)} \tag{16.7}$$

In writing these expressions, we have substituted the expressions for household incomes in (16.4) and (16.5) into the market demand curves for energy and food. Equations (16.6) and (16.7) identify the points at which $S_x = D_x$ and $S_y = D_y$ in Figure 16.9.

(b) The supply curves for labor and capital are the total amount of labor and capital that households provide. Recalling that each of the 100 white-collar households supplies 10 units of labor and 50 units of capital, while each of the 100 blue-collar households supplies 60 units of labor and 0 units of capital, the total labor and capital supplies in this economy are:

$$L = (100 \times 10) + (100 \times 60) = 7{,}000$$
$$K = (100 \times 50) + (100 \times 0) = 5{,}000$$

The supply-equals-demand conditions for the labor and capital markets are thus:

$$7{,}000 = \frac{X}{3}\left(\frac{r}{w}\right)^{\frac{2}{3}} + \frac{Y}{2}\left(\frac{r}{w}\right)^{\frac{1}{2}} \text{ (labor market).} \tag{16.8}$$

$$5{,}000 = \frac{2X}{3}\left(\frac{w}{r}\right)^{\frac{1}{3}} + \frac{Y}{2}\left(\frac{w}{r}\right)^{\frac{1}{2}} \text{ (capital market).} \tag{16.9}$$

(c) We have four supply-equals-demand equations: equations (16.6), (16.7), (16.8), and (16.9). We also have four unknowns: the *prices* of labor and capital and the *quantities* of energy and food. To determine the general equilibrium for the economy, we would solve these four equations to determine these four unknowns. (We will not ask you to do the actual algebra to solve these equations.) Once we had solved these equations, we would then determine the prices of energy and food by plugging the quantities and the input prices into either the demand curves for energy and food or the supply curves for energy and food (i.e., by plugging into either the right-hand sides or the left-hand sides of equations (16.6) and (16.7)). The equilibrium prices and quantities that are shown in Figure 16.9 were actually determined by the process we have just described.

Similar Problem: 16.4

WALRAS' LAW

If you had actually tried to solve the four equations in four unknowns in Learning-By-Doing Exercise 16.2, you would discover something surprising: instead of having four distinct equations in four unknowns, you would really have three equations in four unknowns. That is, one of our four supply-equals-demand equations is redundant.

This is an example of **Walras' Law**, named after the Swiss economist, Leon Walras, who discovered it. Walras' Law states that in a general competitive equilibrium with a total of N markets ($N = 4$ in our simple example), if supply equals demand in the first $N - 1$ markets, then supply will necessarily equal demand in the Nth market as well.

The reason that Walras' Law holds is straightforward. We saw earlier that a household's income is equal to the payments made by firms for the labor and capital services provided by the household. We also know that when consumers maximize their utilities, their budget constraints hold: A consumer's expenditures on goods and services equals a consumer's income. Putting these two observations together implies that total consumer expenditures on goods and services in the economy must therefore equal total payments by firms to purchase inputs. This last condition, coupled with supply-equals-demand in the first $N - 1$ markets in the economy, will ensure that supply-equals-demand in the Nth market as well.

Because of Walras' Law, in the simple economy we analyzed above, we have three market-clearing conditions but four unknowns. This implies that an equilibrium in our economy will determine the prices in just three of our four markets. In the fourth market—which in our example we took to be the capital market—we can set the price equal to any number we want. In our analysis we set that price equal to $1.

What is the significance of Walras' Law? Walras' Law tells us that our general equilibrium analysis determines the prices of labor, energy, and food *relative* to the price of capital, rather than determining the absolute levels of all of these prices. We could have, of course, set the price of capital equal to a number other than $1, perhaps $2 or even $200. Had we done so, all of the other prices in our economy would have changed. However, their ratio to the prespecified price of capital would remain the same and would equal the prices shown in Figure 16.9. For example, the ratio of the price of labor to the price of capital would remain at 0.50, no matter what our prespecified price of capital.

16.3
GENERAL EQUILIBRIUM ANALYSIS: COMPARATIVE STATICS

Now that we have seen how to determine the general competitive equilibrium for a simple economy, how can we apply it? Economists use general equilibrium models to explore the effects of taxes or public policy interventions. Most of these analyses involve performing some kind of comparative statics analysis. For example, they might explore how changes in exogenous variables such as household endowments of labor or capital or tax rates would affect the endogenous variables, prices and quantities, that are determined in equilibrium. The models that economists use for this purpose are much more involved than the simple model we have presented here. In one analysis, economists looked at the effects of motor fuel taxes using a model with more than thirty industries, seven different types of households, and five inputs (capital and four different types of labor).[7] In this section, we will illustrate general equilibrium comparative statics analysis using the model we developed in the previous section. Specifically, we will consider the general equilibrium impact of an excise tax.

Suppose that the government imposes an excise tax in the market for energy in our simple economy. Specifically, the excise tax is $0.20 per unit on energy, and the proceeds are used to buy goods from the food industry, which are then shipped outside the economy (e.g., it is distributed to countries experiencing famines). How does this tax affect prices and quantities in the economy? Also, who is harmed the most by this tax: blue-collar households or white-collar households?

You might think that blue-collar households are likely to be harmed the most. As we can see from Figure 16.10, blue-collar households tend to buy much more energy than they do food in the initial equilibrium. By contrast, white-collar households buy equal portions of both goods. However, when we work through the general equilibrium effects of the energy tax, we will see that this is not necessarily the case.

In performing our comparative statics analysis, we can take advantage of Walras' Law and focus our attention on changes in the prices of energy, food, and labor, keeping the price of capital equal to $1 per unit. The most obvious impact of the tax is that it shifts the supply curve for energy upward by the amount of the tax ($0.20 per unit) from S_x to $S_x + 0.20$. As Figure 16.11 shows, this results in a $0.20 increase in the price of energy. This, in turn, means that the equilibrium quantity of energy demanded will go down. As the equilibrium quantity of energy demanded goes down, the demand for labor by the energy industry goes down. However, because the government spends the proceeds of the tax on food, the aggregate demand for food, which now includes government demand as well as household demand, goes up. This would result in an increase in the demand for labor by food producers.

---

[7]A. Wiese, A. Rose, and G. Shluter, "Motor-Fuel Taxes and Household Welfare: An Applied General Equilibrium Analysis," *Land Economics* (May 1995): 229–243.

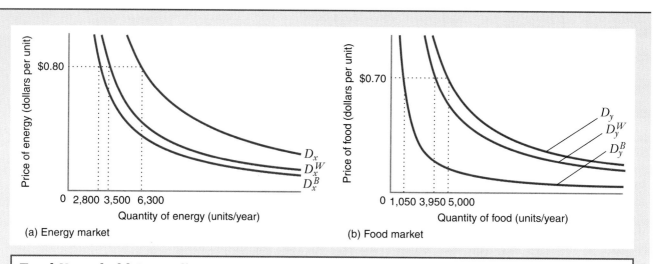

(a) Energy market

(b) Food market

Total Household Expenditures on Energy and Food		
Household	Energy	Food
Blue-collar	2,800 units @ $0.80 per unit = $2,240	1,050 units @ $0.70 per unit = $735
White-collar	3,500 units @ $0.80 per unit = $2,800	3,950 units @ $0.70 per unit = $2,765

FIGURE 16.10   Purchases by Blue-Collar and White-Collar Households at the Initial Equilibrium
Panel (a) shows the demand curves for energy for blue-collar and white-collar households, while Panel (b) shows the demand curves for food by these households. The table below the figures illustrates the amount of money each type of household spends on each good. Blue-collar households spend much more on energy than food, while white-collar households spend about the same amount on each good.

With labor demand by energy producers falling and labor demand by food producers rising, what happens to the overall demand for labor? In other words, does the overall labor demand curve D_L shift to the right or the left? In general, D_L could shift in either direction. In Figure 16.11 we examine the case in which D_L shifts rightward. This case would arise if the food industry uses more labor to produce a given unit of output than the energy industry does.[8] Figure 16.11(c) shows that when D_L shifts to the right, the equilibrium price of labor w goes up. This feeds back to increase the marginal costs of both energy and food, which increases prices in these markets. But this increase in w also increases consumer incomes, particularly among the blue-collar households that derive most of their income from labor. This works to shift demand rightward in both the energy and food markets.

When we account for all of the equilibrium effects, Figure 16.11 shows that the new equilibrium involves a slightly higher price of labor ($w = \$0.55$ versus

[8] In the last section of the Appendix, we show that when we compute the equilibrium using the production functions that generated the supply curves for energy and food in Learning-By-Doing Exercise 16.2, firms in the food industry do, in fact, use more labor to produce a given unit of output than do firms in the energy industry.

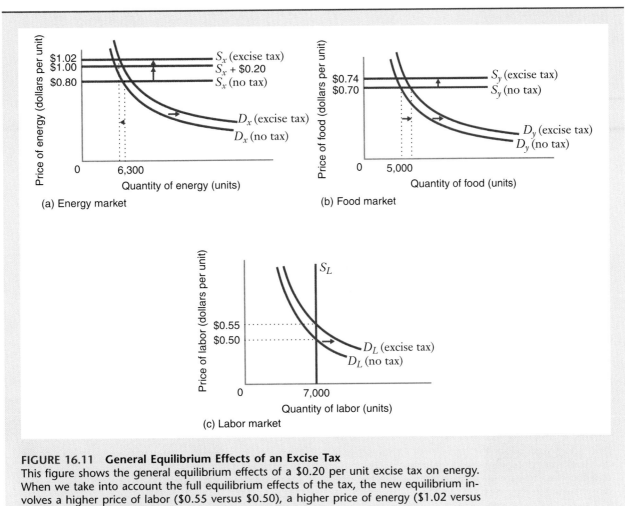

FIGURE 16.11   General Equilibrium Effects of an Excise Tax
This figure shows the general equilibrium effects of a $0.20 per unit excise tax on energy. When we take into account the full equilibrium effects of the tax, the new equilibrium involves a higher price of labor ($0.55 versus $0.50), a higher price of energy ($1.02 versus $0.80), and a higher price of food ($0.74 versus $0.70).

$0.50 initially) and higher prices for both energy and food: (P_x = $1.02 versus $0.80 initially, and P_y = $0.74 versus $0.70 initially). Figure 16.12 summarizes these effects. Because the price of labor has gone up, blue-collar households enjoy a significant increase in income, while white-collar households enjoy a modest increase in income. Both types of households are hurt by the tax. However, blue-collar households are hurt less by the tax than white-collar households because of the boost in income enjoyed by the blue-collar households.

Is the lesson of this analysis that lower-income households will always tend to be harmed less by taxes than higher-income households? No. We constructed the example to make that point for the sake of illustration. The key implication of this example is that the obvious effect of a tax or public policy intervention—which in our example was that the tax would hurt blue-collar households more than white-collar households—might not hold when we consider the full general equilibrium effects of the policy. This is why economists often resort to general equilibrium models when analyzing public policy proposals.

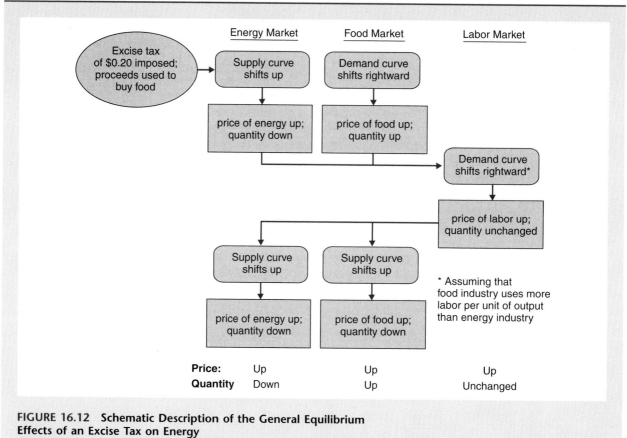

FIGURE 16.12   Schematic Description of the General Equilibrium Effects of an Excise Tax on Energy
This figure summarizes the general equilibrium effects of an excise tax on energy. Start in the upper left portion of the diagram and follow the arrows to trace out the consequences that flow from the imposition of this tax. The final effects on price and quantity are reflected in Figure 16.11.

*E*XAMPLE 16.2   *The General Equilibrium Effects of the Gasoline Excise Tax*

We began the chapter with a question: Who is hurt the most by an increase in the excise tax on gasoline, lower-income households or higher-income households? You might think that the answer is lower-income households. An increase in the excise tax on gasoline increases the price of gasoline, and lower-income households tend to spend a higher fraction of their household income on gasoline than do higher-income households.

Arthur Wiese, Adam Rose, and Gerald Shluter use a general equilibrium analysis to show that this obvious answer might not be correct.[9] They point out that the

[9]Wiese, A., A. Rose, and G. Shluter, "Motor-Fuel Taxes and Household Welfare: An Apllied General Equilibrium Analysis," *Land Economics* (May 1995), pp. 229–243.

proceeds of state gasoline taxes have historically been used by state governments to finance highway construction. When a state collects more revenue from its gasoline tax, it will therefore spend more on construction activities, increasing the demand for the services provided by construction firms. This, in turn, increases construction firms' demand for labor, driving up the wages of the manual labor employed in the construction trades. The increase in the wage of manual labor increases the marginal cost of production in other industries (e.g., manufacturing industries, such as energy, food processing, steel, and automobiles) that also employ manual labor and must compete with the construction industry for the supply of this labor.

As in our simple economy in Figure 16.11, the increase in wages for manual labor feeds through to increase the prices of finished goods in industries that employ manual labor. The increase in the prices of these manufactured goods results in a reduction in the quantity of these goods demanded by households, which means that output in manufacturing industries will go down. As these industries produce less output, they will employ smaller quantities of all types of labor, including white-collar and professional labor. In particular, some of these industries might lay off some of the managers and white-collar professionals that they would have employed had industry output been higher.

The study by Wiese, Rose, and Shluter show that when all is said and done, the effects of an increase in the gasoline tax are rather complicated. All consumers are hurt by higher prices of gasoline and the higher prices of finished goods. Moreover, households of white-collar and other professional labor are hurt by the reduced employment of their labor services. On the other hand, households that supply manual labor benefit from the higher wages that result as construction firms and manufacturing firms compete for their services. Because lower-income households tend to supply a disproportionate share of manual labor, while higher-income households tend to supply a disproportionately higher share of professional services labor, when we consider the full effects of a gasoline tax as its impact ripples through the entire economy, lower-income households are hurt less by a gasoline tax than higher-income households.

The authors of the study go on to point out that state governments now spend a smaller proportion of the proceeds of gasoline taxes on construction programs than they did in the past, and they use more of the proceeds for general state spending (e.g., for education). Given that this is so, the general equilibrium effects of gasoline taxes are different from those just described. Based on a general equilibrium model that relies on recent data on input employment in U.S. industries and spending in U.S. households, Wiese, Rose, and Shluter point out that an increase in the state and local gasoline taxes would hurt the highest-income households and the lowest-income households the most, while hurting middle-income households the least.

Wiese, Rose, and Shluter's analysis is directly relevant for states such as Illinois that in the late spring of 2000 were considering *reductions* in their gasoline taxes. Such cuts would benefit all consumers to some extent, but based on the findings just described, they would be expected to benefit middle-income households the least and low-income and high-income households the most. ◼

16.4
THE EFFICIENCY OF COMPETITIVE MARKETS

In Chapter 10, we saw that the competitive equilibrium in a single competitive market maximizes the net economic surplus that can be generated in that market. That is, the competitive market outcome is economically efficient. In this section, we explore whether economic efficiency arises in an economy in which many competitive markets simultaneously achieve a general equilibrium.

WHAT IS ECONOMIC EFFICIENCY?

Before we can study whether a general competitive equilibrium is efficient, we need to define what efficiency is. At the general competitive equilibrium shown in Figure 16.9, energy and food are consumed by the different households, and labor and capital are used by the different industries. We call this pattern of consumption and input usage an **allocation of goods and inputs.** We say that an allocation of goods and inputs in our economy is **economically efficient** if there is no other feasible allocation of goods and inputs that would make some consumers better off without hurting other consumers. Some books refer to this as **Pareto efficient.** By contrast, an allocation of goods and inputs is **economically inefficient** (or **Pareto inefficient**) if there is an alternative feasible allocation of goods and input that would make all consumers better off as compared with the initial allocation. Put another way, for any inefficient allocation we can always find at least one efficient allocation that consumers would unanimously prefer to the inefficient one. At an inefficient allocation of goods and inputs, the economy is not getting all that it can get from its resources.

Given this definition of efficiency, a competitive equilibrium needs to satisfy three conditions if it is to be efficient:

1. Given the total amounts of energy and food that are consumed by our two types of households, white-collar and blue-collar, there is no way that we can reallocate these amounts among the households to make all households better off than they are at the competitive equilibrium. That is, the allocation must satisfy the condition of **exchange efficiency.** Generally, we have efficiency in exchange when a fixed stock of consumption goods cannot be reallocated among consumers in an economy without making at least some consumers worse off. We have inefficiency in exchange when we can reallocate a fixed basket of consumption goods among consumers in a way that makes all consumers better off.

2. Given the total amounts of capital and labor that are used by our two types of firms, energy producers and food producers, there is no way that we can reallocate these inputs among the firms so that they can produce more energy and more food than they do when they are at the competitive equilibrium. That is, the allocation of inputs must satisfy the condition of **input efficiency.** Generally, we have input efficiency when a fixed stock of inputs cannot be reallocated among firms in an economy without reducing the output of at least one of the goods that is produced in the economy. In other words, we have input efficiency when an expansion of output in one industry (e.g., food) necessitates a reduction in output in another industry (e.g., energy). We have input inefficiency when we can reallocate a fixed stock of inputs among firms so that we can simultaneously expand the output of all of the goods produced in the economy.

3. Given the total amounts of capital and labor that are available in the economy, there is no way that we can make all consumers better off by producing more of one product (e.g., energy) and less of the other (e.g., food). That is, the allocation of goods and inputs in the economy must satisfy the condition of **substitution efficiency.** By contrast, an allocation of goods and inputs is substitution inefficient if we can make all consumers better off by producing more of one product and less of another.

In the next three sections, we explore each of these notions of efficiency in greater detail, and we will show that the general competitive equilibrium in Figure 16.9 satisfies all three efficiency conditions.

EXCHANGE EFFICIENCY

To understand whether the competitive equilibrium satisfies the condition of exchange efficiency, we will need to develop some graphical tools to describe exchange efficiency and inefficiency. Thus, we begin by developing the concept of an Edgeworth box. Having described and explored this tool, we can then determine whether the competitive equilibrium satisfies the condition of exchange efficiency.

Describing Exchange Efficiency Using the Edgeworth Box

In Figure 16.13, we imagine that a given amount of energy and food has been produced—10 units of each product—and is going to be divided among the two representative households in our economy: a white-collar household and a blue-collar household. The diagram in Figure 16.13 is called an **Edgeworth box.** An Edgeworth box shows all of the possible allocations of goods that are possible in our economy, given the total available supply of the goods. The width of the Edgeworth box shows the total amount of energy—10 units—that is available in our economy, while the height of the box shows the total amount of food—10 units—that is available. Each point in the Edgeworth box represents one way to allocate the 10 units of energy and food that are available in our economy among the two households. For example, at point *G*, a white-collar household consumes 5 units of energy and 1 unit of food, while a blue-collar household consumes 5 units of energy and 9 units of food.

Does the allocation represented by point *G* satisfy the condition of exchange efficiency? The answer depends on the preferences of the households. Figure 16.14 takes the Edgeworth box in Figure 16.13 and superimposes upon it the indifference curves for each type of household. To read this diagram, notice that we measure a white-collar household's consumption of energy and food from the lower left-hand corner, and its utility increases as we move toward the upper right-hand corner. By contrast, we measure a blue-collar household's consumption from the upper right-hand corner. For this reason, the blue-collar households's indifference curves are upside down, and its utility increases as it moves toward the lower left-hand corner.

We now can see that point *G* is not efficient. This is because there are other allocations, like point *H*, that simultaneously make both consumers better off than they are at point *G*. We see this because at point *H* both consumers are on higher indifference curves than they are at point *G*. Therefore, if the two households were at point *G*, there is a potential gain from trade: If a white-collar household

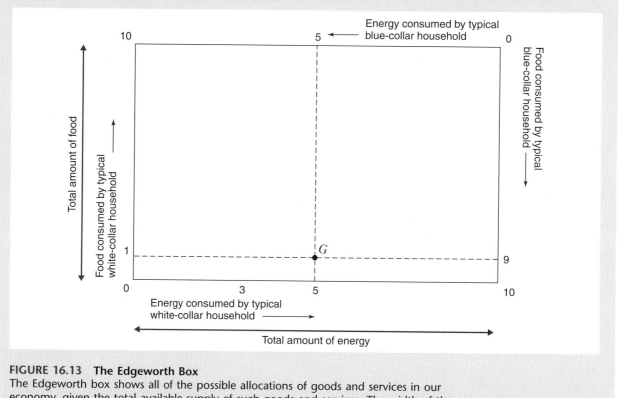

FIGURE 16.13 The Edgeworth Box
The Edgeworth box shows all of the possible allocations of goods and services in our economy, given the total available supply of such goods and services. The width of the Edgeworth box shows the total available amount of energy, while the height of the box shows the total amount of food. Each point in the box represents one way to allocate the food and energy that is available in the economy. For example, at point G, a white-collar household consumes 5 units of energy and 1 unit of food, while a blue-collar household consumes 5 units of energy and 9 units of food.

were to give the blue-collar household 3.5 units of energy in exchange for 3 units of food, both would be better off. This illustrates that an economically inefficient allocation is one in which there is an unexploited, mutually beneficial gain from exchange between the two consumers.

It might strike you as somewhat strange that we use the term *inefficient* to describe a situation in which there is a potential gain from trade. Isn't it a good thing when two individuals are in a position to make both of themselves better off? Indeed it is. The inefficiency is not in the fact that there is a potential gain from exchange. The inefficiency arises if this potential gain is not realized. That is, the inefficiency would arise if, in the process of engaging in market transactions, individuals ended up making decisions that led them to end up at an allocation such as G. We will see that in a competitive market, such inefficiencies will not arise.

If point G is not exchange efficient, which allocations are efficient? Consider a point such as I where a white-collar indifference curve is tangent to a blue-collar indifference curve. If we move from allocation I to any other allocation in the Edgeworth box, at least one of the two consumers will be made worse off.

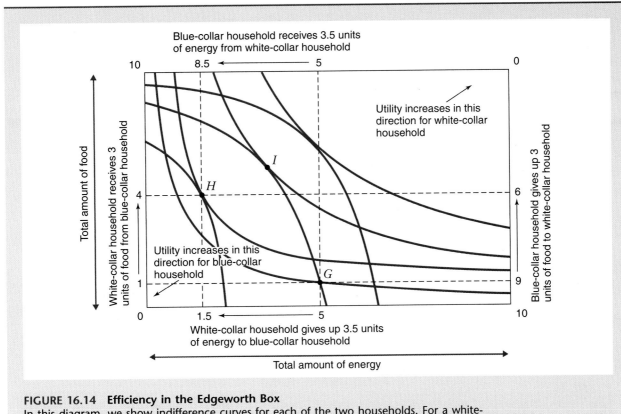

FIGURE 16.14 Efficiency in the Edgeworth Box
In this diagram, we show indifference curves for each of the two households. For a white-collar household, we measure consumption from the lower-left corner, so utility increases as we move toward the northeast. For a blue-collar household, we measure consumption from the upper-right corner, so utility increases as we move toward the southwest. Point G is not efficient. This is because there is another allocation, H, that makes both consumers better off than they are at point G.

Put another way, once the two consumers have reached point *I*, there is no further trade that they can make that would make at least one of them better off without hurting the other party. At point *I*, there are no mutually beneficial gains from trade.

Let's now summarize what we have learned:

- At an inefficient allocation, such as *G*, there are unexploited, mutually beneficial gains from exchange. At such points, consumers' indifference curves cross each other.

- At an efficient allocation, such as *I*, there are no further mutually beneficial gains from exchange. All mutually beneficial gains from exchange have already been exploited. At such allocations, consumers' indifference curves are tangent to each other.

Figure 16.15 highlights the efficient allocations of 10 units of energy and 10 units of food. These are allocations that occur at the points of tangency within the Edgeworth box. The line that connects these efficient allocations in Figure

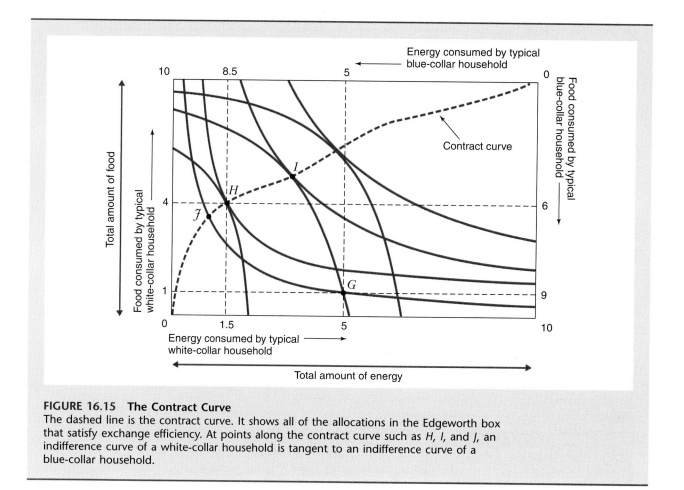

FIGURE 16.15 The Contract Curve
The dashed line is the contract curve. It shows all of the allocations in the Edgeworth box that satisfy exchange efficiency. At points along the contract curve such as *H*, *I*, and *J*, an indifference curve of a white-collar household is tangent to an indifference curve of a blue-collar household.

16.15 is called the **contract curve.** The contract curve shows the allocations of goods in the Edgeworth box that are economically efficient. If the two consumers in Figure 16.15 were free to bargain among themselves and find mutually beneficial gains from exchange, they would bargain their way to some point along the contract curve. Which point they will reach depends on their initial endowments of goods. For example, if the initial allocation of energy and food was point *G*, we would expect that unimpeded trade between our two households would place them somewhere along the portion of the contract curve between *I* and *J*.

LEARNING-BY-DOING EXERCISE 16.3

Checking the Conditions for Exchange Efficiency

Two individuals, Sonia and Anne, together have 10 apples and 6 pears. Let x_S denote the quantity of apples possessed by Sonia and y_S denote the quantity of pears possessed by Sonia. Similarly, let x_A denote the quantity of apples that Anne has and y_A denote the quantity of pears that Anne has. Suppose, further, that for Sonia,

$$MRS_{x,y}^{Sonia} = \frac{2x_S}{y_S},$$

while for Anne

$$MRS_{x,y}^{Anne} = \frac{x_A}{y_A}.$$

Finally, suppose that Sonia has 2 apples and 4 pears, while Anne has 8 apples and 2 pears.

Problem

(a) Does the allocation of apples and pears between Anne and Sonia satisfy the condition of exchange efficiency?
(b) Can you find an exchange between Sonia and Anne that makes both parties better off?

Solution

(a) For this allocation to satisfy the condition of exchange efficiency, the indifference curves of Anne and Sonia must be tangent to one another. To check whether the tangency condition holds, we need to compute the marginal rates of substitution for Sonia and Anne.

When Sonia has 2 apples and 4 pears, her marginal rate of substitution of apples for pears is

$$MRS_{x,y}^{Sonia} = \frac{2(2)}{4} = 1.$$

This tells us that Sonia is willing to give up one pear in order to get one additional apple. Put another way, this also tells us that Sonia is willing to give up one apple to get one additional pear.

When Anne has 8 apples and 2 pears, her marginal rate of substitution of apples for pears is

$$MRS_{x,y}^{Anne} = \frac{8}{2} = 4.$$

This tells us that Anne is willing to give up 4 pears to get 1 additional apple.

We can see from these calculations that for Sonia and Anne the marginal rates of substitution of apples for pears are not equal. Therefore, their indifference curves are not tangent, and the condition of exchange efficiency does not hold.

(b) The fact that the existing allocation of apples and pears is inefficient means that Anne and Sonia can both be made better off by trading with each other. To see why, suppose that Anne gives 2 of her pears to Sonia in exchange for 1 of Sonia's apples. This makes both individuals better off. To see why, recall that Anne was willing to give up four pears to get one additional apple.

Because she only gives up two pears to get that extra apple, Anne is better off. What about Sonia? She was willing to give up one apple to get one additional pear. Under the proposed deal, Sonia gives up one apple to get two extra pears. Thus, Sonia is better off as well. There are many other possible trades between Anne and Sonia that would have made both better off. The key point is that whenever the condition of exchange efficiency does not hold, there is always the possibility of a beneficial gain from trade between individuals in the economy.

Similar Problems: 16.5, 16.6, 16.7

Does the General Competitive Equilibrium Satisfy Exchange Efficiency?

To answer this question, let's recall that at a competitive equilibrium, each household maximizes its utility. This implies that each household type sets its marginal rate of substitution equal to the ratio of the prices:

$$MRS_{x,y}^{W} = MRS_{x,y}^{B} = \frac{P_x}{P_y}.$$

But since the marginal rate of substitution equals the slope of the consumer's indifference curve, this condition tells us that at the equilibrium prices, consumers' indifference curves are tangent to each other—that is, they end up on the contract curve.

Figure 16.16 illustrates this point for the allocation of energy and food that arises in the general equilibrium that we depicted in Figure 16.9. In that equilibrium, firms produced about 63 units of energy per household and about 50 units of food per household. These quantities define the dimensions of our Edgeworth box. At the equilibrium, which is represented by point E in the Edgeworth box, a white-collar household consumes about 35 units of energy and 39 units of food, while a blue-collar household consumes 28 units of energy and about 11 units of food.

At point E, the indifference curves of households are tangent, and these indifference curves are, in turn, tangent to a line whose slope (in absolute value) equals the ratio of the equilibrium prices of energy and food. (Recall these were $0.80 and $0.70, so the slope of this line is 1.14.) This point lies on the contract curve in the Edgeworth box. This means that at the general competitive equilibrium, there are no unexploited gains from exchange between consumers. Notice that all gains from exchange are exhausted even though consumers in our economy did not bargain with each other face-to-face. Instead, all transactions in our economy are between consumers and firms. And yet, despite this, the outcome in a competitive market is the same as the outcome would have been had consumers been able to strike unrestricted bargains with each other when negotiating face-to-face.

INPUT EFFICIENCY

We have just seen that the general competitive equilibrium results in an allocation of consumption goods—energy and food—that is economically efficient. But

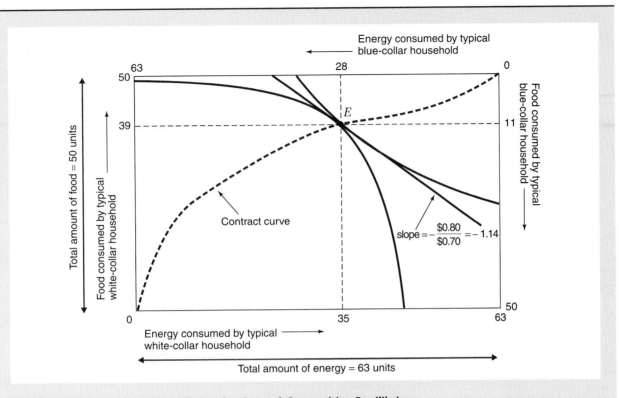

FIGURE 16.16   Exchange Efficiency at the General Competitive Equilibrium
In the general equilibrium depicted in Figure 16.9, firms produced about 63 units of energy per household and about 50 units of food per household. These quantities define the dimensions of this Edgeworth box. At equilibrium, represented by point *E*, a white-collar household consumes about 35 units of energy and 39 units of food, while a blue-collar household consumes 28 units of energy and about 11 units of food. At point *E*, the indifference curves of consumers in the economy are tangent to each other and to a line whose slope (in absolute value) equals the ratio of the equilibrium prices of energy and food, $0.80/$0.70, or about 1.14. This point lies on the contract curve in the Edgeworth box. This means that at the general competitive equilibrium, there are no unexploited gains from exchange between consumers.

what about the allocation of labor and capital that emerges in equilibrium? Does it satisfy the condition of input efficiency?

Describing Input Efficiency Using the Edgeworth Box

To answer this question, we need to draw an **Edgeworth box for inputs,** as shown in Figure 16.17. The Edgeworth box for inputs shows how a fixed quantity of labor and capital can be divided among the production of two different goods—in our example, a producer of energy and a producer of food. The width of the box is the fixed amount of labor to be divided among the producers, while the height of the box is a fixed amount of capital that can be allocated between the two producers. Any point in the box represents an allocation of inputs to the energy producer and the food producer. For example, the Edgeworth box in Figure 16.17 shows how to divide 10 units of labor and 10 units of capital among an energy producer and a food producer. At point *G* in the box, the energy pro-

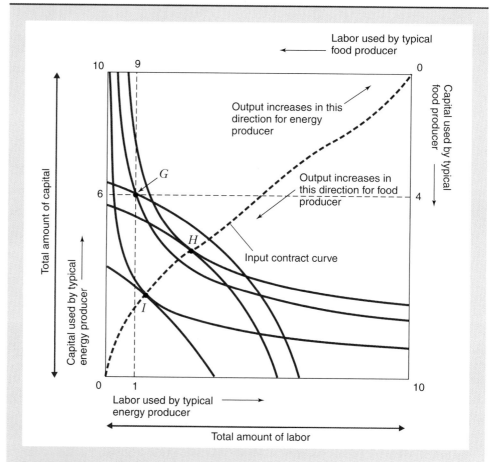

FIGURE 16.17   Input Efficiency in the Edgeworth Box
This diagram shows an Edgeworth Box for inputs. Each point in the box shows a different way to allocate 10 units of labor and 10 units of capital among a typical food producer and a typical energy producer. The allocation represented by point *G* is inefficient: At this point each firm could increase output if it used the input allocation represented by point *H*. Points such as *H* and *I* satisfy the condition of input efficiency. At these points, the firm's isoquants are tangent to each other. The dashed line is the input contract curve: It connects all of the allocations that satisfy input efficiency.

ducer uses 1 unit of labor and 6 units of capital, while the food producer uses 9 units of labor and 4 units of capital.

Inputs in our economy are efficiently allocated between our two industries if there is no feasible reallocation of inputs that allows a firm in one industry to produce more output without reducing the output of a firm in the other industry. The inefficient allocations of inputs occur at the points in the Edgeworth box where the isoquants of the production functions intersect but are not tangent. An input allocation such as *G* in Figure 16.17 is inefficient. By reallocating labor and capital between the energy and food industries to point *H*, we can simultaneously increase output in both industries. Efficient input combinations are points such as *H* and *I* where the isoquants for firms in the two industries are tangent to each other. The entire set of efficient input allocations is described by the **input con-**

tract curve shown in Figure 16.17. The input contract curve shows the set of input allocations that satisfies the condition of input efficiency. That is, the input contract curve connects all of the points of tangency between an isoquant for energy production and an isoquant for food production.

Does the General Competitive Equilibrium Satisfy Input Efficiency?

To answer this question, recall that at a competitive equilibrium, firms in each industry use a combination of labor and capital that minimizes the cost of production, given the prices of labor and capital. As we have seen, this implies that

$$MRTS_{l,k}^x = MRTS_{l,k}^y = \frac{w}{r}$$

Since the marginal rates of technical substitution are the absolute values of the slopes of the isoquants in energy and food production, and since these slopes are brought into equality at a competitive equilibrium, it follows that a general competitive equilibrium satisfies input efficiency. That is, there is no rearrangement of input allocations across industries that would allow one industry to increase its output without reducing output in the other industry.

SUBSTITUTION EFFICIENCY

We have seen that a general competitive equilibrium satisfies the conditions of exchange efficiency and input efficiency. Does it also satisfy our third condition for efficiency, substitution efficiency?

The Production Possibilities Frontier and the Marginal Rate of Transformation

To determine whether the general competitive equilibrium satisfies substitution efficiency, we need to introduce another graph: the **production possibilities frontier.** The production possibilities frontier describes combinations of consumption goods that can be produced in the economy with the economy's available supply of inputs. Figure 16.18 shows a production possibilities frontier for two goods, x and y. When the allocation of inputs across industries satisfies the condition of input efficiency described in the previous section, then if more of good x is produced, less of good y can be produced. This is why the production possibilities frontier is downward sloping. Points such as H, which lie beneath the production possibilities frontier, are inefficient. Indeed, these combinations would not arise in a general competitive equilibrium because we have just seen that the equilibrium satisfies the condition of input efficiency. With input efficiency, firms producing good x are producing as much output as they can given the resources that are devoted to the production of good y.

The slope of the production possibilities frontier shows the amount of good y that the economy must give up in order to gain one additional unit of good x. We call the absolute value of the slope of the production possibilities frontier the **marginal rate of transformation of x for y,** or $MRT_{x,y}$. For example, at point I, the slope of the line tangent to the production possibilities frontier is -2, so the $MRT_{x,y}$ is equal to 2. This tells us that at this point, the economy can get one additional unit of good x only by sacrificing 2 units of good y. In this sense, the

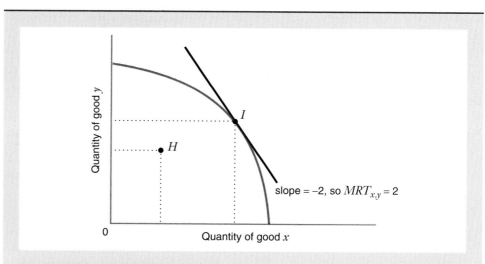

FIGURE 16.18 Production Possibilities Frontier
The production possibilities frontier describes combinations of consumption goods that can be produced in the economy with the economy's available supply of inputs. Points such as *H* that are inside the production possibilities frontier are inefficient: There are other feasible points, such as *I*, that provide larger quantities of both goods. The absolute value of the slope of the production possibilities frontier is the marginal rate of transformation of *x* for *y*, or $MRT_{x,y}$. For example, the $MRT_{x,y} = 2$, which tells us that the economy can get 1 additional unit of good *x* by sacrificing 2 units of good *y*.

$MRT_{x,y}$ tells us the marginal opportunity cost of good *x* in terms of foregone units of good *y*.

The marginal rate of transformation is closely related to the concept of marginal cost. In fact, the marginal rate of transformation is equal to the ratio of the marginal costs of goods *x* and *y*:

$$MRT_{x,y} = \frac{MC_x}{MC_y}.$$

To see why this is so, let's imagine that we want to produce one additional unit of good *x*. The incremental cost of the additional resources (capital and labor) that are needed to produce this extra unit would equal MC_x. Let's suppose that this is equal to $6. Since the supply of resources in our economy is fixed, we need to take away $6 worth of resources from the production of good *y*. Let's suppose that the marginal cost of good *y* is currently equal to $3. This means that we would need to reduce our production of good *y* by 2 units in order to free up $6 worth of resources that we can devote to producing one more unit of good *x*. We have just seen, then, that given that the ratio of the marginal costs is $MC_x/MC_y = \$6/\$3 = 2$, the resulting marginal rate of transformation of *x* for *y* will also be 2. Thus, the marginal rate of transformation equals the ratio of the marginal costs.

In the simple economy whose equilibrium we described in Figure 16.9, every producer had a production function with constant returns to scale, and thus marginal cost was independent of their output. When this is the case, the production possibilities frontier is a straight line, as shown in Figure 16.19. In Figure 16.19, $MRT_{x,y}$ is equal to 0.80/0.70 = 1.14, which is the ratio of the marginal costs that arises in a general equilibrium.

Does the General Competitive Equilibrium Satisfy Substitution Efficiency?

Let's now use the concept of marginal rate of transformation to determine if we have substitution efficiency at a general competitive equilibrium. Suppose that it was the case that $MRT_{x,y} = 1$, but $MRS_{x,y} = 2$ for each household in the economy. If that were the case, then each additional unit of energy produced (good x) would require that one fewer unit of food be produced (good y). However, because $MRS_{x,y} = 2$, each consumer would be willing to give up 2 units of food to get 1 additional unit of energy. In this case, consumer well-being in the economy would go up if more resources were devoted to energy production and fewer resources were devoted to food production. We can use similar reasoning to show that if $MRT_{x,y} > MRS_{x,y}$, consumer utility would go up if fewer resources were devoted to energy production and more resources were devoted to food production. What we learn from this analysis is that in order for the competitive equilibrium to satisfy substitution efficiency, it must be the case that

$$MRT_{x,y} = MRS_{x,y}^{W} = MRS_{x,y}^{B}.$$

Is this condition satisfied at a competitive equilibrium? The answer is yes. Here's why:

- We know that consumer utility maximization implies that $MRS_{x,y}^{W} = MRS_{x,y}^{B} = P_x/P_y$.
- We also know that profit maximization by competitive firms implies that price equals marginal cost in both the energy and food industries (i.e., $P_x = MC_x$ and $P_y = MC_y$, which therefore means that $P_x/P_y = MC_x/MC_y$).
- Finally, we have just seen that $MRT_{x,y} = MC_x/MC_y$.

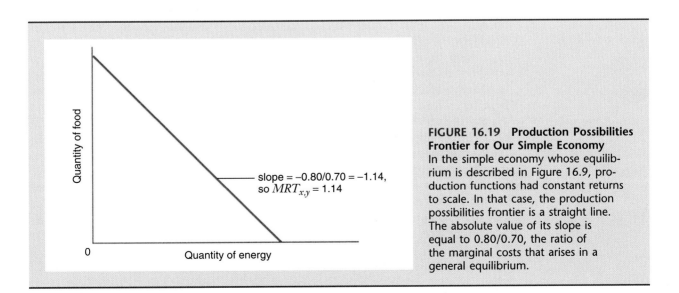

FIGURE 16.19 Production Possibilities Frontier for Our Simple Economy
In the simple economy whose equilibrium is described in Figure 16.9, production functions had constant returns to scale. In that case, the production possibilities frontier is a straight line. The absolute value of its slope is equal to 0.80/0.70, the ratio of the marginal costs that arises in a general equilibrium.

(Figure labels: Quantity of food; Quantity of energy; 0; slope = –0.80/0.70 = –1.14, so $MRT_{x,y} = 1.14$)

Putting these three points together implies:

$$MRT_{x,y} = MRS^W_{x,y} = MRS^B_{x,y}.$$

That is, our condition for substitution efficiency is satisfied at the general competitive equilibrium.

PULLING THE ANALYSIS TOGETHER: THE FUNDAMENTAL THEOREMS OF WELFARE ECONOMICS

In the preceding sections we have seen that the allocation of goods and inputs at a competitive equilibrium satisfies our three criteria for economic efficiency: exchange efficiency, input efficiency, and substitution efficiency. This means that we have just proven the **First Fundamental Theorem of Welfare Economics:**

> *The allocation of goods and inputs that arises in a general competitive equilibrium is economically efficient. That is, given the resources available to the economy, there is no other feasible allocation of goods and inputs that could simultaneously make all consumers better off.*

This theorem is remarkable. Even though households and firms in our economy behave independently and each pursues its own self interest, the First Fundamental Theorem of Welfare Economics tells us that the resulting equilibrium that results from these independent, decentralized, self-interested actions is efficient. It is efficient in the sense that it exploits all of the possible mutually beneficial gains from trade that exist in the economy. This is the essence of the "Invisible Hand" argument made by Adam Smith in his famous 1776 treatise, *An Inquiry into the Nature and Causes of the Wealth of Nations.*[10]

Of course, even though the competitive equilibrium outcome is efficient, there is no guarantee that all consumers fare equally well under the equilibrium. The well-being of an individual consumer depends on his or her endowment of scarce economic resources. For example, we saw that in the equilibrium in Figure 16.9, white-collar households (who supply capital) fared better than blue-collar households (who supply labor) because white-collar households owned the factor of production—capital—that was more scarce and more in demand by producers. Had the pattern of ownership of scarce inputs in the economy been different, the equilibrium distribution of income and utility would have been different.

Figure 16.20 illustrates this point with a graph called the **utility possibilities frontier.** The utility possibilities frontier shows the pattern of utilities that could arise at the various economically efficient allocations of goods and inputs in a simple two-consumer economy. Point E is one pattern of utilities that might arise in the competitive equilibrium. Different economically efficient allocations result in different distributions of utility, such as point F.

Could a social planner, through a suitable redistribution of ownership of scarce resources in the economy, attain any point along this utility possibilities frontier as a general competitive equilibrium? For example, suppose a benevolent planner would like to achieve an economically efficient allocation in which the dis-

---

[10]Adam Smith, *An Inquiry into the Nature and Causes of the Wealth of Nations*, printed for W. Strahan and T. Cadell, London, 1776.

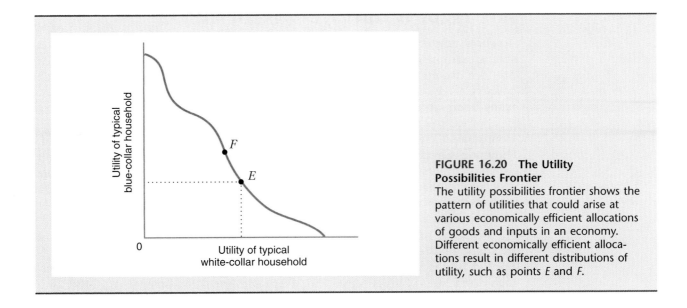

FIGURE 16.20 The Utility Possibilities Frontier
The utility possibilities frontier shows the pattern of utilities that could arise at various economically efficient allocations of goods and inputs in an economy. Different economically efficient allocations result in different distributions of utility, such as points *E* and *F*.

tribution of utilities between white-collar and blue-collar households is somewhat more equal—for example, at equilibrium utilities described by point *F*. Could the planner achieve the desired utility distribution by first redistributing the available stock of labor and capital among the households in the economy and then letting the economy attain a general competitive equilibrium.

The answer, at least in theory, is yes. This is the **Second Fundamental Theorem of Welfare Economics:**

Any economically efficient allocation of goods and inputs can be attained as a general competitive equilibrium through a judicious allocation of the economy's scarce supplies of resources.

The significance of the Second Fundamental Welfare Theorem is that it is at least *possible* to imagine that an economy could simultaneously attain an efficient allocation and one in which the resulting distribution of utility is in some sense equitable or fair. This is not to say that this is easy to do. As we saw in Chapter 10, most of the feasible mechanisms for redistributing wealth in a democratic society (e.g., taxes or subsidies) are themselves costly—that is, they usually distort economic decisions and impair efficiency. Thus, even though the second welfare theorem shows that, in theory, the goals of equity and efficiency are compatible with each other, in practice many public policy choices entail a trade-off between equity and efficiency. The analysis of public policy interventions in Chapter 10 illustrates some of these trade-offs.

In our analysis of exchange efficiency in the previous section, we saw how trade among individuals can make both of them better off. In this section, we will see that trade among countries can make both countries better off. This is the case even though one country is unambiguously more efficient in producing everything than another country.

16.5
GAINS FROM FREE TRADE

FREE TRADE IS MUTUALLY BENEFICIAL

To show that unrestricted free trade can benefit two countries, let's consider a simple example in which two countries—the United States and Mexico—can each produce two goods: computers and clothing. For simplicity, lets assume that each country produces these products with a single input: labor. Table 16.1 shows how many hours of labor are required to produce each good.

For example, Table 16.1 says that in the United States it takes 10 labor hours to produce 1 computer, while in Mexico it takes 60 labor hours to produce that computer. Similarly, in the United States it takes 5 labor hours to produce 1 unit of clothing, while in Mexico it takes 10 labor hours to do so. Notice that Table 16.1 implies that U.S. workers are more productive in both computer and clothing production than their Mexican counterparts since it takes fewer U.S. labor hours to make a unit of either product.

With the numbers in Table 16.1, we can draw the production possibilities frontiers for the United States and Mexico. These are shown in Figure 16.21. For the United States, the marginal rate of transformation of computers for clothing is 10/5, or 2. This is because for every additional computer that is produced, 10 additional labor hours are required. With the supply of labor fixed, these 10 labor hours would have to be diverted from clothing production, which then means that 2 fewer units of clothing can be produced. Put another way, in the United States, the opportunity cost of one additional computer is 2 units of clothing, while the opportunity cost of one additional unit of clothing is 1/2 computer. By contrast, for Mexico, the marginal rate of transformation of computers for clothing is 60/10 = 6. The opportunity cost of one additional computer is 6 units of clothing, while the opportunity cost of one additional unit of clothing is 10/60 or 1/6 of a computer.

Now suppose initially that there is no trade between the United States and Mexico and that in each country there are 100 available labor hours per week. Suppose, further, that 70 U.S. labor hours are devoted to computer production, while the remaining 30 are devoted to clothing production. As shown in Figure 16.21(a), this implies that the U.S. economy operates at point H on its production possibilities frontier: The U.S. economy produces—and U.S. consumers consume—7 computers and 6 units of clothing per week.[11] We assume that this combination of computers and clothing is efficient for the U.S. economy. This

TABLE 16.1
Labor Requirements in the United States and Mexico

	Computers (labor hours per unit)	Clothing (labor hours per unit)
United States	10	5
Mexico	60	10

[11] To see why, note that since each computer requires 10 hours of labor, the United States can produce 70 hours per week/10 hours per unit = 7 units per week if it devotes 70 hours a week to computer production. Further, since each unit of clothing requires 5 hours of labor, the United States can produce 30 hours per week/5 hours per unit = 6 units per week if it devotes 30 hours a week to clothing production.

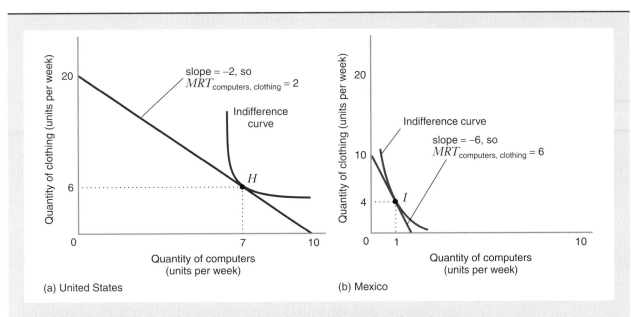

FIGURE 16.21 Production and Consumption in the United States and Mexico: No Trade Situation
The straight line in panel (a) is the production possibilities frontier for the United States, while the straight line in panel (b) is the production possibilities frontier for Mexico. If the countries do not trade, U.S. consumers consume as many computers and units of clothing as U.S. producers produce. Point *H* depicts this outcome. At this point, the utility of a typical U.S. consumer is maximized. Similarly, without trade, Mexican consumers consume as many computers and units of clothing as Mexican producers produce. Point *I* depicts this outcome.

means that at point *H*, a typical U.S. consumer's indifference curve is tangent to the production possibilities frontier.

Let's suppose that in Mexico, 60 out of the 100 available labor hours are devoted to computer production, while the remaining 40 labor hours are devoted to clothing production. As Figure 16.21(b) shows, this means that the Mexican economy operates at point *I* on its production possibility frontier. At this point, the Mexican economy produces—and Mexican consumers consume—1 computer and 4 units of clothing. Let's suppose that this outcome is efficient for Mexican consumers. Thus, at point *I*, a typical consumer's indifference curve is tangent to the Mexican production possibilities frontier. Table 16.2 summarizes the situation for consumers in the United States and Mexico.

TABLE 16.2
Production and Consumption Under No Trade

	Computers (units)	Clothing (units)
United States	7	6
Mexico	1	4
Total	8	10

TABLE 16.3
Production Under Free Trade

	Computers (units)	Clothing (units)
United States	10	0
Mexico	0	10
Total	10	10

We will now see that the two countries can do better by trading with each other. Suppose that the United States specializes in computer production, devoting all 100 hours of its available labor to that activity. Suppose, too, that Mexico specializes in the production of clothes by devoting all 100 of its labor hours to clothing production. Table 16.3 shows the total production of the two countries under this situation, and these outcomes are depicted by points J and K in Figure 16.22.

Now suppose that the United States ships 2 computers per week to Mexico in exchange for 6 units of clothing per week. This means that total consumption in both countries is as shown in Table 16.4.

Trade makes both countries better off. Both countries consume just as many units of clothing as before, but each country now has more computers. As Figure

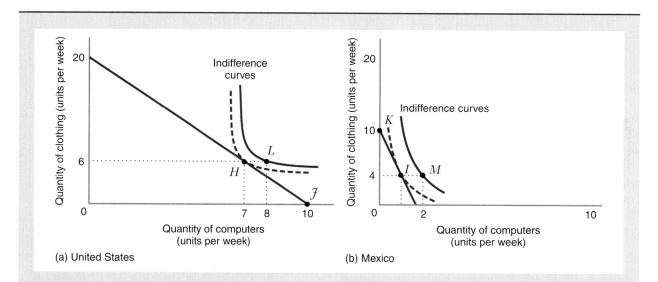

FIGURE 16.22   Production and Consumption in the United States and Mexico: Free Trade
Under free trade, the United States produces 10 computers and no units of clothing (point J), while Mexico specializes in the production of clothing, making no computers and 10 units of clothing (point K). The United States then trades 2 computers for 6 units of clothing. This allows U.S. consumers to consume 8 computers and 6 units of clothing (point L), while Mexican consumers consume 2 computers and 4 units of clothing (point M). Free trade makes consumers in both countries better off than they were before.

TABLE 16.4
Consumption Under Free Trade

	Computers (units)	Clothing (units)
United States	8	6
Mexico	2	4
Total	10	10

16.22 shows, the specialization of production coupled with free trade allows each country to consume "outside" its production possibilities frontier. Thus, when trade between two countries is allowed, both countries can expand their consumption of some goods without reducing their consumption of other goods.

Of course, in practice, not all consumers in the economy benefit equally from the increased consumption opportunities made possible by free trade. In our example, the United States produces less clothing under the free-trade regime than it did in the absence of trade. Workers whose skills are specialized to the textile industry might experience reduced wages or even job losses if trade with Mexico were to commence. Thus, even though the U.S. economy benefits in the aggregate from free trade, those gains are not shared equally, at least in the short run, by all households in the economy.

COMPARATIVE ADVANTAGE

The beneficial effect of free trade is a consequence of a very important idea in microeconomics: **comparative advantage.** One country (say Mexico) has a comparative advantage over another (e.g., the United States) in the production of good X if the opportunity cost of producing an additional unit of good X (e.g., clothing)—expressed in terms of foregone units of good Y (e.g., computers)—is lower in the first country than it is in the second country. In our example, Mexico has a comparative advantage over the United States in the production of clothing. This is because, as we saw above, the opportunity cost of one additional unit of clothing produced in Mexico is one-sixth of a computer, while the opportunity cost of one additional unit of clothing produced in the United States is one-half of a computer.

By the same token, the United States has a comparative advantage over Mexico in the production of computers. This is because, as we can see from Figure 16.21, producing one additional computer in the United States requires a sacrifice of 2 units of clothing, while one additional computer produced in Mexico requires a sacrifice of 6 units of clothing.

Comparative advantage should be contrasted with **absolute advantage.** One country has an absolute advantage over another country in the production of a good X if production of X in the first country requires fewer units of a scarce input (e.g., labor) than it does in the second country. In our example, the United States has an absolute advantage over Mexico in the production of both computers and clothing. Still, as we have just seen, the United States benefits from free trade with Mexico. This is because the benefits from free trade are determined by comparative advantage rather than absolute advantage. In particular, starting from a situation in which two countries are not trading with each other, two countries can make themselves better off by trading when each country specializes in the production of goods for which it has a comparative advantage. In Figure 16.22, we saw that when Mexico specializes in clothing production (its comparative advantage) while the United States specializes in computer production (its comparative advantage), both countries can end up strictly better off through free trade.

EXAMPLE 16.3　　*How Will NAFTA Affect the U.S. Automobile Industry?*

One of the more controversial legislative battles during the first term of the Clinton presidency was the fight to win ratification of the North American Free Trade Agreement (NAFTA) in 1993. NAFTA proposed to eliminate all tariffs between the United States, Mexico, and Canada and to remove many other nontariff barriers to trade over a fifteen-year period. This was an important initiative because by the early 1990s, Canada and Mexico had become the United States's two most important trading partners. NAFTA was approved by a slim majority in the U.S. House of Representatives in the fall of 1993, with many Republicans crossing party lines to support the Clinton administration (which promoted NAFTA) and many Democrats (including then-House Majority Leader Richard Gephardt) voting in opposition to NAFTA.

To the extent that NAFTA creates freer trade between the United States and Mexico, a natural question is how it will affect trade flows within different industries in both countries. The theory of comparative advantage suggests that each country would be expected to increase exports in the industries in which each country has a comparative advantage. Using data on labor productivity and labor wages, Andrew Solocha estimated the extent to which the United States and Mexico enjoyed a comparative advantage in a variety of different industries.[12] One of his most interesting findings is that Mexico might have a comparative advantage vis-à-vis the United States in the production of motor vehicles. He shows that this advantage stems from the high productivity of Mexican workers in the assembly of automobiles and trucks.

An implication of this analysis is that the passage of NAFTA would be expected to result in a shifting of some automobile production facilities from the United States to Mexico. This had already begun to happen during the 1980s, although on a relatively small scale. Does this mean that NAFTA will harm the U.S. auto industry? Solocha argues no. He argues that NAFTA will turn the United States and Mexico (and Canada as well) into a large, integrated trading bloc that will exploit the comparative advantages of each country in specific parts of the automobile and truck

---

[12]Andrew Solocha, "Implications of Comparative Cost Advantage for the NAFTA," *The International Trade Journal*, 8, 1 (Spring 1994), pp. 73–92.

manufacturing businesses, increasing overall industry output. He suggests that while Mexico might have a comparative advantage in the assembly of small cars and light trucks, the United States might have a comparative advantage in the production of larger cars, heavier trucks, and in the parts that go into the production of all motor vehicles. If this is so, while the assembly of small cars and light trucks might be expected to shift from the United States to Mexico, this would be accompanied by an increase in U.S. output of larger vehicles and auto parts. The theory of comparative advantage would tell us that this specialization would result in an increase in the overall output of autos and auto parts throughout North America, benefiting U.S. and Mexican consumers. This specialization would also help to make U.S. firms more effective competitors against the European and Asian firms that are also attempting to sell cars in North America. ■

CHAPTER SUMMARY

• Partial equilibrium analysis studies the determination of price and output in a single market, taking as given the prices in all other markets. By contrast, in general equilibrium analysis, we study the determination of price and output in more than one market at the same time. **(LBD Exercise 16.1)**

• An exogenous event that tends to decrease the price of one good will also tend to decrease the prices of substitute goods. Thus, the prices of substitute goods will tend to be positively correlated. By contrast, an exogenous event that tends to decrease the price of one good will tend to increase the prices of complementary goods. Thus, the prices of complementary goods will tend to be negatively correlated.

• In a general equilibrium, demand for finished products comes from utility maximization by households, while demand for inputs comes from cost minimization by firms. The supply of finished products comes from profit maximization by firms, while the supply of inputs comes from profit maximization by households.

• In a general equilibrium, the prices of all goods are determined simultaneously by supply-equals-demand conditions in every market. **(LBD Exercise 16.2)**

• Walras Law tells us that a general equilibrium only determines the prices of all goods and inputs *relative* to the price of another good or input, rather than determining the absolute levels of all prices.

• To determine the general equilibrium effects of an excise tax on a particular good, we need to analyze the impact of the tax on all markets in the economy, taking into account the interdependencies that exist among those markets.

• An allocation of goods and inputs is economically efficient if there is no other feasible allocation of goods and inputs that would make some consumers better off without hurting other consumers. By contrast, an allocation of goods and inputs is economically inefficient if there is an alternative feasible allocation of goods and inputs that would make all consumers better off as compared with the initial allocation.

• Economy efficiency requires exchange efficiency, input efficiency, and substitution efficiency. **(LBD Exercise 16.3)**

• All three efficiency conditions are satisfied at a general competitive equilibrium. This result is known as the First Fundamental Theorem of Welfare Economics.

• The Second Fundamental Theorem of Welfare Economics says that any economically efficient allocation of goods and inputs can be attained as a general competitive equilibrium through a judicious allocation of the economy's scarce supplies of resources.

• Free trade among two countries can make both countries better off than they would be in the absence of trade.

• A country has a comparative advantage over another in the production of good X if the opportunity cost of producing an additional unit of good X expressed in terms of foregone units of another good Y is lower in the first country than in the second country. Gains from free trade are realized when countries specialize in the production of goods for which they have a comparative advantage.

REVIEW QUESTIONS

1. What is the difference between a partial equilibrium analysis and a general equilibrium analysis? When analyzing the determination of prices in a market, under what circumstances would a general equilibrium analysis be more appropriate than a partial equilibrium analysis?

2. In a general equilibrium analysis with two substitute goods, X and Y, explain what would happen to the price in market X if the supply of good Y increased (i.e., if the supply curve for good Y shifted to the right). How would your answer differ if X and Y were complements?

3. What is the role played by consumer utility maximization in a general equilibrium analysis? What is the role played by firm cost minimization in a general equilibrium analysis?

4. What is Walras' Law? What is its significance?

5. What is an economically efficient allocation? How does an economically efficient allocation differ from an inefficient allocation?

6. What is exchange efficiency? In an Edgeworth box diagram, how are efficient allocations different than inefficient allocations?

7. How does exchange efficiency differ from input efficiency? Could an economy satisfy the conditions for exchange efficiency but not the conditions for input efficiency?

8. Suppose an economy has just two goods, X and Y. *True or False:* If the condition of input efficiency prevails, we can increase the production of X without decreasing the production of Y. Explain your answer.

9. What is the production possibilities frontier? What is the marginal rate of transformation? How does the marginal rate of transformation relate to the concept of the production possibilities frontier?

10. Explain how consumers in an economy can be made better off if the marginal rate of transformation does not equal consumers' marginal rates of substitution.

11. Explain how the conditions of utility maximization, cost minimization, and profit maximization in competitive markets imply that the allocation arising in a general competitive equilibrium is economically efficient.

12. What is comparative advantage? What is absolute advantage? Which of these two concepts is more important for determining the benefits from free trade?

PROBLEMS

16.1. Consider the markets for butter and margarine. The demand curves for butter and margarine are as follows:

$$Q_M^d = 20 - 2P_M + P_B$$
$$Q_B^d = 60 - 6P_B + 4P_M.$$

The supply curves for butter and margarine are:

$$Q_M^s = 2P_M$$
$$Q_B^s = 3P_B.$$

a) Find the equilibrium prices and quantities for butter and margarine.
b) Suppose that an increase in the price of vegetable oil shifts the supply curve of margarine so that it is now

$$Q_M^s = P_M.$$

How does this change affect the equilibrium prices and quantities for butter and margarine? Using words and graphs, explain why a shift in the supply curve for margarine would change the price of butter.

16.2. Suppose that the demand curve for new automobiles is given by

$$Q_A^d = 20 - 0.7P_A - P_G,$$

where Q_A and P_A are the quantity (millions of vehicles) and average price (thousands of dollars per vehicle), respectively, of automobiles in the United States, and P_G is the price of gasoline (dollars per gallon). The supply of automobiles is given by the equation:

$$Q_A^s = 0.3P_A.$$

Suppose that the demand and supply curves for gasoline are

$$Q_G^d = 3 - P_G$$
$$Q_G^s = P_G.$$

a) Find the equilibrium prices of gasoline and automobiles.
b) Sketch a graph that shows how an exogenous increase in the supply of gasoline affects the prices of new cars in the United States.

16.3. Suppose that the demand for steel in Japan is given by the equation

$$Q_S^d = 1,200 - 4P_S + P_A + P_T \text{ (demand curve for steel)},$$

where Q_S is the quantity of steel purchased (millions of tons per year), P_S is the price of steel (yen per ton), P_A is the price of aluminum (yen per ton), and P_T is the price of titanium (yen per ton). The supply curve for steel is given by

$$Q_S^s = 4P_S \text{ (supply curve for steel)}.$$

Similarly, the demand and supply curves for aluminum and for titanium are given by

$$Q_A^d = 1,200 - 4P_A + P_S + P_T \text{ (demand curve for aluminum)}$$

$$Q_A^s = 4P_A \text{ (supply curve for aluminum)}$$

$$Q_T^d = 1,200 - 4P_T + P_S + P_A \text{ (demand curve for titanium)}$$

$$Q_T^s = 4P_T \text{ (supply curve for aluminum)}.$$

a) Find the equilibrium prices of steel, aluminum, and titanium in Japan.
b) Suppose that a strike in the Japanese steel industry shifts the supply curve for steel:

$$Q_S^s = P_S.$$

What does this do to the prices of steel, aluminum, and titanium?
c) Suppose that growth in the Japanese beer industry, a big buyer of aluminum cans, fuels an increase in the demand for aluminum so that the demand curve for aluminum is as follows:

$$Q_A^d = 1,500 - 4P_A + P_S + P_T.$$

How does this affect the prices of steel, aluminum, and titanium?

16.4. Consider a simple economy similar to the one described in the text. This economy produces two goods, beer (denoted by x) and quiche (denoted by y), using labor and capital (denoted by L and K, respectively), that are supplied by two types of households, those consisting of wimps (denoted by W), and those consisting of hunks (denoted by H). Each household of hunks supplies 100 units of labor and no units of capital. Each household of wimps supplies 10 units of capital and no units of labor. There are 100 households of each type. Both beer and quiche are produced with technologies exhibiting constant returns to scale. The market supply curves for beer and quiche are:

$$P_x = w^{\frac{1}{6}}r^{\frac{5}{6}}$$
$$P_y = w^{\frac{3}{4}}r^{\frac{1}{4}},$$

where w denotes the price of labor and r denotes the price of capital. The market demand curves for beer and quiche are given by

$$P_x = \frac{20I_W + 90I_H}{X}.$$

$$P_y = \frac{80I_W + 10I_H}{Y},$$

where X and Y denote the aggregate quantities of beer and quiche demanded in this economy and I_W and I_H are the household incomes of wimps and hunks, respectively. Finally, the market demand curves for labor and capital are given by these equations:

$$L = \frac{X}{6}\left(\frac{r}{w}\right)^{\frac{5}{6}} + \frac{3Y}{4}\left(\frac{r}{w}\right)^{\frac{1}{4}}$$

$$K = \frac{5X}{6}\left(\frac{w}{r}\right)^{\frac{1}{6}} + \frac{Y}{4}\left(\frac{w}{r}\right)^{\frac{3}{4}}.$$

There are four unknowns in our simple economy: the prices of beer and quiche, P_x and P_y, and the prices of labor and capital, w and r. Write down the four equations that determine the equilibrium values of these unknowns.

16.5. Two consumers, Josh and Mary, together have ten apples and four oranges.
a) Draw the Edgeworth box that shows the set of feasible allocations that are available in this simple economy.
b) Suppose Josh has five apples and one orange, while Mary has five apples and three oranges. Identify this allocation in the Edgeworth box.
c) Suppose Josh and Mary have an identical utility function, and assume that this utility function exhibits positive marginal utilities for both apples and oranges and exhibits diminishing marginal rate of substitution of apples for oranges. Could the allocation in part (b)—five apples and one orange for Josh; five apples and three oranges for Mary—be economically efficient?

16.6. Two consumers, Ron and David, together own 1,000 baseball cards and 5,000 Pokémon cards. Let x_R denote the quantity of baseball cards owned by Ron and y_R denote the quantity of Pokémon cards owned by Ron. Similarly, Let x_D denote the quantity of baseball cards owned by David and y_D denote the quantity of Pokémon cards owned by David. Suppose, further, that for Ron, this relation holds:

$$MRS_{x,y}^R = \frac{x_R}{y_R},$$

while for David

$$MRS_{x,y}^D = \frac{2x_D}{y_D}.$$

Finally, suppose $x_R = 800$, $y_R = 800$, while $x_D = 200$, $y_D = 4,200$.
a) Draw an Edgeworth box that shows the set of feasible allocations that are available in this simple economy.
b) Show that the current allocation of cards is not economically efficient.
c) Identify a trade of cards between David and Ron that make both better off. (*Note:* There are many possible answers to this problem.)

16.7. Consider an economy that consists of three individuals, Maureen (M), David (D), and Suvarna (S). Two goods are available in the economy, x and y. The marginal rates of substitution for the three consumers are given by:

$$MRS_{x,y}^{\text{Maureen}} = \frac{2x_M}{y_M}.$$

$$MRS_{x,y}^{\text{David}} = \frac{x_D}{2y_D}.$$

$$MRS_{x,y}^{\text{Suvarna}} = \frac{x_S}{y_S}.$$

Maureen and David are both consuming twice as much of good x as good y, while Suvarna is consuming equal amounts of goods x and y. Are these consumption patterns economically efficient?

16.8. Two firms together employ 20 units of labor and 12 units of capital. For Firm 1, which uses 5 units of labor and 8 units of capital, the marginal products of labor and capital are as follows:

$$MP_l^1 = 20$$
$$MP_k^1 = 40.$$

For Firm 2, which uses 15 units of labor and 4 units of capital, the marginal products are:

$$MP_l^2 = 60$$
$$MP_k^2 = 30.$$

a) Draw an Edgeworth box for inputs that shows the allocation of inputs across these two firms.
b) Is this allocation of inputs economically efficient? Why or why not? If it is not, identify a reallocation of inputs that would allow both firms to increase their outputs.

16.9. Consider an economy that uses labor and capital to produce two goods, beer (x) and peanuts (y), subject to technologies that exhibit constant returns to scale. The marginal cost of a 12-ounce can of beer is $0.50. The marginal cost of a 12-ounce tin of peanuts is $1.00. Currently, the economy is producing 1 million 12-ounce cans of beer and 2 million 12-ounce tins of peanuts. The marginal rates of technical substitution of labor for capital in the beer and peanut industries are the same. Moreover, there are 1 million identical consumers in the economy, each with a marginal rate of substitution of beer for peanuts given by

$$MRS_{x,y} = \frac{x}{3y}.$$

a) Sketch a graph of the economy's production possibilities frontier. Identify the economy's current output on this graph.
b) Does the existing allocation satisfy substitution efficiency? Why or why not?

16.10. The United States and Switzerland can produce automobiles and watches. The labor required to produce a unit of each product is shown on the following page:

U.S. and Swiss Labor Requirements		
	Automobiles (labor hours per unit)	Watches (labor hours per unit)
United States	5	50
Switzerland	20	60

a) Which country has an absolute advantage in the production of watches? In the production of automobiles?
b) Which country has a comparative advantage in the production of watches? In the production of automobiles?

APPENDIX: Deriving the Demand and Supply Curves for the General Equilibrium in Figure 16.9

In this appendix, we will see how to derive the demand and supply curves for the economy whose equilibrium is depicted in Figure 16.9.

DERIVING THE HOUSEHOLD AND MARKET DEMAND CURVES FOR ENERGY AND FOOD

Let's begin by deriving the demand curves for each household type in our economy, and then summing these demand curves to derive market demand curves for energy and food. To do, this, we use the techniques developed in Chapter 5.

Suppose that the utility function for a white-collar household is

$$U^W(x, y) = x^{\frac{1}{2}}y^{\frac{1}{2}}.$$

For this utility function,

$$MU_x^W = \frac{1}{2}\left(\frac{y}{x}\right)^{\frac{1}{2}} \text{ and } MU_y^W = \frac{1}{2}\left(\frac{x}{y}\right)^{\frac{1}{2}}.$$

The marginal rate of substitution is the ratio of the marginal utilities, $MRS_{x,y}^W = MU_x^W/MU_y^W$. Substituting in the above expressions for marginal utility, we have

$$MRS_{x,y}^W = \frac{y}{x}.$$

Assuming that the household maximizes its utility subject to its budget constraint, it will equate $MRS_{x,y}^W$ to the ratio of the prices, P_x/P_y. In addition, the budget constraint is satisfied. Thus utility maximization gives us two equations in two unknowns, x and y.

$$MRS_{x,y}^W = \frac{P_x}{P_y} \text{ implies } \frac{y}{x} = \frac{P_x}{P_y}.$$

The budget constraint implies $xP_x + yP_y = I_W$, where I_W denotes the household's income level (which, recall, depends on the input prices, w and r). When we solve these equations for x and y (treating P_x, P_y, and I_W as constants) we get the following values for x and y:

$$x = \frac{1}{2}\frac{I_W}{P_x}, \text{ and } y = \frac{1}{2}\frac{I_W}{P_y}.$$

These are a typical white-collar household's demand curves for energy and food. Let's suppose that our economy contains 100 such households. If so, we can find the aggregate demand curves for energy and food from white-collar households by multiplying the above expressions by 100. This yields the D_x^W and D_y^W demand curves in Figure 16.5:

$$x^W = \frac{50I_W}{P_x}$$

$$y^W = \frac{50I_W}{P_y}.$$

Let's now turn to the blue-collar households. Suppose that the utility function for a typical blue-collar household is

$$U^B(x, y) = x^{\frac{3}{4}}y^{\frac{1}{4}}.$$

For this utility function,

$$MU_x^B = \frac{3}{4}\left(\frac{y}{x}\right)^{\frac{1}{4}} \text{ and } MU_y^B = \frac{1}{4}\left(\frac{x}{y}\right)^{\frac{3}{4}}.$$

To derive the demand curves for energy and food for a typical blue-collar household, we proceed in the same way as we did for white-collar households. When we do so, we find that the demand curves for a typical blue-collar household are:

$$x = \frac{3}{4}\frac{I_B}{P_x}, \text{ and } y = \frac{1}{4}\frac{I_B}{P_y}.$$

Suppose that there are 100 such households. The aggregate demands for energy and food from blue-collar households is found by multiplying the above expressions by 100. This gives us the D_x^B and D_y^B demand curves in Figure 16.5:

$$x^B = \frac{75I_B}{P_x}$$

$$y^B = \frac{25I_B}{P_y}.$$

We can now find the market demand curves for energy and food by horizontally summing the demand curves for each type of household. Let X be the aggregate amount of energy demanded in the economy. The market demand curve for energy is thus $X = x^W + x^B$, which implies $X = (50I_W + 75I_B)/P_x$. For Learning-By-Doing Exercise 16.2 it will be convenient to write the demand curve for energy in this way:

$$P_x = \frac{50I_W + 75I_B}{X}.$$

Similarly, the market demand curve for food is $Y = y^W + y^B$, so we can also write this demand curve this way:

$$P_y = \frac{50I_W + 25I_B}{Y}.$$

Notice that these market demand curves depend on the income levels of each individual household.

DERIVING THE MARKET DEMAND CURVES FOR LABOR AND CAPITAL

Let's now see how to derive the input demand curves (i.e., the demand curves for labor and capital). Let's begin with the energy industry. Suppose that the production function for a typical energy producer is

$$x = 1.89l^{\frac{1}{3}} k^{\frac{2}{3}}.$$

For this production function,

$$MP_l = \left(\frac{1}{3}\right) 1.89l^{\frac{1}{3}} k^{\frac{2}{3}} l^{-1}, \text{ and } MP_k = \left(\frac{2}{3}\right) 1.89l^{\frac{1}{3}} k^{\frac{2}{3}} k^{-1}.$$

Recall from Chapter 7 that the marginal rate of technical substitution $MRTS^x_{l,k}$ is the ratio of the marginal product of labor to the marginal product of capital, $MRTS^x_{l,k} = MP_l/MP_k$. Substituting in the above expressions for marginal product we have

$$MRTS^x_{l,k} = \frac{1}{2}\frac{k}{l}.$$

When an energy producer minimizes its cost of production, it equates $MRTS^x_{l,k}$ to the ratio of the input prices, w/r. In addition, the quantity of labor and capital must be sufficient to produce the desired amount of output x. Thus cost minimization gives us two equations in two unknowns, k and l.

$$MRTS^x_{l,k} = \frac{w}{r} \text{ implies } \frac{1}{2}\frac{k}{l} = \frac{w}{r}.$$

The production function requires $x = 1.89l^{\frac{1}{3}} k^{\frac{2}{3}}$.

We need to solve these equations for k and l, treating w, r, and x as constants. The easiest way to do this is to solve the first equation for k and substitute it into the second equation, which we then solve for l. Solving the first equation for k gives us

$$k = 2\frac{w}{r}l.$$

Substituting this into the second equation and solving the resulting equation for l gives us:[13]

$$l = \frac{x}{3}\left(\frac{r}{w}\right)^{\frac{2}{3}}.$$

This is the labor demand curve for a typical energy producer. To find the firm's demand curve for capital, we substitute the above expression back into the expression for $k = 2(w/r)l$. Doing this and simplifying gives us the following:[14]

$$k = \frac{2x}{3}\left(\frac{w}{r}\right)^{\frac{1}{3}}.$$

This is the capital demand curve for a typical energy producer.

---

[13] Here are the details on how to simplify this expression. When we substitute in $k = 2(w/r)l$ into the production function, we get:

$$x = 1.89l^{\frac{1}{3}}\left(2\frac{w}{r}l\right)^{\frac{2}{3}}.$$

Rearranging terms gives us:

$$1.89l^{\frac{1}{3}}\left(2\frac{w}{r}l\right)^{\frac{2}{3}} = 1.89(2)^{\frac{2}{3}}\left(\frac{w}{r}\right)^{\frac{2}{3}}l^{\frac{2}{3}}l^{\frac{1}{3}}.$$

Now, using a calculator, we can determine that $1.89 \times (2)^{\frac{2}{3}} = 1.89 \times 1.59 = 3$. Finally, we note that $l^{\frac{2}{3}}l^{\frac{1}{3}} = l^{(\frac{2}{3} + \frac{1}{3})} = l$. Thus,

$$1.89(2)^{\frac{2}{3}}\left(\frac{w}{r}\right)^{\frac{2}{3}}l^{\frac{2}{3}}l^{\frac{1}{3}} = 3\left(\frac{w}{r}\right)^{\frac{2}{3}}l.$$

Pulling all of this together implies:

$$x = 3\left(\frac{w}{r}\right)^{\frac{2}{3}}l$$

Rearranging terms gives us:

$$l = \frac{x}{3}\left(\frac{r}{w}\right)^{\frac{2}{3}}.$$

This is the labor demand curve stated in the text.

[14] Here are the details on how to derive this expression. Substituting the labor demand curve into the equation for k in terms of l that we derived above gives us:

$$k = 2\frac{w}{r}l = 2\frac{w}{r}\left[\frac{x}{3}\left(\frac{r}{w}\right)^{\frac{2}{3}}\right].$$

Rearranging terms we have:

$$k = \frac{2x}{3}\left(\frac{w}{r}\right)^{\frac{1}{3}}$$

This is the capital demand curve stated in the text.

Now consider the food industry. Suppose that the production function for a typical food producer is

$$y = 2\, l^{\frac{1}{2}} k^{\frac{1}{2}}.$$

For this production function,

$$MP_l = \left(\frac{1}{2}\right) 2\, l^{\frac{1}{2}} k^{\frac{1}{2}} l^{-1} \text{ and } MP_k = \left(\frac{1}{2}\right) 2\, l^{\frac{1}{2}} k^{\frac{1}{2}} k^{-1}.$$

To find a firm's demand for labor and capital, we proceed in the same way we did when we solved the typical energy producer's cost-minimization problem. Since we have already seen the key computational details, we will simply state the answer. The labor and capital demand curves for a typical food producer are as follows:

$$l = \frac{y}{2} \left(\frac{r}{w}\right)^{\frac{1}{2}}$$

$$k = \frac{y}{2} \left(\frac{w}{r}\right)^{\frac{1}{2}}.$$

Now, suppose that all energy producers together produce X units of energy, and that all food producers produce Y units of food. What is the overall market demand curve for labor? What is the overall market demand curve for capital? To answer these questions, let's consider the energy industry first. We have just seen that when a typical energy firm produces x units of energy, its demand curve for labor is $l = (x/3)(r/w)^{\frac{2}{3}}$. The energy industry's demand curve for labor is the horizontal summation of this demand curve across all energy producers. For example, if there were 100 identical energy producers, each producing x units of output, the energy industry's overall demand for labor would be 100 times the above expression, or $l^x = 100(x/3)(r/w)^{\frac{2}{3}}$. Now because there are 100 producers, each producing x units of energy, $100x$ is equal to overall energy industry output of X. Thus, the energy industry's demand curve for labor is

$$l^x = \frac{X}{3} \left(\frac{r}{w}\right)^{\frac{2}{3}}.$$

This is the equation for the demand curve D_L^x in Figure 16.6(a). By similar logic, the demand curve for labor for firms in the food industry would be:

$$l^y = \frac{Y}{2} \left(\frac{r}{w}\right)^{\frac{1}{2}}.$$

This is the equation for the demand curve D_L^y in Figure 16.6(a). The overall market demand curve for labor is the sum of labor demands in the energy and food industries. Denoting this overall labor demand by L, we have the following:

$$L = \frac{X}{3} \left(\frac{r}{w}\right)^{\frac{2}{3}} + \frac{Y}{2} \left(\frac{r}{w}\right)^{\frac{1}{2}} \text{ (market demand curve for labor)}.$$

This is the equation for the labor demand curve D_L in Figure 16.6(a).

We can use similar logic to derive the equation for overall demand for capital:

$$k^x = \frac{2X}{3}\left(\frac{w}{r}\right)^{\frac{1}{3}} \text{ (energy industry demand for capital).}$$

$$k^y = \frac{Y}{2}\left(\frac{w}{r}\right)^{\frac{1}{2}} \text{ (food industry demand for capital).}$$

When we add these equations together, we get the overall demand for capital, which we denote by K:

$$K = \frac{2X}{3}\left(\frac{w}{r}\right)^{\frac{1}{3}} + \frac{Y}{2}\left(\frac{w}{r}\right)^{\frac{1}{2}} \text{ (market demand curve for capital).}$$

This is the equation for the capital demand curve D_K in Figure 16.6(b). Notice that the economy-wide demands for labor and capital depend on the ratio of the input prices and on the total output produced in each industry.

DERIVING THE MARKET SUPPLY CURVES FOR ENERGY AND FOOD

Let's now see how to derive the market supply curves for energy and food that are shown in Figure 16.7. Because the market supply curves are the marginal cost curves for energy and food production, the key task is to derive these marginal cost curves. We will do this in two steps.

First, let's derive total cost curves for a typical energy producer and a typical food producer. Recall that we saw problems like this in Chapter 8. The total cost for a typical energy producer is the sum of a producer's costs for labor and capital, $TC = wl + rk$. In the previous section, we derived the cost-minimizing quantities of labor and capital for a typical energy producer. If we substitute these equations for l and k into the TC equation, we get

$$TC = w\left[\frac{x}{3}\left(\frac{r}{w}\right)^{\frac{2}{3}}\right] + r\left[\frac{2x}{3}\left(\frac{w}{r}\right)^{\frac{1}{3}}\right].$$

This simplifies to[15]

$$TC_x = (w^{\frac{1}{3}} r^{\frac{2}{3}})x.$$

---

[15] Here are the details of the simplification of this expression. Let's rearrange terms to get:

$$TC = w\left[\frac{x}{3}\left(\frac{r}{w}\right)^{\frac{2}{3}}\right] + r\left[\frac{2x}{3}\left(\frac{w}{r}\right)^{\frac{1}{3}}\right]$$

$$= \frac{x}{3}\frac{wr^{\frac{2}{3}}}{w^{\frac{2}{3}}} + \frac{2x}{3}\frac{rw^{\frac{1}{3}}}{r^{\frac{1}{3}}}$$

$$= \frac{x}{3}w^1 w^{-\frac{2}{3}}r^{\frac{2}{3}} + \frac{2x}{3}r^1 r^{-\frac{1}{3}}w^{\frac{1}{3}}.$$

Now, note that $w^1 w^{-\frac{2}{3}} = w^{1-\frac{2}{3}} = w^{\frac{1}{3}}$. Similarly, note that $r^1 r^{-\frac{1}{3}} = r^{1-\frac{1}{3}} = r^{\frac{2}{3}}$. Substituting these into the above expression implies that

$$TC_x = \frac{x}{3}w^{\frac{1}{3}}r^{\frac{2}{3}} + \frac{2x}{3}w^{\frac{1}{3}}r^{\frac{2}{3}}$$

$$= xw^{\frac{1}{3}}r^{\frac{2}{3}}.$$

Using similar logic, the total cost curve for a typical food producer has the equation

$$TC_y = (w^{\frac{1}{2}} r^{\frac{1}{2}})y.$$

Now, we will derive the marginal cost curves for a typical energy producer and a typical food producer. Recall that marginal cost is the rate of change of total cost with respect to a change in output. The total cost curve for an energy producer, which we just derived, goes up at a constant rate as the firm's output x goes up. This constant rate is the coefficient for x in the equation for the total cost curve, $(w^{\frac{1}{3}} r^{\frac{2}{3}})$. Thus, the marginal cost curve for an energy producer is

$$MC_x = w^{\frac{1}{3}} r^{\frac{2}{3}}.$$

By the same token, the marginal cost curve for a typical food producer is the coefficient for y in the equation of the total cost curve:

$$MC_y = w^{\frac{1}{2}} r^{\frac{1}{2}}.$$

Note that the marginal cost curves for energy and food producers depend on the input prices for labor and capital. Until we know what these input prices are, we won't know the exact level of marginal cost. Also note that the marginal cost curves for energy and food depend on the input prices in different ways. For example, the marginal cost for energy depends more strongly on the price of capital than it does on the price of labor. Ultimately, this is because of differences in the production functions for energy and capital. Given these production functions, an energy producer uses a higher ratio of capital to labor than does a typical food producer. That is, energy production is more capital-intensive than is food production.

17

Externalities and
Public Goods

In this chapter we consider two kinds of markets that are not likely to allocate resources efficiently, even though they might otherwise be competitive: markets with externalities and markets with public goods. We first encountered externalities in Chapter 5, where we studied network externalities. With network externalities, one consumer's demand depends not only on the price of the good, but also on how many others buy it. More generally, an **externality** arises when the actions of any consumer or producer affect the costs or benefits for other consumers or producers in some way not transmitted by market prices.

A **public good** is a good that benefits all consumers, even though individuals may not pay for the costs of production. A public good has two features: (1) the consumption of the good by one person does not reduce the quantity that can be consumed by others, and (2) a consumer cannot be excluded from the good. Public goods include the provision of such services as national defense, public parks and highways (when they are not congested), and public radio and television. For example, when one viewer tunes in to a public broadcast station, no other consumer is prevented from also watching. To put it another way, the marginal cost of serving an additional viewer is zero. Further, once the signal is provided, viewers cannot be excluded from tuning in to the station.

Why worry about externalities and public goods? The short answer is that, in a competitive market, the *invisible hand* may not guide the market to an economically efficient amount of production when there are externalities or public goods. In Chapter 10, we used partial equilibrium analysis to show that a competitive market maximizes the sum of consumer and producer surplus. Since there are no externalities and public goods in a perfectly competitive market, the private costs and benefits that decision makers face are the same as the social costs and benefits. The invisible hand guides the market to produce the efficient level of output, even though each producer and consumer acts in his own self interest. In Chapter 16 we extended the analysis of competitive markets to a general equilibrium setting, and showed that the allocation of resources in a competitive equilibrium is economically efficient, again with no externalities or public goods.

With an externality or a public good, the costs and benefits affecting at least some decision makers differ from those for society as a whole. The market price may not reflect the social value of the good, and the market may therefore not maximize total surplus. Because they lead to economic inefficiency, public goods and externalities are often identified as sources of *market failure*.

Economist Herbert Mohring has described an example of an externality familiar to all of us. "The users of road and other transportation networks not only experience congestion, they create it. In deciding how and when to travel, most travelers take into account the congestion they expect to experience; few consider the costs their trips impose on others by adding to congestion."[1] The externality arises because commuters bear only *part* of the costs they impose on society when making a trip. As a consumer, you pay for gasoline, wear and tear on your automobile, and parking. You also incur a cost for the time spent in the commute because you could use that time to do something else productive. These are examples of private or *internal* costs, because you take them into account when you decide whether to make the trip.

However, your trip creates other *external* costs that you do *not* bear, adding to traffic congestion and increasing the travel time (and therefore the cost) for other commuters. The social costs of your trip include both your private costs and the external costs imposed on others. As Mohring observes, a commuter rarely worries about these external costs because the consumer does not have to bear them alone.

External costs and benefits can be significant. For example, Mohring has studied the effects of congestion in the rush hour in Minneapolis and St. Paul, Minnesota, using data on patterns of travel in 1990. He found that "the average peak-hour trip imposes costs on other travelers equal to roughly half of the cost directly experienced by those taking the average trip."

A commuter will make a trip by auto when benefits from the trip equal or exceed private costs. However, because the commuter ignores the extra costs imposed on others, the benefits from the trip may be *less* than the social costs. The commuter may therefore travel by auto, even though the social costs significantly exceed the private costs during rush hour. Because individual travelers ignore the external costs, the amount of congestion is higher than would be economically efficient.

We begin by describing how market externalities arise, and then show how they can lead to economic inefficiency. We then examine measures that may improve efficiency when there are externalities. Some measures involve government inter-vention, using taxes, subsidies, or other regulation. For example, policy makers employ several techniques to deal with peak period traffic congestion in major urban areas. The government often subsidizes bus and rapid transit operations, resulting in lower fares that induce commuters to use mass transit instead of automobiles. Municipal authorities frequently reserve special lanes on freeways for buses and, to encourage carpooling, automobiles carrying more than one passenger. And, in some areas highway authorities have employed *congestion pricing* by imposing tolls that increase when congestion is greater. We also show that it may be possible to improve economic efficiency by clearly defining property rights for an externality so that decision makers consider all the social costs and benefits of their actions.

Finally, we consider why the invisible hand will not lead the market to produce an efficient amount of a public good. We will show that a market undersupplies public goods and then describe some of the problems confronting policy makers when they decide whether to provide a public good, and, if so, how much to produce.

17.1

EXTERNAL-ITIES

As we have already observed, externalities can arise in many ways. One consumer's actions may benefit or harm producers or other consumers. Similarly, one producer's actions may benefit or harm consumers or other producers.

Externalities are *positive* if they help other producers or consumers. We frequently observe positive externalities from consumption. For example, when a child is vaccinated to prevent the spread of a contagious disease, that child receives a private benefit because the immunization protects her from contracting the disease. Further, because she is less likely to transmit the disease, other children in the community benefit as well. The *bandwagon effect* we studied in Chap-

---

[1]See H. Mohring, "Congestion," Chapter 6 in *Essays in Transportation Economics and Policy: A Handbook in Honor of John R. Meyer,* eds., J. Gomez-Ibanez, W. Tye, and C. Winston (Washington, D.C.: Brookings Institution Press, 1999).

ter 5 is a positive externality because one consumer's decision to buy a good improves the well-being of other consumers.

There are also many examples of positive externalities from production. The development of a new technology like the laser or the transistor often benefits not only the inventor, but also many other producers and consumers in the economy.

Externalities can also be *negative* if they impose costs on, or reduce benefits for, other producers or consumers. For example, a negative externality from production occurs if a manufacturer of an industrial good causes environmental damage by polluting the air or water. A negative externality from consumption occurs if there is a *snob effect*, as we learned in Chapter 5.

Congestion in the commuter rush hour, as discussed in the introduction to this chapter, is also an example of a negative externality. You are no doubt also familiar with other examples of congestion externalities, including those often encountered on computer networks, telephone systems, and air transportation.

Externalities can occur in a variety of market settings, including not only markets with competition, but also those with monopoly and other imperfect markets we have discussed in earlier chapters. In this chapter we will focus on the effects of externalities in otherwise competitive markets. As you read the chapter, you might think about how you can apply the principles we introduce to study the effects of externalities in markets that are not competitive.

Negative Externality: Congestion on the Internet

EXAMPLE 17.1

If you have ever surfed the Internet, you have no doubt encountered an electronic experience similar to driving on a freeway. Often you are moving quickly from one Web page to another, while at other times you feel as though you are in stop-and-go traffic, waiting for a reply or slowly transmitting or downloading data. Everyone who sends an e-mail or downloads a file shares bandwidth, that is, the capacity for carrying data over the network. Sometimes the capacity is adequate to handle the load without congestion. However, at other times there is so much traffic that the network becomes congested. Additional messages will further slow the flow of traffic.

Often described as an *information superhighway,* the Internet is a very large network connecting millions of computers around the world. The Internet connects computers with communications links that serve as electronic highways or pipelines. The largest pipelines are known as the *Internet backbone.* The backbone is itself a collection of networks belonging to the major Internet service providers (ISPs) such as Sprint, GTE, America Online's ANS, MCI, and UUNet. These networks connect with each other at five points (in Washington, D.C., New Jersey, Chicago, San Francisco, and San Jose, California) to connect computers with each other in the United States and with other computers in the rest of the world. There are also many smaller electronic pipelines, comprised of local and regional ISPs, that often connect individual residential and business customers to the backbone.

When you connect to the Internet, you incur private costs, including costs from network congestion, because your time is valuable. You may also pay charges for each minute you are connected to the network. If your benefits from connecting

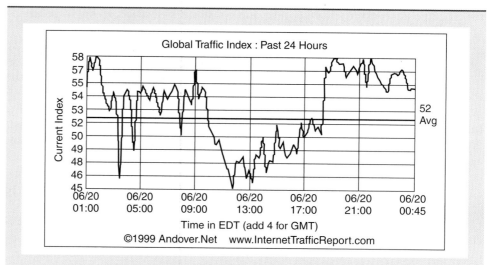

FIGURE 17.1   Congestion on the Internet

Many people time their use of the Internet to avoid congestion. Users often monitor traffic congestion on the Internet, just as they do when they listen to radio reports about the latest traffic conditions on the freeways. The speed with which traffic moves through the Internet varies during the day, depending on the amount of congestion in the network. The graph measures the speed of data flow around the world using an index between 0 and 100, with higher values indicating faster and more reliable connections. The graph shows that, on June 20, 2000, the Internet was generally most congested between 10 A.M. and 6 P.M. (Eastern Daylight Time).

Source: *Internet Traffic Report* of Andover Net (*http://www.internettrafficreport.com/*), June 21, 2000. Copyright © 1998 Andover.Net. All rights reserved. Reproduction in whole or in part in any form or medium without express written permission of Andover.Net is prohibited. Andover.Net and the Andover.Net logo are trademarks of Andover Advanced Technologies, Inc.

exceed these private costs, you will stay online. If your private costs are too high because of congestion, you may decide to delay surfing until another time.

Many users consult Web sites that provide current information on the extent of congestion on the Internet, much as they listen to traffic reports on radio or television stations before deciding whether to make a trip by auto. For example, the Andover News Network posts an Internet Traffic Report on its Web site (www.internettrafficreport.com). The report is based on measurements of the round-trip travel time for messages sent along major paths on the Internet. The amount of congestion is then summarized with an index on a scale from 0 to 100, with a higher number corresponding to a faster transmission time (less congestion). The report measures congestion both by region (e.g., in North America or in Europe) or globally, as Figure 17.1 illustrates.

You may also impose external costs on other users when you surf because your own traffic adds to congestion throughout the network. Like the automobile commuter, while you think about the private costs that you incur because of congestion, you probably do *not* think about the external costs you impose on others as your own traffic adds to congestion. ∎

NEGATIVE EXTERNALITIES AND ECONOMIC EFFICIENCY

Why do firms produce too much in an otherwise competitive market when there are negative externalities? Consider what happens when the production process for a chemical product also generates toxic emissions that harm the environment. Let's assume that there is only one technology available to produce the chemical. That technology produces the chemical and the pollutant in fixed proportion: One unit of pollutant is emitted along with each ton of the chemical produced. Each producer of the chemical is "small" in the market, so that all producers act as price takers.

If the chemical manufacturers do not have to pay for the environmental damage their pollution causes, each firm's private cost will be less than the social cost of producing the chemical. The private cost will include the costs of capital, labor, raw materials, and energy necessary to produce the chemical. However, the private cost will *not* include the cost of the damage that the toxic waste does to the air or water around the plant. The social cost includes both the private cost and the external cost of environmental damage.

Figure 17.2 illustrates the consequences of the externality in a competitive market. With a negative externality, the marginal social cost exceeds the marginal private cost. The marginal private cost curve MPC measures the industry's marginal cost of producing the chemical. Because the technology produces the pollutant and the chemical in a fixed proportion, the horizontal axis measures both the number of units of the pollutant and the number of tons of chemical produced. The marginal external cost of the pollutant is measured by MEC. The marginal external cost curve rises because the incremental damage to the environment increases as more pollution occurs. The social cost, MSC, exceeds the marginal private cost by the amount of the marginal external cost. Thus, $MSC = MPC + MEC$. The marginal social cost curve is the vertical summation of the marginal private cost and the marginal external cost curves.

If firms do not pay for the external costs, the market supply curve is the marginal private cost curve for the industry. The market supply curve is the horizontal sum of the firms' marginal private cost curves. The equilibrium price will be P_1, and the market output will be Q_1.

The table in Figure 17.2 shows the net economic benefits in equilibrium with the negative externality. Consumer surplus is area $A + B + G + K$—that is, the area below the market demand curve and above the equilibrium price P_1. The private producer surplus is area $E + F + R + H + N$, the area below the market price and above the market supply curve. The cost of the externality is area $R + H + N + G + K + M$, which is the same as area $Z + V$. The net social benefits equal the sum of the consumer surplus and the private producer surplus, *minus* the cost of the externality. The net social benefits are therefore represented by the area $A + B + E + F - M$.

Now let's see why the competitive market fails to produce efficiently. In equilibrium the marginal benefit of the last unit produced is P_1, which is *lower* than the marginal social cost of production for that unit. Thus, the net economic benefit from producing that unit is negative.

The efficient amount of output in the market is Q^*, the quantity at which the market demand curve and the marginal social cost curve intersect. There the marginal benefit of the last unit produced (P^*) just equals the marginal social cost. The production of any units beyond Q^* creates a deadweight loss because the marginal social cost curve lies above the demand curve.

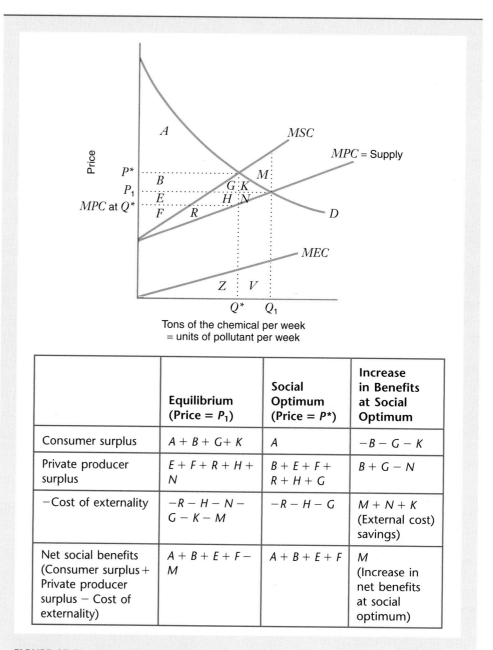

	Equilibrium (Price = P_1)	Social Optimum (Price = P^*)	Increase in Benefits at Social Optimum
Consumer surplus	$A + B + G + K$	A	$-B - G - K$
Private producer surplus	$E + F + R + H + N$	$B + E + F + R + H + G$	$B + G - N$
$-$ Cost of externality	$-R - H - N - G - K - M$	$-R - H - G$	$M + N + K$ (External cost) savings)
Net social benefits (Consumer surplus + Private producer surplus $-$ Cost of externality)	$A + B + E + F - M$	$A + B + E + F$	M (Increase in net benefits at social optimum)

FIGURE 17.2 Negative Externality
With a negative externality, the marginal social cost MSC exceeds the marginal private cost MPC by the amount of the marginal external cost MEC. If firms do not pay for the external costs, the market supply curve is the marginal private cost of the industry MPC. The equilibrium price will be P_1, and the market output will be Q_1. At the social optimum, firms would be required to pay for the external costs, leading to a market price P^* and quantity Q^*. The externality therefore leads to overproduction in the market by the amount ($Q_1 - Q^*$), and to a deadweight loss equal to area M.

If consumers pay the price P^* for the chemical, net economic benefits would increase. Consumer surplus would fall to A, the area under the demand curve and above P^*. Private producer surplus would be the area $B + E + F + R + H + G$. The net social benefits equal consumer surplus plus private producer surplus, *minus* the external cost $(-R - H - G)$. The net social benefits would be the area $A + B + E + F$.

When we add up the net benefits, we find that the market failure arising from the externality creates a deadweight loss equal to area M.

To summarize, the negative externality leads the market to overproduce by the amount $Q_1 - Q^*$. It also reduces the net economic benefits by area M, the deadweight loss arising from the externality.

LEARNING-BY-DOING EXERCISE 17.1

The Efficient Amount of Pollution

This exercise will help you understand why it is *not* generally socially optimal to prohibit industries from using technologies that produce negative externalities.

Problem Evaluate the following argument: "Since pollution is a negative externality, it would be socially optimal to declare illegal the use of any production process that creates pollution."

Solution To answer this question, we refer to Figure 17.2. At the social optimum, net social benefits will be the area $A + B + E + F$. While it is true that there are costs from the externality (area $R + H + G$), the net social benefits from producing the chemical are nevertheless positive, even after taking into account the cost of the externality. If it were illegal to produce the chemical because of the negative externality, society would be deprived of the net benefits represented by the area $A + B + E + F$. Thus, the optimal amount of pollution is not zero.

If we were to outlaw all pollution, we would deprive ourselves of many of the most important products and services in our lives, including gasoline and oil, electric power, many processed foods, goods made from steel, iron, and plastics, and most modern forms of transportation.

Similar Problems: 17.1, 17.3

Emissions Standards

Figure 17.2 is useful in helping us understand why a market fails to produce efficiently with the negative externality. But what can be done to eliminate or reduce economic inefficiency? The government might intervene in the market by restricting the amount of the chemical that can be produced, and therefore the amount of pollution emitted as a byproduct. A governmental limit on the amount of pollution allowed is called an **emissions standard.**

In the United States, the Environmental Protection Agency is the governmental agency primarily responsible for overseeing efforts to keep the air clean. Under the 1990 *Clean Air Act*, the EPA specifies limits on the amount of pollutants allowed in the air anywhere in the United States. The regulation of air quality is a complex undertaking because there are so many kinds of air pollution, and the patterns of pollution change from year to year. The EPA concentrates on emissions that might harm people, including smog, carbon monoxide, lead, particulate matter, sulfur dioxide, and nitrogen dioxide. There are also many other compounds, called air toxins, that can be hazardous to people.

Under the Act, federal and state governments can require large sources of pollution, such as power plants or factories, to apply for a permit to release pollutants into the air. The permit specifies the types and quantities of pollutants that can be emitted, and the steps the source must take to monitor and control pollution. The EPA can assess fines to sources that exceed allowed emissions. Approximately thirty-five states have implemented statewide permit programs for air pollution.

Unfortunately, it is not easy for the government to determine optimal emissions standards. Consider again our example with the chemical manufacturers. To calculate the optimal emissions in the entire market, the government would need to know the market demand curve for the chemical, as well as the marginal private and social cost curves. If the only way to reduce pollution is to cut back on the amount of the chemical produced, the efficient emissions standard in Figure 17.2 would be Q^* units of pollutant (the amount of pollutant released into the air when Q^* tons of the chemical are produced).

Even if the regulator could calculate the optimal size of the emissions in the entire market, it must decide how much pollution each firm will be allowed to release. Some firms will be able to reduce (*abate*) emissions at lower costs than other firms. The determination of the socially optimal pollution allowance for each firm will depend on the costs of abatement for each firm in the market.

To see why abatement costs matter, suppose the government wants to reduce pollution in the market by one unit. Suppose, also, that it would cost Firm *A* $1,000 to reduce pollution by one unit, while Firm *B* could reduce pollution by the same amount at a cost of only $100. It would cost society less to require Firm *B* to cut back its pollution. To some extent the government can simplify the task of determining the efficient allocation of rights to pollute by allowing firms to trade emissions permits. The government could initially allocate rights to pollute, and then let firms trade the rights in a competitive market. Firms with higher abatement costs will attach a higher value to the right to emit a unit of pollution. They would then trade some of their rights to pollute to firms with low abatement costs. In equilibrium, the rights to pollute will be distributed so that the total costs of abatement are as low as possible.

Under the 1990 Clean Air Act it is possible to implement a system of tradeable emissions permits. For example, the program to clean up acid rain includes pollution allowances that can be traded, bought, and sold.

Emissions Fees

The government may also reduce the economic inefficiency from a negative externality by imposing a tax on the firm's output or on the amount of pollutant the firm emits. An **emissions fee** is a tax imposed on pollution that is released into the environment.

Figure 17.3 illustrates the effect of an emissions fee for our example of chemical manufacturing. Suppose the government collects a tax of T on each ton of chemical produced. Because each firm emits one unit of pollutant for each ton of chemical produced, we can also view the tax as an emissions fee of T on each unit of pollutant.

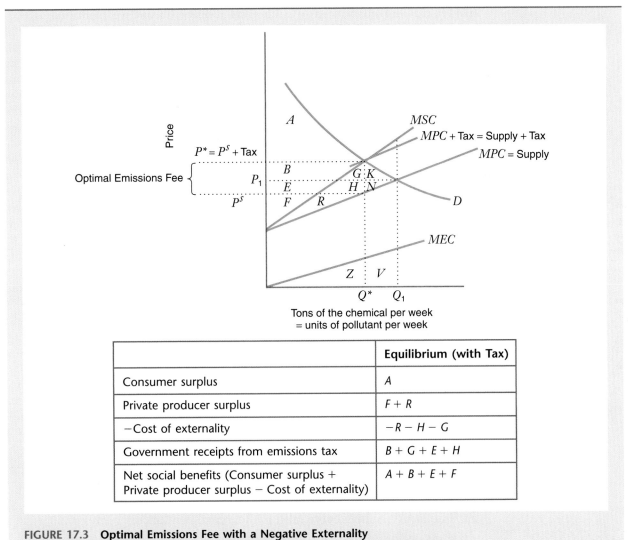

	Equilibrium (with Tax)
Consumer surplus	A
Private producer surplus	$F + R$
−Cost of externality	$-R - H - G$
Government receipts from emissions tax	$B + G + E + H$
Net social benefits (Consumer surplus + Private producer surplus − Cost of externality)	$A + B + E + F$

FIGURE 17.3   Optimal Emissions Fee with a Negative Externality
An optimal emissions fee (or tax) will lead to the economically efficient output Q^* in a competitive market. With an optimal fee, the price consumers pay must cover not only the marginal private cost of production, but also the fee. The curve labeled "Supply + Tax" shows what quantity producers will offer for sale when the price charged to consumers covers the marginal private cost plus the tax. At the optimal tax, the demand curve intersects the "Supply + Tax" curve at the socially optimal quantity, Q^*. Consumers pay P^*, and producers receive a price equal to P^s. The government collects tax revenues equal to the area $B + G + E + H$. There is no deadweight loss with the optimal tax because net benefits are as large as possible ($A + B + E + F$).

One way to understand the effect of the tax is to draw a new curve that adds the amount of the tax vertically to the supply curve, just as we did in Chapter 10 when we studied the effects of an excise tax in a competitive market. The curve labeled "Supply + Tax" in Figure 17.3 tells us how much producers will offer for sale when the price charged to consumers covers the marginal private cost of production *plus* the tax. The equilibrium with the tax is determined at the intersection of the demand curve and the "Supply + Tax" curve.

We have chosen the tax to maximize total surplus in Figure 17.3. The market-clearing quantity is Q^*, the same level of output we identified as economically efficient in Figure 17.2. At Q^* the marginal social benefit is P^*, the price consumers pay for each ton of the chemical. Producers receive P^s, which just covers their marginal private cost of production. The government collects a tax of $P^* - P^s$ per ton of the chemical sold (equivalently viewed as an emissions fee of $P^* - P^s$ per unit of pollutant). As the graph shows, the tax just equals the marginal external cost of the pollution emitted when the industry produces the last ton of the chemical. Thus, the marginal social benefit (P^*) equals the marginal private cost (P^s) plus the marginal external cost.

The table in Figure 17.3 gives us another way to see that the tax in the graph is economically efficient. Consumers pay the price P^* for the chemical, resulting in a consumer surplus equal to area A, the area under the demand curve and above P^*. Private producer surplus is $F + R$, the area below the price producers receive P^s and above the marginal private cost curve. The external cost is area $R + H + G$, which is the same as area Z. The government receives tax revenues equal to area $B + G + E + H$. The net social benefits equal consumer surplus, plus private producer surplus, plus the tax receipts, *minus* the external cost ($-R - H - G$). The net social benefits would be the area $A + B + E + F$. This is the same net benefit that we showed to be socially optimal in Figure 17.2.[2]

LEARNING-BY-DOING EXERCISE 17.2

Emissions Fees

Consider a variation of the chemical manufacturing example. The inverse demand curve for the chemical (which is also the marginal benefit curve) is

$$P^d = 24 - Q,$$

where Q is the quantity consumed (in millions of tons per year) when the price consumers pay (in dollars per ton) is P^d.

The inverse supply curve (also the marginal private cost curve) is

$$MPC = 2 + Q,$$

where MPC is the marginal private cost when the industry produces Q.

---

[2]As we indicated in Chapter 10, one must be careful when using a partial equilibrium analysis like the one in Figure 17.3. A change in the amount of the good consumed in one market may affect market prices, and therefore welfare, elsewhere. Further, there may be additional welfare effects when the government distributes the revenues from the emissions fee somewhere else in the economy. The welfare analysis in Figure 17.3 does not capture these effects.

The industry emits one unit of pollutant for each ton of chemical it produces. As long as there are fewer than 2 million units of pollutant emitted each year, the external cost is zero. But when the pollution exceeds 2 million units, the marginal external cost is positive. The marginal external cost curve is

$$MEC = \begin{cases} 0, & \text{when } Q \le 2 \\ -2 + Q, & \text{when } Q > 2, \end{cases}$$

where MEC is marginal external cost in dollars per unit of pollutant when Q units of pollutant are released.

Problem

(a) Graph the demand, supply, marginal external cost, and marginal social cost curves. What are the equilibrium price and quantity for the chemical when there is no correction for the externality? Determine your answer graphically and algebraically.
(b) At the equilibrium in part (a), how large is consumer surplus? Private producer surplus? External cost? Net social benefit? Show all of these graphically.
(c) How much of the chemical should the market supply at the social optimum?
(d) Suppose the government wants to impose an emissions fee of $\$T$ per unit of emissions. How large should the emissions fee be if the market is to produce the economically efficient amount of the chemical? What price will the consumer pay for a ton of the chemical? What price will the seller receive?
(e) At the equilibrium with the tax in part (d), what is consumer surplus? Private producer surplus? External cost? The impact on the government budget (here a positive number, the government receipts from the emissions fee)? Deadweight loss? Show all of these graphically.
(f) Verify that the following sum is identical when the market operates with no emissions fee and when it operates with the optimal fee you determined in part (d):

> Consumer surplus + private producer surplus − external cost + government receipts from the emissions fee + deadweight loss

Explain why the sum must be the same in both cases.

Solution

(a) See Figure 17.4. The supply curve is the marginal private cost curve in the market. There is a "kink" in the MEC curve (at point G) and in the MSC curve (at point V) because the external cost becomes positive only when there are more than 2 million units of pollution. The marginal external cost curve is OGI. The marginal social cost curve is FVL, the vertical sum of the MPC and MEC curves.

With no emissions fee, the equilibrium is determined by the intersection of the supply (marginal private cost) and demand (marginal benefit) curves, at point H in the graph. The amount consumers pay just equals the marginal private cost for producers in the market.

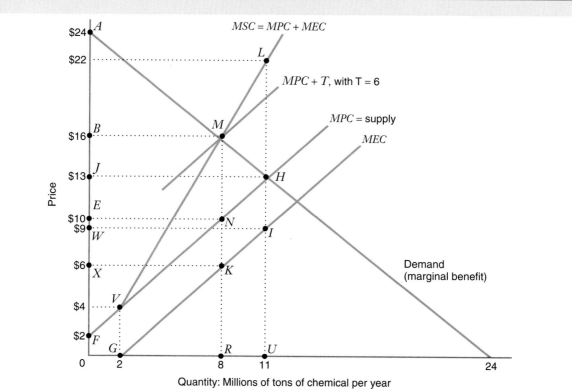

	No Emissions Fee	Emissions Fee of $6 per unit
Consumer surplus	AJH $60.5 million	ABM $32 million
Private producer surplus	FJH $60.5 million	FEN $32 million
−Cost of externality	−VLH (= −GIU) −$40.5 million	−VNM (= −GKR) −$18 million
Government receipts from emissions fee	zero	ENMB $48 million
Net social benefits (Consumer surplus + Private producer surplus − Cost of externality + Government receipts)	AMVF − MLH $80.5 million	AMVF $94 million

FIGURE 17.4   Emissions Fee: Learning-By-Doing Exercise 17.2
The economically efficient output is 8 million tons, determined by the intersection of the demand and *MSC* curves at point *M*. An emissions fee of $6 per unit of pollutant leads to the efficient level of output. With no emissions fee, the price of the chemical is $13 per ton, and 11 million tons are sold each year. The negative externality leads to an inefficiently high level of pollution and a deadweight loss equal to area *MLH*, or $13.5 million per year.

We can find the equilibrium using algebra by setting marginal benefit $(24 - Q)$ equal to marginal private cost $(2 + Q)$. The equilibrium quantity is thus $Q = 11$ million tons of chemical (and therefore 11 million units of pollutant) per year. The equilibrium price can be found by substituting $Q = 11$ into either the marginal benefit or marginal private cost equation. In equilibrium, consumers pay a price of $13 per ton.

(b) Consumer surplus: Area AJH, or $60.5 million per year.

Private producer surplus: Area FJH, or $60.5 million per year.

External costs: We can see the external costs in two places on the graph, area VLH, or, equivalently, area GIU, each representing $40.5 million per year.

Net social benefit: The net social benefit is consumer surplus plus private producer surplus minus external cost, or $80.5 million. The net social benefit is the area $AFH - VLH$, or, equivalently, area $AMVF - MLH$.

(c) Let's first answer the question graphically. The socially optimal level of production would be determined by the intersection of the marginal social cost and demand (marginal benefit) curves, at point M in the graph. The socially optimal level of chemical production is therefore 8 million tons per year. As the graph shows, the 8-millionth ton of the chemical has a marginal benefit of $16. This just equals the marginal social cost of manufacturing the 8-millionth ton of the chemical, including the external cost caused by the emission of the 8-millionth unit of the pollutant.

We can also determine the socially optimal level of production algebraically. The equation representing the marginal benefit curve is $P^d = 24 - Q$. The marginal social cost curve is the sum of the marginal private cost curve ($MPC = 2 + Q$) and marginal external cost curve ($MEC = -2 + Q$ when $Q > 2$). When $Q > 2$, the marginal social cost is therefore $MSC = (2 + Q) + (-2 + Q)$, which simplifies to $MSC = 2Q$. When we set marginal benefit equal to marginal cost, we find that $24 - Q = 2Q$, or that $Q = 8$. Thus, the economically efficient amount of chemical production is 8 million tons per year.

(d) With an emissions fee of T, the equilibrium will be determined by the intersection of the demand curve and the curve labeled $MPC + T$ in the figure. At the optimal fee, the two curves will intersect at the socially optimal quantity of 8 million tons of chemical per year. In other words, the curve labeled $MPC + T$ must run through point M. At M the consumers pay $16 per ton and producers receive $10 per ton. The efficient emissions fee is therefore $6 per ton.

(e) Consumer surplus: Area ABM, or $32 million per year.

Private producer surplus: Area FEN, or $32 million per year.

External cost: We can see the external cost in two places on the graph, area VNM, or, equivalently, area GKR, each representing $18 million per year.

Government receipts from the emissions fee: Area $ENMB$, or $48 million.

Net social benefit: The net social benefit is consumer surplus plus private producer surplus minus external cost plus government receipts, or $94 million. The net social benefit is the area $AMVF$.

Deadweight loss: When we compare the net social benefits with the optimal emissions fee (area $AMVF$) and without the fee (area $AMVF - MLH$), we find that the optimal fee increases net social benefit by area MLH ($13.5 million). This is the deadweight loss from the pollution externality in a competitive market.

(f) With no emissions fee:

Consumer surplus ($60.5 million) + private producer surplus ($60.5 million) − external cost ($40.5 million) + government receipts (zero) + deadweight loss ($13.5 million) = $94 million.

With a $6 emissions fee:

Consumer surplus ($32 million) + private producer surplus ($32 million) − external cost ($18 million) + government receipts ($48 million) + deadweight loss (zero) = $94 million.

The potential net benefit in the market is always $94 million. All of the potential net benefits are captured when there is an efficient emissions fee; there is no deadweight loss. Without the fee, the market performs inefficiently because of the negative externality. Only $80.5 million of the potential net benefits are captured, so $13.5 million in potential benefits have disappeared, becoming a deadweight loss. We recall one of the lessons we learned in Chapter 10: *When the deadweight loss grows by a dollar, the net benefits going to the economy must shrink by that dollar.*

Similar Problem: 17.4

Common Property

Emissions fees and standards are measures that can help correct economic inefficiency arising when a technology produces an undesired byproduct along with some good or service that society values. Negative externalities can also occur in markets that do not involve a byproduct. For example, we have already observed that negative externalities can occur in the use of roadways or the Internet. These are examples of **common property,** that is, resources that anyone can access. No one can be excluded from using common property.

With common property we often observe congestion, a negative externality leading to an overuse of a facility. Figure 17.5 illustrates how congestion generates economic inefficiency. The horizontal axis shows the volume of traffic on a highway, measured in vehicles per hour. When the traffic volume is very low, there is no congestion. In the graph the marginal external cost is zero for traffic volumes below Q_1. Thus, the marginal private cost is the same as the marginal social cost for low volumes.

When the traffic volume exceeds Q_1, congestion sets in. Each new vehicle entering the system adds to the transit time for all vehicles. That is why the marginal external cost rises as traffic volume grows.

Now let's consider the effects of congestion at two different times of the day. In the peak period (rush hour), the demand for use of the highway is high. Absent any government intervention, the equilibrium traffic level would be Q_5, determined by the intersection of the demand curve and the marginal private cost curve. At that traffic level, the marginal benefit for the last vehicle is $5.00 (point A on the demand curve). The marginal private cost is also $5.00. However, the marginal social cost imposed by the last vehicle is $8.00 (point G on the marginal social cost curve). Thus, the marginal external cost is the amount by which the

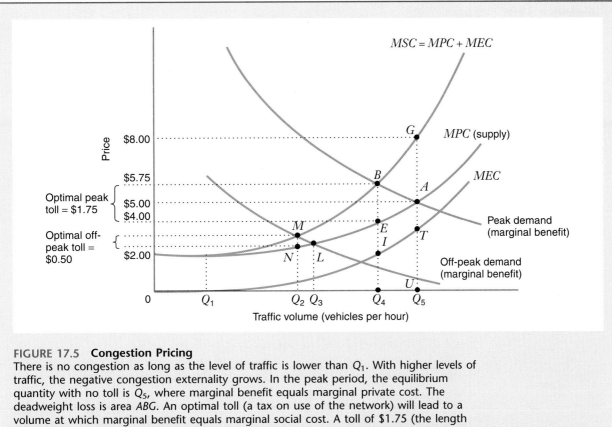

FIGURE 17.5 Congestion Pricing
There is no congestion as long as the level of traffic is lower than Q_1. With higher levels of traffic, the negative congestion externality grows. In the peak period, the equilibrium quantity with no toll is Q_5, where marginal benefit equals marginal private cost. The deadweight loss is area ABG. An optimal toll (a tax on use of the network) will lead to a volume at which marginal benefit equals marginal social cost. A toll of $1.75 (the length of the segment BE) would lead to the social optimum, with a traffic volume Q_4. In the off-peak period, a toll of $0.50 (the length of the segment MN) will lead to the socially optimal level of traffic.

last vehicle increases the costs for *other* vehicles, that is, $3.00, the length of the segment AG (also the length of the segment TU).

The socially optimal level of traffic is Q_4, determined by the intersection of the peak demand curve and the marginal social cost curve. At that traffic level, the marginal benefit and the marginal social cost for the last vehicle are both $5.75 (point B). The marginal private cost is $4.00 (point E). The highway authority could correct for the externality by imposing a toll of $1.75 during the rush hour, bringing the traffic volume to Q_4.

In an off-peak period, the demand for highway use is lower. With the off-peak demand illustrated in Figure 17.5, the efficient off-peak toll would be $0.50. That is the toll that equals the marginal external cost (the length of the segment MN) at the efficient traffic volume Q_2.

The congestion toll, like an emissions fee, is a tax that can be used to correct for negative externalities. Today, most tolls do not vary by hour of the day. The automated collection devices on most toll roads are not capable of collecting tolls that vary during the day. However, as the next example shows, with new technology the widespread use of variable tolls is not far away.

EXAMPLE 17.2   *Congestion Pricing on the Highway*

Traffic congestion has long been a problem in Southern California. In 1995 an innovative toll road opened along Route 91, connecting the major employment centers in Orange and Los Angeles counties with the rapidly growing residential areas in Riverside and San Bernardino counties. The toll road is a ten-mile, four-lane facility, located within the median of the existing eight-lane Riverside Freeway. It is the world's first fully automated toll road.

The project is innovative in two important respects. It is the first U.S. toll road to be privately financed in more than fifty years. It is also the first one to implement *congestion pricing,* with tolls that vary during the day to keep traffic freely moving.

Under a franchise granted by the California Department of Transportation (Caltrans), the $130 million construction cost for the project was financed by a private entity, the California Private Transportation Company (CPTC). Upon completion of construction, the CPTC transferred ownership of the tollway to Caltrans and leased the facility back from the agency for thirty-five years. CPTC collects tolls and pays state agencies to provide law enforcement and road maintenance. The company's profits may not exceed a 17 percent rate of return on its investment, and in the event of a financial failure, the tollway reverts to the state.

Before using the tollway, motorists must obtain a transponder (an electronic device) and prepay money into an account. The transponder functions much like a credit card, containing information on the amount of money that motorists have in their account. Each time a motorist uses the toll road, antennas situated above the highway communicate with the transponder and deduct the toll from that account. There are no toll booths. Tolls range from about $0.40 to $2.75, with higher tolls charged during the periods of peak demand. A system of lasers like those used in jet fighter planes tracks the level of traffic during the day. Electronic signs at the entrance to the toll road inform motorists about traffic conditions and the current size of the toll.   ∎

Besides congestion, there are other examples of negative externalities with common property. For example, most lakes and rivers, and many hunting grounds, are common property. When one person catches fish, a negative externality is imposed on others who would like to fish. The negative externality can become significant when rivalry among commercial fishing enterprises leads to a serious depletion in the stock of fish, jeopardizing fishing harvests in future years. Governments can limit the depletion by imposing taxes or by limiting the quantity of fish that may be caught.

Negative externalities also arise in the petroleum industry, where there are a number of owners of the mineral rights in large reservoirs of oil or natural gas. When one producer extracts a barrel of oil from a reservoir, it depletes the stock of oil available to other producers. The amount of oil that can be successfully recovered from an oil reservoir depends on the way the oil is extracted. If individual producers vigorously compete to extract oil as quickly as they can, they may damage the reservoir, reducing the total amount that producers can ultimately recover. To enhance total recovery, and to minimize the effects of the negative externality, producers often coordinate production. Frequently this involves "unitizing" a field, with production operations carried out through a joint venture.

POSITIVE EXTERNALITIES AND ECONOMIC EFFICIENCY

Positive externalities surround us in everyday life. Examples include education, health care, research and development, public transit, and the bandwagon effect we studied in Chapter 5. With a positive externality, the marginal social benefit from the good or service exceeds the marginal private benefit. Other people around a consumer also benefit when the consumer furthers her education or keeps herself in good health. Similarly, when one firm succeeds in developing a new product or technology with a program of research and development, the benefits often spill over to other firms, and ultimately, to consumers.

Figure 17.6 illustrates why a competitive market produces too little of a good when there are positive externalities. When an individual "consumes" more education, there is an external benefit for other consumers. The more education an individual completes, the more he can contribute to the well-being of others in society.

The figure illustrates the impact of a positive externality in the market. When you decide whether to buy a good, you consider the benefits you will receive (the marginal private benefit), not taking into account the external benefits your purchase will generate. The market demand curve MPB is the horizontal sum of the marginal private benefit curves for all the individuals in the market. The intersection of the MPB (demand) and market MC (supply) curves determines the equilibrium in the market. The price will be P_1, and the market output will be Q_1. In equilibrium, private consumer surplus will be the area below the MPB curve and above the price P_1 (area $B + E + F$). The producer surplus is the area below the market price and above the marginal cost of the industry ($G + R$).

There is also an external benefit in the market. The curve labeled MEB represents the marginal external benefit. With a positive externality, the marginal social benefit exceeds the marginal private benefit by the amount of the marginal external benefit. Thus, $MSB = MPB + MEB$. When the market produces Q_1 units of the good, the size of the external benefit is area $A + H + J$ (which also equals the area $U + V$, the area under the marginal external benefit curve). Thus, the net social benefit when the market produces Q_1 is the sum of the private consumer surplus, the producer surplus, and the external benefits, that is, area $A + B + E + F + G + H + J + R$.

Why does the competitive market fail to produce an economically efficient amount of output? In equilibrium the marginal cost of the last unit produced is P_1, which is *lower* than the marginal social benefit for that unit. Thus, the net social benefit from producing *another* unit is positive. The economically efficient market output is Q^*, where the marginal social benefit *equals* the marginal cost for the last unit produced. Net benefits would increase if the market expands production to Q^*. The failure to produce these additional units introduces a deadweight loss represented by the area $M + N$.

How might public policy correct for the economic inefficiency resulting from underproduction with a positive externality? One possible way would be to

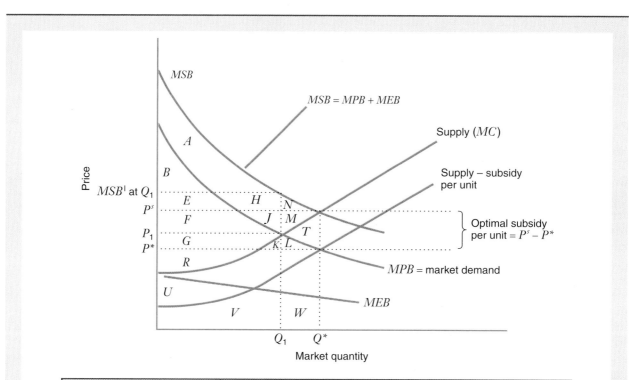

	Equilibrium (No Subsidy)	Social Optimum (Equilibrium with Subsidy)	Increase in Benefits at Social Optimum
Private consumer surplus	$B + E + F$	$B + E + F + G + K + L$	$G + K + L$
Producer surplus	$G + R$	$F + G + R + J + M$	$F + J + M$
Benefit from externality	$A + H + J$	$A + H + J + M + N + T$	$M + N + T$
Government cost from subsidy	zero	$-F - G - J - K - L - M - T$	$-F - G - J - K - L - M - T$
Net social benefits (Private consumer surplus + Producer surplus + Benefit from externality − Government cost)	$A + B + E + F + G + H + J + R$	$A + B + E + F + G + H + J + M + N + R$	$M + N$

FIGURE 17.6 Optimal Subsidy with a Positive Externality

With a positive externality, the marginal social benefit *MSB* equals the marginal private benefit *MPB* plus the marginal external benefit *MEB*. In a competitive market with no correction for the externality, the equilibrium is determined by the intersection of the demand curve (i.e., the marginal private benefit curve *MPB*) and the supply curve. The equilibrium price is P_1 and the quantity is Q_1.

The socially optimal output is Q^*, determined by the intersection of the supply curve and the marginal social benefit curve. The externality leads the market to underproduce by the amount $(Q^* - Q_1)$. The social optimum can be reached with a government subsidy. The optimal subsidy per unit is the difference between the price received by producers P^s and the price paid by consumers P^* at the efficient quantity Q^*. The optimal subsidy eliminates the deadweight loss (area $M + N$) that would arise without the subsidy.

subsidize production of the good. From Chapter 10 you may recall that a subsidy is like a negative tax. We learned there how a subsidy on each unit supplied stimulates production.

How large must the subsidy be to lead the market to produce the efficient output Q^*? To supply the last unit, producers will need to receive the price P^s. However, consumers are willing to pay only P^* for that unit. Thus, there is a gap of $P^s - P^*$ between the price producers require and the one consumers will pay. The government can therefore induce producers to provide that unit and consumers to purchase it if the government provides a subsidy equal to $P^s - P^*$.

We have drawn Figure 17.6 assuming that the subsidy is $P^s - P^*$ for each unit produced. In the table underneath the graph, the column labeled "Social Optimum (Equilibrium with Subsidy)" shows the net benefits with the subsidy. As the table indicates, the optimal subsidy increases the net social benefits by area $M + N$. Thus, with no subsidy, area $M + N$ is the deadweight loss resulting from the positive externality.[3]

Subsidizing Mass Transit   **E**XAMPLE 17.3

Over the last several decades operators of urban mass transit systems have become increasingly dependent on federal subsidies. As ridership declined on most systems in the 1950s and 1960s, transit operators found themselves without the funds necessary to make large capital improvements. In 1964 the Urban Mass Transit Administration (UMTA) began to provide federal subsidies for mass transit. Initially, UMTA required that its subsidies be used to cover capital costs (primarily the costs of major equipment), but not operating costs (such as wages and fuel).

Until 1974, revenues collected by transit authorities covered operating costs for most systems, even though capital costs were heavily subsidized. But in 1975 the federal government began subsidizing operating costs as well as capital costs. Since then, the revenues collected by most mass transit companies have covered only about one-third to one-half of their operating expenses.

Why have such large subsidies for mass transit? As economist Charles Lave notes, the goals of the federal transit subsidy programs seem to have changed over time.

> Federal policy started out with the notion of a one-shot injection of capital to rejuvenate the aging physical plant of our transit systems. A cure, not perpetual hospitalization. It didn't work out that way. The subsidy money encouraged government meddling in transit operations, asking transit systems to undertake a variety of activities unrelated to their traditional goals . . . . The old goal was straightforward: provide a self-supporting service for those who wished to use it. The new goal, assigned by the government, was

---

[3]Once again, we observe that one must use caution when using a partial equilibrium analysis like the one in Figure 17.6. If the government subsidizes one market, it must collect the funds for the subsidy (perhaps introducing a deadweight loss) somewhere else in the economy. The welfare analysis in Figure 17.6 does not capture these effects.

complex and nebulous: use transit service as a tool to solve urban problems, save the central city, provide cheap mobility for the poor, transport the handicapped, and so on.

Lave further observes that " . . . it was more important to expand passenger demand and to provide social services. So routes were extended into inherently unprofitable areas and fares were lowered to the point where no one would find them burdensome."[4]

Lave's comment indicates that there is no precise definition of the goals for mass transit subsidies. But it is clear that positive externalities play an important role in justifying the subsidies.

PROPERTY RIGHTS AND THE COASE THEOREM

So far we have examined how the government might correct for externalities using taxes (emissions fees and tolls) and regulating quantity (emissions standards). As an alternative, the government can assign a **property right,** that is, the exclusive control over the use of an asset or resource, without interference by others.

Why are property rights important in dealing with externalities? Let's return to our example of a chemical manufacturing process that emits pollution as a byproduct. When we described the negative externality, we observed that manufacturers did not have to compensate anyone when they released pollutants into the air. That is why the firms based their production decisions on private marginal costs that did not include the harm that pollution brought to the environment. The costs of pollution were external to the manufacturers.

In that example we also assumed that no one in the surrounding community had a legal right to clean air. If the community owned a property right to clean air, it could have required firms to compensate it for the right to pollute. If a firm were to continue producing the chemical, its marginal private cost would then include the cost of pollution. In other words, the costs of pollution would be internal to the firm instead of external.

In 1960 Ronald Coase developed a fundamental theorem demonstrating how the problem of externalities could be addressed by assigning property rights.[5] He illustrated the idea with an example involving two farms. Farm *A* raises cattle, and the cattle occasionally stray onto the land of a neighboring farm, Farm *B*, which raises crops. Farm *A*'s cattle impose a negative externality by damaging the crops on Farm *B*.

Coase addressed the following issues: Should the cattle be allowed to roam on the property of Farm *B*? Can the owner of Farm *B* require the owner of Farm *A* to construct a fence to restrain the cattle? If so, who should pay for the fence? Does it matter whether the property rights are assigned to the owners of Farm *A* or Farm *B*?

---

[4]C. Lave, "It Wasn't Supposed to Turn Out Like This: Federal Subsidies and Declining Transit Productivity," *Access*, Research at the University of California Transportation Center (Fall 1994), pp. 21–25.

[5]Ronald H. Coase, "The Problem of Social Cost," *Journal of Law and Economics*, 3 (1960): 1–44.

The **Coase Theorem** states that, regardless of how property rights are assigned with an externality, the allocation of resources will be efficient when the parties can costlessly bargain with each other. If the owner of A has the right to let his cattle roam on B's land, B's owner will pay A's owner to build a fence when the damage to B's crops exceeds the cost of the fence. If the cost of the fence exceeds the damage to the crops, it will not be in the interest of owner B to pay for the fence, and the cattle will roam. In other words, when it is socially efficient to construct the fence, the fence will be built to eliminate the externality.

Suppose, instead, that the property rights are assigned to owner B, so that A has to compensate B for any damage. Owner A would build a fence if the damage to B's crops exceeds the cost of the fence. However, if the cost of the fence is greater than the damage to the crops, the owner A will compensate owner B for the damage, and, once again, the cattle will roam.

The example nicely demonstrates the remarkable point of the Coase Theorem. Regardless of whether the property rights are assigned to the owner of Farm A or to the owner of Farm B, the outcome is the same *and* it is socially efficient. The fence will be built when the fence costs less than the damage to the crops, and it will not be built when the fence costs more than the damage.

LEARNING-BY-DOING EXERCISE 17.3

The Coase Theorem

Problem

(a) In the case of the roaming cattle just described, suppose it is costless for the parties to bargain. Verify the Coase Theorem when the cost of the fence is $2,000 and the cost of the damage is $1,000.
(b) Verify the Coase Theorem if the fence costs $2,000 and the damage cost is $4,000.

Solution

(a) Suppose the property rights are assigned to A. Owner B can either pay for a fence costing $2,000, or live with the damage of $1,000. B therefore does not find it worthwhile to pay for a fence, and the cattle will roam. Owner B receives no compensation for the damage of $1,000.

Suppose the property rights are assigned to B. Owner A can either spend $2,000 to build a fence to prevent damage or build no fence and pay $1,000 to owner B to compensate for damage. Owner A does not find it worthwhile to pay for a fence, and the cattle will roam. The damage to B is $1,000, but A will compensate B.

With either property rights assignment, the outcome is the same: the cattle will roam. It is economically efficient to build no fence because the fence costs more than the damage from roaming cattle.
(b) Suppose the property rights are assigned to A. Owner B now finds it worthwhile to pay for a fence, and the cattle will not roam.

Suppose the property rights are assigned to *B*. Owner *A* now finds it worthwhile to pay for a fence, and the cattle will not roam.

Once again, with either assignment of the property right, the outcome is the same: The cattle will not roam. It is economically efficient to pay for the fence because the fence costs less than the damage that would have occurred from roaming cattle.

Similar Problem: 17.7

While the Coase Theorem claims that the allocation of resources will be economically efficient, regardless of the assignment of property rights, the *distribution* of resources very much depends on who hold the property rights. In Learning-By-Doing Exercise 17.3, suppose the cost of the fence is $2,000 and the cost of the damage is $1,000. No one pays for a fence. Either owner will be better off by $1,000 when that person owns the property right.

If the cost of the damage is $4,000, someone will pay for a fence. If *A* owns the property rights, *B* pays for the fence. However, if *B* owns the rights, *A* pays for it. Thus, the owner of the property rights is $2,000 better off than he or she would be without the property rights.

The Coase Theorem with Bargaining

In the simple example just considered, the "bargaining" between the parties is extremely simple once the property rights are defined. If any money is transferred between the parties, the amount of the transfer is the lesser of two amounts: the cost of the fence or the cost of the damage to the crops.

Coase did not explore richer opportunities for bargaining in his work. However, his ideas can be applied to more complex settings where bargaining is possible. Suppose the cost of crop damage is $4,000 if the cattle stray to Farm *B*. Let's add another fencing option. The cost of fencing Owner *A*'s property is $2,000. Alternatively, at a cost of $3,000 owner *B* could build a fence around his property to keep the cattle out.

What happens when we assign the property rights to owner *B*? Owner *A* has three options: (1) fence in his Farm *A* at a cost of $2000, (2) offer owner *B* $3,000 to fence in Farm *B*, or (3) let the cattle roam and pay owner *B* $4,000 to cover crop damage. To minimize his cost, owner *A* will fence in Farm *A*.

Suppose the property rights belong to owner *A*. Owner *B* has three options: (1) fence in Farm at *B* at a cost of $3,000, (2) offer owner *A* $2,000 to fence in Farm *A*, or (3) do nothing and incur $4,000 worth of crop damage. Now there is room for bargaining. Owner *B* would be willing to offer owner *A* up to $3,000 if *A* will fence in his property. (Owner *B* would offer no more than $3,000 to *A* because *B* can fence in Farm *B* at that cost.) At the same time, owner *A* will accept no less than $2,000 to fence in his property. There is an opportunity for both parties to be better off if they agree that *B* will pay *A* some amount between $2,000 and $3,000 to fence Farm *A*. For example, the two parties may agree to split the difference, with owner *A* receiving a payment of $2,500 to build a fence around his farm.

As before, the outcome is the same, regardless of who owns the property right: Farm *A* will be fenced. Further, the outcome is socially efficient because the cost to fence in Farm *A* is less than the cost to fence in Farm *B and* less than the damage caused to the crop farmer if the cattle roam.

To summarize, the Coase Theorem shows that, as long as bargaining is costless, assigning property rights for an externality leads to an efficient outcome, regardless of who owns the rights. However, this powerful proposition depends crucially on the assumption that bargaining is costless. If the bargaining process itself is costly, then the parties might not find it worthwhile to negotiate. Consider our earlier example of the manufacturers who pollute the air as they produce a chemical. If pollution harms thousands of people, it may not be easy for the victims of the negative externality to organize themselves to bargain about compensation. Similarly, if there are many firms in the industry, it may also be costly for them to organize.

There are other potential difficulties with bargaining. If the parties do not know the costs and benefits of reducing the externality, or if they have different perceptions about these costs and benefits, then bargaining may not lead to an efficient outcome. Finally, both parties must be willing to enter into agreements that are mutually beneficial. If one of the parties simply refuses to bargain, or refuses to give the other party an acceptable compensation, it may not be possible to achieve an efficient resource allocation.

17.2 PUBLIC GOODS

We have now learned why a competitive market fails to produce the socially optimal output when there are externalities. For goods with positive externalities, consumers make purchasing decisions based on the marginal private benefits, which are lower than marginal social benefits. Thus, the market produces a lower quantity than the social optimum. Private benefits may be so low that a good is simply not provided at all, even though production of the good would lead to positive net social benefits.

In this section we examine another kind of good that will be undersupplied by the market, public goods. Public goods benefit all consumers even though individual consumers do not pay for the provision of the good. Public goods have two characteristics: They are nonrival goods and nonexclusive goods.

With a **nonrival good,** consumption by one person does not reduce the quantity that can be consumed by others. As we observed in the introduction to this chapter, an example of a nonrival good is public broadcasting. When one viewer tunes in, the number of others who can watch or listen is not diminished. National defense is also a nonrival good. When one person in a community receives protection, the amount of protection available to other consumers is not reduced. The marginal cost of providing output to another consumer of a nonrival good is zero.

By contrast, most goods we encounter in everyday life are **rival goods.** With a given level of production of a rival good, the consumption of the good by one person reduces the amount available to others. For example, when you buy a pair of jeans, a soccer ball, or a computer, you have foreclosed the possibility that anyone else can buy that particular item.

A **nonexclusive good** is a good that, once produced, is accessible to all consumers; no one can be excluded from consuming the good after it is produced. Once a nonexclusive good is produced, a consumer can benefit from the good even if he does not pay for it. Examples of nonexclusive goods are abundant, including national defense, public parks, television and radio signals, and artwork in public places. By contrast, an **exclusive good** is one to which consumers may be denied access.

Many of the goods we observe are both exclusive and rival. Examples include computers, paintings, items of clothing, and automobiles. Suppose a manufacturer makes 1,000 automobiles. When a consumer buys one of them, only 999 are left for others to purchase (i.e., it is rival). In addition, the manufacturer can prevent anyone from access to the automobile. Whoever obtains the vehicle will have to pay for it to enjoy the benefits from consumption.

Some goods are nonexclusive, but rival. Anyone may reserve a picnic table at a public park, but when one person reserves the table on a given day, it is not available to others at that time. Hunting in public game areas is nonexclusive because everyone has access to the game. However, hunters reduce the stock of game left for others when they bag their quarry.

Finally, a good can be nonrival, but exclusive. A pay-TV channel is exclusive because producers can scramble the channel to control access. But the channel is also nonrival. When someone purchases the right to view the channel, this action does not reduce the opportunity for other viewers to do the same.

As we have observed, some goods, like national defense and public broadcasting, are both nonrival and nonexclusive. These are therefore examples of public goods. To avoid confusion as we study public goods, it is important to understand that many goods that are publicly provided are not public goods. Many publicly provided goods are either rival or exclusive, or perhaps even both. Because a public university has a limited capacity, education there can be a rival good. When one student enrolls, another prospective student might be displaced. Further, education at a public university can be an exclusive good because the university can deny admission to an applicant, and because the university can exclude any student who does not pay the required tuition.

EFFICIENT PROVISION OF A PUBLIC GOOD

How much of a public good should be provided to maximize net social benefits? As with other goods, a public good should be provided as long as the marginal benefit of an additional unit is at least as great as the marginal cost of that unit. The marginal cost of a public good is the opportunity cost of using economic resources to produce that good rather than other goods. Because public goods are nonrival, many consumers may enjoy the benefits of an additional unit. The marginal benefit is thus the sum of the benefits of every person who values the additional unit.

Figure 17.7 illustrates the efficient level of production for a public good. For simplicity, let's assume that there are only two consumers in the market. D_1 shows the demand curve for the public good by the first consumer, and D_2 the demand curve for the second consumer. The height of a consumer's demand curve at any quantity shows the marginal benefit of an additional unit of the good to that consumer. For example, the first consumer has a marginal benefit of $30 per year for the 70th unit. The second consumer has the marginal benefit of $130 for the same unit.

How can we determine the marginal social benefit curve for the public good? Because the public good is nonexclusive, both consumers have access to the good. The marginal social benefit of the 70th unit is just the sum of the marginal benefits for the two consumers. The graph shows that the marginal social benefit of

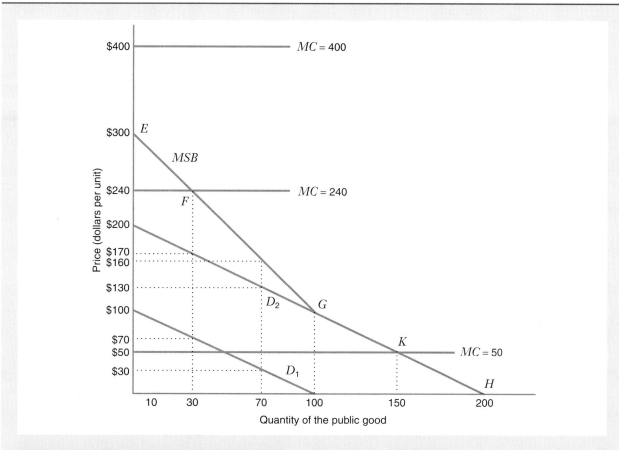

FIGURE 17.7   Efficient Provision of a Public Good
The marginal social benefit of a public good is the vertical summation of the demand
curves for the consumers in the market. The marginal social benefit curve is *EGH*. When
the marginal cost of the public good is $240, the economically efficient level of produc-
tion is 30 units, the output at which the marginal cost and marginal social benefit curves
intersect.
   In Learning-By-Doing Exercise 17.4, we also show that the efficient level of production
is 150 units when the marginal cost is $50, and that it is inefficient to provide the good
at all if the marginal cost is $400.

the 70th unit is $160 ($130 + $30). We can repeat the calculation of the mar-
ginal social benefit at each quantity in the graph. The marginal social benefit
curve is the *vertical summation* of the demand curves for the two individual consumers. In the graph the marginal social benefit curve is the kinked curve *EGH*.
Between *G* and *H* the marginal social benefit curve is the same as D_2 because the
first consumer is not willing to pay anything for these units.
   We can now determine the economically efficient level of production for the
public good. Suppose that the marginal cost of the public good is $240. The eco-
nomically efficient quantity is the quantity at which marginal social benefit equals
marginal cost, or 30 units in the example. It would not be efficient to produce
more than 30 units because the marginal cost exceeds the marginal social benefit for each additional unit produced. For example, as we have already shown, the

marginal social benefit of the 70th unit is $160. However, this is less than the marginal cost, $240. Therefore, it would not be socially efficient to provide the 70th unit of the public good.

Similarly, it would not be efficient to produce less than 30 units of the good. Over this range of production, the marginal social benefit exceeds the marginal cost. Thus, it would be economically efficient to expand production until the marginal social benefit just equals the marginal cost.

At the efficient level of output of 30 units, the marginal benefit for the first consumer is $70, and marginal benefit for the second consumer is $170. Thus, the marginal social benefit of the 30th unit is $240, which just equals the marginal cost of that unit.

This example shows that it may be socially optimal to provide the good, even though no consumer alone is willing to pay enough to cover the marginal cost. Because the good is nonrival, marginal social benefit is the sum of the willingness to pay by all consumers, not simply the willingness to pay by any individual alone.

LEARNING-BY-DOING EXERCISE 17.4

Optimal Provision of a Public Good

This exercise will help you better understand how to find the optimal amount of a public good. It compares the graphical and algebraic solutions. One of the points of the exercise is to understand how to sum demand curves vertically to find the optimum.

In the example we have just considered in Figure 17.7, the demand curves for the two consumers are

Consumer 1: $P_1 = 100 - Q$, and Consumer 2: $P_2 = 200 - Q$

Problem

(a) How would we determine the efficient level of the public good algebraically? Assume the marginal cost of the public good is $240.

(b) Suppose the marginal cost of the public good is $50. What is the efficient level of the public good?

(c) Suppose the marginal cost of the public good is $400. What is the efficient level of the public good?

Solution

(a) As noted in the text, the marginal social benefit curve with a public good is the *vertical* sum of the consumer demand curves. When we sum vertically, we are adding *prices* (i.e., willingness to pay). Therefore, we need to find $P_1 + P_2$. To do this we add the two consumer demand curves in their *inverse* form, with P on the left-hand side and Q on the right-hand side, as they are given above.

Between E and G we know that $P_1 = 100 - Q$ and that $P_2 = 200 - Q$. Then $MSB = P_1 + P_2 = (100 - Q) + (200 - Q) = 300 - 2Q$. To find efficient level of output, we set $MSB = MC$. Thus, $300 - 2Q = 240$, and $Q = 30$. This is the efficient level of output we found graphically in the text.

(b) If the marginal cost is $50, we can determine the efficient level of production graphically by finding the intersection of the *MSB* and marginal cost curves. This occurs at point K in Figure 17.7, at 150 units.

If we attempt to find the optimum with algebra, we must observe that the *MSB* curve between F and G is the same as D_2. Over this region of output, the demand curve for consumer 1 lies along the horizontal axis, so that $P_1 = 0$. Thus, $MSB = 200 - Q$. When we set $MSB = MC$, or $200 - Q = 50$, we find that $Q = 150$.

(c) If the marginal cost is $400, the marginal cost curve lies above the entire marginal social benefit curve, as we show in Figure 17.7. It is therefore not efficient to provide any of the public good. (If you tried to find an algebraic solution by setting $MSC = MB$, or $300 - 2Q = 400$, you would find that $Q = -50$. This tells us that the *MSB* and *MC* curves do not intersect in the positive quadrant. Thus, the algebra tells us that there is no efficient positive level of production of the public good.)

Here is a hint that you may find useful in adding demands. First, you need to know whether you should add the demands vertically or horizontally. As we have shown in this chapter, if you need to find the optimal level of a public good, you need to add demands *vertically*. To add the demands vertically, write the individual demand curves as *inverse* demands and then add them up, as we have just done.

By contrast, in Chapter 5 we showed that, to construct an ordinary market demand curve from individual demand curves, you must add the demands *horizontally* because you want to know the total quantity demanded at any price. The goods we considered in Chapter 5 were *rival* goods. That is why we did not add consumers' willingness to pay to determine the value of an extra unit of the good. To add the demands horizontally, write the individual demand curves in their *normal* form, with Q on the left-hand side and P on the right-hand side. To review how to add demand curves horizontally, you might refer to the discussion following Table 5.3.

Similar Problems: 17.8, 17.10

The Free Rider Problem

There are often thousands, or even millions, of consumers of public goods like a dam, a public park, or public broadcasting. To finance an efficient level of output for a public good, consumers must jointly agree that everyone contributes an amount equal to his own willingness to pay. However, since the provision of a public good is nonexclusive, everyone benefits once the public good is provided. Consequently, individuals have no incentive to pay as much as the good is really worth to them. A consumer can behave as a **free rider,** paying nothing for a good while anticipating that others will contribute.

The free rider problem makes it difficult for a private market to provide public goods efficiently. It is generally easier to organize effective efforts to collect voluntary funding when the number of people involved in paying for a project is small because each person recognizes that her contribution is important. However, when the number of consumers of a public good becomes large, it is more likely that many consumers will act as free riders. Public intervention may be necessary to ensure the provision of a socially beneficial public good. The government therefore often produces a public good itself, or subsidizes the enterprises that produce the good.

EXAMPLE 17.4   *The Free Rider Problem in Public Broadcasting*

As we observed in the introduction to this chapter, public television and public radio are examples of public goods. They are nonrival and nonexclusive. With millions of viewers, it is not surprising that there are many free riders in public broadcasting. In 1997, revenues from public broadcasting totaled $1.94 billion. Only 53 percent of the income is from voluntary private sources such as businesses and subscriber memberships.

According to the Corporation for Public Broadcasting (www.cpb.org/research), more than 92 million Americans watched public television each week during the 1997–98 season. Although more than half of U.S. households tuned in weekly, only 4.9 million individuals contributed to public television during the year. There were also about 20 million public radio listeners, on average tuning in 8 hours per week. Yet only 2 million of them contributed to pubic radio. The average contribution per person, both for television and radio, was about $71 in 1997.

Because of the free rider problem, funds to support public broadcasting must come from many different sources. Subsidies are important. Almost half of the industry's total income comes from tax-based sources, including federal, state, and local governments.

One concern for the industry is the expected decline in future Congressional funding for public broadcasting. In 1999 Congress appropriated $250 million for the Corporation for Public Broadcasting, accounting for 13.4 percent of the industry's total income. Since 1995, Congress has reduced its appropriation for the Corporation of Public Broadcasting by $100 million. As federal funding declines, the industry will need to find funding alternatives to replace tax dollars. ■

CHAPTER SUMMARY

- An externality arises when the actions of any decision maker, either a consumer or a producer, affect the benefits of other consumers or production costs of other firms in the market in ways other than through changes in prices. An externality that reduces the well-being of others is a negative externality. An externality that brings benefit to others is a positive externality.

- Externalities cause *market failure* in competitive markets. With an externality, the *invisible hand* does not lead an otherwise competitive market to produce an economically efficient level of the externality.

- With a negative production externality (like pollution), the private marginal cost to a producer is less than the social marginal cost. With a negative consumption externality (like second-hand smoke from cigarettes), a consumer does not pay for the cost of his own actions imposed on other people. Consequently, a competitive market produces more of the externality than is socially optimal. The government may attempt to improve economic efficiency by reducing the amount of the externality by imposing a quota (such as an emissions standard) or a tax on the externality (such as an emissions tax). **(LBD Exercises 17.1, 17.2)**

• With a positive externality (like education or immunization to prevent the spread of contagious diseases), the private marginal benefit is less than the social marginal benefit. Consequently, a competitive market produces less of the positive externality than is socially optimal. The government may attempt to improve efficiency by stimulating output with a production subsidy.

• Inefficiencies arising from externalities may be eliminated if property rights to externalities are clearly assigned and parties can bargain. The Coase Theorem shows that when parties can costlessly bargain, the outcome of the bargain will be economically efficient, regardless of which party holds the property rights. However, it may be difficult to achieve an efficient outcome with bargaining if there are many parties involved, or if bargaining is a costly process. Although the assignment of the property rights does not affect economic efficiency, it will affect the distribution of income. **(LBD Exercise 17.3)**

• A public good is a good that is nonrival and nonexclusive. The marginal social benefit curve for a public good is the vertical summation of the individual demand curves for that good. A public good is provided efficiently when its marginal social benefit equals its marginal cost.

• It is not easy for a government to determine the optimal amount of a public good because the government lacks information about the amounts individuals are willing to pay for it. Further, a public good is likely to be underproduced because consumers often act as free riders, benefiting from the good but not paying for it. To ensure the provision of a socially beneficial public good, the government often produces the good itself, or subsidizes enterprises that produce the good. **(LBD Exercise 17.4)**

REVIEW QUESTIONS

1. What is the difference between a positive externality and a negative externality? Describe an example of each.

2. Why does an otherwise competitive market with a negative externality produce more output than would be economically efficient?

3. Why does an otherwise competitive market with a positive externality produce less output than would be economically efficient?

4. When do externalities require government intervention, and when is such intervention unlikely to be necessary?

5. How might an emissions fee lead to an efficient level of output in a market with a negative externality?

6. How might an emissions standard lead to an efficient level of output in a market with a negative externality?

7. What is the Coase Theorem, and when is it likely to be helpful in leading a market with externalities to provide the socially efficient level of output?

8. How does a nonrival good differ from a nonexclusive good?

9. What is a public good? How can one determine the optimal level of provision of a public good?

10. Why does the free rider problem make it difficult or impossible for markets to provide public goods efficiently?

PROBLEMS

17.1. Why is it not generally socially efficient to set an emissions standard allowing zero pollution?

17.2. Education is often described as a good with positive externalities. Explain how education might generate positive external benefits. Also suggest a possible action the government might take to induce the market for education to perform more efficiently.

17.3. a) Explain why cigarette smoking is often described as a good with negative externalities.
b) Why might a tax on cigarettes induce the market for cigarettes to perform more efficiently?
c) How would you evaluate a proposal to ban cigarette smoking? Would a ban on smoking necessarily be economically efficient?

17.4. Consider Learning-By-Doing Exercise 17.2, with a socially efficient tax. Suppose a technological improvement shifts the marginal private cost curve down by $1. If the government calculates the optimal tax given the new marginal private cost curve, what will happen to the following?
a) The size of the optimal tax
b) The price consumers pay
c) The price producers receive

17.5. Consider the congestion pricing problem illustrated in Figure 17.5.
a) What is the size of the deadweight loss from the negative externalities if there is no toll imposed during the peak period?
b) Why is the optimal toll during the peak period not $3.00, the difference between the marginal social cost and the marginal private cost when the traffic volume is Q_5?
c) How much revenue will the toll authority collect per hour if it charges the economically efficient toll during the peak period?

17.6. A competitive refining industry produces one unit of waste for each unit of refined product. The industry disposes of the waste by releasing it into the atmosphere. The inverse demand curve for the refined product (which is also the marginal benefit curve) is $P^d = 24 - Q$, where Q is the quantity consumed when the price consumers pay P^d. The inverse supply curve (also the marginal private cost curve) for refining is $MPC = 2 + Q$, where MPC is the marginal private cost when the industry produces Q units. The marginal external cost curve is $MEC = 0.5Q$, where MEC is the marginal external cost when the industry releases Q units of waste.
a) What are the equilibrium price and quantity for the refined product when there is no correction for the externality?
b) How much of the chemical should the market supply at the social optimum?
c) How large is the deadweight loss from the externality?
d) Suppose the government imposes an emissions fee of T per unit of emissions. How large should the emissions fee be if the market is to produce the economically efficient amount of the refined product?

17.7. A chemical producer dumps toxic waste into a river. The waste reduces the population of fish, reducing profits for the local fishing industry by $100,000 per year. The firm could eliminate the waste at a cost of $60,000 per year. The local fishing industry consists of many small firms.

a) Using the Coase Theorem, explain how costless bargaining will lead to a socially efficient outcome, regardless of whether the property rights are owned by the chemical firm or the fishing industry.
b) Why might bargaining not be costless?
c) How would your answer to part a change if the waste reduces the profits for the fishing industry by $40,000? (Assume, as before, that the firm could eliminate the waste at a cost of $60,000 per year.)

17.8. There are three consumers of a public good. The demands for the consumers are as follows:
Consumer 1: $P_1 = 60 - Q$
Consumer 2: $P_2 = 100 - Q$
Consumer 3: $P_3 = 140 - Q$
where Q measures the number of units of the good and P is the price in dollars.
The marginal cost of the public good is $180. What is the economically efficient level of production of the good? Illustrate your answer on a clearly labeled graph.

17.9. Suppose that the good described in Problem 17.8 is not provided at all because of the free rider problem. What is the size of the deadweight loss arising from this market failure?

17.10. In Problem 17.8, how would your answer change if the marginal cost of the public good is $60? What if the marginal cost is $350?

17.11. Some observers have argued that the Internet is overused in times of network congestion.
a) Do you think the Internet serves as common property? Are people ever denied access to the Internet?
b) Draw a graph illustrating why the amount of traffic is higher than the efficient level during a period of peak demand when there is congestion. Let your graph reflect the following characteristics of the Internet:
(1) At low traffic levels, there is no congestion, with marginal private cost equal to marginal external cost.
(2) However, at higher usage levels, marginal external costs are positive, and the marginal external cost increases as traffic grows.
(c) On your graph explain how a tax might be used to improve the economic efficiency in the use of the Internet during a period of congestion.
(d) As an alternative to a tax, one could simply deny access to additional users once the economically efficient volume of traffic is on the Internet. Why might an optimal tax be more efficient than denying access?

Mathematical Appendix

This appendix provides an overview of some of the mathematical concepts that you will find useful as you study microeconomics. In addition to introducing and summarizing the concepts, we will illustrate them by referring to selected examples from the textbook.

A.1 Functional Relationships

Economic analysis often requires that we understand how to relate economic variables to one another. There are three primary ways of expressing the relationships among variables: graphs, tables, and algebraic functions.

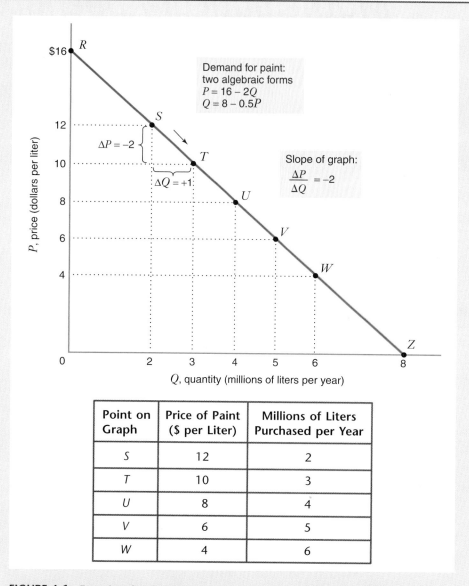

Point on Graph	Price of Paint ($ per Liter)	Millions of Liters Purchased per Year
S	12	2
T	10	3
U	8	4
V	6	5
W	4	6

FIGURE A.1 Functional Relationships: Example with Demand Curve
The graph and table show the relationship between the quantity of paint purchased in a market (Q) and the price of paint (P). For example, the first row of the table indicates that when the price is $12 per liter, 2 million liters would be purchased each year. This corresponds to point S. The functional relationship between quantity and price can be represented algebraically in two ways. If we write price as a function of quantity, the form of the demand curve is $P = 16 - 2Q$. Equivalently, we may write quantity as a function of price, with $Q = 8 - 0.5P$.

For example, Figure A.1 contains information about the demand for paint in a market. The table at the bottom of the figure indicates how much paint consumers would purchase at various prices. For example, if the price of paint is $10 per liter, consumers in the market will buy 3 million liters per year. This information is also shown in the graph at point T. By convention, economists draw demand curves with price on the vertical axis and quantity on the horizontal axis. Since quantity is measured along the horizontal axis (in millions of liters), point T has the coordinates (3,10). Similarly, at a price of $8 per liter, consumers would buy 4 million liters [indicated on the graph at point U, with coordinates (4,8)]. Other points from data in the table are plotted at points S, V, and W. As the figure shows, tables and graphs can be very helpful in showing the relationships among variables.

We also often find it useful to express economic relationships with equations. We can express the relationship between price and quantity using functional notation:

$$Q = f(P), \qquad \text{(A.1)}$$

where the function f tells us Q, the quantity of paint consumed (measured in millions of liters) when the price is P (measured in $ per liter). A specific function that describes the data in Figure A.1 is

$$Q = 8 - 0.5P. \qquad \text{(A.2)}$$

Equation (A.2) is therefore the demand function that contains all of the points shown in Figure A.1. We have written equations (A.1) and (A.2) with Q on the left-hand side and P on the right-hand side. This is the natural way to write a demand function if we want to ask the following question: "How does the number of units sold depend on the price?" The variable on the left-hand side (Q) is the *dependent* variable, and the variable on the right-hand side (P) is the *independent* variable.

Let's use equation (A.2) to find out how much consumers will buy when the price is $8 per liter. When $P = 8$, then $Q = 8 - 0.5(8) = 4$. Thus, consumers will buy 4 million liters per year. To emphasize that Q is a function of P, equation (A.2) might also be written as $Q(P) = 8 - 0.5P$.

We might also use a demand function to answer a different question: "What price will induce consumers to demand any specified quantity?" Now we are asking how the price depends on the quantity we wish to sell.

In other words, how does P depend on Q? We can let P take the role of the dependent variable and Q the independent variable. To see how P depends on Q, we can "invert" equation (A.2) by solving it for P. When we do so, we find that the inverse demand function can be expressed as equation (A.3):

$$P = 16 - 2Q. \qquad \text{(A.3)}$$

Note that all of the combinations of price and quantity in the table in Figure A.1 also satisfy this equation. Let's use equation (A.3) to find out what price will make consumers demand 4 million liters per year. When we substitute $Q = 4$ into the equation, we find that $P = 16 - 2(4) = 8$. Thus, if we want consumers to demand 4 million liters per year, we should set the price at $8 per liter. To emphasize that P is a function of Q, we might also write equation (A.3) as $P(Q) = 16 - 2Q$.

When we draw a demand curve with P on the vertical axis and Q on the horizontal axis, the slope of the graph is just the "rise over the run," that is, the change in price (the vertical distance) divided by the change in quantity (the horizontal distance) as we move along the curve. For example, as we move from point S to point T, the change in price is $\Delta P = -2$, and the change in quantity is $\Delta Q = +1$. Thus, the slope is $\Delta P / \Delta Q = -2$. Since the demand curve in the example is a straight line, the slope is a constant everywhere on the curve. The vertical intercept of the demand curve occurs at point R, at a price of $16 per liter. This means that no paint would be sold at that price or any higher price.[1] If the price of paint were zero, then people would demand 8 million liters. This is the horizontal intercept in the graph, at point Z.

For practice drawing supply and demand curves from an equation, you might review Learning-By-Doing Exercises 2.1 and 2.2.

Learning-By-Doing Exercise A.1
Graphing Total Cost

This example will help you see how to draw a graph and construct a table for a total cost function. Suppose that the function representing the relationship between the total costs of production (C) and the quantity produced (Q) is as follows:

$$C(Q) = Q^3 - 10Q^2 + 40Q. \qquad \text{(A.4)}$$

---

[1]You may recall from a course in algebra that the equation of a straight line is $y = mx + b$, where y is plotted on the vertical axis and x is measured on the horizontal axis. With such a graph m is the slope of the graph and b is the vertical intercept. In Figure A.1 the "y" variable is P because it is plotted on the vertical axis and the "x" variable (the one on the horizontal axis) is Q. Thus, instead of having the equation $y = -2x + 16$, with the example we have $P = -2Q + 16$. The slope is -2 and the vertical intercept is 16.

Problem   In a table, show the total cost of producing each of the amounts of output: $Q = 0$, $Q = 1$, $Q = 2$, $Q = 3$, $Q = 4$, $Q = 5$, $Q = 6$, $Q = 7$. Draw the total cost function on a graph with total cost on the vertical axis and quantity on the horizontal axis.

Solution   The first two columns of Table A.1 show the total cost for each level of output. For example, to produce three units, we evaluate $C(Q)$ when $Q = 3$. We find that $C(3) = (3)^3 - 10(3)^2 + 40(3) = 57$. (Do not worry about the other columns in the table. We will refer to them later.)

The total cost curve is plotted in panel (a) in Figure A.2. (Do not worry about panel (b). We will refer to it later.)

A.2 What Is a "Margin"?

Decision makers are often interested in the **marginal value** of a dependent variable. The marginal value meas-

ures the *change* in a dependent variable associated with a one-unit *change* in an independent variable. The marginal cost therefore measures the rate of change of cost, that is, $\Delta C / \Delta Q$. A decision maker may be interested in the marginal cost because it tells her how much *more* it will cost to produce one *more* unit.

Consider once again Table A.1, which shows the total cost based on equation (A.4). The dependent variable is total cost, and the independent variable is the quantity produced. The table shows two ways of measuring the marginal cost. Column three illustrates the first way by showing how the total cost changes when one more unit is produced. The column is labeled "Arc" Marginal Cost because it measures the change in total cost over an *arc*, or region, over which the quantity increases by one unit. For example, when the quantity increases from $Q = 2$ to $Q = 3$, total cost increases from $C(2) = 48$ to $C(3) = 57$. Thus, the marginal cost over this region of the cost curve is $C(3) - C(2) = 9$. Similarly, the marginal cost over the arc from $Q = 5$ to $Q = 6$ is $C(6) - C(5) = 21$.

TABLE A.1
Relating Total, Average, and Marginal Cost with a Table

(1) Quantity Produced (units) Q	(2) Total Cost ($) C	(3) "Arc" Marginal Cost ($/unit) $C(Q) - C(Q - 1)$	(4) "Point" Marginal Cost ($/unit) dC/dQ	(5) Average Cost ($/unit) C/Q
0	0		40	
		$C(1) - C(0) = 31$		
1	31		23	31
		$C(2) - C(1) = 17$		
2	48		12	24
		$C(3) - C(2) = 9$		
3	57		7	19
		$C(4) - C(3) = 7$		
4	64		8	16
		$C(5) - C(4) = 11$		
5	75		15	15
		$C(6) - C(5) = 21$		
6	96		28	16
		$C(7) - C(6) = 37$		
7	133		47	19

The table shows the values of total cost, marginal cost, and average cost curves when the cost function is $C(Q) = Q^3 - 10Q^2 + 40Q$.

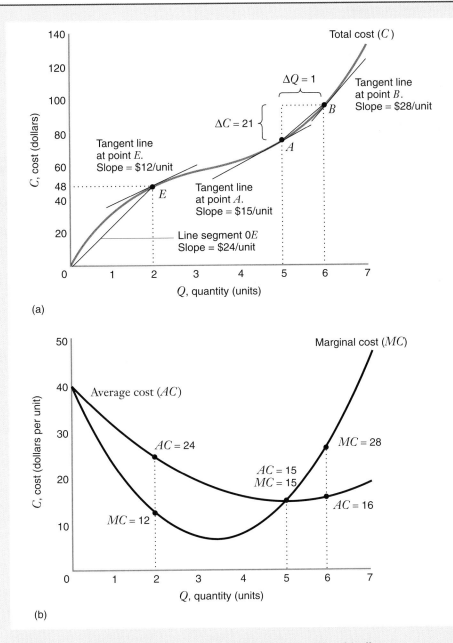

(a)

(b)

FIGURE A.2 Relating Total, Average, and Marginal Cost Graphically
Panel (a) shows the total cost of producing any specified amount of output. The units on the vertical axis of the top graph are monetary (dollars). The bottom graph shows the marginal and average cost curves corresponding to the total cost curve in the top graph. The units on the vertical axis of the bottom graph are dollars per unit. In panel (b), the *value of the marginal cost* at each quantity is the same as the *slope of the total cost* in panel (a).

We can also represent the marginal cost on a graph. Consider Figure A.2(a). The vertical axis measures total cost, and the horizontal axis indicates the quantity produced. We can show that the arc marginal cost approximates the slope of the total cost curve over a region of interest. For example, let's determine the marginal cost when we increase quantity from $Q = 5$ (at point A) to $Q = 6$ (at point B). We can construct a straight line segment connecting points A and B. The slope of this segment is the change in cost (the "rise"), which is 21, divided by the change in the quantity (the "run"), which is 1. Thus, the slope of the segment connecting points *A* and *B* is the arc measure of the marginal cost. Note that over the region the slope of the total cost function changes. The arc marginal cost provides us with an *approximate* value of the slope of the graph over the region of interest.

Instead of approximating the marginal cost by measuring it over an *arc*, we could measure the marginal cost at any specified *point* (that is, at a particular quantity). For example, *at* point *A*, the slope of the total cost curve is the slope of a line tangent to the total cost curve at *A*. The slope of this tangent line measures the rate of change of total cost at point *A*. Thus, *the slope of the line tangent to the total cost curve at point* A *measures the marginal cost at point* A. Similarly, the slope of the line tangent to the total cost curve at point *B* measures the marginal cost there.

How can we determine the value of the marginal cost at a point? One way to do this would be to construct a carefully drawn graph, and then measure the slope of the line tangent to the graph at the point of interest. For example, the slope of the total cost curve at point *B* (when $Q = 6$) is $28 per unit. Thus, the marginal cost when $Q = 6$ is $28 per unit. Similarly, the marginal cost when $Q = 2$ is $12 per unit because that is the slope of the line tangent to the total cost curve at point *E*. Column 4 in Table A.1 shows the exact "point" value of the marginal cost at each quantity.

As we will show later, instead of drawing and carefully measuring the slope of the graph, we can also use calculus to find the marginal cost at a point. (See Learning-By-Doing Exercise A.5.)

Relating Average and Marginal Values

The **average value** is the total value of the dependent variable divided by the value of the independent variable. Table A.1 also shows the average cost, that is, total cost divided by output, C/Q. The average cost is calculated in column 5.

We can also show the average cost curve on a graph. Consider the top graph in Figure A.2. We can show that the average cost at any quantity is the slope of a segment connecting the origin with the total cost curve. For example, let's determine the average cost when the quantity is $Q = 2$ (at point *E*). We can construct a line segment $0E$ connecting the origin to point *E*. The slope of this segment is the total cost (the *rise*), which is 48, divided by the quantity (the *run*), which is 2. Thus, the slope of the segment is the average cost, 24.

Note that the value of the average cost is generally different from the value of the marginal cost. For example, the average cost at $Q = 2$ (again, the slope of the segment connecting the origin to point *E*) is 24, while the marginal cost (the slope of the line tangent to the

total cost curve) is 12. We have plotted the values of the marginal and average cost on Figure A.2(b).

Note that we need one graph to plot the value of the total cost and another to show the values of the average and marginal cost curves. The units of total cost are monetary, for example, dollars. Thus, the units along the vertical axis in the top graph are measured in *dollars*. However, the units of marginal cost, $\Delta C/\Delta Q$, and average cost, C/Q, are *dollars per unit*. The dimensions of total cost differ from the dimensions of average and marginal cost.

It is important to understand the relationship between marginal and average values. Since the marginal value represents the rate of change in the total value, the following statements must be true:

- The average value must *increase* if the marginal value is *greater* than the average value.

- The average value must *decrease* if the marginal value is *less than* the average value.

- The average value will be *constant* if the marginal value *equals* the average value.

These relationships hold for the marginal and average values of *any* measure. For example, suppose the average height of the students in your class is 180 centimeters. Now a new student, Mr. Margin, whose height is 190 centimeters, enters the class. What happens to the average height in the class? Since Mr. Margin's height exceeds the average height, the average height must increase.

Similarly, if Mr. Margin's height is 160 centimeters, the average height in the class must decrease. Finally, if Mr. Margin's height is exactly 180 centimeters, the average height in the class will remain unchanged.

This basic arithmetic insight helps us to understand the relationship between average and marginal product (see Figures 6.3 and 6.4), average and marginal cost (see Figures 8.7, 8.8, 8.9, and 8.10), average and marginal revenues for a monopolist (see Figures 11.2 and 11.5), and average and marginal expenditures for a monopsonist (see Figures 11.19 and 11.20).

Learning-By-Doing Exercise A.2
Relating Average and Marginal Cost

This example will reinforce your understanding of the relationship between marginal and average values. Consider the average and marginal cost curves in Figure A.2(b).

Problem   Use the relationship between marginal and average cost to explain why the average cost curve is rising, falling, or constant at each of the following quantities:

(a) $Q = 2$
(b) $Q = 5$
(c) $Q = 6$

Solution

(a) When $Q = 2$, the marginal cost curve lies *below* the average cost curve. Thus the average cost curve must be falling (have a negative slope).

(b) When $Q = 5$, the marginal cost curve is *equal* to the average cost curve (they intersect). Thus the average cost curve must be constant (have a slope of zero) at that level of output.

(c) When $Q = 6$, the marginal cost curve lies *above* the average cost curve. Thus the average cost curve must be rising (have a positive slope).

A.3 Derivatives

In Figure A.2, we showed that one way to find the marginal cost is to plot the total cost curve and carefully measure the slope at each quantity. This is a tedious process, and it is not always easy to draw a precise tangent line and measure its slope accurately. Instead, we can use the powerful techniques of differential calculus to find the marginal cost or other marginal values we might want to know about.

Let's suppose that y is the dependent variable and x the independent variable in a function:

$$y = f(x).$$

Consider Figure A.3, which depicts the value of the dependent variable on the vertical axis and the value of the independent variable on the horizontal axis.

As we have already discussed, if y measures the *total* value, then the slope of the graph at any point measures the marginal value. (For example, if y measures total cost and x the quantity, then the slope of the cost function is the marginal cost at any quantity.) We can use a concept called a **derivative** to help us find the slope of a function at any point, such as point A in the figure.

We illustrate how a derivative works using Figure A.3. Let's begin with an algebraic approximation of the slope of the graph. The function $y = f(x)$ is curved, so we know that its slope will change as we move along the curve. We might approximate the slope of the graph at F by selecting two points on the curve, E and F. Let's draw a segment connecting these two points and call the segment EF. The slope of the segment is just the rise ($\Delta y = y_3 - y_1$) over the run ($\Delta x = x_3 - x_1$). Thus, the slope of EF is $\Delta y/\Delta x = (y_3 - y_1)/(x_3 - x_1)$. The graph indicates that the slope of EF will not exactly measure the slope of the tangent line at E, but it does give us an approximation of the slope. As the graph is drawn, the slope of EF will be less than the slope of the line tangent to the function at point E.

We can get a better approximation to the slope at E if we choose another point on the graph closer to E,

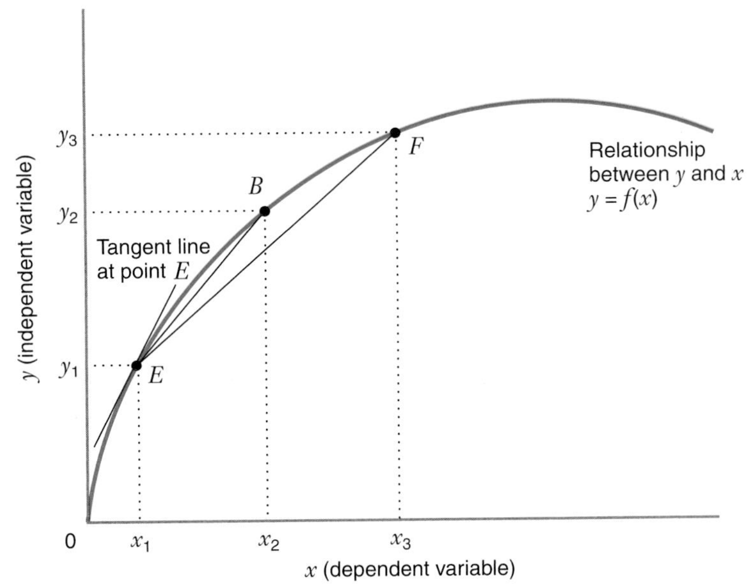

FIGURE A.3 The Meaning of a Derivative
When $x = x_1$, the derivative of y with respect to x (i.e., dy/dx) is the slope of the line tangent to point E.

such as point B. Let's draw a segment connecting these two points and call the segment EB. The slope of the segment EB is $\Delta y/\Delta x = (y_2 - y_1)/(x_2 - x_1)$. Once again, the graph tells us that the slope of EB will not exactly measure the slope of the tangent line at E (it still underestimates the slope at E), but it does give us a better approximation of the slope at E.

If we choose a point very close to E, the approximate calculation of the slope will approach the actual slope at point E. When the two points become very close to each other, Δx approaches zero. The value of the approximation as Δx approaches zero is the derivative, written dy/dx. We express the idea of the derivative mathematically as follows:

$$\frac{dy}{dx} = \lim_{\Delta x \to 0} \frac{\Delta y}{\Delta x}, \qquad (A.5)$$

where the expression "$\lim_{\Delta x \to 0}$" tells us to evaluate the slope $\Delta y/\Delta x$ "in the limit" as Δx approaches zero. The value of the derivative dy/dx at point A is the slope of the graph at that point.

A.4 How to Find a Derivative

In this section we will show you how to find a derivative for a few of the functional forms commonly encountered in economic models. You can refer to any standard calculus book to learn more about derivatives,

including derivatives of other types of functions not included here.

Derivative of a Constant

If the dependent variable y is a constant, its derivative with respect to x is zero. In other words, suppose $y = k$, where k is a constant. Then $dy/dx = 0$.

Consider, for example, the function $y = 4$. Figure A.4 graphs this function. We can find the slope of this function in two ways. First, because the graph is flat, we know that the value of y does not vary as x changes. Thus, by inspection we observe that the slope of the graph is zero.

The second way to find the slope is to take the derivative. Since the derivative of a constant is zero, then $dy/dx = 0$. Since the derivative is always zero, the slope of the graph of the function $y = 4$ is always zero.

Derivative of a Power Function

A power function has the form:

$$y = ax^b, \qquad (A.6)$$

where a and b are constants. For such a function the derivative is:

$$\frac{dy}{dx} = bax^{b-1}. \qquad (A.7)$$

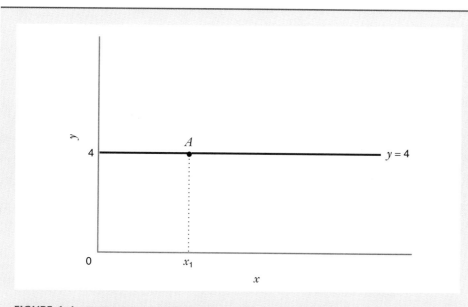

FIGURE A.4   Derivative of a Constant
The graph shows the function $y = 4$. Since the value of y does not vary as x changes, the graph is a horizontal line. The slope of the graph is always 0. The derivative $(dy/dx) = 0$ confirms the fact that the slope of the function is always 0.

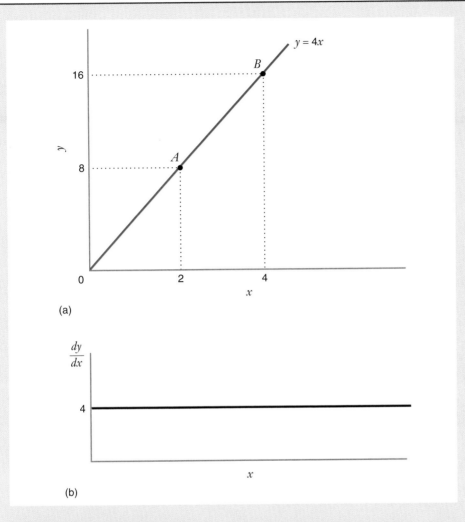

(a)

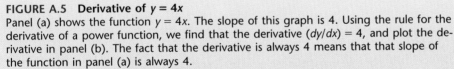

(b)

FIGURE A.5 Derivative of $y = 4x$
Panel (a) shows the function $y = 4x$. The slope of this graph is 4. Using the rule for the derivative of a power function, we find that the derivative (dy/dx) = 4, and plot the derivative in panel (b). The fact that the derivative is always 4 means that that slope of the function in panel (a) is always 4.

Let's consider an example. Suppose $y = 4x$. The top graph of Figure A.5 shows this function. Since the function is a straight line, it has a constant slope. We can find the slope in two ways. First, take any two points on the graph, such as A and B. We find that the slope $\Delta y/\Delta x = (16 - 8)/(4 - 2) = 4$.

The second way to find the slope is to take the derivative. We recognize that $y = 4x$ is a power function like the one in equation (A.6), with $a = 4$ and $b = 1$. As equation (A.5) shows, the derivative is $dy/dx = bax^{b-1} = 4x^0 = 4$. Since the derivative dy/dx is always 4, the slope of the graph of the function $y = 4x$ is always 4.

Learning-By-Doing Exercise A.3
Derivative of a Power Function
Consider the function $y = 3x^2$, shown in Figure A.6(a).

Problem   Find the slope of this function when

(a) $x = -1$
(b) $x = 0$
(c) $x = +2$

Solution

(a) We recognize that $y = 3x^2$ is a power function like the one in equation (A.6), with $a = 3$ and $b = 2$. As

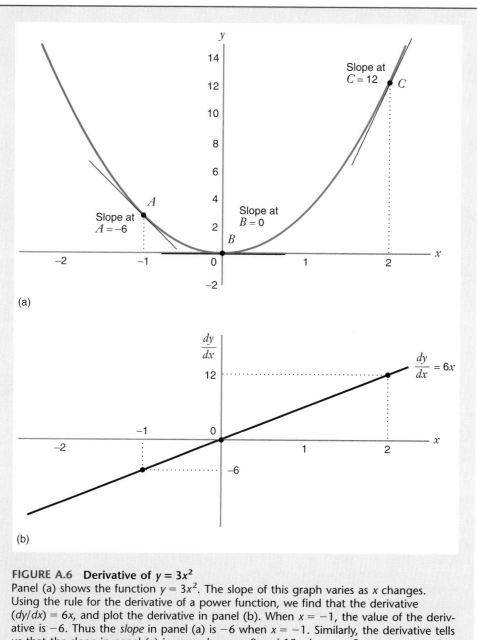

FIGURE A.6   Derivative of $y = 3x^2$

Panel (a) shows the function $y = 3x^2$. The slope of this graph varies as x changes. Using the rule for the derivative of a power function, we find that the derivative $(dy/dx) = 6x$, and plot the derivative in panel (b). When $x = -1$, the value of the derivative is -6. Thus the *slope* in panel (a) is -6 when $x = -1$. Similarly, the derivative tells us that the slope in panel (a) is zero when $x = 0$ and 12 when $x = 2$.

equation (A.7) shows, the derivative is $dy/dx = bax^{b-1} = 6x$. [The graph of the derivative is shown in Figure A.6(b).] Thus, the slope of the function $y = 3x^2$ will be $6x$. When $x = -1$, the value of the derivative is $dy/dx = 6(-1) = -6$. This tells us that the slope of the function $y = 3x^2$ [at point A in panel(a)] is -6.

(b) When $x = 0$, the value of the derivative is $dy/dx = 6(0) = 0$. Thus, the slope of the function $y = 3x^2$ at point B is 0.

(c) When $x = 2$, the value of the derivative is $dy/dx = 6(2) = 12$. Therefore, the slope of the function $y = 3x^2$ at point C is 12.

To summarize one of the uses of derivatives, consider Figure A.6. We could determine the slope of the curve in panel (a) at any point in two ways. First, we could graph the curve carefully, and construct a line segment tangent to the curve. For example, if we want to determine the slope at point A, we could draw a line tangent to A, and then measure the slope of the tangent line. If we did this properly, we would find that the slope at A is -6. However, this is a cumbersome approach and could easily lead to error, especially because the slope of the curve varies as x changes. An easier and more reliable way to find the slope is to find the derivative, and then calculate the value of the derivative for any point at which we want to know the slope.

Learning-By-Doing Exercise A.4
Utility and Marginal Utility
In Chapter 3 (see Table 3.1 and Figure 3.2), we examined the utility function $U(y) = 10\sqrt{y}$. Here U is the dependent variable and y the independent variable. We observed that the corresponding marginal utility function is $MU(y) = 5/\sqrt{y}$.

Problem Show that this marginal utility is correct.

Solution The marginal utility $MU(y)$ is the slope of the utility function, that is, the derivative dU/dy. We can easily find this derivative because $U(y) = 10\sqrt{y}$ is a power function. It may help to rewrite the utility function as $U(y) = 10y^{(1/2)}$. This is a power function with $U = ay^b$, where $a = 10$ and $b = 1/2$. The derivative is then $dU/dy = bay^{b-1} = (1/2)10y^{(1/2)-1} = 5y^{-1/2} = 5/\sqrt{y}$.

Derivatives of a Natural Logarithm
A logarithmic function has the form:

$$y = \ln x, \tag{A.8}$$

where "ln" denotes the natural logarithm of a number. The derivative of the natural logarithm is:

$$\frac{dy}{dx} = \frac{1}{x}. \tag{A.9}$$

Derivatives of Sums and Differences
Suppose $f(x)$ and $g(x)$ are two different functions of x. Suppose further that y is the sum of f and g, that is,

$$y = f(x) + g(x).$$

Then the derivative of y with respect to x is the *sum* of the derivatives of f and g. Thus,

$$\frac{dy}{dx} = \frac{df}{dx} + \frac{dg}{dx}.$$

As an example, assume that $f(x) = 5x^2$ and that $g(x) = 2x$. Both f and g are power functions, with the derivatives $df/dx = 10x$ and $dg/dx = 2$. If $y = f(x) + g(x) = 5x^2 + 2x$, then $dy/dx = (df/dx) + (dg/dx) = 10x + 2$.

Similarly, if y is the difference between f and g, that is,

$$y = f(x) - g(x),$$

then the derivative of y with respect to x is the *difference* of the derivatives of f and g:

$$\frac{dy}{dx} = \frac{df}{dx} - \frac{dg}{dx}.$$

Learning-By-Doing Exercise A.5
Derivatives of Sums and Differences
Consider the cost function from Learning-By-Doing Exercise A.1:

$$C(Q) = Q^3 - 10Q^2 + 40Q.$$

Problem Find the marginal cost when

(a) $Q = 2$
(b) $Q = 5$
(c) $Q = 6$

Solution The marginal cost $MC(Q)$ is the derivative of the total cost function dC/dQ. The total cost function is made up of three terms involving the sums and differences of power functions. Thus, $MC(Q) = 3Q^2 - 20Q + 40$.

(a) When $Q = 2$, the marginal cost is $MC(2) = 3(2)^2 - 20(2) + 40 = 12$. This marginal cost is the slope in panel (a) (the total cost curve) in Figure A.2 when the quantity is 2. The numerical value of the marginal cost is plotted in panel (b) of the same figure.
(b) When $Q = 5$, the marginal cost is $MC(5) = 3(5)^2 - 20(5) + 40 = 15$.
(c) When $Q = 6$, the marginal cost is $MC(6) = 3(6)^2 - 20(6) + 40 = 28$.

Note that the marginal costs calculated in this problem are the ones in column 4 of Table A.1.

Derivatives of Products

Suppose y is the product of $f(x)$ and $g(x)$, that is,

$$y = f(x)g(x).$$

Then the derivative of y with respect to x is

$$\frac{dy}{dx} = f\frac{dg}{dx} + g\frac{df}{dx}.$$

As an example, assume that $f(x) = x^2$ and that $g(x) = (6 - x)$. The function f is a power function, while the function g is the sum of power functions. Their derivatives are thus $df/dx = 2x$ and $dg/dx = -1$. If $y = f(x)g(x) = x^2(6 - x)$, then $dy/dx = f(dg/dx) + g(df/dx) = x^2(-1) + (6 - x)(2x) = -3x^2 + 12x$.

As a check on this answer, we could first expand the function $y = x^2(6 - x) = 6x^2 - x^3$, and then take the derivative of this difference of power functions to get $dy/dx = -3x^2 + 12x$.

Derivatives of Quotients

Suppose y is the quotient of $f(x)$ and $g(x)$, that is,

$$y = \frac{f(x)}{g(x)}.$$

Then the derivative of y with respect to x is:

$$\frac{dy}{dx} = \frac{g\dfrac{df}{dx} - f\dfrac{dg}{dx}}{g^2}.$$

As an example, assume once again that $f(x) = x^2$ and that $g(x) = (6 - x)$. As before, both f and g are power functions, with the derivatives $df/dx = 2x$ and $dg/dx = -1$. If

$$y = \frac{f(x)}{g(x)} = \frac{x^2}{(6 - x)},$$

then

$$\frac{dy}{dx} = \frac{g\frac{df}{dx} - f\frac{dg}{dx}}{g^2} = \frac{(6 - x)(2x) - (x^2)(-1)}{(6 - x)^2}$$

$$= \frac{12x - x^2}{(6 - x)^2}.$$

There are other rules for finding derivatives for many other types of functions. However, the rules we have discussed in this section are the only ones you need to analyze the material covered in this book using calculus.

To sum up, derivatives are useful in helping us to understand and calculate many of the "marginal" concepts in economics. Three of the most commonly encountered marginal concepts are marginal utility, marginal cost, and marginal revenue.

- Suppose the function measuring total utility is $U(Q)$. Then the value of the derivative dU/dQ at any particular Q is the *slope* of the total utility curve *and* the marginal utility at that quantity. (See Learning-By-Doing Exercise A.4, Table 3.1, and Figure 3.2.)
- Suppose the function measuring total cost is $C(Q)$. Then the value of the derivative dC/dQ at any particular Q is the *slope* of the total cost curve *and* the marginal cost at that quantity. (See Learning-By-Doing Exercise A.5, Table A.1, and Figure A.2.)
- Suppose the function measuring total revenue is $R(Q)$. Then the value of the derivative dR/dQ at any particular Q is the *slope* of the total revenue curve *and* the marginal revenue at that quantity.

A.5 Maximization and Minimization Problems

We can use derivatives to find where a function reaches a maximum or minimum. Suppose y, the dependent variable, is plotted on the vertical axis of a graph and x, the independent variable, is measured along the horizontal axis. The main idea is this: *A maximum or a minimum can only occur if the slope of the graph is zero.* In other words, at a maximum or a minimum, the derivative dy/dx must equal zero.

Let's consider an example of a maximum. Figure A.7 shows a graph of the function $y = -x^2 + 6x + 1$. We know that at a maximum of the function, the slope will be zero. Since the slope is just the derivative, we look for the value of x that makes the derivative equal to zero. We observe that y is a sum of power terms, with the derivative $dy/dx = -2x + 6$. At the maximum, the derivative is zero (i.e., $dy/dx = -2x + 6 = 0$). The derivative becomes zero when $x = 3$. Thus, the maximum value of y will then be $y = -3^2 + 6(3) + 1 = 10$.

Now let's consider a function that has a minimum. Consider again Figure A.6, showing a graph of the function $y = 3x^2$. We can use a derivative to verify that the function has its minimum at $x = 0$. We know that at the minimum of the function, the slope will be zero. Since the slope is just the derivative, we need to find the value of x that makes the derivative equal to zero. As we showed above, the derivative is $dy/dx = 6x$. At the minimum, the derivative is zero (i.e., $dy/dx = 6x = 0$). The derivative therefore becomes zero when $x = 0$. Thus, the minimum value of y will occur when $x = 0$.

As the two examples show, when the derivative is zero, we may have either a maximum or a minimum. If we observe that $dy/dx = 0$, from that information alone we cannot distinguish between a maximum and a minimum. To determine whether we have found a maximum

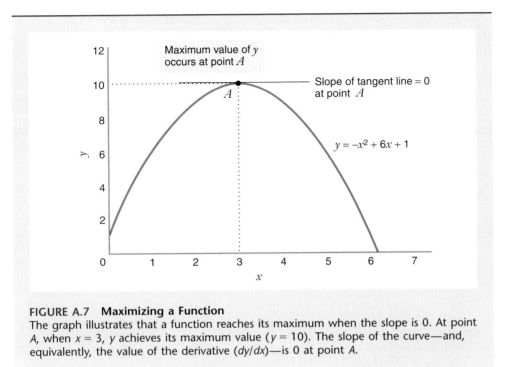

FIGURE A.7 Maximizing a Function
The graph illustrates that a function reaches its maximum when the slope is 0. At point A, when x = 3, y achieves its maximum value (y = 10). The slope of the curve—and, equivalently, the value of the derivative (dy/dx)—is 0 at point A.

or a minimum, we need to examine the *second derivative* of y with respect to x, denoted by d^2y/dx^2. The second derivative is just the derivative of the first derivative dy/dx. In words, the first derivative (dy/dx) tells us the slope of the graph. The second derivative tells us whether the *slope* is increasing or decreasing as x increases. If the second derivative is negative, the slope is becoming less positive (or more negative) as x increases. If the second derivative is positive, the slope is becoming more positive (or less negative) as x increases.

This implies the following results:

- If we are at a point at which $dy/dx = 0$ and $d^2y/dx^2 < 0$, then that point is a maximum point on the function.
- If we are at a point at which $dy/dx = 0$ and $d^2y/dx^2 > 0$, then that point is a minimum point on the function.

To use the second derivative to see if we have found a maximum or a minimum, consider once again the function $y = -x^2 + 6x + 1$, shown in Figure A.7. We have already found that the slope of the graph is zero when

x = 3, the value of x that made the derivative $dy/dx = -2x + 6$ equal to zero. We can verify that the graph reaches a maximum (and not a minimum) by examining the second derivative. The derivative of $-2x + 6$ with respect to x is the second derivative; thus $d^2y/dx^2 = -2$. Since the second derivative is negative, the slope of the graph is becoming less positive as we approach x = 3 from the left, and becomes more negative as we move to the right of x = 3. This verifies that the graph does achieve a maximum when x = 3.

Similarly, we can use a second derivative to show that the graph in Figure A.6 achieves a minimum (not a maximum) when x = 0. We have already found that the slope of the graph is zero when x = 0, the value of x that made the derivative $dy/dx = 6x$ equal to zero. The derivative of 6x with respect to x is the second derivative; thus $d^2y/dx^2 = 6$. Since the second derivative is positive, the slope of the graph is becoming less negative as we approach x = 0 from the left, and becomes ever more positive as we move to the right of x = 0. This verifies that the graph does achieve a minimum when x = 0.[2]

[2]The analysis in this appendix shows how to apply derivatives to find a *local* maximum or a *local* minimum. However, many functions will have more than one maximum or minimum. To find the *global* maximum for a function, you would have to compare the values of all of the local maxima, and then choose the one for which the function attains the highest value. Similarly, to find the *global* minimum for a function, you would have to compare the values of all of the local minima, and then choose the one for which the function attains the lowest value.

Learning-By-Doing Exercise A.6
Using Derivatives to Find a Minimum

Consider once again the total cost function:

$$C(Q) = Q^3 - 10Q^2 + 40Q.$$

The average cost function $AC(Q)$ is then $C(Q)/Q$:

$$AC(Q) = Q^2 - 10Q + 40.$$

The bottom graph of Figure A.2 shows this average cost curve.

Problem

(a) Using a derivative, verify that the minimum of the average cost curve occurs when $Q = 5$. Also show that the value of the average cost is 15 at its minimum.
(b) Using the second derivative, verify that the average cost is minimized (and not maximized) when $Q = 5$.

Solution

(a) The average cost curve reaches its minimum when its slope (and, equivalently, the derivative dAC/dQ) is zero. Observe that $AC(Q)$ is a sum of power functions. Therefore, its derivative is $dAC/dQ = 2Q - 10$. When we set the derivative equal to zero we find that $Q = 5$. This is the quantity that minimizes AC. The value of the average cost at this quantity is $AC(5) = 5^2 - 10(5) + 40 = 15$.
(b) The second derivative of the average cost function is $d^2AC/dQ^2 = 2$. Since the second derivative is positive, the slope of the graph is becoming less negative as we approach $Q = 5$ from the left, and becomes ever more positive as we move to the right of $Q = 5$. This verifies that the graph does achieve a minimum when $Q = 5$.

Optimal Quantity Choice Rules

Once you understand how to use calculus to find a maximum or a minimum, it is easy to see how to apply the technique to economic problems. Let's first develop the optimal quantity choice rule for a profit-maximizing firm that takes all prices as given. We show in Chapter 9 (see equation (9.1)) that a price-taking firm maximizes profit when it chooses its output so that price equals marginal cost. The dependent variable is economic profit, denoted by π. Economic profit is the difference between the firm's revenue (the market price, P, times the quantity it produces, Q) and the firm's total cost, $C(Q)$. Thus,

$$\pi = PQ - C(Q).$$

Because the firm has only a small share of the market, it takes the market price P as given (a constant). To maximize profit, the firm chooses Q so that the slope of the profit curve is zero (see Figure 9.1). In terms of calculus, the firm chooses Q so that $d\pi/dQ = 0$. The derivative of π is

$$\frac{d\pi}{dQ} = P - \frac{dC}{dQ}$$

where dC/dQ is just the marginal cost. Thus, the firm must choose Q so that price equals marginal cost to maximize profits (producing so that $d\pi/dQ = 0$).

Similarly, we show in Chapter 11 (see equation (11.1)) that a profit-maximizing monopolist chooses its output so that marginal revenue equals marginal cost. The dependent variable is economic profit, denoted by π. Economic profit is the difference between the firm's revenue, $R(Q)$, and the firm's total cost, $C(Q)$. Thus,

$$\pi = R(Q) - C(Q).$$

To maximize profit, the firm chooses Q so that the slope of the profit curve is zero (see Figure 11.2). In terms of calculus, the firm chooses Q so that $d\pi/dQ = 0$. The derivative of π is

$$\frac{d\pi}{dQ} = \frac{dR}{dQ} - \frac{dC}{dQ},$$

where dR/dQ is the marginal revenue and dC/dQ is the marginal cost. Thus, the firm must choose Q so that marginal revenue equals marginal cost to maximize profits (again, producing so that $d\pi/dQ = 0$).

A.6 Multivariable Functions

Until now we have been dealing with functions that depend on only one variable. However, in many situations a dependent variable will be related to two or more independent variables. For example, the profit for a firm, π, may depend on the amounts of two outputs, Q_1 being the amount of the first good it produces and Q_2 the amount of the second good. Suppose the profit function for the firm is:

$$\pi = 13Q_1 - 2(Q_1)^2 + Q_1Q_2 + 8Q_2 - 2(Q_2)^2. \quad \textbf{(A.10)}$$

Figure A.8 shows a graph of the profit function. The graph has three dimensions because there are three variables. The dependent variable, profit, is on the vertical axis. The graph shows the two independent variables, Q_1 and Q_2, on the other two axes. As the graph shows, the profit function is a "hill." The firm can maximize its profits at point A, producing $Q_1 = 4$ and $Q_2 = 3$, and then earning profits $\pi = 38$.

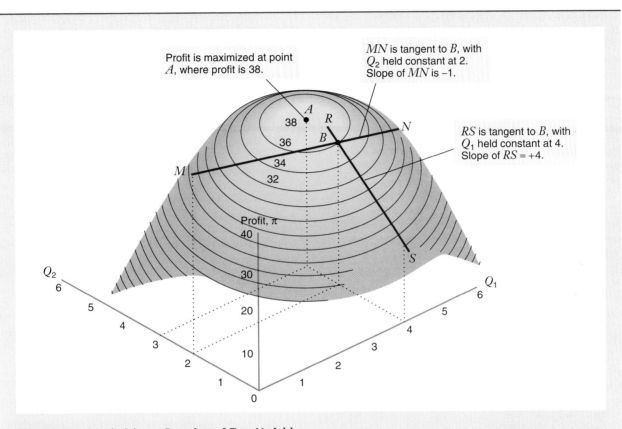

Profit is maximized at point
A, where profit is 38.

MN is tangent to B, with
Q_2 held constant at 2.
Slope of MN is –1.

RS is tangent to B, with
Q_1 held constant at 4.
Slope of $RS = +4$.

FIGURE A.8 Maximizing a Function of Two Variables
A function reaches its maximum when the slope is 0. At point A, when $Q_1 = 4$ and $Q_2 = 3$, the profit function achieves its maximum value of 38. The slope of the profit hill is 0 in all directions (and, equivalently, the values of the partial derivatives $\partial\pi/\partial Q_1$ and $\partial\pi/\partial Q_2$ are zero at point A).

At point B, when $Q_1 = 4$ and $Q_2 = 2$, the profit function achieves a lower value (36). The slope of the profit hill is not 0 in all directions. At B the value of the partial derivative $\partial\pi/\partial Q_2 = +4$. This means that the slope of the profit hill as we increase Q_2 (but hold $Q_1 = 4$) is 4. This is also the slope of the tangent line RS.

At B, the value of the partial derivative $\partial\pi/\partial Q_1 = -1$. This means that the slope of the profit hill as we increase Q_1 (but hold $Q_2 = 2$) is -1. This is also the slope of the tangent line MN.

Let's see how we might use calculus to find the values of the independent variables (Q_1 and Q_2 in this example) that maximize a dependent variable (π in the example). To do so, we need to understand how a change in *each* of the independent variables affects the dependent variable, *holding constant the levels of all other independent variables*.

Consider point B in the graph, where $Q_1 = 4$, $Q_2 = 2$, and $\pi = 36$. As the graph shows, this is *not* the combination of outputs that maximizes profit.

The firm might ask how an increase in Q_2 affects π, holding constant the other independent variable Q_1. To find this information, we find the *partial derivative of π with respect to Q_2*, denoted by $\partial\pi/\partial Q_2$. To obtain this partial derivative, we take the derivative of equation A.10, but treat the level of Q_1 as a constant. When we do this, the first two terms in equation A.10 will be a constant because they depend only on Q_1; therefore the partial derivative of these terms with respect to Q_2 is zero. The partial derivative of the third term (Q_1Q_2) with respect to Q_2 is just Q_1. The partial derivative of the last two terms $[8Q_2 - 2(Q_2)^2]$ with respect to Q_2 will be $8 - 4Q_2$. When we put all of this information together, we learn that

$$\frac{\partial \pi}{\partial Q_2} = Q_1 + 8 - 4Q_2. \qquad \textbf{(A.11)}$$

Equation (A.11) measures the marginal profit (sometimes called marginal profitability) of Q_2. This marginal profit is the rate of change of profit (and the slope of the profit hill) as we vary Q_2, but hold Q_1 constant.

We illustrate what this partial derivative measures in Figure A.8. At point B we have drawn a line tangent to the profit hill (line RS). Along RS we are holding Q_1 constant ($Q_1 = 4$). We can find the slope of RS by evaluating the partial derivative $\partial \pi / \partial Q_2 = Q_1 + 8 - 4Q_2$ when $Q_1 = 4$ and $Q_2 = 2$. The value of the derivative is therefore $\partial \pi / \partial Q_2 = (4) + 8 - 4(2) = 4$. The slope of RS (and therefore the slope of the profit hill at B in the direction of increasing Q_2) is 4.

To help you understand the meaning of a partial derivative, we have provided another view of the profit hill in Figure A.9. This graph shows a cross sectional picture of the profit hill, showing what the profit hill looks like when we vary Q_2, but hold Q_1 constant, with $Q_1 = 4$. Point B in this figure is therefore the same as point B in Figure A.8. We have also drawn RS, the line tangent to the profit hill at point B. (The tangent line RS is the same in Figures A.8 and A.9.) The partial derivative of profit with respect to Q_2 (denoted by $\partial \pi / \partial Q_2$) measures the slope of this tangent line.[3] At point B the slope is 4.

Similarly, we could ask how an increase in Q_1 affects π, holding constant the other independent variable Q_2. To find this information, we find the partial derivative of π with respect to Q_1, denoted by $\partial \pi / \partial Q_1$. We take the derivative of equation (A.10), but treat the level of Q_2 as a constant. When we do this, the last two terms in equation (A.10) will be a constant because they depend only on Q_2; therefore the partial derivative of these terms with respect to Q_1 is zero. The partial derivative

of the third term (Q_1Q_2) with respect to Q_1 is just Q_2. The partial derivative of the first two terms with respect to Q_1 will be $13 - 4Q_1$. When we put all of this information together, we learn that

$$\frac{\partial \pi}{\partial Q_1} = 13 - 4Q_1 + Q_2. \qquad \textbf{(A.12)}$$

Equation (A.12) measures the marginal profit of Q_1, that is, the rate of change of profit as we vary Q_1, but hold Q_2 constant. Let's evaluate this partial derivative at point B in Figure A.8. When $Q_1 = 4$, and $Q_2 = 2$, we find that $\partial \pi / \partial Q_1 = 13 - 4(4) + 2 = -1$. Let's draw the line tangent to the profit hill at point B, holding Q_2 constant ($Q_2 = 2$), and label this line MN. The tangent line will have a slope of -1.

Finding a Maximum or a Minimum

How can we find the top of the profit hill in Figure A.8? At a maximum, the slope of the profit hill will be zero in all directions. This means that at a maximum *the partial derivatives $\partial \pi / \partial Q_1$ and $\partial \pi / \partial Q_2$ must both be zero.* Thus, in the example,

$$\frac{\partial \pi}{\partial Q_1} = 13 - 4Q_1 + Q_2 = 0,$$

$$\frac{\partial \pi}{\partial Q_2} = Q_1 + 8 - 4Q_2 = 0.$$

When we solve these two equations, we find that $Q_1 = 4$ and $Q_2 = 3$. These are the quantities that lead us to the top of the profit hill, point A in Figure A.8.[4] Let's also consider point A in Figure A.9, where $Q_1 = 4$ and $Q_2 = 3$, the outputs that maximize profits. Point A in this figure is therefore the same as point A in Figure A.8. Since we have reached the top of the profit curve, the slope of the profit hill at A in Figure A.9 is zero; this means that the partial derivative $\partial \pi / \partial Q_2$ is zero.

To practice taking partial derivatives, you might try the following exercises.

---

[3]Another way to see the meaning of the partial derivative illustrated in Figure A.9 is to substitute $Q_1 = 4$ into the profit function $\pi = 13Q_1 - 2(Q_1)^2 + Q_1Q_2 + 8Q_2 - 2(Q_2)^2$. Profits then become $\pi = 20 + 12Q - 2(Q_2)^2$. This is the equation of the profit hill in Figure A.9, because we have assumed Q_1 is held constant at 4. The slope of the profit hill in Figure A.9 is therefore $d\pi/dQ_2 = 12 - 4Q_2$. At point B, where $Q_2 = 2$, we find that $d\pi/dQ_2 = 4$, which is the slope of the tangent line RS.

[4]To ensure that we have a maximum, or to distinguish a maximum from a minimum, we would also have to examine the second-order conditions for an optimum. In this appendix we do not present these conditions for a function with more than one independent variable and refer you to any standard calculus text. Also, the techniques we have discussed in this appendix may show you where a local maximum or minimum exists, but you may need to check further to see if the local maximum or minimum is a global optimum (see footnote 2).

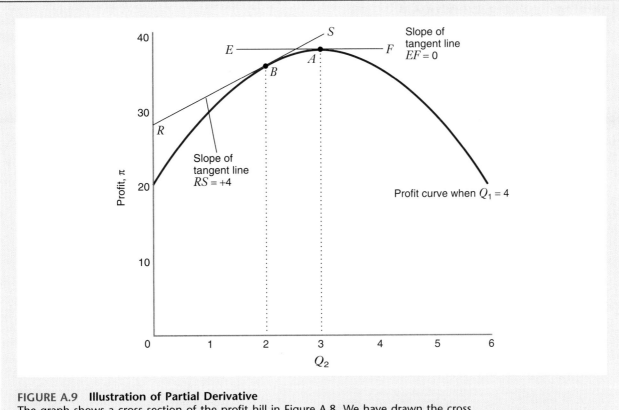

FIGURE A.9   Illustration of Partial Derivative
The graph shows a cross section of the profit hill in Figure A.8. We have drawn the cross section to show what the profit hill looks like when we vary Q_2, but hold Q_1 constant, with $Q_1 = 4$. Point B in this figure is therefore the same as point B in Figure A.8. We have also drawn the line tangent to the profit hill at point B. The value of the partial derivative of profit with respect to Q_2 (denoted by $\partial\pi/\partial Q_2$) measures the slope of this tangent line.

At point A, $Q_1 = 4$ and $Q_2 = 3$, the outputs that maximize profits. Point A is therefore the same as point A in Figure A.8. Since we have reached the top of the profit curve, the slope of the profit hill in Figure A.9 is 0. This means that the partial derivative $\partial\pi/\partial Q_2 = 0$.

Learning-By-Doing Exercise A.7
Marginal Utility with Two Independent Variables

In Chapter 3 (Learning-By-Doing Exercise 3.1), we introduced the utility function $U = \sqrt{xy}$. Here U is the dependent variable and x and y are the independent variables. The corresponding marginal utilities function are $MU_x = \sqrt{y}/(2\sqrt{x})$, and $MU_y = \sqrt{x}/(2\sqrt{y})$.

Problem   Use partial derivatives to verify that these expressions for marginal utilities are correct.

Solution   It may help to rewrite the utility function as $U = x^{1/2}y^{1/2}$. The marginal utility of x is just the partial derivative of U with respect to x, that is, $\partial U/\partial x$. To find

this derivative, we treat y as a constant. Therefore, we only need to find the derivative of the term in brackets: $U = [x^{1/2}]\, y^{1/2}$. (The $y^{1/2}$ is just a multiplicative constant.) We observe that $x^{1/2}$ is a power function, with the derivative $(1/2)x^{-1/2}$, which can be rewritten as $1/(2\sqrt{x})$. The marginal utility is then $MU_x = \sqrt{y}/(2\sqrt{x})$.

Similarly, the marginal utility of y is just the partial derivative of U with respect to y, that is, $\partial U/\partial y$. To find this derivative, we treat x as a constant. Therefore, we only need to find the derivative of the term in brackets: $U = x^{1/2}\, [y^{1/2}]$. We observe that $y^{1/2}$ is a power function, with the derivative $(1/2)y^{-1/2}$, which can be rewritten as $1/(2\sqrt{y})$. The marginal utility is then $MU_y = \sqrt{x}/(2\sqrt{y})$.

Learning-By-Doing Exercise A.8
Marginal Cost with Two Independent Variables

Problem Suppose the total cost C of producing two products is $C = Q_1 + \sqrt{Q_1 Q_2} + Q_2$, where Q_1 measures the number of units of the first product and Q_2 the number of units of the second. When $Q_1 = 16$ and $Q_2 = 1$, find the marginal cost of the first product, MC_1.

Solution It may help to rewrite the total cost function as $C = Q_1 + (Q_1)^{1/2} (Q_2)^{1/2} + Q_2$. The marginal cost of Q_1 is just the partial derivative of C with respect to Q_1, that is, $\partial C / \partial Q_1$. To find this derivative, we treat Q_2 as a constant. Let's consider each of the three terms in the cost function:

1. For the first term, the derivative of Q_1 with respect to Q_1 is 1.
2. For the second term, we only need to find the derivative of the term in brackets: $[(Q_1)^{1/2}] (Q_2)^{1/2}$. (The $(Q_2)^{1/2}$ is just a multiplicative constant.) We observe that $(Q_1)^{1/2}$ is a power function, with the derivative $(1/2) (Q_1)^{-1/2}$, which can be rewritten as $1/(2\sqrt{Q_1})$. The derivative of the second term is therefore $\sqrt{Q_2}/(2\sqrt{Q_1})$.
3. For the third term, Q_2 is being held constant. Since the derivative of a constant is zero, the derivative of the third term is zero.

Thus, the marginal cost of the first product is $MC_1 = 1 + \sqrt{Q_2}/(2\sqrt{Q_1})$. We can evaluate the marginal cost at any level of the outputs. For example, when $Q_1 = 16$ and $Q_2 = 1$, we find that $MC_1 = 1 + \sqrt{1}/(2\sqrt{16}) = 9/8$. In words, when the firm is producing 16 units of the first output and 1 unit of the second, the marginal cost of the first product is 9/8.

A.7 Constrained Optimization

As explained in Chapter 1, economic decision makers often want to extremize (maximize or minimize) the value of an economic variable such as profit, utility, or total production cost. However, they typically face constraints that limit the choices they can make. That is why economics is often described as a science of constrained choice.

Constrained optimization problems can be very large, often involving many decision variables and several constraints. In the next two sections, we present two approaches for solving constrained optimization problems. To facilitate the discussion, we focus here on a problem with two decision variables, x and y, and one constraint, although the principles are easily generalized to more complicated problems.

Let's represent the *objective function* (the function the decision maker wants to maximize or minimize) with the function $F(x, y)$. Let's describe the constraint she must satisfy by the function $G(x, y) = 0$.

For a maximization problem, we write the constrained optimization problem as follows:

$$\max_{(x,y)} F(x,y)$$

$$\text{subject to: } G(x, y) = 0,$$

where the first line identifies the objective function to be maximized. (If the objective function were to be minimized, then the "max" would instead be a "min".) Underneath the "max" is a list of the endogenous variables that the decision maker controls (x and y). The second line represents the constraint the decision maker must satisfy. The decision maker can only choose values of x and y that satisfy $G(x, y) = 0$.

In Chapters 3 and 4 we explore one example of a constrained optimization problem, the consumer choice problem. A consumer may want to maximize his or her satisfaction, but must live within the constraints on available income. For that problem, F would be the utility function and G the budget constraint the consumer faces. In Chapter 7 we examine the cost-minimizing choice of inputs by a producer. A manager wants to minimize production costs, but may be required to supply a specified amount of output. The objective function is total cost, and the constraint is the amount of production required from the firm. In other settings managers often have budgetary constraints that limit the amount of money they can spend on an activity such as advertising.

In this section we show that it may be possible to solve a constrained optimization problem by substituting the constraint into the objective function, and then using calculus to find the maximum or minimum we seek. We illustrate how this might be done with two Learning-By-Doing Exercises.

Learning-By-Doing Exercise A.9
Radio and Beer Advertising

Chapter 1 describes the problem facing a product manager for a small beer company that produces a high-quality microbrewed ale. The manager has a $1 million advertising budget, and could spend the money on ads for TV or for radio. Table 1.1 illustrates new beer sales resulting from advertising. In Chapter 1 we did not give you the function that relates new beer sales to the amount of advertising, instead working with the values given in the table.

Now suppose you know that new beer sales (B, measured in barrels) depend on the amount of advertising on television (T, measured in hundreds of thousands of dollars) and radio (R, measured in hundreds of thousands of dollars) as follows:[5]

$$B(T, R) = 5{,}000T - 250T^2 + 1{,}000R - 50R^2.$$

The function $B(T, R)$ is the objective function because this is the function that the decision maker wants to maximize. However, the manager can spend only $1 million in total advertising. This means that the manager faces a constraint, namely, that $T + R = 10$. We write the maximization problem here as

$$\max_{(T,R)} B(T, R) \qquad \text{(A.13)}$$

$$\text{subject to: } T + R = 10,$$

where T and R are measured in hundreds of thousands of dollars.

Problem Solve this problem for the optimal amounts of radio and television advertising.

Solution The constraint has a simple form in this problem ($T + R = 10$). From the constraint we know that $R = 10 - T$. We can just substitute this expression for R into the objective function as follows:

$$\begin{aligned} B &= 5{,}000T - 250T^2 + 1{,}000R - 50R^2 \\ &= 5{,}000T - 250T^2 + 1{,}000(10 - T) - 50(10 - T)^2 \\ &= 5{,}000T - 300T^2 + 5{,}000. \end{aligned}$$

The key point is the following: The new objective function ($B = 5{,}000T - 300T^2 + 5{,}000$) already has the constraint "built in" because we have substituted the constraint into the original objective function ($B = 5{,}000T - 250T^2 + 1{,}000R - 50R^2$). Now we can choose the optimal amount of TV advertising by setting the first derivative with respect to the amount of television advertising equal to zero:

$$\frac{dB}{dT} = 5{,}000 - 600T = 0.$$

This tells us that $T = 8.33$, that is, the manager should spend about $833,333 on television advertising. We can then use the relationship $R = 10 - T$ to determine the optimal amount of radio advertising, so that $R = 1.67$. The manager should spend about

$166,667 on radio advertising. This "exact" solution is very close to the approximate solution developed in Chapter 1, using only the values displayed in the table.

Learning-By-Doing Exercise A.10
The Farmer's Fencing Problem
Chapter 1 describes a constrained optimization involving the design of a fence for a farm. A farmer wishes to build a rectangular fence for his sheep. He has F feet of fence and cannot afford to purchase more. However, he can choose the dimensions of the pen, which will have a length of L feet and a width of W feet. He wishes to choose L and W to maximize the area of the pen; thus, the objective function is the area LW. He also faces a constraint; he must also make sure that the total amount of fencing he uses (the perimeter of the pen) not exceed F feet. In Chapter 1 we describe the farmer's decision as follows:

$$\max_{(L,W)} LW \qquad \text{(A.14)}$$

$$\text{subject to } 2L + 2W \le F.$$

We know that the farmer will use all of the fence available if he wants to maximize the area of the pen. Therefore, we know that the constraint will be an equality, and the problem is simplified as follows:

$$\max_{(L,W)} LW \qquad \text{(A.15)}$$

$$\text{subject to } 2L + 2W = F.$$

Problem Solve this problem to determine the optimal dimensions of the pen.

Solution The constraint has a simple form in this problem ($2L + 2W = F$). The constraint tells us that $W = (F/2) - L$. We can just substitute this into the original objective function (LW) to find a new form of the objective function that already has the constraint built in:

$$\text{Area} = LW = L\left(\frac{F}{2} - L\right) = \frac{FL}{2} - L^2.$$

Now we can choose the optimal amount length of the pen, L, by setting the first derivative equal to zero:

$$\frac{d\text{Area}}{dL} = \frac{F}{2} - 2L = 0.$$

---

[5]As an independent exercise, you may verify that the function $B(T, R) = 5000T - 250T^2 + 1000R - 50R^2$ gives the values of new beer sales in Table 1.1 for various combinations of television and radio advertising.

This tells us that $L = F/4$. We can then use the relationship $W = (F/2) - L$ to determine the optimal width, so that $W = F/4$. The solution tells us that the rectangle that maximizes the area of the pen will be a square, with sides $F/4$.

Before leaving this example, it is worth observing that we can use the results of the solution to perform *comparative statics* exercises, as described in Chapter 1. The exogenous variable in this problem (the one the farmer takes as given) is F, the amount of fence available to the farmer. The endogenous variables (the ones chosen by the farmer) are the length, L, the width W, and the area (Area $= LW$). We can use derivatives to answer the following questions:

1. How much will the length change when the amount of fence varies? We know that $L = F/4$. Therefore, $dL/dF = 1/4$. The length will increase by one-fourth foot when the perimeter is increased by one foot.

2. How much will the width change when the amount of fence varies? We know that $W = F/4$. Therefore, $dW/dF = 1/4$. The width will increase by one-fourth foot when the perimeter is increased by one foot.

3. How much will the area change when the amount of fence varies? We know that the Area $= LW = F^2/16$. Therefore, $dArea/dF = F/8$. The area will increase by about $F/8$ square feet when the perimeter is increased by one foot.

A.8 Lagrange Multipliers

In the previous section we showed how to solve a constrained optimization problem by solving the constraint for one of the variables and then substituting the constraint into the objective function. This technique is most likely to work when the constraint (or set of constraints) has a simple form. However, it may not be possible to use this approach in more complicated problems.

We now show how to solve constrained optimization problems by constructing an equation, called the *Lagrangian function*, that is a combination of the objective function and the constraint. We begin with a general description of the method, and then illustrate how to use it with two Learning-By-Doing Exercises.

We first construct the Lagrangian function as follows: $\Lambda(x, y, \lambda) = F(x, y) + \lambda G(x, y)$. This function is the sum of two terms: (1) the objective function, and (2) the constraint, multiplied by an unknown factor, λ, which is called the *Lagrange multiplier*. We then set the partial derivatives of the Lagrangian function with respect to the three unknowns (x, y, and λ) equal to zero.

$$\frac{\partial \Lambda}{\partial x} = 0 \longrightarrow \frac{\partial F(x, y)}{\partial x} - \lambda = 0 \qquad \text{(A.16)}$$

$$\frac{\partial \Lambda}{\partial y} = 0 \longrightarrow \frac{\partial F(x, y)}{\partial y} - \lambda = 0 \qquad \text{(A.17)}$$

$$\frac{\partial \Lambda}{\partial \lambda} = 0 \longrightarrow G(x, y) = 0. \qquad \text{(A.18)}$$

We can then use the three equations (A.16, A.17, and A.18) to solve for the three unknowns. To see how to apply this method, consider the following two exercises.

Learning-By-Doing Exercise A.11
Radio and Beer Advertising Revisited

Problem The problem here is the same as in Learning-By-Doing Exercise A.9. Now let's solve the problem using the method of Lagrange.

Solution We define the Lagrangian function

$$\Lambda(T, R, \lambda) = B(T, R) + \lambda(10 - T - R),$$

where λ is the Lagrange multiplier. Note that we have rewritten the constraint so that the right-hand side is zero (i.e., $10 - T - R = 0$). We then place the left-hand side of the constraint in the Lagrangian function.

The conditions for an interior optimum (with $T > 0$ and $R > 0$) are

$$\frac{\partial \Lambda}{\partial T} = 0 \longrightarrow \frac{\partial B(T, R)}{\partial T} - \lambda = 0 \qquad \text{(A.19)}$$

$$\frac{\partial \Lambda}{\partial R} = 0 \longrightarrow \frac{\partial B(T, R)}{\partial R} - \lambda = 0 \qquad \text{(A.20)}$$

$$\frac{\partial \Lambda}{\partial \lambda} = 0 \longrightarrow 10 - T - R = 0 \qquad \text{(A.21)}$$

The partial derivatives in this problem are $\partial B(T, R)/\partial T = 5,000 - 500T$ and $\partial B(T, R)/\partial R = 1,000 - 100T$. Thus, we can write (A.18) as

$$5,000 - 500T = \lambda, \text{ and} \qquad \text{(A.22)}$$

$$1,000 - 100R = \lambda. \qquad \text{(A.23)}$$

Since the right-hand sides of equations (A.22) and (A.23) are the same (λ), we know that at an optimum $5,000 - 500T = 1,000 - 100R$. This is equation A.24).

Equation (A.25) is the same as equation (A.21). Together, equations (A.24) and (A.25) give us two equations in two unknowns, T and R. We now know that the optimal amounts of radio and television advertising are determined by two equations:

$$5,000 - 500T = 1,000 - 100R \quad \text{(A.24)}$$

$$T + R = 10. \quad \text{(A.25)}$$

We then find that $T = \$8.33$ (hundred thousand) and $R = \$1.67$ (hundred thousand), the same solution we found in Learning-By-Doing Exercise A.9.

It is also possible to calculate the value of the Lagrange multiplier λ at the optimum, and this value has an important economic interpretation. We observe that $\lambda = 5,000 - 500T = 5,000 - 500(25/3) = 833.33$. (Alternatively, $\lambda = 1,000 - 100R = 1,000 - 100(5/3) = 833.33$.) The value of λ tells us how much beer sales (the objective function) could be increased if the advertising budget were increased by one "unit" (in this problem a unit of advertising is $100,000). The manager could expect sales to increase by about 833 barrels for every \$100,000 in extra advertising, or by about 0.00833 barrels for each additional dollar of advertising.

Learning-By-Doing Exercise A.12
The Farmer's Fencing Problem Revisited

Problem The problem here is the same as in Learning-By-Doing Exercise A.10. Now let's solve the problem using the method of Lagrange.

Solution We define the Lagrangian

$$\Lambda(L, W, \lambda) = LW + \lambda(F - 2L - 2W),$$

where λ is the Lagrange multiplier. Note that we have rewritten the constraint so that the right-hand side is zero (i.e., $F - 2L - 2W = 0$). We then place the left-hand side of the constraint in the Lagrangian function.

The first-order necessary conditions for an interior optimum (with $L > 0$ and $W > 0$) are

$$\frac{\partial \Lambda}{\partial L} = 0 \longrightarrow \frac{\partial(LW)}{\partial L} - 2\lambda = 0 \quad \text{(A.26)}$$

$$\frac{\partial \Lambda}{\partial W} = 0 \longrightarrow \frac{\partial(LW)}{\partial W} - 2\lambda = 0 \quad \text{(A.27)}$$

$$\frac{\partial \Lambda}{\partial \lambda} = 0 \longrightarrow F - 2L - 2W = 0. \quad \text{(A.28)}$$

The partial derivatives in this problem are $[\partial(LW)/\partial L = W]$ and $[\partial(LW)/\partial W] = L$. Thus, we can write the first-order conditions (A.26) and (A.27) as

$$W = 2\lambda, \text{ and}$$

$$L = 2\lambda.$$

Since the right-hand sides of equations (A.26) and (A.27) are the same (2λ), we know that at an optimum $W = L$. This is equation (A.29). Equation (A.30) is the same as equation (A.28). We now know that the optimal dimensions are determined by two equations:

$$W = L, \text{ and} \quad \text{(A.29)}$$

$$2L + 2W = F. \quad \text{(A.30)}$$

We then find that $L = W = F/4$.

It is also possible to calculate the value of the Lagrange multiplier λ at the optimum. We know that $\lambda = L/2$ and that $L = F/4$. Therefore we know that $\lambda = F/8$. The value of λ tells us how much the area (measured in square feet) could be increased if the perimeter is increased by one unit (that is, one foot). The farmer could expect the area to increase by about $F/8$ square feet for every extra foot of fence.

To see how to use the Lagrange multiplier, let's suppose that the amount of fence were increased from $F = 40$ feet to $F = 41$ feet. The Lagrange multiplier tells us that the area (the objective function) could then be increased by about $F/8$ square feet, or about 5 square feet.

Let's see how good this approximation is. With 40 feet of fence, the optimal dimensions are $L = W = 10$, and the area is $(10)(10) = 100$ square feet. With 41 feet of fence, the optimal dimensions are $L = W = 10.25$, and the area is $(10.25)(10.25) = 105.06$ square feet. Note that the approximation of the increase in the area using the Lagrange multiplier is very close to the actual increase in the area. The smaller the increase in the perimeter, the smaller will be the difference between the approximated and actual increase in the area.

In the text we have shown how Lagrange multipliers can be used to solve selected economic problems involving constrained optimization. In the appendix to Chapter 4, we use this method to solve the problem of consumer choice, where a consumer maximizes utility subject to a budget constraint. Also, in the appendix to Chapter 7 we apply this method to find the combination of inputs that will minimize the costs of producing any required level of output.

SUMMARY

• Economic analysis often requires that we understand how to relate economic variables to one another. There are three primary ways of expressing the relationships among variables: graphs, tables, and algebraic functions. **(LBD Exercise A.1)**

• The *marginal value* of a function measures the *change* in a dependent variable associated with a one-unit *change* in an independent variable. It also measures the slope of the graph of a function with the total value of the dependent variable on the vertical axis and the independent variable on the horizontal axis. The *average value* of a dependent variable is the total value of the dependent variable divided by the value of the independent variable. It is important to understand the relationship between marginal and average values:

• The average value must *increase* if the marginal value is *greater* than the average value.

• The average value must *decrease* if the marginal value is *less than* the average value.

• The average value will be *constant* if the marginal value *equals* the average value.

• Derivatives are useful in helping us to understand and calculate many of the "marginal" values in economics. Three of the most commonly encountered marginal values are marginal utility, marginal cost, and marginal revenue. The derivative of the total utility function is the *slope* of the total utility curve *and* the marginal utility. The derivative of the total cost function is the slope of the total cost curve *and* the marginal cost. The derivative of the total revenue function is the slope of the total revenue curve *and* the marginal revenue. **(LBD Exercises A.3, A.4, and A.5)**

• We can use derivatives to find where a function reaches a maximum or minimum. The function the decision maker wants to maximize or minimize is called the *objective function*. When there is only one dependent variable, the first derivative of the objective function with respect to the decision variable (the endogenous variable) will be zero at a maximum or a minimum. Equivalently, the slope of a graph of the objective function is zero at a maximum or minimum. We must check the second derivative to see if the function is maximized or minimized. **(LBD Exercise A.6)**

• We may also use derivatives to find marginal values (such as marginal cost, marginal revenue, and marginal utility) for a dependent variable that has more than one independent variable. To do so, we take the *partial* derivative of the dependent variable with respect to the independent variable of interest. To maximize or minimize an objective function with more than one dependent variable, we set all of the *partial* derivatives of the function equal to zero. **(LBD Exercises A.7 and A.8)**

• A constrained optimization problem is one in which a decision maker maximizes or minimizes an objective function subject to a set of constraints. There are two techniques for solving constrained optimization problems. Sometimes it may be possible to substitute constraints directly into the objective function, and then use derivatives to find an optimum. In more complex problems, it may not be possible to substitute the constraints into the objective function. One can then use the method of Lagrange multipliers to solve for a constrained optimum. **(LBD Exercises A.9, A.10, A.11, and A.12)**

Solutions to Selected Problems

CHAPTER 1

1.1. The opportunity cost of the CDs is the value of the next best opportunity that is foregone. In this instance, the best that you can do with your CDs if you do not keep them is to sell them for $15. Therefore, the opportunity cost of keeping the CDs is $15.

1.2. While the claim that markets never reach an equilibrium is probably debatable, even if markets do not ever reach equilibrium, the concept is still of central importance. The concept of equilibrium is important because it provides a simple way to predict how market prices and quantities will change as exogenous variables change. Thus, while we may never reach a particular equilibrium price, say because a supply or demand schedule shifts as the market moves toward equilibrium, we can predict with relative ease, for example, whether prices will be rising or falling when exogenous market factors change as we move toward equilibrium. As exogenous variables continue to change we can continue to predict the direction of change for the endogenous variables, and this is not "useless."

1.5. a) With $I_1 = 20$, we had $Q^s = P$ and $Q^d = 30 - P$, which implied an equilibrium price of 15.
With $I_2 = 24$, we have $Q^s = P$ and $Q^d = 34 - P$. Finding the point where $Q^s = Q^d$ yields

$$Q^s = Q^d$$
$$P = 34 - P$$
$$2P = 34$$
$$P = 17.$$

b) Plugging the result from part a) into the equation for Q^s reveals the new equilibrium quantity is $Q = 17$.

1.6. a) Formulate each plan as a function of V, the number of videos to rent.

$$TC_A = 3V$$
$$TC_B = 50 + 2V$$
$$TC_C = 150 + V.$$

Then we have

$$TC_A(75) = 225$$
$$TC_B(75) = 200$$
$$TC_C(75) = 225.$$

Plan B provides the lowest possible cost of $200 if you will purchase 75 videos.
b)
$$TC_A(125) = 375$$
$$TC_B(125) = 300$$
$$TC_C(125) = 275.$$

Plan C provides the lowest possible cost of $275 if you will purchase 125 videos.
c) In this case, the number of videos rented is exogenous because we are choosing a plan given a fixed level of videos.
d) Because you may choose the plan, the plans are endogenous. Note, though, that the details of the individual plans are exogenous.
e) Because you may choose the plan and the plans imply a total cost given a fixed level of videos, you are implicitly choosing the level of total expenditure. Total expenditures are therefore endogenous.

CHAPTER 2

2.1. a) When the price of nuts goes up, quantity demanded falls for all levels of price (demand shifts left). Beer and nuts are demand complements.
b) When income rises, quantity demanded increases for all levels of price (demand shifts rightward).

c)

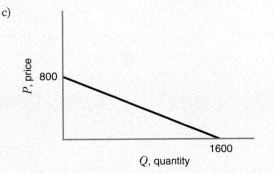

2.3.   a)

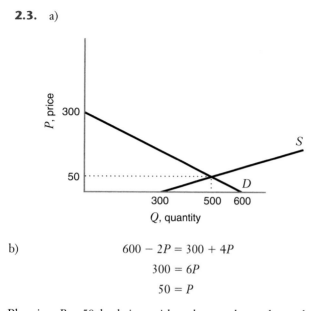

b)

$$600 - 2P = 300 + 4P$$
$$300 = 6P$$
$$50 = P$$

Plugging $P = 50$ back into either the supply or demand equation yields $Q = 500$.

2.6.   a)

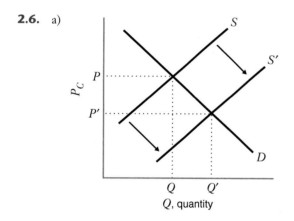

An increase in rainfall will increase supply, lowering the equilibrium price and increasing the equilibrium quantity.

b)

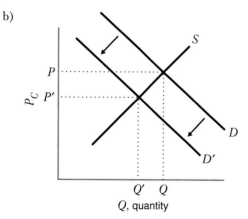

A decrease in disposable income will reduce demand, shifting the demand schedule left, reducing both the equilibrium price and quantity.

2.9.   a) $Q_U^d = 10000 - 100(300) + 99(300)$
$Q_U^d = 9700$
Using $P_U = 300$ and $Q_U^d = 9700$ gives

$$\epsilon_{Q,P} = -100 \left(\frac{300}{9700} \right) = -3.09.$$

b) Market demand is given by $Q^d = Q_U^d + Q_A^d$. Assuming the airlines charge the same price we have

$$Q^d = 10000 - 100P_U + 99P_A + 10000 - 100P_A + 99P_U$$
$$Q^d = 20000 - 100P + 99P - 100P + 99P$$
$$Q^d = 20000 - 2P$$

When $P = 300$, $Q^d = 19400$. This implies an elasticity equal to

$$\epsilon_{Q,P} = -2 \left(\frac{300}{19400} \right) = -0.0309.$$

2.11.   The scare in 1999 would shift demand to the left, identifying a second point on the supply curve. The information implies that price fell \$0.50 while quantity fell 1.5 million. This implies

$$b = \frac{-.5}{-1.5} = \frac{1}{3}.$$

Using a linear supply curve we then have

$$P = a + \frac{1}{3} Q^s$$

$$5 = a + \frac{1}{3} (4)$$

$$a = \frac{11}{3}.$$

Finally, plugging these values for a and b into the supply equation results in

$$P = \frac{11}{3} + \frac{1}{3} Q^s$$

$$3P = 11 + Q^s$$

$$Q^s = -11 + 3P.$$

The floods in 2000 will reduce supply. The shift in supply will identify a second point along the demand curve. Because the scare of 1999 is over, assume that demand has returned to its 1998 state. The change in price and quantity in 2000 imply that price increased $3.00 and that quantity fell 0.5 million.

Performing the same exercise as above we have

$$-b = \frac{3}{-0.5} = -6.$$

Using the 1998 price and quantity information along with this result yields

$$P = a - bQ^d$$
$$5 = a - 6(4)$$
$$a = 29.$$

Finally, plugging these values for a and b into a linear demand curve results in

$$P = 29 - 6Q^d$$
$$6Q^d = 29 - P$$
$$Q^d = \frac{29}{6} - \frac{1}{6}P.$$

CHAPTER 3

3.1. a) Since U increases whenever x or y increases, more of each good is better. This is also confirmed by noting that MU_x and MU_y are both positive for any positive values of x and y.
b) Since $MU_x = (1/2)\sqrt{x}$, as x increases (holding y constant), MU_x falls. Therefore the marginal utility of x is diminishing. However, $MU_y = \sqrt{x}$. As y increases, MU_y is constant. Therefore the preferences exhibit a constant, not diminishing, marginal utility of y.

3.2. a)

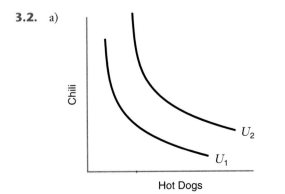

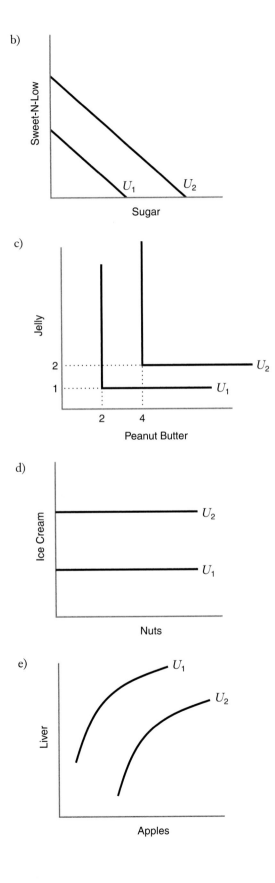

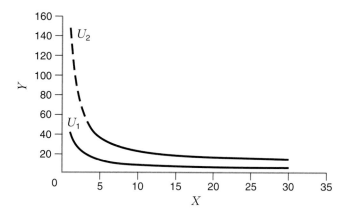

Figure for Problem 3.11

3.7.

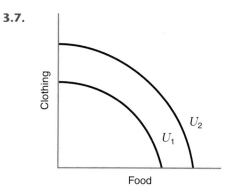

3.8. a) Yes, the "more is better" assumption is satisfied for both goods since $U(x, y)$ increases when the amount of either good increases.
b) The marginal utility of x remains constant at 3.
c) $MRS_{x,y} = 3$
d) The $MRS_{x,y}$ remains constant moving along the indifference curve.
e)

f)

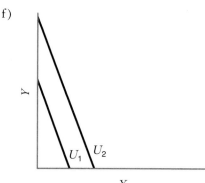

3.11. a) Yes, the "more is better" assumption is satisfied for both goods since $U(x, y)$ increases when the amount of either good increases.
b) The marginal utility of x is positive but declines as the consumer buys more x.
c) $MRS_{x,y} = \dfrac{.4(y^{0.6}/x^{0.6})}{.6(x^{0.4}/y^{0.4})} = \dfrac{0.4y}{0.6x}$
d) As the consumer substitutes x for y, the $MRS_{x,y}$ will decline.
e) See figure.
f) See figure.

3.13. a) Yes, the "more is better" assumption is satisfied for both goods since $U(x,y)$ increases when the amount of either good increases.
b) The marginal utility of x is positive and increases as the consumer buys more x.
c) $MRS_{x,y} = \dfrac{2x}{2y} = \dfrac{x}{y}$
d) As the consumer substitutes x for y, the $MRS_{x,y}$ will increase.

CHAPTER 4

4.1. a) See figure.
b) The tangency condition implies that

$$\frac{MU_F}{MU_C} = \frac{P_F}{P_C}.$$

Plugging in the known information results in

$$\frac{C}{F} = \frac{1}{2}$$

$$2C = F.$$

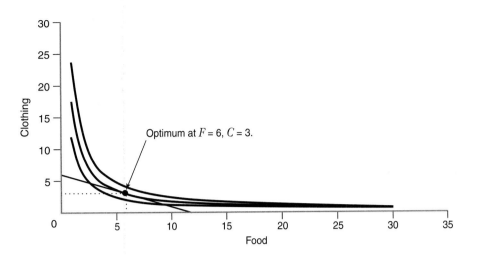

Figure for Problem 4.1a.

Substituting this result into the budget line, $F + 2C = 12$, yields

$$2C + 2C = 12$$
$$4C = 12$$
$$C = 3.$$

Finally, plugging this result back into the tangency condition implies $F = 6$. At the optimum the consumer choose 6 units of food and 3 units of clothing.

c) At the optimum, $MRS_{F,C} = C/F = 3/6 = 1/2$. Note that this is equal to the ratio of the price of food to the price of clothing. This is seen in the graph above as the tangency between the budget line and the indifference curve for $U = 18$.

d) The tangency condition requires

$$\frac{MU_F}{P_F} = \frac{MU_C}{P_C}.$$

If the consumer purchases 4 units of food and 4 units of clothing, then

$$\frac{MU_F}{P_F} > \frac{MU_C}{P_C}.$$

This implies that the consumer could reallocate spending by purchasing more food and less clothing to increase total utility. In fact, at the basket (4,4) total utility is 16 and the consumer spent $12. By giving up one unit of clothing the consumer saves $2 which can than be used to purchase two units of food (they each cost $1). This will result in a new basket (6,3), total utility of 18, and spending of $12. By reallocating spending toward the good with the higher "bang for the buck" the consumer increased total utility while remaining within the budget constraint.

4.3. If Jane is currently at an optimum, the tangency condition must hold. In particular, it must be the case that

$$\frac{MU_H}{MU_M} = \frac{P_H}{P_M}.$$

From the given information we know that $P_H = 3$, $P_M = 1$, and $MRS_{H,M} = 2$. Plugging this into the condition above implies

$$2 < \frac{3}{1}.$$

Since these are not equal, Jane is not currently at an optimum. In addition, since the "bang for the buck" from milkshakes is greater than the "bang for the buck" from hamburgers, Jane can increase her total utility by reallocating her spending to purchase fewer hamburgers and more milkshakes.

4.5. a)

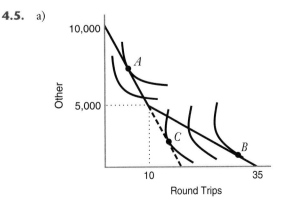

b) Toni is better off with the frequent flyer program than she would be without it at point B. Without the frequent flyer program the best she could achieve is point C on an extension of the budget line without the program with a lower level of total utility. With this set of indifference curves she is better off with the program.

c) Toni is no better off with the frequent flyer program than she would be without it at point A. At this point, her indifference curve is tangent to a portion of the budget line where the frequent flyer program does not apply (less than 10 round trips). With this set of indifference curves she is no better off with the program.

4.7.

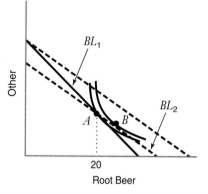

Because the amount of the lump sum tax is equal to the amount of the excise tax the consumer was paying before the change, the new budget line will intersect the old budget line at the old optimum, point A in the graph above. The effect of the change is to rotate the budget line from BL_1 to BL_2. Notice from the graph above that this change allows the consumer to achieve a higher level of utility by moving to point B on the new budget line, consuming more root beer and less of the other goods.

4.9.

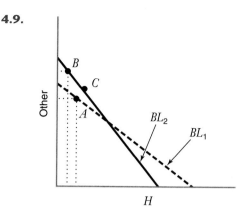

With the initial budget line, BL_1, Sally chooses point A. When her incomes increases and the price of housing increases, the budget line rotates to BL_2 at which time she chooses point B. From this information we can deduce that $B > A$. This is true because (1) B is at least as preferred as C since B was chosen when C cost the same amount as B, and (2) C is strictly preferred to A since C lies to the northeast of A. By transitivity, B must be strictly preferred to A.

CHAPTER 5

5.2.   See figure.

5.5.   a) At the consumer's optimum we must have

$$\frac{MU_x}{P_x} = \frac{MU_y}{P_y}$$

$$\frac{y}{P_x} = \frac{x}{P_y}.$$

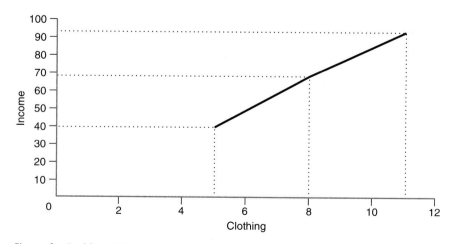

Figure for Problem 5.2.

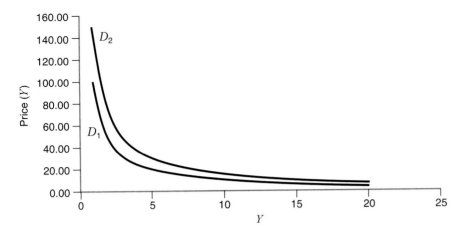

Figure for Problem 5.5b.

Substituting into the budget line, $P_x x + P_y y = I$, gives

$$P_x\left(y\left(\frac{P_y}{P_x}\right)\right) + P_y y = I$$

$$2P_y y = I$$

$$y = \frac{I}{2P_y}.$$

b) Yes, clothing is a normal good. Holding P_y constant, if I increases y will also increase. See figure.

c) The cross-price elasticity of demand of food with respect to the price of clothing must be zero. Note in part (a) that with this utility function the demand for y does not depend on the price of x. Similarly, the demand for x does not depend on the price of y. In fact, the consumer divides her income equally between the two goods regardless of the price of either. Since the demands do not depend on the prices of the other goods, the cross-price elasticity must be zero.

5.6. a)

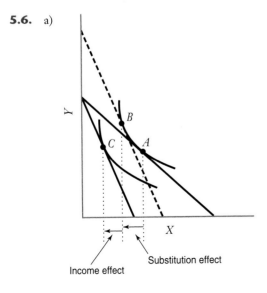

b)

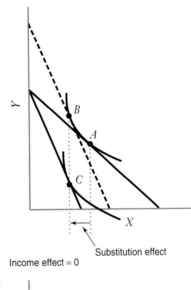

c)

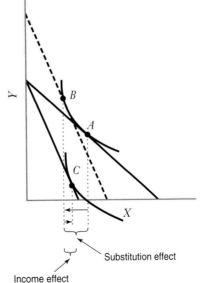

d)

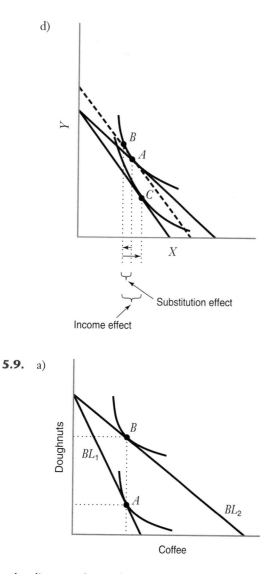

Substitution effect

Income effect

5.9. a)

In the diagram above, the consumer consumes the same amount of coffee and more doughnuts after the price of coffee falls.

b) No, this behavior is not consistent with a quasi-linear utility function. While it is true that there is no income effect with a quasi-linear utility function, the substitution effect would still induce the consumer to purchase more coffee when the price of coffee falls.

5.13. a) If the income consumption curve is vertical, the utility function has no income effect. This will occur, for example, with a quasi-linear utility function. This utility function will have the same marginal rate of substitution for any particular value of tea regardless of the level of total utility. If the price of tea falls, flattening the budget line, the consumer will reach a new optimum where the marginal rate of substitution is equal to the slope of the new budget line. Since the budget line has flattened, this cannot occur at the previ-

ous optimum amount of tea. The substitution effect implies that this new optimum level of tea will be greater than the previous level. Thus, when the price of tea falls, the quantity of tea demanded increases, implying a downward sloping demand curve. This can be seen in the following figure.

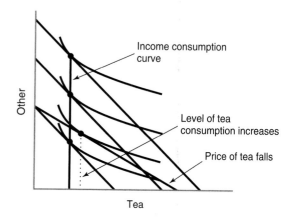

b) Yes, the values will be $30. When the income consumption curve is vertical, the consumer's utility function has no income effect. As stated in the text, when there is no income effect, compensating and equivalent variation will be identical and these will also equal the consumer surplus measured as the area under the demand curve.

CHAPTER 6

6.2. a)

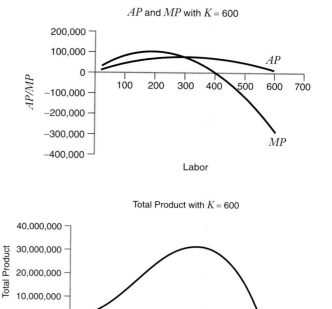

Based on the figure, it appears, that the average product reaches its maximum at $Q = 300$. The marginal product curve appears to reach its maximum at $Q = 200$.

b)

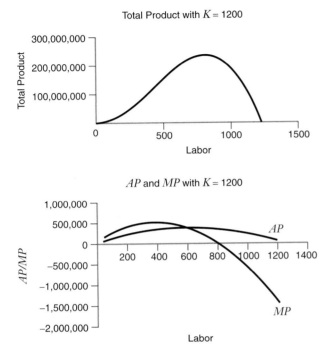

Based on the figure, it appears that the average product curve reaches its maximum at $Q = 600$. The marginal product curve appears to reach its maximum at $Q = 400$.

c) In both instances, for low values of L the total product curve increases at an increasing rate. So in both cases the production function exhibits increasing marginal returns to L over some range.

6.3. a) Incorrect. When $MP > AP$ we know that AP is increasing. When $MP < AP$ we know that AP is decreasing.
b) Incorrect. If MP is negative, $MP < AP$. This only implies that AP is falling. In fact, AP can never be negative because total product can never be negative.
c) Incorrect. Average product is always positive, so this tells us nothing about the change in total product.
d) Incorrect. If total product is increasing, we know that $MP > 0$. If diminishing marginal returns have set in, however, marginal product will be positive but decreasing.

6.5. See figure.
Because these isoquants are convex to the origin, they do exhibit diminishing marginal rate of technical substitution.

6.7. For this production function $MP_L = a$ and $MP_K = b$. The $MRTS_{L,K}$ is therefore

$$MRTS_{L,K} = \frac{MP_L}{MP_K} = \frac{a}{b}.$$

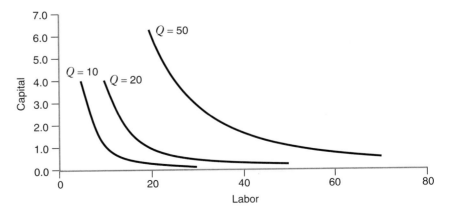

Figure for Problem 6.5.

6.8. a) This isoquants for this situation will be L-shaped as in the following diagram

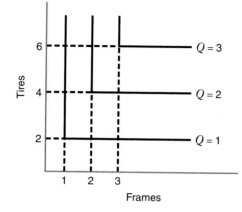

These L-shaped isoquants imply that once you have the correct combination of inputs, say 2 frames and 4 tires, additional units of one resource without more units of the other resource will not result in any additional output.

b) Mathematically, this production function can be written

$$Q = \min\!\left(F, \frac{1}{2}T\right)$$

where F and T represent the number of frames and tires.

6.9. a) To determine the nature of returns to scale, increase all inputs by some factor λ and determine if output goes up by a factor more than, less than, or the same as λ.

$$Q_\lambda = 50\sqrt{\lambda M \lambda L} + \lambda M + \lambda L$$
$$Q_\lambda = 50\lambda\sqrt{ML} + \lambda M + \lambda L$$
$$Q_\lambda = \lambda[50\sqrt{ML} + M + L]$$
$$Q_\lambda = \lambda Q.$$

By increasing the inputs by a factor of λ, output goes up by a factor of λ. Since output goes up by the same factor as the inputs, this production function exhibits constant returns to scale.

(b) The marginal product of labor is

$$MP_L = 25\sqrt{\frac{M}{L}} + 1.$$

Suppose $M > 0$. Holding M fixed, increasing L will have the effect of decreasing MP_L. The marginal product of labor is

decreasing for all level of L. The MP_L, however, will never be negative since both components of the equation above will always be greater than or equal to zero. In fact, for this production function, $MP_L \geq 1$.

6.10. a) For a CES production function of the form $\frac{\sigma-1}{\sigma}$

$$Q = \left[aL^{\frac{\sigma-1}{\sigma}} + bK^{\frac{\sigma-1}{\sigma}}\right]^{\frac{\sigma}{\sigma-1}}$$

the elasticity of substitution is σ. In this example we have a CES production function of the form

$$Q = [K^{0.5} + L^{0.5}]^2.$$

To determine the elasticity of substitution, either set $(\sigma - 1)/\sigma = 0.5$ or $\sigma/(\sigma - 1) = 2$ and solve for σ.

$$\frac{\sigma - 1}{\sigma} = 0.5$$
$$\sigma - 1 = 0.5\sigma$$
$$0.5\sigma = 1$$
$$\sigma = 2.$$

In either case, the elasticity of substitution is 2.

(b)
$$Q_\lambda = [(\lambda K)^{0.5} + (\lambda L)^{0.5}]^2$$
$$Q_\lambda = [(\lambda^{0.5})(K^{0.5} + L^{0.5})]^2$$
$$Q_\lambda = \lambda[K^{0.5} + L^{0.5}]^2$$
$$Q_\lambda = \lambda Q.$$

Since output goes up by the same factor as the inputs, this production function exhibits constant returns to scale.

(c)
$$Q_\lambda = [100 + (\lambda K)^{0.5} + (\lambda L)^{0.5}]^2$$
$$Q_\lambda = [100 + \lambda^{0.5}(K^{0.5} + L^{0.5})]^2$$
$$Q_\lambda = \lambda\left[\frac{100}{\lambda^{0.5}} + K^{0.5} + L^{0.5}\right]^2 < \lambda Q.$$

When the inputs are increased by a factor of λ, output goes up by a factor less than λ, implying decreasing returns to scale. Intuitively, in this production function, while you can increase the K and L inputs, you cannot increase the constant portion. So output cannot go up by as much as the inputs.

CHAPTER 7

7.2. At the optimum we must have

$$\frac{MP_K}{r} = \frac{MP_L}{w}.$$

In this problem we have

$$\frac{200}{0.25} > \frac{1000}{10}$$

$$800 > 100.$$

This implies that the firm receives more output per dollar spent on an additional machine hour of fermentation capacity than for an additional hour spent on labor. Therefore, the firm could lower cost while achieving the same level of output by using fewer hours of labor and more hours of fermentation capacity.

7.3. a) If the price of both inputs changes by the same percentage amount, the slope of the isocost line will not change. Since we are holding the level of output fixed, the isocost line will be tangent to the isoquant at the same point as prior to the price increase. Therefore, the cost-minimizing quantities of the inputs will not change.
b) If the price of capital increases by a larger percentage than the price of labor, then, relatively speaking, the price of labor has become cheaper. The firm will substitute away from capital to labor until

$$\frac{MP_K}{r} = \frac{MP_L}{w}.$$

7.4. No, if the MRTS is diminishing, the expansion path for different input price combinations cannot cross. To understand why, imagine for the moment that they did cross at some point. Recall that the expansion path traces out the cost-minimizing combinations of inputs as output increases. Essentially the expansion path traces out all of the tangencies between the isocost lines and isoquants. These tangencies occur at the point where

$$\frac{MP_L}{MP_K} = \frac{w}{r}.$$

If the expansion paths cross at some point, then the cost minimizing combination of inputs must be identical with both sets of prices. This would require that

$$\frac{MP_K}{r_1} = \frac{MP_L}{w_1},$$

and

$$\frac{MP_K}{r_2} = \frac{MP_L}{w_2}.$$

Unless these pairs of prices are proportional, it is not possible for both of these equations to hold. Therefore, it is not possible for the expansion paths to cross unless the prices are proportional, in which case the two expansion paths will be identical.

7.6. At the optimum

$$\frac{MP_K}{r} = \frac{MP_L}{w}.$$

For this example, that implies

$$\frac{[L^{1/2} + K^{1/2}]K^{-1/2}}{r} = \frac{[L^{1/2} + K^{1/2}]L^{-1/2}}{w}$$

$$\frac{1}{r\sqrt{K}} = \frac{1}{w\sqrt{L}}$$

$$w\sqrt{L} = r\sqrt{K}$$

$$\frac{K}{L} = \frac{w^2}{r^2}.$$

Given that $w = 10$ and $r = 1$, this implies

$$100 = \frac{K}{L}$$

$$100L = K.$$

Returning to the production function and assuming $O = 121,000$ yields

$$121,000 = [L^{1/2} + K^{1/2}]^2$$
$$121,000 = [L^{1/2} + (100L)^{1/2}]^2$$
$$121,000 = [L^{1/2} + 10L^{1/2}]^2$$
$$121,000 = [11L^{1/2}]^2$$
$$121,000 = 121L$$
$$1,000 = L.$$

Since $K = 100L$, $K = 100(1000) = 100,000$. The cost-minimizing quantities of capital and labor to produce 121,000 airframes is $K = 100,000$ and $L = 1,000$.

7.9. The tangency condition requires

$$\frac{MP_L}{MP_K} = \frac{w}{r}.$$

For this Cobb–Douglas production function, $MP_K = L$ and $MP_L = K$. Therefore

$$\frac{K}{L} = \frac{w}{r}$$

$$K = \left(\frac{w}{r}\right)L.$$

Substituting into the production function yields

$$Q = LK$$

$$Q = L\left(\frac{w}{r}\right)L$$

$$Q = \left(\frac{w}{r}\right)L^2$$

$$L = \left(\frac{rQ}{w}\right)^{1/2}.$$

This represents the input demand curve for L. Since

$$K = \left(\frac{w}{r}\right)L,$$

we have

$$K = \left(\frac{w}{r}\right)\left(\frac{rQ}{w}\right)^{1/2}$$

$$K = \left(\frac{wQ}{r}\right)^{1/2}.$$

This represents the input demand curve for K.

CHAPTER 8

8.1. Starting with the tangency condition, we have

$$\frac{MP_L}{MP_K} = \frac{w}{r}$$

$$\frac{K}{L} = \frac{2}{1}$$

$$K = 2L.$$

Substituting into the production function yields

$$Q = LK$$

$$Q = L(2L)$$

$$L = \sqrt{\frac{Q}{2}}.$$

Plugging this into the expression for K above gives

$$K = 2\sqrt{\frac{Q}{2}}.$$

Finally, substituting these into the total cost equation results in

$$TC = 2\left(\sqrt{\frac{Q}{2}}\right) + 2\left(\sqrt{\frac{Q}{2}}\right)$$

$$TC = 4\left(\sqrt{\frac{Q}{2}}\right)$$

$$TC = \sqrt{8Q},$$

and average cost is given by

$$AC = \frac{TC}{Q} = \frac{\sqrt{8Q}}{Q}$$

$$AC = \sqrt{\frac{8}{Q}}.$$

8.3. a) Starting with the tangency condition we have

$$\frac{MP_L}{MP_K} = \frac{w}{r}$$

$$\frac{[L^{1/2} + K^{1/2}]L^{-(1/2)}}{[L^{1/2} + K^{1/2}]K^{-(1/2)}} = \frac{2}{1}$$

$$\frac{K}{L} = 4$$

$$K = 4L.$$

Plugging this into the total cost function yields

$$Q = [L^{1/2} + (4L)^{1/2}]^2$$

$$Q = [3L^{1/2}]^2$$

$$Q = 9L$$

$$L = \frac{Q}{9}.$$

Inserting this back into the solution for K above gives

$$K = \frac{4Q}{9}$$

b)

$$TC = 2\left(\frac{Q}{9}\right) + \frac{4Q}{9}$$

$$TC = \frac{2Q}{3},$$

c)

$$AC = \frac{TC}{Q} = \left(\frac{2Q}{3}\right)\Big/Q$$

$$AC = \frac{2}{3}.$$

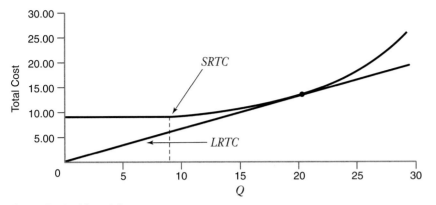

Figure for Problem 8.3.e.

d) When $Q < 9$, the firm needs no labor. If $Q > 9$, the firm does hire labor. Setting $\bar{K} = 9$ and plugging in for capital in the production function yields

$$Q = [L^{1/2} + 9^{1/2}]^2$$
$$Q^{1/2} = L^{1/2} + 3$$
$$L^{1/2} = Q^{1/2} - 3$$
$$L = [Q^{1/2} - 3]^2,$$

Thus,

$$L = \begin{cases} (Q^{1/2} - 3)^2 & \text{when } Q > 9. \\ 0 & \text{when } Q \leq 9 \end{cases}$$

e) $$TC = \begin{cases} 2(Q^{1/2} - 3)^2 + 9 & \text{when } Q > 9. \\ 9 & \text{when } Q \leq 9 \end{cases}$$

Graphically, short-run and long-run total cost are shown in the figure.

8.6. See figure. Since each of these short-run average cost curves reaches a minimum at an average cost of 2.0, the long-run average cost curve associated with these short-run curves will be a horizontal line, tangent to each of these curves, at a long-run average cost of 2.0.

8.7. With some inputs fixed, it is likely that the fixed level is not optimum given the firm's size. Therefore, it may be more expensive to produce additional units in the short run than in the long run when the firm can employ the optimal (i.e., cost minimizing) quantity of the fixed input.

8.8. Economies of scope exist if

$$TC(Q_1, Q_2) - TC(Q_1, 0) < TC(0, Q_2) - TC(0, 0).$$

In this case

$$TC(Q_1, Q_2) = 1000 + 2Q_1 + 3Q_2$$
$$TC(Q_1, 0) = 1000 + 2Q_1$$
$$TC(0, Q_2) = 1000 + 3Q_2$$
$$TC(0, 0) = 0.$$

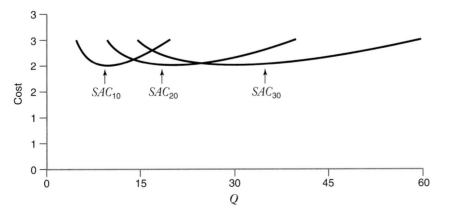

Figure for Problem 8.6.

So, economies of scope exist if

$$(1000 + 2Q_1 + 3Q_2) - (1000 + 2Q_1) < 1000 + 3Q_2$$
$$3Q_2 < 1000 + 3Q_2.$$

Yes, in this case the cost of adding a movie channel when the firm is already providing a sports channel is less costly (by $1000) than a new firm supplying a movie channel from scratch. Economies of scope exist for this satellite TV company.

CHAPTER 9

9.1. a) In order to maximize profit, Ron should operate at the point where $P = MC$.

$$20 = 10 + 0.20Q$$
$$Q = 50.$$

b) Ron's profit is given by $\pi = TR - TC$.

$$\pi = 20(50) - (40 + 10(50) + 0.10(50)^2)$$
$$\pi = 210.$$

c) See figures.

d) First, find the minimum of AVC by setting $AVC = SMC$.

$$AVC = \frac{10Q + 0.1Q^2}{Q} = 10 + 0.1Q$$
$$10 + 0.1Q = 10 + 0.2Q$$
$$Q = 0.$$

The minimum level of AVC is thus 10. For prices below 10 the firm will not produce, and for prices above 10 supply is found by setting $P = SMC$.

$$P = 10 + 0.2Q$$
$$Q = 5P - 50.$$

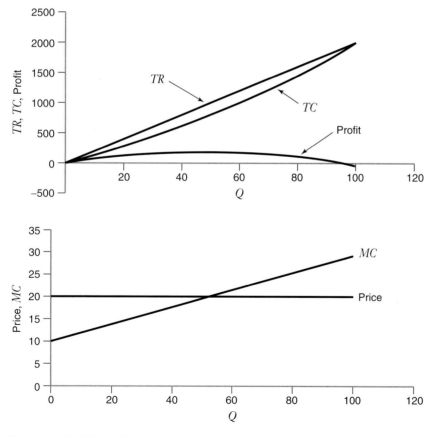

Figures for Problem 9.1.c.

The firm's short-run supply curve is thus

$$s(P) = \begin{cases} 0 & \text{if } P < 10 \\ 5P - 50 & \text{if } P \geq 10. \end{cases}$$

e) If all fixed costs are non-sunk, as in this case, the shutdown rule is $P < SAC$.

$$SAC = \frac{STC}{Q}$$

$$SAC = \frac{40}{Q} + 10 + 0.1Q.$$

The minimum point of SAC occurs where $SAC = SMC$.

$$\frac{40}{Q} + 10 + 0.1Q = 10 + 0.2Q$$

$$Q = 20.$$

The minimum level of SAC is thus 14. For prices below 14, the firm will not produce. For prices above 14, supply is found by setting $P = SMC$ as before.

$$s(P) = \begin{cases} 0 & \text{if } P < 14 \\ 5P - 50 & \text{if } P \geq 14. \end{cases}$$

9.2. a) First, find the minimum of AVC by setting $AVC = SMC$.

$$AVC = \frac{TVC}{Q} = \frac{Q^2}{Q}$$

$$AVC = Q$$

$$Q = 2Q$$

$$Q = 0.$$

The minimum level of AVC is thus 0. When the price is 0 the firm will produce 0, and for prices above 0 find supply by setting $P = SMC$.

$$P = 2Q$$

$$Q = \frac{1}{2}P.$$

Thus,

$$s(P) = \frac{1}{2}P.$$

b) Market supply is found by horizontally summing the supply curves of the individual firms. Since there are 20 identical producers in this market, market supply is given by

$$S(P) = 20s(P)$$

$$S(P) = 10P.$$

c) Equilibrium price and quantity occur at the point where $S(P) = D(P)$.

$$10P = 110 - P$$

$$P = 10.$$

Substituting $P = 10$ back into $D(P)$ implies equilibrium quantity is $Q = 100$. So at the equilibrium, $P = 10$ and $Q = 100$.

9.5. a) Since an individual firm will supply where $P = SMC$,

$$P = 4Q$$

$$Q = \frac{1}{4}P.$$

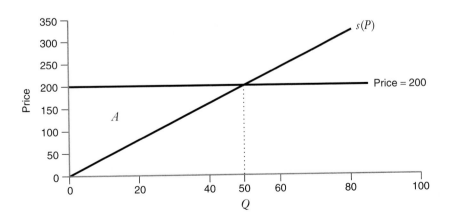

Figure for Problem 9.5.a.

Assuming a firm will supply for any positive price, this implies $s(P) = 1/4\ P$. Graphically we have (see figure).

Producer surplus is given by area A in the figure below, which is $(1/2)(200)50 = 5000$.

(b) Since all firms are identical, overall producer surplus will be $100(5000) = 500,000$.

(c) Economic profit = Producer surplus − Sunk fixed costs. If economic profit for a firm is to be greater than zero, we must have

$$\text{Producer surplus} - \text{Sunk fixed costs} > 0.$$

Since producer surplus is 5000 in this example, this implies that sunk fixed costs must be less than 5000 for the firm to earn positive economic profit.

9.7. a) In a long-run equilibrium all firms earn zero economic profit implying $P = AC$, and each firm produces where $P = MC$. Thus,

$$40 - 12Q + Q^2 = 40 - 6Q + \frac{1}{3}Q^2$$

$$Q = 9.$$

If $Q = 9$, $P = 40 - 12(9) + 9^2 = 13$.

b) At $P = 13$, each firm will produce $Q = 9$ units.

c) Since $D(P) = 2200 - 100P$,

$$D(P) = 2200 - 100(13)$$

$$D(P) = 900.$$

If each firm produces 9 units, the market will have 100 firms in equilibrium.

d) Since each firm is producing 9 units, to double the number of firms in the market to 200, total demand would need to be 1800 units. This implies

$$1800 = A - 100P.$$

Since $P = 13$,

$$1800 = A - 100(13)$$

$$A = 3100.$$

With $A = 3100$, the number of firms in the industry would double.

9.8. For this total cost function, $MC = c$. Since each firm will supply where $P = MC$, in equilibrium $P = c$. If in equilibrium $P = c$,

$$D(P) = a - bc.$$

Equilibrium market quantity is $a - bc$.

In order to determine the number of firms, we need to know the quantity that each individual firm will produce. In this

case marginal cost is constant implying perfectly elastic supply. Thus, at $P = c$ a firm may produce any quantity. Therefore, the number of firms cannot be determined.

9.11. a) Minimum efficient scale occurs at the point where average cost reaches a minimum. This point occurs where $MC = AC$.

$$2Q = \frac{144}{Q} + Q$$

$$Q = 12.$$

At $Q = 12$,

$$AC = \frac{144}{Q} + Q$$

$$AC = 24.$$

b) In the long-run, the equilibrium price will be determined by the minimum level of average cost of firms with average CEOs. Thus, $P = 24$. At this price, firms having average CEOs will earn zero economic profit and firms with exceptional CEOs will earn positive economic profit.

c) At the price, the firms with an average CEO will produce where $P = MC$

$$24 = 2Q$$

$$Q = 12.$$

The firms with an exceptional CEO will also produce where $P = MC$

$$Q = 24.$$

d) At this price

$$D(P) = 7200 - 100P$$

$$D(P) = 4800.$$

e) Since there are 100 exceptional CEOs and assuming they are all employed, the total supply from exceptional CEO firms will be

$$S_E = 100(24)$$

$$S_E = 2400.$$

This leaves $Q = 4800 - 2400 = 2400$ units to be supplied by firms with average CEOs. Thus,

$$N_A = \frac{2400}{12}$$

$$N_A = 200.$$

f) To calculate the exceptional CEO's economic rent, we must compute the highest salary the firm would pay this CEO. This salary is the amount that would drive economic profit to zero. Call this amount S^*. Since the exceptional CEO firm is producing $Q = 24$, the firm's average cost is

$$AC = \frac{144}{24} + \frac{1}{2}(24)$$

$$AC = 18.$$

Since $P = 24$, the exceptional CEO has produced a $6 per unit cost advantage. This implies

$$\frac{S^*}{24} - \frac{144}{24} = 6$$

$$S^* = 288.$$

Economic rent is the difference between this salary, $288,000, and the reservation wage of $144,000. Thus, the exceptional CEO's economic rent is $144,000.

g) Firms that hire exceptional CEOs for $144,000 will gain all of the CEO's economic rent and will therefore earn economic profit of $144,000.

h) In a long-run competitive equilibrium exceptional CEO salaries should be bid up as other firms attempt to split the economic rent with the CEOs. Thus should bid up the salary of the CEOs until economic profits for firms with exceptional CEOs are driven to zero. Thus, exceptional CEO salaries should approach $288,000 in a long-run equilibrium.

CHAPTER 10

10.1. a) The market will clear. The excise tax will alter equilibrium price and quantity, but there will be no excess demand or excess supply.

b) The market will clear. The subsidy will alter equilibrium price and quantity, but there will be no excess demand or excess supply.

c) The market will not clear. A price floor set above the equilibrium price will create excess supply.

d) The market will not clear. A price ceiling set below the equilibrium price will create excess demand.

e) The market will not clear. A quota limiting output below the equilibrium level will create excess supply since the price will be driven above the equilibrium price.

10.3. The incidence of a tax can be summarized quantitatively by

$$\frac{\Delta P^d}{\Delta P^s} = \frac{\epsilon_{Q^s,P}}{\epsilon_{Q^d,P}}.$$

From the given information, $\Delta P_D = 4$, $\Delta P_S = 0$, and $E_D = -0.5$. These price changes imply that 100% of the burden of the tax is borne by the consumer, implying the elasticity of supply must be equal to infinity. Supply is perfectly elastic.

10.5. Therefore, doubling the tax will quadruple the size of the deadweight loss if the supply and demand curves are linear. The height and the base of the deadweight loss triangle have both doubled when the tax doubles. Therefore, the area of the DWL triangle doubles.

10.6. a) Setting $Q^d = Q^s$ results in

$$10 - P = -4 + P$$

$$P = \$7 \text{ per bushel.}$$

Substituting this result into the demand equation gives $Q = 3$ million bushels.

b) At the equilibrium, consumer surplus is $(1/2)(10 - 7)3 = 4.5$ and producer surplus is $(1/2)(7 - 4)3 = 4.5$ (both measured in millions of dollars). There is no deadweight loss in this case, and total net benefits equal $9 million.

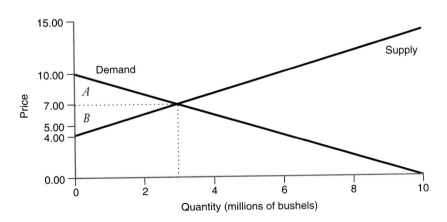

Figure for Problem 10.6.b.

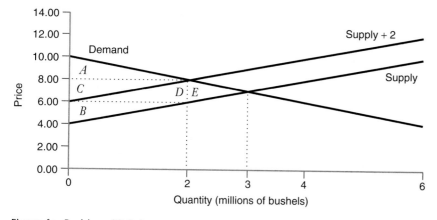

Figure for Problem 10.6.d.

See figure; area A represents consumer surplus, and area B represents producer surplus.

c) If the government imposes an excise tax of $2, the new equilibrium will be

$$10 - (P^s + 2) = -4 + P^s$$
$$P^d = \$6 \text{ per bushel.}$$

Substituting back into the equation for P^d yields $P^d = 8$, and substituting P^s into the supply equation implies $Q = 2$ million.

d) Now the consumer surplus is $(1/2)(10 - 8)2 = 2$, the producer surplus is $(1/2)(6 - 4)2 = 2$, the tax receipts are $2(2) = 4$, and the deadweight loss is $(1/2)(8 - 6)(3 - 2) = 1$ (all measured in millions of dollars).

See figure; area A represents consumer surplus, area B represents producer surplus, areas $C + D$ represent government tax receipts, and area E represents the deadweight loss.

e) If the government provides a subsidy of $1, the new equilibrium will be

$$10 - (P^s - 1) = -4 + P_S$$
$$P^s = \$7.5 \text{ per bushel.}$$

Substituting back into the equation for P^d yields $P^d = 6.5$, and substituting P^s into the supply equation implies $Q = 3.5$ million.

f) Now the consumer surplus is $(1/2)(10 - 6.5)3.5 = 6.125$; the producer surplus is $(1/2)(7.5 - 4)3.5 = 6.125$; the subsidy paid is $-1(3.5) = -3.5$ (negative since the government is paying this amount); and the deadweight loss is $(1/2)(7.5 - 6.5)(3.5 - 3) = 0.25$ (all measured in millions of dollars). See figure; areas $A + B + E$ represent consumer surplus, areas $B + C + F$ represent producer surplus, areas $B + C + D + E$ represent the government subsidy payment, and area D represents the deadweight loss.

g) For part b, potential net benefits are $4.5 + 4.5 + 0 + 0 = 9$; for part d, potential net benefits are $2 + 2 + 4 + 1 = 9$; and for part f, potential net benefits are $6.125 + 6.125 - 3.5 + 0.25 = 9$. Thus, in each case, potential net benefits are the same (and, as above, all are measured in millions of dollars).

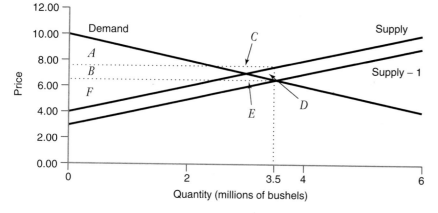

Figure for Problem 10.6.f.

10.7. a) Based on the graph, the government would need to set a tax of $2.00 per unit to achieve the government's target of 600 units sold. By setting a tax at $2.00, the supply curve will shift upward by $2.00 and intersect the demand curve at $P = \$3.00$ and $Q = 600$, the new market equilibrium.

b)

	Tax	Minimum Price
What price per unit would consumers pay?	$3.00	$3.00
What price per unit would producers receive?	$1.00	$3.00
What area represents consumer surplus?	F	F
What area represents the largest producer surplus under the policy?	B	B + C + E
What area represents the smallest producer surplus under the policy?	B	G + H + L + T
What area represents government receipts?	C + E	Zero
What area represents smallest deadweight loss possible under the policy?	G + L	G + L

If demand is perfectly inelastic, the demand curve will be a vertical line. The price will rise by exactly $2 after the tax is imposed and consumers will take on 100% of the tax burden. Consumer surplus will fall by $2 times the market quantity, which will be the same as the pretax quantity given the vertical demand curve. Government tax receipts will increase by $2 times the market quantity, completely offsetting the reduction in consumer surplus. Producer surplus will remain the same because consumers have 100% of the burden of the tax. Thus, since government receipts completely offset the reduction in consumer surplus, there is nothing lost to society. There is no deadweight loss from an excise tax when the demand curve is perfectly inelastic.

CHAPTER 11

11.1. a) If demand is given by $Q = 100 - 5P$, inverse demand is found by solving for P. This implies inverse demand is $P = 20 - (1/5)Q$.

b) Average revenue is given by

$$AR = \frac{TR}{Q} = \frac{PQ}{Q} = P.$$

Therefore, average revenue will be $P = 20 - (1/5)Q$.
c) For a linear demand curve $P = a - bQ$, marginal revenue is given by $MR = a - 2bQ$. In this instance demand is $P = 20 - (1/5)Q$, implying marginal revenue is $MR = 20 - (2/5)Q$.

11.3. If marginal cost is independent of Q, then marginal cost is constant. Assume $MC = c$. Then in the winter the firm will produce where $MR = MC$.

$$a_1 - 2bQ = c$$

$$Q = \frac{a_1 - c}{2b}.$$

At this quantity the price charged will be

$$P = a_1 - b\left(\frac{a_1 - c}{2b}\right)$$

$$P = \frac{a_1 + c}{2}.$$

In the summer the firm will also produce where $MR = MC$.

$$a_2 - 2bQ = c$$

$$Q = \frac{a_2 - c}{2b}.$$

At this quantity the price charged will be

$$P = a_2 - b\left(\frac{a_2 - c}{2b}\right)$$

$$P = \frac{a_2 + c}{2}.$$

Since we are told that $a_2 > a_1$, the price charged during the summer months will be greater than the price charged during the winter months.

11.4. a) If demand is given by $P = 300 - Q$, then $MR = 300 - 2Q$. To find the optimum set $MR = MC$,

$$300 - 2Q = Q$$

$$Q = 100.$$

At $Q = 100$, price will be $P = 300 - 100 = 200$. At this price and quantity, total revenue will be $TR = 200(100) = 20,000$ and total cost will be $TC = 1200 + 0.5(100)^2 = 6,200$. Therefore, the firm will earn a profit of $\pi = TR - TC = 13,800$.

b) The price elasticity at the profit-maximizing price is

$$\epsilon_{Q,P} = \frac{\Delta Q}{\Delta P} \frac{P}{Q}.$$

With the demand curve $Q = 300 - P$, $\Delta Q/\Delta P = -1$. Therefore, at the profit-maximizing price

$$\epsilon_{Q,P} = -1\left(\frac{200}{100}\right)$$

$$\epsilon_{Q,P} = -2.$$

The marginal cost at the profit-maximizing output is $MC = Q = 100$. The inverse elasticity pricing rule states that at the profit-maximizing price and quantity

$$\frac{P - MC}{P} = -\frac{1}{\epsilon_{Q,P}}.$$

In this case we have

$$\frac{200 - 100}{200} = -\frac{1}{-2}$$

$$\frac{1}{2} = \frac{1}{2}.$$

Thus, the IEPR holds for this monopolist.

11.5. a) With demand $P = 210 - 4Q$, $MR = 210 - 8Q$. Setting $MR = MC$ implies

$$210 - 8Q = 10$$

$$Q = 25.$$

With $Q = 25$, price will be $P = 210 - 4Q = 110$. At this price and quantity, total revenue will be $TR = 110(25) = 2,750$.
b) If $MC = 20$, then setting $MR = MC$ implies

$$210 - 8Q = 20$$

$$Q = 23.75.$$

At $Q = 23.75$, price will be $P = 115$. At this price and quantity, total revenue will be $TR = 115(23.75) = 2,731.25$. Therefore, the increase in marginal cost will result in lower total revenue for the firm.
c) If all firms in a competitive market had $MC = 10$, setting $P = MC$ (the optimality condition for a perfectly competitive firm) implies

$$210 - 4Q = 10$$

$$Q = 50.$$

At this quantity, price will be $P = 10$.
d) If all firms in a competitive market had $MC = 20$, then setting $P = MC$ implies

$$210 - 4Q = 20$$

$$Q = 47.50.$$

At this quantity, price will be $P = 20$. When $MC = 10$, $TR = 10(50) = 500$. With $MC = 20$, $TR = 20(47.50) = 950$. Thus, total revenue increases for the perfectly competitive firm after the increase in marginal cost.

11.10. a) Since the profit-maximizing firm will always allocate output among plants so as to keep marginal costs equal, and since the first plant in this example has a constant marginal cost of 8, the profit-maximizing solution will have $MC = 8$ at both plants. To compute total output, set $MR = MC$. With demand $P = 968 - 20Q$, marginal revenue is $MR = 968 - 40Q$. This implies

$$968 - 40Q = 8$$

$$Q = 24.$$

At this quantity, the firm will charge a price of $P = 968 - 20(24) = 488$. Therefore, the price for one razor will be $4.88 and Gillette will supply 24 million blades.

The allocation between plants will require $MC = 8$ at both plants. At plant 2, $MC = 1 + 0.5Q_2$. Setting this equal to 8 implies $Q_2 = 14$. Then, since total output is 24, the firm will produce 10 at plant 1.
b) If $MC = 10$ at plant 1, the setting $MR = MC$ implies

$$968 - 40Q = 10$$

$$Q = 23.95.$$

At this quantity, price will be $4.89. The allocation between plants will require $MC = 10$ at both plants. Setting $MC = 10$ at plant 1 implies $10 = 1 + 0.5Q_2$ implying $Q_2 = 18$. Since total output is 23.95, the firm will produce 5.95 at plant 1.

11.11. a) With demand $P = 100 - 2Q$, $MR = 100 - 4Q$. Setting $MR = MC$ implies

$$100 - 4Q = 0.5Q$$

$$Q = 22.2.$$

At this quantity, price will be $P = 55.6$.
b) With marginal cost pricing the firm sets $P = MC$ as in a competitive environment. In this example

$$100 - 2Q = 0.5Q$$

$$Q = 40$$

At this quantity, price will be $P = 20$.

c) For the monopolist, consumer surplus is $0.5(100 - 55.6)22.2 = 493.83$ and producer surplus is $0.5(11.1)22.2 + (55.6 - 11.1)22.2 = 1,111.11$. For the competitive firm, consumer surplus is $0.5(100 - 20)40 = 1,600$ and producer surplus is $0.5(20)40 = 400$. The sum of consumer and producer surplus under monopoly is 1604.94, and the sum of consumer and producer surplus under competition is 2000. Therefore, the deadweight loss due to monopoly is 395.06.

d) If demand is $P = 180 - 4Q$, $MR = 180 - 8Q$. The monopolist sets $MR = MC$, which gives

$$180 - 8Q = 0.5Q$$
$$Q = 21.18.$$

At this quantity, price will be 95.29. A competitive firm will set $P = MC$, which gives

$$180 - 4Q = 0.5Q$$
$$Q = 40.$$

At this quantity, price will be 20.

With monopoly, consumer surplus will be $0.5(100 - 95.29)21.18 = 49.88$ and producer surplus will be $0.5(10.59)21.18 + (95.29 - 10.59)21.18 = 1906.09$. With perfect competition, consumer surplus will be 1,600 and producer surplus will be 400, as before. Now, the sum of consumer and producer surplus with perfect competition is 2,000 and with monopoly is 1955.97. Therefore, the deadweight loss in this case is 44.03.

Although the competitive solution is identical with both demand curves, the deadweight loss in the first case is far greater. This difference occurs because with the second demand curve demand is less elastic. If consumers are less willing to change quantity as prices change, the firm will be able to extract more surplus from the market. In this example, the demand in the second case implies a Lerner index is 88.9 percent (compared with 80 percent with the first demand curve) indicating extensive market power for this firm.

CHAPTER 12

12.1. a) Third degree—the firm is charging a different price to different market segments, individuals and libraries.
b) First degree—each consumer is paying near his or her maximum willingness to pay.
c) Second degree—the firm is offering quantity discounts. As the number of holes played goes up, the average expenditure per hole falls.
d) Third degree—the firm is charging different prices for different segments. Business customers (M–F) are being charged a higher price than those using the phone on Sunday (e.g., family calls).

e) Second degree—the firm is offering a quantity discount.
f) Third degree—the airline is charging different prices to different segments. Those who can purchase in advance pay one price, while those who must purchase with short notice pay a different price.

12.2. a) If price discrimination is impossible, the firm will set $MR = MC$.

$$20 - 2Q = 2Q$$
$$Q = 5.$$

At this quantity, price will be $P = 15$, total revenue will be $TR = 75$, total cost will be $TC = 49$, and profit will be $\pi = 26$. Producer surplus is just total revenue nonsunk cost, or, in this case total revenue − variable cost. Thus, producer surplus is $75 - 5^2 = 50$.

b) With perfect first-degree price discrimination, the firm sets $P = MC$ to determine the level of output.

$$20 - Q = 2Q$$
$$Q = 6.67.$$

The price charged each consumer, however, will vary. The price charged will be the consumer's maximum willingness to pay and will correspond with the demand curve. Total revenue will be $0.5(20 - 13.33)(6.67) + 13.33(6.67) = 111.16$. Since the firm is producing a total of 6.67 units, total cost will be $TC = 68.49$. Profit is then $\pi = 42.67$, while producer surplus is revenue − variable cost $= 111.16 - 6.67 = 66.67$.

c) By being able to employ perfect first-degree price discrimination, the firm increases profit and producer surplus by 16.67.

12.4. a) With third-degree price discrimination the firm should set $MR = MC$ in each market to determine price and quantity. Thus, in Europe setting $MR = MC$

$$70 - 2Q_E = 10$$
$$Q_E = 30.$$

At this quantity, price will be $P_E = 40$. Profit in Europe is then $\pi_E = (P_E - 10)Q_E = (40 - 10)(30) = 900$. Setting $MR = MC$ in the United States implies

$$110 - 2Q_U = 10$$
$$Q_U = 50.$$

At this quantity, price will be $P_U = 60$. Profit in the U.S. will then be $\pi_U = (P_U - 10)Q_U = (60 - 10)(50) = 2500$. Total profit will be $\pi = 3400$.

b) If the firm can only sell the drug at one price, it will set the price to maximize total profit. The total demand the firm will face is $Q = Q_E + Q_U$. In this case

$$Q = 70 - P + 110 - P$$
$$Q = 180 - 2P.$$

The inverse total demand is then $P = 90 - (1/2)Q$.

Since $MC = 10$, setting $MR = MC$ implies

$$90 - Q = 10$$
$$Q = 80.$$

At this quantity price will be $P = 50$. If the firm sets price at 50, the firm will sell $Q_E = 20$ and $Q_U = 60$. Profit will be $\pi = 50(80) - 10(80) = 3200$.

c) The firm will sell the drug on both continents under either scenario. If the firm can price discriminate, consumer surplus will be $0.5(70 - 40)30 + 0.5(110 - 60)50 = 1700$ and producer surplus (equal to profit) will be 3400. Thus, total surplus will be 5100. If the firm cannot price discriminate, consumer surplus will be $0.5(70 - 50)20 + 0.5(110 - 50)60 = 2000$, and producer surplus will be equal to profit of 3200. Thus, total surplus will be 5200.

12.9. a) Without bundling, the best the firm can do is set the price of airfare at $800 and the price of the hotel at $800. In each case the firm attracts a single customer and earns profit of $500 from each, for a total profit of $1000. The firm could attract two customers for each service at a price of $500, but it would earn profit of $200 on each customer for a total of $800 profit, less profit than the $800 price.

b) With bundling, the best the firm can do is charge a price of $900 for the airfare and hotel. At this price the firm will attract all three customers and earn $300 profit on each, for a total profit of $900. The firm could raise its price to $1000, but then it would only attract one customer and total profit would be $400. Notice that with bundling the firm cannot do as well as it could with mixed bundling. This is because while (a) the demands are negatively correlated, a key to increasing profit through bundling, (b) customer 1 has a willingness to pay for airfare below marginal cost and customer 3 has a willingness to pay for hotel below marginal cost. The firm should be able to do better with mixed bundling.

c) Because customer 1 has a willingness to pay for airfare below marginal cost and customer 3 has willingness to pay for hotel below marginal cost, the firm can potentially earn greater profits through mixed bundling. In this problem, if the firm charges $800 for airfare only, $800 for hotel only, and $1000 for the bundle, then customer 1 will purchase hotel only, customer 2 will purchase the bundle, and customer 3 will purchase airfare only. This will earn the firm

$1400 profit, implying that mixed bundling is the best option in this problem.

12.10. a) Using the inverse elasticity price rule,

$$\frac{P - MC}{P} = -\frac{1}{\epsilon_{Q,P}}$$
$$\frac{P - MC}{P} = -\frac{1}{-3}$$
$$\frac{P}{MC} = 1.5.$$

The firm should set price at about 1.5 times marginal cost.

(b) The optimal advertising-to-sales ratio can be found be equating

$$\frac{A}{PQ} = -\frac{\epsilon_{Q,A}}{\epsilon_{Q,P}}$$
$$\frac{A}{PQ} = -\frac{0.5}{-3}$$
$$\frac{A}{PQ} = 0.167.$$

Thus, advertising expense should be about 16 or 17 percent of sales revenue.

CHAPTER 13

13.1. a) With two firms, demand is given by $P = 300 - 3Q_1 - 3Q_2$. If $Q_2 = 50$, then $P = 300 - 3Q_1 - 150$ or $P = 150 - 3Q_1$. Setting $MR = MC$ implies

$$150 - 6Q_1 = 100$$
$$Q_1 = 8.33.$$

If $Q_2 = 20$, then $P = 240 - 3Q_1$. Setting $MR = MC$ implies

$$240 - 6Q_1 = 100$$
$$Q_1 = 23.33.$$

b) For Firm 1, $P = (300 - 3Q_2) - 3Q_1$. Setting $MR = MC$ implies

$$(300 - 3Q_2) - 6Q_1 = 100$$
$$Q_1 = 33.33 - 0.5Q_2.$$

Since the marginal costs are the same for both firms, symmetry implies $Q_2 = 33.33 - 0.5Q_1$. Graphically, these reaction functions appear as shown in the figure.

c) In equilibrium, both firms will choose the same level of output. Thus, we can set $Q_1 = Q_2$ and solve

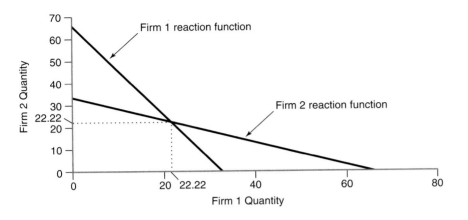

Figure for Problem 13.1.b.

$$Q_2 = 33.33 - 0.5Q_2$$
$$Q_2 = 22.22.$$

Since both firms will choose the same level of output, both firms will produce 22.22 units. Price can be found by substituting the quantity for each firm into market demand. This implies price will be $P = 300 - 3(44.44) = 166.67$.

d) If this market were perfectly competitive, then equilibrium would occur at the point where $P = MC = 100$.

e) If the firms colluded to set the monopoly price, then

$$300 - 6Q = 100$$
$$Q = 33.33.$$

At this quantity, market price will be $P = 300 - 3(200/6) = 200$.

f) If the firms acted as Bertrand oligopolists, the equilibrium would coincide with the perfectly competitive equilibrium of $P = 100$.

g) Suppose Firm 1 has $MC = 100$ and Firm 2 has $MC = 90$. For Firm 1, $P = (300 - 3Q_2) - 3Q_1$. Setting $MR = MC$ implies

$$(300 - 3Q_2) - 6Q_1 = 100$$
$$Q_1 = 33.33 - 0.5Q_2.$$

For Firm 2, $P = (300 - 3Q_1) - 3Q_2$. Setting $MR = MC$ implies

$$(300 - 3Q_1) - 6Q_2 = 90$$
$$Q_2 = 35 - 0.5Q_1.$$

Solving these two reaction functions simultaneously yields $Q_1 = 21.11$ and $Q_2 = 24.44$. With these quantities, market price will be $P = 163.36$.

13.3. a) With four firms, demand is given by $P = 15 - Q_1 - Q_2 - Q_3 - Q_4$. Let X represent total output for Firms 2, 3, and 4. Then demand faced by Firm 1 is $P = (15 - X) - Q_1$. Setting $MR = MC$ implies

$$(15 - X) - 2Q_1 = 5$$
$$Q_1 = 5 - 0.5X.$$

Since all firms have the same marginal cost, the solution will be symmetric. Letting Q^* represent the optimal output for each firm,

$$Q^* = 5 - 0.5(3Q^*)$$
$$Q^* = 2.$$

Thus, total industry output will be 8, with each firm producing 2 units of output. At this quantity, price will be $P = 15 - 8 = 7$. Profits for each firm will be $\pi = TR - TC = 7(2) - 5(2) = 4$.

b) If two firms merge, then the number of firms in the market will fall to three. The new quantity for each firm will be

$$Q^* = 5 - 0.5(2Q^*)$$
$$Q^* = 2.5.$$

Now total industry output will be 7.5, with each of the three firms producing 2.5 units. At this quantity, price will be $P = 15 - 7.5 = 7.5$. Profit per firm will be $\pi = TR - TC = 7.5(2.5) - 5(2.5) = 6.25$.

Thus, while profit per firm does increase after the merger, profits do not double and the merger nets the two firms a smaller total profit. Profit per firm increases after the merger because as the total number of firms falls, each individual firm has greater market power. This greater market power allows the firms to charge a higher price, produce less, and earn greater profit per firm.

13.8. a) When Coca Cola's marginal cost increases, Coke's reaction function will shift away from the origin. This will have the effect of raising both Coke's price and Pepsi's price. See figure.

b) When Pepsi's demand increases, Pepsi's reaction function shifts upward. This will have the effect of increasing both Coke's price and Pepsi's price. See figure.

13.10. a) If American sets a price of $200, we can plug this price into United's demand curve to get United's perceived demand curve.

$$Q_U = 1000 - 2P_U + 200$$
$$P_U = 600 - 0.5Q_U.$$

To find United's profit-maximizing price, set $MR = MC$.

$$600 - Q_U = 10$$
$$Q_U = 590.$$

At this quantity, United will charge a price $P_U = 600 - 0.5(590) = 305$.

b) If American sets a price of $400, then United's perceived demand curve is

$$Q_U = 1000 - 2P_U + 400$$
$$P_U = 700 - 0.5Q_U.$$

Equating MR to MC yields

$$700 - Q_U = 10$$
$$Q_U = 690.$$

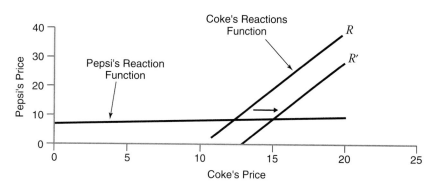

Figure for Problem 13.8.a.

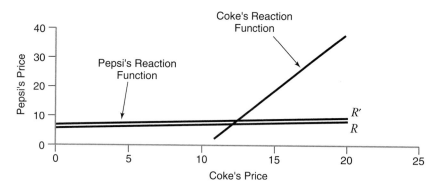

Figure for Problem 13.8.b.

At this quantity, United will charge a price $P_U = 700 - 0.5(690) = 355$.

(c) American's demand can be rewritten as

$$2P_A = (1000 + P_U) - Q_A$$
$$P_A = (500 + 0.5P_U) - 0.5Q_A.$$

Setting $MR = MC$ implies

$$(500 + 0.5P_U) - Q_A = 10$$
$$Q_A = 490 + 0.5P_U.$$

At this quantity, American will charge a price

$$P_A = (500 + 0.5P_U) - 0.5(490 + 0.5P_U)$$
$$P_A = 255 + 0.25P_U.$$

Since the firms have identical marginal cost and symmetric demand curves, United's price reaction function will be $P_U = 255 + 0.25\, P_A$.

d) The Bertrand equilibrium will occur where these price reaction functions intersect. Substituting the expression for P_U into the expression for P_A implies

$$P_A = 255 + 0.25(255 + 0.25P_A)$$
$$P_A = 340.$$

Substituting into the expression for P_U implies $P_A = 340$. So, in the Bertrand equilibrium, each firm charges a price of 340 and attracts a quantity of 660.

CHAPTER 14

14.1.

		Pepsi	
		Aggressive	**Restrained**
Coke	**Aggressive**	$100, $80	$170, $40
	Restrained	$80, $140	$120, $100

In this game, "Aggressive" is a dominant strategy for both firms. Thus, the Nash equilibrium strategy for both firms is to choose "Aggressive."

This game is an example of the prisoners' dilemma. In this game both players have a dominant strategy that leads to an outcome that does not maximize the collective payoffs of the players in the game. If both players chose the "Restrained" strategy, then both players would increase their profits and the collective payoff would be maximized.

14.4.

		Nokia	
		Enter	**Do Not Enter**
Alcatel	**Enter**	−1000, −1000	500, 0
	Do Not Enter	0, 500	0, 0

This game has two Nash equilibria corresponding to the outcomes where one firm chooses "Enter" and the other firm chooses "Do Not Enter." Thus, Alcatel choosing "Enter" and Nokia choosing "Do Not Enter" is a Nash equilibrium, and Alcatel choosing "Do Not Enter" and Nokia choosing "Enter" is a Nash equilibrium.

14.6.

		Boeing	
		P = $5M	**P = $10M**
Airbus	**P = $5M**	30, 30	270, 0
	P = $10M	0, 270	50, 50

a) In this game both players have a dominant strategy to choose "P = $5M." Thus, the Nash equilibrium outcome occurs when Airbus chooses "P = $5M" and Boeing chooses "P = $5M."

b) Airbus's statement implies that it will play "P = $10M" in this quarter and all subsequent quarters as long as Boeing also plays "P = $10M." However, if Boeing ever plays "P = $5M," Airbus will play "P = $5M" in all future quarters.

From Boeing's perspective, if it chooses to continue to play "P = $10M," then in every quarter it will receive a payoff of 50. If it chooses to lower its price to "P = $5M," then in the first quarter it will receive 270. In all subsequent quarters the best Boeing will be able to do is play "P = $5M," as will Airbus, and Boeing will receive 30. Thus, Boeing's two possible payoff streams look like

Boeing	P = $5M	270	30	30	. . . .	30
	P = $10M	50	50	50	. . . .	50

Boeing values a stream of payoffs of $1 starting next quarter as a payoff of $40 in the first quarter. Therefore, Boeing values the two payoff streams as

P = $5M	270 + 40(30) = 1470
P = $10M	50 + 40(50) = 2,050

Therefore, the value of "P = $10M" in current dollars is greater, so Boeing should select "P = $10M" in this quarter and all subsequent quarters.

(c) Now Boeing values the payoff stream differently. In the current situation, Boeing values a stream of payoffs of $1 starting next year as equivalent to $10 received immediately. Thus, Boeing will now value this payoff stream as

$P = \$5M$	$270 + 10(30) = 570$
$P = \$10M$	$50 + 10(50) = 550$

Now "$P = \$5M$" has a higher value in current dollars than "$P = \$10M$." Thus, Boeing should select "$P = \$5M$" this year, receive the high payoff in the current year, and select "$P = \$5M$" thereafter, receiving a stream of payoffs of 30 each year.

14.7.

		Firm 2	
		Aggressive	Passive
Firm 1	**Aggressive**	25, 9	33, 10
	Passive	30, 13	36, 12

a) If both firms choose simultaneously, then Firm 1 will choose its dominant strategy, "Passive." Firm 2, knowing Firm 1 has a dominant strategy, will assume Firm 1 will play this strategy and choose "Aggressive," the best strategy given Firm 1's likely choice. The Nash equilibrium, therefore, has Firm 1 selecting "Passive" and Firm 2 selecting "Aggressive."
b) If Firm 1 can choose first, then if it chooses "Aggressive" Firm 2 will choose "Passive" and Firm 1 will receive 33. If Firm 1 instead chooses "Passive," then Firm 2 will select "Aggressive" and Firm 1 will receive a payoff of 30. Therefore, if Firm 1 can move first, it does best to select "Aggressive" in which case Firm 2 will select its best response "Passive" earning Firm 1 a payoff of 33 and Firm 2 a payoff of 10.

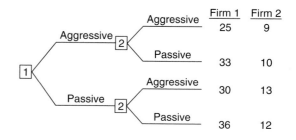

CHAPTER 15

15.1. a) See figure.
b)
$$EV = 0.2(-10) + 0.5(0) + 0.3(20)$$
$$EV = 4.0.$$

c) Variance $= 0.2(-10 - 4)^2 + 0.5(0 - 4)^2 + 0.3(20 - 4)^2$
 Variance $= 124.$

$$\text{Standard deviation} = \sqrt{\text{Variance}}$$
$$\text{Standard deviation} = \sqrt{124}$$
$$\text{Standard deviation} = 11.14$$

15.3. a) See figure.
b)
$$EV = 0.75(0) + 0.25(200)$$
$$EV = 50.$$

c) Expected Utility $= 0.75\sqrt{50(0)} + 0.25\sqrt{50(200)}$
 Expected Utility $= 25.$

d)
$$\text{Utility} = \sqrt{50(50)}$$
$$\text{Utility} = 50$$

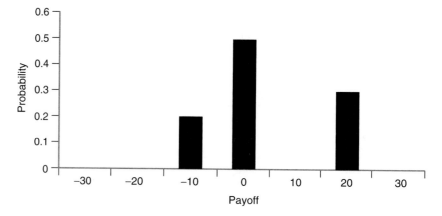

Figure for Problem 15.1.a.

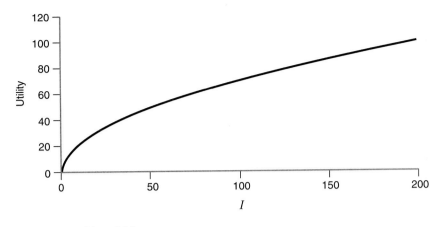

Figure for Problem 15.3.a.

The utility associated with the certain payoff of 50 is higher than the expected utility of the lottery with the same expected payoff. Thus, with this utility function the decision maker is risk averse, since the decision maker prefers the sure thing to a lottery with the same expected payoff.

15.6. If your utility function were $U = \sqrt{I}$, then the risk premium associated with Lottery A would be

$$0.90\sqrt{0} + 0.10\sqrt{400} = \sqrt{40 - RP_A}$$
$$\sqrt{40 - RP_A} = 2$$
$$40 - RP_A = 4$$
$$RP_A = 36.$$

The risk premium associated with Lottery B would be

$$0.50\sqrt{30} + 0.50\sqrt{50} = \sqrt{40 - RP_B}$$
$$\sqrt{40 - RP_B} = 6.27$$
$$40 - RP_B = 39.36$$
$$RP_B = 0.64.$$

Lottery A has a risk premium of 36 and Lottery B has a risk premium of 0.64.

15.8. a)

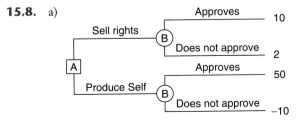

b) The expected payoff for "Sell rights" is $0.20(10) + 0.80(2) = 3.60$. The expected payoff for "Produce yourself"

is $0.20(50) + 0.80(-10) = 2.0$. Therefore, the company should sell the rights with an expected payoff of 3.60.

15.9. If the test indicates the FDA will approve, the company will choose "Produce yourself" and earn a payoff of 50. If the test indicates the FDA will not approve, then the company will choose "Sell the rights" and earn 2. The expected payoff from conducting the costless test is therefore $0.20(50) + 0.80(2) = 11.60$.

The VPI is the difference between the expected payoff with the test and the expected payoff without the test. Thus, VPI $= 11.60 - 3.60 = 8.00$.

CHAPTER 16

16.1. a) In equilibrium we must have quantity supplied equal to quantity demanded in both the butter and margarine markets. This implies in equilibrium we will have

$$Q_M^d = Q_M^s$$
$$Q_B^d = Q_B^s.$$

Substituting in the given curves implies

$$20 - 2P_M + P_B = 2P_M$$
$$60 - 6P_B + 4P_M = 3P_B.$$

Solving for P_B in the first equation and substituting into the second equation imply

$$60 + 4P_M = 9(4P_M - 20)$$
$$60 + 4P_M = 36P_M - 180$$
$$P_M = 7.5.$$

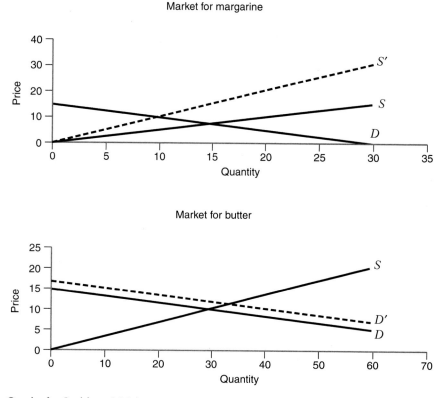

Graphs for Problem 16.1.b.

When $P_M = 7.5$, $P_B = 10$. At these prices, $Q_M = 15$ and $Q_B = 30$.

b) When the supply curve for margarine shifts to $Q_M^s = P_M$, we have

$$20 - 2P_M + P_B = P_M$$
$$60 - 6P_B + 4P_M = 3P_B.$$

Solving the first equation for P_B and substituting into the second equation implies

$$60 + 4P_M = 9(3P_M - 20)$$
$$60 + 4P_M = 27P_M - 180$$
$$P_M = 10.43.$$

When $P_M = 10.43$, $P_B = 11.30$. At these prices, $Q_M = 10.43$ and $Q_B = 33.91$. The increase in the price of vegetable oil increases the price of margarine and decreases the quantity of margarine consumed. As consumers switch to butter, the price of butter rises and the quantity of butter consumed goes up.

The price of butter rises when the price of vegetable oil rises because butter and margarine are substitutes. The effects can be seen in the graphs.

Because the goods are substitutes, when the supply of margarine declines raising the price of margarine, consumers substitute butter for margarine, increasing demand for butter and raising both the equilibrium price and quantity of butter.

16.4. First, in equilibrium, the quantity supplied of beer and quiche must equal the quantity demanded of beer and quiche. This implies

$$w^{1/6}r^{5/6} = \frac{20I_W + 90I_H}{X}$$
$$w^{3/4}r^{1/4} = \frac{80I_W + 10I_H}{Y}.$$

Now, since each hunk supplies 100 units of labor and no units of capital and each wimp supplies 10 units of capital and no units of labor,

$$I_W(w, r) = 10r$$
$$I_H(w, r) = 100w.$$

Substituting these into the conditions above implies

$$w^{1/6}r^{5/6} = \frac{200r + 9000w}{X}$$
$$w^{3/4}r^{1/4} = \frac{800r + 1000w}{Y}.$$

Second, in equilibrium, the quantity supplied of labor and capital must equal the quantity demanded of labor and capital. Since there are 100 households of each type, we will have $L = 100(100) = 10,000$ and $K = 100(10) = 1,000$. Setting these equal to demand implies

$$10,000 = \frac{X}{6}\left(\frac{r}{w}\right)^{5/6} + \frac{3Y}{4}\left(\frac{r}{w}\right)^{1/4}$$

$$1,000 = \frac{5X}{6}\left(\frac{w}{r}\right)^{1/6} + \frac{Y}{4}\left(\frac{w}{r}\right)^{3/4}.$$

16.6. a) See figure.
b) To be economically efficient, the *MRS* for the two consumers must be equal. At this allocation we have

$$MRS_{x,y}^{\text{Ron}} = \frac{x_r}{y_r} = \frac{800}{800} = 1$$

$$MRS_{x,y}^{\text{David}} = \frac{2x_d}{y_d} = \frac{2(200)}{4200} = \frac{2}{21}.$$

Since the *MRS* for the two consumers are not equal, the current allocation is not economically efficient.
c) At the current allocation, Ron is willing to trade one Pokémon card for one baseball card and David is willing to trade 2 Pokémon cards for 21 baseball cards. If David gives Ron 21 baseball cards in exchange for 10 Pokémon cards, both consumers will be better off.

David was willing to give up 21 baseball cards for 2 Pokémon cards, and with this trade he receives 10 Pokémon cards. Thus, David is better off. Ron was willing to trade one Pokémon card for one baseball card. With this trade, he receives 21 baseball cards in exchange for his 10 Pokémon cards. Thus, Ron is better off, too.

16.8. a) See figure.
b) To satisfy input efficiency we must have

$$MRTS_{l,k}^1 = MRTS_{l,k}^2$$

$$\frac{MP_l^1}{MP_k^1} = \frac{MP_l^2}{MP_k^2}.$$

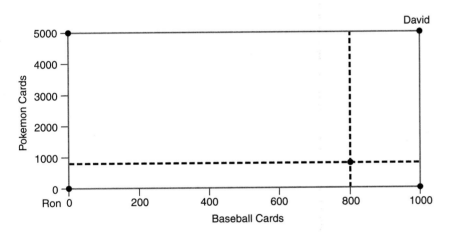

Figure for Problem 16.6.a.

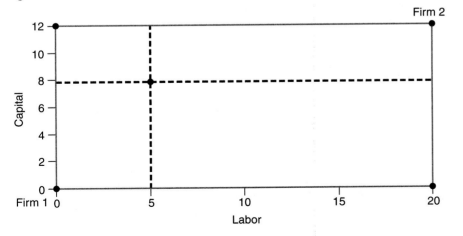

Figure for Problem 16.8.a.

Substituting in the given information implies

$$\frac{20}{40} \neq \frac{60}{30}$$

$$0.5 \neq 2.$$

Since the *MRTS* are not equal, the current allocation of inputs is not economically efficient.

At the current allocation, Firm 1 can trade 2 units of labor for 1 unit of capital without changing output. By giving up one unit of labor to receive one unit of capital the firm can increase its output. At the current allocation Firm 2 can trade two units of capital for one unit of labor without affecting output. By giving up only one unit of capital in exchange for one unit of labor, Firm 2 can increase its output. Therefore, by reallocating one unit of capital from Firm 2 to Firm 1 and one unit of labor, from Firm 1 to Firm 2, both firms can produce more output.

16.10. a) From the information given in the table, the United States has an absolute advantage in the production of watches because the production of one watch takes only 50 hours per watch in the United States, compared with 60 hours per watch in Switzerland.

The United States also has an absolute advantage in the production of automobiles, since the United States spends only 5 hours per auto produced, compared with 20 hours per auto in Switzerland.

b) In the United States the opportunity cost of producing one watch is 10 autos. In Switzerland the opportunity cost of producing one watch is 3 autos. Because the opportunity cost is lower for Switzerland than the United States,

Switzerland has a comparative advantage in the production of watches.

In the United States the opportunity cost of producing one auto is one-tenth of a watch. In Switzerland, the opportunity cost of producing one auto is one-third of a watch. Because the opportunity cost is lower for the United States, the United States has a comparative advantage in the production of autos.

CHAPTER 17

17.1. If the government were to set an emissions standard allowing zero pollution, this standard would not be socially efficient. By setting the standard at zero, the government could reduce pollution by preventing polluting industries from producing goods that society values. By setting the standard at zero, however, the government will also eliminate the benefits to society from production of these goods. In general, the social benefits from producing will likely exceed the social costs up to some nonzero level of production (pollution) implying the socially efficient level of production is nonzero.

17.2. Education is a good that might generate positive external benefits. For example, when an individual furthers her education, she benefits directly in terms of higher income. In addition, this individual, because of her increased education, might be able to develop a new technology that benefits all of society. Thus, while the education helped the individual, by allowing the development of the new technology (because she's smarter!), many people benefitted from her education.

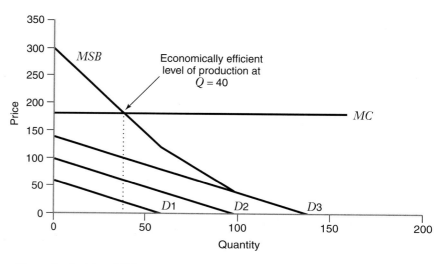

Figure for Problem 17.8.

To induce the market to perform more efficiently, the government would like to entice more individuals to further their education because education generates positive externalities. The government could do this by providing grants, low interest student loans, and so on.

17.5. a) In Figure 17.5, the deadweight loss is area *ABG*. This is deadweight loss because for every vehicle beyond the optimum, Q_4, the marginal social cost exceeds the marginal benefit. Area *ABG* is approximately (assuming the demand and MPC curves are nearly straight lines over this part of the graph) $0.5(Q_5 - Q_4)(8 - 5) = 1.5(Q_5 - Q_4)$.

b) The socially efficient traffic volume occurs where the marginal social cost curve intersects the marginal benefit curve. In Figure 17.5 this occurs at Q_4. At Q_4, the marginal benefit is $5.75 and the marginal private cost is $4.00. To achieve the social optimum the toll should be set so that the marginal benefit equals the marginal private cost plus the toll, effectively forcing the driver to take into account the external cost of entering the highway. At Q_4, this is $5.75 - $4.00 = $1.75.

The toll is not $3.00 because the toll should be set to force the driver at Q_4 to observe the external costs imposed by entering the highway. By setting the toll at $3.00, the difference between the *MPC* and *MB* at Q_5, the toll would be

set to force the driver at Q_4 to observe the external costs imposed from the driver at Q_5 entering the highway. But this cost is unimportant because at the optimum the driver at Q_5 will not be on the highway. The $3.00 toll would create a level of traffic below the social optimum.

c) If the toll authority sets a toll of $1.75, it will earn revenue equal to the toll multiplied by the number of drivers. In this case, revenue will be $1.75 Q_4.

17.8. a) See figure.

The economically efficient level of output occurs where $MSB = MC$. Since this occurs where all three consumers are in the market we have

$$(60 - Q) + (100 - Q) + (140 - Q) = 180$$
$$3Q = 120$$
$$Q = 40$$

17.9. If the good is not provided at all, the deadweight loss would be the area under the demand curve (the *MSB* curve) and above the marginal cost curve, or $0.5(300 - 180)(40) = 2400$. This is a deadweight loss because it measures the potential net economic benefits that would disappear if the good were not offered.

Glossary

Absolute advantage. One country has an absolute advantage over another country in the production of a good X if production of one unit of X in the first country requires fewer units of a scarce input (e.g., labor) than it does in the second country.

Adverse selection. A phenomenon whereby an increase in the insurance premium increases the overall riskiness of the pool of individuals who buy an insurance policy.

Allocation of goods and inputs. A pattern of consumption and input usage that might arise in a general equilibrium in an economy.

Asymmetric information. Situations in which one party knows more about its own actions or characteristics than another party.

Average fixed cost (*AFC*). Total fixed cost per unit of output (i.e., $AFC = TFC/Q$.)

Average nonsunk cost. The sum of average variable cost plus average nonsunk fixed cost.

Average product of labor. The average amount of output per unit of labor.

Average revenue. Total revenue per unit of output that is, the ratio of total revenue to quantity.

Average variable cost (*AVC*). Total variable cost per unit of output, i.e., $AVC = TVC/Q$.

Average value. The total of the dependent variable divided by the independent variable.

Backward induction. A procedure for solving a sequential-move game by starting at the end of the game tree, and for each decision point, finding the optimal decision for the player at that point.

Bandwagon effect. A positive network externality that refers to the increase in the quantity of a good that is demanded as more consumers buy the good.

Barriers to entry. Factors that allow an incumbent firm to earn positive economic profits, while at the same time making it unprofitable for new firms to enter the industry.

Basket. Sometimes called a bundle; a combination of goods and services that an individual might consume.

Block tariff. A block tariff is a form of second-degree price discrimination in which the consumer pays one price for units consumed in the first block of output (up to a given quantity), and a different (usually lower) price for any additional units consumed in the second block.

Budget constraint. The set of baskets that the consumer may purchase given the limited amount of income. All points on or inside the budget line satisfy the budget constraint.

Budget line. The set of baskets that the consumer may purchase when he spends all of his available income.

Bundling. A type of tie-in sale in which a firm requires customers who buy one of its products also to buy another of its products.

Capital-saving technological process. Technological process that causes the marginal product of labor to increase more rapidly than the marginal product of capital.

Capital–labor ratio. The ratio of the quantity of capital to the quantity of labor.

Cardinal ranking. A quantitative measure of the intensity of a preference for one basket over another.

Cartel. A group of producers that collusively determine the price and output in a market.

Choke price. The price at which quantity demanded falls to 0.

Coase theorem. Regardless of how property rights are assigned with an externality, the allocation of resources will be efficient when the parties can costlessly bargain with each other.

Cobb–Douglas production function. A production function of the form $Q = AL^{\alpha}K^{\beta}$, where Q is the quantity of output from L units of labor and K units of capital, and A, α, and β are positive constants.

Cobb–Douglas utility function. A function of the form $U = Ax^{\alpha}y^{\beta}$ where U measures the consumer's utility from x units of one good and y units of another good. A, α, and β are positive constants.

Common property. A resource, such as a public park, a highway, or the Internet, that anyone can access.

Common values. A situation in which an item being sold in an auction has the same intrinsic value to all buyers, but no buyer knows exactly what that value is.

Comparative advantage. One country has a comparative advantage over another country in the production of good X if the opportunity cost of producing an additional unit of good X—expressed in terms of forgone units of some other good Y—is lower in the first country than it is in the second country.

Comparative statics. Analysis used to examine how a change in some exogenous variable will affect the level of some endogenous variable in an economic system.

Compensating variation. A measure of how much money a consumer would be willing to give up *after* a reduction in the price of a good to make her just as well off as she was *before* the price decrease.

Composite good. A good that represents the collective expenditures on every other good except the commodity being considered.

Constant elasticity cost function. A cost function that specifies a multiplicative relationship between total cost, output, and input prices.

Constant elasticity demand curve. A specific demand curve whose formula is $Q = aP^{-b}$ where a and b are positive constants. The term b is the price elasticity of demand along this curve.

Constant elasticity of substitution (CES) production function. A production that includes linear production function, fixed proportions production function, and Cobb–Douglas production function as special cases. It has the form $Q = [aL^{\frac{\sigma-1}{\sigma}} + bK^{\frac{\sigma-1}{\sigma}}]^{\frac{\sigma}{\sigma-1}}$, where a, b, and σ are positive constants, and σ is the elasticity of substitution.

Constant returns to scale. A proportionate increase in all input quantities simultaneously results in the same percentage increase in output.

Constant-cost industry. An industry in which the increase or decrease of industry output does not affect the prices of inputs.

Constrained optimization. An analytical tool for making the best (optimal) choice, taking into account any possible limitations or restrictions on the choices.

Constraints. The restrictions or limits imposed on a decision maker in a constrained optimization problem.

Consumer preferences. Indications of how a consumer would rank (compare the desirability of) any two possible baskets, assuming the baskets were available to the consumer at no cost.

Consumer surplus. The difference between the maximum amount a consumer is willing to pay for a good and the amount he must actually pay when he purchases it.

Contract curve. A curve that shows all the allocations of goods in the Edgeworth box that are economically efficient.

Corner point. A corner point solution to the consumer's optimal choice problem refers to an optimum at which the budget line may not be tangent to an indifference curve. For example, this may occur if the optimal basket is one in which some good is not being consumed at all.

Cost driver. A factor that influences or "drives" total or average costs.

Cost-minimization problem. The problem of finding the input combination that minimizes a firm's total cost of producing a particular level of output.

Cost-minimizing firm. A firm that seeks to minimize the cost of producing a given amount of output.

Cournot equilibrium. An equilibrium in an oligopoly market in which each firm chooses a profit-maximizing output given the output chosen by other firms.

Cross-price elasticity of demand for good i with respect to the price of good j. A measure of the percentage change of the quantity of good i demanded with respect to a one percent change in the price of good j.

Deadweight loss. A reduction in net economic benefits resulting from an inefficient allocation of resources.

Deadweight loss due to monopoly. The difference between the net economic benefit that would arise if the market were perfectly competitive and the net economic benefit attained at the monopoly equilibrium.

Decision tree. A diagram that describes the options available to a decision maker as well as the risky events that can occur at each point in time.

Decreasing-cost industry. An industry in which increases in industry output decreases the prices of some or all inputs.

Decreasing returns to scale. A proportionate increase in all input quantities results in a less than proportionate increase in output.

Demand complements. Two goods related in such a way that if the price of one increases, demand for the other decreases.

Demand substitutes. Two goods related in such a way that if the price of one increases, demand for the other increases.

Derivative. A function describing the slope (or rate of change) of the dependent variable as the independent variable changes at any point on the function.

Derived demand. Demand for a good that is derived from the production and sale of other goods.

Differentiated products oligopoly markets. Markets in which a small number of firms sell products that are substitutes for each other but also differ from each other in significant ways, including attributes, performance, packaging, and image.

Diminishing marginal rate of substitution. Consumer preferences exhibit a diminishing marginal rate of substitution of x for y if the $MRS_{x,y}$ diminishes as the consumption of x increases along an indifference curve.

Diminishing marginal rate of technical substitution. A production function exhibits diminishing marginal rate of technical substitution of labor (L) for capital (K) if $MRTS_{L,K}$ diminishes as the quantity of labor increases along an isoquant.

Diminishing marginal returns to labor. The region along the total product function in which output rises with additional labor but at a decreasing rate.

Diminishing total returns to labor. The region along the total product function where output decreases with additional labor.

Direct demand. Demand for a good that comes from the desire of buyers to directly consume the good itself.

Diseconomies of scale. A range of production in which average cost increases as output goes up.

Dominant firm markets. Markets in which one firm possesses a large share of the market, but competes against numerous small firms, each offering identical products.

Dominant strategy. A strategy that is better than any other a player might choose, no matter what strategy the other player follows.

Dominated strategy. A strategy is dominated when the player has another strategy that gives a higher payoff no matter what the other player does.

Duopoly market. A market in which there are just two firms.

Durable goods. Goods, such as automobiles or airplanes, that provide valuable services over many years.

Dutch descending auction. An auction in which the seller of the object announces a bid, which is then lowered until a buyer announces a desire to buy the item at that price.

Economic costs. The sum of the firm's explicit costs and implicit costs.

Economic profit. The difference between a firm's sales revenue and the totality of its economic costs, including all relevant opportunity costs.

Economic region of production. The region where the isoquants are downward sloping.

Economic rent. The economic return that is attributable to extraordinarily productive inputs whose supply is scarce. The economic rent of a fixed input is the difference between the maximum amount that firms would be willing to pay to acquire the services of the fixed input and the minimum amount that they have to pay to hire the input.

Economically efficient. An allocation of goods and inputs in an economy is economically efficient if there is no other feasible allocation of goods and inputs that would make some consumers better off without hurting other consumers.

Economically inefficient. An allocation of goods and inputs is economically inefficient if there is an alternative feasible allocation of goods and inputs that would make all consumers better off as compared with the initial allocation.

Economies of experience. Cost advantages that result from accumulated experience, or as it is sometimes called, *learning-by-doing*.

Economies of scale. A situation in which average cost decreases as output goes up.

Economies of scope. A situation in which the total cost of producing given quantities of two goods in the same firm is less than the total cost of producing those quantities in two single-product firms.

Edgeworth box for inputs. The Edgeworth box that shows how a fixed quantity of labor and capital can be divided among the production of two different goods.

Edgeworth box. A graphic showing all of the possible allocations of goods that are possible in a two-good economy, given the total available supply of such goods.

Elastic demand. Price elasticity between -1 and $-\infty$.

Elasticity of substitution. A measure of how easy it is for the firm to substitute labor for capital. It is equal to the percentage change in the capital–labor ratio for every 1 percent change in the marginal rate of technical substitution of capital for labor as we move along an isoquant.

Emissions fee. A tax imposed on pollution that is released into the environment.

Emissions standard. A governmental limit on the amount of pollution that may be emitted.

Endogenous variable. A variable whose value is determined within the economic system being studied.

Engel curve. A curve that relates the amount of a commodity purchased to the level of income, holding constant the prices of all goods.

English auction. An auction in which participants cry out their bids, and each participant can increase his bid until the auction ends with the highest bidder winning the object being sold.

Equal access to resources. All firms—those currently in the industry, as well as prospective entrants—have access to the same technology and inputs. This is one of the characteristics of a perfectly competitive industry.

Equilibrium. A state or condition that will continue indefinitely as long as factors exogenous to the system remain unchanged.

Equivalent variation. A measure of how much money we would have to give a consumer *before* a price reduction to keep her as well off as she would be *after* the price change.

Excess demand. A situation in which the quantity demanded at a given price exceeds the quantity supplied.

Excess supply. A situation in which the quantity supplied at a given price exceeds the quantity demanded.

Exchange efficiency. When a fixed stock of consumption goods cannot be reallocated among consumers in an economy without making at least some consumers worse off. We have inefficiency in exchange when we can reallocate a fixed basket of consump-

tion goods among consumers in a way that makes all consumers better off.

Exclusive good. A good to which consumers may be denied access.

Exogenous variable. A variable whose value is taken as given in the analysis of an economic system.

Expansion path. A line that connects the cost-minimizing input combinations as the quantity of output, Q, varies, holding input prices constant.

Expected utility. The expected value of the utility levels that the decision maker receives from the payoffs in a lottery.

Expected value. A measure of the average payoff that a lottery will generate.

Expenditure minimization problem. Consumer choice between goods that will minimize total spending while achieving a given level of utility.

Experience curve. A relationship between average variable cost and cumulative production volume. It is used to describe the economies of experience.

Experience elasticity. The percentage change in average variable cost for every one percent increase in cumulative volume.

Explicit costs. Costs that involve a direct monetary outlay.

Externality. The effect that an action of any decision maker has on the well-being of other consumers or producers, beyond the effects transmitted by changes in prices.

Factors of production. Resources that are used to produce a good.

Fairly priced insurance policy. An insurance policy in which the insurance premium is equal to the expected value of the promised insurance payment.

First fundamental theorem of welfare economics. This theorem tells us that the allocation of goods and inputs that arises in a general competitive equilibrium is economically efficient. That is, given the resources available to the economy, there is no other feasible allocation of goods and inputs that could simultaneously make all consumers better off.

First-degree price discrimination. A seller engages in first-degree price discrimination by attempting to price each unit at the consumer's reservation price (that is, the consumer's maximum willingness to pay for that unit).

First-price sealed-bid auction. An auction in which each bidder submits one bid, not knowing the other bids. The highest bidder wins the object and pays a price equal to his or her bid.

Fixed proportions production function. A production function where the inputs must be combined in a constant ratio to one another.

Fragmented industry. An industry that consists of many small buyers and sellers. This is one of the characteristics of a perfectly competitive industry.

Free entry. An industry is characterized by free entry when any potential entrant has access to the same technology and inputs that existing firms have.

Free rider. A consumer or producer who does not pay for a nonexclusive good, anticipating that others will pay.

Game tree. A diagram that shows the different strategies that each player can follow in the game and the order in which those strategies get chosen.

General equilibrium analysis. An analysis that determines the equilibrium prices and quantities in more than one market simultaneously.

Giffen good. A good so strongly inferior that the income effect outweighs the substitution effect, resulting in an upward-sloping demand curve over some region of prices.

Homogeneous products oligopoly markets. Markets in which a small number of firms sell products that have virtually the same attributes, performance characteristics, image, and (ultimately) price.

Horizontal differentiation. Two products, A and B, are horizontally differentiated when, at equal prices, some consumers view B as a poor substitute for A and thus will continue to buy A even when A's price is higher than B's.

Implicit costs. Costs that do not involve outlays of cash.

Import quota. An upper limit on the amount of a good that may be imported into a country.

Import tariff. A tax imposed on a good that is imported into a country.

Incidence of a tax. A measure of the effect of a tax on the prices consumers pay and sellers receive in a market.

Income consumption curve. The set of utility-maximizing baskets as income varies (and prices are held constant).

Income effect. The change in the amount of a good that a consumer would buy as purchasing power changes, holding all prices constant.

Income elasticity of demand. A measure of the rate of percentage change of quantity demanded with respect to income, holding all prices and other determinants of demand constant.

Increasing marginal returns to labor. The region along the total product function where output rises with additional labor at an increasing rate.

Increasing returns to scale. A proportionate increase in all input quantities results in a greater than proportionate increase in output.

Increasing-cost industry. An industry in which increases in industry output increases the prices of inputs.

Indifference curve. Line connecting a set of consumption baskets that yield the same level of satisfaction to the consumer.

Indivisible input. An input that is available only in a certain minimum size; its quantity cannot be scaled down as the firm's output goes to zero.

Industry-specific inputs. Scarce inputs that are used only by firms in an industry and not by other industries in the economy.

Inelastic Demand. Price elasticity between 0 and -1.

Inferior good. A good that a consumer wants less of as income rises.

Inferior input. An input whose cost-minimizing quantity decreases as the firm produces more output.

Input contract curve. The curve that shows all of the input allocations that satisfy the condition of input efficiency.

Input demand curve. The relationship between the cost-minimizing quantity of an input and the price of that input.

Input efficiency. When a fixed stock of inputs cannot be reallocated among firms in an economy without reducing the output of at least one of the goods that is produced in the economy. In other words, we have input efficiency when an expansion of output in one industry necessitates a reduction in output in another industry. We have input inefficiency when we can reallocate a fixed stock of inputs among firms so that we can simultaneously expand the output of all of the goods produced in the economy.

Inputs. Resources, such as labor, capital equipment, and raw materials, that are combined to produce finished goods.

Interior optimum. An optimal basket at which a consumer will be purchasing positive amounts of all commodities and at which the budget line is tangent to an indifference curve.

Inverse demand curve. An equation for the demand curve that expresses price as a function of quantity.

Inverse elasticity pricing rule (IEPR). The IEPR states that the markup between the profit-maximizing price and marginal cost, expressed as a percentage of price, is equal to minus the inverse of the price elasticity of demand.

Isocost line. The set of combinations of labor and capital that yield the same total cost for the firm.

Isoquant. An isoquant shows all of the combinations of labor and capital that can produce a given level of output.

Labor requirements function. This function tells us the minimum amount of labor that is required to produce a given amount of output.

Labor-saving technological progress. Technological progress that causes the marginal product of capital to increase more rapidly than the marginal product of labor.

Law of demand. The inverse relationship between the price of a good and the quantity demanded, when we hold all other factors that influence demand fixed.

Law of diminishing marginal returns. Principle that as the usage of one input increases, the quantities of other inputs being held fixed, a point will be reached beyond which the marginal product of the variable input will decrease.

Law of one price. All transactions between buyers and sellers occur at a single, common market price.

Law of supply. The positive relationship between price and quantity supplied, holding other factors that influence supply constant.

Legal barriers to entry. Barriers to entry that exist when an incumbent firm is legally protected against competition.

Lerner Index of market power. A measure of monopoly power suggested by the economist Abba Lerner. It equals the percentage markup of price over marginal cost, $(P - MC)/P$.

Limit pricing. A strategy whereby the dominant firm keeps its price below the level that maximizes its current profit in order to reduce the rate of entry by the fringe.

Linear demand curve. A specific demand curve whose formula is $Q = a - bP$.

Linear production function. A production function of the form $Q = aL + bK$, where a and b are positive constants.

Log-linear demand curve. Another expression for constant elasticity demand curve.

Long run. The period of time that is long enough for the firm to vary the quantities of all of its inputs as much as it desires.

Long-run average cost. The firm's total cost per unit of output. It equals long-run total cost divided by Q (i.e., $AC(Q) = TC(Q)/Q$).

Long-run demand curve. The demand curve that pertains to the period of time in which consumers can fully adjust their purchase decisions to changes in price.

Long-run marginal cost. The rate at which long-run total cost changes with respect to output, i.e., $MC(Q) = TC/\Delta Q$.

Long-run market supply curve (or long-run industry supply curve). Indicates total quantity of output that will be supplied at various market prices, assuming that all long-run adjustments (plant size, new entry) take place.

Long-run perfectly competitive equilibrium. A long-run perfectly competitive equilibrium occurs at a price at which supply equals demand, established firms have no incentive to exit, and prospective firms have no incentive to enter the industry.

Long-run supply curve. The supply curve that pertains to the period of time in which producers can fully adjust their supply decisions to changes in price.

Long-run total cost curve. Curve that shows how minimized total cost varies with output, holding input prices fixed.

Lottery. Any event for which the outcome is uncertain.

Managerial diseconomies. A situation in which a given percentage increase in output forces the firm to increase its spending on the services of managers by more than this percentage.

Marginal expenditure on labor. The rate at which the firm's total cost goes up, per unit of labor, as it hires more labor.

Marginal product of labor. The rate at which total output changes as the quantity of labor the firm uses is changed.

Marginal rate of substitution (MRS). The rate at which the consumer will give up one good (y) to get more of another (x), holding the level of utility constant. On a graph with x on the horizontal axis and y on the vertical axis, the $MRS_{x,y}$ at any basket is the negative of the slope of the indifference curve at that basket.

Marginal rate of technical substitution of labor for capital. The rate at which the quantity of capital can be reduced for every one unit increase in the quantity of labor, holding the quantity of output constant.

Marginal rate of transformation of x for y. The absolute value of the slope of the production possibilities frontier (with the quantity of good x measured on the horizontal axis and the quantity of y measured on the vertical axis). The marginal rate of transformation of x for y tells us the marginal opportunity cost of good x in terms of forgone units of good y.

Marginal revenue. The rate at which total revenue changes with respect to output.

Marginal revenue product of labor. The additional revenue that the firm gets when it employs an additional unit of labor.

Marginal utility. The rate at which total utility changes as the level of consumption rises.

Marginal value. The *change* in a dependent variable associated with a one-unit *change* in an independent variable.

Market demand curve. A curve that shows us the quantity of goods that consumers are willing to buy at different prices.

Market power. An individual economic agent has market power if it can affect the price that prevails in the market.

Market supply curve. A curve that shows us the total quantity of goods that their suppliers are willing to sell at different prices.

Minimum efficient scale (MES). The smallest quantity at which the long run average cost curve attains its minimum point.

Mixed strategy. A choice among two or more pure strategies according to prespecified probabilities.

Monopolistic competition. A market in which many firms produce differentiated products that are sold to many buyers.

Monopoly market. A market consisting of a single seller and many buyers.

Monopsony market. A market consisting of a singer buyer and many sellers.

Moral hazard. A phenomenon whereby an insured party exercises less care than he or she would in the absence of insurance.

Multiplant marginal cost curve. The horizontal summation of the marginal cost curves of individual plants.

Nash equilibrium. A situation in which each player chooses a strategy that gives it the highest payoff, given the strategies chosen by the other players in the game.

Natural monopoly. A market in which, for any relevant level of industry output, the total cost incurred by a single firm producing that output is less than the combined total cost that two or more firms would incur if they divided that output among themselves.

Network externalities. A demand characteristic present when the amount of a good demanded by one consumer depends on the number of other consumers who have purchased the good.

Neutral technological process. Technological progress which decreases the amounts of labor and capital needed to produce a given output, without affecting the marginal rate of technical substitution of labor for capital.

Nonexclusive good. A good that, once produced, is accessible to all consumers; no one can be excluded from consuming such a good after it is produced.

Nonlinear outlay schedule. An expenditure schedule in which the average outlay (expenditure) changes with the number of units purchased.

Nonrival good. When a given amount of a nonrival good is produced, consumption by one person does not reduce the quantity that can be consumed by others.

Nonsunk cost. A cost that is incurred only if a particular decision is made.

Nonsunk fixed cost. Fixed costs that must be incurred for a firm to produce any output, but that do not have to be incurred if the firm produces no output.

Normal good. A good that a consumer wants more of as income rises.

Normal input. An input whose cost-minimizing quantity increases as the firm produces more output.

Normative analysis. Analysis that typically focuses on issues of social welfare, examining what will enhance or detract from the common good.

Objective function. The relationship that a decision maker seeks to maximize or minimize.

Opportunity cost. The value of the next best alternative that is forgone when another alternative is chosen.

Optimal choice. Consumer choice of a basket of goods that (1) maximizes satisfaction (utility) while (2) allowing him to live within his budget constraint.

Ordinal ranking. Ranking that states whether a consumer likes one basket more than another, but does not contain quantitative information about the intensity of that preference.

Output elasticity of total cost. The percentage change in total cost per one percent change in output.

Output-insensitive cost. A cost that does not vary with the output of the firm. Equivalent to fixed cost.

Output-sensitive cost. A cost that goes up or down as the firm increases or decreases its output. Equivalent to variable cost.

Output. The good or service produced in a firm.

Pareto efficient. The same as economically efficient.

Pareto superior. A Pareto superior allocation of resources makes at least one participant in the market better off and no one worse off.

Partial equilibrium analysis. An analysis that studies the determination of equilibrium price and output in a single market, taking as given the prices in all other markets.

Perfect complements (in production). Inputs in a fixed-proportions production function.

Perfect complements (in consumption). When two goods are perfect complements, the consumer wants to consume the goods in fixed proportion to one another.

Perfect information about prices. Consumers are fully aware of the prices charged by all sellers in the market. This is one of the characteristics of a perfectly competitive industry.

Perfect substitutes (in production). Inputs in a production function with a constant marginal rate of technical substitution.

Perfect substitutes (in consumption). When two goods are perfect substitutes, the consumer is always willing to substitute a given the amount of one good for a given amount of the other. In other words, the marginal rate of substitution of one good for the other is always constant. The indifference curves therefore will be straight lines.

Perfectly elastic demand. Price elasticity of demand equals minus infinity everywhere along the demand curve.

Perfectly inelastic demand. Price elasticity of demand equals 0 everywhere along the demand curve.

Positive analysis. Analysis that attempts to explain how an economic system works or to predict how it will change over time.

Price consumption curve. The set of utility-maximizing baskets as the price of one good varies (holding constant income and the prices of other goods).

Price discrimination. The practice of charging consumers different prices for the same good or service.

Price elasticity of demand for capital. The percentage change in the cost-minimizing quantity of capital with respect to a one percent change in the price of capital:

Price elasticity of demand for labor. The percentage change in the cost-minimizing quantity of labor with respect to a one percent change in the price of labor.

Price elasticity of demand. A measure of the rate of percentage change of quantity demanded with respect to price, holding all other determinants of demand constant.

Price elasticity of supply. A measure of the rate of percentage change of quantity supplied with respect to price, holding all other determinants of supply constant.

Price taker. A seller or a buyer that takes the price of the product as given when making an output decision (seller) or a purchase decision (buyer).

Principle of diminishing marginal utility. After some point, as consumption of a good increases, the marginal utility of that good will begin to fall.

Prisoners' dilemma. A term that refers to games in which there is a tension between the collective interest of all of the players in the game and the self interest of individual players.

Private values. A situation in which each bidder in an auction has his or her own personalized valuation of the object.

Probability distribution. A depiction of all possible payoffs in a lottery and their associated probabilities.

Probability. The likelihood that a particular outcome of a lottery occurs.

Producer surplus. A monetary measure of the benefit that producers derive from producing a good at a particular price. It is the area between the supply curve and the market price.

Product differentiation. Product differentiation between two or more products exists when the products possess attributes that, in the minds of consumers, set the products apart from one another and make them less than perfect substitutes.

Production function. A mathematical representation that shows the maximum quantity of output the firm can produce given the quantities of inputs that it might employ.

Production possibilities frontier. The curve that describes combinations of consumption goods that can be produced in the economy with the economy's available supply of inputs.

Production set. The set of technically feasible combinations of inputs and outputs.

Profit-maximization condition for a monopolist. The condition that says that a monopolist maximizes profit by producing quantity at which marginal revenue equals marginal cost.

Profit-maximization conditions for a price-taking firm. These are the conditions that $P = MC$ and MC must be increasing. If either of these conditions does not hold, the firm can increase its profits by producing at another level of output.

Property right. The exclusive control over the use of an asset or resource.

Public good. A good, such as national defense, that benefits all consumers even though individual consumers do not pay for the provision of the good. A public good is nonrival and nonexclusive.

Pure strategy. A specific choice of a strategy from the player's possible strategies in a game.

Quasi-Linear utility functions. A utility function that is linear in at least one of the goods consumed, but may be a nonlinear function of the other goods.

Reaction function. A graph that shows a firm's best response (i.e., profit-maximizing choice of output or price) to the action of a rival firm.

Rent-seeking activities. Activity aimed at creating or preserving monopoly power.

Reservation value of an input. The return that the owner of an input could get by deploying the input in its best alternative use outside the industry.

Residual demand curve. In a Cournot model, the residual demand curve traces out the relationship between the market price and a firm's quantity when rival firms hold their outputs fixed. In the dominant firm model, the residual demand curve traces out the relationship between the market price and the dominant firm's demand when fringe firms supply as much as they wish at the market price.

Returns to scale. The concept that tells us by how much output will increase when all inputs are increased by a given percentage amount.

Revealed preference. Analysis that enables us to learn about a consumer's ordinal ranking of baskets by observing how his choices of baskets change as prices and incomes vary.

Revenue equivalence theorem. The revenue equivalence theorem says that when participants in an auction have private values, any auction format will, on average, generate the same revenue for the seller.

Risk averse. A risk-averse decision maker prefers a sure thing to a lottery of equal expected value.

Risk loving. A risk-loving decision maker prefers a lottery to a sure thing that is equal to the expected value of the lottery.

Risk neutral. A risk-neutral decision maker compares lotteries according to their expected value and is therefore indifferent between a sure thing and a lottery with the same expected value.

Risk premium. The necessary difference between the expected value of a lottery and the payoff of a sure thing so that the decision maker is indifferent between the lottery and the sure thing.

Rival good. When a given amount of a nonrival good is produced, consumption by one person reduces the quantity that can be consumed by others.

Screening. A process for sorting consumers based on a consumer characteristic that (1) the firm can see (such as age or status), and (2) that is strongly related to a consumer characteristic that the firm cannot see but would like to observe (such as willingness to pay or elasticity of demand).

Second fundamental theorem of welfare economics. This theorem tells us that any economically efficient allocation of goods and inputs can be attained as a general competitive equilibrium through a judicious allocation of the economy's scarce supplies of resources.

Second-degree price discrimination. A seller engages in second-degree price discrimination by offering consumers a quantity discount.

Second-price sealed-bid auction. An auction in which each bidder submits one bid, not knowing the other bids. The highest bidder wins the object. However, unlike a first-price auction, the winning bidder pays an amount equal to the second-highest bid.

Sequential-move games. Games in which one player (the first mover) takes an action before another player (the second mover). The second mover observes the action taken by the first mover before deciding what action it should take.

Short-run average cost (SAC). The firm's total cost per unit of output when it has one or more fixed inputs (i.e., $SAC(Q) = STC(Q)/Q$).

Short-run cost-minimization problem. The problem of finding a combination of variable inputs to minimize the total cost of producing a particular level of output when one input's quantity is fixed.

Short-run demand curve. The demand curve that pertains to the period of time in which consumers cannot fully adjust their purchase decisions to changes in price.

Short-run marginal cost (SMC). The slope of the short-run total cost curve, i.e., $SMC(Q) = \Delta STC/\Delta Q$.

Short-run market supply curve. The quantity supplied in the aggregate by all firms in the market for each possible market price when the number of firms in the industry is fixed.

Short-run perfectly competitive equilibrium. The market price and quantity at which the quantity demanded equals quantity supplied in the short run.

Short-run supply curve. The short-run supply curve shows how the firm's profit-maximizing output decision changes as the market price changes, assuming that the firm cannot adjust all of its inputs (e.g., quantity of capital or land).

Short-run total cost curve (STC). The short-run total cost curve tells us the minimized total cost of producing a given quantity of output when one or more inputs is fixed.

Short run. The period of time in which at least one of the firm's input quantities cannot be changed.

Shut-down price. The price below which a firm supplies zero output in the short run.

Slope of the experience curve. How much average variable costs go down, as a percentage of an initial level, when cumulative output doubles.

Snob effect. A negative network externality that refers to the decrease in the quantity of a good that is demanded as more consumers buy the good.

Stand-alone cost. The cost of producing a good in a single-product firm.

Standard deviation. The square root of the variance.

Strategic barriers to entry. Barriers to entry that result when the incumbent firm takes explicit steps to deter entry.

Strategic moves. Actions that you take in an early stage of the game that alters your behavior and your competitor's behavior later in the game in a way that is favorable to you.

Strategy. A strategy in a game specifies the actions that a player will take under every conceivable circumstance that the player might face.

Structural barriers to entry. Barriers to entry that exist when incumbent firms have cost or demand advantages that would make it unattractive for a new firm to enter the industry and compete against it.

Subjective probabilities. Probabilities that reflect subjective beliefs about risky events.

Substitution effect. The change in the amount of a good that would be consumed as the price of that good changes, holding constant all other prices and the level of utility.

Substitution efficiency. Given the total amounts of capital and labor that is available in the economy, there is no way to make all consumers better off by producing more of one product (e.g., energy) and less of the other (e.g., food).

Sunk cost. A cost that has already been incurred and cannot be recovered.

Sunk fixed cost. A fixed cost that the firm cannot avoid if it shuts down and produces zero output.

Technically efficient. The set of points in the production set at which the firm is producing as much output as it possibly can given the amount of labor it employs.

Technically inefficient. The set of points in the production set at which the firm is getting less output from its labor than it should.

Technological progress. A change in a production process that enables a firm to achieve more output from a given combination of inputs, or equivalently, the same amount of output from less inputs.

Third-degree price discrimination. A seller practices third-degree price discrimination by charging different uniform prices to different consumer groups or segments in a market.

Tit-for-tat. A strategy in which you do to your opponent this period what your opponent did to you in the last period.

Total cost function. A mathematical relationship that shows how total costs vary with the factors that influence total costs, including the quantity of output and the prices of inputs.

Total fixed cost (TFC). The cost of fixed inputs; does not vary with output.

Total product function. A production function with a single input.

Total product hill. A three-dimensional graph of a production function.

Total revenue. Selling price times the quantity of product it sells, or *PQ*.

Total variable cost (*TVC*). The minimized variable costs; the sum of expenditures on variable inputs, such as labor and materials, at the short-run cost-minimizing input combination. The firm's total variable cost changes as the firm changes its output and is thus the output-sensitive component of its costs.

Translog cost function. A cost function that postulates a quadratic relationship between the log of total cost and the logs of input prices and output. This cost function is more general than the constant elasticity cost function, which is included as a special case.

Tying (tie-in sales). A sales practice that allows a customer to buy one product (the *tying* product) only if she agrees in a *requirements contract* to buy another product (the *tied* product).

Undifferentiated products. Products that consumers perceive as being identical. This is one of the characteristics of a perfectly competitive industry.

Uneconomic region of production. The region of upward-sloping or backward-bending isoquants. In the uneconomic region, at least one input has a negative marginal product.

Uniform price. A seller charges a uniform price when it sells every unit of its output at the same price.

Unitary elastic demand. Price elasticity of -1.

Utility function. A function that measures the level of satisfaction a consumer receives from any basket of goods and services.

Utility possibilities frontier. The curve that shows the pattern of utilities that could arise at the various economically efficient allocations of goods and inputs in an simple two-consumer economy.

Value of perfect information. The increase in a decision maker's expected payoff when the decision maker can—at no cost—conduct a test that will reveal the outcome of a risky event.

Variance. A measure of the riskiness of a lottery. Specifically, it is the expected value of the squared deviation between the possible outcomes of the lottery and the expected value of the lottery.

Vertical differentiation. Two products are vertically differentiated when consumers consider one product better or worse than the other.

Walras' Law. In a general competitive equilibrium with a total of N markets, if supply equals demand in the first $N-1$ markets, then supply will equal demand in the Nth market as well.

Winner's curse. A phenomenon whereby the winning bidder in a common-values auction might bid an amount that exceeds the item's intrinsic value.

Index